柯林斯 COBUILD 初阶
英汉双解学习词典

第3版

英国柯林斯出版公司 编著

Collins COBUILD
PRIMARY LEARNER'S
ENGLISH-CHINESE DICTIONARY
(3rd Edition)

外语教学与研究出版社
FOREIGN LANGUAGE TEACHING AND RESEARCH PRESS
北京 BEIJING

京权图字：01-2019-2756

© HarperCollins Publishers Ltd and Foreign Language Teaching and Research Press (2019) – with copyright in the original English-language content © HarperCollins Publishers (2018)

图书在版编目（CIP）数据

柯林斯 COBUILD 初阶英汉双解学习词典：第 3 版／英国柯林斯出版公司编著．－－ 北京：外语教学与研究出版社，2019.5（2020.10 重印）
ISBN 978-7-5213-0891-4

Ⅰ.①柯… Ⅱ.①英… Ⅲ.①英语－双解词典②双解词典－英、汉 Ⅳ.①H316

中国版本图书馆 CIP 数据核字（2019）第 096992 号

地图审图号：GS（2019）1152 号

出 版 人	徐建忠
责任编辑	谢金霞
责任校对	车云峰　李　云
封面设计	李双双　李　高
版式设计	李　高
出版发行	外语教学与研究出版社
社　　址	北京市西三环北路 19 号（100089）
网　　址	http://www.fltrp.com
印　　刷	紫恒印装有限公司
开　　本	889×1194　1/32
印　　张	21.75
版　　次	2019 年 7 月第 1 版　2020 年 10 月第 3 次印刷
书　　号	ISBN 978-7-5213-0891-4
定　　价	59.00 元

购书咨询：(010) 88819926　电子邮箱：club@fltrp.com
外研书店：https://waiyants.tmall.com
凡印刷、装订质量问题，请联系我社印制部
联系电话：(010) 61207896　电子邮箱：zhijian@fltrp.com
凡侵权、盗版书籍线索，请联系我社法律事务部
举报电话：(010) 88817519　电子邮箱：banquan@fltrp.com
物料号：308910001

出版说明

柯林斯COBUILD系列词典由英国柯林斯出版公司和伯明翰大学资深词典学家共同编写出版。该系列词典首创了以语料库为依托的词典编纂方法，以真实语料代替编写者的直觉来诠释英语用法，成为广受全球英语学习者信赖并推崇的英语词典品牌。

外语教学与研究出版社先前出版了《柯林斯COBUILD高阶英汉双解学习词典》(2011, 2017)和《柯林斯COBUILD中阶英汉双解学习词典》(2017)，受到国内广大英语学习者和英语教师的高度评价。《柯林斯COBUILD初阶英汉双解学习词典》(第3版)的出版，完善了柯林斯COBUILD词典体系，使其成为面向初级至高级英语学习者的全阶段工具书系列。

《柯林斯COBUILD初阶英汉双解学习词典》(第3版)为入门型英语工具书，贴合初级英语学习者实际需求，释义浅显易懂，例证真实自然，译文准确地道。本词典继承了COBUILD系列词典可信赖、易使用等优点，具有以下特色：

1. 收词广泛。收录单词、短语及释义20,000余个。
2. 内容鲜活。依托按月更新的语料库Collins Corpus，提炼新词、新义、新表达。
3. 例证取自语料库，呈现词语真实地道的用法。13,000余条例证均来自英语国家的报纸、期刊、著作等，帮助学习者在真实语境中准确理解词语。
4. 突出标记核心词汇，紧贴初级英语学习者实际需求。详解最常用、最有用的1,500余个核心词汇，便于初级英语学习者重点掌握。

本双解版从策划、翻译、设计、排版、编校到印刷制作，历经多道工序，各方人员耗费了大量心血，力求为学习者呈现一部尽善尽美的词典。然而，我们深知，限于人力、时间和知识水平，词典在出版过程中不免有疏漏之处，在此恳请广大师生朋友不吝赐教，以利修正。

外语教学与研究出版社
综合出版事业部
辞书工作室

Editorial Team
英汉双解版工作人员名单

《柯林斯 COBUILD 初阶英汉双解学习词典（第 3 版）》

项目负责人	姚　虹	申　葳	
责任编辑	谢金霞		
翻　　译	车云峰	冯倩倩	黄希玲
	李　云	刘文竹	谢金霞
	詹莹玥	张　蕾	赵观睿
编　　辑	车云峰	冯倩倩	黄希玲
	李　云	刘文竹	詹莹玥
	张　蕾	赵观睿	

Contents 目录

Guide to dictionary entries 词典条目指南	vi
Grammatical labels used in the dictionary 本词典使用的语法标签	x
Using your dictionary 查词典专项练习	xiii
Punctuation 标点符号	xxi
Times and dates 时间与日期	xxiv
Telling the time 时刻表示法	xxvi
Saying hello and goodbye 问候与道别	xxvii
Pronunciation 发音	xxix

COBUILD Primary Learner's Dictionary A-Z 词典正文   1-641

Reference Pages 附录

Irregular verbs 不规则动词	2
Key words 重点词汇	4
Study vocabulary 学科词汇	10
Classroom vocabulary 课堂语汇	16
Numbers and measurements 数字与度量衡	19

Key Themes in Pictures 专题词汇图解

P1	School and Study 学校与学习
P2	Mathematics 数学
P3	Language 语言
P4	Science 科学
P7	Geography 地理
P10	History and Social Studies 历史与社会科学
P11	Technology 技术
P12	Music 音乐
P13	Art and Design 美术与设计
P14	Sports 体育
P15	Personal, Social and Health Education 个人、社会与健康教育
P16	Jobs 职业

These pictures are in the middle of the dictionary. 这些图片集中插在词典中间。
Credits: The *globe* image on P9 is from **Shutterstock**. 图片鸣谢：第9页 globe（地球仪）的图像来自 Shutterstock。

Guide to dictionary entries 词典条目指南

The main form of the word is in blue. 词的基本形式用蓝色标示。

butterfly /ˈbʌtəflaɪ/ *countable noun* 可数名词 (**butterflies**)
an insect with large coloured wings 蝴蝶: *Butterflies are attracted to the wild flowers.* 蝴蝶流连于野花间。

Plurals: to make a plural form, the general rule is to add 's'. Where a word does not follow this rule, the plural form is shown. 复数形式：一般规则是加 s 构成复数形式。不符合此规则的词给出复数形式。

These symbols show you how to say the word. See page xxix for an explanation of these. 这些符号标注的是词的发音。参见 xxix 页的具体说明。

set¹ /set/ *countable noun* 可数名词
1 a number of things that belong together 一套；一组；一系列: *The table and chairs are normally bought as a set.* 桌椅通常成套购买。□ *I got a chess set for my birthday.* 我生日时给自己买了一副国际象棋。
2 the place where a film is made（电影的）拍摄场地: *The place looked like the set of a James Bond movie.* 这地方看起来像某部詹姆斯·邦德电影的拍摄场地。

This tells you the word class of a word (for example, if it is a noun, an adjective or a verb). 这里标注的是词类（例如，一个词是名词、形容词还是动词）。

set² /set/ *verb* 动词 (**sets, setting, set**)
1 to put something somewhere carefully （小心地）放，置: *She set the vase down gently on the table.* 她轻轻地把花瓶放在桌子上。
2 to make a clock ready to use 设置，调整（钟表）: *I set my alarm clock for seven o'clock every morning.* 我设定了每天早晨 7 点的闹钟。
3 to decide what a date or a price will be 决定，确定（日期或价格）: *They have finally set the date of their wedding.* 他们最终定下了婚礼的日子。
4 when the sun sets, it goes down in the sky（太阳）落山: *They watched the sun set behind the hills.* 他们望着太阳落山。
5 to prepare the table for a meal by putting plates, glasses, knives, forks, and spoons on it 在（桌子）上摆放餐具: *Could you set the table for dinner, please?* 请你摆放餐具准备开饭，好吗？
set fire to something or **set something on fire** to make something burn 放火烧某物: *Angry protestors threw stones and set cars on fire.* 愤怒的抗议者投掷石块并放火焚烧汽车。□ *I struck a match and set fire to the papers.* 我划着一根火柴，将文件点燃。

Blue boxes show the most common and useful words to know. 蓝色底框标注最常用、最有用的词。

Where a word has several meanings, these are ordered according to how common they are. 多义词各义项按使用频率排列。

The forms of all verbs are given. 所有动词都标注了变化形式。

Words with the same spelling but different word classes have different numbers. 拼写相同、词类不同的词以不同的上标数字区分。

Idioms and phrasal verbs are shown below the definitions for the main word. 习语和短语动词排在主词释义之下。

Example sentences show you typical uses of words, and help you to understand them. 例句显示词语典型用法，帮助理解词语。

set off to start going somewhere 动身；出发：*Nick set off for his farmhouse in Connecticut.* 尼克动身前往他在康涅狄格的农舍。
set someone free to cause someone to be free 释放某人：*They agreed to set the prisoners free.* 他们同意释放犯人。
set something up to start or arrange something 创建某事物；建立某事物：*He plans to set up his own business.* 他打算自己创业。

Related words are shown in blue within entries. 相关词以蓝色标示，排在词条之内。

sad /sæd/ *adjective* 形容词 (**sadder, saddest**)
1 unhappy 悲伤的；伤心的：*I'm sad that Jason's leaving.* 贾森要走了，我感到难过。
▶ **sadly** /ˈsædli/ *adverb* 副词：*'My girlfriend is moving away,' he said sadly.* "我女朋友要搬走了。"他伤心地说。
→ Look at picture on P15 参见彩插第 15 页
▶ **sadness** /ˈsædnəs/ *uncountable noun* 不可数名词：*I left with a mixture of sadness and joy.* 我怀着悲喜交加的心情离开了。
2 making you feel unhappy 令人难过的：*It was a sad ending to a great story.* 这个故事很精彩，但结局让人难过。 □ *I have some sad news for you.* 我有个坏消息要告诉你。

Comparative and superlative forms are given, unless they are formed with more or most. 标注比较级、最高级形式，但加 more、most 构成的不予标注。

You will find lots of words in this dictionary to help you with your schoolwork. There is a list of all the school subject words in the reference section on page 10. 本词典收录了大量学校作业中用得到的词语。附录第 10 页列有各学科词表。

baton /ˈbætɒn/ *countable noun* 可数名词
1 a light, thin stick that is used by a conductor (= a person who directs musicians) （乐队指挥的）指挥棒
2 a short stick that one runner passes to another in a race 接力棒

bacteria /bækˈtɪəriə/ *plural noun* 复数名词 very small living things that can make people ill 细菌：*There were high levels of dangerous bacteria in the water.* 这片水域含有大量危险的细菌。
▶ **bacterial** /bækˈtɪəriəl/ *adjective* 形容词：*Tuberculosis is a bacterial disease.* 结核病是一种细菌性疾病。

We use simple words in definitions, but where a difficult word is necessary, a short explanation is given. 本词典使用简单词释义，不得不使用难词时会给出简短解释。

skate¹ /skeɪt/ *countable noun* 可数名词
1 (also 亦作 **ice-skate**) a boot with a long, sharp piece of metal on the bottom, for moving quickly and smoothly on ice 冰鞋
2 (also 亦作 **roller-skate**) a boot with wheels on the bottom, for moving quickly on the ground 轮滑鞋

This information shows that there is another way of expressing the word. 此信息表示该词存在另一种说法。

board² /bɔːd/ *verb* 动词 (**boards, boarding, boarded**)
to get into a train, a ship or an aircraft to travel somewhere (*formal* 正式) 登上（火车、轮船或航空器）: *I boarded the plane to Boston.* 我登上了飞往波士顿的飞机。

A formal label means that this word is usually used in more serious or official situations. "formal 正式"这个标签表示该词通常用于较为严肃或正式的场合。

An informal label means that this word is not usually used in more serious situations or in serious writing. "informal 非正式"这个标签表示该词通常不用于较为严肃的场合和严肃写作中。

stuff¹ /stʌf/ *uncountable noun* 不可数名词
things in general (*informal* 非正式)（泛指）东西，物品: *He pointed to a bag. 'That's my stuff.'* 他指着一个袋子说: "那是我的东西。" □ *There is a huge amount of useful stuff on the Internet.* 因特网上有用的东西非常多。

'shop as,sistant *countable noun* 可数名词 (*American* 美国英语: **clerk**)
a person who works in a shop 店员，售货员
→ Look at picture on P16 参见彩插第 16 页

Common American words are shown. 常用美国英语说法予以标注。

angry /ˈæŋɡri/ *adjective* 形容词 (**angrier, angriest**)
feeling a strong emotion when someone has done something bad, or someone has treated you unfairly 生气的；愤怒的: *We are very angry about the decision to close the school.* 关闭学校这一决定使我们非常愤怒。 □ *An angry crowd gathered.* 愤怒的人群聚集起来。
→ Look at picture on P15 参见彩插第 15 页

LANGUAGE HELP 语言提示
If someone is very angry, you can say they are **furious**. If they are less angry, you can say they are **annoyed** or **irritated**. 表示火气很大，用 furious。表示没那么生气，用 annoyed 或 irritated。

Language Help boxes show related words for vocabulary building. "语言提示"框呈现相关词，帮助积累词汇。

already /ɔːlˈredi/ *adverb* 副词

1 used for showing that one thing happened before another thing 已经（表示一事早于另一事发生）: *The meeting had already finished when we arrived.* 我们到的时候会已经开完了。

2 used for showing that a situation exists now or that it started earlier than expected 已经（表示某情形已然存在或早于预期发生）: *We've already spent most of the money.* 这笔钱我们已花掉大半。◇ *Most of the guests have already left.* 客人已走了大半。

> **LANGUAGE HELP 语言提示**
> **Already** or **yet**? 用 already 还是 yet？
> In British English, you usually use **already** and **yet** with the perfect tenses. 英国英语中，already 和 yet 通常用于完成时: *I've already seen that film.* 我已经看过那部电影了。◇ *Have they arrived yet?* 他们到了吗？
> In American English, people often use a past tense. 美国英语中，常用于过去时: *She already told us about the party.* 她跟我们讲过聚会的事了。◇ *I didn't have any breakfast yet.* 我早饭还什么都没吃呢。

Language Help boxes show differences between words that are often confused. "语言提示"框提供易混词辨析。

Grammatical labels used in the dictionary
本词典使用的语法标签

Nearly all the words that are explained in this dictionary have grammar information given about them. The word class is shown after the headword. Examples of word classes are *adjective, noun, verb* and *preposition*. 本词典所释义的词几乎均配有语法信息。词目后标注了词类，如形容词、名词、动词和介词。

The sections below contain more information about each word class. 下面将具体介绍一下各种词类。

adjective 形容词

An adjective is a word that is used for telling you more about a person or thing. You would use an adjective to talk about appearance, colour, size, or other qualities. 形容词是补充说明人或物的词，用于描述外貌、颜色、大小或其他属性：

> **angry** 生气的：*An **angry** woman appeared at the door.* 一个气呼呼的女人出现在门口。
> **brown** 褐色的：*She has **brown** eyes.* 她有一双褐色的眼睛。
> **wet** 湿的：*My gloves are **wet**.* 我的手套湿了。

adverb 副词

An adverb is a word that gives more information about when, how, or where something happens. 副词是补充说明事情发生时间、方式或场所的词：

> **tomorrow** 明天：*Bye; see you **tomorrow**.* 拜拜，明天见。
> **slowly** 缓慢地：*He spoke **slowly** and clearly.* 他语速缓慢，吐字清晰。
> **down**（放）下：*Danny put **down** his glass.* 丹尼放下玻璃杯。

article 冠词

An article is one of the words *a, an*, or *the* that is used before a noun. It shows whether you are talking about a particular thing or a general example of something. 冠词即 a、an 或 the，用于名词前，表示泛指或特指某事物：

> **a**: *I need **a** drink.* 我得喝一杯。
> **an**: *You'll need **an** umbrella; it's raining outside.* 你得带把伞，外面下雨了。
> **the**: *You should never look directly at the sun.* 绝对不要直视太阳。

auxiliary verb 助动词

An auxiliary verb is a verb that is used with another verb to show its tense, to form questions, or to form the passive. The main auxiliary verbs in English are *be, have* and *do*. 助动词是须与另一动词连用的动词，表示时态、构成疑问句或被动态，英语助动词主要有 be、have 和 do：

> **be**: *Is it snowing?* 下雪了？
> **have**: *I **have** never been to China.* 我从未去过中国。
> **do**: *We **don't** have a computer at home.* 我们家里没电脑。

conjunction 连词

A conjunction is a word such as *and, but, if*, and *since*. Conjunctions are used for linking two words or two parts of a sentence together. 连词是 and、but、if、since 之类的词，用于连接两个词或两个句子成分：

> **but** 但是：*I enjoyed my holiday, **but** it wasn't long enough.* 我假期过得很愉快，可惜假期不够长。
> **and** 和：*James **and** Ewan came to the party.* 詹姆斯和尤安来参加了聚会。
> **if** 如果：***If** you miss your bus, you'll have to walk home.* 你要是错过公交车的话，就只好走回家了。

exclamation 感叹词

An exclamation is a word or phrase which is spoken suddenly or loudly in order to express a strong emotion. 感叹词是突然或大声说出的词或短语，表示强烈的情感：

oh 哦：*'Oh!' Kenny said. 'Has everyone gone?'* "哦！"肯尼说，"大家都走了吗？"
wow 哇：*Wow; this is so exciting!* 哇，这真叫人兴奋！

modal verb 情态动词

A modal verb is a verb such as *may*, *must*, or *would*. A modal verb is used before the infinitive form of a verb. 情态动词是 may、must、would 之类的动词，用于动词原形之前：

*You **must** see a doctor.* 你必须找个大夫看看。

In questions, it comes before the subject. 在疑问句中，情态动词位于主语之前：

***May** we come in?* 我们可以进来吗？

In negatives, it comes before the negative word. 在否定句中，情态动词位于否定词之前：

*I **can't** play the piano.* 我不会弹钢琴。

Modal verbs do not add an *-s* in the third person singular (with *he*, *she*, and *it*). 情态动词用于第三人称单数（如与 he、she 和 it 连用）时不加 s：

*She **must** be at work.* 她一定是在工作。

noun 名词

A noun is a word that refers to a person, a thing, or a quality. In this dictionary, the label *noun* is given to all nouns that can be both countable and uncountable. 名词是表示人、事物或属性的词。本词典中，所有兼具可数和不可数双重属性的名词均标注有"noun 名词"这个标签：

afternoon 下午：*He's arriving in the **afternoon**.* 他今天下午到。

countable noun 可数名词

A countable noun is used for talking about things that can be counted, and that have both singular and plural forms. When a countable noun is used in the singular, it must normally have a word like *a*, *an*, *the*, or *her* in front of it. 可数名词用于表示可以计数的事物，兼具单复数形式。可数名词用作单数时，前面一般必须有 a、an、the、her 之类的词：

accent 口音：*He has an Irish **accent**.* 他有爱尔兰口音。
head 头：*She turned her **head** away.* 她把头扭开了。

uncountable noun 不可数名词

An uncountable noun is used for talking about things that are not normally counted, or that we do not think of as single items. Uncountable nouns do not have a plural form, and they are used with a singular verb. 不可数名词用于表示一般不可计数或人们认为不会单个存在的东西，没有复数形式，与单数动词连用：

help 帮助：*He shouted for **help**.* 他大声呼救。
rain 雨：*We got very wet in the **rain**.* 我们在雨里给浇透了。
beauty 美丽：*The hotel is in an area of natural **beauty**.* 这座宾馆周围环境优美。

plural noun 复数名词

A plural noun is always plural, and it is used with plural verbs. 复数名词只有复数形式，与复数动词连用：

pyjamas 睡衣：*What colour are your **pyjamas**?* 你的睡衣是什么颜色？
scissors 剪刀：*Be careful; these **scissors** are very sharp.* 当心，这把剪刀很锋利。

singular noun 单数名词

A singular noun is always singular and needs a determiner. 单数名词只有单数形式，需要以限定词修饰：

community 社区：*When you live in a small **community**, everyone knows you.* 住在小社区，谁都认识你。
grasp 紧握：*He took her hand in a firm **grasp**.* 他紧紧抓住她的手。

preposition 介词

A preposition is a word such as *by*, *with*, or *from* which is always followed by a noun group or the *-ing* form of a verb. 介词是 by、with、from 之类的词，总是后接名词词组或动词的 -ing 形式：

near 在…附近：*He stood **near** the door.* 他站在门附近。

of 与…有关联：*Alice is a friend of mine.* 艾丽斯是我的朋友。

pronoun 代词

A pronoun is a word that you use instead of a noun, when you do not need or want to name someone or something directly. 代词是替代名词的词，用于不必或不想直接使用人或事物的名称时：

it 它：*John took the book and opened it.* 约翰拿起书翻开书页。
her 她：*He rang Mary and invited her to dinner.* 他打电话给玛丽邀请她共进晚餐。

verb 动词

A verb is a word that is used for saying what someone or something does, or what happens to them, or to give information about them. 动词是表示人或事物做了某事、发生了某事，或提供与其相关信息的词：

sleep 睡觉：*She slept till 10 o'clock in the morning.* 她一直睡到上午 10 点。
eat 吃：*I ate my breakfast quickly.* 我匆匆吃了早饭。

Using your dictionary 查词典专项练习

The exercises in these study pages will help you to understand and use fully all the different features of this dictionary, and to practise your dictionary skills. You will find answers to all the exercises in the Answer Key on pages xix-xx. 以下研习页的专项练习有助于查阅者充分了解并利用本词典的各项不同特色设计，练习个人查阅词典的技能。全部习题答案见 xix—xx 页。

Order of entries 词条顺序

The main part of the dictionary is made up of entries from A to Z. An **entry** is a complete explanation of a word and all its meanings. For example, the first three entries on page 1 are 'a', 'abandon' and 'abbreviation'. You will find each entry under the first letter of that word. 词典正文由 A 至 Z 各字母的词条组成。**词条**是对一个词及其所有义项的完整解释。例如，正文第 1 页前 3 个词条分别是 a、abandon 和 abbreviation。每个词条均排列在其所解释词的首字母之下。

Guide words 引导词

At the top of every page you will see two words. These words are **guide words**. The guide words show what the first and last entry on that page is. For example, on page 2, the first entry is 'about', and the last entry is 'absorb'. 词典正文每页上方可以看到两个词，这便是**引导词**。引导词即当页的起止词条，例如第 2 页的第一个词条是 about，最后一个词条是 absorb。

Exercise 1 练习 1
Put the words on the left between the appropriate guide words. The first one has been done for you as an example. 将左栏单词填写到右栏相应的引导词之间。第 1 题为示例。

1	~~amount~~	a	apart	appendix
2	another	b	administration	adult
3	apparently	c	assembly	asthma
4	assistance	d	among ...... *amount*	analyse
5	admit	e	ankle	answer

Inflected forms 屈折形式

Inflected forms are the different forms that a word can have, such as the past form for a verb, or a plural form for a noun. These forms are shown after the pronunciations. 屈折形式是一个词可以有的不同形式，如动词过去式或名词复数形式。这些形式排在音标之后。

At verb entries, you can see the 3rd person singular, the -*ing* form, the past tense, and, if it is different from the past tense, the past participle. 动词词条标注了第三人称单数形式、-ing 形式、过去式，过去式和过去分词不同时，还会标注过去分词。

give /ɡɪv/ *verb* 动词 (**gives**, **giving**, **gave**, **given**)

At adjective and adverb entries, you can see their comparative and superlative forms. 形容词、副词词条标注了比较级、最高级形式。

pretty /ˈprɪti/ *adjective* 形容词, *adverb* 副词 (**prettier**, **prettiest**)

Most nouns add an -*s* in the plural, but for those that follow a different pattern, you can see their plural forms. 大多数名词后面加 s 变为复数形式，不符合这一变化规则的名词标注有复数形式。

woman /ˈwʊmən/ *countable noun* 可数名词 (**women**)

Exercise 2 练习 2
Which headword would you look at to find these words? The first one has been done for you. 查哪个词目才能找到下列词语？第 1 题为示例。

1 beaches …… beach ……
2 seemed ……………
3 living ……………
4 clearer ……………
5 geese ……………
6 secretaries ……………
7 nicest ……………
8 women ……………
9 forgotten ……………
10 parties ……………

Definitions and examples 释义与例证

Definitions are written using simple words. Examples show typical ways of using the word, and they also give more information about its grammatical patterns. 释义用词浅显易懂。例证说明词目的典型用法，同时呈现其语法模式信息。

Exercise 3 练习 3
Decide what is wrong with each of the following sentences by looking up the word printed in bold. Use the information in the entry to write down the correct sentence. 翻开词典查下列句中的粗体词，看看这些句子错在哪里。借助词条中的信息写出正确的句子。

1 *He hasn't made his **homework**.*

2   The prime minister did a **speech** to the nation.
_____

3   Sally **graduated** Edinburgh University in the summer.
_____

4   He **asked** to me my name.
_____

5   The price of petrol has **fallen** down.
_____

Grammar information 语法信息

Each headword has a label that shows its grammatical word class, for example whether it is a noun, a verb, or an adjective. A list of these labels is shown on pages x-xii. 每个词目均标有词类标签，例如名词、动词、形容词。词类标签详见 x—xii 页。

accent /ˈæksənt/ **countable noun** 可数名词
1 the particular way that someone pronounces words, which shows where the person comes from 口音；腔调: *He had an Irish accent.* 他有爱尔兰口音。
2 a mark written above a letter to show how it is pronounced（字母上方的）音质符号: *The word 'café' has an accent on the 'e'.* 单词 café 中字母 e 上有音质符号。

Exercise 4 练习 4
Write a correct word class from the box next to each word. The first one has been done for you. 从框中选取正确的词类填写在各词后。第 1 题为示例。

| ~~noun~~ | pronoun | modal verb | verb | adjective | countable noun |
| preposition | exclamation | | adverb | adjective | |

1   pool ......noun............   6   accident ....

2   woolly   7   mad ....

3   grind   8   wow ....

4   concerning   9   me ....

5   must   10   hardly ....

Some words have more than one word class. These words have separate 'entries' for each word class. These entries have a small number after the headword, for example, at **answer**. 有些词有不止一个词类，每个词类分立词条，词目后标有上标数字，例如 answer：

answer¹ /ˈɑːnsə/ *verb* 动词 (answers, answering, answered)
1 to say something back to someone who has spoken to you 回答；回复：*I asked him but he didn't answer.* 我问了他，但他没有回答。▫ *Williams answered that he didn't know.* 威廉斯回答说他不知道。
2 to pick up the telephone when it rings 接（电话）：*Why didn't you answer when I phoned?* 我给你打电话为什么不接？ ▫ *She didn't answer the telephone.* 她没有接电话。

answer² /ˈɑːnsə/ *countable noun* 可数名词
1 a way to solve a problem 解决办法：*There are no easy answers to this problem.* 要解决这个问题并非易事。
2 the information that you give when you are doing a test 答案：*I got three answers wrong.* 我有 3 道题答错了。

Exercise 5 练习 5
Read the following sentences. In the first column, write the word class of the bold word. 阅读下列句子。在右边第 1 栏填上粗体词的词类。

Look for the word in the dictionary, and write the headword and its number in the second column. 翻开词典查一下这个词，在右边第 2 栏填上词目及上标数字。

		word class	headword
1	I **hope** you can come to my party.	....verb.......	......hope¹....
2	I don't know the **answer** to this question.	....	....
3	In the afternoon, we looked **around** the shops.	....	....
4	Amy was very **upset** when she heard the news.	....	....
5	I'm **backing** France in the final.	....	....

Style labels 语体标签
Some words are used in particular situations. 有些词用于特定的语境。

In this dictionary, the label *formal* shows that a word is used mainly in official situations such as politics and business. 本词典中，"formal 正式"这个标签表示词语主要用于政治、商务等正式场合。

The label *informal* shows that a word is used mainly in relaxed conversations and personal letters or emails. "informal 非正式"这个标签表示词语主要用于闲谈、私人信件或电子邮件中。

Exercise 6 练习 6
Write the correct style label ('formal' or 'informal') next to these words. Use your dictionary to help you. 查词典，在词后填上正确的语体标签（formal 或 informal）。

1	appliance	....
2	hang out	....
3	exceed	....
4	notify	....
5	weird	....
6	reckon	....

Exercise 7 练习 7

Look at the sentences below. The ***bold italic*** word in each one is informal. Use the dictionary to help you re-write the sentence in a less informal way. 阅读下列句子。各句中的粗斜体词均为非正式用词。借助词典重写句子，使其显得正式一些。

1 *She's had a nasty shock, but she's **okay**.*

   _____

2 *Have you got any **kids**?*

   _____

3 *Who's that **guy** with Katie?*

   _____

4 *Tony was my best **mate** at school.*

   _____

5 *'Remember to turn the computer off.' 'Oh, **yeah**.'*

   _____

Exercise 8 练习 8

This dictionary is written in British English, but it also contains common American English words. 本词典以英国英语编写而成，但同时也收录了常见的美国英语语汇。

Look at the sentences below. For each, say whether the word in ***bold italic*** is British or American English, using the dictionary to help you. Then write the American or British English word with the same meaning (the 'equivalent') next to it in the space provided. 阅读下列句子。借助词典判断各句中的粗斜体词属于英国英语还是美国英语。然后在最右栏空格中填上其在美国英语或英国英语中的同义词（"对等词"）。

Examples	British or American?	Equivalent
1 There was a long **queue** of people at the post office.		

Examples	British or American?	Equivalent
2 Could you take the **garbage** out, please?		
3 I'm wearing a red shirt and black **trousers**.		
4 Please send us your **CV**.		
5 Don't park your car on the **sidewalk**.		

Language Help 语言提示

Language Help boxes give you extra information about words and meanings. For example, they tell you how to avoid common mistakes or when to use a related word. They are the blue boxes that appear after the entry or meaning they relate to. Look at the entry for 'news' to find an example of a Language Help box. "语言提示" 框提供词和义项的额外信息，例如，如何避免常见错误，何时使用相关词。"语言提示" 框为蓝色，出现在相关词条或义项之后，可以翻开词典查看 news 这个词条下的"语言提示"框。

Exercise 9 练习 9
Use the Language Help boxes in the dictionary to help you to correct the mistakes in these sentences. 借助本词典中的"语言提示"框改正下列句中的错误。

1 *My parents **educated** me very strictly.*

2 *Mum was downstairs **hearing** the radio.*

3 *These vegetables need **little** salt to improve their taste.*

4 *How many **luggages** have you got?*

5 *Was anyone **wounded** in the car accident?*

Answer Key 答案

Exercise 1 练习 **1**
1 d, 2 e, 3 a, 4 c, 5 b

Exercise 2 练习 **2**
1 beach
2 seem
3 live
4 clear
5 goose
6 secretary
7 nice
8 woman
9 forget
10 party

Exercise 3 练习 **3**
1 He hasn't **done** his homework.
2 The prime minister **gave** a speech to the nation.
3 Sally **graduated from** Edinburgh University in the summer.
4 He **asked** me my name.
5 The price of petrol has **fallen**.

Exercise 4 练习 **4**
1 noun
2 adjective
3 verb
4 preposition
5 modal verb
6 countable noun
7 adjective
8 exclamation
9 pronoun
10 adverb

Exercise 5 练习 **5**
1 verb, **hope**[1]
2 countable noun, **answer**[2]
3 preposition, **around**[1]
4 adjective, **upset**[1]
5 verb, **back**[3]

Exercise 6 练习 **6**
1 formal
2 informal
3 formal
4 formal
5 informal
6 informal

Exercise 7 练习 **7**
1 She's had a nasty shock, but she's **safe and well**.
2 Have you got any **children**?
3 Who's that **man** with Katie?
4 Tony was my best **friend** at school.

5   'Remember to turn the computer off.' 'Oh, **yes**.'

Exercise 8 练习 8

Examples	British or American?	Equivalent
1 There was a long **queue** of people at the post office.	British	line
2 Could you take the **garbage** out, please?	American	rubbish
3 I'm wearing a red shirt and black **trousers**.	British	pants
4 Please send us your **CV**.	British	résumé
5 Don't park your car on the **sidewalk**.	American	pavement

Exercise 9 练习 9
1   My parents **brought** me **up** very strictly.
2   Mum was downstairs **listening to** the radio.
3   These vegetables need **a little** salt to improve their taste.
4   How many **pieces of luggage** have you got?
5   Was anyone **injured** in the car accident?

Punctuation 标点符号

● **full stop** (*American* 美国英语 : **period**) 句号；句点
A full stop is used at the end of a sentence, unless it is a question or an exclamation. 句号用于句末，疑问句、感叹句除外。

> *It's not your fault.* 这不是你的错。
> *Cook the rice in salted water.* 把米放在盐水里煮。

? **question mark** 问号
If a sentence is a question, you put a question mark at the end. 问号用于疑问句句末。

> *Why did you do that?* 你为什么这么做？
> *He's very good at maths, isn't he?* 他数学很好，不是吗？

! **exclamation mark** (*American* 美国英语 : **exclamation point**) 叹号
You put an exclamation mark at the end of a sentence that expresses surprise, excitement, enthusiasm, or horror. 叹号用于表示惊讶、兴奋、热情或恐惧的句子末尾。

> *What a lovely smell!* 多么好闻的气味！
> *How awful!* 多么可怕啊！

, **comma** 逗号
You put a comma between things on a list. 逗号用于罗列的事物之间。

> *We came to a small, dark room.* 我们来到一个又小又黑的房间。
> *We ate fish, steak and fruit.* 我们吃了鱼、牛排和水果。

You put a comma after or in front of someone's name, or the word you use when you speak to them. 逗号用于人名或称呼的前后。

> *Jenny, I'm sorry.* 珍妮，对不起。
> *I love you, darling.* 我爱你，亲爱的。

You put a comma between the name of a place and the country, state, or county it is in. 逗号用于地名与其所在的国家、州(邦)或郡(县)之间。

> *She was born in Richmond, Surrey, in 1913.* 她于1913年出生在萨里郡的里士满。

You put a comma before a part of a sentence that gives extra information. 逗号用于起补充说明作用的句子成分之前。

> *We sat in the living room, which was rather small.* 我们坐在相当小的起居室里。

You put a comma before a question tag. 逗号用于附加疑问句之前。

> *You're American, aren't you?* 你是美国人，不是吗？

semicolon 分号

You use a semicolon to separate clauses that are closely related. 分号用于分隔密切相关的分句。

He knew everything about me; I knew nothing about him. 他知道我的一切，我对他一无所知。

colon 冒号

You use a colon before a list or explanation, where the list or explanation relates to the previous clause. 冒号用于同前面分句相关的罗列事物或解释说明之前。

These clothes are made of natural materials: cotton, silk, wool, and leather. 这些衣服是由天然材料制成的：棉、丝、毛和皮革。

apostrophe 撇号

You use an apostrophe with *s* to show that a person or thing belongs to someone or something. When the noun is singular, or is plural, but does not end in an *s*, the apostrophe is placed before the *s*. 撇号与 s 连用表示人或物属于何人或何物。不以 s 结尾的名词，无论单复数，撇号一律位于 s 之前。

I stayed at Fiona's house last night. 我昨晚住在菲奥娜家。
Here are the children's rooms. 这几间是儿童房。

When the noun is a regular plural (with an *s*), the apostrophe is placed after the *s*. 名词是规则复数名词（以 s 结尾）时，撇号位于 s 之后。

Those are the dogs' bowls. 那些是狗的碗。

Note 注意: You do not use an apostrophe before the *s* of the possessive pronouns *yours, hers, ours, theirs*, or *its*. 物主代词 yours、hers、ours、theirs 和 its 中的 s 之前勿用撇号。

You use an apostrophe in shortened forms of *be, have, would,* and *not*. 撇号用于 be、have、would 和 not 的缩写形式中。

I'm very sorry. 非常抱歉。
I've got two brothers and two sisters. 我有两个哥哥和两个姐姐。
I'd like a coffee and a ham sandwich, please. 请给我来一杯咖啡、一份火腿三明治。
I can't see anything. 我什么也看不见。

hyphen 连字符

You use a hyphen to join together two words to make another word. 连字符用于连接两个词生成新词。

He was forty-three years old. 他 43 岁。
At half-time, the score was 2-1. 半场时，比分是 2:1。

quotation marks (or 或 quotes, or 或 inverted commas) 引号
You put quotation marks at the beginning and end of direct speech. You start direct speech with a capital letter and you end it with a full stop, a question mark, or an exclamation mark. 引号用于直接引语的头尾。直接引语第一个词首字母要大写，末尾用句号、问号或叹号。

"What happened?" "发生了什么事？"

If you put something like 'he said' after the direct speech, you put a comma in front of the second inverted comma, not a full stop. 直接引语后带有 he said 之类表述的，第二个引号之前用逗号，不用句号。

'We have to go home,' she told him. "我们得回家了。"她告诉他。
'Yes,' he replied. 'He'll be all right.' "是的，"他回答道，"他会没事的。"

Times and dates 时间与日期

Talking about time 谈论时间

If you want to talk about the time that you can see on a clock or a watch, you use the verb be. 谈论钟表上看到的时间，用动词 be。

> What's the time now? It's three thirty. 现在几点了？ 3 点 30 分。
> Can you tell me the time? It's twenty-five past twelve. 你能告诉我现在几点吗？ 12 点 25 分。
> The time **is** six forty-five. 现在是 6 点 45 分。
> It's five to eight and breakfast's at eight o'clock. 现在差 5 分 8 点，早餐在 8 点钟。

You also use these prepositions to indicate a specific time. 还可用下列介词表示具体时间。

at	on	past	to

> I'll meet you **at** seven o'clock. 我 7 点和你见面。
> He mentioned it to me **on** Friday. 他星期五向我提到了这件事。
> It was four minutes **past** midnight. 那是半夜 12 点过 4 分。
> At exactly five minutes **to** nine, Ann left her car. 正好差 5 分 9 点时，安离开了她的车。

You use these prepositions to relate events to a non-specific time. 表示非具体时间用下列介词。

after	before	by	during	following	over

> The match started again **after** lunch. 午饭后比赛又开始了。
> She woke up **during** the night. 她夜里醒了。
> Several demonstrations have been held **over** the past few weeks. 在过去的几周里已经举行了几次示威活动。
> I have to finish this essay **by** Monday. 我必须在星期一之前完成这篇文。
> We arrived **before** lunch. 我们在午饭前到达。
> **Following** the storm, the sun came out. 风暴过后，太阳出来了。

Dates 日期

Writing dates 书写日期

There are several different ways of writing a date. 日期有数种书写方法。

> 20 April   April 20
> 20th April   April 20th

(say 读作 'the twentieth of April' or 'April (the) twentieth')

If you want to give the year, you put it last. 年份位于最后。

> She was born on December 15th 2017. 她出生于 2017 年 12 月 15 日。（读作 'December the fifteenth, twenty seventeen'）

You can write a date in figures. 日期可以写成数字形式。

15/12/17   15.12.17

Note that in American English, you put the month in front of the day. 注意，在美国英语中，月份位于日期之前。

12/15/17   12.15.17

Days of the week 星期

| Monday 星期一 | Tuesday 星期二 | Wednesday 星期三 | Thursday 星期四 |
| Friday 星期五 | Saturday 星期六 | Sunday 星期日 | |

The exam is on Friday afternoon. 考试在星期五下午。
We meet here every Tuesday morning. 我们每周二上午在这里会面。
He took a flight to Nairobi last Thursday. 上周四他乘飞机去了内罗毕。
Aunty Margaret is coming to stay next Tuesday. 玛格丽特姨妈下星期二要来住下。

Months of the year 月份

January 一月	February 二月	March 三月	April 四月	May 五月
June 六月	July 七月	August 八月	September 九月	October 十月
November 十一月	December 十二月			

Here are the most common ways of talking about months. 以下为最常用的月份表示法。

We always have snow in January. 我们1月份总是下雪。
The new shop opens on 5 February. 这家新商店2月5日开业。
I flew to Milan in early March. 我在3月初飞往米兰。
I've been here since last June. 自去年6月以来我一直住在这里。
I'm going to Paris next November. 明年11月我要去巴黎。

Seasons 季节

| spring 春天 | summer 夏天 | autumn 秋天 | winter 冬天 |

Here are the most common ways of talking about seasons. 以下为最常用的季节表示法。

In winter the nights are cold and long. 冬天的夜晚又冷又长。
Richard is starting university next autumn. 理查德明年秋天就要上大学了。
We met again in the spring of last year. 我们去年春天又见面了。

American speakers often use *fall* instead of *autumn*. 美国英语使用者常用 fall 代替 autumn。

He begins teaching in the fall. 他从秋天开始教书。

Telling the time 时刻表示法

Here are the most common ways of saying and writing the time. 以下为时刻最常用的说法和写法。

 four o'clock
four
4.00
4 点

 nine o'clock
nine
9.00
9 点

 twelve o'clock
twelve
12.00
12 点

`04:00` four in the morning
4 a.m.
上午 4 点

`09:00` nine in the morning
9 a.m.
上午 9 点

`12:00` twelve in the morning
12 a.m.
midday
noon
中午 12 点

`16:00` four in the afternoon
4 p.m.
下午 4 点

`21:00` nine in the evening
9 p.m.
晚上 9 点

`00:00` twelve at night
12 p.m.
midnight
午夜 12 点

 half past eleven (*British* 英国英语)
half-eleven (*British* 英国英语)
eleven-thirty
11.30
11 点 30 分

 a quarter to one (*British* 英国英语)
quarter to one (*British* 英国英语)
twelve forty-five
12.45
(a) quarter of one (*American* 美国英语)
12 点 45 分

 a quarter past twelve (*British* 英国英语)
quarter past twelve (*British* 英国英语)
12.15
(a) quarter after twelve (*American* 美国英语)
12 点 15 分

 ten to eight (*British* 英国英语)
ten minutes to eight (*British* 英国英语)
seven-fifty
7.50
ten of eight (*American* 美国英语)
7 点 50 分

 twenty-five past two (*British* 英国英语)
twenty-five minutes past two (*British* 英国英语)
two twenty-five
2.25
twenty-five after two (*American* 美国英语)
2 点 25 分

 twenty to eleven (*British* 英国英语)
twenty minutes to eleven (*British* 英国英语)
ten-forty
10.40
twenty of eleven (*American* 美国英语)
10 点 40 分

Saying hello and goodbye 问候与道别

Saying hello 问候

The usual way of greeting someone is by saying *hello*. After you have greeted someone, you often say their name, or ask how they are. 问候他人通常用 hello。问候完毕，常称呼对方名字或询问其状况。

> '*Hello, it's Molly.*' – '*Oh, hello love.*' "你好，我是莫莉。" —— "哦，你好，亲爱的。"
> '*Hello, Mike.*' – '*Hello. How are you today?*' "你好，迈克。" —— "你好。你今天好吗？"

To greet someone more informally, you can say *hello there* or *hi*. 表示较为随意的问候，可以用 hello there 或 hi。

To greet someone at a particular time of day, you can use the expressions *good morning*, *good afternoon*, and *good evening*. 表示一天中特定时刻的问候，可以用 good morning、good afternoon 和 good evening。

Good morning is used before twelve o'clock midday. *good morning 用于正午 12 点之前。

Good afternoon is used between midday and about six o'clock. *good afternoon 用于正午至午后 6 点左右之间。

Good evening is used after that. *good evening 用于剩余时段。

With people you know, these greetings are often shortened to *morning*, *afternoon*, and *evening*. 这些问候语用于熟人之间时，常简化为 morning、afternoon 和 evening。

Note 注意：*Good night* is only used to say goodbye to someone before you or they go to bed. *good night 仅用于自己或对方睡觉前同对方道别。

Saying goodbye 道别

When two people part, they usually say *goodbye*, *bye*, or *bye bye*. People who know each other are more likely to say *bye* than *goodbye*. People do not usually say *bye* or *bye bye* in very formal situations. 分别时通常说 goodbye、bye 或 bye bye。熟人之间 bye 比 goodbye 更常用。非常正式的场合通常不说 bye 或 bye bye。

To say goodbye more informally, people use the expressions *see you* and *see you later*. They also sometimes say *take care* and *all the best*. 表示较为随意的道别，用 see you 和 see you later，有时也用 take care 和 all the best。

In British English, people sometimes say *cheers* or *look after yourself*. 在英国英语中，有时用 cheers 或 look after yourself。

If you have just met someone for the first time, you can say *it was nice to meet you* when you leave them. 初次见面后分别时，可以说 it was nice to meet you。

> *Thanks for coming along here. It was very nice to meet you.* 谢谢你来这里，很高兴见到你。

Responding to greetings 回应问候

You can respond to a greeting or goodbye by repeating the expression that the other person has used, or with another appropriate expression. 回应问候或道别可以重复对方所使用的表达，也可以选用其他合适的表达。

'Hello Colin.' – 'Hello.' "你好，科林。" —— "你好。"
'Hello Colin.' – 'Good evening, how are you?' "你好，科林。" —— "晚上好，你好吗?"

Pronunciation 发音

In this dictionary the International Phonetic Alphabet (IPA) is used to show how the words are pronounced. The symbols used in the International Phonetic Alphabet are shown in the table below. 本词典采用国际音标标示词语发音。国际音标所用符号见下表。

IPA Symbols 国际音标符号

Vowel sounds 元音

ɑː	calm, ah
æ	act, mass
aɪ	dive, cry
aɪə	fire, tyre
aʊ	out, down
aʊə	flour, sour
e	met, lend, pen
eɪ	say, weight
eə	fair, care
ɪ	fit, win
iː	seem, me
ɪə	near, beard
ɒ	lot, spot
əʊ	note, coat
ɔː	claw, more
ɔɪ	boy, joint
ʊ	could, stood
uː	you, use
ʊə	sure, pure
ɜː	turn, third
ʌ	fund, must
ə	the first vowel in about
i	the second vowel in very
u	the second vowel in actual

Consonant sounds 辅音

b	bed, rub
d	done, red
f	fit, if
g	good, dog
h	hat, horse
j	yellow, you
k	king, pick
l	lip, bill
m	mat, ram
n	not, tin
p	pay, lip
r	run, read
s	soon, bus
t	talk, bet
v	van, love
w	win, wool
z	zoo, buzz
ʃ	ship, wish
ʒ	measure, leisure
ŋ	sing, ring
tʃ	cheap, witch
θ	thin, myth
ð	then, bathe
dʒ	joy, bridge

Notes 注释

Primary and secondary stress are shown by marks above and below the line, in front of the stressed syllable. For example, in the word 'abbreviation' /əˌbriːviˈeɪʃən/, the second syllable has secondary stress and the fourth syllable has primary stress. 主重音和次重音分别以上标和下标标注于重读音节之前。例如，abbreviation /əˌbriːviˈeɪʃən/ 中，第二个音节标有次重音，第四个音节标有主重音。

We do not normally show pronunciations for compound words (words which are made up of more than one word). Pronunciations for the words that make up the compounds are usually found at their entries at other parts of the dictionary. However, compound words do have stress markers. 复合词（由1个以上单词组成的词）一般不标示发音。组成复合词的单词通常可以在本词典中相应的词条下找到其发音。但是，复合词标示了重音符号。

Aa

a /ə/, STRONG 强读 eɪ/ or 或 **an** /ən/, STRONG 强读 æn/ *article* 冠词

> **LANGUAGE HELP 语言提示**
> **An** is used before words that begin with the sound of **a, e, i, o** or **u**. *an 用于以 a、e、i、o、u 所发元音开头的单词之前。

1 used before a noun when people may not know which particular person or thing you are talking about（非特指的人或事物中的）一个：*A waiter came in with a glass of water.* 侍者端着一杯水进来了。 □ *He started eating an apple.* 他开始吃苹果。

2 used when you are talking about any person or thing of a particular type（一类人或事物中的）一个，任何一个：*You should leave it to an expert.* 你应该把它留给专家解决。 □ *Bring a sleeping bag.* 带只睡袋。

3 used instead of the number 'one' before some numbers or measurements（代替数字 one，用于某些数字或度量单位之前）一：*a hundred miles* *100 英里

4 each; for each 每；每一：*Cheryl goes to London three times a month.* 谢里尔每月去伦敦 3 次。 □ *This cheese costs £12.35 a kilo.* 这种奶酪每千克 12.35 英镑。

abandon /əˈbændən/ *verb* 动词 (**abandons, abandoning, abandoned**)

1 to leave a place, a person or a thing, especially when you should not 离弃；遗弃；抛弃：*His parents abandoned him when he was a baby.* 他还是个小宝宝时父母就遗弃了他。

▶ **abandoned** /əˈbændənd/ *adjective* 形容词：*They found an abandoned car.* 他们发现一辆弃置的汽车。

2 to stop doing an activity or a piece of work before it is finished 中止；放弃：*After several hours they abandoned their search.* 几个小时之后，他们放弃了搜索。

abbreviation /əˌbriːviˈeɪʃn/ *countable noun* 可数名词
a short form of a word or phrase 缩写词；缩略形式：*The abbreviation for 'page' is 'p.'.* *page 的缩略形式是 p。

abdomen /ˈæbdəmən/ *countable noun* 可数名词

1 the part of your body below your chest （人的）腹，腹部：*The pain in my abdomen is getting worse.* 我腹部疼得越来越厉害。

▶ **abdominal** /æbˈdɒmɪnl/ *adjective* 形容词：*the abdominal muscles* 腹肌

2 the back part of the three parts that an insect's body is divided into（昆虫的）腹

ability /əˈbɪləti/ *noun* 名词 (**abilities**)
a quality or a skill that makes it possible for you to do something 能力；才能：*Her drama teacher noticed her acting ability.* 戏剧老师发现了她的表演才能。 □ *His mother had strong musical abilities.* 他母亲非常有音乐才华。

able /ˈeɪbl/ *adjective* 形容词
be able to do something

1 to have skills or qualities that make it possible for you to do something（因具有技能或品质而）能够做某事：*A 10-year-old should be able to prepare a simple meal.* *10 岁的孩子应该会做一顿简单的饭。 □ *The company says they're able to keep prices low.* 该公司说他们能够保持低价。

2 to have enough freedom, power, time or money to do something（因有足够的自由、权力、时间、财力等而）能够做某事：*Are you able to help me?* 你能帮我吗？ □ *If I get this job, I'll be able to buy a new car.* 若是这份工作到手，我就能买辆新车了。

abnormal /æbˈnɔːml/ *adjective* 形容词
unusual, especially in a way that is a problem 反常的；异常的；怪异的：*She has an abnormal heartbeat.* 她心跳不正常。

aboard /əˈbɔːd/ *preposition* 介词
on, in or onto a ship, plane, train or bus 在（交通工具）上；上（交通工具）：*He invited us aboard his boat.* 他邀请我们上他的船。 □ *There were about 600 passengers aboard the train.* 大约有 600 名乘客上了火车。

abolish /əˈbɒlɪʃ/ *verb* 动词 (**abolishes, abolishing, abolished**)

to officially end a system or practice 废除，废止（制度或习俗）: *The committee voted on Thursday to abolish the death penalty.* 委员会周四投票决定废除死刑。
▶ **abolition** /ˌæbəˈlɪʃən/ *uncountable noun* 不可数名词: *the abolition of slavery* 奴隶制的废除

about¹ /əˈbaʊt/ *preposition* 介词
used for introducing a particular subject 关于；在…方面: *He knows a lot about architecture.* 他在建筑学方面所知甚多。 □ *He never complains about his wife.* 他从不抱怨妻子。

about² /əˈbaʊt/ *adverb* 副词
used in front of a number to show that the number is not exact 大约；左右: *The child was about eight years old.* 那孩子 8 岁左右。 □ *It got dark at about six o'clock.* *6 点左右天黑了下来。

be about to do something to be going to do something very soon 即将做某事: *I think he's about to leave.* 我觉得他要走了。

> **LANGUAGE HELP** 语言提示
> When you are talking about a number that is not exact, you can use **around** and **round** as well as **about**. 表示概数，除了 about，还可用 around 和 round。

above /əˈbʌv/ *preposition* 介词
1 over or higher than another thing 在…上方；高于: *He lifted his hands above his head.* 他双手举过头顶。 □ *Their flat is above a clothes shop.* 他们的公寓在一家服装店楼上。 □ *There was a mirror above the fireplace.* 壁炉上方有一面镜子。
2 greater than a particular level 高于，超过（某水平）: *The temperature rose to just above 40 degrees.* 温度升至 40 度出头。 □ *I don't want to spend above £5,000 on a new car.* 买新车的费用我想控制在 5,000 英镑以下。
3 in a higher position than you at work, or in a higher class than you at school（在岗位职级或学校年级上）高于: *The bosses above us make all the decisions.* 所有决定都由我们的上司们拍板。 □ *She was in the year above me at school.* 上学时她比我高一个年级。

abroad /əˈbrɔːd/ *adverb* 副词
in or to a foreign country 在国外；到国外: *Many students go abroad to work for the summer.* 很多学生暑期去国外打工。 □ *I* lived abroad for five years when I was a child. 我小时候在国外住过 5 年。

abrupt /əˈbrʌpt/ *adjective* 形容词
very sudden, often in a way that is unpleasant 突然的；意外的: *His career came to an abrupt end last year.* 他的事业在去年陡然画上了句号。
▶ **abruptly** /əˈbrʌptli/ *adverb* 副词: *The horses stopped abruptly.* 马群骤然停下。

absence /ˈæbsəns/ *noun* 名词
the fact of not being present in a particular place 不在；缺席: *Her absence from work is becoming a problem.* 她老是旷工，这成了个问题。

absent /ˈæbsənt/ *adjective* 形容词
not at a place or an event 不在的；缺席的: *Anna was absent from the meeting.* 安娜没有参会。 □ *'Was he at school yesterday?' — 'No, he was absent.'* "他昨天上学了没？" —— "没有，他缺课了。"

absent-minded /ˌæbsəntˈmaɪndɪd/ *adjective* 形容词
often forgetting things or not paying attention to what you are doing 健忘的；心不在焉的: *She looked around the room in an absent-minded dream.* 她心神恍惚地环顾房间。
▶ **absent-mindedly** /ˌæbsəntˈmaɪndɪdli/ *adverb* 副词: *Elliot absent-mindedly scratched his head.* 埃利奥特心不在焉地挠了挠头。

absolute /ˈæbsəluːt/ *adjective* 形容词
total and complete 完全的；彻底的: *No one knows anything with absolute certainty.* 没有谁对什么百分百了解。 □ *We provide French courses for absolute beginners.* 我们为零基础者开设法语课程。

absolutely /ˌæbsəˈluːtli/ *adverb* 副词
1 totally and completely 完全；彻底: *Joan is absolutely right.* 琼完全正确。 □ *I absolutely refuse to get married.* 我是彻底的不婚主义者。
2 used as a way of saying yes or of agreeing with someone strongly（强调同意或赞成）当然，对极了: *'Do you think I should call him?' — 'Absolutely.'* "你觉得我该给他打电话吗？" —— "当然。"

absorb /əbˈzɔːb/ *verb* 动词 (**absorbs, absorbing, absorbed**)
to take in a substance 吸收（物质）: *Cook the rice until it absorbs the water.* 把大米煮到吸收掉水为止。

▶ **absorbent** /əbˈzɔːbənt/ *adjective* 形容词：*A real sponge is softer and more absorbent.* 真正的海绵更软，吸水性更强。

absorbing /əbˈzɔːbɪŋ/ *adjective* 形容词 very interesting and using all your attention and energy 极具吸引力的；引人入胜的：*This is a very absorbing game.* 这游戏太有趣了。

abstract /ˈæbstrækt/ *adjective* 形容词
1 based on general ideas rather than on real things 抽象的：*The students are intelligent and good at abstract thought.* 这些学生很聪明，擅长抽象思维。
2 using shapes and patterns rather than showing people or things 抽象派的：*Mondrian's abstract paintings, with their heavy black lines and bright blocks of colour* 蒙德里安的抽象画，线条粗黑，色块鲜亮

abuse¹ /əˈbjuːs/ *noun* 名词
1 cruel treatment of a person 虐待：*The court found her guilty of child abuse.* 法庭裁定她虐待儿童。
2 *uncountable* 不可数 very rude things that people say when they are angry 辱骂；恶言：*He shouted abuse as the car drove away.* 他冲着开走的汽车破口大骂。
3 the use of something in a wrong way or for a bad purpose 滥用：*This conflict results from their abuse of power.* 这起冲突缘起于他们滥用职权。

abuse² /əˈbjuːz/ *verb* 动词 (**abuses, abusing, abused**)
to treat a person cruelly 虐待：*The film is about a woman who was abused as a child.* 这部电影讲的是一个孩童时遭受虐待的女人的故事。

academic /ˌækəˈdemɪk/ *adjective* 形容词 relating to the work done in schools, universities and colleges 学术的；学业的：*The university has a reputation for academic excellence.* 这所大学学术水平极高，享有盛名。

academy /əˈkædəmi/ *countable noun* 可数名词 (**academies**)
a word that is sometimes used in the names of schools 学院，专科院校（有时用于学校名称）：*She's a second-year student at the Royal Academy of Music.* 她是英国皇家音乐学院二年级的学生。

accelerate /ækˈseləreɪt/ *verb* 动词 (**accelerates, accelerating, accelerated**)
1 to get faster 变快：*Her heartbeat accelerated when she saw him in the crowd.* 她在人群中看到他后，心跳开始加速。
2 to go faster（车辆等）加速行进：*Suddenly the car accelerated.* 汽车突然加速。

accelerator /ækˈseləreɪtə/ *countable noun* 可数名词
the part in a car that you press with your foot to make the car go faster（汽车的）加速踏板，油门踏板：*He took his foot off the accelerator.* 他收脚松开油门踏板。

accent /ˈæksənt/ *countable noun* 可数名词
1 the particular way that someone pronounces words, which shows where the person comes from 口音；腔调：*He had an Irish accent.* 他有爱尔兰口音。
2 a mark written above a letter to show how it is pronounced（字母上方的）音质符号：*The word 'café' has an accent on the 'e'.* 单词 café 中字母 e 上有音质符号。

accept /ækˈsept/ *verb* 动词 (**accepts, accepting, accepted**)
1 to say yes to something that someone offers you, or to agree to take or do something 接受；同意：*She accepted his offer of marriage.* 她接受了他的求婚。 □ *Doctors may not accept gifts.* 医生不可收受礼品。
▶ **acceptance** /ækˈseptəns/ *uncountable noun* 不可数名词：*We listened to his acceptance speech for the Nobel Peace Prize.* 我们听了他领取诺贝尔和平奖时的获奖感言。
2 to recognize that an unpleasant fact or situation cannot be changed 容忍；忍受：*People often accept noise as part of city life.* 人们常默认噪音为城市生活的一部分。
3 to recognize that you are responsible for something 承担，承认（责任）：*Accept the fact that the accident was your fault!* 这起事故责任在你，接受这个事实吧！

acceptable /ækˈseptəbəl/ *adjective* 形容词
1 considered to be normal by most people（大多数人）认同的，认可的：*Asking people for money is not acceptable behaviour.* 向人要钱这种行为不为人们认同。
▶ **acceptably** /ækˈseptəbli/ *adverb* 副词：*They try to teach children to behave acceptably.* 他们尽力教会孩子举止得体。
2 good enough for a particular purpose 尚可的；还可以的：*There was one restaurant that looked acceptable.* 有一家饭店看起来还可以。

access¹ /ˈækses/ *uncountable noun* 不可数名词
1 permission to go into a particular place 进入权；进入许可：*The general public does not have access to the White House.* 公众无权进入白宫。
2 when you are able or allowed to see or use information or equipment（信息、设备的）使用权，享用权：*Patients have access to their medical records.* 病人有权查看病例。

access² /ˈækses/ *verb* 动词 (**accesses, accessing, accessed**)
to find information on a computer 访问，存取（计算机信息）：*Parents can see which sites their children have accessed.* 家长能看到自己的孩子都上过哪些网站。

accessible /əkˈsesɪbəl/ *adjective* 形容词
easy for people to reach or enter 易到达的；易进入的：*The city centre is easily accessible to the general public.* 公众可便捷地进入市中心。□ *Most of the bedrooms and bathrooms are accessible for wheelchairs.* 这些卧室和浴室大多便于轮椅进入。

accessory /əkˈsesəri/ *countable noun* 可数名词 (**accessories**)
a small thing such as a belt or a scarf that you wear with your clothes（衣服的）配饰：*We shopped for handbags, scarves and other accessories.* 我们去买手提包、围巾及其他配饰。

accident /ˈæksɪdənt/ *countable noun* 可数名词
1 when a vehicle hits something and causes injury or damage 交通事故；车祸：*He broke his right leg in a motorbike accident.* 他在一起摩托车事故中右腿骨折。
2 when something bad happens to a person by chance, sometimes causing injury or death 意外事件；事故：*The boy was injured in an accident at a swimming pool.* 男孩在一次泳池事故中受伤。
by accident by chance 偶然；意外地：*We met by accident at a party in Los Angeles.* 我们在洛杉矶的一个派对上偶遇。

accidental /ˌæksɪˈdentəl/ *adjective* 形容词
happening by chance or as the result of an accident 意外的；偶然的：*The police said that the fire was accidental.* 警察称火灾是一起意外。
▶ **accidentally** /ˌæksɪˈdentəli/ *adverb* 副词：*They accidentally removed the names from the computer.* 他们不慎将电脑里的名字删掉了。

accommodation /əˌkɒməˈdeɪʃən/ *uncountable noun* 不可数名词
buildings or rooms where people live or stay 住处；住所：*They always pay extra for luxury accommodation.* 他们总是多付钱住奢华的房间。

accompany /əˈkʌmpəni/ *verb* 动词 (**accompanies, accompanying, accompanied**)
1 to go somewhere with someone (*formal* 正式) 陪伴；陪同：*Ken agreed to accompany me on a trip to Africa.* 肯答应陪我去非洲旅行。
2 to play one part of a piece of music while a singer or a musician sings or plays the main tune 为（歌曲或乐曲）伴奏：*Her singing teacher accompanied her on the piano.* 她的声乐老师用钢琴为她伴奏。

accomplish /əˈkʌmplɪʃ/ *verb* 动词 (**accomplishes, accomplishing, accomplished**)
to succeed in doing something 完成；达成；实现：*If we all work together, I think we can accomplish our goal.* 只要大家齐心协力，我想我们就能实现目标。

accomplishment /əˈkʌmplɪʃmənt/ *countable noun* 可数名词
something unusual or special that you have made or achieved 成就；成绩：*This book is an amazing accomplishment.* 这本书成就斐然。

accord /əˈkɔːd/ *noun* 名词
of your own accord because you want to, and not because someone has asked you 自愿地；主动地：*He left his job of his own accord.* 他主动离职。

acˈcording to *preposition* 介词
1 used when you are saying where some information comes from 据⋯⋯所说：*They drove away in a white van, according to police reports.* 据警方通报，他们驾驶一辆白色厢式汽车离开。
2 used when you are saying which way something should be done 依据；按照：*They played the game according to the British rules.* 他们按照英国规则比赛。
according to plan happening in the way that you intended 按照计划：*Everything is going according to plan.* 一切都按计划进行。

accordion /əˈkɔːdiən/ *countable noun* 可数名词
a musical instrument in the shape of a box, which you hold in your hands. You play it by pressing keys and buttons on the side, while moving the two ends in and out. 手风琴

accordion 手风琴

account[1] /əˈkaʊnt/ *countable noun* 可数名词
1 an arrangement you have with a bank. The bank looks after your money, and you can take some out when you need it.（银行）账户: *I have £3,000 in my bank account.* 我银行账户上有 3,000 英镑。
2 an arrangement you have with a company to use a service they provide（公司提供服务的）账户: *an email account* 电子邮件账户
3 a report of something that has happened 陈述；记述；描述: *He gave the police a detailed account of the events.* 他向警方详细描述了事件经过。
take something into account or **take account of something** to consider something when you are trying to make a decision 考虑到某事物；将某事物考虑进去: *You have to take people's feelings into account.* 你得考虑大家的感受。

account[2] /əˈkaʊnt/ *verb* 动词 (accounts, accounting, accounted)
account for something to explain something or give the reason for it 解释某事物；说明某事物: *How do you account for these differences?* 这些差异你怎么解释？

accountant /əˈkaʊntənt/ *countable noun* 可数名词
a person whose job is to keep financial accounts 会计；会计师

accounts /əˈkaʊnts/ *plural noun* 复数名词
records of all the money that a person or a business receives and spends 账；账目: *He kept detailed accounts of all the money he spent.* 他把每一笔开销都详细地记了账。

accurate /ˈækjʊrət/ *adjective* 形容词
1 correct 精确的；准确的: *I can't give an accurate description of the man because it was too dark.* 我不能很准确地描述那个人的外貌特征，因为当时天太黑了。
▶ **accuracy** /ˈækjʊrəsi/ *uncountable noun* 不可数名词: *Don't trust the accuracy of weather reports.* 天气预报靠不住。
▶ **accurately** /ˈækjʊrətli/ *adverb* 副词: *He described it quite accurately.* 他描述得相当精准。
2 able to work without making a mistake 精准的: *The car's steering is accurate, and the brakes are powerful.* 这辆车转向精准，制动力强。
▶ **accuracy** /ˈækjʊrəsi/ *uncountable noun* 不可数名词: *Your accuracy will improve with practice.* 多加练习，准确性就会提高。
▶ **accurately** /ˈækjʊrətli/ *adverb* 副词: *He hit the golf ball powerfully and accurately.* 他这一杆高尔夫球击得又狠又准。

accuse /əˈkjuːz/ *verb* 动词 (accuses, accusing, accused)
to say that someone did something wrong or dishonest 指责；责备: *They accused her of lying.* 他们指责她说谎。

ache /eɪk/ *verb* 动词 (aches, aching, ached)
to feel a steady pain in a part of your body（身体部位）疼痛: *Her head was hurting and she ached all over (= in every part of her body).* 她不光头疼，浑身都疼。 □ *My leg still aches when I stand for a long time.* 我的腿站久了还是会疼。 ● **ache** *countable noun* 可数名词: *A hot bath will take away all your aches and pains.* 洗个热水澡，周身的酸痛会一扫而空。

achieve /əˈtʃiːv/ *verb* 动词 (achieves, achieving, achieved)
to succeed in doing something, usually after a lot of effort（通常经过努力）实现，达到，获得: *He worked hard to achieve his goals.* 他努力工作以实现自己的目标。

achievement /əˈtʃiːvmənt/ *countable noun* 可数名词
something that you have succeeded in doing, especially after a lot of effort 成就；成绩: *Being chosen for the team was a great achievement.* 能被这个队选上很了不起。

acid /ˈæsɪd/ *noun* 名词
a chemical, usually a liquid, that can burn your skin and cause damage to other substances 酸: *As you can see, the acid damaged the metal bowl.* 如你所见，酸把金属碗腐蚀坏了。

acid rain *uncountable noun* 不可数名词
rain that contains acid that can harm the

acknowledge – action

environment. The acid comes from pollution in the air. 酸雨。

acknowledge /ækˈnɒlɪdʒ/ *verb* 动词 (**acknowledges, acknowledging, acknowledged**)
to agree that something is true or that it exists (*formal* 正式) 承认: *He acknowledged that he was wrong.* 他承认自己错了。□ *At last, the government has acknowledged the problem.* 最终，政府承认了这一问题。

acknowledgments /ækˈnɒlɪdʒmənts/ also 亦作 **acknowledgements** *plural noun* 复数名词
in a book, the part in which the writer thanks all the people who have helped him or her (书的) 致谢，鸣谢: *There are two pages of acknowledgments at the beginning of the book.* 这本书的开头有两页鸣谢。

acquaintance /əˈkweɪntəns/ *countable noun* 可数名词
someone you have met, but who you don't know well 认识的人；泛泛之交: *He spoke to the owner of the bookshop, who was an old acquaintance of his.* 他和书店老板是旧相识，两人聊了几句。

acquire /əˈkwaɪə/ *verb* 动词 (**acquires, acquiring, acquired**)
1 to get or buy something (*formal* 正式) 获得；购得: *The club wants to acquire new sports equipment.* 俱乐部欲购入一些新的体育器材。
2 to learn or develop something 学到；习得；养成: *Students on this programme will acquire a wide range of skills.* 修习这门课程的学生将学到多种技能。

acre /ˈeɪkə/ *countable noun* 可数名词
a unit for measuring an area of land 英亩 (土地面积单位): *William farms a hundred acres of land in Wales.* 威廉在威尔士耕种着 100 英亩土地。

across /əˈkrɒs/ *preposition* 介词
1 from one side of something to the other side of it 穿过；从…的一边到另一边: *She walked across the floor and sat down.* 她穿过地板坐下。□ *He watched Karl run across the street.* 他看着卡尔跑过街道。
● **across** *adverb* 副词: *Richard stood up and walked across to the window.* 理查德站起身走到窗边。
2 going from one side of something to the other side of it 横跨；跨过: *The bridge across the river was closed.* 过河的桥关闭了。□ *He wrote his name across the cheque.* 他在支票上签了名。

acrylic /əˈkrɪlɪk/ *adjective* 形容词
used for describing a type of artist's paint that dries very quickly 丙烯颜料的: *Most people prefer acrylic paint because it dries faster.* 大多数人偏爱丙烯颜料，因为它干得更快。

acrylics /əˈkrɪlɪks/ *plural noun* 复数名词
acrylic paints 丙烯颜料: *This book is a great introduction to painting with acrylics.* 这本书是介绍丙烯颜料作画的入门书，非常棒。

act¹ /ækt/ *verb* 动词 (**acts, acting, acted**)
1 to do something for a particular purpose 行动；做事: *The police acted to stop the fight.* 警方采取行动制止这场争斗。
2 to behave in a particular way 表现；举止: *The youths were acting suspiciously.* 这几个年轻人形迹可疑。□ *He acts as if I'm not there.* 他表现得就好像我不存在一样。
3 to have a part in a play or a film 表演；扮演角色: *He acted in many films.* 他出演过很多电影。

act² /ækt/ *countable noun* 可数名词
1 a single thing that someone does (*formal* 正式) 行为；行动: *I will never forget his act of kindness.* 我永远不会忘记他的善举。□ *This was an appalling act of violence.* 这一暴行令人震惊。
2 a law passed by the government 法案；法令: *The organization was set up by an Act of Congress.* 这一机构是依据一项国会法案设立的。
3 one of the main parts that a play is divided into (戏剧的) 幕: *Act two has a really funny scene.* 第二幕里有一场戏非常搞笑。

acting /ˈæktɪŋ/ *uncountable noun* 不可数名词
the activity or profession of performing in plays or films 表演；演艺业: *I'd like to do some acting some day.* 有朝一日我要从事表演。

action /ˈækʃən/ *noun* 名词
1 *uncountable* 不可数 when you do something for a particular purpose 行动；措施: *The government is taking emergency action.* 政府将采取紧急措施。
2 *countable* 可数 something that you do

on a particular occasion 行为；举动：*Peter could not explain his actions.* 彼得无法对自己的行为作出解释。

active[1] /ˈæktɪv/ *adjective* 形容词
moving around a lot; doing a lot of different things 忙碌的；活跃的：*We've got three very active little kids.* 我们有 3 个非常活泼的小孩。□ *As you get older, it's important to keep active.* 随着年岁增长，要注意保持活力。

active[2] /ˈæktɪv/ *singular noun* 单数名词
in grammar, the form of a verb that you use to show that the subject performs the action. For example, in 'I saw him', the verb **see** is in the active. Compare with **passive**.（动语法）主动式（比较 passive）

activity /ækˈtɪvɪti/ *noun* 名词 (**activities**)
1 *uncountable* 不可数 when people are doing things and there is a lot happening 活跃；热闹；活动：*Once people stop spending, economic activity slows down.* 一旦人们停止消费，经济活动就会放缓。
2 *countable* 可数 something that you spend time doing 活动；行动：*At our hotel, there were lots of activities for small children.* 我们酒店有很多针对小孩的活动。

actor /ˈæktə/ *countable noun* 可数名词
someone whose job is acting in plays or films 演员：*His father was an actor.* 他父亲是个演员。
→ Look at picture on P16 参见彩插第 16 页

actress /ˈæktrəs/ *countable noun* 可数名词 (**actresses**)
a woman whose job is acting in plays or films 女演员：*She's a really good actress.* 她是个非常好的演员。
→ Look at picture on P16 参见彩插第 16 页

actual /ˈæktʃuəl/ *adjective* 形容词
real, exact or genuine 真实的；实际的：*The stories in this book are based on actual people.* 这本书里的故事都是基于真实人物。

LANGUAGE HELP 语言提示
Actual is **not** used for talking about something that is happening now. For this meaning, use **current** or **present**. 表示当前正在发生的事，不用 actual，要用 current 或 present。

actually /ˈæktʃuəli/ *adverb* 副词
really; in fact 事实上；实际上：*People call me Will, but I'm actually called William.* 人们都叫我威尔，实际上我叫威廉。

LANGUAGE HELP 语言提示
Actually is **not** used for talking about something that is happening now. For this meaning, use **currently** or **now**. 表示当前正在发生的事，不用 actually，要用 currently 或 now。

acute /əˈkjuːt/ *adjective* 形容词
very severe or serious 剧烈的；严重的：*He was in acute pain.* 他疼得厉害。

ˌacute ˈaccent *countable noun* 可数名词
a symbol that you put over vowels (= the letters a, e, i, o and u) in some languages to show how to pronounce that vowel. For example, there is an acute accent over the letter 'e' in the French word 'café'. 尖音符

ˌacute ˈangle *countable noun* 可数名词
an angle of less than 90° 锐角

ad /æd/ *countable noun* 可数名词
an advertisement (*informal* 非正式) 广告：*It costs £175 to place an ad in the newspaper for 30 days.* 在那份报纸上登 30 天广告的费用为 175 英镑。

AD /ˌeɪ ˈdiː/ *also* 亦作 **A.D.**
used in dates to show the number of years that have passed since the year in which Jesus Christ was born. Compare with **BC**. 公元（比较 BC）：*The church was built in 600 AD.* 这座教堂建于公元 600 年。

adapt /əˈdæpt/ *verb* 动词 (**adapts, adapting, adapted**)
1 to change your ideas or behaviour in order to deal with a new situation 适应：*The world will be different in the future, and we will have to adapt to the change.* 未来的世界会变得不一样，我们必须适应这一变化。
2 to change something so that you can use it in a different way 使适应；改造：*They adapted the library for use as an office.* 他们将图书馆改造成办公室。

adaptable /əˈdæptəbəl/ *adjective* 形容词
able to deal with new situations 有适应能力的；适应性强的：*Dogs and cats are easily adaptable to new homes.* 猫狗很容易适应新家。

add /æd/ *verb* 动词 (**adds, adding, added**)
1 to put one thing with another thing 加入；添加：*Add the grated cheese to the sauce.* 把干酪丝加到调味汁里。
2 to calculate the total of various numbers or amounts 加；把…相加：*Add all the*

numbers together, and divide by three. 把所有数字相加后除以 3。
3 to say something more 补充说: 'He's very angry,' Mr Smith added. "他气极了。" 史密斯先生补充道。
add something up to find the total of various numbers or amounts 把（数字或数量）相加: *Add up the number of hours you spent on the task.* 把你花在这项任务上的时间加起来。
add up to something to form a total 总计为…；合计达…: *Altogether, the three bills add up to £2,456.* 这 3 张账单总额达 2,456 英镑。

addict /ˈædɪkt/ *countable noun* 可数名词
1 someone who cannot stop doing something harmful or dangerous, such as using drugs 瘾君子；成瘾者: *His girlfriend is a former drug addict.* 他女朋友曾吸毒成瘾。
2 someone who likes a particular activity very much (*informal* 非正式) (对…)入迷的人: *She is a TV addict.* 她是个电视迷。

addicted /əˈdɪktɪd/ *adjective* 形容词
unable to stop taking or doing something that is harmful to you 上瘾的；成瘾的: *Many of the women are addicted to heroin.* 这些女人中有很多吸食海洛因成瘾。

addiction /əˈdɪkʃən/ *noun* 名词
1 when someone is unable to stop taking drugs, alcohol or some other harmful substance 瘾: *She helped him fight his drug addiction.* 她帮助他戒毒。
2 a strong need to do a particular activity for as much time as possible 入迷；嗜好: *We discussed our children's addiction to computer games.* 我们讨论了孩子们沉迷于电脑游戏的问题。

addition /əˈdɪʃən/ *uncountable noun* 不可数名词
the process of calculating the total of two or more numbers 加；加法: *She can count to 100, and do simple addition problems.* 她能数到 100，会做简单的加法。
in addition/in addition to something used when you want to mention another thing relating to the subject you are discussing 此外（还）/除…以外（还）: *In addition to meals, drinks will be provided.* 除膳食外，还将提供饮料。

address[1] /əˈdres/ *countable noun* 可数名词 (**addresses**)
1 the number of the building, the name of the street, and the town or city where you live or work 住址；地址: *'What's your address?' — 'It's 24 Cherry Road, Cambridge, CB1 5AW.'* "您的地址是哪里？"——"剑桥切里路 24 号，邮编 CB1 5AW。"
2 the location of a website on the Internet, for example, http://www.collinsdictionary.com 网址: *Our website address is at the bottom of this page.* 我们的网址在页面底端。

address[2] /əˈdres/ *verb* 动词 (**addresses, addressing, addressed**)
1 to write a person's name and address on a letter 在（信件）上写姓名和地址: *One of the letters was addressed to her.* 其中一封信是写给她的。
2 to speak to a group of people formally 对…讲话；向…发表演说: *He addressed the crowd of 17,000 people.* 他向 17,000 人发表演说。

aˈddress book *countable noun* 可数名词
1 a book in which you write people's names and addresses 通讯录；通讯簿
2 a computer program that you use to record people's email addresses and telephone numbers（计算机）通讯录

adequate /ˈædɪkwət/ *adjective* 形容词
having enough of something; good enough 足够的；合格的: *One in four people worldwide do not have adequate homes.* 全世界有四分之一的人没有足够的住房。 □ *The food in the hotel was adequate, but plain.* 旅馆饭菜充足，但味道一般。

adhesive /ædˈhiːsɪv/ *noun* 名词
a substance used for making things stick together 黏合剂: *Attach the mirror to the wall with a strong adhesive.* 用强力胶将镜子固定到墙上。

adjective /ˈædʒɪktɪv/ *countable noun* 可数名词
a word such as 'big' or 'beautiful' that describes a person or thing. Adjectives usually come before nouns or after verbs like 'be' and 'feel'. 形容词

adjust /əˈdʒʌst/ *verb* 动词 (**adjusts, adjusting, adjusted**)
to make a small change to something 调整；调节: *The company adjusts gas prices once a year.* 这家公司每年调整一次燃气价格。 □ *You can adjust the height of the table.* 桌子高度可以调节。

administration /ædˌmɪnɪˈstreɪʃən/ *noun* 名词
1 *uncountable* 不可数 the job of managing a business or an organization 管理；经营：*A private company took over the administration of the local jail.* 一家私营公司接管了当地监狱的管理工作。
2 *countable* 可数 (*American* 美国英语) the government of a country（国家的）政府：*Three officials in the administration have resigned.* 政府里已有 3 名官员辞职。

administrative /ædˈmɪnɪstrətɪv/ *adjective* 形容词
relating to the management of a business or an organization 管理的；行政的：*Administrative costs were high.* 管理成本很高。

administrator /ædˈmɪnɪstreɪtə/ *countable noun* 可数名词
a person whose job is to help manage a business or an organization 管理者；经营者：*Tom has worked as a university administrator for 20 years.* 汤姆已从事大学管理工作 20 年了。

admiration /ˌædmɪˈreɪʃən/ *uncountable noun* 不可数名词
a strong feeling of liking and respect 钦佩；赞赏；仰慕：*I have great admiration for him.* 我非常钦佩他。

admire /ədˈmaɪə/ *verb* 动词 (**admires, admiring, admired**)
to like and respect someone or something very much 钦佩；赞赏；仰慕：*I admired her when I first met her.* 我第一次见到她时就很钦佩她。
▶ **admirer** /ədˈmaɪərə/ *countable noun* 可数名词：*He was an admirer of her paintings.* 他推崇她的画作。

admission /ædˈmɪʃən/ *noun* 名词
1 *uncountable* 不可数 permission to enter a place 进入许可：*One man was refused admission to the restaurant.* 这家餐馆拒绝一名男子进入。
2 when you admit that you have done something wrong（对过错的）承认，供认：*By the footballer's own admission, he is not playing well this season.* 这名足球队员自己承认本赛季表现欠佳。
3 *uncountable* 不可数 the amount of money that you pay to enter a museum, park or other place 入场费；门票费：*Gates open at 10.30 a.m. and admission is free.* 上午 10 点 30 分开门，免费入场。

admit /ædˈmɪt/ *verb* 动词 (**admits, admitting, admitted**)
1 to agree that you have done something wrong 承认，供认（过错）：*I am willing to admit that I made a mistake.* 我愿意承认我犯了错。
2 to allow someone to enter a place or an organization 准许…进入（或加入）；招收：*She was admitted to law school.* 她被法学院录取。□ *Security officers refused to admit him to the building.* 保安人员拒绝让他进入大楼。

adolescent /ˌædəˈlesənt/ *adjective* 形容词
relating to young people who are no longer children but who have not yet become adults 青少年的；青春期的：*Her music is popular with adolescent girls.* 她的音乐很受青春期少女欢迎。● **adolescent** *countable noun* 可数名词：*Adolescents don't like being treated as children.* 青少年不愿意被当孩子对待。
▶ **adolescence** /ˌædəˈlesəns/ *uncountable noun* 不可数名词：*Adolescence is often a difficult period for young people.* 对于年轻人来说，青春期常是一个问题重重的时期。

adopt /əˈdɒpt/ *verb* 动词 (**adopts, adopting, adopted**)
1 to begin to behave or live in a new way 采用；采纳；采取：*You need to adopt a more positive attitude.* 你需要态度更积极些。□ *Try to adopt a healthy lifestyle.* 生活方式要尽量健康。
2 to take someone else's child into your own family and make them legally your son or daughter 收养；领养：*There are hundreds of people who want to adopt a child.* 有数百人想领养孩子。
▶ **adoption** /əˈdɒpʃən/ *uncountable noun* 不可数名词：*They gave their babies up for adoption.* 他们放弃了自己的宝宝，让别人领养。

adore /əˈdɔː/ *verb* 动词 (**adores, adoring, adored**)
1 to feel strong love and admiration for someone 深爱，爱慕（某人）：*She adored her parents and would do anything to please them.* 她深爱着父母，为让他们高兴她愿意做任何事。
2 to like something very much (*informal* 非正式) 喜爱，热爱（某事）：*Richard adores university life.* 理查德热爱大学生活。

adult /ˈædʌlt/ *countable noun* 可数名词
a fully grown person or animal 成年人；成

年动物：Tickets cost £20 for adults and £10 for children. 成人票价 20 英镑，儿童 10 英镑。● **adult** *adjective* 形容词：*I am the mother of two adult sons.* 我是两个儿子的母亲，他们都已成年。

adult 成年人　　child 儿童

advance¹ /æd'vɑːns/ *verb* 动词 (**advances, advancing, advanced**)
1 to move forward, often in order to attack someone（常指为了进攻而）前进，推进：*Soldiers are advancing towards the capital.* 士兵向首都推进。
2 to make progress, especially in your knowledge of something（尤指知识）发展，进步：*Science has advanced greatly in the last 100 years.* 在过去 100 年里，科学取得了长足进步。

advance² /æd'vɑːns/ *noun* 名词
1 a movement forward, usually as part of a military operation（通常指军事行动中的）前进，推进：*Hitler's army began its advance on Moscow in June 1941.* 1941 年 6 月，希特勒的军队开始向莫斯科推进。
2 progress in understanding a subject or an activity 进步；进展：*There have been many advances in medicine and public health.* 医学和公共卫生方面已有许多进展。
in advance before a particular date or event 提前；事先：*We bought our tickets for the show in advance.* 我们提前买了演出门票。

advanced /æd'vɑːnst/ *adjective* 形容词
1 modern 先进的；现代化的：*This is one of the most advanced phones available.* 这是目前最先进的电话之一。
2 relating to people who are very good at something 高级程度的；高等的：*a dictionary for advanced learners of English* 适合高级英语学习者的词典

advantage /æd'vɑːntɪdʒ/ *countable noun* 可数名词
1 something that puts you in a better position than other people 有利条件；优势：*Being small gives our company an advantage.* 规模小给我们公司带来了优势。
2 a way in which one thing is better than another 优点；好处：*The advantage of home-grown vegetables is their great flavour.* 自种蔬菜的优点是味道好。
take advantage of someone to unfairly get what you want from someone, especially when they are being kind to you 利用某人；占某人便宜：*She took advantage of him — borrowing money and not paying it back.* 她占他的便宜——借他的钱不还。
take advantage of something to make good use of something while you can 利用某事物：*People are taking advantage of lower prices.* 人们趁着降价买进。

adventure /æd'ventʃə/ *noun* 名词
an experience that is unusual, exciting and perhaps dangerous 冒险；探险：*I'm planning a new adventure in Alaska.* 我正计划在阿拉斯加进行一次新的探险。

adverb /'ædvɜːb/ *countable noun* 可数名词
a word such as 'slowly', 'now', 'very' or 'happily' that adds information about an action, event or situation 副词

advert /'ædvɜːt/ *countable noun* 可数名词
information that tells you about something such as a product, an event or a job (*informal* 非正式) 广告：*Have you seen that new advert for Pepsi?* 你看到百事可乐那则新广告了吗？

advertise /'ædvətaɪz/ *verb* 动词 (**advertises, advertising, advertised**)
to tell people about something in newspapers, on television, on signs, or on the Internet 为…做广告；宣传：*They are advertising houses for sale in this magazine.* 他们在这本杂志上为待售的房子刊登广告。 □ *The company advertises on radio stations.* 这家公司在电台上做广告。

advertisement /æd'vɜːtɪsmənt/ *countable noun* 可数名词
information that tells you about something such as a product, an event, or a job (*formal* 正式) 广告；启事：*They saw an advertisement for a job on a farm.* 他们看到一家农场的招聘广告。 □ *an advertisement for a new film* 新电影的广告

advertising /ˈædvətaɪzɪŋ/ *uncountable noun* 不可数名词
the business of creating information that tells people about a product or an event 广告活动；广告业：*I work in advertising.* 我从事广告业。

advice /ædˈvaɪs/ *uncountable noun* 不可数名词
what you say to someone when you are telling them what you think they should do 建议；忠告：*Take my advice and stay away from him!* 听我的，离他远远的！
▫ *I'd like to ask you for some advice.* 我想征求下你的意见。

> **LANGUAGE HELP** 语言提示
> **Advice** is an uncountable noun. You can ask someone for **a piece of advice** or **some advice**. *advice 是不可数名词，可以说 a piece of advice（一条建议）或 some advice（一些建议）。

advise /ædˈvaɪz/ *verb* 动词 (**advises, advising, advised**)
to tell someone what you think they should do 建议；忠告：*Passengers are advised to check in two hours before their flight.* 乘客最好在起飞前两个小时值机。
▫ *His lawyers advised him to plead guilty.* 律师建议他认罪。

adviser /ædˈvaɪzə/ *also* 亦作 **advisor** *countable noun* 可数名词
an expert whose job is to give advice 顾问：*You should ask your financial adviser for advice.* 你应向财务顾问征求意见。

aerial /ˈeəriəl/ *countable noun* 可数名词 (*American* 美国英语：**antenna**)
a piece of equipment that receives television or radio signals 天线

aerobics /eəˈrəʊbɪks/ *uncountable noun* 不可数名词
a form of exercise that makes your heart and lungs stronger 有氧运动；健身操：*I'd like to join an aerobics class to improve my fitness.* 我想参加有氧运动训练班来增强体质。

aeroplane /ˈeərəpleɪn/ *countable noun* 可数名词 (*American* 美国英语：**airplane**)
→ see 见 **plane**

aerosol /ˈeərəsɒl/ *countable noun* 可数名词
a metal container with liquid in it. When you press a button, the liquid comes out strongly in a lot of very small drops. 喷雾器：*an aerosol spray can* 喷雾罐

aesthetic /iːsˈθetɪk/ *adjective* 形容词
relating to beauty and art 审美的；美学的：*We chose the flowers for their aesthetic value.* 我们选这些花是看中它们的审美价值。
▶ **aesthetically** /iːsˈθetɪkli/ *adverb* 副词：*We want our products to be aesthetically pleasing.* 我们希望我们的产品给人美的享受。

affair /əˈfeə/ *noun* 名词
1 *singular* 单数 an event or a group of related events 事情；事件：*She has handled the whole affair badly.* 整个事件她处理得都不好。▫ *Our wedding was a simple affair.* 我们的婚礼很简单。
2 *countable* 可数 a sexual relationship between two people who are not married to each other 私情；风流韵事：*He was having an affair with the woman next door.* 他和隔壁女人有私情。

affairs /əˈfeəz/ *plural noun* 复数名词
1 things in your life that you consider to be private 私事；个人事务：*Why are we so interested in the private affairs of famous people?* 我们为何对名人的私事那么感兴趣？
2 important events and situations 重要事务；大事：*She is an expert on international affairs.* 她是国际事务专家。

affect /əˈfekt/ *verb* 动词 (**affects, affecting, affected**)
to cause someone or something to change in some way 影响：*This problem affects all of us.* 这一问题对我们大家都有影响。
▫ *This area was badly affected by the earthquake.* 这一地区受地震影响严重。

affection /əˈfekʃən/ *uncountable noun* 不可数名词
the feeling of loving or liking someone a lot 爱；喜爱：*She thought of him with affection.* 她深情地想起了他。

affectionate /əˈfekʃənət/ *adjective* 形容词
showing that you love or like someone very much 满怀柔情的；充满爱意的：*She's very affectionate, and she's always hugging the kids.* 她满怀爱意，总是给孩子们拥抱。
▶ **affectionately** /əˈfekʃənətli/ *adverb* 副词：*He looked affectionately at his niece.* 他慈爱地看着外甥女。

afford /əˈfɔːd/ *verb* 动词 (**affords, affording, afforded**)
can afford something to have enough money to pay for something 买得起某物；

负担得起某物: *Some people can't even afford a new TV.* 有些人连一台新电视都买不起。

afloat /əˈfləʊt/ *adverb* 副词
floating 漂浮着: *They tried to keep the ship afloat.* 他们努力让船浮在水面上。

afraid /əˈfreɪd/ *adjective* 形容词
1 worried that something unpleasant may happen 担心的；忧虑的: *I was afraid that nobody would believe me.* 我担心没有人会相信我。
2 frightened because you think that something very unpleasant is going to happen to you 害怕的；恐惧的: *I was afraid of the other boys.* 我害怕其他男孩子。□ *Don't be afraid to ask for help.* 不要害怕求助。

after /ˈɑːftə/ *preposition* 介词
1 happening later than a particular date or event 在（日期或事件）之后: *He died after a long illness.* 他久病后死去。□ *After breakfast, Amy took a taxi to the station.* 早饭后，埃米打车去车站。● **after** *conjunction* 连词: *The phone rang two seconds after we arrived.* 我们到两秒钟电话就响了。
2 following or chasing someone 在…后面；跟随: *Why don't you go after him? He's your son.* 你为什么不跟着他？他是你儿子。

afternoon /ˌɑːftəˈnuːn/ *noun* 名词
the part of each day that begins at lunchtime and ends at about six o'clock 下午: *He's arriving in the afternoon.* 他今天下午到。□ *He stayed in his room all afternoon.* 他整个下午都待在房间里。

aftershave /ˈɑːftəˌʃeɪv/ *uncountable noun* 不可数名词
a liquid with a pleasant smell that men put on their faces after shaving 须后水（男子剃须后抹的润肤液）

afterwards /ˈɑːftəwədz/ *adverb* 副词
in the time after a particular event or time that you have already mentioned 后来；以后: *Shortly afterwards, the police arrived.* 之后不久，警察就来了。

again /əˈɡen, əˈɡeɪn/ *adverb* 副词
1 one more time 再一次；又一次: *He kissed her again.* 他再一次吻了她。□ *Again there was a short silence.* 又是一阵短暂的沉寂。
2 used for saying that something is now in the same state it was in before 又（回到）前的状态）: *He opened his case, took out a folder, then closed it again.* 他打开箱子，取出一个文件夹，然后又把箱子合上了。

against /əˈɡenst, əˈɡeɪnst/ *preposition* 介词
1 touching someone or something 靠；倚；碰: *She leaned against him.* 她靠着他。□ *The rain was beating against the window panes.* 雨水敲打着窗玻璃。
2 used for showing that you think that something is wrong or bad 反对: *He was against the war.* 他反对战争。● **against** *adverb* 副词: *66 people voted in favour of the decision and 34 voted against.* *66人赞成这一决议，34人反对。
3 on the other side in a sports game or a competition 与…对阵；与…竞争: *This is the first of two games against Liverpool.* 这是与利物浦队两场比赛中的第一场。
4 used for talking about who or what you are trying to stop 阻止；预防: *The security forces used violence against opponents of the government.* 安全部队用武力镇压政府反对者。□ *Vitamin E protects against heart disease.* 维生素E可预防心脏疾病。
5 in opposition to 违背；违抗: *She left the hospital against the doctors' advice.* 她不顾医嘱出院了。
against the law/rules not according to a law or a rule 违法／违反规则: *It is against the law to use your mobile phone while you are driving.* 开车时使用手机违法。

age[1] /eɪdʒ/ *noun* 名词
1 the number of years that you have lived 年龄；年纪: *Diana left school at the age of 16.* 戴安娜16岁离校。
2 *uncountable* 不可数 the state of being old 老年: *He refuses to let age slow him down.* 他不愿年纪大了就失去活力。
3 *countable* 可数 a period in history 时代；时期: *the age of silent films* 无声电影时期

age[2] /eɪdʒ/ *verb* 动词 (**ages, aging** or 或 **ageing, aged**)
1 to cause someone to look much older than before 使变老；使显老: *Worry has aged him.* 忧虑使他变老。
2 to start to look older than before 变老: *She has aged dramatically in recent months.* 近几个月她老得很厉害。

aged /eɪdʒd/ *adjective* 形容词
of a particular age *…岁的: *They have two children: Julia, aged 8, and Jackie, aged 10.* 他们有两个孩子：朱莉娅8岁，杰基10岁。

agency /ˈeɪdʒənsi/ *countable noun* 可数名词 (**agencies**)
a business that provides a service 服务机构；代理机构：*I work in an advertising agency.* 我在一家广告公司上班。

agenda /əˈdʒendə/ *countable noun* 可数名词
1 a set of things that you want to do 待办事项；计划：*They support the president's education agenda.* 他们支持总统的教育计划。
2 a list of things to be discussed at a meeting 议程；议事日程：*I'll add it to the agenda for Monday's meeting.* 我会把这一条加进周一的会议议程。

agent /ˈeɪdʒənt/ *countable noun* 可数名词
a person whose job is to do business for another person or company 代理商；中介：*I am buying direct, not through an agent.* 我直接买，不通过中介。

aggressive /əˈɡresɪv/ *adjective* 形容词
behaving angrily or violently towards other people 好斗的；攻击性的：*Some children are much more aggressive than others.* 有些孩子比其他孩子好斗得多。
▶ **aggressively** /əˈɡresɪvli/ *adverb* 副词：*They may react aggressively.* 他们可能会激烈回应。

ago /əˈɡoʊ/ *adverb* 副词
in the past; before now 以前：*I got your letter a few days ago.* 我几天前收到你的信。

agony /ˈæɡəni/ *noun* 名词
great physical or mental pain 剧痛；极度痛苦；折磨：*He tried to move, but screamed in agony.* 他想移动身体，但痛得尖叫起来。

agree /əˈɡriː/ *verb* 动词 (**agrees, agreeing, agreed**)
1 to have the same opinion as someone else about something 赞同；持相同意见：*I agree with you.* 我同意你的意见。 □ *Do we agree that there's a problem?* 我们都认为存在问题，对吧？
2 to say that you will do something, or to accept something 答应；同意：*He agreed to pay me for the drawings.* 他答应向我支付这些画的钱。 □ *She agreed to my suggestion.* 她同意我的建议。

agreement /əˈɡriːmənt/ *countable noun* 可数名词
a plan or a decision that two or more people have made 协议；协定：*After two hours' discussion, they finally reached an agreement.* 经过两个小时的讨论，他们最终达成了协议。

agriculture /ˈæɡrɪkʌltʃər/ *uncountable noun* 不可数名词
the business or activity of taking care of crops and farm animals 农业
▶ **agricultural** /ˌæɡrɪˈkʌltʃərəl/ *adjective* 形容词：*agricultural land* 农田

ah /ɑː/ *exclamation* 感叹词
a word used for showing that you understand something or that you are surprised or pleased（表示明白或惊讶、高兴）啊：*Ah, I see what you mean.* 啊，我明白你的意思了。

aha /ɑːˈhɑː/ *exclamation* 感叹词
a word used for showing that you finally understand something（表示最终弄明白）啊哈：*Aha! Here is the answer to my question.* 啊哈！我找到问题的答案了。

ahead /əˈhed/ *adverb* 副词
1 in front of someone or something 在前面：*The road ahead was blocked.* 前面封路了。 □ *Dad went ahead to fetch the car.* 爸爸到前面取车。
2 directly in front of you 在正前方：*Brett looked straight ahead.* 布雷特盯着正前方。
3 winning in a competition 领先：*Chelsea was ahead all through the game.* 切尔西队在比赛中一直领先。
4 in the future 将来：*There are exciting times ahead.* 未来将是激动人心的时代。
ahead of someone/something in front of a person or thing 在某人／某物前面：*I saw a man thirty metres ahead of me.* 我看到前方30米处有个人。
go ahead used when you are giving someone permission to do something 没问题；可以：*'Can I borrow your dictionary?' — 'Sure, go ahead.'* "我能借一下你的词典吗？"——"行，没问题。"

aid /eɪd/ *uncountable noun* 不可数名词
money, equipment or services that are given to a country or to people, often after something very bad has happened to them 援助；救助；资助：*They have promised billions of dollars in aid.* 他们已许诺援助几十亿美元。
in aid of someone/something in order to make money to help a particular organization 为帮助某人／某事物；为给某人／某事物筹款：*We held a concert in aid of the Red Cross.* 我们为给红十字会筹款举办了一场音乐会。

AIDS /eɪdz/ *uncountable noun* 不可数名词
a disease that destroys the body's ability to fight other diseases 艾滋病；获得性免疫缺陷综合征：*Twenty-five per cent of adults there have AIDS.* 那里四分之一的成人患有艾滋病。

aim¹ /eɪm/ *verb* 动词 (**aims, aiming, aimed**)
1 to plan or hope to do something 计划；希望：*He is aiming for the 100-metre world record.* 他志在打破 100 米世界纪录。 □ *The booklet aims to help pupils choose a career.* 这本小册子旨在帮助学生选择职业。
2 to point something toward a person or a thing 用…瞄准；拿…对准：*He was aiming the gun at Wright.* 他用枪瞄准赖特。

aim² /eɪm/ *countable noun* 可数名词
the purpose of something 目标；目的：*The aim of the event is to bring parents and children together.* 这场活动的目的是把父母和孩子们聚在一起。

ain't /eɪnt/
short for (缩写 =) 'am not', 'are not', 'is not', 'have not' and 'has not'. Many people think this use is wrong. (*informal* 非正式)（很多人认为此用法有误）

air¹ /eə/ *noun* 名词
1 *uncountable* 不可数 the mixture of gases all around us that we breathe 空气：*Keith opened the window and felt the cold air on his face.* 基思打开窗，感受着扑面而来的冷空气。
2 *singular* 单数 the space around things or above the ground 空中；天空：*He was waving his arms in the air.* 他高举双臂挥舞着。

air² /eə/ *adjective* 形容词
involving travel in aircraft 航空的；乘坐飞机的：*Air travel will continue to grow at around 6% per year.* 航空旅行将继续以每年 6% 左右的速度增长。

'air-con,ditioned *adjective* 形容词
having a special piece of equipment that makes the air in a room or a vehicle colder 装有空调的：*All the rooms are air-conditioned, with en suite and satellite TV.* 所有房间都有空调、独立卫生间和卫星电视。

'air-con,ditioning *uncountable noun* 不可数名词
a system for keeping the air cool and dry in a building or a vehicle 空气调节系统

aircraft /'eəkrɑːft/ *countable noun* 可数名词 (**aircraft**)
an aeroplane or a helicopter 飞机；直升机；航空器：*The aircraft landed safely.* 飞机安全着陆。

'air ,force *countable noun* 可数名词
a military force that uses aeroplanes 空军：*the United States Air Force* 美国空军

airline /'eəlaɪn/ *countable noun* 可数名词
a company that carries people or goods in aeroplanes 航空公司：*Most low-cost airlines do not serve food.* 大多数廉价航空公司不提供餐食。

airplane /'eəpleɪn/ *countable noun* 可数名词 (*American* 美国英语)
→ see 见 **aeroplane**

'air po,llution *uncountable noun* 不可数名词
chemicals or other substances that have a harmful effect on the air 空气污染：*We think that air pollution may be the cause of the illness.* 我们认为病因可能是空气污染。

airport /'eəpɔːt/ *countable noun* 可数名词
a place where aeroplanes come and go, with buildings and services for passengers 机场：*Heathrow Airport is one of the busiest international airports in the world.* 希思罗机场是世界上最繁忙的国际机场之一。

aisle /aɪl/ *countable noun* 可数名词
a long narrow passage where people can walk between rows of seats or shelves (座椅或架子间的) 走道，过道：*You'll find the peas in the frozen food aisle.* 豌豆在冷冻食品通道。 □ *Please do not leave bags in the aisle.* 走道上请不要放置行李。

alarm /ə'lɑːm/ *countable noun* 可数名词
1 a piece of equipment that warns you of danger, for example, by making a noise 报警器：*The fire alarm woke us at 5 a.m.* 早晨 5 点钟，我们被火警惊醒。
2 → see 见 **alarm clock**：*Dad set the alarm for eight the next day.* 爸爸定了第二天 8 点的闹钟。

a'larm ,clock *countable noun* 可数名词
a clock that makes a noise to wake you up 闹钟：*I set my alarm clock for 4.30.* 我定了 4 点 30 分的闹钟。

album /'ælbəm/ *countable noun* 可数名词
1 a collection of songs on a CD 歌曲专辑：*The band released their new album on July 1.* 这支乐队 7 月 1 号发行了新专辑。
2 a book in which you keep things that you have collected (用于保存收集物的) 集，册，簿：*Theresa showed me her photo album.* 特雷莎给我看了她的相册。

alcohol /ˈælkəhɒl/ **uncountable noun** 不可数名词
1 drinks that can make people drunk 酒精饮品；酒：*Alcohol will not be served on the flight.* 本次航班不提供酒精饮品。
2 a liquid that is found in drinks such as beer and wine. It is also used as a chemical for cleaning things. 酒精：*Clean the wound with alcohol.* 用酒精清洗伤口。

alcoholic[1] /ˌælkəˈhɒlɪk/ **countable noun** 可数名词
someone who drinks alcohol too often and cannot stop 酗酒者：*He admitted that he is an alcoholic.* 他承认自己酗酒。

alcoholic[2] /ˌælkəˈhɒlɪk/ **adjective** 形容词
containing alcohol 含酒精的：*Wine and beer are alcoholic drinks.* 葡萄酒和啤酒都是酒精饮品。

alert[1] /əˈlɜːt/ **adjective** 形容词
paying attention and being ready to deal with anything that might happen 警觉的；留神的：*We all have to stay alert.* 我们都得保持警觉。

alert[2] /əˈlɜːt/ **verb** 动词 (**alerts, alerting, alerted**)
to tell someone about a dangerous situation 使警觉；使留神：*He wanted to alert people to the danger.* 他想提醒人们当心这种危险。

A level /ˈeɪ ˌlevəl/ **noun** 名词
a British qualification that people take when they are seventeen or eighteen years old（英国）高级水平普通教育证书考试：*Laura is taking her A levels next summer.* 劳拉明年夏天将参加高级证书考试。

algebra /ˈældʒɪbrə/ **uncountable noun** 不可数名词
a type of mathematics in which letters and signs are used to represent numbers 代数（学）

alien /ˈeɪliən/ **countable noun** 可数名词
a creature from another planet 外星人：*Robin Williams plays the part of an alien from the planet 'Ork'.* 罗宾·威廉斯扮演来自"奥克"星的外星人。

alike /əˈlaɪk/ **adjective** 形容词, **adverb** 副词
1 similar 相似的；相像的：*They all look alike to me.* 在我看来他们都差不多。
2 in a similar way 相似地；相像地：*They even dressed alike.* 他们甚至穿得也很像。

alive /əˈlaɪv/ **adjective** 形容词
living; not dead 活着的：*Is your father still alive?* 你父亲仍健在吗？

alkali /ˈælkəˌlaɪ/ **noun** 名词
a substance that is the opposite of an acid, which can burn your skin 碱

all[1] /ɔːl/ **adjective** 形容词
1 used for talking about everyone or everything of a particular type（某类人或事物）每一个的，所有的：*Hugh and all his friends came to the party.* 休和他所有的朋友都来参加了聚会。□ *He loves all literature.* 他热爱一切文学作品。
2 used for talking about the whole of something（某事物）全部的，整体的：*Someone's used all the milk.* 有人把牛奶用完了。□ *Did you eat all of it?* 你都吃光了吗？
all day/all night during the whole day, or the whole night 一整天／一整夜：*He watches TV all day.* 他一整天都在看电视。
at all used for making negative sentences stronger（用于加强否定语气）全然，一点儿，根本：*I never really liked him at all.* 我从未真正喜欢过他。

all[2] /ɔːl/ **adverb** 副词
completely 完全：*I went away and left her all alone.* 我离开了，留下她只身一人。

Allah /ˈælə, ˈælɑː/ **noun** 名词
the name of God in Islam 安拉，真主（伊斯兰教所信奉之神）：*We thank Allah that the boy is safe.* 我们感谢真主，那男孩安全了。

allergic /əˈlɜːdʒɪk/ **adjective** 形容词
becoming ill when you eat, touch or breathe something that does not usually affect people in this way 过敏的：*I'm allergic to cats.* 我对猫过敏。

allergy /ˈælədʒi/ **noun** 名词 (**allergies**)
a condition in which you become ill or get red marks on your skin when you eat, touch or breathe something that does not usually affect people in this way 变态反应；过敏反应：*He has an allergy to nuts.* 他对坚果过敏。

alley /ˈæli/ **countable noun** 可数名词
a narrow street between buildings 小巷；胡同

alliance /əˈlaɪəns/ **countable noun** 可数名词
a group of people, countries, organizations, or political parties that work together 联盟；同盟：*The two parties formed an alliance.* 这两个党派结成联盟。

alligator /ˈælɪɡeɪtə/ **countable noun** 可数名词
a long animal with rough skin, big teeth and short legs 美洲鳄；扬子鳄：*Do not*

feed the alligators. 不要投喂美洲鳄。

alligator 美洲鳄

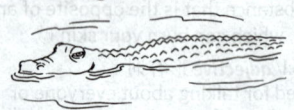

allocate /ˈæləkeɪt/ *verb* 动词 (**allocates, allocating, allocated**)
1 to give something to someone 分发；分派：*Some of the tickets will be allocated to students.* 这些票有一部分会发给学生。
2 to use something for a particular purpose 分配；划拨：*They allocated one billion dollars for malaria research.* 他们划拨了 10 亿美元用于疟疾研究。

allow /əˈlaʊ/ *verb* 动词 (**allows, allowing, allowed**)
1 to give someone permission to do something 允许；准许：*We allow the children to watch TV after school.* 我们允许孩子们放学后看电视。
2 if you are allowed to do or have something, it is all right for you to do or have it 准予；准许得到：*I'm not allowed to go to the party.* 我未获准参加聚会。
3 to give permission for something to happen 允许（某事）发生：*Mobile phone use is not allowed in this carriage.* 本节车厢禁止使用手机。

all ˈright¹ *adjective* 形容词
1 satisfactory or acceptable 令人满意的；还不错的：*'What's your new teacher like?' — 'He's all right.'* "你们新老师怎么样？"——"还不错。"
2 well or safe 健康的；安然无恙的：*Are you all right?* 你还好吧？

all ˈright² *exclamation* 感叹词
used for saying that you agree to something 好的；可以：*'I think you should go now.' — 'All right.'* "我觉得你现在该走了。"——"好的。"

ally /ˈælaɪ/ *countable noun* 可数名词 (**allies**)
1 a country that supports another country, especially in a war（尤指战时的）盟国：*the Western allies* 西方盟国
2 someone who helps and supports another person 盟友；支持者：*He is a close ally of the president.* 他是总统的亲密盟友。

almond /ˈɑːmənd/ *noun* 名词
a type of nut that you can eat or use in cooking 扁桃仁：*She made a cake flavoured with almonds.* 她做了一个扁桃仁风味的蛋糕。

almost /ˈɔːlməʊst/ *adverb* 副词
nearly but not completely 几乎；差不多：*We have been married for almost three years.* 我们结婚快 3 年了。□ *He caught flu, which almost killed him.* 他得了流感，几乎丧命。

alone /əˈləʊn/ *adjective* 形容词, *adverb* 副词
1 without any other people 独自（的）；单独（的）：*She wanted to be alone.* 她想一个人待着。□ *We were alone together.* 就我们两人在一起。□ *He lived alone in this house for almost five years.* 他在这所房子里独自住了近 5 年。
2 without help from other people 独力：*Raising a child alone is very difficult.* 独自养育孩子非常难。

along¹ /əˈlɒŋ/ *preposition* 介词
1 towards one end of a road or other place 沿着；顺着：*Pedro walked along the street.* 佩德罗沿着街走。
2 in or beside a road or another long narrow place 在⋯里；靠着⋯的边：*There were traffic jams all along the roads.* 路上到处都堵车。

along² /əˈlɒŋ/ *adverb* 副词
1 forwards 向前；往前：*He was talking as they walked along.* 他们边向前走他边说着话。
2 with you 一起；一道：*Bring along your friends and family.* 带上亲友。

alongside /əˌlɒŋˈsaɪd/ *preposition* 介词
1 next to 在⋯旁边；沿着⋯边缘：*He crossed the street and walked alongside Central Park.* 他穿过街道，沿着中央公园走。
2 in the same place as 与⋯一起：*He worked alongside Frank and Mark.* 他与弗兰克、马克一处工作。

aloud /əˈlaʊd/ *adverb* 副词
in such a way that other people can hear you 出声地；大声地：*When we were children, our father read aloud to us.* 我们小的时候，父亲给我们朗读。

alphabet /ˈælfəbet/ *countable noun* 可数名词
a set of letters that is used for writing words 字母表：*The modern Russian alphabet has 33 letters.* 现代俄语字母表有 33 个字母。

alphabetical /ˌælfəˈbetɪkl/ *adjective* 形容词
following the normal order of the letters in the alphabet 按字母顺序的：*The books are arranged in alphabetical order.* 这些书

按字母顺序摆放。

already /ɔːlˈredi/ *adverb* 副词
1 used for showing that one thing happened before another thing 已经（表示一事早于另一事发生）: *The meeting had already finished when we arrived.* 我们到的时候会已经开完了。
2 used for showing that a situation exists now or that it started earlier than expected 已经（表示某情形已然存在或早于预期发生）: *We've already spent most of the money.* 这笔钱我们已花掉大半。 □ *Most of the guests have already left.* 客人已走了大半。

> **LANGUAGE HELP** 语言提示
> **Already** or **yet**？用 already 还是 yet？
> In British English, you usually use **already** and **yet** with the perfect tenses. 英国英语中，already 和 yet 通常用于完成时：*I've already seen that film.* 我已经看过那部电影了。□ *Have they arrived yet?* 他们到了吗？
> In American English, people often use a past tense. 美国英语中，常用于过去时：*She already told us about the party.* 她跟我们讲过聚会的事了。□ *I didn't have any breakfast yet.* 我早饭还什么都没吃呢。

also /ˈɔːlsəʊ/ *adverb* 副词
used for giving more information about something 也；还；而且：*The book also includes an index of all US presidents.* 这本书还附有美国历任总统索引。□ *We've got a big table and also some stools and benches.* 我们有一张大桌子，还有一些凳子和长椅。

> **LANGUAGE HELP** 语言提示
> **Also** or **too**？用 also 还是 too？
> **Also** never comes at the end of a sentence. *also 从不用于句尾：*He was also an artist.* 他还是位艺术家。
> **Too** usually comes at the end of a sentence. *too 通常用于句尾：*He's a singer and an actor too.* 他是歌手，也是演员。

alter /ˈɔːltə/ *verb* 动词 (**alters, altering, altered**)
to change 改变；更改：*World War II altered life in many ways.* 第二次世界大战在很多方面改变了生活。□ *His appearance had altered since their last meeting.* 他们上次见面之后，他的样子有了变化。

alternate[1] /ˈɔːltəneɪt/ *verb* 动词
(**alternates, alternating, alternated**)
1 to do one and then the other 交替：*Alternate between walking and running.* 走一会儿，跑一会儿。
2 to repeatedly happen or come one after another 轮流：*Rain alternated with snow.* 雨雪轮番登场。

alternate[2] /ɔːlˈtɜːnət/ *adjective* 形容词
1 repeatedly happening or coming one after another 交替的
2 happening on one day, week, etc, and not on the next day, week, etc 间隔的；每隔（一天、一周等）的：*We go skiing on alternate years.* 我们每隔一年滑一次雪。

alternative[1] /ɔːlˈtɜːnətɪv/ *countable noun* 可数名词
something that you can use or do instead of another thing 替代性事物：*The new treatment may provide an alternative to painkillers.* 这种新疗法可能是止痛药之外的另一种选择。

alternative[2] /ɔːlˈtɜːnətɪv/ *adjective* 形容词
1 different from something that you already have 其他的；备选的：*Alternative methods of travel were available.* 还有其他出行方式可选择。□ *We are working on alternative proposals.* 我们在做备选提案。
2 different from the usual thing 非传统的；另类的：*Have you considered alternative health care?* 你有没有考虑过另类医疗保健？

alternatively /ɔːlˈtɜːnətɪvli/ *adverb* 副词
used for mentioning something different from what you have just said 要不；或者：*Hotels are not too expensive. Alternatively you could stay in a flat.* 酒店费用不是特别高。或者，也可以住公寓。

although /ɔːlˈðəʊ/ *conjunction* 连词
1 used for introducing an idea that may seem surprising 虽然，尽管（表示出乎意料）：*Their system worked, although no one knew how.* 他们的制度起作用了，虽然没有人知道是如何做到的。□ *Although I was only six, I can remember seeing it on TV.* 虽然那时我只有 6 岁，但我依然记得在电视上看到过它。
2 used for introducing information that slightly changes what you have already said 虽然，尽管（表示让步）：*They all play basketball, although on different teams.* 他们都打篮球，虽然身在不同的球队。

altitude /ˈæltɪtjuːd/ *noun* 名词
a measurement of height above the level of the sea 海拔；高度：*The aircraft reached an altitude of about 39,000 feet.* 飞机爬升到约 39,000 英尺的高度。 □ *The illness does not occur in areas of high altitude.* 这种疾病在高海拔地区不会发生。

altogether /ˌɔːltəˈɡeðə/ *adverb* 副词
including everyone or everything 总共；一共：*There were eleven of us altogether.* 我们总共 11 个人。

aluminium /ˌæljʊˈmɪniəm/ *uncountable noun* 不可数名词
a light metal used for making things such as cooking equipment and cans for food and drink 铝：*We recycle aluminium cans.* 我们回收利用铝罐。

always /ˈɔːlweɪz/ *adverb* 副词
1 at all times; every time 总是；每次都是：*She's always late for school.* 她上学总是迟到。 □ *She always gave me socks for my birthday.* 我生日她总是送我袜子。
2 for ever 永远；始终：*I'll always love him.* 我会永远爱他。
3 used when you are talking about something that someone does a lot and which annoys you 老是；一再：*Why are you always interrupting me?* 你为什么老打断我？

am /əm, STRONG 强读 æm/
→ see 见 **be**

a.m. /ˌeɪ ˈem/ also 亦作 **am**
used after a number when you are talking about a time between midnight and noon. Compare with **p.m.** 上午，午前（比较 p.m.）：*I start work at 9 a.m. and I usually finish at 6 p.m.* 我上午 9 点开始工作，通常下午 6 点结束。

amateur /ˈæmətə/ *countable noun* 可数名词
someone who does an activity as a hobby and not as a job 业余爱好者 ● **amateur** *adjective* 形容词：*an amateur golfer* 业余高尔夫球手

amaze /əˈmeɪz/ *verb* 动词 (**amazes, amazing, amazed**)
to surprise someone very much 使大为惊奇；使惊愕：*He amazed us with his knowledge of Italian history.* 他对意大利历史的了解让我们十分惊奇。
▶ **amazed** /əˈmeɪzd/ *adjective* 形容词：*I was amazed at how difficult it was.* 这事难度大得让我吃惊。

amazement /əˈmeɪzmənt/ *uncountable noun* 不可数名词
the feeling you have when something surprises you very much 惊诧；惊愕：*I looked at her in amazement.* 我惊愕地看着她。

amazing /əˈmeɪzɪŋ/ *adjective* 形容词
very surprising, in a way that you like 令人十分惊奇的；惊人的：*It's amazing what we can remember if we try.* 只要愿意尝试，人的记忆力真是惊人。
▶ **amazingly** /əˈmeɪzɪŋli/ *adverb* 副词：*She was an amazingly good cook.* 她厨艺精湛。

ambassador /æmˈbæsədə/ *countable noun* 可数名词
an important official person who lives in a foreign country and represents his or her own country there 大使；使节：*We met the ambassador to Poland.* 我们见了驻波兰大使。

ambition /æmˈbɪʃən/ *noun* 名词
1 *countable* 可数 the feeling that you want very much to do something at some time in the future 梦想；理想：*His ambition is to sail around the world.* 他的梦想是环球航行。
2 *uncountable* 不可数 the desire to be successful, rich or powerful 雄心；抱负；野心：*These young people have hopes for the future and great ambition.* 这些年轻人雄心勃勃，对未来充满希望。

ambitious /æmˈbɪʃəs/ *adjective* 形容词
1 having a strong feeling that you want to be successful, rich or powerful 有雄心的；有抱负的；有野心的：*Chris is very ambitious.* 克里斯雄心勃勃。
2 needing a lot of work or money 规模宏大的；耗资巨大的：*He has ambitious plans for the firm.* 他有宏大的企业规划。

ambulance /ˈæmbjʊləns/ *countable noun* 可数名词
a vehicle for taking people to hospital 救护车；急救车

ambulance 救护车

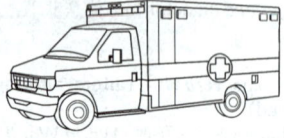

amendment /əˈmendmənt/ *noun* 名词
a change that is added to a law（法令的）修正条款，修正案：*They have proposed an*

amendment to the bill. 他们已提出这一法案的修正案。

among /əˈmʌŋ/ *preposition* 介词
1 in the middle of a group of people or things 在…中间: *There were teenagers sitting among adults.* 成人中坐着一些十几岁的少年。
2 included in a particular group 在(某群体)中间: *We discussed it among ourselves.* 我们内部讨论了一下。 □ *Don't worry; you're among friends.* 别担心，都是自己人。
3 used for saying that most people in a group have a particular opinion or feeling 对(某群体)的大多数人而言: *There is concern among parents about teaching standards.* 家长中大多数对教学质量有顾虑。
4 used for saying that something is given to all of the people in a particular group 在(某群人)中间(分配): *The money will be shared among family members.* 这笔钱将由家庭成员共享。

> **LANGUAGE HELP** 语言提示
> **Among** or **between**? 用 among 还是 between？
> If there are more than two people or things, use **among**. If there are only two people or things, use **between**. 两者以上之间用 among，两者之间用 between。

amount[1] /əˈmaʊnt/ *noun* 名词
how much of something that there is; how much of something that you have, need or get 数量; 数额: *He needs that amount of money to live.* 他需要那么一笔钱维持生计。 □ *I still do a certain amount of work for them.* 我仍然为他们做一些工作。

amount[2] /əˈmaʊnt/ *verb* 动词 (**amounts, amounting, amounted**)
amount to something to add up to a particular total 合计为…; 共计为…: *The payment amounted to £42 billion.* 支付款项共计 420 亿英镑。

amplifier /ˈæmplɪfaɪə/ *countable noun* 可数名词
a piece of electrical equipment that makes sounds louder 声音放大器; 扩音器; 扬声器

amuse /əˈmjuːz/ *verb* 动词 (**amuses, amusing, amused**)
to make you laugh or smile 逗乐; 逗笑: *The thought amused him.* 这种想法把他逗乐了。
amuse yourself to do something so that you do not become bored 自娱; 消遣: *As a child he amused himself listening to the radio.* 他小时候听收音机解闷。

amused /əˈmjuːzd/ *adjective* 形容词
wanting to laugh or smile because of something 被逗乐的; 觉得好笑的: *For a moment, Jackson looked amused.* 有那么一会儿，杰克逊脸上有了笑意。 □ *Alex looked at me with an amused expression on his face.* 亚历克斯看着我，脸上一副愉悦的表情。

amusement /əˈmjuːzmənt/ *noun* 名词
1 *uncountable* 不可数 the feeling that you have when you think that something is funny 有趣; 好笑: *Tom watched them with amusement.* 汤姆饶有兴趣地看着他们。
2 *countable* 可数 a way of passing the time pleasantly 娱乐; 消遣方式: *People did not have many amusements to choose from in those days.* 那时候，人们没有多少娱乐方式可以选择。

aˈmusement ˌpark *countable noun* 可数名词
a place where people pay to ride on machines for fun 游乐场; 游乐园

amusing /əˈmjuːzɪŋ/ *adjective* 形容词
making you laugh or smile 有趣的; 好笑的: *It's an amusing programme that the whole family can enjoy.* 这个节目很有趣，适合全家人观赏。

an /ən, STRONG 强读 æn/ *article* 冠词
used instead of 'a' before words that begin with vowel sounds (用于以元音开头的单词前，代替 a)

anaesthetic /ˌænɪsˈθetɪk/ *noun* 名词
a substance that doctors use to stop you feeling pain 麻醉药: *The operation was performed under a general anaesthetic.* 手术是在全身麻醉的情况下实施的。

analogue /ˈænəlɒg/ also 亦作 **analog** *adjective* 形容词
used for describing a clock or a watch that shows the time using hands (= the long parts that move around and show the time) instead of numbers. Compare with **digital**. (钟表)模拟式的, 指针式的(比较 digital)

analyse /ˈænəˌlaɪz/ *verb* 动词 (**analyses, analysing, analysed**)
to consider something carefully in order to fully understand it or to find out what is in it 分析; 细察: *We need more time to analyse the decision.* 我们需要更多时间来

分析这一决议。▫ *They haven't analysed those samples yet.* 他们尚未分析那些样本。

analysis /əˈnælɪsɪs/ *noun* 名词 (**analyses** /əˈnælɪsiːz/)
1 the process of considering something carefully in order to understand it or explain it（对事物的）分析，细察：*Our analysis shows that the treatment was successful.* 经过我们分析，这一疗法很成功。
2 *uncountable* 不可数 the scientific process of finding out what is in something（对物质成分的）分析，化验：*They collect blood samples for analysis.* 他们采集血液样本进行化验。

ancestor /ˈænsestə/ *countable noun* 可数名词
one of the people in your family who lived before you 祖宗；祖先：*Our daily lives are so different from those of our ancestors.* 我们的日常生活和我们的祖先大差地别。

anchor /ˈæŋkə/ *countable noun* 可数名词
a heavy object that you drop into the water from a boat to stop it moving away 锚

ancient /ˈeɪnʃənt/ *adjective* 形容词
very old, or from a long time ago 古老的；年代久远的：*ancient Jewish traditions* 古老的犹太教传统

and /ənd, STRONG 强读 ænd/ *conjunction* 连词
1 used for connecting two or more words or phrases 和（连接两个或两个以上的词或短语）：*She and Simon have already gone.* 她和西蒙已经走了。▫ *I'm 53 and I'm very happy.* 我53岁，很幸福。
2 used for connecting two words that are the same, in order to make the meaning stronger 接连，越来越（连接两个相同的词，表示强调）：*Learning becomes more and more difficult as we get older.* 随着年纪越来越大，学东西越来越难。▫ *We talked for hours and hours.* 我们谈了很久很久。
3 used when one event happens after another 然后，就（连接两个相继发生的事件）：*I waved goodbye and went down the steps.* 我挥手告别，然后走下台阶。
4 used for showing that two numbers are added together 加（表示两个数字相加）：*Two and two makes four.* *2加2等于4。

angel /ˈeɪndʒəl/ *countable noun* 可数名词
1 a being that some people believe can bring messages from God. In pictures, angels often have wings. 天使
2 someone who is very kind and good 天

使般的人；大好人：*Thank you so much; you're an angel.* 太感谢你了，你就像天使一样。

anger /ˈæŋɡə/ *uncountable noun* 不可数名词
the strong emotion that you feel when you think that someone has behaved badly or has treated you unfairly 愤怒；怒火；怒气：*Parents expressed anger at the decision.* 家长对这一决定表示愤怒。●**anger** *verb* 动词 (**angers, angering, angered**)：*The decision angered some parents.* 这一决定激怒了一些家长。

angle /ˈæŋɡl/ *countable noun* 可数名词
the space between two lines or surfaces that meet in one place. Angles are measured in degrees. 角：*a 30 degree angle* *30度角
at an angle leaning, not straight 斜着；歪着：*He wore his hat at an angle.* 他歪戴着帽子。

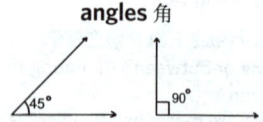

angles 角

angry /ˈæŋɡri/ *adjective* 形容词 (**angrier, angriest**)
feeling a strong emotion when someone has done something bad, or someone has treated you unfairly 生气的；愤怒的：*We are very angry about the decision to close the school.* 关闭学校这一决定使我们非常愤怒。▫ *An angry crowd gathered.* 愤怒的人群聚集起来。
→ Look at picture on P15 参见彩插第15页

> **LANGUAGE HELP 语言提示**
> If someone is very angry, you can say they are **furious**. If they are less angry, you can say they are **annoyed** or **irritated**.
> 表示火气很大，用 furious。表示没那么生气，用 annoyed 或 irritated。

animal /ˈænɪməl/ *countable noun* 可数名词
1 a creature such as a dog or a cat, but not a bird, fish, insect or human 动物，兽（不包括鸟、鱼、昆虫和人类）：*He was attacked by wild animals.* 他被野兽袭击了。
2 any living creature, including a human 动物（包括人类）

animation /ˌænɪˈmeɪʃən/ *uncountable noun* 不可数名词
the process of making films in which

drawings appear to move 动画: *computer animation* 计算机动画

ankle /'æŋkəl/ *countable noun* 可数名词
the part of your body where your foot joins your leg 踝；脚脖子: *John twisted his ankle badly.* 约翰脚踝严重扭伤。

anniversary /ˌænɪ'vɜːsəri/ *countable noun* 可数名词 (**anniversaries**)
a date that is remembered because something special happened on that date in an earlier year 周年纪念日: *They just celebrated their fiftieth wedding anniversary.* 他们刚庆祝了结婚 50 周年纪念日。

announce /ə'naʊns/ *verb* 动词 (**announces, announcing, announced**)
to tell people about something officially 宣布；发布: *He will announce tonight that he is resigning.* 他今晚将宣布辞职。 ▫ *She was planning to announce her engagement.* 她计划宣布订婚。

announcement /ə'naʊnsmənt/ *countable noun* 可数名词
information that someone tells to a lot of people 公告；声明；通告: *The president is expected to make an announcement about his future today.* 预计总统今天将就其未来打算发表声明。 ▫ *An announcement told us that the train was going to be late.* 我们听到了火车将晚点的通知。

announcer /ə'naʊnsə/ *countable noun* 可数名词
someone whose job is to talk between programmes on radio or television（电台、电视台的）广播员，播音员: *The radio announcer said it was nine o'clock.* 电台播音员报时 9 点。

annoy /ə'nɔɪ/ *verb* 动词 (**annoys, annoying, annoyed**)
to make someone angry and upset 使生气；使烦恼: *Rosie said she didn't mean to annoy anyone.* 罗茜说她并不想惹谁生气。 ▫ *It annoyed me that she believed him.* 她相信他说的话，这让我很生气。

annoyed /ə'nɔɪd/ *adjective* 形容词
angry about something 生气的；恼怒的: *She was annoyed that Sasha was there.* 萨莎居然在那儿，她很生气。

annoying /ə'nɔɪɪŋ/ *adjective* 形容词
making you feel angry and upset 气人的；令人恼火的: *It's very annoying when this happens.* 发生这事真让人恼火。

annual /'ænjuəl/ *adjective* 形容词
1 happening once every year 每年的；一年一次的: *They held their annual meeting on 20th May.* 他们 5 月 20 号开了年会。
▶ **annually** /'ænjuəli/ *adverb* 副词: *The prize is awarded annually.* 这个奖项每年颁发一次。
2 for a period of one year 一年的；全年的: *The company has annual sales of about £80 million.* 这家公司年销售额约为 8,000 万英镑。
▶ **annually** /'ænjuəli/ *adverb* 副词: *El Salvador mine produces 100,000 tons of copper annually.* 萨尔瓦多矿每年生产 10 万吨铜。

anonymous /ə'nɒnɪməs/ *adjective* 形容词
without giving your name or saying who you are 匿名的；不透露姓名的: *You can speak to a police officer at any time, and you can choose to remain anonymous.* 你可以随时找警察谈话，并可选择不透露姓名。
▶ **anonymously** /ə'nɒnɪməsli/ *adverb* 副词: *The photographs were sent anonymously to the magazine's offices.* 这些照片是匿名发给杂志社的。

another /ə'nʌðə/ *adjective* 形容词
1 used when talking about one more person or thing of the same type（同类事物中）另一个的，又一个的: *We're going to have another baby.* 我们计划再生个宝宝。
● **another** *pronoun* 代词: *'These biscuits are delicious.' — 'Would you like another?'* "这些饼干真好吃。"——"再来一块？"
2 used when talking about a different person or thing 别的；其他的: *I'll deal with this problem another time.* 我下次再解决这个问题。 ● **another** *pronoun* 代词: *He said one thing and did another.* 他说一套做一套。
one another used for showing that each member of a group does something to or for the other members 互相: *These children are learning to help one another.* 这些孩子在学习互相帮助。

answer[1] /'ɑːnsə/ *verb* 动词 (**answers, answering, answered**)
1 to say something back to someone who has spoken to you 回答；回复: *I asked him but he didn't answer.* 我问了他，但他没有回答。 ▫ *Williams answered that he didn't know.* 威廉斯回答说他不知道。
2 to pick up the telephone when it rings 接（电话）: *Why didn't you answer when I phoned?* 我给你打电话为什么不接？ ▫ *She*

didn't answer the telephone. 她没有接电话。
3 to open the door when you hear a knock or the bell 应(门)：*I knocked and Mary answered the door.* 我敲了敲门，玛丽应了门。● **answer** *countable noun* 可数名词：*I knocked at the front door and there was no answer.* 我敲了敲前门，没有人应答。
4 to write or say what you think is the correct answer to a question in a test 答(题)：*Before you start to answer the questions, read the whole exam carefully.* 开始答题前先把整张考卷仔细看一遍。

answer[2] /ˈɑːnsə/ *countable noun* 可数名词
1 a way to solve a problem 解决办法：*There are no easy answers to this problem.* 要解决这个问题并非易事。
2 the information that you give when you are doing a test 答案：*I got three answers wrong.* 我有3道题答错了。

answering maˌchine *or* 或 **answerphone** /ˈɑːnsəˌfəʊn/ *countable noun* 可数名词
a small machine that records telephone messages 电话答录机

ant /ænt/ *countable noun* 可数名词
a small crawling insect that lives in large groups 蚂蚁

antenna /ænˈtenə/ *countable noun* 可数名词 (**antennae** /ænˈtenɪː/ *or* 或 **antennas**)

> **LANGUAGE HELP** 语言提示
> **Antennas** is the usual plural form for meaning 2. 义项2的复数形式通常为antennas。

1 one of the two long, thin parts attached to the head of an insect that it uses to feel things with (昆虫的)触角 **antenna** 触角
2 (*American* 美国英语) → see 见 **aerial**

antibiotic /ˌæntibaɪˈɒtɪk/ *countable noun* 可数名词
a drug that is used for killing bacteria and treating infections 抗素：*Your doctor may prescribe antibiotics.* 医生可能会给你开抗生素。

anticipate /ænˈtɪsɪpeɪt/ *verb* 动词 (**anticipates, anticipating, anticipated**)
to think about an event and prepare for it before it happens 预料；预计：*Organizers anticipate an even bigger crowd this year.* 组织者预计今年参加人数甚至会更多。

anticipation /ænˌtɪsɪˈpeɪʃən/ *uncountable noun* 不可数名词
a feeling of excitement about something that you know is going to happen 期盼；期待：*The days before Christmas were filled with anticipation and excitement.* 圣诞节前的日子洋溢着期待和兴奋。
in anticipation of something done because you believe that an event is going to happen 因预计到会发生某事：*Some schools were closed in anticipation of the bad weather.* 预计到会出现坏天气，一些学校停课了。

anticlockwise /ˌæntiˈklɒkwaɪz/ *adjective* 形容词, *adverb* 副词
moving in the opposite direction to the direction in which the hands of a clock move 逆时针方向(的)

antiperspirant /ˌæntiˈpɜːspərənt/ *noun* 名词
a substance that you put on your skin to stop you from sweating (= producing liquid through your skin when you are hot) 止汗药：*Try using an antiperspirant for sensitive skin.* 敏感型皮肤可以试用一下止汗药。

antique /ænˈtiːk/ *countable noun* 可数名词
an old object that is valuable because of its beauty or because of the way it was made 古董；古玩：*Jill started collecting antiques as a hobby about a year ago.* 大约1年前，吉尔开始爱好上了收集古董。

antisocial /ˌæntiˈsəʊʃəl/ *adjective* 形容词
not friendly towards other people 反社会的：*antisocial behaviour* 反社会行为

anti-virus /ˌæntiˈvaɪərəs/ *also* 亦作 **antivirus** *adjective* 形容词
protecting a computer from attack by viruses (= programs that enter your computer and stop it from working properly) 杀毒的；防计算机病毒的：*antivirus software* 杀毒软件

antler /ˈæntlə/ *countable noun* 可数名词
one of the two horns that are shaped like branches on the head of a male deer (= a large brown animal with long thin legs) 鹿角

antonym /ˈæntənɪm/ *countable noun* 可数名词
a word that means the opposite of another word 反义词

anus /ˈeɪnəs/ *countable noun* 可数名词 (**anuses**)
the hole from which solid waste matter leaves a person's body 肛门

anxiety /æŋˈzaɪəti/ *noun* 名词 (**anxieties**)
a feeling of being nervous and worried 焦虑；忧虑：*Her voice was full of anxiety.* 她话音里满是焦虑。

anxious /ˈæŋkʃəs/ *adjective* 形容词
nervous or worried about something 焦虑的；忧虑的：*She became very anxious when he didn't come home.* 他没有回家，她非常焦虑。
▶ **anxiously** /ˈæŋkʃəsli/ *adverb* 副词：*They are waiting anxiously for news.* 他们焦急地等待着消息。

any /ˈeni/ *adjective* 形容词
1 used in negative sentences to show that no person or thing is involved（用于否定句）任何的，丝毫的：*I don't have any plans for the summer holidays yet.* 我还没有任何暑假计划。□ *We made this without any help.* 我们做这个没有依靠任何帮助。
● **any** *pronoun* 代词：*The children needed new clothes and we couldn't afford any.* 孩子们需要新衣服，但我们买不起。
2 used in questions to ask if there is some of a particular thing（用于疑问句）任何的：*Do you speak any foreign languages?* 你会说什么外语吗？● **any** *pronoun* 代词：*I will stay and answer questions if there are any.* 如果有问题，我会留下解答。
3 used in positive sentences when you want to say that it does not matter which person or thing you choose（用于肯定句）任何的，所有的：*I'll take any advice.* 任何建议我都接受。

any more or **any longer** used with negative sentences to say that something has stopped happening or is no longer true（用于否定句）再也，再：*I couldn't hide the tears any longer.* 我再也忍不住眼泪。

anybody /ˈenibɒdi/ *pronoun* 代词
→ see 见 **anyone**

anyhow /ˈenihaʊ/ *adverb* 副词
→ see 见 **anyway**

anyone /ˈeniwʌn/ *pronoun* 代词

> **LANGUAGE HELP 语言提示**
> You can also say **anybody**. 也可用 anybody。

1 used in negative statements and questions instead of 'someone' or 'somebody'（用于否定句和疑问句，代替 someone 或 somebody）任何人：*I won't tell anyone I saw you here.* 我不会告诉任何人我在这儿看到了你。□ *Why would anyone want that job?* 怎么会有人想做那份工作？
2 used for talking about someone when the exact person is not important 任何…的人（具体是谁并不重要）：*It's not a job for anyone who is slow with numbers.* 对数字不敏感的人不适合做这份工作。
3 used for talking about all types of people 任何人；无论谁：*Anyone could do what I'm doing.* 我正在做的事情谁都可以做。

anything /ˈeniθɪŋ/ *pronoun* 代词
1 used in negative statements and questions instead of 'something'（用于否定句和疑问句，代替 something）任何事物：*We can't do anything.* 我们什么都做不了。□ *She couldn't see or hear anything at all.* 她什么也看不见，什么也听不见。□ *Did you find anything?* 你找到什么了没？
2 used for talking about something when the exact thing is not important 任何…的事物（具体是什么并不重要）：*More than anything else, he wanted to become a teacher.* 他最想成为一名教师。
3 used for showing that you are talking about a very large number of things 无论什么东西；随便什么事情：*He is young and ready for anything.* 他年轻，什么事情都愿意尝试。

anyway /ˈeniweɪ/ *adverb* 副词

> **LANGUAGE HELP 语言提示**
> You can also say **anyhow**. 也可用 anyhow。

used for suggesting that something is true despite other things that have been said 即便如此；不管怎么说：*I'm not very good at golf, but I play anyway.* 我高尔夫球打得不太好，但我还是打。

anywhere /ˈeniweə/ *adverb* 副词
1 used in negative statements and questions instead of 'somewhere'（用于否定句和疑问句，代替 somewhere）在任何地方：*Did you try to get help from anywhere?* 你有没有试着向什么人求助？□ *I haven't got anywhere to live.* 我没地方住。
2 used for talking about a place, when the exact place is not important 在任何…地方（具体是什么地方并不重要）：*I can meet you*

anywhere you want. 在哪儿见面都行，我随你。

apart /əˈpɑːt/ *adverb* 副词
some distance from each other 相隔地；分开地：*Ray and his sister lived just 25 miles apart.* 雷和妹妹住得相隔仅 25 英里。◻ *Jane and I live apart now.* 现在我和简分开住了。
apart from someone/something except for 除了某人/某事物：*She's feeling better, apart from a slight headache.* 她感觉好些了，只是还有一点轻微的头疼。
take something apart to separate something into parts 拆卸某物：*He likes taking bikes apart and putting them together again.* 他喜欢把自行车拆开再组装起来。

apartment /əˈpɑːtmənt/ *countable noun* 可数名词 (*American* 美国英语)
→ see 见 **flat**

ape /eɪp/ *countable noun* 可数名词
a type of animal like a monkey that lives among trees in hot countries and has long, strong arms and no tail 猿：*wild animals such as monkeys and apes* 猴、猿等野生动物

apologize /əˈpɒlədʒaɪz/ *verb* 动词 (**apologizes, apologizing, apologized**)
to say that you are sorry 道歉；认错：*He apologized to everyone.* 他向所有人道了歉。
I apologize used as a formal or polite way of saying sorry 抱歉（正式或客气的致歉方式）：*I apologize for being late.* 抱歉我迟到了。

apology /əˈpɒlədʒi/ *noun* 名词 (**apologies**)
something that you say or write in order to tell someone that you are sorry 道歉；认错：*I didn't get an apology.* 没有人向我道歉。◻ *We received a letter of apology.* 我们收到一封致歉信。

apostrophe /əˈpɒstrəfi/ *countable noun* 可数名词
the mark (') that shows that one or more letters have been removed from a word, as in "isn't" and "we'll". It is also added to nouns to show possession, as in "Mike's car". 撇号；省字符；所有格符号

app /æp/ *noun* 名词
a computer program with one main purpose, especially one that you use on a mobile phone（尤指手机的）应用程序：*The app translates conversations while you speak.* 这款应用程序可实时翻译说话内容。

apparent /əˈpærənt/ *adjective* 形容词
clear and obvious 明显的；显而易见的：*It's apparent that standards have improved.* 显然水准已提高。

apparently /əˈpærəntli/ *adverb* 副词
used for talking about something that seems to be true, although you are not sure whether it is 好像；似乎；看来：*Apparently he was taken to hospital in the night.* 他好像夜里被送进了医院。

appeal /əˈpiːl/ *verb* 动词 (**appeals, appealing, appealed**)
1 to seem attractive or interesting to someone 有吸引力：*The idea appealed to him.* 他被这个想法吸引。
2 to make a serious and urgent request to someone 呼吁；恳请：*Police appealed to the public for help.* 警方呼吁公众提供帮助。◻ *The president appealed for calm.* 总统呼吁大家保持镇静。● **appeal** *countable noun* 可数名词：*The police made an urgent appeal for help.* 警方紧急呼吁提供援助。

appealing /əˈpiːlɪŋ/ *adjective* 形容词
pleasant and attractive 有吸引力的；讨人喜欢的：*The restaurant serves an appealing mix of Asian dishes.* 这家餐馆供应诱人的亚洲各国菜式。

appear /əˈpɪə/ *verb* 动词 (**appears, appearing, appeared**)
1 to come into sight or begin to be seen 出现；显现：*A woman appeared at the far end of the street.* 一个女人出现在街道的另一头。◻ *These small white flowers appear in early summer.* 这些小白花初夏时节开放。
2 to seem 看起来：*The boy appeared to be asleep.* 那男孩好像睡着了。

appearance /əˈpɪərəns/ *singular noun* 单数名词
the way that someone or something looks 外貌；外表；外观：*She hates it when people make remarks about her appearance.* 她讨厌人们对自己的外表评头论足。

appendix /əˈpendɪks/ *countable noun* 可数名词 (**appendixes** or 或 **appendices**)

> **LANGUAGE HELP** 语言提示
> The plural form **appendices** /əˈpendɪsiːz/ is usually used for meaning 2. 复数形式 appendices 通常用于义项 2，读作 /əˈpendɪsiːz/。

1 a small closed tube in the right side of

your body 阑尾：*They had to remove his appendix.* 他们不得不切除他的阑尾。
2 extra information that is placed after the end of the main text of a book or a document（书末的）附录；（文件的）附件：*an appendix to the main document* 主文件的附件

appetite /ˈæpɪtaɪt/ *noun* 名词
the feeling that you want to eat 食欲；胃口：*He had a healthy appetite, so I cooked huge meals.* 他胃口很好，因此我做饭量很大。

applaud /əˈplɔːd/ *verb* 动词 (**applauds, applauding, applauded**)
to clap your hands together to show that you like something 鼓掌（以示赞赏）：*The audience laughed and applauded.* 观众边笑边鼓掌。

applause /əˈplɔːz/ *uncountable noun* 不可数名词
the noise that a group of people make when they all clap their hands together to show that they like something 掌声：*The crowd greeted the couple with loud applause.* 人们以热烈的掌声欢迎这对夫妇。

apple /ˈæpəl/ *noun* 名词
a firm round fruit with green, red or yellow skin 苹果：*I always have an apple in my packed lunch.* 我自带的午餐里总是放一个苹果。
→ Look at picture on P5 参见彩插第 5 页

appliance /əˈplaɪəns/ *countable noun* 可数名词
a machine that you use to do a job in your home (*formal* 正式)（家用）器具：*You can buy a DVD player from any shop that sells electronic appliances.* 随便一家卖家用电器的商店里都能买到 DVD 播放机。

applicant /ˈæplɪkənt/ *countable noun* 可数名词
someone who formally asks to be considered for a job or a course 申请人；求职者；求学者：*The company keeps records on every job applicant.* 每一个求职者公司都有记录。

application /ˌæplɪˈkeɪʃən/ *countable noun* 可数名词
1 a written request to be considered for a job or a course 申请；申请书：*We have not yet received your application form.* 我们尚未收到你的申请表。
2 a piece of software that is designed to do a particular task in computing（计算机）应用软件：*This is a software application that you can access via the Internet.* 这款应用软件可在因特网上获得。

apply /əˈplaɪ/ *verb* 动词 (**applies, applying, applied**)
1 to write a letter or write on a form in order to ask for something such as a job 申请：*I am applying for a new job.* 我在找新工作。
2 to be about a person or a situation 相关；适用：*This rule does not apply to you.* 这项规定和你没有关系。

appoint /əˈpɔɪnt/ *verb* 动词 (**appoints, appointing, appointed**)
to choose someone for a job or a position 任命；委派：*The bank appointed Kenneth Conley as manager of its office in Birmingham.* 这家银行任命肯尼思·康利为其伯明翰办事处经理。

appointment /əˈpɔɪntmənt/ *countable noun* 可数名词
1 an arrangement to see someone at a particular time 约会；预约：*She has an appointment with her doctor.* 她和医生有预约。
2 a job or a position of responsibility 职位；职务：*I decided to accept the appointment as music director.* 我决定接受音乐总监一职。

appreciate /əˈpriːʃieɪt/ *verb* 动词 (**appreciates, appreciating, appreciated**)
1 to like something 欣赏；赏识：*Everyone can appreciate this kind of art.* 所有人都能欣赏这种艺术。
2 to be grateful for something that someone has done for you 感激；感谢：*Peter helped me so much. I really appreciate that.* 彼得帮了我很大忙，对此我非常感激。
▶ **appreciation** /əˌpriːʃiˈeɪʃən/ *singular noun* 单数名词：*He wants to show his appreciation for her support.* 他想要对她的支持表示感谢。

apprentice /əˈprentɪs/ *countable noun* 可数名词
a young person who works for someone in order to learn their skill 学徒；徒弟：*Their son Dominic is an apprentice woodworker.* 他们的儿子多米尼克是个木工学徒。

approach /əˈprəʊtʃ/ *verb* 动词 (**approaches, approaching, approached**)
1 to move closer to something 靠近；接近；

走近：*He approached the front door.* 他走向前门。▫ *When I approached, the girls stopped talking.* 我一走近，那些女孩子就不说话了。
2 to deal with a task, a problem or a situation, or to think about it in a particular way 探讨；处理；对待：*The bank has approached the situation in a practical way.* 银行已经务实地处理了这一状况。
● **approach** *countable noun* 可数名词 (**approaches**)：*There are two approaches: spend less money or find a new job.* 方法有两种：要么节省开支，要么换个工作。

appropriate /əˈprəʊpriət/ *adjective* 形容词
correct for a particular situation 适当的；合适的：*Is it appropriate that they pay for it?* 由他们付款合适吗？▫ *Wear clothes that are appropriate for the occasion.* 穿适合这一场合的服装。
▸ **appropriately** /əˈprəʊpriətli/ *adverb* 副词：*Try to behave appropriately and ask intelligent questions.* 举止要得体，问问题要动脑子。

approval /əˈpruːvəl/ *uncountable noun* 不可数名词
1 when someone agrees to something 赞成；同意：*The chairman gave his approval for an investigation.* 主席同意进行调查。
2 when you like and admire someone or something 赞许；肯定：*She wanted her father's approval.* 她想得到父亲的肯定。

approve /əˈpruːv/ *verb* 动词 (**approves, approving, approved**)
1 to like someone or something or think they are good 赞许；喜欢；肯定：*My father approves of you.* 我父亲喜欢你。
2 to formally agree to a plan 批准，通过（计划）：*The directors have approved the change.* 董事们已批准这一变动。

approximate /əˈprɒksɪmət/ *adjective* 形容词
near the correct number, time or position, but not exact 大约的；近似的：*The approximate value of the flat is £300,000.* 这套公寓现值 30 万英镑上下。
▸ **approximately** /əˈprɒksɪmətli/ *adverb* 副词：*They've spent approximately £150 million.* 他们已花费约 1.5 亿英镑。

apricot /ˈeɪprɪkɒt/ *noun* 名词
a small, soft, round fruit with yellow flesh and a large seed inside 杏：*a bag of dried apricots* 一袋杏干

April /ˈeɪprɪl/ *noun* 名词
the fourth month of the year 四月：*I'm getting married in April.* 我 4 月份就要结婚了。

apron /ˈeɪprən/ *countable noun* 可数名词
a piece of clothing that you wear over the front of your normal clothes, especially when you are cooking, in order to prevent your clothes from getting dirty 围裙

aquarium /əˈkweəriəm/ *countable noun* 可数名词
1 a building where fish and sea animals live 水族馆；海洋馆
2 a glass box filled with water, in which people keep fish 水族箱；养鱼缸

arch /ɑːtʃ/ *countable noun* 可数名词 (**arches**)
a structure that is curved at the top and is supported on either side 拱；拱形结构：*The bridge is 65 feet high at the top of the main arch.* 这座桥主拱顶有 65 英尺高。

arch 拱

archaeology /ˌɑːkiˈɒlədʒi/ *uncountable noun* 不可数名词
the study of the past that is done by examining the things that remain, such as buildings and tools 考古学
▸ **archaeological** /ˌɑːkiəˈlɒdʒɪkəl/ *adjective* 形容词：*This is one of the region's most important archaeological sites.* 这是该地区最重要的考古遗址之一。
▸ **archaeologist** /ˌɑːkiˈɒlədʒɪst/ *countable noun* 可数名词：*Archaeologists discovered buildings from an ancient culture in Mexico City.* 考古学家们在墨西哥城发现了来自古文明的建筑。
→ Look at picture on P10 参见彩插第 10 页

architect /ˈɑːkɪtekt/ *countable noun* 可数名词
a person whose job is to design buildings 建筑师

architecture /ˈɑːkɪtektʃə/ *uncountable noun* 不可数名词
1 the art of designing buildings 建筑学；建筑术：*He studied architecture in Rome.* 他在罗马学习建筑学。
2 the style of the design of a building 建筑风格；建筑式样：*modern architecture* 现代建筑风格

are /ə, STRONG 强读 ɑː/
→ see 见 **be**

area /ˈeəriə/ *noun* 名词
1 *countable* 可数 a particular part of a town, a country, a region or the world 地区；区域：*There are 11,000 people living in the area.* 这一地区居住有 11,000 人。
2 *countable* 可数 a piece of land or a part of a building that is used for a particular activity（具特殊用途的）场地，区：*We had lunch in the picnic area.* 我们在野餐区吃了午餐。
3 the amount of flat space that a surface covers, measured in square units 面积：*What's the area of this triangle?* 这个三角形的面积有多大？ □ *The islands cover a total area of 400 square miles.* 这些岛屿总面积为 400 平方英里。

arena /əˈriːnə/ *countable noun* 可数名词
a place where sports or entertainments take place 运动场；娱乐场所：*This is the largest indoor sports arena in the world.* 这是世界上最大的室内运动场。

aren't /ɑːnt/
short for（缩写 =）'are not'

argue /ˈɑːɡjuː/ *verb* 动词 (**argues, arguing, argued**)
1 to disagree with someone about something 争吵；争执：*He was arguing with his wife about money.* 他和妻子正为钱的事情吵嘴。 □ *They are arguing over details.* 他们正在细节问题上争来争去。
2 to give the reasons why you think something is true 论证；说理：*Employers argue that the law should be changed.* 雇主们辩称应该修改这项法令。

argument /ˈɑːɡjʊmənt/ *noun* 名词
1 *countable* 可数 a conversation in which people disagree with each other 争论；争吵：*Annie had an argument with one of the other girls.* 安妮和另一个女孩发生了争执。
2 what you say in order to try to convince people that your opinion is correct 理由；论据：*This is a strong argument against nuclear power.* 这是反对核电的一个有力理由。

arise /əˈraɪz/ *verb* 动词 (**arises, arising, arose, arisen**)
to begin to exist 产生；出现：*When the opportunity finally arose, thousands of workers left.* 最终机会出现时，数千名工人离开。

arisen /əˈrɪzən/
→ see 见 **arise**

arithmetic /əˈrɪθmətɪk/ *uncountable noun* 不可数名词
basic number work, for example adding or multiplying 算术：*We teach the young children reading, writing and arithmetic.* 我们教小孩子阅读、写作和算术。

arm¹ /ɑːm/ *countable noun* 可数名词
1 one of the two parts of your body between your shoulders and your hands 手臂；胳膊：*She stretched her arms out.* 她伸开双臂。
→ Look at picture on P4 参见彩插第 4 页
2 the part of a chair on which you rest your arm when you are sitting down（椅子的）扶手：*Mack held the arms of the chair.* 麦克抓住椅子扶手。
3 the part of a piece of clothing that covers your arm 衣袖；袖子：*The coat was short in the arms.* 这件外套袖子短。

arm² /ɑːm/ *verb* 动词 (**arms, arming, armed**)
to provide someone with a weapon 给⋯⋯配备武器：*She was so frightened that she armed herself with a rifle.* 她非常害怕，于是拿了一支步枪。

armchair /ˈɑːmtʃeə/ *countable noun* 可数名词
a big comfortable chair that supports your arms 扶手椅：*She was sitting in an armchair in front of the TV.* 她坐在电视前的扶手椅上。

armed /ɑːmd/ *adjective* 形容词
carrying a weapon, usually a gun 携带武器的；武装的；持枪的：*City police said the man was armed with a gun.* 市警方称那名男子携带了一把枪。 □ *There were armed guards in the street outside their house.* 他们家外面的街道上驻有持枪警卫。

armed ˈforces *plural noun* 复数名词
a country's military forces, who fight on the land, the sea, or in the air（一国的）武装部队：*members of the armed forces* 武装部队士兵

armour /ˈɑːmə/ *uncountable noun* 不可数名词
special metal clothing that soldiers wore in the past for protection in battles 盔甲；铠甲：*a suit of armour* 一套盔甲

armpit /ˈɑːmpɪt/ *countable noun* 可数名词
the area of your body under your arm

where your arm joins your shoulder 腋窝：*The water came up to my armpits.* 水涨到了我腋下。

arms /ɑːmz/ ***plural noun*** 复数名词
weapons, especially bombs and guns 武器；军火：*Soldiers searched the house for illegal arms.* 士兵们搜查了那栋房子看是否藏有非法武器。

army /ˈɑːmi/ ***countable noun*** 可数名词 (**armies**)
a large group of soldiers who are trained to fight battles on land 陆军：*Perkins joined the Army at the age of sixteen.* 珀金斯 16 岁参加陆军。

arose /əˈrəʊz/
→ see 见 **arise**

around¹ /əˈraʊnd/ ***preposition*** 介词
1 surrounding a place or an object or on all sides of it 在⋯周围；围绕：*She looked at the people around her.* 她看着周围的人。
2 along the edge of something, and back to the point where you started 绕⋯一圈；环绕：*We went for a walk around the lake.* 我们环湖散了会儿步。● **around** *adverb* 副词：*They live in a little village with hills all around.* 他们住在一个四面环山的小村庄里。□ *They celebrated their win by running around on the football pitch.* 他们绕足球场奔跑庆祝胜利。
3 to the other side of something 绕过；越过；至⋯的另一边：*The man turned back and hurried around the corner.* 那人转过身，匆匆绕过拐角。
4 on the other side of something 在⋯的另一边：*I looked around the door but the hall was empty.* 我在门口朝里看了看，大厅里空无一人。
5 in different parts of a place or an area 在⋯各处；遍及：*Police say ten people have been arrested around the country.* 警方称全国各地有 10 人被捕。

around² /əˈraʊnd/ ***adverb*** 副词
1 into different places 到处：*She moved things around so the table was under the window.* 她把东西挪到别处，让桌子靠窗摆放。
2 present in a place 在某处：*Have you seen my wife anywhere around?* 你在附近一带见到我太太了吗？
3 approximately 大约：*My salary was around £35,000.* 我的薪水在 35,000 英镑上下。

arrange /əˈreɪndʒ/ ***verb*** 动词 (**arranges, arranging, arranged**)
1 to make plans for an event to happen 安排；筹划：*She arranged an appointment for Friday afternoon.* 她安排了星期五下午会面。□ *I've arranged to see him on Thursday.* 我已经安排好周四见他。
2 to carefully place things in a particular position 整理；排列；布置：*She enjoys arranging dried flowers.* 她喜欢干花插花。

arrangement /əˈreɪndʒmənt/ ***countable noun*** 可数名词
1 a plan that someone makes so that something can happen 安排；筹划：*They're working on final arrangements for the meeting.* 他们正在为会议做最后的准备。
2 a group of things that have been placed in a particular position 排列；布置：*a flower arrangement* 插花

arrest /əˈrest/ ***verb*** 动词 (**arrests, arresting, arrested**)
to take someone to a police station, because they may have broken the law 逮捕；拘捕：*Police arrested five young men in the city.* 警方在城中拘捕了 5 个年轻人。
● **arrest** *noun* 名词：*Police later made two arrests.* 警方后来逮捕了两人。

arrival /əˈraɪvəl/ ***noun*** 名词
when you arrive somewhere 到达；到来：*It was the day after his arrival in Glasgow.* 那是他到格拉斯哥的第二天。

arrive /əˈraɪv/ ***verb*** 动词 (**arrives, arriving, arrived**)
to come to a place from somewhere else 到达；抵达：*Their train arrived on time.* 他们的火车正点到达。□ *After a couple of hours, we arrived at the airport.* 几个小时后，我们到了机场。

arrogant /ˈærəɡənt/ ***adjective*** 形容词
behaving in an unpleasant way towards other people because you believe that you are more important than them 傲慢的；自大的：*Some rather arrogant people think they know everything.* 有些颇为傲慢的人认为他们无所不知。
▶ **arrogance** /ˈærəɡəns/ *uncountable noun* 不可数名词：*the arrogance of powerful people* 强权者的傲慢

arrow /ˈærəʊ/ ***countable noun*** 可数名词
1 a long thin weapon that is sharp and pointed at one end 箭：*They were armed with bows and arrows.* 他们佩带着弓箭。

2 a written sign that points in a particular direction 箭头；箭头符号：*The arrow pointed down to the bottom of the page.* 箭头指向页面底部。

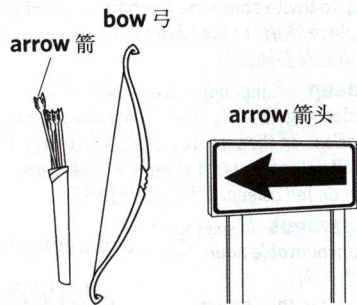
bow 弓
arrow 箭
arrow 箭头

art /ɑːt/ *noun* 名词
1 **uncountable** 不可数 pictures or objects that are created for people to look at 艺术作品；美术作品：*modern American art* 美国现代艺术作品
2 **uncountable** 不可数 the activity of creating pictures or objects for people to look at 艺术；美术：*She decided she wanted to study art.* 她决定学习美术。□ *Edinburgh College of Art* 爱丁堡艺术学院
3 [**arts**] *plural* 复数 activities such as music, painting, literature, film, theatre and dance 艺术活动：*She knew she wanted a career in the arts.* 她知道自己想从事艺术事业。
→ Look at pictures on P13 参见彩图第 13 页

artery /ˈɑːtəri/ *countable noun* 可数名词 (**arteries**)
one of the tubes in your body that carry blood from your heart to the rest of your body. Compare with **vein**. 动脉（比较 vein）：*Many patients suffer from blocked arteries.* 很多病人患有动脉阻塞。

ˈart ˌgallery *countable noun* 可数名词 (**art galleries**)
a place where people go to look at art 美术馆：*It is the most famous art gallery in the world.* 这是世界上最著名的美术馆。

arthritis /ɑːˈθraɪtɪs/ *uncountable noun* 不可数名词
a medical condition in which the joints in your body swell and become painful 关节炎：*I have arthritis in my wrist.* 我手腕患有关节炎。

artichoke /ˈɑːtɪtʃəʊk/ *noun* 名词
a round green vegetable that has thick leaves and looks like a flower 洋蓟（一种绿叶蔬菜）

article /ˈɑːtɪkəl/ *countable noun* 可数名词
1 a piece of writing in a newspaper or magazine（报刊）文章：*I read about it in a newspaper article.* 我是在一篇报纸文章里读到这个的。
2 a word like 'a', 'an' or 'the', which shows whether you are talking about a particular thing or things in general 冠词（即 a、an 和 the）

artificial /ˌɑːtɪˈfɪʃəl/ *adjective* 形容词
made by people, instead of nature 人造的；人工的：*The city has many small lakes, natural and artificial.* 这个城市有很多小型湖泊，有天然的，也有人工的。□ *Try to follow a diet that is free from artificial additives.* 尽量只吃不含人工添加剂的食物。
▶ **artificially** /ˌɑːtɪˈfɪʃəli/ *adverb* 副词：*artificially sweetened lemonade* 加了人造甜味剂的柠檬饮料

ˌartificial inˈtelligence *uncountable noun* 不可数名词
the way in which computers can work in a similar way to the human mind 人工智能

artist /ˈɑːtɪst/ *countable noun* 可数名词
1 someone who draws, paints or creates other works of art 画家；美术家；艺术家：*Each painting is signed by the artist.* 每幅画上都有画家的签名。
2 a performer such as a musician, an actor or a dancer 表演艺术家；艺人：*He was a popular artist, who sold millions of records.* 他是一位很受欢迎的艺人，唱片销量达数百万张。

artistic /ɑːˈtɪstɪk/ *adjective* 形容词
good at drawing or painting 有美术天赋的；善于绘画的：*The boys are sensitive and artistic.* 这些男孩子性格敏感，有美术天分。

as¹ /əz, STRONG 强读 æz/ *conjunction* 连词
1 at the same time as something else happens 当…的时候；随着：*We shut the door behind us as we entered.* 我们进去之后随手关上了门。
2 used for saying how something happens or is done 像…一样；如同：*Today, as usual, he was wearing a suit.* 今天，他穿着西服，一如往常。□ *Please do as you're asked first time.* 有什么指令请马上照办。
3 because 因为：*As I was so young, I didn't have to pay.* 我年龄小，不用付钱。

as² /əz, STRONG 强读 æz/ *preposition* 介词
1 used when you are talking about

someone's job（表示职业）作为: *She works as a nurse.* 她是个护士。
2 used when you are talking about the purpose of something（表示用途）当作: *The fourth bedroom is used as a study.* 第四个卧室用作书房。
as...as used when you are comparing things, or saying how large or small something is 像⋯⋯一样⋯: *It's not as easy as I expected.* 这没有我预期那么简单。▫ *I'm nearly as big as you.* 我块头基本和你一样大。
as if used when you are saying that something appears to be the case 好像；仿佛: *Anne stopped, as if she didn't know what to say next.* 安妮停了下来，仿佛不知道接下来该说什么。

asap /ˌeɪ es eɪ ˈpiː/ *adverb* 副词
short for (缩写 =) 'as soon as possible' 尽快

ash /æʃ/ *noun* 名词 (**ashes**)
the grey powder that remains after something is burned 灰；灰烬: *the cold ashes of a log fire* 原木燃烧后冷却的灰烬

ashamed /əˈʃeɪmd/ *adjective* 形容词
feeling embarrassed or guilty because of someone or something 惭愧的；羞愧的；愧疚的: *I was ashamed of myself for getting so angry.* 我为自己发那么大的火而感到惭愧。

ashore /əˈʃɔː/ *adverb* 副词
from the sea onto the land 上岸；到陆地上: *The hurricane came ashore south of Miami.* 飓风在迈阿密南部登陆。

ashtray /ˈæʃtreɪ/ *countable noun* 可数名词
a small dish for cigarette ash 烟灰缸

aside /əˈsaɪd/ *adverb* 副词
1 to one side of someone 向一边；到一边: *Sarah closed the book and put it aside.* 萨拉合上书放到一边。
2 so that someone can pass you（为闪避而）到旁边，向一旁: *She stepped aside to let them pass.* 她闪到一旁，让他们过去。

ask /ɑːsk/ *verb* 动词 (**asks, asking, asked**)
1 to say something to someone in the form of a question 问；询问: *'How is Frank?' he asked.* "弗兰克怎么样了？"他问道。▫ *I asked him his name.* 我问了他的名字。▫ *She asked me if I was enjoying my dinner.* 她问我对晚餐是否满意。
2 to tell someone that you want them to do something 要求；请求: *We politely asked him to leave.* 我们礼貌地要求他离开。
3 to say that you would like to know or have something 索要；恳求: *She asked for my address.* 她要我的地址。
4 to invite someone to go to an event or a place 邀请: *I asked Juan to the party.* 我邀请胡安参加聚会。

asleep /əˈsliːp/ *adjective* 形容词
sleeping 睡着的；熟睡的: *My daughter was asleep on the sofa.* 我女儿在沙发上睡着了。
fall asleep to start sleeping 入睡: *Sam soon fell asleep.* 萨姆很快就睡着了。

asparagus /əˈspærəɡəs/ *uncountable noun* 不可数名词
a long, thin, green vegetable 芦笋

asparagus 芦笋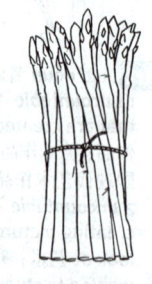

aspect /ˈæspekt/ *countable noun* 可数名词
a quality or a part of something 特性；方面: *He was interested in all aspects of the work here.* 他对这里工作的方方面面都感兴趣。

aspirin /ˈæsprɪn/ *noun* 名词
a mild drug that reduces pain 阿司匹林（镇痛药）

assassinate /əˈsæsɪneɪt/ *verb* 动词 (**assassinates, assassinating, assassinated**)
to murder someone for political reasons 暗杀；行刺: *Robert Kennedy was assassinated in 1968.* 罗伯特·肯尼迪于 1968 年被暗杀。
▶ **assassination** /əˌsæsɪˈneɪʃən/ *noun* 名词: *There were rumours that an assassination attempt was likely.* 有传言称有人可能要行刺。

assault /əˈsɔːlt/ *noun* 名词
a physical attack on a person 攻击；人身侵犯: *There has been a series of assaults in the university area.* 大学区发生了一系列人身侵犯事件。● **assault** *verb* 动词 (**assaults, assaulting, assaulted**): *The gang assaulted him with baseball bats.* 这伙人用棒球棒殴打他。

assemble /əˈsembəl/ *verb* 动词 (**assembles, assembling, assembled**)
1 to come together in a group 集合；聚集: *The students assembled in the hall before classes.* 课前学生们在大厅集合。
2 to collect something together or to fit

the different parts of it together 组装；装配：*Workers were assembling aeroplanes.* 工人们在组装飞机。

assembly /əˈsembli/ *noun* 名词 (**assemblies**)
1 *countable* 可数 a group of people gathered together for a particular purpose 集会：*She made the announcement during a school assembly.* 她在学校集会上通报了这件事。
2 *uncountable* 不可数 the process of fitting the different parts of something together 组装；装配：*a car assembly line* 汽车装配线

assess /əˈses/ *verb* 动词 (**assesses, assessing, assessed**)
to consider a person, thing or situation in order to make a judgment about them 评估；评定：*I looked around and assessed the situation.* 我环顾四周，估计了一下形势。 □ *The doctor is assessing whether I am well enough to travel.* 医生正在评估我的身体状况是否适合出行。
▶ **assessment** /əˈsesmənt/ *noun* 名词：*We carry out an annual assessment of senior managers.* 我们对高级管理人员进行年度考评。

asset /ˈæset/ *countable noun* 可数名词
someone or something that is considered to be useful or valuable 有用的人（或物）；财富：*He is a great asset to the company.* 他是公司的宝贵财富。

assignment /əˈsaɪnmənt/ *countable noun* 可数名词
a task that you are given to do, especially as part of your studies 作业；任务：*We give written assignments as well as practical tests.* 我们会布置书面作业，还会有实践测试。

assist /əˈsɪst/ *verb* 动词 (**assists, assisting, assisted**)
to help someone 帮助；协助：*He was assisting elderly passengers with their luggage.* 他在帮助上了年纪的乘客拿行李。

assistance /əˈsɪstəns/ *uncountable noun* 不可数名词
when you help someone 帮助；协助：*Please let us know if you need any assistance.* 需要什么帮助请尽管和我们说。

assistant /əˈsɪstənt/ *countable noun* 可数名词
a person who helps someone in their work 助理；助手：*Mr Johnson asked his assistant*

to answer the phone while he went out. 约翰逊先生外出期间让助手帮他接听电话。

associate¹ /əˈsəʊsieɪt/ *verb* 动词 (**associates, associating, associated**)
to connect someone or something in some way with something else in your mind 联系；联想：*Some people associate money with happiness.* 有些人把金钱和幸福联系在一起。

associate² /əˈsəʊsiət/ *countable noun* 可数名词
a person you are closely connected with, especially at work 同事；合作伙伴：*business associates* 商业伙伴

association /əˌsəʊsiˈeɪʃn/ *countable noun* 可数名词
an official group of people who have the same job, aim or interest 团体；协会；社团：*We're all members of the National Basketball Association.* 我们都是美国职业篮球联赛的一员。

assorted /əˈsɔːtɪd/ *adjective* 形容词
different from each other in some way 各式各样的；混杂的：*We have a selection of cotton jumpers in assorted colours.* 我们有各种颜色的棉线衫可供选择。

assortment /əˈsɔːtmənt/ *countable noun* 可数名词
a group of things that are different from each other in some way（不同事物的）组合，混合；什锦：*There was an assortment of books on the shelf.* 架子上有各种类型的书。

assume /əˈsjuːm/ *verb* 动词 (**assumes, assuming, assumed**)
to suppose that something is true 假设；假定：*I assumed it was an accident.* 我猜这是一起事故。

assure /əˈʃʊə/ *verb* 动词 (**assures, assuring, assured**)
to tell someone that something is true or will happen 向…保证；使确信：*He assured me that there was nothing wrong.* 他向我保证一切都好。 □ *'Are you sure it's safe?' she asked anxiously. 'It couldn't be safer,' Max assured her.* "你确定这个安全吗？"她不安地问道。"再安全不过了。"马克斯向她保证。

asterisk /ˈæstərɪsk/ *countable noun* 可数名词
the sign * 星号

asthma /ˈæsmə/ *uncountable noun* 不可数名词
a lung condition that causes difficulty in

breathing 哮喘

astonish /əˈstɒnɪʃ/ *verb* 动词 (**astonishes, astonishing, astonished**)
to surprise someone very much 使惊愕；使震惊: *The news astonished them.* 这个消息令他们震惊。
▶ **astonished** /əˈstɒnɪʃt/ *adjective* 形容词: *They were astonished to find the driver was a young boy.* 令他们震惊的是，开车的居然是个小男孩。

astonishing /əˈstɒnɪʃɪŋ/ *adjective* 形容词
very surprising 令人震惊的；非常惊人的: *She found that fact astonishing.* 她觉得这一事实令人震惊。
▶ **astonishingly** /əˈstɒnɪʃɪŋli/ *adverb* 副词: *Andrea was an astonishingly beautiful young woman.* 安德烈娅是个美得惊人的年轻女子。

astonishment /əˈstɒnɪʃmənt/ *uncountable noun* 不可数名词
a feeling of great surprise 震惊；惊愕: *He looked at her in astonishment.* 他惊愕地看着她。

astronaut /ˈæstrənɔːt/ *countable noun* 可数名词
a person who is trained for travelling in space 航天员

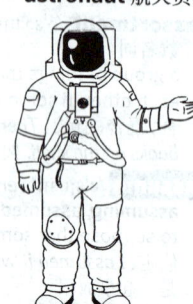

astronaut 航天员

astronomy /əˈstrɒnəmi/ *uncountable noun* 不可数名词
the scientific study of the stars, planets and other natural objects in space 天文学
▶ **astronomer** /əˈstrɒnəmə/ *countable noun* 可数名词: *an amateur astronomer* 天文学爱好者

at /ət, STRONG 强读 æt/ *preposition* 介词
1 used for saying where something happens or is situated 在（某处）: *He will be at the airport to meet her.* 他会到机场去接她。 □ *I didn't like being alone at home.* 我不喜欢独自待在家里。 □ *They agreed to meet at a restaurant.* 他们同意在一家餐馆见面。
2 used for saying when something happens 在（某时间）: *The funeral will take place this afternoon at 3.00 p.m.* 葬礼将于今天下午3点举行。
3 used for saying how fast, how far or how much 以（某一速度、距离或数量）: *I drove back down the motorway at normal speed.* 我以正常车速开车沿高速公路返回。 □ *There were only two houses at that price.* 那个价位的房子只有两栋。
4 used when you direct an action towards someone 朝（某人）: *He looked at Michael and laughed.* 他看着迈克尔笑了。
5 used for saying that someone or something is in a particular state or condition 处于（某状态）: *The two nations are at war.* 那两个国家在交战。
6 used for saying what someone is reacting to 对…（作出反应）: *Mum was annoyed at the mess.* 妈妈看到这一片狼藉很恼火。

good at something doing something well 擅长某事的: *I'm good at my work.* 我很擅长我的工作。

ate /et, eɪt/
→ see 见 **eat**

athlete /ˈæθliːt/ *countable noun* 可数名词
a person who is good at any type of physical sports, exercise or games, especially in competitions 运动员: *Jesse Owens was one of the greatest athletes of the twentieth century.* 杰西·欧文斯是20世纪最伟大的运动员之一。

athletic /æθˈletɪk/ *adjective* 形容词
relating to athletes and athletics 运动员的；体育运动的: *He comes from an athletic family.* 他来自一个运动员家庭。

atlas /ˈætləs/ *countable noun* 可数名词 (**atlases**)
a book of maps 地图册；地图集
→ Look at picture on P9 参见彩插第9页

ATM /ˌeɪ tiː ˈem/ *countable noun* 可数名词 (**ATMs**) (*American* 美国英语)
→ see 见 **cash machine**

atmosphere /ˈætməsfɪə/ *noun* 名词
1 *countable* 可数 the layer of air or other gases around a planet 大气；大气层: *The shuttle Columbia will re-enter the Earth's atmosphere tomorrow morning.* "哥伦比亚"号航天飞机将于明天早晨重返地球大气层。
▶ **atmospheric** /ˌætməsˈferɪk/ *adjective* 形容词: *atmospheric gases* 大气中的气体
2 *singular* 单数 the general feeling that you get when you are in a place 气氛；氛

围: *The rooms are warm and the atmosphere is welcoming.* 这些房间温暖宜人，氛围友好亲切。

atom /ˈætəm/ *countable noun* 可数名词
the very smallest part of something 原子

atomic /əˈtɒmɪk/ *adjective* 形容词
relating to atoms or to power that is produced by splitting atoms 原子的；原子能的: *atomic energy* 原子能 □ *the atomic number of an element* 元素的原子序数

attach /əˈtætʃ/ *verb* 动词 (**attaches, attaching, attached**)
1 to fasten something to an object 绑；系；附: *There is usually a label with instructions attached to the plant.* 植株上通常挂有说明标签。 □ *Please use the form attached to this letter.* 请使用这封信所附的表格。
2 to send a file with an email message (给电子邮件)附上(附件): *I'm attaching the document to this email.* 我会在这封电子邮件中附上这个文件。

attached /əˈtætʃt/ *adjective* 形容词
liking someone or something very much 依恋的；非常喜爱的: *She is very attached to her family and friends.* 她很爱自己的亲友。

attachment /əˈtætʃmənt/ *countable noun* 可数名词
a file that is attached to an email message and sent with it (电子邮件的)附件: *You can send your CV as an attachment to an email.* 你可将简历作为邮件附件发送。

attack[1] /əˈtæk/ *verb* 动词 (**attacks, attacking, attacked**)
1 to try to hurt someone 攻击(人): *I thought he was going to attack me.* 我觉得他要攻击我。 □ *He was in the garden when the dog attacked.* 他待在花园里，那条狗攻击了他。
2 to use violence to enter a building or a town 袭击，进攻(建筑物或城镇): *An armed gang attacked the bank.* 一伙武装分子袭击了银行。

attack[2] /əˈtæk/ *noun* 名词
1 an occasion when someone tries to hurt someone 攻击: *There have been several attacks on police officers.* 袭警事件已有数起。
2 *countable* 可数 when you suffer badly from an illness (疾病的)侵袭, 发作: *an asthma attack* 哮喘发作

attempt /əˈtempt/ *countable noun* 可数名词

an occasion when you try to do something, often without success 尝试；试图: *He made three attempts to rescue his injured colleague.* 他 3 次试图营救受伤的同事。 ● **attempt** *verb* 动词 (**attempts, attempting, attempted**): *She attempted to rescue the boy from the river.* 她试图从河里救出那个男孩。

attend /əˈtend/ *verb* 动词 (**attends, attending, attended**)
1 to be present at an event 出席；参加: *Thousands of people attended the wedding.* 数千人出席了婚礼。 □ *I was invited but I was unable to attend.* 我接到了邀请，但未能出席。
2 to go to a school, college or church regularly 去(教堂、学校); 上(学): *They attended college together.* 他们一起上的大学。
▶ **attendance** /əˈtendəns/ *uncountable noun* 不可数名词: *Attendance at the school is always high.* 这所学校的出勤率一直很高。

attendant /əˈtendənt/ *countable noun* 可数名词
someone whose job is to serve people in a public place 服务员: *Tony Williams was working as a car park attendant in Leeds.* 托尼·威廉斯当时在利兹一家停车场做管理员。

attention /əˈtenʃən/ *uncountable noun* 不可数名词
1 when you look at someone or something, listen to them or think about them carefully 注意；专心: *Can I have your attention?* 请注意听我讲话好吗？
2 when someone is dealing with you or caring for you 照料；护理: *Each year more than two million people need medical attention.* 每年有两百多万人需要治疗。
pay attention to watch and listen carefully 注意；留心: *Are you paying attention to what I'm saying?* 你注意听我说话了吗？

attic /ˈætɪk/ *countable noun* 可数名词
a room at the top of a house just under the roof 顶楼；阁楼

attitude /ˈætɪtjuːd/ *noun* 名词
the way that you think and feel about something 态度；看法: *You need to change your attitude to life.* 你应当改变生活态度。

attract /əˈtrækt/ *verb* 动词 (**attracts, attracting, attracted**)
1 to cause someone or something to come

to a place 吸引：*The museum is attracting many visitors.* 这家博物馆吸引了很多游客。**2** used for describing how one object causes a second object to move towards it 对…产生引力：*Opposite ends of a magnet attract each other.* 磁铁两极相互吸引。
→ Look at picture on P6 参见彩插第 6 页
be attracted to someone/something to like someone or something, and to be interested in knowing more about them 受某人／某事物吸引：*I was attracted to her immediately.* 我立刻被她吸引住了。

attraction /əˈtrækʃən/ *noun* 名词
1 *uncountable* 不可数 a feeling of liking someone 爱慕；喜欢：*His attraction to her was growing.* 他越来越喜欢她。**2** *countable* 可数 something that people can visit for interest or enjoyment 吸引人的地方：*Disney World is an important tourist attraction.* 迪士尼乐园是重要的旅游点。

attractive /əˈtræktɪv/ *adjective* 形容词
pleasant to look at 漂亮的；动人的；有魅力的：*She's a very attractive woman.* 她是个非常漂亮的女人。□ *The flat was small but attractive.* 这所公寓虽小但很温馨。

aubergine /ˈəʊbəʒiːn/ *noun* 名词 (*American* 美国英语：**eggplant**)
a vegetable with a smooth, dark purple skin 茄子

auction /ˈɔːkʃən/ *noun* 名词
a public sale where items are sold to the person who offers the most money 拍卖：*The painting sold for £400,000 at auction.* 这幅画在拍卖会上以 40 万英镑的价格售出。● **auction** *verb* 动词 (**auctions, auctioning, auctioned**)：*Eight drawings by French artist Jean Cocteau will be auctioned next week.* 法国画家让·科克托的 8 幅画作将于下周拍卖。

audience /ˈɔːdiəns/ *countable noun* 可数名词
all the people who are watching or listening to a performance, a film or a television programme 观众；听众：*There was a TV audience of 35 million.* 电视观众人数达 3,500 万。

audio /ˈɔːdiəʊ/ *adjective* 形容词
used for recording and producing sound 录音的；音频的：*audio and video files* 音视频文件

audition /ɔːˈdɪʃən/ *countable noun* 可数名词
a short performance that an actor, a dancer or a musician gives so that someone can decide if they are good enough to be in a play, film or orchestra (演员等的)试镜，试演：*She went to an audition for a Broadway musical.* 她参加了一部百老汇音乐剧的试演。

August /ˈɔːɡəst/ *noun* 名词
the eighth month of the year 八月：*The film comes out in August.* 这部电影 8 月份上映。□ *My new job starts on 22 August.* 我 8 月 22 号开始新工作。

aunt /ɑːnt/ *countable noun* 可数名词
the sister of your mother or father, or the wife of your uncle 姨妈；姑妈；舅妈；婶母；伯母：*She wrote to her aunt in Manchester.* 她给在曼彻斯特的姨妈写了信。□ *Aunt Margaret is coming to visit next week.* 玛格丽特姑妈下周要来做客。

authentic /ɔːˈθentɪk/ *adjective* 形容词
real 真实的；真正的：*They serve authentic Italian food.* 他们供应地道的意大利美食。

author /ˈɔːθə/ *countable noun* 可数名词
1 the person who wrote a piece of writing 作者；著者：*Jill Phillips is the author of the book 'Give Your Child Music'.* 吉尔·菲利普斯是《给孩子音乐》一书的作者。**2** a person whose job is writing books 作家：*Haruki Murakami is Japan's best-selling author.* 村上春树是日本畅销书作家。

authority /ɔːˈθɒrɪti/ *noun* 名词 (**authorities**)
1 *uncountable* 不可数 the power to control other people 权力；权限：*Only the police have the authority to close roads.* 只有警方有权封路。□ *He is now in a position of authority.* 他现在身居权位。**2** [**authorities**] *plural* 复数 the people who are in charge of everyone else 当局；当权者：*The authorities are investigating the attack.* 当局正在调查这起袭击事件。**3** *countable* 可数 an official organization or government department 管理机构：*the Local Education Authority* 地方教育局

authorize /ˈɔːθəraɪz/ *verb* 动词 (**authorizes, authorizing, authorized**)
to give your permission for something to happen 批准；许可：*Only the president could authorize its use.* 这个只有总统能批准使用。
▶ **authorization** /ˌɔːθəraɪˈzeɪʃən/ *uncountable noun* 不可数名词：*We didn't have authorization from the general to*

leave. 我们未得到将军批准，不能离开。

autobiography /ˌɔːtəbaɪˈɒɡrəfi/ *countable noun* 可数名词 (**autobiographies**)
the story of your life, that you write yourself 自传: *He published his autobiography last autumn.* 他去年秋天出版了自传。
▶ **autobiographical** /ˌɔːtəbaɪəˈɡræfɪkəl/ *adjective* 形容词: *an autobiographical novel* 自传体小说

autograph /ˈɔːtəɡrɑːf/ *countable noun* 可数名词
the signature of someone famous (名人的)亲笔签名: *He asked for her autograph.* 他索要她的签名。

automatic /ˌɔːtəˈmætɪk/ *adjective* 形容词
1 an automatic machine works when no one is operating it (机器)自动的，自动化的: *Modern trains have automatic doors.* 现代火车装有自动门。
2 done without thinking 无意识的；不假思索的: *All of the automatic body functions, even breathing, are affected.* 所有无意识的机体功能，甚至呼吸，都受到影响。
▶ **automatically** /ˌɔːtəˈmætɪkli/ *adverb* 副词: *You will automatically wake up after 30 minutes.* 30 分钟后，你会自己醒来。

automobile /ˈɔːtəməbiːl/ *countable noun* 可数名词 (*American* 美国英语)
→ see 见 **car**

autumn /ˈɔːtəm/ *noun* 名词 (*American* 美国英语: **fall**)
the season between summer and winter when the weather becomes cooler and the leaves fall off the trees 秋天；秋季
→ Look at picture on P8 参见彩插第 8 页

auxiliary verb /ɔːɡˈzɪljəri ˌvɜːb/ *countable noun* 可数名词
a verb that you can combine with another verb to change its meaning slightly. In English, 'be', 'have' and 'do' are auxiliary verbs. 助动词(如 be、have、do)

available /əˈveɪləbəl/ *adjective* 形容词
1 that you can find or get 能找到的；可获得的: *Breakfast is available from 6 a.m.* 早上 6 点开始供应早餐。
2 not busy and free to do something 有空的；有闲暇的: *Mr Leach is not available for interviews today.* 利奇先生今天没空接受采访。

avalanche /ˈævəlɑːntʃ/ *countable noun* 可数名词
a large amount of snow or earth that falls down the side of a mountain 雪崩；山崩；

崩塌

avenue /ˈævɪnjuː/ *countable noun* 可数名词
1 sometimes used in the names of streets. The written short form 'Ave.' is also used. 大街，街道(有时用于街名，书面缩写形式为 Ave.): *They live on Park Avenue.* 他们住在公园大道。
2 a straight road, especially one with trees on either side 大道；(尤指)林荫道

average[1] /ˈævərɪdʒ/ *noun* 名词
1 *countable* 可数 the result that you get when you add two or more amounts together and divide the total by the number of amounts you added together 平均数: *'What's the average of 4, 5 and 6?' — '5.'* "4、5、6 的平均数是几？"——"5。" ● **average** *adjective* 形容词: *The average price of goods went up by just 2.2%.* 商品平均价格只上涨了 2.2%。
2 *singular* 单数 the normal amount or quality for a particular group 正常数量；一般水平: *Rainfall was twice the average for this time of year.* 雨量是每年同期平均水平的两倍。 ● **average** *adjective* 形容词: *The average adult man burns 1,500 to 2,000 calories per day.* 普通成年人每天消耗 1,500 到 2,000 卡路里的热量。

average[2] /ˈævərɪdʒ/ *adjective* 形容词
ordinary 普通的；一般的: *He seemed to be a pleasant, average guy.* 他看上去是个和善、普通的男人。

avocado /ˌævəˈkɑːdəʊ/ *noun* 名词
a fruit with dark green skin and a large seed in the middle 鳄梨；油梨: *crab and avocado salad* 蟹肉鳄梨沙拉

avoid /əˈvɔɪd/ *verb* 动词 (**avoids, avoiding, avoided**)
1 to do something in order to stop something unpleasant from happening 避免；防止: *It was a last-minute attempt to avoid a disaster.* 这是为避免灾难发生而做的最后努力。
2 to choose not to do something 回避，避免(做某事): *I avoid working in public places.* 我避免在公共场所工作。
3 to keep away from a person or thing 躲避；避开: *She went to the women's toilets to avoid him.* 她进了女卫生间以躲开他。

> **LANGUAGE HELP** 语言提示
> Remember that you **cannot** say that you 'avoid to do something'. 切记不能说 avoid to do something。

awake – axis

awake /əˈweɪk/ *adjective* 形容词
not sleeping 醒着的；没睡的：*I stayed awake until midnight.* 我到半夜还没睡。

award /əˈbɔːd/ *countable noun* 可数名词
a prize that a person is given for doing something well 奖项；奖品：*He won the National Book Award for fiction.* 他获得了国家图书奖小说类奖项。● **award** *verb* 动词 (**awards, awarding, awarded**)：*She was awarded the prize for both films.* 她两部电影都获了这项奖。

aware /əˈweə/ *adjective* 形容词
knowing about something 意识到的；明白的：*They are well aware of the danger.* 他们充分意识到了这一危险。

▶ **awareness** /əˈweənəs/ *uncountable noun* 不可数名词：*We are trying to raise awareness of the pollution problem.* 我们在尽力提高对污染问题的意识。

away /əˈweɪ/ *adverb* 副词
1 moving in a direction so that you are no longer in a place 离开：*He walked away from his car.* 他从自己的车边走开。
2 not in the place where people expect you to be 不在：*Jason was working away from home for a while.* 贾森外出工作一阵子。
3 due to happen after a particular period of time 距现在；距当时：*Christmas is now only two weeks away.* 再过两个礼拜就是圣诞节了。
4 not near a person or place 不靠近；远离：*Remember to stay a safe distance away from the car in front.* 注意要和前车保持安全距离。
5 at an opponent's sports ground. Compare with **home**.（运动队）在客场（比较 home）：*Canada's Davis Cup team will play away against the Netherlands in February.* 戴维斯杯网球赛加拿大队2月份将客场对阵荷兰队。● **away** *adjective* 形容词：*Charlton are about to play an important away match.* 查尔顿将要打一场重要的客场比赛。

put something away to put something where it should be 收起某物：*I put my book away and went to bed.* 我把书收起来上床睡觉了。

awesome /ˈɔːsəm/ *adjective* 形容词
1 very powerful or frightening 令人惊叹的；使人敬畏的：*I love the awesome power of the ocean waves.* 我喜欢海浪令人惊叹的力量。
2 very good or special (*informal* 非正式)

很棒的；极好的；非常特殊的：*We all agreed the game was awesome.* 我们一致认为这场比赛非常精彩。

awful /ˈɔːfʊl/ *adjective* 形容词
very bad 极坏的；糟糕透顶的：*I thought he was an awful actor.* 我认为他这个演员演技极差。 □ *There was an awful smell of paint.* 有一股非常难闻的油漆味。

awkward /ˈɔːkwəd/ *adjective* 形容词
1 embarrassing and difficult to deal with 令人尴尬的；难处理的：*He kept asking awkward questions.* 他一直问令人尴尬的问题。
▶ **awkwardly** /ˈɔːkwədli/ *adverb* 副词：*There was an awkwardly long silence.* 现场陷入了长时间的沉默，气氛尴尬。
2 difficult to use or carry 不好用的；携带不便的：*The bicycle was small but awkward to carry.* 这辆自行车小是小，但携带不便。
3 looking strange or uncomfortable 笨拙的；别扭的：*Amy made an awkward movement with her hands.* 埃米笨拙地做了个手势。
▶ **awkwardly** /ˈɔːkwədli/ *adverb* 副词：*He fell awkwardly.* 他笨拙地摔倒了。

axe /æks/ *countable noun* 可数名词
a tool with a heavy metal blade and a long handle that is used for cutting wood 斧；斧头
→ Look at picture on P10 参见彩插第 10 页

axis /ˈæksɪs/ *countable noun* 可数名词
(**axes** /ˈæksiːz/)
1 an imaginary line through the middle of something（假想的）轴，轴线：*The Earth spins around its axis.* 地球绕地轴自转。
2 one of the two lines on which you mark points to show measurements or amounts 坐标轴：*We can label the axes: time is on the vertical axis and money is on the horizontal one.* 我们可以标注下坐标轴：纵轴代表时间，横轴代表钱数。

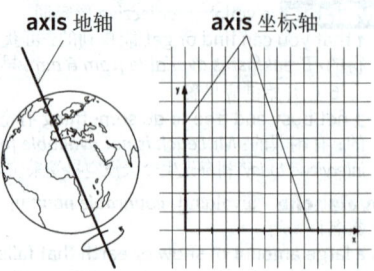

axis 地轴　　**axis** 坐标轴

Bb

baa /bɑː/ *verb* 动词 (**baas, baaing, baaed**)
to make the typical sound of a sheep (羊) 咩咩叫: *He sat by the tent, listening to the lambs baaing.* 他坐在帐篷边，听着羔羊咩的叫声。

baby /ˈbeɪbi/ *countable noun* 可数名词 (**babies**)
a very young child 婴儿: *He bathed the baby and put her to bed.* 他给宝宝洗了澡安顿上床。□ *My wife has just had a baby.* 我妻子刚生了孩子。

babysit /ˈbeɪbisɪt/ *verb* 动词 (**babysits, babysitting, babysat**)
to look after a child while the child's parents are not at home 代人临时照看小孩: *I promised to babysit for Mrs Plunkett.* 我答应替普伦基特太太临时照看孩子。

babysitter /ˈbeɪbiˌsɪtə/ *countable noun* 可数名词
a person who looks after a child while the child's parents are not at home 临时保姆: *It can be difficult to find a good babysitter.* 找一个靠谱的临时保姆可不容易。

bachelor /ˈbætʃələ/ *countable noun* 可数名词
a man who has never married 未婚男子；单身汉

back¹ /bæk/ *adverb* 副词
1 in the direction that is behind you 向后；在后: *She stepped back from the door.* 她从门口退了回来。
2 in or to the place where someone or something was before 在原处；回原处: *I went back to bed.* 我回到床上。□ *I'll be back as soon as I can.* 我会尽快回来。□ *Put the meat back in the freezer.* 把肉放回冰柜。
3 used when you are talking about phoning or writing to someone after they have phoned or written to you 回应（来电、来信）: *I'll call you back after dinner.* 我晚饭后给你回电。□ *I wrote to Anna last week but she hasn't written back yet.* 我上个星期给安娜写了封信，可她到现在也没

回信。

back and forth in one direction and then in the opposite direction 来回地: *He paced back and forth.* 他踱来踱去。

back² /bæk/ *countable noun* 可数名词
1 the part of your body from your neck to your waist that is on the opposite side to your chest 背；后背: *Her son was lying on his back.* 她儿子仰躺着。
→ Look at picture on P4 参见彩插第 4 页
2 the side or part of something that is furthest from the front 背面；后面；后部: *She was in a room at the back of the shop.* 她在店铺后部一个房间里。● **back** *adjective* 形容词: *She opened the back door.* 她打开后门。□ *Ann sat in the back seat of their car.* 安坐在他们汽车后座上。

back to front with the back where the front should be 前后颠倒: *You're wearing your T-shirt back to front.* 你把 T 恤衫前后穿反了。□ *He wears his cap back to front.* 他反戴着帽子。

say/do something behind someone's back to say or do something when someone is not there, so that they do not know what you have said or done 背着某人说某事／做某事: *You shouldn't criticize her behind her back.* 你不该背地里指责她。

back³ /bæk/ *verb* 动词 (**backs, backing, backed**)
1 to move a vehicle backwards 倒（车）；使倒退: *He backed his car out of the driveway.* 他把车倒出车道。
2 to support someone 支持；援助: *We told them what we wanted to do, and they agreed to back us.* 我们跟他们说了想怎么办，他们答应出手相助。

back away to move away from someone or something, often because you are frightened（常指因畏惧而）退缩，退却: *James stood up, but the girl backed away.* 詹姆斯站起身来，女孩却退缩了。

back off to move away from someone or something, in order to avoid problems（为

避开问题而）退让：When she saw me she backed off, looking worried. 她一见我就往后退，一脸担忧。

back out to decide not to do something that you had agreed to do 反悔；退出：They've backed out of the project. 他们退出了项目。

back something up
1 to show evidence to suggest that something is true 支持，证实（说法）：He didn't have any proof to back up his story. 他没有任何证据来印证自己的说法。
2 to make a copy of a computer file so that you can use it if the original file is lost 给（计算机文件）做备份：Make sure you back up your files every day. 每天务必备份一下文件。

backbone /'bækbəʊn/ *countable noun* 可数名词
the line of bones down the middle of your back 脊柱

background /'bækgraʊnd/ *noun* 名词
1 *countable* 可数 the type of family you come from and the type of education and experiences you have had 出身；个人背景：He came from a very poor background. 他出身贫苦。
2 *singular* 单数 sounds, such as music, that you can hear but that you are not listening to with your full attention 背景声音：I heard the sound of music in the background. 我听到了背景音乐声。
3 *countable* 可数 the part of a picture that is behind the main things or people in it. Compare with **foreground**.（图片的）背景（比较 foreground）：I looked at the man in the background of the photograph. 我看着照片背景里的那名男子。

backpack /'bækpæk/ *countable noun* 可数名词
a bag that you carry on your back 背包

backstroke /'bækstrəʊk/ *uncountable noun* 不可数名词
a way of swimming on your back 仰泳：Linda swam backstroke and Isabelle swam breaststroke. 琳达游仰泳，伊莎贝尔游蛙泳。

backup /'bækʌp/ also 亦作 **back-up** *noun* 名词
1 *uncountable* 不可数 extra help that you can get if you need it 增援；额外帮助：If you need backup, just call me. 需要增援就给我打电话。
2 *countable* 可数 a copy of a computer file that you can use if the original file is lost or damaged（计算机文件的）备份：It is very important to make backups of your data. 备份数据事关重大。

backward /'bækwəd/ *adjective* 形容词
1 in the direction that is behind you 向后的；朝后的：He walked away without a backward glance. 他头也不回地走了。
2 without modern industries and machines 落后的：backward nations 落后国家

backwards /'bækwədz/ *adverb* 副词
1 towards the direction that is behind you 向后；朝后：He took two steps backwards. 他后退了两步。
2 in the opposite way to the usual way 倒着；逆向：Kate counted backwards from ten to zero. 凯特从 10 倒数到 0。
backwards and forwards in one direction and then in the opposite direction over and over again 来回地；前后地；来来回回：Jennifer moved backwards and forwards in time with the music. 珍妮弗随着音乐前后晃动。

backyard /ˌbæk'jɑːd/ also 亦作 **back yard** *countable noun* 可数名词（*American* 美国英语）
the land at the back of a house 后院：The house has a large backyard. 这所房子有个很大的后院。

bacon /'beɪkən/ *uncountable noun* 不可数名词
strips of salted or smoked meat that comes from a pig 咸猪肉；熏猪肉：We had bacon and eggs for breakfast. 我们早餐吃了咸猪肉和煎蛋。

bacteria /bæk'tɪərɪə/ *plural noun* 复数名词
very small living things that can make people ill 细菌：There were high levels of dangerous bacteria in the water. 这片水域含有大量危险的细菌。
▶ **bacterial** /bæk'tɪərɪəl/ *adjective* 形容词：Tuberculosis is a bacterial disease. 结核病是一种细菌性疾病。

bad /bæd/ *adjective* 形容词 (**worse, worst**)
1 unpleasant or harmful 坏的；有害的；令人不快的：When the weather was bad, I stayed indoors. 天气不好时，我待在屋里。 ▫ When Ross and Judy heard the bad news, they were very upset. 罗斯和朱迪得知这个坏消息后沮丧万分。 ▫ Too much coffee is bad for you. 喝太多咖啡对你不好。

2 of a very low standard, quality or amount 低劣的；劣质的；少得可怜的: *bad housing* 恶劣的居住条件 ▫ *The school's main problem is that teachers' pay is so bad.* 这所学校的主要问题是教师薪资太低。
3 unable to do something well 差劲的；能力欠佳的: *He's a bad driver.* 他车开得不好。
4 painful or not working properly because of illness or injury 疼痛的；不健康的；受伤的: *Joe has a bad back.* 乔伯背有毛病。
5 rude or offensive 粗鲁的；伤人的: *I don't like to hear bad language in the street.* 我不喜欢在街头听见语言恶语。

be bad at something/be bad at doing something to be unable to do something well 不擅长某事／做不好某事: *I'm bad at football.* 我球踢得不好。▫ *He's bad at making decisions.* 他不擅长拿主意。

feel bad about something to feel sorry or guilty about something 为某事感到难过（或歉疚）: *I feel bad that he's doing most of the work.* 大部分工作都是他在干，我心里过意不去。

go bad to become not fit to eat 变质；变坏: *I think this fish has gone bad.* 我觉得这条鱼已经坏掉了。

not bad quite good (*informal* 非正式) 不错；挺好: *'How are you feeling?' — 'Not bad.'* "你感觉怎么样？"——"不错。"

badge /bædʒ/ *countable noun* 可数名词
a small piece of metal or plastic that you wear on your clothes to show people who you are 徽章，证章（戴在衣服上，表明身份）: *I showed him my police badge.* 我给他看了我的警徽。

badger /'bædʒə/ *countable noun* 可数名词
a wild animal, with a white head with two wide black stripes, that lives beneath the ground and comes out to feed at night 獾

badger 獾

badly /'bædli/ *adverb* 副词 (**worse, worst**)
1 in a way that is not successful or effective 差劲地；拙劣地；不成功地: *I was angry because I played so badly.* 我很生气，因为自己表现太差了。▫ *The whole project was badly managed.* 整个项目管理得很糟糕。
2 seriously or severely 严重地；厉害地: *The fire badly damaged a church.* 大火严重毁坏了一座教堂。▫ *One man was killed and another was badly injured.* 一人遇难，另一人受重伤。
3 very much 非常；十分: *Why do you want to go so badly?* 你为什么这么想走？

badminton /'bædmɪntən/ *uncountable noun* 不可数名词
a game played by two or four players in which the players get points by hitting a small object (= a shuttlecock) across a high net using a racket 羽毛球运动

bag /bæg/ *countable noun* 可数名词
a container made of paper, plastic or leather, used for carrying things 袋；包: *He ate a whole bag of sweets.* 他吃了整整一袋糖果。▫ *The old lady was carrying a heavy shopping bag.* 老太太拎着一个沉重的购物袋。

bags 袋；包

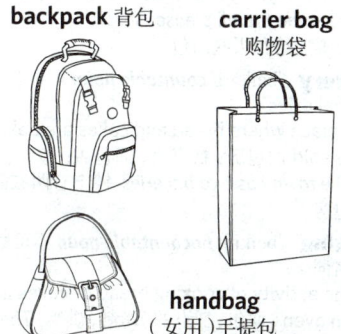

backpack 背包　　carrier bag 购物袋

handbag （女用）手提包

baggage /'bægɪdʒ/ *uncountable noun* 不可数名词
all the bags that you take with you when you travel 行李: *He collected his baggage and left the airport.* 他提取行李后离开了机场。

> **LANGUAGE HELP** 语言提示
> **Baggage** is an uncountable noun. If you want to talk about one bag or suitcase, use **a piece of baggage**. *baggage 是不可数名词，表示一件行李用 a piece of baggage。

baggy /'bægi/ *adjective* 形容词 (**baggier, baggiest**)
big and loose（衣服）宽松的: *He wore baggy trousers and no shirt.* 他穿了条宽松的裤子，没穿衬衫。

bait /beɪt/ *noun* 名词
food that you put on a hook or in a trap to catch fish or animals 饵；诱饵: *This shop*

sells fishing bait. 这家店卖鱼饵。

bake /beɪk/ *verb* 动词 (**bakes, baking, baked**)
to cook food in an oven（在烤炉里）烘烤：*How did you learn to bake cakes?* 你怎么学会的烤蛋糕？ □ *Bake the fish in the oven for 20 minutes.* 把鱼放入烤箱内烤 20 分钟。

baked 'beans *plural noun* 复数名词
small white beans cooked in tomato sauce, sold in a tin 焗豆（白豆配番茄酱做熟，罐装出售）：*baked beans on toast* 焗豆吐司

baker /ˈbeɪkə/ *countable noun* 可数名词
1 a person whose job is to make and sell bread and cakes 面包师；糕点师；面点店老板
2 (also 亦作 **baker's**) a shop where you can buy bread and cakes 面包店；糕点店：*If you're going to the baker's, could you get me some bread, please?* 你要是去面包店，能不能给我买些面包？

bakery /ˈbeɪkəri/ *countable noun* 可数名词 (**bakeries**)
a place where bread and cakes are baked or sold 面包房；糕点房；面包店；糕点店：*The town has two bakeries.* 镇上有两家面包房。

baking /ˈbeɪkɪŋ/ *uncountable noun* 不可数名词
the activity of cooking bread or cakes in an oven（面包、糕点的）烤制，烘焙：*The children want to do some baking.* 孩子们想烘烤些糕点。

balance¹ /ˈbæləns/ *verb* 动词 (**balances, balancing, balanced**)
1 to keep yourself or something else steady, to avoid falling（使）保持平衡：*I balanced on Mark's shoulders.* 我在马克肩头站稳。 □ *She balanced the chair on top of the table.* 她把椅子平稳地放在桌子上。
2 to give the same importance to two different things 同等重视（两个不同的事物）：*Bob has difficulty balancing the demands of his work with the needs of his family.* 鲍勃难以平衡工作要求和家庭需求。

balance² /ˈbæləns/ *noun* 名词
1 *uncountable* 不可数 the ability to stay steady and not to fall over 平衡能力：*Dan lost his balance and started to fall.* 丹失去平衡，开始向下去。
2 *singular* 单数 when all the different parts of something have the same importance 均衡；平衡：*It is important to have a balance between work and play.* 工作和玩耍之间要保持平衡。
3 *countable* 可数 the amount of money you have in your bank account（银行账户）余额：*I'll need to check my bank balance first.* 我得先查一下银行账户余额。

balanced /ˈbælənst/ *adjective* 形容词
fair and reasonable 平衡的；公正合理的：*Journalists should present balanced reports.* 记者应该公平地报道。
a balanced diet a diet containing the right amounts of different foods to keep your body healthy 均衡饮食：*Eat a healthy, balanced diet and get regular exercise.* 饮食要健康、均衡，要经常锻炼。

balcony /ˈbælkəni/ *noun* 名词 (**balconies**)
1 *countable* 可数 a place where you can stand or sit on the outside of a building, above the ground 阳台
2 *singular* 单数 the seats upstairs in a theatre（剧院的）楼厅，楼座

bald /bɔːld/ *adjective* 形容词 (**balder, baldest**)
with no hair, or very little hair, on the top of your head 秃头的；秃顶的：*He rubbed his hand across his bald head.* 他用手揉搓自己的秃头。

ball /bɔːl/ *countable noun* 可数名词
1 a round object that you kick, throw or hit in some sports and games 球：*Two young boys were kicking a ball.* 两个小男孩儿在踢球。 □ *a tennis ball* 网球
2 anything that has a round shape 球状物：*Form the butter into small balls.* 把黄油揉成小球。
3 a large formal party where people dance（大型正式的）舞会：*My parents go to a New Year's ball every year.* 我父母每年都去参加新年舞会。

ballet /ˈbæleɪ/ *noun* 名词
1 *uncountable* 不可数 a type of dancing with carefully planned movements 芭蕾舞：*We saw a film about a boy who becomes a ballet dancer.* 我们看了一部影片，讲述的是一个男孩儿成长为芭蕾舞演员的故事。
2 *countable* 可数 a performance of this type of dancing that tells a story 芭蕾舞剧：*My favourite ballet is 'Swan Lake'.* 我最喜欢的芭蕾舞剧是《天鹅湖》。

balloon /bəˈluːn/ *countable noun* 可数名词
1 a small, thin, brightly-coloured rubber

bag that you blow air into so that it becomes larger. Balloons are used for decoration at parties. 气球: *Large balloons floated above the crowd.* 巨大的气球飘在人群上方。
2 (also 亦作 **hot-air balloon**) a large bag full of hot air, with a basket attached that people can stand in and ride through the air 热气球

ballpark figure /ˈbɔːlpɑːk ˌfɪɡə/ *singular noun* 单数名词
an approximate figure 约数；大概的数字: *I can't tell you the exact cost, but £500 is a ballpark figure.* 我没法告诉你确切的费用，不过大概有 500 英镑。

bamboo /bæmˈbuː/ *uncountable noun* 不可数名词
a tall plant with hard, hollow stems that are sometimes used for making furniture 竹；竹子: *We sat on big bamboo chairs with soft cushions.* 我们坐在垫着软垫的大竹椅上。

ban /bæn/ *verb* 动词 (**bans, banning, banned**)
to say officially that something must not be done, shown or used 明令禁止；取缔: *Ireland was the first country to ban smoking in all workplaces.* 爱尔兰是第一个在所有工作场所禁烟的国家。 □ *The film was banned by the French government.* 这部影片被法国政府禁止上映。 ● **ban** *countable noun* 可数名词: *The report proposes a ban on plastic bags.* 该报告提议颁布禁塑令。

banana /bəˈnɑːnə/ *noun* 名词
a long curved fruit with yellow skin 香蕉: *I bought milk, bread and a bunch of bananas.* 我买了牛奶、面包和一串香蕉。
→ Look at picture on P5 参见彩插第 5 页

band /bænd/ *countable noun* 可数名词
1 a group of people who play music together 乐队: *Matt's a drummer in a rock band.* 马特在一支摇滚乐队当鼓手。
2 a flat, narrow strip of material that you wear around your head or wrists, or that is part of a piece of clothing 带；布条: *Before treatment, doctors and nurses should always check the patient's wristband.* 治疗前，医护人员务必核对患者的腕带。
3 a strip or circle of metal or another strong material that makes something stronger, or that holds several things together (加固或捆绑用的) 条，箍，环: *He took out a white envelope with a rubber band around it.* 他取出一个箍着橡皮筋的白信封。

bandage /ˈbændɪdʒ/ *countable noun* 可数名词
a long strip of cloth that is wrapped around an injured part of your body to protect or support it 绷带: *We put a bandage on John's knee.* 我们给约翰的膝部打了绷带。 ● **bandage** *verb* 动词 (**bandages, bandaging, bandaged**): *Mary finished bandaging her sister's hand.* 玛丽给她妹妹的手打好了绷带。

¹**Band-Aid** also 亦作 **band-aid** *countable noun* 可数名词 (*American* 美国英语) (*British* 英国英语: **plaster**)
a small piece of sticky tape that you use to cover small cuts or wounds on your body (*trademark* 商标) 邦迪创可贴: *She had a Band-Aid on her ankle.* 她脚踝上贴着邦迪创可贴。

bang /bæŋ/ *verb* 动词 (**bangs, banging, banged**)
to hit something hard, making a loud noise 砰然重击: *Lucy banged on the table with her fist.* 露西挥拳砰地砸在桌子上。 □ *The toddler was sitting on the floor, banging two pots together.* 那个刚会走路的小孩儿坐在地上，拿着两个罐子砰砰地撞着玩。 ● **bang** *countable noun* 可数名词: *I heard four or five loud bangs.* 我听到了四五声巨响。

bangs /bæŋz/ *plural noun* 复数名词 (*American* 美国英语)
→ see 见 **fringe**: *Both of them had blond bangs.* 她俩都留着金色刘海。

banister /ˈbænɪstə/ *countable noun* 可数名词
a long narrow piece of wood that you hold on to when you are walking down stairs (楼梯的) 栏杆，扶手

banjo /ˈbændʒəʊ/ *noun* 名词
a musical instrument that looks like a guitar, with a round body, a long neck and four or more strings 班卓琴

¹**bank** /bæŋk/ *countable noun* 可数名词
1 a place where people can keep their money 银行: *He had just £14 in the bank when he died.* 他去世时银行里只有 14 英镑。
2 a raised area of ground along the edge

of a river 岸；堤：*We walked along the east bank of the river.* 我们沿着河东岸走。

bank[2] /bæŋk/ *verb* 动词 (**banks, banking, banked**)
bank on someone/something to rely on someone or something 依赖（或依靠）某人／某事物：*Everyone is banking on his recovery.* 大家都指望着他康复。

ˈbank acˌcount *countable noun* 可数名词
an arrangement with a bank where they look after your money for you 银行账户

ˈbank ˌcard or 或 **ATˈM ˌcard** *countable noun* 可数名词
a plastic card that your bank gives you so that you can get money from your bank account using a cash machine 银行卡；借记卡

bankrupt /ˈbæŋkrʌpt/ *adjective* 形容词
without enough money to pay your debts 破产的；无力偿债的：*If the company cannot sell its products, it will go bankrupt.* 公司产品卖不出去的话，就要破产了。

banner /ˈbænə/ *countable noun* 可数名词
a long strip of cloth or plastic with something written on it 条幅；横幅：*The crowd danced and sang, and waved banners reading 'No War'.* 众人又唱又跳，挥舞着"不要战争"的条幅。

baptism /ˈbæptɪzəm/ *noun* 名词
a Christian ceremony in which a person is baptized（基督教的）洗礼：*Father Wright regularly performs weddings and baptisms.* 赖特神父经常主持婚礼和洗礼。

baptize /bæpˈtaɪz/ *verb* 动词 (**baptizes, baptizing, baptized**)
to touch or cover someone with water, to show that they have become a member of the Christian church（基督教）给…施洗礼：*Mary decided to become a Christian and was baptized.* 玛丽决定皈依基督教，接受了洗礼。

bar /bɑː/ *countable noun* 可数名词
1 a long, straight piece of metal（金属）棒，杆，杠：*The building had bars on all of the windows.* 大楼窗户都加装了防护条。
2 a small block of something 块；条：*What is your favourite chocolate bar?* 你爱吃哪种巧克力条？
3 a place where you can buy and drink alcoholic drinks 酒吧：*Lyndsay met her boyfriend at a local bar.* 林赛在当地酒吧见了男友。
4 a place where you can buy drinks and snacks（出售饮料、小吃的）吧，小食品店：*a coffee bar* 咖啡吧

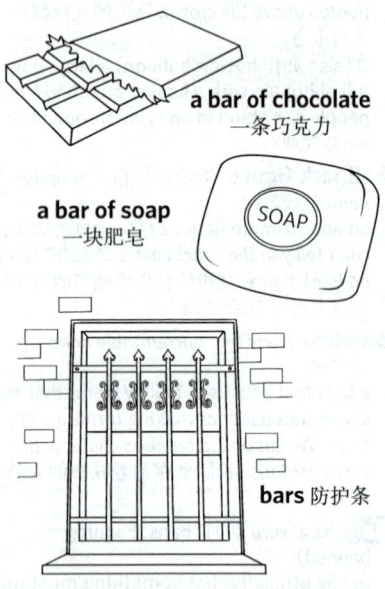

a bar of chocolate 一条巧克力

a bar of soap 一块肥皂

bars 防护条

barbecue /ˈbɑːbɪkjuː/ also 亦作 **barbeque** or 或 **BBQ** *countable noun* 可数名词
1 a piece of equipment that you use for cooking outdoors 露天烤炉；户外烧烤炉
2 a party where you cook food on a barbecue outdoors 露天烧烤：*On Saturday we had a barbecue on the beach.* 星期六我们到海滩烧烤去了。 • **barbecue** *verb* 动词 (**barbecues, barbecuing, barbecued**)：*Tuna can be grilled, fried or barbecued.* 金枪鱼可以烧烤、油炸或烘烤。

barber /ˈbɑːbə/ *countable noun* 可数名词
1 a person whose job is to cut men's hair（为男子服务的）理发师
2 (also 亦作 **barber's**) a shop where men can have their hair cut（为男子服务的）理发店

bare /beə/ *adjective* 形容词 (**barer, barest**)
1 not covered by any clothing 赤裸的；未着衣物的：*Jane's feet were bare.* 简光着脚
2 not covered or decorated with anything 无遮盖的；无装饰的：*The flat has bare wooden floors.* 公寓木地板上什么也没铺。
3 empty 空的：*His refrigerator was bare.* 他的冰箱里空空如也。

barefoot /ˈbeəfʊt/ *adjective* 形容词
not wearing shoes or socks 光脚的；赤脚

的：*He walked 10 miles barefoot to find help.* 他光着脚走了 10 英里去求助。

barely /ˈbeəli/ *adverb* 副词
only just true or possible 刚刚；勉强；几乎不：*Anna could barely remember the ride to the hospital.* 安娜几乎记不得怎么去的医院。

bargain /ˈbɑːɡɪn/ *countable noun* 可数名词
something that is being sold at a lower price than usual 特价品；减价品：*At this price the dress is a bargain.* 这款连衣裙卖这个价属于特惠。

barge /bɑːdʒ/ *countable noun* 可数名词
a long, narrow boat with a flat bottom, used for carrying heavy loads 驳船：*The barges carried water, food and medicines.* 驳船运载着水、食品和药品。

bark¹ /bɑːk/ *verb* 动词 (**barks, barking, barked**)
to make the short, loud noise that a dog makes（犬）吠：*Don't let the dogs bark.* 别让狗叫。● **bark** *countable noun* 可数名词：*Your child may be afraid of a dog's bark, or its size.* 你家孩子可能害怕狗叫，也可能害怕狗的块头。

bark² /bɑːk/ *uncountable noun* 不可数名词
the rough surface of a tree 树皮

barn /bɑːn/ *countable noun* 可数名词
a building on a farm where animals and crops are kept（农场的）畜舍，谷仓

barracks /ˈbærəks/ *countable noun* 可数名词 (**barracks**)
a building where soldiers live and work 兵营；营房：*an army barracks* 陆军军营

barrel /ˈbærəl/ *countable noun* 可数名词
1 a large container, with curved sides and flat ends, for storing liquids 桶：*The U.S. uses about 20 million barrels of oil a day.* 美国每天用掉约 2,000 万桶石油。
2 the long metal part of a gun 枪管

barricade /ˈbærɪkeɪd/ *countable noun* 可数名词
a line of things that have been put across a road to stop people from passing 路障；街垒：*The street was blocked by a barricade.* 街道被路障封锁了。● **barricade** *verb* 动词 (**barricades, barricading, barricaded**)：*Police barricaded all entrances to the square.* 警方设置路障封锁了广场所有入口。

barrier /ˈbæriə/ *countable noun* 可数名词
a fence or a wall that prevents people or things from moving from one area to another 障碍；壁垒；屏障：*A police barrier blocked the road.* 警方设置路障封锁了道路。

bartender /ˈbɑːtendə/ *countable noun* 可数名词
a person who makes and serves drinks in a bar 酒吧招待；调酒师；酒保

base¹ /beɪs/ *countable noun* 可数名词
1 the lowest part of something, or the part that it stands on 底部；基础；底座：*They planted flowers around the base of the tree.* 他们在树底部种了一圈花。□ *The base of the statue weighs four tons.* 雕像底座重 4 吨。
2 a place where soldiers live and work 军事基地：*The army base is close to the airport.* 这个陆军基地靠近机场。
3 the main place where you work or live（工作、生活的）主要地点，基地：*In the summer her base is her home in London.* 夏天她主要待在伦敦的家里。

base² /beɪs/ *verb* 动词 (**bases, basing, based**)
be based on something to be made by using an idea or material from another thing 以某事物为基础：*The film is based on a novel by Alexander Trocchi.* 这部影片改编自亚历山大·特罗基的一部小说。

baseball /ˈbeɪsbɔːl/ *noun* 名词
1 *uncountable* 不可数 a game, played with a bat and a ball on a large field by two teams of nine players, in which players must hit the ball and run around four bases to score 棒球运动
2 *countable* 可数 a small hard ball which is used in the game of baseball 棒球

ˈbaseball ˌcap *countable noun* 可数名词
a cap with a curved part at the front that sticks out above your eyes 棒球帽：*Joe often wears a baseball cap.* 乔常戴一顶棒球帽。

basement /ˈbeɪsmənt/ *countable noun* 可数名词
a part of a building below ground level 地下室：*They put the old toys in the basement.* 他们把旧玩具放在地下室里。

bases
1 /ˈbeɪsɪz/ the plural of **base**（base 的复数形式）
2 /ˈbeɪsiːz/ the plural of **basis**（basis 的复数形式）

bash /bæʃ/ *verb* 动词 (**bashes, bashing, bashed**)
to hit someone or something very hard (*informal* 非正式) 猛击；重击：*I bashed*

him on the head. 我狠狠地打他脑袋。

bashful /ˈbæʃful/ *adjective* 形容词
shy and easily embarrassed 害羞的；腼腆的：*She gave a little bashful smile.* 她腼腆地露出一丝微笑。

basic /ˈbeɪsɪk/ *adjective* 形容词
1 relating to the simplest and most important part of something 基础的；基本的；根本的：*Everyone needs the basic skills of reading and writing.* 每个人都需要具备基本的读写技能。
2 relating to the essential things that everyone needs（需求）基本的：*There were shortages of the most basic foods.* 最基本的食品都短缺。

basically /ˈbeɪsɪkli/ *adverb* 副词
used when you are talking about the most important part of someone or something 基本上；从根本上说：*Basically, he is a nice boy.* 从根本上说，他是个好孩子。 □ *The film is basically a love story.* 这部影片基本上讲了个爱情故事。

basin /ˈbeɪsən/ *countable noun* 可数名词
1 → see 见 **washbasin**
2 a deep bowl used for holding liquids 盆：*Water dripped into a basin at the back of the room.* 水滴进房间后部一个水盆里。

basis /ˈbeɪsɪs/ *noun* 名词 (**bases**)
1 singular 单数 the particular way that something is done 准则；方式：*We meet here for lunch on a regular basis.* 我们定期在此共进午餐。
2 countable 可数 the most important part of something that other things can develop from 基础：*The UN plan is a possible basis for peace talks.* 联合国方案可以作为和平谈判的基础。

basket /ˈbɑːskɪt/ *countable noun* 可数名词
a container made from thin strips of wood, plastic or metal, that is used for carrying or storing objects 篮；篓；筐：*The picnic basket was filled with sandwiches and fruit.* 野餐篮装满了三明治和水果。

basketball /ˈbɑːskɪtbɔːl/ *noun* 名词
1 uncountable 不可数 a game in which two teams of five players each try to throw a large ball through a round net hanging from a high metal ring 篮球运动
2 countable 可数 a large ball which is used in the game of basketball 篮球
→ Look at picture on P14 参见彩插第 14 页

bass /beɪs/ *adjective* 形容词

making a very deep sound 产生低音的：*Dee Murray plays bass guitar in the band.* 迪伊·默里在乐队里弹低音吉他。

bassoon /bəˈsuːn/ *noun* 名词
a large musical instrument, shaped like a tube, that you play by blowing into a curved metal pipe 大管
→ Look at picture on P12 参见彩插第 12 页

bat¹ /bæt/ *countable noun* 可数名词
1 a long piece of wood that is used for hitting the ball in games such as cricket or baseball 球棒；球拍；球板：*a cricket bat* 板球板
2 a small animal, like a mouse with wings, that sleeps upside down during the day and comes out to fly at night 蝙蝠

bat² /bæt/ *verb* 动词 (**bats, batting, batted**)
to hit the ball with a bat in games such as cricket or baseball 击球：*Paxton hurt his elbow while he was batting.* 帕克斯顿击球时伤着了肘部。

batch /bætʃ/ *countable noun* 可数名词 (**batches**)
a group of things or people of the same type 批；批次：*I baked a batch of cakes this morning.* 我今天早上烤了一批蛋糕。

bath¹ /bɑːθ/ *countable noun* 可数名词 (**American** 美国英语：**bathtub**) a long container that you fill with water and sit or lie in to wash your body 浴盆；浴缸：*She was lying in the bath.* 她躺在浴缸里。
have a bath or **take a bath** to sit or lie in a bath filled with water, and wash your body 泡澡；洗盆浴：*He had a bath before he went to bed.* 他睡前泡了个澡。

bath² /bɑːθ/ *verb* 动词 (**baths, bathing, bathed**)
to wash a young child in a bath 用浴盆给（小孩）洗澡：*Would you like me to bath the baby?* 我给宝宝洗个澡怎么样？

bathe /beɪð/ *verb* 动词 (**bathes, bathing, bathed**)
1 to swim in the sea or a lake or river（在海、湖、河中）游泳：*Every morning, we bathed in the river.* 每天早上，我们都下河游泳。
2 to wash a part of your body carefully 清洗（身体部位）：*Bathe the wound in warm water.* 用温水清洗伤口。

bathrobe /ˈbɑːθrəʊb/ *countable noun* 可数名词
a loose coat that you wear indoors after

having a bath or a shower 浴袍；浴衣
bathroom /'bɑːθruːm/ *noun* 名词
  1 *countable* 可数 a room in a house that contains a bath or shower, a washbasin, and sometimes a toilet 浴室
  2 *singular* 单数 (*American* 美国英语)a room that contains a toilet 卫生间；洗手间: *She asked if she could use the bathroom.* 她问他能不能用一下洗手间。
bathtub /'bɑːtʌb/ *countable noun* 可数名词 (*American* 美国英语)
→ see 见 **bath** : *She was lying in a huge pink bathtub.* 她躺在一个巨大的粉红色浴缸里。
baton /'bætɒn/ *countable noun* 可数名词
  1 a light, thin stick that is used by a conductor (= a person who directs musicians) (乐队指挥的)指挥棒
  2 a short stick that one runner passes to another in a race 接力棒
batter /'bætə/ *noun* 名词
  1 *uncountable* 不可数 a mixture of flour, eggs and milk, that is used for making cakes 蛋奶面糊(做蛋糕用): *Pour the cake batter into a round baking tin.* 把做蛋糕用的蛋奶面糊倒进一个圆形烤模里。
  2 *countable* 可数 in sports such as baseball, a person who hits the ball (棒球等运动的)击球员: *The batter hit the ball toward second base.* 击球员将球击向二垒。
battery /'bætəri/ *countable noun* 可数名词 (**batteries**)
  1 a small object that provides electricity for things such as radios 电池: *The game requires two AA batteries.* 这款游戏需要用两节 AA 号电池(即 5 号电池)。
  → Look at picture on P6 参见彩插第 6 页
  2 a box containing acid that provides the electricity that is needed to start a car (汽车的)蓄电池: *Wendy can't take us because her car's battery is flat.* 温迪送不成我们，因为她的汽车电池没电了。
battle /'bætl/ *noun* 名词
  1 a violent fight between groups of people, especially between armies during a war 战斗；战役: *The Battle of Gettysburg took place in July 1863.* 葛底斯堡战役发生于 1863 年 7 月。
  2 *countable* 可数 a struggle for success or control over something (争取成功或控制权的)斗争, 拼搏: *He won his battle against cancer.* 他战胜了癌症。● **battle** *verb* 动词

(**battles, battling, battled**): *Doctors battled all night to save her life.* 大夫们彻夜奋力抢救她。
bay /beɪ/ *countable noun* 可数名词
  a part of a coast where the land goes in and forms a curve 海湾: *We sailed across the bay in the morning.* 我们早上驾船驶过海湾。
BC /ˌbiː 'siː/ *also* 亦作 **B.C.**
  used in dates to show the number of years before the year in which Jesus Christ was born. Compare with **AD**. 公元前 (比较 AD): *He probably lived in the fourth century BC.* 他大概生活在公元前 4 世纪。
BCE /ˌbiː siː 'iː/ *also* 亦作 **B.C.E.**
  used in dates to show the number of years before AD 1 or the year in which Jesus was born. **BCE** is short for (缩写 =) 'Before Common Era'. 公元前: *The temple was built in around 440 BCE.* 这座庙建于公元前 440 年左右。
be¹ /bi, STRONG 强读 biː/ *auxiliary verb* 助动词 (**am, are, is, being, was, were, been**)
  1 used with another verb to form the past or present continuous (与其他动词连用, 构成过去或现在进行时): *This is happening everywhere in the country.* 全国各地都在发生这样的事情。 □ *She was driving to work when the accident happened.* 她开车上班途中发生了事故。
  2 used with another verb to form the passive (与其他动词连用, 构成被动语态): *Her husband was killed in a car crash.* 她丈夫死于车祸。
  3 used with an infinitive to show that something is planned to happen (与不定式连用, 表示将来的安排): *The talks are to begin tomorrow.* 会谈定于明天开始。
be² /bi, STRONG 强读 biː/ *verb* 动词 (**am, are, is, being, was, were, been**)
  1 used for introducing more information about a subject (用于引出更多关于主语的信息): *She's my mother.* 她是我妈妈。 □ *He is a very kind man.* 他是个大好人。 □ *He is fifty years old.* 他 50 岁。 □ *The sky was black.* 天空一片漆黑。 □ *Dad's in the garden.* 爸爸在花园里。
  2 used with 'it' when you are giving your opinion on a situation (与 it 连用, 给出自己对某一状况的看法): *It was too cold for swimming.* 这时候游泳太冷了。
  □ *Sometimes it is necessary to say no.* 有时

beach – beautiful

候必须说不。□ *It's nice having friends to talk to.* 有朋友说说话真好。
3 used in expressions like 'there is' and 'there are' to say that something exists（用于 there is、there are 等表达中，表示存在）: *There is very little traffic this morning.* 今天早上路上车很少。

beach /biːtʃ/ *countable noun* 可数名词 (**beaches**)
an area of sand or stones next to a lake or the sea 滩；湖滩；海滩: *The children played on the beautiful sandy beach.* 孩子们在美丽的沙滩上玩耍。
→ Look at picture on P7 参见彩插第 7 页

bead /biːd/ *countable noun* 可数名词
a small piece of coloured glass, wood or plastic that is used for making jewellery（做首饰用的）珠子: *Victoria was wearing a purple bead necklace.* 维多利亚戴着一条紫色的珠子项链。

beak /biːk/ *countable noun* 可数名词
the hard, pointed part of a bird's mouth 喙；鸟嘴: *She pointed to a black bird with a yellow beak.* 她伸手指着一只黄嘴黑鸟。

beam¹ /biːm/ *verb* 动词 (**beams, beaming, beamed**)
to have a big happy smile on your face 笑容满面；笑逐颜开: *Lucy was waiting at the door, beaming.* 露西在门口迎候，满面笑容。□ *Frances beamed at her friend.* 弗朗西丝笑容满面地看着朋友。

beam² /biːm/ *countable noun* 可数名词
1 a line of light that shines from something bright 光线；光束
2 a long thick bar of wood or metal that supports the roof of a building（房屋的）梁: *The ceilings are supported by oak beams.* 屋顶用橡木梁支撑着。

bean /biːn/ *countable noun* 可数名词
the seed of a plant that you can eat as a vegetable 豆；豆子: *'More green beans, anyone?' Mrs Parkinson asked.* "哪位再来点儿青豆？"帕金森太太问。

bear¹ /beə/ *verb* 动词 (**bears, bearing, bore, borne**)
1 to accept an unpleasant experience 忍受，忍耐（不愉快的经历）: *The loneliness was hard to bear.* 寂寞难耐。
2 to be able to support your weight 承受，支撑（重量）: *The ice was not thick enough to bear their weight.* 冰不够厚，承受不住他们的重量。

can't bear someone/something to dislike someone or something very much 受不了某人／某事物: *I can't bear people being late.* 我受不了谁迟到。□ *I can't bear rudeness.* 我讨厌言行粗鲁。

bear² /beə/ *countable noun* 可数名词
a large, strong wild animal with thick fur and sharp claws 熊

bearable /ˈbeərəbəl/ *adjective* 形容词
that you can deal with without too much difficulty 可忍受的；可应付的: *A cool breeze made the heat bearable.* 一阵凉风吹来，没那么热了。

beard /bɪəd/ *countable noun* 可数名词
the hair that grows on a man's chin and cheeks 络腮胡子: *He's 60 years old, with a long white beard.* 他 60 岁了，蓄着长长的白络腮胡子。

beast /biːst/ *countable noun* 可数名词
a large and dangerous animal 兽；野兽: *He told the children that there were wild beasts in the woods.* 他告诉孩子们森林里有野兽。

beat¹ /biːt/ *verb* 动词 (**beats, beating, beat, beaten**)
1 to hit someone or something very hard 重击；猛击: *They beat him, and left him on the ground.* 他们群殴他，把他打倒在地。□ *We could hear the rain beating against the windows.* 我们能听见雨水敲打窗户的声音。
2 to make a regular sound and movement 有规律地动；搏动: *I felt my heart beating faster.* 我觉得自己心跳加快。● **beat** *countable noun* 可数名词: *He could hear the beat of his heart.* 他能听见自己的心跳声。
3 to mix food quickly with a spoon or a fork（用勺子、叉子）搅拌，搅打: *Beat the eggs and sugar together.* 把鸡蛋和糖混起来搅拌。
4 to defeat someone in a competition or an election 打败，击败（竞赛或竞选对手）: *The Red Sox beat the Yankees 5-2 last night.* 昨晚红袜队以 5 比 2 击败了扬基队。

beat² /biːt/ *countable noun* 可数名词
the rhythm of a piece of music（音乐的）拍，拍子: *Play some music with a steady beat.* 放点儿节拍平稳的音乐。

beaten /ˈbiːtən/
→ see 见 **beat**

beautiful /ˈbjuːtɪfəl/ *adjective* 形容词
1 very attractive to look at 美丽的；漂亮的:

She was a very beautiful woman. 她是个非常漂亮的女人。

> **LANGUAGE HELP 语言提示**
> **Beautiful** is usually used for talking about women and girls. You can describe an attractive man as **handsome** or **good-looking**. *beautiful 通常用来形容女人或女孩，形容男人英俊可以用 handsome 或 good-looking。

2 pleasant to look at, listen to or experience 悦目的；悦耳的；宜人的：*The countryside is beautiful in the autumn.* 秋日的乡间风景宜人。▫ *It was a beautiful morning.* 那是个美妙的早晨。
▶ **beautifully** /ˈbjuːtɪfli/ *adverb* 副词：*Karen sings beautifully.* 卡伦唱歌很好听。

beauty /ˈbjuːti/ *uncountable noun* 不可数名词
the quality of being beautiful 美丽；漂亮：*The hotel is in an area of natural beauty.* 这家宾馆周边自然环境优美。

beaver /ˈbiːvə/ *countable noun* 可数名词
an animal with thick fur, a big flat tail and large teeth 河狸；海狸

became /bɪˈkeɪm/
→ see 见 **become**

because /bɪˈkɒz/ *conjunction* 连词
used when you are giving the reason for something 因为；由于：*He is called Mitch because his name is Mitchell.* 人们叫他 Mitch（米奇），因为他名叫 Mitchell（米切尔）。▫ *I'm sad because he didn't ask me to his birthday party.* 我感到伤心，因为他生日聚会没叫上我。
because of something as a result of something 因为某事物：*He's retiring because of ill health.* 他因为身体不好要退休了。

become /bɪˈkʌm/ *verb* 动词 (**becomes, becoming, became, become**)
to start to be something or someone 变成；成为；变得：*The weather became cold and wet in October.* *10 月天气变得湿冷起来。▫ *Teresa wants to become a teacher.* 特雷莎想当教师。

bed /bed/ *countable noun* 可数名词
1 a piece of furniture that you lie on when you sleep 床：*We went to bed at about 10 p.m.* 我们晚上 10 点左右上床睡觉。▫ *Nina was already in bed.* 尼娜已经睡下了。
2 the ground at the bottom of the sea or of a river 海床；河床

bedroom /ˈbedruːm/ *countable noun* 可数名词
a room that is used for sleeping in 卧室：*Emma, please tidy your bedroom.* 埃玛，请整理一下你的卧室。

bedspread /ˈbedspred/ *countable noun* 可数名词
a decorative cover that you put on a bed 床罩

bedtime /ˈbedtaɪm/ *uncountable noun* 不可数名词
the time when someone usually goes to bed 就寝时间：*It was eight-thirty, Peter's bedtime.* 8 点半了，彼得该睡了。

bee /biː/ *countable noun* 可数名词
a yellow-and-black striped flying insect that makes a sweet food (= honey) and can sting you 蜜蜂：*Bees buzzed in the flowers.* 蜜蜂在花间嗡嗡地飞舞。

beef /biːf/ *uncountable noun* 不可数名词
meat from a cow 牛肉：*We had roast beef for lunch.* 我们午餐吃了烤牛肉。

beefburger /ˈbiːfˌbɜːgə/ *countable noun* 可数名词 (*British* 英国英语)
→ see 见 **hamburger**：*beefburgers and chips* 汉堡包和薯条

beehive /ˈbiːhaɪv/ *countable noun* 可数名词
a container for bees to live in 蜂箱；蜂房

been[1] /bɪn, biːn/
→ see 见 **be**

been[2] /bɪn, biːn/ *verb* 动词
have been to to have visited a place 去过（某地）：*Have you ever been to Paris?* 你去过巴黎吗？

beep[1] /biːp/ *countable noun* 可数名词
1 a short, high sound made by a piece of electronic equipment（电子设备发出的）嘀嘀声：*Please leave a message after the beep.* 听到嘀嘀声后请留言。
2 a short, loud sound made by a car horn（汽车喇叭的）嘟嘟声

beep[2] /biːp/ *verb* 动词 (**beeps, beeping, beeped**)
1 to make a short, high sound（电子设备）发出嘀嘀声：*My mobile phone beeps when I receive a text message.* 我的手机收到短信会嘀地响一下。▫ *When the microwave beeped, he took out his meal and ate it quickly.* 微波炉嘀地响了一声，他取出饭菜快速吃了起来。
2 to make a short, loud sound 使（汽车喇

叭）发出嘟嘟声：*He beeped the horn and waved.* 他边鸣喇叭边挥手。

beer /bɪə/ *uncountable noun* 不可数名词
an alcoholic drink made from grain 啤酒：*He sat in the kitchen drinking beer.* 他坐在厨房里喝啤酒。

beetle /ˈbiːtəl/ *countable noun* 可数名词
an insect with a hard, shiny black body 甲虫

beetroot /ˈbiːtruːt/ *noun* 名词
a dark red root, eaten as a vegetable, that is often preserved in vinegar (= a liquid with a strong sharp taste) 甜菜根（蔬菜）：*Thinly slice the beetroot.* 把甜菜根切成薄片。

before¹ /bɪˈfɔː/ *preposition* 介词
earlier than a particular date, time or event 在⋯之前；早于：*Annie was born a few weeks before Christmas.* 安妮出生于圣诞节前几周。● **before** *conjunction* 连词：*Brush your teeth before you go to bed.* 你刷完牙再上床睡觉。

before² /bɪˈfɔː/ *adverb* 副词
in the past 以前；过去：*I've never been here before.* 我此前从未来过这儿。□ *Have you met Professor Lewis before?* 你之前见过刘易斯教授吗？

beforehand /bɪˈfɔːhænd/ *adverb* 副词
earlier than something else 预先；事先；提前：*If you want to come to the party, please tell me beforehand.* 你想来参加聚会的话，请事先告诉我一下。

beg /beɡ/ *verb* 动词 (begs, begging, begged)
1 to ask someone to do something in a way that shows that you want them to do it very much 乞求；恳求；央求：*I begged him to come to New York with me.* 我恳求他跟我一起来纽约。□ *I begged for help but no one listened.* 我乞求帮助，但没人理。
2 to ask people for food or money because you are very poor 乞讨：*Homeless people were begging on the streets.* 无家可归者在街头乞讨。

began /bɪˈɡæn/
→ see 见 **begin**

beggar /ˈbeɡə/ *countable noun* 可数名词
someone who lives by asking people for money or food 乞丐；叫花子：*There are no beggars on the streets in this city.* 这座城市街头没有乞丐。

begin /bɪˈɡɪn/ *verb* 动词 (begins, beginning, began, begun)
1 to start doing something 开始（做某事）：*Jack stood up and began to move around the room.* 杰克站起来开始在屋里转悠。□ *David began to look angry.* 戴维开始面露怒气。
2 to start to happen, or to start something 开始发生；开始（某物）：*The problems began last November.* 问题在去年11月开始出现。□ *He has just begun his second year at college.* 他刚刚开始大二学年。

beginner /bɪˈɡɪnə/ *countable noun* 可数名词
someone who has just started to do or to learn something 初学者；新手；生手：*The course is for both beginners and advanced students.* 本课程初学者、高级水平学生均适用。

beginning /bɪˈɡɪnɪŋ/ *countable noun* 可数名词
the first part of something 开始；开头；开端：*This was the beginning of her career.* 这是她职业生涯的起点。□ *The wedding will be at the beginning of March.* 婚礼定于3月初举行。

begun /bɪˈɡʌn/
→ see 见 **begin**

behalf /bɪˈhɑːf/ *noun* 名词
on someone's behalf or **on behalf of someone** for somebody; in place of somebody 代表（或代替）某人：*She thanked us all on her son's behalf.* 她代儿子感谢了我们大家。

behave /bɪˈheɪv/ *verb* 动词 (behaves, behaving, behaved)
1 to do and say things in a particular way 表现：*I couldn't believe Molly was behaving in this way.* 我无法相信莫莉会表现成这样。
2 to act in the way that people think is correct and proper 守规矩；表现得体：*Remember to behave yourselves, children!* 记得表现乖些，孩子们！

behaviour /bɪˈheɪvjə/ *uncountable noun* 不可数名词
the way that a person or an animal behaves 行为；表现：*Parents should always reward good behaviour.* 家长应该始终奖励良好的行为。

behind /bɪˈhaɪnd/ *preposition* 介词
1 at the back of someone or something 在⋯后面：*I put a cushion behind his head.* 我给他脑后垫了个垫子。□ *They were*

parked behind the lorry. 它们停放在卡车后面。
2 following someone or something 跟在…后面: *Keith walked along behind them.* 基思尾随着他们走去。 ● **behind** *adverb* 副词: *The other police officers followed behind in a second vehicle.* 其余警察乘另一辆汽车跟在后面。
be behind/be behind schedule to be slower or later doing something than you planned 落后 / 落后于进度安排: *The work is 22 weeks behind schedule.* 这项工作比计划滞后了 22 周。
leave someone/something behind to not take someone or something with you when you go somewhere 丢下某人 / 某物；抛下某人 / 某物: *The soldiers escaped into the mountains, leaving behind their weapons.* 士兵们丢下武器，逃进了山里。

beige /beɪʒ/ *adjective* 形容词
pale brown in colour 米色的；浅褐色的: *The walls are beige.* 墙体是米色的。● **beige** *noun* 名词: *I like beige more than dark brown.* 我喜欢米色胜过深褐色。
→ Look at picture on P13 参见彩插第 13 页

being[1] /ˈbiːɪŋ/
→ see 见 **be**

being[2] /ˈbiːɪŋ/ *countable noun* 可数名词
a person or a living thing 生物；活物: *Remember you are dealing with a living being — consider the horse's feelings too.* 记住，你处理的是一条生命——也要考虑马的感受。

belief /bɪˈliːf/ *noun* 名词
a powerful feeling that something is real or true 信念；信仰；信心: *Benedict has a deep belief in God.* 本尼迪克特对上帝深信不疑。

believable /bɪˈliːvəbl/ *adjective* 形容词
able to be believed 可信的: *Mark's excuse was not very believable.* 马克给的理由不太可信。

believe /bɪˈliːv/ *verb* 动词 (**believes, believing, believed**)
1 to think that something is true (*formal* 正式) 认为: *Scientists believe that life began around 4 billion years ago.* 科学家认为生命起源于大约 40 亿年前。□ *We believe that the money is hidden here in this flat.* 我们认为那笔钱就藏在这所公寓里。
2 to feel sure that someone is telling the truth 相信（某人的话）: *Never believe what you read in the newspapers.* 绝对不要相信报纸上看到的东西。
3 to feel sure that something exists 相信（某物存在）: *I don't believe in ghosts.* 我不相信存在鬼魂。

bell /bel/ *countable noun* 可数名词
1 a metal object that makes a ringing sound 铃；铃铛: *I was eating my lunch when the bell rang.* 我正在吃午饭，门铃响了。
2 a hollow metal object with a loose piece hanging inside it that hits the sides and makes a pleasant sound 钟: *It was a Sunday, and all the church bells were ringing.* 那是个星期天，教堂钟声齐鸣。

belly /ˈbeli/ *countable noun* 可数名词 (**bellies**)
the stomach of a person or an animal 肚子；腹部；胃: *She put her hands on her swollen belly.* 她把双手放在自己隆起的肚子上。

belong /bɪˈlɒŋ/ *verb* 动词 (**belongs, belonging, belonged**)
1 to be owned by someone（所有权上）归属: *The house has belonged to her family for three generations.* 这所房子归她们家所有，已历经三代人了。
2 to be a member of a particular group or organization（组织上）归属: *I used to belong to the tennis club.* 我过去是这家网球俱乐部的会员。
3 to be in the right place 处于正确的地方: *After ten years in New York, I really feel that I belong here.* 在纽约待了 10 年，我打心眼儿里觉得自己属于这里。□ *'Where do these plates belong?' — 'In that cupboard.'* "这些盘子放哪儿？"——"放那个碗柜里。"

belongings /bɪˈlɒŋɪŋz/ *plural noun* 复数名词
the things that you own 个人物品: *I gathered my belongings and left.* 我收拾好个人物品就离开了。

below /bɪˈləʊ/ *preposition* 介词
1 in or to a lower position than someone or something else（位置）在…下面，向…下面: *He came out of the flat below Leonard's.* 他从伦纳德家下面那间公寓里走了出来。□ *We watched the sun sink below the horizon.* 我们看着太阳没入地平线。● **below** *adverb* 副词: *I could see the street below.* 我看得见下面的街道。
2 less than a particular amount, rate or level（数量）少于；（比率或水平）低于: *Night temperatures can drop below zero.* 夜

belt – bet

间气温会降到零度以下。● **below** *adverb* 副词：*Daytime temperatures were at zero or below.* 白天气温在零度或零度以下。

belt /belt/ *countable noun* 可数名词
a strip of leather or cloth that you wear around your waist 腰带；皮带：*He wore a belt with a large brass buckle.* 他系着一条大铜扣腰带。

bench /bentʃ/ *countable noun* 可数名词 (**benches**)
a long seat made of wood or metal 长凳；长椅：*Tom sat down on a park bench.* 汤姆在公园长椅上坐了下来。

bend /bend/ *verb* 动词 (**bends, bending, bent**)
1 to move the top part of your body down and forward 弯腰；俯身：*I bent over and kissed her cheek.* 我俯身亲了她的脸颊。□ *She bent down and picked up the toy.* 她弯腰捡起玩具。
2 to change the position of a part of your body so that it is no longer straight 屈，弯曲（身体部位）：*Remember to bend your legs when you do this exercise.* 做这项锻炼时记住要屈腿。
3 to change direction to form a curve（方向上）弯曲，转弯：*The road bends slightly to the right.* 这条路微微右拐。● **bend** *countable noun* 可数名词：*The accident happened on a sharp bend in the road.* 事故发生在路上一个急转弯处。

beneath /bɪˈniːθ/ *preposition* 介词
below; under 在⋯下面：*She could see the muscles of his shoulders beneath his T-shirt.* 她看得见他T恤衫下双肩的肌肉。□ *There is a car park beneath the shopping centre.* 购物中心下有一个停车场。

benefit /ˈbenɪfɪt/ *verb* 动词 (**benefits, benefiting, benefited**)
to help you or improve your life 惠及；有益于：*These projects will benefit the poor.* 这些项目将惠及穷人。● **benefit** *noun* 名词：*Parents need to educate their children about the benefits of exercise.* 家长得教孩子们了解锻炼的益处。
benefit from something to get help or an advantage from something 受益于某事物：*You would benefit from a change in your diet.* 调整一下饮食，你会从中受益。

bent[1] /bent/
→ see 见 **bend**

bent[2] /bent/ *adjective* 形容词

not straight 弯曲的：*Keep your knees slightly bent.* 双膝微屈。□ *He found a bent nail on the ground.* 他在地上捡到一枚弯曲的钉子。

berry /ˈberi/ *countable noun* 可数名词 (**berries**)
a small, round fruit that grows on a bush or a tree 浆果；莓

beside /bɪˈsaɪd/ *preposition* 介词
next to someone or something 挨着；在⋯旁边：*Can I sit beside you?* 我能坐你边上吗？

besides[1] /bɪˈsaɪdz/ *preposition* 介词
in addition to someone or something 除了⋯以外（还）：*She has many good qualities besides being very beautiful.* 她除了长得非常漂亮，还有许多优秀品质。

besides[2] /bɪˈsaɪdz/ *adverb* 副词
used when you want to give another reason for something 而且；再者：*The house is far too expensive. Besides, I don't want to leave our little apartment.* 这所房子太贵了。再者，我也不想离开我们的小公寓。

best[1] /best/ *adjective* 形容词
a form of the adjective **good**, used to show that one thing is better than all the others（**good** 的最高级）最好的：*Who is your best friend?* 你最要好的朋友是谁？□ *Drink regularly through the day — water is best.* 一天当中经常饮水——水是最好的东西。

best[2] /best/ *adverb* 副词
a form of the adverb **well**, used to show that something is done or happens in a way that is better than all the others（**well** 的最高级）最，最好：*I did best in physics in my class.* 我们班物理数我最好。□ *J. R. R. Tolkien is best known as the author of 'The Hobbit'.* *J. R. R. 托尔金最出名的是他写了《霍比特人》。

best[3] /best/ *noun* 名词
do your best to try very hard to do something as well as possible 尽力；竭尽所能：*If you do your best, no one can criticize you.* 只要尽了力，谁也不能怪罪你。
the best someone or something that is better than all other people or things 最好的人（或事物）：*We offer only the best to our clients.* 我们最好的东西才会提供给客户。

bet /bet/ *verb* 动词 (**bets, betting, bet**)
to give someone some money and say what you think that the result of a race or a sports game will be. If you are correct,

they give you your money back with some extra money, but if you are wrong they keep your money. (以…)打赌; 下(赌注): *Jockeys are forbidden to bet on the outcome of horse races.* 骑手不得参与赛马结果竞猜型博彩。□ *I bet £20 on a horse called Bright Boy.* 我在一匹名叫"机灵小子"的马上下了 20 英镑赌注。● **bet** *countable noun* 可数名词: *Did you make a bet on the horse race?* 这场赛马你下注了吗?
▶ **betting** /ˈbetɪŋ/ *uncountable noun* 不可数名词: *Betting is illegal in many countries.* 赌博在很多国家都违法。
I bet used for showing that you are sure something is true (*informal* 非正式) 我敢说; 我确信: *I bet you were good at sports when you were at school.* 我敢说你上学时体育很好。

better¹ /ˈbetə/ *adjective* 形容词
1 a form of the adjective **good**, used for saying that one thing is of a higher standard than another thing (good 的比较级) 更好的: *This book is better than her last one.* 这部书比她上一部好。
2 no longer ill or injured 康复的; 痊愈的: *When I'm better, I'll talk to him.* 等我好了, 我去找他谈。
3 feeling less ill 病情好转的: *He is feeling much better today.* 他今天感觉好多了。

better² /ˈbetə/ *adverb* 副词
1 a form of the adverb **well**, used to show that one thing is done or happens in a way that is of a higher standard than another thing (well 的比较级) 更好: *You play football better than I do.* 你足球踢得比我好。
2 more 更; 更加: *I like your poem better than mine.* 咱俩的诗我更喜欢你的。
had better should; ought to 应该; 最好: *I think we had better go home.* 我觉得咱们最好回家。

between /bɪˈtwiːn/ *preposition* 介词
1 with one person or thing on one side of you and another person or thing on the other side of you 在(两者)之间: *Nicole was standing between the two men.* 妮科尔站在两名男子中间。
2 from one place to the other and back again 往返于(两地)之间: *I spend a lot of time travelling between Edinburgh and London.* 我有大量时间往返于爱丁堡和伦敦之间。
3 greater than the first amount mentioned and smaller than the second amount 在

(两个数量)之间: *Try to exercise between 15 and 20 minutes every day.* 每天尽量锻炼 15 到 20 分钟。
4 after the first time or date mentioned and before the second time or date 在(两个时间)之间: *The house was built between 1793 and 1797.* 这座房子建于 1793 年至 1797 年之间。□ *I came home between three o'clock and four.* 我 3 点多回家。
5 used to say how many people share something 由…分享(或分担); There is only one bathroom shared between eight people. 8 个人要共用一个浴室。

> **LANGUAGE HELP** 语言提示
> If there are only two people or things, use **between**. If there are more than two people or things, use **among**. 两者之间用 between, 两者以上之间用 among。

beware /bɪˈweə/ *verb* 动词
beware of someone/something to be careful because a person or a thing is dangerous 当心某人/某事物: *Beware of the dangers of swimming in the sea at night.* 夜间在海里游泳要当心危险。

bewildered /bɪˈwɪldəd/ *adjective* 形容词
very confused and unable to decide what to do 不知所措的: *The shoppers looked bewildered by the huge variety of goods for sale.* 琳琅满目的商品使购物者眼花缭乱。

beyond /bɪˈjɒnd/ *preposition* 介词
on the other side of something; further away than something 在…的另一边; 比…远: *On his right was a garden and beyond it a large house.* 他右边是一个花园, 花园那边有一座大房子。● **beyond** *adverb* 副词: *The house had a fabulous view out to the sea beyond.* 这座房子能看到那边大海的壮美景色。

the Bible /ðə ˈbaɪbəl/ *noun* 名词
the holy book of the Christian and Jewish religions《圣经》

biceps /ˈbaɪseps/ *plural noun* 复数名词
the large muscles at the front of the upper part of your arms 二头肌

bicycle /ˈbaɪsɪkəl/ *countable noun* 可数名词
a vehicle with two wheels that you ride by sitting on it and using your legs to make the wheels turn 自行车

bid /bɪd/ *verb* 动词 (**bids, bidding, bid**)
to promise that you will pay a certain amount of money for something that is

big – biological

being sold 出价；投标；竞价：*Lily wanted to bid for the painting.* 莉莉想竞价买这幅画。● **bid** *countable noun* 可数名词：*Bill made the winning £620 bid for the statue.* 比尔出价620英镑拿下了这尊雕像。

big /bɪg/ *adjective* 形容词 (**bigger, biggest**)
1 large in size 块头大的；规模大的：*Australia is a big country.* 澳大利亚是个面积很大的国家。□ *Her husband was a big man.* 她丈夫是个大块头。□ *The crowd included a big group from Cambridge.* 众人中有一大群来自剑桥。
2 important or serious 重要的；严重的：*He owns one of the biggest companies in Italy.* 他拥有一家意大利顶级的大公司。□ *Mandy's problem was too big for her to solve alone.* 曼迪的问题太严重，她一个人解决不了。
3 older 年长的：*I live with my dad and my big brother, John.* 我跟我爸和哥哥约翰一起生活。

big ˈbang ˌtheory *singular noun* 单数名词
a theory that states that the universe was created after an extremely large explosion 大爆炸宇宙论；大爆炸理论

bike /baɪk/ *countable noun* 可数名词
a bicycle or a motorcycle (*informal* 非正式) 自行车；摩托车：*When you ride a bike, you exercise all your leg muscles.* 骑自行车时腿部肌肉都得到了锻炼。

bikini /bɪˈkiːni/ *countable noun* 可数名词
a piece of clothing with two parts that women wear for swimming 比基尼泳装

bilingual /ˌbaɪˈlɪŋgwəl/ *adjective* 形容词
1 able to speak two languages equally well 双语的；能说两门语言的：*He is bilingual in French and English.* 他能说法语、英语两门语言。
2 written or spoken in two languages 使用双语的；双语写（或说）的：*a bilingual dictionary* 双语词典

bill /bɪl/ *countable noun* 可数名词
1 (*American* 美国英语：**check**) a document that shows how much money you must pay for something 账单：*They couldn't afford to pay their bills.* 他们付不起账单。
2 (*American* 美国英语）a piece of paper money 钞票；纸币：*The case contained a large quantity of U.S. dollar bills.* 箱子里装着大量美钞。
3 an official document produced by a government containing a suggestion for a new law 法案；议案：*The bill was approved by a large majority.* 这项法案以绝大多数票获得通过。

billboard /ˈbɪlbɔːd/ *countable noun* 可数名词
a very large board for advertisements at the side of the road（路边）广告牌

billion /ˈbɪljən/

> **LANGUAGE HELP** 语言提示
> The plural form is **billion** after a number. 用在数字后，复数形式为 billion。

the number 1,000,000,000 十亿：*The country's debt has risen to 3 billion dollars.* 该国债务已增至30亿美元。□ *The game was watched by billions of people around the world.* 这场比赛全球有数十亿观众观看。

billionaire /ˌbɪljəˈneə/ *countable noun* 可数名词
an extremely rich person who has money or property worth at least a billion pounds 亿万富翁

bin /bɪn/ *countable noun* 可数名词
1 a container that you put rubbish in 垃圾桶；垃圾箱：*I took the letter and threw it in the bin.* 我接过信扔进了垃圾桶。
→ Look at picture on P1 参见彩插第1页
2 a container that you keep things in 箱子；储物箱：*a plastic storage bin* 塑料储物箱

bind /baɪnd/ *verb* 动词 (**binds, binding, bound**)
to tie rope or string around something to hold it firmly 捆绑；捆扎：*Bind the ends of the rope with thread.* 绳子两头用线扎起来。□ *They bound his hands behind his back.* 他们把他反绑了起来。

binoculars /bɪˈnɒkjʊləz/ *plural noun* 复数名词
special glasses that you use to look at things that are a long distance away 双筒望远镜

binoculars 双筒望远镜

biography /baɪˈɒgrəfi/ *countable noun* 可数名词 (**biographies**)
the story of the life of a person that has been written by another person（人物）传记：*I am reading a biography of Franklin D. Roosevelt.* 我正在读富兰克林·D. 罗斯福的传记。

biological /ˌbaɪəˈlɒdʒɪkəl/ *adjective* 形容词
relating to the scientific study of living

things 生物学的：*biological processes such as reproduction and growth* 生殖、生长等生物过程

biology /baɪˈɒlədʒi/ *uncountable noun* 不可数名词
the scientific study of living things 生物学
▶ **biologist** /baɪˈɒlədʒɪst/ *countable noun* 可数名词：*The marine biologist was killed by a shark while diving.* 这位海洋生物学家潜水时遭鲨鱼攻击遇害。

bird /bɜːd/ *countable noun* 可数名词
an animal with feathers and wings 鸟；禽：*a bird's nest* 鸟窝 □ *The bird flew away as I came near.* 我一靠近鸟就飞走了。

birdhouse /ˈbɜːdhaʊs/ *noun* 名词
a box placed in a tree or other high place that birds can build a nest in 鸟屋；人工巢箱：*He showed us how to build a birdhouse.* 他给我们示范怎么做人工巢箱。

birth /bɜːθ/ *noun* 名词
the moment when a baby is born 出生；诞生：*They are celebrating the birth of their first child.* 他们在庆祝第一个孩子降生。□ *Alice weighed 5 lb 7 oz at birth.* 艾丽斯出生时体重5磅7盎司。
give birth to produce a baby from your body 分娩；生育：*She's just given birth to a baby girl.* 她刚生了一个女孩儿。

birthday /ˈbɜːθdeɪ, -di/ *countable noun* 可数名词
the day of the year that you were born 生日；诞辰：*Mum always sends David a present on his birthday.* 戴维过生日时妈妈总会送上一份礼物。

biscuit /ˈbɪskɪt/ *countable noun* 可数名词
(*American* 美国英语：**cookie**)
a kind of hard, dry cake that is usually sweet and round in shape 饼干：*a chocolate biscuit* 巧克力饼干

bishop /ˈbɪʃəp/ *countable noun* 可数名词
a leader in the Christian church whose job is to look after all the churches in a particular area（基督教的）主教

bit¹ /bɪt/ *countable noun* 可数名词
a unit of information that can be stored on a computer 位，比特（计算机信息量单位）

bit² /bɪt/ *noun* 名词
a bit a small amount of something, or a small part or section of something 一点儿；少量；一小部分：*I do a bit of work at my children's school sometimes.* 有时我在孩子学校干点儿活儿。□ *Only a bit of the cake was left.* 蛋糕只剩下一点儿。
a bit a little 稍微；有点儿：*This girl was a bit strange.* 这个女孩儿有点儿怪。□ *I think people feel a bit happier now.* 我觉得人们现在高兴点儿了。
a bit or **for a bit** for a short time 一会儿；片刻：*Let's wait a bit.* 咱们稍等片刻。
quite a bit quite a lot (*informal* 非正式) 很多；相当于：*Things have changed quite a bit.* 情况变化相当大。

bit³ /bɪt/
→ see 见 **bite**

bite¹ /baɪt/ *verb* 动词 (**bites, biting, bit, bitten**)
1 to use your teeth to cut into or through something 咬：*William bit into his sandwich.* 威廉咬了一口三明治。
2 if a snake or an insect bites, it makes a mark or a hole in your skin with a sharp part of its body（蛇等）咬；（昆虫）叮咬：*Do these flies bite?* 这些苍蝇咬人吗？ □ *He was bitten by a snake last year but made a full recovery.* 去年他被蛇咬了，不过已经痊愈。

bite² /baɪt/ *countable noun* 可数名词
1 a small piece of food that you cut into with your teeth（食物咬下的）一口：*Dan took another bite of apple.* 丹又咬了一口苹果。
2 a painful mark on your body where an animal, a snake or an insect has bitten you（兽、蛇咬的）伤口；（昆虫叮咬的）包块：*A dog bite needs immediate medical attention.* 被狗咬伤后，必须立即就医。

bitten /ˈbɪtən/
→ see 见 **bite**

bitter /ˈbɪtə/ *adjective* 形容词 (**bitterest**)
1 tasting unpleasantly sharp and sour 苦的；酸涩的：*The medicine tasted bitter.* 这种药味道苦。
2 very angry and upset about something that has happened 怨恨的；愤愤不平的：*She is very bitter about the way she lost her job.* 她对自己那样丢掉工作感到愤愤不平。
▶ **bitterly** /ˈbɪtəli/ *adverb* 副词：*'And he didn't even try to help us,' Grant said bitterly.* "他连帮我们的意思都没有。"格兰特气呼呼地说。
3 extremely cold 极冷的；寒冷彻骨的：*A bitter east wind was blowing.* 东风刺骨地吹。
▶ **bitterly** /ˈbɪtəli/ *adverb* 副词：*It's bitterly cold here in Moscow.* 莫斯科这里冷得要命。

bizarre /bɪˈzɑː/ *adjective* 形容词
very strange 怪异的；非常奇怪的：*They were all surprised by their boss's bizarre behaviour.* 他们都对老板古怪的举动感到惊诧。
▶ **bizarrely** /bɪˈzɑːli/ *adverb* 副词：*She dresses bizarrely.* 她的衣着很古怪。

black[1] /blæk/ *adjective* 形容词 (**blacker, blackest**)
1 with the colour of the sky at night 黑色的：*She was wearing a black coat with a white collar.* 她穿着一件白领黑外套。□ *He had thick black hair.* 他有一头浓密的黑发。
→ Look at picture on P13 参见彩插第 13 页
2 belonging to a race of people with dark skins, especially a race originally from Africa（尤指非洲）黑色人种的：*He worked for the rights of black people.* 他努力为黑人争取权利。
3 without milk 不加牛奶的：*A cup of black coffee contains only a few calories.* 一杯黑咖啡仅含几卡路里的热量。

black[2] /blæk/ *noun* 名词
the colour of the sky at night 黑色：*She was wearing black.* 她一袭黑色装束。

ˌblack and ˈwhite also 亦作 **black-and-white** *adjective* 形容词
with the colours black, white and grey only 黑白的：*old black and white films* 老黑白电影 □ *a black-and-white photo* 黑白照片

blackberry /ˈblækbəri/ *countable noun* 可数名词 (**blackberries**)
a small, soft black or dark purple fruit 黑莓

blackboard /ˈblækbɔːd/ *countable noun* 可数名词 (*American* 美国英语：**chalkboard**)
a big, dark-coloured board for writing on in a classroom 黑板
→ Look at picture on P1 参见彩插第 1 页

ˌblack ˈeye *countable noun* 可数名词
a dark-coloured mark around a person's eye because they have been hit there by someone or something（被打造成的）黑眼圈：*Jan arrived at the hospital with a broken nose and a black eye.* 简塌着鼻梁、青着一只眼来到医院。

blackmail /ˈblækmeɪl/ *uncountable noun* 不可数名词
saying that you will say something bad about someone if they do not do what you tell them to do or give you money 勒索；敲诈；讹诈：*Mr Stanley was accused of blackmail.* 斯坦利先生被控敲诈勒索。
● **blackmail** *verb* 动词 (**blackmails, blackmailing, blackmailed**)：*Jeff suddenly realized that Linda was blackmailing him.* 杰夫突然明白了琳达在讹诈他。

blacksmith /ˈblæksmɪθ/ *countable noun* 可数名词
a person whose job is making things out of metal 铁匠

bladder /ˈblædə/ *countable noun* 可数名词
the part of your body where liquid waste is stored until it leaves your body 膀胱

blade /bleɪd/ *countable noun* 可数名词
the flat, sharp part of a knife that is used for cutting 刀身：*The axe blade cut deep into the log.* 斧身深深地劈进了原木。

blame[1] /bleɪm/ *verb* 动词 (**blames, blaming, blamed**)
to say that someone or something made something bad happen 责怪；怪罪；归咎于：*Police blamed the bus driver for the accident.* 警方将事故归咎于公交车司机。

blame[2] /bleɪm/ *noun* 名词
get the blame for something to have people say that you made something bad happen 被责怪干了坏事：*I always got the blame for the trouble that my sister caused.* 妹妹惹的祸总是由我来背黑锅。
take the blame for something to accept that you made something bad happen, even if this is not true 承认自己干了坏事；为坏事承担责任：*Jan always took the blame for Alan's mistakes.* 简老是为艾伦犯的错担责。

bland /blænd/ *adjective* 形容词 (**blander, blandest**)
1 dull and not interesting 枯燥乏味的；沉闷无趣的：*Their music is bland and boring.* 他们的音乐死气沉沉，了无趣味。
2 with very little flavour 味道寡淡的：*The pizza tasted bland, like warm cardboard.* 这份比萨饼吃起来淡而无味，跟加热过的纸板似的。

blank /blæŋk/ *adjective* 形容词
1 with no writing or pictures 空白的；没有图文的：*He tore a blank page from his notebook.* 他从笔记本上撕下一张白页。
2 showing no reaction 漠然的；没有反应的：*Albert looked blank. 'I don't know him, sir.'* 艾伯特一脸漠然。"我不认识他，先生。"
▶ **blankly** /ˈblæŋkli/ *adverb* 副词：*Ellie stared at him blankly.* 埃莉漠然地盯着他。

blanket /ˈblæŋkɪt/ *countable noun* 可数名词
a large, thick piece of cloth that you put on a bed to keep you warm 毯子；毛毯

blast /blɑːst/ *countable noun* 可数名词
a big explosion, especially one caused by a bomb（尤指炸弹引起的）爆炸：*250 people were killed in the blast.* 爆炸中 250 人身亡。

blaze /bleɪz/ *countable noun* 可数名词
a large fire that destroys a lot of things 大火；烈火：*More than 4,000 firefighters are battling the blaze.* 逾 4,000 名消防员在奋力灭火。 ● **blaze** *verb* 动词 (**blazes, blazing, blazed**): *Three people died as the building blazed.* 大楼燃起大火，3 人遇难。

blazer /ˈbleɪzə/ *countable noun* 可数名词
a type of jacket that people wear as part of a uniform（制服的）上衣，夹克

bleach /bliːtʃ/ *uncountable noun* 不可数名词
a chemical that is used for making cloth white, or for making things very clean 漂白剂；漂白粉：*Only use bleach on white fabrics.* 漂白剂只能用于白色织物。
● **bleach** *verb* 动词 (**bleaches, bleaching, bleached**): *I bleached the kitchen sink.* 我用漂白剂清洗了厨房水槽。

bleak /bliːk/ *adjective* 形容词 (**bleaker, bleakest**)
1 not hopeful or likely to be successful 成功无望的；前景惨淡的：*The future looks bleak.* 前景黯淡。
2 cold, dull and unpleasant 阴冷的；凄凉的；萧瑟的：*The weather can be quite bleak here.* 这儿的天气会相当阴冷。

bled /bled/
→ see 见 **bleed**

bleed /bliːd/ *verb* 动词 (**bleeds, bleeding, bled**)
to lose blood from a part of your body 流血；出血：*Ian's lip was bleeding.* 伊恩嘴唇流着血。
▶ **bleeding** /ˈbliːdɪŋ/ *uncountable noun* 不可数名词：*We tried to stop the bleeding from the cut on his arm.* 我们想给他手臂上的伤口止血。

blend /blend/ *verb* 动词 (**blends, blending, blended**)
1 to mix substances together 使混合；掺和：*Blend the butter with the sugar.* 把黄油和糖混合起来。 □ *Blend the ingredients together until you have a smooth mixture.* 把各种配料混合调匀。

2 to look or sound attractive together 协调；融合：*All the colours blend perfectly together.* 所有颜色搭配协调。 ● **blend** *countable noun* 可数名词：*Their music is a blend of jazz and rock'n'roll.* 他们的音乐将爵士乐和摇滚乐糅合在了一起。

bless /bles/ *verb* 动词 (**blesses, blessing, blessed**)
to ask for God's protection for someone or something 为…祈福；祈求上帝保佑：*The pope blessed the crowd.* 教皇为众人祈福。
Bless you something polite that you say to someone when they sneeze (= blow out air through their nose and mouth suddenly and noisily)（对打喷嚏者的礼貌用语）老天保佑

blew /bluː/
→ see 见 **blow**

blind¹ /blaɪnd/ *adjective* 形容词
unable to see 看不见的；盲的；失明的：*My grandfather is going blind.* 我爷爷快失明了。
the blind people who are blind 盲人：*He's a teacher of the blind.* 他是教盲人的。

blind² /blaɪnd/ *countable noun* 可数名词
a piece of cloth or other material that you can pull down over a window to cover it 卷帘；百叶窗：*Susan pulled the blinds up to let the bright sunlight into the room.* 苏珊把百叶窗拉起来让明媚的阳光照进屋里。

blindfold /ˈblaɪndfəʊld/ *countable noun* 可数名词
a strip of cloth that is tied over someone's eyes so that they cannot see 蒙眼布；眼罩
● **blindfold** *verb* 动词 (**blindfolds, blindfolding, blindfolded**): *Mr Li was handcuffed and blindfolded.* 李先生被戴上手铐蒙上了眼。

blink /blɪŋk/ *verb* 动词 (**blinks, blinking, blinked**)
to shut your eyes and very quickly open them again 眨眼：*I stood blinking in bright light.* 我站在明亮的光线下眨眼。

blister /ˈblɪstə/ *countable noun* 可数名词
a raised area of skin filled with a clear liquid 水疱：*I get blisters when I wear these shoes.* 我穿这双鞋脚上会磨出水疱。

blizzard /ˈblɪzəd/ *countable noun* 可数名词
a very bad storm with snow and strong winds 雪暴

blob /blɒb/ *countable noun* 可数名词
a small amount of a thick liquid (*informal*

非正式)(黏稠液体的)一滴,一小团: *Denise wiped a blob of jelly off Edgar's chin.* 丹尼丝擦掉了埃德加下巴上的一星儿果冻。

block¹ /blɒk/ *countable noun* 可数名词
1 a large, solid piece of a substance that has straight sides 方块；块体: *Elizabeth carves animals from blocks of wood.* 伊丽莎白用木块雕刻动物。
2 a large building with offices inside it 办公楼；写字楼: *an office block* 办公楼
3 a group of buildings in a town or a city with streets on all sides 街区: *He walked around the block three times.* 他绕着这个街区走了3圈。□ *She walked four blocks down High Street.* 她沿着大街走了4个街区。

block² /blɒk/ *verb* 动词 (**blocks, blocking, blocked**)
to stop someone or something from passing along a road 阻挡，挡住，堵塞(通道): *The police blocked all the streets in the centre of the city.* 警方封锁了市中心所有街道。□ *A tree fell down and blocked the road.* 一棵树倒了，堵住了道路。

blocked /blɒkt/ or 或 **,blocked 'up** *adjective* 形容词
completely closed so that nothing can get through 堵塞的；阻塞的: *The pipes are blocked and the water can't get through.* 管道堵塞了，水流不过去。

blog /blɒg/ *countable noun* 可数名词
a website that describes the daily life of the person who writes it, and also their thoughts and ideas 博客: *His blog was later published as a book.* 他的博客后来出成了书。
▶ **blogger** /'blɒgə/ *countable noun* 可数名词: *Loewenstein is a freelance author, blogger and journalist.* 勒文施泰因是个自由职业作家、博主和记者。
▶ **blogging** /'blɒgɪŋ/ *uncountable noun* 不可数名词: *Blogging is very popular.* 写博客非常流行。

blogosphere /'blɒgəsfɪə/ or 或 **blogsphere** /'blɒgsfɪə/ *singular noun* 单数名词
all the blogs (= personal records) on the Internet 博客圈；博客世界: *The blogosphere continues to expand.* 博客圈不断壮大。

blonde¹ /blɒnd/ *adjective* 形容词 (**blonder, blondest**)
1 used for describing hair that is pale-coloured (头发)浅色的: *My sister has blonde hair.* 我妹妹头发是浅色的。
2 with blonde hair 有浅色头发的: *He's blonder than his brother.* 他头发颜色比他弟弟浅。

blonde² /blɒnd/ *countable noun* 可数名词
a person, especially a woman, with pale-coloured hair 浅色头发者；(尤指)浅色头发的女子: *She's a blonde with blue eyes.* 她是个金发碧眼的女子。

blood /blʌd/ *uncountable noun* 不可数名词
the red liquid that flows inside your body 血；血液: *His shirt was covered in blood.* 他衬衫上满是血。

blood vessel /'blʌd ˌvesəl/ *countable noun* 可数名词
one of the narrow tubes that your blood flows through 血管

bloom /bluːm/ *verb* 动词 (**blooms, blooming, bloomed**)
to produce flowers; to open out into flowers 开花；(花)开放: *This plant blooms between May and June.* 这种植物五六月间开花。□ *Although it was late autumn, roses were still blooming in the garden.* 虽然已是晚秋，园里的玫瑰依然开放着。

blossom /'blɒsəm/ *uncountable noun* 不可数名词
the flowers that appear on a tree (树上开的)花: *The cherry blossom lasts only a few days.* 樱桃树花期只有几天。● **blossom** *verb* 动词 (**blossoms, blossoming, blossomed**): *The peach trees will blossom soon.* 桃树快开花了。

blouse /blaʊz/ *countable noun* 可数名词
a shirt for a girl or a woman 女衬衫

blow¹ /bləʊ/ *verb* 动词 (**blows, blowing, blew, blown**)
1 when a wind or breeze blows, the air moves (风)吹，刮: *A cold wind was blowing.* 一阵冷风吹着。
2 to move something using the power of the wind (风力)吹动: *The wind blew her hair back from her forehead.* 风把她额前的头发吹到了后面。
3 to send out air from your mouth (用嘴)吹气，哈气: *Danny blew on his fingers to warm them.* 丹尼往手指上哈气取暖。
4 to send air from your mouth into an object so that it makes a sound (用嘴)吹响: *When the referee blows his whistle, the game begins.* 裁判一声哨响，比赛开始。
blow something out to blow at a flame so

that it stops burning 吹灭某物：*I blew out the candle.* 我吹灭蜡烛。

blow something up
1 to destroy something by an explosion 炸毁某物：*He was jailed for trying to blow up a plane.* 他因企图炸毁一架飞机而入狱。 ◻ *Three cars in the car park blew up.* 停车场里3辆汽车被炸毁。
2 to fill something with air 给某物充气：*Can you help me blow up the balloons?* 你能帮我给气球充气吗？

blow your nose to force air out of your nose in order to clear it 擤鼻子：*He took out a handkerchief and blew his nose.* 他掏出手帕擤鼻子。

blow² /bləʊ/ *countable noun* 可数名词
1 a hard hit from someone's hand or from an object 重击；猛击：*He went to the hospital after a blow to the face.* 他脸上被狠狠打了一下，上了医院。
2 an event that makes you feel very unhappy or disappointed 打击；挫折：*The increase in tax was a blow to the industry.* 增税对该产业是个打击。

blown /bləʊn/
→ see 见 **blow**

blue /bluː/ *adjective* 形容词 (**bluer, bluest**)
having the colour of the sky on a sunny day 蓝色的；天蓝色的：*We looked up at the cloudless blue sky.* 我们仰望着晴朗无云的蓝天。◻ *She has pale blue eyes.* 她有一双浅蓝色的眼睛。●**blue** *noun* 名词：*Julie and Angela wore blue.* 朱莉和安杰拉穿着一身蓝。
→ Look at picture on P13 参见彩插第13页

blueberry /ˈbluːbəri/ *countable noun* 可数名词 (**blueberries**)
a small dark blue fruit 蓝莓

the blues /ðə ˈbluːz/ *plural noun* 复数名词
a type of slow, sad music that developed among African-American musicians in the southern United States 布鲁斯音乐；蓝调音乐：*I grew up singing the blues at home with my mum.* 我从小和妈妈在家里唱着布鲁斯音乐长大。

Bluetooth /ˈbluːtuːθ/ *uncountable noun* 不可数名词
a type of technology that allows devices such as mobile phones and computers to communicate with each other without being connected by wires (*trademark* 商标) 蓝牙技术：*This is the latest Bluetooth technology.* 这是最新的蓝牙技术。

blunt /blʌnt/ *adjective* 形容词 (**blunter, bluntest**)
1 saying exactly what you think, without trying to be polite 直率的；直言不讳的
2 not sharp or pointed 钝的；不锋利的：*a blunt pencil* 钝头铅笔

blurred /blɜːd/ *adjective* 形容词
not clear 模糊不清的：*She showed me a blurred photograph.* 她给我看了一张模糊的照片。

blush /blʌʃ/ *verb* 动词 (**blushes, blushing, blushed**)
to become red in the face because you are ashamed or embarrassed（因羞愧或窘迫）脸红：*'Hello, Maria,'he said, and she blushed again.* "你好，玛丽亚。"他说道。她的脸又红了。

board¹ /bɔːd/ *countable noun* 可数名词
1 a flat, thin piece of wood 木板：*There were wooden boards over the doors and windows.* 门窗上封着木板。
2 a flat piece of wood or plastic that you use for a special purpose（特定用途的）板，木板，塑料板：*He wrote a few notes on the board.* 他在黑板上写了几条说明。◻ *A wooden chopping board can be very heavy.* 有的木头案板很重。
3 the group of people who organize and make decisions about a company（公司的）董事会：*The board meets today, and it will announce its decision tomorrow.* 董事会今天开会，明天公布决议。

on board on a train, a ship or an aircraft 在（火车、轮船或航空器）上：*All 25 people on board the plane were killed.* 飞机上25人全部罹难。

board² /bɔːd/ *verb* 动词 (**boards, boarding, boarded**)
to get into a train, a ship or an aircraft to travel somewhere (*formal* 正式) 登上（火车、轮船或航空器）：*I boarded the plane to Boston.* 我登上了飞往波士顿的飞机。

ˈboarding ˌpass *countable noun* 可数名词 (**boarding passes**)
a card that a passenger must show when they are entering an aircraft or a boat 登机牌；登船牌

boast /bəʊst/ *verb* 动词 (**boasts, boasting, boasted**)
to talk about something that you have done or that you own too proudly, in a

boat /bəʊt/ *countable noun* 可数名词
a small ship 船；小船: *One of the best ways to see the area is in a small boat.* 参观这个地区有个极佳的方式就是乘小船。 □ *a fishing boat* 渔船

body /ˈbɒdi/ *countable noun* 可数名词 (**bodies**)
1 all the physical parts of a person or an animal（人、动物的）身体: *Yoga creates a healthy mind in a healthy body.* 瑜伽促进身心健康。
→ Look at pictures on PP4-5 参见彩插第 4 页和第 5 页
2 the main part of a person's or an animal's body, but not their arms, head and legs（人、动物的）躯干: *Lying flat on your back, twist your body onto one side.* 身体躺平，将躯干扭向一侧。
3 a dead person or animal 尸体；死尸: *Two days later, her body was found in a wood.* 两天后，她的尸体在树林中被发现。

bodyguard /ˈbɒdigɑːd/ *countable noun* 可数名词
someone whose job is to protect an important person 保镖；侍卫: *Three of his bodyguards were injured in the attack.* 袭击中他有 3 名保镖受伤。

boil /bɔɪl/ *verb* 动词 (**boils, boiling, boiled**)
1 to produce bubbles and start to change into steam（使）沸腾；烧开: *I stood in the kitchen, waiting for the water to boil.* 我站在厨房里等水开。 □ *Boil the water in the saucepan and add the salt.* 用炖锅把水烧开后放盐。
→ Look at picture on P6 参见彩插第 6 页
2 to cook food in boiling water 煮（食物）: *Wash and boil the rice.* 把米洗一下然后煮饭。 □ *I peeled potatoes and put them in a pot to boil.* 我把土豆削了皮，放到锅里煮。

boiling /ˈbɔɪlɪŋ/ *adjective* 形容词
very hot 滚烫的；酷热的: *It's boiling in here.* 这儿热得要命。

boiling point *uncountable noun* 不可数名词
the temperature at which a liquid starts to change into steam 沸点

bold /bəʊld/ *adjective* 形容词 (**bolder, boldest**)
1 not afraid to do dangerous things; confident 大胆的；自信的: *Their bold plan almost worked.* 他们大胆的计划差点儿奏效。
2 very bright 鲜明的；明亮的: *Jill's dress was patterned with bold flowers.* 吉尔的连衣裙上印着艳丽的花。

bolt /bəʊlt/ *countable noun* 可数名词
1 a long piece of metal that you use with another small piece of metal with a hole in it (= a nut) to fasten things together 螺栓: *Tighten any loose bolts and screws on your bicycle.* 紧紧自行车上松动的螺栓、螺钉。
2 a piece of metal that you move across to lock a door 插销；门闩: *Taylor went to the door and slid the bolt open.* 泰勒走到门口拉开门闩。 ● **bolt** *verb* 动词 (**bolts, bolting, bolted**): *He locked and bolted the kitchen door.* 他锁了厨房门，插上插销。

bomb[1] /bɒm/ *countable noun* 可数名词
a weapon that explodes and damages things nearby 炸弹: *Bombs went off at two London train stations.* 炸弹在伦敦两个火车站爆炸。 □ *The police do not know who planted the bomb.* 警方不清楚是谁安放的炸弹。

bomb[2] /bɒm/ *verb* 动词 (**bombs, bombing, bombed**)
to attack a place with bombs 轰炸；用炸弹攻击: *Military airplanes bombed the airport.* 军机轰炸了机场。
▶ **bombing** /ˈbɒmɪŋ/ *noun* 名词: *There has been a series of car bombings.* 汽车爆炸事件已经发生了一连串。

bond /bɒnd/ *countable noun* 可数名词
a strong feeling of friendship or love between people 情感纽带；关系: *The experience created a special bond between us.* 这段经历使我们建立起了一种特殊关系。 ● **bond** *verb* 动词 (**bonds, bonding, bonded**): *Belinda quickly bonded with her new baby.* 贝琳达很快就和新生宝宝建立起了亲密关系。

bone /bəʊn/ *noun* 名词
one of the hard white parts inside your body 骨；骨头: *Many passengers suffered broken bones in the accident.* 事故造成许多乘客骨折。
→ Look at picture on P5 参见彩插第 5 页

bonfire /ˈbɒnfaɪə/ *countable noun* 可数名词
a large fire that you make outside 篝火；

Bonfires are not allowed in many areas. 很多地区不许点篝火。

bonnet /ˈbɒnɪt/ *countable noun* 可数名词
1 (*American* 美国英语：**hood**) the front part of a car that covers the engine（汽车的）机罩，发动机盖
2 a soft hat that you tie under your chin 系带软帽

bonus /ˈbəʊnəs/ *countable noun* 可数名词 (**bonuses**)
1 an extra amount of money that you earn, usually because you have worked very hard 奖金：*Each member of staff received a £100 bonus.* 每位员工领到 100 英镑奖金。
2 something good that you would not usually expect to get 意外收获：*As a bonus, the CD comes with a free DVD.* 作为特惠，买 CD 免费赠送 DVD。

book[1] /bʊk/ *countable noun* 可数名词
a number of pieces of paper, usually with words printed on them, that are fastened together and fixed inside a cover 书；图书；本子：*Her second book was an immediate success.* 她的第二本书一出版便迅速蹿红。 □ *I've just read a new book by Rosella Brown.* 我刚看过罗塞拉·布朗的一本新书。
→ Look at picture on P1 参见彩插第 1 页

book[2] /bʊk/ *verb* 动词 (**books, booking, booked**)
to arrange to have or use something, such as a hotel room or a ticket to a concert, at a later time 预订；预约：*Laurie booked a flight home.* 劳里订了回家的航班。

bookcase /ˈbʊkkeɪs/ *countable noun* 可数名词
a piece of furniture with shelves that you keep books on 书柜；书橱

booklet /ˈbʊklət/ *countable noun* 可数名词
a very thin book that has a paper cover and that gives you information about something 小册子：*The travel office gave us a booklet about places to visit in Venice.* 旅游局给我们发了一本介绍威尼斯游览景点的小册子。

bookmark /ˈbʊkmɑːk/ *countable noun* 可数名词
the address of a website that you add to a list on your computer so that you can return to it easily 书签（添加到计算机上便于快捷访问的网站地址）：*Use bookmarks to give you quick links to your favourite websites.* 利用书签可以快速链接至自己喜欢上的网站。● **bookmark** *verb* 动词 (**bookmarks, bookmarking, bookmarked**)：*Do you want to bookmark this page?* 你想为本页添加书签吗？

bookshelf /ˈbʊkʃelf/ *countable noun* 可数名词 (**bookshelves** /ˈbʊkʃelvz/)
a shelf that you keep books on 书架

bookshop /ˈbʊkʃɒp/ *countable noun* 可数名词
a shop where books are sold 书店

boom[1] /buːm/ *countable noun* 可数名词
an increase in the number of things that people are buying 繁荣（期）：*an economic boom* 经济繁荣

boom[2] /buːm/ *verb* 动词 (**booms, booming, boomed**)
to make a loud, deep sound 隆隆响；发出响亮深沉的声响：*The wind roared and the thunder boomed above them.* 风声呼啸，他们头顶雷声隆隆。 □ *'Ladies,' boomed Helena. 'We all know why we're here tonight.'* "女士们，"海伦娜瓮声瓮气地说，"我们都清楚今晚自己为什么来这里。"

boost /buːst/ *verb* 动词 (**boosts, boosting, boosted**)
to cause something to increase, improve or be more successful 促进；增算；使增长：*Lower prices will boost sales.* 降价会促进销售。● **boost** *countable noun* 可数名词：*Scoring that goal gave me a real boost.* 这粒进球大大鼓舞了我。
boost someone's confidence to make someone feel more confident 增强某人的信心：*If the team wins, it will boost their confidence.* 球队打赢的话，会提振信心。

boot[1] /buːt/ *countable noun* 可数名词
1 a shoe that covers your whole foot and the lower part of your leg 靴子：*He sat down and took off his boots.* 他坐下来脱掉靴子。
2 (*American* 美国英语：**trunk**) the space at the back of a car that is used for carrying things in（汽车的）行李舱，后备厢

boot[2] /buːt/ *verb* 动词 (**boots, booting, booted**)
(also 亦作 **boot something up**) to make a computer ready to start working 启动（计算机）：*Put the CD into the drive and boot the machine.* 将 CD 插入驱动器，启动机器。 □ *Go over to your computer and boot it up.* 去把你的计算机启动起来。

border /ˈbɔːdə/ *countable noun* 可数名词
1 an imaginary line that divides two

countries 国界线: *They drove across the border.* 他们驾车穿过国界。 □ *Soldiers closed the border between the two countries.* 军队关闭了两国国界。
2 a decoration around the edge of something 饰边: *The curtains were white with a red border.* 窗帘白底红边。

bore¹ /bɔː/
→ see 见 **bear**

bore² /bɔː/ *verb* 动词 (**bores, boring, bored**)
to make someone feel uninterested in something, usually by talking about it too much (通常因唠叨) 使厌烦, 使厌倦: *Dick bored me with stories of his holiday.* 迪克唠叨起他假期的见闻, 让我不胜其烦。

bored /bɔːd/ *adjective* 形容词
not interested in something; having nothing to do 不感兴趣的; 厌倦的; 无聊的: *I am getting very bored with this television programme.* 我逐渐对这个电视节目感到非常厌倦。 □ *Many children get bored during the long school summer holidays.* 漫长的学校暑假中, 许多孩子都感到百无聊赖。
→ Look at picture on P15 参见彩插第 15 页

boring /ˈbɔːrɪŋ/ *adjective* 形容词
not interesting 无趣的; 乏味的: *Washing dishes is boring work.* 刷盘子这活儿很没劲。

born¹ /bɔːn/ *verb* 动词
be born to come out of your mother's body and begin life 出生; 诞生: *She was born in Milan on April 29, 1923.* 她 1923 年 4 月 29 日生于米兰。

born² /bɔːn/ *adjective* 形容词
having a natural ability to do a particular activity or job 天生的: *Jack was a born teacher.* 杰克天生就是当老师的料。

borne /bɔːn/
→ see 见 **bear**

borrow /ˈbɒrəʊ/ *verb* 动词 (**borrows, borrowing, borrowed**)
to use something that belongs to another person for a period of time and then return it 借; 借用: *Can I borrow a pen please?* 请借给我一支钢笔好吗?

boss /bɒs/ *countable noun* 可数名词 (**bosses**)
the person in charge of you at the place where you work 老板; 上司: *He likes his new boss.* 他喜欢新上司。

bossy /ˈbɒsi/ *adjective* 形容词
always telling people what to do, in an annoying way 爱支使人的; 颐指气使的: *Susan is a bossy little girl.* 苏珊是个爱支使人的小姑娘。

botany /ˈbɒtəni/ *uncountable noun* 不可数名词
the scientific study of plants 植物学
▶ **botanical** /bəˈtænɪkəl/ *adjective* 形容词: *The area is of great botanical interest.* 这个地方很有植物学研究价值。

both /bəʊθ/ *adjective* 形容词
used when you are saying that something is true about two people or things 两个 (都…)的: *Stand up straight with both arms at your sides.* 站直身子, 双臂垂在两侧。 □ *Both men were taken to hospital.* 两人都被送进医院。 ● **both** *pronoun* 代词: *Miss Brown and her friend are both from York.* 布朗小姐和她朋友都来自约克。 □ *They both worked at Harvard University.* 他们俩都在哈佛大学工作。 □ *Both of them have to go to London regularly.* 他们两个都得经常去伦敦。

both...and... used to show that each of two facts is true 不但…而且…; 既…又…: *Now women work both before and after having their children.* 现在女性生孩子前后都工作。

bother /ˈbɒðə/ *verb* 动词 (**bothers, bothering, bothered**)
1 to try to talk to someone when they are busy (用言语)打扰: *I'm sorry to bother you, but there's someone here to speak to you.* 不好意思打扰一下, 这儿有个人想跟你说几句话。
2 to make you feel worried or angry 使烦恼; 使生气: *Is something bothering you?* 你有什么烦心事儿吗?

can't be bothered to do something to not want to do something because it is too much work 不想费力做某事: *I can't be bothered to cook this evening; let's order a pizza.* 我今晚不想费劲做饭了; 咱们点个比萨饼吧。

not bother to do something to not do something because you think it is not necessary 懒得做某事: *Lots of people don't bother to get married these days.* 现在很多人都懒得结婚。

bottle /ˈbɒtəl/ *countable noun* 可数名词
a glass or plastic container in which drinks and other liquids are kept 瓶子: *There were two empty water bottles on the table.* 桌上有两个空水瓶。 □ *She drank half a*

bottle of apple juice. 她喝了半瓶苹果汁。

bottom /ˈbɒtəm/ *countable noun* 可数名词
1 the lowest or deepest part of something 底；底部：*He sat at the bottom of the stairs.* 他坐在最下面一级楼梯上。□ *Answers can be found at the bottom of page 8.* 答案见第8页底部。●**bottom** *adjective* 形容词：*There are pencils in the bottom drawer of the desk.* 桌子最下面抽屉里有铅笔。
2 the part of your body that you sit on 屁股；臀部
→ Look at picture on P4 参见彩插第4页

bought /bɔːt/
→ see 见 **buy**

bounce /baʊns/ *verb* 动词 (**bounces, bouncing, bounced**)
1 to hit a surface and immediately move away from it again (使)弹起；(使)弹跳：*The ball bounced across the floor.* 球弹到了地板另一侧。□ *Matthew came into the kitchen bouncing a rubber ball.* 马修拍着橡皮球走进厨房。
2 to jump up and down on a soft surface (在柔软的表面上)蹦：*Some children were playing football; others were riding scooters or bouncing on the trampoline.* 一些孩子在踢足球，其余的在骑滑板车或玩蹦床。

bounce 弹起；蹦

The ball bounced across the floor.
球弹到了地板另一侧。

She is bouncing on the trampoline.
她在蹦床上蹦跳。

3 if an email bounces, it is returned to the person who sent it because of a problem (电子邮件)被退回

bound¹ /baʊnd/
→ see 见 **bind**

bound² /baʊnd/ *adjective* 形容词
bound to certain to happen or to do something 肯定会的；一定会的：*There are bound to be price increases next year.* 明年肯定要涨价。

boundary /ˈbaʊndəri/ *countable noun* 可数名词 (**boundaries**)
an imaginary line that separates one area of land from another area of land (土地的)界线，边界；疆界：*The river forms the western boundary of my farm.* 这条河就是我家农场的西部边界。

bouquet /bəʊˈkeɪ, buː-/ *countable noun* 可数名词
a bunch of flowers that have been cut 花束：*The bride carried a bouquet of roses.* 新娘捧着一束玫瑰。

boutique /buːˈtiːk/ *countable noun* 可数名词
a small shop that sells fashionable clothes, shoes or jewellery 精品店

bow¹ /baʊ/ *verb* 动词 (**bows, bowing, bowed**)
to bend your head or body towards someone as a formal way of greeting them or showing respect 鞠躬：*They bowed low to the king.* 他们向国王深深地鞠了一躬。●**bow** *countable noun* 可数名词：*I gave a bow and waved.* 我鞠了一躬，然后挥了挥手。

bow² /bəʊ/ *countable noun* 可数名词
1 a knot with two round parts and two loose ends that is used in tying shoelaces and ribbons 蝴蝶结：*Add some ribbon tied in a bow.* 加上系成蝴蝶结的丝带。
2 a weapon for shooting arrows 弓：*Some of the men were armed with bows and arrows.* 这些男子中有的佩有弓箭。
3 a long thin piece of wood with threads stretched along it that you move across the strings of a musical instrument (乐器的)弓：*I drew the bow across the strings of the violin.* 我用小提琴琴弓拉动琴弦。

bowels /ˈbaʊəlz/ *plural noun* 复数名词
the tubes in your body where digested food from your stomach is stored before you pass it from your body 肠：*Eating fruit and vegetables can help to keep your bowels healthy.* 吃水果蔬菜有助于保持肠道健康。

bowl¹ /bəʊl/ *countable noun* 可数名词
a round container that is used for mixing and serving food 碗: *Put the soup in a bowl.* 把汤盛进碗里。

bowl² /bəʊl/ *verb* 动词 (**bowls, bowling, bowled**)
to throw the ball in a game of cricket, so that someone can hit it (板球运动中)投(球)

bowling /ˈbəʊlɪŋ/ *uncountable noun* 不可数名词
a game in which you roll a heavy ball down a narrow track toward a group of wooden objects and try to knock down as many of them as possible 保龄球运动: *We go bowling every Saturday afternoon.* 我们每周六下午去打保龄球。

bow tie *countable noun* 可数名词
a tie in the form of a bow (= a knot with two round parts) that men sometimes wear on formal occasions 蝶形领结

box¹ /bɒks/ *countable noun* 可数名词 (**boxes**)
1 a container with a hard bottom, hard sides and usually a lid 箱；盒；匣: *He packed his books into the cardboard box beside him.* 他把书收拾进身旁的纸板箱里。 □ *They sat on wooden boxes.* 他们坐在木箱上。
2 a square shape that is printed on paper 方格；方框: *For more information, just tick the box and send us the form.* 要了解更多信息，请在方框中打钩并将表格发送给我们。

box² /bɒks/ *verb* 动词 (**boxes, boxing, boxed**)
to fight someone according to the rules of boxing 打拳击: *At school I boxed and played baseball.* 上学时我打拳击、打棒球。
▶ **boxer** /ˈbɒksə/ *countable noun* 可数名词: *He wants to be a professional boxer.* 他想成为一名职业拳击手。

boxer shorts *plural noun* 复数名词
loose underwear that boys and men wear on the lower part of their body 男用宽松平脚短内裤: *a pair of boxer shorts* 一条男用平脚短内裤

boxing /ˈbɒksɪŋ/ *uncountable noun* 不可数名词
a sport in which two people fight following special rules 拳击运动

box office also 亦作 **box-office** *countable noun* 可数名词
the place in a theatre where the tickets are sold (剧院的)售票处: *There was a long queue of people outside the box office.* 售票处外排着长长一队人。

boy /bɔɪ/ *countable noun* 可数名词
a male child 男孩: *Did you have any pets when you were a little boy?* 你小时候养过宠物吗？

boycott /ˈbɔɪkɒt/ *verb* 动词 (**boycotts, boycotting, boycotted**)
to refuse to be involved with a country, an organization or an activity because you disapprove of it 抵制: *Some groups threatened to boycott the meeting.* 一些团体威胁抵制此次会议。

boyfriend /ˈbɔɪfrend/ *countable noun* 可数名词
a man or a boy that someone is having a romantic relationship with 男朋友: *Brenda came with her boyfriend, Anthony.* 布伦达和男朋友安东尼一起来的。

Boy Scout *countable noun* 可数名词
→ see 见 **Scout**: *He was a Boy Scout in his youth.* 他年少时参加过童子军。
the Boy Scouts → see 见 **Scout**: *I joined the Boy Scouts when I was ten years old.* 我10岁时加入了童子军。

bra /brɑː/ *countable noun* 可数名词
a piece of underwear that women wear to support their breasts 胸罩；文胸

bracelet /ˈbreɪslɪt/ *countable noun* 可数名词
a piece of jewellery that you wear around your wrist 手镯；手链

brackets /ˈbrækɪts/ *plural noun* 复数名词
curved ( ) or square [ ] marks that you can place around words, letters or numbers when you are writing 括号: *There's a telephone number in brackets under his name.* 他名字下面的括号里有个电话号码。

brain /breɪn/ *countable noun* 可数名词
1 the organ inside your head that controls your body's activities and allows you to think and to feel things 脑
→ Look at picture on P5 参见彩插第5页
2 your mind and the way that you think 头脑: *Sports are good for your brain as well as your body.* 体育运动对大脑和身体均有益。
have brains to have the ability to learn and understand things quickly 有智慧: *These scientists have brains and imagination.* 这些科学家智慧和想象力兼备。

brake /breɪk/ **countable noun** 可数名词
the part in a vehicle that makes it go slower or stop 刹车；车闸；制动器：*He stepped on the brake as the light turned red.* 灯变红了，他踩了刹车。● **brake** **verb** 动词 (**brakes, braking, braked**)：*The driver braked to avoid an accident.* 司机刹车避免了一场事故。

branch /brɑːntʃ/ **countable noun** 可数名词 (**branches**)
1 one of the parts of a tree that have leaves, flowers and fruit 树枝；枝条：*We picked apples from the upper branches of a tree.* 我们摘了高处树枝的苹果。
2 one of the offices or shops that form part of a bigger company 分店；分部；分支机构：*Sadly, we are closing some of our smaller branches.* 遗憾的是，我们要关掉一些小的分店。

brand /brænd/ **countable noun** 可数名词
the name of a product that a particular company makes 品牌：*This shop doesn't sell my favourite brand of biscuits.* 这家商店不卖我最喜欢的那个牌子的饼干。

brand-'new **adjective** 形容词
completely new 全新的；崭新的：*Yesterday he bought a brand-new car.* 昨天他买了一辆崭新的汽车。

brandy /ˈbrændi/ **noun** 名词 (**brandies**)
a strong alcoholic drink made from wine 白兰地 (一种烈酒)

brass /brɑːs/ **noun** 名词
1 uncountable 不可数 a yellow-coloured metal 黄铜：*Ritchie lifted the shiny brass door knocker.* 里奇抓起闪亮的黄铜门环。
2 uncountable 不可数 musical instruments that are made of brass 铜管乐器：*a piece of music for brass* 一支铜管乐器曲子
3 singular 单数 all the musical instruments in an orchestra that are made of brass (管弦乐队的) 铜管乐器组：*Suddenly the brass comes in with great power and intensity.* 突然铜管乐器组高亢激昂地奏响。
→ Look at picture on P12 参见彩插第 12 页

brave /breɪv/ **adjective** 形容词 (**braver, bravest**)
willing to do things that are dangerous, without showing fear 勇敢的；无畏的：*A brave 12-year-old boy tried to help his friends.* 一个勇敢的 12 岁男孩试图帮助朋友。
▶ **bravely** /ˈbreɪvli/ **adverb** 副词：*The army fought bravely.* 全军英勇奋战。

bravery /ˈbreɪvəri/ **uncountable noun** 不可数名词
the ability to do things that are dangerous without showing fear 勇敢；勇气：*He received an award for his bravery.* 他获颁一枚英勇勋章。

bread /bred/ **noun** 名词
a food made mostly from flour and water 面包：*She bought a loaf of bread at the shop.* 她在店里买了一条面包。□ *I usually just have bread and butter for breakfast.* 我一般早餐就吃面包片抹黄油。
→ Look at picture on P5 参见彩插第 5 页

break¹ /breɪk/ **verb** 动词 (**breaks, breaking, broke, broken**)
1 to separate suddenly into pieces often after falling or hitting something 碎裂；断裂：*The plate broke.* 盘子碎了。□ *The plane crashed into the trees and broke into three pieces.* 飞机撞上树丛中断成了三截。□ *Rachel's right arm broke when she was hit by a car.* 蕾切尔被汽车撞后右胳膊骨折。
2 to make something separate into pieces, often by dropping or hitting it 打碎；弄碎；折断：*I'm sorry. I've broken a glass.* 对不起，我打碎了个杯子。□ *After the match, I found out I had broken a bone in my left foot.* 赛后，我发觉自己左脚骨折了。
3 to damage something so that it stops working 损坏；破坏：*I've broken my mobile phone so I need a new one.* 我把手机弄坏了，得换个新的。
4 to do something that you should not do because it is against a law, or because it goes against something that you have agreed or promised to do 违反 (法律)；背弃 (承诺)：*We didn't know we were breaking the law.* 我们不知道违法了。□ *She says you broke a promise to her.* 她说你背弃了对她的承诺。

break down
1 to stop working 损坏；出故障：*Their car broke down.* 他们的车坏了。
2 to start crying 哭起来：*I broke down and cried.* 我失声哭了起来。

break in/break into something to get into a building by force 闯入／强行进入 (建筑物)：*The robbers broke in and stole £8,000.* 窃贼闯进来偷了 8,000 英镑。□ *There was someone trying to break into the house.* 有人企图闯进家里。

break out to begin suddenly 爆发：*He was 29 when war broke out.* 战争爆发那年他 29 岁。

break something off to remove one part of a thing from the rest of it by breaking it 掰下（或折下）某物：*Grace broke off a large piece of bread.* 格雷斯掰了一大块面包。

break up
1 to end a relationship 分手；关系破裂：*I was married for eight years but we broke up last year.* 我结婚 8 年，但去年我们离了。▫ *My girlfriend has broken up with me.* 我女朋友和我闹翻了。
2 to start the school holidays（学校）放假：*We break up at the end of June.* 我们 6 月底放假。

break² /breɪk/ *countable noun* 可数名词
a short period of time when you have a rest 小憩；短休：*We get a 15-minute break for coffee.* 我们有 15 分钟喝咖啡的休息时间。

breakdown /ˈbreɪkdaʊn/ *countable noun* 可数名词
1 the failure of a relationship, a plan or a discussion（关系的）破裂；（计划、讨论的）失败：*Newspapers reported the breakdown of talks between the U.S. and European Union officials.* 报纸上报道了美国和欧盟官员之间的谈判破裂。▫ *Arguments about money led to the breakdown of their marriage.* 为钱争吵导致他们婚姻破裂。
2 when a car or a piece of machinery stops working（汽车、机器的）故障：*You should be prepared for breakdowns and accidents.* 你得为抛锚和事故做好准备。

breakfast /ˈbrekfəst/ *noun* 名词
the first meal of the day 早餐；早饭：*Would you like eggs for breakfast?* 早餐吃鸡蛋好吗？

breakthrough /ˈbreɪkθruː/ *countable noun* 可数名词
an important discovery that is made after a lot of hard work 突破；重大发现：*The scientist described a medical breakthrough in cancer treatment.* 这位科学家描述了一项癌症治疗方面的医学突破。

breast /brest/ *noun* 名词
1 *countable* 可数 one of the two soft, round parts on a woman's chest that can produce milk to feed a baby（女子的）乳房
2 a piece of meat that is cut from the front of a bird（鸟的）胸脯肉：*For dinner I cooked chicken breast with vegetables.* 晚饭我做了蔬菜鸡胸肉。

breaststroke /ˈbreststrəʊk/ *uncountable noun* 不可数名词
a way of swimming in which you pull both of your arms back at the same time, and kick your legs with your knees bent 蛙泳：*I'm learning to swim breaststroke.* 我在学蛙泳。

breath /breθ/ *noun* 名词
the air that you let out through your mouth when you breathe 呼出的气体；气息：*His breath smelled of onion.* 他呼出的气息有洋葱味。

be out of breath to be breathing very quickly because your body has been working hard 气喘吁吁：*She was out of breath from running.* 她跑得上气不接下气。

take a breath to breathe in once 吸口气：*He took a deep breath, and began to climb the stairs.* 他深吸一口气，开始爬楼梯。

breathe /briːð/ *verb* 动词 (**breathes, breathing, breathed**)
to take air into your lungs and let it out again 呼吸：*He was breathing fast.* 他呼吸急促。
▶ **breathing** /ˈbriːðɪŋ/ *uncountable noun* 不可数名词：*Her breathing became slow.* 她的呼吸慢了下来。

breathless /ˈbreθləs/ *adjective* 形容词
having difficulty breathing properly, because you have been running, for example 呼吸困难的；气喘吁吁的：*I was breathless after the race.* 赛后我上气不接下气。

breed¹ /briːd/ *countable noun* 可数名词
a particular type of animal（动物的）品种：*There are about 300 breeds of horse.* 马的品种大概有 300 种。

breed² /briːd/ *verb* 动词 (**breeds, breeding, bred** /bred/)
1 to keep male and female animals so that they will produce babies 繁殖，养殖（动物）：*He breeds dogs for the police.* 他为警方育犬。
2 to produce babies（动物）繁殖，生育：*Birds usually breed in the spring.* 鸟类一般在春天繁殖。

breeze /briːz/ *countable noun* 可数名词
a gentle wind 和风；清风：*We enjoyed the cool summer breeze.* 我们享受着夏日的凉风。

bribe /braɪb/ *verb* 动词 (**bribes, bribing, bribed**)
to offer someone money or something valuable in order to persuade them to do something dishonest 贿赂；收买：*He was*

accused of bribing a bank official. 他被控贿赂一名银行官员。● **bribe** *countable noun* 可数名词: *The police took bribes from criminals.* 警方收受了罪犯的贿赂。

bribery /ˈbraɪbəri/ *uncountable noun* 不可数名词
the act of offering someone money or something valuable in order to persuade them to do something dishonest for you 贿赂；行贿: *He was arrested for bribery.* 他因行贿被捕。

brick /brɪk/ *noun* 名词
a rectangular block used in the building of walls 砖: *a brick wall* 砖墙

bride /braɪd/ *countable noun* 可数名词
a woman on her wedding day, or a woman who is about to get married or has just got married 新娘

bridegroom /ˈbraɪdgruːm/ *countable noun* 可数名词
a man on his wedding day, or a man who is about to get married or has just got married 新郎

bridesmaid /ˈbraɪdzmeɪd/ *countable noun* 可数名词
a woman or a girl who helps the bride on her wedding day 伴娘；女傧相

bridge /brɪdʒ/ *countable noun* 可数名词
a structure that is built over a river or a road so that people or vehicles can cross from one side to the other 桥；桥梁: *He walked over the bridge to get to school.* 他走过桥去上学。

bridge 桥

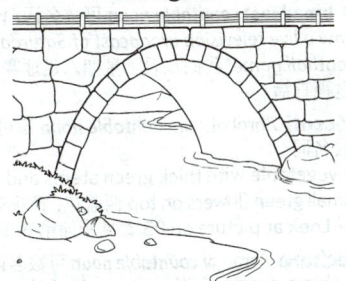

brief /briːf/ *adjective* 形容词 (**briefer, briefest**)
1 lasting for only a short time 短暂的: *She once made a brief appearance on television.* 她曾在电视上短暂露过面。
2 without many words or details 简洁的；简练的: *The book begins with a brief description of his career.* 本书开头简要介绍了他的生涯。

briefcase /ˈbriːfkeɪs/ *countable noun* 可数名词
a small suitcase for carrying business papers 公文包

briefly /ˈbriːfli/ *adverb* 副词
for a very short period of time 短暂地: *He smiled briefly.* 他微微笑了笑。

briefs /briːfs/ *plural noun* 复数名词
men's or women's underwear that they wear on the lower part of their body 内裤: *a pair of briefs* 一条内裤

bright /braɪt/ *adjective* 形容词 (**brighter, brightest**)
1 strong and noticeable in colour（颜色）鲜艳的，鲜明的: *She wore a bright red dress.* 她身着一条鲜艳的红色连衣裙。
2 shining strongly 明亮的；耀眼的: *He looked pale and tired under the bright lights of the TV studio.* 在电视演播室明亮的灯光下，他面色苍白，一脸疲惫。
▶ **brightly** /ˈbraɪtli/ *adverb* 副词: *The sun shone brightly in the sky.* 艳阳当空。
3 full of light 光线充足的: *There was a bright room where patients could sit with their visitors.* 有一间明亮的屋子，患者可以坐下来会客。
4 clever and able to learn things quickly 聪明的: *He seems brighter than most boys.* 他好像比大多数男孩都聪明。

brighten /ˈbraɪtən/ *verb* 动词 (**brightens, brightening, brightened**)
1 to suddenly look happier 突然快乐起来: *Seeing him, she seemed to brighten a little.* 看见他，她似乎露出了点儿喜色。
2 to make something more colourful and attractive 使生色；为⋯增色: *Pots planted with flowers brightened the area outside the door.* 盆栽花给门外这块地方增色不少。

brilliant /ˈbrɪliənt/ *adjective* 形容词
1 very clever or skilful 聪颖的；技艺高超的: *She had a brilliant mind.* 她聪明伶俐。 □ *He was a brilliant pianist.* 他是位才华横溢的钢琴家。
▶ **brilliantly** /ˈbrɪliəntli/ *adverb* 副词: *The film was brilliantly written and acted — a really great production.* 这部影片写得精彩，演得漂亮——一部异彩纷呈的制作。
2 extremely bright in light or colour（光线或颜色）非常明亮的: *The woman had brilliant*

green eyes. 这个女人眼睛碧绿碧绿的。
3 very good (*informal* 非正式) 非常好的：*That film was brilliant.* 那部影片棒极很。

brim /brɪm/ *countable noun* 可数名词
the part of a hat that sticks out around the bottom 帽檐：*Rain dripped from the brim of his old hat.* 雨水从他旧帽子的帽檐上滴落下来。

bring /brɪŋ/ *verb* 动词 (**brings, bringing, brought**)
1 to have someone or something with you when you come to a place（造访某地时）带上：*Remember to bring an old shirt to wear when we paint.* 粉刷时记得带件旧衬衫穿。 □ *Can I bring Susie to the party?* 我能带上苏茜来参加聚会吗？
2 to get something that someone wants and take it to them 带给，拿来（他人索要之物）：*He poured a glass of milk for Sarah and brought it to her.* 他给萨拉倒了一杯牛奶，端到她面前。
bring someone up to take care of a child until it is an adult 把某人养大：*She brought up four children.* 她把4个孩子拉扯大。□ *He was brought up in Nebraska.* 他在内布拉斯加长大。
bring something back to return something 返还（或退还）某物：*Please could you bring back those books that I lent you?* 请把我借给你的那些书还回来好吗？
bring something in to earn money 挣（钱）：*My job brings in about £24,000 a year.* 我的职位每年大概能挣24,000英镑。
bring something up to introduce a particular subject into a conversation 提起（某个话题）：*Her mother brought up the subject of going back to work.* 她妈妈提起重返工作的话题。

> **LANGUAGE HELP 语言提示**
> **Bring** or **take**? 用 bring 还是 take？
> **Bring** gives the idea of movement towards the speaker and **take** gives the idea of movement away from the speaker. *bring 有朝说话人而来之意，take 有离说话人而去之意。

brisk /brɪsk/ *adjective* 形容词 (**brisker, briskest**)
quick and using a lot of energy 利落的；矫健的：*He gave me a brisk handshake.* 他利落地用力握了握我的手。
▶ **briskly** /ˈbrɪskli/ *adverb* 副词：*Eve walked briskly through the park.* 伊夫步伐矫健地穿过公园。

bristle /ˈbrɪsəl/ *countable noun* 可数名词
1 one of the short hairs that grow on a man's face（男子脸上的）短髭
2 a short thick hair on a brush（刷子上的）毛

brittle /ˈbrɪtəl/ *adjective* 形容词
hard but easily broken 脆的：*I have very brittle fingernails.* 我的指甲很脆。

broad /brɔːd/ *adjective* 形容词 (**broader, broadest**)
1 wide 宽的；宽阔的：*His shoulders were broad and his waist was narrow.* 他肩宽腰细。
a broad smile/grin a big, happy smile or grin 灿烂的笑／咧嘴大笑：*He greeted them with a wave and a broad smile.* 他挥了挥手，笑容满面地向他们致意。
2 including a large number of different things 广泛的；涉及面广的：*The library had a broad range of books.* 这座图书馆藏书宏富。

broadband /ˈbrɔːdbænd/ *uncountable noun* 不可数名词
a method of sending many electronic messages at the same time over the Internet 宽带（因特网中用于传输信息的系统）：*They've announced big price cuts for broadband customers.* 他们宣布为宽带用户大幅降价。

broadcast /ˈbrɔːdkɑːst/ *verb* 动词 (**broadcasts, broadcasting, broadcast**)
to send out a programme so that it can be heard on the radio or seen on television 播送，播出（节目）：*The concert will be broadcast live on television and radio.* 这场音乐会将通过电视和广播现场直播。
● **broadcast** *countable noun* 可数名词：*We saw a live television broadcast of Saturday's football game.* 我们观看了星期六足球赛的电视直播。

broccoli /ˈbrɒkəli/ *uncountable noun* 不可数名词
a vegetable with thick green stems and small green flowers on top 西蓝花；青花菜
→ Look at picture on P5 参见彩插第5页

brochure /ˈbrəʊʃə/ *countable noun* 可数名词
a thin magazine with pictures that gives you information about a product or a service（介绍产品或服务的）小册子，宣传册：*The city looked beautiful in the travel brochures.* 这座城市从旅游宣传册上看很漂亮。

broke¹ /brəʊk/
→ see 见 **break**

broke² /brəʊk/ *adjective* 形容词
without any money (*informal* 非正式) 不名一文的; 身无分文的: *I don't have a job, and I'm broke.* 我没有工作，一个子儿也没有。

broken¹ /ˈbrəʊkən/
→ see 见 **break**

broken² /ˈbrəʊkən/ *adjective* 形容词
in pieces or not working 破碎的; 折断的; 损坏的: *She was taken to hospital with a broken leg.* 她一条腿骨折, 被送进了医院。 □ *a broken window* 破损的窗户 □ *My watch is broken.* 我的手表坏了。

bronze¹ /brɒnz/ *uncountable noun* 不可数名词
a yellowish-brown metal that is a mixture of copper and tin 青铜: *a bronze statue of a ballet dancer* 一尊芭蕾舞演员的青铜雕塑

bronze² /brɒnz/ *adjective* 形容词
yellowish-brown in colour 青铜色的; 黄褐色的: *The sky began to fill with bronze light.* 天空开始布满黄褐色的光。

bronze medal *countable noun* 可数名词
an award made of brown metal that you get as third prize in a competition 铜牌

brooch /brəʊtʃ/ *countable noun* 可数名词 (**brooches**)
a piece of jewellery that has a pin on the back so that you can fasten it to your clothes 饰针; 胸针

brood /bruːd/ *verb* 动词 (**broods, brooding, brooded**)
to feel sad or worry a lot about something 忧虑; 闷闷不乐: *She constantly broods about having no friends.* 她一直为没有朋友感到郁闷。

broom /bruːm/ *countable noun* 可数名词
a type of brush with a long handle used for sweeping the floor 扫帚; 笤帚

brother /ˈbrʌðə/ *countable noun* 可数名词
a boy or a man who has the same parents as you (同父母的) 兄弟, 哥哥, 弟弟: *Are you Peter's brother?* 你是彼得的弟弟吗？

brother-in-law *countable noun* 可数名词 (**brothers-in-law**)
the brother of your husband or wife, or the man who is married to your sister 大伯子; 小叔子; 大舅子; 小舅子; 姐夫; 妹夫

brought /brɔːt/
→ see 见 **bring**

brow /braʊ/ *countable noun* 可数名词
your forehead 额; 额头: *He wiped his brow with the back of his hand.* 他用手背擦了擦前额。

brown /braʊn/ *adjective* 形容词 (**browner, brownest**)
having the colour of earth or wood 褐色的; 棕色的: *He looked into her brown eyes.* 他盯着她褐色的眼睛。● **brown** *noun* 名词: *Colours such as dark brown and green will be popular in the fashion world this autumn.* 深褐色、绿色等颜色将是今秋时尚界的流行色。
→ Look at picture on P13 参见彩插第 13 页

brownie /ˈbraʊni/ *countable noun* 可数名词
a small flat chocolate cake 布朗尼蛋糕 (一种小方块巧克力蛋糕): *She put a tray of chocolate brownies on the table.* 她把一盘巧克力布朗尼蛋糕放到桌上。

Brownie /ˈbraʊni/ *countable noun* 可数名词
a girl who is a member of the Brownies 幼年女童子军队员
the Brownies an organization for girls between the ages of seven and ten 幼年女童子军 (成员为 7—10 岁女孩)

browse /braʊz/ *verb* 动词 (**browses, browsing, browsed**)
1 to look at things in a shop, without buying anything (在店铺里) 随便看看: *I stopped in several bookshops to browse.* 我在几家书店停下来随便看看。
2 to look through a book or a magazine 浏览, 翻阅 (书刊): *She was sitting on the sofa browsing through the TV magazine.* 她坐在沙发上浏览电视杂志。
3 to search for information on the Internet (在因特网上) 浏览: *The software allows you to browse the Internet on your mobile phone.* 这款软件可以让你在手机上浏览网页。

browser /ˈbraʊzə/ *countable noun* 可数名词
a piece of computer software that allows you to search for information on the Internet (上网使用的) 浏览器: *You need an up-to-date Web browser.* 你需要用最新的网页浏览器。

bruise /bruːz/ *verb* 动词 (**bruises, bruising, bruised**)
to injure a part of your body so that a purple mark appears there 挫伤; 擦伤; 碰伤: *I bruised my knee on a desk drawer.* 我的膝盖碰到书桌抽屉擦伤了。● **bruise**

brush – buckle

countable noun 可数名词: *How did you get that bruise on your arm?* 你胳膊那儿怎么青了一块?
▶ **bruised** /bruːzd/ *adjective* 形容词: *a bruised knee* 擦伤的膝盖

brush[1] /brʌʃ/ *countable noun* 可数名词 (**brushes**)
an object with a lot of bristles or hairs attached to it that you use for painting, cleaning things and making your hair tidy 刷子; 毛刷; 画笔: *We gave him paint and brushes.* 我们给了他颜料和几支画笔。□ *He brought soapy water and brushes to clean the floor.* 他弄来肥皂水和刷子清理地面。

brushes 刷子

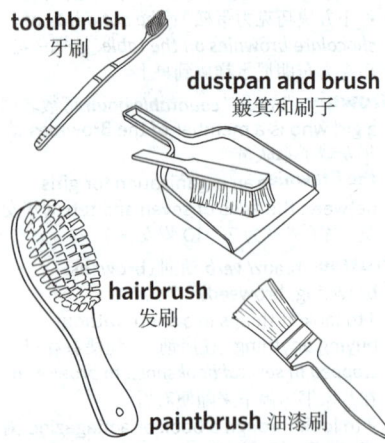

brush[2] /brʌʃ/ *verb* 动词 (**brushes, brushing, brushed**)
1 to clean something or make it tidy using a brush (用刷子)刷，扫: *Have you brushed your teeth?* 你刷牙了吗? □ *You need to brush your hair.* 你的头发得梳一梳。
2 to remove something with movements of your hands (用手)拂，掸: *He brushed the snow off his suit.* 他掸掉套装上的雪。
3 to touch something lightly 轻触; 轻擦: *The cat brushed against her leg.* 猫蹭了蹭她的腿。

Brussels sprout /ˌbrʌsəlz 'spraʊt/ *countable noun* 可数名词
a small round vegetable made of many leaves 抱子甘蓝; 球芽甘蓝

brutal /'bruːtəl/ *adjective* 形容词
very cruel and violent 残暴的; 野蛮的: *a brutal military dictator* 残暴的军事独裁者 □ *brutal punishment* 残酷的惩罚
▶ **brutally** /'bruːtəli/ *adverb* 副词: *Her parents were brutally murdered.* 她父母被残忍杀害了。

BTW
short for (缩写 =) 'by the way' in an email or a text message (用于电子邮件或手机短信) 另, 对了, 顺便提一句

bubble[1] /'bʌbəl/ *countable noun* 可数名词
1 a small ball of air or gas in a liquid 泡; 气泡: *Air bubbles rise to the surface.* 气泡升到表面。
2 a hollow ball of soapy liquid that is floating in the air or standing on a surface 肥皂泡: *With soap and lots of bubbles children love bathtime.* 有了肥皂和大量的肥皂泡, 孩子们爱上洗澡。

bubble[2] /'bʌbəl/ *verb* 动词 (**bubbles, bubbling, bubbled**)
to produce bubbles 冒泡; 起泡: *Heat the soup until it is bubbling.* 把汤加热至沸腾。

bubbly /'bʌbli/ *adjective* 形容词
1 very lively and cheerful 活泼开朗的: *Sue is a bubbly girl who loves to laugh.* 休是个活泼爱笑的女孩儿。
2 with a lot of bubbles 多泡的: *When the butter is melted and bubbly, add the flour.* 黄油熔化并大量起泡时, 加入面粉。

bucket /'bʌkɪt/ *countable noun* 可数名词
a round metal or plastic container with a handle, used for holding and carrying water 桶; 水桶: *She threw a bucket of water on the fire.* 她朝火上泼了一桶水。

bucket 桶

buckle /'bʌkəl/ *countable noun* 可数名词
a piece of metal or plastic on one end of a belt or a shoe that is used for fastening it (皮带或鞋的)搭扣, 扣环: *He wore a belt with a large silver buckle.* 他系了条带大银扣的皮带。● **buckle** *verb* 动词 (**buckles, buckling, buckled**): *The girl sat down to buckle her shoes.* 女孩儿坐下来系鞋扣。

buckle 皮带扣
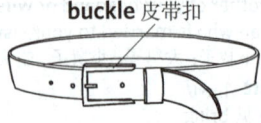

bud /bʌd/ *countable noun* 可数名词
a new growth on a tree or plant that develops into a leaf or flower 芽；苞；蕾：*Small pink buds were beginning to form on the bushes.* 灌木丛开始萌出粉色的小花蕾。

Buddhism /ˈbʊdɪzəm/ *uncountable noun* 不可数名词
a religion that teaches that the way to end suffering is by controlling your desires 佛教

Buddhist /ˈbʊdɪst/ *countable noun* 可数名词
a person whose religion is Buddhism 佛教徒 ● **Buddhist** *adjective* 形容词：*Buddhist monks* 佛教僧侣

budge /bʌdʒ/ *verb* 动词 (**budges, budging, budged**)
not budge
1 to refuse to change your mind about something 不动摇；不让步：*The government will not budge on this point.* 政府在这一点上不会让步。
2 to be impossible to move 无法移动：*I tried to open the window, but it wouldn't budge.* 我试图打开窗户，可是窗户纹丝不动。

budget¹ /ˈbʌdʒɪt/ *countable noun* 可数名词
1 the amount of money that you have available to spend 预算：*She will design a new kitchen for you within your budget.* 她会给你设计一个新厨房，花费不超出你的预算。□ *The actress will star in a low-budget film.* 这位女演员将主演一部低成本影片。
2 the financial plan made by a government in some countries about how much money it will spend on services in the next year 政府年度预算

budget² /ˈbʌdʒɪt/ *verb* 动词 (**budgets, budgeting, budgeted**)
to decide how much money you can afford to spend 做预算；将…编入预算：*The company has budgeted £10 million for advertising.* 公司做了 1,000 万英镑的广告预算。

buffalo /ˈbʌfələʊ/ *countable noun* 可数名词 (**buffalo**)
a wild animal like a large cow with horns that curve upwards 水牛；北美野牛

buffet /ˈbʌfeɪ/ *countable noun* 可数名词
a meal at a party where the food is arranged on a long table and guests serve themselves 自助餐：*After the event, there will be a buffet.* 活动后将会有自助餐。

bug /bʌɡ/ *countable noun* 可数名词
1 an insect (*informal* 非正式) 虫子；昆虫
2 a mild illness (*informal* 非正式) 小病：*I think I have a stomach bug.* 我觉得胃有点儿不舒服。
3 a mistake in a computer program（计算机程序的）错误，缺陷：*There is a bug in the software.* 软件里有一处错误。

buggy /ˈbʌɡi/ *countable noun* 可数名词 (**buggies**)
a chair with four wheels that you use for pushing a small child along 婴儿车

build¹ /bɪld/ *verb* 动词 (**builds, building, built**)
to make something by joining different things together 建造；建筑：*They are going to build a hotel here.* 他们要在这儿建一座宾馆。□ *The house was built in the early 19th century.* 这座房子建于 19 世纪早期。

build² /bɪld/ *noun* 名词
the particular shape of a person's body 体形；身材；体格：*He's six feet tall and of medium build.* 他身高 6 英尺，中等身材。

builder /ˈbɪldə/ *countable noun* 可数名词
a person whose job is to build or repair houses and other buildings 建筑工人；建造者：*The builders have finished the roof.* 建筑工人已经盖好了房顶。
→ Look at picture on P16 参见彩插第 16 页

building /ˈbɪldɪŋ/ *countable noun* 可数名词
a structure that has a roof and walls 建筑物：*They lived on the top floor of the building.* 他们住在大楼顶层。

built /bɪlt/
→ see 见 **build**

bulb /bʌlb/ *countable noun* 可数名词
1 the glass part inside a lamp that gives out light 灯泡：*A single bulb hangs from the ceiling.* 一只灯泡孤零零地悬在天花板上。
→ Look at picture on P6 参见彩插第 6 页
2 a root of a flower or a plant 鳞茎：*tulip bulbs* 郁金香鳞茎

bulge /bʌldʒ/ *verb* 动词 (**bulges, bulging, bulged**)
to stick out 凸起；鼓起：*His pockets were bulging with coins.* 他口袋里装着硬币，鼓鼓囊囊的。● **bulge** *countable noun* 可数名词：*The police officer noticed a bulge under the man's coat and realized that he had a gun.* 警察注意到那名男子外套鼓起一块，意识到他有枪。

bulk /bʌlk/ *noun* 名词
in bulk in large amounts 批量地：*It is cheaper to buy supplies in bulk.* 批量采购日用品要便宜些。

the bulk of something most of 某物的大部分：*The bulk of the money will go to the children's hospital in Dublin.* 大部分钱将用于都柏林的儿童医院。

bulky /ˈbʌlki/ *adjective* 形容词 (**bulkier, bulkiest**)
large and heavy 笨重的；又大又沉的：*The shop can deliver bulky items like lawnmowers.* 割草机之类笨重的物件店铺可以送货上门。

bull /bʊl/ *countable noun* 可数名词
a male animal of the cow family, and some other animals 公牛；雄兽

bulldog /ˈbʊldɒg/ *countable noun* 可数名词
a short dog with a large square head 斗牛犬

bulldozer /ˈbʊldəʊzə/ *countable noun* 可数名词
a large vehicle with a broad metal blade at the front that is used for moving large amounts of earth 推土机

bullet /ˈbʊlɪt/ *countable noun* 可数名词
a small piece of metal that is shot out of a gun 枪弹；子弹：*A bullet hit the wall behind him, narrowly missing him.* 一颗子弹打到了他身后的墙上，险些打中他。

bulletin board /ˈbʊlɪtɪn ˌbɔːd/ *countable noun* 可数名词
in computing, a system that allows users to send and receive messages（计算机的）公告板系统：*The Internet is the largest computer bulletin board in the world.* 因特网是世界上最大的计算机公告板系统。

bully /ˈbʊli/ *countable noun* 可数名词 (**bullies**)
someone who often hurts or frightens other people 恶霸；恃强凌弱者：*He was the class bully.* 他是班上一霸。● **bully** *verb* 动词 (**bullies, bullying, bullied**)：*I wasn't going to let him bully me.* 我不会由着他欺负我。

bumblebee /ˈbʌmbəlˌbiː/ also 亦作 **bumble bee** *countable noun* 可数名词
a large bee 熊蜂；大黄蜂

bump¹ /bʌmp/ *verb* 动词 (**bumps, bumping, bumped**)
to accidentally hit something or someone while you are moving（无意地）碰，撞：*They stopped walking and I almost bumped into them.* 他们停下来不走了，我差点儿撞上他们。□ *She bumped her head on a low branch.* 她的头撞到了一根低矮的树枝上。

bump into someone to meet someone you know by chance 偶遇（或撞见）某人：*I bumped into Lisa in the supermarket yesterday.* 我昨天在超市里撞见了莉萨。

bump² /bʌmp/ *countable noun* 可数名词
an injury that you get if you hit something or if something hits you 撞伤；（碰撞造成的）肿包：*She fell over and got a large bump on her head.* 她摔倒了，头上撞了个大包。

bumper /ˈbʌmpə/ *countable noun* 可数名词
a heavy bar at the front and back of a vehicle that protects the vehicle if it hits something（车辆的）保险杠：*I felt something hit the rear bumper of my car.* 我感到有个东西撞上了车后保险杠。

bumpy /ˈbʌmpi/ *adjective* 形容词 (**bumpier, bumpiest**)
not smooth or flat 不平的；坑坑洼洼的：*We rode our bicycles down the bumpy streets.* 我们骑着自行车穿过坑坑洼洼的街道。

bun /bʌn/ *countable noun* 可数名词
1 a small bread roll 小圆面包：*He had a bun and a glass of milk.* 他吃了个小圆面包，喝了一杯牛奶。
2 a style of arranging your hair so that it is attached tightly at the back of your head in the shape of a ball 圆发髻

bunch /bʌntʃ/ *countable noun* 可数名词 (**bunches**)
1 a number of flowers with their stems held together 花束：*He left a huge bunch of flowers in her hotel room.* 他在她宾馆房间里留下一大束花。
2 a number of bananas or grapes growing together（香蕉或葡萄的）串
3 a group or a number of people or things (*informal* 非正式)（人或物的）群：*They're a great bunch of kids.* 那群孩子人很多。

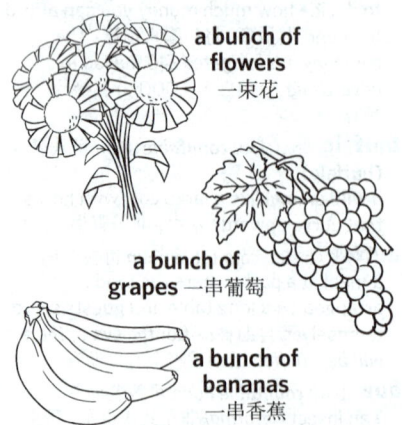

a bunch of flowers 一束花

a bunch of grapes 一串葡萄

a bunch of bananas 一串香蕉

bundle /ˈbʌndəl/ *countable noun* 可数名词
a number of things that are tied or wrapped together so that they can be carried or stored 捆；束；包：*He left a bundle of papers on the floor.* 他在地上留了一捆文件。

bungalow /ˈbʌŋɡələʊ/ *countable noun* 可数名词
a house that has only one level, and no stairs 平房

bunk /bʌŋk/ *countable noun* 可数名词
a narrow bed that is usually attached to a wall, especially in a ship（尤指轮船的）卧铺，铺位：*Sally was lying on her narrow wooden bunk.* 萨莉躺在狭窄的木板床上。

bunk beds *plural noun* 复数名词
two single beds that are built one on top of the other 双层床；上下床：*The children slept in bunk beds.* 孩子们睡在上下床上。

bunny /ˈbʌni/ *countable noun* 可数名词 (**bunnies**)
a child's word for a rabbit (*informal* 非正式) 兔子（儿语）

buoy /bɔɪ/ *countable noun* 可数名词
an object floating in the sea or a lake that shows ships and boats where they can go safely 浮标；航标

burden /ˈbɜːdən/ *countable noun* 可数名词
something that causes people a lot of worry or hard work 负担；累赘：*I don't want to become a burden on my family when I get old.* 我不想老了以后成为家人的累赘。

burger /ˈbɜːɡə/ *countable noun* 可数名词
(*also* 亦作 **hamburger**) meat that is cut into very small pieces and pressed into a flat round shape, often eaten between two pieces of bread 汉堡包；汉堡肉饼：*I ordered a burger for lunch.* 我午饭点了个汉堡包。

burglar /ˈbɜːɡlə/ *countable noun* 可数名词
someone who enters a building by force in order to steal things 入室窃贼：*Specially-trained dogs often help the police to catch burglars.* 经过专门训练的狗经常帮警察抓入室窃贼。

burglary /ˈbɜːɡləri/ *noun* 名词 (**burglaries**)
the crime of entering a building by force and stealing things 入室盗窃（罪）：*An 11-year-old boy committed a burglary.* 一个11岁男孩儿犯了入室盗窃罪。

burgle /ˈbɜːɡəl/ *verb* 动词 (**burgles, burgling, burgled**)
to enter a building by force and steal things 闯入…行窃：*My flat was burgled today.* 我家公寓今天失盗了。

burial /ˈberiəl/ *noun* 名词
the act or ceremony of putting a dead body into a grave in the ground 埋葬；葬礼：*Charles and his two sons attended the burial.* 查尔斯携二子参加了葬礼。

burn /bɜːn/ *verb* 动词 (**burns, burning, burned** or 或 **burnt**)
1 to destroy or damage something with fire 烧毁；烧掉：*She burned her old love letters.* 她烧掉了过去的情书。
2 to injure a part of your body by fire or by something very hot 烧伤，灼伤（身体部位）：*Take care not to burn your fingers.* 注意别烧着手指。● **burn** *countable noun* 可数名词：*She suffered burns to her back.* 她背部被烧伤。
3 to produce heat or fire 燃烧；着火：*A massive forest fire was burning in Alberta yesterday.* 昨天艾伯塔省发生了巨大的森林火灾。
4 to be destroyed by fire 被烧毁；被焚烧：*When I arrived, one of the vehicles was still burning.* 我赶到时，其中一辆车还在燃烧。
5 to copy something onto a CD 刻录（光盘）：*I have the equipment to burn audio CDs.* 我有刻录音频光盘的设备。

burnt /bɜːnt/
→ see 见 **burn**

burp /bɜːp/ *verb* 动词 (**burps, burping, burped**)
to make a noise because air from your stomach has been forced up through your throat 打嗝 ● **burp** *countable noun* 可数名词：*a loud burp* 响嗝

burqa /ˈbɜːkə/ *also* 亦作 **burka** *countable noun* 可数名词
a long dress that covers the head and body and is traditionally worn by some women in Islamic countries 布卡罩袍（伊斯兰国家某些女性穿的蒙面长袍）

burst /bɜːst/ *verb* 动词 (**bursts, bursting, burst**)
to suddenly break open and release air or another substance 爆裂；胀破：*The driver lost control of his car when a tyre burst.* 爆胎后，司机失去了对车的控制。

burst out to suddenly start laughing,

crying or making another noise 突然开始（大笑、大哭等）: *The class burst out laughing.* 全班突然大笑起来。

bury /ˈberi/ *verb* 动词 (**buries, burying, buried**)
1 to put something into a hole in the ground and cover it up 埋；埋藏: *Some animals bury nuts and seeds.* 有些动物会把坚果和种子埋起来。
2 to put the body of a dead person into a grave and cover it with earth 埋葬（死者）: *Soldiers helped to bury the dead.* 士兵们帮着掩埋死者。

bus /bʌs/ *countable noun* 可数名词 (**buses**)
a large motor vehicle that carries passengers 公共汽车；巴士: *He missed his last bus home.* 他错过了回家的末班公交车。

bush /bʊʃ/ *countable noun* 可数名词 (**bushes**)
a plant with leaves and branches that is smaller than a tree 灌木: *a rose bush* 蔷薇丛
the bush an area in a hot country that is far from cities and where very few people live（热带国家的）荒野: *the Australian bush* 澳大利亚荒野

busily /ˈbɪzɪli/ *adverb* 副词
in a very active way 忙碌地: *Workers were busily trying to repair the damage.* 工人们忙着修复破损处。

business /ˈbɪznɪs/ *noun* 名词 (**businesses**)
1 *uncountable* 不可数 work that is related to producing, buying and selling things 商业；商务: *He had a successful career in business.* 他在商界混得风生水起。 □ *She attended Harvard Business School.* 她上了哈佛商学院。
2 *countable* 可数 an organization that produces and sells goods or that provides a service 企业: *The bakery is a family business.* 这家面包店是个家族企业。

businessman /ˈbɪznɪsmən/ *countable noun* 可数名词 (**businessmen** /ˈbɪznɪsmen/)
a man who works in business 商人；企业家: *He's a rich businessman.* 他是位富商。
→ Look at picture on P16 参见彩插第 16 页

businesswoman /ˈbɪznɪswʊmən/ *countable noun* 可数名词 (**businesswomen** /ˈbɪznɪswɪmɪn/)
a woman who works in business 女商人；女企业家: *She's a successful businesswoman who manages her own company.* 她管理自己的公司，是位成功的女企业家。
→ Look at picture on P16 参见彩插第 16 页

busy /ˈbɪzi/ *adjective* 形容词 (**busier, busiest**)
1 working hard, so that you are not free to do anything else 忙的；忙碌的: *What is it? I'm busy.* 什么事儿？我忙着呢。 □ *They are busy preparing for a party on Saturday.* 他们忙着筹备星期六的聚会。
2 full of people who are doing things 热闹的；繁忙的: *We walked along a busy city street.* 我们走在一条繁忙的城市街道上。
3 when a telephone line is busy, it is being used by someone else（电话线）忙的，占线的: *I tried to reach him, but the line was busy.* 我打电话联系他，可是占线。

but¹ /bət, STRONG 强读 bʌt/ *conjunction* 连词
used to introduce something that is different from what you have just said 但是；可是；不过: *I really enjoyed my holiday, but now it's time to get back to work.* 我假期过得特别快活，不过现在得回去上班了。 □ *Heat the milk until it is very hot, but not boiling.* 把牛奶加热到特别烫，但不要沸腾。

but² /bət, STRONG 强读 bʌt/ *preposition* 介词
except 除了: *You've done nothing but complain all day.* 你整天除了牢骚啥也没干。

butcher /ˈbʊtʃə/ *countable noun* 可数名词
1 someone who cuts up and sells meat 屠夫；肉贩
2 (also 亦作 **butcher's**) a shop where you can buy meat 肉铺；肉店

butter /ˈbʌtə/ *uncountable noun* 不可数名词
a soft yellow food made from cream that you spread on bread or use in cooking 黄油: *The waitress brought us bread and butter.* 女服务生给我们端来了抹了黄油的面包片。 ● **butter** *verb* 动词 (**butters, buttering, buttered**): *She put two pieces of bread on a plate and buttered them.* 她把两片面包放到盘子里，抹上黄油。

butterfly /ˈbʌtəflaɪ/ *countable noun* 可数名词 (**butterflies**)
an insect with large coloured wings 蝴蝶: *Butterflies are attracted to the wild flowers.* 蝴蝶流连于野花间。

butterscotch /ˈbʌtəˌskɒtʃ/ *uncountable noun* 不可数名词
a type of hard brown sweet made from butter and sugar 奶油硬糖

button¹ /ˈbʌtən/ *countable noun* 可数名词
1 a small hard object that you push through holes (= buttonholes) to fasten your clothes 纽扣；扣子：*I bought a blue jacket with silver buttons.* 我买了一件蓝色夹克，上面有银色的扣子。
2 a small object on a piece of equipment that you press to make it work 按钮：*He put in a DVD and pressed the 'play' button.* 他插进一张 DVD 盘，按了"播放"按钮。

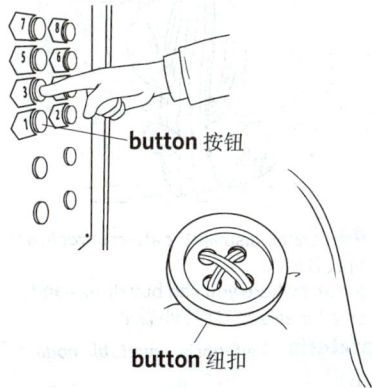

button 按钮

button 纽扣

button² /ˈbʌtən/ *verb* 动词 (**buttons, buttoning, buttoned**)
to fasten a piece of clothing by pushing its buttons through the buttonholes 扣上…的纽扣：*Ferguson stood up and buttoned his coat.* 弗格森站起来，扣上大衣扣子。

buy /baɪ/ *verb* 动词 (**buys, buying, bought**)
to get something by paying money for it 买；购买：*He could not afford to buy a house.* 他买不起房子。 □ *Lizzie bought herself a bike.* 莉齐给自己买了一辆自行车。
▶ **buyer** /ˈbaɪə/ *countable noun* 可数名词：*Car buyers are more interested in safety than speed.* 购车者更关注安全，而不是速度。

buzz /bʌz/ *verb* 动词 (**buzzes, buzzing, buzzed**)
to make a sound like a bee 嗡嗡响；发出嗡嗡声：*There was a fly buzzing around my head.* 有只苍蝇围着我的头嗡嗡飞。 ● **buzz**

countable noun 可数名词：*The annoying buzz of an insect kept us awake.* 一只虫子恼人地嗡嗡叫着，吵得我们睡不着。

by /baɪ/ *preposition* 介词
1 used for showing which person or thing did or made something（引出施动者）由，被，出自：*The dinner was served by his mother and sisters.* 晚餐是他母亲和姐妹们做的。 □ *She was woken by a loud noise in the street.* 她被街上一声巨响吵醒了。 □ *Here's a painting by Van Gogh.* 这是一幅凡高的画。
2 used for showing what you use to do something（引出所用物）用，靠，借助：*We usually travel by car.* 我们一般驾车出行。 □ *You can pay by credit card, cheque or cash.* 你可以用信用卡、支票或现金支付。
3 beside; close to 在…旁边；在…附近：*Judith was sitting in a chair by the window.* 朱迪丝坐在窗边的椅子上。 □ *Jack stood by the door, ready to leave.* 杰克站在门边，准备离开。
4 past 经过；经由：*He waved as he drove by the house.* 他开车经过房子时挥了挥手。
● **by** *adverb* 副词：*They were very polite and would always say hello as they walked by.* 他们很有礼貌，走路经过时都会问声好。
5 at or before a particular time 在（特定时间）；在（特定时间）之前：*I'll be home by eight o'clock.* 我8点前到家。

by yourself
1 alone 独自；单独：*A man was sitting by himself in a corner.* 一名男子独自坐在角落里。
2 without help from anyone else 独立；独自：*I can do it by myself.* 我自己一个人就能做。

bye /baɪ/ or 或 **bye-bye**
a way of saying goodbye (*informal* 非正式) 拜拜；再见：*Bye, Daddy.* 拜拜，老爸。

byte /baɪt/ *countable noun* 可数名词
a unit of information in computing 字节（计算机信息量单位）：*two million bytes of data* 200 万字节数据

Cc

cab /kæb/ *countable noun* 可数名词
a **taxi** 出租车；的士

cabbage /ˈkæbɪdʒ/ *noun* 名词
a round vegetable with white, green or purple leaves 甘蓝；卷心菜
→ Look at picture on P5 参见彩插第 5 页

cabin /ˈkæbɪn/ *countable noun* 可数名词
1 a small wooden house in the woods or mountains（林间或山中的）小木屋：*We stayed in a log cabin.* 我们待在了一个原木小屋里。
2 a small room on a boat（船上的）隔间，舱室：*He showed her to a small cabin.* 他把她领到了一个小舱室。
3 the part of a plane where people sit（飞机的）座舱，客舱：*He sat in the first-class cabin.* 他坐在头等舱。

cabinet /ˈkæbɪnɪt/ *countable noun* 可数名词
1 a piece of furniture with shelves, used for storing things in 柜子；储藏柜：*I looked in the medicine cabinet.* 我朝药品柜里看了看。
2 a group of important members of the government who give advice to the prime minister 内阁：*The issue was discussed at the cabinet's weekly meeting.* 内阁的周例会讨论了此议题。

cable /ˈkeɪbəl/ *noun* 名词
1 a very strong, thick rope, made of metal 缆绳；缆索：*They used a cable made of steel wire.* 他们使用了钢缆。
2 a thick wire that carries electricity 电缆：*The island gets its electricity from underground power cables.* 这座岛通过地下电力电缆供电。

cable television *uncountable noun* 不可数名词
a television system in which signals travel along wires 有线电视：*We don't have cable TV.* 我们没有有线电视。

cactus /ˈkæktəs/ *countable noun* 可数名词 (**cacti** /ˈkæktaɪ/)
a plant with lots of sharp points that grows in hot, dry places 仙人掌

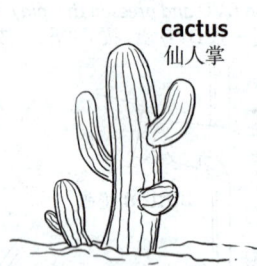
cactus
仙人掌

café /ˈkæfeɪ/ also 亦作 **cafe** *countable noun* 可数名词
a place where you can buy drinks and small meals 咖啡屋；小餐馆

cafeteria /ˌkæfɪˈtɪəriə/ *countable noun* 可数名词
a restaurant in a school or a place of work where you buy a meal and carry it to the table yourself（学校或单位的）自助餐厅，自助食堂

caffeine /ˈkæfiːn/ *uncountable noun* 不可数名词
a chemical in coffee and tea that makes you more active 咖啡碱；咖啡因

cage /keɪdʒ/ *countable noun* 可数名词
a structure made of metal bars where you keep birds or animals（养鸟或兽的）笼子：*I hate to see birds in cages.* 我见不得把鸟关笼子里。

cake /keɪk/ *noun* 名词
a sweet food that you make from flour, eggs, sugar and butter 蛋糕：*He ate a piece of chocolate cake.* 他吃了一块巧克力蛋糕。□ *We baked her a birthday cake.* 我们给她烤了个生日蛋糕。

calculate /ˈkælkjuleɪt/ *verb* 动词 (**calculates, calculating, calculated**)
to find out an amount by using numbers 计算；算出：*Have you calculated the cost of your trip?* 你算过你这趟出行的费用了吗？

calculation /ˌkælkjuˈleɪʃən/ *noun* 名词
when you find out a number or an amount by using mathematics 计算：*Ryan made a*

quick calculation in his head. 瑞安在心里迅速地算了一下。

calculator /ˈkælkjʊˌleɪtə/ *countable noun* 可数名词
a small electronic machine that you use to calculate numbers 计算器: *He takes a pocket calculator to school.* 他带着袖珍计算器去上学。
→ Look at picture on P1 参见彩插第 1 页

calendar /ˈkælɪndə/ *countable noun* 可数名词
a list of days, weeks and months for a particular year 日历: *There was a calendar on the wall.* 墙上挂着日历。

calf /kɑːf/ *countable noun* 可数名词 (**calves** /kɑːvz/)
1 a young cow 小牛；牛犊
2 the thick part at the back of your leg, between your ankle and your knee 腓肠；小腿肚
→ Look at picture on P4 参见彩插第 4 页

call /kɔːl/ *verb* 动词 (**calls, calling, called**)
1 to give someone or something a particular name 称呼；给⋯起名字: *I wanted to call the dog Mufty.* 我想给这只狗取名为穆夫季。 □ *Her daughter is called Charlotte.* 她女儿叫夏洛特。
2 to say something in a loud voice 喊；叫: *Someone called his name.* 有人喊他的名字。
3 to telephone someone 给⋯打电话: *Would you call me as soon as you find out?* 你弄清楚之后马上给我打电话好吗？ □ *I think we should call the doctor.* 我觉得我们应该打电话叫医生。 ● **call** *countable noun* 可数名词: *I made a phone call to my grandmother.* 我给外婆打了个电话。
4 to make a short visit somewhere 拜访；短暂停留: *A salesman called at the house.* 一名销售人员入户推销。 ● **call** *countable noun* 可数名词: *The doctor was out on a call.* 医生出门应诊了。

call for someone to go to someone's home so that you can both go somewhere else together (去)某人人: *I'll call for you at seven o'clock.* 我 7 点钟来接你。

call on someone to visit someone for a short time 拜访某人；看望某人: *Sofia was intending to call on Miss Kitts.* 索菲娅打算去拜访基茨小姐。

call someone back to telephone someone in return for a call they made to you 给某人回电话: *I'll call you back.* 我会给你回电话。

call something off to cancel an event that has been planned 取消某事: *He called off the trip.* 他取消了行程。

caller /ˈkɔːlə/ *countable noun* 可数名词
a person who is making a telephone call 打电话的人: *A caller told police what happened.* 有人打电话告诉警方事件经过。

calm¹ /kɑːm/ *adjective* 形容词 (**calmer, calmest**)
1 not worried, angry or excited 镇定的；镇静的；冷静的: *She is a calm, patient woman.* 她冷静而有耐心。 □ *Try to keep calm.* 尽量保持冷静。
▶ **calmly** /ˈkɑːmli/ *adverb* 副词: *Alan said calmly, 'I don't believe you.'* 艾伦平静地说：''我不相信你。''
2 not moving much (水面) 平静的: *The sea was very calm and the stars were bright.* 大海上风平浪静，天空中星光灿烂。
3 without much wind 无风的；没什么风的: *It was a fine, calm day.* 那天天气晴朗，没有风。

calm² /kɑːm/ *verb* 动词 (**calms, calming, calmed**)

calm down to become less upset or excited 平静下来；镇定下来: *Calm down and listen to me.* 冷静一下，听我说。

calm someone down to make someone less upset or excited 使某人平静 (或镇定) 下来: *I'll try to calm him down.* 我会尽量让他平静下来。

calorie /ˈkæləri/ *countable noun* 可数名词
a unit that is used for measuring the amount of energy in food 卡，卡路里 (热量单位): *These sweet drinks have a lot of calories in them.* 这些甜饮热量很高。

came /keɪm/
→ see 见 **come**

camel /ˈkæməl/ *countable noun* 可数名词
an animal with one or two large lumps on its back 骆驼

camel 骆驼

camera /ˈkæmrə/ *countable noun* 可数名词
a piece of equipment for taking photographs or making films 照相机；摄影机: *a digital camera* 数码相机

¹**camera phone** *countable noun* 可数名词
a mobile phone that can take photographs 拍照手机

camp[1] /kæmp/ *countable noun* 可数名词
a place where people live or stay in tents 营地: *an army camp* 军营

camp[2] /kæmp/ *verb* 动词 (**camps, camping, camped**)
to stay somewhere in a tent 宿营; 露营: *We camped near the beach.* 我们在海滩附近露营。
▶ **camping** /ˈkæmpɪŋ/ *uncountable noun* 不可数名词: *They went camping in Devon.* 他们去德文露营了。

campaign /kæmˈpeɪn/ *countable noun* 可数名词
a number of things that you do over a period of time in order to get a particular result (为达到特定目的的)活动, 运动: *January marks the start of the election campaign.* 1月份标志着选举活动拉开帷幕。● **campaign** *verb* 动词 (**campaigns, campaigning, campaigned**): *We are campaigning for better health services.* 我们在为争取更好的医疗服务奔走呼号。

camper /ˈkæmpə/ *countable noun* 可数名词
a person who is staying in a tent, for example on holiday 宿营者; 露营者: *The campers packed up their tents.* 露营者将帐篷收了起来。

campfire /ˈkæmpfaɪə/ *countable noun* 可数名词
a fire that you light outdoors when you are camping 营火; 篝火

campsite /ˈkæmpsaɪt/ *countable noun* 可数名词
a place where you can stay in a tent 营地; 宿营地; 露营地

campus /ˈkæmpəs/ *countable noun* 可数名词 (**campuses**)
an area of land that contains the main buildings of a university or college (大学)校园

can[1] /kən, STRONG 强读 kæn/ *modal verb* 情态动词

LANGUAGE HELP 语言提示
Use the form **cannot** in negative statements. When you are speaking, you can use the short form **can't**, pronounced /kɑːnt/. *can 的否定形式是 cannot, 口语中可用其缩写形式 can't, 读作 /kɑːnt/。

1 used for saying that you have the ability to do something (表示有能力)能, 会, 可以: *I can take care of myself.* 我能照顾自己。□ *Can you swim yet?* 你会游泳了吗?
2 used for showing that something is sometimes true (表示有时属实)会, 可能: *Exercising alone can be boring.* 一个人锻炼有时会感到无聊。
3 used with words like 'smell', 'see' and 'hear' (和 smell、see、hear 等连用)能: *I can smell smoke.* 我能闻到烟味儿。
4 used for saying that you are allowed to do something (表示得到许可)能, 可以: *Can I go to the party at the weekend?* 我周末能去参加聚会吗? □ *Sorry. We can't answer any questions.* 对不起, 我们无法回答任何问题。
5 used for making requests or offers (用于提出请求或建议)能: *Can I have a look at that book?* 我能看一下那本书吗? □ *Can I help you?* 需要我帮忙吗?

can[2] /kæn/ *countable noun* 可数名词
a metal container for food, drink or paint (储存食品、饮料或油漆的)金属罐, 听: *a can of cola* 一听可乐

canal /kəˈnæl/ *countable noun* 可数名词
a long narrow river made by people for boats to travel along 运河; (人工)水道: *The canals of Venice are very beautiful.* 威尼斯的水道风景迷人。

cancel /ˈkænsəl/ *verb* 动词 (**cancels, cancelling, cancelled**)
to say that something that has been planned will not happen 取消: *We cancelled our trip to Washington.* 我们取消了华盛顿之行。
▶ **cancellation** /ˌkænsəˈleɪʃən/ *noun* 名词: *The cancellation of his visit upset many people.* 他取消了访问行程, 很多人感到失落。

cancer /ˈkænsə/ *noun* 名词
a serious disease that makes groups of cells in the body grow when they should not 癌; 癌症: *Jane had cancer when she was 25.* 简 25 岁得了癌症。

candidate /ˈkændɪdeɪt/ *countable noun* 可数名词
someone who is trying to get a particular job, or trying to win a political position 求职者; 候选人: *He is a candidate for the job.* 他是这个职位的候选人。

candle /ˈkændəl/ *countable noun* 可数名词
a long stick of wax with a piece of string through the middle, that you burn to give

you light 蜡烛: *The only light in the bedroom came from a candle.* 卧室里仅有一支蜡烛照明。

candlestick /ˈkændlˌstɪk/ *countable noun* 可数名词
an object that holds a candle 烛台

candy /ˈkændi/ *noun* 名词 (**candies**)
(*American* 美国英语)
sweet food such as chocolate or toffee 糖果: *I gave him a piece of candy.* 我给了他一块糖。

cane /keɪn/ *noun* 名词
the long hollow stem of a plant such as bamboo(竹子等的)茎, 秆, 藤: *cane furniture* 藤条家具

cannon /ˈkænən/ *countable noun* 可数名词
a large heavy gun on wheels that was used in battles in the past(旧时装在轮子上的)加农炮, 大炮: *The soldiers stood beside the cannons.* 士兵们站在大炮旁边。

cannot /ˈkænɒt/
the negative form of **can**(can 的否定形式)

canoe /kəˈnuː/ *countable noun* 可数名词
a small, narrow boat that you move through the water using a short pole (= a paddle) 划艇

canoe 划艇

can't /kɑːnt/
short for (缩写 =) 'cannot'

canteen /kænˈtiːn/ *countable noun* 可数名词
a place in a school or college where students can buy and eat lunch(学校的)食堂: *Rebecca ate her lunch in the canteen.* 丽贝卡在食堂吃了午饭。

canvas /ˈkænvəs/ *noun* 名词 (**canvases**)
1 *uncountable* 不可数 a strong, heavy material that is used for making tents and bags 帆布: *a canvas bag* 帆布包
2 a piece of this material that you paint on 画布: *an artist's canvas* 画家用的画布
→ Look at picture on P13 参见彩插第 13 页

canyon /ˈkænjən/ *countable noun* 可数名词
a long, narrow valley with very steep sides 峡谷: *the Grand Canyon* 大峡谷

cap /kæp/ *countable noun* 可数名词
1 a soft, flat hat with a curved part at the front(有帽舌的)帽子: *He wore a dark blue baseball cap.* 他头戴一顶深蓝色棒球帽。
2 the lid of a bottle 瓶盖: *She took the cap off her water bottle and drank.* 她打开水瓶盖子喝了起来。

capable /ˈkeɪpəbəl/ *adjective* 形容词
1 able to do something 有⋯能力的; 能够⋯的: *He was not even capable of standing up.* 他甚至都无法站起来。
2 able to do something well 胜任的; 有能力的: *She's a very capable teacher.* 她是位能力很强的老师。

capacity /kəˈpæsɪti/ *noun* 名词 (**capacities**)
1 the maximum amount that something can hold 容量: *The stadium has a capacity of 50,000.* 这座体育场可容纳 5 万人。
2 *uncountable* 不可数 someone's ability to do something 能力; 才能: *Every human being has the capacity for love.* 每个人都有爱的能力。

cape /keɪp/ *countable noun* 可数名词
1 a large piece of land that sticks out into the sea 地角; 岬角: *the Cape of Good Hope* 好望角
2 a long coat without sleeves, that covers your body and arms 披肩; 斗篷

capital /ˈkæpɪtəl/ *noun* 名词
1 *countable* 可数 the city where the government of a country meets 首都: *Berlin is the capital of Germany.* 柏林是德国的首都。
→ Look at picture on P9 参见彩插第 9 页
2 *countable* 可数 the large letter that you use at the beginning of sentences and names 大写字母: *He wrote his name in capitals.* 他用大写字母写了名字。

LANGUAGE HELP 语言提示
Note that you must always use a capital letter with days of the week and months of the year. 注意, 表示星期几和月份的词首字母必须大写。

→ Look at picture on P3 参见彩插第 3 页
3 *uncountable* 不可数 money that you use to start a business 资金; 资本: *They provide capital for small businesses.* 他们为小型企业提供资金。

capitalism /ˈkæpɪtəˌlɪzəm/ *uncountable noun* 不可数名词
an economic and political system in which property, business and industry are privately owned and not owned by the state 资本主义(制度)

capitalist /ˈkæpɪtəlɪst/ *countable noun* 可数名词
someone who believes in a system where industry is owned by private companies rather than by the government 资本家；资本主义者 ● **capitalist** *adjective* 形容词: *Banks play an important part in the capitalist system.* 银行在资本主义制度中发挥重要作用。

ˌcapital ˈpunishment *uncountable noun* 不可数名词
when a criminal is killed legally as a punishment 死刑: *Capital punishment is not used in some countries.* 有些国家没有死刑。

captain /ˈkæptɪn/ *countable noun* 可数名词
1 an officer of middle rank in the army or navy (陆军的)上尉；(海军的)上校: *He was a captain in the army.* 他是陆军上尉。
2 the leader of a sports team (运动队的)队长: *Mickey Thomas is the captain of the tennis team.* 米基·托马斯是这支网球队的队长。
3 the person who is in charge of an aeroplane or a ship 机长；舰长；船长: *Who is the captain of this boat?* 谁是这艘船的船长？

caption /ˈkæpʃən/ *countable noun* 可数名词
a piece of writing next to a picture, that tells you something about the picture (图片旁的)说明文字: *The photo had the caption 'John, aged 6 years'.* 照片上写着"约翰，6岁"这几个字。

captive /ˈkæptɪv/ *countable noun* 可数名词
a person or an animal who is kept in a place and not allowed to leave 俘虏；囚犯；被关的动物: *The captives were treated with respect.* 俘虏受到尊重。 ● **captive** *adjective* 形容词: *Scientists are studying the behaviour of the captive birds.* 科学家在研究鸟儿被关笼中时的行为表现。

captivity /kæpˈtɪvɪti/ *uncountable noun* 不可数名词
when a person or an animal is kept in a place and not allowed to leave 囚禁；关押；拘禁: *The birds were kept in captivity.* 这些鸟儿是笼养的。

capture /ˈkæptʃə/ *verb* 动词 (**captures, capturing, captured**)
to catch someone or something and keep them somewhere so that they cannot leave 俘虏；擒获: *The enemy shot down the aeroplane and captured the pilot.* 敌军击落飞机，俘虏了飞行员。

car /kɑː/ *countable noun* 可数名词
1 (*American* 美国英语: **automobile**) a motor vehicle with space for about 5 people 汽车；轿车: *They arrived by car.* 他们是坐汽车来的。
2 (*American* 美国英语) → see 见 **carriage**

caramel /ˈkærəml/ *uncountable noun* 不可数名词
a type of sweet food made from burnt sugar, butter and milk 焦糖牛奶糖

caravan /ˈkærəvæn/ *countable noun* 可数名词 (*American* 美国英语: **trailer**)
a large vehicle that is pulled by a car. You can sleep and eat in a caravan on holiday. 旅居挂车(由汽车牵引，内置起居用具，可供度假使用)

carbohydrate /ˌkɑːbəʊˈhaɪdreɪt/ *noun* 名词
a substance in food that provides the body with energy, or foods that contain this substance, such as sugar and bread 糖类；碳水化合物；含碳水化合物的食物: *You need to eat more carbohydrates such as bread, pasta or potatoes.* 你需要多吃些含碳水化合物的食物，如面包、意大利面或土豆。

carbon dioxide /ˌkɑːbən daɪˈɒksaɪd/ *uncountable noun* 不可数名词
a gas that animals and people produce when they breathe out 二氧化碳

carbon monoxide /ˌkɑːbən məˈnɒksaɪd/ *uncountable noun* 不可数名词
a poisonous gas that is produced by engines that use petrol 一氧化碳

card /kɑːd/ *noun* 名词
1 *countable* 可数 a piece of stiff paper with a picture and a message, that you send to someone on a special occasion 卡；卡片: *She sends me a card on my birthday.* 我生日她送我一张贺卡。
2 *countable* 可数 a small piece of cardboard or plastic that has information about you written on it 身份证；工作证: *Please remember to bring your membership card.* 请记得带上您的会员卡。
3 *countable* 可数 a small piece of plastic that you use to pay for things 银行卡；购物卡: *He paid the bill with a credit card.* 他用信用卡结了账。
4 *countable* 可数 a piece of stiff paper with numbers or pictures on it that you use for playing games 扑克牌；纸牌: *They*

enjoy playing cards. 他们喜欢打牌。
5 uncountable 不可数 strong, stiff paper 卡纸；硬纸: You will need three pieces of strong card. 你会用到 3 张硬卡纸。

cards 卡片；银行卡；纸牌

birthday card
生日贺卡

credit card
信用卡

playing card
扑克牌

cardboard /ˈkɑːdbɔːd/ **uncountable noun** 不可数名词
thick, stiff paper that is used for making boxes（硬）纸板: a cardboard box 纸箱

cardigan /ˈkɑːdɪɡən/ **countable noun** 可数名词
a jumper that opens at the front like a jacket 开襟毛衣；开襟针织衫

care¹ /keə/ **verb** 动词 (**cares, caring, cared**)
to be interested in someone or something, or to think they are very important 在意；关注；关心: We care about the environment. 我们关注环境。

care for someone

1 to love someone 爱某人: He still cares for you. 他仍然在乎你。
2 to look after someone 照顾某人: A nurse cares for David in his home. 戴维在家有护士照顾。

care² /keə/ **uncountable noun** 不可数名词
when you do something very carefully so that you do not make any mistakes 仔细；细心；小心: He chose his words with care. 他措辞谨慎。

take care of someone/something to look after someone or something 照顾某人／某物: There was no one to take care of the children. 孩子们没人照顾。

career /kəˈrɪə/ **countable noun** 可数名词
a job that you do for a long time, or the years of your life that you spend working 工作；事业；职业生涯: She had a long career as a teacher. 她教龄很长。

careful /ˈkeəfʊl/ **adjective** 形容词
thinking a lot about what you are doing so that you do not make any mistakes 小心的；仔细的；谨慎的: Be very careful with this liquid, it can be dangerous. 接触这种液体要格外小心，可能有危险。
▶ **carefully** /ˈkeəfʊli/ **adverb** 副词: Have a nice time, and drive carefully. 玩得开心，小心开车。

careless /ˈkeələs/ **adjective** 形容词
not giving enough attention to what you are doing, and so making mistakes 粗心的；大意的: Some of my students were very careless with homework. 我有一些学生写作业很不认真。

caretaker /ˈkeəteɪkə/ **countable noun** 可数名词
someone who looks after a building such as a school and the area around it（学校等建筑物的）管理员，看管人

cargo /ˈkɑːɡəʊ/ **noun** 名词 (**cargoes**)
the things that a ship or a plane is carrying（轮船或飞机所运载的）货物: The ship was carrying a cargo of bananas. 这艘轮船装着一批香蕉。

carnation /kɑːˈneɪʃən/ **countable noun** 可数名词
a plant with white, pink or red flowers 康乃馨；香石竹

carnival /ˈkɑːnɪvəl/ **countable noun** 可数名词
a celebration in the street, with music and dancing 狂欢节；嘉年华

carnivore /ˈkɑːnɪvɔː/ **countable noun** 可数名词
an animal that eats mainly meat. Compare with **herbivore** and **omnivore**. 食肉动物（比较 herbivore 和 omnivore）

carol /ˈkærəl/ **countable noun** 可数名词
a song that Christians sing at Christmas 圣诞颂歌: The children all sang carols as loudly as they could. 孩子们全都放声高唱圣诞颂歌。

ˈcar ˌpark **countable noun** 可数名词
an area of ground or a building where

people can leave their cars for a period of time 停车场；停车库

carpenter /ˈkɑːpɪntə/ ***countable noun*** 可数名词
a person whose job is to make and repair wooden things 木工；木匠
→ Look at picture on P16 参见彩插第 16 页

carpet /ˈkɑːpɪt/ ***noun*** 名词
a thick, soft covering for the floor 地毯: *He picked up the clothes and vacuumed the carpets.* 他捡起衣服，用吸尘器清理地毯。

carriage /ˈkærɪdʒ/ ***countable noun*** 可数名词 (*American* 美国英语: **car**)
one of the sections of a train where people sit（客运列车的）车厢: *He found his seat in the carriage and sat down.* 他在车厢中找到自己的座位坐了下来。

carrier bag /ˈkæriə ˌbæg/ ***countable noun*** 可数名词
a plastic or paper bag with handles that you use for carrying shopping 购物袋

carrot /ˈkærət/ ***noun*** 名词
a long, thin, orange-coloured vegetable 胡萝卜: *We had chicken with potatoes, peas and carrots.* 我们吃了鸡肉配土豆、豌豆和胡萝卜。
→ Look at picture on P5 参见彩插第 5 页

carry /ˈkæri/ ***verb*** 动词 (**carries, carrying, carried**)
1 to hold something in your hand and take it with you 拿；提；拎；搬: *He was carrying a briefcase.* 他拎着公文包。
2 to always have something with you 携带；随身带: *You have to carry a passport.* 你得随身带着护照。
3 to take someone or something somewhere 运送；运载: *Lorries carrying food and medicine left the capital city yesterday.* 运送食品和药品的卡车昨天离开了首都。

carry on to continue to do something 接着；继续；坚持: *The teacher carried on talking.* 老师继续说下去。

carry something out to do something 做某事；实施某事；执行某事: *They carried out tests in the laboratory.* 他们在实验室里做了测试。

cart /kɑːt/ ***countable noun*** 可数名词
1 an old-fashioned wooden vehicle that is usually pulled by a horse（旧时的）马车
2 (*American* 美国英语)→ see 见 **trolley**

carton /ˈkɑːtən/ ***countable noun*** 可数名词 a plastic or cardboard container for food or drink（装食品或饮品的）塑料盒, 纸盒: *a carton of milk* 一盒牛奶

cartoon /kɑːˈtuːn/ ***countable noun*** 可数名词
1 a funny drawing, often in a magazine or newspaper 漫画；卡通画: *cartoon characters* 漫画人物
2 a film that uses drawings for all the characters and scenes instead of real people or objects 卡通片；动画片: *We watched children's cartoons on TV.* 我们在电视上看了儿童动画片。

carve /kɑːv/ ***verb*** 动词 (**carves, carving, carved**)
1 to cut an object out of wood or stone 雕；刻: *He carved the statue from one piece of rock.* 他用一块石头雕出了这座雕像。
2 to cut slices from meat 切，分割（肉）: *Andrew began to carve the chicken.* 安德鲁开始切鸡肉。

case /keɪs/ ***countable noun*** 可数名词
1 a particular situation, especially one that you are using as an example 事例；案例；特定情况: *In some cases, it can be very difficult.* 这在某些情况下会很有难度。
2 a crime that police are working on 案件；案子: *a murder case* 谋杀案
3 a container that is designed to hold or protect something 盒；箱；匣: *He uses a black case for his glasses.* 他用一个黑色的盒子装眼镜。

in any case said when you are adding another reason for something（用于补充理由）不管怎样，无论如何: *The concert was sold out, and in any case, most of us could not afford a ticket.* 音乐会的票卖光了，不过反正我们大多数人也买不起票。

in case or **just in case** because a particular thing might happen 以防万一: *I've brought some food in case we get hungry.* 我带了些吃的来，万一我们饿了呢。

in that/which case if that is the situation 那样的话；在那种情况下: *'It's raining.'—'Oh, in that case we'll have to stay in.'* "下雨了。"——"哦，那样的话，我们就出不去了。"

cash¹ /kæʃ/ ***uncountable noun*** 不可数名词
money in the form of notes and coins 现金: *two thousand pounds in cash* 2,000 英镑现金

cash² /kæʃ/ ***verb*** 动词 (**cashes, cashing, cashed**)
to take a cheque to a bank and get money

for it 兑现(支票): *I stopped at the bank to cash a cheque.* 我中途去银行把支票兑了。

'cash ,desk *countable noun* 可数名词
the place in a shop where you pay 收银台

cashew /kəˈʃuː, ˈkæʃuː/ *countable noun* 可数名词
(also 亦作 **cashew nut**) a curved nut that you can eat 腰果

cashier /kæˈʃɪə/ *countable noun* 可数名词
a person whose job is to take customers' money in shops or banks 收银员;银行柜员

'cash ma,chine *countable noun* 可数名词
(*American* 美国英语: **ATM**)
(also 亦作 **cash dispenser**) a machine in the wall outside a bank or other building where you can get money, using a special plastic card 自动柜员机;自助取款机

casino /kəˈsiːnəʊ/ *countable noun* 可数名词
a place where people gamble (= risk money) by playing games 赌场

cassette /kəˈset/ *countable noun* 可数名词
a small, flat plastic case containing tape that is used for recording and playing sound or pictures 盒式磁带: *a small cassette recorder* 小型盒式录音机

cast /kɑːst/ *countable noun* 可数名词
1 all the people who act in a play or a film (一部戏剧或电影的)全体演员: *The show is very amusing and the cast is very good.* 演出妙趣横生,演员表现出色。
2 a hard cover for protecting a broken arm or leg(保护骨折手臂或腿的)石膏: *His arm is in a cast.* 他胳膊打着石膏。

castle /ˈkɑːsəl/ *countable noun* 可数名词
a large building with thick, high walls that was built in the past to protect people during wars and battles 城堡
→ Look at picture on P10 参见彩插第 10 页

casual /ˈkæʒuəl/ *adjective* 形容词
1 relaxed and not worried about what is happening 漫不经心的;随意的: *She tried to sound casual, but she was frightened.* 她尽量让声音听上去满不在乎,但其实她很害怕。
▸ **casually** /ˈkæʒuəli/ *adverb* 副词: *'No need to hurry,' Ben said casually.* "不用着急。"本漫不经心地说。
2 worn at home or on holiday, and not on formal occasions(服装)休闲的,随便的: *I also bought some casual clothes for the weekend.* 我还买了些周末穿的休闲装。
▸ **casually** /ˈkæʒuəli/ *adverb* 副词: *They were casually dressed.* 他们穿得很休闲。

casualty /ˈkæʒuəlti/ *noun* 名词 (**casualties**)
1 *countable* 可数 a person who is injured or killed in a war or in an accident(战争或事故中的)伤亡者: *Helicopters bombed the town, causing many casualties.* 直升机轰炸了该镇,造成大量伤亡。
2 *uncountable* 不可数 the place in a hospital where people go for emergency treatment if they have a bad accident or a sudden illness 急诊室;急救室;抢救室

cat /kæt/ *countable noun* 可数名词
a small animal covered with fur that people in some countries keep as a pet 猫: *The cat sat on my lap, purring.* 猫坐在我的大腿上,发出呜呜声。

cat 猫
tail 尾巴
fur 软毛
claw 爪(zhǎo, 指趾甲)
paw 爪(zhuǎ, 指脚)

catalogue /ˈkætəlɒɡ/ *countable noun* 可数名词
a list of things you can buy from a particular company(商品)目录: *The website has an on-line catalogue of products.* 这个网站有在线产品目录。

catastrophe /kəˈtæstrəfi/ *countable noun* 可数名词
a sudden event that causes a lot of suffering or damage 灾变;灾难: *They learn how to deal with major catastrophes, including earthquakes.* 他们学习如何应对地震等重大灾难。
▸ **catastrophic** /ˌkætəˈstrɒfɪk/ *adjective* 形容词: *A storm caused catastrophic damage to the houses.* 一场风暴严重毁坏了这些房屋。

catch /kætʃ/ *verb* 动词 (**catches, catching, caught**)
1 to find a person or an animal and hold them 抓获;逮到: *Police say they are confident of catching the man.* 警方说他们有信心抓到那名男子。 □ *Where did you catch the fish?* 你在哪儿抓到的鱼?

2 to take and hold an object that is moving through the air 接住；截住（空中移动的物体）: *I jumped up to catch the ball.* 我跳起来去接球。● **catch** *countable noun* 可数名词 (**catches**): *That was a great catch.* 那个球接得漂亮。

3 to get part of your body stuck somewhere accidentally 使（身体部位）意外卡住: *I caught my finger in the car door.* 我手指让车门给夹了。

4 to get on a bus, train or plane in order to travel somewhere 乘坐；搭乘: *We caught the bus on the corner of the street.* 我们在街角上了公交车。

5 to see or find someone doing something wrong 撞见，当场抓住（某人做坏事）: *They caught him with £30,000 cash in a briefcase.* 他们抓住他时，在一个公文包里发现 3 万英镑现金。

6 to become ill with an illness 染上，患，得（疾病）: *Keep warm, or you'll catch a cold.* 注意保暖，不然你会感冒的。

catch up/catch up with someone
1 to reach someone by walking faster than they are walking 追上／赶上某人: *I stopped and waited for her to catch up.* 我停下来，等她赶上来。□ *She hurried to catch up with him.* 她急匆匆地去追他。
2 to reach the same level as someone else 追上／赶上某人的水平: *You'll have to work hard to catch up.* 你得努力才能追上。

categorize /ˈkætɪɡəˌraɪz/ *verb* 动词 (**categorizes, categorizing, categorized**) to say which group or type people or things belong to 把⋯⋯分组；将⋯⋯分类: *Their music is usually categorized as jazz.* 他们的音乐通常被归为爵士乐。

category /ˈkætɪɡri/ *countable noun* 可数名词 (**categories**) a group of people or things that are similar 种类；类别: *Their music falls into the category of 'jazz'.* 他们的音乐被归入爵士乐这一类别。

caterpillar /ˈkætəpɪlə/ *countable noun* 可数名词 a small animal with a long body that develops into a butterfly (= an insect with large coloured wings) 毛虫，蠋（蝴蝶的幼虫）

cathedral /kəˈθiːdrəl/ *countable noun* 可数名词 a large and important church 大教堂；主教座堂: *We visited some of the great cathedrals of Madrid.* 我们参观了马德里一些宏伟的大教堂。

Catholic /ˈkæθlɪk/ *adjective* 形容词 (also 亦作 **Roman Catholic**) belonging to a section of the Christian Church that has the Pope as its leader 天主教的: *a Catholic priest* 天主教神父 ● **Catholic** *countable noun* 可数名词: *His parents are Catholics.* 他父母是天主教徒。

cattle /ˈkætəl/ *plural noun* 复数名词 cows that are kept for their milk or meat 牛

caught /kɔːt/
→ see 见 **catch**

cauliflower /ˈkɒlɪflaʊə/ *noun* 名词 a large, round, white vegetable surrounded by green leaves 花椰菜；花果

cause¹ /kɔːz/ *countable noun* 可数名词
1 what makes an event happen 原因；诱因: *We still don't know the exact cause of the accident.* 我们仍不清楚事故的确切原因。
2 an aim that some people support or fight for 事业；目标；理想: *A strong leader will help our cause.* 强势的领导者对我们的事业会有帮助。

cause² /kɔːz/ *verb* 动词 (**causes, causing, caused**) to make something happen 导致；造成: *Stress can cause headaches.* 压力会造成头疼。

caution /ˈkɔːʃən/ *uncountable noun* 不可数名词 great care to avoid danger 谨慎；慎重: *Always cross the street with caution.* 过马路时一定要小心。

cautious /ˈkɔːʃəs/ *adjective* 形容词 very careful, because there might be danger 谨慎的；慎重的: *Doctors are cautious about using this new medicine.* 医生对使用这种新药态度慎重。
▶ **cautiously** /ˈkɔːʃəsli/ *adverb* 副词: *David moved cautiously forward and looked down into the water.* 戴维一边小心向前走，一边低头看下方的水。

cave /keɪv/ *countable noun* 可数名词 a large hole in the side of a hill or under the ground 山洞；洞穴
→ Look at picture on P10 参见彩插第 10 页

caveman /ˈkeɪvmæn/ *countable noun* 可数名词 (**cavemen** /ˈkeɪvmen/) a person in the past who lived mainly in caves 穴居人

cc /ˌsiː ˈsiː/
used at the beginning of emails or at the end of a business letter to show that a copy is being sent to another person（用于电子邮件开头或商业信函末尾）抄送: *cc j.jones@harpercollins.co.uk* * 抄送 j.jones@harpercollins.co.uk

CD /ˌsiː ˈdiː/ *countable noun* 可数名词 (**CDs**)
a disc for storing music or computer information. **CD** is short for（缩写 =）**compact disc**. 光碟；光盘
→ Look at picture on P11 参见彩插第 11 页

CD burner /ˌsiː ˈdiː ˌbɜːnə/ *countable noun* 可数名词
a piece of equipment that you use for copying information or music from a computer onto a CD 光盘刻录机

C'D ˌplayer *countable noun* 可数名词
a machine that plays CDs 光碟播放机；光碟播放机
→ Look at picture on P11 参见彩插第 11 页

CD-ROM /ˌsiː diː ˈrɒm/ *countable noun* 可数名词 (**CD-ROMs**)
a CD that stores a very large amount of information that you can read using a computer 只读光碟；只读光盘

CE /ˌsiː ˈiː/ also 亦作 **C.E.**
used in dates to show the number of years after AD 1 or the year in which Jesus was born. **CE** is short for（缩写 =）'Common Era'. 公元（用于年份中）: *Sweden did not become Christian until around 1000 CE.* 瑞典直到公元 1000 年左右才改为基督教国家。

cease /siːs/ *verb* 动词 (**ceases, ceasing, ceased**)
to stop (*formal* 正式) 停止；终止: *At one o'clock the rain ceased.* *1 点的时候雨停了。

cease-fire /ˈsiːsˌfaɪə/ also 亦作 **ceasefire** *countable noun* 可数名词
an agreement to stop fighting a war 停火（协定）: *They have agreed to a ceasefire after three years of war.* *3 年战争之后，他们已同意停火。

ceiling /ˈsiːlɪŋ/ *countable noun* 可数名词
the top inside part of a room 天花板: *The rooms all had high ceilings.* 这些房间的天花板都很高。

celebrate /ˈselɪˌbreɪt/ *verb* 动词 (**celebrates, celebrating, celebrated**)
to do something enjoyable for a special reason 庆祝: *I passed my test and wanted to celebrate.* 我考试过了，想庆祝下。
□ *Dick celebrated his 60th birthday on Monday.* 迪克周一庆祝了 60 岁生日。
▶ **celebration** /ˌselɪˈbreɪʃən/ *noun* 名词: *There was a celebration in our house that night.* 那晚我们家开了个庆祝会。

celebrity /sɪˈlebrɪti/ *countable noun* 可数名词 (**celebrities**)
someone who is famous 名人；明星: *Kylie Minogue was our celebrity guest.* 凯莉·米诺格做过我们的明星嘉宾。

celery /ˈseləri/ *uncountable noun* 不可数名词
a vegetable with long, pale-green sticks that you can cook or eat raw (= without cooking) 芹菜: *Cut a stick of celery into small pieces.* 把一根芹菜切成小段。

cell /sel/ *countable noun* 可数名词
1 the smallest part of an animal or a plant 细胞: *We are studying blood cells.* 我们在研究血细胞。
2 a small room with a lock in a prison or a police station 牢房；监舍；（警察局的）留置室: *How many prisoners were in the cell?* 牢房里有多少犯人？

cellar /ˈselə/ *countable noun* 可数名词
a room underneath a building 地窖；地下室: *He kept the boxes in the cellar.* 他把那些箱子存放在地窖里。

cello /ˈtʃeləʊ/ *noun* 名词
a musical instrument that is like a large violin. You sit behind it and rest it on the floor. 大提琴
→ Look at picture on P12 参见彩插第 12 页
▶ **cellist** /ˈtʃelɪst/ *countable noun* 可数名词: *He is a great cellist.* 他是位出色的大提琴手。

cellphone /ˈselfəʊn/ *countable noun* 可数名词 (*American* 美国英语)
→ see 见 **mobile phone**

Celsius /ˈselsiəs/ *adjective* 形容词
used for describing a way of measuring temperature. Water freezes at 0° Celsius and boils at 100° Celsius. 摄氏温标的（0 摄氏度为水的冰点，100 摄氏度为水的沸点）: *11° Celsius is around 52° Fahrenheit.* *11 摄氏度约等于 52 华氏度。

cement /sɪˈment/ *uncountable noun* 不可数名词
a grey powder that becomes very hard when you mix it with sand and water and leave it to dry 水泥

cemetery /ˈsemətri/ *countable noun* 可数名词 (**cemeteries**)
a place where dead people are buried 公墓；墓地；墓园

census /ˈsensəs/ *countable noun* 可数名词 (**censuses**)
an occasion when a government counts all the people in a country 人口普查: *That census counted a quarter of a billion Americans.* 美国那次人口普查的总人口为2.5亿人。

cent /sent/ *countable noun* 可数名词
a small coin that is used in many countries. There are one hundred cents in a dollar or a euro. 分（货币单位）: *The book cost six dollars and fifty cents.* 这本书花了6.5美元。

centilitre /ˈsentɪˌliːtə/ *countable noun* 可数名词
a unit for measuring liquid. There are ten millilitres in a centilitre and one hundred centilitres in a litre. 厘升（液量单位，1厘升 = 10毫升，1升 = 100厘升）

centimetre /ˈsentɪˌmiːtə/ *countable noun* 可数名词
a unit for measuring length. There are ten millimetres in a centimetre and one hundred centimetres in a metre. 厘米（长度单位，1厘米 = 10毫米，1米 = 100厘米）: *This tiny plant is only a few centimetres high.* 这株小小的植物只有几厘米高。
→ Look at picture on P2 参见彩插第2页

central /ˈsentrəl/ *adjective* 形容词
in the middle part of a place 中央的；中心的: *They live in Central America.* 他们住在中美洲。

central heating *uncountable noun* 不可数名词
a heating system that uses hot air or water to heat every part of a building 集中供暖；中央供暖

centre /ˈsentə/ *countable noun* 可数名词
1 the middle of something 中央；中心: *We sat in the centre of the room.* 我们坐在房间中央。
2 a place where people can take part in a particular activity, or get help 活动中心；救助中心: *The building is now a health centre.* 这栋建筑现在是保健中心。

centrifugal force /ˌsentrɪˌfjuːgəl ˈfɔːs/ *uncountable noun* 不可数名词
the force that makes objects move away from the centre when they are moving around a central point 离心力: *The juice is removed by centrifugal force.* 果汁在离心力作用下分离出来。

century /ˈsentʃəri/ *countable noun* 可数名词 (**centuries**)
one hundred years 世纪: *The story started a century ago.* 这个故事始于1个世纪前。 □ *She was one of the most important painters of the nineteenth century.* 她是19世纪最重要的画家之一。

ceramic /sɪˈræmɪk/ *adjective* 形容词
made from clay (= a type of earth) that has been heated to a very high temperature so that it becomes hard 陶瓷的: *The wall is covered with ceramic tiles.* 这堵墙贴了瓷砖。

ceramics /sɪˈræmɪks/ *plural noun* 复数名词
objects made from clay (= a type of earth) that has been heated to a very high temperature so that it becomes hard 瓷器；陶瓷（制品）: *The museum has a huge collection of Chinese ceramics.* 这座博物馆有数量庞大的中国瓷器藏品。

cereal /ˈsɪəriəl/ *noun* 名词
1 *uncountable* 不可数 a food made from grain, that you can mix with milk and eat for breakfast（可混合牛奶作早餐的）谷类食物，麦片: *I have a bowl of cereal every morning.* 我每天早上吃一碗麦片糊。
→ Look at picture on P5 参见彩插第5页
2 *countable* 可数 a plant that produces grain for food 谷类作物；谷物: *Rice is similar to other cereal grains such as corn and wheat.* 水稻和玉米、小麦等谷物类似。

ceremonial /ˌserɪˈməʊniəl/ *adjective* 形容词
used or done at a ceremony 仪式的；礼节的；礼仪的: *The children watched the ceremonial dances.* 孩子们观看了仪式舞蹈。

ceremony /ˈserɪməni/ *countable noun* 可数名词 (**ceremonies**)
a formal event 仪式；典礼: *a wedding ceremony* 结婚典礼

certain /ˈsɜːtən/ *adjective* 形容词
1 sure 肯定的；有把握的；确定的: *She's absolutely certain that she's going to recover.* 她坚信自己会恢复的。 □ *One thing is certain, both players are great sportsmen.* 有一点可以肯定，两名选手都是伟大的运动员。
2 particular 特定的: *He calls me at a certain time every day.* 他每天都会在特定

时间给我打电话。
for certain without any doubt at all 确定；无疑：*She didn't know for certain if he was at home.* 她不确定他是否在家。
make certain to check something so that you are sure 确保：*Parents should make certain that children do their homework.* 家长要确保孩子完成家庭作业。

certainly /ˈsɜːtənli/ *adverb* 副词
1 definitely, without any doubt 肯定；确定；无疑：*The meeting will certainly last an hour.* 这次会议肯定要开1个小时。
2 used when you are agreeing or disagreeing strongly with what someone has said（用于强调同意或不同意）当然：*'Are you still friends?' — 'Certainly.'* "你们还是朋友吗？" —— "当然。" □ *'Perhaps I should go now.' — 'Certainly not!'* "也许我现在该走了。" —— "绝对不行！"

certainty /ˈsɜːtənti/ *uncountable noun* 不可数名词
the feeling of having no doubts at all about something 确定；有把握：*I can tell you this with absolute certainty.* 我可以十分肯定地这么告诉你们。

certificate /səˈtɪfɪkət/ *countable noun* 可数名词
an official document that proves that the facts on it are true 证书；证明：*You must show your birth certificate.* 你必须出示出生证明。 □ *I have a certificate signed by my teacher.* 我有老师签过字的证明。

chain¹ /tʃeɪn/ *countable noun* 可数名词
a line of metal rings that are connected together 链条；链子：*He wore a gold chain around his neck.* 他脖子上戴着一条金链子。

chain² /tʃeɪn/ *verb* 动词 (**chains, chaining, chained**)
to attach a person or thing to something with a chain 用链子拴住：*The dogs were chained to a fence.* 那些狗被拴在了栅栏上。

chair¹ /tʃeə/ *countable noun* 可数名词
a piece of furniture for one person to sit on, with a back and four legs 椅子：*He suddenly got up from his chair.* 他突然从椅子上站了起来。
→ Look at picture on P1 参见彩插第1页

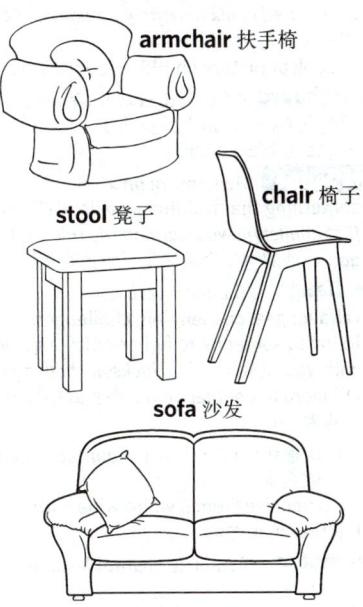

chairs 椅类
armchair 扶手椅
stool 凳子
chair 椅子
sofa 沙发

chair² /tʃeə/ *verb* 动词 (**chairs, chairing, chaired**)
to be the person who controls a meeting 主持（会议）：*They asked him to chair the committee meeting.* 他们请他主持此次委员会会议。

chairman /ˈtʃeəmən/ *countable noun* 可数名词 (**chairmen** /ˈtʃeəmən/)
the person who controls a meeting or an organization（会议或机构的）主席：*He is chairman of the committee that wrote the report.* 由他任主席的委员会撰写了本报告。

chairperson /ˈtʃeəpɜːsən/ *countable noun* 可数名词
the person who controls a meeting or an organization（会议或机构的）主席：*She's the chairperson of the planning committee.* 她是计划委员会主席。

chairwoman /ˈtʃeəwʊmən/ *countable noun* 可数名词 (**chairwomen** /ˈtʃeəwɪmɪn/)
the woman who controls a meeting or an organization（会议或机构的）女主席：*The chairwoman welcomed us and opened the meeting.* 女主席向我们致了欢迎辞并宣布会议开幕。

chalk /tʃɔːk/ *uncountable noun* 不可数名词
1 a type of soft white rock 白垩
2 small sticks of chalk that you use for

chalkboard – chaos

writing or drawing 粉笔: *Now use a piece of coloured chalk to write your name.* 现在用一根彩色粉笔写下你的名字。
→ Look at picture on P13 参见彩插第 13 页

chalkboard /ˈtʃɔːkbɔːd/ *countable noun* 可数名词 (*American* 美国英语)
→ see 见 **blackboard**

challenge¹ /ˈtʃælɪndʒ/ *noun* 名词
something that is difficult to do 挑战: *His first challenge was learning the rules of the game.* 他的第一个挑战是了解比赛规则。

challenge² /ˈtʃælɪndʒ/ *verb* 动词 (**challenges, challenging, challenged**)
to invite someone to fight or play a game with you 挑战（某人）: *Jackson challenged O'Meara to another game.* 杰克逊挑战奥马拉再赛一场。

champagne /ʃæmˈpeɪn/ *uncountable noun* 不可数名词
an expensive French white wine with bubbles in it 香槟

champion /ˈtʃæmpiən/ *countable noun* 可数名词
the winner of a sports competition or game 冠军: *He was the Commonwealth champion twice.* 他两次获得英联邦运动会冠军。□ *Kasparov became the world champion.* 卡斯帕罗夫获得了世界冠军。

championship /ˈtʃæmpiənʃɪp/ *countable noun* 可数名词
a competition to find the best player or team in a particular sport or game 冠军赛；锦标赛: *The world chess championship was on TV last night.* 昨晚电视上转播了世界国际象棋冠军赛。

chance /tʃɑːns/ *noun* 名词
1 a possibility that something will happen 可能（性）；机会: *There is a good chance that we can win the game against Australia.* 我们很有希望赢下与澳大利亚的比赛。
2 *singular* 单数 a time when you can do something 机会；机遇: *Everyone gets a chance to vote.* 人人都有一次投票机会。□ *Millions of children never get the chance to go to school.* 数百万儿童从未有机会上学。
by chance not planned by anyone 偶然；碰巧: *He met Justin by chance in the street.* 他在街上巧遇贾斯廷。

change¹ /tʃeɪndʒ/ *noun* 名词
1 an occasion when something becomes different 变化；改变；变革: *There will soon be some big changes in our company.* 我们公司很快会发生一些重大变革。
2 *uncountable* 不可数 the money that you get back when you pay with more money than something costs 找零: '*There's your change.*' — '*Thanks very much.*' "这是您的找零。" —— "多谢。"
3 *uncountable* 不可数 coins 硬币: *I need 36 pence. Do you have any change?* 我需要 36 便士。你有硬币吗？

change² /tʃeɪndʒ/ *verb* 动词 (**changes, changing, changed**)
1 to become different 改变；变化: *The colour of the sky changed from pink to blue.* 天空的颜色从粉色变成了蓝色。□ *She changed into a happy woman.* 她变得快乐起来。
2 to make something different 使改变；使变化: *They should change the law.* 他们应该修订法律。
3 to replace something with something new or different 更换；替换: *They decided to change the name of the band.* 他们决定给乐队换个名字。□ *He changed to a different medication.* 他换了一种药。
4 to put on different clothes 换（衣服）；更衣: *Ben changed his shirt.* 本换了件衬衫。□ *They let her shower and change.* 他们让她冲澡换了衣服。□ *You can get changed in the bedroom.* 你可以在卧室里换衣服。
5 to get off one bus, train or plane, and get on to another in order to continue your journey 换乘；转（车）；转（机）: *I changed planes in Chicago.* 我在芝加哥转了机。

channel /ˈtʃænəl/ *countable noun* 可数名词
1 a television station 电视台；电视频道: *There is a huge number of television channels in America.* 美国电视频道为数众多。
2 a narrow passage that water can flow along 水道；沟渠: *a shipping channel* 航道

chant /tʃɑːnt/ *countable noun* 可数名词
a word or group of words that is repeated again and again 不断重复的话: *Then the crowd started the chant of 'U-S-A!'* 然后众人开始一遍遍地喊"美国！"。● **chant** *verb* 动词 (**chants, chanting, chanted**): *The people chanted his name.* 人们反复呼唤他的名字。□ *The crowd chanted 'We are with you.'* 众人反复呼喊"我们支持你"。

chaos /ˈkeɪɒs/ *uncountable noun* 不可数名词
when there is no order or organization 混乱；无秩序: *The race ended in chaos.* 这场

比赛在一片混乱中结束。

chaotic /keɪˈɒtɪk/ *adjective* 形容词
completely confused and without order 混乱的；无秩序的：*The city seemed to be a chaotic place to me.* 我认为这座城市没有秩序可言。

chapel /ˈtʃæpəl/ *countable noun* 可数名词
a room or part of a church that people pray in 小礼拜堂；小教堂：*She went to the chapel on the hillside to pray.* 她去山坡上的小礼拜堂做祷告。

chapter /ˈtʃæptə/ *countable noun* 可数名词
a part of a book（书的）章，回，篇：*For more information, see Chapter 4.* 详细信息请见第 4 章。

character /ˈkærɪktə/ *countable noun* 可数名词
1 all the things that make a person or place different from other people or places 性格；特点；特色：*It's difficult to understand the change in her character.* 她性格的转变让人费解。
2 one of the people in a story 角色；人物：*Collard himself plays the main character.* 科勒德亲自出演主角。

characteristic /ˌkærɪktəˈrɪstɪk/ *countable noun* 可数名词
a quality that is typical of someone or something 特色；特点；特征：*The twins already had their own characteristics.* 这对双胞胎已经各有各的特点。

charcoal /ˈtʃɑːkəʊl/ *uncountable noun* 不可数名词
burnt wood that you can use for drawing 木炭（可用于绘画）：*We all did charcoal drawings of the building.* 我们都画过那栋建筑的炭笔画。
→ Look at picture on P13 参见彩插第 13 页

charge[1] /tʃɑːdʒ/ *verb* 动词 (**charges, charging, charged**)
1 to ask someone to pay money for something 向⋯收费；收取（费用）：*The driver only charged us £2 each.* 司机仅收我们每人 2 英镑。□ *How much do you charge for printing photos?* 打印照片怎么收费？
2 to formally tell someone that they have done something wrong 控告；指控：*The police have enough evidence to charge him.* 警方有足够的证据指控他。
3 to put electricity into a battery 给⋯充电：*Alex forgot to charge his mobile phone.* 亚历克斯忘了给手机充电。□ *I left my MP3 player charging.* 我把 MP3 播放器放那儿充电。

charge something to something to pay for something you are buying using your credit card (= a plastic card that you use to buy things and pay for them later) 用（信用卡）为某物付钱：*I'll charge it to my Visa.* 我用维萨卡付账。

charge[2] /tʃɑːdʒ/ *countable noun* 可数名词
1 an amount of money that you have to pay for a service 服务费：*We can arrange this for a small charge.* 我们可以安排这项服务，只收少许费用。
2 the amount or type of electrical force that something has 电荷；电量：*an electrical charge* 电荷
in charge of someone/something to be responsible for someone or something 主管某人／负责某事物：*Who is in charge here?* 这里谁是负责人？□ *He was in charge of the campaign.* 他是此次活动的负责人。

charity /ˈtʃærɪti/ *noun* 名词 (**charities**)
an organization that collects money for people who need help 慈善机构；慈善组织：*Michael is working for a children's charity.* 迈克尔目前就职于一家儿童慈善机构。

charm /tʃɑːm/ *uncountable noun* 不可数名词
the quality of being pleasant and attractive 魅力；吸引力：*This hotel has real charm.* 这家宾馆很吸引人。

charming /ˈtʃɑːmɪŋ/ *adjective* 形容词
very pleasant and attractive 有魅力的；吸引人的：*He seemed to be a charming young man.* 他似乎是个迷人的年轻人。

chart /tʃɑːt/ *countable noun* 可数名词
a diagram or graph that shows information 图表：*See the chart on next page for more details.* 详细信息见下页图表。

charter /ˈtʃɑːtə/ *countable noun* 可数名词
a formal document that describes the rights or principles of an organization 章程；宪章：*the United Nations Charter*《联合国宪章》

chase /tʃeɪs/ *verb* 动词 (**chases, chasing, chased**)
to run after someone in order to catch them 追；追赶：*She chased the boys for 100 yards.* 她追了那些男孩 100 码远。
● **chase** *countable noun* 可数名词：*The*

chase ended at about 10.30 p.m. on the M1 motorway. 这场追逐于晚上 10 点 30 分左右在 1 号高速公路上结束。

chase 追

She chased the boys for 100 yards. 她追了那些男孩 100 码远。

chat /tʃæt/ ***verb*** 动词 (**chats, chatting, chatted**)

1 to talk in an informal, friendly way 聊天；闲聊：*The women sit and chat at coffee time.* 女人们在咖啡时间坐着聊天。 ▫ *I was chatting to him the other day.* 前几天我正和他闲聊。 ● **chat** *countable noun* 可数名词：*I had a chat with John.* 我和约翰聊了聊。 ▫ *The author took part in a live web chat.* 作者参与了一次网络直播聊天。

2 to exchange written messages on a website or on your phone (通过网站或手机) 聊天：*There are instant messaging apps you can use to chat with your friends.* 可以通过即时通信应用与朋友们聊天。

¹chat ˌroom also 亦作 **chatroom** *countable noun* 可数名词

a website where people can exchange messages (网络) 聊天室

chatter /ˈtʃætə/ ***verb*** 动词 (**chatters, chattering, chattered**)

1 to talk quickly about things that are not important 唠叨；喋喋不休：*Erica chattered about her grandchildren.* 埃丽卡喋喋不休地聊着她的孙子孙女们。 ● **chatter** *uncountable noun* 不可数名词：*The students stopped their noisy chatter.* 学生们停止了叽叽喳喳。

2 used for describing how your teeth keep knocking together if you are cold (牙齿) 打战：*She was so cold her teeth chattered.* 她冷得牙齿直打战。

chauffeur /ˈʃəʊfə, ʃəʊˈfɜː/ *countable noun* 可数名词

a person whose job is to drive for another person (私人) 司机

cheap /tʃiːp/ *adjective* 形容词 (**cheaper, cheapest**)

1 costing little money or less than you expected 便宜的；不贵的：*I'm going to rent a room if I can find somewhere cheap enough.* 如果能找到足够便宜的地方，我打算租间屋子。 ▫ *People who own cars are demanding cheaper petrol.* 有车的人想让汽油便宜些。

▶ **cheaply** /ˈtʃiːpli/ *adverb* 副词：*You can deliver more food more cheaply by ship.* 走海路可以运更多食品，费用也更便宜。

2 costing less money than similar products but often of bad quality 廉价的：*Don't buy any of those cheap watches.* 不要买那种廉价手表。

cheat /tʃiːt/ ***verb*** 动词 (**cheats, cheating, cheated**)

to do something that is not honest or fair, often because you want to get something 作弊；舞弊；弄虚作假：*Students sometimes cheated in order to get into top schools.* 为了进入名校，学生有时会作弊。 ● **cheat** *countable noun* 可数名词：*Are you calling me a cheat?* 你说我是骗子？

check¹ /tʃek/ ***verb*** 动词 (**checks, checking, checked**)

1 to make sure that something is correct 检查；审查；核实：*Check the meanings of the words in a dictionary.* 去词典里查查这些词的意思。 ▫ *I think there is an age limit, but I'll check.* 我觉得有年龄限制，不过我会核实一下。 ▫ *She checked whether she had a clean shirt.* 她看了看自己是否有干净的衬衫。

2 (*American* 美国英语) → see 见 **tick**

check in to tell the person at the desk of an airport or a hotel that you have arrived (在机场) 办理登机手续；(在宾馆) 办理入住手续：*We checked in early and walked around the airport.* 我们早早办好了登机手续，在机场逛了逛。 ▫ *I checked in at a small hotel on the village square.* 我在乡村广场的一家小旅馆登记入住。

check out to pay the bill at a hotel and leave (在宾馆) 办理结账手续，结账退房：*They packed and checked out of the hotel.* 他们收拾好行李，退房离开了宾馆。 ▫ *They checked out yesterday morning.* 他们昨天早上退房走的。

check² /tʃek/ *countable noun* 可数名词
1 when you make sure that something is correct 检查；审查；核实: *We need to do some quick checks before the plane leaves.* 飞机起飞前我们需要快速检查下。
2 (*American* 美国英语) the **bill** in a restaurant (餐馆的) 结账单
3 (*American* 美国英语) → see 见 **cheque**

checked /tʃekt/ *adjective* 形容词
with a pattern of small squares, usually of two colours 有 (双色) 格子图案的: *The waiter had a checked shirt.* 服务员穿着格子衬衫。

'check-,in *countable noun* 可数名词
the counter or desk at an airport where you show your ticket and give someone your luggage (机场的) 值机柜台

'checking a,ccount *countable noun* 可数名词 (*American* 美国英语)
→ see 见 **current account**

'check ,mark *countable noun* 可数名词 (*American* 美国英语)
→ see 见 **tick**

checkout /tʃekaʊt/ *countable noun* 可数名词
the place where you pay in a supermarket or other shop (超市等的) 收银台

'check-,up *countable noun* 可数名词
a general examination by your doctor or dentist 体检；牙科检查

cheek /tʃiːk/ *countable noun* 可数名词
one of the two sides of your face below your eyes 脸颊；脸蛋儿: *The tears started rolling down my cheeks.* 眼泪开始顺着我的脸颊滚落。

cheeky /tʃiːki/ *adjective* 形容词 (**cheekier, cheekiest**)
rude, often in an amusing way 调皮的；厚脸皮的: *David was a very cheeky little boy who loved to play jokes on people.* 戴维是个很调皮的小男孩，喜欢捉弄人。

cheer /tʃɪə/ *verb* 动词 (**cheers, cheering, cheered**)
to shout loudly to show that you are pleased or to encourage someone 喝彩；欢呼: *We cheered as she went up the steps to the stage.* 她迈上台阶登台时我们欢呼起来。● **cheer** *countable noun* 可数名词: *The audience gave him a loud cheer.* 观众为他大声欢呼。

cheer someone up to make someone feel happier 使某人高兴起来；使某人振作起来: *Stop trying to cheer me up.* 不要再给我打气了。

cheer up to become happier 高兴起来；振作起来: *Cheer up. Life could be worse.* 打起精神来，日子还不算太糟。

cheerful /tʃɪəfʊl/ *adjective* 形容词
happy 欢快的；高兴的；兴高采烈的: *Paddy was always smiling and cheerful.* 帕迪总是面带笑容，乐呵呵的。
▶ **cheerfully** /tʃɪəfʊli/ *adverb* 副词: *'We've got good news,' Pat said cheerfully.* "我们有好消息。" 帕特高兴地说。
▶ **cheerfulness** /tʃɪəfʊlnəs/ *uncountable noun* 不可数名词: *I liked his natural cheerfulness.* 我喜欢他乐呵呵的天性。

cheerleader /tʃɪəliːdə/ *countable noun* 可数名词
one of a group of people who encourage the crowd to shout support for their team at a sports event 啦啦队队员

cheers /tʃɪəz/ *exclamation* 感叹词
1 used just before people drink to celebrate something (*informal* 非正式) 干杯
2 goodbye (*informal* 非正式) 再见
3 thank you (*informal* 非正式) 谢谢

cheese /tʃiːz/ *noun* 名词
a solid food made from milk which is usually white or yellow 奶酪；干酪: *We had bread and cheese for lunch.* 我们午饭吃了面包配奶酪。 □ *This shop sells delicious French cheeses.* 这家商店有美味的法式干酪出售。
→ Look at picture on P5 参见彩插第 5 页

chef /ʃef/ *countable noun* 可数名词
a cook in a restaurant 厨师
→ Look at picture on P16 参见彩插第 16 页

chemical¹ /kemɪkəl/ *adjective* 形容词
relating to chemistry or chemicals 化学的；化学品的: *Do you know what caused the chemical reaction?* 你知道为什么会发生这种化学反应吗？ □ *Almost all of the natural chemical elements are found in the ocean.* 海洋中几乎含有所有天然化学元素。

chemical² /kemɪkəl/ *countable noun* 可数名词
a substance that is used in a chemical process or made by a chemical process 化学品: *The programme was about the use of chemicals in farming.* 这个节目讲的是化学品在农业中的使用。

chemist /kemɪst/ *countable noun* 可数名词
1 a person who prepares and sells medicines 药剂师

2 (also 亦作 **chemist's**) a shop that sells medicines, make-up and some other things 药妆店
3 a scientist who studies chemistry 化学家

chemistry /ˈkemɪstri/ *uncountable noun* 不可数名词
the science of the structure of gases, liquids and solids, and how they change 化学

cheque /tʃek/ *countable noun* 可数名词
(*American* 美国英语：**check**)
a printed piece of paper from a bank. You write an amount of money on it and use it to pay for things. 支票：*He gave me a cheque for £1,500.* 他给了我一张 1,500 英镑的支票。

chequebook /ˈtʃekbʊk/ *countable noun* 可数名词
a book containing a number of cheques 支票簿

cherry /ˈtʃeri/ *countable noun* 可数名词
(**cherries**)
a small, round fruit with red skin 樱桃

chess /tʃes/ *uncountable noun* 不可数名词
a game for two people, played on a board with black and white squares on it, using different shaped pieces 国际象棋：*He was playing chess with his uncle.* 他正和叔叔下国际象棋。

chest /tʃest/ *countable noun* 可数名词
1 the top part of the front of your body 胸；胸部；胸膛：*He folded his arms across his broad chest.* 他双臂交叠于宽阔的胸前。□ *He was shot in the chest.* 他胸部中弹。
→ Look at picture on P4 参见彩插第 4 页
2 a large, strong box for storing things（存放东西的）大箱子：*We know she has money locked in a chest somewhere.* 我们知道她把钱锁在某处的箱子里。

chest of ˈdrawers *countable noun* 可数名词
a piece of furniture with drawers that you use for keeping clothes in 五斗橱；带抽屉的衣柜

chew /tʃuː/ *verb* 动词 (**chews, chewing, chewed**)
to break up food with your teeth 嚼；咀嚼：*Always chew your food well.* 食物要细细咀嚼。

ˈchewing ˌgum *uncountable noun* 不可数名词
a type of sweet that you can chew for a long time 口香糖：*a packet of chewing gum* 一包口香糖

chick /tʃɪk/ *countable noun* 可数名词
a baby bird 雏鸟；小鸟；小鸡

chicken /ˈtʃɪkɪn/ *noun* 名词
1 *countable* 可数 a bird that is kept on a farm for its eggs and meat 鸡
2 *uncountable* 不可数 the meat of this bird 鸡肉：*We had chicken sandwiches.* 我们吃了鸡肉三明治。

chief[1] /tʃiːf/ *countable noun* 可数名词
the leader of a group 首领；领导人：*The police chief has said very little.* 警察局长透露的信息非常少。

chief[2] /tʃiːf/ *adjective* 形容词
most important 最主要的；首要的：*Sunburn is the chief cause of skin cancer.* 晒伤是皮肤癌的首要病因。

chiefly /ˈtʃiːfli/ *adverb* 副词
not completely, but especially or mostly 主要；首要：*Rhodes is chiefly known for her fashion designs.* 罗兹主要以时装设计出名。

child /tʃaɪld/ *countable noun* 可数名词
(**children**)
1 a young boy or girl 小孩；孩子；儿童：*When I was a child I lived in a village.* 我小时候生活在一个村庄里。□ *The show is free for children age 6 and under.* *6 岁及以下儿童可免费观看这场演出。
2 someone's sons and daughters 子女；儿女：*They have three young children.* 他们有 3 个年幼的孩子。

childhood /ˈtʃaɪldˌhʊd/ *noun* 名词
the time when someone is a child 童年；孩童时期：*She had a happy childhood.* 她有个幸福的童年。

childish /ˈtʃaɪldɪʃ/ *adjective* 形容词
behaving like a child 孩子气的；幼稚的：*Paco had a childish smile on his face.* 帕科脸上露出孩子气的笑容。

children /ˈtʃɪldrən/
the plural of **child**（child 的复数形式）

chill /tʃɪl/ *verb* 动词 (**chills, chilling, chilled**)
to make something cold 使冷却；使凉下来：*Chill the fruit salad in the fridge.* 把水果沙拉放冰箱里冰一下。

chill out to relax (*informal* 非正式) 放松：*After school, we chill out and watch TV.* 放学后，我们休息放松，看看电视。

chilli /ˈtʃɪli/ also 亦作 **chili** *noun* 名词
(**chillies** or 或 **chillis**)
a small red or green pepper that tastes

very hot 辣椒

chilly /'tʃɪli/ *adjective* 形容词 (**chillier, chilliest**)
rather cold 寒冷的: *It was a chilly afternoon.* 那是个寒冷的下午。

chimney /'tʃɪmni/ *countable noun* 可数名词
a pipe above a fire that lets the smoke travel up and out of the building 烟囱: *Smoke from chimneys polluted the skies.* 烟囱冒出的烟污染了天空。

chimpanzee /ˌtʃɪmpæn'ziː/ *countable noun* 可数名词
a type of small African animal, like a monkey with no tail 黑猩猩

chin /tʃɪn/ *countable noun* 可数名词
the part of your face below your mouth 颏; 下巴

china /'tʃaɪnə/ *uncountable noun* 不可数名词
a hard white substance that is used for making cups and plates 瓷: *He ate from a small bowl made of china.* 他用一个小瓷碗吃饭。

chip[1] /tʃɪp/ *countable noun* 可数名词
1 (*American* 美国英语: **fries**) a long thin piece of potato, cooked in oil and eaten hot 薯条: *fish and chips* 炸鱼薯条
2 (*American* 美国英语) → see 见 **crisp**
3 a very small part that controls a piece of electronic equipment 芯片: *a computer chip* 电脑芯片
4 a small piece that has been broken off something 碎屑; 碎片; 碎块: *It contains real chocolate chips.* 它含有真正的巧克力碎粒。

chip[2] /tʃɪp/ *verb* 动词 (**chips, chipping, chipped**)
to break a small piece off something 使脱落; 削落; 凿落; 剥落: *The toffee chipped the woman's tooth.* 太妃糖把那名女子的牙硌掉了一块儿。
▶ **chipped** /tʃɪpt/ *adjective* 形容词: *The paint on the door was badly chipped.* 门上的漆剥落严重。

chocolate /'tʃɒklət/ *noun* 名词
1 *uncountable* 不可数 a sweet food made from cocoa 巧克力: *We shared a bar of chocolate.* 我们分吃了一条巧克力。
2 (also 亦作 **hot chocolate**) a hot drink made from chocolate 巧克力热饮: *The visitors can buy tea, coffee and chocolate.* 有茶、咖啡和巧克力热饮供游客购买。
3 *countable* 可数 a small sweet or nut covered with chocolate 巧克力糖: *The class gave the teacher a box of chocolates.* 全班送给老师一盒巧克力糖。

choice /tʃɔɪs/ *countable noun* 可数名词
1 a situation when there are several things and you can choose the one you want 选择; 挑选; 选择范围: *It comes in a choice of colours.* 有多种颜色可供选择。 □ *There's a choice between meat or fish.* 可以选择肉或鱼。
2 the thing or things that you choose 选定的东西: *Her mother didn't really agree with her choice.* 她妈妈并不太认同她的选择。
have no choice to be unable to choose to do something else 别无选择: *We had to agree — we had no choice.* 我们只好同意——别无选择。

choir /'kwaɪə/ *countable noun* 可数名词
a group of people who sing together 唱诗班; 合唱队; 合唱团: *He sang in his church choir for years.* 他在教堂唱诗班唱了多年。

choke /tʃəʊk/ *verb* 动词 (**chokes, choking, choked**)
to be unable to breathe because there is not enough air, or because something is blocking your throat (使)窒息; (使)噎住: *A small child may choke on the toy.* 这个玩具可能会让年龄小的孩子窒息。 □ *The smoke was choking her.* 烟呛得她要喘不过气来。

cholesterol /kə'lestərɒl/ *uncountable noun* 不可数名词
a substance that exists in your blood. Too much cholesterol in the blood can cause heart disease. 胆固醇: *He has a dangerously high cholesterol level.* 他的胆固醇水平高得危险。

choose /tʃuːz/ *verb* 动词 (**chooses, choosing, chose, chosen**)
1 to decide to have a person or thing 选择; 挑选; 选取: *Each group will choose its own leader.* 每组要选出自己的组长。 □ *You can choose from several different patterns.* 你可以从几个不同的图案中挑选。
2 to do something because you want to 决定; 甘愿: *Many people choose to eat meat at dinner only.* 很多人只愿意晚饭吃肉。 □ *You can remain silent if you choose.* 你愿意的话, 可以保持沉默。

chop /tʃɒp/ *verb* 动词 (**chops, chopping, chopped**)
(also 亦作 **chop something up**) to cut something into pieces with a knife 剁碎;

切碎；砍；劈：*Chop the butter into small pieces.* 把黄油切成小块。▫ *We started chopping wood for a fire.* 我们开始劈柴生火。

chop something down to cut through the trunk of a tree with an axe 砍倒（树）：*Sometimes they chop down a tree for firewood.* 有时他们砍树当柴烧。

chop something off to remove something using scissors or a knife 剪下某物；切掉某物：*Chop off the fish's heads and tails.* 切掉鱼头和鱼尾。

chop something up same meaning as **chop** 同 chop

chopsticks /'tʃɒpstɪks/ *plural noun* 复数名词
a pair of thin sticks that people in some Asian countries use for eating food 筷子：*She had no idea how to use chopsticks.* 她不会用筷子。

chord /kɔːd/ *countable noun* 可数名词
a number of musical notes played or sung at the same time 和弦：*I can play a few chords on the guitar.* 我会用吉他弹几个和弦。

chore /tʃɔː/ *countable noun* 可数名词
a job that you have to do, for example, cleaning the house 任务；家务活儿：*After I finished my chores, I could go outside and play.* 等做完家务，我就能出去玩了。

chorus /'kɔːrəs/ *countable noun* 可数名词 (**choruses**)
1 a part of a song that you repeat several times 副歌：*Caroline sang two verses and the chorus of her song.* 卡罗琳唱了她那首歌中的两段和副歌部分。
2 a large group of people who sing together 合唱团；合唱队：*The Harvard orchestra and chorus performed Beethoven's Ninth Symphony.* 哈佛大学管弦乐团和合唱团表演了贝多芬的《第九交响曲》。

chose /tʃəʊz/
→ see 见 **choose**

chosen /'tʃəʊzən/
→ see 见 **choose**

christen /'krɪsən/ *verb* 动词 (**christens, christening, christened**)
to give a baby a name during a Christian ceremony 给…施洗；（施洗时）为…命名：*She was born in March and christened in June.* 她 3 月出生，6 月受洗。

christening /'krɪsənɪŋ/ *countable noun* 可数名词
a ceremony in which members of a church welcome a baby and it is officially given its name（基督教的）洗礼：*I cried at my granddaughter's christening.* 孙女洗礼上我哭了。

Christian /'krɪstʃən/ *countable noun* 可数名词
someone who believes in Jesus Christ, and follows what he taught 基督徒
● **Christian** *adjective* 形容词：*the Christian Church* 基督教会

Christianity /ˌkrɪstiˈænɪti/ *uncountable noun* 不可数名词
a religion that believes in Jesus Christ and follows what he taught 基督教

Christmas /'krɪsməs/ *noun* 名词 (**Christmases**)
the period around the 25th December, when Christians celebrate the birth of Jesus Christ 圣诞节；圣诞节期间：*'Merry Christmas!'* "圣诞快乐！" ▫ *We're staying at home for the Christmas holidays.* 我们待在家里过圣诞节。

chromosome /'krəʊməˌsəʊm/ *countable noun* 可数名词
the part of a cell in an animal or a plant that controls characteristics such as hair and eye colour 染色体：*Each cell of our bodies contains 46 chromosomes.* 我们人体的每个细胞都包含 46 条染色体。

chubby /'tʃʌbi/ *adjective* 形容词 (**chubbier, chubbiest**)
slightly fat 微胖的；胖乎乎的：*Do you think I'm too chubby?* 你觉得我是不是太胖乎了？

chuckle /'tʃʌkəl/ *verb* 动词 (**chuckles, chuckling, chuckled**)
to laugh quietly 低声笑；轻声地笑：*He chuckled and said 'Of course not.'* 他轻声笑着说："当然不。" ● **chuckle** *countable noun* 可数名词：*He gave a little chuckle.* 他轻声一笑。

chunk /tʃʌŋk/ *countable noun* 可数名词
a thick, solid piece of something 厚块；大块：*Large chunks of ice floated past us.* 大块大块的冰从我们身边漂过。

chunky /'tʃʌŋki/ *adjective* 形容词 (**chunkier, chunkiest**)
large and heavy 粗重的；厚实的；大而重的：*She was wearing a chunky gold necklace.* 她戴着一条沉甸甸的金项链。

church /tʃɜːtʃ/ *noun* 名词 (**churches**)
a building where Christians go to pray（基督教的）教堂，礼拜堂：*We got married in Coburn United Methodist Church.* 我们在科本联合卫理公会教堂结的婚。▫ *The family has gone to church.* 这家人去教堂做礼拜了。

cider /ˈsaɪdə/ *uncountable noun* 不可数名词
an alcoholic drink made from apples 苹果酒：*He ordered a glass of cider.* 他点了一杯苹果酒。

cigar /sɪˈɡɑː/ *countable noun* 可数名词
a brown roll of dried tobacco leaves that some people smoke 雪茄烟

cigarette /ˌsɪɡəˈret/ *countable noun* 可数名词
a small tube of paper containing tobacco that some people smoke 香烟

cinema /ˈsɪnɪmə, ˈsɪnɪmɑː/ *countable noun* 可数名词
(*American* 美国英语：**movie theater**) a building where people go to watch films 电影院：*There is a shopping arcade with a multiplex cinema (= a cinema with several screens).* 有一个购物中心，里面有一家多厅影院。

the cinema (*American* 美国英语：**the movies**) films in general（泛指）电影

cinnamon /ˈsɪnəmən/ *uncountable noun* 不可数名词
a sweet spice used for adding flavour to food 肉桂皮，桂皮（香料）

circle /ˈsɜːkəl/ *countable noun* 可数名词
a round shape 圆；圆形；圆圈：*The Japanese flag is white, with a red circle in the centre.* 日本国旗是白底中央有一个红色的圆。▫ *She drew a mouth, a nose and two circles for eyes.* 她画了一张嘴、一个鼻子、两个代表眼睛的圆圈。
→ Look at picture on P2 参见彩插第 2 页

circuit /ˈsɜːkɪt/ *countable noun* 可数名词
1 a track that cars race around 赛车道；环形赛道：*the grand prix circuit* 大奖赛的赛车道
2 a complete path that electricity can flow around 电路；回路：*The electrical circuit was broken.* 电路受损。
→ Look at picture on P6 参见彩插第 6 页

circular /ˈsɜːkjʊlə/ *adjective* 形容词
shaped like a circle 圆形的：*The circular walk around the castle can be done in 20 minutes.* 20 分钟内就能绕这座城堡走一圈。

circulate /ˈsɜːkjʊleɪt/ *verb* 动词 (**circulates, circulating, circulated**)
to move easily and freely in a place 循环；流通：*The blood circulates through the body.* 血液在身体内循环。
▶ **circulation** /ˌsɜːkjʊˈleɪʃən/ *uncountable noun* 不可数名词：*the circulation of air* 空气循环

circulation /ˌsɜːkjʊˈleɪʃən/ *uncountable noun* 不可数名词
the movement of blood through your body（血液的）循环：*Regular exercise is good for the circulation.* 经常锻炼对血液循环有益。

circumference /səˈkʌmfrəns/ *uncountable noun* 不可数名词
the distance around the edge of a circle 圆周；圆周长：*Think of a way to calculate the Earth's circumference.* 想个能测量地球周长的方法。

circumstance /ˈsɜːkəmstæns/ *countable noun* 可数名词
a fact about a particular situation 情况；情形；形势：*You're doing really well, considering the circumstances.* 考虑到目前的情形，你做得很好。▫ *Under normal circumstances, this trip would only take about 20 minutes.* 正常情况下，这趟行程只需 20 分钟左右。

circus /ˈsɜːkəs/ *countable noun* 可数名词 (**circuses**)
a group of people and animals that travels around to different places and performs shows in a big tent 马戏团：*I always wanted to work as a clown in a circus.* 我一直想去马戏团当小丑。

citizen /ˈsɪtɪzən/ *countable noun* 可数名词
1 a person who legally belongs to a particular country 公民；国民：*We are proud to be American citizens.* 我们为自己是美国公民而自豪。
2 the people who live in a town or city 城镇居民；市民：*He travelled to Argentina to meet the citizens of Buenos Aires.* 为了见见布宜诺斯艾利斯的市民，他去阿根廷旅游过。

citrus /ˈsɪtrəs/ *adjective* 形容词
from a family of juicy fruits with a sharp taste such as an orange or a lemon 柑橘类的：*Citrus fruits are a good source of vitamin C.* 柑橘类果实富含维生素 C。

city /ˈsɪti/ *countable noun* 可数名词 (**cities**)
a large town 城市：*We visited the city of*

Los Angeles. 我们访问了洛杉矶市。

civil /ˈsɪvəl/ *adjective* 形容词
1 used for talking about the people of a country and their activities 公民的；国民的：*The American Civil War is also called the War Between the States.* 美国内战又称南北战争。□ *civil rights* 公民权利
2 used for talking about people or things that are connected with the state, and not the army or the church 平民的；民用的；世俗的：*We had a civil wedding in the town hall.* 我们在市政厅举行了一场世俗婚礼。
3 polite, although not very friendly (*formal* 正式) 有礼貌的；客气的：*Please try to be a little more civil to people.* 请尽量对人再客气些。

civilian /sɪˈvɪliən/ *countable noun* 可数名词
a person who is not a member of the armed forces 平民；老百姓：*The soldiers were not shooting at civilians.* 士兵不会射击平民。● **civilian** *adjective* 形容词：*The men were wearing civilian clothes.* 那些人穿着便装。

civilization /ˌsɪvɪlaɪˈzeɪʃn/ *noun* 名词
a group of people with their own organization and culture 文明：*We learned about the ancient civilizations of Greece.* 我们了解了古希腊文明。

civilized /ˈsɪvɪlaɪzd/ *adjective* 形容词
1 with a high level of social organization and cultural development 文明的：*Boxing should be illegal in a civilized society.* 文明社会不应给予拳击合法地位。
2 polite and reasonable 举止得体的；通情达理的：*She was very civilized about it.* 她对此很开通。

civil rights *plural noun* 复数名词
the legal rights that all people have to fair treatment 公民权：*She never stopped fighting for civil rights.* 她争取民权的斗争从未停歇。

civil war *countable noun* 可数名词
a war between different groups of people who live in the same country 内战：*When did the American Civil War begin?* 美国内战何时开始的？

claim¹ /kleɪm/ *verb* 动词 (**claims, claiming, claimed**)
1 to say that something is true 声称；断言：*She claimed that she was not responsible for the mistake.* 她声称此次出错的责任不在她。□ *The man claimed to be very rich.* 那个男人自称很有钱。
2 to say that something belongs to you 索要；索取：*If nobody claims the money, you can keep it.* 如果没人来认领这笔钱，你就自己留着吧。

claim² /kleɪm/ *countable noun* 可数名词
1 something that someone says, which may or may not be true 声称；断言：*Most people just don't believe their claims.* 大多数人根本就不相信他们的说法。
2 something that you ask for because you think you should have it 索要物；索赔物：*an insurance claim* 保险索赔

clam /klæm/ *countable noun* 可数名词
a type of shellfish 蛤；蛤蜊

clamp /klæmp/ *countable noun* 可数名词
a piece of equipment that holds two things together 夹具；夹子；夹钳 ● **clamp** *verb* 动词 (**clamps, clamping, clamped**)：*Clamp the microphone to the stand.* 用夹具把麦克风固定到架子上。

clamp 夹钳

clap /klæp/ *verb* 动词 (**claps, clapping, clapped**)
to hit your hands together, usually to show that you like something 鼓掌；拍手：*The men danced and the women clapped.* 男人们跳起舞，女人们拍手应和。□ *Margaret clapped her hands.* 玛格丽特鼓了几下掌。

clarify /ˈklærɪfaɪ/ *verb* 动词 (**clarifies, clarifying, clarified**)
to make something easier to understand, usually by explaining it (*formal* 正式) 阐明；澄清：*I would like to clarify those remarks I made.* 我想澄清一下我说的那番话。

clarinet /ˌklærɪˈnet/ *noun* 名词
a musical instrument that you blow. It is a long black wooden tube with keys on it that you press, and a single reed (= small flat part that moves and makes a sound when you blow). 单簧管；黑管
→ Look at picture on P12 参见彩插第 12 页

clarity /ˈklærɪti/ *uncountable noun* 不可数名词
the quality of being clear and easy to understand 清楚；清晰易懂：*This new law will bring some clarity to the situation.* 这部新法将比较清楚地解释这种情况。

clash /klæʃ/ *verb* 动词 (**clashes, clashing, clashed**)
1 to fight or argue with someone else 打斗；冲突；争执：*He often clashed with his staff.* 他常与员工发生争论。● **clash** *countable noun* 可数名词 (**clashes**)：*There have been a number of clashes between police and students.* 警方和学生之间有一些冲突。
2 to look horrible with another thing 不协调；不搭配：*His pink shirt clashed with his red hair.* 他的粉衬衫和红头发太不搭了。

clasp[1] /klɑːsp/ *verb* 动词 (**clasps, clasping, clasped**)
to hold someone or something tightly 抓紧；握紧；抱紧：*She clasped the children to her.* 她紧紧地搂住孩子们。

clasp[2] /klɑːsp/ *countable noun* 可数名词
a small object that fastens something 搭扣；扣环：*Kathryn undid the metal clasp of her handbag.* 凯瑟琳打开了手提包的金属搭扣。

class /klɑːs/ *noun* 名词 (**classes**)
1 *countable* 可数 a group of students who learn at school together 班；班级：*He spent six months in a class with younger students.* 他和比自己年纪小的学生在一个班里上了 6 个月的课。
2 *countable* 可数 a time when you learn something at school 课堂；上课：*Classes start at 9 o'clock.* *9 点开始上课。□ *We do lots of reading in class.* 我们在课堂上做大量阅读。
3 *countable* 可数 a group of things that are the same in some way 类别；种类；等级：*These vegetables all belong to the same class of plants.* 这些蔬菜都属于同一植物类别。
4 a group of people with the same economic and social position in a society 社会等级；阶级；阶层：*These programs only help the middle class.* 这些方案仅对中产阶级有帮助。

classic[1] /ˈklæsɪk/ *adjective* 形容词
of very good quality, and popular for a long time 经典的；典范的：*Fleming directed the classic film 'The Wizard of Oz'.* 弗莱明执导了经典电影《绿野仙踪》。

classic[2] /ˈklæsɪk/ *countable noun* 可数名词
something that is of very good quality, and has been popular for a long time 经典作品；名著：*'Jailhouse Rock' is one of the classics of modern popular music.* 《监狱摇滚》是现代流行音乐经典作品之一。

classical /ˈklæsɪkəl/ *adjective* 形容词
traditional in form, style or content 传统的；古典的：*I like listening to classical music and reading.* 我喜欢听古典音乐和阅读。

Classics /ˈklæsɪks/ *plural noun* 复数名词
the study of the languages, literature and cultures of ancient Greece and Rome 古典学（研究古代希腊罗马的语言、文学及文化的学问）：*She studied Classics at Cambridge University.* 她在剑桥大学读古典学。

classify /ˈklæsɪfaɪ/ *verb* 动词 (**classifies, classifying, classified**)
to divide things into groups or types 把…分类；为…归类：*Vitamins can be classified into two categories.* 维生素可分为两类。

classmate /ˈklɑːsmeɪt/ *countable noun* 可数名词
a student who is in the same class as someone at school 同班同学

classroom /ˈklɑːsruːm/ *countable noun* 可数名词
a room in a school where lessons take place 教室

clause /klɔːz/ *countable noun* 可数名词
a group of words that contains a verb 分句；小句；从句

claw /klɔː/ *countable noun* 可数名词
the thin, hard, pointed part at the end of the foot of a bird or an animal（禽兽的）爪：*Lions have very sharp claws and teeth.* 狮子的爪和牙齿都很锋利。

clay /kleɪ/ *uncountable noun* 不可数名词
a type of earth that is soft when it is wet and hard when it is dry. Clay is used for making things such as pots and bricks. 黏土；陶土：*a clay pot* 陶罐
→ Look at picture on P13 参见彩插第 13 页

clean[1] /kliːn/ *adjective* 形容词 (**cleaner, cleanest**)
not dirty 干净的：*Make sure the children's hands are clean before they eat.* 要保证孩子们吃饭前洗干净手。□ *This floor is easy to keep clean.* 这地板容易保持干净。

clean[2] /kliːn/ *verb* 动词 (**cleans, cleaning, cleaned**)
to remove the dirt from something 打扫；使干净：*He fell from a ladder while he was cleaning the windows.* 他擦窗户时从梯子上掉了下来。
clean something up to clean a place

completely 清理某事物: *Hundreds of workers are cleaning up the beaches.* 数百名工人在清理海滩。 ◻ *Who is going to clean up this mess?* 谁来收拾下这一片狼藉？

cleaner /ˈkliːnə/ *countable noun* 可数名词
a person whose job is to clean the rooms and furniture inside a building（大楼的）保洁员，清洁工: *This is the hospital where Sid worked as a cleaner.* 锡德就是在这家医院做保洁员。

clear¹ /klɪə/ *adjective* 形容词 (**clearer, clearest**)
1 easy to understand, see or hear 清楚的；明白的；明显的: *The instructions are clear and readable.* 这份操作指南清楚易懂。 ◻ *It is clear that things will have to change.* 很明显，情况将不得不改变。 ◻ *This camera takes very clear pictures.* 这台相机拍照非常清晰。
▶ **clearly** /ˈklɪəli/ *adverb* 副词: *Clearly, the police cannot break the law.* 显然，警方不能违法。
2 used for describing a substance that has no colour, and that you can see through 透明的；清澈的: *a clear plastic bag* 透明的塑料袋
3 without anything blocking the way 无障碍的；通畅的: *The runway is clear — you can land.* 跑道通畅——可以降落。
4 with no clouds 无云的；晴朗的: *It was a beautiful day with a clear blue sky.* 那天天气很好，湛蓝的天空万里无云。

clear² /klɪə/ *verb* 动词 (**clears, clearing, cleared**)
1 to remove things from a place because you do not want or need them there 清除；清理: *Can someone clear the table, please?* 谁来收拾下桌子好吗？
2 when the sky clears, it stops raining 转晴；放晴: *The sky cleared and the sun came out.* 天空放晴，太阳出来了。

clear away/clear something away to put the things that you have been using back in their proper place 收拾干净 / 收拾某物: *The waitress cleared away the plates.* 那名女服务员收拾走了盘子。 ◻ *He helped to clear away after dinner.* 晚饭后他帮忙收拾餐具。

clear something out to tidy a cupboard or a place, and to throw away the things in it that you no longer want 清理某处；整理某处: *I cleared out my desk before I left.* 离开前我整理了下书桌。

clear up to make a place tidy 整理；收拾: *The children played while I cleared up in the kitchen.* 我打扫厨房时，孩子们在玩耍。

clerk /klɑːk/ *countable noun* 可数名词
1 a person whose job is to work with numbers or documents in an office 文员；文书；簿记员: *She works as a clerk in a travel agency.* 她是一家旅行社的文员。
2 (*American* 美国英语) → see 见 **shop assistant**

clever /ˈklevə/ *adjective* 形容词 (**cleverer, cleverest**)
intelligent and able to think and understand quickly 聪明的: *He's a very clever man.* 他非常聪明。
▶ **cleverly** /ˈklevəli/ *adverb* 副词: *The garden has been cleverly designed.* 这个花园设计得很巧妙。

click /klɪk/ *verb* 动词 (**clicks, clicking, clicked**)
1 to make or cause something to make a short, sharp sound（使）发出咔嗒声；（使）咔嚓作响: *Hundreds of cameras clicked as she stepped out of the car.* 她从车上下来那一刻，数百台照相机咔嚓咔嚓响成一片。 ◻ *She clicked the switch on and off.* 她把开关咔嗒咔嗒地开了又关。 ● **click** *countable noun* 可数名词: *I heard a click and then her recorded voice.* 我听到咔嗒一声，接着就是她的录音。
2 to press one of the buttons on the mouse of a computer in order to make something happen on a part of a computer screen（用鼠标）点击，单击: *I clicked on a link.* 我点击了一个链接。 ● **click** *countable noun* 可数名词: *You can check your email with a click of your mouse.* 点击鼠标就可以查看电子邮件。

client /ˈklaɪənt/ *countable noun* 可数名词
a person who pays someone for a service 委托人；客户: *The lawyer and her client were sitting at the next table.* 律师和她的委托人坐在邻桌。

> **LANGUAGE HELP 语言提示**
> See note at **customer**. 见 customer 的语言提示。

cliff /klɪf/ *countable noun* 可数名词
a high area of land with a very steep side next to the sea（海边的）悬崖，峭壁: *The car rolled over the edge of a cliff.* 汽车从悬崖边翻了下去。
→ Look at picture on P7 参见彩插第 7 页

climate /ˈklaɪmət/ *uncountable noun* 不可数名词
the normal weather in a place 气候: *She loves the hot and humid climate of Florida.* 她喜欢佛罗里达的湿热气候。

ˈclimate ˌchange *uncountable noun* 不可数名词
changes in the earth's climate, especially the fact that it is getting warmer because of high levels of certain gases 气候变化（尤指过度排放某些气体造成的全球气候变暖）: *Species are becoming extinct because of climate change.* 由于气候变化，物种正在灭绝。

climax /ˈklaɪmæks/ *countable noun* 可数名词 (**climaxes**)
the most exciting or important moment, near the end of something 高潮: *The climax of the story is when Romeo and Juliet die.* 罗密欧和朱丽叶之死是这个故事的高潮。

climb /klaɪm/ *verb* 动词 (**climbs, climbing, climbed**)
1 to move towards the top of something 爬; 攀登: *It took half an hour to climb the hill.* 爬那座山花了半个小时。 □ *Climb up the steps onto the bridge.* 沿着台阶爬到桥上。 ● **climb** *countable noun* 可数名词: *It was a hard climb to the top of the mountain.* 费了好大劲才爬上山顶。
2 to move into or out of a small space（由于空间小而）爬行: *The girls climbed into the car and drove off.* 女孩子们钻进车里，开车走了。 □ *He climbed out of his bed.* 他从床上爬了起来。
3 to increase in value or amount（价值或数量）上升，增加: *The price of petrol has been climbing steadily.* 汽油价格一直稳定上行。

climber /ˈklaɪmə/ *countable noun* 可数名词
a person who climbs rocks or mountains 登山者; 攀登者: *A climber was rescued yesterday after falling 300 metres.* 昨天，一名登山者跌落 300 米后获救。

climbing /ˈklaɪmɪŋ/ *uncountable noun* 不可数名词
the activity of climbing rocks or mountains 攀登; 登山运动; 攀岩运动

cling /klɪŋ/ *verb* 动词 (**clings, clinging, clung**)
to hold someone or something tightly 抓紧; 握紧; 抱紧: *The man was rescued as he clung to the boat.* 那名男子紧紧抓住了船，最终获救。

clinic /ˈklɪnɪk/ *countable noun* 可数名词
a place where people receive medical advice or treatment 诊所; 医务室

clinical /ˈklɪnɪkəl/ *adjective* 形容词
involving medical treatment or testing people for illnesses 临床的: *She received her clinical training in Chicago.* 她在芝加哥接受了临床培训。

clip[1] /klɪp/ *countable noun* 可数名词
1 a small object for holding things together 夹子; 回形针: *She took the clip out of her hair.* 她取下头发上的发夹。
2 a short piece of a film that is shown separately（影片）片段，剪辑: *They showed a film clip of the Apollo moon landing.* 他们播放了"阿波罗"号登月的影像片段。

clip[2] /klɪp/ *verb* 动词 (**clips, clipping, clipped**)
to fasten things together using a clip（用夹子）夹住: *Clip the rope onto the ring.* 把绳子夹在环上。

cloakroom /ˈkloʊkruːm/ *countable noun* 可数名词 (**cloakrooms**)
a room in a building where you can leave your coat 衣帽间

clock /klɒk/ *countable noun* 可数名词
a device that shows you what time it is 钟; 时钟: *He could hear a clock ticking.* 他能听到时钟嘀嗒不停。
aˌround the ˈclock all day and all night without stopping 不分昼夜; 日以继夜: *Firemen have been working around the clock.* 消防员不眠不休地工作着。

clockwise /ˈklɒkwaɪz/ *adjective* 形容词, *adverb* 副词
moving in a circle in the same direction as the hands on a clock 顺时针方向（的）: *Move your right arm around in a clockwise direction.* 按顺时针方向挥动右臂。 □ *The children started moving clockwise around the room.* 孩子们开始在屋子里按顺时针方向绕圈。

close[1] /kloʊz/ *verb* 动词 (**closes, closing, closed**)
1 to shut a door or a window 关; 关上: *If you are cold, close the window.* 你要是觉得冷，就关上窗户吧。 □ *David closed the door quietly.* 戴维轻轻地关上了门。
2 to stop being open, so that people cannot come and buy things 关门: *The*

shop closes on Sundays and public holidays. 这家商店周日和公共假日都不营业。
close down/close something down to stop all work in a place, usually for ever 停业；倒闭：*That shop closed down years ago.* 那家商店几年前倒闭了。

close² /kləʊs/ *adjective* 形容词 (**closer, closest**)
1 near to something else 近的；靠近的：*The apartment is close to the beach.* 这个公寓在海滩附近。▫ *The man moved closer.* 那个人走近了些。
▶ **closely** /ˈkləʊsli/ *adverb* 副词：*They crowded closely around the fire.* 他们紧紧地挤在炉火边。
2 liking each other very much and knowing each other well 亲近的；亲密的：*She was close to her sister, Gail.* 她和姐姐盖尔关系好。▫ *We were close friends at school.* 上学时我们是好朋友。
3 careful and complete 仔细的；彻底的：*Let's have a closer look.* 咱们再仔细地看一下吧。
4 won by only a small amount 实力不相上下的；优势微弱的：*It was a close contest for a Senate seat.* 参议院席位之争势均力敌。

closed /kləʊzd/ *adjective* 形容词
not open so that people cannot buy or do anything there 停业的；关门的：*The supermarket was closed when we got there.* 我们到的时候超市已经关门了。

closet /ˈklɒzɪt/ *countable noun* 可数名词 (*American* 美国英语)
→ see 见 **wardrobe**

cloth /klɒθ/ *noun* 名词
1 *uncountable* 不可数 material that is used for making clothing 布；布料：*You need two metres of cloth.* 你需要两米布。
2 *countable* 可数 a piece of cloth that you use for cleaning, drying or protecting things（用于清洁、吸水或起保护作用的）布：*Clean the surface with a damp cloth.* 用湿布擦净表面。

clothes /kləʊðz/ *plural noun* 复数名词
the things that people wear, such as shirts, coats, trousers and dresses 衣服；服装：*Milly went upstairs to change her clothes.* 米利上楼去换衣服。

LANGUAGE HELP 语言提示
Clothes is always plural. For a single shirt, dress or skirt, for example, use a **piece of clothing** or an **item of clothing**.

*clothes 始终是复数形式。表示一件衣服用 **a piece of clothing** 或 **an item of clothing**。

clothing /ˈkləʊðɪŋ/ *uncountable noun* 不可数名词
the things that people wear 衣服；服装：*She works in a women's clothing shop.* 她在一家女装店工作。

cloud /klaʊd/ *noun* 名词
1 a white or grey thing in the sky that is made of drops of water 云：*Clouds began to form in the sky.* 天空中开始出现云朵。
2 *countable* 可数 an amount of smoke or dust floating in the air（烟或尘土的）一团：*A cloud of black smoke spread across the sky.* 一团黑烟在天空中散开。

cloudy /ˈklaʊdi/ *adjective* 形容词 (**cloudier, cloudiest**)
with a lot of clouds in the sky 多云的：*It was a windy, cloudy day.* 那天风大多云。
→ Look at picture on P8 参见彩插第 8 页

clown /klaʊn/ *countable noun* 可数名词
a performer who wears funny clothes and does silly things to make people laugh 小丑

club /klʌb/ *countable noun* 可数名词
1 an organization for people who all like doing a particular activity 俱乐部：*He joined the local golf club.* 他加入了当地的高尔夫俱乐部。
2 a place where the members of a club meet 俱乐部会所：*I stopped at the club for a drink.* 我在俱乐部停下来喝了一杯。
3 → see 见 **nightclub**：*The streets are full of bars, clubs and restaurants.* 街上到处都是酒吧、夜总会和饭店。
4 a long, thin, metal stick that you use to hit the ball in the game of golf 高尔夫球杆
5 a thick, heavy stick that can be used as a weapon 棍棒（用作武器）：*The men were carrying knives and clubs.* 这些人拿着刀和棍棒。

clue /kluː/ *countable noun* 可数名词
information that helps you to find an answer 线索；提示：*I'll give you a clue; the answer begins with the letter 'p'.* 我提示你一下：答案以字母 p 开头。

clumsy /ˈklʌmzi/ *adjective* 形容词 (**clumsier, clumsiest**)
not moving in a very easy way and often breaking things 笨拙的：*As a child she was very clumsy.* 她小时候笨手笨脚的。▫ *Dad*

was rather clumsy on his skates. 爸爸滑冰的样子很笨拙。
▶ **clumsily** /ˈklʌmzɪli/ *adverb* 副词: *He fell clumsily onto the bed.* 他笨拙地往床上一倒。

clung /klʌŋ/
→ see 见 **cling**

cluster /ˈklʌstə/ *countable noun* 可数名词
a small group of people or things close together(人的)一小群；(事物的)一组，一簇: *There was a cluster of houses near the river.* 河边有一小片房子。

clutch¹ /klʌtʃ/ *verb* 动词 (**clutches, clutching, clutched**)
to hold something very tightly 抓紧；握紧；抱紧: *Michelle clutched my arm.* 米歇尔紧紧抓住我的胳膊。

clutch² /klʌtʃ/ *countable noun* 可数名词 (**clutches**)
the part of a vehicle that you press with your foot before you move the gear stick (= the part that changes the engine speed)(车辆的)离合器

clutter /ˈklʌtə/ *uncountable noun* 不可数名词
a lot of things that you do not need in a messy state 杂乱的东西: *I'm a very tidy person, and I hate clutter.* 我特别爱干净，讨厌乱放东西。● **clutter** *verb* 动词 (**clutters, cluttering, cluttered**): *Empty cans clutter the desks.* 空金属罐胡乱地堆在书桌上。

cm
short for (缩写 =) **centimetre** or **centimetres**

coach¹ /kəʊtʃ/ *countable noun* 可数名词 (**coaches**)
1 a comfortable bus that travels between cities or takes people on long journeys 长途汽车；长途客车
2 a **carriage** on a train (火车的)旅客车厢
3 someone who is in charge of teaching a person or a sports team 教练: *She's the women's football coach at Durham University.* 她是达勒姆大学女子足球队的教练。
4 a vehicle with four wheels that is pulled by horses 四轮大马车

coach² /kəʊtʃ/ *verb* 动词 (**coaches, coaching, coached**)
to help someone to become better at a particular sport or skill 训练；指导: *She coached a golf team in San José.* 她在圣何塞执教一支高尔夫球队。

coal /kəʊl/ *uncountable noun* 不可数名词
a hard black substance that comes from under the ground and is burned to give heat 煤: *Put some more coal on the fire.* 再往火里加些煤。

coarse /kɔːs/ *adjective* 形容词 (**coarser, coarsest**)
feeling dry and rough 粗糙的: *His skin was coarse and dry.* 他的皮肤又糙又干。

coast /kəʊst/ *countable noun* 可数名词
the land that is next to the sea 海滨；海岸: *We stayed at a camp site on the coast.* 我们待在海滨营地。
▶ **coastal** /ˈkəʊstəl/ *adjective* 形容词: *Coastal areas have been flooded.* 海滨地区已被洪水淹没。

coastline /ˈkəʊstlaɪn/ *noun* 名词
the edge of a country's coast 海岸线

coat¹ /kəʊt/ *countable noun* 可数名词
1 a piece of clothing with long sleeves that you wear over other clothes when you go outside 外套；大衣: *He put on his coat and walked out.* 他穿上外套走了出去。
2 an animal's fur or hair (动物的)皮毛
3 a thin layer of paint 涂料层: *The front door needs a new coat of paint.* 前门需要新刷一层漆。

coat² /kəʊt/ *verb* 动词 (**coats, coating, coated**)
to cover something with a thin layer of a substance 给⋯涂上(或裹上): *Coat the fish with flour.* 将鱼裹上面粉。

cobweb /ˈkɒbweb/ *countable noun* 可数名词
the fine net that a spider makes for catching insects 蜘蛛网: *The windows are cracked and covered in cobwebs.* 窗户残破不全，布满了蜘蛛网。

cockpit /ˈkɒkpɪt/ *countable noun* 可数名词
the part of an aeroplane or a racing car where the pilot or driver sits (飞机的)驾驶舱；(赛车的)驾驶座

cockroach /ˈkɒkrəʊtʃ/ *countable noun* 可数名词 (**cockroaches**)
a large brown insect that likes to live in places where food is kept 蟑螂

cocoa /ˈkəʊkəʊ/ *uncountable noun* 不可数名词
1 a brown powder used for making chocolate 可可粉
2 a hot drink made from cocoa powder and milk or water 可可热饮: *Let's have a cup of cocoa.* 咱们喝杯可可吧。

coconut /ˈkəʊkəˌnʌt/ *noun* 名词
1 *countable* 可数 a very large nut with a hairy shell that grows on trees in warm countries 椰子
2 *uncountable* 不可数 the white flesh of a coconut 椰子肉: *Add two cups of grated coconut.* 加两杯椰蓉。

cocoon /kəˈkuːn/ *countable noun* 可数名词
a case that some insects make around themselves before they grow into adults 茧: *The butterfly slowly breaks out of its cocoon.* 蝴蝶慢慢破茧而出。

cod /kɒd/ *noun* 名词 (**cod**)
1 a large sea fish with white flesh 鳕鱼
2 *uncountable* 不可数 this fish eaten as food 鳕鱼(指菜品): *We had cod and chips for dinner.* 我们晚饭吃的鳕鱼配薯条。

code /kəʊd/ *noun* 名词
1 *countable* 可数 a set of rules for people to follow 行为准则；规则；法规: *We keep a strict dress code (= people must wear particular clothes).* 我们遵守着严格的着装规定。
2 a secret way to replace the words in a message with other words or symbols, so that some people will not understand the message 密码；代码: *They sent messages using codes.* 他们用密码发送消息。
3 *uncountable* 不可数 a set of instructions that a computer can understand (计算机)代码: *a few lines of simple computer code* 几行简单的计算机代码
4 *countable* 可数 a group of numbers or letters that gives information about something (邮政)编码；(电话)区号: *The dialling code for Oxford is 01865.* 牛津的电话区号是01865。

coffee /ˈkɒfi/ *noun* 名词
1 the beans (= seeds) of the coffee plant, which can also be made into a powder 咖啡豆: *The island produces plenty of coffee.* 这座岛盛产咖啡豆。
2 *uncountable* 不可数 a drink made from boiling water and coffee beans 咖啡(饮料): *Would you like some coffee?* 你要来点咖啡吗？
3 *countable* 可数 a cup of this drink 一杯咖啡: *I'd like three coffees and a tea, please.* 请给我3杯咖啡和1杯茶。

coffin /ˈkɒfɪn/ *countable noun* 可数名词
a box that you put a dead person in when you bury them 棺材；灵柩

coil /kɔɪl/ *countable noun* 可数名词
a piece of rope or wire that forms a series of rings (绳子或金属线绕成的)卷，圈: *He was carrying a coil of rope.* 他拿着一卷绳子。

coin /kɔɪn/ *countable noun* 可数名词
a small round piece of metal money 硬币: *She put the coins in her pocket.* 她把硬币放进了口袋里。
→ Look at picture on P10 参见彩插第10页

coins 硬币

coincidence /kəʊˈɪnsɪdəns/ *noun* 名词
when similar or related events happen at the same time without planning 巧合: *It is a coincidence that they arrived at the same time.* 他们同时到达是个巧合。 □ *We met by coincidence several years later.* 几年之后我们巧遇了。

cold¹ /kəʊld/ *adjective* 形容词 (**colder, coldest**)
1 feeling uncomfortable because you are not warm enough 感觉冷的: *I was freezing cold.* 我快冻僵了。 □ *Put on a jumper if you're cold.* 你要是觉得冷，就把套头衫穿上。
2 without any warmth 冰凉的；寒冷的: *He washed his face with cold water.* 他用凉水洗脸。 □ *We went out into the cold, dark night.* 我们出门走进寒冷漆黑的夜里。

> **LANGUAGE HELP** 语言提示
> If something is very cold, you can say that it is **freezing**. 表示非常冷可以用 freezing。

3 not showing emotion and not friendly 冷淡的；不友好的: *Her mother was an angry, cold woman.* 她妈妈脾气大，待人冷漠。

cold² /kəʊld/ *countable noun* 可数名词
an illness that makes liquid flow from your nose, and makes you cough 感冒；伤风: *I have a bad cold.* 我得了重感冒。

catch cold or **catch a cold** to become ill with a cold 患感冒: *Dry your hair so you don't catch cold.* 弄干头发以防感冒。

Cold War *noun* 名词
the difficult relationship between the Soviet Union and the Western powers after the Second World War 冷战: *This was the first major crisis of the post-Cold War era.* 这是后冷战时期的首个重大危机。

coleslaw /ˈkəʊlslɔː/ *uncountable noun* 不可数名词
a salad made from pieces of raw carrot and cabbage (= a round vegetable with white or green leaves), mixed with a special sauce (= mayonnaise) 卷心菜沙拉 (生胡萝卜丝和卷心菜丝中拌入蛋黄酱)

collage /ˈkɒlɑːʒ/ *countable noun* 可数名词
a picture that you make by sticking pieces of paper or cloth on a surface 拼贴画: *The children made a collage of words and pictures from magazines.* 孩子们从杂志上剪下词和图片做成了拼贴画。

collapse /kəˈlæps/ *verb* 动词 (**collapses, collapsing, collapsed**)
to fall very suddenly (突然) 倒塌，昏倒: *The bridge collapsed last October.* 那座桥去年 10 月塌了。 □ *He collapsed at his home last night.* 他昨晚在家里昏倒了。

collar /ˈkɒlə/ *countable noun* 可数名词
1 the part of a shirt or coat that goes around someone's neck 领子；衣领: *He pulled up his jacket collar in the cold wind.* 冷风吹来，他竖起了夹克衫的领子。
2 a band of leather or plastic that you put around the neck of a pet dog or cat (宠物狗或猫的) 项圈，颈圈

collarbone /ˈkɒləˌbəʊn/ *countable noun* 可数名词
one of the two long bones between your throat and your shoulders 锁骨: *Harold had a broken collarbone.* 哈罗德的锁骨骨折了。

colleague /ˈkɒliːɡ/ *countable noun* 可数名词
a person someone works with 同事: *She's busy talking to a colleague.* 她正忙着和同事讲话。

collect /kəˈlekt/ *verb* 动词 (**collects, collecting, collected**)
1 to bring things together from several places or people 收集；采集: *Two young girls collected wood for the fire.* 两个小女孩拾了木柴生火。
▶ **collection** /kəˈlekʃən/ *uncountable noun* 不可数名词: *Computers can help with the collection of information.* 计算机可以帮助收集信息。

2 to go and get someone or something from a place where they are waiting for you 接走；领取: *She babysits for us and collects the children from school.* 她临时替我们看孩子，接孩子放学。
3 to get things and save them over a period of time because you like them 收藏；搜集: *I collect stamps.* 我集邮。

collection /kəˈlekʃən/ *countable noun* 可数名词
a group of similar or related things 收藏品；收集物: *He has a large collection of paintings.* 他收藏了大量绘画作品。

collector /kəˈlektə/ *countable noun* 可数名词
someone who collects things that they like, such as stamps or old furniture 收集者；收藏家: *Her parents were both art collectors.* 她父母都是艺术品收藏家。

college /ˈkɒlɪdʒ/ *noun* 名词
a place where students study after they leave secondary school 大学；学院；专科学校: *I have one son in college.* 我有个儿子在上大学。 □ *Joan is attending a local college.* 琼正在当地一所学院念书。

collide /kəˈlaɪd/ *verb* 动词 (**collides, colliding, collided**)
to crash into another person or vehicle 碰撞；相撞: *The two cars collided.* 两辆车撞到了一起。 □ *He ran up the stairs and collided with Susan.* 他跑上楼梯，撞到了苏珊。

collie /ˈkɒli/ *countable noun* 可数名词
(also 亦作 **collie dog**) a dog with long hair and a long, narrow nose 柯利犬

collision /kəˈlɪʒən/ *noun* 名词
when two moving objects hit each other 碰撞；相撞: *Many passengers were killed in the collision.* 这起相撞事故造成许多乘客身亡。

colon /ˈkəʊlən/ *countable noun* 可数名词
1 a mark (:) that you can use to join parts of a sentence 冒号
2 the lower part of the tube that takes waste out of your body 结肠: *colon cancer* 结肠癌

colony /ˈkɒləni/ *countable noun* 可数名词 (**colonies**)
an area or a group of people that is controlled by another country 殖民地: *Massachusetts was a British colony.* 马萨诸塞州曾是英国殖民地。

colour[1] /ˈkʌlə/ *countable noun* 可数名词
the way that something looks in the light.

Red, blue and green are colours. 颜色：*'What colour is the car?'* — *'It's red.'* "那辆车是什么颜色的？" — "红色。" □ *Judy's favourite colour is pink.* 朱迪最喜欢粉色。

colour² /ˈkʌlə/ *adjective* 形容词
used for describing a television or photograph that shows things in all their colours, and not just in black, white and grey（电视画面或照片）彩色的：*The book is illustrated with colour photos.* 这本书有彩色照片的插图。

colour³ /ˈkʌlə/ *verb* 动词 (**colours, colouring, coloured**)
colour something or **colour something in** to use pens or pencils to add colour to a picture 为某物上色；给某物填色：*The children coloured in their pictures.* 孩子们给自己的画儿涂上了颜色。

coloured /ˈkʌləd/ *adjective* 形容词
having a particular colour or colours 有颜色的；彩色的：*They wore brightly coloured hats.* 她们戴着颜色艳丽的帽子。

colourful /ˈkʌləfʊl/ *adjective* 形容词
having bright colours or a lot of different colours 色彩鲜艳的；五颜六色的：*The people wore colourful clothes.* 人们穿着五颜六色的衣服。

column /ˈkɒləm/ *countable noun* 可数名词
1 a tall, solid structure that supports part of a building（支撑建筑物的）柱，柱子：*The house has six white columns across the front.* 这栋房子正面有6根白色的柱子。
2 a narrow section of writing on one side or part of a page, for example in a newspaper（报纸等的）栏：*The left column contains a list of names.* 左栏有一份名单。

column 栏   **column** 柱

coma /ˈkəʊmə/ *countable noun* 可数名词
when someone is not conscious for a long time 昏迷：*She was in a coma for seven weeks.* 她昏迷了7周。

comb /kəʊm/ *countable noun* 可数名词
a thin piece of plastic or metal with teeth (= narrow, pointed parts). You use a comb to make your hair tidy. 梳子● **comb** *verb* 动词 (**combs, combing, combed**)：*He combed his hair carefully.* 他仔细梳了梳头发。

combat¹ /ˈkɒmbæt/ *uncountable noun* 不可数名词
fighting during a war 战斗：*More than 16 million men died in combat.* *1,600 多万人阵亡。

combat² /ˈkɒmbæt/ *verb* 动词 (**combats, combating** or 或 **combatting, combated** or 或 **combatted**)
to try to stop something from happening 与⋯斗争；打击：*They've introduced new laws to combat crime.* 他们推行新法打击犯罪。

combination /ˌkɒmbɪˈneɪʃən/ *countable noun* 可数名词
a mixture of things 结合；混合；联合：*That is an interesting combination of colours.* 那是多种颜色的奇妙混合。

combine /kəmˈbaɪn/ *verb* 动词 (**combines, combining, combined**)
1 to join two or more things together 使混合；使合并：*Combine the flour with 3 tablespoons of water.* 往面粉里加3大汤匙水。
2 to exist together 并存：*Disease and hunger combine to kill thousands of people.* 疾病肆虐再加上饥荒，成千上万的人因此丧命。

come /kʌm/ *verb* 动词 (**comes, coming, came, come**)
1 used for saying that someone or something arrives somewhere, or moves toward you 来；来到：*Two police officers came into the hall.* 两名警察来到大厅。
□ *He came to a door.* 他来到一扇门前。
□ *Eleanor came to see her.* 埃莉诺来看她。
□ *Come here, Tom.* 来这里，汤姆。
2 to happen 发生：*The announcement came after a meeting at the White House.* 白宫召开会议之后发布了这则通告。
3 used for talking about the particular position of someone or something 处于；位列：*I came last in the race.* 这场赛跑我得了最后一名。

come across someone/something to find something or someone, or meet them by

chance 偶然发现某人 / 某物；偶遇某人 / 某物：*I came across a photo of my grandparents when I was looking for my diary.* 我找日记本的时候发现了一张祖父母的合照。

come back to return to a place 返回：*He wants to come back to London.* 他想回伦敦。

come down
1 to fall to the ground 落下；降落：*The rain came down for hours.* 雨下了好几个小时。
2 to become less than before 下降；降低：*Interest rates should come down.* 利率应该下调。

come from something used for saying that someone or something started in a particular place 来自某地：*Nearly half the students come from other countries.* 近乎半数学生来自其他国家。□ *Most of Germany's oil comes from the North Sea.* 德国大部分石油来自北海。

come in to enter a place 进入；进来：*Come in and sit down.* 进来坐下。

come off to be removed 被移走；被移开：*This lid won't come off.* 这盖子打不开。

come on used for encouraging someone to do something or to be quicker 快点儿；加把劲儿：*Come on, or we'll be late.* 快点儿，要不我们会迟到的。

come out when the sun comes out, it appears in the sky because the clouds have moved away（太阳）出现，露出来：*Oh, look! The sun's coming out!* 噢，看！太阳要出来了！

come to something to add up to a particular amount 总计为（某数量）：*Lunch came to £80.* 午餐一共 80 英镑。

come true used when something that you wish for or dream actually happens（愿望或梦想）实现，成真：*My life-long dream has just come true.* 我一生的梦想刚刚实现了。

come up
1 to be mentioned in a conversation 被提及：*The subject came up at work.* 工作中有人提到了这个问题。
2 when the sun comes up, it rises（太阳）升起：*It will be so great watching the sun come up.* 看太阳冉冉升起将是多么美好的事情。

comedian /kəˈmiːdiən/ *countable noun* 可数名词
a person whose job is to make people laugh 喜剧演员：*Who is your favourite comedian?* 你最喜欢哪个喜剧演员？

comedy /ˈkɒmədi/ *countable noun* 可数名词 (**comedies**)
a play, film or television programme that is intended to make people laugh 喜剧：*The film is a romantic comedy.* 这是部浪漫喜剧电影。

comet /ˈkɒmɪt/ *countable noun* 可数名词
a bright object that has a long tail and travels around the sun 彗星

comfort¹ /ˈkʌmfət/ *uncountable noun* 不可数名词
being relaxed, and having no pain or worry 舒适；舒服：*You can sit in comfort while you are watching the show.* 你可以舒服地坐着看演出。
▸ **in comfort** having a pleasant life in which you have everything you need 安逸地；顺心地：*He lived in comfort for the rest of his life.* 他的余生过得很舒心。

comfort² /ˈkʌmfət/ *verb* 动词 (**comforts, comforting, comforted**)
to make someone feel less worried or unhappy 安慰；抚慰：*Ned tried to comfort her.* 内德试着安慰她。

comfortable /ˈkʌmftəbəl/ *adjective* 形容词
1 making you feel physically relaxed 让人舒服的；舒适的：*This is a really comfortable chair.* 这把椅子特别舒服。□ *A home should be comfortable and warm.* 家应该舒适而温暖。
2 feeling physically relaxed 放松的；舒服的：*Lie down on your bed and make yourself comfortable.* 躺到床上，身体放松。
▸ **comfortably** /ˈkʌmftəbli/ *adverb* 副词：*Are you sitting comfortably?* 你坐得舒服吗？

comic¹ /ˈkɒmɪk/ *adjective* 形容词
funny 滑稽的；好笑的：*It is one of the greatest comic films.* 这是最伟大的喜剧电影之一。

comic² /ˈkɒmɪk/ *countable noun* 可数名词
a magazine that contains stories told in pictures 连环画杂志；漫画书

comical /ˈkɒmɪkəl/ *adjective* 形容词
funny or silly, and making you want to laugh 滑稽的；搞笑的：*They had slightly comical smiles on their faces.* 他们脸上的笑容有点儿搞笑。

comma /ˈkɒmə/ *countable noun* 可数名词
the punctuation mark (,) 逗号

command¹ /kəˈmɑːnd/ *countable noun* 可数名词
1 an official instruction to do something 命令：*He shouted a command at his*

soldiers. 他吼着向士兵下达了命令。 □ He obeyed the command. 他服从了命令。
2 an instruction that you give to a computer （向计算机下达的）命令，指令: The keyboard command 'Ctrl+S' saves your document. 键盘命令 Ctrl 键加 S 键可以保存文件。

command² /kəˈmɑːnd/ verb 动词 (**commands, commanding, commanded**)
to tell someone that they must do something 命令: He commanded his soldiers to attack. 他命令士兵进攻。

commence /kəˈmens/ verb 动词 (**commences, commencing, commenced**)
to begin, or begin something (formal 正式) 开始；开始做: The school year commences in the autumn. 学年秋季开始。 □ The company commenced production in August. 公司于 8 月开始生产。

comment /ˈkɒment/ verb 动词 (**comments, commenting, commented**)
to give your opinion or say something about something 发表意见；作出评论: Mr Cooke has not commented on these reports. 库克先生还未对这些报道发表看法。
● **comment** noun 名词: It is difficult to make a comment about the situation. 这种局面不好评论。

commerce /ˈkɒmɜːs/ uncountable noun 不可数名词
the buying and selling of large amounts of things 贸易；商业: There are rules for international commerce. 国际贸易有规可依。

commercial¹ /kəˈmɜːʃəl/ adjective 形容词
relating to the buying and selling of things 贸易的；商业的: New York is a centre of commercial activity. 纽约是商业活动中心。

commercial² /kəˈmɜːʃəl/ countable noun 可数名词
an advertisement on television or radio （电视或广播中的）商业广告: There are too many commercials on TV these days. 如今电视上的商业广告太多了。

commit /kəˈmɪt/ verb 动词 (**commits, committing, committed**)
to do something illegal 犯（罪）；做（坏事）: I have never committed a crime. 我从来没犯过罪。

commitment /kəˈmɪtmənt/ noun 名词
1 uncountable 不可数 the work you do for something that you think is important 奉献；投入: They praised him for his commitment to peace. 他献身于和平事业，受到了他们

的赞扬。
2 countable 可数 a promise to do something 承诺；保证: We made a commitment to work together. 我们承诺要一起工作。

committee /kəˈmɪti/ countable noun 可数名词
a group of people who meet to make decisions or plans for a larger group 委员会: I was on the tennis club committee for 20 years. 我在网球俱乐部委员会工作了 20 年。

common /ˈkɒmən/ adjective 形容词
1 found in large numbers or happening often 常见的；普遍的: Hansen is a common name in Norway. 汉森在挪威是个常见的名字。 □ What is the most common cause of road accidents? 道路交通事故最常见的原因是什么？
▶ **commonly** /ˈkɒmənli/ adverb 副词: Parsley is a commonly used herb. 欧芹是一种常用香草。
2 shared by two or more people or groups 共有的；共同的: The United States and Canada share a common language. 美国和加拿大说同一种语言。
in common with similar qualities or interests 相似；相像: He had nothing in common with his sister. 他和他姐姐一点儿都不像。

common sense also 亦作 **commonsense** uncountable noun 不可数名词
the ability to make good judgements and to be sensible 常识: Use common sense: don't leave valuable items in your car. 要有常识：不要把贵重物品留在车内。

communicate /kəˈmjuːnɪkeɪt/ verb 动词 (**communicates, communicating, communicated**)
to share information with other people, for example by speaking or writing 交流；沟通: They communicate with their friends by mobile phone. 他们用手机和朋友们交流。 □ They use email to communicate with each other. 他们通过电子邮件互相交流。
▶ **communication** /kəˌmjuːnɪˈkeɪʃən/ uncountable noun 不可数名词: Good communication is important in business. 做生意善于沟通很重要。

communications /kəˌmjuːnɪˈkeɪʃənz/ plural noun 复数名词
a way of sending or receiving information

通信: *a communications satellite* 通信卫星

communism /ˈkɒmjʊˌnɪzəm/ also 亦作 **Communism** *uncountable noun* 不可数名词
the political idea that all people are equal and workers should control how things are produced 共产主义

communist /ˈkɒmjʊnɪst/ also 亦作 **Communist** *countable noun* 可数名词
someone who supports the ideas of communism 共产主义者: *He was a committed communist and an economics student at the University of Gdansk.* 他是坚定的共产主义者，就读于格但斯克大学经济学专业。• **communist** *adjective* 形容词: *She is a member of the Communist Party.* 她是一名共产党员。

community /kəˈmjuːnɪti/ *noun* 名词 (**communities**)
1 *singular* 单数 a group of people who live in a particular area 社区: *When you live in a small community, everyone knows you.* 住在小社区，人人都认识你。
2 *countable* 可数 a group of people who are similar in some way, or have similar interests 群体；团体: *These results are of great interest to the scientific community.* 科学界对这些结果特别感兴趣。

commute /kəˈmjuːt/ *verb* 动词 (**commutes, commuting, commuted**)
to travel to work or school 乘车上下班（或上下学）；通勤: *Mike commutes to Miami every day.* 迈克每天坐车去迈阿密上班。
▶ **commuter** /kəˈmjuːtə/ *countable noun* 可数名词: *In Tokyo, most commuters travel to work on trains.* 在东京，大多数通勤者搭乘火车上班。

compact /kəmˈpækt/ *adjective* 形容词
small, or taking up very little space 小型的；袖珍的: *The garden is compact and easy to manage.* 花园很小，容易打理。

compact disc *countable noun* 可数名词
a small shiny disc that contains music or information. The short form **CD** is also used. 小型光碟，光盘，激光唱片（缩写形式为 CD）

companion /kəmˈpænjən/ *countable noun* 可数名词
someone who you spend time with or travel with 伴侣；同伴；同行者: *Her travelling companion was her father.* 她的旅伴是她爸爸。

company /ˈkʌmpəni/ *noun* 名词 (**companies**)
1 *countable* 可数 a business that sells goods or services 公司: *Her mother works for an insurance company.* 她妈妈在一家保险公司上班。
2 *uncountable* 不可数 having another person or other people with you 陪伴: *I always enjoy Nick's company.* 我一向喜欢有尼克陪着我。

keep someone company to spend time with someone and stop them from feeling lonely or bored 陪伴某人: *I'll stay here and keep Emma company.* 我会待在这里陪着埃玛。

comparable /ˈkɒmpərəbəl/ *adjective* 形容词
similar 类似的；同类的: *House prices here are comparable to prices in Paris and Tokyo.* 这里的房价与巴黎和东京的差不多。

comparative /kəmˈpærətɪv/ *adjective* 形容词
used in grammar when talking about the form of an adjective or adverb that shows that one thing has more of a particular quality than something else has. For example, 'bigger' is the comparative form of 'big'. Compare with **superlative**.（语法中）比较级的（比较 superlative）
• **comparative** *countable noun* 可数名词: *The comparative of 'pretty' is 'prettier'.* *pretty 的比较级为 prettier。

compare /kəmˈpeə/ *verb* 动词 (**compares, comparing, compared**)
to consider how things are different and how they are similar 比较: *I use the Internet to compare prices.* 我通过因特网比较价格。

comparison /kəmˈpærɪsən/ *noun* 名词
a study of the differences between two things 比较；对照: *The information helps parents to make comparisons between schools.* 该信息有助于家长比较各所学校。

compartment /kəmˈpɑːtmənt/ *countable noun* 可数名词
1 a separate part inside a box or a bag where you keep things（盒、包的）格，隔层: *The case has a separate compartment for camera accessories.* 这个盒子有单独的隔层放相机配件。
2 one of the separate spaces in a railway carriage (= section of a train)（火车车厢的）隔间: *The family always sat in the first-class compartment.* 这家人总是坐一

等包厢。

compass /ˈkʌmpəs/ *countable noun* 可数名词 (**compasses**)
a thing that people use for finding directions (north, south, east and west), with a needle that always points north 指南针；罗盘：*You'll need a map and a compass.* 你会用到地图和指南针。
→ Look at picture on P9 参见彩插第 9 页

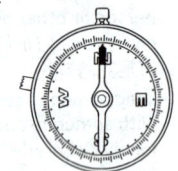
compass 指南针

compasses /ˈkʌmpəsɪz/ *plural noun* 复数名词
a piece of equipment that you use for drawing circles. It is made of two long thin parts, joined together at the top in the shape of the letter V. 圆规
→ Look at picture on P1 参见彩插第 1 页

compatible /kəmˈpætɪbəl/ *adjective* 形容词
1 able to work well together 兼容的：*Is your MP3 player compatible with your computer?* 你的 MP3 播放器和电脑兼容吗？
2 having a good relationship with someone because you have similar opinions and interests 合得来的；相处融洽的：*Hannah and I are very compatible.* 汉娜和我非常合得来。

compete /kəmˈpiːt/ *verb* 动词 (**competes, competing, competed**)
to participate in a contest or a game 竞争；参加比赛：*He will compete in the 10km road race again this year.* 他今年将再次参加 10 公里公路赛跑。

competence /ˈkɒmpɪtəns/ *uncountable noun* 不可数名词
the ability to do something well 能力；才干：*No one doubts his competence.* 没有人质疑他的能力。

competent /ˈkɒmpɪtənt/ *adjective* 形容词
able to do something well 有能力的；有才干的：*He is a confident, competent driver.* 他开起车来很自信，并且车艺了得。

competition /ˌkɒmpɪˈtɪʃən/ *noun* 名词
an event in which people try to show that they are best at an activity 竞赛；比赛：*The two boys entered a surfing competition.* 这两个男孩报名参加了冲浪比赛。

competitive /kəmˈpetɪtɪv/ *adjective* 形容词
wanting to be more successful than other people 好胜的：*He has always been very competitive.* 他一直很好胜。

competitor /kəmˈpetɪtə/ *countable noun* 可数名词
a person who takes part in a competition 选手；参赛者：*One of the oldest competitors won the silver medal.* 最年长选手中的一位赢得了银牌。

complain /kəmˈpleɪn/ *verb* 动词 (**complains, complaining, complained**)
to say that you are not satisfied with someone or something 抱怨；发牢骚：*Voters complained about the election result.* 选民对选举结果有怨言。□ *I shouldn't complain; I've got a good job.* 我不该抱怨的，我已经找到了一份好工作。□ *'Someone should do something about it,' he complained.* "应该有人来管管。"他抱怨道。
complain of something to say that you have a pain or an illness 主诉（病情）：*He went to the hospital, complaining of a sore neck.* 他去了医院，说脖子疼。

complaint /kəmˈpleɪnt/ *noun* 名词
when you say that you are not satisfied 抱怨；投诉：*The police received several complaints about the noise.* 警方收到数起噪音投诉。

complete¹ /kəmˈpliːt/ *adjective* 形容词
1 in every way 完全的；全部的：*His birthday party was a complete surprise.* 他的生日聚会完全是个惊喜。
▶ **completely** /kəmˈpliːtli/ *adverb* 副词：*Thousands of homes have been completely destroyed.* 数千房屋彻底被毁。
2 finished 完成的；结束的：*The project is not yet complete.* 这个项目尚未结束。

complete² /kəmˈpliːt/ *verb* 动词 (**completes, completing, completed**)
1 to finish a task 完成；结束：*We hope to complete the project by January.* 我们希望到 1 月份能完成这个项目。
2 to write the necessary information on a form 填写（表格）：*Complete the first part of the application form.* 填写申请表的第一部分。

complex¹ /ˈkɒmpleks/ *adjective* 形容词
having many parts and difficult to understand 复杂的：*Crime is a complex problem.* 犯罪是个复杂的问题。

complex² /ˈkɒmpleks/ *countable noun* 可数名词 (**complexes**)
a group of buildings used for a particular purpose 综合楼，建筑综合体（有特定用途的建筑群）：*a large industrial complex* 大型

工业综合楼

complexion /kəmˈplekʃən/ *countable noun* 可数名词
the natural colour of the skin on someone's face 面色；脸色：*She had a pale complexion.* 她面色苍白。

complicate /ˈkɒmplɪˌkeɪt/ *verb* 动词 (**complicates, complicating, complicated**)
to make something more difficult to understand or deal with 使复杂；使难以理解；使难以处理：*Please don't complicate the situation.* 请不要把局面复杂化。

complicated /ˈkɒmplɪˌkeɪtɪd/ *adjective* 形容词
having many parts, and difficult to understand 复杂的；难懂的：*The situation is very complicated.* 情况非常复杂。

complication /ˌkɒmplɪˈkeɪʃən/ *countable noun* 可数名词
a problem or difficulty 问题；困难：*There were a number of complications.* 有不少问题。

compliment /ˈkɒmplɪmənt/ *countable noun* 可数名词
something nice that you say to someone, for example about their appearance 赞美；称赞：*He was very nice to me and paid me several compliments.* 他对我很友善，夸了我好几句。● **compliment** /ˈkɒmplɪˌment/ *verb* 动词 (**compliments, complimenting, complimented**)：*They complimented me on the way I looked.* 他们夸我好看。

compose /kəmˈpəʊz/ *verb* 动词 (**composes, composing, composed**)
to write a piece of music, a speech or a letter 创作（音乐）；写（讲稿或信）：*Vivaldi composed a large number of concertos.* 维瓦尔第创作了大量协奏曲。
be composed of something to be made or formed from different parts or members 由某事物构成：*Water is composed of oxygen and hydrogen.* 水由氧和氢构成。

composer /kəmˈpəʊzə/ *countable noun* 可数名词
a person who writes music 作曲家：*Mozart and Beethoven were great composers.* 莫扎特和贝多芬是伟大的作曲家。

composition /ˌkɒmpəˈzɪʃən/ *noun* 名词
1 *countable* 可数 a piece of music or writing 音乐作品；文章；作文
2 *uncountable* 不可数 the parts or members of something 组成；构成：*They study the chemical composition of the food we eat.* 他们研究我们所吃食物的化学构成。

compound /ˈkɒmpaʊnd/ *countable noun* 可数名词
1 a substance that is made from two or more elements 化合物：*Dioxins are chemical compounds that are produced when material is burned.* 二噁英是物质燃烧时形成的化合物。
2 a word that is made from two or more other words, for example 'fire engine' 复合词（如 fire engine） ● **compound** *adjective* 形容词：*a compound noun* 复合名词

comprehend /ˌkɒmprɪˈhend/ *verb* 动词 (**comprehends, comprehending, comprehended**)
to understand something (*formal* 正式)理解；领悟：*I don't think you fully comprehend what's happening.* 我觉得你没有完全弄清楚目前的情况。

comprehension /ˌkɒmprɪˈhenʃən/ *uncountable noun* 不可数名词
the ability to understand something (*formal* 正式) 理解力；领悟力：*a reading comprehension test* 阅读理解测试

comprehensive school /ˌkɒmprɪˈhensɪv ˌskuːl/ *countable noun* 可数名词
in the UK, a school for students aged 11-18 （英国面向 11—18 岁学生的）综合中学

compromise /ˈkɒmprəˌmaɪz/ *noun* 名词
a situation in which people accept something slightly different from what they really want 妥协；让步；折中：*Try to reach a compromise between the demands of work and family life.* 尽量在工作需要和家庭生活之间找到一个折中点。

compulsory /kəmˈpʌlsəri/ *adjective* 形容词
used for saying that you must do something 义务的；强制的：*In Australia, voting is compulsory.* 在澳大利亚，投票是强制的。

computer /kəmˈpjuːtə/ *countable noun* 可数名词
an electronic machine that can store and deal with large amounts of information 计算机；电脑：*He watched the concert on his computer through the Internet.* 他用电脑在网上观看了那场音乐会。□ *The company installed a £650,000 computer system.* 这家公司安装了一个价值 65 万英镑的计算机系统。
→ Look at picture on P11 参见彩插第 11 页

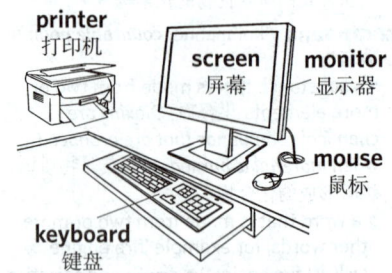

computer 计算机
- **printer** 打印机
- **screen** 屏幕
- **monitor** 显示器
- **mouse** 鼠标
- **keyboard** 键盘

computing /kəm'pju:tɪŋ/ *uncountable noun* 不可数名词
the activity of using a computer and writing programs for it 计算（指计算机应用及编程）: *They offer a course in business and computing.* 他们开设有商业和计算机应用方面的课程。

conceal /kən'si:l/ *verb* 动词 (**conceals, concealing, concealed**)
to hide something or keep it secret 掩盖；隐藏；遮住；掩饰: *The hat concealed her hair.* 帽子遮住了她的头发。□ *Robert could not conceal his happiness.* 罗伯特无法掩饰自己的喜悦之情。

conceive /kən'si:v/ *verb* 动词 (**conceives, conceiving, conceived**)
1 to be able to imagine something or believe it 设想；想象；构思: *I can't even conceive of that amount of money.* 那么多钱我甚至都无法想象。
2 used for describing the moment when a woman becomes pregnant 怀孕；受孕: *They have been trying to conceive for three years now.* 3年来他们一直想要个孩子。□ *The baby was conceived naturally, and is due in October.* 这个宝宝是自然受孕的，预产期在10月份。

concentrate /'kɒnsən,treɪt/ *verb* 动词 (**concentrates, concentrating, concentrated**)
to give something all your attention 全神贯注；聚精会神: *He should concentrate on his studies.* 他应该专心于学业。□ *She had to concentrate hard to win the race.* 要想赢得比赛，她的注意力必须高度集中。

concentration /,kɒnsən'treɪʃən/ *uncountable noun* 不可数名词
giving something all your attention 全神贯注；专心；专注: *At first there is greater concentration on speaking skills.* 起初，更

多的注意力放在讲话技巧上。

concept /'kɒnsept/ *countable noun* 可数名词
an idea about something 概念；观念: *Our laws are based on the concept of fairness.* 我们的法律以公平这个理念为基础。

concern /kən'sɜːn/ *verb* 动词 (**concerns, concerning, concerned**)
1 to worry someone 使担心；使不安: *It concerns me that she hasn't telephoned.* 她没来电话，这让我不安。● **concern** *uncountable noun* 不可数名词: *She expressed concern about my grandfather's health.* 她表达了对我祖父健康状况的关心。
2 to be about a particular subject 涉及；关于: *The book concerns Sandy's two children.* 这本书讲述了桑迪的两个孩子。

concerned /kən'sɜːnd/ *adjective* 形容词
worried 担心的；不安的: *I've been concerned about you recently.* 我最近一直担心你。
be concerned with something to be about something 涉及某事物；关于某事物: *Randolph's work is concerned with the effects of pollution.* 伦道夫的著作论述了污染的影响。

concerning /kən'sɜːnɪŋ/ *preposition* 介词
about something or someone (*formal* 正式) 关于: *Contact Mr Coldwell for more information concerning the class.* 班级详情请联系科德韦尔先生了解。

concert /'kɒnsət/ *countable noun* 可数名词
a performance of music 音乐会: *We attended a concert by the great jazz pianist Harold Mabern.* 我们聆听了伟大爵士钢琴家哈罗德·马本的音乐会。□ *The weekend began with an outdoor rock concert.* 一场室外摇滚音乐会拉开了周末的大幕。

conclude /kən'klu:d/ *verb* 动词 (**concludes, concluding, concluded**)
1 to make a decision after thinking about something carefully 断定；总结；得出（结论）: *We've concluded that it's best to tell her the truth.* 我们最终认为最好告诉她真相。□ *So what can we conclude from this experiment?* 那么我们从这个实验中可以得出什么结论？
2 to end (*formal* 正式) 结束；终止: *The evening concluded with dinner and speeches.* 晚宴和讲话之后，这个夜晚结束了。

conclusion /kən'klu:ʒən/ *noun* 名词
1 *countable* 可数 a decision that you make after thinking carefully about something 结论；推论: *I've come to the conclusion*

concrete – cone

that she's a great musician. 我的结论是她是位伟大的音乐家。

2 *singular* 单数 the ending of a story（故事的）结局，结尾：*What do you understand from the conclusion of the story?* 你从故事结局悟到了什么？
→ Look at picture on P3 参见彩插第 3 页

concrete /ˈkɒŋkriːt/ *uncountable noun* 不可数名词
a hard substance made by mixing a grey powder (= cement) with sand and water. Concrete is used for building. 混凝土：*The hotel is constructed from steel and concrete.* 这家酒店是钢筋混凝土结构。□ *We sat on the concrete floor.* 我们坐在混凝土地面上。

condemn /kənˈdem/ *verb* 动词 (**condemns, condemning, condemned**)
1 to say that something is not acceptable 谴责；指责：*Police condemned the recent violence.* 警方谴责了近期的暴力事件。
2 to give someone a severe punishment 重判（某人）：*He was condemned to life in prison.* 他被判终身监禁。

condition /kənˈdɪʃən/ *noun* 名词
1 *singular* 单数 the state that someone or something is in 状态；状况：*Doctors expect his condition to improve.* 医生预计他情况能好转。□ *The old house is in terrible condition.* 这栋老房子破败不堪。
2 [**conditions**] *plural* 复数 the things that affect people's comfort and safety 条件；环境：*People are living in terrible conditions with little food or water.* 人们缺吃少喝，生活环境恶劣。
3 *countable* 可数 a medical problem 疾病；健康问题：*Doctors think he may have a heart condition.* 医生认为他可能有心脏病。

conditional /kənˈdɪʃənəl/ *singular noun* 单数名词
a type of sentence used for talking about a situation that may exist or happen. Most conditional sentences begin with 'if'. For example 'If you work hard, you'll pass your exams'. 条件句

conduct¹ /kənˈdʌkt/ *verb* 动词 (**conducts, conducting, conducted**)
1 to organize and do an activity or a task 进行；组织；实施：*I decided to conduct an experiment.* 我决定做个实验。
2 to allow heat or electricity to pass through 传导（热或电）：*Clay conducts electricity very well.* 黏土导电性能出色。
3 to stand in front of musicians and direct their performance 指挥（乐队）：*The new musical work was composed and conducted by Leonard Bernstein.* 这部新的音乐作品由伦纳德·伯恩斯坦创作并指挥演奏。

conduct yourself to behave in a particular way 表现：*The way he conducts himself embarrasses the family.* 他的行为让家人难堪。

conduct² /ˈkɒndʌkt/ *uncountable noun* 不可数名词
the way someone behaves (*formal* 正式) 行为；举止：*She won a prize for good conduct in school.* 她因在学校表现优异获得奖励。

conductor /kənˈdʌktə/ *countable noun* 可数名词
1 a person who stands in front of a group of musicians and directs their performance（乐队的）指挥
2 a person on a train whose job is to help passengers and check tickets 列车员

cone /kəʊn/ *countable noun* 可数名词
1 a solid shape with one flat round end and one pointed end 圆锥；锥体：*Orange traffic cones stop people from parking on the bridge.* 橙色交通锥阻止人们在桥上停车。
2 a thin biscuit in the shape of a cone that you put ice cream into and eat 冰激凌脆皮筒：*an ice-cream cone* 一个冰激凌脆皮筒
3 the fruit of a tree such as a pine or fir（松树、冷杉等的）球果：*a pine cone* 一颗松球

cones 圆锥；冰激凌脆皮筒；球果

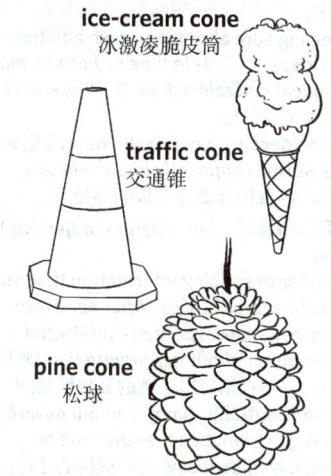

ice-cream cone 冰激凌脆皮筒

traffic cone 交通锥

pine cone 松球

conference /ˈkɒnfrəns/ *countable noun* 可数名词
a long meeting about a particular subject 专题讨论会；研讨会：*We attended a conference on education last month.* 我们上个月参加了一场教育研讨会。

confess /kənˈfes/ *verb* 动词 (**confesses, confessing, confessed**)
to admit that you did something wrong 承认；坦白；供认：*He confessed to seventeen murders.* 他供认了17起谋杀案。 □ *Ed confessed that he broke the window.* 埃德承认他打碎了窗户。

confession /kənˈfeʃən/ *countable noun* 可数名词
when you admit that you have done something wrong 承认；坦白；供认：*I have a confession to make. I lied about my age.* 我有件事要坦白。我谎报了年龄。

confidence /ˈkɒnfɪdəns/ *uncountable noun* 不可数名词
1 the feeling that you can trust someone 信任；信赖：*I have great confidence in you.* 我特别信任你。
2 the feeling of being sure about your own abilities and ideas 自信；信心：*The team is full of confidence.* 全队上下信心满满。
in confidence told as a secret 私下；秘密地：*We told you all these things in confidence.* 这些事我们都是私下跟你说的。

confident /ˈkɒnfɪdənt/ *adjective* 形容词
1 certain that the result of something will be good 坚信的；有信心的：*I am confident that I'll get the job.* 我坚信我会得到那份工作。
2 feeling sure about your own abilities and ideas 自信的：*In time he became more confident and relaxed.* 最终，他变得越来越自信，越来越放松。
▶ **confidently** /ˈkɒnfɪdəntli/ *adverb* 副词：*She walked confidently into the boss's office.* 她自信地走进老板的办公室。

confidential /ˌkɒnfɪˈdenʃəl/ *adjective* 形容词
used for describing information that must be kept secret 机密的：*After her death, some newspapers printed confidential information about her private life.* 她去世以后，一些报纸登出了她的私生活秘闻。
▶ **confidentially** /ˌkɒnfɪˈdenʃəli/ *adverb* 副词：*Any information they give will be treated confidentially.* 他们提供的任何信息都将被当作机密。

confine /kənˈfaɪn/ *verb* 动词 (**confines, confining, confined**)
to keep a person or an animal in a particular place so that they cannot leave it 监禁；关押；把…关起来：*The animals are confined in tiny cages.* 这些动物被关在多个小笼子里。
▶ **confinement** /kənˈfaɪnmənt/ *uncountable noun* 不可数名词：*He read a lot during his two-year confinement in prison.* 狱中两年，他读了不少书。

confirm /kənˈfɜːm/ *verb* 动词 (**confirms, confirming, confirmed**)
1 to say that something is true 证实；证明：*The doctor confirmed that my nose was broken.* 医生证实我的鼻子骨折了。
2 to say that a meeting or an arrangement will definitely happen 确认，确定（会议或安排）：*He called at seven to confirm our appointment.* 他7点钟打电话确认了我们的预约事宜。
▶ **confirmation** /ˌkɒnfəˈmeɪʃən/ *uncountable noun* 不可数名词：*You will receive confirmation of your order by email.* 你会收到确认订单的电子邮件。

conflict[1] /ˈkɒnflɪkt/ *noun* 名词
a fight or an argument between people or countries 冲突；争执：*The military conflict lasted many years.* 这场军事冲突持续了很多年。

conflict[2] /kənˈflɪkt/ *verb* 动词 (**conflicts, conflicting, conflicted**)
to be very different from 冲突；相互矛盾：*His opinions usually conflicted with mine.* 他常与我意见相左。

conform /kənˈfɔːm/ *verb* 动词 (**conforms, conforming, conformed**)
1 to follow a rule or a law 遵守，遵从（规则或法律）：*The lamp conforms to new safety standards.* 这盏灯符合新的安全标准。
2 to behave in a way that most people think is correct or normal 按规矩行事：*At her age, it is important to conform.* 在她这个年纪，行事不出格很重要。

confuse /kənˈfjuːz/ *verb* 动词 (**confuses, confusing, confused**)
1 to think that one thing or person is another thing or person 混淆；搞错：*I always confuse my left with my right.* 我总是左右不分。
▶ **confusion** /kənˈfjuːʒən/ *uncountable*

noun 不可数名词: *Use different colours to avoid confusion.* 用不同的颜色以避免混淆。
2 to make it difficult for someone to understand something 使困惑；把⋯弄糊涂: *My words confused him.* 我的话把他弄糊涂了。

confused /kənˈfjuːzd/ *adjective* 形容词
not understanding what is happening, or not knowing what to do 困惑的；糊涂的: *People are confused about what's going to happen.* 人们搞不懂会发生什么事。
→ Look at picture on P15 参见彩插第 15 页

confusing /kənˈfjuːzɪŋ/ *adjective* 形容词
difficult to understand, making it difficult for people to know what to do 难懂的；令人费解的: *The directions are really confusing.* 这个用法说明真是让人一头雾水。

confusion /kənˈfjuːʒən/ *uncountable noun* 不可数名词
1 a situation in which the facts about something are not clear 困惑；不明: *There's still confusion about the number of students.* 学生人数依然不明。
2 a situation in which a lot of things are happening in a badly organized way 混乱；杂乱: *People were pushing and shouting, and there was confusion everywhere.* 人们推搡吵嚷，到处乱哄哄的。

congratulate /kənˈɡrætʃuˌleɪt/ *verb* 动词 (congratulates, congratulating, congratulated)
to express pleasure about something good that has happened to someone 祝贺；向⋯道贺: *She congratulated him on the birth of his son.* 她祝贺他喜得贵子。
▶ **congratulation** /kənˌɡrætʃuˈleɪʃən/ *uncountable noun* 不可数名词: *We received several letters of congratulation.* 我们收到了几封贺信。

congratulations /kənˌɡrætʃuˈleɪʃənz/ *plural noun* 复数名词
used for congratulating someone 恭喜；祝贺: *Congratulations on your new job.* 恭喜你找到新工作。

conjunction /kənˈdʒʌŋkʃən/ *countable noun* 可数名词
a word that joins together parts of sentences. For example, 'and' and 'or' are conjunctions. 连词

connect /kəˈnekt/ *verb* 动词 (connects, connecting, connected)
to join one thing to another (使)连接: *Next, connect the printer to your computer.* 接下来，把打印机连到电脑上。

connected /kəˈnektɪd/ *adjective* 形容词
used for describing a relationship between things 有关的；有联系的: *She described the problems connected with a high-fat diet.* 她讲了一下高脂饮食会造成的问题。

connection /kəˈnekʃən/ *noun* 名词
1 a relationship between two things, people or groups 关系；联系: *I felt a strong connection between us.* 我感觉我们的关系牢不可破。 □ *Children need to understand the connection between energy and the environment.* 孩子们需要弄清楚能源和环境的关系。
2 *countable* 可数 a way of communicating using the telephone or a computer (通过电话或计算机的)连接，接通: *You'll need a fast Internet connection to view this site.* 网速够快才能浏览这个网站。
3 *countable* 可数 a train, a bus or a plane that leaves after another one arrives and allows you continue your journey by changing from one to the other 联运列车（或巴士、航班）: *My flight was late and I missed the connection.* 航班晚点，我没赶上转机。

conquer /ˈkɒŋkə/ *verb* 动词 (conquers, conquering, conquered)
1 to take complete control of the land of another country or group of people 占领；征服: *Germany conquered France in 1940.* 德国于 1940 年占领了法国。
2 to manage to deal with a problem 克服；攻克: *I've conquered my fear of spiders.* 我已经不再害怕蜘蛛。

conscience /ˈkɒnʃəns/ *countable noun* 可数名词
the part of your mind that tells you if what you are doing is wrong 良心；良知: *My conscience is clear about everything I have done.* 我做的每件事都问心无愧。
have a guilty conscience to feel bad because you know you did something wrong 感到内疚；心怀愧疚: *They have no guilty conscience about downloading music from the Internet without paying.* 他们对不付费就从网上下载音乐没有半点儿愧疚。

conscientious /ˌkɒnʃiˈenʃəs/ *adjective* 形容词
careful to follow rules and do things

conscious – considerate

correctly 认真的；一丝不苟的: *She is very conscientious about doing her homework.* 她做家庭作业很认真。
- ▶ **conscientiously** /ˌkɒnʃiˈenʃəsli/ *adverb* 副词: *He conscientiously exercised every night.* 他每晚都认真锻炼。

conscious /ˈkɒnʃəs/ *adjective* 形容词
awake, and not asleep or unconscious 清醒的；有知觉的: *She was fully conscious soon after the operation.* 手术刚结束不久她就完全恢复了意识。

conscious of something
1 noticing something 注意到某事物的: *She was conscious of Nick watching her across the room.* 她注意到尼克在房间那头看着自己。
2 thinking about something a lot because you think it is important 关注某事物的: *I'm very conscious of my weight.* 我非常关注自己的体重。

consent /kənˈsent/ *verb* 动词 (**consents, consenting, consented**)
to agree to do something or to allow it to happen (*formal* 正式) 同意；允许: *She consented to marry him.* 她同意嫁给他。
- ● **consent** *uncountable noun* 不可数名词: *Pollard finally gave his consent to the police search.* 波拉德最终同意让警方搜查。

consequence /ˈkɒnsɪkwəns/ *countable noun* 可数名词
a result or effect of something that has happened 结果；后果；影响: *She understood the consequences of her actions.* 她明白自己这么做的后果。

consequently /ˈkɒnsɪkwəntli/ *adverb* 副词
as a result (*formal* 正式) 因此；所以: *He worked all night, and consequently he slept during the day.* 他工作了一宿，所以白天补了觉。

conservation /ˌkɒnsəˈveɪʃən/ *uncountable noun* 不可数名词
the activity of taking care of the environment (对环境的) 保护: *wildlife conservation* 野生生物保护

conservative /kənˈsɜːvətɪv/ *adjective* 形容词
not liking changes and new ideas 保守的；守旧的: *People often become more conservative as they get older.* 人常常年纪越大越保守。

Conservative /kənˈsɜːvətɪv/ *adjective* 形容词

belonging to or voting for the Conservative Party in the UK and in some other countries 保守党的；支持保守党的: *Conservative MPs* 下院保守党议员
- ● **Conservative** *countable noun* 可数名词: *The Conservatives won the election.* 保守党赢得了选举。

Con'servative ˌParty *singular noun* 单数名词
one of the three main political parties in the UK (英国) 保守党

conserve /kənˈsɜːv/ *verb* 动词 (**conserves, conserving, conserved**)
1 to use energy or water carefully so that it lasts for a long time 节约（能源或水）: *The factories have closed for the weekend to conserve energy.* 这些工厂周末停工以节约能源。
2 to take care of the environment 保护（环境）: *World leaders agreed to work together to conserve forests.* 各国领导人同意共同努力保护森林。

consider /kənˈsɪdə/ *verb* 动词 (**considers, considering, considered**)
1 to have a particular opinion of a person or thing 认为；看待: *The police consider him to be dangerous.* 警方认为他是危险人物。
2 to think about something carefully 仔细考虑；斟酌: *The president says he's still considering the situation.* 总统说他还在仔细考虑目前的局面。 □ *You should consider the feelings of other people.* 你应该考虑他人的感受。
- ▶ **consideration** /kənˌsɪdəˈreɪʃən/ *uncountable noun* 不可数名词: *After careful consideration, we've decided that a change is necessary.* 经过一番认真思考，我们决定必须要有所改变。

considerable /kənˈsɪdərəbəl/ *adjective* 形容词
great or large (*formal* 正式) 多的；大的: *The land cost a considerable amount of money.* 这块地花了一大笔钱。
- ▶ **considerably** /kənˈsɪdərəbli/ *adverb* 副词: *The king was considerably taller and larger than he was.* 国王比他高不少，也壮很多。

considerate /kənˈsɪdərət/ *adjective* 形容词
thinking and caring about the feelings of other people 体贴的；替人着想的: *He's the most considerate man I know.* 他是我认识的人中最能体谅人的。

consideration /kənˌsɪdəˈreɪʃən/ **uncountable noun** 不可数名词
when you think about and care about the feelings of other people 体贴；替人着想: *Show consideration for your neighbours.* 要体谅邻居。

consist /kənˈsɪst/ **verb** 动词 (**consists, consisting, consisted**)
consist of something to be made up of particular things or people 由…构成；由…组成: *My diet consisted of biscuits and milk.* 我吃饼干，喝牛奶。

consistent /kənˈsɪstənt/ **adjective** 形容词
always behaving in the same way 一致的；一贯的: *Oakley is one of the team's most consistent players.* 奥克利是队中发挥最稳定的队员之一。
▶ **consistency** /kənˈsɪstənsi/ **uncountable noun** 不可数名词: *She scores goals with great consistency.* 她能十分稳定地进球得分。
▶ **consistently** /kənˈsɪstəntli/ **adverb** 副词: *The airline consistently wins awards for its service.* 这家航空公司连续因服务获得嘉奖。

console¹ /kənˈsəʊl/ **verb** 动词 (**consoles, consoling, consoled**)
to try to make someone who is unhappy feel more cheerful 安慰；安抚: *She started to cry and I tried to console her.* 她哭了起来，我努力安抚她。

console 安慰

console² /ˈkɒnsəʊl/ **countable noun** 可数名词
a part of a machine that has many switches and lights. You use these switches to operate the machine, for example to play a computer game. (机器的)操纵台，控制台，仪表板: *A light flashed on the console.* 控制台上有个灯闪了。

consonant /ˈkɒnsənənt/ **countable noun** 可数名词
1 one of the letters of the alphabet that is not a, e, i, o or u 辅音字母: *The word 'book' contains two consonants and two vowels.* *book 这个单词有两个辅音字母和两个元音字母。
2 a sound such as the ones written as **p**, **f**, **n** or **t** 辅音

constant /ˈkɒnstənt/ **adjective** 形容词
happening all the time or always there 持续不断的；一直存在的: *Doctors say she is in constant pain.* 医生说她一直疼。
▶ **constantly** /ˈkɒnstəntli/ **adverb** 副词: *The direction of the wind is constantly changing.* 风向一直在变。

constituency /kənˈstɪtʃuənsi/ **countable noun** 可数名词 (**constituencies**)
an area, and the people who live in it. At an election, the people in the constituency choose one person for the government. 选区: *The two MPs represent very different constituencies.* 这两位下院议员代表两个迥异的选区。

constitution /ˌkɒnstɪˈtjuːʃən/ **countable noun** 可数名词
the laws of a country or an organization 宪法；章程: *The government has to write a new constitution this year.* 政府今年需要新修一部宪法。

construct /kənˈstrʌkt/ **verb** 动词 (**constructs, constructing, constructed**)
to build something 建造；修建: *His company constructed an office building in Nottingham.* 他的公司在诺丁汉建了一栋办公楼。

construction /kənˈstrʌkʃən/ **noun** 名词
1 uncountable 不可数 the process of building something 建造；修建: *He has started construction on a swimming pool.* 他开始修建游泳池。
2 countable 可数 something that has been built 建筑物: *The new theatre is an impressive steel and glass construction.* 新剧院是座恢宏的钢构玻璃建筑。

consult /kənˈsʌlt/ **verb** 动词 (**consults, consulting, consulted**)
to ask someone for their advice 咨询；请教: *Perhaps you should consult a lawyer.* 也许你应该找个律师咨询下。
▶ **consultation** /ˌkɒnsəlˈteɪʃən/ **noun** 名词: *I had a consultation with a doctor.* 我咨询了一位医生。

consultant /kənˈsʌltənt/ **countable noun** 可数名词
someone who gives expert advice on a

subject 顾问；咨询师：*Alex is a young management consultant from Glasgow.* 亚历克斯来自格拉斯哥，是位年轻的管理顾问。

consume /kənˈsjuːm/ *verb* 动词 (**consumes, consuming, consumed**)
1 to eat or drink something (*formal* 正式) 吃；喝：*Martha consumed a box of biscuits every day.* 玛莎每天吃一盒饼干。
2 to use fuel, energy or time 消耗，耗费（燃料、能源或时间）：*Airlines consume huge amounts of fuel every day.* 航空公司每天都要消耗大量燃料。

consumer /kənˈsjuːmə/ *countable noun* 可数名词
a person who buys something or uses a service 消费者；顾客；客户：*What are my consumer rights?* 我作为消费者有哪些权利？

contact¹ /ˈkɒntækt/ *uncountable noun* 不可数名词
meeting or communicating with someone 联系；联络：*I don't have much contact with teenagers.* 我和青少年接触不多。□ *Anita has not been in contact with us since last year.* 去年开始，安尼塔没再联系过我们。

contact² /ˈkɒntækt/ *verb* 动词 (**contacts, contacting, contacted**)
to telephone someone or send them a message or letter（通过电话、邮件等）联系，联络：*The girl's parents contacted the police.* 这名女孩的父母报了警。

ˈ**contact ˌlens** *countable noun* 可数名词 (**contact lenses**)
a small, very thin piece of plastic that you put on your eyes to help you see better 隐形眼镜

contagious /kənˈteɪdʒəs/ *adjective* 形容词
used for describing a disease that passes easily from one person to another when they touch. Compare with **infectious**.（病）接触传染的（比较 infectious）：*The disease is highly contagious.* 这种病传染性很强。

contain /kənˈteɪn/ *verb* 动词 (**contains, containing, contained**)
to have other things inside 包含；含有：*The envelope contained a Christmas card.* 信封里有一张圣诞贺卡。

container /kənˈteɪnə/ *countable noun* 可数名词
a box that is used for holding or storing things 容器：*Store the food in a plastic container.* 把食物保存在一个塑料容器里。

contemporary¹ /kənˈtemprəri/ *adjective* 形容词
existing now, or at the same time as someone or something else 当代的；同时期的；同时代的：*contemporary art* 当代艺术

contemporary² /kənˈtemprəri/ *countable noun* 可数名词 (**contemporaries**)
a person who is, or was, alive at the same time as someone else 同时期的人；同时代的人

content /kənˈtent/ *adjective* 形容词
happy or satisfied 开心的；满足的；满意的：*He says his daughter is quite content.* 他说他女儿相当满意。

contented /kənˈtentɪd/ *adjective* 形容词
happy and satisfied 满足的；满意的：*Richard was a very contented baby.* 理查德是个非常好哄的宝宝。

contents /ˈkɒntents/ *plural noun* 复数名词
1 the things inside a container（容器的）内容：*Empty the contents of the can into a bowl.* 把罐里的东西倒进碗里。
2 the different chapters and sections of a book 目录：*There is no table of contents.* 没有目录。

contest /ˈkɒntest/ *countable noun* 可数名词
a competition or a game 比赛；竞赛：*It was an exciting contest.* 这是一场精彩的比赛。

contestant /kənˈtestənt/ *countable noun* 可数名词
a person who takes part in a competition or a game 选手；参赛者：*Contestants on the TV show have to answer six questions correctly.* 该电视节目的参赛者需要答对6道题。

context /ˈkɒntekst/ *noun* 名词
1 the situation in which an event happens（事件的）背景，情景：*Don't use this sort of language in a business context.* 商务活动中不要使用这类语言。
2 the words and sentences that come before and after a particular word or sentence, that help you to understand its meaning 语境；上下文

continent /ˈkɒntɪnənt/ *countable noun* 可数名词
a very large area of land, such as Africa or Asia 洲；大陆
→ Look at picture on P9 参见彩插第9页
▶ **continental** /ˌkɒntɪˈnentəl/ *adjective* 形容词：*Mount Whitney is the highest*

mountain in continental United States. 惠特尼山是美国本土最高峰。

continual /kənˈtɪnjuəl/ *adjective* 形容词
happening without stopping, or happening very often 不间断的；不停的: *The team has had almost continual success since last year.* 自从去年起，这支队伍几乎连战连捷。
▶ **continually** /kənˈtɪnjuəli/ *adverb* 副词: *Gemma cried almost continually when she was a baby.* 杰玛婴儿时几乎哭个不停。 ☐ *Malcolm was continually changing his mind.* 马尔科姆不停地改变主意。

continuation /kənˌtɪnjuˈeɪʃən/ *uncountable noun* 不可数名词
the fact that something continues to happen or to exist 不间断；延续: *We do not support the continuation of the war.* 我们不支持继续打仗。

continue /kənˈtɪnjuː/ *verb* 动词 (continues, continuing, continued)
1 to not stop 持续: *The war continued for another four years.* 这场仗又打了 4 年。
2 to not stop doing something 持续做: *They continue to fight for justice.* 他们一直为正义而斗争。
3 to start again 再开始: *The trial continues today.* 审判今天继续进行。
4 to start doing something again 继续做；接着做: *She looked up for a minute and then continued drawing.* 她抬起头看了一会儿，然后又接着画起来。
5 to keep going in a particular direction (顺着某方向)一直走，延伸: *He continued rapidly up the path.* 他沿着这条小路快速往前走。

continuous /kənˈtɪnjuəs/ *adjective* 形容词
1 happening over a long time without stopping 不间断的；持续的: *They heard continuous gunfire.* 他们听到持续的炮火声。
▶ **continuously** /kənˈtɪnjuəsli/ *adverb* 副词: *The police are working continuously on the case.* 警方一直在调查这起案件。
2 with no spaces 没有间隔的；连续的: *There was a continuous queue of cars outside in the street.* 外面街上小汽车一辆接着一辆排起了长队。
3 used for describing a form of the verb that is made using the auxiliary 'be' and the present participle, as in 'I'm going on holiday'(动词)进行式的

contract /ˈkɒntrækt/ *countable noun* 可数名词
an official agreement between two companies or two people 合同；合约: *He signed a contract to play for the team for two years.* 他和该队签了两年合同。

contraction /kənˈtrækʃən/ *countable noun* 可数名词
a short form of a word or words (词的)缩约形式: *'It's' (with an apostrophe) can be used as a contraction for 'it is'.* 带撇号的 it's 可用作 it is 的缩约形式。

contradict /ˌkɒntrəˈdɪkt/ *verb* 动词 (contradicts, contradicting, contradicted)
to say that what someone has just said is wrong 反驳；否认；驳斥: *She looked surprised, but she did not contradict him.* 她面露惊讶，但是并没有反驳他。

contrary /ˈkɒntrəri/ *adjective* 形容词
completely different from something else 相反的: *Contrary to what people think, light exercise makes you less hungry.* 与大家的认知相反，轻度锻炼可减轻饥饿感。
on the contrary used when you disagree with something and you are going to say that the opposite is true 相反: *'People just don't do things like that.' — 'On the contrary, they do them all the time.'* "人们根本不会做那样的事。"——"相反，人们一直在做。"

contrast¹ /ˈkɒntrɑːst/ *noun* 名词
a clear difference between two or more people or things 反差；对照；对比: *There is a clear contrast between the two men.* 那两个人反差明显。

contrast² /kənˈtrɑːst/ *verb* 动词 (contrasts, contrasting, contrasted)
to show the differences between things 对比；对照: *In this section we contrast four different ideas.* 我们在这部分要对比 4 种不同的观点。

contribute /kənˈtrɪbjuːt/ *verb* 动词 (contributes, contributing, contributed)
to help to pay for something 捐助；捐献；援助: *The U.S. is contributing $4 billion to the project.* 美国将为该项目出资 40 亿美元。☐ *If you are buying her a present, you must let me contribute.* 要是你打算买礼物给她，一定让我也凑个份子。
▶ **contributor** /kənˈtrɪbjətər/ *countable noun* 可数名词: *The financial services industry is a major contributor to the economy.* 金融服务业为经济发展作出了重要贡献。

contribution /ˌkɒntrɪˈbjuːʃən/ ***countable noun*** 可数名词
money that someone gives to help to pay for something 捐款；捐资：*He made a £5,000 contribution to the charity.* 他向慈善机构捐款 5,000 英镑。

control[1] /kənˈtrəʊl/ ***noun*** 名词
1 ***uncountable*** 不可数 the power to make all the important decisions about something 控制权；支配权：*He took control of every situation.* 任何情况都要听他指挥。
2 ***uncountable*** 不可数 the ability to make a person or machine do what you want them to do（对人或机器的）控制力，支配力：*He lost control of his car.* 他的车失控了。
3 ***countable*** 可数 a switch you use in order to operate a machine 控制器；开关；闸：*You operate the controls without looking at them.* 你没有看着开关进行操作。
in control having the power to make all the important decisions about something 有控制权的；有支配权的：*She feels that she's in control of her life again.* 她觉得生活又在自己的掌控中了。
out of control used for describing something that people cannot deal with 失去控制的；不受控制的：*The fire was out of control.* 火势失控。
under control used for describing something that people can deal with 受控制的；在控制之下的：*The situation is under control.* 局面在掌控之中。

control[2] /kənˈtrəʊl/ ***verb*** 动词 (**controls, controlling, controlled**)
1 to have the power to make all the important decisions about something 控制；掌管；支配：*He controls the largest company in California.* 他掌管着加利福尼亚最大的公司。
2 to make a person or machine do what you want them to do 操纵，控制（人或机器）：*There was a computer system to control the gates.* 大门由电脑系统控制。
▫ *My parents couldn't control me.* 我爸妈管不了我。

controversial /ˌkɒntrəˈvɜːʃəl/ ***adjective*** 形容词
used for describing people or things that people argue about or disagree with 有争议的；引起争议的：*In business, I try to stay away from controversial subjects.* 工作中我尽量避开有争议的话题。

controversy /ˈkɒntrəvɜːsi, kənˈtrɒvəsi/ ***uncountable noun*** 不可数名词
when people argue about something, or disapprove of it 争议；争论：*The TV show caused controversy when it was shown last year.* 这档电视节目去年播出时引发了争论。

convenience /kənˈviːniəns/ ***countable noun*** 可数名词
a piece of equipment designed to make your life easier 便利设施：*This flat includes all the modern conveniences.* 这套公寓里现代化便利设施一应俱全。
for your convenience done in a way that is helpful for you 为了方便您：*We include an envelope for your convenience.* 我们附上了信封以方便您回复。

convenient /kənˈviːniənt/ ***adjective*** 形容词
1 useful for a particular purpose 方便的；便利的：*This is a convenient place to get coffee before work.* 这里上班前买杯咖啡很方便。
▶ **convenience** /kənˈviːniəns/ ***uncountable noun*** 不可数名词：*They may use a credit card for convenience.* 方便起见，他们可能会使用信用卡。
▶ **conveniently** /kənˈviːniəntli/ ***adverb*** 副词：*The house is conveniently located close to the railway station.* 这所房子位于火车站附近，出行便利。
2 used for describing a time when you are available to do something（时间上）方便的，合适的：*She will try to arrange a convenient time.* 她将尽量安排一个合适的时间。

conventional /kənˈvenʃənəl/ ***adjective*** 形容词
1 behaving in a way that is considered to be normal by most people 传统的；遵循惯例的：*I've always been quite conventional; I work hard and behave properly.* 我一直来挺循规蹈矩的：努力工作，规矩做人。
2 used for describing a method or product that is usually used（方法或产品）常用的，常规的：*In a conventional oven, bake at 200°C for 30 minutes.* 用常规烤箱以 200 摄氏度烤 30 分钟。

conversation /ˌkɒnvəˈseɪʃən/ ***countable noun*** 可数名词
an occasion when you talk to someone about something 交谈；谈话：*I had an interesting conversation with him.* 我和他有一番有趣的谈话。

convert /kən'vɜ:t/ *verb* 动词 (**converts, converting, converted**)
to change something into a different form 改变；转变：*The signal will be converted into electronic form.* 信号会被转化为电子形式。□ *He wants to convert the building into a hotel.* 他想把这栋建筑改成宾馆。

convict /kən'vɪkt/ *verb* 动词 (**convicts, convicting, convicted**)
to find someone guilty of a crime in a court of law 给…定罪；宣判…有罪：*He was convicted of murder.* 他被判谋杀罪名成立。

convince /kən'vɪns/ *verb* 动词 (**convinces, convincing, convinced**)
1 to persuade someone to do something 说服；劝服：*He convinced her to marry Tom.* 他说服她嫁给汤姆。
2 to make someone believe that something is true or that it exists 使相信；使确信；使信服：*The new players have convinced me of their ability.* 新队员已经向我证明了他们的能力。
▶ **convinced** /kən'vɪnst/ *adjective* 形容词：*She was convinced that the diamonds were real.* 她相信了那些是真钻石。

cook¹ /kʊk/ *verb* 动词 (**cooks, cooking, cooked**)
to prepare and heat food 烹调；烹饪：*I have to go and cook dinner.* 我得去做晚饭。□ *Let the vegetables cook for about 10 minutes.* 让蔬菜炖上 10 分钟左右。

> **LANGUAGE HELP 语言提示**
> **Cooking verbs:** You **roast** meat in an oven. You **bake** bread and cakes. You can **boil** vegetables in hot water. You can **fry** meat and vegetables in oil. You can also **grill** meat directly under or over a flame. 烹饪类动词：烤箱烤肉用 roast，烘焙糕点用 bake，热水煮菜用 boil，油里煎炸肉或蔬菜用 fry，直接在火上下烤肉用 grill。

cook² /kʊk/ *countable noun* 可数名词
a person who prepares and cooks food 厨师；做饭的人：*I'm a terrible cook.* 我做饭很难吃。

cookbook /'kʊkbʊk/ *countable noun* 可数名词
a book that tells you how to prepare different meals 食谱；烹饪书

cooker /'kʊkə/ *countable noun* 可数名词
a piece of kitchen equipment that is used for cooking food 炉灶；灶具

cookie /'kʊki/ *countable noun* 可数名词
(*American* 美国英语)
→ see 见 **biscuit**

cooking /'kʊkɪŋ/ *uncountable noun* 不可数名词
1 the activity of preparing food 做饭：*He did the cooking and cleaning.* 他负责做饭和打扫卫生。
2 food that is cooked in a particular way 饭菜；菜肴：*The restaurant specializes in Italian cooking.* 这家饭店专门做意大利菜。

cool¹ /ku:l/ *adjective* 形容词 (**cooler, coolest**)
1 having a low temperature, but not cold 凉的；凉爽的：*I felt the cool air on my neck.* 我脖子感觉到了凉风。□ *The water was cool.* 水是凉的。
2 calm 沉着的；冷静的；平静的：*You have to remain cool in very difficult situations.* 面对十分困难的局面，你得保持冷静。
3 fashionable and interesting (*informal* 非正式) 酷的；时尚的：*I met some really cool people last night.* 昨晚我遇见了一些特别酷的人。□ *She had really cool boots.* 她穿着非常时尚的靴子。

cool² /ku:l/ *verb* 动词 (**cools, cooling, cooled**)
to become lower in temperature 变凉；冷却；降温：*Drain the meat and allow it to cool.* 把肉沥干水，让它冷却。

cool down
1 to become lower in temperature 变凉；冷却；降温：*Once it cools down, you'll be able to touch it.* 等温度降下来，你就可以摸了。
2 to become less angry 平静下来；冷静下来：*He has had time to cool down.* 他有时间平静下来。

cooperate /kəʊ'ɒpəˌreɪt/ *verb* 动词 (**cooperates, cooperating, cooperated**)
to work with or help someone 合作；协作：*He finally agreed to cooperate with the police.* 他最终同意和警方合作。
▶ **cooperative** /kəʊ'ɒpərətɪv/ *adjective* 形容词：*I made an effort to be cooperative.* 我尽力配合。
▶ **cooperation** /kəʊˌɒpə'reɪʃən/ *uncountable noun* 不可数名词：*Thank you for your cooperation.* 感谢您合作。

coordinate /kəʊ'ɔ:dɪˌneɪt/ *verb* 动词 (**coordinates, coordinating, coordinated**)
1 to organize an activity 协调组织：*She*

coordinates the weekend activities. 她协调组织周末的活动。
2 to make the parts of your body work together efficiently 协调（身体部位）: *You need to coordinate legs, arms and breathing.* 你需要协调腿、手臂和呼吸。
▶ **coordination** /kəʊˌɔːdɪˈneɪʃən/ *uncountable noun* 不可数名词: *You need great hand-eye coordination to hit the ball.* 你得手眼协调好才能打到球。

cop /kɒp/ *countable noun* 可数名词
a policeman or policewoman (*informal* 非正式) 警察: *The cops know where to find him.* 警察知道哪里能找到他。

cope /kəʊp/ *verb* 动词 (**copes, coping, coped**)
to deal with a problem or task in a successful way 成功处理；顺利应付: *The group has helped her cope with a serious illness.* 这个团队助她战胜了重病。

copper /ˈkɒpə/ *uncountable noun* 不可数名词
a soft reddish-brown metal 铜: *Chile produces much of the world's copper.* 全球大量铜产自智利。

copy[1] /ˈkɒpi/ *countable noun* 可数名词 (**copies**)
1 something that is produced that looks exactly like another thing 复制品；复印件: *I made a copy of Steve's letter.* 我复印了一份史蒂夫的信。
2 one of many books or newspapers that are exactly the same (书的)册，本；(报纸的)份: *Did you get a copy of 'The Guardian'?* 你买《卫报》了吗？

copy[2] /ˈkɒpi/ *verb* 动词 (**copies, copying, copied**)
1 to make or write something that is exactly like another thing 复制；拷贝；复印: *Copy files from your old computer to your new one.* 把文件从旧电脑拷贝到新电脑。
2 to try to do what another person does 模仿；效法；仿效: *Children try to copy the behaviour of people they admire.* 孩子们总想模仿偶像的举止。

coral /ˈkɒrəl/ *uncountable noun* 不可数名词
a hard substance formed from the bones of very small sea animals 珊瑚: *She was wearing a coral necklace.* 她戴着一串珊瑚项链。

cord /kɔːd/ *uncountable noun* 不可数名词
strong, thick string 粗线；绳: *She was carrying a package tied with heavy cord.* 她扛着一个用粗绳捆着的包袱。

core /kɔː/ *countable noun* 可数名词
1 the central part of a fruit that contains the seeds (水果的)核: *Annie put her apple core in the bin.* 安妮把苹果核扔进了垃圾箱。
2 the central part of the Earth 地核: *What is the temperature in the Earth's core?* 地核温度有多少度？

cork /kɔːk/ *countable noun* 可数名词
an object that you push into the top of a bottle to close it 瓶塞；软木塞: *He took the cork out of the bottle.* 他把瓶塞取了下来。

corkscrew /ˈkɔːkskruː/ *countable noun* 可数名词
a tool for pulling corks out of bottles 瓶塞钻；瓶塞起子

corn /kɔːn/ *uncountable noun* 不可数名词
crops such as wheat or barley, or their seeds 谷物；谷粒: *grinding corn and baking bread* 磨碎谷物烤面包

corner /ˈkɔːnə/ *countable noun* 可数名词
a point where two sides of something meet, or where a road meets another road 角；墙角；街角: *There was a table in the corner of the room.* 屋子角落里有张桌子。 □ *He stood on the street corner, waiting for a taxi.* 他站在街角等出租车。

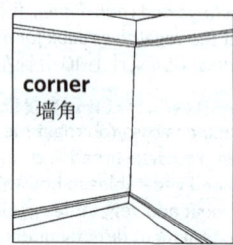
corner 墙角

corner 街角

cornflakes /ˈkɔːnfleɪks/ *plural noun* 复数名词
a type of dried food that people eat with milk for breakfast 玉米片: *a bowl of*

cornflakes 一碗玉米片

corporate /ˈkɔːprət/ *adjective* 形容词
relating to large companies（大）公司的；企业的：*Our city flats are popular with private and corporate customers.* 我们的城市公寓很受私人客户和公司客户欢迎。

corporation /ˌkɔːpəˈreɪʃn/ *countable noun* 可数名词（*American* 美国英语）
a large business or company（大）公司；企业：*Her father works for a big corporation.* 她爸爸在一家大公司上班。

corpse /kɔːps/ *countable noun* 可数名词
a dead body 尸体：*Police found the corpse in a nearby river.* 警察在附近的河里找到了尸体。

correct¹ /kəˈrekt/ *adjective* 形容词
right or true 正确的；无误的：*The correct answers can be found on page 8.* 正确答案见第 8 页。
▸ **correctly** /kəˈrektli/ *adverb* 副词：*Did I pronounce your name correctly?* 你的名字我念对了吗？

correct² /kəˈrekt/ *verb* 动词 (**corrects, correcting, corrected**)
to make a problem or a mistake right 改正；纠正：*There is another way you can correct the problem.* 这个问题还有一个纠正办法。□ *Students are given a chance to correct mistakes.* 学生们得到一次改正错误的机会。
▸ **correction** /kəˈrekʃn/ *noun* 名词：*You may make corrections to your final test.* 你们可以给自己的期末试卷改错。

correspond /ˌkɒrɪˈspɒnd/ *verb* 动词 (**corresponds, corresponding, corresponded**)
1 to be very similar to something or closely connected with something 相似；相关；相对应：*The rise in food prices corresponds closely to rises in oil prices.* 食品价格上涨和油价上涨密切相关。□ *The two maps correspond closely.* 这两张地图十分相似。
2 to write letters or emails to someone 通信：*She still corresponds with her American friends.* 她仍与美国朋友通信。□ *We corresponded regularly.* 我们定期通信。

correspondence /ˌkɒrɪˈspɒndəns/ *uncountable noun* 不可数名词
the letters or emails that someone receives or sends 通信；往来信件；往来邮件：*The website contains copies of Einstein's personal correspondence.* 这个网站上有爱因斯坦个人信件的复印件。

correspondent /ˌkɒrɪˈspɒndənt/ *countable noun* 可数名词
a person who writes news reports 记者；通讯员：*He's the White House correspondent for The Times.* 他是《泰晤士报》驻白宫记者。

corridor /ˈkɒrɪdɔː/ *countable noun* 可数名词
a long passage in a building 走廊；走道：*There were doors on both sides of the corridor.* 走廊两侧都有门。

corrupt¹ /kəˈrʌpt/ *adjective* 形容词
behaving in a dishonest way in order to gain money or power 腐败的；腐化的：*We know that there are some officials who are corrupt.* 我们知道有些官员腐败。

corrupt² /kəˈrʌpt/ *verb* 动词 (**corrupts, corrupting, corrupted**)
to cause a computer file or program to stop working properly, so that it may not be safe to use 损坏（计算机文件或程序）：*The files were corrupted by a virus.* 这些文件被病毒破坏了。

cosmetics /kɒzˈmetɪks/ *plural noun* 复数名词
products that you put on your face to make yourself look more beautiful 化妆品：*She wears nail polish and cosmetics.* 她涂了指甲油并且化了妆。

cost¹ /kɒst/ *countable noun* 可数名词
the amount of money you need in order to buy, do or make something 费用；花费；价格：*The cost of a loaf of bread has gone up.* 一条面包的价格上涨了。□ *There will be an increase in the cost of posting a letter.* 寄信要涨价了。

cost² /kɒst/ *verb* 动词 (**costs, costing, cost**)
to have as a price 价钱为；需要（某人）支付：*This course costs £150 per person.* 这门课每人 150 英镑。□ *It will cost us over £100,000 to buy new lorries.* 我们买新卡车要花 10 多万英镑。

costly /ˈkɒstli/ *adjective* 形容词 (**costlier, costliest**)
very expensive 昂贵的；代价大的：*We must try to avoid such costly mistakes.* 我们必须尽量避免犯这种损失惨重的错误。

costume /ˈkɒstjuːm/ *noun* 名词
a set of clothes that someone wears in a performance 戏服；演出服装：*The costumes and scenery were designed by Robert Rauschenberg.* 演出服装和舞台布景

由罗伯特·劳申伯格设计。

cosy /ˈkəʊzi/ *adjective* 形容词 (**cosier, cosiest**)
comfortable and warm 温暖舒适的：*Hotel guests can relax in the cosy lounge.* 宾馆的客人可以在温暖舒适的休息室里放松休息。

cot /kɒt/ *countable noun* 可数名词 (*American* 美国英语：**crib**)
a bed for a baby 婴儿床

cottage /ˈkɒtɪdʒ/ *countable noun* 可数名词
a small house, usually in the country（乡村）小屋；村舍：*She lived in a little white cottage in the woods.* 她住在林中一栋白色小屋里。

cotton /ˈkɒtən/ *uncountable noun* 不可数名词
1 cloth or thread that is made from the cotton plant 棉布；棉线：*He's wearing a cotton shirt.* 他穿着一件棉衬衫。□ *a reel of cotton* 一卷棉线
2 a plant that is used for making cloth 棉；棉花；棉株：*They own a large cotton plantation in Tennessee.* 他们在田纳西有一大片棉花种植园。
3 (*American* 美国英语) → see 见 **cotton wool**

cotton wool *uncountable noun* 不可数名词 (*American* 美国英语：**cotton**)
soft cotton material used for cleaning your skin or putting cream on it 药棉；脱脂棉（用于清洁皮肤或涂抹乳霜）：*cotton wool balls* 脱脂棉球

couch /kaʊtʃ/ *countable noun* 可数名词 (**couches**)
a long, comfortable seat for two or three people 长沙发（可坐 2—3 人）

cough¹ /kɒf/ *verb* 动词 (**coughs, coughing, coughed**)
to suddenly force air out of your throat with a noise 咳嗽：*James began to cough violently.* 詹姆斯开始剧烈咳嗽。

cough² /kɒf/ *countable noun* 可数名词
1 when you suddenly force air out of your throat with a noise 咳嗽：*They were interrupted by a quiet cough.* 他们被一声轻咳打断了。
2 an illness that makes you cough 咳嗽（病）：*I had a cough for over a month.* 我咳嗽了一个多月。

could /kəd, STRONG 强读 kʊd/ *modal verb* 情态动词
1 used for saying that you were able to do something 能；会：*I could see that*

something was wrong. 我能感觉到有什么事不太对劲儿。□ *It was so dark that I couldn't see where I was going.* 太黑了，我看不清自己在往哪儿走。
2 used for showing that something is possibly true, or that it may possibly happen 有可能；可能会：*It could snow again tonight.* 今晚可能还下雪。□ *'Where's Jack?' — 'I'm not sure; he could be in the toilet.'* "杰克在哪儿？"——"我不确定，他可能在厕所。"
3 used in questions to make polite requests（用于疑问句，表示礼貌地请求）能，可以：*Could I stay tonight?* 我今晚可以留下吗？□ *He asked if he could have a cup of coffee.* 他问是否可以来杯咖啡。

couldn't /ˈkʊdənt/
short for（缩写 =）'could not'

could've /ˈkʊdəv/
short for（缩写 =）'could have'

council /ˈkaʊnsəl/ *countable noun* 可数名词
a group of people who are chosen to control a particular area 政务委员会；地方议会：*The city council has decided to build a new school.* 市政务委员会已经决定要建一所新学校。

count¹ /kaʊnt/ *verb* 动词 (**counts, counting, counted**)
1 to say all the numbers in order 数数：*Nancy counted slowly to five.* 南希慢慢数到了 5。
2 to see how many there are in a group 数出（总数）：*I counted the £5 notes.* 我把这些面额 5 英镑的纸币数了数。□ *I counted 34 sheep on the hillside.* 我数了数，山坡上有 34 只羊。
3 to be important 重要：*Every penny counts if you want to be a millionaire.* 如果你想成为百万富翁，每一分钱都不能浪费。
count on someone/something to feel sure that someone or something will help you 指望某人／某事物：*You can count on us to keep your secret.* 我们会替你保守秘密的，你放心。□ *Can we count on your support for Ms Ryan?* 我们能把你算作瑞安女士的支持者吗？

count² /kaʊnt/ *noun* 名词
keep count of something to know how many things there are 记录某事物的数目：*Keep count of the number of hours you work.* 记下你的工作时长。
lose count of something to not know how many things there are 记不清某事物的数

目：*I lost count of the number of times she called.* 我记不清她打过多少次电话了。

countable noun /ˈkaʊntəbəl ˈnaʊn/ *countable noun* 可数名词
a noun such as 'bird', 'chair' or 'year' that has a singular and a plural form 可数名词

counter /ˈkaʊntə/ *countable noun* 可数名词
1 a long flat surface in a shop or café where customers are served（商店或咖啡馆的）柜台：*That man works behind the counter at the DVD rental shop.* 那个人是 DVD 出租店的柜员。
2 a very small object that you use in board games（棋盘游戏的）筹码，棋子：*Move your counter one square for each spot on the dice.* 骰子显示几点，就把代表你的棋子移动几格。

counterfeit /ˈkaʊntəfɪt/ *adjective* 形容词
used for describing money, goods or documents that are not real, but look exactly like real ones 仿造的；假冒的：*He admitted using counterfeit notes.* 他承认使用假钞。

country /ˈkʌntri/ *noun* 名词 (countries)
1 *countable* 可数 an area of the world with its own government and people 国；国家：*This is the largest country in the world.* 这是世界上最大的国家。□ *We crossed the border between the two countries.* 我们跨过了这两个国家间的边境。
→ Look at picture on P9 参见彩插第 9 页
2 *singular* 单数 land that is away from cities and towns 乡下；乡村：*You can live a healthy life in the country.* 在乡下可以过上健康的生活。□ *She was cycling along a country road.* 她沿着乡村道路骑车。□ *She lived alone in a small house in the country.* 她独居在乡下的一座小房子里。
3 *uncountable* 不可数 a style of popular music from the southern United States（源自美国南部的）乡村音乐：*I always wanted to play country music.* 我一直想演奏乡村音乐。

countryside /ˈkʌntriˌsaɪd/ *uncountable noun* 不可数名词
land that is away from cities and towns 乡下；乡村：*I've always loved the English countryside.* 我一直都喜欢英格兰乡村。

LANGUAGE HELP 语言提示
Countryside or **nature**? 用 countryside 还是 nature？
Countryside is land that is away from towns and cities. **Nature** is used for talking about animals and plants.
*countryside 指远离城镇的乡间，nature 则用于动植物语境。

county /ˈkaʊnti/ *countable noun* 可数名词 (counties)
a part of a state or country 郡；县：*Maidstone is an English town in the county of Kent.* 梅德斯通是英国肯特郡的一个镇。

couple /ˈkʌpəl/ *countable noun* 可数名词
two people who are married or having a romantic relationship 夫妻；情侣：*The couple have no children.* 这对夫妻没有孩子。
a couple two or around two people or things 两个；几个：*There are a couple of police officers outside.* 外面有几个警察。□ *Things should get better in a couple of days.* 过几天情况应该会好转。

coupon /ˈkuːpɒn/ *countable noun* 可数名词
a piece of paper that allows you to pay less money than usual for a product, or to get it free 优惠券：*Cut out the coupon on page 2 and take it to your local supermarket.* 剪下第 2 页的优惠券，拿到你们当地的超级市场。

courage /ˈkʌrɪdʒ/ *uncountable noun* 不可数名词
the quality someone shows when they are not afraid 勇气：*The girl had the courage to tell the police.* 那个女孩有勇气报警。

courageous /kəˈreɪdʒəs/ *adjective* 形容词
showing courage 勇敢的：*The courageous girl saved her baby sister from a house fire.* 那个勇敢的女孩从着火的房子中救出了还是婴儿的妹妹。

courgette /kʊəˈʒet/ *countable noun* 可数名词 (*American* 美国英语：zucchini)
a long, thin vegetable with a dark green skin 小胡瓜

course /kɔːs/ *noun* 名词
1 *countable* 可数 a series of lessons on a particular subject 课程：*I'm taking a course in business administration.* 我正在上一门商业管理的课程。
2 *countable* 可数 one part of a meal 一道菜：*Lunch was excellent, especially the first course.* 午餐特别好吃，尤其是第一道菜。
3 *countable* 可数 an area of land for racing or for playing golf 竞速运动场地；高尔夫球场：*The hotel complex has a swimming pool, tennis courts and a golf course.* 这个

酒店综合体含一个游泳池、几个网球场和一个高尔夫球场。
4 uncountable 不可数 the direction in which someone or something is going 航向；航线；路线：*The pilot changed course to land in Chicago.* 飞行员改变了航线在芝加哥降落。

court /kɔːt/ **countable noun** 可数名词
1 a place where a judge and a group of people (= a jury) decide if someone has done something wrong 法庭：*The man will appear in court later this month.* 该男子本月晚些时候将出庭。
2 an area for playing a game such as tennis or basketball（网球、篮球等的）球场：*The hotel has several tennis courts.* 这家酒店有几个网球场。

courteous /ˈkɜːtiəs/ **adjective** 形容词
polite 有礼貌的；客气的；谦恭的：*He was a kind and courteous man.* 他为人谦和有礼。
▶ **courteously** /ˈkɜːtiəsli/ **adverb** 副词：*He nodded courteously to me.* 他礼貌地向我点了点头。

courtesy /ˈkɜːtɪsi/ **uncountable noun** 不可数名词
polite behaviour and consideration for other people (*formal* 正式) 礼貌；谦恭；彬彬有礼：*Showing courtesy to other drivers costs nothing.* 对其他司机以礼相待并不难做到。

courtyard /ˈkɔːtjɑːd/ **countable noun** 可数名词
an open area that is surrounded by buildings or walls 庭院；院子：*The second bedroom overlooked the courtyard.* 第二间卧室俯瞰庭院。

cousin /ˈkʌzən/ **countable noun** 可数名词
the child of your uncle or your aunt 堂兄（弟）；堂姐（妹）；表兄（弟）；表姐（妹）：*Do you know my cousin Alex?* 你认识我表兄亚历克斯吗？

cover¹ /ˈkʌvə/ **verb** 动词 (**covers, covering, covered**)
1 to put something over something else to protect it 遮挡：*Cover the dish with a heavy lid.* 用一个重点儿的盖子把菜罩住。
2 to form a layer over the surface of something else 覆盖：*Snow covered the city.* 城市银装素裹。 □ *The desk was covered with papers.* 书桌上铺满了文件。

cover² /ˈkʌvə/ **countable noun** 可数名词
1 something that is put over an object to protect it 盖子；罩子；遮挡物：*Keep a plastic cover on your computer when you are not using it.* 不用电脑的时候往上套个塑料罩。
2 the outside part of a book or a magazine 封面：*She appeared on the cover of last week's magazine.* 她登上了上周杂志的封面。

cow /kaʊ/ **countable noun** 可数名词
a large female animal that is kept on farms for its milk 奶牛：*Dad went out to milk the cows.* 爸爸去外面给奶牛挤奶。

coward /ˈkaʊəd/ **countable noun** 可数名词
someone who has no courage 懦夫；胆小者：*They called him a coward because he refused to fight.* 因为他拒绝打架，他们叫他胆小鬼。

cowardly /ˈkaʊədli/ **adjective** 形容词
not brave and easily frightened 懦弱的；胆小的：*I was too cowardly to complain.* 我太懦弱，不敢抱怨。

cowboy /ˈkaʊbɔɪ/ **countable noun** 可数名词
a man who rides a horse and takes care of cows in North America（北美的）牛仔，骑马牧牛人

crab /kræb/ **noun** 名词
1 countable 可数 a sea animal with a shell and ten legs. Crabs usually move sideways. 蟹；螃蟹
2 uncountable 不可数 the meat of this animal 蟹肉：*I'll have the crab salad, please.* 请给我来份蟹肉沙拉。

crack¹ /kræk/ **verb** 动词 (**cracks, cracking, cracked**)
to become slightly broken, with lines on the surface, but not in separate pieces 裂开；破裂：*The plane's windscreen cracked.* 这架飞机的挡风玻璃裂了。 □ *a cracked mirror* 有裂痕的镜子

crack² /kræk/ **countable noun** 可数名词
1 a very narrow gap between two things 缝隙；窄缝：*Kathryn saw him through a crack in the curtains.* 凯瑟琳从窗帘缝里看到了他。
2 a line that appears on the surface of something when it is slightly broken 裂缝：*The plate had a crack in it.* 这个盘子有道裂缝。
3 a sharp sound, like the sound of a piece of wood breaking 爆裂声；噼啪声：*Suddenly there was a loud crack.* 突然传来噼啪一声巨响。

cracker /ˈkrækə/ *countable noun* 可数名词
a thin, hard piece of baked bread that people sometimes eat with cheese 薄脆面包干（可配奶酪食用）

crackle /ˈkrækəl/ *verb* 动词 (**crackles, crackling, crackled**)
to make a lot of short, sharp noises 发出爆裂声；噼啪作响: *The radio crackled again.* 收音机又劈啦作响。

cradle /ˈkreɪdəl/ *countable noun* 可数名词
a baby's bed that you can move from side to side 摇篮

craft /krɑːft/ *countable noun* 可数名词
an activity that involves making things skilfully with your hands 手艺；工艺: *We want to teach our children about native crafts and culture.* 我们想教会孩子们本地的手工艺和文化。

crafty /ˈkrɑːfti/ *adjective* 形容词 (**craftier, craftiest**)
getting what you want in a clever way, perhaps by being dishonest 巧妙的；狡猾的；诡计多端的: *She was so crafty, nobody ever suspected her.* 她非常狡猾，从没有人怀疑过她。

cramp /kræmp/ *noun* 名词
a sudden strong pain in a muscle 痛性痉挛；抽筋: *Mike was complaining of stomach cramps.* 迈克说自己胃部痉挛。

crane /kreɪn/ *countable noun* 可数名词
a large machine with a long arm that can lift very heavy things 起重机；吊车

crash¹ /kræʃ/ *countable noun* 可数名词 (**crashes**)
1 an accident in which a vehicle hits something 碰撞；相撞: *His son was killed in a car crash.* 他儿子死于一场车祸。
2 a sudden loud noise 突然的巨响: *People said they heard a loud crash at about 1.30 a.m.* 人们说凌晨1点30分左右听到一声巨响。

crash² /kræʃ/ *verb* 动词 (**crashes, crashing, crashed**)
1 to hit something 碰撞；撞击: *Her car crashed into the back of a lorry.* 她的车撞上了一辆卡车的车尾。
2 used for saying that a computer or a computer program suddenly stops working（计算机或计算机程序）崩溃，瘫痪: *My computer crashed for the second time that day.* 那天我的电脑第二次崩溃。

crate /kreɪt/ *countable noun* 可数名词
a large box for moving or storing things 大箱子: *The pictures are packed in wooden crates.* 照片被打包进几个大木箱子里。

crater /ˈkreɪtə/ *countable noun* 可数名词
a very large hole in the top of a volcano (= a mountain that forces hot gas and rocks into the air) 火山口: *Rocks shot up three miles from the volcano's crater.* 岩块从火山口喷出3英里高。

crawl¹ /krɔːl/ *verb* 动词 (**crawls, crawling, crawled**)
to move on your hands and knees 爬: *I began to crawl toward the door.* 我开始朝门爬去。

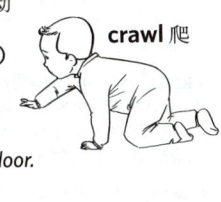
crawl 爬

crawl² /krɔːl/ *uncountable noun* 不可数名词
a way of swimming in which you lie on your front and move one arm over your head and then the other, while kicking your legs 自由泳: *Neil is learning to swim the crawl.* 尼尔在学自由泳。

crayon /ˈkreɪɒn/ *countable noun* 可数名词
a stick of coloured wax that you use for drawing 蜡笔

crazy /ˈkreɪzi/ *adjective* 形容词 (**crazier, craziest**)
very strange or not at all sensible (*informal* 非正式) 疯狂的；不理智的: *People obviously thought we were crazy.* 大家显然觉得我们疯了。
▶ **crazily** /ˈkreɪzɪli/ *adverb* 副词: *He ran crazily around in circles.* 他疯了似的转圈跑。
be crazy about someone/something to like someone or something very much (*informal* 非正式) 迷恋某人/热衷于某事物: *He's still crazy about his job.* 他对工作依然充满激情。 □ *We're crazy about each other.* 我们深爱对方。
go crazy to be extremely bored or upset, or feel that you cannot wait for something any longer (*informal* 非正式) 极度无聊；特别烦闷；等不下去了: *Annie thought she might go crazy if she didn't find out soon.* 安妮觉得要是不能很快弄清楚，她就要疯了。

creak /kriːk/ *verb* 动词 (**creaks, creaking, creaked**)
to make a short, high sound when moved 嘎吱作响: *The stairs creaked under his feet.* 楼梯在他脚下嘎吱作响。 □ *The door*

creaked open. 门嘎吱一声开了。● **creak** countable noun 可数名词: *The door opened with a creak.* 门嘎吱一声开了。

cream[1] /kri:m/ *noun* 名词
1 uncountable 不可数 a thick liquid that is made from milk 奶油: *She went to the shop to buy some cream.* 她去商店里买些奶油。
2 a substance that you rub into your skin 护肤霜；药膏；乳膏: *hand cream* 护手霜
3 yellowish-white in colour 奶油色；淡黄色；米色: *Many women say they can't wear cream.* 很多女人说自己不适合米色。

cream[2] /kri:m/ *adjective* 形容词
of a yellowish-white colour 奶油色的；淡黄色的；米色的: *She wore a cream silk shirt.* 她穿了一件米色丝绸衬衫。

creamy /'kri:mi/ *adjective* 形容词 (**creamier, creamiest**)
1 with a lot of cream or milk 富含奶油（或奶）的: *I like rich, creamy coffee.* 我喜欢味道浓郁的奶香咖啡。
2 soft and smooth 柔软平滑的: *We had pasta in a rich, creamy sauce.* 我们吃了酱汁浓郁细滑的意面。

crease[1] /kri:s/ *countable noun* 可数名词
a line that appears in cloth or paper when it has been folded 褶痕；皱痕: *Dad always wears trousers with sharp creases.* 爸爸总是穿裤线笔直的裤子。

crease[2] /kri:s/ *verb* 动词 (**creases, creasing, creased**)
to form lines when pressed or folded 起皱；起褶: *Most clothes crease a bit when you are travelling.* 旅行中大多数衣服都会有点儿起褶。
▶ **creased** /kri:st/ *adjective* 形容词: *His clothes were terribly creased.* 他的衣服皱得厉害。

create /kri'eɪt/ *verb* 动词 (**creates, creating, created**)
to make something happen or exist 创造；创作: *It's great for a group of schoolchildren to create a show like this.* 一群小学生创作出这样的节目真是了不起。 □ *Could this solution create problems for us in the future?* 这个解决方案以后会不会给我们带来麻烦？
▶ **creator** /kri'eɪtə/ *countable noun* 可数名词: *Matt Groening, creator of The Simpsons* 马特·格罗宁——《辛普森一家》的创作者

creation /kri'eɪʃən/ *countable noun* 可数名词
something that someone has made 创造物；作品: *The new bathroom is my own creation.* 这间新浴室是我自己的杰作。

creative /kri'eɪtɪv/ *adjective* 形容词
1 good at having new ideas 有创造力的: *When you don't have much money, you have to be creative.* 没什么钱的时候，你得有创造力。
2 using something in a new way 有创意的: *He is famous for his creative use of words.* 他因创造性地使用词语而出名。

creature /'kri:tʃə/ *countable noun* 可数名词
a living thing that is not a plant 生物；动物: *Like all living creatures, birds need plenty of water.* 和所有有生命的生物一样，鸟儿也需要大量的水。

credit /'kredɪt/ *noun* 名词
1 uncountable 不可数 an arrangement that allows someone to buy something and pay for it later 赊购；赊欠: *We buy everything on credit.* 我们买东西都是赊账。
2 uncountable 不可数 praise that people give you because they think that you are responsible for something good that has happened 赞扬；称赞；认可: *I can't take all the credit myself.* 我不能一个人把功劳都揽了。
3 [**credits**] plural 复数 the list of all the people who made a film or a television programme（电影或电视节目的）演职人员表: *It was great to see my name in the credits.* 能在演职人员表里看到我的名字真是太棒了。

'**credit card** *countable noun* 可数名词
a plastic card that you use to buy something and pay for it later 信用卡: *Call this number to order by credit card.* 信用卡订购请拨打这个号码。

creep /kri:p/ *verb* 动词 (**creeps, creeping, crept**)
to move somewhere quietly and slowly 蹑手蹑脚地移动: *He crept up the stairs.* 他蹑手蹑脚地上了楼梯。

creepy /'kri:pi/ *adjective* 形容词 (**creepier, creepiest**)
making you feel nervous or frightened (*informal* 非正式) 令人不安的；令人毛骨悚然的: *This place is really creepy at night.* 这个地方到了晚上非常吓人。

crept /krept/
→ see 见 **creep**

crescent /ˈkresənt, ˈkrez-/ *countable noun* 可数名词
a curved shape like the shape of a new moon 新月形；月牙形

crew /kruː/ *countable noun* 可数名词
the people who work on a ship or an aircraft（轮船或飞机上的）全体工作人员：*He was new on the crew of the space shuttle.* 他刚成为航天飞机的机组人员。□ *These ships carry small crews of about twenty men.* 这些船上只有 20 来个船员。

crib /krɪb/ *countable noun* 可数名词
(*American* 美国英语)
→ see 见 **cot**

cricket /ˈkrɪkɪt/ *uncountable noun* 不可数名词
an outdoor game played by two teams who try to score runs (= points) by hitting a ball with a wooden bat 板球运动：*During the summer term we played cricket.* 夏季学期我们打过板球。

crime /kraɪm/ *noun* 名词
an illegal act 犯罪活动：*The police are searching the scene of the crime.* 警方正在勘察犯罪现场。

criminal /ˈkrɪmɪnəl/ *countable noun* 可数名词
a person who does something illegal 罪犯：*We want to protect ourselves against dangerous criminals.* 我们想保护自己免受危险罪犯的伤害。

cripple /ˈkrɪpəl/ *verb* 动词 (**cripples, crippling, crippled**)
to stop someone from ever moving their body normally again 使跛；使成瘸子：*Mr Easton was crippled in an accident.* 伊斯顿先生一次事故后瘸了腿。

crisis /ˈkraɪsɪs/ *noun* 名词 (**crises** /ˈkraɪsiːz/)
a situation that is very serious or dangerous 危机：*This is a worldwide crisis that affects us all.* 这是一场影响我们所有人的全球危机。

crisp¹ /krɪsp/ *adjective* 形容词 (**crisper, crispest**)
pleasantly hard 脆的；酥脆的：*Bake the potatoes for 15 minutes, until they're nice and crisp.* 将土豆烤 15 分钟，直至酥脆。□ *crisp lettuce* 脆口生菜

crisp² /krɪsp/ *countable noun* 可数名词
(*American* 美国英语：**potato chip**)
a very thin slice of potato, which is cooked in oil and eaten as a snack 薯片：*a bag of crisps* 一包薯片

critic /ˈkrɪtɪk/ *countable noun* 可数名词
a person who writes and gives their opinion about books, films, music or art 评论家；批评家；评论员：*Mather was a film critic for many years.* 马瑟是个从业多年的影评家。

critical /ˈkrɪtɪkəl/ *adjective* 形容词
1 very serious and dangerous 严重的；危急的：*The economic situation may soon become critical.* 经济形势可能很快会变得危急。
▶ **critically** /ˈkrɪtɪkli/ *adverb* 副词：*Food supplies are critically low.* 食品供给严重不足。
2 saying that a person or thing is wrong or bad 挑剔的；批评的：*His report is critical of the judges.* 他的报道批评了法官。
▶ **critically** /ˈkrɪtɪkli/ *adverb* 副词：*She spoke critically about Lara.* 她说起拉腊来颇有微词。

criticism /ˈkrɪtɪˌsɪzəm/ *noun* 名词
1 *uncountable* 不可数 when someone expresses disapproval of someone or something 批评；批判；指责：*The president faced strong criticism for his remarks.* 该总统因其言论遭到强烈批评。
2 *countable* 可数 a statement that expresses disapproval 批判的话；指责的话：*Teachers should say something positive before making a criticism.* 老师在提出批评之前应该先说些鼓励的话。

criticize /ˈkrɪtɪˌsaɪz/ *verb* 动词 (**criticizes, criticizing, criticized**)
to express your disapproval of someone or something 批评；批判；指责：*His mother rarely criticized him.* 他妈妈很少批评他。

crocodile /ˈkrɒkəˌdaɪl/ *countable noun* 可数名词
a large animal with a long body, a long mouth and sharp teeth. Crocodiles live in rivers in hot countries. 鳄鱼

crooked /ˈkrʊkɪd/ *adjective* 形容词
not straight 弯曲的；不直的：*I looked at his crooked broken nose.* 我看了看他骨折的歪鼻子。

crop /krɒp/ *countable noun* 可数名词
a plant that people grow for food 庄稼：*Rice farmers here still plant their crops by hand.* 这里的水稻种植户仍然人工种植庄稼。

cross¹ /krɒs/ *verb* 动词 (**crosses, crossing, crossed**)
1 to move to the other side of a place 穿过；

越过: *She crossed the road without looking.* 她过马路时没注意看。
2 to put one of your arms, legs or fingers on top of the other 使交叉; 使交叠: *Jill crossed her legs.* 吉尔翘着二郎腿。
cross something out to draw a line through words 画掉某事物: *He crossed out her name and added his own.* 他画掉她的名字, 加上了自己的。

cross² /krɒs/ *countable noun* 可数名词 (**crosses**)
1 the act of hitting or kicking the ball from one side of a sports field to a person on the other side (球的) 横传
2 a shape like ✝, the most important Christian symbol 十字形, 十字架 (基督教最重要的标记): *She wore a cross around her neck.* 她脖子上戴着一个十字架。
3 a written mark in the shape of an X ✕叉形符号: *Put a cross next to those activities you like.* 在你喜欢的活动旁画叉。

cross³ /krɒs/ *adjective* 形容词 (**crosser, crossest**)
angry 生气的; 愤怒的: *I'm terribly cross with him.* 我很生他的气。
▶ **crossly** /ˈkrɒsli/ *adverb* 副词: *'No, no, no,' Morris said crossly.* "不行, 不行, 不行。" 莫里斯生气地说。

crossroads /ˈkrɒsrəʊdz/ *countable noun* 可数名词
a place where two roads cross each other 十字路口: *Turn right at the first crossroads.* 在第一个十字路口右转。

crosswalk /ˈkrɒswɔːk/ *countable noun* 可数名词 (*American* 美国英语)
→ see 见 **pedestrian crossing**

crossword /ˈkrɒswɜːd/ *countable noun* 可数名词
(*also* 亦作 **crossword puzzle**) a printed word game that consists of a pattern of black and white squares. You write the answers down or across on the white squares. 纵横字谜; 纵横填字游戏: *He could do The New York Times crossword puzzle in 15 minutes.* 他能在 15 分钟内完成《纽约时报》上的纵横字谜。

crouch /kraʊtʃ/ *verb* 动词 (**crouches, crouching, crouched**)
to bend your legs and body so that you are close to the ground 蹲; 蹲伏: *We crouched in the bushes to hide.* 我们蹲伏在灌木丛里。

crouch 蹲伏

crow¹ /krəʊ/ *countable noun* 可数名词
a large black bird that makes a loud noise 乌鸦

crow² /krəʊ/ *verb* 动词 (**crows, crowing, crowed**)
to make the loud sound of a cock (= male chicken), often early in the morning (公鸡) 打鸣: *We had to get up when the cock crowed.* 公鸡一打鸣, 我们就得起床。

crowd¹ /kraʊd/ *countable noun* 可数名词
a large group of people who have gathered together 人群: *A huge crowd gathered in the town square.* 一大群人聚集在镇广场上。

crowd² /kraʊd/ *verb* 动词 (**crowds, crowding, crowded**)
to move closely together around someone or something 聚在…周围: *The children crowded around him.* 孩子们聚在他周围。
crowd into something to enter a place so that it becomes very full 大批涌入某地: *Thousands of people crowded into the city centre to see the president.* 数千人涌入市中心一睹总统风采。

crowded /ˈkraʊdɪd/ *adjective* 形容词
full of people 人多的; 拥挤的: *He looked slowly around the small crowded room.* 他慢慢地环视着这个拥挤的小房间。 ▫ *This is a crowded city of 2 million.* 这个拥挤的城市有 200 万人口。

crown¹ /kraʊn/ *countable noun* 可数名词
a gold or silver circle that a king or queen wears on their head 王冠; 皇冠

crown² /kraʊn/ *verb* 动词 (**crowns, crowning, crowned**)
to put a crown on a person's head as a sign that they have officially become a new king or queen 为…加冕: *Two days later, Juan Carlos was crowned king.* 两天

后，胡安·卡洛斯加冕为国王。

crude /kruːd/ *adjective* 形容词 (**cruder, crudest**)
1 simple and rough 粗糙的；简陋的：*We sat on crude wooden boxes.* 我们坐在简陋的木箱子上。
▶ **crudely** /ˈkruːdli/ *adverb* 副词：*Someone has crudely painted over the original sign.* 有人草草地在原标志上涂抹了几笔。
2 rude or offensive 粗鲁的；冒犯的：*The boys sang loudly and told crude jokes.* 男孩子们高声唱歌，讲粗俗的笑话。▫ *Please don't be so crude.* 请不要如此粗鲁。
▶ **crudely** /ˈkruːdli/ *adverb* 副词：*He hated it when she spoke so crudely.* 他不喜欢她说脏话。

cruel /kruːəl/ *adjective* 形容词 (**crueller, cruellest**)
deliberately making people suffer 残忍的：*Children can be very cruel.* 孩子有时可能很残忍。
▶ **cruelly** /ˈkruːəli/ *adverb* 副词：*Douglas was often treated cruelly by his sisters.* 道格拉斯常被姐妹们整得很惨。
▶ **cruelty** /ˈkruːəlti/ *uncountable noun* 不可数名词：*There are laws against cruelty to animals.* 有禁止虐待动物的法律。

cruise[1] /kruːz/ *countable noun* 可数名词
a holiday that you spend on a ship or boat 乘船游览；航游：*He and his wife went on a world cruise.* 他和妻子乘船环游世界去了。

cruise[2] /kruːz/ *verb* 动词 (**cruises, cruising, cruised**)
to move at a steady comfortable speed 悠闲地移动；缓慢地行驶：*A black and white police car cruised past.* 一辆黑白相间的警车缓缓开过。

crumb /krʌm/ *countable noun* 可数名词
a small piece that falls from bread when someone breaks it 面包屑：*I stood up, brushing crumbs from my trousers.* 我站起来掸掉裤子上的面包屑。

crumble /ˈkrʌmbəl/ *verb* 动词 (**crumbles, crumbling, crumbled**)
1 to have pieces breaking off it 坍塌：*The stone wall was crumbling away in places.* 这堵石墙有些地方在逐渐坍塌。
2 to break something into a lot of small pieces 使成碎屑：*Crumble the goat's cheese into a salad bowl.* 把山羊奶酪弄碎，放入沙拉碗里。

crumple /ˈkrʌmpəl/ *verb* 动词 (**crumples, crumpling, crumpled**)
(also 亦作 **crumple something up**) to press paper or cloth, making a lot of lines and folds in it 使变皱；使起皱：*She crumpled the paper in her hand.* 她把那张纸在手里揉成一团。▫ *She crumpled up the note.* 她把那张便条揉成一团。
▶ **crumpled** /ˈkrʌmpəld/ *adjective* 形容词：*His uniform was crumpled and dirty.* 他的制服又皱又脏。

crunch /krʌntʃ/ *verb* 动词 (**crunches, crunching, crunched**)
1 used for describing the noise that a lot of small stones make when someone walks or drives over them（石子）嘎吱作响：*The gravel crunched under his boots.* 他的靴子踩在砾石上发出嘎吱嘎吱的声响。
● **crunch** *countable noun* 可数名词 (**crunches**)：*We heard the crunch of tyres on the road up to the house.* 我们听到轮胎轧在这条通往房子的马路上，发出嘎吱嘎吱的声音。
2 to noisily break something into small pieces between your teeth 嘎吱嘎吱地嚼：*She crunched an ice cube loudly.* 她嘎嘣嘎嘣地大声嚼着冰块。

crunchy /ˈkrʌntʃi/ *adjective* 形容词 (**crunchier, crunchiest**)
pleasantly hard, and making a noise when eaten（食物）硬脆的，松脆的：*We enjoyed the fresh, crunchy vegetables.* 我们爱吃鲜脆的蔬菜。

crush /krʌʃ/ *verb* 动词 (**crushes, crushing, crushed**)
to press something very hard so that it breaks or loses its shape 压坏；压碎；把…压变形：*Andrew crushed his empty can.* 安德鲁把他的空罐子捏扁了。▫ *The drinks were full of crushed ice.* 这些饮料里加满了碎冰。

crust /krʌst/ *countable noun* 可数名词
1 the hard outer part on a loaf of bread 面包皮：*Cut the crusts off the bread.* 把面包皮从面包上切下来。
2 the outer layer of the Earth 地壳：*Earthquakes damage the Earth's crust.* 地震会破坏地壳。

crutch /krʌtʃ/ *countable noun* 可数名词 (**crutches**)
a long stick that you put under your arm to help you to walk if you have hurt your leg or your foot 拐杖：*I can walk without crutches now.* 我现在不拄拐杖也能走了。

cry – culture

cry¹ /kraɪ/ *verb* 动词 (**cries, crying, cried**)
1 to have tears coming from your eyes 哭；哭泣：*I hung up the phone and started to cry.* 我挂断电话哭了起来。
2 (also 亦作 **cry out**) to say something very loudly 喊叫；高声说：*'Nancy Drew,' she cried, 'you're under arrest!'* "南希·德鲁，"她喊道，"你被捕了！"
cry out to say something very loudly 喊叫；高声说：*'You're wrong, you're all wrong!' Henry cried out.* "你错了，你大错特错！"亨利大喊道。

cry² /kraɪ/ *countable noun* 可数名词 (**cries**)
1 a loud, high sound that you make when you feel a strong emotion (表达强烈感情的) 叫喊，叫声：*She saw the spider and let out a cry of horror.* 她看到了蜘蛛，吓得叫一声。
2 the loud, high sound that a bird or an animal makes (鸟的) 鸣叫，啼鸣；(动物的) 嗥叫，吠：*The cry of a strange bird sounded like a whistle.* 有种奇怪的鸟叫起来像吹哨。

crystal /ˈkrɪstəl/ *noun* 名词
1 *countable* 可数 a small, hard piece of a natural substance 晶体；结晶：*salt crystals* 盐晶体 □ *ice crystals* 冰晶
2 *uncountable* 不可数 a transparent rock used in jewellery 水晶：*Liza wore a crystal necklace at her wedding.* 莉莎在婚礼上戴了一条水晶项链。
3 *uncountable* 不可数 high-quality glass 水晶玻璃：*Their drinking glasses were made from crystal.* 他们的水杯是水晶玻璃做的。

cub /kʌb/ *countable noun* 可数名词
a young wild animal such as a bear (熊等的) 幼兽，崽：*young lion cubs* 幼狮

cube /kjuːb/ *countable noun* 可数名词
1 a solid object with six square surfaces 立方体：*She took a tray of ice cubes from the freezer.* 她从冰柜里拿出一盘冰块。□ *He dropped two sugar cubes into his coffee.* 他往咖啡里加了两块糖。
2 the number that you get if you multiply a number by itself twice 立方；三次幂：*The cube of 2 is 8.* 2 的立方等于 8。
→ Look at picture on P2 参见彩插第 2 页

cubic /ˈkjuːbɪk/ *adjective* 形容词
used for talking about units of volume. For example, a cubic metre is a space that is one metre long on each side. 立方的：*They moved 3 billion cubic metres of earth.* 他们移走了 30 亿立方米的土。

cucumber /ˈkjuːkʌmbə/ *noun* 名词
a long dark-green vegetable that you eat raw 黄瓜：*We had cheese and cucumber sandwiches for lunch.* 我们午餐吃的奶酪黄瓜三明治。

cuddle /ˈkʌdəl/ *verb* 动词 (**cuddles, cuddling, cuddled**)
to put your arms around someone and hold them close 拥抱；搂抱：*Everybody wanted to cuddle the baby.* 大家都想抱抱那个小宝宝。● **cuddle** *countable noun* 可数名词：*I just wanted to give him a cuddle.* 我只是想抱一抱他。

cuddly /ˈkʌdəli/ *adjective* 形容词 (**cuddlier, cuddliest**)
looking soft and pleasant, and making you want to put your arms around them 令人想拥抱的；惹人怜爱的：*a big, cuddly teddy bear* 让人想搂在怀里的大玩具熊

cue /kjuː/ *countable noun* 可数名词
1 an action or a statement that tells someone that they should do something 提示；暗示：*The church bell struck eleven. That was my cue to leave.* 教堂的钟敲了 11 下。这意味着我该离开了。
2 a long, thin wooden stick that you use to hit the ball across the table in some games 球杆：*a snooker cue* 斯诺克球杆

cuff /kʌf/ *countable noun* 可数名词
the end of the sleeve of a shirt 袖口：*He was wearing a blue shirt with a white collar and white cuffs.* 他身穿一件白领白袖口的蓝衬衫。

cultivate /ˈkʌltɪˌveɪt/ *verb* 动词 (**cultivates, cultivating, cultivated**)
to grow plants on a piece of land 耕；耕作；种植：*She cultivated a small garden of her own.* 她开垦了一个属于自己的小园子。

cultural /ˈkʌltʃərəl/ *adjective* 形容词
1 relating to the arts 艺术的：*We've organized a range of sports and cultural events.* 我们组织了一系列体育和艺术活动。
2 relating to ideas and customs of a particular society 文化的：*As a nation we are proud of our cultural diversity.* 从国家层面看，我们为自己的文化多样性感到骄傲。

culture /ˈkʌltʃə/ *noun* 名词
1 *uncountable* 不可数 activities such as art, music, literature and theatre 文化 (指艺术、音乐、文学、戏剧等活动)：*Films are part of our popular culture.* 电影是我们流

行文化的一部分。
2 countable 可数 the way of life, the traditions and beliefs of a particular group of people 文化，文明（指特定群体的生活方式、传统和信仰）: *I live in the city among people from different cultures.* 我生活的城市住着来自不同文化背景的人。

cunning /ˈkʌnɪŋ/ *adjective* 形容词
clever and possibly dishonest 狡猾的；奸诈的: *Police described the man as cunning and dangerous.* 警方称此人狡猾且危险。

cup /kʌp/ *noun* 名词
1 countable 可数 a small round container that you drink from 杯子: *Let's have a cup of coffee.* 咱们喝杯咖啡吧。
2 countable 可数 a large round metal container that is given as a prize to the winner of a competition 奖杯: *I think New Zealand will win the cup.* 我认为新西兰将荣获奖杯。
3 used in the names of some competitions that have a cup as a prize *…杯（用于设奖杯的体育比赛名称中）: *the Ryder Cup* 莱德杯

cups 杯
cup and saucer 一套杯碟
mug 马克杯
glass 玻璃杯
cup 奖杯

cupboard /ˈkʌbəd/ *countable noun* 可数名词
a piece of furniture with doors and shelves for storing things like food or dishes 橱柜: *The kitchen cupboard was full of cans of soup.* 厨房的橱柜里全是汤罐头。

cure /kjʊə/ *verb* 动词 (**cures, curing, cured**)
to make someone become well again 治愈；治好: *The new medicine cured her headaches.* 这种新药治好了她的头痛。 ▫ *Almost overnight I was cured.* 我几乎在一夜之间被治愈。 ● **cure** *countable noun* 可数名词: *There is still no cure for a cold.* 依然没有治愈感冒的药物。

curiosity /ˌkjʊəriˈɒsɪti/ *uncountable noun* 不可数名词
a desire to know about something 好奇心；求知欲: *The children show a lot of curiosity about the past.* 孩子们对过去的事情表现得很好奇。

curious /ˈkjʊəriəs/ *adjective* 形容词
wanting to know more about something 好奇的；求知欲强的: *Steve was curious about the place I came from.* 史蒂夫对我的家乡感到很好奇。
▶ **curiously** /ˈkjʊəriəsli/ *adverb* 副词: *The woman in the shop looked at them curiously.* 商店里的那个女人好奇地看着他们。

curl¹ /kɜːl/ *countable noun* 可数名词
a piece of hair shaped in curves 鬈发: *She was talking to a little girl with blonde curls.* 她正在和一个满头金色鬈发的小女孩讲话。

curl² /kɜːl/ *verb* 动词 (**curls, curling, curled**)
to form curved shapes（使）拳曲；（使）卷曲: *Her hair curled around her shoulders.* 她头发拳曲，披在肩上。 ▫ *Maria curled her hair for the party.* 玛丽亚为参加聚会卷了下头发。
curl up to move your head, arms and legs close to your body 蜷缩: *She curled up next to him.* 她蜷缩在他身旁。

curly /ˈkɜːli/ *adjective* 形容词 (**curlier, curliest**)
shaped in curves 卷曲的: *I've got naturally curly hair.* 我的头发是自然鬈。

currency /ˈkʌrənsi/ *noun* 名词 (**currencies**)
the money that is used in a particular country 货币: *The plans were for a single European currency.* 这些计划是为了实现单一欧洲货币。

current¹ /ˈkʌrənt/ *countable noun* 可数名词
a steady flow of water, air or energy 水流；气流；电流: *The fish move with the currents of the sea.* 鱼顺着洋流游动。 ▫ *I felt a current of cool air.* 我感到一阵凉风。 ▫ *The wires carry a powerful electric current.* 这些电线可传输强大的电流。
→ Look at picture on P6 参见彩插第 6 页

current² /ˈkʌrənt/ *adjective* 形容词
happening now 目前的；现在的：*The current situation is different from the one five years ago.* 现在的情况和 5 年前的不同。
▶ **currently** /ˈkʌrəntli/ *adverb* 副词：*He is currently unmarried.* 他目前未婚。

ˌcurrent acˈcount *countable noun* 可数名词 (*American* 美国英语：**checking account**)
a personal bank account that you can take money from at any time 活期存款账户；往来账户

curriculum /kəˈrɪkjʊləm/ *countable noun* 可数名词 (**curriculums** or 或 **curricula** /kəˈrɪkjʊlə/)
all the subjects that students learn about in a school or college (学校或学院的) 全部课程：*Business skills should be part of the school curriculum.* 商业技能应该成为学校课程的一部分。

curriculum vitae /kəˌrɪkjʊləm ˈviːtaɪ/ *countable noun* 可数名词
→ see 见 **CV**

curry¹ /ˈkʌri/ *noun* 名词 (**curries**)
a dish, originally from Asia, that is cooked with hot spices 咖喱菜：*Our favourite dish is the vegetable curry.* 我们最爱吃的菜是咖喱蔬菜。 □ *Shall we go for a curry tonight?* 咱们今晚去吃咖喱菜怎么样？

curse¹ /kɜːs/ *verb* 动词 (**curses, cursing, cursed**)
to use very impolite or offensive language (*formal* 正式) 咒骂；辱骂：*Jake nodded, but he was cursing silently.* 杰克点了点头，但是心里骂了一句。

curse² /kɜːs/ *countable noun* 可数名词
1 something very impolite or offensive that someone says 咒骂；辱骂：*Shouts and curses came from all directions.* 叫喊声和咒骂声从四面八方涌来。
2 a strange power that seems to cause unpleasant things to happen to someone 咒语；诅咒：*He believes that an evil spirit has put a curse on his business.* 他认为自己的生意受到了恶魔的诅咒。

cursor /ˈkɜːsə/ *countable noun* 可数名词
a small line on a computer screen that shows where you are working (计算机屏幕上的) 光标，游标：*He moved the cursor and clicked the mouse.* 他移动光标之后点击了鼠标。
→ Look at picture on P11 参见彩插第 11 页

curtain /ˈkɜːtən/ *noun* 名词
1 *countable* 可数 a piece of material that hangs from the top of a window to cover it at night 窗帘：*She closed her bedroom curtains.* 她拉上了卧室的窗帘。
2 *singular* 单数 the large piece of material that hangs at the front of the stage in a theatre until a performance begins (舞台上的) 幕，帷幕：*The curtain fell, and the audience stood and clapped.* 幕布落下，观众起立鼓掌。

curve¹ /kɜːv/ *countable noun* 可数名词
a smooth, bent line 曲线；弧线：*She carefully drew the curve of his lips.* 她仔细地画出他嘴唇的曲线。

curve² /kɜːv/ *verb* 动词 (**curves, curving, curved**)
to have the shape of a curve or move in a curve 呈曲线状；沿曲线运动：*Her spine curved forward.* 她的脊柱向前弯曲。 □ *The ball curved through the air.* 球在空中划出一道弧线。
▶ **curved** /kɜːvd/ *adjective* 形容词：*curved lines* 曲线

cushion /ˈkʊʃən/ *countable noun* 可数名词
a bag of soft material that you put on a seat to make it more comfortable 坐垫；垫子：*The baby lay on a velvet cushion.* 婴儿躺在天鹅绒垫子上。

custard /ˈkʌstəd/ *uncountable noun* 不可数名词
a sweet yellow sauce made of milk, eggs and sugar 蛋奶沙司：*We had apple pie and custard for dessert.* 我们的餐后甜点是苹果馅饼加蛋奶沙司。

custom /ˈkʌstəm/ *noun* 名词
something that is usual or traditional among a particular group of people 风俗；习俗：*This is an ancient Japanese custom.* 这是日本一种古老的风俗。 □ *It was the custom to give presents.* 送礼物是风俗。

customer /ˈkʌstəmə/ *countable noun* 可数名词
someone who buys something from a shop or a website 顾客：*I was a very satisfied customer.* 我这个顾客很满意。

LANGUAGE HELP 语言提示
When you buy something from a shop, you are a **customer**. When you use a service, you are a **client**. 表示店铺顾客用 customer，表示所服务的客户用 client。

customs /ˈkʌstəmz/ *uncountable noun* 不可数名词
the place at an airport, for example, where people have to show certain goods that they have bought abroad（机场等的）海关: *He walked through customs.* 他走过海关。

cut /kʌt/ *verb* 动词 (**cuts, cutting, cut**)
1 to use something sharp to remove part of something, or to break it 切；割；砍；剪: *Mrs Haines cut the ribbon.* 海恩斯夫人剪了彩。□ *Cut the tomatoes in half.* 把这些西红柿切成两半。□ *You've had your hair cut, it looks great.* 你剪头发了，真好看。• **cut** *countable noun* 可数名词: *Carefully make a cut in the fabric.* 小心地在这块布料上剪一个口儿。
2 to accidentally injure yourself on a sharp object so that you bleed 割破；划伤: *I started to cry because I cut my finger.* 我因为割破手指哭了起来。□ *He cut himself shaving.* 他刮胡子把脸刮破了。• **cut** *countable noun* 可数名词: *He had a cut on his left eyebrow.* 他左眉毛处有个伤口。
3 to reduce something 削减；缩减；裁减: *We need to cut costs.* 我们需要降低成本。• **cut** *countable noun* 可数名词: *The government announced a 2% cut in interest rates.* 政府宣布利率下调2%。

cut down on something to use or do less of something 削减某物；减少某物: *He cut down on coffee.* 他喝咖啡喝得少了。
cut something down to cut through a tree so that it falls to the ground 砍倒（树木）: *They cut down several trees.* 他们砍倒了几棵树。
cut something off to remove something using scissors or a knife 剪掉某物；切掉某物: *Mrs Johnson cut off a large piece of meat.* 约翰逊夫人切下一大块肉。
cut something out to remove something from what surrounds it using scissors or a knife 剪下某物；切下某物: *I cut the picture out and stuck it on my wall.* 我剪下那张图，贴到了我的墙上。
cut something up to cut something into several pieces 切碎某物；剁碎某物；剪碎某物: *Cut up the tomatoes.* 把西红柿切成小块儿。

cut and paste *verb* 动词 (**cuts and pastes, cutting and pasting, cut and pasted**)
to remove words or pictures on a computer from one place and copy them to another place（在计算机上）剪切复制: *You can cut and paste words, phrases, sentences or even paragraphs from one part of your document to another.* 你可以把文件某处的词、短语、句子甚至段落剪切复制到另一处。

cute /kjuːt/ *adjective* 形容词 (**cuter, cutest**)
pretty or attractive (*informal* 非正式) 可爱的；漂亮迷人的: *Oh, look at that dog! He's so cute.* 哦，快看那只狗狗！它好可爱。□ *I thought that girl was really cute.* 我觉得那个女孩儿特别迷人。

cutlery /ˈkʌtləri/ *uncountable noun* 不可数名词
knives, forks and spoons 餐具: *We had to eat our breakfast with plastic cutlery.* 我们只好用塑料餐具吃早饭。

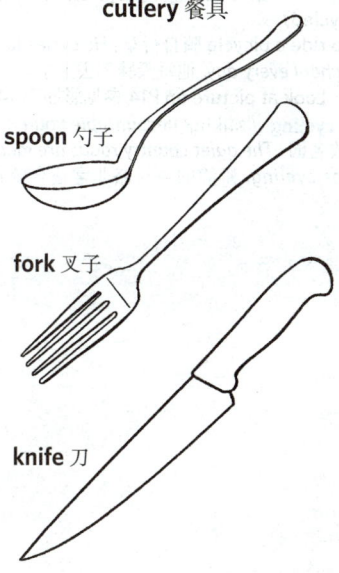

cutlery 餐具
spoon 勺子
fork 叉子
knife 刀

CV /ˌsiː ˈviː/ *countable noun* 可数名词 (**CVs**) (*American* 美国英语: **résumé**)
a written list of your education and work experience that you send when you are trying to get a new job. **CV** is short for (缩写 =) **curriculum vitae**. 简历；履历: *Please send your CV to the following address.* 请将您的简历发送到下面的地址。

cyberbully /ˈsaɪbəˌbʊli/ *verb* 动词 (**cyberbullies, cyberbullying, cyberbullied**)
to deliberately try to frighten or upset someone by sending or posting messages

cyberspace – cynical

on the Internet 网络欺凌: *Some kids tried to cyberbully me.* 有几个小孩子想要在网络上恐吓我。

cyberspace /ˈsaɪbəˌspeɪs/ **uncountable noun** 不可数名词
the imaginary place where electronic communications take place 网络空间: *Our cyberspace communications started in an Internet chat room.* 我们在因特网聊天室开始的网聊。

cycle¹ /ˈsaɪkəl/ **countable noun** 可数名词
1 → see 见 **bicycle**: *a cycle ride* 骑自行车出行
2 a process that is repeated again and again 周期；循环: *We are studying the life cycle of the plant.* 我们正在研究这种植物的生命周期。

cycle² /ˈsaɪkəl/ **verb** 动词 (**cycles, cycling, cycled**)
to ride a bicycle 骑自行车: *He cycles to school every day.* 他每天骑车去上学。
→ Look at picture on P14 参见彩插第 14 页
▶ **cycling** /ˈsaɪklɪŋ/ **uncountable noun** 不可数名词: *The quiet country roads are ideal for cycling.* 僻静的乡村路非常适合骑自行车。

cyclist /ˈsaɪklɪst/ **countable noun** 可数名词
someone who rides a bicycle 骑自行车的人: *We must have better protection for cyclists.* 我们须为骑自行车的人提供更好的保护。

cylinder /ˈsɪlɪndə/ **countable noun** 可数名词
a shape or container with circular ends and long straight sides 圆柱；圆柱体；圆筒: *Never store or change gas cylinders near a flame.* 切勿在火源附近存放或更换燃气罐。
→ Look at picture on P2 参见彩插第 2 页

cymbal /ˈsɪmbəl/ **countable noun** 可数名词
a flat, round, metal musical instrument that makes a loud noise when you hit it, or when you hit two of them together 钹，铙钹（打击乐器）
→ Look at picture on P12 参见彩插第 12 页

cynical /ˈsɪnɪkəl/ **adjective** 形容词
believing that people are usually bad or dishonest 认为人性为恶的；对人性悲观的: *He has a cynical view of the world.* 他愤世嫉俗。
▶ **cynically** /ˈsɪnɪkəli/ **adverb** 副词: *He laughed cynically.* 他嘲讽地大笑。

Dd

dad /dæd/ *countable noun* 可数名词
father (*informal* 非正式) 爸爸: *Don't tell my mum and dad about this!* 这件事不要告诉我爸妈!

daddy /ˈdædi/ *countable noun* 可数名词 (**daddies**)
father (used mainly by young children) (*informal* 非正式) 爸爸 (主要为儿语): *Look at me, Daddy!* 爸爸,快看我! □ *My daddy always reads me stories and helps me with my homework.* 我爸爸总是给我读故事,辅导我做作业。

daffodil /ˈdæfədɪl/ *countable noun* 可数名词
a yellow flower with a long stem that appears in spring 黄水仙

daily /ˈdeɪli/ *adjective* 形容词, *adverb* 副词
appearing or happening every day 每日(的); 每天(的): *the French daily newspaper 'Le Monde'* 法国日报《世界报》 □ *The students use this dictionary almost daily.* 这些学生几乎每天都要用这本词典。

dainty /ˈdeɪnti/ *adjective* 形容词 (**daintier, daintiest**)
small, delicate and pretty 小巧的; 精致的; 秀丽的: *Did you walk here in those dainty little shoes?* 你穿着那双精致小巧的鞋子走来的?
▶ **daintily** /ˈdeɪntɪli/ *adverb* 副词: *She walked daintily down the steps.* 她优雅地走下台阶。

dairy /ˈdeəri/ *adjective* 形容词
used for talking about foods such as butter and cheese that are made from milk 奶制的; 乳制的: *He can't eat dairy products.* 他吃不了乳制品。

daisy /ˈdeɪzi/ *countable noun* 可数名词 (**daisies**)
a small wild flower with a yellow centre and white petals 雏菊

dam /dæm/ *countable noun* 可数名词
a wall that is built across a river in order to hold back water 水坝: *Before the dam was built, the Campbell River often flooded.* 大坝修成之前, 坎贝尔里弗经常发生水灾。

damage[1] /ˈdæmɪdʒ/ *verb* 动词 (**damages, damaging, damaged**)
to break or harm something 破坏; 损害: *He damaged a car with a baseball bat.* 他用棒球棒砸坏了一辆车。 □ *The new tax will badly damage Australian industries.* 新征税费将严重损害澳大利亚的工业。
▶ **damaging** /ˈdæmɪdʒɪŋ/ *adjective* 形容词: *We can see the damaging effects of pollution in cities.* 我们能看到污染对城市造成的破坏性影响。

damage[2] /ˈdæmɪdʒ/ *uncountable noun* 不可数名词
physical harm that happens to an object 损坏; 破坏: *The explosion caused a lot of damage to the house.* 爆炸对这栋房屋造成严重破坏。

damp /dæmp/ *adjective* 形容词 (**damper, dampest**)
slightly wet 潮湿的: *Her hair was still damp.* 她的头发还湿漉漉的。 □ *We went out into the damp, cold air.* 我们出门走进寒冷潮湿的空气中。

dance[1] /dɑːns/ *verb* 动词 (**dances, dancing, danced**)
to move your body to music 跳舞: *She turned on the radio and danced around the room.* 她打开收音机, 在房间里跳起舞来。 □ *Shall we dance?* 能和我跳支舞吗?
▶ **dancing** /ˈdɑːnsɪŋ/ *uncountable noun* 不可数名词: *Let's go dancing tonight.* 咱们今晚去跳舞吧。

dance[2] /dɑːns/ *countable noun* 可数名词
1 a particular series of movements that you usually do in time to music 舞蹈: *a traditional Scottish dance* 苏格兰传统舞蹈
2 a party where people dance with each other 舞会: *At the school dance he talked to her all evening.* 学校舞会上他整晚都在和她交谈。

dancer /ˈdɑːnsə/ *countable noun* 可数名词
a person who earns money by dancing, or a person who is dancing 舞蹈演员; 舞者:

dandelion - dash

She's a dancer with Ballet Rambert. 她是兰伯特芭蕾舞团的舞蹈演员。

dandelion /ˈdændɪˌlaɪən/ **countable noun** 可数名词
a wild plant with yellow flowers that turn into balls of soft white seeds 蒲公英

danger /ˈdeɪndʒə/ **noun** 名词
1 uncountable 不可数 the possibility that something unpleasant will happen, or that you may be harmed or killed 危险：*I'm worried. I think Mary's in danger.* 我很担心，我觉得玛丽有危险。
2 countable 可数 something or someone that can hurt or harm you 危险因素；危险的人；威胁：*They warned us about the dangers of driving too fast.* 他们警告我们开车过快有诸多危险。

dangerous /ˈdeɪndʒərəs/ **adjective** 形容词
able or likely to harm you 危险的；不安全的：*We are in a very dangerous situation.* 我们的情况非常危险。□ *He owns a dangerous dog.* 他养了一条很危险的狗。
▶ **dangerously** /ˈdeɪndʒərəsli/ **adverb** 副词：*He is dangerously ill.* 他病得很重。

dare /deə/ **verb** 动词 (**dares, daring, dared**)
to be brave enough to do something 敢于；有胆量：*Most people don't dare to disagree with Harry.* 大多数人都不敢和哈里有不同意见。 □ *I didn't dare open the door.* 我不敢开门。 • **dare modal verb** 情态动词：*She dare not leave the house.* 她不敢离开房子。
dare someone to do something to ask someone to do something dangerous in order to prove that they are brave enough to do it 激某人做（危险的）某事：*They dared me to jump into the water but I refused.* 他们激我往水里跳，但我拒绝了。
how dare you used for showing that you are very angry about something that someone has done 你竟敢，你怎么敢（表示愤怒）：*How dare you say that about my mother!* 你怎么敢那样说我母亲！

> **LANGUAGE HELP** 语言提示
> You can leave out the word **to** after **dare**.
> *dare 后可省去 to：Nobody dared complain.* 没有人敢发牢骚。

daring /ˈdeərɪŋ/ **adjective** 形容词
willing to do dangerous things 大胆的；敢于冒险的：*He made a daring escape from the island in a small boat.* 他冒险划一艘小船从岛上逃离。

dark¹ /dɑːk/ **adjective** 形容词 (**darker, darkest**)
1 with no light, or very little light 黑暗的；昏暗的：*It was too dark to see much.* 天太黑了，看不见太多东西。
▶ **darkness** /ˈdɑːknəs/ **uncountable noun** 不可数名词：*The light went out, and we were in total darkness.* 灯灭了，我们完全在黑暗之中。
▶ **darkly** /ˈdɑːkli/ **adverb** 副词：*a darkly lit hall* 灯光昏暗的大厅
2 having the colour black or a colour close to black 黑色的；深色的：*He wore a dark suit.* 他穿了一套深色西装。□ *a dark blue dress* 深蓝色连衣裙
▶ **darkly** /ˈdɑːkli/ **adverb** 副词：*His skin was darkly tanned.* 他的皮肤晒得黝黑。
3 with brown or black hair, eyes, or skin （头发、眼睛或皮肤）黑色的，深色的：*He had dark, curly hair.* 他有一头卷曲的黑发。
get dark to become night（天）变黑：*We shut the curtains when it got dark.* 天黑了，我们拉上窗帘。

dark² /dɑːk/ **uncountable noun** 不可数名词
the dark the lack of light in a place 黑；黑暗：*Children are often afraid of the dark.* 孩子们通常怕黑。

darling /ˈdɑːlɪŋ/ **noun** 名词
a name that you call someone that you love very much 亲爱的（用作爱称）：*Thank you, darling.* 谢谢你，亲爱的。

dart¹ /dɑːt/ **verb** 动词 (**darts, darting, darted**)
to move suddenly and quickly 猛冲；飞奔：*Ingrid darted across the street.* 英格丽德飞奔着穿过街道。

dart² /dɑːt/ **countable noun** 可数名词
a small, narrow object with a sharp point that you can throw or shoot 镖；飞镖

darts /dɑːts/ **uncountable noun** 不可数名词
a game in which you throw darts (= small pointed objects) at a round board that has numbers on it 掷镖游戏：*I enjoy playing darts.* 我喜欢掷镖游戏。

dash¹ /dæʃ/ **verb** 动词 (**dashes, dashing, dashed**)
to go somewhere quickly and suddenly 飞奔；急奔：*She dashed downstairs when the doorbell rang.* 门铃响了，她冲下楼。 • **dash singular noun** 单数名词：*She screamed and made a dash for the door.* 她尖叫一声，朝

门口冲去。

dash² /dæʃ/ *countable noun* 可数名词 (**dashes**)
a short, straight, horizontal line that you use in writing 破折号: *Sometimes people use a dash (—) where they could use a colon (:).* 有时人们用破折号（——）代替冒号（：）。

dashboard /ˈdæʃbɔːd/ *countable noun* 可数名词
the part of a car in front of the driver, where most of the controls are (汽车的) 仪表板: *The clock on the dashboard showed two o'clock.* 仪表板上时钟显示2点。

data /ˈdeɪtə/ *noun* 名词
1 *plural* 复数 information, especially when it is in the form of facts or numbers 数据; 资料: *Government data shows that unemployment is going up.* 政府提供的数据表明失业率在攀升。
2 *uncountable* 不可数 information that can be used by a computer program (计算机程序可用的) 数据: *A memory stick can hold huge amounts of data.* 优盘能储存大量数据。

database /ˈdeɪtəˌbeɪs/ *countable noun* 可数名词
a collection of information on a computer that is stored in such a way that you can use it and add to it easily (存储于计算机中的) 数据库: *Searching the database is quick and simple.* 搜索数据库简便快捷。

date¹ /deɪt/ *countable noun* 可数名词
1 a particular day and month or a particular year 日期; 日子: *'What's the date today?' — '23rd July.'* "今天是几号？" —— "7月23号。"
2 an arrangement to meet a boyfriend or a girlfriend (男女间的) 约会: *I have a date with Bob tonight.* 我今晚要和鲍勃约会。
3 a small, dark-brown, sticky fruit with a stone inside 海枣 (果实)

date² /deɪt/ *verb* 动词 (**dates, dating, dated**)
to go out with someone regularly because you are having a romantic relationship with them 约会; 与…约会: *They've been dating for three months.* 他们已经约会3个月了。 *I once dated a woman who was a teacher.* 我曾和一位女老师约会过。

daughter /ˈdɔːtə/ *countable noun* 可数名词
a person's female child 女儿: *We met Flora and her daughter Catherine.* 我们遇到了弗洛拉和她的女儿凯瑟琳。 *She's the daughter of a university professor.* 她是一位大学教授的女儿。

daughter-in-law *countable noun* 可数名词 (**daughters-in-law**)
the wife of a person's son 儿媳妇

dawn /dɔːn/ *noun* 名词
the time when the sky becomes light in the morning 黎明; 拂晓: *Nancy woke at dawn.* 南希黎明时分醒来。

day /deɪ/ *noun* 名词
1 *countable* 可数 a period of twenty-four hours from one midnight to the next midnight 一天; 一日: *They'll be back in three days.* 他们3天后回来。 *It snowed every day last week.* 上周每天都下雪。 *'What day is it today?' — 'It's Thursday.'* "今天星期几？" —— "星期四。"
2 the time when it is light outside 白天; 白昼: *We spent the day watching tennis.* 我们白天看网球比赛。 *The streets are busy during the day.* 这些街道白天很热闹。

one day
1 at some time in the future (将来) 有一天; 有朝一日: *I dream of living in Australia one day.* 我梦想着将来有一天能在澳大利亚居住。 *I hope one day you will make someone who will make you happy.* 我希望有一天你能找到给你幸福的人。
2 at some time in the past (过去) 有一天: *One day, he came home from work, and she wasn't there.* 一天，他下班回家，发现她不在家。

the other day a few days ago 几天前: *I saw Fiona in town the other day.* 我几天前在城里看到菲奥娜。

these days at this time; not in the past 现在; 目前: *These days, I have enough money to do what I want.* 现在，我有足够的钱做我想做的事。

daydream /ˈdeɪdriːm/ *verb* 动词 (**daydreams, daydreaming, daydreamed**)
to think about pleasant things for a period of time 做白日梦; 空想; 幻想: *I was daydreaming about a job in France.* 我幻想着在法国工作。 ● **daydream** *countable noun* 可数名词: *She was looking out the window in a daydream.* 她望着窗外，陷入遐想。

daydream 做白日梦

I was daydreaming about a job in France. 我幻想着在法国工作。

daylight /ˈdeɪlaɪt/ *uncountable noun* 不可数名词
the natural light that there is during the day 日光：*A little daylight came through a crack in the wall.* 一线日光透过墙上的裂缝照射进来。

daytime /ˈdeɪtaɪm/ *singular noun* 单数名词
the part of a day between the time when it gets light and the time when it gets dark 白天；日间：*He rarely went anywhere in the daytime; he was always out at night.* 他白天很少出门，一直都是晚上出去。

dead /ded/ *adjective* 形容词
1 not alive 死亡的；去世的：*She told me her husband was dead.* 她告诉我她丈夫去世了。 □ *They put the dead body into the ambulance.* 他们将尸体放进救护车。
2 not working 不运转的；失灵的：*I answered the phone but the line was dead.* 我接起电话，但电话掉线了。
the dead people who have died 死去的人；亡者：*Two soldiers were among the dead.* 死者中有两名士兵。

deadline /ˈdedlaɪn/ *countable noun* 可数名词
a particular time or date before which you must do or finish something 截止日期；最后期限：*We missed the deadline because of several problems.* 因遇到几个问题，我们没能赶上最后期限。

deadly /ˈdedli/ *adjective* 形容词 (**deadlier, deadliest**)
able or likely to kill a person or an animal 致命的；致死的：*This deadly disease killed 70 people in Malaysia last year.* 这种致命的疾病去年在马来西亚导致 70 人死亡。

deaf /def/ *adjective* 形容词 (**deafer, deafest**)
unable to hear anything or unable to hear very well 聋的；失聪的：*She is now totally deaf.* 她现在彻底失聪了。

deafen /ˈdefən/ *verb* 动词 (**deafens, deafening, deafened**)
to make someone unable to hear anything else because of a very loud noise 使听不见；震聋：*The noise of the engine deafened her.* 发动机的声响吵得她什么都听不见。

deafening /ˈdefənɪŋ/ *adjective* 形容词
very loud 震耳欲聋的：*All we could hear was the deafening sound of gunfire.* 我们只能听到震耳欲聋的枪炮声。

deal¹ /diːl/ *verb* 动词 (**deals, dealing, dealt**) (also 亦作 **deal something out**) to give playing cards to the players in a game of cards（纸牌游戏中）发（牌），给…发牌：*She dealt each player a card.* 她给每位玩家发了 1 张牌。 □ *Dalton dealt out five cards to each player.* 多尔顿给每位玩家发了 5 张牌。
deal in something to buy or sell a particular type of goods 经营（或买卖）某物：*They deal in antiques.* 他们做古董买卖。
▶ **dealer** /ˈdiːlə/ *countable noun* 可数名词：*an antique dealer* 古董商
deal something out same meaning as **deal** 同 deal
deal with someone/something to give your attention to someone or something 应付某人 / 处理某事：*Could you deal with this customer, please?* 你来为这位顾客服务好吗？

deal² /diːl/ *countable noun* 可数名词
a business agreement 协议；交易：*They made a deal to share the money between them.* 他们达成协议，双方分这笔钱。
a great deal of something or **a good deal of something** a lot of a particular thing 许多某物；大量某物：*You can earn a great deal of money in this job.* 做这份工作能挣很多钱。

dealt /delt/
→ see 见 **deal**

dear¹ /dɪə/ *adjective* 形容词 (**dearer, dearest**)
1 used for describing someone that you love 亲爱的；心爱的：*Mrs Cavendish is a dear friend of mine.* 卡文迪什夫人是我的密友。
2 used at the beginning of a letter or an email before the name of the person you are writing to（用于书信或电子邮件开头

的收信人姓名之前）亲爱的: *Dear Peter, How are you?* 亲爱的彼得，你好吗？◇ *Dear Sir or Madam...* 敬启者…

dear² /dɪə/ *exclamation* 感叹词
oh dear used for showing that you are surprised or upset（表示吃惊或难过）天哪，哎呀: *Oh dear! Poor Max.* 天哪！可怜的马克斯。

death /deθ/ *noun* 名词
the end of a person's or an animal's life 死；死亡: *1.5 million people are in danger of death from hunger.* 150 万人有饿死的危险。 ◇ *It's the thirtieth anniversary of her death.* 这是她 30 周年祭日。

debate /dɪˈbeɪt/ *noun* 名词
a long discussion or argument 辩论；讨论: *The debate will continue until they vote on Thursday.* 这场辩论将一直继续，直到他们周四投票表决。 ◇ *There has been a lot of debate among teachers about this subject.* 这个问题老师之间有很多讨论。● **debate** *verb* 动词 (**debates, debating, debated**): *The committee will debate the issue today.* 委员会今天将讨论这个问题。 ◇ *They were debating which team would win.* 他们在讨论哪个队会获胜。

debit card /ˈdebɪt ˌkɑːd/ *countable noun* 可数名词
a bank card that you can use to pay for things 借记卡

debris /ˈdeɪbriː, ˈdebriː/ *uncountable noun* 不可数名词
pieces from something that has been destroyed 碎片；残骸: *Debris from the plane was found over an area the size of a football pitch.* 飞机残骸散落在一块足球场大小的区域。

debt /det/ *noun* 名词
an amount of money that you owe someone 债务；欠款: *He is still paying off his debts.* 他仍在还欠款。
be in debt or **get into debt** to owe money 欠债；负债: *Many students get into debt.* 很多学生都负债。

decade /ˈdekeɪd/ *countable noun* 可数名词
a period of ten years 十年: *She spent a decade studying in London.* 她曾在伦敦求学 10 年。

decay /dɪˈkeɪ/ *verb* 动词 (**decays, decaying, decayed**)
to gradually be destroyed by a natural process; to become bad 腐烂；腐朽: *The bodies slowly decayed.* 尸体慢慢地腐烂了。 ◇ *Brush your teeth every day so that they don't decay.* 每天刷牙以防牙齿蛀蚀。 ● **decay** *uncountable noun* 不可数名词: *Eating too many sweets causes tooth decay.* 吃太多糖果会导致蛀牙。

deceive /dɪˈsiːv/ *verb* 动词 (**deceives, deceiving, deceived**)
to deliberately make someone believe something that is not true 欺骗；蒙骗: *She accused the government of trying to deceive the public.* 她指控政府试图欺骗公众。

December /dɪˈsembə/ *noun* 名词
the twelfth and last month of the year 十二月: *I arrived on a bright morning in December.* 我在 12 月一个明媚的早晨抵达。

decent /ˈdiːsənt/ *adjective* 形容词
1 acceptable or good enough 像样的；尚好的: *Without decent housing, poor health and poverty will not be defeated.* 没有像样的住房，就无法战胜疾病和贫穷。 ◇ *If the weather is decent, we'll have a barbecue at the weekend.* 周末天气好的话，我们就在户外烧烤。
▶ **decently** /ˈdiːsəntli/ *adverb* 副词: *They treated their prisoners decently.* 他们优待囚犯。
2 morally right or polite 正派的；正直的；得体的: *He's a really nice, decent guy.* 他是个非常和善、正派的人。 ◇ *It was very decent of him to ring and explain.* 他打电话解释的做法很得体。

deception /dɪˈsepʃən/ *uncountable noun* 不可数名词
when someone deliberately makes you believe something that is not true 欺骗: *Lies and deception are not a good way to start a marriage.* 靠谎言和欺骗结婚非明智之举。

deceptive /dɪˈseptɪv/ *adjective* 形容词
making you believe something that is not true 欺骗性的；误导的: *The sea looked warm, but appearances can be deceptive: it was absolutely freezing!* 海水看似温暖，但表象是有欺骗性的：实际上海水冰冷刺骨！
▶ **deceptively** /dɪˈseptɪvli/ *adverb* 副词: *The atmosphere in the hall was deceptively peaceful.* 大厅里的氛围看似平和，但只是假象。

decide /dɪˈsaɪd/ *verb* 动词 (**decides, deciding, decided**)
1 to choose to do something after thinking

decimal – decoration

about it for some time 决定: *She decided to take a course in philosophy.* 她决定修一门哲学课。 □ *Think about it very carefully before you decide.* 作决定之前要仔细考虑。
2 to choose how something should happen or be done 确定; 选定: *Schools need to decide the best way of testing students.* 学校要选定测试学生的最佳方式。
3 to form your opinion about something 断定; 判定: *He decided Franklin was lying to him.* 他断定富兰克林在向他撒谎。

decimal[1] /ˈdesɪməl/ *countable noun* 可数名词
part of a number that is written in the form of a dot followed by one or more numbers 小数: *The interest rate is shown as a decimal, such as 0.10, which means 10%.* 利率以小数显示，如 0.10, 即 10%。

decimal[2] /ˈdesɪməl/ *adjective* 形容词
using a system that counts in units of ten 十进位的: *The mathematics of ancient Egypt used a decimal system.* 古埃及的数学用十进制。

decimal ˈpoint *countable noun* 可数名词
the dot that you use when you write a number as a decimal 小数点: *A waiter forgot to put the decimal point in the £45.00 bill and they were charged £4500.* 服务员忘了加小数点，他们 45.00 英镑的账单收了 4500 英镑。
→ Look at picture on P2 参见彩插第 2 页

decision /dɪˈsɪʒən/ *countable noun* 可数名词
a choice about what to do 决定: *I don't want to make the wrong decision and regret it later.* 我不想作出错误的决定又事后后悔。

deck /dek/ *countable noun* 可数名词
1 one of the floors of a bus or a ship (公共汽车、船的) 一层: *We went on a luxury ship with five passenger decks.* 我们登上有 5 层客舱的豪华轮船。
2 a flat wooden area attached to a house, where people can sit (房屋旁的) 木制平台: *A deck leads into the main room of the home.* 一个木制平台通到房子的客厅。
3 a complete set of playing cards (纸牌的) 一副: *Matt picked up the cards and shuffled the deck.* 马特把牌拢起来洗牌。

declaration /ˌdekləˈreɪʃən/ *countable noun* 可数名词
an official statement 宣言; 声明: *We consider these attacks to be a declaration of war.* 我们认为这几次袭击是在宣战。

declare /dɪˈkleə/ *verb* 动词 (declares, declaring, declared)
1 to say that something is true in a firm, clear way 宣称; 声称: *Melinda declared that she was leaving home.* 梅琳达宣称她要离开家。
2 to officially state that something is the case 宣布; 宣告: *The president finally declared an end to the war.* 总统最终宣告战争结束。 □ *The judges declared Mr Stevens innocent.* 法官宣布史蒂文斯先生无罪。
3 to say what you have bought during a visit to another country, so that you can pay tax on it in your own country 申报 (纳税品): *Please declare all food, plants and animal products.* 所有的食品、植物及动物产品都要申报。 □ *At the airport, I was asked if I had anything to declare.* 在机场，我被询问是否有物品要申报。

decline /dɪˈklaɪn/ *verb* 动词 (declines, declining, declined)
1 to become less in amount, importance or strength 下降; 减少; 衰退: *The local population is declining.* 当地人口数量在减少。
2 to politely refuse to accept something (*formal* 正式) 婉拒; 谢绝: *He declined their invitation.* 他婉拒了他们的邀请。 □ *She offered me a cup of tea, but I declined.* 她提议给我倒杯茶，但我谢绝了。

decorate /ˈdekəreɪt/ *verb* 动词 (decorates, decorating, decorated)
1 to make something look more attractive by adding things to it 装饰; 装点: *He decorated his room with pictures of sports stars.* 他用体育明星的照片装饰房间。
2 to put new paint or paper on the walls and ceiling of a room 粉刷; (给…) 贴墙纸: *They were decorating Jemma's bedroom.* 他们正在粉刷耶马的卧室。 □ *She loves decorating.* 她喜欢粉刷房间。
▶ **decorating** /ˈdekəreɪtɪŋ/ *uncountable noun* 不可数名词: *I did a lot of the decorating myself.* 许多粉刷的活儿都是我自己干的。

decoration /ˌdekəˈreɪʃən/ *noun* 名词
1 an object that you use to make something look more attractive 装饰品; 点缀物: *Colourful paper decorations were hanging from the ceiling.* 天花板上悬挂着彩纸装饰。
2 *uncountable* 不可数 the furniture and

the paint or paper on the walls of a room
（室内的）装饰，装潢：*The decoration was practical for a family home.* 装潢很实用，适合家居生活。

decorative /ˈdekərətɪv/ *adjective* 形容词
intended to look pretty or attractive 装饰性的：*The curtains are only decorative — they do not open or close.* 这些窗帘只是装饰性的，不能开合。

decrease¹ /dɪˈkriːs/ *verb* 动词 (**decreases, decreasing, decreased**)
to become less in amount, size or strength 减少；降低：*Last year the average price of property in this area decreased from £134,000 to £126,000.* 去年，这个地区的房产均价从13.4万英镑降到12.6万英镑。 ◻ *Property may start to decrease in value.* 房产或许开始贬值。

decrease² /ˈdiːkriːs/ *countable noun* 可数名词
the process of growing less in amount, size or strength 减少；降低：*There has been a decrease in the number of people without a job.* 失业人数有所下降。

dedicate /ˈdedɪkeɪt/ *verb* 动词 (**dedicates, dedicating, dedicated**)
to say on the first page of a book, a play or a piece of music that you have written it for a particular person 把（书、戏剧或音乐）题献（给）：*She dedicated her first book to her sons.* 她把第一本书题献给了几个儿子。
▶ **dedication** /ˌdedɪˈkeɪʃən/ *countable noun* 可数名词：*I read the dedication at the beginning of the book.* 我读了这本书开头的献词。

deduct /dɪˈdʌkt/ *verb* 动词 (**deducts, deducting, deducted**)
to take away a particular amount from a total 减去；扣除：*The company deducted £50 from his wages.* 公司从他的薪水中扣掉50英镑。

deed /diːd/ *countable noun* 可数名词
something that is done, especially something that is very good or very bad 行为；（尤指）功绩，劣迹：*The people who did this evil deed must be punished.* 做这件坏事的人必须得到惩罚。

deep /diːp/ *adjective* 形容词, *adverb* 副词 (**deeper, deepest**)
1 going down a long way 深的（地）：*The water is very deep.* 水很深。 ◻ *The kids dug a deep hole in the middle of the garden.* 孩子们在花园中央挖了个深坑。 ◻ *She put her hands deep into her pockets.* 她把双手深深插进口袋。
2 used for emphasizing the seriousness or strength of something 严重的；深切的：*He expressed his deep sympathy to the family.* 他向这家人表达了深切的同情。
▶ **deeply** /ˈdiːpli/ *adverb* 副词：*He loved his brother deeply.* 他深爱自己的哥哥。
3 having a low, usually strong, sound（声音）深沉的，低沉的：*He spoke in a deep, warm voice.* 他的嗓音低沉而温暖。
4 strong and dark in colour（颜色）深的，浓的：*The sky was deep blue and starry.* 深蓝色的天空中繁星点点。
5 if you are in a deep sleep, you are sleeping so soundly that it is difficult for someone to wake you（睡眠）沉的，酣的：*Una fell into a deep sleep.* 尤娜沉沉睡去。
▶ **deeply** /ˈdiːpli/ *adverb* 副词：*She slept deeply, but woke early.* 她睡得很沉，但醒得很早。

take a deep breath to breathe in so that your lungs are completely filled with air 深吸一口气：*Cal took a long, deep breath, as he tried to control his emotions.* 卡尔深深地吸了一口气，努力控制自己的情绪。

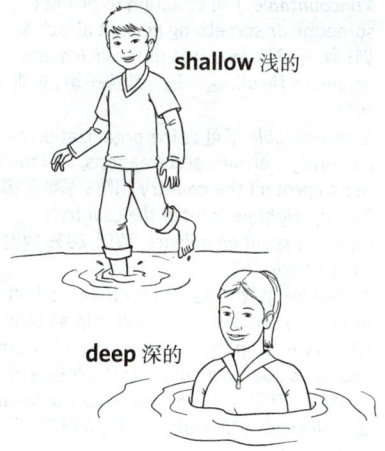

shallow 浅的

deep 深的

deepen /ˈdiːpən/ *verb* 动词 (**deepens, deepening, deepened**)
to become stronger 加深；深化：*These friendships will probably deepen in your teenage years.* 到你十几岁的时候，这几段友谊可能会更深厚。

deer /dɪə/ *countable noun* 可数名词 (**deer**)
a large wild animal that eats grass and

leaves, the male of which usually has large horns that look like branches 鹿

default /dɪˈfɔːlt/ *uncountable noun* 不可数名词
the way that something will be done if you do not give any other instruction 缺省；默认：*The default setting on the printer is for colour.* 这台打印机的默认设置是彩打。

defeat /dɪˈfiːt/ *verb* 动词 (**defeats, defeating, defeated**)
to beat someone in a battle, a game or a competition 击败；战胜：*They defeated the French army in 1954.* 1954 年他们打败了法军。● **defeat** *noun* 名词：*He was prime minister until his party's defeat in the general election this summer.* 今年夏天他所在的政党在大选中落败，此后他不再担任首相。□ *The team suffered a 2-1 defeat in the semi-finals.* 球队在半决赛中以 1 比 2 落败。

defective /dɪˈfektɪv/ *adjective* 形容词
not working properly 有缺点的；有缺陷的：*If the product is defective, you can demand your money back.* 产品若有缺陷，可要求退款。

defence /dɪˈfens/ *noun* 名词
1 *uncountable* 不可数 action to protect someone or something against attack 防御；保卫：*The land was flat, which made defence difficult.* 这一地区地势平坦，很难防御。
2 *uncountable* 不可数 the organization of a country's armies and weapons, and their use to protect the country 国防；军事防御：*Twenty-eight per cent of the country's money is spent on defence.* 该国 28% 的财力用于国防。
3 *singular* 单数 in games such as football or hockey, the group of players in a team who try to stop the opposing players from scoring a goal or a point（足球、曲棍球等中的）防守（队员）：*Their defence was weak and allowed in 12 goals.* 他们防守薄弱，失了 12 个球。

defend /dɪˈfend/ *verb* 动词 (**defends, defending, defended**)
1 to take action in order to protect someone or something 防御；保卫：*The army must be able to defend its own country against attack.* 军队须能保卫国家，抵御进攻。
2 in sports, to try to stop the other team from getting points（体育运动中）防守：*The team scored three excellent goals and defended superbly.* 球队进了 3 个漂亮的球，防守也极为稳固。
3 to argue in support of a decision 为（某决定）辩护；维护：*The president defended his decision to go to war.* 总统为自己开战的决议辩护。
4 to argue, in a law court, that a person is not guilty of a particular crime（法庭上）为（某人）辩护：*He has hired a lawyer to defend him in court.* 他请了一位律师在法庭上为自己辩护。

defender /dɪˈfendə/ *countable noun* 可数名词
a sports player whose main task is to try and stop the other side from scoring（体育运动中的）防守队员：*Lewis was the team's top defender.* 刘易斯是队里顶尖的防守队员。

defiant /dɪˈfaɪənt/ *adjective* 形容词
refusing to obey someone 违抗的；反抗的：*She stood looking at her father with a defiant expression on her face.* 她站在那里看着父亲，脸上一副不服气的神情。
▶ **defiantly** /dɪˈfaɪəntli/ *adverb* 副词：*They defiantly refused to accept the plan.* 他们轻蔑地拒绝了这个计划。

deficit /ˈdefəsɪt/ *countable noun* 可数名词
the amount by which something is less than the amount that is needed 差额；赤字，亏损：*The budget showed a deficit of five billion pounds.* 预算赤字达 50 亿英镑。

define /dɪˈfaɪn/ *verb* 动词 (**defines, defining, defined**)
to say clearly what something is and what it means 给⋯下定义：*The government defines a household as 'a group of people who live in the same house'.* 政府给"家庭"下的定义是"同住一栋房子的人们"。

definite /ˈdefɪnɪt/ *adjective* 形容词
1 firm and clear, and unlikely to change 明确的；确定的：*I need a definite answer soon.* 我需要尽快得到一个明确的答复。□ *I want to make some definite plans for the future.* 我想针对未来制订一些明确的计划。
2 true, rather than just being an opinion or a guess 确凿的；确切的：*We didn't have any definite proof.* 我们没有任何确凿的证据。

definite article countable noun 可数名词
the word 'the' 定冠词（即 the）: Place names often have a definite article, as in 'The Alps'. 地名前常加定冠词，如 The Alps（阿尔卑斯山）。

definitely /'defɪntli/ adverb 副词
certainly; without any doubt 肯定地；无疑地: I'll definitely come to your birthday party. 我肯定要去你的生日派对。▫ The extra money will definitely help. 额外的那笔钱肯定会有所帮助。

definition /ˌdefɪ'nɪʃən/ countable noun 可数名词
the meaning of a word or an expression that you find in a dictionary（词典里词或短语的）释义，定义: What is the definition of 'an adult'? 'adult' 的定义是什么？

deform /dɪ'fɔːm/ verb 动词 (deforms, deforming, deformed)
to cause a person's body to have an unnatural shape 使（身体部位）变形；使成畸形: The disease deforms the arms and the legs. 这种疾病会导致四肢变形。
▶ **deformed** /dɪ'fɔːmd/ adjective 形容词: He had a deformed right leg. 他右腿畸形。

defy /dɪ'faɪ/ verb 动词 (defies, defying, defied)
to refuse to obey someone or something 违抗，反抗: This was the first time I defied my mother. 这是我第一次违抗母亲。

degree /dɪ'griː/ countable noun 可数名词
1 a unit for measuring temperatures that is often written as °*度，度数（温度单位，常写作°）: It's over 35° Celsius outside. 户外温度超过 35 摄氏度。▫ Bake the cake at 180 degrees Celsius for 25 minutes or until light brown. 将蛋糕在 180 摄氏度下烘烤 25 分钟，或烤至浅棕色。
2 a unit for measuring angles that is often written as °*度，度数（角的量度单位，常写作°）: It was pointing outward at an angle of 45 degrees. 它向外指着 45 度角的方向。▫ Angles smaller than a right angle (less than 90°) are called acute angles. 比直角小的角，即小于 90° 的角，叫作锐角。
3 a qualification that you receive when you have successfully completed a course of study at a university or a college 学位: He has an engineering degree. 他有工程学位。▫ She has a degree in Russian. 她有俄语学位。

delay /dɪ'leɪ/ verb 动词 (delays, delaying, delayed)
1 to not do something immediately or at the planned time, but to do it later 推迟；延迟: Many women delay motherhood because they want to have a career. 很多女性因想拥有自己的事业而推迟要孩子。
2 to make someone or something late 使耽搁；使延误: Passengers were delayed at the airport for five hours. 乘客在机场被耽搁了 5 个小时。▫ Our flight was delayed for three hours. 我们的航班延误了 3 个小时。● **delay** noun 名词: He apologized for the delay. 他为这次延误道歉。

delegate /'delɪɡət/ countable noun 可数名词
a person who represents a group of other people at a meeting, for example（会议等的）代表: About 750 delegates attended the conference. 约 750 个代表参会。

delete /dɪ'liːt/ verb 动词 (deletes, deleting, deleted)
to remove or put a line through something that has been written down or stored in a computer 删除；删掉: He deleted files from the computer. 他从电脑里删掉了文件。

deliberate /dɪ'lɪbərət/ adjective 形容词
planned and not done by accident 故意的；蓄意的: They told deliberate lies in order to sell newspapers. 为了卖报纸，他们故意说谎。
▶ **deliberately** /dɪ'lɪbərətli/ adverb 副词: He started the fire deliberately. It wasn't an accident. 他是蓄意纵火，并非意外。

delicate /'delɪkət/ adjective 形容词
1 easily broken or damaged 易碎的；脆弱的: The machine even washes delicate glassware. 这台机器甚至能清洗易碎的玻璃制品。▫ Do not rub the delicate skin around the eyes. 不要揉眼周娇嫩的皮肤。
2 pleasant and light in colour, taste or smell（颜色）柔和的；（味道）清淡可口的；（气味）清香的: The beans have a delicate flavour. 这些豆子味道清香。▫ The sheets were a delicate shade of pink. 床单带一点儿淡淡的粉色。

delicatessen /ˌdelɪkə'tesən/ countable noun 可数名词
a shop that sells food such as cold meats and cheeses（出售冷盘肉、干酪等的）熟食店

delicious /dɪ'lɪʃəs/ adjective 形容词
very good to eat 美味的；可口的: There was a wide choice of delicious meals. 有很

delight - demonstrate

多美味可口的饭菜可以选择。
▶**deliciously** /dɪˈlɪʃəsli/ *adverb* 副词: *This yogurt has a deliciously creamy flavour.* 这酸奶有一种香甜的奶油味。

delight /dɪˈlaɪt/ *uncountable noun* 不可数名词
a feeling of great pleasure 高兴；愉快: *He expressed delight at the news.* 听到这一消息，他很开心。□ *Andrew laughed with delight.* 安德鲁开心地大笑。

delighted /dɪˈlaɪtɪd/ *adjective* 形容词
extremely pleased 高兴的；愉快的: *Frank was delighted to see her.* 见到她，弗兰克很开心。

deliver /dɪˈlɪvər/ *verb* 动词 (**delivers, delivering, delivered**)
to take something to a particular place 递送；运送: *Only 90% of first-class post is delivered on time.* 仅 90% 的一级邮件是按时递送的。□ *The Canadians plan to deliver more food to Somalia.* 加拿大计划向索马里运送更多食品。

delivery /dɪˈlɪvəri/ *noun* 名词 (**deliveries**)
1 *uncountable* 不可数 when someone brings letters, packages or other goods to a particular place (信件、包裹等的) 递送，投递: *Please allow 28 days for delivery of your order.* 您的订单配送需 28 天。
2 *countable* 可数 the goods that are delivered 递送之物；投送之物: *I got a delivery of fresh eggs this morning.* 我今天早上收到了送来的新鲜鸡蛋。

deluxe /dɪˈlʌks/ *adjective* 形容词
very high quality and expensive 豪华的；高级的: *She only stays in deluxe hotel suites.* 她只住豪华酒店套房。

demand¹ /dɪˈmɑːnd/ *verb* 动词 (**demands, demanding, demanded**)
to ask for something in a very firm way 强烈要求: *The victim's family is demanding an investigation into the shooting.* 受害者家属强烈要求调查这起枪击事件。□ *He demanded that I give him an answer.* 他坚决要求我给他一个答复。

demand² /dɪˈmɑːnd/ *countable noun* 可数名词
a firm request for something (强烈的) 要求: *There were demands for better services.* 有客户要求提供更好的服务。
in (great) demand very popular and wanted by a lot of people 很受欢迎；有很大需求: *Maths teachers are always in demand.* 数学老师总是很抢手。

democracy /dɪˈmɒkrəsi/ *uncountable noun* 不可数名词
a system of government in which people choose their leaders by voting for them in elections 民主制度；民主政体: *We're studying democracy in Eastern Europe.* 我们正在研究东欧的民主政体。

democrat /ˈdeməkræt/ *countable noun* 可数名词
a person who believes in and wants democracy 民主主义者: *This is the time for democrats and not dictators.* 现在需要的是民主主义者，不是独裁者。

democratic /ˌdeməˈkrætɪk/ *adjective* 形容词
1 having or relating to a political system in which the leaders are elected by the people that they govern 民主制度的；民主政体的: *Bolivia returned to democratic rule in 1980s.* 玻利维亚于 20 世纪 80 年代恢复民主政体。
2 based on the idea that everyone has equal rights and should be involved in making important decisions 民主的；有民主精神的: *Education is the basis of a democratic society.* 教育是民主社会的基础。

demolish /dɪˈmɒlɪʃ/ *verb* 动词 (**demolishes, demolishing, demolished**)
to destroy something completely 摧毁；拆除: *The storm demolished buildings and flooded streets.* 暴风雨摧毁了建筑，淹没了街道。
▶**demolition** /ˌdeməˈlɪʃən/ *uncountable noun* 不可数名词: *The bomb caused the total demolition of the old bridge.* 那枚炸弹彻底炸毁了那座古老的桥。

demonstrate /ˈdemənˌstreɪt/ *verb* 动词 (**demonstrates, demonstrating, demonstrated**)
1 to show people how something works or how to do something 示范；演示: *Several companies were demonstrating their new products.* 几家公司正在演示新产品。
▶**demonstration** /ˌdemənˈstreɪʃən/ *countable noun* 可数名词: *We watched a cooking demonstration.* 我们观看了一场烹饪示范。
2 to march or gather somewhere to show that you oppose or support something 示威: *Ten thousand people demonstrated against the war.* 1 万人进行了反战示威。

▶**demonstration** /ˌdemənˈstreɪʃən/ *countable noun* 可数名词: *Soldiers broke up an anti-government demonstration.* 士兵们驱散了反政府示威的人群。

▶**demonstrator** /ˈdemənˌstreɪtə/ *countable noun* 可数名词: *Police were dealing with a crowd of demonstrators.* 警方正在应对示威人群。

den /den/ *countable noun* 可数名词
the home of some types of wild animal (野生动物的) 穴, 窝

denial /dɪˈnaɪəl/ *noun* 名词
when you say that something is not true or that it does not exist 否认: *There have been many official denials of the government's involvement.* 官方已多次否认政府参与此事。

denim /ˈdenɪm/ *uncountable noun* 不可数名词
a thick cotton cloth, usually blue, which is used for making clothes 蓝粗棉布; 牛仔布: *a denim jacket* 牛仔布夹克衫

dense /dens/ *adjective* 形容词 (**denser, densest**)
1 with a lot of things or people in a small area 稠密的; 密集的: *The road runs through a dense forest.* 这条公路穿过一片茂密的森林。
▶**densely** /ˈdensli/ *adverb* 副词: *Java is a densely populated island.* 爪哇岛人口稠密。
2 very thick and difficult to see through 浓的; 浓密的: *The planes came close to each other in dense fog.* 飞机在浓雾中相互靠近。
3 having great weight in relation to size 密度大的: *Ice is less dense than water, and so it floats.* 冰的密度小于水, 因此会浮在水面。

density /ˈdensɪti/ *noun* 名词 (**densities**)
how heavy a substance or an object is in relation to its size 密度: *Jupiter's moon Io has a density of about 3.5 grams per cubic centimetre.* 木星的卫星木卫一密度约为每立方厘米 3.5 克。

dent /dent/ *verb* 动词 (**dents, denting, dented**)
to make a hollow area in the surface of something by hitting it or pressing it too hard 使凹陷; 使产生凹痕: *The stone dented the car door.* 石头把车门砸出一块凹陷。● **dent** *countable noun* 可数名词: *There was a dent in the side of the car.* 车身侧面有一处凹陷。

dent 凹陷

dental /ˈdentəl/ *adjective* 形容词
relating to teeth 牙齿的: *Regular dental care is important.* 定期护理牙齿很重要。

dentist /ˈdentɪst/ *countable noun* 可数名词
1 a person whose job is to examine and treat people's teeth 牙医: *Visit your dentist twice a year for a checkup.* 每年去牙医处做两次牙齿检查。
2 (also 亦作 **dentist's**) the place where a dentist works 牙科诊所: *I'm going to the dentist's after school.* 我放学后要去看牙医。
→ Look at picture on P16 参见彩插第 16 页

deny /dɪˈnaɪ/ *verb* 动词 (**denies, denying, denied**)
to say that something is not true 否认: *Robby denied stealing the bike.* 罗比否认偷了自行车。□ *He denied that he was involved in the crime.* 他否认自己参与了这起罪案。

deodorant /diˈəʊdərənt/ *noun* 名词
a substance that you can put on your skin to hide or prevent bad smells 除臭剂, 香体剂 (用于消除或预防体臭)

depart /dɪˈpɑːt/ *verb* 动词 (**departs, departing, departed**)
to leave 离开; 启程; 动身: *Flight 43 will depart from Newcastle at 11.45 a.m.* *43 次航班将于上午 11 点 45 分从纽卡斯尔起飞。□ *In the morning, Mr McDonald departed for Sydney.* 麦克唐纳先生上午启程前往悉尼。

department /dɪˈpɑːtmənt/ *countable noun* 可数名词
1 one of the sections in an organization such as a government, a business or a university (政府的) 部, 局, 科; (企业的) 部门; (大学的) 系, 所: *She works for the Department of Health.* 她在卫生部工作。
2 one of the sections in a large shop (大型商场的) 货品区: *He works in the shoe department.* 他负责卖鞋的区域。

de·partment ˌstore countable noun 可数名词
a large shop that sells many different types of goods 百货商场；百货公司

departure /dɪˈpɑːtʃə/ noun 名词
the act of going away from somewhere 离开；启程；出发：*Illness delayed the president's departure for Helsinki.* 总统抱病，前往赫尔辛基的行程推迟。

departures /dɪˈpɑːtʃəz/ singular noun 单数名词
the place in an airport where passengers wait before they get onto their plane（机场的）候机厅

depend /dɪˈpend/ verb 动词 (**depends, depending, depended**)
can depend on someone/something to know that someone or something will support you or help you when you need them 可以指望某人／某事物；可以信赖某人／某事物：*'You can depend on me,' I assured him.* "有我你就放心吧。"我向他保证。
depend on someone/something to need someone or something in order to do something 依靠某人／某事物；依赖某人／某事物：*I'm depending on you to protect me.* 我指望你保护我。□ *He depended on his writing for his income.* 他靠写作赚取收入。
depend on something to be decided by something 取决于某事物：*The cooking time depends on the size of the potato.* 所需的烹饪时间取决于土豆的大小。
it depends or **that depends** used for showing that you cannot give an answer to a question because you need more information 视情况而定；看情况：*'How long can you stay?' — 'I don't know. It depends.'* "你能待多久？" ——"不知道，得看情况。"

dependable /dɪˈpendəbəl/ adjective 形容词
helpful and sensible 可靠的；可信赖的：*He was a dependable friend.* 他是个可靠的朋友。

dependent /dɪˈpendənt/ adjective 形容词
needing someone or something in order to succeed or to be able to survive 依靠的；依赖的：*The young gorillas are completely dependent on their mothers.* 大猩猩幼崽完全依赖母亲照顾。

▶ **dependence** /dɪˈpendəns/ uncountable noun 不可数名词：*We discussed the city's dependence on tourism.* 我们讨论了这个城市对旅游业的依赖。

deposit /dɪˈpɒzɪt/ countable noun 可数名词
1 a sum of money that is part of the full price of something, and that you pay when you agree to buy it 订金；预付款：*He paid a £500 deposit for the car.* 他付了500英镑的购车订金。
2 an amount of a substance that has been left somewhere as a result of a chemical or geological process 堆积物；沉积物：*underground deposits of gold* 地下金矿
3 an amount of money that you put into a bank account 存款：*I made a deposit every week.* 我每周存一笔款。

depot /ˈdepəʊ/ countable noun 可数名词
a place where goods or vehicles are kept until they are needed 仓库；车库：*The food is stored in a depot at the airport.* 食物储存在机场仓库。□ *a bus depot* 公交场站

depress /dɪˈpres/ verb 动词 (**depresses, depressing, depressed**)
to make you feel sad 使抑郁；使沮丧：*This time of year always depresses me.* 每年这个时候我总是很郁闷。

depressed /dɪˈprest/ adjective 形容词
feeling very sad and unable to enjoy anything for a long time 抑郁的；沮丧的：*She was very depressed after her husband died.* 丈夫死后，她非常消沉。

depressing /dɪˈpresɪŋ/ adjective 形容词
making you feel sad 令人抑郁的；使人沮丧的：*The view from the window was grey and depressing.* 从窗户望出去，所见皆是灰蒙蒙的，令人沮丧。

depression /dɪˈpreʃən/ uncountable noun 不可数名词
a state of mind in which you are very sad and you feel that you cannot enjoy anything 抑郁；沮丧：*Mr Thomas was suffering from depression.* 托马斯先生患有抑郁症。

deprive /dɪˈpraɪv/ verb 动词 (**deprives, depriving, deprived**)
to take something away from someone, or prevent them from having something 剥夺；使丧失：*They were deprived of fuel to heat their homes.* 他们家里没有燃料取暖。

▶ **deprived** /dɪˈpraɪvd/ adjective 形容词：*These are some of the most deprived children in the country.* 这些是这个国家最

贫穷的一些孩子。

depth /depθ/ *noun* 名词
how deep something is; the distance from the top to the bottom of something 深度：*The average depth of the sea is around 4,000 metres.* 海洋的平均深度约为 4,000 米。
in depth in a very detailed way 深入地；彻底地：*We will discuss these three areas in depth.* 我们将深入探讨这 3 个领域。

deputy /'depjuti/ *countable noun* 可数名词 (**deputies**)
the second most important person in an organization 副职；副手；副主管：*Dr Amin is the museum's deputy director.* 阿明博士是这家博物馆的副馆长。

descend /dɪ'send/ *verb* 动词 (**descends, descending, descended**)
to move down from a higher level to a lower level (*formal* 正式) 下来；下降；下去：*We descended to the basement.* 我们下到地下室。

describe /dɪ'skraɪb/ *verb* 动词 (**describes, describing, described**)
to say what something is like 描述；描写；形容：*She described what she did in her spare time.* 她描述了她在业余时间做的事情。□ *The poem describes their life together.* 这首诗描述了他们在一起的生活。

description /dɪ'skrɪpʃən/ *noun* 名词
an explanation of what someone looks like, or what something is 描述；描写；形容：*Police have given a description of the man.* 警方已描述了这名男子的特征。□ *He gave a detailed description of how the new system will work.* 他详细说明了新系统将如何运行。

desert[1] /'dezət/ *noun* 名词
a large area of land where there is almost no water, trees or plants 沙漠：*They travelled through the Sahara Desert.* 他们穿过撒哈拉沙漠。

desert[2] /dɪ'zɜːt/ *verb* 动词 (**deserts, deserting, deserted**)
1 to leave a place so that it becomes empty 离弃，舍弃(某地)：*Poor farmers are deserting their fields and coming to the cities to find jobs.* 穷苦农民正舍弃土地，来城市寻找工作。
▶ **deserted** /dɪ'zɜːtɪd/ *adjective* 形容词 *She led them into a deserted street.* 她带他们走进一条空寂无人的街道。
2 to leave or abandon someone who needs your help or support 抛弃，遗弃(某人)：*Sadly, most of her friends have deserted her.* 不幸的是，她的朋友大多离开了她。

deserve /dɪ'zɜːv/ *verb* 动词 (**deserves, deserving, deserved**)
to be worthy of something because of your actions or qualities 值得；应得：*These people deserve to get more money.* 这些人应该拿到更多的钱。□ *This is a serious crime, and it deserves a severe punishment.* 这起案件情节严重，应给予严厉处罚。

design[1] /dɪ'zaɪn/ *verb* 动词 (**designs, designing, designed**)
to make a detailed plan or drawing to show how something should be made 设计；规划：*They wanted to design a machine that was both attractive and practical.* 他们想要设计一种既美观又实用的机器。

design[2] /dɪ'zaɪn/ *noun* 名词
1 *uncountable* 不可数 the process of planning and drawing things 设计；规划：*He had a talent for design.* 他有设计天赋。
→ Look at picture on P13 参见彩插 P13 页
2 *countable* 可数 a drawing that shows how something should be built or made 设计图；图纸：*They drew the design for the house.* 他们绘制了这栋房子的设计图。
3 *countable* 可数 a pattern of lines or shapes that is used for decorating something 图案；花纹：*The table cloths come in three different designs.* 桌布有 3 种纹样。

designer /dɪ'zaɪnə/ *countable noun* 可数名词
a person whose job is to design things by making drawings of them 设计师；设计者：*Caroline is a fashion designer.* 卡罗琳是一名时装设计师。

desirable /dɪ'zaɪərəbəl/ *adjective* 形容词
so useful or attractive that everyone wants to have it 合意的；理想的；可取的：*The house is in a desirable neighbourhood, close to schools.* 这栋房子所在社区很理想，离学校很近。

desire[1] /dɪ'zaɪə/ *countable noun* 可数名词
a strong wish to do or have something 渴望；热望；欲望：*I had a strong desire to help people.* 我非常渴望能帮助他人。

desire[2] /dɪ'zaɪə/ *verb* 动词 (**desires, desiring, desired**)
to want something very much (*formal* 正

式）渴望；想望；想要：*This house is ideal for someone who desires a bit of peace.* 若寻求宁静的环境，这处房子很理想。
▶ **desired** /dɪˈzaɪəd/ *adjective* 形容词：*This will produce the desired effect.* 这样会产生理想的效果。

desk /desk/ *noun* 名词
1 countable 可数 a table that you sit at to write or work 书桌；写字台；办公桌
→ Look at picture on P1 参见彩插第 1 页
2 singular 单数 a place in a public building where you can get information 服务台；问询台：*They asked for Miss Minton at the reception desk.* 他们在服务台说要找明顿小姐。

desktop[1] /ˈdesktɒp/ *adjective* 形容词
of a convenient size for using on a desk or a table 台式的：*A $1,000 desktop personal computer can perform about 450 calculations per second.* 一台 1,000 美元的台式个人电脑每秒钟能进行约 450 次计算。

desktop[2] /ˈdesktɒp/ also 亦作 **desk-top** *countable noun* 可数名词
the images that you see on a computer screen when the computer is ready to use（计算机的）桌面：*You can rearrange the icons on the desktop.* 你可以重新排列桌面上的图标。

despair /dɪˈspeə/ *uncountable noun* 不可数名词
the feeling that everything is wrong and that nothing will improve 绝望：*I looked at my wife in despair.* 我绝望地看着妻子。
● **despair** *verb* 动词 (**despairs, despairing, despaired**)：*'Oh, I despair sometimes,' she said, looking at the mess.* "哦，我有时会感到绝望。"她看着一片狼藉说道。

desperate /ˈdespərət/ *adjective* 形容词
1 willing to try anything to change your situation 不顾一切的；孤注一掷的：*He was desperate to get back to the city.* 他不顾一切地要回到那座城市。□ *There were hundreds of patients desperate for his help.* 有数百名患者极度渴望得到他的帮助。
▶ **desperately** /ˈdespərətli/ *adverb* 副词：*Thousands of people are desperately trying to leave the country.* 数千人不顾一切地要离开这个国家。
2 very difficult, serious or dangerous 极困难的；极严重的；极危险的：*The situation in the area is desperate — there is no food.* 这个地区形势极为严峻——没有食物。

desperation /ˌdespəˈreɪʃən/ *uncountable noun* 不可数名词
the feeling that you have when you are in such a bad situation that you will try anything to change it 绝望；不顾一切；孤注一掷：*There was a look of desperation in her eyes.* 她的眼神里有一丝绝望。

despise /dɪˈspaɪz/ *verb* 动词 (**despises, despising, despised**)
to dislike someone or something very much 鄙视；憎恨；厌恶：*She despises dishonesty, and she hated lying to Dave.* 她厌恶欺骗，不愿跟戴夫说谎。

despite /dɪˈspaɪt/ *preposition* 介词
used for introducing a fact that makes something surprising 尽管；虽然：*The barbecue was a success, despite the rain.* 虽说下了雨，烧烤活动还是很成功。

dessert /dɪˈzɜːt/ *noun* 名词
something sweet that you eat at the end of a meal（饭后）甜点：*We had ice cream for dessert.* 我们餐后甜点吃了冰激凌。

dessertspoon /dɪˈzɜːtspuːn/ *countable noun* 可数名词
a spoon that you use for eating desserts 点心匙

destination /ˌdestɪˈneɪʃən/ *countable noun* 可数名词
the place you are going to 目的地：*He wanted to arrive at his destination before dark.* 他想天黑前赶到目的地。

destiny /ˈdestɪni/ *countable noun* 可数名词 (**destinies**)
everything that happens to you during your life, including what will happen in the future 命运：*Do we control our own destiny?* 我们掌握着自己的命运吗？

destroy /dɪˈstrɔɪ/ *verb* 动词 (**destroys, destroying, destroyed**)
to cause so much damage to something that it cannot be used any longer, or does not exist any longer 毁灭；摧毁：*The original house was destroyed by fire.* 原来的房子被大火烧毁了。
▶ **destruction** /dɪˈstrʌkʃən/ *uncountable noun* 不可数名词：*We must stop the destruction of our forests.* 我们必须停止破坏森林。

destructive /dɪˈstrʌktɪv/ *adjective* 形容词
causing great damage 破坏性的；毁灭性的：*a destructive storm* 破坏性的风暴

detach /dɪˈtætʃ/ *verb* 动词 (**detaches, detaching, detached**)
to remove something from another thing to which it was attached (*formal* 正式) 拆卸；使分开：*Detach the card and post it to this address.* 撕下卡片，寄到这个地址。

detached /dɪˈtætʃt/ *adjective* 形容词
not joined to any other building (建筑) 独立式的：*We have a house with a detached garage.* 我们的房子有独立车库。

detail /ˈdiːteɪl/ *countable noun* 可数名词
one of the small, individual parts of something 细节：*We discussed the details of the letter.* 我们讨论了信件的一些细节。
in detail in a way that considers all the different facts or parts of something 详细地；细致地：*Examine the contract in detail before signing it.* 在合同上签字之前要仔细审读。

detailed /ˈdiːteɪld/ *adjective* 形容词
containing a lot of details 详细的；细致的：*She gave us a detailed description of the man.* 她向我们详细描述了那个人的特征。

details /ˈdiːteɪlz/ *plural noun* 复数名词
the facts about someone or something 详情；信息；资料：*See the bottom of this page for details of how to apply for this offer.* 有关如何申请这份工作，详情请参阅本页底部。

detect /dɪˈtekt/ *verb* 动词 (**detects, detecting, detected**)
to find or notice something 觉察；发现：*One of the hotel guests detected the smell of smoke.* 旅馆的一位客人闻到了烟味。
□ *Arnold could detect sadness in the old man's face.* 阿诺德能觉察到那个老人脸上有一丝悲伤。
▶ **detection** /dɪˈtekʃən/ *uncountable noun* 不可数名词：*The process is used in the detection of cancer.* 这一方法被用于癌症筛查。

detective /dɪˈtektɪv/ *countable noun* 可数名词
someone whose job is to discover what has happened in a crime, and to find the people who did the crime 侦探：*Detectives are still searching for the four men.* 侦探仍在搜索那 4 个人的行踪。

detergent /dɪˈtɜːdʒənt/ *noun* 名词
a chemical substance that you use for washing things such as clothes or dishes 洗涤剂；清洁剂：*Hand-wash the gloves in warm water, using a mild detergent.* 用温水的洗涤剂在温水中用手清洗手套。

deteriorate /dɪˈtɪəriəˌreɪt/ *verb* 动词 (**deteriorates, deteriorating, deteriorated**)
to get worse 恶化；变坏：*Her eyesight is rapidly deteriorating.* 她的视力急剧下降。
▶ **deterioration** /dɪˌtɪəriəˈreɪʃən/ *noun* 名词：*Too little sleep can cause a deterioration in your health.* 睡眠严重不足会导致健康状况恶化。

determination /dɪˌtɜːmɪˈneɪʃən/ *uncountable noun* 不可数名词
the feeling you have when you have firmly decided to do something 决心；坚决；坚定：*Everyone behaved with courage and determination.* 所有人都表现得勇敢坚定。

determine /dɪˈtɜːmɪn/ *verb* 动词 (**determines, determining, determined**)
1 to control what will happen (*formal* 正式) 是…的决定因素：*The size of the chicken pieces will determine the cooking time.* 烹饪时间的长短取决于鸡块的大小。
2 to discover something (*formal* 正式) 确定；查明：*The investigation will determine what really happened.* 此次调查会查明到底发生了什么。

determined /dɪˈtɜːmɪnd/ *adjective* 形容词
certain that you want to do something, no matter how difficult it is 坚决的；坚定的：*He is determined to win gold in the final.* 他下定决心要在决赛中夺金。

detest /dɪˈtest/ *verb* 动词 (**detests, detesting, detested**)
to dislike someone or something very much 厌恶；憎恶：*You are probably aware that I detest smoking.* 你可能察觉到我讨厌抽烟。

devastate /ˈdevəˌsteɪt/ *verb* 动词 (**devastates, devastating, devastated**)
to damage an area or a place very badly, or to destroy it completely 毁坏；破坏；摧毁：*The earthquake devastated parts of Indonesia.* 地震摧毁了印度尼西亚的部分地区。
▶ **devastation** /ˌdevəˈsteɪʃən/ *uncountable noun* 不可数名词：*The war brought massive devastation to the area.* 战争使该地区遭到大面积破坏。

develop /dɪˈveləp/ *verb* 动词 (**develops, developing, developed**)
1 to grow or change over a period of time 发育；成长；发展：*Children need time to*

develop. 孩子需要时间来成长。▫ By then, their friendship had developed into love. 到那时，他们的友谊已经发展成了爱情。
▶**developed** /dɪˈveləpt/ *adjective* 形容词: *Their bodies were well developed and very fit.* 他们的身体发育得很好，非常健壮。
2 to begin to occur 出现；产生: *A problem developed aboard the space shuttle.* 航天飞机上出了个问题。
3 to design and produce a new product 研制，研发(新产品): *Scientists have developed a car paint that changes colour.* 科学家研发出了一种能变色的汽车喷漆。

development /dɪˈveləpmənt/ *noun* 名词
1 *uncountable* 不可数 change or growth over a period of time 发展；成长；发育: *We've been studying the development of language.* 我们一直在研究语言的发展。
2 *uncountable* 不可数 the process of creating a new product (新产品的)研发，研制: *The company is spending £850 million on research and development.* 这家公司在研发上的投入是 8.5 亿英镑。
3 *countable* 可数 an event or an incident that has recently happened and has an effect on an existing situation (事态的)发展，进展: *Police say this is an important development in the investigation.* 警方称这是调查过程中的一个重大进展。

device /dɪˈvaɪs/ *countable noun* 可数名词 something that has been invented for a particular purpose 器具；仪器；设备: *He used an electronic device to measure the rooms.* 他用电子设备测量房间尺寸。

devil /ˈdevəl/ *noun* 名词 an evil spirit who, according to some people, makes bad things happen 魔鬼；恶魔

devise /dɪˈvaɪz/ *verb* 动词 (**devises, devising, devised**) to invent a plan 策划；设计；想出: *We devised a plan to help him.* 我们想出了一个帮他的方案。

devote /dɪˈvəʊt/ *verb* 动词 (**devotes, devoting, devoted**)
  devote yourself to something to spend all or most of your time or energy on something 全身心投入某事；致力于某事: *She devoted herself to her art.* 她全身心投入到她的艺术中。

devoted /dɪˈvəʊtɪd/ *adjective* 形容词 feeling deep love for someone 深爱的；挚爱的: *He was devoted to his mother.* 他深爱母亲。

dew /djuː/ *uncountable noun* 不可数名词 small drops of water that form on the ground during the night 露水；露珠: *The dew formed on the leaves.* 露珠在叶子上凝结。

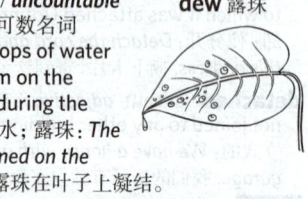
dew 露珠

diagnose /ˈdaɪəgnəʊz/ *verb* 动词 (**diagnoses, diagnosing, diagnosed**) to find out what is wrong with someone who is ill 诊断；确诊: *His son was diagnosed with diabetes.* 他儿子经诊断患有糖尿病。 ▫ *Her GP has diagnosed pneumonia.* 她的全科医生已诊断是肺炎。

diagnosis /ˌdaɪəgˈnəʊsɪs/ *noun* 名词 (**diagnoses** /ˌdaɪəgˈnəʊsiːz/) when a doctor finds out what is wrong with someone who is ill 诊断；确诊: *I had a second test to confirm the diagnosis.* 我又做了一次检查以确诊。

diagonal /daɪˈægənəl/ *adjective* 形容词 going from one corner of a square across to the opposite corner 斜线的；对角线的: *The screen showed a pattern of diagonal lines.* 屏幕上是斜纹图案。
▶**diagonally** /daɪˈægənəli/ *adverb* 副词: *He ran diagonally across the field.* 他斜穿着跑过田地。

diagram /ˈdaɪəˌgræm/ *countable noun* 可数名词 a simple drawing of lines used, for example, to explain how a machine works 简图；示意图: *He showed us a diagram of the inside of a computer.* 他给我们看了计算机内部结构的示意图。

dial¹ /ˈdaɪəl/ *countable noun* 可数名词
1 the part of a machine or a piece of equipment that shows you the time or a measurement 表盘；刻度盘；仪表盘: *The dial on the clock showed five minutes to seven.* 时钟的钟面显示差 5 分 7 点。
2 a small wheel on a piece of equipment that you can move in order to control the way it works (设备的)旋钮: *He turned the dial on the radio.* 他转动收音机旋钮。

dial² /ˈdaɪəl/ *verb* 动词 (**dials, dialling, dialled**) to press the buttons on a telephone in order to call someone 拨，按(电话号码): *Dial the number, followed by the hash (#).*

sign. 拨打号码，再按井号键。

dialect /ˈdaɪəlekt/ **countable noun** 可数名词
a form of a language that people speak in a particular area 方言；地方话：*They were speaking in the local dialect.* 他们说的是当地方言。

dialogue /ˈdaɪəlɒɡ/ **noun** 名词
a conversation between two people in a book, a film or a play（书、电影或戏剧中的）对话，对白：*He writes great dialogues.* 他对白写得特别好。□ *The film contains some very funny dialogue.* 这部电影的一些对白特别逗。

ˈdialogue ˌbox also 亦作 **dialog box countable noun** 可数名词
a small area that appears on a computer screen, containing information or questions（计算机屏幕上的）对话框：*Clicking here brings up another dialogue box.* 点击这里会生成一个新的对话框。

diameter /daɪˈæmɪtə/ **countable noun** 可数名词
the length of a straight line that can be drawn across a round object, passing through the middle of it 直径：*The tube is much smaller than the diameter of a human hair.* 这根导管比人头发的直径还要细得多。

diamond /ˈdaɪəmənd/ **noun** 名词
1 a hard, clear stone that is very expensive, and is used for making jewellery 钻石；金刚石：*a pair of diamond earrings* 一对钻石耳环
2 countable 可数 the shape ♦ *菱形：A baseball field is in the shape of a diamond.* 棒球场是菱形的。

diaper /ˈdaɪəpə/ **countable noun** 可数名词
(*American* 美国英语)
→ see 见 **nappy**: *She fed the baby and changed its diaper.* 她给宝宝喂食后又换了尿片。

diarrhoea /ˌdaɪəˈriːə/ **uncountable noun** 不可数名词
an illness that makes all the waste products come out of your body as liquid 腹泻；拉肚子：*Many team members suffered from diarrhoea.* 很多队员腹泻。

diary /ˈdaɪəri/ **countable noun** 可数名词
(**diaries**)
a book with a separate space for each day of the year that you use to write down things that you plan to do, or to record what happens in your life 记事簿；日记本：

I read the entry in his diary for July 10, 1940. 我读了他日记里 1940 年 7 月 10 日的那一篇。

dice /daɪs/ **countable noun** 可数名词 (**dice**)
a small block of wood or plastic with spots on its sides, used for playing games 色子；骰子：*I threw both dice and got a double 6.* 我掷出两个色子，点数都是 6。

dice 色子

dictate /dɪkˈteɪt/ **verb** 动词 (**dictates, dictating, dictated**)
to say or record something onto a machine, so that someone else can write it down for you 口授；口述；听写：*He dictated a moving letter to his mother.* 他给母亲口述了一封感人的信。

dictation /dɪkˈteɪʃən/ **uncountable noun** 不可数名词
when one person speaks and someone else writes down what they are saying 口授；口述；听写：*She was taking dictation from her boss.* 她正在记录老板的口述。

dictator /dɪkˈteɪtə/ **countable noun** 可数名词
a ruler who has complete power in a country 独裁者；专政者：*The country was ruled by a dictator for more than twenty years.* 这个国家被一个独裁者统治了 20 多年。

dictionary /ˈdɪkʃənri/ **countable noun** 可数名词 (**dictionaries**)
a book in which the words and phrases of a language are listed, together with their meanings 词典；字典：*We checked the spelling in the dictionary.* 我们在词典里查证了这个拼写。
→ Look at picture on P3 参见彩插第 3 页

did /dɪd/
→ see 见 **do**

didn't /ˈdɪdənt/
short for (缩写 =) 'did not'

die /daɪ/ **verb** 动词 (**dies, dying, died**)
1 to stop living 死；死亡：*My dog died last week.* 我的狗上周死了。□ *Sadly, my mother died of cancer.* 不幸的是，我的母亲死于癌症。
2 to gradually becomes weaker and then stop 消亡；逐渐消失：*My love for you will*

never die. 我对你的爱永远不灭。
be dying for something to want something very much (*informal* 非正式) 非常想要某物；渴望某物：*I'm dying for some fresh air.* 我非常渴望能呼吸到新鲜空气。
be dying to do something to want to do something very much (*informal* 非正式) 非常想做某事；渴望做某事：*I was dying to get home and relax.* 我特别想回家放松一下。

diesel /ˈdiːzəl/ **uncountable noun** 不可数名词
a fuel that is used in the engines of some vehicles instead of petrol 柴油

diet /ˈdaɪət/ **noun** 名词
the type of food that you regularly eat 日常饮食；日常食物：*It's never too late to improve your diet.* 什么时候改善饮食都为时不晚。● **diet** *verb* 动词 (**diets, dieting, dieted**)：*I've been dieting since the birth of my child.* 孩子出生后我就开始节食。
be on a diet to eat special types of food, or eat less food than usual 在节食；在按规定饮食：*Have you been on a diet? You've lost a lot of weight.* 你瘦了很多，是在节食吗？

differ /ˈdɪfə/ *verb* 动词 (**differs, differing, differed**)
to be different from another thing 有区别；不同于：*The story he told police differed from the one he told his mother.* 他在警方和母亲那里说辞不一。

difference /ˈdɪfrəns/ *noun* 名词
1 countable 可数 the way in which two things are different from each other 差别；差异；不同之处：*The main difference between the two computers is the price.* 这两台电脑最主要的差别就是价格。
2 singular 单数 the amount by which one quantity is more or less than another quantity 差量；差额：*The difference between 8,532 and 8,522 is 10.* *8,532 和 8,522 之间差 10。
make a difference to have an important effect on you 有影响；起作用：*Where you live makes a difference to the way you feel.* 居住地点会影响你的感受。
make no difference to have no effect on what you are doing; to have no importance 没有影响；不重要：*It makes no difference to me what you do.* 你做什么我都无所谓。

different /ˈdɪfrənt/ *adjective* 形容词
1 not alike 不同的；有差别的：*Although they are twins, they are so different!* 他们是双胞胎，但差别很大！□ *London was different from most European capital cities.* 伦敦和大多数欧洲国家的首都城市不同。
▶ **differently** /ˈdɪfrəntli/ *adverb* 副词：*Every person learns differently.* 每个人的学习方式都不一样。
2 used for showing that you are talking about two or more separate things of the same type 各种的；各样的：*Different countries export different products.* 不同国家出口不同的产品。
3 unusual 不同寻常的；与众不同的：*Her taste in clothes is interesting and different.* 她的穿衣品味有趣而独特。

difficult /ˈdɪfɪkəlt/ *adjective* 形容词
1 not easy to do, understand or deal with 困难的；不容易的：*The homework was too difficult for us.* 这家庭作业对我们来说太难了。□ *It was a very difficult decision to make.* 这是一个非常艰难的决定。
2 behaving in a way that is not reasonable or helpful 难相处的；难取悦的：*My son is 10 years old and a very difficult child.* 我儿子 10 岁，特别不听话。

difficulty /ˈdɪfɪkəlti/ **countable noun** 可数名词 (**difficulties**)
a problem 难题；困难：*There's always the difficulty of getting information.* 获取信息一直都是个难题。
have difficulty doing something to be unable to do something easily 做某事有困难：*Do you have difficulty walking?* 你走路有困难吗？

dig /dɪɡ/ *verb* 动词 (**digs, digging, dug**)
to make a hole in the ground 挖；掘：*I took the shovel and started digging.* 我拿过铁锹，挖了起来。□ *First, dig a large hole in the ground.* 首先，在地上挖个大洞。

dig 挖

digest /daɪˈdʒest/ *verb* 动词 (**digests, digesting, digested**)
to process food in your stomach, so that your body can use it for energy 消化：*Rice is easy to digest.* 米饭很好消化。□ *Do not swim for an hour after a meal to allow time to digest your food.* 饭后 1 小时之内不要游泳，要留出时间消化食物。

▶ **digestion** /daɪˈdʒestʃən/ *uncountable noun* 不可数名词: Peppermint helps digestion. 薄荷助消化。

digit /ˈdɪdʒɪt/ *countable noun* 可数名词
a written symbol for any of the ten numbers from 0 to 9 *（0 到 9 的任一）数字: Her telephone number differs from mine by one digit. 她的电话号码和我的只差 1 位数字。

digital /ˈdɪdʒɪtəl/ *adjective* 形容词
1 using information in the form of thousands of very small signals 数字的；数码的: Most people now have digital television. 现在多数人都买数字电视。
2 giving information in the form of numbers. Compare with **analogue**. 数字的，数字显示的（比较 analogue）: I've got a new digital watch. 我有一块新的数字式手表。

dignified /ˈdɪgnɪˌfaɪd/ *adjective* 形容词
calm, serious, and deserving respect 有尊严的；庄重的；可敬的: He was a very dignified and charming man. 他举止庄重，富有魅力。

dignity /ˈdɪgnɪti/ *uncountable noun* 不可数名词
serious, calm and controlled behaviour 庄严；庄重；端庄: She received the news with quiet dignity. 她听到这一消息时表现得沉稳庄重。

dilemma /daɪˈlemə/ *countable noun* 可数名词
a difficult situation in which you have to make a choice between two things 进退两难；两难的困境: He was facing a dilemma: should he return to his country or stay in Europe? 他进退两难，该回国还是留在欧洲？

diligent /ˈdɪlɪdʒənt/ *adjective* 形容词
hard-working, in a careful and thorough way 勤奋的；勤勉的: She's a diligent student. 她是个勤奋的学生。
▶ **diligence** /ˈdɪlɪdʒəns/ *uncountable noun* 不可数名词: He performed his duties with diligence. 他勤勤恳恳，尽职尽责。
▶ **diligently** /ˈdɪlɪdʒəntli/ *adverb* 副词: He was diligently searching the house. 他仔细搜查着房子的每个角落。

dilute /daɪˈluːt/ *verb* 动词 (dilutes, diluting, diluted)
to add water to another liquid 冲淡；稀释: This juice is quite strong, but you can dilute it with water. 这果汁很浓，但可加水稀释。
▫ The liquid is then diluted. 之后液体被稀释。

dim¹ /dɪm/ *adjective* 形容词 (**dimmer, dimmest**)
not bright 昏暗的；暗淡的: She waited in the dim light. 她在昏暗的光线下等待。
▶ **dimly** /ˈdɪmli/ *adverb* 副词: Two lamps burned dimly. 两盏灯暗淡地发着光。

dim² /dɪm/ *verb* 动词 (**dims, dimming, dimmed**)
to become less bright 变昏暗；变暗淡: The theatre lights dimmed and the orchestra started to play. 剧场的灯暗下来，管弦乐队开始演奏。 ▫ Could someone dim the lights, please? 劳驾，谁能把灯光调暗一点？

dimensions /daɪˈmenʃənz/ *plural noun* 复数名词
the measurements of something 尺寸；大小: We do not yet know the exact dimensions of the room. 我们还不知道这个房间的具体面积。

dine /daɪn/ *verb* 动词 (**dines, dining, dined**)
to have dinner (*formal* 正式) 进餐；吃饭: He drives a nice car and dines at the best restaurants. 他开着辆好车，去最高档的餐馆吃饭。

'dining ˌroom *countable noun* 可数名词
a room where people eat their meals 餐厅；饭厅

dinner /ˈdɪnə/ *noun* 名词
1 the main meal of the day, usually served in the evening 正餐；主餐；晚餐: She invited us for dinner. 她邀请我们吃晚餐。 ▫ Would you like to stay and have dinner? 你留下来一起吃饭好吗？
2 *countable* 可数 a formal social event in the evening at which a meal is served 晚宴；宴会: a series of official dinners 一系列的正式晚宴

dinnertime /ˈdɪnətaɪm/ also 亦作 **dinner time** *uncountable noun* 不可数名词
the time of the day when most people have their dinner 正餐时间；晚餐时间: The telephone call came just before dinnertime. 正要吃晚餐时，电话来了。

dinosaur /ˈdaɪnəˌsɔː/ *countable noun* 可数名词
a large animal that lived millions of years ago 恐龙

dinosaur 恐龙

dip[1] /dɪp/ **verb** 动词 (**dips**, **dipping**, **dipped**) to put something in a liquid and then quickly take it out again 浸；蘸：*Dip each apple in the syrup.* 每个苹果蘸一下糖浆。

dip[2] /dɪp/ **countable noun** 可数名词 a thick sauce that you dip pieces of food into before eating them 蘸酱；调味酱汁：*We sat and watched TV with a huge plate of crisps and dips.* 我们一边坐着看电视，一边吃着一大盘薯片蘸酱。

diploma /dɪˈpləʊmə/ **countable noun** 可数名词 a qualification that a student who has completed a course of study may receive 文凭；毕业证书：*He was awarded a diploma in social work.* 他获得了社会福利工作文凭。

diplomacy /dɪˈpləʊməsi/ **uncountable noun** 不可数名词 the activity or profession of managing relations between the governments of different countries 外交：*If diplomacy fails, there could be a war.* 如果外交失败，可能会发生战争。

diplomat /ˈdɪpləˌmæt/ **countable noun** 可数名词 a senior official whose job is to discuss international affairs with officials from other countries 外交官：*Sir Harold is a Western diplomat with experience in Asia.* 哈罗德先生是一位在亚洲事务上很有经验的西方外交家。

diplomatic /ˌdɪpləˈmætɪk/ **adjective** 形容词
1 relating to diplomacy and diplomats 外交的；外交官的：*The two countries enjoy good diplomatic relations.* 两国外交关系良好。
2 careful to say or do things without offending people 圆通的；讲究策略的：*She is very direct, but I prefer a more diplomatic approach.* 她很直接，但我喜欢比较圆通的方式。

▶**diplomatically** /ˌdɪpləˈmætɪkəli/ **adverb** 副词：*'Of course,' agreed Sloan diplomatically.* "当然。"斯隆客套地应和道。

direct[1] /daɪˈrekt, dɪˈrekt/ **adjective** 形容词, **adverb** 副词
1 toward a place or an object, without changing direction and without stopping 直达的；径直：*They took a direct flight to Athens.* 他们搭乘去雅典的直飞航班。 □ *You can fly direct from New York to London.* 你可以从纽约直飞伦敦。
▶**directly** /daɪˈrektli, dɪˈrektli/ **adverb** 副词：*She rushed home and went directly to her room.* 她快速赶回家，径直进了自己房间。
2 with nothing or no-one else in between 直接的(地)；直接接触的(地)：*Protect your plants from direct sunlight.* 避免植物直接受阳光照射。□ *More farms are selling direct to consumers.* 更多的农场直接把产品卖给消费者。
▶**directly** /daɪˈrektli, dɪˈrektli/ **adverb** 副词：*Never look directly at the sun.* 千万不要直视太阳。
3 honest and open, and saying exactly what you mean 坦率的；直截了当的：*He avoided giving a direct answer.* 他避免直接作答。
▶**directly** /daɪˈrektli, dɪˈrektli/ **adverb** 副词：*Explain simply and directly what you hope to achieve.* 请简要直接地说明您想要达成的目标。

direct[2] /daɪˈrekt, dɪˈrekt/ **verb** 动词 (**directs**, **directing**, **directed**)
1 to be responsible for organizing a project or a group of people 领导；管理：*Christopher will direct everyday operations.* 日常运营将由克里斯托弗管理。
▶**direction** /daɪˈrekʃən, dɪˈrekʃən/ **uncountable noun** 不可数名词：*Organizations need clear direction.* 各组织机构需要条理清晰的指导。
▶**director** /daɪˈrektə, dɪˈrektə/ **countable noun** 可数名词：*The company has a new director.* 这家公司换了新经理。
2 to be responsible for the way in which a film, play or television programme is performed 导演；执导：*Branagh himself will direct the movie.* 布拉纳本人将执导这部影片。

direction /daɪˈrekʃən, dɪˈrekʃən/ **noun** 名词 the general line that someone or something is moving or pointing in 方向；

方位：*The nearest town was ten miles in the opposite direction.* 最近的城镇在相反方向上 10 英里处。□ *He started walking in the direction of Larry's shop.* 他开始朝拉里店铺的方向走去。

directions /daɪˈrekʃənz, dɪˈrekʃənz/ *plural noun* 复数名词
instructions that tell you what to do, how to do something, or how to get somewhere 指示；说明；指示：*She stopped the car to ask for directions.* 她停下车问路。

directly /daɪˈrektli, dɪˈrektli/ *adverb* 副词
with nothing else separating you from something that is above, below or in front of you 直接地；正好：*They live in the flat directly above us.* 他们就住在我们公寓的正上方。

di‚rect ˈobject *countable noun* 可数名词
the person or thing that is affected by or involved in the action carried out by the subject. Compare with **indirect object**. 直接宾语（比较 indirect object）

director /daɪˈrektə, dɪˈrektə/ *countable noun* 可数名词
1 one of the people who control a company or an organization（公司的）董事，理事；（机构的）主任，主管：*We wrote to the directors of the bank.* 我们给银行主管写了信。
2 the person who tells the actors and technical staff of a play, a film or a television programme what to do 导演

directory /daɪˈrektəri, dɪˈrektəri/ *countable noun* 可数名词 (**directories**)
a book containing lists of people's names, addresses and telephone numbers 通讯录；电话簿：*You'll find our number in the telephone directory.* 你可以在电话簿里找到我们的号码。

dirt /dɜːt/ *uncountable noun* 不可数名词
1 dust or mud 灰尘；污垢：*I started to clean the dirt off my hands.* 我开始清洗手上的泥。
2 the earth on the ground 泥土：*They all sat on the dirt under a tree.* 他们都坐在树下的泥土地上。

dirty /ˈdɜːti/ *adjective* 形容词 (**dirtier, dirtiest**)
not clean 肮脏的；污秽的：*She collected the dirty plates from the table.* 她收拾了桌上的脏盘子。

disability /ˌdɪsəˈbɪlɪti/ *countable noun* 可数

名词 (**disabilities**)
a permanent injury or condition that makes it difficult for you to work or live normally（身体上的）残疾，伤残，缺陷：*We're building a new classroom for people with disabilities.* 我们正在修建残障人士适用的新教室。

disabled /dɪˈseɪbəld/ *adjective* 形容词
having an injury or a condition that makes it difficult for you to move around 有残疾的；残障的：*parents of disabled children* 残疾儿童的父母

disadvantage /ˌdɪsədˈvɑːntɪdʒ/ *countable noun* 可数名词
something that makes things more difficult for you 不利条件；缺点：*The big disadvantage of this computer is its size.* 这台电脑的一大缺点就是它的尺寸。
be at a disadvantage to have a difficulty that many other people do not have 处于不利境地：*Children from poor families were at a disadvantage.* 贫困家庭的孩子处于不利地位。

disagree /ˌdɪsəˈɡriː/ *verb* 动词 (**disagrees, disagreeing, disagreed**)
1 to have a different opinion from someone else 不同意；有分歧：*I really have to disagree with you here.* 在这一点上我实在不能苟同。□ *O'Brien disagreed with the suggestion that his team played badly.* 对于他的球队打得不好这种说法，奥布赖恩并不认同。□ *They always disagreed about politics.* 他们的政治观点总是相左。
2 to disapprove of an action or a decision 不赞成；反对：*I respect the president but I disagree with his decision.* 我尊敬总统，但我反对他的这个决议。

disagreement /ˌdɪsəˈɡriːmənt/ *noun* 名词
when people do not agree with something or with each other 意见不一；分歧：*Mum and Dad had a disagreement about money.* 爸妈在钱的问题上有分歧。□ *Britain and France have expressed disagreement with the plan.* 英国和法国反对这个计划。

disappear /ˌdɪsəˈpɪə/ *verb* 动词 (**disappears, disappearing, disappeared**)
to go away 消失；失踪：*The sun disappeared and it started raining again.* 太阳不见了，又下起雨来。□ *His daughter disappeared thirteen years ago.* 他女儿 13 年前失踪。

▶ **disappearance** /ˌdɪsəˈpɪərəns/ *noun* 名

词：*Investigators suspect a thunderstorm in the area may have had something to do with the plane's disappearance.* 调查人员怀疑这架飞机的失踪和该地区发生的雷暴有关。

disappoint /ˌdɪsəˈpɔɪnt/ **verb** 动词 (**disappoints, disappointing, disappointed**)
to make you feel sad because something that you wanted did not happen, or was not as good as you hoped 使失望：*He apologized to fans left disappointed by the cancellation of last week's concerts.* 他向因上周音乐会取消而失望的粉丝致歉。

▶ **disappointing** /ˌdɪsəˈpɔɪntɪŋ/ **adjective** 形容词：*The restaurant looked great, but the food was disappointing.* 这家餐馆看上去不错，但饭菜让人不敢恭维。

disappointed /ˌdɪsəˈpɔɪntɪd/ **adjective** 形容词
sad because something has not happened or because something is not as good as you hoped 失望的；沮丧的：*I was disappointed that John was not there.* 约翰不在那里，我很失望。

disappointment /ˌdɪsəˈpɔɪntmənt/ **noun** 名词
1 *uncountable* 不可数 the feeling you have when you are disappointed 失望；沮丧：*She couldn't hide the disappointment in her voice.* 她掩饰不住声音里的失望。
2 *countable* 可数 something or someone that is not as good as you hoped 令人失望的事物（或人）：*Their team's defeat was a huge disappointment for the fans.* 球队的失利令粉丝大失所望。

disapproval /ˌdɪsəˈpruːvəl/ *uncountable noun* 不可数名词
when you show that you think that someone or something is bad or wrong 不赞同；反对：*He stared at Marina with disapproval.* 他不以为然地盯着玛丽娜。

disapprove /ˌdɪsəˈpruːv/ **verb** 动词 (**disapproves, disapproving, disapproved**)
to think that someone or something is bad or wrong 不赞成；反对：*Most people disapprove of violence.* 多数人反对暴力行为。

disaster /dɪˈzɑːstə/ *countable noun* 可数名词
1 a very bad accident or event that may hurt many people 灾难；灾害：*It was the second air disaster (= plane crash) that month.* 这是那个月的第 2 次空难。

2 something that is not at all successful 非常糟糕的事；彻底的失败：*The party was a total disaster — everyone went home early.* 这场聚会太失败了——大家都提前回家了。

disastrous /dɪˈzɑːstrəs/ *adjective* 形容词
causing a lot of problems for many people 灾难性的；极为严重的：*The country suffered a disastrous earthquake in July.* 这个国家 7 月份遭遇了一场灾难性的地震。

disbelief /ˌdɪsbɪˈliːf/ *uncountable noun* 不可数名词
when you do not believe that something is true or real 不相信；怀疑：*She looked at him in disbelief.* 她疑惑地看着他。

disc /dɪsk/ *countable noun* 可数名词
a flat, circular object 圆盘状物：*The food processor has three slicing discs.* 这个食物料理机有三个圆盘状削片。 □ *The earrings are made of silver discs.* 这副耳环由银质圆片做成。

discard /dɪsˈkɑːd/ **verb** 动词 (**discards, discarding, discarded**)
to get rid of something 丢弃；抛弃：*Do not discard your receipt.* 收据不要扔。

discipline /ˈdɪsɪplɪn/ *uncountable noun* 不可数名词
1 the practice of making people obey rules 纪律；管束：*Children need discipline in order to feel secure and safe.* 孩子们需要纪律约束，这样才有安全感。
2 the quality of being able to obey particular rules and standards 自制力；遵守纪律：*He was impressed by the team's speed and discipline.* 这支队伍的速度和自制力给他留下深刻印象。

'disc ˌjockey *countable noun* 可数名词
someone whose job is to play music and talk on the radio. The short form **DJ** is also used. (电台) 音乐节目主持人 (缩写形式为 **DJ**)

disclose /dɪsˈkləʊz/ **verb** 动词 (**discloses, disclosing, disclosed**)
to tell people about something 透露；披露；泄露：*They refused to disclose details of the deal.* 他们拒绝披露交易细节。

disco /ˈdɪskəʊ/ *countable noun* 可数名词
a place or an event where people dance to pop music 迪斯科舞厅；迪斯科舞会：*Fridays and Saturdays are regular disco nights.* 每周五和周六定期举行迪斯科晚会。

discomfort /dɪsˈkʌmfət/ *uncountable noun* 不可数名词
an unpleasant feeling in part of your body 不舒服；不适：*Steve had some discomfort, but no real pain.* 史蒂夫有些不适，但算不上病痛。

disconnect /ˌdɪskəˈnekt/ *verb* 动词 (**disconnects, disconnecting, disconnected**)
to stop electricity, gas or water from going into a piece of equipment or a building 切断（电、煤气或水的供应）：*If you don't pay your phone bill, the phone company will disconnect your phone.* 不交电话费，你的电话将被电话公司停机。

discount /ˈdɪskaʊnt/ *countable noun* 可数名词
a reduction in the usual price of something 减价；折扣：*All staff get a 20% discount.* 所有员工享受 8 折优惠。

discourage /dɪsˈkʌrɪdʒ/ *verb* 动词 (**discourages, discouraging, discouraged**)
to make you feel less keen or confident about something 使泄气；使灰心：*Learning a language may be difficult at first. Don't let this discourage you.* 刚开始学习一门语言会很难，但不要因此灰心。
▶ **discouraged** /dɪsˈkʌrɪdʒd/ *adjective* 形容词：*He felt discouraged by his lack of progress.* 他没什么进步，感到很灰心。

discover /dɪsˈkʌvə/ *verb* 动词 (**discovers, discovering, discovered**)
1 to become aware of something that you did not know about before 发现，发觉（之前未知之事）：*After a short conversation, she discovered the reason for his unhappiness.* 短短几句对话之后，她发现了他不开心的原因。
2 to find something 找到；发现：*The car was discovered on a roadside outside the city.* 这辆车在城外的路边被发现。
3 to be the first person to find or use a new place, substance or method（第一个）发现：*Who was the first European to discover America?* 第一个发现美洲大陆的欧洲人是谁？

discovery /dɪsˈkʌvəri/ *noun* 名词 (**discoveries**)
when you become aware of something that you did not know about before 发现；发觉：*The man was arrested after the discovery of stolen paintings.* 偷盗的画作被发现之后，这个人被捕了。

make a discovery to be the first person to find or become aware of something that no one knew about before 有发现：*In that year, two important scientific discoveries were made.* 那一年有两项重大科学发现。

discreet /dɪsˈkriːt/ *adjective* 形容词
polite and careful in what you do or say 言行谨慎的；周到得体的：*He was a real gentleman, and he was always very discreet.* 他是个真正的绅士，事事周到得体。

discriminate /dɪsˈkrɪmɪneɪt/ *verb* 动词 (**discriminates, discriminating, discriminated**)
to treat a person or a group of people unfairly 区别对待；歧视：*They believe the law discriminates against women.* 他们认为这项法律歧视女性。

discrimination /dɪsˌkrɪmɪˈneɪʃən/ *uncountable noun* 不可数名词
the practice of treating one person or group unfairly 区别对待；歧视：*Many companies are breaking age discrimination laws.* 很多公司都未执行具年龄歧视的诸项法规。

discus /ˈdɪskəs/ *singular noun* 单数名词
the sport of throwing a heavy round object 铁饼运动：*He won the discus at the world championships.* 他在世界锦标赛的铁饼项目中夺冠。

discuss /dɪsˈkʌs/ *verb* 动词 (**discusses, discussing, discussed**)
to talk about something 讨论；谈论：*We are meeting next week to discuss plans for the future.* 我们将于下周碰面讨论对未来的规划。

> **LANGUAGE HELP 语言提示**
> You **cannot** say *discuss about* something. Instead, you can say that you **discuss** something **with** someone. 不能说 discuss about something，可以说 discuss something with someone：*I discussed the problem with my parents.* 我同父母讨论了这个问题。

discussion /dɪsˈkʌʃən/ *noun* 名词
a conversation about a subject 讨论；商讨：*Managers are having informal discussions later today.* 经理们今天晚些时候将进行非正式会谈。

disease /dɪˈziːz/ *noun* 名词
an illness that affects people, animals or plants 疾病；病：*There are no drugs*

available to treat this disease. 这种病现在无药可治。□ *heart disease* 心脏病

disgrace /dɪsˈgreɪs/ *singular noun* 单数名词
something that is very bad or wrong 丢脸的事；耻辱：*His behaviour was a disgrace.* 他的行为真丢脸。

disgraceful /dɪsˈgreɪsfʊl/ *adjective* 形容词
very bad or wrong 丢脸的；可耻的：*The way they treated him was disgraceful.* 他们对待他的方式真可耻。
▶ **disgracefully** /dɪsˈgreɪsfʊli/ *adverb* 副词：*His brother behaved disgracefully.* 他哥哥的行为很不光彩。

disguise¹ /dɪsˈgaɪz/ *noun* 名词
in disguise to have changed the way you look so that people will not recognize you 以乔装方式：*He travelled in disguise, dressed as an old man.* 他扮成一位老人乔装出行。

disguise² /dɪsˈgaɪz/ *verb* 动词 (**disguises, disguising, disguised**)
1 to hide something or make it appear different so that people will not recognize it 掩盖；掩饰：*I tried to disguise the fact that I was ill.* 我尽力掩饰自己生病的事情。
2 if you disguise yourself, you change how you look so that people will not recognize you 假扮；伪装：*We disguised ourselves as a group of tourists.* 我们假扮成一群游客。
▶ **disguised** /dɪsˈgaɪzd/ *adjective* 形容词：*The robber was disguised as a medical worker.* 抢劫者伪装成医务工作者。

disgust /dɪsˈgʌst/ *uncountable noun* 不可数名词
a very strong feeling of not liking or not approving of something 厌恶；憎恶：*At first I felt sorry for Mr Hart, but now I feel disgust for him.* 起初我为哈特先生难过，但现在我讨厌他。

disgusted /dɪsˈgʌstɪd/ *adjective* 形容词
feeling strongly that you do not like or do not approve of something 厌恶的；憎恶的：*I'm disgusted by the way that he was treated by his employers.* 他受到雇主如此对待真让我气愤。

disgusting /dɪsˈgʌstɪŋ/ *adjective* 形容词
extremely unpleasant or unacceptable 令人厌恶的；令人反感的：*The food tasted disgusting.* 这食物的味道令人作呕。

dish /dɪʃ/ *countable noun* 可数名词 (**dishes**)
1 a shallow container for cooking or serving food 盘；碟：*Pour the mixture into a square glass dish.* 把混合物倒入玻璃方碟中。
2 food that is prepared in a particular way 一盘菜；菜肴：*There were plenty of delicious dishes to choose from at the party.* 聚会上有很多美味的菜肴可供选择。

dishonest /dɪsˈɒnɪst/ *adjective* 形容词
not honest and unable to be trusted 不诚实的；不可靠的：*I admit that I was dishonest with him.* 我承认我那时欺骗了他。
▶ **dishonesty** /dɪsˈɒnɪsti/ *uncountable noun* 不可数名词：*She accused the government of dishonesty.* 她指责政府有欺骗行为。

dishwasher /ˈdɪʃwɒʃə/ *countable noun* 可数名词
a machine that washes and dries dishes 洗碗机

disinfect /ˌdɪsɪnˈfekt/ *verb* 动词 (**disinfects, disinfecting, disinfected**)
to clean something using a substance that kills bacteria 为…消毒（或杀菌）：*Chlorine is used for disinfecting water.* 氯用于给水消毒。

disinfectant /ˌdɪsɪnˈfektənt/ *noun* 名词
a substance that kills bacteria 消毒剂：*They washed their hands with disinfectant.* 他们用消毒剂洗手。

disk /dɪsk/ also 亦作 **disc** *countable noun* 可数名词
the part of a computer where information is stored 磁盘；光盘：*The program uses 2.5 megabytes of disk space.* 这个程序占用2.5兆的磁盘空间。

ˈdisk ˌdrive *countable noun* 可数名词
the part of a computer that holds a disk （计算机）磁盘驱动器

dislike /dɪsˈlaɪk/ *verb* 动词 (**dislikes, disliking, disliked**)
to not like someone or something 不喜欢；厌恶：*Many children dislike the taste of green vegetables.* 很多孩子不喜欢绿叶蔬菜的味道。● **dislike** *countable noun* 可数名词：*Make a list of your likes and dislikes about your job.* 列出工作中哪些是自己喜欢的，哪些是不喜欢的。

dismay /dɪsˈmeɪ/ *uncountable noun* 不可数名词
a strong feeling of fear, worry or sadness (*formal* 正式) 惊恐；焦虑；哀伤：*Local people reacted with dismay.* 当地人对此惊恐万状。
▶ **dismayed** /dɪsˈmeɪd/ *adjective* 形容词：*Glen was shocked and dismayed at her reaction.* 格伦对她的反应感到震惊错愕。

dismiss /dɪsˈmɪs/ *verb* 动词 (**dismisses, dismissing, dismissed**)
1 to say that something is not important enough for you to consider 不考虑；不理会：*Perry dismissed the suggestion as nonsense.* 佩里把这个建议视为胡说八道而不予理会。
2 to tell someone junior to you that they can leave 让…离开；解散：*The teacher dismissed us early, and I hurried to my locker.* 老师提前让我们散了，我急忙赶到储物柜前。

disobey /ˌdɪsəˈbeɪ/ *verb* 动词 (**disobeys, disobeying, disobeyed**)
to not do what you have been told to do 不服从；违抗：*He often disobeyed his mother and father.* 他经常不听父母的话。

disorganized /dɪsˈɔːɡənaɪzd/ *adjective* 形容词
1 badly arranged, planned or managed 缺乏组织的；杂乱无章的；混乱的：*He walked into the large, disorganized office.* 他走进乱糟糟的大办公室。
2 very bad at organizing things in your life 缺乏条理的；计划不周的：*My boss is completely disorganized.* 我老板做事毫无条理可言。

dispenser /dɪsˈpensə/ *countable noun* 可数名词
a machine or a container from which you can get something 自助取物装置；自动售货机：*a soap dispenser* 皂液器

display[1] /dɪsˈpleɪ/ *verb* 动词 (**displays, displaying, displayed**)
to put something in a place where people can see it 展示；陈列：*Old soldiers proudly displayed their medals.* 老兵们骄傲地展示自己的勋章。

display[2] /dɪsˈpleɪ/ *countable noun* 可数名词
an arrangement of things that have been put in a particular place, so that people can see them easily 展示；展览；陈列：*In the second gallery, there was a display of World War II aircraft.* 第二陈列室展出了第二次世界大战中的飞机。
on display in a public place for people to see 在展出：*The artist's work is on display in New York next month.* 这位艺术家的作品下月将在纽约展出。

disposable /dɪsˈpəʊzəbəl/ *adjective* 形容词
designed to be thrown away after use 用后即可丢弃的；一次性的：*disposable nappies* 一次性尿布 □ *a disposable razor* 一次性剃须刀

disposal /dɪsˈpəʊzəl/ *uncountable noun* 不可数名词
when you get rid of something that you no longer want or need（废物的）丢弃，处理，清理：*waste disposal* 废物处理

dispose /dɪsˈpəʊz/ *verb* 动词 (**disposes, disposing, disposed**)
dispose of something to get rid of something 清理某物；处理某物：*How do they dispose of nuclear waste?* 他们是怎么处理核废料的？

dispute /dɪsˈpjuːt/ *noun* 名词
when two people or groups cannot agree about something 争论；争端：*The government had to do something to end the dispute.* 政府不得不采取举措结束争端。

disqualify /dɪsˈkwɒlɪfaɪ/ *verb* 动词 (**disqualifies, disqualifying, disqualified**)
to stop someone from taking part in a competition 取消…的参赛资格：*Thomson was disqualified from the race.* 汤姆森被取消了比赛资格。

disrupt /dɪsˈrʌpt/ *verb* 动词 (**disrupts, disrupting, disrupted**)
to cause difficulties that prevent an event from continuing 扰乱，打断（事件进程）：*A fire broke out last night, disrupting preparations for tonight's pop concert.* 昨晚发生了火灾，打乱了今晚流行音乐会的准备工作。
▶ **disruption** /dɪsˈrʌpʃən/ *uncountable noun* 不可数名词：*The bad weather caused disruption at many airports.* 恶劣的天气导致很多机场航班取消。

disruptive /dɪsˈrʌptɪv/ *adjective* 形容词
preventing something from continuing in a normal way 破坏性的；制造混乱的：*We have a lot of difficult, disruptive children.* 我们有很多孩子难以管教，爱捣乱。

dissatisfied /dɪsˈsætɪsˌfaɪd/ *adjective* 形容词
not happy about something 不满意的：*Thousands of dissatisfied customers called the company to complain.* 数千名不满意的客户给公司打电话投诉。

dissect /daɪˈsekt, dɪ-/ *verb* 动词 (**dissects, dissecting, dissected**)
to cut open a dead body in order to examine it 解剖：*We dissected a frog in our biology class.* 我们在生物课上解剖了一只青蛙。

▶ **dissection** /daɪˈsekʃən, dɪ-/ *uncountable noun* 不可数名词: *The dissection of the tiny insect took place under a microscope.* 这只小昆虫的解剖工作在显微镜下进行。

dissolve /dɪˈzɒlv/ *verb* 动词 (**dissolves, dissolving, dissolved**)
to become completely mixed with a liquid 溶解: *Heat the mixture gently until the sugar dissolves.* 慢慢加热混合物直至糖溶解。

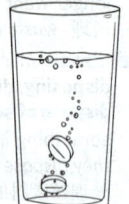
dissolve 溶解

distance /ˈdɪstəns/ *noun* 名词
the amount of space between two places 距离; 间距: *Measure the distance between the wall and the table.* 量一下墙和桌子之间的距离。
from a distance from a long way away 从远处; 远远地: *From a distance, the lake looked beautiful.* 这片湖从远处看非常美。
in the distance a long way away from you 在远处; 在远方: *We had a beautiful view of the countryside with the mountains in the distance.* 远山映衬下的乡村美景我们尽收眼底。

distant /ˈdɪstənt/ *adjective* 形容词
1 very far away 遥远的; 远距离的: *The mountains were on the distant horizon.* 群山坐落在远处的地平线上。
2 not closely related to you 远房的; 远亲的: *I received a letter from a distant cousin.* 我收到一个远房表亲的来信。

distinct /dɪˈstɪŋkt/ *adjective* 形容词
with an individual sound, appearance or taste 不同的; 有区别的: *Each vegetable has its own distinct flavour.* 每种蔬菜都有自己独特的味道。
distinct from something quite different from another thing 和某物截然不同的: *Quebec is quite distinct from the rest of Canada.* 魁北克和加拿大其他地方截然不同。

distinction /dɪˈstɪŋkʃən/ *noun* 名词
draw a distinction or **make a distinction** to say clearly that two things are different 区分; 区别: *He makes a distinction between art and culture.* 他分析了艺术和文化的不同。

distinguish /dɪˈstɪŋgwɪʃ/ *verb* 动词 (**distinguishes, distinguishing, distinguished**)
to be able to see or understand how two things are different 区分; 辨别; 分清: *When do babies learn to distinguish between men and women?* 小宝宝何时学会辨别男性和女性?

distinguished /dɪˈstɪŋgwɪʃt/ *adjective* 形容词
very successful and with a good reputation 杰出的; 著名的: *He came from a distinguished academic family.* 他来自一个优秀的学者家庭。

distract /dɪˈstrækt/ *verb* 动词 (**distracts, distracting, distracted**)
to take your attention away from what you are doing 使分心; 分散…的注意力: *I'm easily distracted by noise.* 一有声音我就很容易分心。

distraction /dɪˈstrækʃən/ *noun* 名词
something that turns your attention away from something else that you want to concentrate on 使人分心的事; 分散注意力的事: *Mobile phones in cars are a dangerous distraction for drivers.* 车里有手机会让开车的人分心，这很危险。

distress /dɪˈstres/ *uncountable noun* 不可数名词
a strong feeling of sadness or pain 悲伤; 痛苦; 忧虑: *The condition can cause great distress in young people.* 这种疾病会给年轻人带来极大的痛苦。
▶ **distressing** /dɪˈstresɪŋ/ *adjective* 形容词: *It is very distressing when your baby is ill.* 宝宝生病很让人闹心。

distribute /dɪˈstrɪbjuːt/ *verb* 动词 (**distributes, distributing, distributed**)
to give things to a number of people 分发; 分配: *They distributed free tickets to young people.* 他们给年轻人分发免费入场券。
▶ **distribution** /ˌdɪstrɪˈbjuːʃən/ *uncountable noun* 不可数名词: *They are trying to stop the illegal distribution of music over the Internet.* 他们在尽力阻止音乐在网上的非法传播。

district /ˈdɪstrɪkt/ *countable noun* 可数名词
a particular area of a city or a country 地区; 区域: *I drove around the business district.* 我开着车在商业区转了转。

disturb /dɪˈstɜːb/ *verb* 动词 (**disturbs, disturbing, disturbed**)
1 to interrupt someone or something by talking to them or making a noise 打扰; 干扰: *Sorry, am I disturbing you?* 抱歉，没打扰到你吧? □ *Only the occasional*

passing car disturbed the silence. 只有偶尔驶过的汽车打破这片宁静。 **2** to make someone feel upset or worried 使不安；使焦虑：*He was disturbed by the news of the attack.* 这起袭击的消息让他不安。

disturbance /dɪˈstɜːbəns/ ***countable noun*** 可数名词
an event in which people behave violently in public 骚乱；动乱：*During the disturbance, three men were hurt.* 这一骚乱中有 3 名男子受伤。

disturbing /dɪˈstɜːbɪŋ/ ***adjective*** 形容词
making you feel worried or upset 使人焦虑的；令人不安的：*We've received some disturbing news.* 我们收到一些让人不安的消息。

disused /ˌdɪsˈjuːzd/ ***adjective*** 形容词
empty and no longer used 不再使用的；废弃的：*a disused petrol station* 废弃的加油站

ditch /dɪtʃ/ ***countable noun*** 可数名词 (**ditches**)
a deep, long, narrow hole that carries water away from a road or a field（道路、田边的）沟，渠：*Both vehicles landed in a ditch.* 两辆车都掉进了沟里。

dive /daɪv/ ***verb*** 动词 (**dives, diving, dived**)
1 to jump into water with your arms and your head going in first 跳水：*Ben dived into the water.* 本跳入水中。 • **dive *countable noun*** 可数名词：*Pam walked out and did another perfect dive.* 帕姆走了出来，又跳出完美的一跳。
▶ **diving** /ˈdaɪvɪŋ/ ***uncountable noun*** 不可数名词：*Shaun won medals in diving and swimming.* 肖恩获得了跳水和游泳项目的奖牌。

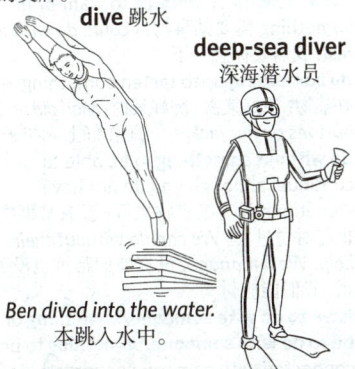

dive 跳水

deep-sea diver 深海潜水员

Ben dived into the water. 本跳入水中。

2 to go under the surface of the sea or a lake, using special equipment for breathing 潜水：*We were diving to look at fish.* 我们潜水去看鱼。 • **dive *countable noun*** 可数名词：*He is already planning the next dive.* 他已经在计划下一次潜水了。
▶ **diver** /ˈdaɪvə/ ***countable noun*** 可数名词：*a deep-sea diver* 深海潜水员
▶ **diving** /ˈdaɪvɪŋ/ ***uncountable noun*** 不可数名词：*equipment for diving* 潜水设备

diverse /daɪˈvɜːs/ ***adjective*** 形容词
made up of many different people or things 形形色色的；各式各样的：*We have a very diverse group of students this year.* 今年我们的这群学生特点迥异，各不相同。

diversion /daɪˈvɜːʃən/ ***countable noun*** 可数名词
an activity that takes your attention away from what you are doing 分心的事；分散注意力的事：*The trip was a welcome diversion from their troubles at home.* 这次旅行让他们从家里的烦心事中暂时抽身，很是开心。

divert /daɪˈvɜːt/ ***verb*** 动词 (**diverts, diverting, diverted**)
to make vehicles or people use a different route 使转向；使改道：*The plane was diverted to Edinburgh Airport.* 飞机改变航线飞往爱丁堡机场。

divide /dɪˈvaɪd/ ***verb*** 动词 (**divides, dividing, divided**)
1 to separate into smaller parts（使）分开；（使）分裂；（使）分散：*Divide the pastry in half.* 把油酥面团一分为二。 ▫ *The class was divided into two groups of six.* 这个班被分为两组，每组 6 人。 ▫ *Half a mile upstream, the river divides.* 在上游半英里处，河水分流。
2 to find out how many times one number can fit into another bigger number 除：*Measure the floor area and divide it by six.* 测量地面面积，再除以 6。
→ Look at picture on P2 参见彩插第 2 页
3 to separate two areas 分隔；分开：*The border divides Mexico from the United States.* 这条分界线将墨西哥和美国分隔开来。
4 to cause disagreement between people 使产生分歧；使意见不一：*Several major issues divided the country.* 这个国家在几个大的议题上有分歧。

divide something up to separate something into smaller groups 划分某事

物；分割某事物：*They divided the country up into four areas.* 他们将这个国家分成4个区。

'diving ,board *countable noun* 可数名词 a board at the edge of a swimming pool from which people can jump into the water 跳板

division /dɪˈvɪʒən/ *noun* 名词
1 *uncountable* 不可数 when someone or something separates something into parts 分开；分割；划分：*the division of land after the war* 战后土地的分割
2 *uncountable* 不可数 the process of dividing one number by another smaller number 除；除法：*I taught my daughter how to do division.* 我教女儿除法。
3 *countable* 可数 a group of departments in a large organization（大机构的）部门：*She manages the bank's Latin American division.* 她主管该银行的拉丁美洲分部。

divorce /dɪˈvɔːs/ *noun* 名词 the legal ending of a marriage 离婚：*Many marriages end in divorce.* 很多婚姻以离婚收场。● **divorce** *verb* 动词 (**divorces, divorcing, divorced**)：*Jack and Lillian got divorced last year.* 杰克和莉莲去年离了婚。 □ *He divorced me and married my friend.* 他和我离婚，娶了我的朋友。

divorced /dɪˈvɔːst/ *adjective* 形容词 no longer legally married to your former husband or wife 离婚的；离异的：*He is divorced, with a young son.* 他离婚了，带着一个年幼的儿子。

DIY /ˌdiː aɪ ˈwaɪ/ *uncountable noun* 不可数名词 the activity of making or repairing things yourself, especially in your home. **DIY** is short for（缩写=）'do-it-yourself'.（尤指在家里）自己动手，自行维修：*a DIY project* *DIY 项目

dizzy /ˈdɪzi/ *adjective* 形容词 (**dizzier, dizziest**) having the feeling that you are losing your balance and that you are about to fall 头晕目眩的；眩晕的：*Her head hurt, and she felt slightly dizzy.* 她头疼，还有点头晕。
▸ **dizziness** /ˈdɪzinəs/ *uncountable noun* 不可数名词：*His head injury caused dizziness.* 他头部受伤，引起头晕。

DJ /ˌdiː ˈdʒeɪ/ *also* 亦作 **D.J.** *or* 或 **dj** *countable noun* 可数名词 someone whose job is to play music and talk on the radio. **DJ** is short for（缩写=）*disc jockey*.（电台）音乐节目主持人

do^1 /də, STRONG 强读 duː/ *auxiliary verb* 助动词 (**does, did**)

LANGUAGE HELP 语言提示
When you are speaking, you can use the negative short forms **don't** for **do not** and **didn't** for **did not**. 口语中，否定形式 do not 可缩作 don't，did not 可缩作 didn't。

1 used with 'not' to form the negative of main verbs（与 not 连用构成主动词的否定式）：*They don't work very hard.* 他们工作不怎么努力。 □ *I did not know Jamie had a car.* 我不知道杰米有辆车。
2 used with another verb to form questions（与另一动词连用构成疑问句）：*Do you like music?* 你喜欢音乐吗？ □ *What did he say?* 他说什么了？
3 used instead of repeating a verb when you are answering a question（回答问题时用于代替动词，避免重复）：*'Do you think he is telling the truth?' — 'Yes, I do.'* "你认为他说的是实话吗？"——"我觉得是。"

do^2 /də, STRONG 强读 duː/ *verb* 动词 (**does, doing, did, done**)
1 to take some action or perform an activity or a task 做；干：*I was trying to do some work.* 我当时正想干点活儿。 □ *After lunch Elizabeth and I did the dishes.* 午饭后，我和伊丽莎白洗了碗。
2 used when you are asking someone what their job is 做，从事（用于询问职业）：*'What does your father do?' — 'He's a doctor.'* "你父亲是做什么的？"——"他是个医生。"
3 to be good enough 适合；足够：*It doesn't matter what you wear — anything warm will do.* 穿什么都可以，暖和就行。
could do with something to want or need something 需要某事物：*I could do with a rest.* 我需要休息一下。
do something up to fasten something 扣好某物；系好某物；绑好某物：*Mari did up the buttons on her jacket.* 玛丽扣好上衣扣子。
do without something to be able to continue, although you do not have something 没有某事物也行；没有某事物也能对付过去：*We can do without their help. We'll manage.* 没有他们帮忙也没关系，我们能应付。
have to do with someone/something or **be to do with someone/something** to be connected with someone or something 和

某人／某事物相关：*Clarke insists all this has nothing to do with him.* 克拉克坚持说所有这一切都和他无关。

dock /dɒk/ *countable noun* 可数名词
an area of water beside land where ships go so that people can get on or off them 船坞；码头 ● **dock** *verb* 动词 (**docks, docking, docked**): *The ferry docked and the passengers disembarked onto the island.* 渡轮靠岸，乘客们下船登岛。

doctor /ˈdɒktə/ *countable noun* 可数名词
1 a person whose job is to treat people who are ill or injured 医生；大夫：*Be sure to speak to your doctor before planning your trip.* 安排行程前一定要和医生谈一谈。
2 (also 亦作 **doctor's**) the place where a doctor works 诊所：*I went to the doctor today.* 我今天去了诊所。
→ Look at picture on P16 参见彩插第 16 页
3 someone who has been awarded the highest academic degree by a university 博士：*He is a doctor of philosophy.* 他是哲学博士。

document /ˈdɒkjəmənt/ *countable noun* 可数名词
1 an official piece of paper with important information on it 文件；公文：*Always read legal documents carefully before you sign them.* 在法律文件上签字前一定要仔细阅读。
2 a piece of text that is stored on a computer（计算机）文件，文档：*Remember to save your document before you send it.* 发送文件前一定要记得保存。

documentary /ˌdɒkjəˈmentri/ *countable noun* 可数名词 (**documentaries**)
a television programme or a film that provides information about a particular subject 纪实节目；纪录片：*Did you see that documentary on TV last night?* 你昨晚在电视上看那个纪录片了吗？

dodge /dɒdʒ/ *verb* 动词 (**dodges, dodging, dodged**)
1 to move suddenly, especially to avoid something 闪躲；躲避：*I dodged back behind the tree and waited.* 我闪身躲到树后等待。
2 to avoid something by moving 闪身躲开；避开：*He dodged a speeding car.* 他闪身躲开一辆飞驰的汽车。

does /dəz, STRONG 强读 dʌz/
→ see 见 **do**

doesn't /ˈdʌzənt/
short for（缩写 =）'does not'

dog /dɒɡ/ *countable noun* 可数名词
an animal that is sometimes kept by people as a pet, or used to guard buildings 狗；犬：*He was walking his dog.* 他在遛狗。

doll /dɒl/ *countable noun* 可数名词
a child's toy that looks like a small person or a baby 玩偶；玩具娃娃

dollar /ˈdɒlə/ *countable noun* 可数名词
the unit of money ($) that is used in the U.S., Canada, and some other countries. There are 100 cents in a dollar. 元（美国、加拿大等国货币单位，符号为 $）：*She earns seven dollars an hour.* 她每小时挣 7 美元。

dolphin /ˈdɒlfɪn/ *countable noun* 可数名词
a large, grey or black-and-white intelligent animal that lives in the sea 海豚

dolphin 海豚

domain name /dəˈmeɪn ˌneɪm/ *countable noun* 可数名词
the main part of a website address that tells you who the website belongs to（网址的）域名：*I've just bought the domain name 'adamwilson.com'.* 我刚买下了域名 adamwilson.com。

dome /dəʊm/ *countable noun* 可数名词
a round roof 穹顶；圆屋顶：*Kiev is known as 'the city of golden domes'.* 基辅被称作"金色穹顶之城"。

domestic /dəˈmestɪk/ *adjective* 形容词
1 happening or existing within one particular country 国内的；本国的：*The airline offers over 100 domestic flights a day.* 这家航空公司每天有超过 100 架次国内航班。
2 relating to the home and family 家的；家庭的：*In our family we all share the domestic chores.* 在我们家，大家一起分担家务活儿。

dominate /ˈdɒmɪˌneɪt/ *verb* 动词 (**dominates, dominating, dominated**)
to have power over another country or person 控制；统治；支配：*Women are no longer dominated by men.* 女性不再受男性支配。

dominoes /ˈdɒmɪnəʊz/ *uncountable noun* 不可数名词
a game that uses small rectangular blocks, called dominoes, that are marked

with spots 多米诺骨牌游戏

donate /dəʊˈneɪt/ *verb* 动词 (**donates, donating, donated**)
1 to give something to an organization 捐赠；赠送：*He often donates large amounts of money to charity.* 他经常向慈善机构捐赠大笔钱款。
▶ **donation** /dəʊˈneɪʃən/ *noun* 名词：*Employees make regular donations to charity.* 员工定期向慈善机构捐赠。
2 to allow doctors to use some of your blood or a part of your body to help someone who is ill 献(血)；捐献(器官)：*If you are able to donate blood, you should do it.* 如果身体状况允许，就应该献血。

done /dʌn/
→ see 见 **do**

donkey /ˈdɒŋki/ *countable noun* 可数名词
an animal like a small horse with long ears 驴

donor /ˈdəʊnə/ *countable noun* 可数名词
a person who gives a part of their body or some of their blood so that doctors can use them to help someone who is ill 器官捐献者；献血者：*a blood donor* 献血者

don't /dəʊnt/
short for (缩写 =) 'do not'

door /dɔː/ *countable noun* 可数名词
1 a piece of wood, glass or metal that fills an entrance 门：*I knocked at the front door, but there was no answer.* 我敲了敲前门，但没有回应。
2 the space in a wall when a door is open 门口；出入口：*She looked through the door of the kitchen.* 她从厨房门口看过去。
answer the door to open a door because someone has knocked on it or rung the bell 应门：*Carol answered the door as soon as I knocked.* 我一敲门，卡萝尔就应门了。
go door to door to go along a street stopping at each house, for example to sell something or to collect money for charity 挨户挨户：*They are going from door to door collecting money.* 他们挨家挨户筹钱。
next door in the next room or building 在隔壁：

Who lives next door? 隔壁住的是谁？

doorbell /ˈdɔːbel/ *countable noun* 可数名词
a bell next to a door that you can ring to tell the people inside that you are there 门铃

doorknob /ˈdɔːnɒb/ *countable noun* 可数名词
a round handle on a door that you use to open and close it 球形门把手

doorstep /ˈdɔːstep/ *countable noun* 可数名词
a step in front of a door outside a building 门阶；门前台阶：*I went and sat on the doorstep.* 我走过去坐在门前台阶上。

doorway /ˈdɔːweɪ/ *countable noun* 可数名词
a space in a wall where a door opens and closes 门口；门道：*David was standing in the doorway.* 戴维站在门口。

dorm /dɔːm/ *countable noun* 可数名词 (*informal* 非正式)
→ see 见 **dormitory**

dormitory /ˈdɔːmɪtri/ *countable noun* 可数名词 (**dormitories**)
a large bedroom where several people sleep 宿舍；寝室

dose /dəʊs/ *countable noun* 可数名词
the particular amount of a medicine or a drug that you take at one time (药物的) 剂量：*You can treat the infection with one big dose of antibiotics.* 你可以用大剂量的抗生素治疗感染。 □ *Do not exceed the stated dose.* 不要超过规定剂量。

dot /dɒt/ *countable noun* 可数名词
a very small round mark, like the one on the letter 'i' or in the names of websites 点；小圆点：*He makes paintings with little tiny dots of colour.* 他用极小的彩色圆点作画。

dot com /ˌdɒt ˈkɒm/
used when you are saying someone's email or website address. For the address 'katiegreen@harpercollins.com', you say 'Katie Green at harpercollins dot com'. (电子邮件或网址末尾的).com

dotted /ˈdɒtɪd/ *adjective* 形容词
made up of a row of dots 由点组成的：*Cut along the dotted line.* 沿虚线裁开。

double¹ /ˈdʌbəl/ *adjective* 形容词
1 with two parts 成双的；成对的：*This room has double doors opening on to a balcony.* 这个房间有一道双扇门通向阳台。

door 门

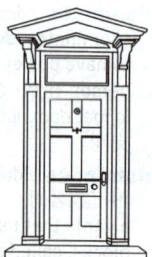

2 twice the normal size 两倍的；双倍的：*I gave him a double portion of ice cream.* 我给了他双份冰激凌。
3 intended for two people 双人的；供两人用的：*The hotel charges £180 for a double room.* 这家酒店双人间要 180 英镑。▫ *One of the bedrooms has a double bed.* 其中一个卧室有一张双人床。

double² /ˈdʌbəl/ **verb** 动词 (**doubles, doubling, doubled**)
to become twice as big 加倍；翻番：*The number of students has doubled from 50 to 100.* 学生人数翻了一番，从 50 名增加到 100 名。

double bass **noun** 名词 (**double basses**)
a very big wooden musical instrument with four strings 低音提琴
→ Look at picture on P12 参见彩插第 12 页

double-click **verb** 动词 (**double-clicks, double-clicking, double-clicked**)
to press one of the buttons on a computer mouse (= the part that you move around with your hand) twice quickly in order to make something happen（用鼠标）双击：*Double-click on a file to start the application.* 双击文件，启动应用程序。

doubt¹ /daʊt/ **noun** 名词
the feeling of not being certain about something 怀疑；疑虑：*Rendell had doubts about the plan.* 伦德尔对这一计划心存疑虑。▫ *There is no doubt that the Earth's climate is changing.* 毫无疑问，地球气候正在变化。
in doubt not certain 不确定的；不肯定的：*If you are in doubt about anything, please get in touch with us.* 对任何事情有疑问都请和我们联系。
no doubt used for showing that you feel certain about something 无疑；肯定：*She will no doubt be here soon.* 她肯定很快就到。

doubt² /daʊt/ **verb** 动词 (**doubts, doubting, doubted**)
1 to think that something is probably not true or will probably not happen 怀疑（某事的真实性或可能性）：*I doubt if I'll learn anything new from this lesson.* 我怀疑是否能从这门课程中学到新知识。▫ *I doubt he will come to the party.* 我怀疑他不来参加聚会。
2 to think that someone may be saying something that is not true 质疑，不相信

（某人的话）：*No one doubted him.* 没有人怀疑他。

doubtful /ˈdaʊtfʊl/ **adjective** 形容词
1 not likely 未必的；不大可能的：*It is doubtful that he will marry again.* 他是否会再婚还很难说。
2 not certain 怀疑的；疑惑的；没把握的：*Sophie sounded doubtful about the idea.* 索菲听上去对这个想法心存疑惑。

dough /dəʊ/ **uncountable noun** 不可数名词
a mixture of flour, water and other things that can be cooked to make bread and cakes 生面团：*Leave the dough in a cool place overnight.* 将面团放至阴凉处过夜。

doughnut /ˈdəʊnʌt/ **countable noun** 可数名词
a sweet round cake with a hole in the middle 甜甜圈；多纳圈

dove /dʌv/ **countable noun** 可数名词
a bird that is used as a symbol of peace 鸽子

down¹ /daʊn/ **preposition** 介词
1 toward a lower level or in a lower place 往⋯下面；在⋯下面：*A man came down the stairs to meet them.* 一个男人走下楼梯迎接他们。▫ *He was halfway down the hill.* 他下到半山腰。● **down adverb** 副词：*She went down to the kitchen.* 她下楼来到厨房。
2 along a road or a river 沿着，顺着（路、河流）：*They walked quickly down the street.* 他们沿着街道快步走去。

down² /daʊn/ **adverb** 副词
onto a surface（放）下：*Danny put down his glass.* 丹尼放下玻璃杯。

down³ /daʊn/ **adjective** 形容词
1 unhappy or depressed (*informal* 非正式) 闷闷不乐的；情绪低落的：*You sound really down. What's wrong?* 你听上去情绪非常低落。出什么事了？
2 not working 出故障的；死机的：*The computer's down again.* 电脑又死机了。

downhill /ˌdaʊnˈhɪl/ **adjective** 形容词, **adverb** 副词
down, towards the bottom of a slope 向山下（的）：*downhill ski runs* 下坡滑雪道 ▫ *He walked downhill toward the river.* 他往山下走，朝河边去了。

download /ˌdaʊnˈləʊd/ **verb** 动词 (**downloads, downloading, downloaded**)
to copy a file, a program or other information from a bigger computer, a

downloadable - dragon

network or the Internet to your own computer 下载: *You can download the software from the Internet.* 你可以从因特网上下载这款软件。● **download** *countable noun* 可数名词: *The file is available as a free download.* 这个文件可免费下载。

downloadable /ˌdaʊnˈləʊdəbl/ *adjective* 形容词
able to be copied onto your computer 可下载的: *More information is available in the downloadable files below.* 更多信息请见以下可下载文件。

downpour /ˈdaʊnpɔː/ *countable noun* 可数名词
a sudden heavy fall of rain 倾盆大雨; 暴雨; 骤雨: *The heavy downpours caused problems for motorists last night.* 昨晚的倾盆大雨给驾车者带来了麻烦。

downstairs /ˌdaʊnˈsteəz/ *adjective* 形容词, *adverb* 副词
1 to a lower floor of a building 往楼下: *Denise went downstairs and made some tea.* 丹尼丝下楼泡了些茶。□ *She went downstairs to the kitchen.* 她下楼来到厨房。
2 on a lower floor of a building 在楼下(的): *She painted the downstairs rooms.* 她粉刷了楼下的几个房间。

downtown /ˌdaʊnˈtaʊn/ *adjective* 形容词, *adverb* 副词 (*American* 美国英语)
belonging to the part of a city where the large shops and businesses are 在商业区(的); 在闹市区(的): *He works in an office in downtown Chicago.* 他在芝加哥闹市区的一家办事处上班。□ *He worked downtown for an insurance firm.* 他在闹市区的一家保险公司上班。

downward /ˈdaʊnwəd/ *adjective* 形容词
moving or looking down 向下的: *John waved his hand in a downward motion.* 约翰向下挥了下手。

downwards /ˈdaʊnwədz/ *adverb* 副词
towards the ground or a lower level 向下; 往下: *Ben pointed downwards with his stick.* 本用拐杖向下指了指。

doze /dəʊz/ *verb* 动词 (**dozes, dozing, dozed**)
to sleep lightly or for a short period 小睡; 打盹儿: *She dozed for a while in the cabin.* 她在客舱里打了个盹儿。
doze off to fall into a light sleep 打瞌睡; 打盹儿: *I closed my eyes and dozed off.* 我闭上眼睛打了个盹儿。

dozen /ˈdʌzən/

> **LANGUAGE HELP** 语言提示
> The plural form is **dozen** after a number. 用在数字后，复数形式为 dozen。

twelve 一打; 十二个: *Will you buy me a loaf of bread and a dozen eggs please?* 你给我买一条面包、一打鸡蛋可以吗？
dozens of a lot of 许多; 大量: *The storm destroyed dozens of buildings.* 这场风暴摧毁了大量建筑。

Dr
short for (缩写 =) **doctor**

drab /dræb/ *adjective* 形容词 (**drabber, drabbest**)
dull and boring 单调乏味的; 缺乏生气的: *He was living in a small, drab apartment in Tokyo.* 他住在东京一个乏味的小公寓里。

draft /drɑːft/ *countable noun* 可数名词
a piece of writing that you have not finished working on 草稿; 草案: *I emailed a first draft of the article to him.* 我把文章初稿用电子邮件发给他。

drag /dræɡ/ *verb* 动词 (**drags, dragging, dragged**)
1 to pull something along the ground 拖; 拉; 拽: *He dragged his chair toward the table.* 他把椅子往桌边拉了拉。
2 to use a computer mouse (= the part that you move around with your hand) to move an image on the screen (用鼠标)拖动: *Simply drag and drop the file into the desired folder.* 把文件拖放到目标文件夹即可。
3 to seem to last a long time 过得很慢; 显得拖沓: *The minutes dragged past while I waited for him to arrive.* 我等着他来的时候，每分钟都过得很慢。

drag and ˈdrop also 亦作 **drag-and-drop** *verb* 动词 (**drags and drops, dragging and dropping, dragged and dropped**)
to move computer files or images from one place to another on a computer screen 拖放(文件、图片): *Drag and drop the folder to the hard drive.* 把文件夹拖放到硬盘上。

dragon /ˈdræɡən/ *countable noun* 可数名词
in stories, an animal with rough skin that has wings and breathes out fire (西方传说中的)龙

dragon 龙

dragonfly /ˈdræɡənˌflaɪ/ *countable noun* 可数名词 (**dragonflies**)
an insect that flies near water, with a long thin body and four wings 蜻蜓

drain¹ /dreɪn/ *verb* 动词 (**drains, draining, drained**)
1 to remove a liquid by making it flow somewhere else 排放（液体）；使流走：*They built the tunnel to drain water out of the mines.* 他们建造坑道，将矿井里的水排出。
2 to remove the liquid surrounding food 控干（食物）的水分；把（食物）沥干：*Drain the pasta well.* 充分沥干意大利面的水分。

drain² /dreɪn/ *countable noun* 可数名词
an opening that carries a liquid away from a place 排液口；排水口：*A piece of soap was clogging the drain.* 下水口卡了块肥皂。

drama /ˈdrɑːmə/ *noun* 名词
1 *countable* 可数 a serious play or film 戏剧：*The film is a drama about a woman searching for her children.* 这部电影讲述了一个女人找寻她的孩子的故事。
2 a real situation that is exciting 戏剧性情景：*This novel is full of drama.* 这部小说充满了戏剧性情节。
3 *uncountable* 不可数 the study of plays and acting 戏剧（学）：*drama classes* 戏剧课

dramatic /drəˈmætɪk/ *adjective* 形容词
happening suddenly 突如其来的；急剧的：*There's been a dramatic change in the way we shop.* 我们的购物方式发生了巨变。
▶ **dramatically** /drəˈmætɪkli/ *adverb* 副词：*The climate has changed dramatically.* 气候急剧变化。

dramatist /ˈdræmətɪst/ *countable noun* 可数名词
a person who writes plays 剧作家；编剧

drank /dræŋk/

→ see 见 **drink**

drape /dreɪp/ *verb* 动词 (**drapes, draping, draped**)
to put a piece of cloth somewhere so that it hangs down 悬挂，搭放（织物）：*He draped the damp towel over a chair.* 他把湿毛巾搭在椅子上。

drastic /ˈdræstɪk/ *adjective* 形容词
having a very big effect 猛烈的；激烈的；极端的：*Drastic measures are needed to improve the situation.* 要改善这种状况，需要采取强有力的措施。

draught /drɑːft/ *countable noun* 可数名词
a stream of cold air that comes into a room 穿堂风；通风气流：*Block draughts around doors and windows.* 挡住门窗处的穿堂风。

draw¹ /drɔː/ *verb* 动词 (**draws, drawing, drew, drawn**)
1 to use a pencil or a pen to make a picture 画；描绘；绘图：*She was drawing with a pencil.* 她在用铅笔画画。 □ *I've drawn a picture of you.* 我给你画了张像。
▶ **drawing** /ˈdrɔːɪŋ/ *uncountable noun* 不可数名词：*I like dancing, singing, and drawing.* 我喜欢跳舞、唱歌、画画。
2 to move somewhere 移动；行进：*The taxi was drawing away.* 出租车开走了。 □ *The train was drawing into the station.* 火车正在进站。
3 to move someone or something somewhere 拉；拖：*He drew his chair nearer the fire.* 他把椅子往炉火边拉了拉。 □ *He drew Caroline close to him.* 他把卡罗琳拉近自己。 □ *He drew an envelope from his pocket.* 他从口袋里抽出一个信封。
4 to finish a game with the same number of points as the other player or team 打成平局：*We drew 2-2 last weekend.* 我们上周末 2 比 2 战平。
5 to take money out of a bank account, so that you can use it 提取，支取（存款）：*A few months ago he drew out nearly all his savings.* 几个月前，他取出了几乎所有存款。

draw something up to write or type a list or a plan 拟定（清单）；制订（计划）：*They drew up a formal agreement.* 他们拟定了一份正式协议。

draw the curtains to pull the curtains across a window 拉上窗帘：*He went to the window and drew the curtains.* 他走到窗边拉上窗帘。

draw² /drɔː/ *countable noun* 可数名词
the result of a game when both players or teams score the same number of points 平局: *The match ended in a draw.* 比赛以平局结束。

drawback /ˈdrɔːbæk/ *countable noun* 可数名词
a part of something that makes it less useful than you would like 缺点; 缺陷: *The flat's only drawback was that it was too small.* 这套公寓唯一的缺点就是太小了。

drawer /ˈdrɔːə/ *countable noun* 可数名词
the part of a desk, for example, that you can pull out and put things in 抽屉: *She opened her desk drawer and took out the book.* 她拉开书桌抽屉取出书。

drawing /ˈdrɔːɪŋ/ *countable noun* 可数名词
a picture made with a pencil or a pen 图画; 素描; 图样: *She did a drawing of me.* 她给我画了张像。
→ Look at picture on P13 参见彩插第 13 页

drawn /drɔːn/
→ see 见 **draw**

dread /dred/ *verb* 动词 (**dreads, dreading, dreaded**)
to feel very anxious about something because you think that it will be unpleasant or upsetting 恐惧; 非常担心: *I've been dreading this moment for a long time.* 我担心这一刻已经很久了。

dreadful /ˈdredfʊl/ *adjective* 形容词
very unpleasant or very poor in quality 糟糕透顶的; 劣质的: *They told us the dreadful news.* 他们告诉了我们这个糟糕透顶的消息。 □ *I didn't enjoy the film; the acting was dreadful.* 我不喜欢这部电影,演得太差了。

dream¹ /driːm/ *countable noun* 可数名词
1 a series of events that you see in your mind while you are asleep 梦: *He had a dream about Claire.* 他梦到了克莱尔。
2 something that you often think about because you would like it to happen 梦想; 理想; 愿望: *After all these years, my dream has finally come true.* 这么多年过去了,我的梦想终于实现了。

dream² /driːm/ *verb* 动词 (**dreams, dreaming, dreamed** or 或 **dreamt**)
1 to see events in your mind while you are asleep 做梦; 梦见: *Richard dreamed that he was on a bus.* 理查德梦见自己在一辆公交车上。 □ *She dreamed about her baby.* 她梦见了自己的宝宝。
2 to often think about something that you would like to do or to be 梦想; 渴望: *She dreamed of becoming an actress.* 她梦想成为一名演员。

dreamt /dremt/
→ see 见 **dream**

dress¹ /dres/ *noun* 名词 (**dresses**)
1 *countable* 可数 a piece of clothing that covers the body and part of the legs of a woman or a girl 连衣裙: *She was wearing a short black dress.* 她穿着一条黑色短连衣裙。
2 *uncountable* 不可数 a particular type of clothing 衣服: *He wore formal evening dress to the dinner.* 他穿着正式的晚礼服去参加宴会。

dress² /dres/ *verb* 动词 (**dresses, dressing, dressed**)
1 (also 亦作 **get dressed**) to put clothes on yourself 穿衣服: *Sarah got dressed quickly.* 萨拉很快穿好了衣服。
2 to put clothes on another person 给⋯穿衣服: *I washed and dressed the children.* 我给孩子们洗完澡穿好衣服。

dress up
1 to put on formal clothes 穿上正装; 精心打扮: *You do not need to dress up for dinner.* 你们不必穿正装赴宴。
2 to put on clothes that make you look like someone else, for fun 装扮; 乔装打扮: *He dressed up like a cowboy for the fancy dress party.* 他装扮成牛仔参加化装派对。

dressed /drest/ *adjective* 形容词
wearing clothes 穿着衣服的: *He threw her into a swimming pool, fully dressed.* 他把她和衣扔进游泳池里。 □ *Are you dressed yet?* 你穿好衣服了吗?

dresser /ˈdresə/ *countable noun* 可数名词
a piece of furniture with cupboards or drawers in the lower part and shelves in the upper part, used for storing plates and dishes 碗橱; 餐具柜

dressing gown *countable noun* 可数名词
a long, loose garment that you wear over your night clothes when you are not in bed 晨衣, 晨服(起床后穿在睡衣外面的宽松外衣)

drew /druː/
→ see 见 **draw**

dribble /ˈdrɪbəl/ *verb* 动词 (**dribbles, dribbling, dribbled**)
1 to flow in a thin stream 滴淌; 成细流;

Blood dribbled down Harry's face. 血顺着哈里的脸颊滴淌。
2 in a game or sport, to keep the ball moving by using your hand or foot 运（球）、带（球）：*Owen dribbled the ball toward Ferris.* 欧文把球带向费里斯。

dried /draɪd/ *adjective* 形容词
with all the water removed 干的；脱水的：*dried herbs* 干草药

drift /drɪft/ *verb* 动词 (**drifts, drifting, drifted**)
to be carried by the wind or by water 飘；漂移；漂流：*We drifted up the river.* 我们漂向河上游。
drift off to gradually fall asleep 迷迷糊糊地睡去；逐渐入睡：*He finally drifted off to sleep.* 他最后迷迷糊糊地睡着了。

drill /drɪl/ *countable noun* 可数名词
a tool for making holes 钻；钻机：*an electric drill* 电钻 ● **drill** *verb* 动词 (**drills, drilling, drilled**)：*You'll need to drill a hole in the wall.* 你得在墙上钻个孔。

drink¹ /drɪŋk/ *verb* 动词 (**drinks, drinking, drank, drunk**)
1 to take liquid into your mouth and swallow it 喝；饮：*He drank his cup of coffee.* 他喝他那杯咖啡。
2 to drink alcohol 喝酒；饮酒：*He drinks too much.* 他饮酒过量。
▶ **drinker** /ˈdrɪŋkə/ *countable noun* 可数名词：*I'm not a heavy drinker.* 我酒喝得不多。

drink² /drɪŋk/ *countable noun* 可数名词
an amount of a liquid that you drink 一杯，一份（饮品）：*I'll get you a drink of water.* 我给你拿杯水。

drip /drɪp/ *verb* 动词 (**drips, dripping, dripped**)
1 to fall in small drops 滴下；滴落：*The rain dripped down my face.* 雨水顺着我的脸颊滴落。
2 to produce small drops of liquid 滴水：*The kitchen tap was dripping.* 厨房水龙头在滴水。

drive¹ /draɪv/ *verb* 动词 (**drives, driving, drove, driven**)
1 to control the movement and direction of a car or another vehicle 开车；驾驶：*I drove into town.* 我开车进了城。 □ *She has never learned to drive.* 她从没学过开车。 □ *We drove the car to Bristol.* 我们开车去布里斯托尔。
▶ **driving** /ˈdraɪvɪŋ/ *uncountable noun* 不可

数名词：*a driving instructor* 驾驶教练
2 to take someone somewhere in a car 开车送（某人）：*She drove him to the station.* 她开车送他去车站。

drive² /draɪv/ *countable noun* 可数名词
1 a trip in a car 驾车出行；开车兜风：*Let's go for a drive in the country on Sunday.* 咱们周日开车去乡下兜风吧。
2 the part of a computer that reads and stores information（计算机）驱动器，盘：*Save your work on drive C.* 把你做的工作存在 C 盘里。

driven /ˈdrɪvən/
→ see 见 **drive**

driver /ˈdraɪvə/ *countable noun* 可数名词
a person who drives a bus, a car or a train, for example 驾驶员；司机：*The driver got out of his truck.* 司机下了卡车。 □ *a taxi driver* 出租车司机

driveway /ˈdraɪvweɪ/ *countable noun* 可数名词
a small road that leads from the street to the front of a building 私家车道：*There is a driveway and a garage at the front of the house.* 房子前面有私家车道和车库。

ˈdriving ˌlicence *countable noun* 可数名词
a document that shows that you have passed a driving test and that you are allowed to drive 驾照；驾驶执照

droop /druːp/ *verb* 动词 (**droops, drooping, drooped**)
to hang or lean downward 低垂；下垂：*His eyelids drooped and he yawned.* 他眼皮垂下来，打起了哈欠。

drop¹ /drɒp/ *verb* 动词 (**drops, dropping, dropped**)
1 to quickly become less in level or amount（快速）下降，降低：*Temperatures can drop to freezing at night.* 夜间气温会跌至冰点。● **drop** *countable noun* 可数名词：*There was a sudden drop in the number of visitors to the site.* 去这一地点的游客数量陡然下降。
2 to let something fall 使掉下；使落下：*I dropped my glasses and broke them.* 我把眼镜弄掉摔碎了。
3 (also 亦作 **drop someone off**) to take someone somewhere in a car and leave them there 中途放下（某人）：*He dropped me outside the hotel.* 他把我放在酒店外面。
drop by or **drop in** to visit someone informally 非正式拜访：*She will drop by*

later. 她晚点儿会过来坐坐。□ *Why not drop in for a chat?* 过来聊聊吧。

drop off to go to sleep (*informal* 非正式) 睡着：*Jimmy dropped off and started to snore.* 吉米睡着了，打起了呼噜。□ *I lay on the bed and dropped off to sleep.* 我在床上躺着躺着就睡着了。

drop out to stop attending school, or taking part in a race, before you have completed your studies or the race 退学；退赛：*He dropped out of high school at the age of 16.* 他16岁从中学辍学。

drop someone off to take someone somewhere in a car and leave them there 中途放下某人：*Dad dropped me off at school on his way to work.* 爸爸上班路上把我放到了学校。

drop² /drɒp/ *countable noun* 可数名词
a very small amount of liquid that is shaped like a little ball 滴：*a drop of water* 一滴水

ˈdrop-down ˌmenu *countable noun* 可数名词
a list of choices on a computer screen that appears when you click on an arrow or a piece of text 下拉菜单：*If you click on the search box, a drop-down menu appears.* 点击搜索框，会出现下拉菜单。

drought /draʊt/ *noun* 名词
a long period of time with no rain 干旱；旱灾：*The drought has killed all their crops.* 他们的庄稼都旱死了。

drove /drəʊv/
→ see 见 **drive**

drown /draʊn/ *verb* 动词 (**drowns, drowning, drowned**)
to die under water because you cannot breathe 淹死；溺亡：*A child can drown in only a few inches of water.* 儿童在几英寸深的水里都有可能溺亡。

drowsy /ˈdraʊzi/ *adjective* 形容词 (**drowsier, drowsiest**)
tired and unable to think clearly 困倦的；昏昏欲睡的：*He felt pleasantly drowsy.* 他感觉很舒适，昏昏欲睡。

drug /drʌɡ/ *countable noun* 可数名词
1 a chemical that is used as a medicine 药品；药物：*The new drug is too expensive for most countries.* 对大多数国家来说，这种新药太贵了。

2 a type of illegal substance that some people take because they enjoy its effects 毒品：*She was sure Leo was taking drugs.* 她确信利奥在吸毒。

ˈdrug ˌaddict *countable noun* 可数名词
someone who cannot stop using illegal drugs 吸毒者；瘾君子

drum /drʌm/ *countable noun* 可数名词
a simple musical instrument that you hit with sticks or with your hands 鼓
→ Look at picture on P12 参见彩插第12页
▶ **drummer** /ˈdrʌmə/ *countable noun* 可数名词：*He was a drummer in a band.* 他是一支乐队的鼓手。

drunk¹ /drʌŋk/
→ see 见 **drink**

drunk² /drʌŋk/ *adjective* 形容词
having drunk too much alcohol 喝醉的：*He got drunk and fell down the stairs.* 他喝醉了，从楼梯上摔了下来。

dry¹ /draɪ/ *adjective* 形容词 (**drier, driest**)
1 having no water or any other liquid in it or on it 干的；干燥的：*Clean the metal with a soft dry cloth.* 用柔软的干布擦拭金属。
2 without any rain 干旱的；无雨的：*The Sahara is one of the driest places in Africa.* 撒哈拉沙漠是非洲最干旱的地区之一。

dry² /draɪ/ *verb* 动词 (**dries, drying, dried**)
1 to become dry 变干：*Let your hair dry naturally if possible.* 可能的话让头发自然晾干。
2 to remove the water from something 弄干；擦干：*Mrs Mason picked up a towel and began drying dishes.* 梅森夫人拿起一块毛巾开始擦干盘子。

dry up to become completely dry 干透；干涸：*The river dried up.* 河干了。

ˌdry-ˈclean *verb* 动词 (**dry-cleans, dry-cleaning, dry-cleaned**)
to clean clothes with a special chemical rather than with water 干洗：*The suit must be dry-cleaned.* 这套衣服得干洗。

ˌdry ˈcleaner *countable noun* 可数名词 (also 亦作 **dry cleaner's**) a shop where things can be dry-cleaned 干洗店

dryer /ˈdraɪə/ also 亦作 **drier** *countable noun* 可数名词
a machine for drying things 烘干机；干燥机：*Put the clothes in the dryer for a few minutes.* 把衣服放进干衣机里烘几分钟。

duck /dʌk/ *noun* 名词
a bird that lives near water 鸭子：*A few ducks were swimming around in the shallow water.* 几只鸭子在浅水中游来游去。

duck 鸭子

due /djuː/ *adjective* 形容词
1 expected to happen or arrive at a particular time 到期的；预期的；预定到达的：*The results are due at the end of the month.* 预计月底会有结果。▫ *Her second baby is due in six weeks.* 她的第二个宝宝预计在 6 周后出生。
2 needing to be paid（钱）应付的，到期的：*When is the next payment due?* 下一笔款项什么时候支付？
due to something as a result of something; because of something 由于某事；因为某事：*She couldn't do the job, due to pain in her hands.* 由于双手疼痛，她做不了这份工作。

duet /djuːˈet/ *countable noun* 可数名词
a piece of music performed by two people 二重唱（曲）；二重奏（曲）：*She sang a duet with Maurice Gibb.* 她和莫里斯·吉布表演了二重唱。

dug /dʌɡ/
→ see 见 **dig**

duke /djuːk/ *countable noun* 可数名词
a man with a very high social rank in some countries 公爵：*the Duke of Edinburgh* 爱丁堡公爵

dull /dʌl/ *adjective* 形容词 (**duller, dullest**)
1 not interesting or exciting 乏味的；无聊的；沉闷的：*I thought he was boring and dull.* 我觉得他既无趣又沉闷。
2 not bright in colour 暗淡的；晦暗的：*the dull grey sky of London* 伦敦晦暗的天空

dumb /dʌm/ *adjective* 形容词 (**dumber, dumbest**)
1 (*informal* 非正式) stupid（人）蠢的，笨的：*He's so clever that he makes me feel really dumb.* 他太聪明了，让我觉得自己很笨。
2 (*American* 美国英语, *informal* 非正式) silly and annoying（事情）愚蠢的, 恼人的：*He had this dumb idea.* 他出的这个馊主意。

dummy /ˈdʌmi/ *countable noun* 可数名词 (**dummies**)
1 a model of a person, often used in safety tests 假人，人体模型（常用于安全测试）：*a crash-test dummy* 碰撞试验用假人
2 an object that you put in a baby's mouth to stop it from crying 安抚奶嘴

dump¹ /dʌmp/ *verb* 动词 (**dumps, dumping, dumped**)
1 to leave something somewhere quickly and carelessly (*informal* 非正式) 丢；乱放：*We dumped our bags at the hotel and went to the market.* 我们把行李包扔在酒店就去市场了。
2 to put or leave something somewhere because you no longer want it (*informal* 非正式) 丢弃；扔掉：*The robbers' car was dumped near the motorway.* 劫匪开的车被丢弃在高速公路附近。
3 to end a relationship with a boyfriend or girlfriend (*informal* 非正式) 与…分手；甩掉（恋人）：*My boyfriend dumped me last night.* 昨晚男朋友和我分了手。

dump² /dʌmp/ *countable noun* 可数名词
1 a place where you can take things that you no longer want 垃圾场；废物堆：*I've got to take the garden waste to the dump.* 我得把园林废弃物运到垃圾场。
2 an ugly and unpleasant place (*informal* 非正式) 脏地方；令人讨厌的地方：*'What a dump!' Amy said, looking at the house.* "真像个垃圾堆一样！"埃米看着房子说道。

dune /djuːn/ *countable noun* 可数名词
a hill of sand near the sea or in a desert 沙丘：*Behind the beach is an area of sand dunes and grass.* 海滩后面是一片沙丘和草地。

duo /ˈdjuːəʊ/ *countable noun* 可数名词
a pair of musicians, singers or other performers 一对表演者；表演搭档：*a famous singing duo* 一对著名的歌唱搭档

during /ˈdjʊərɪŋ/ *preposition* 介词
between the beginning and the end of a period of time 在…期间：*Storms are common during the winter.* 冬季风暴很常见。▫ *I fell asleep during the performance.* 演出期间我睡着了。

> **LANGUAGE HELP 语言提示**
> If you want to say how long something lasts, use **for**. 表示某事持续的时间，用 for：*I went to Wales for two weeks.* 我去了威尔士两周。

dusk /dʌsk/ *uncountable noun* 不可数名词
the time just before night when it is not completely dark 黄昏；傍晚：*We arrived home at dusk.* 我们黄昏时分到了家。

dust¹ /dʌst/ *uncountable noun* 不可数名词
a fine powder of dry earth or dirt 灰尘；尘土：*I could see a thick layer of dust on the furniture.* 我能看到家具上有一层厚厚的尘土。

dust² /dʌst/ *verb* 动词 (**dusts, dusting, dusted**)
to remove dust from furniture with a cloth（用布）擦去(…的)灰尘：*I dusted and polished the furniture in the living room.* 我拭去客厅家具上的灰尘，并把它们擦亮。
□ *I was dusting in his study.* 我正在打扫他书房的灰尘。

dustbin /'dʌstbɪn/ *countable noun* 可数名词 (*American* 美国英语 : **garbage can**)
a large container for rubbish that you keep outside（户外的）垃圾桶，垃圾箱

duster /'dʌstə/ *countable noun* 可数名词
a cloth that you use for removing dust from furniture 抹布

dustman /'dʌstmən/ *countable noun* 可数名词 (**dustmen** /'dʌstmen/)
a person whose job is to take away rubbish from outside people's houses 垃圾清运工

dusty /'dʌsti/ *adjective* 形容词 (**dustier, dustiest**)
covered with dust 布满灰尘的：*a dusty room* 满是灰尘的房间

duty /'djuːti/ *noun* 名词 (**duties**)
1 work that you have to do 职责；任务：*I did my duties without complaining.* 我毫无怨言地履行自己的职责。
2 *singular* 单数 something that you feel that you have to do 责任；义务：*I consider it my duty to warn you of the dangers.* 我觉得我有义务提醒你存在的危险。
off duty not working 下班；不值勤：*The two police officers were off duty when the accident happened.* 事故发生时那两名警察并未当值。
on duty working 上班；值勤：*How many nurses were on duty last night?* 昨晚有几名护士值班？

duty-free *adjective* 形容词
sold at airports or on airplanes or ships at a cheaper price than usual because no tax has to be paid 免关税的：*duty-free perfume* 免税香水

duvet /'duːveɪ/ *countable noun* 可数名词
a thick warm cover for a bed 羽绒被

DVD /ˌdiː viː 'diː/ *countable noun* 可数名词
short for (缩写 =) 'digital video disk': a disk on which a film or music is recorded 数字光碟
→ Look at picture on P11 参见彩插第 11 页

DVD burner /ˌdiː viː diː 'bɜːnə/ *or* 或 **DVD writer** *countable noun* 可数名词
a piece of computer equipment that you use for putting information onto a DVD 数字光碟刻录机

DVD player *countable noun* 可数名词
a machine for showing films that are stored on a DVD 数字光碟播放机
→ Look at picture on P11 参见彩插第 11 页

dwarf /dwɔːf/ *countable noun* 可数名词 (**dwarves** /dwɔːvz/, **dwarfs**)
1 an animal or a plant that is much smaller than usual 矮生动物（或植物）
2 in children's stories, a small man who sometimes has magical powers（童话故事中会魔法的）小矮人

dye /daɪ/ *verb* 动词 (**dyes, dyeing, dyed**)
to change the colour of something by putting it in a special liquid 给…染色：*The actor had to dye his hair for the film.* 为了出演这部电影，这个演员不得不染发。
● **dye** *uncountable noun* 不可数名词：*a bottle of hair dye* 一瓶染发剂

dynamic /daɪ'næmɪk/ *adjective* 形容词
full of energy and always having new and exciting ideas 精力充沛的；生气勃勃的：*He was a dynamic and energetic leader.* 他是一位富有干劲、精力充沛的领导。

Ee

each /iːtʃ/ *adjective* 形容词
every 每；每一：*Each book is beautifully illustrated.* 每本书都配有精美插图。□ *The library buys 2,000 new books each year.* 图书馆每年购入 2,000 本新书。● **each** *pronoun* 代词：*We each have different needs and interests.* 我们每个人都有不同的需求和爱好。● **each** *adverb* 副词：*Tickets are six dollars each.* 每张票 6 美元。
each of every one of * (…中的) 每一个：*He gave each of them a book.* 他给了他们每人一本书。□ *Each of these exercises takes one or two minutes to do.* 这些练习每一项做起来需要一两分钟。
each other used for showing that each member of a group does something to or for the other members 彼此；互相：*We looked at each other in silence.* 我们默默地看着对方。

We looked at each other in silence.
我们默默地看着对方。

eager /ˈiːɡə/ *adjective* 形容词
wanting to do something very much 热切的；急切的；渴望的：*The children are all very eager to learn.* 孩子们都非常渴望学习。
▶ **eagerly** /ˈiːɡəli/ *adverb* 副词：*'So what do you think will happen?' he asked eagerly.* "那你觉得会发生什么？"他急切地问。

eagle /ˈiːɡəl/ *countable noun* 可数名词
a large bird that eats small animals 雕

ear /ɪə/ *countable noun* 可数名词
one of the two parts of your body that you hear sounds with 耳；耳朵：*He whispered something in her ear.* 他在她耳边嘀咕了几句。

→ Look at picture on P4 参见彩插第 4 页

earache /ˈɪəreɪk/ *uncountable noun* 不可数名词
a pain inside your ear 耳痛：*I woke up in the morning with terrible earache.* 我早上醒来时耳朵疼得要命。

eardrum /ˈɪədrʌm/ also 亦作 **ear drum** *countable noun* 可数名词
the part inside your ear that reacts when sound waves reach it 耳膜；鼓膜：*The explosion burst Ollie Williams' eardrum.* 爆炸震裂了奥利·威廉斯的耳膜。

early /ˈɜːli/ *adverb* 副词 (**earlier, earliest**)
before the usual time 早；提早；提前：*I had to get up early this morning.* 我今天早晨不得不早起。□ *She arrived early to get a place at the front.* 她早早就到了，想占个前排座位。● **early** *adjective* 形容词：*I want to get an early start in the morning.* 我今天早上想早点动身。

earn /ɜːn/ *verb* 动词 (**earns, earning, earned**)
1 to receive money for work that you do 挣（钱）：*She earns £27,000 a year.* 她一年挣 27,000 英镑。
2 to get something because you deserve it 赢得，博得（应得之物）：*A good manager earns the respect of his team.* 优秀的主教练会赢得团队的尊重。

earphones /ˈɪəfəʊnz/ *plural noun* 复数名词
things that you wear in your ears so that you can listen to music or the radio without anyone else hearing 耳机

earring /ˈɪərɪŋ/ *countable noun* 可数名词
a piece of jewellery that you wear on your ear 耳环：*The woman wore large, gold earrings.* 那个女人戴着大金耳环。

earth /ɜːθ/ *noun* 名词
1 the planet that we live on 地球：*The space shuttle returned safely to Earth today.* 航天飞机今天安全返回地球。□ *The Earth travels round the sun.* 地球绕着太阳转。
2 *uncountable* 不可数 the substance in

which plants grow 土；土地；土壤：*a huge pile of earth* 一大堆土
on earth used in questions that begin with 'how', 'why', 'what' or 'where', to show that you are very surprised（用于以 how、why、what 或 where 开头的问句中，表示非常惊讶）到底，究竟：*How on earth did that happen?* 那件事儿到底是怎么发生的？

earthquake /ˈɜːθkweɪk/ *countable noun* 可数名词
a sudden strong movement of the Earth's surface 地震：*the San Francisco earthquake of 1906* 1906 年旧金山地震

ease /iːz/ *uncountable noun* 不可数名词
at ease confident and relaxed 自在的；轻松自信的：*It is important that you feel at ease with your doctor.* 在医生面前一定要放松。
with ease without difficulty or effort 轻松地；不费力地：*Anne passed her exams with ease.* 安妮轻松通过了考试。

easel /ˈiːzəl/ *countable noun* 可数名词
a stand that supports a picture while an artist is working on it 画架
→ Look at picture on P13 参见彩插第 13 页

east¹ /iːst/ also 亦作 **East** *uncountable noun* 不可数名词
the direction that is in front of you when you look at the sun in the morning 东；东方：*The city lies to the east of the river.* 这座城市位于河东。● **east** *adjective* 形容词：*There is a line of hills along the east coast.* 沿东海岸有一列山丘。
→ Look at picture on P9 参见彩插第 9 页
the East the southern and eastern part of Asia, including India, China and Japan 东方（指东亚、南亚）

east² /iːst/ also 亦作 **East** *adjective* 形容词, *adverb* 副词
1 towards the east 朝东；向东：*Go east on Route 9.* 上 9 号公路向东行驶。
2 coming from the east 自东方来的：*A cold east wind was blowing.* 寒冷的东风刮着。

Easter /ˈiːstə/ *noun* 名词
a Christian festival in March or April when people celebrate Jesus Christ's return to life（基督教的）复活节

easterly /ˈiːstəli/ *adjective* 形容词
1 to the east or towards the east 东的；向东的：*We sailed in an easterly direction.* 我们向东航行。
2 blowing from the east 东方吹来的；东风的：*It was a beautiful September day, with cool easterly winds.* 那是 9 月一个晴好的日子，凉爽的东风吹拂着。

eastern /ˈiːstən/ *adjective* 形容词
1 in or from the east of a place 在东边的；来自东部的：*Eastern Europe* 东欧
2 used for describing things or ideas that come from the countries of the East, such as India, China or Japan（事物、思想）东方的：*Exports to Eastern countries have gone down.* 面向东方国家的出口已经下降了。

easy /ˈiːzi/ *adjective* 形容词（**easier**, **easiest**）
not difficult to do 容易的；简单的：*Losing weight is not easy.* 减肥不容易。□ *The software is easy to use.* 这款软件简单易用。
▶ **easily** /ˈiːzɪli/ *adverb* 副词：*Most students found jobs easily at the end of the course.* 课程结束后大多数学生轻松找到了工作。
take it easy to relax and not worry（*informal* 非正式）放松；别紧张：*I suggest you take it easy for a week or two.* 我建议你放松一两周。

eat /iːt/ *verb* 动词（**eats**, **eating**, **ate**, **eaten**）
to put something into your mouth and swallow it 吃：*What did you eat last night?* 你昨晚吃的什么？□ *I ate slowly and without speaking.* 我慢慢吃，一言不发。

eaten /ˈiːtən/
→ see 见 **eat**

e-book /ˈiːbʊk/ *noun* 名词
a digital book that you can read on a screen 电子书

echo /ˈekəʊ/ *countable noun* 可数名词（**echoes**）
a sound that you hear again because it hits a surface and then comes back 回声：*I heard the echo of someone laughing across the hall.* 我听见大厅里荡着谁的笑声。● **echo** *verb* 动词（**echoes**, **echoing**, **echoed**）：*His feet echoed on the stone floor.* 他的脚踩在石头地面上发出回响。

eclipse /ɪˈklɪps/ *countable noun* 可数名词
an occasion when the light from the sun or the moon is blocked for a short time because of the position of the sun, the moon and the Earth 日食；月食：*The last total solar eclipse was in November.* 上一次日全食发生在 11 月。

eco-friendly /ˌiːkəʊ ˈfrendli/ *adjective* 形容词
less harmful to the environment than other similar products or services 生态友

好的: *eco-friendly washing powder* 生态友好型洗衣粉

ecology /ɪˈkɒlədʒi/ *uncountable noun* 不可数名词
the study of the relationships between living things and their environment 生态学: *He is professor of ecology at the university.* 他是这所大学的生态学教授。
▶ **ecologist** /ɪˈkɒlədʒɪst/ *countable noun* 可数名词: *Ecologists are concerned that these chemicals will pollute lakes.* 生态学家担心这些化学品会污染湖泊。
▶ **ecological** /ˌiːkəˈlɒdʒɪkəl/ *adjective* 形容词: *How can we save the Earth from ecological disaster?* 我们怎样才能拯救地球免于生态灾难?

economic /ˌiːkəˈnɒmɪk, ˌek-/ *adjective* 形容词
connected with the organization of the money and industry of a country 经济的; 经济方面的: *The economic situation is very bad.* 经济形势非常糟糕。

economical /ˌiːkəˈnɒmɪkəl, ˌek-/ *adjective* 形容词
not needing a lot of money or other things in order to work well 经济的; 节约的: *People are driving smaller and more economical cars.* 人们开着更小、更经济的车型。
▶ **economically** /ˌiːkəˈnɒmɪkəli, ˌek-/ *adverb* 副词: *Services need to operate more economically.* 运营服务项目需要提高经济性。

economics /ˌiːkəˈnɒmɪks, ˌek-/ *uncountable noun* 不可数名词
the study of the way in which money and industry are organized in a society 经济学: *His sister is studying economics.* 他姐姐在读经济学。

economist /ɪˈkɒnəmɪst/ *countable noun* 可数名词
a person who studies economics 经济学家

economy /ɪˈkɒnəmi/ *countable noun* 可数名词 (**economies**)
the system for organizing the money and industry of the world, a country or local government 经济; 经济体: *The Indian economy is changing fast.* 印度经济发展变化快。

ecosystem /ˈiːkəʊˌsɪstəm/ *countable noun* 可数名词
the relationship between all the living things in a particular area together 生态系统: *These industries are destroying whole ecosystems.* 这些产业正在毁灭整个生态系统。

edge /edʒ/ *countable noun* 可数名词
1 the part of something that is farthest from the middle 边; 边缘: *We lived in a block of flats on the edge of town.* 我们住在城边一栋公寓楼里。□ *She was standing at the water's edge.* 她站在水边。
2 the sharp side of a knife (刀的)刃, 锋: *His hand touched the edge of the sword.* 他的手碰到了剑刃。

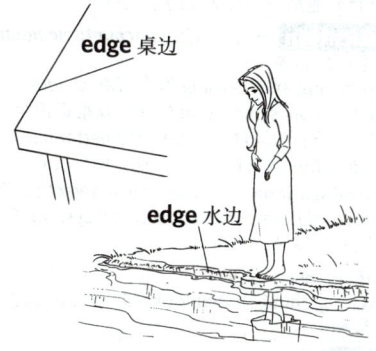
edge 桌边
edge 水边

edible /ˈedɪbəl/ *adjective* 形容词
safe to eat 可食用的; 能吃的: *The flowers are edible, and they look wonderful in salads.* 这些花可以吃, 拌在沙拉里很好看。

edit /ˈedɪt/ *verb* 动词 (**edits, editing, edited**)
to check a text and correct the mistakes in it 编辑: *She helped him edit his essay.* 她帮他编辑文章。

edition /ɪˈdɪʃən/ *countable noun* 可数名词
one of a number of books, magazines or newspapers that is printed at one time (图书、报刊的)版本, 版次: *The second edition was published in Canada.* 第二版在加拿大出版。

editor /ˈedɪtə/ *countable noun* 可数名词
a person who checks and corrects texts 编辑: *He works as an editor of children's books.* 他是童书编辑。

educate /ˈedʒʊˌkeɪt/ *verb* 动词 (**educates, educating, educated**)
1 to teach someone at a school or college 教, 教育(学生): *He was educated at Yale and Stanford.* 他在耶鲁和斯坦福念的书。
2 to teach people better ways of doing something 指导; 教导: *We want to educate people about healthy eating.* 我们想指导人

们健康饮食。

LANGUAGE HELP 语言提示
If you want to talk about the way parents look after their children and teach them about the world, use the verb **bring up**. 表示父母养育子女及教导其认知世界的方式，用 bring up：*His parents brought him up very strictly.* 他父母对他管教很严。

educated /ˈedʒʊˌkeɪtɪd/ *adjective* 形容词
having a lot of knowledge 有文化的；受过教育的：*He was an educated and honest man.* 他是一个有文化的正人君子。

▶ **education** /ˌedʒʊˈkeɪʃən/ *uncountable noun* 不可数名词
teaching and learning 教育：*My children's education is important to me.* 我很重视我家孩子们的教育。 □ *We need better health education.* 我们需要提高健康教育水平。

▶ **educational** /ˌedʒʊˈkeɪʃənəl/ *adjective* 形容词：*the American educational system* 美国教育体制

eel /iːl/ *noun* 名词
a long, thin fish that looks like a snake 鳗；鳗鲡

effect /ɪˈfekt/ *noun* 名词
a change or a reaction that is the result of something 效果；效应；影响：*Parents worry about the effect of junk food on their child's health.* 家长担心垃圾食品对子女健康的影响。

effective /ɪˈfektɪv/ *adjective* 形容词
producing the results that you want 有效的；奏效的：*Massage is effective against back pain.* 按摩能有效缓解背痛。

▶ **effectively** /ɪˈfektɪvli/ *adverb* 副词：*We need to use water more effectively.* 我们得提高用水效率。

efficient /ɪˈfɪʃənt/ *adjective* 形容词
able to do tasks successfully, without wasting time or energy 高效的；有效率的：*The engine is efficient and powerful.* 这款发动机效率高、马力大。

▶ **efficiency** /ɪˈfɪʃənsi/ *uncountable noun* 不可数名词：*We must think of ways to improve efficiency.* 我们必须想办法提高效率。

▶ **efficiently** /ɪˈfɪʃəntli/ *adverb* 副词：*We want people to use energy more efficiently.* 我们想要人们提高能源使用效率。

effort /ˈefət/ *noun* 名词
when you try very hard to do something

努力；奋力：*You should make an effort to speak the local language when you go abroad.* 出国后要努力说当地话。

e.g. /ˌiː ˈdʒiː/
for example 例如；譬如：*We need professionals of all types, e.g. teachers.* 我们需要各种类型的专业技术人才，比如教师。

egg /eg/ *noun* 名词
1 countable 可数 a round object that contains a baby bird, insect, snake or fish 蛋；卵
2 a hen's egg, that people eat as food in many countries 鸡蛋：*Break the eggs into a bowl.* 把鸡蛋打到碗里。 □ *Brush the top with egg.* 上面刷一层鸡蛋液。
→ Look at picture on P5 参见彩插第 5 页

eggplant /ˈegplɑːnt/ *noun* 名词（American 美国英语）
→ see 见 **aubergine**

eight /eɪt/
the number 8 八

eighteen /ˌeɪˈtiːn/
the number 18 十八

▶ **eighteenth** /ˌeɪˈtiːnθ/ *adjective* 形容词, *adverb* 副词：*I had a big party for my eighteenth birthday.* 我办了个大派对庆祝 18 岁生日。

eighth[1] /eɪtθ/ *adjective* 形容词, *adverb* 副词
the item in a series that you count as number eight 第八：*Shekhar was the eighth prime minister of India.* 谢卡尔是印度第 8 位总理。

eighth[2] /eɪtθ/ *countable noun* 可数名词
one of eight equal parts of something (1/8) 八分之一：*We walked for an eighth of a mile.* 我们走了八分之一英里。

eighty /ˈeɪti/
the number 80 八十

▶ **eightieth** /ˈeɪtiəθ/ *adjective* 形容词, *adverb* 副词：*Mr Stevens recently celebrated his eightieth birthday.* 史蒂文斯先生刚庆祝了自己 80 岁生日。

either[1] /ˈaɪðə, ˈiːðə/ *adjective* 形容词
1 each（两者中）每个，各个：*He couldn't remember either man's name.* 两个男子的名字他都记不得。 □ *There are no simple answers to either of those questions.* 两个问题每个都不容易回答。
2 one of two things or people（两者中）任何一个的：*You can choose either date.* 你可以从两个日子中选一个。 ● **either** *pronoun* 代词：*She wants a big house and a new car.*

I don't want either. 她想要大房子、新汽车、我哪个也不想要。

either² /ˈaɪðə, ˈiːðə/ *adverb* 副词
used in negative sentences to mean also (用于否定句) 也：He said nothing, and she did not speak either. 他一言不发，她也沉默不语。

either...or... used for showing that there are two possibilities to choose from (表示二选一) 要么…要么…：I will either walk or take the bus. 我要么走路，要么乘公交车。
□ You can contact him either by phone or by email. 你可以打电话或发电子邮件联系他。

eject /ɪˈdʒekt/ *verb* 动词 (**ejects, ejecting, ejected**)
to remove something or push it out 移除；推出；使弹出：You can eject the disc from the camera and put it into a DVD player. 你可以把光碟从摄像机里取出来，放进 DVD 播放器。

elastic /ɪˈlæstɪk/ *uncountable noun* 不可数名词
a rubber material that stretches when you pull it, and then returns to its original size and shape 橡皮筋；松紧带：The hat has a piece of elastic that goes under the chin. 这顶帽子有一根松紧带可以扣在下巴下面。

elbow /ˈelbəʊ/ *countable noun* 可数名词
the part in the middle of your arm where it bends 肘；肘部：She leaned forward, with her elbows on the table. 她身体前倾，双肘支在桌上。
→ Look at picture on P4 参见彩插第 4 页

elderly /ˈeldəli/ *adjective* 形容词
used as a polite way of saying that someone is old 年长的；上年纪的：An elderly couple lived in the house next door. 一对老夫妇住在隔壁房子里。

elect /ɪˈlekt/ *verb* 动词 (**elects, electing, elected**)
to choose a person to do a particular job by voting for them 选举：The people have elected a new president. 人民选出了新总统。

election /ɪˈlekʃən/ *noun* 名词
a process in which people vote to choose a person who will hold an official position 选举：She won her first election in May. *5 月她赢得了第一次选举。

electric /ɪˈlektrɪk/ *adjective* 形容词
1 working using electricity 电动的；用电作的：Kelly loves to play the electric guitar. 凯利喜欢弹电吉他。

2 carrying electricity 导电的；输电的；通电的：It is not safe to play near electric power lines. 在输电线附近玩儿不安全。

electrical /ɪˈlektrɪkəl/ *adjective* 形容词
using or relating to electricity 电的；用电的：an electrical appliance 电器

electrician /ɪˌlekˈtrɪʃən, ˌelek-/ *countable noun* 可数名词
a person whose job is to repair electrical equipment 电工
→ Look at picture on P16 参见彩插第 16 页

electricity /ɪˌlekˈtrɪsɪti, ˌelek-/ *uncountable noun* 不可数名词
energy that is used for producing heat and light, and to provide power for machines 电

eˌlectric ˈshock *countable noun* 可数名词
the sudden painful feeling that someone gets when electricity goes through their body 电击；触电

electronic /ɪˌlekˈtrɒnɪk, ˌelek-/ *adjective* 形容词
using electricity and small electrical parts 电子的：Please do not use electronic equipment on the plane. 飞机上请勿使用电子设备。

▶ **electronically** /ɪˌlekˈtrɒnɪkəli, ˌelek-/ *adverb* 副词：The gates are operated electronically. 这些门是电子控制的。

elegant /ˈelɪɡənt/ *adjective* 形容词
beautiful in a simple way 优雅的；雅致的：Our room was elegant, with high ceilings and tall, narrow windows. 我们的房间很雅致，高高的天花板，狭长的窗户。

element /ˈelɪmənt/ *countable noun* 可数名词
1 one of the different parts of something 部分；要素：Good health is an important element in our lives. 好身体是我们生活中很重要的一部分。
2 a basic chemical substance such as gold, oxygen or carbon (化学) 元素

elementary /ˌelɪˈmentri/ *adjective* 形容词
very easy and basic 基础的；简单的：It's a simple system that uses elementary mathematics. 这个系统很基础，只用到基础数学。

elephant /ˈelɪfənt/ *countable noun* 可数名词
a very large grey animal with a long nose called a trunk 象

elevator /ˈelɪveɪtə/ *countable noun* 可数名词 (American 美国英语)
→ see 见 **lift**

eleven /ɪˈlevən/
the number 11 十一

elf /elf/ *countable noun* 可数名词 (**elves** /elvz/)
a very small person with pointed ears and magic powers in children's stories 小精灵（童话故事中的尖耳小人儿，有魔力）

eligible /ˈelɪdʒɪbəl/ *adjective* 形容词
allowed to do something 有资格的；符合条件的: *Almost half the population are eligible to vote.* 将近半数人口有选举资格。

eliminate /ɪˈlɪmɪˌneɪt/ *verb* 动词
(**eliminates, eliminating, eliminated**)
to remove something completely (*formal* 正式) 根除；彻底去除: *The touch screen eliminates the need for a keyboard.* 触摸屏彻底淘汰了键盘。

else /els/ *adjective* 形容词, *adverb* 副词
1 more; extra 别的；其他的: *What else did you get for your birthday?* 你生日还收到了什么东西？
2 different 不同的；其他: *If you don't like this, try something else.* 你不喜欢这个的话，可以试试别的。 □ *I never wanted to live anywhere else.* 我从未想过换个地方住。
or else used for saying what will happen if someone does not do something（引出不做某事的后果）否则，要不然: *Do as I say, or else I won't help you.* 照我说的办，否则我不帮你。

elsewhere /ˌelsˈweə/ *adverb* 副词
in other places or to another place 在别处；到别处: *80 per cent of the city's residents were born elsewhere.* 该市 8 成居民出生于外地。

email /ˈiːmeɪl/ also 亦作 **e-mail** *noun* 名词
a system of sending written messages from one computer to another. *Email* is short for (缩写 =) 'electronic mail'. 电子邮件 ● **email** *verb* 动词 (**emails, emailing, emailed**): *Jamie emailed me to say he couldn't come.* 杰米发邮件给我说他来不了。
→ Look at picture on P11 参见彩插 11 页

embarrass /ɪmˈbærəs/ *verb* 动词
(**embarrasses, embarrassing, embarrassed**)
to make someone feel shy or ashamed 使窘迫；使羞愧；使尴尬: *His mother's behaviour embarrassed him.* 母亲的举动令他难堪。
▶ **embarrassing** /ɪmˈbærəsɪŋ/ *adjective* 形容词: *He always found Judith a bit embarrassing.* 他始终觉得朱迪丝有点儿让

人难为情。

embarrassed /ɪmˈbærəst/ *adjective* 形容词
feeling shy, ashamed or guilty about something 窘迫的；羞愧的；尴尬的: *He looked a bit embarrassed when he noticed his mistake.* 他注意到自己的错误后略显窘迫。

embarrassment /ɪmˈbærəsmənt/ *uncountable noun* 不可数名词
the feeling you have when you are embarrassed 窘迫；羞愧；尴尬: *I feel no embarrassment at making mistakes.* 我不会为犯错感到羞愧。

embrace /ɪmˈbreɪs/ *verb* 动词 (**embraces, embracing, embraced**)
to put your arms around someone to show that you love or like them 拥抱；搂抱: *Pam embraced her sister.* 帕姆拥抱了妹妹。
□ *People were crying with joy and embracing.* 人们喜极而泣，相拥在一起。

embroider /ɪmˈbrɔɪdə/ *verb* 动词
(**embroiders, embroidering, embroidered**)
to sew a pattern of threads onto clothing or cloth 绣；在…上刺绣: *The dress was embroidered with small red flowers.* 这条裙子绣着小红花。

embroidery /ɪmˈbrɔɪdəri/ *uncountable noun* 不可数名词
a pattern of threads that is sewn onto cloth for decoration 刺绣；绣花；绣品: *The shorts had blue embroidery over the pockets.* 短裤口袋上绣着蓝色图案。

embryo /ˈembriəʊ/ *countable noun* 可数名词
an animal or a human that is starting to grow, before it is born 胚；胚胎

emerald /ˈemərəld/ *countable noun* 可数名词
a bright green stone that is used in jewellery 翡翠；绿宝石；祖母绿

emerge /ɪˈmɜːdʒ/ *verb* 动词 (**emerges, emerging, emerged**)
to come out from a place 出来；出现: *Richard was waiting when she emerged from her house.* 她从房子里出来时，理查德正在外面等着。

emergency[1] /ɪˈmɜːdʒənsi/ *countable noun* 可数名词 (**emergencies**)
a serious situation, such as an accident, when people need help quickly 紧急情况；突发事件: *Come quickly. This is an emergency!* 快来。有紧急情况！

emergency[2] /ɪˈmɜːdʒənsi/ *adjective* 形容词
done or arranged quickly, because an

emergency has happened 紧急的；应急的：*The board held an emergency meeting.* 董事会召开了紧急会议。

emigrate /'emɪˌɡreɪt/ *verb* 动词 (**emigrates, emigrating, emigrated**)
to leave your own country and go to live in another country 移居国外；移民他国：*His parents emigrated to the U.S. in 1954.* 他爸妈 1954 年移居美国。

emoji /ɪ'məʊdʒi/ *countable noun* 可数名词
a small picture that you can use in an Internet or a phone message to express a feeling or an idea（因网上或手机信息中所用的）表情符号：*I sent her a sleeping face emoji.* 我给她发送了一个睡觉表情符号。

emotion /ɪ'məʊʃən/ *noun* 名词
a feeling such as joy or love 情绪；情感：*Andrew never shows his emotions in public.* 安德鲁从不公开表露情绪。 □ *Jill's voice was full of emotion.* 吉尔的声音饱含情感。

emotional /ɪ'məʊʃənəl/ *adjective* 形容词
1 concerned with feelings 情绪的；情感的：*After her death, I needed some emotional support.* 她去世后，我需要些情感上的支撑。
▶ **emotionally** /ɪ'məʊʃənəli/ *adverb* 副词：*By the end of the show, I was physically and emotionally exhausted.* 节目结束时，我身心俱疲。
2 often showing your feelings, especially when you are upset（尤指苦恼时）情绪化的，情绪外露的：*He is a very emotional man.* 他这个人非常情绪化。

emperor /'empərə/ *countable noun* 可数名词
a man who rules a group of countries (= an empire) 皇帝：*the Emperor Napoleon* 拿破仑皇帝

emphasis /'emfəsɪs/ *noun* 名词 (**emphases** /'emfəsiːz/)
1 special importance that is given to something 重视；重要性：*Schools should place more emphasis on health education.* 学校应提高对健康教育的重视程度。
2 extra force that you put on a word or part of a word when you are speaking 重读；强调：*The emphasis is on the first syllable of the word 'elephant'.* *elephant 这个词第一个音节重读。

emphasize /'emfəˌsaɪz/ *verb* 动词 (**emphasizes, emphasizing, emphasized**)
to show that something is especially important 强调；着重；重视：*He emphasizes the importance of reading to young children.* 他强调给儿童读书的重要性。

empire /'empaɪə/ *countable noun* 可数名词
a number of separate nations that are all controlled by the ruler of one particular country 帝国：*the Roman Empire* 罗马帝国

employ /ɪm'plɔɪ/ *verb* 动词 (**employs, employing, employed**)
to pay someone to work for a person or a company 聘用；雇用：*The company employs 18 workers.* 公司雇了 18 个工人。

employee /ɪm'plɔɪiː/ *countable noun* 可数名词
a person who is paid to work for another person or a company 员工；雇员：*The police believe that airport employees were involved.* 警方认为机场雇员涉案。

employer /ɪm'plɔɪə/ *countable noun* 可数名词
the person or the company that you work for 雇主；用人单位：*Your employer should agree to pay you for this work.* 你们单位应该答应向你支付这项工作的报酬。

employment /ɪm'plɔɪmənt/ *uncountable noun* 不可数名词
work that you are paid for 工作：*She was unable to find employment.* 她找不到工作。

empty¹ /'empti/ *adjective* 形容词 (**emptier, emptiest**)
used for describing a place or container that has no people or things in it 空的：*The room was cold and empty.* 房间里很冷，空荡荡的。 □ *There were empty cans all over the floor.* 地板上到处都是空罐子。

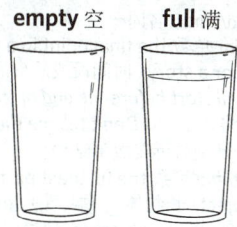

empty 空　　full 满

empty² /'empti/ *verb* 动词 (**empties, emptying, emptied**)
to remove the contents of a container 清空；倒空：*I emptied the rubbish bin.* 我把垃圾桶倒干净。 □ *Empty the noodles into a bowl.* 把面条倒进碗里。

enable /ɪn'eɪbəl/ *verb* 动词 (**enables, enabling, enabled**)
to make it possible for someone to do

enclose – energetic

something 使能够；使得以：*The new test will enable doctors to treat the disease early.* 这项新检测将使医生能够提早治疗这种病。

enclose /ɪnˈkləʊz/ *verb* 动词 (**encloses, enclosing, enclosed**)
1 to completely surround a place or an object 包围；围住：*The park is enclosed by a wooden fence.* 公园围了一圈木栅栏。
2 to put something in the same envelope as a letter 随信附上：*I have enclosed a cheque for £100.* 我随信附上了一张 100 英镑的支票。

encourage /ɪnˈkʌrɪdʒ/ *verb* 动词 (**encourages, encouraging, encouraged**)
1 to give someone hope or confidence 鼓励；鼓舞：*When things aren't going well, he encourages me.* 不顺的时候，他鼓励我。
2 to try to persuade someone to do something 鼓动；努力说服：*We want to encourage people to take more exercise.* 我们想鼓励人们多锻炼。

encouragement /ɪnˈkʌrɪdʒmənt/ *noun* 名词
the act of encouraging someone 鼓励；鼓舞：*Friends gave me a lot of encouragement.* 朋友给了我很多鼓励。

encouraging /ɪnˈkʌrɪdʒɪŋ/ *adjective* 形容词
giving people hope or confidence 令人鼓舞的；振奋人心的：*The results have been encouraging.* 结果令人振奋。

encyclopedia /ɪnˌsaɪkləˈpiːdiə/ *countable noun* 可数名词
a book or a CD-ROM containing facts about many different subjects 百科全书

end¹ /end/ *noun* 名词
1 *singular* 单数 the final point in a period of time or a story（时间段或故事的）末尾：*Work will start before the end of the year.* 年底前将开工。▫ *Don't tell me the end of the story!* 别告诉我故事结局！
2 *countable* 可数 the furthest part of a long object（长物体的）端，头：*Both ends of the tunnel were blocked.* 地道两头都封上了。
▸ **for hours/days/weeks on end** for a long time 一连几个小时／几天／几周：*We can talk for hours on end.* 我们能一聊就是几个小时。
▸ **make ends meet** to have enough money for the things you need 勉强维持生计；使收支相抵：*With Betty's salary they couldn't make ends meet.* 靠贝蒂的薪水，他们入不敷出。

end² /end/ *verb* 动词 (**ends, ending, ended**)
to reach the final point and stop 结束；终止：*The meeting quickly ended.* 会议很快开完了。
▸ **end up** to be in a particular place or situation after a series of events 最终落得：*We ended up back at the house again.* 我们到头来又回到了这座房子。

endangered species /ɪnˈdeɪndʒəd spiːʃiːz/ *countable noun* 可数名词 (**endangered species**)
a type of animal that may soon disappear from the world 濒危种；濒危物种：*These African beetles are on the list of endangered species.* 这些非洲甲虫被列入濒危物种名录。

ending /ˈendɪŋ/ *countable noun* 可数名词
the last part of a book or a film（书或影片的）结尾，结局：*The film has a happy ending.* 影片结局圆满。

endless /ˈendləs/ *adjective* 形容词
lasting for a very long time 无尽的；无休止的：*The morning classes seemed endless.* 上午的课好像没完没了。
▸ **endlessly** /ˈendləsli/ *adverb* 副词：*They talk about it endlessly.* 他们无休止地谈着那件事。

endurance /ɪnˈdjʊərəns/ *uncountable noun* 不可数名词
the ability to continue with a difficult activity over a long period of time 耐力：*The exercise will improve strength and endurance.* 这项锻炼能够增强力量和耐力。

endure /ɪnˈdjʊə/ *verb* 动词 (**endures, enduring, endured**)
to experience a difficult situation 遭受；忍耐：*She endured great pain in her life.* 她一生遭受了巨大的痛苦。

enemy /ˈenəmi/ *noun* 名词 (**enemies**)
1 *countable* 可数 someone who hates a person, and wants to harm them 仇敌；敌人：*His enemies hated and feared him.* 他的敌人对他又恨又怕。
2 *singular* 单数 an army that is fighting against you in a war 敌军；敌兵：*We are going to attack the enemy tomorrow morning.* 我们计划明早向敌军发起攻击。

energetic /ˌenəˈdʒetɪk/ *adjective* 形容词
having a lot of energy 精力旺盛的：*Young children are very energetic.* 小孩子精力非常旺盛。

energy /ˈenədʒi/ *uncountable noun* 不可数名词
1 the ability and strength to do active physical things 力气；力量：*He's saving his energy for next week's race.* 他在为下周的赛跑养精蓄锐。
2 the power from electricity or the sun, for example, that makes machines work or provides heat 能；能量：*These machines are powered with energy from the sun.* 这些机器使用的是太阳能。

engaged /ɪnˈɡeɪdʒd/ *adjective* 形容词
if two people are engaged, they have agreed to marry each other 订婚的：*We got engaged on my 26th birthday.* 我 26 岁生日当天我们订了婚。

engagement /ɪnˈɡeɪdʒmənt/ *countable noun* 可数名词
an agreement to get married to somebody 婚约；订婚：*We announced our engagement in November.* 我们 11 月宣布订婚。

engine /ˈendʒɪn/ *countable noun* 可数名词
1 the part of a car that produces the power to make it move（汽车的）发动机，引擎：*He got into the driving seat and started the engine.* 他坐进驾驶座，发动了引擎。
2 the front part of a train that pulls the rest of it 机车；火车头：*In 1941, trains were pulled by steam engines.* 1941 年，火车是由蒸汽机车牵引的。

engineer /ˌendʒɪˈnɪə/ *countable noun* 可数名词
1 a person who designs, builds and repairs machines, or structures such as roads, railways and bridges 工程师
2 a person who repairs mechanical or electrical machines 机修工；维修人员：*They sent an engineer to fix the computer.* 他们派了位维修人员来修电脑。

engineering /ˌendʒɪˈnɪərɪŋ/ *uncountable noun* 不可数名词
the work of designing and constructing machines or structures such as roads and bridges 工程；工程学：*She studies science and engineering at college.* 她在大学读理工科。

English¹ /ˈɪŋɡlɪʃ/ *uncountable noun* 不可数名词
the language spoken by people who live in Great Britain and Ireland, the United States, Canada, Australia and many other countries 英语：*Do you speak English?* 你说英语吗？
the English the people who come from or live in England 英格兰人

English² /ˈɪŋɡlɪʃ/ *adjective* 形容词
belonging to or relating to England 英格兰的：*He began to enjoy the English way of life.* 他开始喜欢上了英格兰的生活方式。

enhance /ɪnˈhɑːns/ *verb* 动词 (**enhances, enhancing, enhanced**)
to improve the quality of something 增进；增强：*A little sugar enhances the flavour of the peas.* 加少许糖能给豆子提味儿。

enjoy /ɪnˈdʒɔɪ/ *verb* 动词 (**enjoys, enjoying, enjoyed**)
to like doing something 喜欢，享受（做某事）：*I enjoyed playing basketball.* 我喜欢打篮球。
enjoy yourself to have a good time doing something 过得愉快：*I am really enjoying myself at the moment.* 我此刻感到非常快活。

enjoyable /ɪnˈdʒɔɪəbəl/ *adjective* 形容词
giving you pleasure 令人愉悦的：*The film was much more enjoyable than I expected.* 影片比我想象的要好看得多。

enjoyment /ɪnˈdʒɔɪmənt/ *uncountable noun* 不可数名词
the feeling of pleasure that you have when you do something that you like 愉悦；快乐；乐趣：*We get a lot of enjoyment from our garden.* 我们从园子里获得很多乐趣。

enlarge /ɪnˈlɑːdʒ/ *verb* 动词 (**enlarges, enlarging, enlarged**)
to make something bigger 增大；扩大；使变大：*You can enlarge these photographs.* 你可以放大这些照片。

enormous /ɪˈnɔːməs/ *adjective* 形容词
extremely large in size or amount 巨大的；极多的：*The main bedroom is enormous.* 主卧非常大。
▶ **enormously** /ɪˈnɔːməsli/ *adverb* 副词：*I admired him enormously.* 我特别仰慕他。

enough /ɪˈnʌf/ *adjective* 形容词
as much as you need 充足的；足够的：*They had enough cash for a one-way ticket.* 他们有足够的现金买张单程票。 ● **enough** *adverb* 副词：*I was old enough to work and earn money.* 我长大了，可以工作赚钱了。
● **enough** *pronoun* 代词：*They are not doing enough.* 他们做得不够。

enquire /ɪnˈkwaɪə/ also 亦作 **inquire** verb 动词 (**enquires, enquiring, enquired**)
to ask for information about something 询问；打听：*He called them to enquire about the job.* 他打电话向他们询问职位情况。

enquiry /ɪnˈkwaɪəri/ also 亦作 **inquiry** countable noun 可数名词 (**enquiries**)
a question you ask in order to get some information about something 询问；打听：*He made some inquiries and discovered she had gone to Canada.* 他打听了一番，发现她已经去加拿大了。

enrol /ɪnˈrəʊl/ verb 动词 (**enrols, enrolling, enrolled**)
to officially join a class 注册（课程）；招收，录取（学生）：*He has already enrolled at medical college.* 他已经在医学院注册入学了。 □ *Already, 46 students are enrolled in the two classes.* 已有 46 名学生被这两个班录取。

ensure /ɪnˈʃʊə/ verb 动词 (**ensures, ensuring, ensured**)
to make sure that something happens (*formal* 正式) 保证；确保；保障：*The school ensures the safety of all students.* 学校保障全体学生的安全。 □ *We will work hard to ensure that this doesn't happen again.* 我们会努力确保此类事件不再发生。

enter /ˈentə/ verb 动词 (**enters, entering, entered**)
1 to go into a place such as a room or building (*formal* 正式) 进入（房间、楼宇等）：*He entered the room and stood near the door.* 他进了房间，站在门口附近。
2 to state that you will be a part of a competition, a race or an exam 报名参加（竞赛、考试等）：*To enter the competition, go to our website and fill in the details.* 报名比赛请登录我们网站填写详细信息。
3 to write or type information in a form or a book, or into a computer 填写，录入（信息）：*They enter the addresses into the computer.* 他们将地址录入计算机。

enterprise /ˈentəˌpraɪz/ countable noun 可数名词
a company or a business 企业；公司：*We provide help for small and medium-sized enterprises.* 我们为中小企业提供帮助。

entertain /ˌentəˈteɪn/ verb 动词 (**entertains, entertaining, entertained**)
1 to do something that amuses or interests people 娱乐；使快乐：*They were entertained by singers and dancers.* 他们观看了歌舞演员的娱乐表演。
▶ **entertaining** /ˌentəˈteɪnɪŋ/ adjective 形容词：*His show is entertaining, intelligent and funny.* 他的节目兼具娱乐性、知识性和趣味性。
2 to invite guests to your home and give them food and drink 招待；款待：*This is the season for entertaining outdoors.* 这是露天待客的季节。

entertainer /ˌentəˈteɪnə/ countable noun 可数名词
a person whose job is to entertain audiences, for example, by telling jokes, singing or dancing（以说笑话、唱歌、跳舞等娱乐他人的）演员，艺人：*Chaplin was possibly the greatest entertainer of the twentieth century.* 卓别林可能是 20 世纪最伟大的演员。

entertainment /ˌentəˈteɪnmənt/ uncountable noun 不可数名词
performances of plays and films, and activities such as reading and watching television, that give people pleasure 娱乐演出；娱乐活动：*At the party, there was children's entertainment and a swimming competition.* 派对上安排有儿童娱乐活动和游泳比赛。

enthusiasm /ɪnˈθjuːziˌæzəm/ uncountable noun 不可数名词
a feeling that you have when you really enjoy something or want to do something 热情；热忱；热衷：*Does your girlfriend share your enthusiasm for sports?* 你女朋友和你一样热爱体育吗？

enthusiastic /ɪnˌθjuːziˈæstɪk/ adjective 形容词
showing how much you like or enjoy something 热情的；热忱的；热衷的：*Tom was not very enthusiastic about the idea.* 汤姆对这个主意不怎么热衷。

entire /ɪnˈtaɪə/ adjective 形容词
whole or complete 全部的；完全的：*He spent his entire life in China.* 他一生都在中国度过。

entirely /ɪnˈtaɪəli/ adverb 副词
completely and not just partly 全部；完全：*I agree entirely.* 我完全同意。 □ *I'm not entirely sure what to do.* 对于要做些什么，我没有十足的把握。

entitle /ɪnˈtaɪtəl/ verb 动词 (**entitles, entitling, entitled**)
be entitled to something to be allowed to

have or do something 获准拥有某物；有资格做某事：*They are entitled to first class travel.* 他们有权乘坐头等舱出行。

entrance /'entrəns/ *noun* 名词
1 *countable* 可数 the door or gate where you go into a place 门；入口：*He came out of a side entrance.* 他从边门走了出来。
2 *countable* 可数 the moment when someone arrives in a room 入室；进屋：*She didn't notice her father's entrance.* 她没有注意到父亲进屋。
3 *uncountable* 不可数 permission to go into a place 进入权；进入许可：*We tried to go in, but we were refused entrance.* 我们想进去，但被拒绝了。

entry /'entri/ *uncountable noun* 不可数名词 when you go into a particular place 进入；入内：*Entry to the museum is free.* 这家博物馆参观免费。
no entry used on signs to show that you are not allowed to go into a particular area（公示语）禁止入内

envelope /'envələʊp/ *countable noun* 可数名词
the paper cover in which you put a letter before you send it to someone 信封：*She put the letter back into the envelope and gave it to me.* 她把信塞回信封交给我。

envelope 信封

envious /'enviəs/ *adjective* 形容词 wanting something that someone else has 羡慕的；嫉妒的：*I'm not envious of your success.* 我不羡慕你成功。
▶ **enviously** /'enviəsli/ *adverb* 副词：*People talked enviously about his good luck.* 人们谈论着他的好运气，都很羡慕。

environment /ɪn'vaɪərənmənt/ *noun* 名词
1 the conditions in which someone lives or works（生活或工作的）环境：*The children are taught in a safe and happy environment.* 孩子们在安全幸福的环境中接受教育。
2 *uncountable* 不可数 the natural world of land, the seas, the air, plants and animals（自然）环境：*Please respect the environment by recycling.* 请尊重环境，回收利用。
▶ **environmental** /ɪnˌvaɪərən'mentəl/ *adjective* 形容词：*Environmental groups protested loudly during the conference.* 大会期间环保组织大声抗议。
▶ **environmentally** /ɪnˌvaɪərən'mentəli/ *adverb* 副词：*environmentally friendly cleaning products* 环境友好型清洁产品

envy /'envi/ *verb* 动词 (**envies, envying, envied**)
to wish that you had the same things that someone else has 羡慕；嫉妒：*I don't envy young people these days.* 我不羡慕如今的年轻人。● **envy** *uncountable noun* 不可数名词：*She was full of envy when she heard their news.* 得知他们的消息后，她心中充满了妒意。

epic /'epɪk/ *countable noun* 可数名词 a long book, poem or film about important events 史诗；史诗般的作品：*We read Homer's epics about the Trojan war.* 我们读了讲述特洛伊战争的荷马史诗。● **epic** *adjective* 形容词：*This is an epic story of love and war.* 这是一个讲述爱情与战争的史诗级故事。

epidemic /ˌepɪ'demɪk/ *countable noun* 可数名词
when a particular disease affects a large number of people（疾病的）流行：*a flu epidemic* 流感

epilogue /'epɪˌlɒɡ/ *countable noun* 可数名词 an extra part that is added at the end of a piece of writing 跋；后记；尾声

episode /'epɪsəʊd/ *countable noun* 可数名词 one of the parts of a story on television or radio（电视剧、广播剧的）集：*The final episode will be shown next Sunday.* 最后一集下周日播出。

equal¹ /'iːkwəl/ *adjective* 形容词
1 being the same in size, number or value 同样的；相等的：*There are equal numbers of men and women.* 男女人数相等。
▶ **equally** /'iːkwəli/ *adverb* 副词：*The money will be divided equally among his three children.* 这笔钱将由他的 3 个子女平分。
2 used for saying that different groups of people have the same rights or are treated in the same way 平等的：*We want equal rights at work.* 我们想要平等的工作权利。
▶ **equally** /'iːkwəli/ *adverb* 副词：*The system should treat everyone equally.* 制度应对大家一视同仁。

equal² /'iːkwəl/ *countable noun* 可数名词 someone who has the same ability or rights as someone else (能力或权利) 相同者: *You and I are equals.* 你我不相上下。

equal[3] /ˈiːkwəl/ *verb* 动词 (**equals, equalling, equalled**)
to be the same as a particular number or amount 等于: *9 minus 7 equals 2.* *9 减 7 等于 2.
→ Look at picture on P2 参见彩插第 2 页

equality /ɪˈkwɒlɪti/ *uncountable noun* 不可数名词
the fair treatment of all the people in a group 平等: *Few people really believed in racial equality in the 1800s.* *19 世纪鲜有人真正相信种族平等。

ˈequals ˌsign *countable noun* 可数名词
the sign =, which is used in mathematics to show that two numbers are equal 等号

equation /ɪˈkweɪʒən/ *countable noun* 可数名词
a mathematical statement that two amounts or values are the same 方程;等式

equator /ɪˈkweɪtə/ *singular noun* 单数名词
a line that is shown on maps around the middle of the world 赤道

equator 赤道

equatorial /ˌekwəˈtɔːriəl/ *adjective* 形容词
at or near the equator 赤道上的;赤道附近的: *The cassava plant grows in most equatorial regions.* 木薯在大部分赤道地区均有分布。

equip /ɪˈkwɪp/ *verb* 动词 (**equips, equipping, equipped**)
be equipped with something to have the things that you need to do a particular job 配备(或装备)某物: *The army is equipped with 5,000 tanks.* 陆军装备了 5,000 辆坦克。 □ *The phone is equipped with a camera.* 这部电话配有一个摄像头。

equipment /ɪˈkwɪpmənt/ *uncountable noun* 不可数名词
all the things that are used for a particular purpose 装备;设备: *tractors and other farm equipment* 拖拉机和其他农场设备

equivalent /ɪˈkwɪvələnt/ *singular noun* 单数名词
something that is the same as another thing, or used in the same way 等同物;对等物: *The Internet has become the modern equivalent of the phone.* 目前因特网已经等同于电话。 ● **equivalent** *adjective* 形容词: *an equivalent amount* 相等的量

era /ˈɪərə/ *countable noun* 可数名词
a period of time that is considered as a single unit 代;纪元;时代: *Their leader promised them a new era of peace.* 他们的领导人向他们许诺开创一个新的和平时代。

erase /ɪˈreɪz/ *verb* 动词 (**erases, erasing, erased**)
to remove something such as writing or a mark 消除,清除(字迹等): *She erased his name from her address book.* 她把他的名字从通讯录中抹掉了。

eraser /ɪˈreɪzə/ *countable noun* 可数名词
(*American* 美国英语)
→ see 见 **rubber**

erect[1] /ɪˈrekt/ *verb* 动词 (**erects, erecting, erected**)
to build something such as a building or a bridge (*formal* 正式): 建造;建筑: *The building was erected in 1900.* 这座建筑建于 1900 年。

erect[2] /ɪˈrekt/ *adjective* 形容词
straight and upright 竖直的;直立的: *Stand erect, with your arms hanging naturally.* 挺身站直,双臂自然下垂。

erode /ɪˈrəʊd/ *verb* 动词 (**erodes, eroding, eroded**)
if the wind or sea erodes land, it gradually destroys it (风、海洋) 侵蚀 (陆地): *The sea is gradually eroding the coastline.* 海慢慢地侵蚀着海岸线。
▶ **erosion** /ɪˈrəʊʒən/ *uncountable noun* 不可数名词: *The storms caused soil erosion and flooding.* 风暴引发土壤侵蚀和洪水。

errand /ˈerənd/ *countable noun* 可数名词
a short trip to do a job or to buy something (办事或购物的) 差事;跑腿儿: *We ran errands and took her meals when she was sick.* 她生病时我们替她跑腿儿、打饭。

error /ˈerə/ *noun* 名词
a mistake 差错;错误: *You should check your work for errors in grammar or spelling.* 你要检查下自己作业有没有语法或拼写错误。

erupt /ɪˈrʌpt/ *verb* 动词 (**erupts, erupting, erupted**)
when a volcano erupts, it throws out hot, melted rock (= lava) (火山) 喷发: *Krakatoa erupted in 1883.* 喀拉喀托火山

1883年喷发过。

▶ **eruption** /ɪˈrʌpʃən/ *noun* 名词: *The country's last volcanic eruption was 600 years ago.* 该国最近一次火山喷发发生在600年前。

escalate /ˈeskəˌleɪt/ *verb* 动词 (**escalates, escalating, escalated**)
to become worse 恶化; 加剧: *Nobody wants the situation to escalate.* 谁也不希望形势恶化下去。

escalator /ˈeskəˌleɪtə/ *countable noun* 可数名词
a set of moving stairs 自动扶梯: *Take the escalator to the third floor.* 乘自动扶梯上4楼。

escalator 自动扶梯

escape /ɪˈskeɪp/ *verb* 动词 (**escapes, escaping, escaped**)
1 to manage to get away from a place 逃跑; 逃脱: *A prisoner has escaped from a jail in northern Texas.* 一名囚犯从得克萨斯州北部的一座监狱越狱。● **escape** *countable noun* 可数名词: *He made his escape at night.* 他趁夜逃走。
2 to avoid an accident 避免, 躲过(事故): *The two officers escaped serious injury.* 两名警察伤势不重。● **escape** *countable noun* 可数名词: *I had a narrow escape on the bridge.* 我在桥上险些出事儿。

especially /ɪˈspeʃəli/ *adverb* 副词
used for showing that something is more important or true 特别; 尤其: *Millions of wild flowers grow in the valleys, especially in April and May.* 山谷里生长着不计其数的野花, 尤其是在四月份和五月份。

essay /ˈeseɪ/ *countable noun* 可数名词
a short piece of writing on a subject (关于特定主题的)短文, 论说文: *We asked Jason to write an essay about his home town.* 我们要贾森写一篇介绍他家乡的短文。
→ Look at picture on P3 参见彩插第 3 页

essential /ɪˈsenʃəl/ *adjective* 形容词
necessary 必需的; 必要的: *Play is an essential part of a child's development.* 玩耍是儿童成长不可或缺的一部分。

establish /ɪˈstæblɪʃ/ *verb* 动词 (**establishes, establishing, established**)
to create an organization 建立, 创立, 设立(机构): *He established the business five years ago.* 他 5 年前创立了这家企业。

establishment /ɪˈstæblɪʃmənt/ *noun* 名词
1 *countable* 可数 an organization in a building in a particular place (*formal* 正式) 机构: *an educational establishment* 教育机构
2 *singular* 单数 the people who have power in a country 当权派; 权势集团: *the American establishment* 美国权势集团

estate /ɪˈsteɪt/ *countable noun* 可数名词
a large house in a large area of land in the country, owned by a person or an organization 地产; 庄园: *He spent the holidays at his aunt's 300-acre estate.* 他在姑妈家 300 英亩的庄园里度假。

eˈstate ˌagent *countable noun* 可数名词
a person whose job is to sell buildings or land 房地产经纪人

estimate /ˈestɪˌmeɪt/ *verb* 动词 (**estimates, estimating, estimated**)
to say how much you think there is of something 估计; 估算: *It's difficult to estimate how much money he has.* 他有多少钱难以估算。● **estimate** /ˈestɪmət/ *countable noun* 可数名词: *She made an estimate of the lorry's speed.* 她估计了一下卡车的速度。

estuary /ˈestʃuri/ *countable noun* 可数名词 (**estuaries**)
the wide part of a river where it meets the sea 河口

etc. /etˈsetrə/
used at the end of a list to show that there are other things that you have not mentioned. Etc. is short for (缩写 =) 'etcetera'. 等; 等等

etcetera /etˈsetrə/ *also* 亦作 **et cetera**
→ see 见 **etc.**

eternal /ɪˈtɜːnəl/ *adjective* 形容词
lasting forever 永久的; 永恒的; 恒久的: *What's the secret of eternal happiness?* 实现永久幸福的诀窍是什么?

ethical /ˈeθɪkəl/ *adjective* 形容词
1 relating to beliefs about right and wrong

道德的；伦理的：*Heather is now a vegetarian for ethical reasons.* 希瑟现在出于道德因素吃素。
2 morally right or morally acceptable 合乎道德的；伦理上可接受的：*ethical business practices* 符合道德规范的商业行为

ethnic /ˈeθnɪk/ *adjective* 形容词
relating to groups of people that have the same culture or belong to the same race 民族的：*Most of their friends come from other ethnic groups.* 他们的大多数朋友都是其他民族的。

euro /ˈjʊərəʊ/ *countable noun* 可数名词
a unit of money that is used by many countries in the European Union (= an organization that encourages trade) 欧元

European /ˌjʊərəˈpiːən/ *adjective* 形容词
belonging to or coming from Europe 欧洲的：*European countries* 欧洲国家
● **European** *countable noun* 可数名词：*When did Europeans first arrive in America?* 欧洲人首次抵达美洲是什么时候？

evacuate /ɪˈvækjuˌeɪt/ *verb* 动词 (**evacuates, evacuating, evacuated**)
to move people out of a place because it is dangerous 疏散；转移；使撤离：*Families were evacuated from the area because of the fighting.* 住户因战争从该地区撤离。

evaluate /ɪˈvæljuˌeɪt/ *verb* 动词 (**evaluates, evaluating, evaluated**)
to consider something or someone in order to decide how good or bad they are 评估；评价：*We need to evaluate the situation very carefully.* 我们得认真地评估一下局势。
▶ **evaluation** /ɪˌvæljuˈeɪʃən/ *noun* 名词：*The programme includes an evaluation of students' writing skills.* 本项目涵盖学生写作技能评估。

evaporate /ɪˈvæpəˌreɪt/ *verb* 动词 (**evaporates, evaporating, evaporated**)
to change from a liquid into a gas 蒸发：*Boil the sauce until most of the liquid evaporates.* 熬煮调味汁直至收去大部分汁水。
→ Look at picture on P6 参见彩插第 6 页

eve /iːv/ *countable noun* 可数名词
the day before a particular event or occasion 前一天；前夕：*The story begins on the eve of her birthday.* 故事始于她生日的前一天。

even[1] /ˈiːvən/ *adjective* 形容词
1 used for describing numbers that can be divided exactly by two, for example 4, 8 and 24 *偶数的；双数的
2 smooth and flat 平滑的；平坦的：*You will need a table with an even surface.* 你需要一张表面平滑的桌子。
3 equally balanced between two sides 不相上下的；势均力敌的：*It was an even game.* 这是一场平分秋色的比赛。

even[2] /ˈiːvən/ *adverb* 副词
1 used for saying that something is rather surprising（表示令人意外）连，甚至，哪怕：*Rob still seems happy, even after the bad news.* 罗布看上去依旧很快乐，即便是听到了那则坏消息之后。
2 used for making another word stronger（表示强调）更加，愈发：*Our car is big, but theirs is even bigger.* 我们家的车很大，可他们家的更大。
even if used for showing that a particular fact does not change anything 即使；纵然：*I'm going to the party, even if you won't come.* 就算你不去参加聚会，我也要去。
even so used for adding a surprising fact 即便如此；尽管这样：*The bus was nearly empty. Even so, the man sat down next to her.* 公交车上几乎空无一人。即便如此，那名男子还是挨着她坐下了。
even though although, despite the fact that 虽然；尽管：*She wasn't embarrassed, even though she made a mistake.* 她不觉得尴尬，虽然自己犯了错误。

evening /ˈiːvnɪŋ/ *noun* 名词
the part of each day between the end of the afternoon and midnight 傍晚；晚上：*That evening he went to see a movie.* 那天晚上他去看电影了。□ *We usually have dinner at seven in the evening.* 我们晚上一般 7 点钟吃饭。

event /ɪˈvent/ *countable noun* 可数名词
1 something that happens 事件：*This terrible event caused death and injury to many.* 此次惨痛事件造成多人死伤。
2 an organized activity or celebration（有组织的）活动；庆典：*Several sports events were cancelled.* 数项体育赛事被取消。

eventually /ɪˈventʃuəli/ *adverb* 副词
at some later time, especially after a lot of delays or problems（尤指几经延误或磨难后）最终，终于：*They eventually married in May.* 他们最终于 5 月完婚。□ *Eventually your child will leave home.* 你的孩子终有一天要离开家。

ever /ˈevə/ *adverb* 副词
at any time. Ever is usually used in questions and negative sentences.（通常用于疑问句、否定句）在任何时候: *I don't think I'll ever trust people again.* 我觉得自己再也不会相信别人了。□ *Have you ever seen anything like it?* 你见过类似的东西吗？□ *The country is more powerful than ever before.* 该国比以往任何时候都强大。

every /ˈevri/ *adjective* 形容词
1 used for showing that you are talking about all the members of a group 每一个: *Every room has a window facing the sea.* 每个房间都有一个朝海的窗户。□ *Every child gets a free piece of fruit.* 每个孩子都有一块免费水果吃。
2 used for saying how often something happens（表示发生频率）每: *We had to attend meetings every day.* 我们每天都要开会。□ *He saw his family once every two weeks.* 他每两个星期见一次家人。
every other day or **every second day** happening one day, then not happening the next day, and continuing in this way 每隔一天: *I called my mother every other day.* 我每隔一天给妈妈打个电话。

everybody /ˈevriˌbɒdi/ *pronoun* 代词
→ see 见 **everyone**

everyday /ˈevriˌdeɪ/ *adjective* 形容词
ordinary, a regular part of your life 日常的；平常的: *They were doing everyday activities around the house.* 他们像平常一样在家里活动着。□ *Computers are a central part of everyday life.* 计算机是日常生活的中心。

everyone /ˈevriˌwʌn/ *pronoun* 代词

> **LANGUAGE HELP** 语言提示
> You can also say **everybody**. 也可用 everybody。

all people, or all the people in a particular group 每个人；所有人: *Everyone on the street was shocked when they heard the news.* 听到消息，街上的每个人都惊了。□ *Not everyone thinks that the government is acting fairly.* 不是每个人都觉得政府办事公道。

everything /ˈevriθɪŋ/ *pronoun* 代词
used when you are talking about all the objects, actions or facts in a situation 所有事物；一切: *Everything in his life has changed.* 他生活中的一切都变了。□ *Susan*

and I do everything together. 我和苏珊什么事儿都一起做。□ *Is everything all right?* 一切都好吗？

everywhere /ˈevriˌweə/ *adverb* 副词
used when you are talking about a whole area or all the places in a particular area 四处；各处；到处: *People everywhere want the same things.* 各地的人都想要相同的东西。□ *We went everywhere together.* 我们到哪儿都一起。

evidence /ˈevɪdəns/ *uncountable noun* 不可数名词
an object or a piece of information that makes you believe that something is true or has really happened 证据；佐证；根据: *There is no evidence that he stole the money.* 没有证据表明他偷了那笔钱。□ *Evidence shows that most of us are happy with our lives.* 证据表明我们大多数人对自己的生活感到满意。

evident /ˈevɪdənt/ *adjective* 形容词
easy to notice or understand 明显的；显而易见的: *Changes are evident across the country.* 全国各地变化明显。□ *It was evident that she was not feeling well.* 显然她感觉不舒服。

evidently /ˈevɪdəntli/ *adverb* 副词
clearly 明显地；显而易见地: *The two men evidently knew each other.* 这两名男子显然彼此认识。

evil /ˈiːvəl/ *adjective* 形容词
morally very bad 邪恶的；道德败坏的: *Who's the most evil person in all of history?* 史上头号大坏蛋是谁？

evolution /ˌiːvəˈluːʃən, ˌev-/ *uncountable noun* 不可数名词
a process in which animals or plants slowly change over many years 进化；演化；演变: *The evolution of mammals involved many changes in the body.* 哺乳动物的进化涉及身体上的诸多改变。

evolve /ɪˈvɒlv/ *verb* 动词 (**evolves, evolving, evolved**)
to gradually develop over a period of time into something different 进化；演化；演变: *Popular music evolved from folk songs.* 流行乐由民歌演化而来。□ *The theory is that humans evolved from apes.* 该学说称人由猿进化而来。

exact /ɪɡˈzækt/ *adjective* 形容词
correct and complete in every way 确切的；精确的: *I don't remember the exact words.*

我记不得确切的话了。▫ *Can you tell me the exact date of the incident?* 你能告诉我事件发生的确切日期吗？

exactly /ɪɡˈzæktli/ *adverb* 副词
1 correctly and completely 确切地；精确地：*The tower was exactly a hundred metres in height.* 这座塔刚好高 100 米。
2 in every way, or with all the details 完全：*I came to exactly the same conclusion.* 我得出了完全相同的结论。
3 said when you are agreeing with someone（表示同意）正是，确实如此：*Eve nodded. 'Exactly.'* 伊芙点了点头说："正是。"

exaggerate /ɪɡˈzædʒəˌreɪt/ *verb* 动词
(**exaggerates, exaggerating, exaggerated**) to say that something is bigger, worse or more important than it really is 夸张；夸大：*He thinks I'm exaggerating.* 他觉得我是夸大其词。▫ *Try not to exaggerate the risks of travelling alone.* 不要夸大独自出行的风险。
▶ **exaggeration** /ɪɡˌzædʒəˈreɪʃən/ *noun* 名词：*It's not an exaggeration, it's a fact.* 这不是夸张，这是事实。

exam /ɪɡˈzæm/ *countable noun* 可数名词
a formal test that you take to show your knowledge of a subject 考试：*I don't want to take any more exams.* 我不想再参加考试了。

LANGUAGE HELP 语言提示
If you do an exam, you can say that you **take** an exam or **sit** an exam. If you do not pass an exam, you **fail** it. 参加考试用 take 或 sit，考试未通过用 fail。

examination /ɪɡˌzæmɪˈneɪʃən/ *countable noun* 可数名词
1 (*formal* 正式)→ see 见 **exam**
2 an occasion when a doctor looks at your body in order to check how healthy you are 诊察；（身体）检查：*She is waiting for the results of a medical examination.* 她在等医学检查结果。

examine /ɪɡˈzæmɪn/ *verb* 动词 (**examines, examining, examined**)
to look at something or someone carefully 审视；检查；细看：*He examined her documents.* 他仔细看看了她的文件。▫ *A doctor examined her and could find nothing wrong.* 一位大夫给她做了检查，没有发现任何问题。
▶ **examination** /ɪɡˌzæmɪˈneɪʃən/ *noun* 名

词：*The government said the plan needed careful examination.* 政府称该方案需要认真审查。

examine 检查

A doctor examined her and could find nothing wrong. 一位大夫给她做了检查，没有发现任何问题。

example /ɪɡˈzɑːmpəl/ *countable noun* 可数名词
something that shows what other things in a particular group are like 例子；例证；示例：*The building is a fine example of 19th-century architecture.* 这座房子是 19 世纪建筑的范例。
for example used for introducing an example of something 例如；比如：*The technique can be used for treating diseases like cancer, for example.* 比如，这种技术可以用于治疗癌症之类的疾病。

exceed /ɪkˈsiːd/ *verb* 动词 (**exceeds, exceeding, exceeded**)
to be greater than a particular amount (*formal* 正式) 逾，超过（特定数量）：*The cost of a new boat exceeded £100,000.* 新船花费逾 10 万英镑。

excellence /ˈeksələns/ *uncountable noun* 不可数名词
the quality of being extremely good in some way 优秀；卓越；杰出：*She won an award for excellence in teaching.* 她获得了一项教育杰出成就奖。

excellent /ˈeksələnt/ *adjective* 形容词
extremely good 优秀的；卓越的；杰出的：*The printing quality is excellent.* 印刷质量出类拔萃。

except /ɪkˈsept/ *preposition* 介词
used for showing that you are not including a particular thing or person 除…之外：*The shops are open every day except Sunday.* 店铺除了周日，每天都开门。

□ The room was empty except for a television. 房间里除了一台电视机，什么也没有。● **except** conjunction 连词: I'm much better now, except that I still have a headache. 我现在好多了，只是还有点儿头疼。

exception /ɪk'sepʃən/ countable noun 可数名词
a particular thing, person or situation that is not included in what you say 例外；特例: Not many musicians can sing well and play well, but Eddie is an exception. 弹唱俱佳的音乐人不多，但埃迪是个特例。

exceptional /ɪk'sepʃənəl/ adjective 形容词
used for describing someone or something that is better than others in some way 优异的；非凡的: He is a player with exceptional ability. 他是个能力超群的选手。

▶ **exceptionally** /ɪk'sepʃənəli/ adverb 副词: She's an exceptionally talented dancer. 她是位非常有天赋的舞者。

excess /'ekses/ adjective 形容词
more than is usual or necessary 过多的；过量的: After cooking the fish, pour out any excess fat. 做完鱼后，倒出多余的油。

excessive /ɪk'sesɪv/ adjective 形容词
more than is necessary 过多的；过量的: Their spending on clothes is excessive. 他们花在衣服上的钱太多了。

exchange /ɪks'tʃeɪndʒ/ verb 动词 (exchanges, exchanging, exchanged)
1 to give something to someone at the same time as they give something to you 交换；互换: We exchanged addresses. 我们交换了地址。● **exchange** countable noun 可数名词: There will be a meal, followed by the exchange of gifts. 会安排一顿饭，饭后互换礼物。
2 to take something back to a shop and get a different thing 更换，调换（商品）: If you are unhappy with the product, we will exchange it. 如对产品不满意，我们给退换。

ex'change rate countable noun 可数名词
the amount of another country's money that you can buy with a country's money 汇率: The exchange rate is around 3.7 pesos to the dollar. 比索兑美元的汇率约为 3.7 比 1。

excited /ɪk'saɪtɪd/ adjective 形容词
very happy or enthusiastic 兴奋的；激动的: I was excited about playing football again. 又能踢球了，我很兴奋。
→ Look at picture on P15 参见彩插第 15 页

excitement /ɪk'saɪtmənt/ noun 名词
the feeling you have when you are excited 兴奋；激动: He shouted with excitement. 他兴奋地喊叫。

exciting /ɪk'saɪtɪŋ/ adjective 形容词
making you feel very happy or enthusiastic 令人兴奋的；激动人心的: The film is exciting, and also very scary. 影片很刺激，也很吓人。

exclaim /ɪks'kleɪm/ verb 动词 (exclaims, exclaiming, exclaimed)
to speak suddenly or loudly, often because you are excited or shocked（常因兴奋或惊愕而）呼喊，大叫: 'Fantastic!' Jackson exclaimed delightedly. "太好了！"杰克逊高兴地大叫道。

exclamation /ˌeksklə'meɪʃən/ countable noun 可数名词
something that you say suddenly and loudly, showing that you are excited or angry（兴奋或愤怒的）呼喊，大叫: Sue gave an exclamation when she saw the house. 休看见房子时惊叹了一声。

excla'mation ˌmark countable noun 可数名词
a mark (!) used in writing for showing surprise or excitement 叹号

exclude /ɪk'skluːd/ verb 动词 (excludes, excluding, excluded)
1 to prevent someone from entering a place or doing an activity 不让…进入；将…排除在外: The public was excluded from both meetings. 这两场会议不对公众开放。
2 to not use or consider something 不使用；不考虑: The price excludes taxes. 这个价格不含税。

exclusive /ɪk'skluːsɪv/ adjective 形容词
available only to people who are rich or powerful 高档的；高级的: It was a private, exclusive club. 那是一家高级私人俱乐部。

exclusively /ɪk'skluːsɪvli/ adverb 副词
involving only the place or thing mentioned, and nothing else 仅仅；唯独: This perfume is available exclusively from selected David Jones stores. 这款香水只从几家戴维·琼斯的精品店有售。

excuse[1] /ɪk'skjuːs/ countable noun 可数名词
a reason that you give in order to explain why you did something 理由；借口: They

are trying to find excuses for their failure. 他们想给自己的失败找借口。

excuse² /ɪkˈskjuːz/ *verb* 动词 (excuses, excusing, excused)
to forgive someone for doing something 原谅；宽恕：*I'm not excusing him for what he did.* 我不会原谅他的所作所为。
excuse me used for politely getting someone's attention（用于礼貌地引起对方注意）请问，劳驾：*Excuse me, but are you Mr Hess?* 请问，您是赫斯先生吗？

executive /ɪɡˈzekjʊtɪv/ *countable noun* 可数名词
someone who has an important job at a company（公司的）高管，经理：*She loved her job as an advertising executive.* 她热爱自己广告主管的工作。

exempt /ɪɡˈzempt/ *adjective* 形容词
not having to obey a rule or perform a duty 被免除的；被豁免的：*Men in college were exempt from military service.* 大学在校男生免服兵役。

exercise¹ /ˈeksəˌsaɪz/ *countable noun* 可数名词
1 a movement that you do in order to stay healthy and strong 锻炼；运动：*I do special neck and shoulder exercises every morning.* 我每天早上都做专门的颈部和肩部锻炼。
2 an activity that you do in order to practise a skill（技能）练习，训练：*Dennis said that the writing exercise was very useful.* 丹尼斯说写作练习非常有用。

exercise² /ˈeksəˌsaɪz/ *verb* 动词 (exercises, exercising, exercised)
to move your body in order to stay healthy and strong 锻炼；运动：*You should exercise at least two or three times a week.* 你每周至少要运动两三次。● **exercise** *uncountable noun* 不可数名词：*Lack of exercise can cause sleep problems.* 缺乏锻炼会引起睡眠问题。

ˈexerciseˌbook *countable noun* 可数名词
a book that you use at school for writing in 练习本；练习簿
→ Look at picture on P1 参见彩插第 1 页

exhaust¹ /ɪɡˈzɔːst/ *verb* 动词 (exhausts, exhausting, exhausted)
to make someone very tired 使疲惫不堪；使精疲力竭：*We were worried that the trip would exhaust him.* 我们担心此行会让他吃不消。
▶ **exhausted** /ɪɡˈzɔːstɪd/ *adjective* 形容词：

She was too exhausted to talk. 她累得都没力气说话了。
▶ **exhausting** /ɪɡˈzɔːstɪŋ/ *adjective* 形容词：*It was an exhausting climb to the top of the hill.* 爬到山顶累得要命。
▶ **exhaustion** /ɪɡˈzɔːstʃən/ *uncountable noun* 不可数名词：*He fainted from exhaustion.* 他累得晕倒在地。

exhaust² /ɪɡˈzɔːst/ *uncountable noun* 不可数名词
the gas or steam that the engine of a vehicle produces（车辆发动机的）废气，尾气：*The vehicle's exhaust fumes began to fill the garage.* 车的尾气开始在车库里弥散开来。

exˈhaustˌpipe *countable noun* 可数名词
a pipe that carries gases or steam out of a car's engine（汽车的）排气管

exhibit /ɪɡˈzɪbɪt/ *verb* 动词 (exhibits, exhibiting, exhibited)
to put an object in a public place such as a museum so that people can come to look at it 展览；展出：*The paintings were exhibited in Paris in 1874.* 这些画作于 1874 年在巴黎展出。

exhibition /ˌeksɪˈbɪʃən/ *countable noun* 可数名词
a public event where art or interesting objects are shown 展览（会）：*The Museum of the City of New York has an exhibition of photographs.* 纽约市博物馆有一个摄影展。

exist /ɪɡˈzɪst/ *verb* 动词 (exists, existing, existed)
to be a real thing or situation 存在：*It is clear that a serious problem exists.* 显然存在一个严重问题。

existence /ɪɡˈzɪstəns/ *uncountable noun* 不可数名词
the fact that something is a real thing or situation 存在：*We can understand the existence of stars and planets.* 我们能理解恒星和行星的存在。□ *The club is still in existence.* 这家俱乐部仍然存在。

existing /ɪɡˈzɪstɪŋ/ *adjective* 形容词
in this world or available now 现存的；现有的：*There is a need to improve existing products.* 现有产品需要改进。

exit /ˈeksɪt/ *countable noun* 可数名词
the door that you use to leave a public building 出口：*He walked towards the exit.* 他朝出口走去。

exit 出口

exotic /ɪɡˈzɒtɪk/ *adjective* 形容词
unusual and interesting, usually because it comes from another country 奇异有趣的；异国风情的：*The house has a garden with exotic plants.* 房子有一个花园，里面栽种着奇花异草。

expand /ɪkˈspænd/ *verb* 动词 (**expands, expanding, expanded**)
to become larger 变大；扩大；增加：*The industry expanded in the 19th century.* 该产业在 19 世纪得到了发展。 □ *We want to expand children's knowledge of the world.* 我们想扩宽孩子对世界的认识。
▶ **expansion** /ɪkˈspænʃən/ *uncountable noun* 不可数名词：*Local people are against the expansion of the airport.* 当地人反对扩建机场。

expect /ɪkˈspekt/ *verb* 动词 (**expects, expecting, expected**)
to believe that something will happen 预期；预料；预计：*He expects to lose his job.* 他预料要丢工作。 □ *We expect the price of bananas to rise.* 我们预计香蕉价格会上涨。
be expecting to have a baby growing inside you 怀孕：*She announced that she was expecting another child.* 她宣布她又怀孕了。
be expecting something/someone to believe that something or someone will arrive soon 预计某事物／某人将至：*I wasn't expecting a visitor.* 我没想到会有人登门。
expect someone to do something to believe that it is someone's duty to do something 指望某人做某事：*I expect you to help around the house.* 我指望你帮忙做家务。
I expect used for showing that you think something is true or will probably happen 我猜想；我预计：*I expect you're hungry.* 我估计你饿了。 □ *I expect she'll be here soon.* 我猜她一会儿就到。

expectation /ˌekspekˈteɪʃən/ *countable noun* 可数名词
a belief someone has about how something should happen 期望；期待；预期：*Young people have high expectations for the future.* 年轻人对未来抱有很高的期望。

expel /ɪkˈspel/ *verb* 动词 (**expels, expelling, expelled**)
to officially tell someone to leave a school or an organization 开除；将…除名：*Two students were expelled for cheating.* 两名学生因作弊被开除。

expense /ɪkˈspens/ *noun* 名词
1 the cost or price of something 价格；价钱；成本：*He bought a big television at great expense.* 他花大价钱买了一台大电视。
2 [**expenses**] *plural* 复数 amounts of money that you spend on things 费用；花费：*Her hotel expenses were paid by the company.* 她的宾馆住宿费由公司支付。

expensive /ɪkˈspensɪv/ *adjective* 形容词
costing a lot of money 昂贵的：*People thought that healthy food was more expensive than fast food.* 人们觉得健康食品比快餐贵。

experience¹ /ɪkˈspɪəriəns/ *noun* 名词
1 *uncountable* 不可数 knowledge or skill in a job or activity that you have done for a long time 经验：*No teaching experience is necessary.* 教学经验不限。
▶ **experienced** /ɪkˈspɪəriənst/ *adjective* 形容词：*He is an experienced pilot.* 他是位经验丰富的飞行员。
2 *countable* 可数 something important that happens to you (重要的)经历：*What has been your most enjoyable experience?* 你最愉快的经历是什么？

experience² /ɪkˈspɪəriəns/ *verb* 动词 (**experiences, experiencing, experienced**)
to have something happen to you 经历；体验：*I have never experienced true love.* 我从未遇到过真爱。

experiment¹ /ɪkˈsperɪmənt/ *noun* 名词
1 a scientific test that you do in order to discover what happens to something (科学)实验：*Laboratory experiments show that vitamin D slows cancer growth.* 实验室实验显示，维生素 D 可延缓肿瘤生长。
2 when you test a new idea or method 试验；测试：*They started the magazine as an*

experiment. 他们办刊搞试验。

experiment[2] /ɪkˈsperɪmənt/ *verb* 动词 (**experiments, experimenting, experimented**)
1 to do a scientific test on something 做实验: *The scientists have experimented on mice.* 科学家在老鼠身上做了实验。
2 to test a new idea or method 尝试；测试: *I like cooking, and I have the time to experiment.* 我喜欢做饭，而且也有时间尝试新菜。

experimental /ɪkˌsperɪˈmentəl/ *adjective* 形容词
new, or using new ideas or methods 实验性的；试验性的: *an experimental musician* 实验音乐家

expert /ˈekspɜːt/ *countable noun* 可数名词
a person who knows a lot about a particular subject 专家；行家: *His brother is a computer expert.* 他弟弟是计算机专家。

expertise /ˌekspɜːˈtiːz/ *uncountable noun* 不可数名词
special skill or knowledge 专业知识；专业技能；专长: *We're looking for someone with expertise in foreign languages.* 我们在寻找具备外语专长的人。

expire /ɪkˈspaɪə/ *verb* 动词 (**expires, expiring, expired**)
to not be able to be used any more 到期；期满；失效: *My contract expires in July.* 我的合同 7 月到期。

explain /ɪkˈspleɪn/ *verb* 动词 (**explains, explaining, explained**)
1 to describe something to someone so that they can understand it 解释；说明: *He explained the law in simple language.* 他用简单的语言解释了这项法律。 □ *Professor Griffiths explained how the drug works.* 格里菲思教授说明了这种药物的作用原理。
2 to give reasons for something that happened 为…辩解；说明…的理由: *She left a note explaining her actions.* 她留了张字条解释自己的举动。 □ *Can you explain why you didn't telephone?* 能解释一下你为什么没打电话吗？

explanation /ˌekspləˈneɪʃən/ *countable noun* 可数名词
information that you give someone to help them to understand something 解释；说明: *There was no explanation for the car accident.* 没有关于车祸情况的说明。

explicit /ɪkˈsplɪsɪt/ *adjective* 形容词

expressed or shown clearly, without hiding anything 明确的；清晰的；毫不隐瞒的: *Many parents worry about explicit violence on television.* 许多家长对电视上赤裸裸的暴力场面感到担忧。

explode /ɪkˈspləʊd/ *verb* 动词 (**explodes, exploding, exploded**)
to burst with great force 爆炸；引爆: *A second bomb exploded in the capital yesterday.* 昨天第二枚炸弹在首都爆炸。

exploit /ɪkˈsplɔɪt/ *verb* 动词 (**exploits, exploiting, exploited**)
to treat someone unfairly by using their work or ideas 剥削；压榨: *They said that he exploited other musicians.* 他们说他压榨其他音乐人。

explore /ɪkˈsplɔː/ *verb* 动词 (**explores, exploring, explored**)
to travel around a place to find out what it is like 探索；考察；在…探险: *The best way to explore the area is in a boat.* 考察这一地区最好是乘船去。
▸ **exploration** /ˌekspləˈreɪʃən/ *noun* 名词: *He led the first English exploration of North America.* 他领导了英格兰人的首次北美考察。
▸ **explorer** /ɪkˈsplɔːrə/ *countable noun* 可数名词: *Who was the US explorer who discovered the Titanic shipwreck?* 发现"泰坦尼克"号残骸的那位美国探险家是谁？

explosion /ɪkˈspləʊʒən/ *countable noun* 可数名词
when something suddenly bursts with a loud sound 爆炸: *Six soldiers were injured in the explosion.* 爆炸中有 6 名士兵受伤。

explosive /ɪkˈspləʊsɪv/ *noun* 名词
a substance or an object that can cause an explosion 炸药；爆炸物: *The explosives were packaged in yellow bags.* 炸药装在黄色袋子里面。 ● **explosive** *adjective* 形容词: *No explosive device was found.* 未发现爆炸装置。

export[1] /ɪkˈspɔːt/ *verb* 动词 (**exports, exporting, exported**)
to sell products to another country 出口: *They also export cars.* 他们也出口汽车。 □ *The company now exports to Japan.* 公司产品现在出口至日本。 ● **export** /ˈekspɔːt/ *uncountable noun* 不可数名词: *A lot of our land is used for growing crops for export.* 我们许多土地用来种植出口作物。
▸ **exporter** /ˈekspɔːtə/ *countable noun* 可数

名词：*Brazil is a big exporter of coffee.* 巴西是咖啡出口大国。

export² /ˈekspɔːt/ *countable noun* 可数名词
a product that one country sells to another country 出口产品；输出品：*Last year our main export was cars.* 去年我们的主要出口产品是汽车。

expose /ɪkˈspəʊz/ *verb* 动词 (exposes, exposing, exposed)
to show something so that people can see it 使暴露；使显露：*Vitamin D is made when the skin is exposed to sunlight.* 皮肤受到阳光照射生成维生素 D。

express¹ /ɪkˈspres/ *verb* 动词 (expresses, expressing, expressed)
to show what you think or feel 表达；表示；表现：*Only one company expressed an interest in his plan.* 只有一家公司对他的计划表示有兴趣。

express² /ɪkˈspres/ *adjective* 形容词
used for describing a service that sends or receives things faster than usual 快递的；快速的；特快的：*An express postal service is available.* 邮政速递服务可用。

expression /ɪkˈspreʃən/ *noun* 名词
1 the way that your face looks at a particular moment 表情；神情：*There was an expression of sadness on his face.* 他神情忧伤。
2 *countable* 可数 a word or phrase 表达；措辞；说法：*Try to learn a few words and expressions in the language.* 努力学会这门语言的一些词汇和表达。

expressive /ɪkˈspresɪv/ *adjective* 形容词
clearly showing a person's feelings 清楚表现情感的；富于表现力的：*He has a very expressive face, so you always know what he's thinking.* 他的喜怒哀乐全都写在脸上，所以始终可以了解他在想什么。

extend /ɪkˈstend/ *verb* 动词 (extends, extending, extended)
to make something longer 延长；使变长：*These treatments have extended the lives of people with cancer.* 这些治疗手段延长了癌症患者的生命。

extension /ɪkˈstenʃən/ *countable noun* 可数名词
1 an extra period of time for which something lasts 展期；延长期：*He was given a six-month extension to his visa.* 他获得了 6 个月的签证延期。
2 a telephone that connects to the main telephone line in a building（电话）分机：*She can talk to me on extension 308.* 她可以打分机 308 找我谈。
3 an extra part that is added to a building to make it bigger（建筑物的）扩建部分：*Mr Patel has built an extension to his home.* 帕特尔先生扩建了住宅。

extensive /ɪkˈstensɪv/ *adjective* 形容词
covering a wide area 广大的；广阔的：*It is a four-bedroom house with extensive gardens.* 这是一座四居室的房子，还有很大的园子。

extent /ɪkˈstent/ *singular noun* 单数名词
the importance or seriousness of a situation 程度；地步：*The government has information on the extent of industrial pollution.* 政府了解工业污染的程度。 □ *He soon discovered the extent of the damage.* 他不久就弄清了毁损程度。

exterior¹ /ɪkˈstɪəriə/ *countable noun* 可数名词
the outside surface of something 外表面；外部；外观：*They are going to paint the exterior of the building.* 他们打算把大楼外部粉刷一下。

exterior² /ɪkˈstɪəriə/ *adjective* 形容词
used for talking about the outside parts of something 外部的；外面的：*exterior walls* 外墙

external /ɪkˈstɜːnəl/ *adjective* 形容词
on or relating to the outside of a place, person or area 外面的；外部的：*You lose a lot of heat through external walls.* 大量热量透过外墙流失。

extinct /ɪkˈstɪŋkt/ *adjective* 形容词
not existing any more 灭绝的；不复存在的：*Many animals could become extinct in less than 10 years.* 许多动物可能在 10 年内灭绝。

extinction /ɪkˈstɪŋkʃən/ *uncountable noun* 不可数名词
the death of all the living members of a species of animal or plant（物种的）灭绝：*We are trying to save these animals from extinction.* 我们努力拯救这些动物，使其免于灭绝。

extinguish /ɪkˈstɪŋgwɪʃ/ *verb* 动词 (extinguishes, extinguishing, extinguished)
to stop a fire from burning (*formal* 正式) 扑灭；熄灭：*It took about 50 minutes to extinguish the fire.* 灭火用了 50 分钟左右。

extra /ˈekstrə/ *adjective* 形容词
more than the normal amount 额外的；附

加的：*He used the extra time to check his work.* 他额外花时间检查自己的工作。
● **extra** *adverb* 副词：*You may be charged £10 extra for this service.* 这项服务可能要加收 10 英镑。

extract /ɪkˈstrækt/ *verb* 动词 (**extracts, extracting, extracted**)
to take or pull something out 取出；拔出：*A dentist may decide to extract the tooth.* 牙医可能会决定拔掉这颗牙。

extraordinary /ɪkˈstrɔːdənri/ *adjective* 形容词
1 extremely good or special 非凡的；卓越的；非同寻常的：*He's an extraordinary musician.* 他是一位杰出的音乐家。
2 very unusual or surprising 异乎寻常的；大出所料的：*An extraordinary thing just happened.* 刚刚发生了一件特别蹊跷的事儿。

extravagant /ɪkˈstrævəgənt/ *adjective* 形容词
1 spending too much money 奢侈的；铺张的；奢靡的：*He was extravagant in all things — his clothing and his partying.* 他凡事都大事铺张——着装如此，搞派对也是如此。
2 costing too much money 昂贵的；花费不菲的：*He came home with extravagant gifts for everyone.* 他回家给每个人都带了价值不菲的礼物。

extreme /ɪkˈstriːm/ *adjective* 形容词
very great in degree 极端的；极度的：*You should use any drug with extreme care.* 用任何药物都务必格外谨慎。
▶ **extremely** /ɪkˈstriːmli/ *adverb* 副词：*My mobile phone is extremely useful.* 我的手机特别有用。

eye /aɪ/ *countable noun* 可数名词
one of the two parts of your body with which you see 眼；眼睛：*I opened my eyes and looked.* 我睁开眼睛看。 □ *Mrs Brooke was a tall lady with dark brown eyes.* 布鲁克太太个子高高的，双眼深褐色。
→ Look at picture on P4 参见彩插第 4 页

catch someone's eye
1 to attract someone's attention 吸引某人的注意力：*A movement across the garden caught her eye.* 有个东西穿过园子，吸引了她的注意力。
2 to make someone notice you, so that you can speak to them（为攀谈）引起某人的注意：*He tried to catch Annie's eye.* 他想引起安妮的注意。

have your eye on something to want to have something (*informal* 非正式）看上某物：*I've had my eye on that dress for a while now.* 我刚才就看上那条连衣裙了。

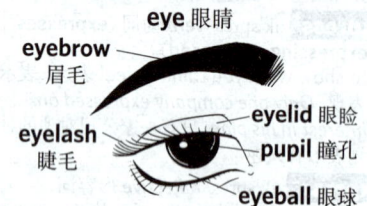

eye 眼睛
eyebrow 眉毛
eyelash 睫毛
eyelid 眼睑
pupil 瞳孔
eyeball 眼球

eyeball /ˈaɪbɔːl/ *countable noun* 可数名词
one of the two parts of your eyes that are like white balls 眼球；眼珠

eyebrow /ˈaɪbraʊ/ *countable noun* 可数名词
one of the two lines of hair that grow above your eyes 眉；眉毛
→ Look at picture on P4 参见彩插第 4 页

eyeglasses /ˈaɪglɑːsɪz/ *plural noun* 复数名词（*American* 美国英语）
→ see 见 **glasses**

eyelash /ˈaɪlæʃ/ *countable noun* 可数名词 (**eyelashes**)
one of the hairs that grow on the edges of your eyelids 睫毛
→ Look at picture on P4 参见彩插第 4 页

eyelid /ˈaɪlɪd/ *countable noun* 可数名词
one of the pieces of skin that cover your eyes when they are closed 眼睑

eyesight /ˈaɪsaɪt/ *uncountable noun* 不可数名词
your ability to see 视力：*He cannot get a driving licence because he has poor eyesight.* 他无法取得驾照，因为他视力不好。

fable /ˈfeɪbəl/ *noun* 名词
a type of story, usually about animals, that teaches people a lesson 寓言: *Here is a children's fable about love and honesty.* 这是一则关于爱与诚实的儿童寓言。

fabric /ˈfæbrɪk/ *noun* 名词
cloth that you use for making things like clothes and bags 织物；布料: *The shirt is made from beautiful soft fabric.* 这件衬衫由漂亮柔软的布料制成。

fabulous /ˈfæbjʊləs/ *adjective* 形容词
very good (*informal* 非正式) 极好的；绝妙的: *The flat offers fabulous views of the city.* 这间公寓视野极好，城市美景尽收眼底。

face¹ /feɪs/ *countable noun* 可数名词
1 the front part of your head 脸；面部: *She had a beautiful face.* 她容貌秀丽。
2 the front or a vertical side of something 正面；坡面: *the south face of Mount Qomolangma* 珠穆朗玛峰南坡面 □ *a clock face* 钟面

face to face looking at someone directly 面对面；当面: *I got off the bus and came face to face with my teacher.* 我下了公交车，迎面碰上了我的老师。

to make a face or **to pull a face** to change your face into an ugly expression 扮鬼脸；做怪相: *She made a face at the horrible smell.* 闻到恶臭味，她表情都扭曲了。

face² /feɪs/ *verb* 动词 (**faces, facing, faced**)
1 to look in a particular direction 面向；面对: *They stood facing each other.* 他们面面站着。 □ *Our house faces south.* 我们的房子朝南。
2 to have to deal with something unpleasant 面临，面对（不好的事）: *Williams faces life in prison.* 威廉斯面临终身监禁。 □ *I can't face telling my girlfriend.* 我真不想和女朋友说这事儿。

facilities /fəˈsɪlɪtiz/ *plural noun* 复数名词
something such as rooms, buildings or pieces of equipment that are used for a particular purpose 设施；设备: *The hotel has excellent sports facilities, including a golf course.* 这家酒店有着一流的体育设施，其中就有一个高尔夫球场。

fact /fækt/ *countable noun* 可数名词
something that you know is true 事实；真相: *He doesn't hide the fact that he wants to win.* 他没有隐瞒他想赢这一事实。

in fact used when you are giving more information about something that you have just said 实际上，确切地说（用于补充说明前面所说的话）: *I don't watch television; in fact, I no longer own a TV.* 我不看电视；实际上，我现在没有电视了。

factor /ˈfæktə/ *countable noun* 可数名词
something that helps to produce a result 因素；要素: *Exercise is an important factor in a healthy lifestyle.* 在健康的生活方式中，锻炼身体是一个重要因素。

factory /ˈfæktri/ *countable noun* 可数名词 (**factories**)
a large building where people use machines to make goods 工厂

fade /feɪd/ *verb* 动词 (**fades, fading, faded**)
to become lighter in colour（使）褪色: *The colour suddenly faded from her cheeks.* 她突然面色苍白。 □ *Sunlight has faded the carpets and curtains.* 阳光的照射让地毯和窗帘褪了色。

▶ **faded** /ˈfeɪdɪd/ *adjective* 形容词: *Michael was wearing faded jeans and a green cotton shirt.* 迈克尔穿着褪了色的牛仔裤和绿色的棉质衬衫。

Fahrenheit /ˈfærənˌhaɪt/ *adjective* 形容词
used for describing a way of measuring how hot something is. It is shown by the symbol °F. Water freezes at 32°F (0°C) and boils at 212°F (100°C). 华氏的；华氏温标的: *The temperature was above 100°F.* 气温在 100 华氏度以上。

fail /feɪl/ *verb* 动词 (**fails, failing, failed**)
1 not to pass an exam or a test 不及格；未通过: *75 per cent of secondary school students failed the exam.* *75% 的中学生这次考试不及格。

2 not to succeed when you try to do something 失败；未能做成：*The Republicans failed to get the 60 votes they needed.* 共和党未能得到他们所需要的 60 票。
without fail always 总是；一直：*Andrew attended every board meeting without fail.* 安德鲁每次董事会都参加，从不缺席。

failure /ˈfeɪljə/ *noun* 名词
1 *uncountable* 不可数 when you do not succeed in doing something 失败：*Brian was depressed after the failure of his business.* 布赖恩生意失败后很沮丧。□ *The project ended in failure.* 这个项目以失败告终。
2 *countable* 可数 something which is not a success 失败的事物：*His first novel was a failure.* 他的第一部小说是个失败的作品。

faint¹ /feɪnt/ *adjective* 形容词 (**fainter, faintest**)
1 not strong or clear 微弱的；不清晰的：*I could hear the faint sound of traffic in the distance.* 我可以听到远处隐约传来车辆声。□ *There was still the faint hope that Kimberly might return.* 金伯利还有一线希望会回来。
▶ **faintly** /ˈfeɪntli/ *adverb* 副词：*The room smelled faintly of paint.* 这屋子有隐隐的油漆味。
2 feeling that you are going to fall, usually because you are ill or very tired（通常因生病或疲惫而）虚弱的，快要晕倒的：*Ryan was unsteady on his feet and felt faint.* 瑞安站不稳，感觉自己要晕倒了。

faint² /feɪnt/ *verb* 动词 (**faints, fainting, fainted**)
to become unconscious for a short time 昏厥；晕厥：*She suddenly fell forward and fainted.* 她突然向前栽倒，昏了过去。

fair¹ /feə/ *adjective* 形容词 (**fairer, fairest**)
1 treating everyone in the same way 公正的；公平的：*It's not fair; she's got more than me!* 这不公平；她得到的比我多！□ *I wanted everyone to get fair treatment.* 我想让每个人都得到公正的待遇。
▶ **fairly** /ˈfeəli/ *adverb* 副词：*We solved the problem quickly and fairly.* 我们快速公正地解决了这一问题。
▶ **fairness** /ˈfeənəs/ *uncountable noun* 不可数名词：*There were concerns about the fairness of the election campaign.* 有人担忧这次选举活动是否公正。
2 having light-coloured hair or skin（头发）浅色的；（皮肤）白皙的：*My mother is very fair.* 我妈妈皮肤白皙。□ *Eric had thick fair hair.* 埃里克有着一头浓密的浅色头发。
3 not bad, but not very good 一般的；尚可的：*'What did you think of the film?'* — *'Hmm. Fair.'* "你觉得这部电影怎么样？" —— "嗯，一般般。"

fair² /feə/ *countable noun* 可数名词
1 a place where you can play games to win prizes, and you can ride on special, big machines for fun 游乐场
2 an event where people show, buy and sell goods, or share information 商品交易会；展销会：*US Airways is organizing a job fair to hire new workers.* 全美航空公司正在组织一场招聘会来招募新员工。

fairly /ˈfeəli/ *adverb* 副词
quite 相当；比较：*The team have been playing fairly well lately.* 这支队伍最近打得还可以。□ *She's fairly good at maths and science.* 她的数学和科学学得还不错。

fairy /ˈfeəri/ *countable noun* 可数名词 (**fairies**)
a very small person with wings, who can do magic. Fairies appear in children's stories, and they are not real. 仙女；小精灵

ˈfairy ˌtale *countable noun* 可数名词
a story for children about magic and fairies 童话

faith /feɪθ/ *noun* 名词
1 *uncountable* 不可数 the belief that someone or something is good or honest, or that a thing works 信赖；相信：*I have faith in the honesty of my employees.* 我相信我的员工是诚实的。
2 *countable* 可数 a particular religion 宗教：*The children will learn about a variety of faiths such as Islam and Judaism.* 孩子们将了解到各种各样的宗教，如伊斯兰教和犹太教。

faithful /ˈfeɪθfʊl/ *adjective* 形容词
always supporting your family and friends 忠实的；忠诚的：*Help your brothers and sisters, and be faithful to your friends.* 帮助你的兄弟姐妹，忠于你的朋友。

faithfully /ˈfeɪθfʊli/ *adverb* 副词
Yours faithfully words you write at the end of a formal letter, before your name, when you start the letter with the words 'Dear Sir' or 'Dear Madam' 忠实于您的（用于正式信件结尾处写信人的名字前，信件开头的称呼语为 Dear Sir 或 Dear Madam）

fake¹ /feɪk/ **adjective** 形容词
used for describing a copy of something, especially something that is valuable 假的；伪造的：*The men used fake passports to get into the country.* 这些人用假护照进入了这个国家。

fake² /feɪk/ **countable noun** 可数名词
something that is a copy of something, especially something valuable 假货；赝品：*Art experts think that the painting is a fake.* 艺术品专家认为这幅画是赝品。

fall¹ /fɔːl/ **verb** 动词 (**falls, falling, fell, fallen**)
1 to move quickly towards the ground by accident 坠落；跌倒；落下：*Tyler fell from his horse and broke his arm.* 泰勒坠马摔断了胳膊。 ▫ *Jacob lost his balance and fell backwards.* 雅各布失去了平衡，向后摔倒了。 ▫ *There was a huge crash as a large painting fell off the wall.* 一大幅画从墙上掉下来，发出一声巨响。
2 when rain or snow falls, it comes down from the sky（雨、雪）降落，落下：*More than 30 inches of rain fell in 6 days.* *6 天里降水量超过了 30 英寸。
3 to become less or lower 减少；降低：*Unemployment fell to 4.6 per cent in May.* 5 月份的失业率降到了 4.6%。 ▫ *Here, temperatures at night can fall below freezing.* 这里的夜间气温会降到零度以下。
fall apart to break into pieces 破碎；破裂：*Gradually, the old building fell apart.* 渐渐地，这栋老房子塌了。
fall asleep to start to sleep 睡着：*He fell asleep in front of the fire.* 他在炉火前睡着了。
fall behind to fail to make progress or move forward as fast as other people 落后；跟不上：*Some of the students fell behind in their work.* 有些学生的课业跟不上了。
fall down to fall to the ground 摔倒：*The wind hit Chris so hard, he fell down.* 风太大，把克里斯吹倒了。
fall ill to become ill 生病：*Emily suddenly fell ill and was rushed to hospital.* 埃米莉突然生病，被火速送往医院。
fall off something to come away from the thing it was fixed to 从某物上掉下（或脱落）：*An engine fell off the wing of the aeroplane.* 一个引擎从机翼上掉了下来。
fall out
1 to come out（头发、牙齿等）掉落，脱落：*His first tooth fell out when he was six.* 他 6 岁时掉了第 1 颗牙。 ▫ *My hair is starting to fall out.* 我开始脱发了。
2 to have an argument with someone and stop being friendly with them（与某人）吵架，闹翻：*Ashley has fallen out with her boyfriend.* 阿什莉和男朋友闹翻了。

fall² /fɔːl/ **noun** 名词
1 countable 可数 when you fall to the ground 摔倒：*Grandpa broke his right leg in a bad fall.* 爷爷有一次摔得很重，摔断了右腿。
2 countable 可数 when something becomes less or lower 减少；下降：*There has been a sharp fall in the value of the dollar.* 美元大幅贬值。
3 (*American* 美国英语) → see 见 **autumn**

fallen /ˈfɔːlən/
→ see 见 **fall**

false /fɔːls/ **adjective** 形容词
1 wrong or not true 错误的；不正确的：*The president received false information from his advisers.* 总统从顾问那里得到了错误信息。
▶ **falsely** /ˈfɔːlsli/ **adverb** 副词：*She was falsely accused of stealing.* 她被诬告偷窃。
2 not real or not natural 假的；非自然的：*My grandma has false teeth.* 我奶奶戴假牙。

fame /feɪm/ **uncountable noun** 不可数名词
when you are very well known by a lot of people 名声；名望：*Connery gained fame as Agent 007 in the Bond films.* 康纳利因在詹姆斯·邦德系列电影中扮演特工 007 而成名。

familiar /fəˈmɪliə/ **adjective** 形容词
used for describing someone or something that you have seen or heard before 熟悉的；熟知的：*That boy's face looks familiar.* 那个男孩的模样看上去很眼熟。 ▫ *Her name sounds familiar to me.* 她的名字我听着很熟悉。

family /ˈfæmɪli/ **countable noun** 可数名词 (**families**)
a group of people who are related to each other, usually parents and their children 家庭；家人：*William and his family live in Hawaii.* 威廉和他的家人住在夏威夷。 ▫ *A ticket for a family of four costs £68.* 四口之家的票价是 68 英镑。

famine /ˈfæmɪn/ **noun** 名词
a time when there is not enough food for people to eat, and many people die 饥荒：*Their country is suffering from*

famine and war. 他们的国家正遭受饥荒和战争。

famous /ˈfeɪməs/ *adjective* 形容词
very well known 有名的；著名的：*Edvard Munch's painting 'The Scream' is one of the world's most famous paintings.* 爱德华·蒙克的作品《呐喊》是世界上最有名的画作之一。

fan[1] /fæn/ *countable noun* 可数名词
1 someone who likes someone or something very very much 粉丝；迷：*If you're a Johnny Depp fan, you'll love this film.* 如果你是约翰尼·德普的粉丝，你会喜欢这部电影的。
2 a piece of equipment that moves the air around a room to make you cooler 风扇
3 a flat object that you move backwards and forwards in front of your face to make you cooler 扇子

fan[2] /fæn/ *verb* 动词 (**fans, fanning, fanned**)
to move a fan or another flat object around in front of yourself, to make yourself feel cooler 给…扇风：*Jessica fanned herself with a newspaper.* 杰茜卡用报纸给自己扇风。

fanatic /fəˈnætɪk/ *countable noun* 可数名词
someone whose behaviour or opinions are very extreme 狂热分子：*I am not a religious fanatic but I am a Christian.* 我不是宗教狂热分子，但我是基督徒。

fancy[1] /ˈfænsi/ *adjective* 形容词 (**fancier, fanciest**)
not simple or ordinary 花哨的；精致的：*fancy jewellery* 精致的珠宝

fancy[2] /ˈfænsi/ *verb* 动词 (**fancies, fancying, fancied**)
to want to have something or do something (*informal* 非正式) 想要；想做：*I fancied a piece of chocolate cake.* 我想要一块巧克力蛋糕。 □ *Do you fancy going to the cinema tonight?* 你今晚想去看电影吗？

fantastic /fænˈtæstɪk/ *adjective* 形容词
very good (*informal* 非正式) 极好的：*Sarah has a fantastic social life — she's always out.* 萨拉的社交生活很精彩——她总不在家待着。

fantasy /ˈfæntəsi/ *countable noun* 可数名词 (**fantasies**)
an imaginary story or thought that is very different from real life 幻想；想象：*Everyone has had a fantasy about winning the lottery.* 每个人都幻想过中彩票。 □ *a*

fantasy novel 一部幻想小说

FAQ /ˌef eɪ ˈkjuː/ *countable noun* 可数名词 (**FAQs**)
often written on websites, and is short for (缩写 =) 'frequently asked questions' 常见问题 (常用于网站)

far /fɑː/ *adverb* 副词 (**farther** or 或 **further, farthest** or 或 **furthest**)
1 a long way from somewhere 远；遥远地：*We've gone too far to go back now.* 我们走得太远了，现在已经回不去了。 □ *My sister moved even farther away from home.* 我姐姐搬得离家更远了。
2 used in questions and statements about distances (用于与距离相关的疑问句和陈述句中) 远：*How far is it to San Francisco?* 到旧金山有多远？

> **LANGUAGE HELP** 语言提示
> Use **far** in questions about distance, and after 'too'. You can also say that a place is **a long way away**, or that it is **a long way from** another place. *far 用于有关距离的疑问句中，也可用于 too 后。可以用* **a long way away** *表示某地很远，* **a long way from** *表示离某地很远：Anna was still a long way away.* 安娜离得还很远。 □ *Dubai is a long way from London.* 迪拜距离伦敦很远。

3 used for saying 'very much' when you are comparing things (用于在比较时强调程度) 远，非常：*Your essay is far better than mine.* 你的文章比我的好得多。
by far used for saying that someone or something is the biggest, the best or the most important (用于强调最高程度) 显然：*Unemployment is by far the most important issue.* 失业无疑是最重要的问题。
far from not at all 根本不：*What they said was far from the truth.* 他们说的根本不是事实。
so far up until now 到目前为止；迄今为止：*So far, they have failed.* 到目前为止，他们已经失败了。

fare /feə/ *countable noun* 可数名词
the money that you pay for a trip in a bus, a train, an aeroplane or a taxi (交通工具的) 票价；车费；飞机票价：*The fare is £11 one way.* 单程票价为 11 英镑。

farewell /ˌfeəˈwel/ *countable noun* 可数名词
goodbye 告别；再见：*We said our farewells and got in the car.* 我们说了再见，然后上了

车。□ He said farewell to us at the station. 他在车站与我们告了别。● **farewell** *adjective* 形容词: Before she left, she organized a farewell party for family and friends. 在离开之前，她为家人和朋友开了一场告别派对。

farm /fɑːm/ *countable noun* 可数名词
an area of land and buildings where people grow crops and keep animals 农场；养殖场: Both boys like to work on the farm. 两个男孩都喜欢在农场工作。

farmer /ˈfɑːmə/ *countable noun* 可数名词
a person who owns or works on a farm 农场主；农民
→ Look at picture on P16 参见彩插第 16 页

farmhouse /ˈfɑːmhaʊs/ *countable noun* 可数名词
the house on a farm where the farmer lives 农舍；农场住宅

farming /ˈfɑːmɪŋ/ *uncountable noun* 不可数名词
the job of growing crops or keeping animals on a farm 耕作；养殖

farther /ˈfɑːðə/
→ see 见 **far**

farthest /ˈfɑːðɪst/
→ see 见 **far**

fascinate /ˈfæsɪneɪt/ *verb* 动词 (**fascinates, fascinating, fascinated**)
to interest someone very much 使着迷: American history fascinates me. 美国历史令我着迷。

fascinated /ˈfæsɪneɪtɪd/ *adjective* 形容词
thinking that something is very interesting 很感兴趣的；入迷的: My brother is fascinated by racing cars. 我兄弟对赛车很感兴趣。

fascinating /ˈfæsɪneɪtɪŋ/ *adjective* 形容词
very interesting 非常有趣的；迷人的: Madagascar is a fascinating place. 马达加斯加是个迷人的地方。

fashion /ˈfæʃn/ *noun* 名词
1 *uncountable* 不可数 the activity or business that involves styles of clothing and appearance 时装领域；时尚业: The magazine contains 20 full-colour pages of fashion. 这本杂志中有 20 面关于时装的彩色插页。
2 *countable* 可数 a style of clothing that is popular at a particular time（服装等）流行款式: Long dresses were the fashion when I was a child. 我小时候流行长裙。
in/out of fashion popular or not popular at a particular time 流行／过时: Short skirts were in fashion back then. 那时流行短裙。

fashionable /ˈfæʃənəbəl/ *adjective* 形容词
1 popular at a particular time 时兴的；流行的: Long dresses will be very fashionable this year. 今年长裙会非常流行。
2 wearing fashionable clothes 时髦的；时尚的
▶ **fashionably** /ˈfæʃənəbli/ *adverb* 副词: Katie is always fashionably dressed. 凯蒂总是穿得很时髦。

fast[1] /fɑːst/ *adjective* 形容词, *adverb* 副词 (**faster, fastest**)
1 quick 快的；迅速的: Jane has always loved fast cars. 简一向喜欢高速轿车。□ I'm a fast reader. 我阅读速度快。□ The underground is the fastest way to get around London. 乘地铁是游转伦敦最快的方式。
2 showing a time that is later than the real time 走得快的；偏快的: That clock is an hour fast. 那个表快了一个小时。
3 quickly 快地；迅速地: James drives too fast. 詹姆斯开得太快了。□ Can't you run any faster? 你不能跑得再快一点儿吗？
4 without any delay 立即；马上: You need to see a doctor — fast! 你需要去看医生 — 马上！
fast asleep deeply asleep 睡熟的: Anna climbed into bed and five minutes later she was fast asleep. 安娜爬上床，5 分钟之后就睡熟了。

fast[2] /fɑːst/ *verb* 动词 (**fasts, fasting, fasted**)
to not eat any food for a period of time 斋戒；禁食 ● **fast** *countable noun* 可数名词: The fast ends at sunset. 日落时分斋戒结束。

fasten /ˈfɑːsən/ *verb* 动词 (**fastens, fastening, fastened**)
1 to join the two sides of something together so that it is closed 扣上；系上: Heather got quickly into her car and fastened the seat-belt. 希瑟快速上了车，系上安全带。
2 to attach one thing to another 固定: There was a notice fastened to the gate. 大门上贴着一则通告。

fasten 系上

fast food uncountable noun 不可数名词
hot food that is served quickly in a restaurant 快餐：*He likes fast food like hamburgers, pizzas and hot dogs.* 他喜欢吃汉堡、比萨、热狗这样的快餐。

fat¹ /fæt/ adjective 形容词 (**fatter, fattest**)
1 weighing too much 肥胖的：*I ate too much and I began to get fat.* 我吃得太多，开始长胖了。
2 very thick or wide 非常厚的；非常宽的：*Emily picked up a fat book and handed it to me.* 埃米莉拿起一本非常厚的书递给了我。

fat² /fæt/ uncountable noun 不可数名词
1 a substance containing oil that is found in some foods（食物中的）脂肪：*Cream contains a lot of fat.* 奶油中含有大量脂肪。
2 the soft substance that people and animals have under their skin（动物或人的）脂肪，肥肉

fatal /ˈfeɪtəl/ adjective 形容词
1 having very bad results 后果严重的；毁灭性的：*Justin made the fatal mistake of lending her some money.* 贾斯廷犯了个极严重的错误，就是借了一些钱给她。
2 causing someone's death 致命的：*The TV star was attacked in a fatal stabbing.* 那位电视明星被捅了致命的一刀。
▶ **fatally** /ˈfeɪtəli/ adverb 副词：*The soldier was fatally wounded in the chest.* 这位士兵的胸部受了致命伤。

fatality /fəˈtælɪti/ countable noun 可数名词 (**fatalities**)
a death that is caused by an accident or by violence (formal 正式)（事故或暴力导致的）死亡：*Yesterday's fatality is the 36th this year.* 昨天的死亡事件是今年的第 36 起。

fate /feɪt/ noun 名词
1 uncountable 不可数 a power that some people believe controls everything that happens in the world 命运；天意：*I think it was fate that Andy and I met.* 我觉得安迪和我相遇是天意。
2 countable 可数 what happens to someone or something 遭际；境遇：*Frank was never seen again, and we never knew his fate.* 大家再也没有见过弗兰克，我们不知道他遭遇了什么。

father /ˈfɑːðə/ countable noun 可数名词
your male parent 父亲：*His father was an artist.* 他父亲是个艺术家。

ˈfather-in-ˌlaw countable noun 可数名词 (**fathers-in-law**)
the father of your husband or wife 公公；岳父

fatigue /fəˈtiːɡ/ uncountable noun 不可数名词
a feeling of being extremely tired 疲惫；疲劳：*He was taken to hospital suffering from extreme fatigue.* 他疲劳过度，被送进医院。

faucet /ˈfɔːsɪt/ countable noun 可数名词
(American 美国英语)
→ see 见 **tap**

fault /fɔːlt/ noun 名词
1 singular 单数 if something bad is your fault, you made it happen 过失；过错：*The accident was my fault.* 这场事故是我的过错。
2 countable 可数 a weakness in someone or something 弱点；缺点：*Gavin's worst fault is his temper.* 加文最大的缺点就是脾气不好。

faulty /ˈfɔːlti/ adjective 形容词
not working well 出故障的；有问题的：*The car had worn tyres and faulty brakes.* 这辆车的轮胎已磨损，刹车也出了故障。

favour /ˈfeɪvə/ countable noun 可数名词
something that you do to help someone 帮助：*Please would you do me a favour and give David a message for me?* 能请你帮个忙，替我给戴维带个信儿吗？
in favour thinking that something is a good thing 赞许的；支持的：*I'm in favour of income tax cuts.* 我赞同削减所得税。

favourable /ˈfeɪvərəbl/ adjective 形容词
right or good 肯定的；有利的：*The president's speech received favourable reviews.* 总统的演讲获得了肯定的评价。 □ *We hope that the weather will be favourable.* 我希望明天有个好天气。

favourite /ˈfeɪvərɪt/ adjective 形容词
used for describing the thing or person that you like more than all the others 最喜爱的：*What is your favourite film?* 你最

喜欢哪部电影？● **favourite** *countable noun* 可数名词：*Of all the seasons, autumn is my favourite.* 所有的季节中，我最喜欢秋天。

fax /fæks/ *countable noun* 可数名词 (**faxes**)
1 (also 亦作 **fax machine**) a special machine that is joined to a telephone line. You use a fax to send and receive documents. 传真机
2 a copy of a document that you send or receive using a fax machine 传真件：*I sent Daniel a long fax this morning.* 今早我给丹尼尔发了一份长长的传真。● **fax** *verb* 动词 (**faxes, faxing, faxed**)：*I faxed a copy of the letter to my boss.* 我用传真把信件发给我的老板。

fear /fɪə/ *noun* 名词
1 the unpleasant feeling you have when you think that you are in danger 恐惧；惧怕：*My whole body was shaking with fear.* 我因恐惧而浑身发抖。
2 a thought that something unpleasant might happen 担心；害怕：*Many young people have a fear of failure.* 很多年轻人害怕失败。● **fear** *verb* 动词 (**fears, fearing, feared**)：*Many people fear flying.* 许多人害怕坐飞机。

fearful /ˈfɪəfʊl/ *adjective* 形容词
afraid of something (*formal* 正式) 担心的；害怕的：*They were all fearful of losing their jobs.* 他们都担心失业。

fearless /ˈfɪələs/ *adjective* 形容词
not afraid of anything 无所畏惧的：*He was a brave and fearless man — a true hero.* 他是一个勇敢的、无所畏惧的男人——一个真正的英雄。

feast /fiːst/ *countable noun* 可数名词
a large and special meal for a lot of people 宴会；盛宴：*On Friday night, they had a wedding feast for 1,000 guests.* 周五晚上他们有一场婚宴，要宴请 1,000 名宾客。

feat /fiːt/ *countable noun* 可数名词
a very brave or difficult act 壮举；功绩：*The men performed feats of physical bravery.* 这些人展现出了异常强悍的体格。

feather /ˈfeðə/ *countable noun* 可数名词
one of the light soft things that cover a bird's body 羽毛：*peacock feathers* 孔雀羽毛

feather 羽毛

feature /ˈfiːtʃə/ *countable noun* 可数名词
1 an important part of something 特征；特色；特点：*The house has many attractive features, including a swimming pool.* 这房子有许多吸引人的特色，比如它有一个游泳池。
2 a special story in a newspaper or magazine (报刊的) 特写，专题：*There was a feature on Tom Cruise in The New York Times.*《纽约时报》上有关于汤姆·克鲁斯的专题。
3 your eyes, your nose, your mouth or any other part of your face 面貌的一部分：*Emily's best feature is her dark eyes.* 埃米莉五官中最好看的是她黑色的眼睛。

February /ˈfebjuəri/ *noun* 名词
the second month of the year 二月：*The band's U.S. tour starts on February 7.* 这支乐队 2 月 7 号开始美国巡演。

fed /fed/
→ see 见 **feed**

fed up *adjective* 形容词
unhappy or bored (*informal* 非正式) 不满的；厌烦的：*My brother soon became fed up with city life.* 我兄弟很快便厌倦了城市生活。

fee /fiː/ *countable noun* 可数名词
1 the money that you pay to be allowed to do something 费；费用：*We paid the small entrance fee and drove inside.* 我们付了少许入场费之后驱车进入。
2 the money that you pay a person or an organization for advice or for a service 咨询费；服务费：*We had to pay the lawyer's fees ourselves.* 我们需要自付律师费。

feeble /ˈfiːbəl/ *adjective* 形容词 (**feebler, feeblest**)
weak 虚弱的：*My uncle was old and feeble, and was not able to walk far.* 我叔叔年迈虚弱，走不了太远。
▶ **feebly** /ˈfiːbli/ *adverb* 副词：*Her left hand moved feebly at her side.* 她的左手在身侧无力地动着。

feed /fiːd/ *verb* 动词 (**feeds, feeding, fed**)
to give food to a person or an animal 喂；饲养：*It's time to feed the baby.* 该喂宝宝了。□ *It's usually best to feed a small dog twice a day.* 通常，小狗最好一天喂两次。

feedback /ˈfiːdbæk/ *uncountable noun* 不可数名词
a situation when someone tells you how well or badly you are doing 反馈：*Ask your*

teacher for feedback on your work. 向老师询问有关你功课的反馈。

feel /fi:l/ *verb* 动词 (**feels, feeling, felt**)
1 to experience a particular emotion or physical feeling 感觉；感到：*I am feeling really happy today.* 我今天真的很开心。□ *I felt a sharp pain in my shoulder.* 我感到肩膀一阵剧痛。□ *How do you feel?* 你感觉怎么样？□ *She felt guilty about spending so much money on clothes.* 花这么多钱买衣服，她感到愧疚。
2 used for describing the way that something seems when you touch it or experience it 摸起来；有…感觉：*The blanket feels soft.* 这条毯子摸起来很柔软。□ *The sun felt hot on my back.* 太阳火辣辣地照在我的背上。□ *The room felt rather cold.* 这个房间相当冷。
3 to touch something with your hand, so that you can find out what it is like 摸；触摸：*The doctor felt my pulse.* 医生诊了诊我的脉。□ *Feel how soft this leather is.* 摸一下这皮革有多柔软。
4 to be aware of something because you touch it or it touches you（身体）感觉到，觉察出：*Anna felt something touching her face.* 安娜感觉有东西碰着自己的脸。
5 to have an opinion about something 以为；认为：*We feel that this decision is fair.* 我们认为这个决定很公平。

feel for someone to have sympathy for someone 同情某人；可怜某人：*Nicole was crying, and I really felt for her.* 妮科尔在哭，我真的很同情她。

feel like doing something to want to do something 想要做某事：*'I just don't feel like going out tonight,' Rose said quietly.* "我今晚不想出去。"罗丝平静地说。

feeling /'fi:lɪŋ/ *noun* 名词
1 [countable] 可数 something that you feel in your mind or your body 感觉；感触：*I had feelings of sadness and loneliness.* 我感到又难过又孤独。
→ Look at picture on P15 参见彩插第 15 页
2 [countable] 可数 when you think that something is probably going to happen 预感：*I have a feeling that everything will be all right.* 我预感一切都会好起来。
3 [feelings] *plural* 复数 what you think and feel about something 看法；感受：*They have strong feelings about politics.* 他们对政治有着强烈的看法。
4 [uncountable] 不可数 the ability to feel

things in part of your body（身体的）感觉：*After the accident, Jason had no feeling in his legs.* 事故之后，贾森的双腿失去了知觉。

hurt someone's feelings to say or do something that makes someone upset 伤害某人的感情：*I'm really sorry if I hurt your feelings.* 如果伤害了你的感情，我很抱歉。

feet /fi:t/
the plural of **foot**（**foot** 的复数形式）

fell /fel/
→ see 见 **fall**

fellow /'feləʊ/ *adjective* 形容词
used for describing people who are like you or from the same place as you（人）有共同点的，来自同一个地方的：*Richard was just 18 when he married fellow student Barbara.* 理查德 18 岁时就和同学芭芭拉结了婚。

felt¹ /felt/
→ see 见 **feel**

felt² /felt/ *uncountable noun* 不可数名词
a type of soft thick cloth 毛毡：*Amy was wearing an old felt hat.* 埃米戴了一顶旧毛毡帽。

felt-'tip *countable noun* 可数名词
(also 亦作 **felt-tip pen**) a pen with a soft point 毡头笔：*a pack of felt-tip pens* 一盒毡头笔
→ Look at picture on P1 参见彩插第 1 页

female /'fi:meɪl/ *countable noun* 可数名词
1 any animal, including humans, that can give birth to babies or lay eggs 女性；雌性动物：*Each female will lay just one egg.* 每个雌体只产一枚卵。● **female** *adjective* 形容词：*female gorillas* 雌猩猩
2 a woman or a girl 女人；女孩：*This disease affects males more than females.* 这种疾病对于男性的影响大于女性。
● **female** *adjective* 形容词：*Who is your favourite female singer?* 你最喜欢的女歌手是谁？

feminine /'femɪnɪn/ *adjective* 形容词
1 considered to be typical of women 女性特有的；有女人味儿的：*I love feminine clothes, so I wear skirts a lot.* 我喜欢有女人味儿的衣服，所以我常穿裙子。□ *His voice was strangely feminine.* 他的声音有点儿像女人，怪怪的。
2 used for describing a noun, pronoun or adjective that has a different form from other forms (such as 'masculine' forms)

in some languages. Compare with **masculine**.（名词、代词或形容词）阴性的（比较 masculine）

feminism /ˈfemɪˌnɪzəm/ **uncountable noun** 不可数名词
the belief that women should have the same rights and opportunities as men 女权主义

feminist /ˈfemɪnɪst/ **countable noun** 可数名词
a person who believes in feminism 女权主义者: *Feminists argue that women should not have to choose between children and a career.* 女主义者认为女性不应该被迫在孩子和职业之间作选择。● **feminist** **adjective** 形容词: *feminist writer Simone de Beauvoir* 女权主义作家西蒙娜·德·波伏瓦

fence /fens/ **countable noun** 可数名词
a wooden or metal wall around a piece of land 栅栏；围栏

fern /fɜːn/ **noun** 名词
a plant that has long stems with leaves that look like feathers 蕨；蕨类植物

ferry /ˈferi/ **countable noun** 可数名词 (**ferries**)
a boat that regularly takes people or things a short distance across water 渡船；轮渡: *They crossed the River Gambia by ferry.* 他们乘坐渡船过了冈比亚河。

fertile /ˈfɜːtaɪl/ **adjective** 形容词
1 used for describing land or soil where plants grow very well（土地或土壤）肥沃的
2 able to have babies 能生育的
▶ **fertility** /fɜːˈtɪlɪti/ **uncountable noun** 不可数名词: *There are natural remedies to improve fertility.* 有提高生育力的自然疗法。

fertilizer /ˈfɜːtɪlaɪzə/ also 亦作 **fertiliser uncountable noun** 不可数名词
a substance that you put on soil to make plants grow better 肥料

festival /ˈfestɪvəl/ **countable noun** 可数名词
1 a series of special events such as concerts or plays（音乐、戏剧等的）节、会演: *The actress was in Rome for the city's film festival.* 这位女演员在罗马参加该城市的电影节。
2 a time when people celebrate a special event 节日: *Shavuot is a two-day festival for Jews.* 五旬节是犹太教节日，为期两天。

fetch /fetʃ/ **verb** 动词 (**fetches, fetching, fetched**)
to go somewhere and bring something or someone back 去拿；去取: *Sylvia fetched a towel from the bathroom.* 西尔维娅去浴室拿了条毛巾。□ *Please could you fetch me a glass of water?* 请帮我拿杯水好吗？

fever /ˈfiːvə/ **noun** 名词
when your body is too hot because you are ill 发热；发烧: *Jim had a high fever.* 吉姆发高烧了。

feverish /ˈfiːvərɪʃ/ **adjective** 形容词
having a fever 发热的；发烧的: *Joshua was feverish and wouldn't eat anything.* 乔舒亚发烧了，什么都吃不下。

few /fjuː/ **adjective** 形容词 (**fewer, fewest**)
not many 少数的；很少的: *She had few friends.* 她朋友很少。
a few some, but not many 一些；几个: *I'm having a dinner party for a few close friends.* 我要为几个密友办晚宴。□ *Here are a few ideas that might help you.* 这几个想法或许能帮到你。□ *Most were Americans but a few were British.* 大多数都是美国人，但有几个是英国人。
a few of some, but not many 一些: *I met a few of her friends at the party.* 在派对上我见到了她的几个朋友。
few of not many 不多: *Few of the houses still had lights on.* 只有几栋房子还亮着灯。

> **LANGUAGE HELP 语言提示**
> If you say *I have a few friends*, you mean that you have some friends. If you say *I have few friends*, you mean that you do not have many friends. *I have a few friends* 意为"我有一些朋友"。I have few friends 意为"我没几个朋友"。

fiancé /fiˈɒnseɪ/ **countable noun** 可数名词
the man that a woman is going to marry 未婚夫

fiancée /fiˈɒnseɪ/ **countable noun** 可数名词
the woman that a man is going to marry 未婚妻

fibre /ˈfaɪbə/ **noun** 名词
1 **countable** 可数 a thin thread that is used for making cloth or rope（用于织布或编绳索的）纤维: *We only sell clothing made from natural fibres.* 我们只出售天然纤维制成的衣服。
2 **uncountable** 不可数 the part of a fruit or vegetable that helps all the food you eat to move through your body（水果、蔬菜中的）膳食纤维: *Most vegetables contain fibre.* 大部分蔬菜都含有膳食纤维。

fiction /ˈfɪkʃən/ *uncountable noun* 不可数名词
books and stories about people and events that are not real 小说；虚构类文学作品
▶ **fictional** /ˈfɪkʃənəl/ *adjective* 形容词：*Harry Potter, the fictional hero of J.K. Rowling's books* 哈利·波特，J.K. 罗琳书中虚构的主角

fidget /ˈfɪdʒɪt/ *verb* 动词 (**fidgets, fidgeting, fidgeted**)
to keep moving slightly, because you are nervous or bored 坐立不安；躁动：*Brenda fidgeted in her seat.* 布伦达在座位上坐立不安。

field /fiːld/ *countable noun* 可数名词
1 a piece of land where crops are grown, or where animals are kept 田地；田野：*We drove past fields of sunflowers.* 我们驱车经过向日葵田。
2 a piece of land where sports are played 运动场：*a football field* 足球场
3 a subject that someone knows a lot about 领域：*Professor Greenwood is an expert in the field of international law.* 格林伍德教授是国际法领域的专家。

fielder /ˈfiːldə/ *countable noun* 可数名词
a player in some sports who has to pick up or catch the ball after a player from the other team has hit it 守field员；外场手：*He hit 10 home runs and he's also a good fielder.* 他打了 10 个本垒打，而且还是个优秀的守场员。

fierce /fɪəs/ *adjective* 形容词 (**fiercer, fiercest**)
1 very angry and likely to attack 狂怒的；凶猛的
▶ **fiercely** /ˈfɪəsli/ *adverb* 副词：*'Go away!' she said fiercely.* "走开！"她怒气冲冲地说。
2 very strong or enthusiastic 强烈的；激烈的：*There's fierce competition for places in the team.* 这个队的名额竞争激烈。

fifteen /fɪfˈtiːn/
the number 15 十五
▶ **fifteenth** /fɪfˈtiːnθ/ *adjective* 形容词, *adverb* 副词：*the fifteenth century* *15 世纪

fifth¹ /fɪfθ/ *adjective* 形容词, *adverb* 副词
the item in a series that you count as number five 第五：*This is his fifth trip to Australia.* 这是他第 5 次去澳大利亚。

fifth² /fɪfθ/ *countable noun* 可数名词
one of five equal parts of something (1/5) 五分之一：*The machine allows us to do the job in a fifth of the usual time.* 使用机器可以让我们用往常五分之一的时间完成工作。

fifty /ˈfɪfti/
the number 50 五十
▶ **fiftieth** /ˈfɪftiəθ/ *adjective* 形容词, *adverb* 副词：*He's just celebrated his fiftieth birthday.* 他刚过了 50 岁生日。

fig /fɪɡ/ *countable noun* 可数名词
a soft sweet fruit full of tiny seeds. Figs grow on trees in hot countries. 无花果

fig 无花果

fight¹ /faɪt/ *verb* 动词 (**fights, fighting, fought**)
1 to try to hurt someone by using physical force 打斗；扑架：*'Stop fighting!' Mum shouted.* "别打了！"妈妈喊道。□ *Susan fought a lot with her younger sister.* 苏珊经常和妹妹打架。
2 to take part in a war 战斗：*He fought in the war and was taken prisoner.* 他参与作战，后被俘。
3 to try very hard to stop something unpleasant 与…作斗争：*It is very hard to fight forest fires.* 森林火灾很难扑灭。
4 to try very hard to get something 斗争；争取：*Lee had to fight hard for his place on the team.* 李必须努力拼搏为自己在队中争取一席之地。
5 to argue (*informal* 非正式) 争吵：*Robert's parents fight all the time.* 罗伯特的父母总是吵架。

fight² /faɪt/ *countable noun* 可数名词
a situation in which people try to hurt each other with words or by using physical force 打斗；扑架；吵架：*I had a fight with Simon at the party last night.* 我昨晚在派对上和西蒙打了一架。

fighter /ˈfaɪtə/ *countable noun* 可数名词
a person who fights another person, especially as a sport 战斗者；(尤指)拳击手：*He was a professional fighter for 17 years.* 他做了 17 年的职业拳击手。

figure /ˈfɪɡə/ *countable noun* 可数名词
1 one of the symbols from 0 to 9 that you use to write numbers 数字：*They've put the figures in the wrong column.* 他们把数字放错列了。□ *John earns a six-figure salary — £100,000 at least.* 约翰挣着 6 位数的薪水——至少 10 万英镑。

2 an amount or a price expressed as a number 数额；数据：*Can I see your latest sales figures?* 我可以看你最近的销售额吗？
3 the shape of a person you cannot see clearly 人影；身影：*Two figures moved behind the thin curtain.* 薄薄的窗帘后面有两个人影在动。
4 the shape of someone's body 体形；身材：*Lauren has a very good figure.* 劳伦身材很好。

file¹ /faɪl/ ***countable noun*** 可数名词
1 a box or a type of envelope that you keep papers in 文件盒；文件夹：*The file contained letters and reports.* 文件盒里有信件和报告。
→ Look at picture on P1 参见彩插第 1 页
2 a collection of information that you keep on your computer（计算机的）文件：*I deleted the files by mistake.* 我误删了这些文件。
3 a tool that you use for rubbing rough objects to make them smooth 锉刀：*a nail file* 指甲锉
in single file walking or standing in a line, one behind the other 成一路纵队：*We walked past him in single file.* 我们排成一列，从他身边走过。

file² /faɪl/ ***verb*** 动词 (**files, filing, filed**)
1 to put a document in the correct place 把…归档：*The letters are all filed alphabetically.* 这些信件全部按照字母顺序归档了。
2 to make something smooth using a special tool (= a file) 锉平：*Mum was filing her nails.* 妈妈在锉指甲。
3 to walk somewhere in a line, one behind the other 排成纵队行走：*More than 10,000 people filed past the dead woman's coffin.* 一万多人排成纵队走过这位女逝者的灵柩。

filename /ˈfaɪlneɪm/ ***countable noun*** 可数名词
the name that you give to a particular computer file 文件名

ˈfile-ˌsharing also 亦作 **file sharing** ***uncountable noun*** 不可数名词
a way of sharing computer files among a large number of users 计算机文件共享

fill /fɪl/ ***verb*** 动词 (**fills, filling, filled**)
1 (also 亦作 **fill up**) to cause a container to become full of something 装满；填满：*Rachel went to the bathroom and filled a glass with water.* 蕾切尔去浴室装了一杯水。□ *The bath was filling up quickly.* 浴缸很快就满了。
2 (also 亦作 **fill up**) to cause a space to be full of something 挤满；占满：*Rows of desks filled the office.* 办公室里摆满了一排排桌子。
▶ **filled** /fɪld/ ***adjective*** 形容词：*The museum is filled with historical objects.* 博物馆里古物琳琅满目。
3 (also 亦作 **fill in**) to put a substance into a hole to make the surface smooth again 填平；填补：*Fill the cracks between walls and window frames.* 填平墙和窗框之间的缝隙。□ *Start by filling in any cracks.* 从填补裂隙开始。

fill something in or **fill something out** to write information in the spaces on a form 填写（表格）：*When you have filled in the form, send it to your employer.* 填完表格之后，发给雇主。

fill up to cause a container or space to be full of something 装满；挤满：*Filling up your car's petrol tank these days is very expensive.* 如今要给车加满一箱油可不便宜。

filling /ˈfɪlɪŋ/ ***noun*** 名词
1 ***countable*** 可数 a small amount of plastic or metal that fills a hole in a tooth（补牙用的）填料：*The dentist said I needed two fillings.* 牙医说我需要两块填料。
2 what is inside a cake, a pie or a sandwich（蛋糕、馅饼或三明治等的）馅：*Next, make the pie filling.* 接下来做馅饼中的馅料。

film¹ /fɪlm/ ***noun*** 名词
1 (*American* 美国英语：**movie**) ***countable*** 可数 a story that is told using moving pictures on the television or at a cinema 电影；影片：*I'm going to see a film tonight.* 我今晚要去看场电影。
2 the roll of plastic that is used for taking photographs in some older cameras 胶卷：*Emily put a new roll of film into the camera.* 埃米莉往相机里装了一卷新胶片。

film² /fɪlm/ ***verb*** 动词 (**films, filming, filmed**)
to use a camera to take moving pictures of something 把…拍成电影：*He filmed her life story.* 他把她的生平拍成了电影。

filter /ˈfɪltə/ ***countable noun*** 可数名词
an object that only allows liquid or air to pass through it, and that holds back solid parts such as dirt or dust 过滤器：*The water filters are available in different styles, colours and designs.* 各种风格、颜色和式样

的滤水器都有。● **filter** *verb* 动词 (**filters, filtering, filtered**): *The device cleans and filters the air.* 这个设备净化并过滤空气。

filthy /ˈfɪlθi/ *adjective* 形容词 (**filthier, filthiest**)
very dirty 肮脏的: *He always wore a filthy old jacket.* 他总是穿着一件脏兮兮的旧夹克。

fin /fɪn/ *countable noun* 可数名词
one of the flat parts like a wing that helps a fish to swim 鳍

final¹ /ˈfaɪnəl/ *adjective* 形容词
1 last 最后的；最终的: *The team's final game of the season will be tomorrow.* 该队这个赛季的最后一场比赛将在明天举行。
2 used for describing something that cannot be changed 不可更改的: *The judges' decision is final.* 法官的判决不可更改。

final² /ˈfaɪnəl/ *noun* 名词
1 *countable* 可数 the last game or race in a series, that decides who is the winner 决赛: *He played in the final of the US Open.* 他参加了美国公开赛的决赛。
2 [**finals**] *plural* 复数 the exams taken by British university students at the end of their final year (英国的)大学毕业考试: *Anna took her finals in the summer.* 安娜夏天参加了大学毕业考试。

finalist /ˈfaɪnəlɪst/ *countable noun* 可数名词
someone who reaches the final of a competition 参加决赛者；决赛选手: *My brother was a regional finalist.* 我弟弟参加了地区决赛。

finally /ˈfaɪnəli/ *adverb* 副词
1 after a long time 终于；总算: *The letter finally arrived at the end of last week.* 上周末信总算到了。
2 said before you say the last thing in a list 最后(用于引出最后的话题): *Combine the flour and the cheese, and finally, add the cream.* 把面粉和芝士混合，最后加奶油。

finance¹ /ˈfaɪnæns/ *verb* 动词 (**finances, financing, financed**)
to provide the money to pay for something 给…提供资金: *The government used the money to finance the war.* 政府利用这笔钱资助战争。

finance² /ˈfaɪnæns/ *noun* 名词
1 *uncountable* 不可数 money, or the activity of managing large amounts of money 资金；财政；金融: *Professor Buckley teaches finance at Princeton University.* 巴克利教授在普林斯顿大学教

授金融学。
2 [**finances**] *plural* 复数 the money that someone has 财力；财源: *Take control of your finances now and save thousands of pounds.* 现在打理好财务，能省下好几千英镑。

financial /faɪˈnænʃəl, fɪ-/ *adjective* 形容词
relating to money 财务的；金融的: *The company is in financial difficulties.* 该公司面临着财务困难。

find /faɪnd/ *verb* 动词 (**finds, finding, found**)
1 to see something after you have been looking for it 找到，发现(在寻找的东西): *The police searched the house and found a gun.* 警察搜查了这栋房子，找到一把枪。
□ *David has finally found a job.* 戴维终于找到了一份工作。
2 to see or discover something by chance 碰巧发现: *If you find my purse, can you let me know?* 你要是看到了我的钱包，请告诉我一声。
3 used for expressing your opinion about something 觉得；认为: *I find his behaviour extremely rude.* 我觉得他的行为极其粗鲁。
□ *We all found the film very funny.* 我们都觉得这部电影非常有趣。

find someone guilty/not guilty to say that someone is guilty or not guilty of a crime 裁定某人有罪 / 无罪: *The woman was found guilty of murdering her partner.* 这个女人被判谋杀伴侣罪名成立。

find something out to learn the facts about something 查明，弄清(某事物的真相): *I'll watch the next episode to find out what happens.* 我要看下一集，弄清发生了什么。

find your way to get somewhere by choosing the right way to go 找到(去某处的)路: *We lost our dog, but he found his way home.* 我们的狗丢了，但它找到了回家的路。

fine¹ /faɪn/ *adjective* 形容词 (**finer, finest**)
1 very good 很好的: *There is a fine view of the countryside.* 乡村美景映入眼帘。
2 well or happy 健康的；幸福的: *Linda is fine and sends you her love.* 琳达安好，她让我转达对你的爱。
3 satisfactory or acceptable 令人满意的；可以接受的: *Everything is going to be just fine.* 一切都会好起来的。
4 very thin 纤细的: *fine hairs* 纤细的毛发
5 used for describing the weather when the sun is shining (天气)晴朗的

fine² /faɪn/ *countable noun* 可数名词 money that someone has to pay because they have done something wrong 罚金；罚款 ● **fine** *verb* 动词 (**fines, fining, fined**)：*She was fined £300 for driving dangerously.* 她因危险驾驶被罚了 300 英镑。

ˌfine ˈart *uncountable noun* 不可数名词 (also 亦作 **fine arts**) the paintings and objects that artists produce for other people's pleasure, rather than for a particular use 美术（品）；艺术（品）：*the Museum of Fine Arts* 美术博物馆

finger /ˈfɪŋɡə/ *countable noun* 可数名词 one of the long thin parts at the end of each hand 手指：*Amber had a huge diamond ring on her finger.* 安伯手指上戴着一枚大钻戒。
cross your fingers or **keep your fingers crossed** to put one finger on top of another and hope for good luck（交叉手指）祈求好运

fingernail /ˈfɪŋɡəˌneɪl/ *countable noun* 可数名词 one of the thin hard parts at the end of each of your fingers 手指甲

fingerprint /ˈfɪŋɡəˌprɪnt/ *countable noun* 可数名词 the mark that your finger makes when it touches something 指纹：*His fingerprints were found on the gun.* 枪上发现了他的指纹。

fingertip /ˈfɪŋɡəˌtɪp/ also 亦作 **finger-tip** *countable noun* 可数名词 the end of your finger 指尖：*He plays the drum very lightly with his fingertips.* 他用指尖轻敲着鼓。

finish¹ /ˈfɪnɪʃ/ *verb* 动词 (**finishes, finishing, finished**)
1 to stop doing something 结束，停止（做某事）：*Dad finished eating, and left the room.* 爸爸吃完离开了房间。
2 to end 结束；完成：*The concert finished just after midnight.* 音乐会刚过午夜就结束了。

finish² /ˈfɪnɪʃ/ *singular noun* 单数名词 the end of something or the last part of it 结尾；最后一部分：*There was an exciting finish to the women's 800-metre race.* 女子 800 米跑最后的赛程激动人心。

finished /ˈfɪnɪʃt/ *adjective* 形容词 no longer using something 不再用…的：*When you are finished with the book,* *please give it back to your teacher.* 你要是不用这本书了，请把它还给你的老师。

fir /fɜː/ or 或 **fir ˈtree** *noun* 名词 a tall tree with thin leaves (= needles) that do not fall in winter 冷杉

fire¹ /faɪə/ *noun* 名词
1 *uncountable* 不可数 the hot, bright flames that come from things that are burning 火；火焰：*We learned how to make fire and hunt for fish.* 我们学会了生火和捕鱼。
2 flames that destroy buildings or forests 火灾：*87 people died in a fire at the theatre.* *87 人在剧场火灾中丧生。*□ *a forest fire* 森林火灾
3 *countable* 可数 a burning pile of wood or coal that you make 炉火；灶火：*There was a fire in the fireplace.* 壁炉里燃着火。
catch fire to start burning 着火；失火：*Several buildings caught fire in the explosion.* 几座建筑物在爆炸中着了火。
on fire burning and being damaged by a fire 着火的：*Quick! My car's on fire!* 快点！我的车着火了！
set fire to something or **set something on fire** to make something start to burn 点着某物

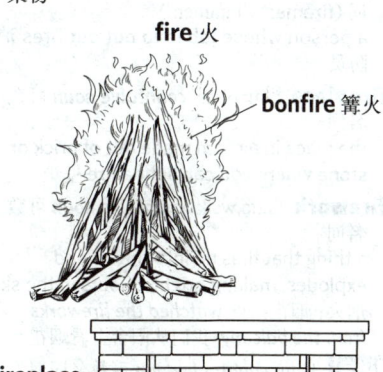
fire 火 — bonfire 篝火

fireplace 壁炉 — fire 炉火

fire² /faɪə/ *verb* 动词 (**fires, firing, fired**)
1 to shoot a gun or a bullet 开（枪或炮）；射出（子弹）：*Have you ever fired a gun before?* 你之前开过枪吗？
2 to tell someone to leave their job 开除；解雇：*She was fired from that job in August.*

*8月份她被解雇了。

fire a׳larm *countable noun* 可数名词
a piece of equipment that makes a loud noise to warn people when there is a fire 火灾警报器

firearm /ˈfaɪɑːm/ *countable noun* 可数名词
a gun (*formal* 正式) 枪: *The guards were carrying firearms.* 警卫持着枪。

fire brigade /ˈfaɪə brɪˌɡeɪd/ *countable noun* 可数名词
an organization that has the job of putting out fires 消防署；消防队

׳fire ˌengine *countable noun* 可数名词
a large vehicle that carries people and equipment for putting out fires 消防车

fire extinguisher /ˈfaɪər ɪkˌstɪŋɡwɪʃə/ *countable noun* 可数名词
a metal container with water or chemicals inside for stopping fires 灭火器

firefighter /ˈfaɪəfaɪtə/ *countable noun* 可数名词
a person whose job is to put out fires 消防员
→ Look at picture on P16 参见彩插第16页

fireman /ˈfaɪəmən/ *countable noun* 可数名词 (firemen /ˈfaɪəmən/)
a person whose job is to put out fires 消防员

fireplace /ˈfaɪəpleɪs/ *countable noun* 可数名词
the place in a room made out of brick or stone where you can light a fire 壁炉

firework /ˈfaɪəˌwɜːk/ *countable noun* 可数名词
a thing that flies up into the air and explodes, making bright colours in the sky 烟火；烟花: *We watched the fireworks from the balcony.* 我们从阳台上看烟花。

firm¹ /fɜːm/ *countable noun* 可数名词
a group of people who work together 公司: *Kevin works for a Chicago law firm.* 凯文就职于芝加哥一家律师事务所。

firm² /fɜːm/ *adjective* 形容词 (**firmer**, **firmest**)
1 not soft 硬的；坚实的: *When you buy fruit, make sure it is firm.* 买水果要买硬的。
2 strong 结实的；强有力的: *His handshake was firm.* 他握手有力。
▶ **firmly** /ˈfɜːmli/ *adverb* 副词: *She held me firmly by the elbow.* 她紧紧地抓住我的胳膊肘儿。

3 not changing your mind 坚定的；坚决的: *She was firm with him. 'I don't want to see you again.'* 她对他的态度很坚决：“我不想再见到你。”
▶ **firmly** /ˈfɜːmli/ *adverb* 副词: *'You must go to bed now, kids,' he said firmly.* "孩子们，得上床睡觉了。"他不容反驳地说。

first /fɜːst/ *adjective* 形容词, *adverb* 副词
1 coming before all the others 最早(的)；第一(的): *January is the first month of the year.* 一月是一年中的第一个月。 ▫ *Who came first in the race?* 这场比赛谁得了第一？
2 before doing anything else 先，首先(做某事): *First I went to the police and told them what had happened.* 首先，我去了警察局告诉他们发生了什么。
3 before anyone else 最先，最早(表示早于其他人): *The people who lived nearby arrived first.* 住在附近的人到得最早。
at first used for talking about what happened at the beginning of an event 起初；开始时: *At first, he seemed surprised by my questions.* 起初，他似乎对我的问题感到惊讶。
first or **first of all** used for introducing the first thing that you want to say 第一，首先(用于引出想说的话): *First of all, I'd like to thank you for coming.* 首先，我要感谢你们的到来。

ˌfirst ˈaid *uncountable noun* 不可数名词
simple medical treatment that you give to an ill or injured person 急救: *Each group leader must do a course in basic first aid.* 每个组长必须参加一个基本急救课程。

ˌfirst-ˈclass also 亦作 **first class** *adjective* 形容词
1 of the highest standard 一流的；优等的: *The Altea is a newly-built first-class hotel.* 阿尔特亚酒店是一家新建的一流酒店。
2 used for describing the best and most expensive seats on a train or an aeroplane (火车或飞机座位)头等的: *He won two first-class tickets to fly to Dublin.* 他赢得了两张飞往都柏林的头等舱机票。● **first-class** *adverb* 副词: *We never fly first class.* 我们从没坐过飞机的头等舱。
3 used for describing the fastest and most expensive way of sending letters (信函)优先投递的，第一类的: *a first-class letter* 一封一类信件 ● **first-class** *adverb* 副词: *I sent the letter first-class, but it hasn't arrived.* 我把这封信按第一类邮件投递的，但还没寄到。

first floor *countable noun* 可数名词
1 the floor of a building just above the floor that is level with the street 二楼；二层
2 (*American* 美国英语)→ see 见 **ground floor**

firstly /ˈfɜːstli/ *adverb* 副词
used when you mention the first thing in a list 首先；第一：*Firstly, you're late, and secondly, you've forgotten your homework.* 首先，你迟到了；其次，你忘记做作业了。

first name *countable noun* 可数名词
the name that comes before your family name 名字(置于姓氏前)：*'What's Dr Wright's first name?' 'It's Emma. Emma Wright.'* "赖特医生叫什么名字？" "叫埃玛，埃玛·赖特。"

fish[1] /fɪʃ/ *countable noun* 可数名词 (**fish** or 或 **fishes**)
an animal that lives and swims in water, that people eat as food 鱼：*Dave caught a huge fish this morning.* 戴夫今早抓到一条大鱼。□ *This fish is delicious.* 这条鱼很好吃。→ Look at picture on P5 参见彩插第 5 页

fish 鱼
scales 鳞
fin 鳍

fish[2] /fɪʃ/ *verb* 动词 (**fishes, fishing, fished**)
to try to catch fish 捕鱼；钓鱼：*Brian learned to fish in the Colorado River.* 布赖恩在科罗拉多河学会钓鱼。

fisherman /ˈfɪʃəmən/ *countable noun* 可数名词 (**fishermen** /ˈfɪʃəmən/)
a person who catches fish as a job or for sport 渔夫；垂钓者

fishing /ˈfɪʃɪŋ/ *uncountable noun* 不可数名词
the sport or business of catching fish 钓鱼；捕鱼

fishing rod *countable noun* 可数名词
a long thin stick with a thread and a hook, that is used for catching fish 钓竿

fist /fɪst/ *countable noun* 可数名词
your hand with your fingers closed tightly together 拳；拳头：*Steve stood up and shook an angry fist at Patrick.* 史蒂夫站起身，愤怒地向帕特里克挥舞着拳头。

fit[1] /fɪt/ *verb* 动词 (**fits, fitting, fitted**)
1 to be the right size for someone or something 大小适合(某物)；合(某人)的身：*The costume fitted the child perfectly.* 这件演出服穿在这个孩子身上正合适。□ *The game is small enough to fit into your pocket.* 这款游戏机很小，可以装进口袋里。
2 to attach something somewhere 固定；安装：*He fits locks on the doors.* 他在门上安了锁。
fit someone/something in to find time or space for someone or something 找出时间见某人 / 做某事；可容纳某人 / 某物：*The dentist can fit you in just after lunch.* 牙医午餐后就可以见你。□ *We can't fit any more children in the car.* 这辆车多一个孩子都装不下了。

fit[2] /fɪt/ *adjective* 形容词 (**fitter, fittest**)
1 healthy and strong 健康的；健壮的：*You're looking very fit. I can tell you exercise regularly.* 你看上去很健壮，我看得出你经常锻炼身体。
▶ **fitness** /ˈfɪtnəs/ *uncountable noun* 不可数名词：*Sophie is a fitness instructor.* 索菲是一名健身教练。
2 good enough for a particular purpose 合适的：*Only two of the bicycles were fit for the road.* 这些自行车中只有两辆适合在这条路上骑。

fit[3] /fɪt/ *countable noun* 可数名词
1 when someone suddenly starts coughing or laughing (咳嗽或笑的)发作，一阵：*I suddenly had a fit of coughing.* 我突然一阵咳嗽。
2 when someone suddenly becomes unconscious and their body makes violent movements 昏厥抽搐

five /faɪv/
the number 5 五

fix /fɪks/ *verb* 动词 (**fixes, fixing, fixed**)
1 to repair something 修理：*This morning, a man came to fix my washing machine.* 今早来了一个男人帮我修洗衣机。
2 to attach something firmly or securely to a particular place 固定；安装：*The clock is fixed to the wall.* 钟固定在墙上。

fizzy /ˈfɪzi/ *adjective* 形容词 (**fizzier, fizziest**)
containing small bubbles 起泡的：*fizzy water* 汽水

flag /flæɡ/ *countable noun* 可数名词
a piece of coloured cloth with a pattern on it that is used as a symbol for a country or an organization 旗；旗帜：*The crowd was*

shouting and waving American flags. 人群大声呼喊并挥舞着美国国旗。

flake¹ /fleɪk/ **countable noun** 可数名词
a small thin piece of something 小薄片：*Large flakes of snow began to fall.* 大片雪花开始飘落下来。

flake² /fleɪk/ **verb** 动词 **(flakes, flaking, flaked)**
(also 亦作 **flake off**) when paint flakes, small thin pieces of it come off（油漆等）剥落，脱落：*The paint was flaking off the walls.* 墙上的漆脱落了。

flame /fleɪm/ **noun** 名词
the bright burning gas that comes from a fire 火焰：*The flames almost burned her fingers.* 火焰几乎烧到了她的手指。
burst into flames to suddenly start burning strongly 突然燃起大火；突然烈火熊熊：*The plane crashed and burst into flames.* 飞机坠毁起火，烈焰冲天。
in flames burning 燃烧的；起火的：*When we arrived, the house was in flames.* 我们到达时，房子在燃烧。

flammable /ˈflæməbəl/ **adjective** 形容词
burning easily 易燃的：*Always store paint and flammable liquids away from the house.* 始终要将油漆和易燃液体存放在远离房屋的地方。

flap¹ /flæp/ **verb** 动词 **(flaps, flapping, flapped)**
1 to move quickly up and down or from side to side 摆动；抖动：*Sheets flapped on the clothes line.* 床单在晾衣绳上飘摆。
2 when a bird flaps its wings, it moves them up and down quickly 拍打，振动（翅膀）：*The birds flapped their wings and flew across the lake.* 鸟儿振翅飞过湖面。

flap² /flæp/ **countable noun** 可数名词
a flat piece of something that can move up and down or from side to side（可上下移动或左右翻动的）片状物：*I opened the flap of the envelope and took out the letter.* 我拆开信封封舌取出了信。

flash¹ /flæʃ/ **countable noun** 可数名词 **(flashes)**
a sudden bright light 闪光：*There was a flash of lightning.* 一道闪电划过天空。

flash² /flæʃ/ **verb** 动词 **(flashes, flashing, flashed)**
to shine on and off very quickly 闪光；闪烁：*They could see a lighthouse flashing through the fog.* 他们能看到一座灯塔在雾中闪烁。

'flash drive countable noun 可数名词
a small object for storing computer information that you can carry with you and use in different computers 优盘；闪存盘

flat¹ /flæt/ **adjective** 形容词 **(flatter, flattest)**
1 level or smooth 平的；平坦的：*Tiles can be fixed to any flat surface.* 瓷砖可贴在任何平整的表面上。 □ *a flat roof* 平屋顶
2 used for describing a tyre or ball that does not have enough air in it（轮胎、球等）瘪的，没气的
3 used for describing a note that is slightly lower than another note. Compare with **sharp**. 降半音的（比较 sharp）：*This is how to sing a B flat.* 降 B 调就是这样唱。

flat² /flæt/ **countable noun** 可数名词
(*American* 美国英语：**apartment**)
a set of rooms for living in, usually on one floor and part of a larger building 公寓；单元房

flatten /ˈflætən/ **verb** 动词 **(flattens, flattening, flattened)**
to make something flat 使变平：*Flatten the bread dough with your hands.* 用手将面包面团压平。

flatter /ˈflætə/ **verb** 动词 **(flatters, flattering, flattered)**
to say nice things to someone because you want them to like you 奉承；讨好：*Everyone likes to be flattered, to be told that they're beautiful.* 每个人喜欢听恭维的话，被夸赞长得美。

flattering /ˈflætərɪŋ/ **adjective** 形容词
making someone look or seem attractive or important 使人显得更漂亮（或更重要）的：*It was a very flattering photograph — he looked like a film star.* 这张照片显得人很漂亮——他看上去就像个电影明星。

flavour /ˈfleɪvə/ **noun** 名词
the taste of a food or drink 味道：*I added some pepper for extra flavour.* 我加了些胡椒粉提味儿。● **flavour verb** 动词 **(flavours, flavouring, flavoured)**：*Flavour your favourite dishes with herbs and spices.* 加点儿香草和香料给你最喜欢的菜调味。

flaw /flɔː/ **countable noun** 可数名词
something that is wrong with something 错误：*There are a number of flaws in his theory.* 他的理论中有许多错误。

flea /fliː/ *countable noun* 可数名词
a very small insect that jumps. Fleas live on the bodies of humans or animals, and drink their blood as food. 跳蚤: *Our dog has fleas.* 我们的狗身上有跳蚤。

fled /fled/
→ see 见 **flee**

flee /fliː/ *verb* 动词 (**flees, fleeing, fled**)
to run away from something or someone (*formal* 正式) 逃离；逃避: *He slammed the door behind him and fled.* 他砰的一声关上门逃走了。

fleece /fliːs/ *countable noun* 可数名词
1 the coat of wool that covers a sheep 羊毛
2 a jacket or a jumper made from a soft warm cloth 绒头织物上衣: *He was wearing tracksuit trousers and a dark blue fleece.* 他穿着运动裤和深蓝色羊毛衫。

fleet /fliːt/ *countable noun* 可数名词
a large group of boats, aircraft or cars 船队；机群；车队: *The fleet sailed out to sea.* 船队驶向了大海。

flesh /fleʃ/ *uncountable noun* 不可数名词
1 the soft part of your body that is between your bones and your skin (身上的)肉: *The bullet went straight through the flesh of his arm.* 子弹径直穿过他胳膊上的肉。
2 the soft part that is inside a fruit or vegetable (水果或蔬菜的)肉

flew /fluː/
→ see 见 **fly**

flexible /ˈfleksɪbəl/ *adjective* 形容词
1 bending easily without breaking 易弯曲的；柔韧的: *These children's books have flexible plastic covers.* 这些儿童读物有柔韧的塑料封面。
2 able to change easily 易变通的；灵活的: *I'm very lucky to have flexible working hours.* 很幸运，我工作时间很灵活。
▶ **flexibility** /ˌfleksɪˈbɪlɪti/ *uncountable noun* 不可数名词: *It's possible to go there by bus, but a car gives more flexibility.* 可以坐公共汽车到那里，但开汽车更自由些。

flick /flɪk/ *countable noun* 可数名词
a quick, sharp movement 轻弹；轻快的移动: *The pony gave a quick flick of its tail.* 小马快速地甩了甩尾巴。 ● **flick** *verb* 动词 (**flicks, flicking, flicked**): *He shook his head to flick hair out of his eyes.* 他晃了晃脑袋，把头发从眼前甩开。

flicker /ˈflɪkə/ *verb* 动词 (**flickers, flickering, flickered**)
to shine in a way that is not steady (光)闪烁，摇曳: *The lights flickered, and suddenly it was dark.* 灯闪了闪，突然四周一片漆黑。
● **flicker** *countable noun* 可数名词: *He could see the flicker of flames.* 他能看到火光摇曳。

flight /flaɪt/ *noun* 名词
1 *countable* 可数 a trip in an aircraft 飞行；航程: *The flight to New York will take four hours.* 飞到纽约需要4个小时。 □ *Our flight was two hours late.* 我们的航班晚点两个小时。
2 *countable* 可数 a set of stairs that go from one level to another 梯段: *Ashley walked up the short flight of steps.* 阿什莉走上那一小段台阶。
3 *uncountable* 不可数 the action of flying 飞行；飞翔: *The photograph showed an eagle in flight.* 照片上有一只雕在飞翔。

fling /flɪŋ/ *verb* 动词 (**flings, flinging, flung**)
to throw something somewhere using a lot of force 猛掷；用力抛: *She flung down the magazine and ran from the room.* 她把杂志一摔，从房间里跑了出来。

flip /flɪp/ *verb* 动词 (**flips, flipping, flipped**)
to turn over quickly 快速翻转: *The car flipped over and burst into flames.* 汽车突然翻车并起火。
flip through something to turn the pages of a book quickly 快速翻阅，浏览(书): *He was flipping through a magazine in the living room.* 他在起居室里翻看着杂志。

flipper /ˈflɪpə/ *countable noun* 可数名词
a long, flat rubber shoe that you wear to help you to swim faster (帮助加速游泳的)脚蹼，鸭脚板

flirt¹ /flɜːt/ *verb* 动词 (**flirts, flirting, flirted**)
to behave towards someone in a way that shows that you think they are attractive 调情；打情骂俏: *My brother was flirting with all the girls.* 我哥哥在跟所有的女孩调情。

flirt² /flɜːt/ *countable noun* 可数名词
a person who likes to flirt a lot 爱调情的人: *I'm not a flirt. I'm only interested in my boyfriend.* 我不是爱调情的人，我只对我男朋友感兴趣。

float¹ /fləʊt/ *verb* 动词 (**floats, floating, floated**)
1 to stay on the surface of a liquid, and not sink 漂浮: *A plastic bottle was floating in the water.* 水上漂着一个塑料瓶。

2 to move slowly and gently through the air 飘浮: *A yellow balloon floated past.* 一个黄色的气球飘过。

float 漂浮；飘浮

A yellow balloon floated past. 一个黄色的气球飘过。

A plastic bottle was floating in the water. 水上漂着一个塑料瓶。

float² /fləʊt/ ***countable noun*** 可数名词
an object that stays on the surface of the water and supports your body while you are learning to swim (学游泳用的) 浮板

flock /flɒk/ ***countable noun*** 可数名词
a group of birds, sheep or goats (鸟或羊) 群: *A flock of birds flew overhead.* 一群鸟儿从头顶飞过。

flood¹ /flʌd/ ***noun*** 名词
an occasion when a lot of water covers land that is usually dry 洪水；水灾: *More than 70 people died in the floods.* 逾 70 人在这次洪灾中丧生。
→ Look at picture on P8 参见彩插第 8 页
in floods of tears crying a lot 泪如雨下的

flood² /flʌd/ ***verb*** 动词 (**floods, flooding, flooded**)
to fill an area with water 淹没: *The water tank burst and flooded the house.* 水箱爆裂，房屋被淹。
▶ **flooding** /ˈflʌdɪŋ/ ***uncountable noun*** 不可数名词: *The flooding is the worst in sixty-five years.* 这次水灾是 65 年来最严重的一次。

floodlight /ˈflʌdlaɪt/ ***countable noun*** 可数名词
a very powerful light that is used outside for lighting public buildings and sports grounds at night 泛光灯；投光灯

floor /flɔː/ ***countable noun*** 可数名词
1 the part of a room that you walk on 地板；地面: *There were no seats, so we sat on the floor.* 没有座位，我们就坐在了地板上。

2 all the rooms that are on a particular level of a building 层；楼层: *The café was on the seventh floor.* 咖啡馆在 8 层。

> **LANGUAGE HELP 语言提示**
> In British English, the **ground floor** of a building is the floor that is level with the street. The floor on the next level is called the **first floor**. In American English, the **first floor** is the floor that is level with the street, and the next floor up is the **second floor**. 英国英语中，ground floor 意为建筑物的 "一层"，"二层" 称作 first floor。美国英语中，first floor 意为 "一层"，"二层" 称作 second floor。

flop /flɒp/ ***verb*** 动词 (**flops, flopping, flopped**)
to sit or lie down suddenly and heavily because you are so tired (因疲倦) 猛然坐下 (或躺下): *Ben flopped down on to the bed and fell asleep at once.* 本一头倒在床上，马上就睡着了。

floppy /ˈflɒpi/ ***adjective*** 形容词 (**floppier, floppiest**)
loose, and hanging down 松软的；下垂的: *Stephanie was wearing a blue floppy hat.* 斯蒂芬妮戴着一顶垂边软帽。

florist /ˈflɒrɪst/ ***countable noun*** 可数名词
1 a person who owns or works in a shop that sells flowers 花店店主；花店店员
2 (also 亦作 **florist's**) a shop where you can buy flowers 花店

flour /ˈflaʊə/ ***uncountable noun*** 不可数名词
a fine powder that is used for making bread, cakes and pastry 面粉

flourish /ˈflʌrɪʃ/ ***verb*** 动词 (**flourishes, flourishing, flourished**)
to grow or develop very well 长势茂盛；繁荣: *This plant flourishes in warm climates.* 这种植物在气候温暖的地方长势很好。
□ *Heckart's career really flourished in the 1950s.* 赫卡特的事业在 20 世纪 50 年代蒸蒸日上。

flow /fləʊ/ ***verb*** 动词 (**flows, flowing, flowed**)
to move somewhere in a steady and continuous way 流；流动: *A stream flowed gently down into the valley.* 小溪缓缓流入山谷。● **flow** ***uncountable noun*** 不可数名词: *Vicky tried to stop the flow of blood.* 维基试图止血。□ *The new tunnel will speed up traffic flow.* 新隧道将加快车流通行。

flower¹ /ˈflaʊə/ *countable noun* 可数名词
the brightly coloured part of a plant 花: *Dad gave Mum a huge bunch of flowers.* 爸爸送给妈妈一大束花。

flower² /ˈflaʊə/ *verb* 动词 (**flowers, flowering, flowered**)
to produce flowers 开花: *These plants will flower soon.* 这些植物很快就要开花了。

flown /fləʊn/
→ see 见 **fly**

flu /fluː/ *uncountable noun* 不可数名词
an illness that is like a very bad cold; short for (缩写 =) 'influenza' 流感

fluent /ˈfluːənt/ *adjective* 形容词
able to speak a particular language easily and correctly 流利的；流畅的: *Jose is fluent in Spanish and English.* 乔斯能说一口流利的西班牙语和英语。
▶ **fluently** /ˈfluːəntli/ *adverb* 副词: *He spoke three languages fluently.* 他能流利地说3种语言。

fluffy /ˈflʌfi/ *adjective* 形容词 (**fluffier, fluffiest**)
very soft 松软的: *I dried myself with a big fluffy towel.* 我用一条柔软的大毛巾把身上擦干。

fluid /ˈfluːɪd/ *noun* 名词
a liquid (*formal* 正式) 流体；液体: *Make sure that you drink plenty of fluids.* 一定要摄入足量的水。

flung /flʌŋ/
→ see 见 **fling**

flush /flʌʃ/ *verb* 动词 (**flushes, flushing, flushed**)
1 to clean a toilet with water by pressing or pulling a handle 冲 (抽水马桶): *I heard someone flushing the toilet.* 我听到有人在冲马桶。
2 if you flush, your face becomes red because you are hot, ill, embarrassed or angry 脸红: *Amanda flushed with embarrassment.* 阿曼达尴尬得红了脸。
▶ **flushed** /flʌʃt/ *adjective* 形容词: *Her face was flushed with anger.* 她气得脸通红。

flute /fluːt/ *noun* 名词
a musical instrument that you play by blowing. You hold it sideways to your mouth. 长笛
→ Look at picture on P12 参见彩插第 12 页

flutter /ˈflʌtə/ *verb* 动词 (**flutters, fluttering, fluttered**)
to make a lot of quick, light movements 颤动；振动: *The butterfly fluttered its wings.* 蝴蝶震颤着翅膀。

fly¹ /flaɪ/ *countable noun* 可数名词 (**flies**)
a small insect with two wings 苍蝇

fly² /flaɪ/ *verb* 动词 (**flies, flying, flew, flown**)
1 to move through the air 飞；飞行: *The planes flew through the clouds.* 飞机飞过云层。
2 to travel somewhere in an aircraft 乘飞机: *Jerry flew to Los Angeles this morning.* 杰里今早乘飞机飞往洛杉矶。
3 to make an aircraft move through the air 驾驶 (飞机): *He flew a small plane to Cuba.* 他开一架小飞机去古巴。□ *I learnt to fly in Vietnam.* 我在越南学会了开飞机。

flyer /ˈflaɪə/ also 亦作 **flier** *countable noun* 可数名词
a small printed notice that advertises something 广告传单: *A tall girl gave us a flyer for the concert.* 一个高个子女孩给了我们一张音乐会宣传单。

foam /fəʊm/ *uncountable noun* 不可数名词
the mass of small bubbles that you sometimes see on the surface of a liquid 泡沫: *He drank his coffee, and wiped the foam off his moustache.* 他喝了口咖啡，然后抹去胡子上的泡沫。

focus¹ /ˈfəʊkəs/ *verb* 动词 (**focuses, focusing, focused**)
1 to give all your attention to something 集中注意力；专注: *Voters are now focusing on the war.* 选民现在都将注意力聚焦到了战争上。
2 to make changes to a camera so that you can see clearly through it 给 (相机) 调焦；使聚焦: *The camera was focused on his terrified face.* 相机聚焦到了他惊恐的脸上。

focus² /ˈfəʊkəs/ *countable noun* 可数名词 (**foci** /ˈfəʊsaɪ/ or 或 **focuses**)
the person or thing that everyone is looking at 焦点: *Wherever she goes, she's the focus of attention.* 不管去哪儿，她都是关注的焦点。
in focus clear and sharp 清晰的；对焦准确的: *Make sure that the subject of the photo is in focus.* 确保焦点对准拍摄对象。
out of focus unclear 模糊的；失焦的: *The photo was out of focus.* 照片没拍清楚。

foetus /ˈfiːtəs/ *countable noun* 可数名词 (**foetuses**)
an animal or a human being before it is born 胎；胎儿

fog /fɒg/ *uncountable noun* 不可数名词
thick cloud that is close to the ground 雾：*The car crash happened in thick fog.* 车祸发生在浓雾中。
▶ **foggy** /ˈfɒgi/ (**foggier, foggiest**) *adjective* 形容词：*a foggy day* 雾天
→ Look at picture on P8 参见彩插第 8 页

foil /fɔɪl/ *uncountable noun* 不可数名词
very thin metal sheets that you use for covering food 箔（用于包裹食物）：*Cover the turkey with foil and cook it for another 20 minutes.* 用箔纸将火鸡裹起来，再烹饪 20 分钟。

fold /fəʊld/ *verb* 动词 (**folds, folding, folded**)
to bend a piece of paper or cloth so that one part covers another part 折叠；对折：*He folded the paper carefully.* 他小心翼翼地把纸折起来。□ *I folded the towels and put them in the cupboard.* 我把毛巾叠起来放进橱柜里。

fold your arms
交叉双臂

● **fold** *countable noun* 可数名词：*Make another fold down the middle of the paper.* 将纸张再次对折。

fold your arms to put one arm under the other and hold them over your chest 交叉双臂

folder /ˈfəʊldə/ *countable noun* 可数名词
1 a folded piece of cardboard or plastic that you keep papers in 文件夹：*Liz carried her work folders into the study.* 利兹拿着她的工作文件夹进了书房。
2 a group of files that are stored together on a computer（计算机系统中的）文件夹：*I deleted the folder by mistake.* 我误删了这个文件夹。

folk¹ /fəʊk/ *plural noun* 复数名词
1 people 人们：*Most folk around here think she's a bit crazy.* 这里大多数人都觉得她有点儿疯狂。
2 your mother and father (*informal* 非正式) 爸妈：*I'll introduce you to my folks.* 我会把你介绍给我的爸妈。

folk² /fəʊk/ *adjective* 形容词
used for describing art, customs and music that belong to a particular group of people or country 民间的；民俗的：*This is a collection of traditional folk music from nearly 30 countries.* 这里收集了近 30 个国家的传统民间音乐。

ˈfolk ˌmusic *uncountable noun* 不可数名词
music that is traditional or typical of a particular group of people or country 民间音乐：*I listen to a variety of music including classical and folk music.* 我听各类音乐，包括古典乐和民间音乐。

follow /ˈfɒləʊ/ *verb* 动词 (**follows, following, followed**)
1 to move along behind someone 跟随；跟着：*We followed him up the steps.* 我们跟着他上了楼梯。□ *Please follow me, madam.* 女士，请跟着我。□ *She realized that the car was following her.* 她意识到那辆车在跟着她。
2 to go somewhere using a path to direct you 沿着（小径）行进：*All we had to do was follow the road.* 我们所要做的就是沿着这条路走。
3 to do something in the way that an instruction says 听从；遵循：*Follow the instructions carefully.* 要严格遵从指示。
4 to understand an explanation or a film 理解；跟得上：*Can you follow the story so far?* 目前为止这故事你能看懂吗？□ *I'm sorry, I don't follow.* 对不起，我没明白。

as follows used for introducing a list or an explanation 如下：*The winners are as follows: E. Walker; R. Foster; R. Gates.* 获胜者如下：E. 沃克、R. 福斯特、R. 盖茨。

following /ˈfɒləʊɪŋ/ *adjective* 形容词
used for describing the day, week or year after the one you have just mentioned 接下来的（一天、一周或一年）：*We had dinner together on Friday and then met for lunch the following day.* 我们周五共进了晚餐，第二天又一起吃了午餐。

fond /fɒnd/ *adjective* 形容词 (**fonder, fondest**)
liking someone or something very much 喜爱…的；酷爱…的：*I am very fond of Michael.* 我非常喜欢迈克尔。□ *Dad's fond of singing.* 爸爸喜欢唱歌。□ *Mrs Johnson was very fond of cats.* 约翰逊太太非常喜欢猫。

font /fɒnt/ *countable noun* 可数名词
a set of letters of the same style and size 字体：*You can change the font so that it's easier to read.* 你可以调整一下字体以便阅读。

food /fuːd/ *noun* 名词
what people and animals eat 食品；食物：

The waitress brought our meal and said, 'Enjoy your food!' 女服务员给我们上完菜说:"用餐愉快!" □ *The people were starving — there was no food to eat.* 人们都饿坏了——没有东西可吃。

food chain *singular noun* 单数名词
the natural process by which one living thing is eaten by another, which is then eaten by another, and so on 食物链

fool¹ /fuːl/ *countable noun* 可数名词
a stupid or silly person 傻子;笨蛋: *I didn't understand anything. I felt like a fool.* 我什么都不懂,感觉自己像个傻子。
make a fool of someone to make someone seem silly by telling people about something stupid that they have done, or by tricking them 愚弄某人: *Your brother is making a fool of you.* 你弟弟在戏弄你。

fool² /fuːl/ *verb* 动词 (**fools, fooling, fooled**)
to make someone believe something that is not true 欺骗;愚弄: *Harris fooled people into believing she was a doctor.* 哈里斯骗得人们相信她是一名医生。
fool around to behave in a silly way 吊儿郎当;瞎胡闹: *They fool around and get into trouble at school.* 他们在学校里瞎混、惹麻烦。

foolish /ˈfuːlɪʃ/ *adjective* 形容词
stupid or silly 愚蠢的;傻的: *It would be foolish to ignore the risks.* 忽略风险是愚蠢的。
▶ **foolishly** /ˈfuːlɪʃli/ *adverb* 副词: *He knows that he acted foolishly.* 他知道自己做得很蠢。

foot /fʊt/ *noun* 名词 (**feet**)
1 *countable* 可数
the part of your body that is at the end of your leg, and that you stand on 足;脚: *We danced until our feet were sore.* 我们跳舞跳到脚痛。 □ *He's suffering from a foot injury.* 他正承受脚伤的痛苦。
→ Look at picture on P4 参见彩插第 4 页

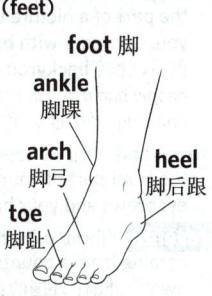

foot 脚
ankle 脚踝
arch 脚弓
heel 脚后跟
toe 脚趾

2 *countable* 可数 a unit for measuring length. A foot is equal to 30.48 centimetres. There are 12 inches in a foot. The plural form is **feet** or **foot**. 英尺(长度单位,1 英尺 = 12 英寸或 30.48 厘米): *We were six thousand feet above sea level.* 我们当时在海拔 6,000 英尺的地方。 □ *The room is 10 foot long and 6 foot wide.* 这个房间长 10 英尺,宽 6 英尺。
3 *singular* 单数 the part of something that is furthest from its top 底部;下端: *He was waiting at the foot of the stairs.* 他在楼梯下面等着。
on foot walking 步行: *We explored the island on foot.* 我们步行游岛。
on your feet standing up 站立着: *Everyone was on their feet shouting and clapping.* 所有人都站着欢呼鼓掌。
put your feet up to have a rest(架起脚)休息: *I'll do the chores, so you can put your feet up.* 我来做家务,你可以休息了。

football /ˈfʊtbɔːl/ *noun* 名词
1 *uncountable* 不可数 a game for two teams of eleven players. Each team tries to win points by kicking the ball into an area at the other end of the field. 足球运动: *Paul loves playing football.* 保罗喜欢踢足球。
2 *countable* 可数 a ball that is used for playing football 足球: *Antonio kicked the football off the pitch.* 安东尼奥把足球踢出了球场。
→ Look at picture on P14 参见彩插第 14 页

footballer /ˈfʊtbɔːlə/ *countable noun* 可数名词
a person who plays football 足球运动员

footpath /ˈfʊtpɑːθ/ *countable noun* 可数名词
a path for people to walk on, especially in the countryside(尤指乡间的)人行小径

footprint /ˈfʊtprɪnt/ *countable noun* 可数名词
the mark that your foot makes on the ground 脚印

footstep /ˈfʊtstep/ *countable noun* 可数名词
the sound that you make each time your foot touches the ground when you are walking 脚步声: *I heard footsteps outside.* 我听到外面有脚步声。

for /fə, STRONG 强读 fɔː/ *preposition* 介词
1 used for saying who will have or use something 给;对;供: *These flowers are for you.* 这些花是给你的。 □ *I reserved a table for two at the restaurant.* 我在饭店预定了一张两人桌。
2 used for saying which person or company employs you 受雇于: *He works for a bank.* 他在一家银行工作。
3 done so that someone else does not

have to do it 为了；以帮助: *I held the door open for the next person.* 我为下一个进出的人把着门。

4 used for describing a word that has the same meaning as another word（意思）相当于，等于: *In French, the word for 'love' is 'amour'.* 在法语中用 amour 表示"爱"。

5 used for describing the purpose of an object（表示用途或目的）为了，用来: *This knife is for slicing bread.* 这把刀是用来切面包的。

6 used for saying where a bus, train, plane or boat is going 去往；前往: *They took the train for Rio early the next morning.* 他们第二天一早乘火车去里约。

7 used when you are saying how long something lasts（表示时间）持续: *We talked for about half an hour.* 我们谈了约一个小时。

8 used for saying how far someone or something goes（表示距离）达，计: *We continued to drive for a few miles.* 我们继续往前开了几英里。

9 used for giving the price of something that you buy（表示价格）以…的价钱: *The Martins sold their house for £1.4 million.* 马丁一家以 140 万英镑的价格卖掉了他们的房子。

10 agreeing with or supporting someone or something 赞成；支持: *Well, are you for us or against us?* 嗯，你是支持我们还是反对我们？

11 as part of a particular team（作为队伍中的一员）效力于: *Kerry plays hockey for the school team.* 克里在校队打曲棍球。

forbade /fəˈbeɪd/
→ see 见 **forbid**

forbid /fəˈbɪd/ *verb* 动词 (**forbids, forbidding, forbade, forbidden**)
to tell someone that they must not do something 禁止；不准: *My parents have forbidden me to see my boyfriend.* 我父母不许我见男朋友。

forbidden¹ /fəˈbɪdən/
→ see 见 **forbid**

forbidden² /fəˈbɪdən/ *adjective* 形容词
not allowed 禁止的: *Pets are forbidden here.* 这里禁止宠物入内。

force¹ /fɔːs/ *verb* 动词 (**forces, forcing, forced**)

1 to make someone do something when they do not want to 强迫；迫使: *They forced him to give them the money.* 他们逼他给钱。

2 to break the lock of a door or a window 强行打开（门或窗）: *Police forced the door of the flat and arrested Mr Roberts.* 警察撞开公寓门抓捕了罗伯茨先生。

force² /fɔːs/ *noun* 名词

1 uncountable 不可数 strength used for doing something 力；力量: *Police used force to break up the fight.* 警察用武力制止了这场打斗。

2 uncountable 不可数 the power or strength that something has 影响力；威力: *The force of the explosion destroyed the building.* 爆炸产生的威力摧毁了这座建筑物。

3 countable 可数 a group of people, for example soldiers or police officers, who do a particular job 部队；武装部队: *Russian forces entered the region.* 俄罗斯军队进入了该地区。

forecast¹ /ˈfɔːkɑːst/ *countable noun* 可数名词
what someone expects will happen in the future 预测；预报: *Did you see the weather forecast?* 你看天气预报了吗？

forecast² /ˈfɔːkɑːst/ *verb* 动词 (**forecasts, forecasting, forecast** or 或 **forecasted**)
to say what you think is going to happen in the future 预测；预言: *Economists were forecasting higher oil prices.* 经济学家预测油价将上涨。

▶ **forecaster** /ˈfɔːkɑːstə/ *countable noun* 可数名词: *David worked for 34 years as a weather forecaster.* 戴维做了 34 年的天气预报员。

foreground /ˈfɔːɡraʊnd/ *noun* 名词
the part of a picture that seems nearest to you. Compare with **background**.（图片的）前景（比较 background）: *There are five people and a dog in the foreground of the painting.* 画中前景里有 5 个人和 1 只狗。

forehead /ˈfɒhed/ *countable noun* 可数名词
the front part of your head between your eyebrows and your hair 额；前额

foreign /ˈfɒrɪn/ *adjective* 形容词
coming from a country that is not your own 国外的；外国的: *It's good to learn a foreign language.* 学一门外语很好。

foreigner /ˈfɒrɪnə/ *countable noun* 可数名词
someone who comes from a different country 外国人

foresee /fɔːˈsiː/ *verb* 动词 (**foresees, foreseeing, foresaw, foreseen**)
to expect and believe that something will

happen 预见；预料: *He did not foresee any problems.* 他没有料到会出现问题。

forest /ˈfɒrɪst/ *noun* 名词
a large area where trees grow close together 森林；林区: *a forest fire* 森林火灾
→ Look at picture on P7 参见彩插第 7 页

forever /fəˈrevə/ *adverb* 副词
used for saying that something will never change 永远: *I think that we will live together forever.* 我觉得我们会永远生活在一起。 □ *His pain was gone forever.* 他的痛苦永远消失了。

foreword /ˈfɔːwɜːd/ *countable noun* 可数名词
an introduction to a book (书的) 前言，序言: *She has written the foreword to a cookbook.* 她为一本烹饪书写了前言。

forgave /fəˈɡeɪv/
→ see 见 **forgive**

forge /fɔːdʒ/ *verb* 动词 (**forges, forging, forged**)
to make illegal copies of paper money, a document or a painting in order to cheat people 伪造，假冒 (纸币、文件、画作等): *He admitted to forging passports.* 他承认伪造护照。 □ *They used forged documents to leave the country.* 他们利用假文件离开了这个国家。
▶ **forger** /ˈfɔːdʒə/ *countable noun* 可数名词: *He's an expert art forger.* 他是个艺术品造假高手。

forgery /ˈfɔːdʒəri/ *noun* 名词 (**forgeries**)
1 *countable* 可数 something that has been forged 伪造品；赝品: *The letter was a forgery.* 这封信是伪造的。
2 *uncountable* 不可数 the crime of forging money, documents or paintings 伪造罪: *He was convicted of forgery.* 他犯了伪造罪。

forget /fəˈɡet/ *verb* 动词 (**forgets, forgetting, forgot, forgotten**)
1 to not remember something 忘记；遗忘: *He never forgets his dad's birthday.* 他从没忘记过爸爸的生日。 □ *I forgot to lock the door.* 我忘记锁门了。
2 to not bring something with you 忘记带: *When we reached the airport, I realized I'd forgotten my passport.* 我们到达机场之后，我发现自己忘带护照了。
3 to deliberately put something out of your mind 不把…放在心上；不去想: *You will soon forget the bad experience you had today.* 你很快就会忘掉今天的糟心事儿的。

LANGUAGE HELP 语言提示
If you want to say that you put something somewhere and left it there, use the verb **leave**. 表示把某物落在某处，用动词 leave: *I left my bag on the bus.* 我把包落在公交车上了。

forgetful /fəˈɡetful/ *adjective* 形容词
often forgetting things 健忘的: *My mother became very forgetful and confused when she got old.* 我妈妈年纪大了之后非常健忘，人迷迷糊糊的。

forgive /fəˈɡɪv/ *verb* 动词 (**forgives, forgiving, forgave, forgiven**)
to stop being angry with someone who has done something bad or wrong 原谅；宽恕: *Hopefully Jane will understand and forgive you.* 希望简能理解并原谅你。 □ *Irene forgave Terry for stealing her money.* 艾琳原谅了特里偷她钱的事。

forgiven /fəˈɡɪvn/
→ see 见 **forgive**

forgot /fəˈɡɒt/
→ see 见 **forget**

forgotten /fəˈɡɒtən/
→ see 见 **forget**

fork /fɔːk/ *countable noun* 可数名词
1 a tool with long metal points, used for eating food 叉；餐叉: *Please use your knife and fork.* 请使用刀叉。
2 a place where a road, path or river divides into two parts and forms a 'Y' shape 岔路；分岔处: *We arrived at a fork in the road.* 我们到了一个岔路口。 ● **fork** *verb* 动词 (**forks, forking, forked**): *Jan stopped where the path forked.* 简在小路分岔处停了下来。

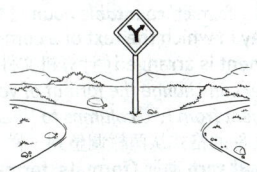

fork 岔路

form¹ /fɔːm/ *countable noun* 可数名词
1 a type of something 类型；种类: *She has a rare form of the disease.* 她得了此病中罕见的一种。 □ *I am against violence in any form.* 我反对任何形式的暴力。
2 the shape of something or the way it appears 形状；外形: *The dress fits the form of her body exactly.* 这条连衣裙完美贴合她

的身形。

3 a piece of paper with questions on it and spaces where you should write the answers 表格；调查表：*Please fill in this form and sign it at the bottom.* 请填写这份表格并在下面签字。

4 a class in a school 年级：*He's in the sixth form of the local school.* 他在当地学校读六年级。

5 the way that a noun or a verb is spelled or spoken when it is used for talking about the plural, the past or the present, for example（表示单复数、时态等的）形式；词形

form² /fɔːm/ *verb* 动词 (**forms, forming, formed**)
1 to make a particular shape 呈现…形状：*Form a diamond shape with your legs.* 双腿摆成菱形。
2 to make something 形成；构成：*These articles formed the basis of Randolph's book.* 这些文章构成了伦道夫这本书的基础。
3 to start an organization 建立，组成（组织、机构）：*They tried to form a study group on human rights.* 他们尝试建立一个人权研究小组。

formal /ˈfɔːməl/ *adjective* 形容词
very correct and serious rather than relaxed and friendly 规范的；正式的：*We received a very formal letter of apology.* 我们收到了一封非常正式的道歉信。
▶ **formally** /ˈfɔːməli/ *adverb* 副词：*He spoke formally, and without expression.* 他说得很正式，而且面无表情。
▶ **formality** /fɔːˈmæləti/ *uncountable noun* 不可数名词：*Lilly's formality and seriousness amused him.* 莉莉的庄重与严肃让他觉得好笑。

format /ˈfɔːmæt/ *countable noun* 可数名词
the way in which the text of a computer document is arranged（计算机文件的）格式：*You can change the format of your document from two columns to three.* 你可以将文件的格式从两栏调整到三栏。
● **format** *verb* 动词 (**formats, formatting, formatted**)：*The software can automatically format the text in a document as you type it.* 当您在文件中键入文本时，这个软件可以自动为文本排版。

formation /fɔːˈmeɪʃən/ *uncountable noun* 不可数名词
the beginning of the existence of something 形成；构成：*The vitamin is essential for the formation of red blood cells.* 维生素对红细胞的生成是必不可少的。

former¹ /ˈfɔːmə/ *adjective* 形容词
used for saying that a person or thing was something in the past, but is not that thing now 以前的；曾经的：*There was an interview with the former president, Richard Nixon.* 前总统理查德·尼克松接受了一次采访。

former² /ˈfɔːmə/ *pronoun* 代词
used for talking about the first of two people or things that have just been mentioned 前者；前一个：*Both the seeds and the leaves are useful — the former for soups, and the latter for salads.* 种子和叶子都有用——前者可以煲汤，后者可以做沙拉。

formerly /ˈfɔːməli/ *adverb* 副词
in the past, but not now 以前；从前：*He was formerly in the navy.* 他以前是海军。

formidable /ˈfɔːmɪdəbəl, fəˈmɪd-/ *adjective* 形容词
making you feel slightly frightened 令人生畏的；可怕的：*We have a formidable task ahead of us.* 我们面临着一项艰巨任务。

formula /ˈfɔːmjʊlə/ *countable noun* 可数名词 (**formulae** /ˈfɔːmjʊliː/ or 或 **formulas**)
1 a group of letters, numbers or other symbols that represents a scientific rule 公式：*This mathematical formula describes the distances of the planets from the Sun.* 这个数学公式可计算行星与太阳的距离。
2 a description of the chemical elements that a substance contains 化学式：*Glucose and fructose have the same chemical formula.* 葡萄糖和果糖的化学式相同。

fort /fɔːt/ *countable noun* 可数名词
a strong building that is used as a military base 堡垒

fortnight /ˈfɔːtnaɪt/ *countable noun* 可数名词
a period of two weeks 两星期：*I'll be back in a fortnight.* 我两星期之后回来。

fortress /ˈfɔːtrɪs/ *countable noun* 可数名词 (**fortresses**)
a castle or other large strong building that is difficult for enemies to enter 城堡；堡垒

fortunate /ˈfɔːtʃʊnɪt/ *adjective* 形容词
lucky 幸运的：*He was extremely fortunate to survive.* 他能活下来真是太幸运了。

fortunately /ˈfɔːtʃʊnɪtli/ *adverb* 副词
said when you start to talk about an event

or a situation that is good 幸运地；幸亏： *Fortunately, the weather last winter was good.* 很幸运，去年冬天的天气很好。

fortune /ˈfɔːtʃuːn/ *noun* 名词
1 *countable* 可数 a very large amount of money 大笔钱；巨款： *He made a fortune buying and selling houses.* 他通过买卖房屋挣了一大笔钱。
2 *uncountable* 不可数 luck 运气： *Patrick still can't believe his good fortune.* 帕特里克仍然无法相信他有这么好的运气。

forty /ˈfɔːti/
the number 40 四十
▶**fortieth** /ˈfɔːtiəθ/ *adjective* 形容词, *adverb* 副词： *It was the fortieth anniversary of his death.* 这是他逝世 40 周年的日子。

forward /ˈfɔːwəd/ *verb* 动词 (**forwards, forwarding, forwarded**)
to send a letter or an email to someone after you have received it 转发： *He asks each person to forward the email to 10 other people.* 他要求每个人都将这封电子邮件转发给另外 10 个人。

forwards /ˈfɔːwədz/ or 或 **forward** /ˈfɔːwəd/ *adverb* 副词
1 in a direction that is in front of you 向前： *He came forward and asked for help.* 他走向前来寻求帮助。 □ *She fell forwards on to her face.* 她脸朝地仆倒了。
2 in a position near the front of something 靠前： *Try to get a seat as far forwards as possible.* 找一个尽量靠前的座位。

forward slash *countable noun* 可数名词 (**forward slashes**)
the sloping line / that separates letters, words or numbers, for example in Internet addresses 斜线号；正斜杠

fossil /ˈfɒsəl/ *countable noun* 可数名词
the part of a plant or an animal that died a long time ago and has turned into rock 化石

fossil fuel *noun* 名词
a substance such as coal or oil that is found in the ground and used for producing power 化石燃料： *When we burn fossil fuels, we use oxygen and produce carbon dioxide.* 化石燃料燃烧时，消耗氧气，产生二氧化碳。

foster /ˈfɒstə/ *adjective* 形容词
used for describing someone who is paid by the government to take care of other people's children for a period of time 寄养的；代养的： *living with foster parents* 和养

父母生活在一起

fought /fɔːt/
→ see 见 **fight**

foul¹ /faʊl/ *adjective* 形容词 (**fouler, foulest**)
1 dirty, and smelling or tasting unpleasant 肮脏的；难闻的；难吃的： *foul, polluted water* 恶臭的脏水
2 offensive and containing rude words（言语）冒犯的，粗鲁的： *The play was full of foul language.* 这部剧满是脏话。

foul² /faʊl/ *countable noun* 可数名词
a move in a game or a sport that is not allowed according to the rules（比赛、体育运动中的）犯规： *He has committed more fouls than any other player this season.* 这个赛季他犯规的次数比其他选手都多。

found¹ /faʊnd/
→ see 见 **find**

found² /faʊnd/ *verb* 动词 (**founds, founding, founded**)
to start an organization 建立；成立： *The charity was founded in 1892.* 这个慈善机构成立于 1892 年。
▶**founder** /ˈfaʊndə/ *countable noun* 可数名词： *He was one of the founders of the United Nations.* 他是联合国的创始人之一。

foundation /faʊnˈdeɪʃən/ *noun* 名词
1 [**foundations**] *plural* 复数 the bricks, stones or concrete that a building is built on 地基： *the building's foundations* 这座楼的地基
2 *countable* 可数 an organization that provides money for a special purpose 基金会： *We applied for support from the National Foundation for Educational Research.* 我们申请国家教育研究基金会的支持。

fountain /ˈfaʊntɪn/ *countable noun* 可数名词
1 a structure in a pool or a lake where water is forced up into the air and falls down again 喷泉；喷水池
2 a piece of equipment that you can drink water from in a public place 饮水喷头

four /fɔː/
the number 4 四

fourteen /ˌfɔːˈtiːn/
the number 14 十四
▶**fourteenth** /ˌfɔːˈtiːnθ/ *adjective* 形容词, *adverb* 副词： *The festival is now in its fourteenth year.* 今年是这个艺术节举办的第 14 年了。

fourth /fɔːθ/ *adjective* 形容词, *adverb* 副词 the item in a series that you count as number four 第四： *Last year's winner is in fourth place in today's race.* 去年的冠军在今天的比赛中取得了第 4 名。

fowl /faʊl/ *countable noun* 可数名词 (**fowl**) a bird that can be eaten as food, such as a chicken 家禽

fox /fɒks/ *countable noun* 可数名词 (**foxes**) a wild animal that looks like a dog, has red fur and a thick tail 狐狸

fraction /ˈfrækʃən/ *countable noun* 可数名词
1 a part of a whole number. For example, 1/2 and 1/3 are both fractions. 分数
2 a very small amount of something 一点儿；少量： *She hesitated for a fraction of a second.* 她微微犹豫了一下。

fracture[1] /ˈfræktʃə/ *countable noun* 可数名词 a break in something, especially a bone 断裂；(尤指)骨折： *She suffered a hip fracture.* 她髋部骨折了。

fracture[2] /ˈfræktʃə/ *verb* 动词 (**fractures, fracturing, fractured**) to develop a crack or a break in a bone 使断裂；使骨折： *He fractured several of his ribs.* 他断了几根肋骨。

fragile /ˈfrædʒaɪl/ *adjective* 形容词 easily broken or damaged 脆弱的；易损坏的： *His fragile bones are the result of a bad diet.* 他骨头易脆是不良饮食造成的。

fragment /ˈfrægmənt/ *countable noun* 可数名词 a small piece of something 碎片： *We tried to pick up the tiny fragments of glass.* 我们试着捡起那些小玻璃碎片。

fragrance /ˈfreɪɡrəns/ *noun* 名词 a pleasant or sweet smell 香气；香味： *The cream is easy to apply and has a pleasant fragrance.* 这种乳霜容易涂抹，而且香味宜人。

frail /freɪl/ *adjective* 形容词 (**frailer, frailest**) not very strong or healthy 虚弱的；衰弱的： *He looked very frail in his hospital bed.* 他躺在医院的病床上，看上去很虚弱。

frame /freɪm/ *countable noun* 可数名词 the wood, metal or plastic around a picture (画作等的)边框： *She had a photograph of her mother in a silver frame.* 她有一张母亲的照片，镶着银色的边框。
● **frame** *verb* 动词 (**frames, framing, framed**)： *The picture has already been framed and hung on the wall.* 这幅画已经镶好框挂在墙上了。

framework /ˈfreɪmwɜːk/ *countable noun* 可数名词 a structure that forms a support for something 框架；构架： *The wooden shelves sit on a steel framework.* 木架子放在一个钢架上。

frank /fræŋk/ *adjective* 形容词 (**franker, frankest**) saying things in an open and honest way 坦白的；坦诚的： *My husband has not been frank with me.* 我丈夫没对我坦白。
▶ **frankly** /ˈfræŋkli/ *adverb* 副词： *You can talk frankly to me.* 你可以坦诚地跟我讲。

frankly /ˈfræŋkli/ *adverb* 副词 used when you are going to say something that may be surprising or direct 坦白说；坦率地说： *Frankly, this whole thing is getting boring.* 坦白说，这整件事越来越无聊了。

frantic /ˈfræntɪk/ *adjective* 形容词 very frightened or worried, and not knowing what to do 害怕的；忧虑的；慌乱的： *They became frantic when their 4-year-old son did not return.* 他们 4 岁的儿子没有回来，他们慌了。
▶ **frantically** /ˈfræntɪkli/ *adverb* 副词： *Two people were waving frantically from the boat.* 船上两个人疯狂地挥手。

fraud /frɔːd/ *noun* 名词 the crime of getting money by not telling the truth 诈骗；欺骗： *He was jailed for two years for fraud.* 他因诈骗罪入狱两年。

freak[1] /friːk/ *adjective* 形容词 very unusual 反常的；怪异的： *James broke his leg in a freak accident playing golf.* 詹姆斯打高尔夫球时离奇地发生意外，摔断了腿。

freak[2] /friːk/ *countable noun* 可数名词
1 an unfriendly word for someone whose behaviour or appearance is very different or unusual 怪ticky；怪人： *I'm not a freak — I'm just like you guys.* 我不是怪胎——我和你们这些人一样。
2 someone with a very strong interest in something (*informal* 非正式) (对某事物痴迷的)…狂： *a health freak* 保健狂

freckle /ˈfrekəl/ *countable noun* 可数名词 a small light-brown spot on your skin, especially on your face (尤指脸上的)雀斑： *He had short red hair and freckles.* 他一头红色的短发，脸上有雀斑。

free¹ /friː/ *adjective* 形容词 (**freer, freest**)
1 used for describing things that you do not have to pay for 免费的: *The classes are free, with lunch provided.* 这些课程不收费，而且提供午餐。
2 not controlled by rules or other people 自由的；不受约束的: *They are free to bring their friends home at any time.* 他们可以随时带朋友到家里来。
▶ **freely** /ˈfriːli/ *adverb* 副词: *They all express their opinions freely in class.* 他们都在课堂上自由发表意见。
3 used for describing someone who is not a prisoner (人身) 自由的；不受监禁的: *He walked from the court a free man.* 他以一个自由人的身份走出法庭。
4 not busy 空闲的；有空的: *She spent her free time shopping.* 她空闲时间用来逛街。
5 not being used by anyone 不在使用的；空着的: *Is this seat free?* 这个座位有人吗？

free² /friː/ *verb* 动词 (**frees, freeing, freed**)
to help someone or something to get out of a place 解救；使解脱: *Rescue workers freed him from the car.* 救援人员将他从车里解救了出来。

freedom /ˈfriːdəm/ *uncountable noun* 不可数名词
the state of being able to do what you want to do 自由: *They enjoy the freedom to spend their money as they wish.* 他们享受着随心所欲花钱的自由。 □ *We are fighting for freedom of choice.* 我们在争取选择自由。

freeze /friːz/ *verb* 动词 (**freezes, freezing, froze, frozen**)
1 to become solid because the temperature is low 冻结；结冰: *If the temperature drops below 0°C, water freezes.* 气温降到零摄氏度以下，水就会结冰。 □ *The ground froze solid.* 地面冻住了。
→ Look at picture on P6 参见彩插第 6 页
▶ **freezing** /ˈfriːzɪŋ/ *uncountable noun* 不可数名词: *The damage was caused by freezing and thawing.* 损坏是由冻融造成的。
2 to make food or drink very cold in order to preserve it 冷冻，冷藏 (食物、饮料)
3 to stand completely still 呆住；僵住: '*Freeze*,' *shouted the police officer.* "站住。" 警察喊道。

freezer /ˈfriːzə/ *countable noun* 可数名词
a large container or part of a fridge used for freezing food 冰柜；(冰箱的) 冷冻室

freezing /ˈfriːzɪŋ/ *adjective* 形容词
1 very cold 极冷的: *The cinema was freezing.* 影院里极冷。
2 feeling very cold (人) 感到极冷的: '*You must be freezing,*' *she said.* "你一定冻坏了。" 她说道。

freight /freɪt/ *uncountable noun* 不可数名词
goods that are moved by lorries, trains, ships or aeroplanes (货运) 货物: *a freight train* 货运火车

French fries /ˌfrentʃ ˈfraɪz/ *plural noun* 复数名词 (*American* 美国英语)
→ see 见 **chip**

French horn /ˌfrentʃ ˈhɔːn/ *noun* 名词
a musical instrument shaped like a long round metal tube with one wide end, that is played by blowing into it 法国号；圆号
→ Look at picture on P12 参见彩插第 12 页

frequency /ˈfriːkwənsi/ *noun* 名词 (**frequencies**)
1 *uncountable* 不可数 the number of times an event happens 频率 (特定时间段内发生的次数): *The frequency of Kara's phone calls increased.* 卡拉打电话更频繁了。
2 the number of times a sound wave or a radio wave vibrates (= moves quickly up and down) within a period of time (声波或无线电波的) 频率: *You can't hear waves of such a high frequency.* 这么高频率的声波是听不到的。

frequent /ˈfriːkwənt/ *adjective* 形容词
happening often 经常的；频繁的: *There are frequent trains from London to Paris.* 从伦敦到巴黎的列车来往频繁。
▶ **frequently** /ˈfriːkwəntli/ *adverb* 副词: *He was frequently unhappy.* 他经常不开心。

fresh /freʃ/ *adjective* 形容词 (**fresher, freshest**)
1 picked, caught or produced recently 新鲜的: *We only sell fresh fish that has been caught locally.* 我们只卖当地捕捞的鲜鱼。
2 done, made or experienced recently 新近的: *There were fresh car tracks in the snow.* 雪地里有新留下的车辙。
▶ **freshly** /ˈfreʃli/ *adverb* 副词: *We bought some freshly-baked bread.* 我们买了一些新出炉的面包。
3 used for describing something that smells, tastes or feels clean or cool 清新的；凉爽的: *The air was fresh and she immediately felt better.* 空气清新，她立即感觉好多了。

Friday – from

4 replacing or added to an existing thing or amount 替代的；外加的：*The waiter placed a fresh glass on the table.* 服务员在桌上重新放了一个杯子。

Friday /ˈfraɪdeɪ, -di/ *noun* 名词
the day after Thursday and before Saturday 星期五：*He is going home on Friday.* 他周五回家。 □ *Friday 6 November* *11 月 6 日，星期五

fridge /frɪdʒ/ or 或 **refrigerator** *countable noun* 可数名词
a large container that is kept cool inside, usually by electricity, so that the food and drink in it stays fresh 冰箱

friend¹ /frend/ *countable noun* 可数名词
someone who you like and know well 朋友：*She's my best friend.* 她是我最好的朋友。 □ *She was never a close friend of mine.* 她从来都不是我的密友。
be friends if you are friends with someone, you are their friend and they are yours（和某人）是朋友：*I still wanted to be friends with Alison.* 我依然想和艾莉森做朋友。 □ *We remained good friends.* 我们一直是好朋友。
make friends to meet someone and become their friend 交朋友：*He has made friends with the kids on the street.* 他跟街头的孩子成了朋友。 □ *Dennis made friends easily.* 丹尼斯很容易就能交到朋友。

friend² /frend/ *verb* 动词 (**friends, friending, friended**)
to ask someone to be your friend on a social media website, so you can see each other's posts（社交网络上）加⋯为好友：*Never friend people you don't know.* 不要加不认识的人为好友。

friendly /ˈfrendli/ *adjective* 形容词 (**friendlier, friendliest**)
behaving in a pleasant, kind way 友好的；友善的：*Godfrey was friendly to me.* 戈弗雷对我很友好。 □ *The man had a pleasant, friendly face.* 这个男人面容和蔼可亲。

friendship /ˈfrendʃɪp/ *noun* 名词
a relationship between two or more friends 友谊；友情：*Their friendship has lasted more than sixty years.* 他们的友谊持续了 60 多年。

fries /fraɪz/ *plural noun* 复数名词 (*American* 美国英语)
→ see 见 **chip**

fright /fraɪt/ *noun* 名词
1 *uncountable* 不可数 a sudden feeling of fear 惊骇；恐惧：*There was a loud noise, and Franklin jumped with fright.* 一声巨响，富兰克林吓得跳了起来。
2 *countable* 可数 an experience that makes you suddenly afraid 惊吓；恐怖的经历：*The snake raised its head, which gave everyone a fright.* 那条蛇昂起头来，大家都吓了一跳。

frighten /ˈfraɪtən/ *verb* 动词 (**frightens, frightening, frightened**)
to make you suddenly feel afraid, anxious or nervous 使惊恐；使害怕：*He knew that Soli was trying to frighten him.* 他知道索利在吓唬他。

frightened /ˈfraɪtənd/ *adjective* 形容词
anxious or afraid 受惊的；害怕的：*She was frightened of making a mistake.* 她害怕犯错。
→ Look at picture on P15 参见彩插第 15 页

frightening /ˈfraɪtənɪŋ/ *adjective* 形容词
making you feel afraid, anxious or nervous 令人害怕的；骇人的：*It was a very frightening experience.* 这是一次极为恐怖的经历。

frill /frɪl/ *countable noun* 可数名词
a long narrow strip of cloth or paper with a lot of folds in it, used as a decoration 褶边；饰边：*She loves party dresses with ribbons and frills.* 她喜欢带丝带和褶边的宴会礼服。

fringe /frɪndʒ/ *countable noun* 可数名词
1 (*American* 美国英语：**bangs**) hair which is cut so that it hangs over your forehead 刘海：*a short fringe* 短刘海
2 a row of hanging threads that is used for decorating a piece of cloth 穗；流苏：*The jacket had leather fringes on the sleeves.* 这件夹克的袖子上有皮革流苏。

frog /frɒg/ *countable noun* 可数名词
a small animal with smooth skin, big eyes and long back legs that it uses for jumping. Frogs live in or near water. 蛙

from /frəm, STRONG 强读 frɒm/ *preposition* 介词
1 used for saying who has sent or given something to you 出自；得自：*I received a letter from Mary yesterday.* 昨天我收到了玛丽的来信。 □ *The watch was a present from his wife.* 这块手表是妻子送给他的礼物。
2 used for saying where someone lives or was born（人）来自：*I come from New*

Zealand. 我来自新西兰。

3 leaving a place 离开: *Everyone watched as she ran from the room.* 大家看着她从房间里跑了出去。 ▫ *Mr Baker travelled from Washington to London for the meeting.* 贝克先生从华盛顿到伦敦参加会议。

4 used when you are talking about how far away something is (表示距离) 离: *The park is only a hundred yards from the centre of town.* 公园离市中心仅有 100 码远。 ▫ *How far is the hotel from here?* 这儿离酒店有多远?

5 used for saying what was used for making something (表示原料) 由: *This bread is made from white flour.* 这种面包是用白面粉做的。 ▫ *The cans are made from steel.* 这些罐子是铁的。

6 used for saying that something stops being the first thing and becomes the second thing (表示变化) 从…(变成…): *Unemployment fell from 7.5 to 7.2%.* 失业率从 7.5% 降到了 7.2%。

7 used for talking about the beginning of a period of time (表示时间) 从, 自: *Breakfast is available from 6 a.m.* 早餐 6 点开始供应。

front¹ /frʌnt/ *countable noun* 可数名词
the part of something that faces you, or that is nearest the direction it faces 前部; 前面: *Stand at the front of the queue.* 站到队伍前面。 ▫ *Children under the age of three may not sit in the front of the car.* 3 岁以下儿童不得坐在汽车前座。

in front
1 ahead of others in a moving group 在前面: *Don't drive too close to the car in front.* 不要和前车靠得太近。
2 winning a competition 领先: *Richard Dunwoody is in front in the race.* 理查德•邓伍迪在比赛中领先。

in front of someone when someone is present 在某人面前: *They never argued in front of their children.* 他们从来不在孩子面前吵架。

in front of something facing a particular thing, ahead of it or close to the front part of it 在某物前面: *She sat down in front of her mirror.* 她在镜子前坐了下来。 ▫ *A child ran in front of my car.* 一个小孩跑到了我的车前。

front² /frʌnt/ *adjective* 形容词
in or on the front of something 前面的; 前部的: *Helen came to the front door.* 海伦来到门前。 ▫ *I've broken my front tooth.* 我的门牙断了。

frontier /ˈfrʌntɪə, frʌnˈtɪə/ *countable noun* 可数名词
the border between two countries 国界; 边境: *They showed their passports at the Russian frontier.* 他们在俄罗斯边境出示了护照。

frost /frɒst/ *uncountable noun* 不可数名词
ice like white powder that forms outside when the weather is very cold 霜: *There was frost on my windscreen this morning.* 今早我的挡风玻璃上有霜。
▶ **frosty** /ˈfrɒsti/ (**frostier, frostiest**) *adjective* 形容词: *a cold and frosty night* 一个下了霜的寒冷夜晚

frown /fraʊn/ *verb* 动词 (**frowns, frowning, frowned**)
to move your eyebrows together because you are annoyed, worried or confused, or because you are concentrating 皱眉: *Nancy shook her head, frowning.* 南希皱着眉摇了摇头。 ▫ *He frowned at her anxiously.* 他不安地朝她皱了皱眉头。 ● **frown** *countable noun* 可数名词: *There was a deep frown on the boy's face.* 男孩眉头紧锁。

frown 皱眉

froze /froʊz/
→ see 见 **freeze**

frozen¹ /ˈfroʊzən/
→ see 见 **freeze**

frozen² /ˈfroʊzən/ *adjective* 形容词
1 hard because the weather is very cold 冻硬的: *It was extremely cold and the ground was frozen hard.* 天气极冷, 地面都冻硬了。
2 used for describing food that has been stored at a very low temperature (食物) 冷冻的, 冷藏的: *Frozen fish is a healthy convenience food.* 冷冻鱼是一种健康的方便食品。
3 very cold (人) 冻坏的, 冻僵的: *I'm frozen out here.* 我在这儿都冻僵了。

fruit /fruːt/ *noun* 名词 (**fruit**)

LANGUAGE HELP 语言提示
If you are talking about different types of fruit, you can refer to these as **fruits**. 表示不同种类的水果, 可以用 fruits。

the part of a tree or plant that contains seeds, covered with a substance that you can often eat 水果；果实: *Fresh fruit and vegetables provide fibre and vitamins.* 新鲜蔬果含纤维和维生素。 □ *We grow bananas and other tropical fruits here.* 我们在这里种植香蕉及其他热带水果。

frustrate /frʌˈstreɪt/ *verb* 动词 (**frustrates, frustrating, frustrated**)
to upset someone or make them angry because there is nothing they can do about a problem 使沮丧；使懊恼: *His lack of ambition frustrated me.* 他缺乏雄心壮志，这让我很恼火。
▶ **frustrated** /frʌˈstreɪtɪd/ *adjective* 形容词: *Roberta felt frustrated and angry.* 罗伯塔感到沮丧和愤怒。
▶ **frustrating** /frʌˈstreɪtɪŋ/ *adjective* 形容词: *This situation is very frustrating for us.* 这种形势令我们很沮丧。
▶ **frustration** /frʌˈstreɪʃən/ *uncountable noun* 不可数名词: *The team was showing signs of frustration.* 这支队伍露出受挫的迹象。

fry /fraɪ/ *verb* 动词 (**fries, frying, fried**)
to cook food in hot fat or oil 油煎；油炸: *Fry the onions until they are brown.* 把洋葱煎至呈褐色。

ˈfrying ˌpan *countable noun* 可数名词
a flat metal pan with a long handle, in which you fry food 长柄平底锅

fuel /ˈfjuːəl/ *noun* 名词
a substance such as coal or oil that is burned to provide heat or power 燃料: *They bought some fuel on the motorway.* 他们在高速公路上加了些油。

fulfil /fʊlˈfɪl/ *verb* 动词 (**fulfils, fulfilling, fulfilled**)
to manage to do what you said or hoped you would do 实现（诺言、希望等）: *She fulfilled her dream of starting law school.* 她实现了读法学院的梦想。

full /fʊl/ *adjective* 形容词 (**fuller, fullest**)
1 containing as much liquid or as many people or things as possible 满的；装满的: *The petrol tank was full.* 油箱是满的。 □ *Her case was full of clothes.* 她的箱子里装满了衣服。 □ *Sorry. The bus is full. You'll have to get the next one.* 抱歉，这辆公交车已满。你得坐下一辆了。
2 feeling that you do not want any more food 吃饱的: *You should stop eating when you're full.* 饱了就不要再吃了。
3 complete, with nothing missing 完全的；完整的: *For full details of the event, visit our website.* 欲了解活动详情，请访问我们的网站。
4 used when you are saying that something is as big, loud, strong, fast, etc. as possible 最大（强度）的；最大量的: *The car crashed into the wall at full speed.* 汽车以全速撞到墙上。
a full moon when the moon looks like a complete circle 满月；圆月
full name your first name, other names that you may have and your family name 全名；全称: *'May I have your full name?' — 'Yes, it's Patricia Mary White.'* "能告诉我你的全名吗？"——"好的，帕特里夏·玛丽·怀特。"
in full completely, giving every detail 完整地；全面地: *Mr Thompson signed his name in full.* 汤普森先生签了全名。

ˌfull ˈstop *countable noun* 可数名词 (*American* 美国英语: **period**)
the mark (.) used in writing at the end of a sentence when it is not a question or an exclamation 句号；句点

ˌfull-ˈtime also 亦作 **full time** *adjective* 形容词
for all of each normal working week 全职的；专职的: *I'm looking for a full-time job.* 我在找一份全职工作。● **full-time** *adverb* 副词: *Deirdre works full time.* 戴尔德丽做全职工作。

fully /ˈfʊli/ *adverb* 副词
completely 完全地；彻底地: *We are fully aware of the problem.* 我们充分意识到了这个问题。 □ *He promised to answer fully and truthfully.* 他答应会全面如实作答。

fun[1] /fʌn/ *uncountable noun* 不可数名词
pleasure and enjoyment 趣事；乐趣: *It could be fun to watch them.* 看他们会很有趣。 □ *Liz was always so much fun.* 利兹总是那么有趣。
for fun as a joke, without wanting to cause any harm 为了好玩: *Don't say such things, even for fun.* 即使是闹着玩，也不能说这种话。
make fun of someone/something to laugh at someone or something, or make jokes about them 嘲弄某人／某物；拿某人／某物开玩笑: *Don't make fun of me.* 别拿我开玩笑。

fun² /fʌn/ *adjective* 形容词
pleasant and enjoyable 令人开心的；令人愉悦的: *The course is interesting and it's also fun.* 这门课程很有趣，也很好玩儿。

function¹ /ˈfʌŋkʃən/ *countable noun* 可数名词
1 the purpose of a thing or a person（事物的）功能；（人的）职责: *One of the main functions of the skin is protection.* 皮肤的主要功能之一就是起保护作用。
2 a large formal dinner or party 宴会；大型聚会: *He attended a private function hosted by one of his students.* 他参加了由他的一个学生组织的私人聚会。

function² /ˈfʌŋkʃən/ *verb* 动词 (functions, functioning, functioned)
to work well 起作用；正常运转: *Your heart is functioning normally.* 你的心脏功能正常。

functional /ˈfʌŋkʃənəl/ *adjective* 形容词
1 useful rather than decorative 实用的: *I like modern, functional furniture.* 我喜欢现代、实用的家具。
2 working properly 运转正常的: *We have fully functional smoke alarms on all staircases.* 我们在各层的楼梯都安装了运转完全正常的烟雾报警器。

fund¹ /fʌnd/ *noun* 名词
1 [funds] *plural* 复数 amounts of money that are available to be spent 资金: *We're having a concert to raise funds for cancer research.* 我们要举办一场音乐会，为癌症研究筹集资金。
2 *countable* 可数 an amount of money that people save for a particular purpose 基金；专款: *There is a scholarship fund for engineering students.* 有一个为工程学专业学生服务的奖学金基金。

fund² /fʌnd/ *verb* 动词 (funds, funding, funded)
to provide money for something 为…提供资金: *The Foundation has funded a variety of projects.* 这个基金会已经资助了各种各样的项目。

fundamental /ˌfʌndəˈmentəl/ *adjective* 形容词
very important and necessary 重要的；不可或缺的；基本的: *We all have a fundamental right to protect ourselves.* 我们都有保护自己的基本权利。

funding /ˈfʌndɪŋ/ *uncountable noun* 不可数名词
money that a government or organization provides for a particular purpose（政府或机构为特定目的提供的）资金，款项: *They are hoping to get government funding for the programme.* 他们希望政府给这个项目拨款。

ˈfund-raising also 亦作 **fundraising** *uncountable noun* 不可数名词
the activity of collecting money for a particular use 募捐；筹款

funeral /ˈfjuːnərəl/ *countable noun* 可数名词
a ceremony that takes place when the body of someone who has died is buried or cremated (= burned) 葬礼: *The funeral will be in Edinburgh.* 葬礼将在爱丁堡举行。

fungus /ˈfʌŋɡəs/ *noun* 名词 (fungi /ˈfʌŋɡiː, ˈfʌndʒaɪ/ or 或 funguses)
a plant that has no flowers, leaves or green colour, and grows in wet places 真菌: *There were mushrooms and other fungi growing out of the wall.* 墙上长出了蘑菇和其他真菌。 □ *This fungus likes living in warm, wet places.* 这种真菌喜欢生长在温暖、潮湿的地方。

funnel /ˈfʌnəl/ *countable noun* 可数名词
1 a tube with a wide, round top, used for pouring liquids into a container such as a bottle 漏斗
2 a tube on the top of a ship or railway engine where steam can escape（轮船或蒸汽机车上的）烟囱

funny /ˈfʌni/ *adjective* 形容词 (funnier, funniest)
1 amusing and likely to make you smile or laugh 有趣的；令人发笑的: *I'll tell you a funny story.* 我给你讲一个好玩的故事。
2 strange, surprising or confusing 古怪的；奇怪的；令人困惑的: *Children get some very funny ideas sometimes!* 小孩子的想法有时候真是稀奇古怪！ □ *There's something funny about him.* 他有点儿古怪。
3 slightly ill (*informal* 非正式) 不适的；微恙的: *My head began to ache and my stomach felt funny.* 我开始头疼，胃也有点不适。

fur /fɜː/ *uncountable noun* 不可数名词
the thick hair that grows on the bodies of many animals（许多动物身上的）软毛: *This creature's fur is short and silky.* 这种动物的毛短而柔滑。

furious /ˈfjʊəriəs/ *adjective* 形容词
extremely angry 暴怒的: *He is furious at the way he has been treated.* 他受到的待遇令他大为光火。

furnace /ˈfɜːnɪs/ *countable noun* 可数名词
a container with a very hot fire inside it, used for making glass or heating metal 火炉；熔炉: *The iron bars glow in the red-hot furnace.* 铁条在炽热的熔炉里发着光。

furniture /ˈfɜːnɪtʃə/ *uncountable noun* 不可数名词
large objects such as tables, chairs or beds 家具: *Each piece of furniture matched the style of the house.* 每一件家具都和房子的风格很相配。

> **LANGUAGE HELP** 语言提示
> **Furniture** is an uncountable noun. If you want to talk about a table, a chair, or a bed in general terms, you can say a **piece of furniture** or an **item of furniture**.
> *furniture 是不可数名词。泛指一件家具可用 a piece of furniture 或 an item of furniture。

furry /ˈfɜːri/ *adjective* 形容词 (**furrier, furriest**)
1 covered with thick, soft hair 毛茸茸的: *I love little furry animals.* 我喜欢毛茸茸的小动物。
2 feeling similar to fur 软毛般的: *The leaves are soft and furry.* 这些叶子软软的、毛茸茸的。

further /ˈfɜːðə/
→ see 见 **far**

furthest /ˈfɜːðɪst/
→ see 见 **far**

fury /ˈfjʊəri/ *uncountable noun* 不可数名词
violent or very strong anger 狂怒；暴怒: *Her eyes were full of fury.* 她的眼睛里满是怒火。

fuse /fjuːz/ *countable noun* 可数名词
a small wire in a piece of electrical equipment that stops it from working when too much electricity passes through it (电器中的)保险丝: *The fuse blew as he pressed the button to start the motor.* 他按下按钮启动马达时保险丝烧断了。

fuss¹ /fʌs/ *singular noun* 单数名词
anxious or excited behaviour that is not useful 慌乱；大惊小怪: *I don't know what all the fuss is about.* 我不知道为什么要这样大惊小怪的。

fuss² /fʌs/ *verb* 动词 (**fusses, fussing, fussed**)
to worry or behave in a nervous, anxious way about things that are not important 慌乱；大惊小怪: *Carol fussed about getting me a drink.* 卡罗尔手忙脚乱地要给我弄一杯喝的。
fuss over someone to pay someone a lot of attention and do things to make them happy or comfortable 对某人关爱备至: *Aunt Laura fussed over him all afternoon.* 劳拉姑妈一整个下午都对他宠爱有加。

fussy /ˈfʌsi/ *adjective* 形容词 (**fussier, fussiest**)
very difficult to please and interested in small details 挑剔的；爱计较的: *She is very fussy about her food.* 她非常挑食。

future¹ /ˈfjuːtʃə/ *noun* 名词
1 singular 单数 the time that will come after now 将来；未来: *He was making plans for the future.* 他在为未来制订计划。
2 countable 可数 what will happen to someone after the present time 前途；前景: *His future depends on the result of the election.* 他的前途取决于这次选举结果。
in (the) future used when you are talking about what will happen after now 今后: *I asked her to be more careful in the future.* 我要求她今后要更加谨慎。

future² /ˈfjuːtʃə/ *adjective* 形容词
happening or existing after the present time 未来的；将来的: *The lives of future generations will be affected by our decisions.* 我们的决定将会影响后代的生活。

future tense *countable noun* 可数名词
the form of the verb that is used for talking about the time that will come after the present (动词的)将来式

Gg

gadget /ˈgædʒɪt/ *countable noun* 可数名词
a small machine or useful object 小器具: *The shop sells computers and other electronic gadgets.* 店里出售电脑和其他小电子产品。

gain /geɪn/ *verb* 动词 (gains, gaining, gained)
1 to get something 获得；得到: *You can gain access to the website for £14 a month.* 每月支付 14 英镑便可登录该网站。□ *Students can gain valuable experience by working during their holidays.* 学生在假期工作可以获得宝贵的经验。
2 to have more of something 增加；使增长: *Some women gain weight after they have a baby.* 一些女性生了宝宝后体重会增加。□ *The car was gaining speed as it came toward us.* 汽车朝我们驶来时正在加速。

galaxy /ˈgæləksi/ *countable noun* 可数名词 (galaxies)
a very large group of stars and planets 星系: *Astronomers have discovered a distant galaxy.* 天文学家发现了一个遥远的星系。

gale /geɪl/ *countable noun* 可数名词
a very strong wind 大风: *A strong gale was blowing.* 狂风大作。

gallery /ˈgæləri/ *countable noun* 可数名词 (galleries)
a place where people go to look at art 美术馆；画廊: *We visited an art gallery.* 我们参观了一家美术馆。

gallon /ˈgælən/ *countable noun* 可数名词
a unit for measuring liquids. There are eight pints in a gallon. In Britain, it is equal to around 4.546 litres, whereas in America, it is equal to around 3.785 liters. 加仑（液量单位，1 加仑 = 8 品脱，1 英制加仑 ≈ 4.546 升，1 美制加仑 ≈ 3.785 升): *The tank holds 1,000 gallons of water.* 罐里能装下 1,000 加仑水。

gallop /ˈgæləp/ *verb* 动词 (gallops, galloping, galloped)
to run very fast 奔腾；飞奔: *The horses galloped away.* 马儿奔腾而去。

gallop 奔腾

gamble¹ /ˈgæmbəl/ *countable noun* 可数名词
a risk that you take because you hope that something good will happen 冒险: *She took a gamble and started up her own business.* 她放手一搏，创办了自己的公司。

gamble² /ˈgæmbəl/ *verb* 动词 (gambles, gambling, gambled)
1 to take a risk because you hope that something good will happen 冒险；碰运气: *Companies sometimes have to gamble on new products.* 公司有时候不得不拿新产品赌一把。
2 to risk money in a game or on the result of a race or competition 赌博: *John gambled heavily on horse racing.* 约翰沉迷于赌马。
▶ **gambling** /ˈgæmblɪŋ/ *uncountable noun* 不可数名词: *The gambling laws are quite tough.* 和赌博相关的法律非常严厉。

gambler /ˈgæmblə/ *countable noun* 可数名词
someone who risks money regularly, for example in card games or horse racing 赌徒: *Her father was a heavy gambler.* 她父亲嗜赌如命。

game /geɪm/ *countable noun* 可数名词
1 an activity or a sport in which you try to win 游戏；运动；比赛: *Football is a popular game.* 足球是一项很受欢迎的运动。□ *We played a game of cards.* 我们打牌了。
2 one particular occasion when you play a game（游戏、比赛等的）局，盘，场: *It was the first game of the season.* 这是本赛季第一场比赛。

¹game ˌconsole or 或 **¹games ˌconsole** countable noun 可数名词
a piece of electronic equipment that is used for playing computer games on a television screen 游戏机: *More than half of six- to ten-year-olds have a games console.* *6 到 10 岁的孩子中，一半以上都有一台游戏机。
→ Look at picture on P11 参见彩插第 11 页

gang /ɡæŋ/ countable noun 可数名词
1 a group of people, especially young people, who go around together and often deliberately cause trouble（尤指青年）团伙: *They had a fight with another gang.* 他们和另一个团伙打了一架。
2 an organized group of criminals 犯罪团伙: *Police are hunting for a gang that has stolen several cars.* 警方正在追捕一个盗窃多辆汽车的犯罪团伙。

gap /ɡæp/ countable noun 可数名词
a space between two things, or a hole in something 缝隙；缺口: *There was a narrow gap between the curtains.* 窗帘之间有一条窄缝。□ *His horse escaped through a gap in the fence.* 他的马从围栏的缺口处跑掉了。

garage /ˈɡærɑːʒ, -rɪdʒ/ countable noun 可数名词
1 a building where you keep a car 车库；停车房: *The house has a large garage.* 这所房子有一个很大的车库。
2 a place where you can have your car repaired, and sometimes buy petrol and oil 汽车修理厂（有时兼营加油业务）: *Nancy took her car to a local garage.* 南希把车开到当地一家汽车修理厂。

garbage /ˈɡɑːbɪdʒ/ uncountable noun 不可数名词 (*American* 美国英语)
→ see 见 **rubbish**

¹garbage ˌcan countable noun 可数名词 (*American* 美国英语)
→ see 见 **dustbin**

garden¹ /ˈɡɑːdən/ noun 名词
1 (*American* 美国英语: **yard**) countable 可数 the part of the land by your house where you grow flowers and vegetables（住宅旁的）花园，菜园，园子: *She had a beautiful garden.* 她有一个美丽的花园。
2 [**gardens**] plural 复数 places with plants, trees and grass, that people can visit 公园: *The gardens are open from 10.30 a.m. until 5.00 p.m.* 公园开放时间为上午 10 点半到下午 5 点。

garden² /ˈɡɑːdən/ verb 动词 (**gardens, gardening, gardened**)
to do work in your garden 做园艺工作: *Jim gardened at the weekends.* 吉姆周末打理庭园。
▶ **gardening** /ˈɡɑːdənɪŋ/ uncountable noun 不可数名词: *My favourite hobby is gardening.* 我最大的爱好就是做园艺活儿。

gardener /ˈɡɑːdnə/ countable noun 可数名词
a person who works in a garden 园丁；花匠: *She employed a gardener.* 她雇了一名园艺工人。

garlic /ˈɡɑːlɪk/ uncountable noun 不可数名词
a plant like a small onion with a strong flavour, which you use in cooking 蒜；大蒜: *When the oil is hot, add a clove of garlic.* 油热后，加入一瓣蒜。

garment /ˈɡɑːmənt/ countable noun 可数名词
a piece of clothing（一件）衣服: *Exports of garments to the U.S. fell by 3%.* 对美国的服装出口额下降了 3%。

gas /ɡæs/ noun 名词 (**gases**)
1 any substance that is not a liquid or a solid 气体: *Hydrogen is a gas, not a metal.* 氢是一种气体，不是金属。
→ Look at picture on P6 参见彩插第 6 页
2 uncountable 不可数 a substance with a strong smell that is used for producing heat and for cooking 燃气；天然气；煤气: *a gas fire* 燃气采暖炉
3 uncountable 不可数 (*American* 美国英语) → see 见 **petrol**

gasoline /ˈɡæsəliːn/ uncountable noun 不可数名词 (*American* 美国英语)
→ see 见 **petrol**

gasp /ɡɑːsp/ verb 动词 (**gasps, gasping, gasped**)
to take a short, quick breath through your mouth 急喘气；喘息: *She gasped for air.* 她大口喘着气。● **gasp** countable noun 可数名词: *There was a gasp from the crowd as he scored the goal.* 他进球得分后，人群中传来一声惊呼。

gate /ɡeɪt/ countable noun 可数名词
1 a structure like a door that you use to enter a field, or the area around a building（田地或庭院的）大门: *He opened the gate and walked up to the house.* 他打开院门朝房子走去。
2 a place where passengers leave an airport and get on an aeroplane 登机门；

登机口: Please go to gate 15. 请到 15 号登机口。

gather /ˈɡæðə/ *verb* 动词 (**gathers, gathering, gathered**)
1 to come together in a group 聚集；集合: *We gathered around the fireplace and talked.* 我们聚在壁炉边聊天。
2 to collect things together so that you can use them 收集；收拢: *They gathered enough firewood to make a fire.* 他们捡了足够多的木柴来生火。□ *He used a hidden microphone to gather information.* 他用窃听器来搜集信息。

gathering /ˈɡæðərɪŋ/ *countable noun* 可数名词
an occasion when people meet together for a particular purpose 聚会；集会: *They held a large family gathering.* 他们举办了一次大型家庭聚会。

gauge^1 /ɡeɪdʒ/ *verb* 动词 (**gauges, gauging, gauged**)
to measure or judge something 测量；判断: *She found it hard to gauge his mood.* 她发现他的情绪很难揣摩。

gauge^2 /ɡeɪdʒ/ *countable noun* 可数名词
a piece of equipment that measures the amount or level of something 测量仪器；计量仪: *The temperature gauge showed that the water was boiling.* 温度计显示水在沸腾。

gave /ɡeɪv/
→ see 见 **give**

gay /ɡeɪ/ *adjective* 形容词
attracted to people of the same sex 同性恋的: *The quality of life for gay men has improved.* 男同性恋的生活质量有了改善。

gaze /ɡeɪz/ *verb* 动词 (**gazes, gazing, gazed**)
to look steadily at someone or something for a long time 凝视；盯着看: *She was gazing at herself in the mirror.* 她凝视着镜中的自己。□ *He gazed into the fire.* 他凝视着炉火。

gear /ɡɪə/ *noun* 名词
1 *countable* 可数 a part of an engine that changes engine power into movement 传动装置；排挡: *On a hill, use low gears.* 在山上挂低挡。□ *The car was in fourth gear.* 车挂的是 4 挡。
2 *uncountable* 不可数 the equipment or special clothing that you use for a particular activity (某项活动的)装备: *He took his fishing gear with him.* 他带上他的钓鱼装备。□ *camping gear* 露营装备

ˈgear ˌstick *countable noun* 可数名词
the handle that you use to change gear in a car or other vehicle 变速杆；换挡杆

geese /ɡiːs/
the plural of **goose** (goose 的复数形式)

gel /dʒel/ *uncountable noun* 不可数名词
a thick substance like jelly, especially one that you use to keep your hair in a particular style or for washing your body 凝胶；(尤指)发胶，沐浴露: *shower gel* 沐浴露

gem /dʒem/ *countable noun* 可数名词
a valuable stone that is used in jewellery 宝石: *precious gems* 名贵的宝石

gender /ˈdʒendə/ *noun* 名词
the fact of being male or female 性别: *We do not know the children's ages and genders.* 我们不知道孩子们的年龄和性别。

gene /dʒiːn/ *countable noun* 可数名词
the part of a cell that controls a person's, an animal's or a plant's physical characteristics, growth and development 基因: *He carries the gene for red hair.* 他携带红发基因。

general^1 /ˈdʒenrəl/ *adjective* 形容词
involving most people and things 普遍的；一般的: *There is not enough general understanding of this problem.* 人们对这个问题的了解不够普遍。
in general used for talking about something as a whole, rather than part of it 整体上；总的来说: *We need to improve our educational system in general.* 我们需要从整体上改进我们的教育体系。

general^2 /ˈdʒenrəl/ *countable noun* 可数名词
an officer with a high rank in the army (陆军)将军: *The troops received a visit from the general.* 将军对部队进行了视察。

ˌgeneral eˈlection *countable noun* 可数名词
a time when people choose a new government 大选；普选

generalize /ˈdʒenrəˌlaɪz/ *verb* 动词 (**generalizes, generalizing, generalized**)
to say something that is usually, but not always, true 概括；归纳: *You shouldn't generalize and say that all men are the same.* 你不该一概而论, 说所有男人都一样。

generally /ˈdʒenrəli/ *adverb* 副词
1 used for describing something without

giving any particular details 大体上: *He was generally a good man.* 他总的来说是个好人。
2 used for saying that something usually happens, but not always 通常；一般: *It is generally believed that darker fruits contain more iron.* 大家普遍认为颜色较深的水果含铁量较高。

general practitioner /ˌdʒenrəl prækˈtɪʃənə/ *countable noun* 可数名词
→ see 见 **GP**

generate /ˈdʒenəˌreɪt/ *verb* 动词 (**generates, generating, generated**)
1 to cause something to exist 引起；导致: *The reforms will generate new jobs.* 改革会带来新的就业机会。
2 to produce a form of energy or power 产生（能量）；发（电）: *We use oil to generate electricity.* 我们利用石油发电。

generation /ˌdʒenəˈreɪʃən/ *countable noun* 可数名词
all the people in a group or country who are of a similar age 一代人；一辈人: *The current generation of teens are the richest in history.* 现在的青少年比以往任何时候都要有钱。

generator /ˈdʒenəˌreɪtə/ *countable noun* 可数名词
a machine that produces electricity 发电机: *The house has its own power generators.* 房子有自用发电机。

generous /ˈdʒenərəs/ *adjective* 形容词
giving you more than you expect of something 慷慨的；大方的: *He is generous with his money.* 他出手阔绰。
▶ **generosity** /ˌdʒenəˈrɒsɪti/ *uncountable noun* 不可数名词: *Diana was surprised by his kindness and generosity.* 他的善良和慷慨让黛安娜惊讶。
▶ **generously** /ˈdʒenərəsli/ *adverb* 副词: *We would like to thank everyone who generously gave their time.* 我们要向每位慷慨付出自己时间的人表示感谢。

genetic /dʒɪˈnetɪk/ *adjective* 形容词
related to genetics or genes 遗传学的；基因的: *a rare genetic disease* 罕见的基因疾病

genetically modified /dʒɪˌnetɪkli ˈmɒdɪfaɪd/ *adjective* 形容词
used for describing plants and animals that have had their genetic structure (= pattern of chemicals in cells) changed in order to make them more suitable for a particular purpose. The short form **GM** is also used. 转基因的 (缩写形式为 GM)

genetics /dʒɪˈnetɪks/ *uncountable noun* 不可数名词
the study of how qualities are passed on from parents to children 遗传学: *Genetics is changing our understanding of cancer.* 遗传学正改变我们对癌症的认识。

genius /ˈdʒiːniəs/ *countable noun* 可数名词 (**geniuses**)
a very skilled or intelligent person 天才: *Chaplin was a comic genius.* 卓别林是喜剧天才。

gentle /ˈdʒentəl/ *adjective* 形容词 (**gentler, gentlest**)
1 kind, mild and calm 温和的；和蔼的: *My husband was a quiet and gentle man.* 我丈夫是个文静而温和的人。
▶ **gently** /ˈdʒentli/ *adverb* 副词: *She smiled gently at him.* 她温柔地冲他微笑。
2 slow or soft 徐缓的；轻柔的: *Rest and gentle exercise will make you feel better.* 休息以及舒缓的运动会让你感到更舒适。
▶ **gently** /ˈdʒentli/ *adverb* 副词: *Patrick took her gently by the arm.* 帕特里克轻轻地挽着她的手臂。

gentleman /ˈdʒentəlmən/ *countable noun* 可数名词 (**gentlemen** /ˈdʒentəlmen/)
1 a man who is polite, educated and kind to other people 绅士；有教养的人: *He was always such a gentleman.* 他总是如此彬彬有礼。
2 used for talking to men or for talking about them in a polite way (对男性的礼貌称呼) 先生: *This way, please, ladies and gentlemen.* 女士们、先生们，这边请。

the gents /ðə ˈdʒents/ *singular noun* 单数名词
a public toilet for men (*informal* 非正式) 男厕所: *Excuse me, can you tell me where the gents is, please?* 请问男厕所在哪里？

genuine /ˈdʒenjuɪn/ *adjective* 形容词
true and real 真正的；真实的: *He's a genuine American hero.* 他是真正的美国英雄。 □ *We have a genuine friendship.* 我们拥有真挚的友谊。

genus /ˈdʒenəs/ *countable noun* 可数名词 (**genera** /ˈdʒenərə/)
a type of animal or plant (动植物的) 属: *a genus of plants called 'Lonas'* 名为"黄蓍香"的一属植物

geography /dʒiˈɒgrəfi/ *uncountable noun* 不可数名词
the study of the countries of the world and things such as the land, seas, weather, towns, and population 地理学
→ Look at pictures on PP7-9 参见彩插第 7 页至第 9 页

geology /dʒiˈɒlədʒi/ *uncountable noun* 不可数名词
the study of the Earth's structure, surface and origins 地质学: *He was professor of geology at the University of Georgia.* 他是佐治亚大学地质学教授。
▶ **geologist** /dʒiˈɒlədʒɪst/ *countable noun* 可数名词: *Geologists have studied the way that heat flows from the Earth.* 地质学家已经研究过地球如何散热。

geometry /dʒiˈɒmɪtri/ *uncountable noun* 不可数名词
a type of mathematics relating to lines, angles, curves and shapes 几何(学): *They're studying basic geometry.* 他们正在学习基础几何学。

germ /dʒɜːm/ *countable noun* 可数名词
a very small living thing that can cause disease or illness 细菌; 病菌: *This chemical is used for killing germs.* 这种化学品用于杀菌。

gesture /ˈdʒestʃə/ *countable noun* 可数名词
a movement that you make with a part of your body, especially your hands, to express emotion or information 示意动作; (尤指)手势: *Sarah made a gesture with her fist.* 萨拉挥拳示意。● **gesture** *verb* 动词 (**gestures, gesturing, gestured**): *I gestured toward the house.* 我朝那房子示意。

get[1] /get/ *auxiliary verb* 助动词 (**gets, got**)
used with another verb to show that something happens to someone (*informal* 非正式) (与另一动词连用) 被: *He got arrested for possession of drugs.* 他因持有毒品被捕。

get[2] /get/ *verb* 动词 (**gets, getting, got, got** or 或 **gotten**)
1 to become 变得: *The boys were getting bored.* 男孩们开始觉得无聊起来。 □ *Don't worry. Things will get better.* 不用担心。事情会好起来的。
2 to make someone do something 使…做; 让…做: *They got him to give them a lift in his car.* 他们让他载他们一程。
3 to arrange for someone to do something for you 使做好: *Why don't you get your car fixed?* 你为什么不找人修车呢?
4 to arrive somewhere 到达: *He got home at 4 a.m.* 他凌晨 4 点到的家。 □ *How do I get to your place from here?* 我从这儿怎么去你那里?
5 to buy or obtain something 买; 获得: *Dad needs to get a birthday present for Mum.* 爸爸得给妈妈买个生日礼物。 □ *I got a job at the shop.* 我在这家商店得到了一份工作。
6 to receive something 收到; 接到: *I'm getting a bike for my birthday.* 我生日会收到一辆自行车。 □ *He gets a lot of letters from fans.* 他收到许多粉丝来信。
7 to go and bring someone or something to a particular place 去接; 去取: *I went downstairs to get the post.* 我下楼去取邮件。 □ *It's time to get the kids from school.* 该接孩子们放学了。
8 to understand something 理解: *Dad laughed, but I didn't get the joke.* 爸爸笑了, 但我没听懂这个笑话。
9 to become ill with an illness or a disease 染, 患(病): *I've got flu.* 我得了流感。
10 to leave a place on a particular train, bus, aeroplane or boat 搭乘; 乘坐: *I got the train home at 10.45 p.m.* 我搭乘晚上 10 点 45 分的列车回家。

get along with someone to have a friendly relationship with someone 和某人友好相处: *It's impossible to get along with him.* 根本没法和他和睦相处。

get away to escape 逃跑; 逃脱: *The thieves got away through an upstairs window.* 窃贼从楼上的窗户逃走了。

get away with something to not be punished for doing something wrong 逃脱某事的惩罚: *Criminals know how to steal and get away with it.* 罪犯们知道如何在偷窃后逃脱惩罚。

get back to return somewhere 返回; 回来: *I'll call you when we get back from Scotland.* 我们从苏格兰回来后, 我会打电话给你。

get by to have just enough of something 勉强够; 勉强应付: *We have enough money to get by.* 我们有足够的钱维持生计。

get down to make your body lower until you are sitting, resting on your knees, or lying on the ground 坐下; 跪下; 趴下; 躺下: *Everybody got down on the ground and started looking for my earring.* 所有人都蹲

ghetto - gigantic

在地上开始找寻我的耳环。

get in to reach a station or an airport（火车）到站；（飞机）抵达：*Our flight got in two hours late.* 我们的航班晚了两个小时抵达。

get into something to climb into a car 上，进（汽车）：*We said goodbye and I got into the taxi.* 我们互道再见之后，我上了出租车。

get off something to leave a bus, train, or bicycle 下（公共汽车、火车或自行车）：*He got off the train at Central Station.* 他在中央车站下了火车。

get off 下（车）

He got off the train at Central Station. 他在中央车站下了火车。

get on
1 to have a friendly relationship with someone 友好相处：*He's always complaining. I can't get on with him.* 他总是牢骚不断。我没法和他好好相处。 □ *We all get on well.* 我们都相处得非常愉快。
2 to enter a train or bus or sit on a bicycle 上（火车、公共汽车或自行车）：*She got on the train just before it left.* 她刚上去，火车就开动了。
3 to continue doing or start doing something 继续做；开始做：*Jane got on with her work.* 简接着干活儿。

get out
1 to leave a place because you want to escape from it 逃离：*They got out of the country just in time.* 他们刚好及时逃离了这个国家。
2 to leave a car（从车中）下来：*A man got out of the van and ran away.* 一个男人从厢式货车里出来，然后跑掉了。

get over something to become happy or well again after an unhappy experience or an illness 从（不快或疾病）中恢复过来：*It took me a long time to get over her death.*

她离世后，我过了很久才缓过来。

get through something to complete a task or an amount of work 完成，做完（任务或一定量的工作）：*We got through plenty of work today.* 我们今天完成了许多工作。

get together to meet in order to talk about something or to spend time together 聚集；相聚：*Christmas is a time for families to get together.* 圣诞节是家庭团聚的时刻。

get up
1 to move your body so that you are standing 起身；站起：*I got up and walked over to the window.* 我站起来走向窗户。
2 to get out of bed 起床：*They have to get up early in the morning.* 他们得起个大早。

ghetto /ˈɡetəʊ/ **countable noun** 可数名词
(**ghettos** or 或 **ghettoes**)
a part of a city where many poor people live 贫民区：*They came from the inner-city ghettos.* 他们来自城中心贫民窟。

ghost /ɡəʊst/ **countable noun** 可数名词
the spirit of a dead person that some people believe they can see or feel 鬼魂：*He saw the ghost of a dead man.* 他看见了死人的鬼魂。

giant[1] /ˈdʒaɪənt/ *adjective* 形容词
very large or important 巨大的；十分重要的：*America's giant car makers are located in Detroit.* 美国大型汽车制造商位于底特律。 □ *They watched the concert on a giant TV screen.* 他们透过巨大的电视屏幕观看音乐会。

giant[2] /ˈdʒaɪənt/ **countable noun** 可数名词
a very big and strong man, especially one that appears in children's stories（尤指童话故事中的）巨人

gift /ɡɪft/ **countable noun** 可数名词
1 something that you give to someone as a present 礼物：*We gave her a birthday gift.* 我们送给她一份生日礼物。
2 a natural ability to do something 天赋；天资：*He had a gift for teaching.* 他有教学天赋。

gigabyte /ˈɡɪɡəˌbaɪt/ **countable noun** 可数名词
one thousand and twenty-four megabytes (= a unit for measuring the size of a computer's memory) 吉字节；(计算机信息量单位, 1 吉字节 = 1,024 兆字节)

gigantic /dʒaɪˈɡæntɪk/ *adjective* 形容词
extremely large 巨大的；庞大的；极大的：*There are gigantic rocks along the roadside.*

路旁巨石林立。

giggle /ˈgɪgəl/ **verb** 动词 (**giggles, giggling, giggled**)
to laugh in a silly way, like a child 傻笑；咯咯笑: *The girls began to giggle.* 女孩们咯咯笑了起来。● **giggle** *countable noun* 可数名词: *He gave a little giggle.* 他咯咯笑了一声。

ginger /ˈdʒɪndʒə/ *uncountable noun* 不可数名词
the root of a plant with a sweet, spicy flavour that you use in cooking 姜

giraffe /dʒɪˈrɑːf/ *countable noun* 可数名词
a large African animal with a very long neck, long legs and dark spots on its body 长颈鹿

girl /gɜːl/ *countable noun* 可数名词
a female child 女孩: *They have two girls and a boy.* 他们有两个女儿一个儿子。

girlfriend /ˈgɜːlfrend/ *countable noun* 可数名词
1 a girl or woman who someone is having a romantic relationship with 女朋友: *Does he have a girlfriend?* 他有女朋友吗？
2 a female friend 女性朋友: *I had lunch with my girlfriends.* 我和几位女性朋友共进了午餐。

Girl ˈGuide *countable noun* 可数名词
a member of the Girl Guides (= an organization that teaches girls practical skills, and encourages them to help other people) 女童子军队员: *If you are aged between ten and fifteen, you can become a Girl Guide.* 年龄在 10 岁至 15 岁之间，就可以成为女童子军队员。

give /gɪv/ *verb* 动词 (**gives, giving, gave, given**)
1 to let someone have something 给；给予: *My parents gave me a watch for my birthday.* 我父母送给我一块手表作为生日礼物。□ *They gave him the job.* 他们给了他这份工作。□ *I gave him my phone number.* 我把我的电话号码给了他。
2 to pass an object to someone, so that they can take it 递给: *Give me that pencil.* 把那支铅笔递给我。□ *Please give me your bag to carry.* 请把你的包递给我来拿。
3 used with nouns when you are talking about actions or sounds. For example, 'She gave a smile' means 'She smiled'. 做出（动作）；发出（声音）: *She gave me a big kiss.* 她热情地亲了我一下。□ *He gave a*

shout when the box fell on his foot. 盒子落在他的脚上，他大喊了一声。
give in to agree to do something although you do not really want to do it 屈服；让步: *After saying 'no' a hundred times, I finally gave in and said 'yes'.* 说了很多次"不行"之后，我最终屈从表示"可以"。
give something away to give something that you own to someone 赠送某物: *She likes to give away plants from her garden.* 她喜欢拿自己花园里的植物送人。
give something back to return something to the person who gave it to you 返还某物；归还某物: *I gave the book back to him.* 我把书还给了他。□ *Give me back my camera.* 把相机还给我。
give something out to give one of a number of things to each person in a group of people 分发某物: *Our teacher gave out papers, pencils and calculators for the maths test.* 我们老师把数学测验用的考卷、铅笔和计算器分发下来。
give something up to stop doing or having something 停止做某事；放弃某物: *We gave up hope of finding the fishermen.* 我们对找到那些渔民不抱任何希望了。
give up to decide that you cannot do something and stop trying to do it 放弃: *I give up. I'll never understand this.* 我认输了。这个我永远也弄不明白。

given /ˈgɪvən/
→ see 见 **give**

glacier /ˈglæsiə/ *countable noun* 可数名词
a very large amount of ice that moves very slowly, usually down a mountain 冰川
→ Look at picture on P7 参见彩插第 7 页

glad /glæd/ *adjective* 形容词
happy and pleased about something 开心的；愉快的: *They seemed glad to see me.* 他们见到我似乎很开心。□ *I'm glad you like the present.* 我很高兴你喜欢这个礼物。
▶ **gladly** /ˈglædli/ *adverb* 副词: *Malcolm gladly accepted the invitation.* 马尔科姆愉快地接受了邀请。

glamorous /ˈglæmərəs/ *adjective* 形容词
very attractive, exciting or interesting 富有魅力的；迷人的: *She looked glamorous in a white dress.* 她穿着白色连衣裙，风姿绰约。

glance /glɑːns/ *verb* 动词 (**glances, glancing, glanced**)
to look at something or someone very

quickly 瞥视；扫视：*He glanced at his watch.* 他匆匆看了一眼手表。● **glance** *countable noun* 可数名词：*Trevor and I exchanged glances.* 特雷弗和我迅速交换了一下眼神。

glare[1] /gleə/ *verb* 动词 (**glares, glaring, glared**)
1 to look at someone with an angry expression on your face 怒目而视；瞪视：*The old woman glared at him.* 老妇人瞪着他。
2 to shine with a very bright light 发出耀眼的光：*The sun glared down on us.* 耀眼的阳光照在我们身上。

glare[2] /gleə/ *noun* 名词
1 *countable* 可数 an angry look 怒视；瞪视：*She gave him a furious glare.* 她怒不可遏地瞪了他一眼。
2 *uncountable* 不可数 very bright light that is difficult to look at 眩光；刺眼的光：*the glare from a car's lights* 汽车灯的强光

glass /glɑːs/ *noun* 名词 (**glasses**)
1 *uncountable* 不可数 a hard, transparent substance that is used for making things such as windows and bottles 玻璃：*He served the salad in a glass bowl.* 他把沙拉装在玻璃碗中端上来。
2 *countable* 可数 a container made from glass, which you can drink from 玻璃杯：*He picked up his glass and drank.* 他拿起玻璃杯喝了起来。□ *I drink a glass of milk every day.* 我每天喝一杯牛奶。

glass 玻璃

glasses /ˈglɑːsɪz/ *plural noun* 复数名词 (*American* 美国英语：**eyeglasses**)
two pieces of glass or plastic (= **lenses**) in a frame, that some people wear in front of their eyes to help them to see better 眼镜：*He took off his glasses.* 他摘下眼镜。

gleam /gliːm/ *verb* 动词 (**gleams, gleaming, gleamed**)
to shine with a soft light 发出柔光：*His black hair gleamed in the sun.* 他的黑发在阳光下泛着光。

glide /glaɪd/ *verb* 动词 (**glides, gliding, glided**)
to move somewhere quietly and easily 滑动；轻盈地移动：*Waiters glide between the tables carrying trays.* 侍者端着托盘在餐桌间自如穿行。□ *Geese glide over the lake.* 鹅在湖面悠然滑行。

glimmer[1] /ˈglɪmə/ *verb* 动词 (**glimmers, glimmering, glimmered**)
to shine with a weak light 发出微光：*The moon glimmered through the mist.* 月亮透过薄雾发出朦胧的光。

glimmer[2] /ˈglɪmə/ *countable noun* 可数名词
1 a weak light 微光：*In the east there was a glimmer of light.* 东边有一抹微光。
2 a small sign of something 一丝；一线少许：*The new drug offers a glimmer of hope for patients.* 这种新药给患者带来一线希望。

glimpse /glɪmps/ *countable noun* 可数名词
when you see someone or something for a very short amount of time 一瞥；扫视：*Fans waited outside the hotel to catch a glimpse of the star.* 粉丝守在酒店外想一睹这位明星的风采。● **glimpse** *verb* 动词 (**glimpses, glimpsing, glimpsed**)：*She glimpsed something in the water.* 她瞥见水里有什么东西。

glisten /ˈglɪsən/ *verb* 动词 (**glistens, glistening, glistened**)
to shine, often because of being wet (常因湿而)闪亮，发亮：*The ocean glistened in the sunlight.* 阳光下海面波光粼粼。□ *David's face was glistening with sweat.* 戴维脸上汗珠晶莹发亮。

glitter /ˈglɪtə/ *verb* 动词 (**glitters, glittering, glittered**)
to shine with small flashes of light 闪烁；闪闪发光：*The ring glittered on Andrea's finger.* 那枚戒指在安德烈娅的手指上闪闪发光。

global /ˈgləʊbəl/ *adjective* 形容词
relating to the whole world 全球的；全世界的：*American businesses compete in a global economy.* 美国公司参与全球经济竞争。
▶ **globally** /ˈgləʊbəli/ *adverb* 副词：*The company employs 5,800 people globally, including 2,000 in London.* 这家公司在全球有 5,800 名雇员，其中 2,000 人在伦敦。

global economy *singular noun* 单数名词
the way in which the nations of the world work together through international trade and financial matters 全球经济：*We will soon see the effect of rising oil prices on the global economy.* 我们很快就会看到油价上涨对全球经济的影响。

globalization /ˌgləʊbəlaɪˈzeɪʃən/ uncountable noun 不可数名词
the idea that the world is developing a single economy as a result of modern technology and communications 全球化: *The report focuses on the globalization of business activities around the world.* 这篇报道着眼于世界商业活动的全球化。

global ˈwarming uncountable noun 不可数名词
the gradual rise in the Earth's temperature caused by high levels of certain gases 全球变暖: *If we use less energy, we can help to reduce global warming.* 我们减少能源消耗有助于减缓全球变暖。

globe /gləʊb/ noun 名词
1 countable 可数 an object shaped like a ball with a map of the world on it 地球仪: *A large globe stood on his desk.* 他书桌上放着一个大地球仪。
→ Look at picture on P1 and P9 参见彩插第1页和第9页
2 singular 单数 the world 地球；世界: *Thousands of people across the globe took part in the survey.* 全球范围内有成千上万人参与了这项调查。

gloomy /ˈgluːmi/ adjective 形容词 (gloomier, gloomiest)
1 almost dark so that you cannot see very well 昏暗的；阴暗的: *Inside it's gloomy after all that sunshine.* 外面阳光明媚，里面一片昏暗。
2 sad and without much hope of success or happiness 阴郁的；无望的: *He is gloomy about the future of the country.* 他对这个国家的未来颇为悲观。□ *The economic prospects for next year are gloomy.* 来年经济前景黯淡。

glorious /ˈglɔːriəs/ adjective 形容词
1 very beautiful; making you feel very happy 壮丽的；美好的: *We saw a glorious rainbow.* 我们看到了一道绚丽的彩虹。□ *He has glorious memories of his days as a champion.* 他心中保留着作为冠军时的美好回忆。
▶ **gloriously** /ˈglɔːriəsli/ adverb 副词: *It was a gloriously sunny morning.* 那是一个阳光灿烂的早上。
2 involving great fame or success 辉煌的；荣耀的: *He had a glorious career as a broadcaster and writer.* 他有辉煌的播音、写作生涯。
▶ **gloriously** /ˈglɔːriəsli/ adverb 副词: *The mission was gloriously successful.* 任务完成得非常出色。

glory /ˈglɔːri/ uncountable noun 不可数名词
the fame and admiration from other people that you get by doing something great 辉煌；荣耀: *He had his moment of glory when he won the cycling race.* 他夺得自行车赛冠军的那一刻无比荣耀。

glossary /ˈglɒsəri/ countable noun 可数名词 (glossaries)
a list of difficult words that are used in a book or special subject, with explanations of their meanings 词汇表；术语表

glossy /ˈglɒsi/ adjective 形容词 (glossier, glossiest)
smooth and shiny 光滑的；有光泽的: *She had glossy black hair.* 她有一头乌黑光亮的秀发。

glove /glʌv/ countable noun 可数名词
a piece of clothing that you wear on your hand, with a separate part for each finger 手套: *He put his gloves in his pocket.* 他把手套塞进口袋里。

glow /gləʊ/ countable noun 可数名词
a soft, steady light, for example the light from a fire when there are no flames 柔和稳定的光: *She saw the red glow of a fire.* 她看见柔和的红色火光。● **glow** verb 动词 (glows, glowing, glowed): *The lantern glowed softly in the darkness.* 灯笼在黑暗中发出柔和的光。

glue /gluː/ uncountable noun 不可数名词
a sticky substance used for joining things together 胶；胶水: *You will need scissors and a tube of glue.* 你需要剪刀和一管胶水。
● **glue** verb 动词 (glues, glueing or 或 gluing, glued): *She glued the pieces of newspaper together.* 她把报纸碎片用胶水粘起来。

GM /ˌdʒiː ˈem/ adjective 形容词
short for (缩写 =) genetically modified

go¹ /gəʊ/ verb 动词 (goes, going, went, gone)
1 to move or travel somewhere 去；行进: *We went to Rome on holiday.* 我们假期去了罗马。□ *I went home for the weekend.* 我回家过周末了。□ *It took an hour to go three miles.* 走3英里路花了1个小时。
2 to leave the place where you are 离开；走: *It's time for me to go.* 我该走了。
3 to leave a place in order to do something 去（做某事）: *We went swimming early this morning.* 我们今天一大早去游泳了。□ *They've gone shopping.*

他们去购物了。◻ He went for a walk. 他去散步了。◻ I'll go and make breakfast. 我去做早餐吧。
4 to visit school, work or church regularly 去（学校、单位或教堂）：Does your daughter go to school yet? 你女儿还上学吗？
5 to lead to a place 通往：This road goes from Blairstown to Millbrook Village. 这条路从布莱尔斯敦通向米尔布鲁克村。
6 used for describing where you usually keep something（通常）放于：The shoes go on the shoe shelf. 鞋放在鞋架上。
7 to become 变得；变成：I'm going crazy. 我快要疯了。◻ The meat has gone bad. 肉已经坏了。
8 used for talking about the way that something happens 进展；进行：How's your job going? 你的工作怎样？◻ Everything is going wrong. 事事都不顺。
9 to be working 工作；运行：Can you get my car going again? 你能把我的车修好吗？
go ahead to take place 发生；进行：The wedding went ahead as planned, about 14 hours after the accident. 在事故发生后约 14 个小时，婚礼按计划进行。

go away
1 to leave a place or a person 离开；走开：Just go away and leave me alone! 快走开，别烦我！
2 to leave a place and spend time somewhere else, especially as a holiday 外出（尤指度假）：Why don't we go away this weekend? 我们这个周末何不出去度假呢？
go back to return somewhere 返回；回来：He'll be going back to college soon. 他很快就会重返大学。
go by to pass 过去；流逝：The week went by so quickly. 这周过得飞快。

go down
1 to become less 下降；下跌：House prices went down last month. 上月房价降了。
2 when the sun goes down, it goes below the line between the land and the sky（太阳）落下：It gets cold after the sun goes down. 日落后天气变冷。

go off
1 to explode 爆炸：A bomb went off, destroying the vehicle. 一枚炸弹爆炸，摧毁了这辆车。
2 to no longer be good to eat or drink（食物或饮料）变质，坏掉：This fish has gone off. 这条鱼已经变质了。

go on
1 to continue to do something 继续：She just went on laughing. 她只是一个劲儿笑。
2 to be happening 发生：While this conversation was going on, I just listened. 这番谈话进行着，我只是聆听。

go out
1 to leave your home to do something enjoyable 外出娱乐：I'm going out tonight. 我今晚要出去玩。
2 to have a romantic relationship with someone 交往；谈恋爱：I've been going out with my girlfriend for three months. 我和女友已经交往了 3 个月。
3 to stop shining or burning 熄灭：The bedroom light went out after a moment. 卧室的灯过了一会儿就灭了。◻ The fire went out and the room became cold. 炉火熄灭，屋里冷了起来。
go over something to look at something or think about it very carefully 仔细查看某事物；认真考虑某事物：We went over the details again. 我们又仔细核查了一下细节。
go through something to experience something difficult 经历（困苦）：He went through a difficult time when he lost his job. 他失业后度过了一段艰难时期。
go together to look or taste good together 相称；（食物）相搭：Cheese and tomato go together well. 奶酪和番茄搭配非常美味。
go up to become greater 上涨；上升：The cost of calls went up to £1.00 a minute. 话费涨至每分钟 1 英镑。
go with something to look or taste good with something else 与某物相称；与某物搭配美味：Those trousers would go with my blue shirt. 那条裤子应该可以搭我的蓝衬衣。

go^2 /gəʊ/ *countable noun* 可数名词 (**goes**) the time when someone should do something in a game or activity（游戏或活动中）轮到的机会：Whose go is it now? 现在该谁了？
have a go to try to do something (*informal* 非正式) 尝试：Children should have a go at playing a musical instrument. 孩子们应该尝试演奏一种乐器。

goal /gəʊl/ *countable noun* 可数名词
1 the place, in games such as football, where the players try to put the ball in order to win a point for their team 球门：The ball went straight into the goal. 球直接入门。
2 a point that is scored when the ball goes into the goal in games such as football 进

球得分: *He scored five goals in one game.* 他一场比赛有 5 粒进球。
3 the aim or purpose that you have when you do something 目标；目的: *Our goal is to make patients comfortable.* 我们的目标是让病人舒适。

goal 球门
net 球门网
goalpost 球门柱
crossbar 横梁
goalkeeper 守门员

goalkeeper /ˈɡəʊlkiːpə/ *countable noun* 可数名词
the player on a sports team whose job is to guard the goal 守门员

goalpost /ˈɡəʊlpəʊst/ *countable noun* 可数名词
one of the two wooden posts that form the goal in games such as football 球门柱

goat /ɡəʊt/ *countable noun* 可数名词
an animal that is about the size of a sheep. Goats have horns, and hairs on their chin that look like a beard. 山羊

gobble /ˈɡɒbəl/ *verb* 动词 (**gobbles, gobbling, gobbled**)
(also 亦作 **gobble up**) to eat food very quickly 狼吞虎咽地吃: *Don't gobble your food.* 别狼吞虎咽地吃东西。▫ *Pete hungrily gobbled up the rest of the sandwiches.* 皮特饿得几口就把剩下的三明治一扫而光。

god /ɡɒd/ *countable noun* 可数名词
a spirit that people in many religions believe has power over a particular part of the world or nature (宗教中主宰某个领域的)神: *Poseidon was the Greek god of the sea.* 波塞冬是希腊海神。

God /ɡɒd/ *noun* 名词
the name given to the spirit that people in many religions believe created the world 上帝；天主；真主: *He believes in God.* 他信上帝。

goddess /ˈɡɒdɪs/ *countable noun* 可数名词 (**goddesses**)
a female god 女神: *There was a statue of a goddess in the temple.* 庙里有一尊女神像。

goggles /ˈɡɒɡəlz/ *plural noun* 复数名词
large glasses that fit closely to your face around your eyes to protect them 护目镜: *a pair of swimming goggles* 一副泳镜

going /ˈɡəʊɪŋ/ *verb* 动词
be going to
1 used for talking about something that will probably happen in the future 可能会: *I think it's going to be successful.* 我认为它会成功的。▫ *You're going to enjoy this.* 你会乐在其中的。
2 used for saying that you intend to do something 打算: *I'm going to go to bed.* 我要上床睡觉了。▫ *He announced that he's going to resign.* 他宣布打算辞职。

gold¹ /ɡəʊld/ *uncountable noun* 不可数名词
1 a valuable, yellow-coloured metal that is used for making jewellery, ornaments and coins 金: *a ring made of gold* 金戒指 ▫ *The price of gold was going up.* 金价在上涨。
2 jewellery and other things that are made of gold 黄金饰品；黄金制品: *We handed over all our gold and money.* 我们把所有的黄金饰品和钱都交了出来。

gold² /ɡəʊld/ *adjective* 形容词
bright yellow in colour, and often shiny 金色的: *He wore a black and gold shirt.* 他穿了一件黑金两色的衬衣。

golden /ˈɡəʊldən/ *adjective* 形容词
1 bright yellow in colour 金色的；金黄色的: *She combed her golden hair.* 她梳了梳她的金发。
2 made of gold 金的；金质的: *He wore a golden chain.* 他戴了条金链子。

goldfish /ˈɡəʊldfɪʃ/ *countable noun* 可数名词 (**goldfish**)
a small orange fish that people often keep as a pet 金鱼

gold 'medal *countable noun* 可数名词
an award made of gold metal that you get as first prize in a competition 金牌；金质奖章: *Her dream is to win a gold medal in the next competition.* 她的梦想是在下次比赛中赢得金牌。

golf /ɡɒlf/ *uncountable noun* 不可数名词
a game in which you use long sticks (= golf clubs) to hit a small, hard ball into holes 高尔夫球运动: *Do you play golf?* 你打高尔夫球吗？

▶ **golfer** /ˈɡɒlfə/ *countable noun* 可数名词: *He is one of the world's best golfers.* 他是世界顶级高尔夫球手之一。

▶**golfing** /ˈgɒlfɪŋ/ *uncountable noun* 不可数名词: *You can play tennis or go golfing.* 你可以打网球，也可以打高尔夫球。

ˈ**golf** ˌ**club** *countable noun* 可数名词
a long, thin metal stick with a piece of wood or metal at one end that you use to hit the ball when you play golf 高尔夫球杆

ˈ**golf** ˌ**course** *countable noun* 可数名词
a large area of grass where people play golf 高尔夫球场

gone /gɒn/
→ see 见 **go**

good¹ /gʊd/ *adjective* 形容词 (**better, best**)
1 pleasant or enjoyable 令人愉快的；美好的: *We had a really good time.* 我们玩得非常开心。□ *These people want a better life for their children.* 这些人想让子女过上更好的生活。
2 of a high quality or level 好的；优质的: *Good food is important for your health.* 优质食品对健康非常重要。□ *Our customers want the best possible quality at a low price.* 我们的顾客想要以低价买到尽可能好的东西。
3 suitable for an activity 合适的: *This room is a good place for relaxing and reading.* 这个房间非常适合放松和阅读。□ *What would be a good time to meet?* 什么时候见面合适？
4 sensible 合理的；明智的: *It's a good idea to keep your desk tidy.* 保持书桌整洁是应该的。□ *There was a good reason for his strange behaviour.* 他的古怪行为情有可原。
5 skilful at doing something 擅长的；精通的: *I'm not very good at singing.* 我唱歌不怎么样。
6 behaving well 行为良好的；有礼貌的: *The children were very good.* 这些孩子非常懂事。
7 kind and thoughtful 好心的；体贴的: *You are good to me.* 你对我很好。

good² /gʊd/ *uncountable noun* 不可数名词
what people consider to be morally right 善行: *They should know the difference between good and bad, right and wrong.* 他们应该知善恶、明对错。
do someone good to help someone to feel better 于某人有益: *The fresh air will do you good.* 新鲜空气对你有好处。
for good used for saying that something has disappeared and will never come back 永远；彻底: *These forests may be gone for good.* 这些森林可能会永远消失。
no good used for saying that something will not bring any success 没用；没好处: *I asked her to repeat the question, but it was no good – I couldn't understand her.* 我让她重复一遍问题，但还是无济于事——我听不懂她的话。□ *It's no good worrying about it now.* 现在担心也没用。

ˌ**good after**ˈ**noon**
said to someone when you see or speak to them in the afternoon (*formal* 正式) 下午好

goodbye /ˌgʊdˈbaɪ/ also 亦作 **good-bye**
said to someone when you or they are leaving a place, or at the end of a telephone conversation 再见；再会

ˌ**good** ˈ**evening**
said the first time you see or speak to someone in the evening (*formal* 正式) 晚上好

ˌ**good-**ˈ**looking** *adjective* 形容词 (**better-looking, best-looking**)
having an attractive face 漂亮的；好看的: *Katy noticed him because he was good-looking.* 凯蒂因他长得帅气注意到了他。

ˌ**good** ˈ**morning**
said the first time you see or speak to someone in the morning (*formal* 正式) 早上好

goodness /ˈgʊdnəs/ *uncountable noun* 不可数名词
the quality of being kind, helpful and honest 善良: *He believes in human goodness.* 他相信人性善良。
for goodness' sake used for showing that you are annoyed or worried (表示生气或担心) 天哪: *For goodness' sake, do something!* 天哪，做点什么吧！
thank goodness used for showing that you are happy that something bad has not happened 谢天谢地: *Thank goodness you're here; I've been so worried.* 谢天谢地你来了，我担心死了。

ˌ**good** ˈ**night**
said to someone late in the evening before you go home or go to bed 晚安

goods /gʊdz/ *plural noun* 复数名词
things that you can buy or sell 商品: *Companies sell goods or services.* 公司销售商品或服务。

Google /ˈguːgəl/ *noun* 名词
a computer program that you can use to search for information on the Internet (*trademark* 商标) 谷歌搜索引擎: *Why don't you look him up on Google?* 你为什么

不到谷歌上去搜一下他？● **Google** *verb* 动词 (**Googles, Googling, Googled**)：*We Googled her name, and found her website.* 我们用谷歌搜索了她的名字，发现了她的网站。

goose /guːs/ *countable noun* 可数名词 (**geese**)
a large bird like a duck with a long neck 鹅；雁：*The Canada Goose is a beautiful bird.* 加拿大黑雁是一种漂亮的鸟。

gorgeous /ˈɡɔːdʒəs/ *adjective* 形容词
very pleasant or attractive (*informal* 非正式) 迷人的；非常漂亮的；令人非常愉快的：*It's a gorgeous day.* 天气非常好。□ *You look gorgeous.* 你看上去漂亮极了。

gorilla /ɡəˈrɪlə/ *countable noun* 可数名词
a very large animal like a monkey with long arms, black fur and a black face 大猩猩

gossip /ˈɡɒsɪp/ *uncountable noun* 不可数名词
informal conversation about other people 闲聊；闲谈；流言：*There has been gossip about the reasons for his absence.* 关于他缺席的原因有一些传言。● **gossip** *verb* 动词 (**gossips, gossiping, gossiped**)：*They sat at the kitchen table gossiping about Jenny.* 他们坐在餐桌旁说珍妮的闲话。

gotten /ˈɡɒtən/ (*American* 美国英语)
→ see 见 **get**

govern /ˈɡʌvən/ *verb* 动词 (**governs, governing, governed**)
to officially control and organize a country 统治；治理：*The people choose who they want to govern their country.* 人们选择由谁来治理他们的国家。

government /ˈɡʌvənmənt/ *countable noun* 可数名词
the group of people who control and organize a country, a state or a city 政府：*The government has decided to make changes.* 政府已经决定变革。
▶ **governmental** /ˌɡʌvənˈmentəl/ *adjective* 形容词：*She works for a governmental agency.* 她为政府机构工作。

> **LANGUAGE HELP** 语言提示
> In Britain, the head of the government is the **Prime Minister**. 英国政府首脑称作 Prime Minister（首相）。

gown /ɡaʊn/ *countable noun* 可数名词
1 a long dress that women wear on formal occasions（正式场合穿的）长裙，女礼服：*She was wearing a ball gown.* 她穿着一件舞会礼服。 **2** a loose black piece of clothing that students wear at their graduation ceremony (= the ceremony where they receive their degree) 学位服：*He was wearing a university graduation gown.* 他穿着一件学士服。

GP /ˌdʒiː ˈpiː/ *countable noun* 可数名词 (**GPs**)
a general doctor who treats all types of illnesses and does not work in a hospital. GP is short for (缩写 =) **general practitioner**. 全科医生；家庭医生

grab /ɡræb/ *verb* 动词 (**grabs, grabbing, grabbed**)
to take something suddenly and roughly 抓住；抢夺：*I grabbed her hand.* 我抓住她的手。

graceful /ˈɡreɪsfəl/ *adjective* 形容词
moving in a smooth and attractive way 优雅的；优美的：*His movements were smooth and graceful.* 他的动作流畅而优美。
▶ **gracefully** /ˈɡreɪsfəli/ *adverb* 副词：*She stepped gracefully onto the stage.* 她优雅地登上舞台。

grade[1] /ɡreɪd/ *countable noun* 可数名词
1 the mark that a teacher gives you to show how good your work is 分数；成绩：*The best grade you can get is an A.* 最好的成绩是 A。 **2** the level of quality of a product 等级；品级：*The price of all grades of petrol has gone up.* 各种品级的汽油都涨价了。

grade[2] /ɡreɪd/ *verb* 动词 (**grades, grading, graded**)
to judge the quality of something 评定；给⋯评级：*Teachers grade the students' work from A to F.* 老师给学生作业打出 A 至 F 几个分档。

gradual /ˈɡrædʒuəl/ *adjective* 形容词
happening slowly, over a long period of time 逐渐的；渐进的：*Losing weight is a gradual process.* 减肥是一个循序渐进的过程。
▶ **gradually** /ˈɡrædʒuəli/ *adverb* 副词：*We are gradually learning to use the new computer system.* 我们在逐步学习使用新计算机系统。

graduate[1] /ˈɡrædʒuət/ *countable noun* 可数名词
a student who has completed a course at a college or university 大学毕业生：*His parents are both college graduates. They studied at Cornell.* 他父母都是大学毕业生，曾就读于康奈尔大学。

graduate² /ˈɡrædʒueɪt/ *verb* 动词 (graduates, graduating, graduated)
to complete your studies at college or university 大学毕业: *Her son has just graduated from Oxford.* 她儿子刚从牛津大学毕业。

graduation /ˌɡrædʒuˈeɪʃən/ *countable noun* 可数名词
a special ceremony for students when they have completed their studies at a university or college（大学）毕业典礼: *Her parents came to her graduation.* 她父母来参加了她的毕业典礼。

graffiti /ɡrəˈfiːti/ *uncountable noun* 不可数名词
words or pictures that people write or draw on walls or in public places 涂鸦: *There was graffiti all over the walls.* 墙上到处都是涂鸦。

grain /ɡreɪn/ *countable noun* 可数名词
1 a single seed from a particular crop 谷粒: *He was grateful for every single grain of rice.* 他感激每一粒米。
2 a tiny, hard piece of something such as sand or salt 颗粒；细粒: *How many grains of sand are there in the desert?* 沙漠里有多少粒沙子？

gram /ɡræm/ also 亦作 **gramme** *countable noun* 可数名词
a unit of weight. There are one thousand grams in a kilogram. 克（重量单位）: *A football weighs about 400 grams.* 足球重约 400 克。
→ Look at picture on P2 参见彩插第 2 页

grammar /ˈɡræmə/ *uncountable noun* 不可数名词
a set of rules for a language that describes how words go together to form sentences 语法: *You need to know the basic rules of grammar.* 你需要了解基本的语法规则。

grammatical /ɡrəˈmætɪkəl/ *adjective* 形容词
1 relating to grammar 语法的: *He studied a book of grammatical rules.* 他学习了一本讲语法规则的书。
2 correct, obeying the rules of grammar 符合语法规则的: *We want to see if students can write grammatical English.* 我们想要了解学生能否写出合乎语法规则的英语。

gran /ɡræn/ *countable noun* 可数名词 (*informal* 非正式)
→ see 见 **grandmother**

grand /ɡrænd/ *adjective* 形容词 (grander, grandest)
very impressive in size or appearance 宏伟的；壮丽的: *The town hall is a grand building in the centre of town.* 市政厅位于市中心，气象宏伟。

grandad /ˈɡrændæd/ also 亦作 **granddad** *countable noun* 可数名词 (*informal* 非正式)
→ see 见 **grandfather**

grandchild /ˈɡræntʃaɪld/ *countable noun* 可数名词 (**grandchildren** /ˈɡræntʃɪldrən/)
the child of your son or daughter（外）孙子；（外）孙女: *You're grandma's favourite grandchild.* 你是奶奶最喜欢的孙子。

granddaughter /ˈɡrændɔːtə/ *countable noun* 可数名词
the daughter of your son or daughter（外）孙女: *This is my granddaughter, Amelia.* 这是我孙女阿梅莉亚。

grandfather /ˈɡrænfɑːðə/ *countable noun* 可数名词
the father of your father or mother（外）祖父: *His grandfather was a professor.* 他祖父是位教授。

grandma /ˈɡrænmɑː/ *countable noun* 可数名词 (*informal* 非正式)
→ see 见 **grandmother**: *Grandma was from Scotland.* 奶奶家在苏格兰。

grandmother /ˈɡrænmʌðə/ *countable noun* 可数名词
the mother of your father or mother（外）祖母: *My grandmothers were both teachers.* 我祖母和外祖母都是教师。

grandpa /ˈɡrænpɑː/ *countable noun* 可数名词 (*informal* 非正式)
→ see 见 **grandfather**: *Grandpa was sitting in the garden.* 爷爷坐在花园里。

grandparent /ˈɡrænpeərənt/ *countable noun* 可数名词
the parent of your father or mother（外）祖父；（外）祖母: *Tammy lives with her grandparents.* 塔米和祖父母住在一起。

grandson /ˈɡrænsʌn/ *countable noun* 可数名词
the son of your son or daughter（外）孙子: *My grandson's birthday was on Tuesday.* 我孙子的生日在星期二。

granny /ˈɡræni/ *countable noun* 可数名词 (**grannies**) (*informal* 非正式)
→ see 见 **grandmother**: *I hugged my granny.* 我拥抱了奶奶。

grant[1] /grɑːnt/ *countable noun* 可数名词
an amount of money that a government gives to a person or to an organization for a special purpose 拨款：*They got a grant to research the disease.* 他们获得一笔拨款来研究这种疾病。

grant[2] /grɑːnt/ *verb* 动词 (**grants, granting, granted**)
to allow someone to have something (*formal* 正式) 准予；给予：*France granted him political asylum.* 法国给予了他政治庇护。
take someone for granted to not show that you are grateful for anything that someone does 对某人不知感激；不把某人的付出当回事：*She feels that her family take her for granted.* 她觉得家人对她是予取予求。

grape /ɡreɪp/ *countable noun* 可数名词
a small green or purple fruit that grows in bunches and is used to make wine 葡萄：*I bought six oranges and a small bunch of grapes.* 我买了6个橙子和一小串葡萄。

grapefruit /ˈɡreɪpfruːt/ *noun* 名词 (**grapefruit**)

> **LANGUAGE HELP 语言提示**
> The plural can also be **grapefruits**. 复数形式也可以用 grapefruits。

a large, round, yellow fruit that has a slightly sour taste 葡萄柚；西柚

graph /ɡrɑːf/ *countable noun* 可数名词
a picture that shows information about sets of numbers or measurements 图表：*The graph shows that prices went up about 20 per cent last year.* 图表显示去年价格上涨了20%左右。

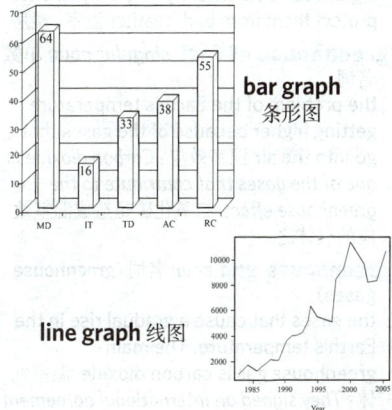
graphs 图表
bar graph 条形图
line graph 线图

graphics /ˈɡræfɪks/ *plural noun* 复数名词
drawings, pictures or symbols, especially when they are produced by a computer (尤指计算机制作的) 图形：*The game's graphics are very good, so you can see things clearly.* 这款游戏画面精良，成像非常清楚。

grasp[1] /ɡrɑːsp/ *verb* 动词 (**grasps, grasping, grasped**)
1 to take something in your hand and hold it very firmly 抓紧；抓牢：*He grasped both my hands.* 他抓紧我的双手。
2 to understand something that is complicated 理解；领会：*I don't think you have grasped how serious this problem is.* 我觉得你没有认识到这个问题的严重性。

grasp[2] /ɡrɑːsp/ *singular noun* 单数名词
1 a very firm hold or grip 紧握；紧抓：*He took her hand in a firm grasp.* 他紧紧抓住她的手。
2 an understanding of a subject 理解；领会：*She has a good grasp of geometry.* 她几何学得很好。

grass /ɡrɑːs/ *uncountable noun* 不可数名词
a plant with thin, green leaves that cover the surface of the ground 草；青草：*We sat on the grass and ate our picnic.* 我们坐在草地上吃野餐。

grasshopper /ˈɡrɑːsˌhɒpə/ *countable noun* 可数名词
an insect that jumps high into the air and makes a sound with its long back legs 蚱蜢

grassy /ˈɡrɑːsi/ *adjective* 形容词 (**grassier, grassiest**)
covered in grass 长满草的：*a grassy hillside* 长满青草的山坡

grateful /ˈɡreɪtfʊl/ *adjective* 形容词
wanting to thank someone for something that they give you or do for you 感激的：*She was grateful to him for being so helpful.* 他帮了这么大的忙，她心怀感激。
▶ **gratefully** /ˈɡreɪtfʊli/ *adverb* 副词：*He said that any help would be gratefully received.* 他说对于任何帮助都将心存感激。

gratitude /ˈɡrætɪˌtjuːd/ *uncountable noun* 不可数名词
the feeling you have when you want to thank someone 感激之情：*He expressed gratitude to everyone for their help.* 他向所有帮助他的人表示感谢。

grave[1] /ɡreɪv/ *countable noun* 可数名词
a place in the ground where a dead person

is buried 坟墓: *They visit her grave twice a year.* 他们每年给她扫两次墓。

grave² /greɪv/ *adjective* 形容词 (**graver, gravest**)
very serious and important 严重的；重大的: *These weapons are a grave danger to the world.* 这些武器对于世界是重大威胁。

graveyard /ˈgreɪvjɑːd/ *countable noun* 可数名词
an area of land where dead people are buried 墓地: *They went to the graveyard to put flowers on her grave.* 他们去墓地给她的墓献花。

gravity /ˈgrævɪti/ *uncountable noun* 不可数名词
the force that makes things fall to the ground 重力: *The force of gravity pulls everything down.* 重力使一切物体落向地面。
→ Look at picture on P6 参见彩插第 6 页

gravy /ˈgreɪvi/ *uncountable noun* 不可数名词
a sauce made from the juices that come from meat when it cooks 肉汁；肉卤

grease /griːs/ *uncountable noun* 不可数名词
1 a thick substance like oil 油脂状物: *His hands were covered in grease.* 他双手沾满了油渍。
2 animal fat that is produced when you cook meat (烹饪肉时产生的) 动物油脂: *The plates were all covered in grease.* 这些盘子上面全都油乎乎的。

greasy /ˈgriːsi/ *adjective* 形容词 (**greasier, greasiest**)
used for describing something that has grease on it or in it 有油渍的；油腻的: *He wiped the greasy counter.* 他擦拭了满是油污的柜台。

great¹ /greɪt/ *adjective* 形容词 (**greater, greatest**)
1 very large 非常大的；巨大的: *She had a great big smile on her face.* 她脸上露出了灿烂的笑容。
2 large in amount or degree (数量) 大的；(程度) 深的: *She lived to a great age.* 她很长寿。
▶ **greatly** /ˈgreɪtli/ *adverb* 副词 (*formal* 正式): *He will be greatly missed.* 大家会非常怀念他。
3 important, famous or exciting 重大的；伟大的: *They made great scientific discoveries.* 他们取得了重大科学发现。
□ *He has the ability to be a great player.* 他具备成为优秀球员的能力。

▶ **greatness** /ˈgreɪtnəs/ *uncountable noun* 不可数名词: *She dreamed of achieving greatness.* 她梦想能取得卓越成就。
4 very good (*informal* 非正式): *We had a great time.* 我们玩得很开心。
□ *It's great to meet you.* 见到你很高兴。

great² /greɪt/ *exclamation* 感叹词
very good 太好了；棒极了: *Oh great! You made a cake.* 哦，太棒了！你做了个蛋糕。

greed /griːd/ *uncountable noun* 不可数名词
the feeling that you want to have more of something than you need 贪婪；贪心: *People say that the world economy is based on greed.* 人们说世界经济建立在贪婪这个基础之上。

greedy /ˈgriːdi/ *adjective* 形容词 (**greedier, greediest**)
wanting to have more of something than you need 贪婪的；贪心的: *They still want more money? I think that's a bit greedy.* 他们还想要更多的钱？我觉得那有点儿贪心了。
▶ **greedily** /ˈgriːdɪli/ *adverb* 副词: *He raised the bottle to his lips and drank greedily.* 他把瓶子举到嘴边大口喝了起来。

green /griːn/ *adjective* 形容词 (**greener, greenest**)
1 having the colour of grass or leaves 绿色的: *She wore a green dress.* 她穿了一条绿色连衣裙。● **green** *noun* 名词: *I've never looked good in green.* 绿色一向不适合我。
→ Look at picture on P13 参见彩插第 13 页
2 relating to the protection of the environment 环保的: *the Green Party* 绿党

greenhouse /ˈgriːnhaʊs/ *countable noun* 可数名词
a glass building where you grow plants to protect them from bad weather 温室；暖房

ˈgreenhouse efˌfect *singular noun* 单数名词
the problem of the Earth's temperature getting higher because of the gases that go into the air 温室效应: *Carbon dioxide is one of the gases that contribute to the greenhouse effect.* 二氧化碳是造成温室效应的气体之一。

ˌgreenhouse ˈgas *noun* 名词 (**greenhouse gases**)
the gases that cause a gradual rise in the Earth's temperature. The main greenhouse gas is carbon dioxide. 温室气体: *They signed an international agreement*

to limit greenhouse gases. 他们签署了一项控制温室气体的国际协议。

greet /griːt/ *verb* 动词 (**greets, greeting, greeted**)
to say 'Hello' or shake hands with someone 同…打招呼；向…问好；欢迎: *She greeted him when he came in from school.* 她欢迎放学回家的他。

greeting /ˈɡriːtɪŋ/ *noun* 名词
something friendly that you say or do when you meet someone 问候；致意: *We exchanged friendly greetings.* 我们互致友好的问候。

grew /ɡruː/
→ see 见 **grow**

grey /ɡreɪ/ *adjective* 形容词 (**greyer, greyest**)
having the colour of ashes or clouds on a rainy day 灰色的: *a grey suit* 灰色套装 ● **grey** *noun* 名词: *She was dressed in grey.* 她穿着灰色的衣服。
→ Look at picture on P13 参见彩插第 13 页

grid /ɡrɪd/ *countable noun* 可数名词
a pattern of straight lines that cross over each other to make squares. On maps, you can use the grid to help you find a particular thing or place. 网格；(地图的)坐标方格: *The number puzzle uses a grid of nine squares.* 数独游戏在九宫格内进行。

grief /ɡriːf/ *uncountable noun* 不可数名词
a feeling of great sadness 悲伤；悲痛: *We all experience grief at some point in our lives.* 我们一生中都会有某个悲伤的时刻。

grieve /ɡriːv/ *verb* 动词 (**grieves, grieving, grieved**)
to feel very sad about something, especially someone's death (尤指因某人去世而)悲伤，悲痛: *He's grieving over his dead wife.* 他在为死去的妻子哀悼。

grill¹ /ɡrɪl/ *countable noun* 可数名词
1 part of a cooker that cooks food placed under it using strong heat (灶具内的)烤架: *Put the meat under a grill until it is brown.* 把肉放在烤架下烤至棕色。
2 a flat frame of metal bars that you can use to cook food over a fire (置于火上的)烤架: *We cooked the fish on a grill over the fire.* 我们把鱼放在烤架上用火烤。

grill² /ɡrɪl/ *verb* 动词 (**grills, grilling, grilled**)
to cook food on metal bars above a fire or barbecue or under a grill (用烤架)烤炙: *Grill the steaks for about 5 minutes each side.* 把牛排两面各烤 5 分钟左右。
□ *grilled fish* 烤鱼

grin /ɡrɪn/ *verb* 动词 (**grins, grinning, grinned**)
to have a big smile on your face 咧嘴大笑: *He grinned with pleasure.* 他开心地咧嘴笑了起来。 □ *Phillip grinned at her.* 菲利普冲她咧嘴一笑。 ● **grin** *countable noun* 可数名词: *She had a big grin on her face.* 她笑容满面。

grind /ɡraɪnd/ *verb* 动词 (**grinds, grinding, ground**)
to rub a substance against something hard until it becomes a fine powder 磨碎，碾碎: *Grind some pepper into the sauce.* 将一些胡椒磨成粉放进调味汁中。

grip /ɡrɪp/ *verb* 动词 (**grips, gripping, gripped**)
to take something with your hand and hold it firmly 握紧；抓紧: *She gripped the rope.* 她抓紧绳子。 ● **grip** *countable noun* 可数名词: *Keep a tight grip on your purse.* 要把钱包紧紧抓在手里。

groan /ɡrəʊn/ *verb* 动词 (**groans, groaning, groaned**)
to make a long, low sound because you are feeling pain, or because you are unhappy about something 呻吟；叹息: *He began to groan with pain.* 他开始疼得直哼哼。 □ *The man on the floor was groaning.* 那个男子在地板上呻吟着。 ● **groan** *countable noun* 可数名词: *I heard a groan from the crowd.* 我听到人群中传来一声叹息。

groceries /ˈɡrəʊsəriz/ *plural noun* 复数名词
the things that you buy at a grocery or at a supermarket 食品杂货: *a small bag of groceries* 一小袋日用品

groom¹ /ɡruːm/ *countable noun* 可数名词
1 a person whose job is to look after horses 马倌；马夫
2 a man on the day of his wedding, or a man who is about to get married or has just got married 新郎

groom² /ɡruːm/ *verb* 动词 (**grooms, grooming, groomed**)
to clean an animal's fur, usually by brushing it 刷洗(动物)；给(动物)梳毛: *She groomed the horses regularly.* 她定期刷洗马匹。

groove /ɡruːv/ *countable noun* 可数名词
a deep line that is cut into a surface 沟；槽: *He used a knife to cut a groove in the stick.*

他用刀在木棍上挖了个槽。

grope /ɡrəʊp/ *verb* 动词 (**gropes, groping, groped**)
to use your hands to try to find something that you cannot see 摸索: *He groped for the door handle in the dark.* 他在黑暗中摸索着找门把手。

gross national product /ˌɡrəʊs ˌnæʃənəl ˈprɒdʌkt/ *noun* 名词
the total value of all of a country's income in a particular year 国民生产总值

ground[1] /ɡraʊnd/
→ see 见 **grind**

ground[2] /ɡraʊnd/ *noun* 名词
1 *singular* 单数 the surface of the Earth or the floor of a room 地; 地面: *He fell to the ground.* 他摔到地上。
2 *countable* 可数 an area of land that is used for a particular activity (某种活动的) 场地: *a sports ground* 运动场
3 [**grounds**] *plural* 复数 the garden or area of land around a large or important building (大型或重要建筑物周围的) 庭院, 花园: *the palace grounds* 皇家花园

ˌground ˈfloor *countable noun* 可数名词 (*American* 美国英语: **first floor**)
the part of a building that is at the same level as the ground 底层; 一楼: *His office is on the ground floor.* 他的办公室在一楼。

group /ɡruːp/ *countable noun* 可数名词
1 a number of people or things that are together 组; 群; 批: *A small group of people stood on the street corner.* 一小群人站在街角。
2 a number of people who play music together 乐队; 乐团: *He played guitar in a rock group.* 他在一支摇滚乐队担任吉他手。

grow /ɡrəʊ/ *verb* 动词 (**grows, growing, grew, grown**)
1 to gradually become bigger 长大; 长高; 发育: *All children grow at different rates.* 每个孩子的发育速度不同。
2 used for saying that a plant or a tree lives in a particular place (植物) 生长: *There were roses growing by the side of the door.* 门边长着玫瑰花。
3 to put seeds or young plants in the ground and take care of them 栽种; 种植: *I always grow a few red onions.* 我总是会种几株红洋葱。
▶ **grower** /ˈɡrəʊə/ *countable noun* 可数名词: *apple growers* 苹果种植者

4 to gradually become longer 变长; 长长: *My hair grows really fast.* 我的头发长得非常快。
5 to gradually change 变成; 变得: *He's growing old.* 他渐渐老去。

grow out of something
1 to stop behaving in a particular way as you get older (因长大而) 改掉 (习惯): *Most children who bite their nails grow out of it.* 大多数咬指甲的小孩长大以后就不咬了。
2 to become too big to wear a piece of clothing 长大而穿不下 (原来的衣服): *You've grown out of your shoes again.* 你的鞋又小了。

grow up to gradually change from being a child into being an adult 长大成人: *She grew up in Tokyo.* 她在东京长大。

growl /ɡraʊl/ *verb* 动词 (**growls, growling, growled**)
to make a low noise in the throat, usually because of anger 低声吼叫: *The dog was growling and showing its teeth.* 那条狗龇着牙, 低声吼叫。● **growl** *countable noun* 可数名词: *The animal gave a growl.* 那只动物发出一声低吼。

grown /ɡrəʊn/
→ see 见 **grow**

ˈgrown-up also 亦作 **ˈgrownup** *countable noun* 可数名词
a child's word for an adult 成年人, 大人 (儿语): *Archie's almost a grown-up now.* 阿奇现在几乎是个成年人了。● **ˌgrown-ˈup** *adjective* 形容词: *She has two grown-up children who both live nearby.* 她的两个孩子长大成人, 都住在附近。

growth /ɡrəʊθ/ *uncountable noun* 不可数名词
1 development 发展; 增长: *The city's population growth slowed to 1.6% last year.* 去年这个城市的人口增长降至1.6%。 □ *The government expects strong economic growth.* 政府期望经济增长势头强劲。
2 the process of a person, an animal or a plant getting bigger 发育; 成长: *Milk is important for a baby's growth and development.* 奶对于婴儿的生长发育很重要。

grudge /ɡrʌdʒ/ *countable noun* 可数名词
a feeling of anger with someone because of something they did in the past 积怨; 不满: *He seems to have a grudge against me.* 他似乎对我心怀怨恨。

grumble /ˈɡrʌmbəl/ *verb* 动词 (**grumbles, grumbling, grumbled**)
to complain about something 抱怨；发牢骚: *They grumble about how hard they have to work.* 他们抱怨不得不非常辛苦地工作。▫ *Dad grumbled that we never cleaned our rooms.* 爸爸抱怨我们从来不打扫自己的房间。● **grumble** *countable noun* 可数名词: *The high prices have brought grumbles from some customers.* 高定价引起一些顾客的不满。

grumpy /ˈɡrʌmpi/ *adjective* 形容词 (**grumpier, grumpiest**)
a little angry 脾气坏的；不悦的: *He's getting grumpy and depressed.* 他变得脾气暴躁、郁郁寡欢。
▸ **grumpily** /ˈɡrʌmpɪli/ *adverb* 副词: *'Go away, I'm busy,' said Ken grumpily.* "走开，我忙着呢。"肯没好气地说道。

grunt /ɡrʌnt/ *verb* 动词 (**grunts, grunting, grunted**)
to make a low sound, especially because you are annoyed or not interested in something (尤指因生气或不感兴趣而)咕哝，嘟囔: *When I said hello he just grunted.* 我和他打招呼，他却只是咕哝了一声。▫ *'Huh,' he grunted.* "呵。"他哼了一声。● **grunt** *countable noun* 可数名词: *Barbara replied with a grunt.* 芭芭拉嘟囔着应了一声。

guarantee[1] /ˌɡærənˈtiː/ *verb* 动词 (**guarantees, guaranteeing, guaranteed**)
1 to promise that something will happen 保证；担保: *We guarantee the safety of our products.* 我们保证产品的安全性。▫ *I guarantee that you will enjoy this film.* 我保证你会喜欢这部电影的。
2 to provide a written promise that the product will be repaired or the customer will be given a new one if it has anything wrong with it 为⋯提供质量保证: *All our computers are guaranteed for 12 months.* 我们所有的计算机都有 12 个月的质保期。

guarantee[2] /ˌɡærənˈtiː/ *countable noun* 可数名词
1 a promise 保证；承诺: *He gave me a guarantee he would finish the job.* 他向我保证过会完成这项工作。
2 a written promise by a company to repair a product or give you a new one if it has anything wrong with it 质保单；保修单: *Keep the guarantee in case something goes wrong.* 把质保单留好，以防出了什么问题。

guard[1] /ɡɑːd/ *verb* 动词 (**guards, guarding, guarded**)
1 to stand near a place, a person or an object to watch and protect them 守卫；护卫: *Armed police guarded the court.* 武装警察守卫着法庭。
2 to watch someone and keep them in a particular place to stop them from escaping 看守；看管: *Marines with rifles guarded them.* 手持步枪的海军陆战队士兵看守着他们。

guard[2] /ɡɑːd/ *countable noun* 可数名词
someone such as a soldier or a police officer, who is guarding a particular place or person 卫兵；警卫；看守: *The prisoners attacked their guards.* 囚犯袭击了狱警。

guardian /ˈɡɑːdiən/ *countable noun* 可数名词
someone who is legally responsible for another person, often a child 监护人: *Diana's grandmother was her legal guardian.* 黛安娜的祖母曾是她的法定监护人。

guerrilla /ɡəˈrɪlə/ *also* 亦作 **guerilla** *countable noun* 可数名词
a person who fights for a military group that does not form part of the regular army 游击队员: *Five soldiers were killed in a guerrilla attack.* 在一次游击队袭击中，5 名士兵丧生。

guess /ɡes/ *verb* 动词 (**guesses, guessing, guessed**)
to give an answer or provide an opinion when you do not know if it is true 猜；猜测: *Yvonne guessed that he was around 40 years old.* 伊冯娜猜测他的年纪在 40 岁上下。▫ *Guess what I just did!* 猜猜我刚才做了什么！● **guess** *countable noun* 可数名词 (**guesses**): *He made a guess at her age.* 他猜了猜她的年纪。▫ *If you don't know, just have a guess.* 你要是不知道，就猜猜吧。

guest /ɡest/ *countable noun* 可数名词
1 someone who you invite to your home or to an event 客人；宾客: *She was a guest at the wedding.* 她是参加婚礼的宾客。
2 someone who is staying in a hotel (宾馆的)客人，房客: *A few guests were having breakfast.* 几位酒店客人在用早餐。

guest house *countable noun* 可数名词
a small hotel 小旅馆

guidance /ˈɡaɪdəns/ *uncountable noun* 不可数名词
help and advice 指导；指点: *My tennis game improved under his guidance.* 我的网

球水平在他的指导下提高了。

guide¹ /gaɪd/ *countable noun* 可数名词
1 a book or a website that gives you information to help you to do or understand something 指导手册；网上指南：*He found a step-by-step guide to building your own home.* 他找到了一本手把手教你建造自己房屋的指导手册。
2 a book or a website that gives tourists information about a town, an area, or a country 旅游手册；网上旅游指南：*The guide to Paris lists hotel rooms for as little as £25 a night.* 这份巴黎旅游指南列出了房价低至每晚 25 英镑的酒店房间。
3 someone who shows tourists around places such as museums or cities 导游：*A guide will take you on a tour of the city.* 导游会带你游览这座城市。

guide² /gaɪd/ *verb* 动词 (**guides, guiding, guided**)
to go somewhere with someone to show them the way 给…带路；为…引路：*He took her by the arm and guided her toward the door.* 他拉着她的胳膊，领她向门口走去。

Guide /gaɪd/ *countable noun* 可数名词
a **Girl Guide** 女童子军队员

guidebook /ˈgaɪdbʊk/ *countable noun* 可数名词
(also 亦作 **guide**) a book for tourists that gives information about a town, an area or a country 旅游指南；旅游手册

guilt /gɪlt/ *uncountable noun* 不可数名词
1 an unhappy feeling that you have when you think that you have done something wrong 内疚、愧疚：*She felt a lot of guilt about her children's unhappiness.* 孩子们不快乐，这让她非常内疚。
2 the fact that you have done something wrong or illegal 有过失；有罪：*There is not enough evidence to prove his guilt.* 没有足够的证据证明他有罪。

guilty /ˈgɪlti/ *adjective* 形容词 (**guiltier, guiltiest**)
1 feeling unhappy because you think that you have done something wrong 内疚的；愧疚的：*I feel so guilty, leaving all this work to you.* 把这些工作都交给你做，我非常愧疚。
2 having committed a crime or an offence 有罪的；犯罪的：*The jury found them guilty of murder.* 陪审团裁定他们的谋杀罪成立。

guinea pig /ˈgɪni ˌpɪg/ *countable noun* 可数名词
1 a person who is used in an experiment 实验对象；实验品：*The doctor used himself as a guinea pig in his research.* 医生把自己当作研究中的实验品。
2 a small animal with fur and no tail. People often keep guinea pigs as pets. 豚鼠；天竺鼠

guitar /gɪˈtɑː/ *noun* 名词
a musical instrument with strings 吉他
→ Look at picture on P12 参见彩插第 12 页

guitarist /gɪˈtɑːrɪst/ *countable noun* 可数名词
a person who plays the guitar 吉他演奏者；吉他手：*He's one of the world's best jazz guitarists.* 他是世界上最优秀的爵士乐吉他手之一。

gulf /gʌlf/ *countable noun* 可数名词
a large area of sea that has land almost all the way around it 海湾：*A storm is crossing the Gulf of Mexico.* 风暴正横扫墨西哥湾。

gulp /gʌlp/ *verb* 动词 (**gulps, gulping, gulped**)
to eat or drink something very quickly 大口吃（或喝）；狼吞虎咽地吃：*She gulped her orange juice.* 她大口喝下橙汁。 ● **gulp** *countable noun* 可数名词：*She took a gulp of fresh air.* 她深吸了一大口新鲜空气。

gum /gʌm/ *noun* 名词
1 *uncountable* 不可数 a sweet sticky substance that you keep in your mouth for a long time but do not swallow 口香糖：*I do not chew gum in public.* 我不在公共场合嚼口香糖。
2 *countable* 可数 one of the areas of firm, pink flesh inside your mouth, where your teeth grow 牙龈；齿龈：*Gently brush your teeth and gums.* 要轻轻地刷牙齿和齿龈。

gun /gʌn/ *countable noun* 可数名词
a weapon that shoots bullets 枪：*He pointed the gun at the police officer.* 他拿枪指向那名警察。

gunman /ˈgʌnmən/ *countable noun* 可数名词 (**gunmen** /ˈgʌnmen/)
a criminal who uses a gun 持枪歹徒：*A gunman fired at police.* 一名持枪歹徒向警察开了枪。

gush /gʌʃ/ *verb* 动词 (**gushes, gushing, gushed**)
to flow very quickly and strongly 喷；涌：*Gallons of water gushed out of the tank.* 大量的水从水箱里喷了出来。 ● **gush** *singular noun* 单数名词：*I heard a gush of water.* 我听到水喷涌而出的声音。

gust /gʌst/ *countable noun* 可数名词
a short, strong, sudden rush of wind 阵风：*A gust of wind came down the valley.* 一阵风刮过山谷。

gut /gʌt/ *singular noun* 单数名词
the tube inside the body of a person or an animal that food passes through after it has been in the stomach 肠；肠道：*The food then passes into the gut.* 食物接着进入肠道。

have the guts to do something to have the courage to do something that is difficult or unpleasant (*informal* 非正式) 有勇气做某事：*She has the guts to say what she thinks.* 她敢于说出自己的想法。

gutter /ˈgʌtə/ *countable noun* 可数名词
1 the edge of a road, where water collects and flows away when it rains (路边的) 排水沟：*His hat fell into the gutter.* 他的帽子掉进排水沟里。
2 a pipe under

gutter 天沟

the edge of a roof that carries water away when it rains (屋顶的) 天沟, 檐沟：*We need to fix the gutters.* 我们需要修一下檐沟。

guy /gaɪ/ *countable noun* 可数名词
a man (*informal* 非正式) 男人；家伙：*I was working with a guy from Birmingham.* 我当时和一个来自伯明翰的家伙一起工作。

gym /dʒɪm/ *countable noun* 可数名词
a club, building or large room with equipment for doing physical exercises 健身会所；健身房；体育馆：*I go to the gym twice a week.* 我一周去两次健身房。

gymnasium /dʒɪmˈneɪziəm/ *countable noun* 可数名词 (**gymnasiums** or 或 **gymnasia** /dʒɪmˈneɪziə/) (*formal* 正式)
→ see 见 **gym**

gymnastics /dʒɪmˈnæstɪks/ *uncountable noun* 不可数名词
a sport that consists of physical exercises that develop your strength and your ability to move easily 体操：*The women's gymnastics team won a silver medal.* 女子体操队赢得了一块银牌。
→ Look at picture on P14 参见彩插第 14 页

Hh

ha /hɑː/ *exclamation* 感叹词
used for showing that you are surprised, annoyed or pleased(用以表示惊奇、恼怒或高兴)哈: *'Ha!' said James. 'Did you really believe me?'* "哈!"詹姆斯说道,"你真的相信我吗?"

habit /ˈhæbɪt/ *noun* 名词
something that you do often or regularly 习惯: *He has many bad habits, such as biting his nails.* 他有很多坏习惯,比如咬指甲。
in the habit of used for saying that someone does something regularly 有⋯的习惯: *They were in the habit of watching TV every night.* 他们习惯每天晚上看电视。

habitat /ˈhæbɪtæt/ *noun* 名词
the environment in which an animal or a plant lives or grows (动植物的)生境, 栖息地: *In its natural habitat, the plant will grow up to 25 feet.* 在原生境中,这种植物能长到 25 英尺高。

had /hæd/
→ see 见 **have**

hadn't /ˈhædənt/
short for (缩写 =) 'had not'

ha ˈha *exclamation* 感叹词
used in writing to show the sound that people make when they laugh(书写中用以表示大笑声)哈哈: *'Ha ha!' he laughed.* "哈哈!"他大笑起来。

hail /heɪl/ *uncountable noun* 不可数名词
small balls of ice that fall like rain from the sky 雹;冰雹: *There will be storms with heavy rain and hail.* 将会有风暴天气,伴有大雨和冰雹。

hair /heə/ *noun* 名词
1 *uncountable* 不可数 the fine threads that grow on your head 头发: *I wash my hair every night.* 我每天晚上洗头。
2 the short threads that grow on the bodies of humans and animals(人、动物的)毛发: *Most men have hair on their chest.* 大多数男人长有胸毛。 ▫ *There were dog hairs all over the sofa.* 沙发上满是狗毛。

haircut /ˈheəkʌt/ *countable noun* 可数名词
an occasion when someone cuts your hair for you 理发: *You need a haircut.* 你需要理发了。

hairdresser /ˈheədresə/ *countable noun* 可数名词
1 a person whose job is to cut and style people's hair 理发师;美发师: *She works as a hairdresser.* 她是个理发师。
2 (also 亦作 **hairdresser's**) a place where you go to have your hair cut 理发店
→ Look at picture on P16 参见彩插第 16 页

hairdryer /ˈheədraɪə/ *countable noun* 可数名词
a machine that you use to dry your hair 吹风机

hairstyle /ˈheəstaɪl/ *countable noun* 可数名词
the style in which your hair has been cut or arranged 发型;发式: *I think her new hairstyle looks great.* 我认为她的新发型很好看。

hairy /ˈheəri/ *adjective* 形容词 (**hairier, hairiest**)
covered with hairs 多毛的: *He was wearing shorts that showed his hairy legs.* 他穿着短裤,露出长满汗毛的双腿。

halal /hɑːl/ *adjective* 形容词
used for describing meat from animals that have been killed according to Muslim law (肉)清真的: *a halal butcher's shop* 清真肉铺

half¹ /hɑːf/ *noun* 名词 (**halves**)
one of two equal parts of a number, an amount or an object 半;一半: *More than half of all U.S. houses are heated with gas.* 美国所有的住宅中有一半以上采用天然气供暖。 ▫ *We sat and talked for half an hour.* 我们坐下来谈了半个小时。 ▫ *They only received half the money.* 他们仅收到一半的钱。 ● **half** *adjective* 形容词: *I'll stay with you for the first half hour.* 前半个小时我会和你待在一起。
→ Look at picture on P2 参见彩插第 2 页

half² /hɑːf/ *adverb* 副词
used for saying that something is only partly in the state that you are describing 部分地；不完全地：*The glass was half empty.* 玻璃杯空了一半。

half-term also 亦作 **half term** *uncountable noun* 不可数名词
a short holiday in the middle of a school term (= a three-month period of school) (学校的)期中假：*the half-term holidays* 期中假

halftime /ˌhɑːfˈtaɪm/ *uncountable noun* 不可数名词
the period between the two parts of a sports event, when the players take a short rest (体育比赛的)中场休息：*We bought something to eat during halftime.* 中场休息时我们买了点儿吃的。

halfway /ˌhɑːfˈweɪ/ *adverb* 副词
1 in the middle of a place or between two points (空间上)在中间：*He was halfway up the ladder.* 他爬到梯子一半的位置。
2 in the middle of an event or period of time 在(事件的)中途；(时间上)到一半：*We were more than halfway through our tour.* 我们的旅程已过半。

hall /hɔːl/ *countable noun* 可数名词
1 the area that connects one room in a house or a flat to another 门厅；过道：*The hall leads to a large living room.* 正门过道通向一间很大的客厅。
2 a large room or building that is used for public events such as concerts and meetings 礼堂；大厅：*We went into the dance hall.* 我们走进了舞厅。

hallo /hæˈləʊ/
→ see 见 **hello**

Halloween /ˌhæləʊˈiːn/ also 亦作 **Hallowe'en** *uncountable noun* 不可数名词
the night of 31st October when children wear special clothes, and walk from house to house asking for sweets 万圣节前夕(10月31日晚，孩子们身穿奇装异服，挨家挨户讨糖吃)

hallway /ˈhɔːlweɪ/ *countable noun* 可数名词
an area in a building with doors that lead into other rooms (大楼内的)走廊：*They walked along the quiet hallway.* 他们沿着寂静的走廊走去。

halt¹ /hɔːlt/ *verb* 动词 (**halts, halting, halted**)
to stop something 使停止；使停下：*Officials halted the race at 5.30 p.m. yesterday.* 官员于昨天下午5点30分叫停了那场比赛。

halt² /hɔːlt/ *noun* 名词
come to a halt to stop moving 停下来：*The lift came to a halt at the first floor.* 电梯在二楼停了下来。

halves /hɑːvz/
the plural of **half** (**half** 的复数形式)

ham /hæm/ *uncountable noun* 不可数名词
meat from a pig that has been prepared with salt and spices 火腿肉

hamburger /ˈhæmbɜːɡə/ *countable noun* 可数名词
a type of food made from small pieces of meat that have been shaped into a flat circle. Hamburgers are fried or grilled and are often eaten in a round piece of bread (= a roll). 汉堡包

> **LANGUAGE HELP** 语言提示
> **Beefburger** is also used in British English. 英国英语也用 beefburger。

hammer /ˈhæmə/ *countable noun* 可数名词
a tool that is made from a heavy piece of metal attached to the end of a handle. It is used for hitting nails into wood. 锤子；榔头：*She got a hammer and a nail and two pieces of wood.* 她拿来一把锤子、一个钉子和两块木头。
● **hammer** *verb* 动词 (**hammers, hammering, hammered**)：*She hammered a nail into the window frame.* 她把一枚钉子钉到窗框上。

hammer 锤子

hamper /ˈhæmpə/ *verb* 动词 (**hampers, hampering, hampered**)
to make it difficult for someone to do what they are trying to do 妨碍；阻碍：*The bad weather hampered the rescue operation.* 恶劣天气妨碍了营救行动。

hamster /ˈhæmstə/ *countable noun* 可数名词
a small animal that is similar to a mouse and is often kept as a pet 仓鼠(常作宠物)

hand¹ /hænd/ *countable noun* 可数名词
1 the part of your body at the end of your arm that you use for holding things 手：*I put my hand into my pocket and took out the letter.* 我把手伸进口袋里，拿出了那封信。
→ Look at picture on P4 参见彩插第4页

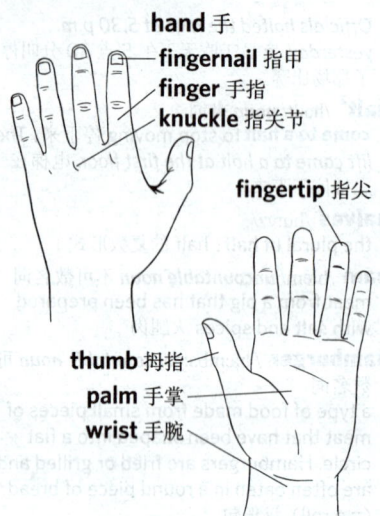

hand 手
fingernail 指甲
finger 手指
knuckle 指关节
fingertip 指尖
thumb 拇指
palm 手掌
wrist 手腕

2 one of the long thin parts on a clock or a watch that move to show the time 指针
by hand done or made using your hands rather than a machine 用手工：*The dress was made by hand.* 那件连衣裙是手工做的。
give someone a hand to help someone 帮助某人；协助某人：*Come and give me a hand in the kitchen.* 来厨房帮我一下。
hand in hand holding each other by the hand 手拉手：*They go everywhere hand in hand.* 他们到哪儿都手拉着手。
on hand near and ready to be used 在手头；现成可用：*There are experts on hand to give you all the help you need.* 随时都有专家为您提供所需要的一切帮助。
on the one hand used for talking about the first of two different ways of looking at something（用以引导出两个不同视角中的第一个）一方面：*On the one hand, the body cannot survive without fat. On the other hand, if the body has too much fat, our health starts to suffer.* 一方面，人体没有脂肪就无法存活；另一方面，体内脂肪过多又会开始损害健康。
on the other hand used for talking about the second of two different ways of looking at something（用以引导出两个不同视角中的第二个）另一方面：*The film lost money. Reviews, on the other hand, were mostly favourable.* 电影亏本了，然而影评却多是褒扬。
out of hand no longer able to be controlled 失去控制的：*The argument got out of hand*

when her boyfriend hit her. 她男友动手打了她，之后争吵变得一发不可收拾。

hand² /hænd/ *verb* 动词 (hands, handing, handed)
to put something into someone's hand 交；递：*He handed me a piece of paper.* 他递给我一张纸。
hand something in to take something to someone and give it to them 提交某物；上交某物：*I need to hand in my homework today.* 我今天得交家庭作业。 □ *They found £7,500 in cash on the street and handed it in to police.* 他们在大街上捡到了 7,500 英镑的现金，然后交给了警察。
hand something out to give one thing to each person in a group 分发某物：*My job was to hand out the prizes.* 我的任务是发奖品。

handbag /ˈhændbæg/ *countable noun* 可数名词 (*American* 美国英语：*purse*)
a small bag that a woman uses for carrying things such as money and keys（女用）小手提包

handbook /ˈhændbʊk/ *countable noun* 可数名词
a book that gives you advice and instructions about a particular subject 手册；指南：*The staff handbook says we get two weeks of holiday.* 员工手册上写着我们有两个星期的假期。

handcuffs /ˈhændkʌfs/ *plural noun* 复数名词
two connected metal rings that can be locked around someone's wrists 手铐：*He was taken to prison in handcuffs.* 他被铐住双手带进了监狱。● **handcuff** /ˈhændkʌf/ *verb* 动词 (**handcuffs, handcuffing, handcuffed**)：*Police tried to handcuff him but he ran away.* 警察想铐住他，但他跑掉了。

handful /ˈhændfʊl/ *noun* 名词
1 *singular* 单数 a small number of people or things（人或物的）少数，少量：*Only a handful of people knew his secret.* 只有少数人知道他的秘密。
2 *countable* 可数 the amount of something that you can hold in your hand 一把（的量）：*She threw a handful of sand into the water.* 她把一把沙子扔进了水里。

handkerchief /ˈhæŋkətʃɪf/ *countable noun* 可数名词
a small square piece of cloth that you use

for blowing your nose 手帕

handle¹ /ˈhændəl/ *countable noun* 可数名词
1 an object that is attached to a door or drawer, used for opening and closing it （门或抽屉的）把手，拉手：*I turned the handle and the door opened.* 我转动把手，门开了。
2 the part of a tool, a bag or a cup that you hold（工具的）柄，把；（包或杯子的）把手：*I held the knife handle tightly.* 我紧紧地握着刀柄。

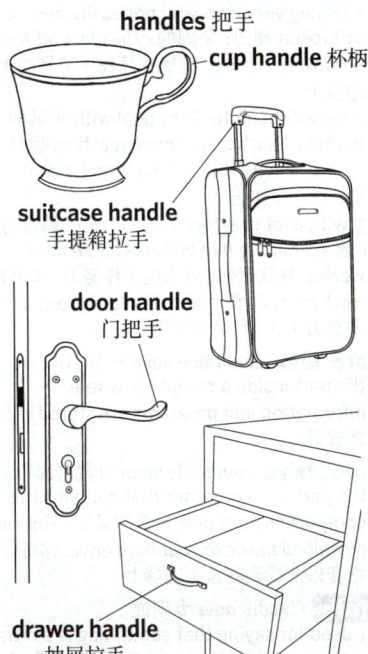

handles 把手
cup handle 杯柄
suitcase handle 手提箱拉手
door handle 门把手
drawer handle 抽屉拉手

handle² /ˈhændəl/ *verb* 动词 (handles, handling, handled)
1 to deal with a situation 处理；应付：*I think I handled the meeting very badly.* 我认为我把这次会谈搞得一团糟。
2 to hold something or move it with your hands（用手）拿，搬动：*Wash your hands before handling food.* 拿食物前请先洗手。

handmade /ˌhændˈmeɪd/ also 亦作 **hand-made** *adjective* 形容词
made by someone without using machines 手工制作的：*The shop sells beautiful handmade jewellery.* 这家商店出售漂亮的手工珠宝。

handout /ˈhændaʊt/ *countable noun* 可数名词
a piece of paper containing information that is given to people in a meeting or a class（发给参会者或学生的）讲义，提纲：*The instructions are all written in the handout.* 操作说明都写在讲义中了。

handshake /ˈhændʃeɪk/ *countable noun* 可数名词
when you take someone's right hand with your own right hand and move it up and down as a way of greeting them or showing that you have agreed about something 握手：*He has a strong handshake.* 他握手很有力。

handsome /ˈhænsəm/ *adjective* 形容词
having an attractive face 英俊的；相貌堂堂的：*The photo showed a tall, handsome soldier.* 照片上是一位身材高大、相貌英俊的士兵。

handwriting /ˈhændraɪtɪŋ/ *uncountable noun* 不可数名词
your style of writing with a pen or a pencil 笔迹；字迹：*The address was in Anna's handwriting.* 地址是安娜的笔迹。

handy /ˈhændi/ *adjective* 形容词 (**handier**, **handiest**)
1 useful 有用的：*The book gives handy ideas on growing plants.* 这本书就种植花草提供了有用的建议。
2 nearby and easy to reach 手头的；近便的：*Make sure you have a pencil and paper handy.* 要确保手头有铅笔和纸。

hang /hæŋ/ *verb* 动词 (**hangs**, **hanging**, **hung** or 或 **hanged**)

> **LANGUAGE HELP 语言提示**
> Use **hangs**, **hanging**, **hanged** for the sense **be hanged**. *hang 作"绞死"解时屈折变化形式为 hangs、hanging 和 hanged。

1 to be attached somewhere without touching the ground（某物）悬挂，吊：*Flags hang at every entrance.* 每个入口处都悬挂着旗子。
2 to attach something somewhere so that it does not touch the ground 悬挂，吊起（某物）：*She hung her clothes outside to dry.* 她把衣服挂在外面晾干。

be hanged to be killed by having a rope tied around your neck 被绞死：*The five men were hanged on Tuesday.* 那5个人在星期二被处以绞刑。

hang on
1 to wait (*informal* 非正式) 稍等: *Can you hang on for a minute?* 你能稍等一下吗？
2 to hold something very tightly 抓紧；握紧: *He hung on to the rail as he went downstairs.* 他下楼时紧紧地抓住扶手。

hang out
to spend a lot of time somewhere (*informal* 非正式) 常去，泡在（某处）: *I often hang out at the shopping arcade.* 我常在购物街闲逛。

hang up
to end a phone call 挂断电话: *Don't hang up on me!* 不要挂断我的电话！

happen /ˈhæpən/ *verb* 动词 (happens, happening, happened)
1 to take place without being planned（偶然）发生，出现: *We don't know what will happen.* 我们不知道将会发生什么。
2 to take place and affect someone 发生（在…身上）: *What's the worst thing that has ever happened to you?* 你所遇到最糟糕的事情是什么？

happen to do something
to do something by chance 碰巧做某事: *I happened to be at the library at the same time as Jim.* 碰巧我和吉姆同时都在图书馆。

happily /ˈhæpɪli/ *adverb* 副词
added to something you say in order to show that you are glad that something happened 幸运地: *Happily, this situation will soon get much easier.* 幸好，这种情况很快就会变得容易很多。

happy /ˈhæpi/ *adjective* 形容词 (happier, happiest)
1 feeling pleased and satisfied 快乐的；高兴的: *Marina was a happy child.* 玛丽娜是个快乐的孩子。
▶ **happily** /ˈhæpɪli/ *adverb* 副词: *The children played happily together all day.* 孩子们在一起快乐地玩耍了一整天。
→ Look at picture on P15 参见彩插第 15 页
▶ **happiness** /ˈhæpɪnəs/ *uncountable noun* 不可数名词: *I think she was looking for happiness.* 我想她在寻找幸福。
2 full of happy feelings and pleasant experiences 使人幸福的；让人幸福的: *She had a very happy childhood.* 她有一个非常幸福的童年。 □ *Grandma's house was always a happy place.* 奶奶家总是一个令人快乐的地方。
3 used in some expressions to say that you hope someone will enjoy a special occasion（表示祝愿）: *Happy Birthday!* 生日快乐！

happy to do something
very willing to do something 愿意（或乐意）做某事的: *I'm happy to answer any questions.* 我愿意回答任何问题。

harbour /ˈhɑːbə/ *countable noun* 可数名词
an area of water next to the land where boats can safely stay 海港；港口；港湾: *The fishing boats left the harbour and went out to sea.* 渔船离开港湾出海了。

hard /hɑːd/ *adjective* 形容词, *adverb* 副词 (harder, hardest)
1 feeling very firm, and not easily bent, cut or broken 硬的；坚固的: *The glass hit the hard wooden floor.* 玻璃杯摔在了坚硬的木地板上。
2 very difficult to do or deal with 难做的；困难的: *That's a very hard question.* 那是个很难回答的问题。 □ *She's had a hard life.* 她一生艰苦。
3 with a lot of effort 努力的（地）；勤奋的（地）: *I admire him because he's a hard worker.* 我钦佩他，因为他工作努力。 □ *If I work hard, I'll finish the job tomorrow.* 如果我努力工作，我明天能完成任务。

ˈhard ˌdisk *countable noun* 可数名词
the part inside a computer where information and programs are stored 硬盘；硬磁盘

ˈhard ˌdrive *countable noun* 可数名词
the part of a computer that contains the computer's hard disk 硬盘驱动器: *You can download music to your hard drive.* 你可以把音乐下载到硬盘驱动器上。

hardly /ˈhɑːdli/ *adverb* 副词
1 used for saying that something is almost not true or only just true 几乎不；将将: *I hardly know you.* 我不怎么认识你。 □ *I've hardly slept for three days.* 我差不多 3 天没睡觉了。
2 used in expressions such as **hardly ever** and **hardly any** to mean almost never or almost none（用于 hardly ever、hardly any 等短语中）几乎从不，几乎没有: *We hardly ever eat fish.* 我们几乎从不吃鱼。 □ *They hire young workers with hardly any experience.* 他们聘用几乎没有任何经验的年轻工人。

hardware /ˈhɑːdweə/ *uncountable noun* 不可数名词
1 things in computer systems such as the computer, the keyboard and the screen, rather than the software programs that tell the computer what to do. Compare

with **software**. 硬件（比较 software）: *The hardware costs about £200.* 硬件要花费大约 200 英镑。
2 tools and equipment that are used in the home and garden（家庭及园艺用）五金制品: *He bought a hammer and some nails at a hardware shop.* 他在一家五金店买了一把锤子和一些钉子。

harm /hɑːm/ *verb* 动词 (**harms, harming, harmed**)
to injure or damage someone or something 伤害；损害: *The boys didn't mean to harm anyone.* 男孩子们没想要伤害任何人。□ *This product may harm the environment.* 该产品可能损害环境。
● **harm** *uncountable noun* 不可数名词: *Don't worry. He won't do you any harm.* 不要担心，他不会伤害你的。

harmful /ˈhɑːmfʊl/ *adjective* 形容词
having a bad effect on someone or something 有害的: *People should know about the harmful effects of the sun.* 人们应该了解阳光的危害。

harmless /ˈhɑːmləs/ *adjective* 形容词
not having any bad effects 无害的: *These insects are harmless.* 这些昆虫是无害的。

harmony /ˈhɑːməni/ *noun* 名词 (**harmonies**)
1 *uncountable* 不可数 when people are living together without harming anyone or anything 融洽；和睦；和谐: *People have lived in harmony with nature for centuries.* 数百年来，人们与自然和谐相处。
2 the pleasant combination of different notes of music played at the same time 和声: *The children were singing in harmony.* 孩子们在唱和声。

harp /hɑːp/ *noun* 名词
a large musical instrument that has strings stretched from the top to the bottom of a frame. You play the harp with your fingers. 竖琴
→ Look at picture on P12 参见彩插第 12 页

harsh /hɑːʃ/ *adjective* 形容词 (**harsher, harshest**)
1 hard and unpleasant 恶劣的；艰苦的: *We met during the first harsh winter after the war.* 我们在战后第一个寒冷的冬天相遇。
2 unkind 严厉的；无情的: *She said many harsh things about her brother.* 她说了她哥哥许多坏话。
▶ **harshly** /ˈhɑːʃli/ *adverb* 副词: *He was harshly treated in prison.* 他在监狱里遭受虐待。
3 unpleasant because of being too hard, bright or rough 强烈的；刺眼的；粗糙的: *The leaves can burn badly in harsh sunlight.* 树叶在太阳的强光照射下会严重灼伤。

harvest /ˈhɑːvɪst/ *singular noun* 单数名词
the gathering of a farm crop 收割；收获: *Wheat harvests were poor in both Europe and America last year.* 去年欧洲和美洲的小麦收成不好。● **harvest** *verb* 动词 (**harvests, harvesting, harvested**): *Farmers here still plant and harvest their crops by hand.* 这里的农民仍然手工种植和收割农作物。

has /həz, STRONG 强读 hæz/
→ see 见 **have**

hasn't /ˈhæzənt/
short for（缩写 =）'has not'

haste /heɪst/ *uncountable noun* 不可数名词
when you do things too quickly 仓促；匆忙: *He almost fell down the stairs in his haste to get to the phone.* 他匆忙去接电话时险些摔下楼梯。

hasty /ˈheɪsti/ *adjective* 形容词 (**hastier, hastiest**)
done suddenly or quickly 草率的；草草了事的: *Perhaps I was too hasty when I said she couldn't come.* 我说她来不了也许太草率了。
▶ **hastily** /ˈheɪstɪli/ *adverb* 副词: *A meeting was hastily arranged to discuss the problem.* 为了讨论这个问题匆忙安排了一次会议。

hat /hæt/ *countable noun* 可数名词
a thing that you wear on your head 帽子: *Look for a woman in a red hat.* 找一位戴红帽子的女士。

hatch /hætʃ/ *verb* 动词 (**hatches, hatching, hatched**)
when a baby bird, insect or other animal hatches, it comes out of its egg. You can also say that an egg hatches.（雏鸟、幼虫或其他动物）孵出，出壳；（蛋）孵化: *The young birds died soon after they hatched.* 雏鸟出壳后很快就死掉了。□ *The eggs hatch after a week.* 蛋在 1 周后孵化。

hate /heɪt/ *verb* 动词 (**hates, hating, hated**)
to have a strong feeling of dislike for someone or something 厌恶；憎恨；讨厌: *She thinks that everyone hates her.* 她认为每个人都憎恨她。□ *He hates losing.* 他讨厌失败。● **hate** *uncountable noun* 不可数

名词: He spoke of the hate that he felt for some people. 他谈到他对一些人的憎恨。

haul /hɔːl/ *verb* 动词 (**hauls, hauling, hauled**)
to move something somewhere using a lot of effort (用力) 拖，拉，拽: *They hauled the car out of the water.* 他们把汽车从水里拖了出来。

haunted /ˈhɔːntɪd/ *adjective* 形容词
used for describing a building where people believe ghosts (= spirits of dead people) appear (建筑物被认为) 闹鬼的，有鬼魂出没的: *Tracy said the house was haunted.* 特蕾西说那栋房子闹鬼。

have¹ /həv, STRONG 强读 hæv/ *auxiliary verb* 助动词 (**has, had**)

> **LANGUAGE HELP 语言提示**
> When you are speaking, you can use the short forms **I've** for **I have** and **hasn't** for **has not**. 口语中，I have 可缩作 I've，has not 可缩作 hasn't。

used with another verb to form perfect tenses (与另一动词连用构成完成时): *Alex hasn't left yet.* 亚历克斯还没有离开。 □ *What have you found?* 你发现了什么？ □ *Frankie hasn't been feeling well today.* 弗朗姬今天感觉不舒服。

have² /həv, STRONG 强读 hæv/ *verb* 动词 (**has, having, had**)
1 used with a noun to talk about an action or an event (与名词连用，描述某一动作或事件): *Come and have a look at this!* 过来看看这个！ □ *We had a long talk last night.* 昨晚我们谈了很长时间。 □ *Come and have a meal with us tonight.* 今晚来和我们一起吃饭吧。 □ *We are having a meeting to decide what to do.* 我们将开会决定做什么。 □ *I had an accident and broke my wrist.* 我出了事故，摔断了手腕。
2 (also 亦作 **have got**) used for saying that someone or something owns something 有；拥有: *Billy has a new bicycle.* 比利有一辆新自行车。 □ *Have we got enough chairs?* 我们有足够的椅子吗？
3 used for talking about people's relationships (表示人际关系) 有: *Do you have any brothers or sisters?* 你有兄弟姐妹吗？
4 (also 亦作 **have got**) used when you are talking about a person's appearance or character 具有 (某种外貌或性格): *You*

have beautiful eyes. 你有一双美丽的眼睛。 □ *George has a terrible temper.* 乔治脾气暴躁。
5 used for saying that something is in a particular position or state 使处于 (某位置或状态): *Mary had her eyes closed.* 玛丽双目紧闭。

have something done used for saying that someone does something for you 请人做某事: *He had his hair cut yesterday.* 他昨天理发了。

have to do something or **have got to do something** used when you are saying that someone must do something, or that something must happen. If you do not have to do something, it is not necessary for you to do it. 必须做某事；不得不做某事: *I have to go home soon.* 我必须马上回家。 □ *You've got to tell me the truth.* 你必须告诉我真相。 □ '*You don't have to explain.*' "你不用解释。"

haven't /ˈhævənt/
short for (缩写 =) 'have not'

hawk /hɔːk/ *countable noun* 可数名词
a large bird that catches and eats small birds and animals 鹰

hay /heɪ/ *uncountable noun* 不可数名词
grass that has been cut and dried so that it can be used for feeding animals (作饲料用的) 干草，草料

hazard /ˈhæzəd/ *countable noun* 可数名词
something that could be dangerous 危险；危害: *Too much salt may be a health hazard.* 吃过多的盐会危害健康。

HDTV /ˌeɪtʃ diː tiː ˈviː/ *uncountable noun* 不可数名词
a television system that provides a very clear image. **HDTV** is short for (缩写 =) 'high-definition television'. 高清晰度电视；高画质电视: *The quality of digital TV is better, especially HDTV.* 数字电视的质量较好，特别是高清电视。

he /hi, STRONG 强读 hiː/ *pronoun* 代词
used for talking about a man, a boy or a male animal 他；它 (指雄性动物): *John was my boss, but he couldn't remember my name.* 约翰是我的老板，但他记不住我的名字。

head¹ /hed/ *countable noun* 可数名词
1 the top part of your body that has your eyes, mouth and brain in it 头；头部: *The ball came down and hit him on the head.* 球

落下来砸到了他的头上。
→ Look at picture on P4 参见彩插第 4 页
2 your mind 头脑；脑筋：*I just said the first thing that came into my head.* 我只是脑子里想到什么说什么。
3 the person who is in charge of a company or an organization 主管；负责人：*I spoke to the head of the department.* 我和部门经理谈过了。
4 the top, the start or the most important end of something 顶端；前端；最重要的位置：*She sat at the head of the table.* 她坐在桌子的上首。
a head or **per head** used for describing the cost or amount for one person 每人：*This simple meal costs less than £4 a head.* 这顿简餐每人花费不到 4 英镑。

head² /hed/ **verb** 动词 (**heads, heading, headed**)
to be the person who is in charge of a department, a company or an organization 掌管；主管；负责：*Michael Williams heads the department's Office of Civil Rights.* 迈克尔·威廉斯负责该部民权处。
be heading for to be going towards a particular place 向（某地）行进：*He is heading for the bus stop.* 他朝公交车站走去。

headache /ˈhedeɪk/ **countable noun** 可数名词
a pain in your head 头痛：*I have a terrible headache.* 我头痛得厉害。

headfirst /ˌhedˈfɜːst/ also 亦作 **head-first** *adverb* 副词
with your head in front of your body when you are moving 头向前：*Chee dived headfirst into the water.* 奇一头扎进水里。

headfirst 头向前

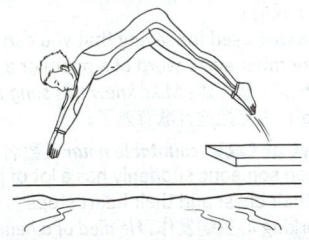

heading /ˈhedɪŋ/ **countable noun** 可数名词
a title that is written at the top of a page（页首的）标题：*When you read the book, notice the chapter headings.* 读这本书时要注意章节的标题。

headlight /ˈhedlaɪt/ **countable noun** 可数名词
one of the large lights at the front of a vehicle（汽车的）头灯，前灯：*He turned on the car's headlights when the rain started.* 雨下起来的时候，他把车前灯打开了。

headline /ˈhedlaɪn/ *noun* 名词
1 *countable* 可数 the title of a newspaper story, printed in large letters（报纸的）大字标题：*The headline said: 'New Government Plans'.* 报纸标题写着："政府新计划"。
2 [**headlines**] *plural* 复数 the important parts of the news that you hear first on radio or television news reports（广播或电视的）新闻摘要：*Claudia Polley read the news headlines.* 克劳迪娅·波利播报了新闻摘要。

headphones /ˈhedfəʊnz/ *plural noun* 复数名词
things that you wear on your ears so that you can listen to music or the radio without anyone else hearing 耳机：*I listened to the programme on headphones.* 我戴耳机收听节目。

headphones 耳机

headquarters /ˈhedkwɔːtəz/ *singular noun* 单数名词
the main offices of an organization 总部；总公司：*The news broadcast came from Chicago's police headquarters.* 这则新闻广播来自芝加哥警察总局。

head teacher **countable noun** 可数名词
a teacher who is in charge of a school 校长

heal /hiːl/ *verb* 动词 (**heals, healing, healed**)
to become healthy again 康复；痊愈：*It took six months for her injuries to heal.* 她伤口愈合用了 6 个月。

health /helθ/ *uncountable noun* 不可数名词
the condition of a person's body 身体状况；健康：*Too much fatty food is bad for your health.* 太多高脂食物对健康有害。

'health care also 亦作 **healthcare**
uncountable noun 不可数名词
services for preventing and treating illnesses and injuries 医疗卫生；卫生保健：*Nobody wants to pay more money for health care.* 没有人愿意为医疗保健多花钱。

healthy /ˈhelθi/ *adjective* 形容词 (**healthier, healthiest**)
1 well, and not often ill 健康的；健壮的：*People need to exercise to be healthy.* 人们需要运动来保持健康。
2 good for your health 有益健康的：*Try to eat a healthy diet.* 尽量做到健康饮食。

heap /hiːp/ *countable noun* 可数名词
a messy pile of things (凌乱的) 一堆：*There was a heap of clothes in the corner of the room.* 房间角落里有一堆衣服。● **heap** *verb* 动词 (**heaps, heaping, heaped**)：*His mother heaped more carrots onto Michael's plate.* 他的妈妈给迈克尔的盘子里添了些胡萝卜。

hear /hɪə/ *verb* 动词 (**hears, hearing, heard**)
1 to become aware of a sound through your ears 听见；听到：*She could hear music in the distance.* 她能听见远处的音乐声。□ *I heard him say, 'Thanks.'* 我听见他说："谢谢。"
2 to find out about something by someone telling you, or from the radio or television 听说；得知：*My mother heard about the school from Karen.* 我妈妈是从卡伦那里知道这所学校的。□ *I hear that Bruce Springsteen is playing at Madison Square Garden tomorrow evening.* 我听说布鲁斯·斯普林斯廷明晚将在麦迪逊广场花园演出。
3 to know about something or someone 听说过：*I've heard of him, but I've never met him.* 我听说过他，但从未见过。

hear from someone to receive a letter, an email or a telephone call from someone 接到某人的来信（或电子邮件、电话）：*It's always great to hear from you.* 收到你的来信我总是很高兴。

LANGUAGE HELP 语言提示
Hear or **listen**? 用 hear 还是 listen？
Use **hear** to talk about sounds that you notice when they reach your ears. *hear 表示被动听到：*I heard a noise downstairs.* 我听到楼下有声响。
Use **listen** when you are paying attention to something you can hear. *listen 表示用心倾听：*He turned on the radio and listened to the news.* 他打开收音机听新闻。

---

heard /hɜːd/
→ see 见 **hear**

hearing /ˈhɪərɪŋ/ *uncountable noun* 不可数名词
the sense that makes it possible for you to be aware of sounds 听觉；听力：*His hearing was excellent.* 他的听力极好。

'hearing aid *countable noun* 可数名词
a small piece of equipment that people wear in their ear to help them to hear better 助听器

heart /hɑːt/ *noun* 名词
1 *countable* 可数 the part inside your chest that makes the blood move around your body 心；心脏：*His heart was beating fast.* 他的心跳得很快。
→ Look at picture on P5 参见彩插第 5 页
2 *countable* 可数 your deep feelings 内心：*Anne's words filled her heart with joy.* 安妮的话使她的心中充满了喜悦。
3 *singular* 单数 the middle part of a place 中心；中央：*They own a busy hotel in the heart of the city.* 他们在市中心拥有一家业务繁忙的酒店。
4 *countable* 可数 the shape ♥ 心形

heart 心脏   heart 心形

break someone's heart to make someone very unhappy 使某人伤心；使某人心碎：*I fell in love on holiday but the girl broke my heart.* 我度假时坠入了爱河，但那个女孩伤透了我的心。

by heart used for saying that you can remember every word of a poem or a song 凭记忆；靠背诵：*Mike knew this song by heart.* 迈克把这首歌背熟了。

'heart at,tack *countable noun* 可数名词
when someone suddenly has a lot of pain in their chest and their heart stops working 心脏病发作：*He died of a heart attack.* 他死于心脏病发作。

heartbeat /ˈhɑːtbiːt/ *singular noun* 单数名词
the regular movement of your heart as it pushes blood through your body 心搏；心跳：*The doctor listened to her heartbeat.* 医

heat /hiːt/ *uncountable noun* 不可数名词
when something is hot 热: *Our clothes dried quickly in the heat of the sun.* 我们的衣服在太阳的高温下很快就晒干了。● **heat** *verb* 动词 (**heats, heating, heated**): *Heat the tomatoes and oil in a pan.* 把西红柿和油放平底锅里加热。

heater /ˈhiːtə/ *countable noun* 可数名词
a piece of equipment that is used for making a room warm 加热器；暖气装置: *There's an electric heater in the bedroom.* 卧室里有一个电热器。

heating /ˈhiːtɪŋ/ *uncountable noun* 不可数名词
the equipment that is used for keeping a building warm 供暖设备: *She turned on the heating.* 她打开了供暖设备。

heaven /ˈhevən/ *noun* 名词
the place where some people believe good people go when they die 天堂；天国: *I believe that when I die I will go to heaven.* 我想我死后会去天堂。

heavy /ˈhevi/ *adjective* 形容词 (**heavier, heaviest**)
1 weighing a lot 重的；沉的: *This bag is very heavy. What's in it?* 这个袋子很重。里面是什么？
2 used for asking about how much someone or something weighs (用于询问重量) 有…重的: *How heavy is your suitcase?* 你的手提箱有多重？
3 great in amount 大量的；多的: *We drove through heavy traffic for two hours.* 我们在拥挤的车流中开了两个小时的车。
▶ **heavily** /ˈhevɪli/ *adverb* 副词: *It rained heavily all day.* 下了一整天的大雨。

hectic /ˈhektɪk/ *adjective* 形容词
very busy and involving a lot of activity 忙碌的；繁忙的: *Ben had a hectic work schedule.* 本的工作日程排得很紧。

he'd /hɪd, STRONG 强读 hiːd/
1 short for (缩写 =) 'he had'
2 short for (缩写 =) 'he would'

hedge /hedʒ/ *countable noun* 可数名词
a row of small trees growing close together around a garden or a field 绿篱；树篱

hedgehog /ˈhedʒhɒɡ/ *countable noun* 可数名词
a small brown animal with sharp points covering its back 刺猬

heel /hiːl/ *countable noun* 可数名词
1 the back part of your foot, just below your ankle 足跟；脚跟: *I have a big blister on my heel.* 我脚跟上有一个大水疱。
2 the raised part on the bottom at the back of a shoe 鞋跟: *She always wears shoes with high heels.* 她总是穿着高跟鞋。

height /haɪt/ *noun* 名词
1 the size of a person or thing from the bottom to the top 身高；高度: *Her weight is normal for her height.* 她的体重就她的身高来说是正常的。□ *I am five feet six inches in height.* 我身高 5 英尺 6 英寸。
2 the distance that something is above the ground (自地面算起的) 高度: *You can change the height of the seat.* 你可以调整座位的高度。

heir /eə/ *countable noun* 可数名词
someone who will receive a person's money or property when that person dies (财产的) 继承人: *Elizabeth was her father's heir.* 伊丽莎白是她父亲的继承人。

held /held/
→ see 见 **hold**

helicopter /ˈhelɪkɒptə/ *countable noun* 可数名词
an aircraft with long blades on top that go around very fast. It is able to stay still in the air and to move straight upwards or downwards as well as forwards and backwards. 直升机

hell /hel/ *noun* 名词
the place where some people believe bad people go when they die 地狱: *My mother says I'll go to hell if I lie.* 我妈妈说如果我撒谎便会去地狱。

he'll /hɪl, STRONG 强读 hiːl/
short for (缩写 =) 'he will'

hello /heˈləʊ/ also 亦作 **hallo**
1 said to someone when you meet them (见面问候语) 喂，你好: *Hello, Trish. How are you?* 喂，特里什，你好吗？
2 said when you answer the phone (接电话用语) 喂: *Cohen picked up the phone and said 'Hello?'* 科恩拿起电话说道："喂？"

helmet /ˈhelmɪt/ *countable noun* 可数名词
a hat made of a hard material, which you wear to protect your head 头盔；安全帽

help /help/ *verb* 动词 (**helps, helping, helped**)
1 to make it easier for someone to do something 帮助；帮忙: *Can somebody help me, please?* 请问有人能帮我吗？ □ *You*

can help by giving them some money. 你可以帮衬他们一些钱。 ●**help** *uncountable noun* 不可数名词: *Thanks very much for your help.* 非常感谢你的帮助。
2 to improve a situation 有帮助；有用: *Thanks for your advice. That helps.* 谢谢你的建议，很有帮助。
can't help something to be unable to stop the way you feel or behave 忍不住做某事: *I couldn't help laughing when I saw her face.* 我看到她的脸时忍不住大笑起来。
help yourself to take what you want of something 自便；随便取用: *There's bread on the table. Help yourself.* 桌子上有面包，随便拿吧。

helpful /ˈhelpfʊl/ *adjective* 形容词
helping you by being useful or willing to work for you 有帮助的；愿意帮忙的: *The staff in the hotel are very helpful.* 旅馆的工作人员非常乐于助人。

helpless /ˈhelpləs/ *adjective* 形容词
not having the strength or ability to do anything useful 无助的；无力的: *Parents often feel helpless when their children are ill.* 孩子生病时父母往往感到很无助。
▶ **helplessly** /ˈhelpləsli/ *adverb* 副词: *They watched helplessly as the house burned to the ground.* 他们无奈地看着房子被烧成平地。

hemisphere /ˈhemɪˌsfɪə/ *noun* 名词
1 *countable* 可数 one half of the Earth（地球的）半球: *These animals live in the northern hemisphere.* 这些动物生活在北半球。
2 one half of a sphere (= an object that is shaped like a ball)（球体的）半球

hen /hen/ *countable noun* 可数名词
a female chicken 母鸡

her¹ /hə, STRONG 强读 hɜː/ *pronoun* 代词
used for talking about a woman, a girl or a female animal 她；它（指雌性动物）: *I told her that dinner was ready.* 我告诉她饭做好了。

her² /hə, STRONG 强读 hɜː/ *adjective* 形容词
used for showing that something belongs to or relates to a girl or a woman 她的: *She took her coat off and sat down.* 她脱下外套坐了下来。 □ *She travelled around the world with her husband.* 她和丈夫环游了世界。

herb /hɜːb/ *countable noun* 可数名词
a plant whose leaves are used in cooking to add flavour to food, or as a medicine 香草；药草: *Fry the mushrooms in a little olive oil and add the chopped herbs.* 用少许橄榄油煎一下蘑菇，然后加入切碎的香草。
▶ **herbal** /ˈhɜːbəl/ *adjective* 形容词: *Do you know any herbal remedies for colds?* 你知道治疗感冒的草药吗？

herbivore /ˈhɜːbɪvɔː/ *countable noun* 可数名词
an animal that eats only plants. Compare **carnivore** and **omnivore**. 食草动物，食植动物（比较 carnivore 和 omnivore）

herd /hɜːd/ *countable noun* 可数名词
a large group of one type of animal that lives together 兽群；牧群: *Herds of elephants crossed the river each day.* 每天成群的大象渡过这条河。

here /hɪə/ *adverb* 副词
1 used when you are talking about the place where you are 在这里；在这儿: *I can't stay here all day.* 我不能一整天都待在这儿。 □ *Come and sit here.* 过来坐这儿。
2 used when you are offering or giving something to someone（用于给人东西时）: *Here's your coffee.* 这是您的咖啡。

here's /hɪəz/
short for (缩写 =) 'here is'

hero /ˈhɪərəʊ/ *countable noun* 可数名词 (**heroes**)
1 the main male character of a story（故事的）男主人公，男主角: *The actor Daniel Radcliffe plays the hero in the Harry Potter films.* 演员丹尼尔·拉德克利夫在《哈利·波特》系列电影中担任男主角。
2 someone who has done something brave or good 英雄: *Mr Mandela is a hero who has inspired millions.* 曼德拉先生是一位鼓舞了数百万民众的英雄。

heroic /hɪˈrəʊɪk/ *adjective* 形容词
used for saying that you admire a person or their actions because they have been very brave 英勇的: *He made a heroic effort to save the boy from the fire.* 他英勇地从大火中救出了那个男孩。

heroin /ˈherəʊɪn/ *uncountable noun* 不可数名词
a strong illegal drug 海洛因（毒品）

heroine /ˈherəʊɪn/ *countable noun* 可数名词
1 the main female character of a story（故事的）女主人公，女主角: *The heroine of the book is a young doctor.* 这本书的女主人公是一名年轻的医生。

2 a woman who has done something brave or good 女英雄：China's first gold medal winner became a national heroine. 中国首位金牌获得者成了民族女英雄。

hers /hɜːz/ *pronoun* 代词
used for showing that something belongs to a woman, girl or female animal 她的（东西）：She admitted that the bag was hers. 她承认包是她的。

herself /həˈself/ *pronoun* 代词
1 used for talking about a woman, girl or female animal that you have just mentioned 她自己；它自己（指雌性动物）：She looked at herself in the mirror. 她看着镜子里的自己。□ If she's not careful, she'll hurt herself. 她若不小心会伤到自己。
2 used for saying that something is done by a woman or girl, and not by anyone else（用于强调）她自己，亲自：She doesn't go to the hairdresser's. She cuts her hair herself. 她不去理发店。她自己给自己剪头发。

he's /hiz, STRONG 强读 hiːz/
1 short for（缩写 =）'he is'
2 short for（缩写 =）'he has'

hesitate /ˈhezɪˌteɪt/ *verb* 动词（**hesitates, hesitating, hesitated**）
to not act quickly, usually because you are not sure about what to say or do 犹豫；迟疑：Catherine hesitated before answering. 凯瑟琳迟疑了一下才回答。
▶ **hesitation** /ˌhezɪˈteɪʃən/ *noun* 名词：After some hesitation, she replied, 'I'll have to think about that.' 一番犹豫后，她答道："我得考虑一下。"

hexagon /ˈheksəɡən/ *countable noun* 可数名词
a shape with six straight sides 六边形；六角形
→ Look at picture on P2 参见彩插第 2 页

hey /heɪ/
1 used in informal situations to attract someone's attention（用于非正式场合，引起他人注意）嘿：'Hey! Be careful!' shouted Patty. "嘿！小心点！"帕蒂喊道。
2 used in informal situations to greet someone（非正式招呼语）嘿：He smiled and said 'Hey, Kate.' 他笑着说道："嘿，凯特。"

hi /haɪ/
used in informal situations to greet someone（非正式招呼语）嗨：'Hi, Liz,' she said. "嗨，利兹。"她说道。

hibernation /ˌhaɪbəˈneɪʃən/ *uncountable noun* 不可数名词
the time when some animals sleep through the winter 冬眠：The animals consume three times more calories to prepare for hibernation. 这些动物摄入 3 倍于平时的热量为冬眠做准备。

hiccup /ˈhɪkʌp/ *countable noun* 可数名词
a sudden short sound in your throat that often happens because you have been eating or drinking too quickly 嗝；呃逆：Do you know how to cure hiccups? 你知道如何治疗打嗝吗？□ Babies can get hiccups in the womb. 婴儿能在子宫里打嗝。● **hiccup** *verb* 动词（**hiccups, hiccuping** or 或 **hiccupping, hiccuped** or 或 **hiccupped**）：He laughed so hard he started hiccuping. 他笑得太厉害，打起了嗝。

hid /hɪd/
→ see 见 **hide**

hidden¹ /ˈhɪdən/
→ see 见 **hide**

hidden² /ˈhɪdən/ *adjective* 形容词
not easy to see or know about 隐藏的；潜藏的：There are hidden dangers on the beach. 海滩上有隐藏的危险。

hide /haɪd/ *verb* 动词（**hides, hiding, hid, hidden**）
1 to put something or someone in a place where they cannot easily be seen or found 藏；隐藏：He hid the bicycle behind the wall. 他把自行车藏在墙后。
2 to go somewhere where people cannot easily find you 躲藏；藏匿：The little boy hid in the wardrobe. 小男孩藏在衣柜里。
3 to cover something so that people cannot see it 遮住；遮挡：She hid her face in her hands. 她用手捂住了脸。
4 to not let people know what you feel or know 掩饰；隐瞒：Lee tried to hide his excitement. 李竭力掩饰自己的兴奋。

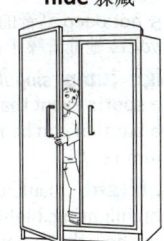

hide 躲藏

The little boy hid in the wardrobe.
小男孩藏在衣柜里。

hideous /ˈhɪdiəs/ *adjective* 形容词
very ugly or unpleasant 十分丑陋的；非常讨厌的：She saw a hideous face at the

window. 她看到窗口有一张十分丑陋的脸。 □ He was injured in a hideous knife attack. 他在一次可怕的持刀袭击中受伤。
▶ **hideously** /'hɪdɪəsli/ *adverb* 副词: *I was convinced that I was hideously ugly.* 我确信自己长得很丑。

high /haɪ/ *adjective* 形容词, *adverb* 副词 (**higher, highest**)
1 extending a long way from the bottom to the top（由下至上）高的: *They lived in a house with a high wall around it.* 他们住在一栋高墙环绕的房子内。 □ *Mount Qomolangma is the highest mountain in the world.* 珠穆朗玛峰是世界上最高的山。

> **LANGUAGE HELP** 语言提示
> When you are describing people, use **tall**. 形容人时，用 tall: *She was a tall woman.* 她个子很高。

2 used for talking or asking about how much something measures from the bottom to the top 有…高的: *The grass in the garden was a foot high.* 花园里的草有 1 英尺高。
3 a long way above the ground（离地面）高的（地）: *I looked down from the high window.* 我从高高的窗口往下看。 □ *The sun was high in the sky.* 太阳高挂在天上。 □ *She can jump higher than other people.* 她能比其他人跳得高。
4 great in amount or strength（数量或力量）大的: *High winds destroyed many trees and buildings.* 大风摧毁了许多树木和建筑物。
5 not deep 高音的: *She spoke in a high voice.* 她扯着嗓子说话。

'high ,jump *singular noun* 单数名词
a sports event that involves jumping over a bar that can be raised higher after each jump 跳高

highlight[1] /'haɪlaɪt/ *verb* 动词 (**highlights, highlighting, highlighted**)
to show that a point or problem is important 突出；强调: *Her talk highlighted the problems of homeless people.* 她的讲话强调了无家可归者的问题。

highlight[2] /'haɪlaɪt/ *countable noun* 可数名词
one of the most interesting parts of an event 亮点；精华；最有趣的部分: *That tennis game was one of the highlights of the tournament.* 那局网球比赛是本次锦标赛的亮点之一。

highly /'haɪli/ *adverb* 副词
1 used before some adjectives to mean 'very' 很；非常: *Mr Singh was a highly successful salesman.* 辛格先生是个非常成功的推销员。
2 used for saying that you think something or someone is very good 极为赞赏地: *Michael thought highly of the school.* 迈克尔对这所学校评价很高。

high-tech /,haɪ'tek/ also 亦作 **high tech** or 或 **hi tech** *adjective* 形容词
using modern methods and computers 高技术的；高科技的: *high-tech camera equipment* 高科技摄影器材

hijab /'hɪdʒæb/ *countable noun* 可数名词
a scarf that some Muslim women wear, that covers their hair and neck（穆斯林妇女戴的）头巾，盖头: *Leila wears a hijab but her sister doesn't.* 莱拉戴着头巾，但她姐姐没戴。

hijack /'haɪdʒæk/ *verb* 动词 (**hijacks, hijacking, hijacked**)
to illegally take control of a plane or other vehicle while it is travelling from one place to another 劫持（飞机等交通工具）: *Two men hijacked the plane.* 两名男子劫持了那架飞机。

hike[1] /haɪk/ *countable noun* 可数名词
a long walk, especially in the countryside（尤指乡间的）远足，徒步旅行: *We went for a hike in the Campsie Hills.* 我们去坎普西丘陵远足了。

hike[2] /haɪk/ *verb* 动词 (**hikes, hiking, hiked**)
to go for a long walk 去远足；徒步旅行: *We hiked to the top of the mountain.* 我们登上了山顶。
▶ **hiker** /'haɪkə/ *countable noun* 可数名词: *The hikers spent the night in the mountains.* 远足者在山中过夜。
▶ **hiking** /'haɪkɪŋ/ *uncountable noun* 不可数名词: *I love hiking in the mountains.* 我喜欢登山远足。
→ Look at picture on P14 参见彩插第 14 页

hilarious /hɪ'leərɪəs/ *adjective* 形容词
very funny 很好笑的；非常滑稽的: *He told me a hilarious story.* 他给我讲了一个令人捧腹的故事。

hill /hɪl/ *countable noun* 可数名词
an area of land that is higher than the land around it 小山；山丘；丘陵: *The castle is on a hill above the old town.* 城堡位于俯瞰老城的一座小山上。

hillside /ˈhɪlsaɪd/ *countable noun* 可数名词
the slope of a hill 小山坡

hilly /ˈhɪli/ *adjective* 形容词 (**hillier, hilliest**)
with a lot of hills 多小山的；多丘陵的：*The countryside in this area is quite hilly.* 这个地区的乡村丘陵起伏。

him /hɪm/ *pronoun* 代词
used for talking about a man, a boy or a male animal 他；它(指雄性动物)：*Elaine met him at the railway station.* 伊莱恩在火车站遇到了他。 □ *Is Sam there? Let me talk to him.* 萨姆在吗？让我和他讲话。

himself /hɪmˈself/ *pronoun* 代词
1 used for talking about a man, a boy or a male animal that you have just mentioned 他自己；它自己(指雄性动物)：*He poured himself a cup of coffee.* 他给自己倒了一杯咖啡。 □ *He was talking to himself.* 他在自言自语。
2 used for saying that something is done by a man or a boy, and not by anyone else (用于强调)他自己，亲自：*He made your card himself.* 他亲自为你做的贺卡。 □ *He'll probably tell you about it himself.* 他很可能会亲自告诉你那件事。

Hindu /ˈhɪnduː, hɪnˈduː/ *countable noun* 可数名词
a person who believes in Hinduism 印度教教徒 ● **Hindu** *adjective* 形容词：*We visited a Hindu temple.* 我们参观了一座印度教庙宇。

Hinduism /ˈhɪnduːˌɪzəm/ *uncountable noun* 不可数名词
an Indian religion that has many gods and teaches that people have another life on earth after they die 印度教(印度宗教，敬奉多神，相信轮回转世)

hinge /hɪndʒ/ *countable noun* 可数名词
a piece of metal that is used for joining two pieces of wood together so that they open and shut 铰链；合页：*The hinge is broken and the door won't shut.* 合页坏了，门关不上了。

hint¹ /hɪnt/ *countable noun* 可数名词
1 a suggestion that is not made directly 暗示；示意：*Has he given you any hints about what he wants for his birthday?* 他暗示过你他想要什么生日礼物了吗？
2 a helpful piece of advice 有益的建议：*Here are some helpful hints to make your trip easier.* 这儿有几条有用的建议可以让你的旅途更轻松。

hint² /hɪnt/ *verb* 动词 (**hints, hinting, hinted**)
to suggest something in a way that is not direct 暗示；示意：*She has hinted at the possibility of having a baby.* 她暗示了要生孩子的可能性。

hip /hɪp/ *countable noun* 可数名词
one of the two areas or bones at the sides of your body between the tops of your legs and your waist 臀；髋：*Tracey put her hands on her hips and laughed.* 特蕾西双手叉腰大笑了起来。
→ Look at picture on P4 参见彩插第 4 页

hip-hop *uncountable noun* 不可数名词
a type of music and dance that developed among African-American people in the United States in the 1970s and 1980s 嘻哈音乐(20世纪七八十年代在美国黑人中兴起的一种音乐和舞蹈形式)

hippo /ˈhɪpəʊ/ *countable noun* 可数名词
a hippopotamus (*informal* 非正式) 河马

hippopotamus /ˌhɪpəˈpɒtəməs/ *countable noun* 可数名词 (**hippopotamuses**)
a very large animal with short legs and thick skin that lives in and near rivers 河马

hire /haɪə/ *verb* 动词 (**hires, hiring, hired**)
to pay someone to do a job for you 雇用；聘用：*He just hired a new secretary.* 他刚刚雇用了一名新秘书。

his /hɪz/ *adjective* 形容词
used for showing that something belongs or relates to a man, a boy or a male animal 他的；它的(指雄性动物)：*He spent part of his career in Hollywood.* 他在好莱坞度过了部分职业生涯。 □ *He went to the party with his girlfriend.* 他和女朋友去参加了聚会。 ● **his** *pronoun* 代词：*Henry said the decision was his.* 亨利说这是他的决定。

hiss /hɪs/ *verb* 动词 (**hisses, hissing, hissed**)
to make a sound like a long 's' 发嘶声：*My cat hisses when I step on its tail.* 我踩到猫尾巴时，它发出嘶嘶声。 ● **hiss** *countable noun* 可数名词 (**hisses**)：*The hiss of steam came from the kitchen.* 厨房里传来蒸汽的嘶嘶声。

history /ˈhɪstəri/ *uncountable noun* 不可数名词
1 events that happened in the past 历史：*The film showed great moments in football history.* 这部电影展现了足球史上的伟大时刻。
2 the study of events that happened in the

past 历史学：*He studied history at Indiana University.* 他在印第安纳大学读历史。
→ Look at picture on P10 参见彩插第 10 页

hit¹ /hɪt/ *verb* 动词 (**hits, hitting, hit**)
1 to touch someone or something with a lot of force 打；击；撞：*She hit the ball hard.* 她用力击球。▫ *The car hit a traffic sign.* 汽车撞到一个交通标志上了。
2 to affect a person, place or thing very badly 打击；危害：*The earthquake hit northern Peru.* 地震袭击了秘鲁北部。

hit² /hɪt/ *countable noun* 可数名词
1 a CD, film or play that is very popular and successful 风行一时的唱片（或电影、戏剧）：*The song was a big hit in Japan.* 这首歌风靡日本。
2 a single visit to a web page（网页的）点击，浏览，访问：*The company has had 78,000 hits on its website.* 该公司网站有 7.8 万次的点击量。
3 when someone finds a website that contains the information they are looking for（在网站上的）查询结果，检索结果

hitchhike /ˈhɪtʃhaɪk/ *verb* 动词 (**hitchhikes, hitchhiking, hitchhiked**)
to travel by getting rides from passing vehicles without paying 搭便车；搭顺风车：*Neil hitchhiked to Scotland during his holiday.* 尼尔假期搭便车去了苏格兰。
▶ **hitchhiker** /ˈhɪtʃhaɪkə/ *countable noun* 可数名词：*On my way to Newcastle I picked up a hitchhiker.* 我在去纽卡斯尔的途中捎上了一个搭便车的人。

HIV /ˌeɪtʃ aɪ ˈviː/ *uncountable noun* 不可数名词
a virus (= a harmful thing that can make you ill) that reduces the ability of people's bodies to fight illness and that can cause **AIDS** 人类免疫缺陷病毒；艾滋病病毒
HIV negative not infected with the HIV virus 人类免疫缺陷病毒检测呈阴性
HIV positive infected with the HIV virus 人类免疫缺陷病毒检测呈阳性

hive /haɪv/ *countable noun* 可数名词
a structure in which bees live 蜂房；蜂箱

hoax /həʊks/ *countable noun* 可数名词 (**hoaxes**)
an occasion when someone says that something bad is going to happen, when this is not true 骗局；恶作剧：*Police say that the bomb alert was a hoax.* 警方说炸弹警报是个恶作剧。

hob /hɒb/ *countable noun* 可数名词
the top part of a cooker (= a piece of equipment that you use for cooking food) where you put pans 炉盘

hobby /ˈhɒbi/ *countable noun* 可数名词 (**hobbies**)
an activity that you enjoy doing in your free time 业余爱好：*My hobbies are music and tennis.* 我的业余爱好是音乐和网球。

hockey /ˈhɒki/ *uncountable noun* 不可数名词
a sport for two teams of eleven players, in which players use long curved sticks to hit a small hard ball 曲棍球运动
→ Look at picture on P14 参见彩插第 14 页

ˈhockey ˌstick *countable noun* 可数名词
a long curved stick that is used for hitting a small ball in the game of hockey 曲棍球球棍

hold¹ /həʊld/ *verb* 动词 (**holds, holding, held**)
1 to have something in your hands or your arms 拿着；抓住；握；抱：*She held his hand tightly.* 她紧紧地握着他的手。▫ *I held the baby in my arms.* 我把婴儿抱在怀里。
2 to put something into a particular position and keep it there 使保持（某种姿势）：*Hold your hands up.* 把双手举起来。▫ *Try to hold the camera steady.* 尽量拿稳相机。
3 to be able to contain a particular amount of something 容纳；包含：*One CD-ROM can hold over 100,000 pages of text.* 一张只读光盘可存储超过 10 万页的文本。
4 used with nouns such as 'party' and 'meeting' to talk about particular activities that people are organizing 召开；举办；举行：*The country will hold elections within a year.* 该国将在一年内举行选举。
5 (also 亦作 **hold the line**) to wait for a short time when you are making a telephone call（打电话时）等待，不挂断：*Please can you hold, sir?* 先生，请您等一会儿好吗？

hold on/hold onto something to keep your hand on or around something 抓住／抓紧某物：*The thief pulled me to the ground but I held onto my handbag.* 小偷把我拖倒在地，但我抓住手提包不松手。▫ *You must hold on tightly. Don't fall!* 你必须紧紧抓住，不要掉下去！

hold someone up to make someone late 耽搁某人；使某人延误：*I won't hold you up — I just have one quick question.* 我不会

耽误你的——我只有一个简单的问题。
hold something/someone back to stop something or someone from moving forwards or from doing something 阻挡某事物／某人: *The police held back the crowd.* 警察把人群拦住了。

hold² /həʊld/ *countable noun* 可数名词
1 when you have something in your hands or your arms 抓；握；拿: *Cooper took hold of the rope and pulled on it.* 库珀抓住绳子用力拉。
2 the place in a ship or an aeroplane where goods or luggage are stored（船或飞机的）货舱，底舱
get hold of someone to succeed in speaking to someone 跟某人联系上: *I've called him several times but I can't get hold of him.* 我给他打了几次电话，但都找不到他。
get hold of something to find something, usually after some difficulty（通常指经历困难后）找到某物: *It is hard to get hold of medicines in some areas of the country.* 在这个国家的一些地区很难弄到药品。

holdup /ˈhəʊldʌp/ *also 亦作* **hold-up** *countable noun* 可数名词
when someone uses a weapon to make someone give them money or other valuable things 持械抢劫: *Police are looking for a man after a hold-up in a local bank.* 当地一家银行发生持械抢劫案后，警方正在寻找一名男子。

hole /həʊl/ *countable noun* 可数名词
an opening or an empty space in something 洞；孔；坑: *He dug a hole 45 feet wide and 15 feet deep.* 他挖了一个 45 英尺宽、15 英尺深的坑。 □ *I've got a hole in my jeans.* 我的牛仔裤破了一个洞。

holiday /ˈhɒlɪˌdeɪ/ *countable noun* 可数名词 (*American* 美国英语: **vacation**)
1 a time when you do not go to work or school 假期: *I can't wait for the summer holidays.* 我等暑假都等不及了。
2 a time when you go somewhere away from home and stay there for a while（外出）度假期: *We're going on holiday in July.* 我们打算 7 月份去度假。

hollow /ˈhɒləʊ/ *adjective* 形容词
having an empty space inside 中空的；空心的: *a hollow tree* 中空的树

holly /ˈhɒli/ *noun* 名词 (**hollies**)
a plant that has hard, shiny leaves with sharp points, and red berries (= small round fruit) in winter 冬青

holocaust /ˈhɒləkɔːst/ *noun* 名词
the Holocaust the organized killing by the Nazis of millions of Jews during the Second World War（二战期间纳粹对数百万犹太人有组织的）大屠杀

holy /ˈhəʊli/ *adjective* 形容词 (**holier, holiest**)
connected with God or a particular religion 与上帝（或神）有关的；神圣的: *This is a holy place.* 这是个神圣的地方。

home /həʊm/ *noun* 名词
1 *countable* 可数 the house or flat where someone lives 家: *He died from a fall at his home in London.* 他在伦敦的家中摔死了。 □ *Hi, Mum, I'm home!* 嗨，妈妈，我回来了！
● **home** *adverb* 副词: *She wasn't feeling well and she wanted to go home.* 她感到不舒服，想回家。
2 *uncountable* 不可数 the town or country where someone lives or was born 家乡；故乡: *I'm going home to Scotland for the holidays.* 我假期准备回家乡苏格兰。
3 *countable* 可数 a building where people who cannot care for themselves live and are cared for 养老院；养老院: *It's a home for elderly people.* 这是一个养老院。
at home
1 in the place where you live 在家: *She stayed at home, waiting for him to call.* 她待在家里，等他来电话。
2 used for saying that a sports team is playing on its own ground. Compare with **away**.（运动队）在主场（比较 **away**）: *Manchester United are playing at home tonight.* 曼联今晚将主场作战。 ● **home** *adjective* 形容词: *Nolan may return for Saturday's home game against the New York Rangers.* 诺兰可能回来参加周六主场迎战纽约游骑兵队的比赛。

homeless /ˈhəʊmləs/ *adjective* 形容词
having nowhere to live 无家的: *There are a lot of homeless families in the city.* 该市有许多无家可归的家庭。
the homeless homeless people 无家可归者: *We're collecting money for the homeless.* 我们在为无家可归者募款。

homemade /ˌhəʊmˈmeɪd/ *adjective* 形容词
made in someone's home, rather than in a shop or factory 自制的；自家做的：*I miss my mother's homemade bread.* 我怀念我妈妈自己做的面包。

¹home page *countable noun* 可数名词
the main page of a person's or an organization's website（网站）主页：*The company offers a number of services on its home page.* 该公司在其主页上提供了一些服务。

homesick /ˈhəʊmsɪk/ *adjective* 形容词
feeling unhappy because you are away from home and missing your family and friends 想家的；思乡的：*He was homesick for his family.* 他思念家人。

homework /ˈhəʊmwɜːk/ *uncountable noun* 不可数名词
school work that teachers give to students to do at home in the evening or at the weekend 家庭作业：*Have you done your homework, Gemma?* 杰玛，你做家庭作业了没有？

homosexual /ˌhɒməʊˈsekʃuəl, ˌhəʊ-/ *adjective* 形容词
sexually attracted to people of the same sex 同性恋的：*The study found that 4 to 10 per cent of American men are homosexual.* 这项研究发现 4% 至 10% 的美国男性是同性恋。● **homosexual** *countable noun* 可数名词：*The organization wants equal treatment for homosexuals.* 该组织希望同性恋者获得平等对待。

honest /ˈɒnɪst/ *adjective* 形容词，*adverb* 副词
1 always telling the truth and not stealing or cheating 诚实的；老实的；正直的：*She's honest, and I trust her.* 她为人诚实，我信任她。
▶ **honestly** /ˈɒnɪstli/ *adverb* 副词：*Please try to answer these questions honestly.* 请老实回答这些问题。
2 used before or after a statement to show that you want people to believe you (*informal* 非正式)说真的（用于句首或句末）：*I'm not sure, honest.* 我没把握，说真的。
▶ **honestly** /ˈɒnɪstli/ *adverb* 副词：*Honestly, I don't know anything about it.* 说实话，我对此一无所知。

honesty /ˈɒnɪsti/ *uncountable noun* 不可数名词
the quality of being honest 诚实：*I admire his courage and honesty.* 我敬佩他的勇气和诚实。

honey /ˈhʌni/ *noun* 名词
1 a sweet, sticky food that is made by bees (= black-and-yellow insects) 蜂蜜
2 a name you call someone as a sign of affection（爱称）亲爱的，宝贝儿：*Honey, I don't think that's a good idea.* 宝贝儿，我认为那不是个好主意。

honeymoon /ˈhʌniˌmuːn/ *countable noun* 可数名词
a holiday taken by a man and a woman who have just got married 蜜月：*We went to Florida on our honeymoon.* 我们去佛罗里达度蜜月。

honour¹ /ˈɒnə/ *countable noun* 可数名词
a special award that is given to someone 荣誉：*He won many honours — among them an award for his film performance.* 他赢得了许多荣誉——其中一项是表彰他的电影表演的。

honour² /ˈɒnə/ *verb* 动词 (**honours, honouring, honoured**)
to give someone public praise for something they have done 表扬；表彰：*Maradona was honoured with an award from Argentina's football association.* 马拉多纳获得了阿根廷足协的嘉奖。

hood /hʊd/ *countable noun* 可数名词
1 the part of a coat that you can pull up to cover your head（外套的）风帽，兜帽：*Put up your hood — it's starting to rain.* 戴上你的风帽——下起雨了。
2 (*American* 美国英语) the **bonnet** of a car（汽车的）机罩

hoodie /ˈhʊdi/ *noun* 名词
a jacket or top with a hood 连兜帽外套（或上衣）：*She wore jeans and a hoodie.* 她穿着牛仔裤和连帽上衣。

hoof /huːf/ *countable noun* 可数名词 (**hoofs** or 或 **hooves**)
one of the hard parts of the feet of horses, cows and some other animals（马、牛等动物的）蹄：*He heard the sound of horses' hooves behind him.* 他听见身后传来马蹄声。

hook /hʊk/ *countable noun* 可数名词
1 a curved piece of metal or plastic that you use for hanging things on 钩；挂钩：*His jacket hung from a hook.* 他的夹克挂在衣钩上。
2 a curved piece of metal with a sharp point that you tie to the end of a fishing line to catch fish with 鱼钩：*Mr Kruger*

removed the hook from the fish's mouth. 克鲁格先生取出了鱼嘴里的鱼钩。

hoop /huːp/ *countable noun* 可数名词
1 a ring made of wood, metal or plastic 箍；环；圈：*Jessica was wearing jeans, trainers and gold hoop earrings.* 杰茜卡穿着牛仔裤、运动鞋，戴着环形金耳环。
2 the ring that players try to throw the ball into in basketball in order to score points for their team（篮球）篮圈

hoot /huːt/ *verb* 动词 (**hoots**, **hooting**, **hooted**) to make the loud noise of an owl（猫头鹰）鸣叫：*An owl hooted in the distance.* 一只猫头鹰在远处鸣叫。● **hoot** *countable noun* 可数名词：*Suddenly, he heard the loud hoot of a train.* 突然，他听见了火车的轰鸣声。

hooves /huːvz/
a plural of **hoof**（hoof 的复数形式之一）

hop /hɒp/ *verb* 动词 (**hops**, **hopping**, **hopped**)
1 to move by jumping on one foot（人）单脚跳
2 used when birds and animals move by jumping on both of their feet or all four of their feet together（鸟兽）齐足跳：*A small brown bird hopped in front of them.* 一只褐色的小鸟在他们面前蹦跳。
3 to move somewhere quickly or suddenly (*informal* 非正式) 快速（或突然）移动：*We hopped on the train.* 我们跳上了火车。

hope¹ /həʊp/ *verb* 动词 (**hopes**, **hoping**, **hoped**)
to want something to be true or to happen 希望；期望：*The team are hoping to win a medal.* 该队希望赢得一枚奖牌。◻ *I hope that you get better soon.* 希望你早日康复。◻ *We're all hoping for some good weather.* 我们都希望有个好天气。◻ *'I hope we'll meet again soon.' 'I hope so, too.'* "我希望我们很快再见面。" "我也是。"

hope² /həʊp/ *noun* 名词
the feeling of wanting something good to happen, and believing that it will happen 希望；期望：*What are your hopes for the future?* 你对未来有什么期望？ ◻ *This medicine will give new hope to millions of people around the world.* 该药将给全世界数百万人带来新的希望。◻ *As time passes, the police are losing hope of finding the men alive.* 随着时间流逝，警察渐渐失去了找到这些人存活的希望。

hopeful /ˈhəʊpfʊl/ *adjective* 形容词
thinking that something that you want will probably happen 抱有希望的；满怀希望的：*The doctors are hopeful that Grandma will get better soon.* 医生们对奶奶很快好转满怀希望。

hopefully /ˈhəʊpfʊli/ *adverb* 副词
1 said when you are talking about something that you hope will happen 希望；但愿：*Hopefully, you won't have any more problems.* 但愿你别再遇到问题。
2 hoping that something good will happen 怀着希望地：*David looked hopefully at the coffee pot.* 戴维满怀希望地看着咖啡壶。

hopeless /ˈhəʊpləs/ *adjective* 形容词
1 having no chance of success 没有希望成功的；无望的：*I don't believe the situation is hopeless.* 我认为形势并非毫无希望。
2 very bad 极差的；糟糕透顶的：*I'm hopeless at sport.* 我体育差得很。
▶ **hopelessly** /ˈhəʊpləsli/ *adverb* 副词：*Harry realized that he was hopelessly lost.* 哈里意识到自己完全迷路了。

horizon /həˈraɪzən/ *singular noun* 单数名词
the line that appears between the sky and the land or the sea 地平线：*A small boat appeared on the horizon.* 一艘小船出现在地平线上。

horizontal /ˌhɒrɪˈzɒntəl/ *adjective* 形容词
flat and level with the ground 水平的；横的：*She was wearing a grey sweater with black horizontal stripes.* 她穿着一件带黑色横条纹的灰色毛衣。

hormone /ˈhɔːməʊn/ *countable noun* 可数名词
a chemical substance in your body that affects the way your body works 激素；荷尔蒙：*This hormone is present in both sexes.* 这种激素在两性体内都存在。

horn /hɔːn/ *countable noun* 可数名词
1 one of the hard pointed things that grow from an animal's head（动物头上的）角
2 an object in a car or another vehicle that makes a loud noise, and that you use as a warning of danger（汽车等的）喇叭：*I could hear the sound of a car horn outside.* 我能听见外面有辆汽车鸣喇叭。
3 a musical instrument with a long metal tube that you play by blowing into it 号，号角（一种乐器）：*Joshua started playing the horn when he was eight.* 乔舒亚8岁开始吹号。

horoscope /ˈhɒrəˌskəʊp/ *countable noun* 可数名词
what some people believe will happen to

horrible – hot

you in the future, using the position of the stars when you were born 星象；占星预言：*I always read my horoscope in the newspaper.* 我经常在报纸上看我的星座运势。

horrible /ˈhɒrɪbəl/ *adjective* 形容词
very unpleasant (*informal* 非正式) 糟糕的；十分讨厌的：*The smell was horrible.* 那气味很难闻。□ *It was a horrible experience.* 那是一次糟糕的经历。□ *Stop being horrible to me!* 别对我那么凶！
▶ **horribly** /ˈhɒrɪbli/ *adverb* 副词：*Sam was feeling horribly ill.* 萨姆感觉自己病得厉害。

horrify /ˈhɒrɪfaɪ/ *verb* 动词 (**horrifies, horrifying, horrified**)
to shock someone greatly 使震惊，惊吓：*His family was horrified by the news.* 他家人被这个消息吓坏了。
▶ **horrifying** /ˈhɒrɪfaɪɪŋ/ *adjective* 形容词：*It was a horrifying sight.* 这是一幅可怕的景象。

horror[1] /ˈhɒrə/ *uncountable noun* 不可数名词
a feeling of great shock and fear when you see or experience something very unpleasant 震惊；恐惧：*I felt sick with horror.* 我吓得要命。

horror[2] /ˈhɒrə/ *adjective* 形容词
used about a film that is very frightening that you watch for entertainment (电影) 恐怖的：*I'm not a fan of horror films.* 我不喜欢恐怖片。

horse /hɔːs/ *countable noun* 可数名词
a large animal that people can ride 马：*Have you ever ridden a horse?* 你骑过马吗？

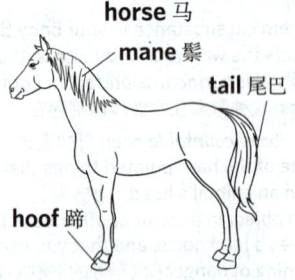

horse 马
mane 鬃
tail 尾巴
hoof 蹄

ˈhorse ˌracing *uncountable noun* 不可数名词
a sport in which people ride horses in races 赛马运动

ˈhorse ˌriding *uncountable noun* 不可数名词
the sport or activity of riding a horse 马术；骑马
→ Look at picture on P14 参见彩插第 14 页

horseshoe /ˈhɔːʃuː/ *countable noun* 可数名词
a piece of metal in the shape of a U, that is fixed to a horse's foot 马蹄铁；马掌

hose /həʊz/ *countable noun* 可数名词
a long rubber or plastic pipe that you use to put water on plants or on a fire 软管；水龙带

hospital /ˈhɒspɪtəl/ *noun* 名词
a place where doctors and nurses care for people who are ill or injured 医院：*The two men were taken to hospital after the car crash.* 车祸发生后那两名男子被送往医院。

host /həʊst/ *countable noun* 可数名词
the person at a party who has invited the guests 主人：*I didn't know anyone at the party, except the host.* 除了主人外，参加聚会的人我一个也不认识。

hostage /ˈhɒstɪdʒ/ *countable noun* 可数名词
someone who is kept as a prisoner by people until the people get what they want 人质：*The two hostages were freed yesterday.* 两名人质昨日获释。

hostess /ˈhəʊstɪs/ *countable noun* 可数名词 (**hostesses**)
the woman at a party who has invited the guests 女主人：*She's the perfect hostess, making sure that all her guests are relaxed and happy.* 她是完美的女主人，尽心让所有的客人放松、开心。

hostile /ˈhɒstaɪl/ *adjective* 形容词
very unfriendly 怀有敌意的；敌对的：*A large, hostile crowd surrounded him.* 一大群怀有敌意的人围住了他。

hot /hɒt/ *adjective* 形容词 (**hotter, hottest**)
1 having a high temperature 温度高的；热的：*When the oil is hot, add the sliced onion.* 油热后放入切好的洋葱。□ *Have some hot coffee. That will warm you up.* 喝些热咖啡，你会暖和起来。□ *I was too hot and tired to eat.* 我太热、太累了，吃不下东西。
2 describing the weather when the temperature is high (天气) 炎热的：*It's too hot to play tennis.* 天气太热了，不能打网球。
3 having a strong, burning taste 辣的：*I love eating hot curries.* 我喜欢吃辛辣的咖喱菜。

LANGUAGE HELP 语言提示
If the weather is **boiling** or **scorching**, it is very hot. If the weather is **warm**, it is pleasant, and not too hot. 形容天气时，

boiling 和 scorching 表示非常热，warm 表示温暖舒适：*We sat in the garden on warm evenings.* 在温暖的夜晚，我们坐在园子里。

hot dog *countable noun* 可数名词
a long piece of bread with a hot sausage (= a long thin piece of hot cooked meat) inside it 热狗（香肠面包）：*The children ate hot dogs and ice cream at Melissa's birthday party.* 孩子们在梅利莎的生日晚会上吃了热狗和冰激凌。

hotel /həˈtel/ *countable noun* 可数名词
a building where people pay to sleep and eat meals 旅馆；酒店：*Janet stayed the night in a small hotel near the harbour.* 珍妮特在港口附近一家小旅馆过的夜。

hour /aʊə/ *countable noun* 可数名词
a period of sixty minutes 小时；钟头：*They waited for about two hours.* 他们等了大约两个小时。 □ *I only slept about half an hour last night.* 我昨晚只睡了大约半个小时。

hourly /ˈaʊəli/ *adjective* 形容词, *adverb* 副词
happening once every hour 每小时一次（的）：*He listened to the hourly news programme on the radio.* 他收听了整点新闻广播。 □ *The buses run hourly between the two cities.* 公共汽车每小时一趟往返于两个城市之间。

house /haʊs/ *countable noun* 可数名词
a building where people live 房屋；房子；住宅：*Amy's invited me to her house for dinner.* 埃米邀请我去她家吃晚饭。 □ *Grandma has moved to a small house in the country.* 奶奶搬到乡下一处小房子了。

household /ˈhaʊshəʊld/ *countable noun* 可数名词
all the people who live together in a house 户；家庭；人家：*I grew up in a large household, with three brothers and three sisters.* 我在一个大家庭里长大，有 3 个兄弟和 3 个姐妹。

housewife /ˈhaʊswaɪf/ *countable noun* 可数名词 (**housewives** /ˈhaʊswaɪvz/)
a woman who does not have a paid job, but spends most of her time looking after her house and family 家庭主妇：*Sarah's a housewife and mother of four children.* 萨拉是家庭主妇，4 个孩子的母亲。

housework /ˈhaʊswɜːk/ *uncountable noun* 不可数名词
the work that you do to keep a house clean and tidy 家务活：*Men are doing more housework nowadays.* 现今男人做的家务多起来了。

hover /ˈhɒvə/ *verb* 动词 (**hovers, hovering, hovered**)
to stay in one place in the air, and not move forwards or backwards 悬停；盘旋；翱翔：*Helicopters hovered over the scene of the accident.* 直升机悬停在事故现场上方。

how /haʊ/ *adverb* 副词
1 used for asking about the way that something happens or is done 怎样；如何：*How do you spell his name?* 他的名字怎么拼写？ □ '*How do you get to work?*' '*By bus.*' "你怎么上班？" "坐公交。" □ *How does a mobile phone work?* 手机是如何工作的？
2 used for asking questions about time, or the amount or age of something（询问时间、数量或年龄）：*How much money do you have?* 你有多少钱？ □ *How many people will be at the dinner?* 将有多少人出席晚宴？ □ *How long will you stay?* 你待多长时间？ □ *How old is your son?* 你儿子多大了？
3 used when you are asking someone whether something was good（询问事物的好坏）怎么样：*How was your trip to Orlando?* 你的奥兰多之行怎么样？
4 used for asking if someone is well（询问身体好坏）怎么样：*Hi! How are you doing?* 嗨！你好吗？ □ *How's Rosie?* 罗西怎么样？

LANGUAGE HELP 语言提示
If you ask '**How is Susan?**', you are asking about her health. If you want to know about her appearance, ask '**What does Susan look like?**'. If you want to know about her personality, ask '**What is Susan like?**'. *"How is Susan?"用于询问健康状况。询问其外貌特征，用"What does Susan look like?"。询问其性格特点，用"What is Susan like?"。

how about... said when you are suggesting something to someone（用于提出建议）…怎么样：*How about a cup of coffee?* 喝杯咖啡怎么样？ □ *How about meeting tonight?* 今晚见面怎么样？

How do you do? used in order to be polite when you meet someone for the first time. The other person answers by saying '**How do you do?**' also. 你好（初次见面时的问候语，对方亦应以 How do you do? 回答）

however¹ /haʊˈevə/ *adverb* 副词
used when you are saying something that is not expected because of what you have just said 但是；然而；不过: *The flat is rather small. It is, however, much nicer than our old flat.* 这套公寓相当小，但比我们的旧公寓好多了。

however² /haʊˈevə/ *conjunction* 连词
used when you want to say that it makes no difference how something is done 不管怎样；无论如何: *Wear your hair however you want.* 你想怎么梳头就怎么梳。

howl /haʊl/ *verb* 动词 (**howls, howling, howled**)
to make a long, loud, crying sound 嚎叫；呼啸: *A dog suddenly howled.* 一条狗突然嚎叫起来。 □ *Daniel fell to the ground, howling with pain.* 丹尼尔摔倒在地，疼得直叫喊。● **howl** *countable noun* 可数名词: *The dog gave a long howl.* 那条狗发出一声长长的嚎叫。

HTML /ˌeɪtʃ tiː em ˈel/ *uncountable noun* 不可数名词
the standard way of preparing documents so that people can read them on the Internet. **HTML** is short for (缩写 =) 'hypertext markup language'. 超文本标记语言

hub /hʌb/ *countable noun* 可数名词
a very important centre for a particular activity (某活动的) 中心，核心: *They say that New York is the hub of the art world.* 他们说纽约是艺术世界的中心。

hug /hʌɡ/ *verb* 动词 (**hugs, hugging, hugged**)
to put your arms around someone and hold them tightly, to show your love or friendship 拥抱；搂抱: *Crystal hugged him and invited him to dinner the next day.* 克里斯特尔拥抱了他，邀请他第二天来吃晚饭。
● **hug** *countable noun* 可数名词: *She gave him a hug and said 'Well done.'* 她给了他一个拥抱，说："做得好。"

huge /hjuːdʒ/ *adjective* 形容词 (**huger, hugest**)
very large 非常大的；巨大的: *Emily was wearing huge dark sunglasses.* 埃米莉戴着大大的黑色太阳镜。
▶ **hugely** /ˈhjuːdʒli/ *adverb* 副词: *This hotel is hugely popular.* 这家旅馆人气很旺。

hum /hʌm/ *verb* 动词 (**hums, humming, hummed**)
1 to make a low continuous noise 发嗡嗡声: *The birds sang and the bees hummed.* 鸟儿喳喳唱，蜜蜂嗡嗡叫。● **hum** *singular noun* 单数名词: *I could hear the distant hum of traffic.* 我能听见远处车辆的嗡嗡声。
2 to sing a tune with your lips closed 哼 (曲子): *Barbara began humming a song.* 芭芭拉开始哼一支歌曲。

human /ˈhjuːmən/ *adjective* 形容词
relating to people, and not animals or machines 人的: *What is the smallest bone in the human body?* 人体中哪块骨头最小？
● **human** *countable noun* 可数名词: *Humans are capable of some wonderful achievements.* 人类有能力取得一些了不起的成就。

human being *countable noun* 可数名词
a man, a woman or a child 人: *Every human being has the right to freedom.* 每一个人都有自由的权利。

humanity /hjuːˈmænɪti/ *uncountable noun* 不可数名词
1 all the people in the world (统称) 人；人类: *Can humanity survive the future?* 人类能在未来存活吗？
2 the quality of being kind and thoughtful 人道；仁慈: *Her speech showed great humanity.* 她的演讲洋溢着仁爱精神。

human nature *uncountable noun* 不可数名词
the way that most people behave 人性: *It is human nature to worry about your children.* 为孩子操心是人之常情。

human race *singular noun* 单数名词
all the people living in the world 人类: *Some people believe that the human race is destroying the Earth.* 一些人认为人类正在摧毁地球。

human rights *plural noun* 复数名词
basic rights that all people should have 人权: *Both armies promised to respect human rights.* 双方军队都承诺会尊重人权。

humble /ˈhʌmbəl/ *adjective* 形容词 (**humbler, humblest**)
1 not believing that you are better than other people 谦逊的；虚心的: *He remains humble about his achievements.* 他从不张扬自己的成就。
2 ordinary and not special in any way 简朴的；不起眼的: *Ms Cruz comes from a humble background.* 克鲁兹女士出身平凡。

humid /ˈhjuːmɪd/ *adjective* 形容词
wet and warm 温暖潮湿的；湿热的:

Tomorrow, we can expect hot and humid conditions. 预计明天天气湿热。

humidity /hjuːˈmɪdɪti/ *uncountable noun* 不可数名词
the amount of water in the air 湿度：*The humidity is relatively low at the moment.* 目前湿度相对较低。

humorous /ˈhjuːmərəs/ *adjective* 形容词
making you laugh or smile 滑稽有趣的；幽默的：*He usually likes to write humorous poems.* 他通常喜欢写幽默的诗。
▶ **humorously** /ˈhjuːmərəsli/ *adverb* 副词：*Mr Stevenson smiled humorously.* 史蒂文森先生幽默地笑了。

humour /ˈhjuːmə/ *uncountable noun* 不可数名词
the quality of being funny 幽默；诙谐：*I laughed when I saw the humour of the situation.* 看到当时的滑稽情景，我笑了。

hump /hʌmp/ *countable noun* 可数名词
1 a small hill or raised area 小丘；隆起物
2 the large lump on a camel's back 驼峰：*Camels store water in their hump.* 骆驼把水储存在驼峰里。

hump 驼峰

hump 小丘

hundred /ˈhʌndrəd/

LANGUAGE HELP 语言提示
The plural form is **hundred** after a number. 用在数字后，复数形式为 hundred。

the number 100 一百：*More than a hundred people were there.* 那里有100多人。
▶ **hundredth** /ˈhʌndrədθ/ *adjective* 形容词, *adverb* 副词：*The bank's hundredth anniversary is in December.* 这家银行的百年纪念日在十二月。
▶ **hundreds of** a lot of things or people 许多：*He received hundreds of letters.* 他收到了许多信。

hung /hʌŋ/
→ see 见 **hang**

hunger /ˈhʌŋɡə/ *uncountable noun* 不可数名词
the feeling that you get when you need something to eat 饥饿(感)：*Hunger is the body's signal that you need to eat.* 饥饿是需要吃东西时身体发出的信号。

hungry /ˈhʌŋɡri/ *adjective* 形容词 (**hungrier**, **hungriest**)
wanting to eat 饿的；饥饿的：*My friend was hungry, so we drove to a supermarket to get some food.* 我朋友饿了，我们就开车去超市买了些食物。
▶ **hungrily** /ˈhʌŋɡrɪli/ *adverb* 副词：*James ate hungrily.* 詹姆斯狼吞虎咽地吃着。

hunt /hʌnt/ *verb* 动词 (**hunts**, **hunting**, **hunted**)
1 to chase and kill wild animals for food or as a sport 打猎；狩猎：*I learned to hunt and fish when I was a child.* 我小时候学会了打猎和捕鱼。 ● **hunt** *countable noun* 可数名词：*Dad went on a fox hunt last year.* 爸爸去年去猎狐了。
▶ **hunting** /ˈhʌntɪŋ/ *uncountable noun* 不可数名词：*He went deer hunting with his cousins.* 他和堂兄弟们去猎鹿。
2 to try to find something or someone by searching carefully 搜寻；寻找：*Police are still hunting for clues at the victim's flat.* 警方仍在受害者的公寓内搜寻线索。 ● **hunt** *countable noun* 可数名词：*Many people helped in the hunt for the missing children.* 很多人帮忙寻找失踪儿童。
▶ **hunting** /ˈhʌntɪŋ/ *uncountable noun* 不可数名词：*Job hunting is not easy.* 找工作不容易。

hunter /ˈhʌntə/ *countable noun* 可数名词
a person who hunts wild animals for food or as a sport 猎人；狩猎者：*Hundreds of deer hunters will visit the area this season.* 这个季节会有数百名猎鹿人来到这个地区。

hurdle /ˈhɜːdəl/ *countable noun* 可数名词
a difficulty that may stop you from doing something 难关；障碍：*Writing a CV is the first hurdle in a job search.* 写简历是求职的第一道难关。

hurdles /ˈhɜːdəlz/ *countable noun* 可数名词
a race in which people have to jump over a number of fences 跨栏比赛

hurricane /ˈhʌrɪkən/ *countable noun* 可数名词
a storm with very strong winds and rain 飓风

hurry¹ /ˈhʌri/ *verb* 动词 (**hurries, hurrying, hurried**)
to move or do something as quickly as you can 赶快；匆忙：*Claire hurried along the road.* 克莱尔沿路匆匆而行。▫ *Everyone hurried to find a seat.* 大家急忙找座位坐下。
hurry up to do something more quickly 赶快；赶紧：*Hurry up and get ready, or you'll miss the school bus!* 赶快准备好，否则会误了校车！

hurry² /ˈhʌri/ *noun* 名词
in a hurry needing or wanting to do something quickly 急忙；匆忙：*I'm sorry, I'm in a hurry and I have to go!* 抱歉，我赶时间，得走了！

hurt /hɜːt/ *verb* 动词 (**hurts, hurting, hurt**)
1 to make someone or something feel pain 使疼痛；使受伤：*Yasin hurt himself while he was playing football.* 亚辛踢足球时伤了自己。▫ *I fell over and hurt my leg yesterday.* 昨天我摔伤了腿。● **hurt** *adjective* 形容词：*How badly are you hurt?* 你伤得有多重？
2 used for saying that you feel pain in a part of your body 感到疼痛：*His arm hurt.* 他胳膊疼。
3 to say or do something that makes someone unhappy 使不快：*I'm really sorry if I hurt your feelings.* 如果伤害了你的感情，我真的很抱歉。● **hurt** *adjective* 形容词：*She was deeply hurt by what Smith said.* 史密斯的话深深伤害了她。

husband /ˈhʌzbənd/ *countable noun* 可数名词
the man that someone is married to 丈夫：*Eva married her husband in 1957.* 伊娃和丈夫于1957年结的婚。

hush¹ /hʌʃ/
used when you are telling someone to be quiet（用于让他人安静）嘘：*Hush! The teacher's talking.* 嘘！老师在讲课。

hush² /hʌʃ/ *singular noun* 单数名词
when everything is quiet in a place 寂静：*There was a sudden hush in the room.* 房间里突然变得鸦雀无声。

hut /hʌt/ *countable noun* 可数名词
a small simple building, especially one made of wood 简陋小屋；(尤指)小木屋

hygiene /ˈhaɪdʒiːn/ *uncountable noun* 不可数名词
the practice of keeping yourself and the things you use clean 卫生：*The key to good hygiene is washing your hands before touching food.* 良好卫生的关键在于接触食物前要洗手。
▶ **hygienic** /haɪˈdʒiːnɪk/ *adjective* 形容词：*This kitchen is easy to keep clean and hygienic.* 这个厨房很容易保持清洁卫生。

hymn /hɪm/ *countable noun* 可数名词
a religious song that Christians (= people who believe in Jesus Christ) sing in church (基督教的)圣歌：*I like singing hymns.* 我喜欢唱圣歌。

hyperlink /ˈhaɪpəlɪŋk/ *countable noun* 可数名词
a link to another part of a document on a computer or to another document 超链接：*Web pages are full of hyperlinks.* 网页上到处都是超链接。

hyphen /ˈhaɪfən/ *countable noun* 可数名词
the punctuation sign (-) that you use to join two words together, as in 'left-handed'. You also use a hyphen to show that a word continues on the next line. 连字符

hypnosis /hɪpˈnəʊsɪs/ *uncountable noun* 不可数名词
when someone is in a sort of deep sleep, but they can still see, hear and speak 催眠(状态)：*Ms Chorley uses hypnosis to help her clients relax.* 乔利女士通过催眠帮助客户放松。

Ii

I /aɪ/ *pronoun* 代词
used for talking about yourself as the subject of a verb (用作动词的主语) 我: *I live in Arizona.* 我住在亚利桑那州。▫ *Jim and I are getting married.* 我和吉姆要结婚了。

ice /aɪs/ *uncountable noun* 不可数名词
frozen water 冰: *The ground was covered with ice.* 地上结着冰。▫ *Do you want ice in your drink?* 你的饮料要加冰吗？

iceberg /ˈaɪsbɜːg/ *countable noun* 可数名词
a very large piece of ice that floats in the sea 冰山

ice ˈcream *noun* 名词
1 a very cold sweet food that is made from frozen cream 冰激凌: *Serve the pie warm with vanilla ice cream.* 趁热把馅饼端上桌，配上香草冰激凌。
2 *countable* 可数 a portion of ice cream 一份冰激凌: *Do you want an ice cream?* 你要来一份冰激凌吗？

ˈice ˌcube *countable noun* 可数名词
a small block of ice that you put into a drink to make it cold (加入饮料中的)冰块

ˈice ˌhockey *uncountable noun* 不可数名词
a game that is played on ice by two teams. They use long curved sticks to try to hit a small rubber disc (= a puck) into a goal. 冰球运动

ˈice-ˌskate also 亦作 **ice skate** *countable noun* 可数名词
a boot with a thin metal bar underneath that people wear to move quickly on ice 冰鞋；溜冰鞋

ˈice-ˌskating *uncountable noun* 不可数名词
the activity or sport of moving about on ice wearing ice-skates 滑冰: *I love watching ice-skating on television.* 我喜欢在电视上看滑冰。

icicle /ˈaɪsɪkəl/ *countable noun* 可数名词
a long pointed piece of ice that hangs down from a surface 冰锥；冰柱；冰溜子

icicle 冰锥

icing /ˈaɪsɪŋ/ *uncountable noun* 不可数名词
a sweet substance that you use for decorating cakes 糖霜

icon /ˈaɪkɒn/ *countable noun* 可数名词
a picture on a computer screen that you can choose, in order to open a particular program (计算机屏幕上的)图标: *Kate clicked on the mail icon on her computer screen.* 凯特点击了计算机屏幕上的邮件图标。
→ Look at picture on P11 参见彩插第 11 页

icy /ˈaɪsi/ *adjective* 形容词 (**icier, iciest**)
1 extremely cold 冰冷的；极冷的: *An icy wind was blowing.* 刺骨的风吹着。
2 covered in ice 结冰的；冰冻的: *an icy road* 结冰的道路
→ Look at picture on P8 参见彩插第 8 页

ID /ˌaɪ ˈdiː/ *uncountable noun* 不可数名词
a document that shows who you are 身份证件；身份证明: *I had no ID so I couldn't prove that it was my car.* 我没有身份证件，无法证明这是我的车。

I'd /aɪd/
1 short for (缩写 =) 'I had': *I was sure I'd seen her before.* 我确信之前见过她。
2 short for (缩写 =) 'I would': *There are some questions I'd like to ask.* 我想问一些问题。

idea /aɪˈdɪə/ *noun* 名词
1 *countable* 可数 a thought, especially a new one (尤指新的)想法，点子，主意: *These people have a lot of great ideas.* 这些人有很多好点子。▫ *'Let's have something to eat.' — 'Good idea.'* "咱们弄点儿吃的

吧。"——"好。"
2 singular 单数 how much you know or understand about something 了解；认识：*We had no idea what was happening.* 我们不清楚怎么回事儿。
3 singular 单数 the aim or purpose of something 目的；目标：*The idea is to have fun.* 目的是玩得开心。

ideal¹ /aɪˈdiːəl/ *adjective* 形容词
1 best possible 最佳的；理想的：*You are the ideal person to do the job.* 你是这个职位的最佳人选。
2 perfect 完美的；理想的：*Imagine for a moment that you're living in an ideal world.* 想象一下，你生活在一个理想的世界里。

ideal² /aɪˈdiːəl/ *countable noun* 可数名词
a principle or an idea that people try to achieve 理想：*We must defend the ideals of liberty and freedom.* 我们必须捍卫自由的理想。

identical /aɪˈdentɪkəl/ *adjective* 形容词
exactly the same 一模一样的；完全相同的：*The houses were almost identical.* 这些房子几乎一模一样。

identification /aɪˌdentɪfɪˈkeɪʃən/ *uncountable noun* 不可数名词
a document that proves who you are 身份证件；身份证明：*The police asked him to show some identification.* 警察要他出示证件。

identify /aɪˈdentɪfaɪ/ *verb* 动词 (**identifies, identifying, identified**)
to be able to say who or what a person or thing is 识别；鉴定；确认：*Now we have identified the problem, we must decide how to fix it.* 我们已经发现了问题，必须决定怎么解决问题。□ *The handbook tells you how to identify the different birds.* 手册教你识别不同的鸟。
▶ **identification** /aɪˌdentɪfɪˈkeɪʃən/ *uncountable noun* 不可数名词：*Early identification of the disease is important.* 这种病做到早发现很重要。

identity /aɪˈdentɪti/ *countable noun* 可数名词 (**identities**)
who you are 身份：*He uses the name Abu to hide his identity.* 他化名阿布掩饰自己的身份。

idiom /ˈɪdiəm/ *countable noun* 可数名词
a group of words that have a particular meaning when you use them together. For example, 'to hit the roof' is an idiom that means to become very angry. 习语；成语；惯用语

idiot /ˈɪdiət/ *countable noun* 可数名词 someone who is very stupid 白痴；傻子：*I felt like an idiot.* 我觉得自己像个白痴。

idol /ˈaɪdəl/ *countable noun* 可数名词
a famous person who is greatly admired or loved 偶像：*The crowd cheered when their idol waved to the cameras.* 看到偶像朝摄像机挥手，人群欢呼起来。

if /ɪf/ *conjunction* 连词
1 used for talking about things that might happen 如果；要是；倘若：*You can go if you want.* 你要是想去可以去。□ *He might win — if he's lucky.* 他可能会赢——要是他走运的话。
2 used when you are talking about a question that someone has asked (用于谈论提问) 是否：*He asked if I wanted some water.* 他问我是否想来点水。
as if used for comparing one thing with another (用于比较) 好像，仿佛：*He moved his hand as if he was writing something.* 他移动着手，好像在写字。
if only used for expressing a strong wish (表示强烈愿望) 要是⋯多么好：*If only I had a car.* 我要是有辆车多好啊。

ignorant /ˈɪɡnərənt/ *adjective* 形容词
not knowing things 无知的；不知情的：*People don't want to appear ignorant.* 人们不想显得自己无知。□ *Most people are ignorant of these facts.* 大多数人不了解这些事实。
▶ **ignorance** /ˈɪɡnərəns/ *uncountable noun* 不可数名词：*I feel embarrassed by my ignorance of world history.* 我为自己对世界史的无知感到难堪。

ignore /ɪɡˈnɔː/ *verb* 动词 (**ignores, ignoring, ignored**)
to not pay any attention to someone or something 忽视；不理会：*He completely ignored the 'No Parking' sign.* 他全然无视"禁止停车"的标识。

ignore 忽视

He completely ignored the 'No Parking' sign.
他全然无视"禁止停车"的标识。

ill /ɪl/ *adjective* 形容词
not in good health 生病的；有病的：*He is seriously ill with cancer.* 他得了癌症，病得很重。

I'll /aɪl/
short for（缩写 =）'I will' or 'I shall'

illegal /ɪˈliːɡəl/ *adjective* 形容词
not allowed by law 非法的；违法的：*It is illegal for the interviewer to ask your age.* 访谈者询问你年龄是不合法的。□ *I have done nothing illegal.* 我没做过犯法的事。
▶ **illegally** /ɪˈliːɡəli/ *adverb* 副词：*He received a fine for parking illegally.* 他违法停车吃了罚单。

illness /ˈɪlnəs/ *noun* 名词 (**illnesses**)
1 *countable* 可数 a particular disease or a period of bad health 病；疾病；患病期：*She is recovering from a serious illness.* 她患了重病，正在康复。
2 *uncountable* 不可数 the fact or experience of being ill 生病；有病：*He was away from school because of illness.* 他因病离校。

illusion /ɪˈluːʒən/ *noun* 名词
1 a false idea or belief 错误想法；错误观念：*He's under the illusion that money makes people happy.* 他误以为金钱使人幸福。
2 *countable* 可数 something that seems to exist 错觉；幻觉：*Large windows can give the illusion of more space.* 大窗户给人以空间变大的错觉。

illustrate /ˈɪləstreɪt/ *verb* 动词 (**illustrates, illustrating, illustrated**)
to put pictures into a book 给（图书）添加插图：*She illustrates children's books.* 她给童书画插图。
▶ **illustration** /ˌɪləˈstreɪʃən/ *countable noun* 可数名词：*It's a book with beautiful illustrations.* 这本书插图精美。

IM /ˌaɪ ˈem/ *noun* 名词
short for（缩写 =）**instant messaging**：*The device lets you chat via IM.* 这款设备让你可以通过即时消息聊天。

I'm /aɪm/
short for（缩写 =）'I am'

image /ˈɪmɪdʒ/ *countable noun* 可数名词
1 a picture of someone or something (*formal* 正式) 图像；影像；图片：*The image on screen changes every 10 seconds.* 屏幕上的图像每 10 秒钟变换一次。
2 a picture or an idea of someone or something in your mind 印象：*If you talk about California, people have an image of sunny blue skies.* 说到加利福尼亚，人们就会联想到阳光明媚的蓝天。
3 the way that a person, a group or an organization appears to other people（人、团体或机构的）形象：*The government does not have a good public image.* 政府公众形象不佳。

imaginary /ɪˈmædʒɪnəri/ *adjective* 形容词
existing only in your mind or in a story, and not in real life 想象的；假想的：*Lots of children have imaginary friends.* 许多孩子都会凭空想象出一些朋友。

imagination /ɪˌmædʒɪˈneɪʃən/ *noun* 名词
your ability to invent pictures or ideas in your mind 想象力：*You must use your imagination to find an answer to this problem.* 你必须发挥想象力找到这个问题的答案。

imagine /ɪˈmædʒɪn/ *verb* 动词 (**imagines, imagining, imagined**)
1 to form a picture or an idea of something in your mind 想象；设想：*He could not imagine a more peaceful scene.* 他想象不出更祥和的景象。
2 to think that you have seen, heard or experienced something, when in fact you have not 幻想；臆想：*I realize that I imagined the whole thing.* 我意识到整件事都是我臆想出来的。

imitate /ˈɪmɪteɪt/ *verb* 动词 (**imitates, imitating, imitated**)
to copy what someone does or produces 模仿；仿效；模拟：*I didn't like the way he imitated my voice.* 我不喜欢他模仿我声音的样子。

imitation[1] /ˌɪmɪˈteɪʃən/ *countable noun* 可数名词
a copy of something 模仿；仿制品：*He tried to do an imitation of an English accent.* 他想模仿英音。□ *Make sure you get the real thing — don't buy an imitation.* 一定要买正牌货——别买仿品。

imitation[2] /ˌɪmɪˈteɪʃən/ *adjective* 形容词
made to look like another more expensive product 仿制的；仿造的：*The books are covered in imitation leather.* 这些书封面用的是人造革。

immature /ˌɪməˈtjʊə/ *adjective* 形容词
behaving in a silly way that is more typical of young people（人）表现不成熟的：*He's too immature to get married.* 他太不成熟，不适合结婚。

immediate /ɪˈmiːdiət/ *adjective* 形容词
happening next or very soon 立即的；即刻的：*There is no immediate solution to the problem.* 这个问题没有一蹴而就的解决办法。

immediately /ɪˈmiːdiətli/ *adverb* 副词
happening without any delay 立即；即刻；马上：*'Call the police immediately!' she shouted.* "快报警！"她叫道。

immense /ɪˈmens/ *adjective* 形容词
extremely large 极大的；巨大的：*We still need to do an immense amount of work.* 我们仍需做海量的工作。

immensely /ɪˈmensli/ *adverb* 副词
very much 非常；十分：*I enjoyed the film immensely.* 我非常喜欢这部影片。

immigrant /ˈɪmɪɡrənt/ *countable noun* 可数名词
a person who comes to live in a country from another country（外国来的）移民：*The company employs several immigrants.* 公司聘用了几个移民。

immigration /ˌɪmɪˈɡreɪʃən/ *uncountable noun* 不可数名词
when people come into a country to live and work there 移民：*The government is changing the immigration laws.* 政府正在修改移民法。

immoral /ɪˈmɒrəl/ *adjective* 形容词
bad or wrong 不道德的；道德败坏的：*Some people think that it's immoral to earn a lot of money.* 有些人认为挣大钱不道德。

immortal /ɪˈmɔːtəl/ *adjective* 形容词
living or lasting forever 永生的；永存的：*They prayed to their immortal gods.* 他们向自己永生的神灵祷告。 □ *When you're young, you think you're immortal.* 年轻时，你觉得自己不会老。

immune /ɪˈmjuːn/ *adjective* 形容词
safe from being affected by a particular disease 免疫的；有免疫力的：*Some people are naturally immune to measles.* 有些人天生对麻疹有免疫力。

impact /ˈɪmpækt/ *noun* 名词
1 *countable* 可数 a strong effect 影响；作用：*The experience had a huge impact on her.* 这段经历对她影响巨大。
2 the action of one object hitting another 碰撞；撞击：*The impact of the crash turned the lorry over.* 事故撞击力致使卡车翻覆。

impatient /ɪmˈpeɪʃənt/ *adjective* 形容词
1 annoyed because you have to wait too long for something 不耐烦的；等不及的：*People are impatient for the war to be over.* 人们迫不及待地希望战争结束。
▶ **impatiently** /ɪmˈpeɪʃəntli/ *adverb* 副词：*She waited impatiently for the post to arrive.* 她焦急地等待邮件到来。
2 becoming annoyed very quickly 急躁的；没耐心的：*Try not to be impatient with your kids.* 尽量不要跟孩子急。
▶ **impatience** /ɪmˈpeɪʃəns/ *uncountable noun* 不可数名词：*She tried to hide her growing impatience with him.* 她对他越来越不耐烦，但尽力不表现出来。

imperative /ɪmˈperətɪv/ *singular noun* 单数名词
the base form of a verb, usually without a subject. The imperative is used for telling someone to do something. Examples are 'Go away' and 'Please be careful'.（动词的）祈使式

imperfect /ɪmˈpɜːfɪkt/ *adjective* 形容词
having faults (*formal* 正式) 不完美的：*We live in an imperfect world.* 我们生活在一个不完美的世界里。

imperialism /ɪmˈpɪəriəlɪzəm/ *uncountable noun* 不可数名词
a system in which a powerful country controls other countries 帝国主义：*These nations are victims of imperialism.* 这些国家是帝国主义的受害者。
▶ **imperialist** /ɪmˈpɪəriəlɪst/ *countable noun* 可数名词：*She accused me of being a Western imperialist.* 她指责我是西方帝国主义者。

import[1] /ɪmˈpɔːt/ *verb* 动词 (imports, importing, imported)
to buy goods from another country for use in your own country 进口：*The U.S. imports over half of its oil.* 美国逾半石油靠进口。
▶ **importer** /ɪmˈpɔːtə/ *countable noun* 可数名词：*The UK is the world's biggest importer of champagne.* 英国是全球第一大香槟进口国。

import[2] /ˈɪmpɔːt/ *countable noun* 可数名词
a product bought from another country for use in your own country 进口产品：*Cheap imports are adding to the problems of our farmers.* 廉价进口产品使我国农民的问题雪上加霜。

important /ɪmˈpɔːtənt/ *adjective* 形容词
1 that you feel you must do, have or think

about 重要的；重大的；必要的：*The most important thing in my life is my career.* 我人生第一要务是事业。▫ *It's important to answer her questions honestly.* 如实回答她的问题很重要。

▶ **importance** /ɪmˈpɔːtəns/ *uncountable noun* 不可数名词：*The teacher stressed the importance of doing our homework.* 老师强调了做家庭作业的重要性。

▶ **importantly** /ɪmˈpɔːtəntli/ *adverb* 副词：*I was hungry and, more importantly, my children were hungry.* 我饿了，更要紧的是，我的孩子们饿了。

2 having influence or power 有影响力的；有权势的：*She's an important person in the world of television.* 她是电视界的大腕儿。

impossible /ɪmˈpɒsɪbəl/ *adjective* 形容词
unable to be done or to happen 不可能的：*It is impossible for me to get another job at my age.* 我这个年纪不可能再找一份工作。▫ *The snow made it impossible to play the game.* 因为下雪，这场比赛没法打。

impractical /ɪmˈpræktɪkəl/ *adjective* 形容词
not sensible or realistic 不明智的；不现实的：*She was wearing impractical high-heeled shoes.* 她穿着离谱的高跟鞋。

impress /ɪmˈpres/ *verb* 动词 (**impresses, impressing, impressed**)
to make you feel great admiration 使钦佩，使赞赏：*Their speed impressed everyone.* 他们的速度人人称赞。

▶ **impressed** /ɪmˈprest/ *adjective* 形容词：*I was very impressed by his lecture.* 我十分欣赏他的课。

impression /ɪmˈpreʃən/ *countable noun* 可数名词
what you feel or think about someone or something 印象；感想：*What were your first impressions of college?* 你对大学的第一印象如何？

make an impression have a strong effect 产生影响；发挥作用：*It's her first day at work and she has already made an impression.* 这是她第一天上班，她就已经有所作为。

under the impression believing that something is true 以为；觉得：*I was under the impression that you were moving to New York.* 我以为你要搬到纽约去。

impressive /ɪmˈpresɪv/ *adjective* 形容词
making you feel strong admiration 令人钦佩的；使人赞赏的：*They collected an impressive amount of cash: $390.8 million.* 他们筹得了一笔可观的现金：3.908亿美元。

improve /ɪmˈpruːv/ *verb* 动词 (**improves, improving, improved**)
to get better 改进；改善：*Your general health will improve if you drink more water.* 多喝水，总体健康状况就会改善。▫ *Their French improved during their trip to Paris.* 巴黎之行期间他们的法语水平有提高。▫ *We are trying to improve our services to customers.* 我们在努力改进客户服务。

▶ **improvement** /ɪmˈpruːvmənt/ *noun* 名词：*There have been some great improvements in technology in recent years.* 近年来技术大有进步。

impulse /ˈɪmpʌls/ *noun* 名词
a sudden feeling that you must do something 冲动：*I felt a sudden impulse to tell her that I loved her.* 我突然涌起一股冲动，要告诉她我爱她。

on impulse suddenly deciding to do something 冲动之下；一时冲动：*Sean usually acts on impulse.* 肖恩一般都是意气用事。

impulsive /ɪmˈpʌlsɪv/ *adjective* 形容词
doing things suddenly, without thinking about them carefully first 冲动的；意气用事的：*He is too impulsive to be a good leader.* 他太冲动，难以成为优秀的领导人。

in¹ /ɪn/ *preposition* 介词
1 used when you are saying where someone or something is（表示所在处所）在：*My brother was playing in the garden.* 我弟弟在花园里玩。▫ *Mark now lives in Singapore.* 马克现在生活在新加坡。▫ *Are you still in bed? It's almost lunchtime!* 你还在床上？快吃午饭了！

2 used for saying that you are wearing a particular piece of clothing 穿着：*Who is the woman in the red dress?* 那个穿红裙的女人是谁？

3 used for talking about the job that someone does（表示职业）在…中：*John's son is in the navy.* 约翰的儿子在海军服役。▫ *Dad works in the music industry.* 爸爸在音乐行业工作。

4 used for talking about a particular period of time（表示特定时间段）：*He was born in 1996.* 他生于1996年。▫ *Sales improved in April.* 4月份销售额上涨。

5 used for talking about how long something takes（表示所用时长）在…内：*He walked two hundred miles in eight days.*

他 8 天走了 200 英里。
6 used for talking about a state or situation (表示状态或形势) 在…中: *Dave was in a hurry to get back to work.* 戴夫急着回去上班。□ *The kitchen's in a mess.* 厨房里一片狼藉。
7 used for talking about the way that something is done or said (表示言行方式) 用，以: *Please do not write in pencil — use a pen.* 请不要用铅笔写——用钢笔。□ *The men were speaking in Russian.* 这些男子说俄语。□ *She always talks in a loud voice.* 她说话总是大嗓门儿。

in² /ɪn/ *adjective* 形容词, *adverb* 副词
1 to a place, from outside 进入；至内: *I knocked on the door, and went in.* 我敲了敲门，走了进去。
2 at your home 在家: *Maria isn't in just now.* 玛丽亚此刻不在家。
3 inside the area of play in games such as tennis or basketball. Compare with **out**. (网球、篮球运动中) 界内的 (比较 out): *The line judge signalled that the ball was in.* 司线裁判员示意球落在界内。

inability /ˌɪnəˈbɪlɪti/ *uncountable noun* 不可数名词
the fact that someone cannot do something 无能；无法: *Her inability to concentrate could cause an accident.* 她无法集中注意力，这可能会造成事故。

inaccurate /ɪnˈækjʊrət/ *adjective* 形容词
not completely correct 不精确的；不准确的: *Her comments are inaccurate and untrue.* 她的评论不准确，也不符合事实。

inappropriate /ˌɪnəˈprəʊpriət/ *adjective* 形容词
wrong or bad in a particular situation 不适宜的；不适合的: *The film is inappropriate for young children.* 这部影片少儿不宜。

inbox /ˈɪnbɒks/ also 亦作 **in-box** *countable noun* 可数名词 (**inboxes**)
the place where your computer stores emails that have arrived for you (电子邮件的) 收件箱: *I went home and checked my inbox.* 我回家查看了收件箱。

incapable /ɪnˈkeɪpəbəl/ *adjective* 形容词
unable to do something 无能力的: *She is incapable of making sensible decisions.* 她作不出明智的决定。

incentive /ɪnˈsentɪv/ *noun* 名词
something that makes you want to do something 激励；奖励；诱因: *We want to give our employees an incentive to work hard.* 我们想采取激励措施让员工卖力工作。

inch /ɪntʃ/ *countable noun* 可数名词 (**inches**)
a unit for measuring length. There are about 2.54 centimetres in an inch. There are twelve inches in a foot. 英寸 (长度单位，1 英寸 ≈ 2.54 厘米，12 英寸 = 1 英尺): *Dig a hole 18 inches deep.* 挖一个 18 英寸深的洞。

incident /ˈɪnsɪdənt/ *countable noun* 可数名词
something unpleasant that happens (*formal* 正式) 事故；(不好的) 事件: *The incident happened in the early hours of Sunday morning.* 事故发生在星期天凌晨。

inclined /ɪnˈklaɪnd/ *adjective* 形容词
having a particular opinion, but without feeling strongly about it 有…想法 (或意向) 的: *I am inclined to agree with Alan.* 我倾向于赞同艾伦的看法。

include /ɪnˈkluːd/ *verb* 动词 (**includes, including, included**)
to have something as one part 包括；包含: *The trip will include a day at the beach.* 此行将有一天待在海滩。

including /ɪnˈkluːdɪŋ/ *preposition* 介词
part of a particular group of people or things 包括；包含: *Thousands were killed, including many women and children.* 数千人被杀，包括许多妇女和儿童。

income /ˈɪŋkʌm/ *noun* 名词
the money that a person earns or receives 收入；所得；收益: *Many of the families here are on low incomes.* 这儿许多家庭收入都很低。

ˈincome tax *noun* 名词 (**income taxes**)
a part of your income that you have to pay regularly to the government 所得税: *You pay income tax every month.* 你按月缴纳所得税。

incompetent /ɪnˈkɒmpɪtənt/ *adjective* 形容词
unable to do a job properly 能力不足的；不能胜任的；不称职的: *He always fires incompetent employees.* 他总是解雇不称职的员工。

incomplete /ˌɪnkəmˈpliːt/ *adjective* 形容词
not yet finished, or not having all the parts that are needed 未完成的；未结束的；不完整的: *The data we have is incomplete.* 我们拥有的数据不完整。

inconsiderate /ˌɪnkənˈsɪdərət/ *adjective* 形容词
not thinking enough about how your behaviour will affect other people 不体贴的；不体谅人的；不为人着想的: *It was inconsiderate of her to come without calling.* 她考虑欠妥，没打个电话就来了。

inconvenient /ˌɪnkənˈviːniənt/ *adjective* 形容词
causing difficulties for someone 不方便的；造成困难的: *I know it's inconvenient, but I have to see you now.* 我知道你不方便，可我现在就得见你。

incorrect /ˌɪnkəˈrekt/ *adjective* 形容词
wrong or untrue 不正确的；不真实的: *The answer he gave was incorrect.* 他给的答案不对。
▶ **incorrectly** /ˌɪnkəˈrektli/ *adverb* 副词: *The article suggested, incorrectly, that he was sick.* 文章错误地暗示他生病了。

increase /ɪnˈkriːs/ *verb* 动词 (**increases, increasing, increased**)
to get bigger in some way 增加；增大；增长: *The population continues to increase.* 人口持续增长。 □ *Japanese exports increased by 2% last year.* 去年日本出口增长了 2%。 ● **increase** /ˈɪnkriːs/ *countable noun* 可数名词: *There was a sudden increase in the cost of oil.* 油价骤升。

increasingly /ɪnˈkriːsɪŋli/ *adverb* 副词
more and more 日益；越来越: *He was finding it increasingly difficult to make decisions.* 他发现作决定越来越难。

incredible /ɪnˈkredɪbəl/ *adjective* 形容词
1 used for saying how good something is, or to make what you are saying stronger 极好的；（用于加强语气）惊人的: *The food was incredible.* 饭菜棒得很。 □ *I work an incredible number of hours.* 我工作时长惊人。
▶ **incredibly** /ɪnˈkredɪbli/ *adverb* 副词: *It was incredibly hard work.* 那是异常艰苦的工作。
2 used for saying that you cannot believe that something is really true 不可思议的；难以置信的: *It seems incredible that nobody saw the danger.* 没有人看到危险，似乎有点儿不可思议。

indeed /ɪnˈdiːd/ *adverb* 副词
1 used for making something you have said stronger（用于加强语气）的确，确实: *He admitted that he had indeed paid him.* 他承认他的确向他付过钱了。
2 used for making the word 'very' stronger（用于加强 very 语气）真的，实在: *The results were very strange indeed.* 结果着实非常奇怪。

indefinite /ɪnˈdefɪnɪt/ *adjective* 形容词
without a fixed finishing time 无限期的；期限不定的: *He was sent to jail for an indefinite period.* 他被无限期关在监狱里。
▶ **indefinitely** /ɪnˈdefɪnətli/ *adverb* 副词: *We cannot allow this situation to continue indefinitely.* 我们不能任由当前局势无限期持续下去。

inˌ**definite** ˈ**article** *countable noun* 可数名词
the words 'a' and 'an' 不定冠词（即 a 和 an）

independence /ˌɪndɪˈpendəns/ *uncountable noun* 不可数名词
1 when one country is not ruled by another country（国家的）独立: *In 1816, Argentina declared its independence from Spain.* *1816 年，阿根廷宣布脱离西班牙独立。
2 the fact that a person does not need help from other people（人的）独立，自立: *He was afraid of losing his independence.* 他害怕失去自己的独立性。

independent /ˌɪndɪˈpendənt/ *adjective* 形容词
1 not affected by, or not needing help from other people 独立的；不受他人影响的；无需他人协助的: *We need an independent review.* 我们需要一场独立评审。
▶ **independently** /ˌɪndɪˈpendəntli/ *adverb* 副词: *We have groups of people working independently in different parts of the world.* 我们有多个群组在全球不同地方独立开展工作。
2 able to take care of yourself without needing help or money from anyone else（人）独立的，自立的: *Children become more independent as they grow.* 孩子们越长大越独立。
▶ **independently** /ˌɪndɪˈpendəntli/ *adverb* 副词: *We want to help students with disabilities to live independently.* 我们想帮助残障学生实现生活自立。
3 not ruled by other countries, but having a separate government（国家）独立的: *Papua New Guinea became independent from Australia in 1975.* 巴布亚新几内亚 1975 年脱离澳大利亚独立。

index /ˈɪndeks/ *countable noun* 可数名词 (**indices** /ˈɪndɪsiːz/ or 或 **indexes**)
a list printed at the back of a book that tells you what is included in it and on which pages you can find each item（图书的）索引: *There's a subject index at the back of the book.* 本书最后有主题索引。

indicate /ˈɪndɪkeɪt/ *verb* 动词 (**indicates, indicating, indicated**)
1 to show that something is true 显示；表明: *The report indicates that most people agree.* 报告显示大多数人赞同。
2 to show someone where something is （*formal* 正式）指示: *He indicated a chair. 'Sit down.'* 他指着一把椅子说: "坐下。"

indication /ˌɪndɪˈkeɪʃən/ *noun* 名词
a sign that suggests something 迹象；表示: *This statement is a strong indication that the government is changing its mind.* 此番表态释放了政府改弦易辙的强烈迹象。

indicator /ˈɪndɪkeɪtə/ *countable noun* 可数名词
a flashing light on a car that tells you when the car is going to turn left or right（汽车的）转向灯，转向指示灯

indifferent /ɪnˈdɪfərənt/ *adjective* 形容词
not at all interested in something 毫无兴趣的；漠不关心的: *We have become indifferent to the suffering of other people.* 我们已经对他人的苦难漠然置之。

indigestion /ˌɪndɪˈdʒestʃən/ *uncountable noun* 不可数名词
pains in your stomach because of something that you have eaten 消化不良

indirect /ˌɪndaɪˈrekt/ *adjective* 形容词
1 not caused directly by the person or thing mentioned, but happening because of them（因果关系）间接的，非直接的: *Millions could die of hunger as an indirect result of the war.* 数百万人可能死于饥饿，这是战争的间接结果。
▸ **indirectly** /ˌɪndaɪˈrektli/ *adverb* 副词: *The government is indirectly responsible for the violence.* 政府对此次暴力事件负有间接责任。
2 not the shortest route between two places（路线）非直达的，迂回的: *He took an indirect route back home.* 他绕道回了家。
3 suggesting something, without stating it clearly（话语）委婉的，含蓄的，拐弯抹角的: *It was an indirect criticism of the president.* 这是对总统委婉的批评。

▸ **indirectly** /ˌɪndaɪˈrektli/ *adverb* 副词: *She indirectly suggested that he should leave.* 她含蓄地暗示他应该离开。

indirect object *countable noun* 可数名词
the thing or person that something is done to in a sentence. For example, in 'She gave him her address', 'him' is the indirect object. Compare with **direct object**. 间接宾语（比较 **direct object**）

individual¹ /ˌɪndɪˈvɪdʒuəl/ *adjective* 形容词
relating to one person or thing, rather than to a large group 个体的；单个的: *We ask each individual customer for suggestions.* 我们向每一位顾客单独征求建议。
▸ **individually** /ˌɪndɪˈvɪdʒuəli/ *adverb* 副词: *You can remove each seat individually.* 你可以把每个座位单独拆下来。

individual² /ˌɪndɪˈvɪdʒuəl/ *countable noun* 可数名词
a person 个体；个人: *We want to reward individuals who do good things.* 我们想奖励做好事的个人。

indoor /ˈɪndɔː/ *adjective* 形容词
done or used inside a building 室内的；户内的: *The hotel has an indoor pool.* 宾馆有个室内游泳池。

indoors /ˌɪnˈdɔːz/ *adverb* 副词
in or to the inside of a building 在室内；向室内: *They warned us to close the windows and stay indoors.* 他们警告我们关上窗户待在室内。

industrial /ɪnˈdʌstriəl/ *adjective* 形容词
1 describing things that relate to industry（事物）工业的，产业的: *The company sells industrial machinery and equipment.* 公司出售工业机械与设备。
2 used for describing a city or a country in which industry is very important（城市或国家）工业化的，工业发达的: *Western industrial countries* 西方工业化国家

industry /ˈɪndəstri/ *noun* 名词 (**industries**)
1 *uncountable* 不可数 the work of making things in factories 工业: *The meeting was for leaders in banking and industry.* 这次会议与会者为银行界和工业界的领袖。
2 *countable* 可数 all the people and activities involved in making a particular product or providing a particular service 产业；行业: *The country depends on its tourism industry.* 该国依赖旅游业。

inefficient /ˌɪnɪˈfɪʃənt/ *adjective* 形容词
not using time or energy in the best way

低效的；没效率的：inefficient work methods 低效的工作方法

inequality /ˌɪnɪˈkwɒlɪti/ **uncountable noun** 不可数名词
when people do not have the same social position, wealth or chances 不平等；不均等：Now there is even greater inequality between the rich and the poor. 目前贫富不均问题愈发严重。

inevitable /ɪnˈevɪtəbəl/ **adjective** 形容词
impossible to prevent or avoid 不可避免的；无法规避的：Suffering is an inevitable part of life. 苦难是人生必修课。
▶ **inevitably** /ɪnˈevɪtəbli/ **adverb** 副词
Advances in technology will inevitably lead to unemployment. 技术进步不可避免地造成失业。

inexperienced /ˌɪnɪkˈspɪəriənst/ **adjective** 形容词
having little knowledge or experience of a particular subject 没经验的；缺乏经验的：She was treated by an inexperienced young doctor. 给她治疗的是一位年轻大夫，没什么经验。

infant /ˈɪnfənt/ **countable noun** 可数名词
a baby or very young child (formal 正式) 婴儿；幼儿：He held the infant in his arms. 他怀里抱着那个婴儿。

infect /ɪnˈfekt/ **verb** 动词 (infects, infecting, infected)
to give a person or an animal a disease or an illness 感染；传染：A single mosquito can infect a large number of people. 单单一只蚊子就可以传染一大群人。
▶ **infection** /ɪnˈfekʃən/ **uncountable noun** 不可数名词：Even a small cut can lead to infection. 哪怕一个小伤口也可能造成感染。

infection /ɪnˈfekʃən/ **countable noun** 可数名词
an illness that is caused by bacteria 感染；传染病：Ear infections are common in young children. 耳部感染是幼童常见病。

infectious /ɪnˈfekʃəs/ **adjective** 形容词
passed easily from one person to another. Compare with **contagious**. (病)传染性的 (比较 contagious)：The disease is highly infectious. 这种病具有很强的传染性。

inferior /ɪnˈfɪəriə/ **adjective** 形容词
not as good as something else 次的；较差的：If you buy it somewhere else, you'll get an inferior product. 你上别的地方买，会买到劣质产品。

infertile /ɪnˈfɜːtaɪl/ **adjective** 形容词
1 unable to produce babies (人或动物)不育的：Ten per cent of couples are infertile. 有10%的夫妇不育。
2 used for describing soil that is of poor quality (土壤)贫瘠的：Nothing grew on the land, which was poor and infertile. 这块地什么也不长，很贫瘠。

infinite /ˈɪnfɪnɪt/ **adjective** 形容词
having no limit, end or edge 无限的；无穷的；无边的：There is an infinite number of stars. 恒星数量无穷无尽。

infinitive /ɪnˈfɪnɪtɪv/ **countable noun** 可数名词
the basic form of a verb, for example, 'do', 'be', 'take' and 'eat'. The infinitive is often used with 'to' in front of it. (动词的)不定式，原形

inflatable /ɪnˈfleɪtəbəl/ **adjective** 形容词
needing to be filled with air before being used 需充气的：The children were playing on the inflatable castle. 孩子们在充气城堡上玩。

inflate /ɪnˈfleɪt/ **verb** 动词 (inflates, inflating, inflated)
to fill something with air 给…充气(或打气)：You should inflate tyres to the level recommended by the manufacturer. 你得给轮胎充气充到制造商推荐的程度。

inflate 给…打气

inflation /ɪnˈfleɪʃən/ **uncountable noun** 不可数名词
a general increase in the prices of goods and services in a country 通货膨胀：The whole world is suffering from rising inflation. 全球都承受着通胀水平走高之苦。

influence[1] /ˈɪnfluəns/ **uncountable noun** 不可数名词
the power to make other people agree with you or do what you want 势力；权势；影响力：He used his influence to get his son into medical school. 他利用自己的影响力把儿子弄进了医学院。

have an influence on someone/something
to affect what someone does or what happens 对某人／某事物有影响：*Alan had a big influence on my career.* 艾伦对我的事业影响很大。

influence² /ˈɪnfluəns/ *verb* 动词 (**influences, influencing, influenced**)
to use your power to make someone agree with you or do what you want 影响；左右：*The newspapers tried to influence public opinion.* 报界试图左右舆论。

influential /ˌɪnfluˈenʃəl/ *adjective* 形容词
having a lot of influence over people or events 有影响力的；有势力的：*He was influential in changing the law.* 他对于修法很有影响力。

info /ˈɪnfəʊ/ *uncountable noun* 不可数名词
short for (缩写 =) **information** (*informal* 非正式)

inform /ɪnˈfɔːm/ *verb* 动词 (**informs, informing, informed**)
to tell someone about something 通知；告知：*We will inform you of any changes.* 如有变化，我们会通知你。 □ *My daughter informed me that she was leaving home.* 我女儿告诉我她要离开家。

informal /ɪnˈfɔːml/ *adjective* 形容词
relaxed and friendly, rather than serious or official 非正式的；轻松友好的：*Her style of writing is very informal.* 她的文风非常轻松随意。 □ *The house has an informal atmosphere.* 这所房子有一种让人轻松自在的氛围。

▶ **informally** /ɪnˈfɔːməli/ *adverb* 副词：*She was chatting informally to the children.* 她在跟孩子们亲切地闲聊。

information /ˌɪnfəˈmeɪʃən/ *uncountable noun* 不可数名词
facts about someone or something. The short form **info** is also used. 信息，资料（缩写形式为 info）：*Pat did not give her any information about Sarah.* 帕特没有给她关于萨拉的任何资料。 □ *We can provide information on training.* 我们可以提供培训信息。

> **LANGUAGE HELP** 语言提示
> **Information** is an uncountable noun. You can say a **piece of information** when you are talking about a particular fact.
> *information 是不可数名词，表示一则信息时可用 a piece of information。

information technology *uncountable noun* 不可数名词
the study and practice of using computers. The short form **I.T.** is often used. 信息技术（缩写形式为 I.T.）：*He works in the information technology industry.* 他从事信息技术行业。

informative /ɪnˈfɔːmətɪv/ *adjective* 形容词
giving you useful information 提供有用信息的；长知识的：*The meeting was friendly and informative.* 这场会议气氛友好，又增进了知识。

ingredient /ɪnˈɡriːdiənt/ *countable noun* 可数名词
one of the things that you use to make something, especially when you are cooking 成分；（尤指）食材：*Mix together all the ingredients.* 把所有食材混合起来。

inhabit /ɪnˈhæbɪt/ *verb* 动词 (**inhabits, inhabiting, inhabited**)
to live in a particular place 居住于；栖居于：*The people who inhabit these islands do not use money.* 这些岛的居民不用钱。

inhabitant /ɪnˈhæbɪtənt/ *countable noun* 可数名词
the people who live in a particular place 居民；栖居者：*The inhabitants of the town wrote a letter to the president.* 该镇居民给总统写了一封信。

inhale /ɪnˈheɪl/ *verb* 动词 (**inhales, inhaling, inhaled**)
to breathe in 吸入；吸气：*He took a long slow breath, inhaling deeply.* 他缓慢而深长地吸了口气。 □ *The men inhaled the poisonous gas and began to feel sick.* 这几名男子吸入有毒气体，开始感到恶心。

inherit /ɪnˈherɪt/ *verb* 动词 (**inherits, inheriting, inherited**)
1 to receive money or property from someone who has died 继承（遗产）：*He has no child to inherit his house.* 他没有子女继承房产。
2 to be born with a personal quality because other members of your family had it 遗传（个人特性）：*Her children have inherited her love of sports.* 她的子女遗传了她对体育的热爱。

inheritance /ɪnˈherɪtəns/ *noun* 名词
money or property that you receive from someone who has died 遗产；继承财产：*She used her inheritance to buy a house.* 她用继承来的遗产买了一座房子。

initial¹ /ɪˈnɪʃəl/ *adjective* 形容词
happening at the beginning of a process 初始的；最初的：*The initial reaction has been excellent.* 初始反应很好。

initial² /ɪˈnɪʃəl/ *countable noun* 可数名词
the capital letter that begins a name（名字的）大写首字母：*She drove a silver car with her initials on the side.* 她开着一辆银色轿车，车身涂有她的姓名首字母。

initially /ɪˈnɪʃəli/ *adverb* 副词
near the beginning of a process or situation 最初；开始时：*The list initially included 11 players.* 名单最初包括 11 名选手。

inject /ɪnˈdʒekt/ *verb* 动词 (injects, injecting, injected)
to put a substance into someone's body using a special type of needle 注射：*The drug was injected into patients four times a week.* 每周给患者注射 4 次这种药物。

injection /ɪnˈdʒekʃən/ *countable noun* 可数名词
the act of putting a substance into someone's body using a special type of needle 注射：*They gave me an injection to help me sleep.* 他们给我打了一针帮我入睡。

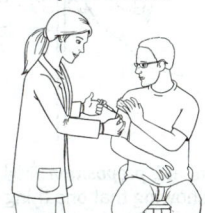
injection 注射

injure /ˈɪndʒə/ *verb* 动词 (injures, injuring, injured)
to damage part of someone's body 弄伤；使受伤：*The bomb seriously injured five people.* 炸弹造成 5 人重伤。

injured /ˈɪndʒəd/ *adjective* 形容词
having suffered damage to part of the body 受伤的；有伤的：*Nurses helped the injured man.* 护士救助了伤者。

> **LANGUAGE HELP** 语言提示
> See note at **wound**. 见 wound 的语言提示。

the injured people who have been injured 伤者；伤员：*Army helicopters moved the injured (= injured people).* 陆军直升机运送伤员。

injury /ˈɪndʒəri/ *noun* 名词 (injuries)
damage to a person's or an animal's body（对肉体的）损伤，伤害：*He was suffering from serious head injuries.* 他头部多处受伤严重。

injustice /ɪnˈdʒʌstɪs/ *uncountable noun* 不可数名词
when a situation is not fair or right 不公平；不公正；非正义：*They have fought injustice all their lives.* 他们毕生同不公正现象斗争。

ink /ɪŋk/ *noun* 名词
the coloured liquid that you use for writing or printing 墨；墨水：*The letter was written in blue ink.* 这封信是用蓝墨水写的。

inland /ˈɪnlænd/ *adjective* 形容词
not beside the sea, but in or near the middle of a country 内陆的；内地的：*inland lakes* 内陆湖 ● **inland** /ɪnˈlænd/ *adverb* 副词：*Most of the population lives inland.* 人口大多分布在内地。

in-laws *plural noun* 复数名词
the parents of your husband or wife 公婆；岳父母：*At Christmas, we had lunch with my in-laws.* 圣诞节我们和公婆一起吃了午饭。

inner /ˈɪnə/ *adjective* 形容词
used for describing the parts inside something, or the parts closest to its centre 内部的；内侧的：*James has an infection of the inner ear.* 詹姆斯内耳感染。

inner city *countable noun* 可数名词 (inner cities)
the poor areas near the centre of a big city（大城市的）内城（系贫民区）：*Samuel grew up in an inner-city neighbourhood in Houston.* 塞缪尔在休斯敦内城区长大。

innocence /ˈɪnəsəns/ *uncountable noun* 不可数名词
1 the quality of having no experience or knowledge of the more difficult aspects of life 天真；纯真；单纯：*Ah! The sweet innocence of youth!* 啊！青春甜美的纯真！
2 not being guilty of a crime 无罪；清白；无辜：*This information could prove your brother's innocence.* 这个信息可以证明你弟弟无罪。

innocent /ˈɪnəsənt/ *adjective* 形容词
1 not guilty of a crime 无罪的；清白的；无辜的：*The jury found him innocent of murder.* 陪审团认定他未犯谋杀罪。
2 having no experience or knowledge of the more difficult aspects of life 天真的；纯真的；单纯的：*They seemed so young and innocent.* 他们看上去这么年轻、这么天真。

innovation /ˌɪnəˈveɪʃən/ **countable noun** 可数名词
a new thing or a new way of doing something 创新；新事物；新方法：*They showed us some of their latest technological innovations.* 他们给我们看了一些他们最新的技术创新成果。

innovative /ˈɪnəvətɪv, -veɪtɪv/ **adjective** 形容词
1 new and different 新颖的；革新的；创新性的：*The company produces innovative car designs.* 该公司制作创新性的汽车设计。
2 having new ideas and doing different things 有创意的；有创新精神的：*He is one of America's most innovative film-makers.* 他是美国最具创新精神的电影制作人之一。

input /ˈɪnpʊt/ **noun** 名词
1 the help, information or advice that one person gives to another person 投入（指援助、信息或建议）：*There has been a lot of hard work and input from the public.* 这中间有公众大量的辛苦努力和投入。
2 uncountable 不可数 information that you type into a computer（计算机信息的）输入：*Who is responsible for data input here?* 这儿谁负责数据输入？● **input verb** 动词 (**inputs, inputting, input**)：*We need more staff to input the data.* 我们需要增加人手输入数据。

inquisitive /ɪnˈkwɪzɪtɪv/ **adjective** 形容词
wanting to find out about things 好探问的；爱打听的：*Amy was very inquisitive, always wanting to know how things worked.* 埃米非常爱刨根问底，遇到东西总想弄个明白。

insane /ɪnˈseɪn/ **adjective** 形容词
1 seriously mentally ill 疯的；精神错乱的：*For a while, I thought I was going insane.* 有一会儿，我觉得自己要疯了。
2 very foolish 非常愚蠢的；荒唐的：*I thought the idea was completely insane.* 我觉得这个想法太荒唐了。

insect /ˈɪnsekt/ **countable noun** 可数名词
a very small animal that has six legs. Most insects have wings. 昆虫

insecure /ˌɪnsɪˈkjʊə/ **adjective** 形容词
1 thinking that you are not good enough 缺乏自信的；自我认同度低的：*Most people are a little insecure about their looks.* 大多数人都对自己的长相有点儿不自信。
▶ **insecurity** /ˌɪnsɪˈkjʊərɪti/ **uncountable noun** 不可数名词：*Both men and women can have feelings of shyness and insecurity.* 男人和女人都会感到害羞和不自信。
2 not firm or steady 不结实的；不稳当的：*Don't take risks with an insecure ladder.* 不要冒险上不稳当的梯子。

insensitive /ɪnˈsensɪtɪv/ **adjective** 形容词
not thinking about or caring about other people's feelings 冷漠的；不敏感的；不考虑他人感受的：*My husband is very insensitive to my problem.* 我丈夫对我的问题不管不问。
▶ **insensitivity** /ɪnˌsensɪˈtɪvɪti/ **uncountable noun** 不可数名词：*I'm sorry about my insensitivity towards her.* 很抱歉，我没有考虑到她的感受。

insert /ɪnˈsɜːt/ **verb** 动词 (**inserts, inserting, inserted**)
to put an object inside something 插入；嵌入：*Mike took a key from his pocket and inserted it into the lock.* 迈克从兜里掏出一把钥匙插进锁孔里。

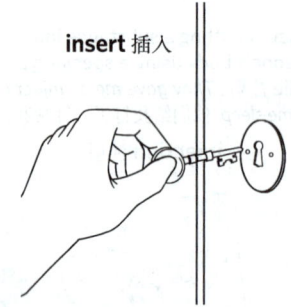
insert 插入

inside¹ /ˌɪnˈsaɪd/ **preposition** 介词
used for showing that one thing is in another 在…里面；在…内侧：*Inside the envelope was a photograph.* 信封里面是一张照片。● **inside adjective** 形容词：*Josh took his mobile phone from the inside pocket of his jacket.* 乔希从外套内兜里掏出手机。

inside² /ˌɪnˈsaɪd/ **adverb** 副词
into a building 至室内：*The couple chatted on the doorstep before going inside.* 这两口子在门阶上聊了会儿才进去。

inside³ /ˌɪnˈsaɪd/ **countable noun** 可数名词
the inner part of something 内部；里面：*I've painted the inside of the house.* 我已经粉刷完了房子内部。

inside out with the part that is normally inside on the outside 里面朝外；里外颠倒：*I didn't realize that my T-shirt was inside out.* 我没有意识到T恤衫里外穿反了。

inside out 里外颠倒

I didn't realize that my T-shirt was inside out. 我没有意识到T恤衫里外穿反了。

insight /ˈɪnsaɪt/ *noun* 名词
a good understanding of something 洞悉；深入见解：*This book provides fascinating insights into the way the mind works.* 本书呈现了对头脑工作方式的深入见解，饶有趣味。

insignificant /ˌɪnsɪɡˈnɪfɪkənt/ *adjective* 形容词
not important 不重要的；无足轻重的：*In 1949, Bonn was a small, insignificant city.* *1949 年，波恩还是一个名不见经传的小城。

insist /ɪnˈsɪst/ *verb* 动词 (**insists, insisting, insisted**)
1 to say firmly that something must happen 坚持；执意：*Rob insisted on driving them to the station.* 罗布执意要开车送他们到车站。 □ *He insisted that I stay for dinner.* 他坚持要我留下来吃晚饭。
2 to say very firmly that something is true 坚称；坚持认为：*Clarke insisted that he was telling the truth.* 克拉克坚称自己说的都是实话。

inspect /ɪnˈspekt/ *verb* 动词 (**inspects, inspecting, inspected**)
to look at something very carefully 检查；审视：*Dad inspected the car carefully before he bought it.* 爸爸仔细检查后才买下那辆汽车。
▶ **inspection** /ɪnˈspekʃən/ *noun* 名词：*Dixon still makes weekly inspections of all his shops.* 狄克逊每周仍要视察一遍旗下所有店铺。

inspector /ɪnˈspektə/ *countable noun* 可数名词
1 a person whose job is to check that people do things correctly 检查员；督察员：*a fire inspector* 消防检查员

2 an officer in the police (警察系统的)督察：*Police Inspector John Taylor* 警队督察约翰·泰勒

inspiration /ˌɪnspəˈreɪʃən/ *uncountable noun* 不可数名词
a feeling of enthusiasm and new ideas that you get from someone or something 灵感：*My inspiration as a writer comes from poets like Walt Whitman.* 我的写作灵感来自沃尔特·惠特曼这样的诗人。

inspire /ɪnˈspaɪə/ *verb* 动词 (**inspires, inspiring, inspired**)
1 to give you new ideas and a strong feeling of enthusiasm 启发；给…以灵感：*Singer and songwriter Bob Dylan inspired a generation of young people.* 歌手兼词作者鲍勃·迪伦启发了一代年轻人。
▶ **inspiring** /ɪnˈspaɪərɪŋ/ *adjective* 形容词：*She was one of the most inspiring people I ever met.* 她是我所遇到过的最能启发人的人之一。
2 to make someone feel a particular way 激起，激发(特定情感)：*A teacher has to inspire confidence in the students.* 老师得激起学生的信心。

install /ɪnˈstɔːl/ *verb* 动词 (**installs, installing, installed**)
to put something somewhere so that it is ready to be used 安装；布设：*They installed a new telephone line in the flat.* 他们在公寓里新布了一条电话线。
▶ **installation** /ˌɪnstəˈleɪʃən/ *uncountable noun* 不可数名词：*The installation of smoke alarms could save hundreds of lives.* 安装烟雾报警器可能会拯救数百条生命。

instalment /ɪnˈstɔːlmənt/ *countable noun* 可数名词
1 one of several small regular payments that you make over a period of time (分期付款的)一期付款：*She is repaying the loan in monthly instalments of £30.* 她在分期还这笔贷款，每月 30 英镑。
2 one part of a story in a magazine, or on TV or radio (杂志、电视或广播连载故事的)一期，一部：*Charles Dickens' novel, The Old Curiosity Shop, was published in weekly instalments.* 查尔斯·狄更斯的小说《老古玩店》是按周连载发表的。

instance /ˈɪnstəns/ *noun* 名词
for instance used for giving an example of what you are talking about 例如；比如：*I want to talk about environmental issues,*

for instance, global warming. 我想谈谈环境问题，比如全球变暖。

instant[1] /ˈɪnstənt/ *countable noun* 可数名词
a very short period of time 瞬间；刹那；一小会儿：*For an instant, I wanted to cry.* 有一瞬间，我想哭。

instant[2] /ˈɪnstənt/ *adjective* 形容词
1 immediate 立即的；即刻的：*Her book was an instant success.* 她那本书迅速蹿红。
▸ **instantly** /ˈɪnstəntli/ *adverb* 副词：*The man was killed instantly.* 男子当场殒命。
2 prepared very quickly and easily 速食的；速溶的：*He stirred instant coffee into a mug of hot water.* 他把速溶咖啡搅进了一杯热水里。

ˈinstant ˌmessaging *uncountable noun* 不可数名词
the activity of sending written messages from one computer to another. The message appears immediately on the screen of the computer you send it to if this computer is also using the service. The short form **IM** is also used. 即时通信，即时消息传送（缩写形式为 IM）：*Instant messaging is my favourite way to communicate with friends.* 我最喜欢通过即时通信和朋友交流。

instead /ɪnˈsted/ *adverb* 副词
in the place of someone or something 代替：*Robert didn't want to go bowling. He went to the cinema instead.* 罗伯特不想打保龄球。他去看电影了。
▸ **instead of someone/something** in the place of someone or something 代替某人／某事物：*Why don't you walk to work, instead of driving?* 你何不走路去上班，别开车了？

instinct /ˈɪnstɪŋkt/ *noun* 名词
the natural way that a person or an animal behaves or reacts 本能：*My first instinct was to laugh.* 我第一反应是大笑。

instinctive /ɪnˈstɪŋktɪv/ *adjective* 形容词
felt or done without consideration 本能的：*Smiling is instinctive to all human beings.* 微笑是全人类的本能。
▸ **instinctively** /ɪnˈstɪŋktɪvli/ *adverb* 副词：*When the phone rang, Jane instinctively knew something was wrong.* 电话铃响起时，简本能地意识到出事儿了。

institute /ˈɪnstɪtjuːt/ *countable noun* 可数名词
an organization or a place where people study a particular subject in detail in order to discover new facts 学院；学会；研究所：*My uncle works at the National Cancer Institute.* 我叔叔在国家癌症研究所工作。

institution /ˌɪnstɪˈtjuːʃən/ *countable noun* 可数名词
a large organization such as a school, a bank or a church 机构（如学校、银行、教会）：*Most financial institutions offer interest-only loans for home-buyers.* 大多数金融机构为购房者提供停本还息贷款。

instruct /ɪnˈstrʌkt/ *verb* 动词 (**instructs, instructing, instructed**)
1 to formally tell someone to do something (*formal* 正式) 吩咐；指示；命令：*Grandpa's doctor instructed him to get more fresh air.* 大夫嘱咐爷爷多呼吸新鲜空气。
2 to teach someone a particular subject 教录；讲授：*Our teachers instruct the children in music, dance and physical education.* 我们老师教授孩子们音乐、舞蹈和体育。

instruction /ɪnˈstrʌkʃən/ *noun* 名词
1 *countable* 可数 something that someone tells you to do 吩咐；指示；命令：*We had instructions from our teacher not to leave the building.* 老师嘱咐我们不要离开大楼。
2 [**instructions**] *plural* 复数 information on how to do something 说明；指南：*The cookbook uses simple instructions and photographs.* 这本菜谱采用了简单说明配照片的形式。

instructor /ɪnˈstrʌktə/ *countable noun* 可数名词
someone whose job is to teach a skill or an activity 教练；指导者：*Rachel is a swimming instructor.* 蕾切尔是一位游泳教练。

instrument /ˈɪnstrəmənt/ *countable noun* 可数名词
1 a tool that you use for doing a particular job 工具；器械；器具；仪器：*scientific instruments* 科学仪器
2 an object that you use for making music 乐器：*Tim plays four musical instruments, including piano and guitar.* 蒂姆会演奏 4 种乐器，包括钢琴和吉他。

instrumental /ˌɪnstrəˈmentəl/ *adjective* 形容词
1 helping to make something happen 有助益的；起促进作用的：*Mr Johnson was instrumental in the company's success.* 约

翰逊先生对公司走向成功起到了推动作用。**2** for musical instruments only, and not for voices 乐器的：*We welcomed the visitors with traditional dance and instrumental music.* 我们用传统舞蹈和器乐欢迎来客。

insulate /ˈɪnsjuleɪt/ ***verb*** 动词 (**insulates, insulating, insulated**)
to cover something with rubber or plastic to prevent electricity from passing through 使绝缘：*insulated wire* 绝缘线

insult¹ /ɪnˈsʌlt/ ***verb*** 动词 (**insults, insulting, insulted**)
to say or do something to someone that is rude or offensive 辱骂；侮辱：*I'm sorry. I didn't mean to insult you.* 对不起。我无意侮辱你。
▶ **insulted** /ɪnˈsʌltɪd/ ***adjective*** 形容词：*I was really insulted by the way he spoke to me.* 他那样跟我说话，我受到了深深的侮辱。
▶ **insulting** /ɪnˈsʌltɪŋ/ ***adjective*** 形容词：*Don't use insulting language.* 切勿使用侮辱性语言。

insult² /ˈɪnsʌlt/ ***countable noun*** 可数名词
something rude that a person says or does 辱骂；侮辱性言行：*The boys shouted insults at each other.* 男孩子们互相谩骂。

insurance /ɪnˈʃʊərəns/ ***uncountable noun*** 不可数名词
an agreement that you make with a company in which you pay money to them regularly, and they pay you if something bad happens to you or your property 保险：*I pay about £40 per month for car insurance.* 我每月交 40 英镑左右的汽车保险。

insure /ɪnˈʃʊə/ ***verb*** 动词 (**insures, insuring, insured**)
to pay money regularly to a company so that, if you become ill, or if your property is damaged or stolen, the company will pay you an amount of money 为…投保；给…上保险：*It costs a lot of money to insure your car.* 给汽车上保险很花钱。

intellectual /ˌɪntəˈlektʃuəl/ ***adjective*** 形容词
involving a person's ability to think and to understand ideas and information 智力的：*Dr Miller is an expert on the intellectual development of children.* 米勒博士是研究儿童智力发育的专家。

intelligence /ɪnˈtelɪdʒəns/ ***uncountable noun*** 不可数名词
1 the ability to understand and learn things quickly and well 聪颖；聪慧；智慧：*Stephanie's a woman of great intelligence.* 斯蒂芬妮是个有大智慧的女子。
2 information that is collected by the government or the army about other countries' activities 情报：*There is a need for better military intelligence.* 需要提升搜集军事情报的水平。

intelligent /ɪnˈtelɪdʒənt/ ***adjective*** 形容词
able to think, understand and learn things quickly and well 聪颖的；聪慧的；有智慧的：*Susan's a very intelligent woman.* 苏珊是个非常聪明的女子。
▶ **intelligently** /ɪnˈtelɪdʒəntli/ ***adverb*** 副词：*William can talk intelligently on many different subjects.* 威廉对很多不同的话题都能发表一番高论。

intend /ɪnˈtend/ ***verb*** 动词 (**intends, intending, intended**)
1 to plan to do something 有意；打算；计划：*We're intending to stay in Philadelphia for four years.* 我们打算在费城待 4 年。□ *What do you intend to do when you leave college?* 你大学毕业后打算干什么？
2 to plan or make something for a particular purpose（计划）使…用于特定目的：*This money is intended for schools.* 这笔钱是用于学校的。□ *The big windows were intended to make the room brighter.* 大窗户意在使房间亮堂些。

intense /ɪnˈtens/ ***adjective*** 形容词
very great or strong 巨大的；非常强的：*The intense heat made him sweat.* 酷热令他汗流不止。
▶ **intensely** /ɪnˈtensli/ ***adverb*** 副词：*The fast-food business is intensely competitive.* 快餐业竞争激烈。

intensive /ɪnˈtensɪv/ ***adjective*** 形容词
involving a lot of effort or many people 强化的；大强度的；密集的：*The course begins with sixteen weeks of intensive training.* 这门课开始有 16 周强化培训。
▶ **intensively** /ɪnˈtensɪvli/ ***adverb*** 副词：*Dan is working intensively on his new book.* 丹在紧锣密鼓地创作新书。

intention /ɪnˈtenʃən/ ***noun*** 名词
something that you plan to do 意图；意向；打算：*It is my intention to retire later this year.* 我打算今年晚些时候退休。□ *Karen has no intention of getting married again.* 卡伦无意再婚。

intentional /ɪnˈtenʃənəl/ *adjective* 形容词
done on purpose, and not by mistake 有意的；故意的：*I'm sorry if I hurt him — it wasn't intentional.* 要是伤害了他，我感到抱歉——我不是故意的。
▶ **intentionally** /ɪnˈtenʃənəli/ *adverb* 副词：*He intentionally crashed his car to collect insurance money.* 他故意撞车骗取保险赔偿金。

interactive /ˌɪntərˈæktɪv/ *adjective* 形容词
used for describing something that allows direct communication between itself and the user 交互式的；互动式的：*Press the red button on your interactive TV to vote for your favourite singer.* 按下交互式电视上的红色按钮，为你最喜爱的歌手投票。

interactive whiteboard *countable noun* 可数名词
an electronic board in a classroom. Teachers and students can write on it using a special pen, or by touching it with their finger. 交互式电子白板
→ Look at picture on P1 参见彩插第 1 页

interest¹ /ˈɪntrəst, -tərest/ *noun* 名词
1 *uncountable* 不可数 a feeling that you want to know more about something 兴趣；兴致；兴味：*There is a lot of interest in making the book into a film.* 很多人对把这本书改编成电影兴趣浓厚。 □ *She liked Jason at first, but she soon lost interest in him.* 她起初喜欢贾森，不过不久就没兴趣了。
2 *countable* 可数 something that you like doing 爱好：*'What are your interests?' 'I enjoy riding horses and I also play tennis.'* "你有什么爱好？""我喜欢骑马，也打网球。"
3 *uncountable* 不可数 the extra money that you pay if you have borrowed money, or the extra money that you receive if you have money in some types of bank account 利息：*Do you earn much interest on that account?* 你那个账户利息多吗？ □ *How much interest do you have to pay on the loan?* 你那笔贷款得付多少利息？

interest² /ˈɪntrəst, -tərest/ *verb* 动词
(**interests, interesting, interested**)
to make you feel that you want to know more about something 使感兴趣；引起…的兴趣：*Fashion does not interest her.* 时尚引不起她的兴趣。

interested /ˈɪntrestɪd/ *adjective* 形容词
wanting to know more about something 感兴趣的；有兴趣的：*I thought you might be interested in this article in the newspaper.* 我觉得你可能对报上这篇文章感兴趣。

interesting /ˈɪntrestɪŋ/ *adjective* 形容词
making you want to know more about something 有趣的；令人感兴趣的：*It was interesting to be in a new town.* 置身一座新城很有意思。
▶ **interestingly** /ˈɪntrestɪŋli/ *adverb* 副词：*Interestingly, there are no British writers on the list.* 有意思的是，名单上没有英国作家。

interfere /ˌɪntəˈfɪə/ *verb* 动词 (**interferes, interfering, interfered**)
1 to get involved in a situation when other people do not want you to 干涉；干预；介入：*I wish everyone would stop interfering and just leave me alone.* 我希望大家别再多管闲事，让我一个人静一静。
▶ **interference** /ˌɪntəˈfɪərəns/ *uncountable noun* 不可数名词：*She didn't appreciate her mother's interference in her life.* 她不喜欢妈妈干涉自己的生活。
2 to stop an activity from going well 干扰；扰乱；妨碍：*Mobile phones can interfere with aircraft equipment.* 手机会干扰机上设备。

interior /ɪnˈtɪəriə/ *countable noun* 可数名词
the inside part of something 内部：*The interior of the house was dark and old-fashioned.* 房子内部昏暗而陈旧。● **interior** *adjective* 形容词：*They painted the interior walls of the house white.* 他们把房子内墙刷成了白色。

intermediate /ˌɪntəˈmiːdiət/ *adjective* 形容词
in the middle level, between two other levels 中级的；中等水平的：*We teach beginner, intermediate and advanced level students.* 我们教初级、中级以及高级水平的学生。

internal /ɪnˈtɜːnəl/ *adjective* 形容词
existing or happening on the inside of something 内部的：*After the accident, Aaron suffered internal bleeding.* 事故后，阿龙出现了内出血。

international /ˌɪntəˈnæʃənəl/ *adjective* 形容词
involving different countries 国际的：*The best way to end poverty is through international trade.* 消灭贫困最好的途径是国际贸易。
▶ **internationally** /ˌɪntəˈnæʃənəli/ *adverb*

副词: *Bruce Lee is an internationally famous film star.* 李小龙是国际知名影星。

Internet /ˈɪntənet/ also 亦作 **internet** *noun* 名词
the network that allows computer users to connect with computers all over the world, and that carries email 因特网；互联网: *Do you have Internet access at home?* 你家里能上网吗？

interpret /ɪnˈtɜːprɪt/ *verb* 动词 (**interprets, interpreting, interpreted**)
1 to decide what something means 解释；阐释: *You can interpret the data in different ways.* 你可以用不同的方式解读这些数据。
2 to put the words that someone says into another language 口译
▶ **interpreter** /ɪnˈtɜːprɪtə/ *countable noun* 可数名词: *Speaking through an interpreter, he said that he was very happy to be in the UK.* 他通过口译员表示，自己非常高兴来到英国。

interrogate /ɪnˈterəˌɡeɪt/ *verb* 动词 (**interrogates, interrogating, interrogated**)
to ask someone questions for a long time in order to get some information from them 讯问；审问；询问: *Mr Wright was interrogated by police for eight hours on Thursday night.* 星期四夜里赖特先生被警察讯问了8个小时。
▶ **interrogation** /ɪnˌterəˈɡeɪʃən/ *noun* 名词: *He confessed during an interrogation by police.* 他接受警方审问时招供了。

interrupt /ˌɪntəˈrʌpt/ *verb* 动词 (**interrupts, interrupting, interrupted**)
1 to say or do something that causes someone to stop what they are doing 打断；打岔: *Don't interrupt the teacher when she's speaking.* 老师说话时不要打岔。 □ *I'm sorry to interrupt, but there's a phone call for you.* 不好意思，打断一下，有您的电话。
▶ **interruption** /ˌɪntəˈrʌpʃən/ *noun* 名词: *I can't concentrate on my work — there are too many interruptions.* 我没法集中精力工作——老有人打岔。
2 to cause an activity to stop for a period of time 中止；中断；使暂停: *Rain interrupted the tennis match for two hours.* 下雨使得本场网球赛中断了两小时。
▶ **interruption** /ˌɪntəˈrʌpʃən/ *noun* 名词: *The meeting continued with no more interruptions.* 会议继续进行，没有再生枝节。

interval /ˈɪntəvəl/ *countable noun* 可数名词
the period of time between two events 间隔期: *We met again after an interval of 12 years.* 时隔12年，我们再次见面。

interview¹ /ˈɪntəˌvjuː/ *noun* 名词
a formal meeting in which someone asks you questions to find out if you are the right person for a job 面试: *The interview went well, so I hope that I've got the job.* 面试顺利，我希望自己得到了这个职位。

interview² /ˈɪntəˌvjuː/ *verb* 动词 (**interviews, interviewing, interviewed**)
to ask someone questions to find out if they are the right person for a particular job 面试: *Anna was interviewed for a job at The New York Times yesterday.* 安娜昨天去面试了《纽约时报》的一个职位。
▶ **interviewer** /ˈɪntəˌvjuːə/ *countable noun* 可数名词: *The interviewer asked me why I wanted the job.* 面试官问我为什么申请这个职位。

intestine /ɪnˈtestɪn/ *countable noun* 可数名词
the tube in your body that food passes through when it has left your stomach 肠

intimate /ˈɪntɪmət/ *adjective* 形容词
knowing someone very well and liking them a lot 亲密的；密切的: *I told my intimate friends I wanted to have a baby.* 我告诉密友自己想要个孩子。
▶ **intimately** /ˈɪntɪmətli/ *adverb* 副词: *He knows the family fairly well, but not intimately.* 他跟这家人相当熟，不过算不上亲密。

intimidate /ɪnˈtɪmɪˌdeɪt/ *verb* 动词 (**intimidates, intimidating, intimidated**)
to frighten someone in order to make them do what you want 恐吓；威胁；胁迫: *Many people feel intimidated by these teenage gangs.* 许多人感觉受到了这些少年帮派的威胁。
▶ **intimidation** /ɪnˌtɪmɪˈdeɪʃən/ *uncountable noun* 不可数名词: *Witnesses are often afraid of intimidation.* 证人往往害怕恐吓。

into /ˈɪntə, ˈɪntu, STRONG 强读 ˈɪntuː/ *preposition* 介词
1 inside 在⋯里面: *Put the apples into a dish.* 把苹果放在盘子里。
2 to the inside from the outside 到⋯里面: *Mum got into the car and started the engine.* 妈妈钻进汽车启动了发动机。

intolerant - invent

3 against（碰）上；（撞）上：*A train crashed into the barrier at the end of the track.* 一列火车撞上了铁轨尽头的挡车器。
4 used for talking about putting a different piece of clothing on（换）上（衣服）：*I'm cold — I'll change into some warmer clothes.* 我觉得冷——我要换件暖和些的衣服。
5 used for talking about things changing to a different form（变）成（另一形式）：*The book has been made into a film.* 这本书已经被改编成电影。
6 used for talking about how something is divided（分）成：*I cut the cake into 12 slices.* 我把蛋糕切成了 12 块。
7 used when you are dividing one number by another number 除：*5 into 15 is 3.* *5 除 15 等于 3。

intolerant /ɪnˈtɒlərənt/ *adjective* 形容词
not accepting people who behave and think differently to you 不包容的；不宽容的：*They are intolerant of the opinions of others.* 他们容不得别人的意见。
▶ **intolerance** /ɪnˈtɒlərəns/ *uncountable noun* 不可数名词：*They worry about people's intolerance toward foreigners.* 他们对人们不包容外国人感到忧虑。

intranet /ˈɪntrənet/ *countable noun* 可数名词
a network of computers in a particular organization 内联网

intransitive /ɪnˈtrænsɪtɪv/ *adjective* 形容词
used for describing a verb that does not have an object（动词）不及物的

introduce /ˌɪntrəˈdjuːs/ *verb* 动词
(**introduces, introducing, introduced**)
1 to tell people each other's names so that they can get to know each other 介绍；引见：*Tim, may I introduce you to my wife, Jennifer?* 蒂姆，我给你介绍一下，这位是我的夫人珍妮弗。
2 to bring something new to a place; to make something exist for the first time 引入；推行：*The airline introduced a new direct service from Houston last month.* 这家航空公司上个月新推出了一项自休斯敦出发的直航服务。
▶ **introduction** /ˌɪntrəˈdʌkʃən/ *uncountable noun* 不可数名词：*Did the introduction of the euro affect prices?* 推行欧元影响价格了吗？

introduce yourself to tell someone your name 做自我介绍：*Before the meeting, we all introduced ourselves.* 会前我们每个人都做了自我介绍。

introduction /ˌɪntrəˈdʌkʃən/ *countable noun* 可数名词
the part at the beginning of a book that tells you what the book is about 引言；导言：*J.D. Salinger wrote the introduction to the book.* *J.D. 塞林格为本书撰写了导言。
→ Look at picture on P3 参见彩插第 3 页

intuition /ˌɪntjuˈɪʃən/ *noun* 名词
an ability to know or understand something through your feelings 直觉：*My intuition told me that I could trust him.* 直觉告诉我可以信任他。

invade /ɪnˈveɪd/ *verb* 动词 (**invades, invading, invaded**)
to attack and enter a country 侵略；侵犯；入侵：*In 1944 the Allies invaded the Italian mainland.* *1944 年，盟军攻入意大利本土。

invalid[1] /ˈɪnvəlɪd/ *countable noun* 可数名词
someone who needs to be cared for by another person because they are very sick or badly injured 病人；病残者；伤病员：*Both of Mary's parents were invalids.* 玛丽爸妈都是病号。

invalid[2] /ɪnˈvælɪd/ *adjective* 形容词
used for describing a document that cannot be accepted, because it breaks an official rule（文件等）无效的：*He was trying to board a flight for the Philippines with an invalid passport.* 他企图使用无效护照登机前往菲律宾。

invasion /ɪnˈveɪʒən/ *noun* 名词
an occasion when an army enters a country and attacks it 侵略；侵犯；入侵：*Cyprus has been divided since an invasion in 1974.* 塞浦路斯自从 1974 年遭受入侵之后一直处于分裂状态。

invent /ɪnˈvent/ *verb* 动词 (**invents, inventing, invented**)
1 to be the first person to think of something or to make it 发明；首创：*The ballpoint pen was invented by the Hungarian, Laszlo Biro.* 圆珠笔是匈牙利人拉斯洛·比罗发明的。
▶ **inventor** /ɪnˈventə/ *countable noun* 可数名词：*Who was the inventor of the telephone?* 电话是谁发明的？
2 to try to make other people believe that something is true when it is not 编造；捏造：*Heather invented an excuse not to attend Ryan's birthday party.* 希瑟编了个借口，不去参加瑞安的生日派对。

invention /ɪnˈvenʃən/ *noun* 名词
1 countable 可数 something that has been invented by someone 发明物；首创物：*Paper was a Chinese invention.* 纸是中国人发明的。
2 uncountable 不可数 when something is invented 发明；首创：*The invention of the telescope led to the discovery of Uranus in 1781.* 望远镜的发明促成了 1781 年天王星的发现。

invertebrate /ɪnˈvɜːtɪbrət/ *countable noun* 可数名词
an animal that does not have a spine (= bones in its back). Compare with **vertebrate**. 无脊椎动物（比较 vertebrate）
● **invertebrate** *adjective* 形容词：*Ponds contain many invertebrate species.* 池塘里有很多种无脊椎动物。

inverted commas /ɪnˌvɜːtɪd ˈkɒməz/ *plural noun* 复数名词
marks that are used in writing to show what someone said. You write them as ' ' or " ". 引号（写作' '或" "）

invest /ɪnˈvest/ *verb* 动词 (**invests, investing, invested**)
to put money into a business or a bank, in order to try to make a profit from it 投资：*He invested millions of dollars in the business.* 他在这家企业投资了数百万美元。

investigate /ɪnˈvestɪɡeɪt/ *verb* 动词 (**investigates, investigating, investigated**)
to try to find out how something happened 调查：*Police are investigating how the accident happened.* 警方正在调查事故起因。
▶ **investigation** /ɪnˌvestɪˈɡeɪʃən/ *noun* 名词：*We have begun an investigation into the man's death.* 我们已经开始调查这名男子之死。

investigator /ɪnˈvestɪɡeɪtə/ *countable noun* 可数名词
a person whose job is to find out about something 调查员；调查者：*Investigators have been questioning the survivors.* 调查人员一直在询问幸存者。

investment /ɪnˈvesmənt/ *noun* 名词
1 uncountable 不可数 the activity of investing money 投资：*John's an investment advisor in Chicago.* 约翰是芝加哥的一位投资顾问。
2 an amount of money that you invest, or the thing that you invest your money in 投资额；投资对象：*Anthony made a $1 million investment in the company.* 安东尼往公司投了 100 万美元。

invisible /ɪnˈvɪzɪbəl/ *adjective* 形容词
impossible to see 隐形的；不可见的；看不见的：*In the story, Matilda becomes invisible after eating blue sweets.* 故事中，玛蒂尔达吃了蓝色糖果之后隐形了。

invitation /ˌɪnvɪˈteɪʃən/ *countable noun* 可数名词
when someone asks you to go to an event 邀请：*I accepted Sarah's invitation to her birthday party.* 我接受了萨拉参加她生日派对的邀请。

invite /ɪnˈvaɪt/ *verb* 动词 (**invites, inviting, invited**)
to ask someone to come to an event 邀请：*She invited him to her 26th birthday party.* 她邀请他参加自己 26 岁生日聚会。

invoice /ˈɪnvɔɪs/ *countable noun* 可数名词
a document that shows how much money you must pay for goods you have ordered or the work that someone has done for you 发票；发货清单：*We sent them an invoice for £11,000 four months ago.* 我们 4 个月前寄给他们一张 11,000 英镑的发票。
● **invoice** *verb* 动词 (**invoices, invoicing, invoiced**)：*You will not be invoiced for the work until January.* 你干的这个活儿要到 1 月份才开具发票。

involve /ɪnˈvɒlv/ *verb* 动词 (**involves, involving, involved**)
1 to have something as a necessary part 需要；包含；须有：*Running a household involves lots of different skills.* 持家需要许多不同技能。
2 if an activity involves someone, they take part in it 涉及；牵涉：*The scandal involved a former senator.* 这桩丑闻牵涉一位前参议员。
3 to get someone to take part in something 使参与；使介入：*We involve the children in everything we do.* 我们让孩子们参与我们所做的每一件事。

involved /ɪnˈvɒlvd/ *adjective* 形容词
taking part in something 参与的；介入的：*All of their children are involved in the family business.* 他们所有子女都加入了家族企业。

involvement /ɪnˈvɒlvmənt/ *uncountable noun* 不可数名词
when you take part in something 参与；介

iris – irritate

入：*Edwards has always denied any involvement in the crime.* 爱德华兹始终否认涉案。

iris /ˈaɪərɪs/ *countable noun* 可数名词 (**irises**)
the round coloured part of a person's eye 虹膜

iron[1] /ˈaɪən/ *noun* 名词
1 *uncountable* 不可数 a hard, dark grey metal 铁：*We waited for the iron gates to open.* 我们等待铁门打开。
2 *countable* 可数 a piece of electrical equipment with a flat metal base that you heat and move over clothes to make them smooth 电熨斗

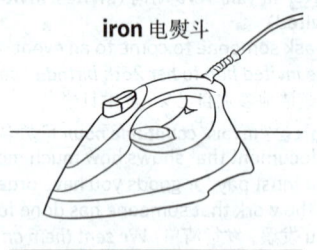

iron 电熨斗

iron[2] /ˈaɪən/ *verb* 动词 (**irons, ironing, ironed**)
to make clothes smooth using an iron 熨烫：*I began to iron some shirts.* 我开始熨几件衬衣。
▶ **ironing** /ˈaɪənɪŋ/ *uncountable noun* 不可数名词：*I was doing the ironing when she called.* 她来电时我在熨衣服。

ironic /aɪˈrɒnɪk/ or 或 **ironical** /aɪˈrɒnɪkəl/ *adjective* 形容词
strange or funny; very different from what people expect 荒诞的；可笑的；具讽刺意味的：*It is ironic that we lie in the sun to make our skin look more attractive.* 为了拥有更迷人的肤色，我们躺在太阳底下晒，这真是好笑。
▶ **ironically** /aɪˈrɒnɪkli/ *adverb* 副词：*His enormous dog is ironically called 'Tiny'.* 可笑的是，他那条大狗居然叫"小小"。

irony /ˈaɪərəni/ *uncountable noun* 不可数名词
a type of humour where you say the opposite of what you really mean 反语；反话：*'You're early!' he said, as we arrived two hours late, his voice full of irony.* "你来得真早！" 我们迟到了两个小时，他满口讥讽地说。

irrational /ɪˈræʃənəl/ *adjective* 形容词 not based on sensible, clear thinking 非理性的；无理性的：*I think hatred is often irrational.* 我认为仇恨往往都是不理性的。
▶ **irrationally** /ɪˈræʃənəli/ *adverb* 副词：*My husband is irrationally jealous and possessive.* 我丈夫爱吃醋，占有欲很强，不可理喻。

irregular /ɪˈregjʊlə/ *adjective* 形容词
1 used for describing something that happens at different times 不定时的；不规律的：*The tests showed that his heartbeat was irregular.* 检查显示他心律不齐。
▶ **irregularly** /ɪˈregjʊləli/ *adverb* 副词：*He was eating irregularly and losing weight.* 他吃饭有一顿没一顿的，在减肥。
2 not following the usual rules of grammar. For example, 'run' is an irregular verb, because the past form is 'ran' (and not 'runned'). Compare with **regular**.（动词等）不规则的（比较 regular）

irrelevant /ɪˈreləvənt/ *adjective* 形容词
not connected with what you are talking about or doing 无关的；不相干的：*Remove any irrelevant details from your essay.* 删掉文章中所有无关细节。

irresponsible /ˌɪrɪˈspɒnsɪbəl/ *adjective* 形容词
not thinking about the possible results of your actions 不负责任的；无责任感的：*There are still too many irresponsible drivers who use their mobile phones while driving.* 开车玩手机这种不负责任的司机还有很多。

irritable /ˈɪrɪtəbəl/ *adjective* 形容词
becoming angry very easily 易怒的；暴躁的：*After waiting for him for over an hour, Amber was feeling irritable.* 安伯等了他1个多小时，心里开始冒火了。
▶ **irritably** /ˈɪrɪtəbli/ *adverb* 副词：*'Why are you talking so loudly?' he asked irritably.* "你说话干吗这么大声？" 他生气地问。

irritate /ˈɪrɪteɪt/ *verb* 动词 (**irritates, irritating, irritated**)
1 to repeatedly annoy someone 反复激怒：*His voice really irritates me.* 他那嗓门让我气不打一处来。
▶ **irritated** /ˈɪrɪteɪtɪd/ *adjective* 形容词：*He has become increasingly irritated by questions about his retirement.* 他越来越反感人家问他退休的事。
▶ **irritating** /ˈɪrɪteɪtɪŋ/ *adjective* 形容词：*The children have an irritating habit of*

leaving the door open. 孩子们老不关门，这个毛病真叫人恼火。

2 to make a part of your body slightly painful 刺激（身体部位）: *The smoke from the fire irritated his eyes, nose and throat.* 火上升起的烟刺激他的眼睛、鼻子和喉咙。

irritation /ˌɪrɪˈteɪʃən/ ***noun*** 名词
1 uncountable 不可数 the feeling you have when you are annoyed 恼火；气恼: *David tried not to show his irritation.* 戴维尽量不表露出恼火。

2 a feeling of slight pain in a part of your body（对身体部位的）刺激: *These oils may cause irritation to sensitive skins.* 这些油可能会刺激敏感型皮肤。

is /ɪz/
→ see 见 **be**

Islam /ˈɪzlɑːm/ ***uncountable noun*** 不可数名词
the religion that was started by Muhammed 伊斯兰教: *My cousin Michael converted to Islam at the age of 16.* 我表弟迈克尔 16 岁皈依了伊斯兰教。
▶ **Islamic** /ɪzˈlæmɪk/ ***adjective*** 形容词: *He's an expert in Islamic law.* 他是伊斯兰教教法专家。

island /ˈaɪlənd/ ***countable noun*** 可数名词
a piece of land that is completely surrounded by water 岛；岛屿: *They live on the Caribbean island of Barbados.* 他们生活在加勒比海巴巴多斯岛上。
→ Look at picture on P7 参见彩插第 7 页

island 岛

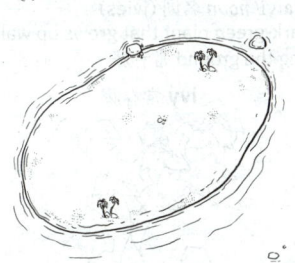

isle /aɪl/ ***countable noun*** 可数名词
an island 岛；岛屿: *Ireland is sometimes called 'the Emerald Isle'.* 爱尔兰有时被称为"翡翠岛"。

isn't /ˈɪzənt/
short for（缩写 =）'is not'

isolate /ˈaɪsəˌleɪt/ ***verb*** 动词 (**isolates, isolating, isolated**)
to keep someone away from other people 使孤立；使隔离: *Julie was quickly isolated from other patients in the hospital.* 朱莉很快与同院其他患者隔离开来。

isolated /ˈaɪsəˌleɪtɪd/ ***adjective*** 形容词
far away from other places 孤立的；偏僻的: *Mark and his girlfriend have bought an isolated farmhouse in Spain.* 马克和女友已经在西班牙买下了一座与世隔绝的农舍。

ISP /ˌaɪ es ˈpiː/ ***countable noun*** 可数名词
a company that provides Internet and email services. ISP is short for（缩写 =）'Internet service provider'. 因特网服务提供者；因特网服务提供商

issue¹ /ˈɪsjuː, ˈɪʃuː/ ***countable noun*** 可数名词
1 an important subject that people are talking about（重要的）问题，议题: *Climate change is a major environmental issue.* 气候变化是一大环境问题。

2 the copy of a magazine or newspaper that is published in a particular month or on a particular day（报刊的）期: *Have you read the latest issue of the 'Scientific American'?* 你看过最新一期《科学美国人》吗？

issue² /ˈɪsjuː, ˈɪʃuː/ ***verb*** 动词 (**issues, issuing, issued**)
to officially say or give something（正式）发布，发放: *The government issued a warning of possible attacks.* 政府发布预警称可能发生袭击。 □ *The embassy has stopped issuing visas to journalists.* 大使馆已经停止发放记者签证。

it /ɪt/ ***pronoun*** 代词
1 used when you are talking about an object, an animal, a thing or a situation that you have already mentioned 它（指代已经提到过的物体、动物、事情或局势）: *They live in a beautiful cottage. Here's a photo of it.* 他们住在一座漂亮的乡间小屋中。这儿有一张小屋的照片。 □ *She has a problem but she's too embarrassed to talk about it.* 她有一个问题，不过羞于启齿。

2 used before certain nouns, adjectives and verbs to talk about your feelings（用于某些名词、形容词和动词前，表示个人情感）: *It was nice to see Steve again.* 再次见到史蒂夫真好。 □ *It's a pity you can't come to the party, Sarah.* 你不能来参加派对真遗憾，萨拉。

3 used when you are talking about the time, the date, the weather or the

distance to a place（用于表示时间、日期、天气或距离）: *It's three o'clock.* 现在是 3 点。 ロ *It was Saturday, so she was at home.* 那天是周六，所以她在家。 ロ *It was snowing yesterday.* 昨天下着雪。 ロ *It's ten miles to the next petrol station.* 下一座加油站距此 10 英里。
4 used when you are saying who someone is（用于告知身份）: *'Who's that on the phone?' — 'It's Mrs Williams.'* "哪位？" —— "威廉斯太太。"

I.T. /ˌaɪ ˈtiː/
short for (缩写 =) information technology

italic /ɪˈtælɪk/ *plural noun* 复数名词
letters that slope to the right. The examples in this dictionary are printed in italics. 斜体字 • **italic** *adjective* 形容词: *italic type* 斜体字

itch¹ /ɪtʃ/ *verb* 动词 (**itches, itching, itched**)
to have an unpleasant feeling on your skin that makes you want to scratch it 发痒: *Her perfume made my eyes itch.* 她的香水让我眼睛发痒。
▶ **itchy** /ˈɪtʃi/ *adjective* 形容词: *My eyes feel itchy and sore.* 我眼睛又疼又痒。

itch² /ɪtʃ/ *countable noun* 可数名词 (**itches**)
an unpleasant feeling on your skin that makes you want to scratch it 痒: *Can you scratch my back? I've got an itch.* 你给我挠挠背好吗？有点痒。

it'd /ˈɪtəd/
1 short for (缩写 =) 'it would'
2 short for (缩写 =) 'it had'

item /ˈaɪtəm/ *countable noun* 可数名词
1 one thing in a list or a group of things（列表或群组的）项，单件: *The most valuable item in the sale was a Picasso drawing.* 拍卖中最值钱的一件是毕加索的一幅素描。
2 a piece of news in a newspaper or a magazine, or on television or radio（报刊、电视、广播的）一则新闻: *There was an item in the paper about him.* 报上有一条他的新闻。

it'll /ˈɪtəl/
short for (缩写 =) 'it will'

its /ɪts/ *adjective* 形容词
used for showing that something belongs or relates to a thing, a place or an animal that has just been mentioned 它的: *He held the knife by its handle.* 他手握着刀柄。

> **LANGUAGE HELP 语言提示**
> **Its** or **it's**? 用 its 还是 it's？
> **Its** means 'belonging to it'. *its 意为 "它的"*: *The horse raised its head.* 那匹马昂起头。
> **It's** is short for 'it is' or 'it has'. *it's 是 it is 或 it has 的缩写形式*: *It's hot in here.* 这儿很热。 ロ *It's stopped raining.* 雨停了。

it's /ɪts/
1 short for (缩写 =) 'it is'
2 short for (缩写 =) 'it has'

itself /ɪtˈself/ *pronoun* 代词
1 used as the object of a verb or preposition when an animal or a thing is both the subject and the object of the verb（用作动词、介词的宾语）它自己，它本身: *The kitten washed itself, then lay down by the fire.* 猫咪洗了洗脸，然后躺在了炉火边。
2 used for making a word stronger（用于加强语气）自身，本身: *There are lots of good restaurants on the road to Wilmington, and in Wilmington itself.* 去威尔明顿的路上和威尔明顿当地都有很多好饭店。
by itself without any help 自己；独自；自动: *The company is working on a car that can drive by itself.* 公司正在研制一款自动驾驶汽车。

I've /aɪv/
short for (缩写 =) 'I have'

ivy /ˈaɪvi/ *noun* 名词 (**ivies**)
a dark-green plant that grows up walls or along the ground 常春藤

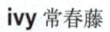
ivy 常春藤

Jj

jacket /ˈdʒækɪt/ *countable noun* 可数名词
a short coat with long sleeves 短上衣；夹克衫: *He wore a black leather jacket.* 他身穿一件黑色皮夹克。

jacket 短上衣

jackpot /ˈdʒækpɒt/ *countable noun* 可数名词
a large sum of money that is the most valuable prize in a game 头奖；最高奖: *She won the jackpot of £5 million.* 她赢得了 500 万英镑的头奖。

jagged /ˈdʒægɪd/ *adjective* 形容词
having a rough edge with lots of sharp points 锯齿状的；有尖突的: *There were sharp jagged rocks just below the surface of the water.* 水面下就是些尖突不平的石头。

jail /dʒeɪl/ *noun* 名词
a place where criminals have to stay as a punishment 监狱: *He went to jail for 15 years.* 他入狱 15 年。□ *Three prisoners escaped from a jail.* *3 名犯人越狱了。

jam¹ /dʒæm/ *verb* 动词 (**jams, jamming, jammed**)
to push something somewhere hard 硬推；硬塞: *He jammed the key into the lock.* 他使劲把钥匙插进锁里。

jam² /dʒæm/ *noun* 名词
1 *uncountable* 不可数 a sweet food that contains soft fruit and sugar 果酱: *Kate spread the strawberry jam on her toast.* 凯特往吐司上抹了草莓酱。
2 *countable* 可数 a situation when there are so many vehicles on a road that they cannot move 交通拥堵: *The lorries sat in a traffic jam for ten hours.* 卡车堵了 10 小时。

January /ˈdʒænjuəri/ *noun* 名词
the first month of the year 一月: *We always have snow in January.* 我们这儿 1 月份总会下雪。

jar /dʒɑː/ *countable noun* 可数名词
a glass container, with a lid, that is used for storing food (带盖子的)玻璃罐: *There were several glass jars filled with sweets.* 有几个装满了糖果的玻璃罐。

javelin /ˈdʒævlɪn/ *countable noun* 可数名词
a long pointed stick that is thrown in sports competitions (体育比赛中的)标枪

jaw /dʒɔː/ *countable noun* 可数名词
the top and bottom bones of a person's or an animal's mouth 颌: *Andrew broke his lower jaw.* 安德鲁下颌骨折了。

jazz /dʒæz/ *uncountable noun* 不可数名词
a style of music that has strong rhythms 爵士乐: *The club plays live jazz on Sundays.* 这家俱乐部每周日现场演奏爵士乐。

jealous /ˈdʒeləs/ *adjective* 形容词
1 feeling angry because you think that another person is trying to take away someone or something that you love 吃醋的: *He got jealous and there was a fight.* 他吃醋了，结果打了一架。
2 feeling angry or unhappy because you do not have something that someone else has 忌妒的: *She was jealous of her sister's success.* 她忌妒姐姐的成功。
▶ **jealously** /ˈdʒeləsli/ *adverb* 副词: *Gloria looked jealously at his new car.* 格洛丽亚看着他的新车，很是忌妒。

jealousy /ˈdʒeləsi/ *uncountable noun* 不可数名词
1 the feeling of anger that someone has when they think that another person is trying to take away someone or something that they love 醋意: *He could not control his jealousy when he saw me with my new partner.* 看到我和新交往的男

友在一起，他无法控制自己的醋意。
2 the feeling of anger or sadness that someone has when they want something that another person has 忌妒

jeans /dʒiːnz/ *plural noun* 复数名词
trousers that are made of strong cotton cloth 牛仔裤: *We saw a young man in jeans and a T-shirt.* 我们看到一个穿着牛仔裤和T恤衫的年轻人。

Jeep /dʒiːp/ *countable noun* 可数名词
a type of car that can travel over rough ground (*trademark* 商标) 吉普（一种越野车）: *a U.S. Army Jeep* 美国军用吉普

jelly /ˈdʒeli/ *uncountable noun* 不可数名词
a soft sweet food made from fruit juice and sugar that moves from side to side when you touch it 果冻: *After dinner, we had jelly with ice cream.* 晚饭后，我们吃了冰激凌果冻。

jellyfish /ˈdʒeliˌfɪʃ/ *countable noun* 可数名词 (jellyfish)
a sea animal that has a clear soft body and that can sting you 水母

jerk /dʒɜːk/ *verb* 动词 (jerks, jerking, jerked)
to move a short distance very suddenly and quickly 猝然一动: *The train jerked violently from side to side.* 火车晃得厉害。
☐ *Sam jerked his head in my direction.* 萨姆突然扭头看向我。● **jerk** *countable noun* 可数名词: *He gave a jerk of his head to the other two men.* 他突然扭头看向另两个人。

jerky /ˈdʒɜːki/ *adjective* 形容词 (jerkier, jerkiest)
very sudden and quick 急促的；不平稳的: *Avoid any sudden or jerky movements.* 避免突然移动或晃动。

jersey /ˈdʒɜːzi/ *noun* 名词
a piece of clothing with sleeves that you wear on the top part of your body 套头衫: *The boys wore baseball caps and jerseys.* 那些男孩子头戴棒球帽，身穿套头衫。

jet /dʒet/ *countable noun* 可数名词
1 an aircraft with jet engines 喷气式飞机: *He arrived from Key West by jet.* 他从基韦斯特坐喷气式飞机抵达。
2 a strong, fast, thin stream of liquid or gas（液体或气体的）射流，急流: *A jet of water poured through the windows.* 一道水柱从窗户射入。

Jew /dʒuː/ *countable noun* 可数名词
a person who practises the religion of Judaism 犹太人；犹太教徒

jewel /ˈdʒuːəl/ *countable noun* 可数名词
a valuable stone, such as a diamond 宝石: *The box was filled with precious jewels and gold.* 盒子里装满了贵重宝石和金子。

jeweller /ˈdʒuːələ/ *countable noun* 可数名词
1 a person who makes, sells and repairs jewellery and watches 钟表首饰商；钟表首饰匠
2 (also 亦作 **jeweller's**) a shop where you can buy jewellery and watches 钟表首饰店: *We went to a jeweller's on Oxford Street.* 我们去了牛津街的一家钟表首饰店。

jewellery /ˈdʒuːəlri/ *uncountable noun* 不可数名词
decorations that you wear on your body, such as a ring that you wear on your finger 首饰: *She sold all her gold jewellery.* 她把金首饰全卖了。
→ Look at picture on P10 参见彩插第 10 页

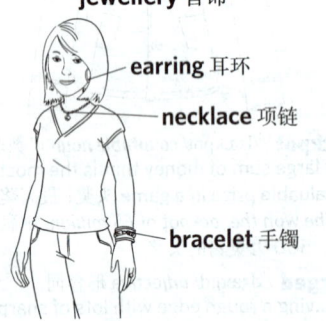
jewellery 首饰
— **earring** 耳环
— **necklace** 项链
— **bracelet** 手镯

Jewish /ˈdʒuːɪʃ/ *adjective* 形容词
1 belonging or relating to the religion of Judaism 犹太教的: *We celebrated the Jewish festival of Passover.* 我们庆祝了犹太教节日逾越节。
2 believing in and practising the religion of Judaism 信奉犹太教的: *She was from a traditional Jewish family.* 她来自一个传统犹太教家庭。

jigsaw /ˈdʒɪɡsɔː/ *countable noun* 可数名词
(also 亦作 **jigsaw puzzle**) a picture on cardboard or wood that has been cut up into different shapes that you have to put back together again 拼图: *The children put the last pieces in the jigsaw puzzle.* 孩子们把拼图的最后几块拼了上去。

jingle /ˈdʒɪŋɡəl/ *verb* 动词 (jingles, jingling, jingled)
to make a gentle sound like small bells (使)发出叮当声: *Her bracelets jingled on*

her thin wrist. 她纤细的手腕上手镯叮当作响。□ *Brian put his hands in his pockets and jingled some coins.* 布赖恩把手插进兜里, 把几枚硬币拨弄得叮当作响。

job /dʒɒb/ *countable noun* 可数名词
1 the work that someone does to earn money 工作: *I want to get a job.* 我想找份工作。□ *Terry was looking for a new job.* 特里正在重新找工作。
2 a particular task 任务; 活儿: *I have some jobs to do in the house today.* 我今天在家有些活儿要做。
do a good job to do something well 干得好: *Most of our teachers are doing a good job in the classroom.* 我们大部分老师在课堂教学方面表现出色。
→ Look at picture on P16 参见彩插第 16 页

jobless /ˈdʒɒbləs/ *adjective* 形容词
without a job 失业的; 无工作的: *The number of jobless people went up last month.* 上个月失业人数上升。

jockey /ˈdʒɒki/ *countable noun* 可数名词
someone who rides a horse in a race 赛马骑师

jog /dʒɒg/ *verb* 动词 (jogs, jogging, jogged)
to run slowly, often as a form of exercise 慢跑; 健身跑: *They went jogging every morning.* 他们每天早上都去慢跑。● **jog** *countable noun* 可数名词: *He went for an early-morning jog.* 他去晨跑了。
▶ **jogger** /ˈdʒɒgə/ *countable noun* 可数名词: *The park was full of joggers.* 公园里到处都是慢跑的人。
▶ **jogging** /ˈdʒɒgɪŋ/ *uncountable noun* 不可数名词: *The jogging helped him to lose weight.* 慢跑帮他减了肥。
→ Look at picture on P14 参见彩插第 14 页

join /dʒɔɪn/ *verb* 动词 (joins, joining, joined)
1 to become a member of an organization 加入; 成为……一员: *He joined the Army five years ago.* 他 5 年前参了军。
2 to stand at the end of a queue so that you are part of it 排(队): *He joined the queue of people waiting to get on the bus.* 他排队等着上车。
3 to attach or fasten two things together 使接合: *'And' is often used for joining two sentences.* *and 常用来连接两个句子。□ *Join the two squares of fabric to make a bag.* 将这两块方布料缝成袋子。

joint¹ /dʒɔɪnt/ *countable noun* 可数名词
a part of your body, such as your elbow or your knee, where two bones meet and are able to move together 关节: *Her joints ache if she exercises.* 她一锻炼关节就疼。

joint² /dʒɔɪnt/ *adjective* 形容词
shared by two or more people 共同的; 共享的: *We opened a joint bank account.* 我们开了个联名账户。

joke /dʒəʊk/ *countable noun* 可数名词
something that someone says to make you laugh 笑话: *He made a joke about it.* 他拿它开了个玩笑。● **joke** *verb* 动词 (jokes, joking, joked): *She often joked about her big feet.* 她常拿自己的大脚开玩笑。□ *I was only joking! I didn't mean it.* 我只是开个玩笑! 我没那个意思。

jolly /ˈdʒɒli/ *adjective* 形容词 (jollier, jolliest)
happy and cheerful 快乐的; 高兴的: *She was a jolly, kind woman.* 她整天乐呵呵, 心肠也好。

jolt /dʒəʊlt/ *verb* 动词 (jolts, jolting, jolted)
to move suddenly and quite violently (使)摇动; (使)颠簸: *She was jolted awake by a crash of thunder.* 她被一声炸雷震醒了。□ *The train jolted again.* 火车又晃了一下。● **jolt** *countable noun* 可数名词: *The plane hit the runway with a jolt.* 飞机颠了一下, 撞上了跑道。

jot /dʒɒt/ *verb* 动词 (jots, jotting, jotted)
jot something down to write something down quickly 匆匆写下某事物: *David jotted down the address on a notepad.* 戴维在记事本上匆匆写下地址。

journal /ˈdʒɜːnəl/ *countable noun* 可数名词
1 a magazine or a newspaper that deals with a special subject (专门学科的) 报刊, 杂志, 刊物: *The results were published in scientific journals.* 这些结果刊登在了科学杂志上。
2 a notebook or a diary 笔记本; 日记本: *Sara wrote her private thoughts in her journal.* 萨拉在日记中写下自己的心声。

journalist /ˈdʒɜːnəlɪst/ *countable noun* 可数名词
a person whose job is to collect news stories and write about them for newspapers, magazines, television or radio 新闻记者; 新闻工作者: *The president spoke to an audience of two hundred journalists.* 总统对两百名记者讲了话。
▶ **journalism** /ˈdʒɜːnəlɪzəm/ *uncountable noun* 不可数名词: *He began a career in journalism.* 他开始从事新闻工作。

journey /ˈdʒɜːni/ *countable noun* 可数名词
an occasion when you travel from one place to another 旅行；行程：*Their journey took them from Paris to Brussels.* 他们从巴黎到了布鲁塞尔。

joy /dʒɔɪ/ *uncountable noun* 不可数名词
a feeling of great happiness 高兴；愉快；喜悦：*She shouted with joy.* 她高兴地大喊。

joyful /ˈdʒɔɪfʊl/ *adjective* 形容词
causing happiness and pleasure (*formal* 正式) 令人高兴的；使人愉快的：*A wedding is a joyful occasion.* 婚礼是个喜庆的场合。
▶ **joyfully** /ˈdʒɔɪfʊli/ *adverb* 副词：*The children cheered joyfully.* 孩子们高兴地欢呼起来。

Judaism /ˈdʒuːdeɪˌɪzəm/ *uncountable noun* 不可数名词
the religion of the Jewish people 犹太教

judge¹ /dʒʌdʒ/ *countable noun* 可数名词
1 the person in a court of law who decides how criminals should be punished 法官：*The judge sent him to jail for 100 days.* 法官判他入狱 100 天。
2 a person who decides who will be the winner of a competition 裁判员；评委：*A panel of judges will choose the winner.* 一个裁判小组负责评出获胜者。

judge² /dʒʌdʒ/ *verb* 动词 (**judges, judging, judged**)
1 to decide who is the winner of a competition 裁判；评判：*He will judge the contest and award the prize.* 他将担任比赛的裁判并颁奖。
2 to form an opinion about someone or something 评价；判断：*People should wait, and judge the film when they see it for themselves.* 大家应该等亲自看过这部电影之后再评价。

judgment /ˈdʒʌdʒmənt/ *also* 亦作 **judgement** *noun* 名词
1 *uncountable* 不可数 the ability to make sensible decisions about what to do 判断力：*I respect his judgment, and I'll follow his advice.* 我尊重他的判断力，会听从他的建议。
2 a decision made by a judge or by a court of law 判决；裁决：*The judge has promised to deliver a full written judgment next Tuesday.* 法官已承诺在下周二作出完整的书面判决。

judo /ˈdʒuːdəʊ/ *uncountable noun* 不可数名词
a sport in which two people fight without weapons 柔道：*He was also a black belt in judo.* 他也是柔道黑带。

jug /dʒʌg/ *countable noun* 可数名词
a container with a handle used for holding and pouring liquids (有把的) 罐，壶

juggle /ˈdʒʌgəl/ *verb* 动词 (**juggles, juggling, juggled**)
to keep several objects in the air by throwing and catching them repeatedly 玩杂耍抛接 (数件物品)：*She was juggling five balls.* 她在抛接 5 个球。
▶ **juggler** /ˈdʒʌglə/ *countable noun* 可数名词：*He was a professional juggler.* 他是专业的杂耍抛接艺人。
▶ **juggling** /ˈdʒʌgəlɪŋ/ *uncountable noun* 不可数名词：*It's a children's show, with juggling and comedy.* 这是个儿童节目，包括杂耍抛接和喜剧表演。

juggle 玩抛接杂耍

juice /dʒuːs/ *noun* 名词
1 *uncountable* 不可数 the liquid from a fruit or a vegetable 果汁；蔬菜汁：*He had a large glass of fresh orange juice.* 他喝了一大玻璃杯鲜榨橙汁。
2 [**juices**] *plural* 复数 the liquid that comes out of a piece of meat when you cook it 肉汁：*Pour the cooking juices into a pan, and add the cream.* 把烹饪用的肉汁倒入平底锅里，然后加入奶油。

juicy /ˈdʒuːsi/ *adjective* 形容词 (**juicier, juiciest**)
containing a lot of juice and very enjoyable to eat 多汁的：*The waiter brought a thick, juicy steak to the table.* 服务员端来一份厚实多汁的牛排。

July /dʒʊˈlaɪ/ *noun* 名词
the seventh month of the year 七月：*In July 1969, Neil Armstrong walked on the moon.* 1969 年 7 月，尼尔·阿姆斯特朗在月球上行走。

jump /dʒʌmp/ *verb* 动词 (**jumps, jumping, jumped**)
1 to bend your knees, push against the ground with your feet, and move quickly upwards into the air 跳；跳跃：*I jumped over the fence.* 我跳过了栅栏。● **jump** *countable noun* 可数名词：*She set a world record for the longest jump by a woman.* 她创造了女子跳远的世界纪录。
2 to move quickly and suddenly 突然快速移动：*Adam jumped up when he heard the doorbell.* 亚当听到门铃后一跃而起。
jump at something to accept an offer or an opportunity quickly and with enthusiasm 迫不及待地接受（提议或机会）：*She jumped at the chance to be on TV.* 她迫不及待地接受了上电视的机会。
make someone jump to make someone move suddenly because they are frightened or surprised 把某人吓（或惊）一跳：*The phone rang and made her jump.* 电话铃响了，把她吓了一跳。

jumper /ˈdʒʌmpə/ *countable noun* 可数名词
a warm piece of clothing that covers the top part of your body 套头衫；套头毛衣

June /dʒuːn/ *noun* 名词
the sixth month of the year 六月：*He spent two weeks with us in June.* 他6月份和我们一起待了两周。

jungle /ˈdʒʌŋgəl/ *noun* 名词
a forest in a tropical country where large numbers of tall trees and plants grow very close together（热带）丛林，密林：*The trail led them deeper into the jungle.* 这条小路把他们带入了丛林深处。

junior /ˈdʒuːniə/ *adjective* 形容词
having one of the lower positions in an organization 职级低的：*His father was a junior officer in the army.* 他爸爸是陆军连级军官。

junk /dʒʌŋk/ *uncountable noun* 不可数名词
old and useless things that you do not want or need (*informal* 非正式)垃圾：*What are you going to do with all that junk?* 你打算怎么处理那些垃圾？

jury /ˈdʒʊəri/ *countable noun* 可数名词 (**juries**)
the group of people in a court of law who listen to the facts about a crime and decide if a person is guilty or not 陪审团：*The jury decided she was not guilty of murder.* 陪审团裁定她谋杀罪名不成立。

just /dʒʌst/ *adjective* 形容词, *adverb* 副词
1 a very short time ago 刚刚；刚才：*I just had the most awful dream.* 我刚刚做了个特别可怕的梦。
2 at this moment; very soon 此刻；正在；正要：*I'm just making some coffee.* 我正在做咖啡。▫ *I'm just going to bed.* 我正要上床睡觉。
3 only 仅仅；只是：*It costs just a few dollars.* 这只需花费几美元。
4 used to make the next thing that you say stronger（强调接下来说的话）请，就：*Just stop talking and listen to me!* 先别讲话，听我说！
5 exactly 正好；恰好：*They are just like the rest of us.* 他们恰好和我们中的其他人一样。
6 fair or right (*formal* 正式) 公正的；正当的；恰当的：*I think he got his just punishment.* 我认为他得到了应有的惩罚。
just about almost 几乎；差不多：*All our money is just about gone.* 我们所有的钱几乎一分没剩。
just a minute or **just a moment** or **just a second** used when you are asking someone to wait for a short time 稍候；稍等一下：*Just a moment. What did you say?* 稍等，您刚才说什么？

justice /ˈdʒʌstɪs/ *uncountable noun* 不可数名词
the fair treatment of people 公平；公正；正义：*We want freedom, justice and equality.* 我们渴望自由、公平和平等。

justified /ˈdʒʌstɪˌfaɪd/ *adjective* 形容词
reasonable and acceptable 合理的；正当的：*In my opinion, the decision was justified.* 在我看来，这个决定是合理的。▫ *I work very hard, so I feel justified in asking for more money.* 我工作非常努力，所以我认为我要求多拿钱理所应当。

justify /ˈdʒʌstɪˌfaɪ/ *verb* 动词 (**justifies, justifying, justified**)
to show that a decision or an action is reasonable or necessary 证明…合理；证明…正当：*Is there anything that can justify a war?* 有什么理由可以为战争开脱吗？

Kk

kangaroo /ˌkæŋɡəˈruː/ *countable noun* 可数名词
a large Australian animal, the female of which carries her baby in a pocket on her stomach 袋鼠

karate /kəˈrɑːti/ *uncountable noun* 不可数名词
a Japanese sport in which people fight using their hands and feet 空手道

KB or 或 **K**
in writing, short for (书面缩写 =) **kilobyte** or **kilobytes**

keen /kiːn/ *adjective* 形容词 (**keener, keenest**)
1 wanting to do something or very interested in something 渴望的；热衷的：*Charles was keen to show his family the photos.* 查尔斯热切地想要给家人展示照片。 □ *Father was always a keen golfer.* 爸爸一直热衷于打高尔夫球。 □ *I'm not keen on TV game shows.* 我不喜欢看电视游戏节目。
2 very strong or good 强烈的；浓厚的；非常好的：*For this job, you need to have a keen sense of adventure.* 要做这份工作，你需要极富冒险精神。
keen on someone/something liking someone or something a lot 非常喜欢某人／某事物的：*I'm not keen on physics and chemistry.* 我不喜欢物理和化学。

keep /kiːp/ *verb* 动词 (**keeps, keeping, kept**)
1 to remain in a particular state or place 保持；留在；处于：*Keep away from the doors while the train is moving.* 列车运行中要远离车门。 □ *We burned wood to keep warm.* 我们烧木头取暖。 □ *'Keep still!'* "别动！"
2 to make someone or something stay in a particular state or place 使保持；使处于：*The noise of the traffic kept him awake.* 车来车往的噪音吵得他一直没睡着。 □ *He kept his head down, hiding his face.* 他低着头，藏起了脸。
3 to continue to have something 保有；留

着：*I want to keep these clothes, and I want to give these away.* 这些衣服我想留着，这些想送人。
4 to store something in a particular place 存放；储存：*She kept her money under the bed.* 她把钱放在床下。
keep a promise to do what you said you would do 信守诺言：*He kept his promise to come to my birthday party.* 他信守诺言参加我的生日聚会。
keep doing something to do something many times or continue to do something 重复做某事；继续做某事：*I keep forgetting the password for my computer.* 我总是记不住电脑密码。 □ *She kept running although she was exhausted.* 她尽管已筋疲力尽，仍继续跑着。
keep something up to continue to do something 继续做某事：*I could not keep the diet up for longer than a month.* 我节食最多坚持1个月。
keep up with someone to move as fast as another person so that you are moving together 跟上某人：*Sam walked faster to keep up with his father.* 萨姆加快了脚步，以便跟上他爸爸。

kennel /ˈkenəl/ *countable noun* 可数名词
a small house for a dog 狗窝：*Dad built a kennel for our dog in the garden.* 爸爸给我们家狗在花园里搭了个窝。

kept /kept/
→ see 见 **keep**

kerb /kɜːb/ *countable noun* 可数名词
the edge of a pavement (= a path next to a road) that is nearest to the road 道牙；马路牙子：*I pulled over to the kerb.* 我把车停靠在路边。

ketchup /ˈketʃʌp/ *noun* 名词
a thick, red sauce made from tomatoes 番茄酱：*He was eating a burger with ketchup.* 他就着番茄酱吃汉堡。

kettle /ˈketəl/ *countable noun* 可数名词
a metal container with a lid and a handle, that you use for boiling water (烧水用的)

壶，水壶：*I'll put the kettle on and make us some tea.* 我来烧水给咱们沏点茶。

key¹ /kiː/ *noun* 名词
1 *countable* 可数 a specially shaped piece of metal that opens or closes a lock 钥匙：*They put the key in the door and entered.* 他们用钥匙打开门进去了。
2 *countable* 可数 one of the buttons that you press in order to operate a computer keyboard（计算机键盘的）键：*Now press the 'Delete' key.* 现在按下 Delete（删除）键。
3 *countable* 可数 one of the white and black bars that you press in order to play a piano（钢琴的）键
4 a particular scale of musical notes（音乐的）调：*the key of A minor* *A 小调

keys 钥匙

key² /kiː/ *adjective* 形容词
most important 关键的；最重要的：*He's a key player on the team.* 他是队里的核心选手。

keyboard /ˈkiːbɔːd/ *countable noun* 可数名词
1 the set of keys that you press in order to operate a computer（计算机的）键盘
2 the set of black and white keys that you press when you play a piano（钢琴的）键盘
3 (also 亦作 **keyboards**) an electronic musical instrument that has a keyboard 键盘乐器
→ Look at picture on P11 参见彩插 11 页

keyhole /ˈkiːhəʊl/ *countable noun* 可数名词
the part of a lock where you put a key 锁眼；钥匙孔：*I looked through the keyhole, but I couldn't see anything inside.* 我从锁眼朝里看，但是什么也看不到。

key ring *countable noun* 可数名词
a metal ring on which you keep keys 钥匙环：*He pulled his key ring from his pocket.* 他从口袋里掏出钥匙环。

keyword /ˈkiːwɜːd/ also 亦作 **key word** *countable noun* 可数名词
a word or a phrase that you can use when you are searching for a particular document in an Internet search（因特网搜索时用的）关键词，关键字：*Users can search by title, by author, by subject and by keyword.* 用户可以根据标题、作者、主题及关键词进行搜索。

kg (**kg** or 或 **kgs**)
in writing, short for（书面缩写 =）**kilogram** or **kilograms**

khaki /ˈkɑːki/ *adjective* 形容词
greenish-brown or yellowish-brown in colour 卡其色的；土黄色的；黄褐色的：*He was dressed in khaki trousers.* 他穿着卡其裤。

kHz
short for（缩写 =）**kilohertz**

kick¹ /kɪk/ *verb* 动词 (**kicks, kicking, kicked**)
1 to hit someone or something with your foot 踢；踹：*He kicked the door hard.* 他使劲踢门。□ *He kicked the ball away.* 他把球踢开了。
2 to move your legs up and down quickly 踢蹬；踢（腿）：*Abby was taken away, kicking and screaming.* 阿比被带走时又踢又叫的。□ *The baby smiled and kicked her legs.* 宝宝笑了，踢了踢腿。

kick² /kɪk/ *noun* 名词
1 *countable* 可数 an act of hitting someone or something with your foot 踢；踹：*He went over to the door and gave it a kick.* 他走到门口踹了门一脚。
2 *singular* 单数 a feeling of pleasure or excitement (*informal* 非正式) 快乐；兴奋：*I love acting. I get a big kick out of it.* 我热爱表演。表演让我感到很快乐。

kid¹ /kɪd/ *countable noun* 可数名词
a child (*informal* 非正式) 小孩：*They have three kids.* 他们有 3 个孩子。

kid² /kɪd/ *verb* 动词 (**kids, kidding, kidded**)
to say something that is not really true, as a joke (*informal* 非正式) 开玩笑：*I thought he was kidding but he was serious.* 我以为他在开玩笑，但是他是认真的。□ *I'm just kidding.* 我只是开个玩笑。

kidnap /ˈkɪdnæp/ *verb* 动词 (**kidnaps, kidnapping, kidnapped**)
to take someone away by force and keep them as a prisoner, often until their friends or family pay a large amount of money 绑架：*The tourists were kidnapped by a group of men with guns.* 游客被一伙儿持枪分子绑架了。

▶ **kidnapper** /ˈkɪdnæpə/ *countable noun* 可数名词：*His kidnappers have threatened to kill him.* 绑匪已威胁要杀了他。

▶ **kidnapping** /ˈkɪdnæpɪŋ/ *noun* 名词：*Williams was jailed for eight years for the kidnapping.* 威廉斯因绑架入狱 8 年。

kidney /ˈkɪdni/ *countable noun* 可数名词
one of the two organs in your body that remove waste liquid from your blood 肾；肾脏：*She urgently needs a kidney transplant.* 她急需肾移植。

kill /kɪl/ *verb* 动词 (kills, killing, killed)
to make a person, an animal or other living thing die 杀死；导致死亡：*More than 1,000 people have been killed.* *1,000 多人被杀.* □ *These viruses can kill.* 这些病毒能致命。
▶ **killing** /ˈkɪlɪŋ/ *uncountable noun* 不可数名词：*The TV news reported the killing of seven people.* 电视新闻报道有 7 人被杀。

killer /ˈkɪlə/ *countable noun* 可数名词
1 a person who has killed someone 杀人者；杀手：*The police are searching for the killer.* 警方正在搜捕凶手。
2 something that causes death 导致死亡的事物：*Heart disease is the biggest killer of men in some countries.* 在一些国家，心脏病是男性的头号杀手。

kilo /ˈkiːləʊ/ *countable noun* 可数名词
→ see 见 **kilogram**：*He's lost ten kilos in weight.* 他减了 10 公斤体重。

kilobyte /ˈkɪləˌbaɪt/ *countable noun* 可数名词
a unit for measuring information in computing (1 kilobyte = 1,024 bytes) 千字节（计算机信息量单位，1 千字节 = 1,024 字节）

kilogram /ˈkɪləˌɡræm/ *also* 亦作 **kilogramme** *countable noun* 可数名词
a unit for measuring weight (1 kilogram is equal to around 2.2 pounds, and 1,000 grams is equal to 1 kilogram) 千克, 公斤（重量单位, 1 千克 ≈ 2.2 磅）: *The box weighs 4.5 kilograms.* 这个箱子重 4.5 千克。
→ Look at picture on P2 参见彩插第 2 页

kilohertz /ˈkɪləˌhɜːts/ *countable noun* 可数名词 (kilohertz)
a unit for measuring radio waves 千赫（兹）（频率单位）: *The frequency of the radio waves slowly increased to 4 kilohertz.* 无线电波的频率慢慢升到了 4 千赫。

kilometre /ˈkɪləˌmiːtə, kɪˈlɒmɪtə/ *countable noun* 可数名词
a unit for measuring distance (1 kilometre is equal to around 0.62 miles and 1,000 metres is equal to 1 kilometre) 千米, 公里（长度单位, 1 千米 ≈ 0.62 英里）: *We're now only one kilometre from the border.* 我们现在距离边界只有 1 千米。
→ Look at picture on P2 参见彩插第 2 页

kilowatt /ˈkɪləˌwɒt/ *countable noun* 可数名词
a unit of power 千瓦（功率单位）: *The system produced only 25 kilowatts of power.* 这个系统的功率只有 25 千瓦。

kind¹ /kaɪnd/ *countable noun* 可数名词
a type of person or thing 种类：*What kind of car do you drive?* 你开哪种车？ □ *He travels a lot, and sees all kinds of interesting things.* 他游历甚广，见识各种有趣的事。
kind of a little; in some way (*informal* 非正式) 有点儿；稍微：*I'm kind of thirsty.* 我有点儿渴。

kind² /kaɪnd/ *adjective* 形容词 (kinder, kindest)
friendly and helpful 友善的；乐于助人的：*Thank you for being so kind to me.* 谢谢你对我这么好。
▶ **kindly** /ˈkaɪndli/ *adverb* 副词：*The woman smiled kindly at her.* 那名女子朝她友善地笑了笑。
▶ **kindness** /ˈkaɪndnəs/ *uncountable noun* 不可数名词：*I'll never forget his generosity and kindness.* 我永远也不会忘记他的慷慨和善良。

kindly /ˈkaɪndli/ *adjective* 形容词
kind and caring 友善的；体贴的：*He gave her a kindly smile.* 他冲她友善地笑了下。

king /kɪŋ/ *noun* 名词
a man from a royal family, who is the head of state of that country 君主；国王：*the king and queen of Spain* 西班牙国王和王后
→ Look at picture on P10 参见彩插第 10 页

kingdom /ˈkɪŋdəm/ *countable noun* 可数名词
a country that is ruled by a king or a queen 王国：*the Kingdom of Denmark* 丹麦王国

kiosk /ˈkiːɒsk/ *countable noun* 可数名词
a small building with a window where people can buy things like newspapers （出售报纸等的）小亭；售货亭：*I was getting a newspaper at the kiosk.* 我正在报刊亭买报纸。

kiss /kɪs/ *verb* 动词 (kisses, kissing, kissed)
to touch someone with your lips to show love or to greet them 吻，亲吻：*She smiled*

and kissed him on the cheek. 她笑了笑，亲吻了他的面颊。▫ *The woman gently kissed her baby.* 那名女子温柔地亲吻了自己的小宝宝。▫ *We kissed goodbye at the airport.* 我们在机场吻别。● **kiss** *countable noun* 可数名词 (**kisses**): *I put my arms around her and gave her a kiss.* 我搂住她亲了一口。

kit /kɪt/ *countable noun* 可数名词
1 a group of items that are kept and used together for a particular purpose (具特定用途的) 成套物件: *a first aid kit* 急救箱 ▫ *She's just got her first drum kit.* 她刚刚得到自己的第一套架子鼓。
2 a set of parts that you can put together in order to make something 拼装套具: *a model aeroplane kit* 一套飞机拼装模型

kitchen /ˈkɪtʃɪn/ *countable noun* 可数名词
a room that is used for cooking 厨房

kite /kaɪt/ *countable noun* 可数名词
a toy that you fly in the wind at the end of a long string 风筝: *We went to the beach to fly kites.* 我们去海滩放风筝。

kitten /ˈkɪtən/ *countable noun* 可数名词
a very young cat 小猫

kiwi fruit /ˈkiːwiː ˌfruːt/ *noun* 名词

> **LANGUAGE HELP** 语言提示
> The plural can also be **kiwi fruits**. 复数形式也可用 kiwi fruits。

a small fruit with brown skin, black seeds, and bright green flesh 猕猴桃；奇异果

km (**km** or 或 **kms**)
in writing, short for (书面缩写 =) **kilometre** or **kilometres**

knead /niːd/ *verb* 动词 (**kneads, kneading, kneaded**)
to press and stretch dough (= a mixture of flour, water and other things) when you are making bread 揉，捏(面团): *Knead the dough for a few minutes.* 把面团揉上几分钟。

knee /niː/ *countable noun* 可数名词
the part in the middle of your leg where it bends 膝；膝盖；膝关节: *Lie down and bring your knees up toward your chest.* 躺下，膝盖朝胸部收起。
→ Look at picture on P4 参见彩插第 4 页

kneel /niːl/ *verb* 动词 (**kneels, kneeling, kneeled** or 或 **knelt**)
(also 亦作 **kneel down**) to bend your legs and rest with one or both of your knees on the ground 跪；跪下: *She knelt by the bed* *and prayed.* 她跪在床边祈祷。▫ *Other people were kneeling, but she just sat.* 其他人跪着，而她只是坐着。▫ *She kneeled down beside him.* 她在他旁边跪下。

kneel 跪

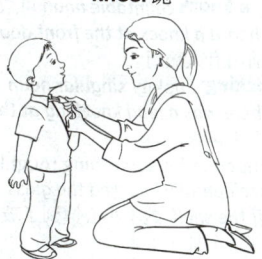

knelt /nelt/
→ see 见 **kneel**

knew /njuː/
→ see 见 **know**

knickers /ˈnɪkəz/ *plural noun* 复数名词
a piece of underwear that girls and women wear on the lower part of their body 女式短衬裤

knife /naɪf/ *countable noun* 可数名词 (**knives**)
a sharp flat piece of metal with a handle, that you can use to cut things or as a weapon 刀: *I stopped eating and put down my knife and fork.* 我停住嘴，放下刀叉。

knight /naɪt/ *countable noun* 可数名词
in the past, a special type of soldier who rode a horse (旧时的) 骑士: *King Arthur's knights* 亚瑟王的骑士
→ Look at picture on P10 参见彩插第 10 页

knit /nɪt/ *verb* 动词 (**knits, knitting, knitted**)
to make a piece of clothing from wool by using two long sticks (= needles) 编织；针织: *I had many hours to knit and sew.* 我又织又缝，弄了好多个小时。▫ *I have already started knitting baby clothes.* 我已经开始织小宝宝的衣服了。
▶ **knitting** /ˈnɪtɪŋ/ *uncountable noun* 不可数名词: *My favourite hobbies are knitting and reading.* 我最大的爱好是编织和看书。

knives /naɪvz/
the plural of **knife** (knife 的复数形式)

knob /nɒb/ *countable noun* 可数名词
a round handle or switch 球形把手；旋钮: *He turned the knob and pushed the door.* 他转动把手推了推门。▫ *a volume knob* 音量旋钮

knock /nɒk/ *verb* 动词 (**knocks, knocking, knocked**)
1 to hit something in order to make a noise 敲：*She went to Simon's flat and knocked on the door.* 她去西蒙的公寓敲了敲门。● **knock** *countable noun* 可数名词：*They heard a knock at the front door.* 他们听到前门有人敲门。
▶ **knocking** /'nɒkɪŋ/ *singular noun* 单数名词：*There was a loud knocking at the door.* 有人在大声敲门。
2 to touch or hit something roughly 碰；撞：*She accidentally knocked the glass and it fell off the shelf.* 她不小心撞到了玻璃杯，它从架子上掉了下来。
knock someone out to hit someone hard on the head so that they fall, go into a kind of deep sleep and cannot get up again 打晕某人：*He was knocked out in a fight.* 他在一场打斗中被打晕了。
knock someone/something over to hit someone or something so that they fall over 撞倒某人/某物：*The third wave was so strong it knocked me over.* 第 3 个浪头大，把我拍倒了。□ *She stood up suddenly, knocking over a glass of milk.* 她突然站起来，打翻了一杯牛奶。
knock something down to destroy a building or part of a building 推倒, 拆毁（建筑物）：*We're knocking down the wall between the kitchen and the dining room.* 我们正在拆厨房和餐厅之间的墙。

knot /nɒt/ *verb* 动词 (**knots, knotting, knotted**)
to tie two pieces of string or rope together 把…打成结：*He knotted the laces securely together.* 他系紧鞋带。● **knot** *countable noun* 可数名词：*Tony wore a bright-red scarf tied in a knot around his neck.* 托尼脖子上系着一条亮红色围巾。

know /nəʊ/ *verb* 动词 (**knows, knowing, knew, known**)
1 to have a fact or an answer in your mind 知道：*You should know the answer to that question.* 你应该知道那道题的答案。□ *I don't know his name.* 我不知道他的名字。□ *'How old is he?' — 'I don't know.'* "他多大年纪？" —— "我不知道。"
2 to be familiar with a person or a place 认识；熟悉：*I've known him for nine years.* 我认识他 9 年了。□ *I know Leeds well. I used to live there.* 我很熟悉利兹。我以前住在那里。
3 to understand something 理解；明白：*I know how you feel.* 我明白你的感受。
I know used when you are agreeing with what someone has just said 我知道（用于表示同意对方所说）：*'The weather is awful.' — 'I know.'* "天气真差。" —— "我知道。"
you know used when you want someone to listen to what you are saying (*informal* 非正式) 你要知道（用于引起对方注意）：*I'm doing this for you, you know.* 我这么做是为了你，你要知道。

knowledge /'nɒlɪdʒ/ *uncountable noun* 不可数名词
information and understanding about a subject 知识；学问：*He has a wide knowledge of sports.* 他有丰富的体育知识。□ *Scientists have very little knowledge of the disease.* 科学家们对这种疾病所知甚少。

knowledgeable /'nɒlɪdʒəbəl/ *also* 亦作 **knowledgable** *adjective* 形容词
knowing a lot about a particular subject 博学的；有见识的；知识渊博的：*Our staff are all extremely knowledgeable about our products.* 我们的员工对我们的产品都了如指掌。

known[1] /nəʊn/
→ see 见 **know**

known[2] /nəʊn/ *adjective* 形容词
familiar to a particular group of people 知名的；著名的：*Hawaii is known for its beautiful beaches.* 夏威夷以美丽的海滩而闻名。

knuckle /'nʌkəl/ *countable noun* 可数名词
one of the parts of your body where your fingers join your hands, and where your fingers bend 指节；指关节：*She tapped on the door with her knuckles.* 她用指关节轻轻敲门。

the Koran /ðə kɔː'rɑːn/ *noun* 名词
the most important book in the religion of Islam《古兰经》

kph
written after a number to show the speed of something; short for（缩写 =）'kilometres per hour' 千米每小时（用于数字后，表示速度）

kW
in writing, short for（书面缩写 =）**kilowatt** or **kilowatts**

Ll

lab /læb/ *countable noun* 可数名词
→ see 见 **laboratory**

label /ˈleɪbəl/ *countable noun* 可数名词
a piece of paper or plastic that is attached to an object to give information about it 标签；标记: *Always read the label on the bottle.* 一定要看瓶上的标签。● **label** *verb* 动词 (**labels, labelling, labelled**): *All foods must be clearly labelled.* 所有食品必须标明标签。

label 标签

laboratory /ləˈbɒrətri/ *countable noun* 可数名词 (**laboratories**)
a building or a room where scientific work is done 实验室: *He works in a research laboratory at Columbia University.* 他在哥伦比亚大学的一个研究实验室工作。

labour /ˈleɪbə/ *uncountable noun* 不可数名词
1 very hard work, usually physical work 劳动；体力劳动: *The punishment for refusing to fight was a year's hard labour.* 拒绝战斗的惩罚是一年的苦役。
2 the workers of a country or an industry 劳动力: *Employers want cheap labour.* 雇主想要廉价劳动力。

'Labour Party *singular noun* 单数名词
one of the three main political parties in the UK 工党（英国三大政党之一）

lace /leɪs/ *noun* 名词
1 *uncountable* 不可数 a delicate cloth with a design made of fine threads 网眼织物；花边；蕾丝: *She wore a blue dress with a lace collar.* 她穿着一条有花边领的蓝裙。
2 *countable* 可数 one of two thin pieces of material that are used for fastening shoes 鞋带: *Barry put on his shoes and tied the laces.* 巴里穿上鞋子，系上鞋带。● **lace** *verb* 动词 (**laces, lacing, laced**): *I laced my shoes tightly.* 我把鞋带系紧。

lack /læk/ *uncountable noun* 不可数名词
when there is not enough of something or it does not exist 缺乏；短缺: *I was tired from lack of sleep.* 我因睡眠不足而感到疲倦。● **lack** *verb* 动词 (**lacks, lacking, lacked**): *The meat lacked flavour.* 这肉味道寡淡。

lad /læd/ *countable noun* 可数名词
a young man or boy (*informal* 非正式) 小伙子；男孩: *When I was a lad, we used to go to Yorkshire every summer.* 我小的时候，我们每年夏天都去约克郡。

ladder /ˈlædə/ *countable noun* 可数名词
a piece of equipment used for reaching high places. It is made of two long pieces of wood or metal with short steps between them. 梯子: *He climbed the ladder so he could see over the wall.* 他爬上梯子好看到墙那边。

the ladies /ðə ˈleɪdiz/ *singular noun* 单数名词
a public toilet for women (*informal* 非正式) 女厕所；女卫生间: *Excuse me, can you tell me where the ladies is, please?* 请问女厕所在哪里？

ladle /ˈleɪdəl/ *countable noun* 可数名词
a large, round, deep spoon with a long handle, used for serving soup 长柄勺；汤勺

lady /ˈleɪdi/ *countable noun* 可数名词 (**ladies**)
used when you are talking about a woman in a polite way (对女子的礼貌称呼) 女士，小姐，夫人: *She's a very sweet old lady.* 她是个非常可爱的老太太。

ladybird /ˈleɪdiˌbɜːd/ *countable noun* 可数名词
a small round insect that is red or yellow with black spots 瓢虫

laid /leɪd/
→ see 见 **lay**

laid-'back *adjective* 形容词
behaving in a calm, relaxed way (*informal* 非正式) 放松的；无忧的；悠闲的: *Everyone here is really laid-back.* 这里每人都非常悠闲。

lain /leɪn/
→ see 见 **lie**

lake /leɪk/ *countable noun* 可数名词
a large area of water with land around it 湖；湖泊：*They went fishing in the lake.* 他们去湖里钓鱼。
→ Look at picture on P7 参见彩插第 7 页

lamb /læm/ *noun* 名词
1 *countable* 可数 a young sheep 羔羊；小羊
2 *uncountable* 不可数 the flesh of a lamb eaten as food 羔羊肉：*For supper she served lamb and vegetables.* 晚饭她端上了羔羊肉和蔬菜。

lame /leɪm/ *adjective* 形容词 (**lamer, lamest**)
1 not able to walk very well 瘸的；跛的：*The horses were lame and the men were tired.* 马跛了，人也累了。
2 used about an excuse that is not very good (借口) 站不住脚的，无说服力的：*He gave me some lame excuse about being too busy to call me.* 他找了个蹩脚的借口，说太忙没时间给我打电话。

lamp /læmp/ *countable noun* 可数名词
a light that works using electricity or by burning oil or gas 灯：*She switched on the lamp by her bed.* 她打开床边的灯。

land¹ /lænd/ *uncountable noun* 不可数名词
an area of ground, especially one that is used for a particular purpose such as farming or building (尤指农业、建设等特定用途的) 土地：*There is not enough good farm land.* 良田不足。

land² /lænd/ *verb* 动词 (**lands, landing, landed**)
1 to come down to the ground after moving through the air 降落；落地：*The ball landed 20 feet away.* 球落在 20 英尺外。
2 to arrive somewhere 抵达；着陆：*The plane landed just after 10 pm.* 飞机刚过晚上 10 点就着陆了。
▶ **landing** /ˈlændɪŋ/ *noun* 名词：*The pilot made an emergency landing into the sea.* 飞行员紧急迫降到海里。

landform /ˈlændfɔːm/ also 亦作 **land form** *countable noun* 可数名词
a natural feature of the Earth's surface, such as a hill, a lake or a beach 地貌：*This small country has a wide variety of landforms.* 这个小国地貌复杂。

landing /ˈlændɪŋ/ *countable noun* 可数名词
the flat area at the top of the stairs in a house or building 楼梯平台

landlady /ˈlændleɪdi/ *countable noun* 可数名词 (**landladies**)
a woman who owns a building and allows people to live there in return for rent 女房东：*There was a note under the door from my landlady.* 女房东在我们下留了一张便条。

landlord /ˈlændlɔːd/ *countable noun* 可数名词
a man who owns a building and allows people to live there in return for rent 房东：*His landlord doubled the rent.* 他的房东把租金提高了一倍。

landmark /ˈlændmɑːk/ *countable noun* 可数名词
a building or other object that helps people to know where they are 地标；标志性建筑；标志性物体：*The Empire State Building is a New York landmark.* 帝国大厦是纽约的一个地标。

landscape /ˈlændskeɪp/ *noun* 名词
1 everything you can see when you look across an area of land 风景；景观：*We travelled through the beautiful landscape of northern Scotland.* 我们游览了苏格兰北部的美丽风景。
2 *countable* 可数 a painting that shows a scene in the countryside 乡村风景画：*She paints landscapes of hills and river valleys.* 她画丘陵河谷风景画。

lane /leɪn/ *countable noun* 可数名词
1 a narrow road, especially in the countryside 小路；(尤指) 乡间小路：*Our house was on a quiet country lane.* 我们家房子在一条僻静的乡间小路上。
2 a part of a road that is marked by a painted line 车道：*The lorry was travelling at 20 mph in the slow lane.* 卡车在慢车道上以 20 英里的时速行驶着。

language /ˈlæŋɡwɪdʒ/ *noun* 名词
1 *countable* 可数 a system of sounds and written symbols that people of a particular country or region use in talking or writing 语言：*The English language has over 500,000 words.* 英语有 50 多万个单词。□ *Students must learn to speak a second language.* 学生必须学会说第二语言。
2 *uncountable* 不可数 the use of a system of communication that has a set of sounds or written symbols 语言表达：*Some children develop language more quickly than others.* 有些孩子语言发展比其他孩子快。
→ Look at picture on P3 参见彩插第 3 页

lantern /ˈlæntən/ *countable noun* 可数名词
a light in a metal frame with glass sides 提灯；灯笼

lap¹ /læp/ *countable noun* 可数名词
1 the flat area formed by the tops of your legs when you are sitting down（坐着时的）大腿面: *Ravi was sitting on his dad's lap.* 拉维坐在爸爸大腿上。
2 one turn around a race course（跑道的）一圈: *He was not able to run the last lap of the race.* 他没能跑完比赛的最后一圈。

lap 大腿面
Ravi was sitting on his dad's lap. 拉维坐在爸爸大腿上。

lap² /læp/ *verb* 动词
(**laps, lapping, lapped**)
to use short quick movements of the tongue to take liquid up into the mouth 舔食；舔着喝: *The cat lapped milk from a dish.* 猫舔食盘子里的牛奶。

lapel /ləˈpel/ *countable noun* 可数名词
the folds on the front of a jacket or coat（夹克或外套胸前的）翻领: *He wore a flower in his lapel.* 他胸前翻领上别着一朵花。

laptop /ˈlæptɒp/ *countable noun* 可数名词
a small computer that you can carry with you 笔记本电脑: *She was working at her laptop.* 她在笔记本电脑前工作。
→ Look at picture on P11 参见彩插第 11 页

large /lɑːdʒ/ *adjective* 形容词 (**larger, largest**)
1 greater in size than most other things of the same type（尺寸）大的: *This fish lives mainly in large rivers and lakes.* 这种鱼主要生活在大型河流和湖泊里。□ *In the largest room a few people were sitting on the floor.* 在最大的房间里，有几个人坐在地板上。
2 more than the average amount or number 大量的；大规模的: *The robbers got away with a large amount of cash.* 劫匪抢走了大量现金。□ *A large number of people are still looking for jobs.* 许多人仍在找工作。

largely /ˈlɑːdʒli/ *adverb* 副词
used for saying that something is mostly true 主要地；很大程度上；多半: *The project is largely paid for by taxes.* 这项工程费用大部分由税收支付。□ *The government is largely to blame for this.* 政府在很大程度上对此负有责任。

laser /ˈleɪzə/ *countable noun* 可数名词
a strong light that is produced by a special machine 激光: *Doctors are trying new laser technology to help patients.* 医生们正在尝试新的激光技术来救治病人。

laser printer *countable noun* 可数名词
a computer printer that produces clear words and pictures on paper using laser beams (= strong lines of light) 激光打印机

last¹ /lɑːst/ *adjective* 形容词, *adverb* 副词
1 the most recent 刚过去的；最近的: *I got married last July.* 我去年 7 月结的婚。□ *He didn't come home last night.* 他昨晚没有回家。□ *A lot has changed since my last visit.* 自我上次到访，发生了许多变化。
2 happening or coming after all the others of the same type 最后的；最末的: *I read the last three pages of the chapter.* 我读了这一章的最后 3 页。
3 at the end, or after everyone else 最后: *I arrived home last.* 我最后到的家。● **last** *pronoun* 代词: *Rosa was the last to go to bed.* 罗莎最后一个上床睡觉。
4 the only one that is left 唯一剩下的: *Can I have the last piece of pizza?* 最后一块比萨饼我吃了行吗？
at last finally; after you have been waiting for a long time 最终；终于: *I'm so glad that we've found you at last!* 真高兴我们终于找到你了！

last² /lɑːst/ *verb* 动词 (**lasts, lasting, lasted**)
1 to continue to exist for a particular length of time 持续；延续: *The marriage lasted for less than two years.* 这段婚姻持续了不到两年。
2 to be able to be used for a particular length of time 够用；足够维持: *One tube of glue lasts for a long time.* 一管胶水可以用很长时间。

lasting /ˈlɑːstɪŋ/ *adjective* 形容词
continuing to exist for a very long time 持久的；耐久的: *Everyone wants lasting peace.* 每个人都想要持久的和平。

lastly /ˈlɑːstli/ *adverb* 副词
used when you want to mention a final item 最后；最后一点: *Lastly, can I ask about your future plans?* 最后，我能问一下你未来的计划吗？

last name *countable noun* 可数名词
the name of your family. In English, your last name comes after all your other

names. 姓（英语中的姓放在名字之后）: *'What is your last name?'* — *'Garcia.'* "你姓什么？"——"加西亚。"

latch /lætʃ/ *countable noun* 可数名词 (**latches**)
a metal bar that you use to fasten a door or a gate. You lift the bar to open the door or gate. 门闩；插销: *She lifted the latch and pushed the door open.* 她拉起门闩推开门。

late /leɪt/ *adjective* 形容词, *adverb* 副词 (**later, latest**)
1 near the end of a period of time 末期（的）；晚期（的）: *He was in his late 20s.* 他当时快 30 岁了。□ *It was late in the afternoon.* 那是傍晚。□ *He married late in life.* 他结婚很晚。
2 near the end of the day 天色晚的；深夜的: *It was very late and the streets were empty.* 天色很晚了，街上空荡荡的。
3 after the time that something should start or happen 迟；晚: *The train was 40 minutes late.* 火车晚点了 40 分钟。
□ *Steve arrived late for his class.* 史蒂夫上课迟到了。

lately /ˈleɪtli/ *adverb* 副词
used for talking about events that happened recently 最近；近来: *Dad's health hasn't been good lately.* 爸爸最近身体不好。

later /ˈleɪtə/ *adverb* 副词
used for talking about a time that is after the one that you have been talking about 以后；后来；随后: *He joined the company straight from school and left his job ten years later.* 他从学校一毕业就进了这家公司，10 年后辞职。

latest /ˈleɪtɪst/ *adjective* 形容词
1 most recent 最近的: *I really liked her latest book.* 我特别喜欢她的新书。
2 new and modern 最新的: *That shop sells only the latest fashions.* 那家商店只卖最新的款式。

latitude /ˈlætɪtjuːd/ *noun* 名词
the distance of a place from the equator (= the line around the middle of the Earth). Compare with **longitude**. 纬度（比较 longitude）: *The evenings are already long at this northern latitude.* 在北半球这个纬度，傍晚已经很长了。
→ Look at picture on P9 参见彩插第 9 页

latter /ˈlætə/ *pronoun* 代词

the second of two things that have been mentioned. The first of them is called the **former**. 后者: *He found his cousin and uncle. The latter was sick.* 他找到了堂弟和叔叔。他叔叔病了。● **latter** *adjective* 形容词: *Some people like speaking in public and some don't. Mike belongs in the latter group.* 有些人喜欢在公共场合讲话，有些人不喜欢。迈克属于后者。

laugh /lɑːf/ *verb* 动词 (**laughs, laughing, laughed**)
1 to make a sound while smiling to show that you think something is funny 笑；发笑: *When I saw what he was wearing, I started to laugh.* 我看到他穿的衣服时，笑了起来。□ *Some of the boys laughed at his jokes.* 一些男孩听到他讲的笑话后笑了起来。● **laugh** *countable noun* 可数名词: *Len gave a loud laugh.* 莱恩大笑了一声。
2 to make jokes about someone or something 嘲笑；讥笑: *People used to laugh at me because I was so small.* 以前我因个子小常受人嘲笑。

laughter /ˈlɑːftə/ *uncountable noun* 不可数名词
the sound of people laughing 笑声: *Their laughter filled the room.* 房间里洋溢着他们的笑声。

launch /lɔːntʃ/ *verb* 动词 (**launches, launching, launched**)
1 to send a spacecraft (= a vehicle that goes into space) away from Earth 发射（航天器）: *NASA plans to launch a new satellite.* 美国航空航天局计划发射一颗新卫星。
2 to put a ship or a boat into water 使（船）下水: *The Titanic was launched in 1911.* 泰坦尼克号于 1911 年下水。
3 to start a large and important activity 发起，发动，推出（重大活动）: *The police have launched a search for the missing girl.* 警方已开始寻找失踪的女孩。

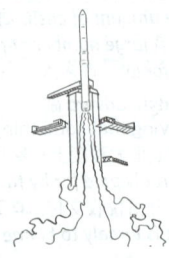

launch 发射

launderette /ˌlɔːndəˈret/ *countable noun* 可数名词
a place where people pay to use machines to wash and dry their clothes 自助洗衣店

laundry /ˈlɔːndri/ *noun* 名词 (**laundries**)
1 *uncountable* 不可数 clothes and other things that are going to be washed 待洗衣物: *I'll do your laundry.* 我给你洗衣服。
2 *countable* 可数 a business that washes and irons clothes and other things for people 洗衣店: *He takes his shirts to the laundry.* 他把衬衫拿到洗衣店去洗。

lava /ˈlɑːvə/ *uncountable noun* 不可数名词 the very hot liquid rock that comes out of a volcano (= a mountain with a hole at the top that throws out hot substances) (火山的)熔岩: *Lava poured from the volcano.* 熔岩从火山喷涌而出。

lavatory /ˈlævətri/ *countable noun* 可数名词 (**lavatories**)
a toilet 厕所

law /lɔː/ *noun* 名词
1 *singular* 单数 a system of rules that a society or government develops to deal with things like crime 法律: *Driving too fast is against the law.* 超速驾驶是违法的。 □ *These companies are breaking the law.* 这些公司正在做违法的事。
2 *countable* 可数 one of the rules in a system of law 法律；法规；法令: *The government has introduced a new law to protect young people.* 政府颁行了一部保护青少年的新法律。

lawful /ˈlɔːfʊl/ *adjective* 形容词 allowed by law (*formal* 正式) 法定的；合法的: *We want fair and lawful treatment of prisoners.* 我们要求公正合法地对待囚犯。
▶ **lawfully** /ˈlɔːfʊli/ *adverb* 副词: *Did the police act lawfully in shooting him?* 警方向他开枪合法吗？

lawn /lɔːn/ *noun* 名词
an area of short grass around a house or other building (房屋等周围的)草地，草坪: *They were sitting on the lawn.* 他们坐在草坪上。

lawnmower /ˈlɔːnməʊə/ *countable noun* 可数名词
a machine for cutting grass 割草机；剪草机

lawsuit /ˈlɔːsuːt/ *countable noun* 可数名词
a case that a court of law deals with (*formal* 正式) 诉讼: *The lawsuit accuses him of theft and kidnapping.* 诉讼指控他盗窃和绑架。

lawyer /ˈlɔɪə/ *countable noun* 可数名词
a person whose job is to advise people about the law and to represent them in court 律师: *His lawyers say that he is not guilty.* 他的律师们说他无罪。

lay¹ /leɪ/
→ see 见 **lie**

lay² /leɪ/ *verb* 动词 (**lays, laying, laid**)
1 to put something somewhere carefully 放置；安放: *He laid the newspaper on the desk.* 他把报纸放在桌子上。 □ *She gently laid the baby in her cot.* 她轻轻地把宝宝放在小床上。
2 when a female bird lays an egg, it pushes an egg out of its body 下(蛋)

layer /ˈleɪə/ *countable noun* 可数名词
a substance or a material that covers a surface, or that lies between two other things 层；表层；夹层: *A fresh layer of snow covered the street.* 街上新落了一层雪。

layout /ˈleɪaʊt/ *countable noun* 可数名词
the way the parts of a place are arranged 布局；布置；设计；安排: *He tried to remember the layout of the farmhouse.* 他试图记住农舍的布局。

lazy /ˈleɪzi/ *adjective* 形容词 (**lazier, laziest**)
not wanting to work 不愿工作的；懒惰的: *I'm not lazy; I like to be busy.* 我不是个懒人，我喜欢忙一点儿。
▶ **laziness** /ˈleɪzinəs/ *uncountable noun* 不可数名词: *Too much TV encourages laziness.* 看电视太多助长惰性。

lb.

> **LANGUAGE HELP** 语言提示
> The plural is **lbs.** or **lb.** 复数形式是 lbs. 或 lb.。

short for (缩写 =) **pound**, when you are talking about weight 磅

lead¹ /liːd/ *verb* 动词 (**leads, leading, led**)
1 to go in front of a group of people 走在⋯前列；给⋯开路: *A jazz band led the parade.* 一支爵士乐队引领着游行队伍。
2 to take someone to a place 带领；引领: *I took his hand and led him into the house.* 我拉起他的手领他进了屋子。
3 used for describing where a road or path goes (道路)通向，通往: *This path leads down to the beach.* 这条小路通向海滩。
4 to be winning in a race or competition (比赛中)领先: *The Eagles led by three*

points at half-time. 老鹰队在半场结束时领先3分。
5 to be in control of a group of people 领导；率领；掌管: *Chris leads a large team of salespeople.* 克里斯领导着一个庞大的销售团队。
6 used for describing someone's life 过（某种生活）: *She led a normal, happy life.* 她过着平常、快乐的生活。
7 to cause a particular situation 导致；造成: *Every time we talk about money it leads to an argument.* 每次我们谈起钱都会争论一番。

lead² /liːd/ *countable noun* 可数名词
a long thin piece of leather or a chain, that you use to control a dog 牵狗绳；束犬链: *All dogs in public places should be on a lead.* 在公共场所所有狗都应该套上牵狗绳。
in the lead winning in a race or competition（比赛中）领先: *Harvard were already in the lead after ten minutes.* *10 分钟后，哈佛队已经领先了。

lead³ /led/ *noun* 名词
1 *uncountable* 不可数 a soft, grey, heavy metal 铅: *In the past, most water pipes were made of lead.* 过去，大多数水管是铅制的。
2 *countable* 可数 the grey part in the middle of a pencil that makes a mark on paper 铅笔芯: *He started writing, but his pencil lead immediately broke.* 他开始写字，但铅笔芯一写就断了。

leader /ˈliːdə/ *countable noun* 可数名词
1 the person who is in charge of a group of people or an organization 领导者；领袖: *Members today will elect a new leader.* 今天会员们将选出一位新领导人。
2 the person who is in front of all the others in a race or competition, or who is winning（比赛中的）领先者: *The leader came in two minutes before the other runners.* 领先者比其他赛跑选手早两分钟完赛。

leadership /ˈliːdəʃɪp/ *noun* 名词
1 *countable* 可数 the people who are in control of a group or an organization 领导: *He attended a meeting with the Croatian leadership.* 他出席了与克罗地亚领导人的会议。
2 *uncountable* 不可数 someone's position of being in control of a group of people 领导地位: *The company doubled in size under her leadership.* 在她的领导下，公司规模扩大了一倍。

leading /ˈliːdɪŋ/ *adjective* 形容词
1 most important or successful in a particular area 最重要的；一流的: *a leading violin player* 一流的小提琴手
2 used for describing the person or team that is winning a race or competition（比赛中）领先的: *It always feels good to be in the leading team.* 身为榜首球队的一员总是感觉不错。

leaf /liːf/ *countable noun* 可数名词 (**leaves**)
the parts of a tree or plant that are flat, thin, and usually green 叶；叶子: *A brown, dry oak leaf fell into the water.* 一片褐色的干橡树叶掉进水里。

leaflet /ˈliːflət/ *countable noun* 可数名词
a piece of paper containing information about a particular subject 传单；宣传页: *My doctor gave me a leaflet about healthy eating.* 医生给了我一张健康饮食宣传页。

league /liːɡ/ *countable noun* 可数名词
1 a group of people, clubs or countries that have joined together for a particular purpose 联盟；同盟: *The League of Nations was formed after World War I.* 国际联盟是在第一次世界大战后成立的。
2 a group of teams that play against each other（体育俱乐部）联合会；（体育运动）联赛: *the football league* 足球联赛

leak /liːk/ *verb* 动词 (**leaks, leaking, leaked**)
1 to let liquid or gas escape 漏（液体或气体）: *The roof leaks every time it rains.* 每次下雨屋顶都漏水。 ● **leak** *countable noun* 可数名词: *A gas leak caused the explosion.* 燃气泄漏引起了爆炸。
2 when liquid or gas leaks, it escapes from something 漏；（液体）渗漏；（气体）泄漏: *The water is leaking out from the bottom of the bucket.* 水正从桶底漏出来。

leak 漏

The water is leaking out from the bottom of the bucket. 水正从桶底漏出来。

lean¹ /liːn/ *verb* 动词 (**leans, leaning, leaned** or 或 **leant**)
1 to bend your body from your waist in a

particular direction 探身；(上身)倾斜：
The driver leaned across and opened the passenger door. 司机探身打开了乘客门。
2 to rest on someone or something 靠着，倚靠：*She was feeling tired and leaned against him.* 她感到累了，靠在他身上。

lean 探身

The driver leaned across and opened the passenger door. 司机探身打开了乘客门。

lean² /liːn/ *adjective* 形容词 (**leaner, leanest**)
1 used for describing meat that does not have very much fat (肉)瘦的
2 thin, but fit and healthy 瘦而健康的：*He was lean and strong.* 他精瘦健壮。

leant /lent/
→ see 见 **lean**

leap /liːp/ *verb* 动词 (**leaps, leaping, leaped** or 或 **leapt**)
1 to jump high in the air or to jump a long distance 跳；跳跃：*He leaped in the air and waved his hands.* 他腾跃起来，挥动双手。
●**leap** *countable noun* 可数名词：*Powell won the long jump with a leap of 8 metres 95 centimetres.* 鲍威尔以 8.95 米赢得了跳远比赛。
2 to move somewhere suddenly and quickly 迅猛移动：*The two men leapt into the car and drove away.* 那两个人跳进汽车开走了。

leapt /lept/
→ see 见 **leap**

learn /lɜːn/ *verb* 动词 (**learns, learning, learned** or 或 **learnt**)
to get knowledge or a skill by studying, training, or through experience 学；学习；学会：*Where did you learn English?* 你在哪里学的英语？ □ *He is learning to play the piano.* 他正在学习弹钢琴。

▶**learner** /ˈlɜːnə/ *countable noun* 可数名词：*Clint is a quick learner; he's one of my smarter students.* 克林特学东西很快，他是我相对聪明的学生之一。

ˈlearning ˌdifficulty *countable noun* 可数名词
a condition that makes it difficult for someone to learn as quickly or in the same way as most other people 学习困难：*She works supporting pupils with learning difficulties.* 她帮助有学习困难的学生。

learnt /lɜːnt/
→ see 见 **learn**

lease /liːs/ *verb* 动词 (**leases, leasing, leased**)
1 to pay someone to allow you to use their property 租用；租赁：*He leased an apartment in Toronto.* 他在多伦多租了一套公寓。
2 to allow someone to use your property in exchange for money 出租：*She's going to lease the building to students.* 她打算把这栋楼租给学生。

least /liːst/ *adjective* 形容词, *adverb* 副词
a smaller amount than anyone or anything else, or the smallest amount possible 最少(的)；最小(的)：*He wants to spend the least amount of money possible on a car.* 他想在车上尽量少花钱。 □ *He is one of the least friendly people I have ever met.* 他是我遇到的最不友好的人之一。 ●**least** *pronoun* 代词：*The report found that teenage girls exercised the least.* 报告发现十几岁的女孩锻炼最少。
at least not less than a particular number or amount 至少：*Drink at least half a pint of milk each day.* 每天至少喝半品脱牛奶。

leather /ˈleðə/ *noun* 名词
animal skin that is used for making shoes, clothes, bags and furniture 皮革：*She bought a leather jacket.* 她买了一件皮夹克。

leave¹ /liːv/ *verb* 动词 (**leaves, leaving, left**)
1 to go away from a place or person 离开：*He left the country yesterday.* 他昨天离开了这个国家。 □ *My flight leaves in less than an hour.* 我的航班 1 小时内起飞。
2 to not bring something with you 没带：*I left my bags in the car.* 我把行李放车上了。
3 to not use all of something 留下；剩下：*Please leave some cake for me!* 请给我留些蛋糕！
4 to give something to someone when you die 遗赠；遗留：*He left everything to his children when he died.* 他死后把一切都

留给了孩子们。
5 to forget to bring something with you 忘了带；落下：*I left my purse in the petrol station.* 我把钱包落在加油站了。
leave someone alone to stop annoying someone 不打扰某人：*Please just leave me alone!* 请别烦我！
leave something alone to stop touching something 不碰某物：*Leave my purse alone!* 别碰我的钱包！
leave someone/something out to not include someone or something 不包括某人/某物；漏掉某人/某物：*Why did they leave her out of the team?* 她们为什么把她排除在队伍之外？

leave² /liːv/ *uncountable noun* 不可数名词
a period of time when you are away from work 假期；休假：*Why don't you take a few days' leave?* 你为什么不休几天假呢？
on leave not working at your job 休假：*She has gone on leave for a week.* 她休假一个星期了。

leaves /liːvz/
1 the plural form of **leaf**（leaf 的复数形式）
2 → see 见 **leave**

lecture /ˈlektʃə/ *countable noun* 可数名词
a talk that someone gives in order to teach people about a particular subject 讲座；讲课；演讲：*We attended a lecture by Professor Eric Robinson.* 我们听了埃里克·鲁宾逊教授的讲座。● **lecture** *verb* 动词 (**lectures, lecturing, lectured**)：*She invited him to Atlanta to lecture on the history of art.* 她邀请他去亚特兰大做艺术史讲座。

lecturer /ˈlektʃərə/ *countable noun* 可数名词
a teacher at a university or college 讲师：*a lecturer in law* 法学讲师

led /led/
→ see 见 **lead**

ledge /ledʒ/ *countable noun* 可数名词
1 a narrow shelf of rock on the side of a mountain 岩架；岩脊
2 a narrow shelf along the bottom edge of a window（窗）台：*a window ledge* 窗台

leek /liːk/ *noun* 名词
a long, thin vegetable that is white at one end and has long green leaves 韭葱

left¹ /left/
→ see 见 **leave**

left² /left/ *adjective* 形容词, *adverb* 副词
1 still there after everything else has gone or been used 留下的；剩下的：*Is there any*

milk left? 还有牛奶吗？
2 opposite the side that most people write with 左边的；向左地：*I've broken my left leg.* 我左腿断了。□ *Turn left at the corner.* 拐角处左转。● **left** *singular noun* 单数名词：*The bank is on the left at the end of the road.* 银行在马路尽头的左边。□ *There is a high brick wall to the left of the building.* 建筑物左边有一堵高高的砖墙。

left-hand *adjective* 形容词
positioned on the left of something 左手的；左边的：*The Japanese drive on the left-hand side of the road.* 日本人靠路左侧开车。

left-handed *adjective* 形容词
using your left hand rather than your right hand for activities such as writing and sports 惯用左手的；左撇子的：*A left-handed tennis player won the tournament.* 一个左手执拍的网球选手赢得了锦标赛。

leftover /ˈleftəʊvə/ *adjective* 形容词
used for describing an amount of something that remains after the rest of it has been used or eaten 剩下的：*If you have any leftover chicken, use it to make this delicious pie.* 如果你有剩下的鸡肉，就拿来做这种美味的馅饼。

leftovers /ˈleftəʊvəz/ *plural noun* 复数名词
food that has not been eaten after a meal 吃剩的食物；残羹剩饭：*Put any leftovers in the fridge.* 把剩饭菜放进冰箱。

left-wing *adjective* 形容词
supporting the ideas of the political left 左翼的；左派的：*I'm not going to vote for him because he is too left-wing.* 我不会投他，他太左了。

leg /leg/ *countable noun* 可数名词
1 one of the long parts of a person's or an animal's body that they use for walking and standing 腿：*He broke his right leg in a motorcycle accident.* 他在一起摩托车事故中摔断了右腿。
→ Look at picture on P4 参见彩插第 4 页
2 one of the parts of a pair of trousers that cover your legs 裤腿；裤管：*Anthony dried his hands on the legs of his jeans.* 安东尼在牛仔裤裤腿上擦干了双手。
3 one of the long parts of a table or a chair that it stands on（桌椅）腿：*a broken chair leg* 断了的椅子腿

legal /ˈliːɡəl/ *adjective* 形容词
1 used for describing things that relate to

the law 法律的；与法律有关的：*He promised to take legal action.* 他承诺提起法律诉讼。 □ *the legal system* 法律体系
2 allowed by law 合法的：*My actions were completely legal.* 我的行为完全合法。

legalize /ˈliːɡəˌlaɪz/ *verb* 动词 (**legalizes, legalizing, legalized**)
to pass a law to make something legal 使合法化；使得到法律认可：*They made a case for legalizing file-sharing.* 他们提出了文件共享合法化的理由。

legend /ˈledʒənd/ *noun* 名词
a very old and popular story 传说；传奇故事：*The play is based on an ancient Greek legend.* 这出戏是根据古希腊的一个传说改编的。

leisure /ˈleʒə/ *uncountable noun* 不可数名词
the time when you are not working, when you can relax and do things that you enjoy 空闲；闲暇：*They spend their leisure time painting or drawing.* 他们用业余时间画画。

leisurely /ˈleʒəli/ *adjective* 形容词
done in a relaxed way 不慌不忙的；慢悠悠的：*Lunch was a leisurely meal.* 午饭吃得很悠闲。

lemon /ˈlemən/ *noun* 名词
a yellow fruit with very sour juice 柠檬：*I like a slice of lemon in my tea.* 我喜欢在茶里放一片柠檬。

lemonade /ˌleməˈneɪd/ *noun* 名词
a drink that is made from lemons, sugar and water 柠檬饮料：*They ordered two lemonades.* 他们点了两杯柠檬饮料。

lend /lend/ *verb* 动词 (**lends, lending, lent**)
1 to give someone money that they must give back after a certain amount of time 贷(款)给；借(钱)给：*The government will lend you money at very good rates.* 政府将以很优惠的利率贷款给你。
2 to allow someone to use something of yours for a period of time 借给；借出：*Will you lend me your pen?* 把你的钢笔借给我好吗？

length /leŋθ/ *noun* 名词
1 the measurement from one end of something to the other 长度：*The table is about a metre in length.* 这张桌子大约1米长。
→ Look at picture on P2 参见彩ँ第2页
2 how long an event lasts 持续时间；时长：*The average length of a patient's stay in hospital is about 48 hours.* 病人住院的平均时长约为48小时。
at length for a long time or in great detail 长时间地；详尽地：*They spoke at length about their families.* 他们详细地谈了他们的家庭。

lengthen /ˈleŋθən/ *verb* 动词 (**lengthens, lengthening, lengthened**)
to make or become longer (使)变长：*The sun went down and the shadows lengthened.* 太阳下山，影子变长了。 □ *This exercise will lengthen the muscles in your legs.* 这种锻炼会拉伸腿部肌肉。

lengthy /ˈleŋθi/ *adjective* 形容词 (**lengthier, lengthiest**)
1 lasting for a long time 很长的；漫长的：*There was a lengthy meeting to decide the company's future.* 决定公司未来的会议开了很长时间。
2 containing a lot of words 长篇的；冗长的：*The United Nations produced a lengthy report on the subject.* 联合国就这个问题发表了一份长篇报告。

lens /lenz/ *countable noun* 可数名词 (**lenses**)
a thin, curved piece of glass or plastic used in things such as cameras and glasses. A lens makes things look larger, smaller or clearer. 透镜；镜片：*I bought a powerful lens for my camera.* 我为照相机买了一个功能强大的镜头。

lent /lent/
→ see 见 **lend**

lentil /ˈlentɪl/ *countable noun* 可数名词
a small, round dried seed that you use in cooking, for example to make soups 小扁豆；兵豆

leopard /ˈlepəd/ *countable noun* 可数名词
a large wild cat. Leopards have yellow fur with black spots, and live in Africa and Asia. 豹

leotard /ˈliːəˌtɑːd/ *countable noun* 可数名词
a tight piece of clothing that covers the top part of your body. People wear leotards when they practise dancing or do exercises. (跳舞或锻炼时穿的)紧身衣

lesbian /ˈlezbiən/ *noun* 名词
a woman who is sexually attracted to other women 女同性恋者：*The main character in the novel is a lesbian.* 这部小说的主角是个女同性恋。 ● **lesbian** *adjective* 形容词：*The organization supports lesbian and gay members.* 该组织支持女同性恋和男同性恋会员。

less /les/ *adjective* 形容词
a smaller amount of something 较少的；更少的：*People should eat less fat.* 人们应减少脂肪摄入。□ *He earns less money than his brother.* 他挣的钱比他哥哥少。□ *The population of the country is less than 12 million.* 这个国家的人口不足 1,200 万。
• **less** *pronoun* 代词：*He thinks people should spend less and save more.* 他认为人们应该少花钱、多储蓄。

lessen /ˈlesən/ *verb* 动词 (lessens, lessening, lessened)
to make something smaller 使减少；使降低；使减轻：*A change in diet might lessen your risk of heart disease.* 改变饮食也许能降低患心脏病的风险。

lesson /ˈlesən/ *countable noun* 可数名词
a time when you learn about a particular subject 课：*Johanna has started taking piano lessons.* 约翰娜开始上钢琴课了。

let /let/ *verb* 动词 (lets, letting, let)
1 to not try to stop something from happening 让；任由…发生：*I just let him sleep.* 我任由他睡个够。
2 to give someone your permission to do something 准许；许可；同意：*I love sweets but Mum doesn't let me eat them very often.* 我喜欢糖果，但妈妈不让我经常吃。
3 to allow someone to enter or leave a place 允许（某人进入或离开某处）：*I went down and let them into the building.* 我下来让他们进入大楼。
4 to allow someone to live in your property in exchange for money 出租：*When I moved to London, I let my flat in New York.* 我搬到伦敦后，把纽约的公寓租了出去。
5 used when you are offering to do something 让，由（用于主动提出做某事）：*Let me hang up your coat.* 让我把你的大衣挂起来。

let go of someone/something to stop holding a person or a thing 放开某人／某物：*She let go of Mona's hand.* 她放开了莫纳的手。

let someone know to tell someone about something 让某人知道：*I want to let them know that I'm safe.* 我想给他们报个平安。

let someone off to give someone a lighter punishment than they expect or no punishment at all 放某人；饶恕某人：*He thought that if he said he was sorry, the judge would let him off.* 他以为说句对不起法官就会放过他。

let's short for (缩写 =) 'let us'; used when you are making a suggestion 让我们（用于提出建议）

lethal /ˈliːθəl/ *adjective* 形容词
used for describing something that can kill people or animals 致命的：*She swallowed a lethal dose of sleeping pills.* 她吞下了致命剂量的安眠药。

letter /ˈletə/ *countable noun* 可数名词
1 a message that you write or type on paper and send to someone 信；信件：*I received a letter from a friend.* 我收到一封朋友的来信。□ *Mrs Franklin sent a letter offering me the job.* 富兰克林夫人寄来一封信，提出让我做那份工作。
2 a written symbol that represents a sound in a language 字母：*The children practised writing the letters of the alphabet.* 孩子们练习写字母表中的字母。

ˈletter box *countable noun* 可数名词 (letter boxes) (American 美国英语：mailbox)
a hole in a door for putting letters through（门上的）投信口

lettering /ˈletərɪŋ/ *uncountable noun* 不可数名词
writing or printing（书写或印刷的）文字：*On the door was a small blue sign with white lettering.* 门上有一块蓝色的小牌子，上面写着白色的字。

lettuce /ˈletɪs/ *noun* 名词
a plant with large green leaves that is eaten mainly in salads 莴苣；生菜

level[1] /ˈlevəl/ *noun* 名词
1 *countable* 可数 used for describing the amount or quality of something 水平（用于描述数量或品质）：*We have the lowest level of inflation for 20 years.* 我们的通货膨胀率是 20 年来最低的。
2 *singular* 单数 the height of something 高度：*The water level was 6.5 feet below normal.* 水位比正常值低 6.5 英尺。

level[2] /ˈlevəl/ *adjective* 形容词
1 at the same height as another thing 等高的；齐平的：*He sat down so his face was level with the boy's.* 他坐下来以便能平视那个男孩。
2 completely flat 平的；平坦的：*Make sure the ground is level before you start building.* 在开始建造之前，要确保地面平整。

lever /ˈliːvə/ *countable noun* 可数名词
1 a handle that you push or pull to operate

a machine 操纵杆；控制杆：*Push the lever to switch the machine on.* 推操纵杆启动机器。
2 a bar that you use to lift something heavy. You put one end of it under the heavy object, and then push down on the other end. 杠杆：*Joseph found a stick to use as a lever and lifted up the stone.* 约瑟夫找了一根棍子作杠杆，把石头撬了起来。

liable /ˈlaɪəbəl/ *adjective* 形容词
liable to very likely 很可能…的：*Some of this old equipment is liable to break down.* 这批旧设备中有一些很容易坏。

liar /ˈlaɪə/ *countable noun* 可数名词
someone who tells lies 说谎者；撒谎者：*He's a liar and a cheat.* 他说谎成性，是个骗子。

liberal /ˈlɪbərəl/ *adjective* 形容词
understanding and accepting that other people have different ideas and beliefs, and may therefore behave differently 开明的；开通的：*My parents are very liberal and relaxed.* 我父母非常开明，管得很松。

liberty /ˈlɪbəti/ *uncountable noun* 不可数名词
the freedom to live in the way that you want to 自由：*We must do all we can to defend liberty and justice.* 我们必须尽我们所能捍卫自由和正义。

librarian /laɪˈbreəriən/ *countable noun* 可数名词
a person who works in a library 图书馆管理员

library /ˈlaɪbrəri/ *countable noun* 可数名词 (**libraries**)
a place where books, newspapers, DVDs and music are kept for people to use or borrow 图书馆：*I found the book I needed at the local library.* 我在当地图书馆找到了我需要的那本书。

lice /laɪs/
the plural of **louse** (louse 的复数)

licence /ˈlaɪsəns/ *countable noun* 可数名词
an official document that gives you permission to do, use or own something 执照；许可证：*You need a licence to drive a car.* 你得有驾照才能开车。

lick /lɪk/ *verb* 动词 (**licks, licking, licked**)
to move your tongue across the surface of something 舔：*She licked the stamp and pressed it onto the envelope.* 她舔了舔邮票，把它贴在信封上。 ● **lick** *countable noun*

可数名词：*Can I have a lick of your ice cream?* 我能舔一口你的冰激凌吗？

licorice /ˈlɪkərɪs/ *uncountable noun* 不可数名词
a firm black substance with a strong taste that is used for making a type of sweet 甘草（用于制糖果）

lid /lɪd/ *countable noun* 可数名词
the top of a container that can be removed 盖；盖子：*She lifted the lid of the box.* 她掀起箱盖。

lie¹ /laɪ/ *verb* 动词 (**lies, lying, lay, lain**)
1 to be in a flat position, and not standing or sitting 躺；平躺；平卧：*There was a man lying on the ground.* 有一个人躺在地上。
2 to be in a flat position on a surface 平放：*His clothes were lying on the floor by the bed.* 他的衣服丢在床边的地板上。

> **LANGUAGE HELP 语言提示**
> **Lie** or **lay**? 用 lie 还是 lay？
> **Lie** does not have an object. *lie 后不接宾语：*Lie on the floor with your arms by your sides.* 躺在地板上，双臂置于身体两侧。
> **Lay** has an object. *lay 后接宾语：*Lay the baby on the bed.* 把宝宝放在床上。

3 to say something that you know is not true 说谎；撒谎：*I know he's lying.* 我知道他在撒谎。 □ *Never lie to me again.* 别再跟我撒谎了。
lie down to move your body so that it is flat on something, usually when you want to rest or sleep 躺下：*Why don't you go upstairs and lie down?* 你为什么不上楼躺下呢？

lie² *countable noun* 可数名词
something that someone says or writes that they know is not true 谎言；谎话：*You told me a lie!* 你撒谎骗我！ □ *'How old are you?' — 'Eighteen.' — 'That's a lie.'* "你多大了？"——"18。"——"撒谎。"

lieutenant /lefˈtenənt/ *countable noun* 可数名词
an officer in the army or navy 陆军中尉；海军上尉：*Lieutenant Campbell ordered the men to stop firing.* 坎贝尔中尉命令士兵停止射击。

life /laɪf/ *noun* 名词 (**lives**)
1 *countable* 可数 someone's state of being alive, or the period of time when they are alive 生命；人生：*Your life is in danger.* 你有生命危险。 □ *A nurse tried to save his life.*

lifebelt - light bulb

一名护士试图救他的命。▫ *He spent the last fourteen years of his life in France.* 他在法国度过了人生中的最后14年。
2 *uncountable* 不可数 the quality of being interesting and full of energy 活力；生命力：*The town was full of life.* 这个城镇充满了生机。

lifebelt /'laɪfbelt/ *countable noun* 可数名词
a large ring that you can hold onto to stop you from going under water 救生圈

lifeboat /'laɪfbəʊt/ *countable noun* 可数名词
a boat that is used for saving people who are in danger at sea 救生艇

'life cycle *countable noun* 可数名词
the series of changes that happen to an animal or a plant from the beginning of its life until its death 生命周期；生活周期：*This plant completes its life cycle in a single season.* 这种植物在一个季节就完成了它的生命周期。

lifeguard /'laɪfgɑːd/ *countable noun* 可数名词
a person who works at a beach or a swimming pool and helps people when they are in danger (海滩或泳池的)救生员

'life jacket *countable noun* 可数名词
a jacket that helps you to float when you have fallen into deep water 救生衣

lifestyle /'laɪfstaɪl/ *also* 亦作 **life-style** *or* 或 **life style** *noun* 名词
the way someone has chosen to live and behave 生活方式：*She talked about the benefits of leading a healthier lifestyle.* 她谈了改善生活方式的好处。

lifetime /'laɪftaɪm/ *countable noun* 可数名词
the length of time that someone is alive 一生；终生；寿命：*He travelled a lot during his lifetime.* 他一生中游历了很多地方。

lift¹ /lɪft/ *verb* 动词 (**lifts, lifting, lifted**)
(*also* 亦作 **lift something up**) to take something and move it upwards 举起；提起；抬起：*He lifted the bag onto his shoulder.* 他把包扛上肩。▫ *She lifted the baby up and gave him to me.* 她把宝宝举起来给了我。

lift² /lɪft/ *countable noun* 可数名词
1 (*American* 美国英语：**elevator**) a machine that carries people or things up and down inside tall buildings 电梯；直梯：*We took the lift to the fourteenth floor.* 我们乘电梯到了15楼。
2 when you take someone somewhere in your car 免费搭车；搭便车：*He often gave me a lift home.* 他经常让我搭车回家。

light¹ /laɪt/ *noun* 名词
1 *uncountable* 不可数 the energy that comes from the sun, that lets you see things (阳)光；光线：*He opened the curtains, and suddenly the room was filled with light.* 他拉开窗帘，房间里一下子洒满了阳光。
2 *countable* 可数 something such as an electric lamp that produces light 灯：*Remember to turn the lights out when you leave.* 离开时记得关灯。

light 灯

light² /laɪt/ *verb* 动词 (**lights, lighting, lit** *or* 或 **lighted**)
1 to produce light for a place 照亮；使明亮：*The room was lit by only one light.* 房间里只有一盏灯照明。
2 to start something burning 使燃烧；点燃：*Stephen took a match and lit the candle.* 斯蒂芬划了一根火柴点燃蜡烛。

light³ /laɪt/ *adjective* 形容词 (**lighter, lightest**)
1 full of natural light during the day 明亮的；光线充足的：*Here it gets light at about 6 a.m.* 这里早上6点左右天就亮了。
2 not heavy; easy to lift or move 轻的；不重的：*The printer is quite light, so it's easy to move around.* 打印机很轻，容易移动。
3 not very great in amount or power 少量的；轻微的：*She had a light lunch of salad and fruit.* 她午饭只吃了少量的沙拉和水果。▫ *There was a light wind that day.* 那天有微风。
4 pale in colour 浅色的：*He was wearing jeans and a light-blue T-shirt.* 他穿着牛仔裤和浅蓝色T恤衫。

'light bulb *countable noun* 可数名词
the glass part that you put in an electric

light to produce light 电灯泡

lighten /ˈlaɪtən/ *verb* 动词 (**lightens, lightening, lightened**)
to make something less dark 使变亮；使颜色变浅：*She lightened her hair with a special cream.* 她用一种特殊霜剂把头发染成浅色。

lighter /ˈlaɪtə/ *countable noun* 可数名词
a small object that produces a flame. It is used for lighting things such as candles or fires. 打火机

lighthouse /ˈlaɪthaʊs/ *countable noun* 可数名词
a tower that is built near or in the sea. It has a flashing lamp that warns ships of danger. 灯塔

lighting /ˈlaɪtɪŋ/ *uncountable noun* 不可数名词
the way that a place is lit 照明；灯光：*The kitchen had bright overhead lighting.* 厨房有明亮的顶灯。

lightning /ˈlaɪtnɪŋ/ *uncountable noun* 不可数名词
the very bright flashes of light in the sky that happen during a storm 闪电：*One man died when he was struck by lightning.* 一名男子被闪电击中身亡。 □ *A flash of lightning lit up the house.* 一道闪电照亮了房子。
→ Look at picture on P8 参见彩插第 8 页

like¹ /laɪk/ *preposition* 介词
1 similar to another person or thing 像；和…相似：*He looks like my uncle.* 他长得像我叔叔。 □ *His house is just like yours.* 他的房子和你的很相似。
2 used when you are talking about how a thing or person seems to you 像（用于谈论印象）：*What does Maria look like?* 玛丽亚长什么样？ □ *'What was the party like?' — 'Great!'* "聚会怎么样？"——"棒极了！"
3 used for giving an example 例如；譬如：*large cities like New York and Chicago* 像纽约和芝加哥这样的大城市

like² /laɪk/ *verb* 动词 (**likes, liking, liked**)
to think a thing or a person is interesting, enjoyable or attractive 喜欢；喜爱：*He likes baseball.* 他喜欢棒球。 □ *Do you like swimming?* 你喜欢游泳吗？

I'd like used for saying politely that you want something（礼貌用法）我想要，我希望：*I'd like to ask you a few questions.* 我想问你几个问题。 □ *I'd like a cup of tea and a cheese sandwich, please.* 请给我来一杯茶和一份奶酪三明治。

if you like used when you are suggesting something to someone in an informal way 你要是愿意的话（用于非正式地提出建议）：*You can stay here if you like.* 你愿意的话可以留在这里。

Would you like...? used for politely offering something（礼貌用法）要…吗？：*Would you like some coffee?* 要来点儿咖啡吗？

likeable /ˈlaɪkəbəl/ also 亦作 **likable** *adjective* 形容词
pleasant and easy to be with 可爱的；讨人喜欢的：*He was a clever and likable guy.* 他是个聪明可爱的家伙。

likelihood /ˈlaɪkliˌhʊd/ *uncountable noun* 不可数名词
how probable something is 可能性：*The likelihood of getting the disease is small.* 得这种病的可能性很小。

likely /ˈlaɪkli/ *adjective* 形容词 (**likelier, likeliest**)
1 probably true in a particular situation 可能的：*A gas leak was the most likely cause of the explosion.* 这次爆炸最可能的原因是燃气泄漏。
2 used for saying that a person or thing will probably do something 可能的；有希望的：*Eric is a bright young man who is likely to succeed in life.* 埃里克是个聪明的年轻人，很有希望成为人生赢家。

likewise /ˈlaɪkwaɪz/ *adverb* 副词
the same 同样地；一样：*He gave money to charity and encouraged others to do likewise.* 他捐钱给慈善机构，并鼓励其他人也这样做。

liking /ˈlaɪkɪŋ/ *noun* 名词
to your liking used when something suits you 合人胃口的；让人中意的：*London was more to his liking than Rome.* 伦敦比罗马更合他的意。

lilac¹ /ˈlaɪlək/ *noun* 名词
1 a purple, pink or white flower that grows on a small tree 丁香：*Lilac grew against the garden wall.* 丁香贴着花园的墙生长。
2 pale purple 淡紫色；丁香紫：*Would you prefer lilac or yellow for your bedroom?* 卧室你想用淡紫色还是黄色？

lilac² /ˈlaɪlək/ *adjective* 形容词
pale purple in colour 淡紫色的：*The bride*

wore a lilac dress. 新娘穿着淡紫色的连衣裙。

lily /ˈlɪli/ noun 名词 (lilies)
a plant with large sweet-smelling flowers 百合

limb /lɪm/ countable noun 可数名词
an arm or a leg 肢；臂，腿：*She stretched out her aching limbs.* 她伸展疼痛的四肢。

lime /laɪm/ noun 名词
a round, green fruit that tastes like a lemon 来檬：*Use fresh lime juice and fresh herbs in this recipe.* 这份食谱要用新鲜的来檬汁和香草。

limit¹ /ˈlɪmɪt/ countable noun 可数名词
1 the greatest amount or degree of something 限度；限制：*There is no limit to how much fresh fruit you should eat in a day.* 一天应该吃多少新鲜水果是没有限制的。
2 the largest or smallest amount of something that is allowed 极限；限量；限额：*He was driving 40 miles per hour over the speed limit.* 他以超出限速达 40 英里的时速行驶。

limit² /ˈlɪmɪt/ verb 动词 (limits, limiting, limited)
to stop something from becoming greater than a particular amount 限制；限定：*Try to limit the amount of time you spend on the Internet.* 尽量限制上网时间。

limousine /ˌlɪməˈziːn/ countable noun 可数名词
(also 亦作 **limo**) a large and very comfortable car 大型高级轿车；豪华轿车：*As the president's limousine approached, the crowd began to cheer.* 总统的豪华轿车驶近时，人群开始欢呼起来。

limp¹ /lɪmp/ verb 动词 (limps, limping, limped)
to walk with difficulty because you have hurt one of your legs or feet 瘸着走；跛行；蹒跚：*James limps because of a hip injury.* 詹姆斯髋部受伤，走路一瘸一拐。● **limp** countable noun 可数名词：*Anne walks with a limp.* 安妮走路一瘸一拐的。

limp² /lɪmp/ adjective 形容词 (limper, limpest)
soft or weak 绵软的；虚弱的：*Her body was limp and she was too weak to move.* 她身体绵软虚弱，动弹不得。

line¹ /laɪn/ noun 名词
1 countable 可数 a long, thin mark on something 线；线条：*Draw a line at the bottom of the page.* 在这一页的底部画一条线。
2 countable 可数 a series of words written or printed in a row（文字的）行：*Now read the next line of the poem.* 现在读这首诗的下一行。
3 a long piece of string or rope that you use for a particular purpose（有专门用途的）线，绳：*Melissa was outside, hanging the clothes on the line.* 梅利莎在外面往绳子上晾衣服。
4 countable 可数 a route that trains move along 轨道；铁道：*We stayed on the train to the end of the line.* 我们待在火车上，直到铁轨的尽头。
5 countable 可数 a very long wire for telephones or electricity 电话线；电线：*Suddenly the telephone line went dead.* 突然电话线没电了。
6 countable 可数 a number of people or vehicles that are waiting one behind the other 排；行；列：*There was a line of people waiting to go into the cinema.* 有一队人等着进电影院。
stand in line or **wait in line** (*American* 美国英语) to be in a line of people or vehicles that are waiting for something（人、车辆）排队：*For the homeless, standing in line for meals is part of the daily routine.* 对于无家可归的人来说，排队领饭是他们日常生活的一部分。

line² /laɪn/ verb 动词 (lines, lining, lined)
1 to stand in lines along a road 沿（道路）站成排：*Thousands of local people lined the streets to welcome the president.* 成千上万当地人夹道欢迎总统。
2 to cover the inside of a container with something 给…做衬里：*Line the box with newspaper.* 在盒子里衬上报纸。

linen /ˈlɪnɪn/ uncountable noun 不可数名词
a type of strong cloth 亚麻布：*She wore a white linen suit.* 她穿着一套白色亚麻套装。

liner /ˈlaɪnə/ countable noun 可数名词
a large ship in which people travel long distances, especially on holiday 客轮；邮轮：*a luxury ocean liner* 豪华远洋客轮

lingerie /ˈlænʒəri/ uncountable noun 不可数名词
women's underwear 女式内衣：*The shop sells expensive designer lingerie.* 这家商店出售昂贵的名牌女式内衣。

lining /ˈlaɪnɪŋ/ noun 名词
a piece of cloth that is attached to the

inside of a piece of clothing or a curtain 衬里；内衬：*She wore a black jacket with a red lining.* 她穿着一件有红色衬里的黑色夹克。

link[1] /lɪŋk/ *countable noun* 可数名词
1 a connection between two things, often because one of them causes the other 联系；关联：*Scientists believe there is a link between poor diet and cancer.* 科学家认为不良饮食和癌症之间有联系。
2 an area on a computer screen that allows you to move from one web page or website to another（网页的）链接：*The website has links to other tourism sites.* 该网站有转到其他旅游网站的链接。
3 one of the rings in a chain（链条的）链节：*She was wearing a chain of heavy gold links.* 她戴着一条沉甸甸的金链子。

link[2] /lɪŋk/ *verb* 动词 (**links, linking, linked**)
to make a connection between two things, often because one of them causes the other 使有关联：*Studies have linked television violence with aggressive behaviour.* 研究表明，电视暴力与攻击性行为有关。

lion /ˈlaɪən/ *countable noun* 可数名词
a large wild cat that lives in Africa. Lions have yellow fur, and male lions have long hair on their head and neck (= a mane). 狮；狮子

lip /lɪp/ *countable noun* 可数名词
one of the two outer parts of the edge of your mouth 嘴唇：*He kissed her gently on the lips.* 他轻轻地吻了吻她的嘴唇。
→ Look at picture on P4 参见彩插第 4 页

lipstick /ˈlɪpstɪk/ *noun* 名词
a coloured substance that women sometimes put on their lips 口红；唇膏：*She was wearing red lipstick.* 她涂着红色口红。

liquid /ˈlɪkwɪd/ *noun* 名词
a substance that is not a solid or a gas. Liquids flow and can be poured. Water and oil are liquids. 液体：*She took out a small bottle of clear liquid.* 她拿出一小瓶透明液体。□ *Drink plenty of liquids while you are flying and after you land.* 飞行中和着陆后要多喝水。
→ Look at picture on P6 参见彩插第 6 页

list[1] /lɪst/ *countable noun* 可数名词
a set of names or other things that are written or printed one below the other 名单；清单：*I added coffee to my shopping list.* 我在购物单上添加了咖啡。□ *There were six names on the list.* 名单上有 6 个名字。

list[2] /lɪst/ *verb* 动词 (**lists, listing, listed**)
to write or say names or other things one after another 列举；列出：*The students listed the sports they liked best.* 学生们列出了他们最喜欢的运动。

listen /ˈlɪsən/ *verb* 动词 (**listens, listening, listened**)
1 to give your attention to a sound, or to what someone is saying 听；倾听：*He spends his time listening to the radio.* 他把时间花在听收音机上。
2 used when you want someone to pay attention to you because you are going to say something 听着（用于引起注意）：*Listen, there's something I should warn you about.* 听着，我要提醒你一件事。
→ Look at picture on P3 参见彩插第 3 页

LANGUAGE HELP 语言提示
See note at **hear**. 见 **hear** 的语言提示。

listener /ˈlɪsnə/ *countable noun* 可数名词
someone who is listening to a speaker 听者：*When he finished talking, his listeners applauded loudly.* 他讲完后，听众们掌声雷动。

lit /lɪt/
→ see 见 **light**

literacy /ˈlɪtərəsi/ *uncountable noun* 不可数名词
the ability to read and write 读写能力：*The library's adult literacy programme helps about 2,000 people a year.* 图书馆的成人识字计划每年帮助大约 2,000 人。

literally /ˈlɪtərəli/ *adverb* 副词
1 saying what each word means in another language 按字面；字面上：*Volkswagen literally means 'people's car'.* *Volkswagen 的字面意思是"人民的汽车"。
2 used for emphasizing what you are saying（表示强调）真，确实：*The view is literally breathtaking.* 这景色真令人叹为观止。

literature /ˈlɪtrətʃə/ *uncountable noun* 不可数名词
books, plays and poetry that most people consider to be of high quality 文学：*Chris is studying English literature at Leeds University.* 克里斯在利兹大学学习英国文学。

litre /ˈliːtə/ *countable noun* 可数名词
a unit for measuring liquid. There are

1,000 millilitres in a litre. 升（液量单位，1 升 = 1,000 毫升）: *Adults should drink about two litres of water each day.* 成年人每天应该喝大约两升水。
→ Look at picture on P2 参见彩插第 2 页

litter¹ /ˈlɪtə/ *noun* 名词
1 uncountable 不可数 paper or rubbish that people leave lying on the ground in public places（公共场所的）垃圾，废弃物: *I hate it when I see people dropping litter.* 我讨厌看到人们乱扔垃圾。

litter 垃圾

2 countable 可数 all the babies that are born to an animal at the same time（动物一胎所生的）一窝幼崽: *Our cat has just given birth to a litter of three kittens.* 我们家猫刚刚一窝生了 3 只小猫。

litter² /ˈlɪtə/ *verb* 动词 (litters, littering, littered)
to be lying around or over a place in a messy way 使凌乱；使乱七八糟: *Broken glass littered the pavement.* 碎玻璃散落在人行道上。
▶ **littered** /ˈlɪtəd/ *adjective* 形容词: *The room was littered with toys.* 房间里乱七八糟地丢着些玩具。

little /ˈlɪtl/ *adjective* 形容词, *adverb* 副词 (littler, littlest)
1 small 小的: *We all sat at a little table.* 我们都坐在一张小桌旁。
2 short 短的: *Go down the road a little way and then turn left.* 沿着这条路走一小段，然后左拐。□ *We waited for a little while, and then we went home.* 我们等了一小会儿，然后就回家了。
3 not much 不多的；少的: *I have little money and little free time.* 我没有多少钱，也没有多少空闲。□ *I get very little sleep these days.* 这些天我睡得很少。● **little** *pronoun* 代词: *He ate little, and drank less.*

他吃得少，喝得更少。
4 not very often or not very much 不经常；不多: *They spoke very little.* 他们很少说话。
5 rather; to a small degree 稍微；略微: *He was a little bit afraid of the dog.* 他有点儿怕那条狗。

a little a small amount of something 少量；少许: *I need a little help sometimes.* 我有时需要一点帮助。

> **LANGUAGE HELP 语言提示**
> **A little** or **little**? 用 a little 还是 little？
> If you say *I have a little money*, you are saying that you have some money. If you say *I have little money*, you are saying that you do not have much money. *I have a little money* 表示有一些钱；I have little money 表示没有多少钱。

live¹ /lɪv/ *verb* 动词 (lives, living, lived)
1 to have your home in a particular place 住；居住: *She lived in New York for 10 years.* 她在纽约住了 10 年。□ *Where do you live?* 你住在哪里？
2 to have a particular type of life 以（某种方式）生活；过…生活: *Pete lives a quiet life in Cornwall.* 皮夫在康沃尔过着平静的生活。
3 to be alive 活命；生存: *We all need water to live.* 我们都需要水来生存。
4 to stay alive until you are a particular age 活: *He lived to 103.* 他活到了 103 岁。
live on something to eat a particular type of food 以食某物为生: *Sheep live mainly on grass.* 绵羊主要吃草。

live² /laɪv/ *adjective* 形容词, *adverb* 副词
1 not dead 活的: *The local market sells live animals.* 当地市场出售活的动物。
2 used for describing a television or radio programme that you watch at the same time that it happens 实况转播的；通过现场播: *They watch all the live football games on TV.* 他们在电视上观看所有现场直播的足球比赛。□ *The president's speech was broadcast live.* 总统的演讲进行了现场直播。

lively /ˈlaɪvli/ *adjective* 形容词 (livelier, liveliest)
cheerful; having a lot of energy 生气勃勃的；活跃的: *Amy is a lively, sociable little girl.* 埃米是一个活泼、合群的小女孩。

liver /ˈlɪvə/ *noun* 名词
1 countable 可数 the large organ in your body that cleans your blood 肝脏: *liver*

disease 肝病
2 the liver of some animals that you can cook and eat（动物的可食用的）肝：*They ate lamb's liver for dinner.* 他们晚饭吃了羊肝。

lives /laɪvz/
the plural of **life**（life 的复数）

living¹ /'lɪvɪŋ/ *adjective* 形容词
alive, and not dead 活的；活着的：*He is perhaps the world's most famous living artist.* 他也许是世界上在世的最著名的艺术家。□ *He has no living relatives.* 他没有健在的亲戚。

living² /'lɪvɪŋ/ *noun* 名词
1 *singular* 单数 the way you earn money 生计；谋生：*What does she do for a living?* 她做什么来谋生？□ *Scott earns a living as a lawyer.* 斯科特以当律师为生。
2 *uncountable* 不可数 the way that people live 生活方式：*Mum believes in healthy living.* 妈妈相信健康的生活方式。

'living ˌroom *countable noun* 可数名词
a room where people sit together and talk or watch television 起居室；客厅：*We were sitting in the living room watching TV.* 我们坐在客厅里看电视。

LANGUAGE HELP 语言提示
Lounge is also used in British English. 英国英语也用 lounge。

lizard /'lɪzəd/ *countable noun* 可数名词
a small animal with a long tail and rough skin 蜥蜴

load¹ /ləʊd/ *verb* 动词 (**loads, loading, loaded**)
to put a large amount of things into a vehicle or a container 给⋯装东西：*The men finished loading the van.* 那些男人装好了车。

load² /ləʊd/ *countable noun* 可数名词
something heavy that is being carried 负载；负荷：*This car can take a big load.* 这辆车能装很多东西。

loaf /ləʊf/ *countable noun* 可数名词
(**loaves**)
bread that has been shaped and baked in one piece 一条（面包）：*He bought a loaf of bread and some cheese.* 他买了一条面包和一些奶酪。

loan¹ /ləʊn/ *countable noun* 可数名词
an amount of money that you borrow 借款；贷款：*Right now it's very difficult to get a loan from a bank.* 现在很难从银行贷到款。

loan² /ləʊn/ *verb* 动词 (**loans, loaning, loaned**)
to lend something to someone 出借；借给：*Brandon loaned his girlfriend £6,000.* 布兰登借给女朋友 6,000 英镑。

loathe /ləʊð/ *verb* 动词 (**loathes, loathing, loathed**)
to dislike someone very much (*formal* 正式) 厌恶；嫌恶：*The two men loathe each other.* 这两个人互相厌恶。

loaves /ləʊvz/
the plural of **loaf**（loaf 的复数）

lobby /'lɒbi/ *countable noun* 可数名词
(**lobbies**)
the area inside the entrance to a big building（大型建筑物的）大厅，门厅：*I met her in the hotel lobby.* 我在酒店大堂遇见了她。

lobster /'lɒbstə/ *noun* 名词
a sea animal that has a hard shell and eight legs 龙虾：*She sold me two live lobsters.* 她卖给我两只活龙虾。

local /'ləʊkəl/ *adjective* 形容词
in, or relating to, the area where you live 当地的；本地的；地方的：*Susan put an advertisement in the local paper.* 苏珊在当地报纸上登了一则广告。
▶ **locally** /'ləʊkəli/ *adverb* 副词：*I prefer to shop locally.* 我喜欢购买本地产品。

located /ləʊ'keɪtɪd/ *adjective* 形容词
in a particular place 位于⋯的：*The gym and beauty salon are located on the second floor.* 健身房和美容院位于 3 层。

location /ləʊ'keɪʃən/ *countable noun* 可数名词
the place where something is 地点；位置：*For dates and locations of the meetings, call this number.* 请拨打这个号码咨询会议的日期和地点。

lock¹ /lɒk/ *verb* 动词 (**locks, locking, locked**)
1 to close a door or a container with a key 锁；锁上：*Are you sure you locked the front door?* 你确定你锁了前门吗？
2 to put a thing or a person somewhere and to close the door or the lid with a key 把⋯锁（在某处）：*She locked the case in the cupboard.* 她把箱子锁在橱柜里。
lock something away to put something in a container and to close it with a key 把某物锁起来：*She cleaned her jewellery and locked it away in a case.* 她把首饰擦干净锁好放在盒子里。

进箱子里。
lock up to lock all the windows and doors of a house or a car 锁好门窗：*Don't forget to lock up before you leave.* 走之前别忘了锁好门窗。

lock² /lɒk/ *countable noun* 可数名词
the part of a door or a container that you use to keep it shut and to make sure that no-one can open it. You can open a lock with a key. 锁：*She turned the key in the lock and opened the door.* 她转动锁上的钥匙打开了门。

locker /ˈlɒkə/ *countable noun* 可数名词
a small cupboard with a lock, that you keep things in at a school or at a sports club（学校或体育俱乐部的）存物柜，寄存柜

loft /lɒft/ *countable noun* 可数名词
the space directly under the roof of a building 闷顶；阁楼：*The loft was filled with boxes of old photos.* 阁楼里堆满了成箱的老照片。

log¹ /lɒg/ *countable noun* 可数名词
a thick piece of wood that has been cut from a tree 原木：*a log fire* 原木炉火

log² /lɒg/ *verb* 动词 (**logs, logging, logged**)
to write something down as a record of the event 记录：*They log everything that comes in and out of the warehouse.* 所有进出仓库的物品他们都有记录。
log in or **log on** to type a special secret word so that you can start using a computer or a website 登录（计算机或网站）：*She turned on her computer and logged in.* 她打开电脑登录进去。
log out or **log off** to stop using a computer or website by clicking on an instruction 退出，注销（计算机或网站）：*I logged off and went out for a walk.* 我下了网出去散步。

logic /ˈlɒdʒɪk/ *uncountable noun* 不可数名词
a way of working things out, by saying that one fact must be true if another fact is true 逻辑：*The students study philosophy and logic.* 学生们学习哲学和逻辑。

logical /ˈlɒdʒɪkəl/ *adjective* 形容词
reasonable or sensible 合乎逻辑的；合乎情理的：*There must be a logical explanation for his behaviour.* 他的行为一定有合乎逻辑的解释。

logo /ˈləʊɡəʊ/ *countable noun* 可数名词
the special design that an organization puts on all its products or advertisements（组织的）标识，标志：*The company's logo is a penguin.* 该公司的标志是一只企鹅。

LOL
short for（缩写 =）'laughing out loud'; often used in email and text messages 大笑（常用于电邮和短信）

lollipop /ˈlɒlɪˌpɒp/ *countable noun* 可数名词
a hard sweet on the end of a stick 棒棒糖：*What's your favourite flavour of lollipop?* 你最喜欢什么口味的棒棒糖？

lollipop 棒棒糖

lonely /ˈləʊnli/ *adjective* 形容词 (**lonelier, loneliest**)
1 unhappy because you are alone 孤独的；寂寞的：*Mr Garcia has been lonely since his wife died.* 加西亚先生自从妻子去世后一直很孤独。
▶ **loneliness** /ˈləʊnlinɪs/ *uncountable noun* 不可数名词：*I have a fear of loneliness.* 我害怕孤独。
2 used for describing a place where very few people go 偏僻的：*Her car broke down on a lonely country road.* 她的汽车在一条偏僻的乡间公路上抛锚了。

long¹ /lɒŋ/ *adjective* 形容词, *adverb* 副词 (**longer** /ˈlɒŋɡə/, **longest** /ˈlɒŋɡɪst/)
1 a lot of time 长时间地；长期地：*Cleaning up didn't take too long.* 清理工作没花多长时间。□ *Have you been waiting long?* 你等很久了吗？
2 lasting for a lot of time 长时间的；长期的：*We had a long meeting.* 我们开了个长会。□ *She is planning a long holiday in Europe.* 她正在计划去欧洲度一个长假。□ *'How long is the film?'* — *'About two hours.'* "电影有多长？" —— "大约两个小时。"
3 measuring a great distance from one end to the other（长度）长的：*There was a long table in the middle of the kitchen.* 厨房中央有一张长桌。□ *Lucy had long dark hair.* 露西有一头长长的黑发。
4 used for describing a great distance（距离）长的：*The long trip made him tired.* 长途旅行使他疲惫不堪。

as long as or **so long as** if 只要：*They can do what they want as long as they are not breaking the law.* 只要不犯法，他们可以想干什么就干什么。
no longer or **not any longer** used when something was true in the past, but is not true now 不再：*Ben and I are no longer in*

the same class. 我和本不在同一个班了。

long² /lɒŋ/ verb 动词 (longs, longing, longed)
to want something very much 渴望: *I'm longing to meet her.* 我渴望遇见她。

long-ˈdistance adjective 形容词
used for talking about travel or communication between places that are a long way from each other (行程或通信)长途的, 长距离的: *Long-distance travel can be very tiring.* 长途旅行可能会很累。 □ *Stacey makes a lot of long-distance calls on her mobile phone.* 斯泰茜用手机打了很多长途电话。

longitude /ˈlɒndʒɪtjuːd/ noun 名词
how far a place is to the west or east of an imaginary line that goes from the North Pole to the South Pole. Compare with **latitude**. 经度 (比较 latitude)
→ Look at picture on P9 参见彩插第9页

ˈlong ˌjump singular noun 单数名词
a sports event that involves jumping as far as you can 跳远

loo /luː/ countable noun 可数名词
a toilet (*informal* 非正式) 厕所; 洗手间: *I asked if I could go to the loo.* 我问能不能上厕所。

look¹ /lʊk/ verb 动词 (looks, looking, looked)
1 to turn your eyes in a particular direction so that you can see what is there 看; 瞧: *I looked out of the window.* 我向窗外望去。 □ *If you look over there, you'll see a lake.* 你往那边看, 会看到一个湖。 □ *Look at me!* 看我!

> **LANGUAGE HELP 语言提示**
> **Look** or **watch**? 用 look 还是 watch?
> You **look at** something that is not moving. 看静止的物体用 look at: *I asked him to look at the picture.* 我让他看图片。
> You **watch** something that is moving or changing. 看正在运动或变化的物体用 watch: *He watched the children playing outside.* 他看着外面玩耍的孩子。

2 to try to find someone or something 寻找; 寻求: *I'm looking for a child.* 我在找一个孩子。 □ *I looked everywhere for my purse.* 我到处找我的钱包。
3 seem 看上去; 看似; 显得: *'You look lovely, Marcia!'* "你模样很可爱, 马西娅!" □ *Sheila was looking sad.* 希拉显得很伤心。
4 used when you want someone to pay

attention to you (引起注意) 喂: *Look, I'm sorry. I didn't mean it.* 喂, 我很抱歉。我不是故意的。

look after someone to take care of someone 照料某人; 照看某人: *Maria looks after the kids while I'm at work.* 玛丽亚在我上班时照看孩子们。

look forward to something to want something to happen because you think you will enjoy it 盼望某事; 期待某事: *She's looking forward to her holiday in Hawaii.* 她盼望着到夏威夷度假。

look out used when you are warning someone that they are in danger 小心; 当心: *'Look out!' somebody shouted, as the lorry started to move towards us.* "当心!" 当卡车开始向我们驶来时有人喊道。

look out for something to pay attention so that you see something if it happens 留心某事物; 留神某事物: *Officers are looking out for the stolen vehicle.* 警察正在寻找失窃车辆。

look something up to find a fact or piece of information by looking in a book or on a computer (在书中或电脑上) 查找, 查阅(信息等): *I looked up your number in my address book.* 我在通讯录里查到了你的电话号码。

look² /lʊk/ singular noun 单数名词
1 when you turn your eyes in a particular direction so that you can see what is there 看; 瞧: *Lucille took a last look in the mirror.* 露西尔最后照了了照镜子。
2 a particular appearance or expression 样子; 外观; 表情: *He saw the look of surprise on her face.* 他看到她脸上惊讶的表情。 □ *Be very careful. I don't like the look of those guys.* 要多加小心。我不喜欢那些家伙的样子。

loom /luːm/ countable noun 可数名词
a machine that is used for making cloth 织布机

loop /luːp/ countable noun 可数名词
a shape like a circle in a piece of string or rope 圈; 环; 套: *On the ground beside them was a loop of rope.* 他们旁边的地上有一个绳套。

loose /luːs/ adjective 形容词 (looser, loosest)
1 not firmly fixed to something else 松的; 未固定牢的: *One of Hannah's top front teeth is loose.* 汉娜有一颗上门牙松动了。

loosen – lot

▶ **loosely** /ˈluːsli/ *adverb* 副词: *He held the gun loosely in his hand.* 他手里握着枪，握得不牢。
2 used when a person or an animal escapes from the place where they are held 不受约束的；无束缚的；自由的: *Our dog got loose and ran away yesterday.* 我们家狗昨天挣脱跑掉了。
3 not fitting closely 宽松的: *Wear loose, comfortable clothing when exercising.* 运动时穿宽松舒适的衣服。
▶ **loosely** /ˈluːsli/ *adverb* 副词: *A scarf hung loosely around his neck.* 他脖子上松松地系着一条围巾。

loosen /ˈluːsən/ *verb* 动词 (**loosens, loosening, loosened**)
to make something less tight 使变松: *He loosened his tie around his neck.* 他松了松脖子上的领带。

lord /lɔːd/ *noun* 名词
1 countable 可数 a man with a high position in society 勋爵；贵族: *Kathleen Kennedy married Lord Cavendish in 1944.* 凯瑟琳·肯尼迪于1944年嫁给卡文迪什勋爵。
2 God or Jesus Christ 神；上帝；基督: *She prayed now. 'Lord, help me to find courage.'* 她此刻祈祷起来。"主啊，求你帮助我找到勇气。"

lorry /ˈlɒri/ *countable noun* 可数名词 (**lorries**) (*American* 美国英语: **truck**)
a large vehicle that is used for transporting goods by road 卡车

lose /luːz/ *verb* 动词 (**loses, losing, lost**)
1 to not win a game 输掉（比赛）；被打败: *Our team lost the game by one point.* 我们队以1分之差输了比赛。 □ *No one likes to lose.* 没有人喜欢失败。
2 to not know where something is 遗失；丢失: *I've lost my keys.* 我把钥匙丢了。
3 to not have something any more because someone has taken it away from you 损失；丧失；失去: *I lost my job when the company shut down.* 公司倒闭后，我失业了。
lose money used when a business earns less money than it spends 亏损: *The company has been losing money for the last three years.* 这家公司过去3年来一直在亏损。
lose weight to become less heavy 减肥: *His doctor told him to lose weight.* 医生告诉他要减肥。

loser /ˈluːzə/ *countable noun* 可数名词
the person who does not win a game（比赛的）输家，败方: *In any game, there's always a winner and a loser.* 在任何比赛中，总是有赢家和输家。
bad loser a person who does not like losing, and complains about it 输不起的人
good loser a person who accepts that they have lost a game without complaining 输得起的人: *I try to be a good loser.* 我努力做一个输得起的人。

loss /lɒs/ *noun* 名词 (**losses**)
1 when you do not have something that you used to have, or when you have less of it than before 丧失；遗失；丢失: *The first symptoms are a slight fever and a loss of appetite.* 最初的症状是轻微发热和食欲不振。
2 uncountable 不可数 the death of a friend or relative 去世；逝世: *He is mourning the loss of his mother and father.* 他在哀悼逝去的父母。
3 when a business earns less money than it spends 亏损: *The company made a loss again last year.* 这家公司去年又亏损了。

lost¹ /lɒst/
→ see 见 **lose**

lost² /lɒst/ *adjective* 形容词
1 not knowing where you are; unable to find your way 迷路的；迷失方向的: *I realized I was lost.* 我意识到迷路了。
2 used for talking about something that you cannot find 丢失的；找不到的: *We complained to the airline about our lost luggage.* 我们向航空公司投诉行李丢失。

lost property *uncountable noun* 不可数名词
things that people have lost or accidentally left in a public place 失物: *Lost property should be handed to the driver.* 失物应交给司机。

lot¹ /lɒt/ *pronoun* 代词
(*also* 亦作 **lots**) a large amount 大量；许多: *I learned a lot from him.* 我从他身上学到了很多。
a lot of something or **lots of something** a large amount of something 大量…；许多…: *A lot of our land is used for growing crops.* 我们大量土地用于种庄稼。 □ *He drank lots of milk.* 他喝了很多牛奶。

lot² /lɒt/ *adverb* 副词
a lot very much or very often 很；非常；经

常：*I like you a lot.* 我非常喜欢你。▫ *Matthew goes out quite a lot.* 马修经常外出。

lotion /ˈləʊʃən/ *noun* 名词
a liquid that you use to clean or to protect your skin 洁肤液；护肤液；润肤乳：*Remember to put on some suntan lotion.* 记得涂点防晒霜。

lottery /ˈlɒtəri/ *countable noun* 可数名词 (**lotteries**)
a type of game where people buy tickets with numbers on them. If the numbers on your ticket are chosen, you win a prize. 抽奖；抽彩；乐透：*She has won the national lottery twice.* 她中了两次国家彩票。

loud /laʊd/ *adjective* 形容词 (**louder, loudest**)
with a high level of sound 大声的；响亮的；喧闹的：*The music was so loud that I couldn't hear what she was saying.* 音乐太吵了，我听不见她在说什么。
▸ **loudly** /ˈlaʊdli/ *adverb* 副词：*The cat rolled onto its back, purring loudly.* 猫翻过个身仰躺着，呼噜呼噜地喘。
out loud so that other people can hear 大声地：*Parts of the book made me laugh out loud.* 这本书有些部分让我捧腹大笑。

lounge /laʊndʒ/ *countable noun* 可数名词
1 a room in a hotel or an airport where people can sit (旅馆的) 休息室；(机场的) 候机厅：*an airport lounge* 候机厅
2 (*British* 英国英语) → see 见 **living room**

louse /laʊs/ *countable noun* 可数名词 (**lice**)
a small insect that lives on the bodies of people or animals 虱；虱子

lousy /ˈlaʊzi/ *adjective* 形容词 (**lousier, lousiest**)
very bad (*informal* 非正式) 极坏的；非常糟糕的：*The weather was lousy all weekend.* 整个周末天气都很糟糕。▫ *I was a lousy secretary.* 我是个差劲的秘书。

lovable /ˈlʌvəbəl/ *adjective* 形容词
easy to love 可爱的；讨人喜欢的：*He is a sweet, lovable dog.* 它是一只乖巧可爱的狗。

love[1] /lʌv/ *verb* 动词 (**loves, loving, loved**)
1 to care very much about someone, or to have strong romantic feelings for them 爱；关爱：*Oh, Amy, I love you.* 哦，埃米，我爱你。▫ *You will love your baby from the moment she is born.* 你从宝宝出生的那一刻起就会爱上她。
2 to like something very much 喜欢；喜爱：*I love food, I love cooking and I love eating.* 我爱食物，我爱烹饪，我爱吃。▫ *Sophie loves to play the piano.* 索菲喜欢弹钢琴。

love[2] /lʌv/ *uncountable noun* 不可数名词
1 the very strong warm feeling that you have when you care very much about someone, or you have strong romantic feelings for them 爱；关爱：*In the four years since we married, our love has grown stronger.* 结婚4年来，我们的爱情日益牢固了。▫ *a love story* 爱情故事
2 used at the end of a letter to a friend or relative (信末结语) 爱你的：*The letter ended, 'love from Anna.'* 信的结尾是："爱你的安娜。"
fall in love to start to love someone in a romantic way 爱上：*Maria fell in love with Danny as soon as she met him.* 玛丽亚一见到丹尼就爱上了他。

lovely /ˈlʌvli/ *adjective* 形容词 (**lovelier, loveliest**)
beautiful, very nice or very enjoyable 可爱的；迷人的；漂亮的；极好的：*You look lovely, Marcia.* 你模样很可爱，马西娅。▫ *Sam has a lovely voice.* 萨姆有一副好嗓子。▫ *'Thank you for a lovely evening!'* "谢谢你，我们度过了一个愉快的夜晚！"

lover /ˈlʌvə/ *countable noun* 可数名词
1 a person who has a sexual relationship, but is not married 情人；情侣：*Every Thursday she met her lover Leon.* 每周四她都会和情人利昂相见。
2 a person who likes something very much 爱好者：*The website is for music lovers.* 这个网站是为音乐爱好者创建的。

loving /ˈlʌvɪŋ/ *adjective* 形容词
feeling or showing love for other people 有爱的；充满爱的：*My parents had a loving relationship.* 我父母关系很好。
▸ **lovingly** /ˈlʌvɪŋli/ *adverb* 副词：*Brian looked lovingly at Mary.* 布赖恩深情地看着玛丽。

low /ləʊ/ *adjective* 形容词, *adverb* 副词 (**lower, lowest**)
1 close to the ground 低的 (地)；矮的 (地)；接近地面的 (地)：*It was late afternoon and the sun was low in the sky.* 那是傍晚时分，太阳低垂。▫ *An aeroplane flew low over the beach.* 一架飞机在海滩上低空飞行。
2 small in amount (数量) 低的，少的：*House prices are still very low.* 房价仍然很低。
3 very bad 不好的；差的：*The hospital was criticized for its low standards of care.* 这家医院因护理水平低下而受到批评。

4 deep and quiet 低沉的；轻声的：*His voice was so low she couldn't hear him.* 他声音太低了，她听不见。

lower¹ /ˈləʊə/ *adjective* 形容词
used for describing something that is under another thing 下面的：*Emily bit her lower lip nervously.* 埃米莉紧张地咬着下唇。

lower² /ˈləʊə/ *verb* 动词 (**lowers, lowering, lowered**)
1 to move something down 放下；使下降：*They lowered the coffin into the grave.* 他们将棺材放到墓穴中。
2 to make something less 减少；降低：*The Central Bank lowered interest rates yesterday.* 中央银行昨天下调了利率。

ˌlower ˈcase *uncountable noun* 不可数名词
small letters, not capital letters. Compare with **upper case**. 小写字母（比较 upper case）：*Type your user name and password in lower case.* 用小写字母输入用户名和密码。

loyal /ˈlɔɪəl/ *adjective* 形容词
keeping your friends or your beliefs, even in difficult times 忠诚的；忠实的：*They have always stayed loyal to the Republican Party.* 他们一直忠于共和党。
▶ **loyally** /ˈlɔɪəli/ *adverb* 副词：*The staff loyally supported their boss.* 员工们一心一意地支持他们的老板。

loyalty /ˈlɔɪəlti/ *uncountable noun* 不可数名词
when you continue to be someone's friend, or to believe in something, even in difficult times 忠诚；忠实；忠心：*I believe in family loyalty.* 我相信要忠于家庭。

Ltd
a written short form of（书面缩写＝）'Limited', used after the name of a company 有限（责任）公司（用于公司名称之后）：*Holmes Healthfoods Ltd* 霍姆斯健康食品有限公司

luck /lʌk/ *uncountable noun* 不可数名词
the good things that happen to you, that have not been caused by yourself or other people 好运；幸运：*Before the game, we shook hands and wished each other luck.* 比赛前，我们握手互祝好运。
▶ **bad luck** the bad things that happen to you, that have not been caused by yourself or other people 倒霉；厄运：*We had a lot of bad luck during the first half of this season.* 我们在本赛季上半段运气很不好。

good luck or **best of luck** used for telling someone that you hope they will be successful in something they are trying to do (*informal* 非正式) 祝好运；祝成功

luckily /ˈlʌkɪli/ *adverb* 副词
used when you want to say that it is good that something happened 幸好；幸而：*Luckily, nobody was seriously injured in the accident.* 幸运的是，事故中没有人受重伤。

lucky /ˈlʌki/ *adjective* 形容词 (**luckier, luckiest**)
1 having good luck 运气好的；幸运的：*I am luckier than most people here. I have a job.* 我比这里的大多数人都幸运。我有工作。
□ *Rob is very lucky to be alive after that accident.* 罗布在那次事故后还活着，真是幸运。
2 bringing success or good luck 带来好运的：*I'm wearing my lucky shirt. How can I lose?* 我穿着幸运衫。我怎么会输呢？

luggage /ˈlʌɡɪdʒ/ *uncountable noun* 不可数名词
the bags that you take with you when you travel 行李：*Do you have any luggage?* 你有行李吗？

> **LANGUAGE HELP** 语言提示
> **Luggage** is an uncountable noun. If you want to talk about one bag or suitcase, use **a piece of luggage** or **some luggage**.
> *luggage 是不可数名词，表示单件行李可用 a piece of luggage 或 some luggage。

luggage 行李

ˈluggage ˌrack *countable noun* 可数名词
a shelf for putting luggage on in a train or a bus（火车或公共汽车上的）行李架

lukewarm /ˌluːkˈwɔːm/ *adjective* 形容词
slightly warm 微温的；不冷不热的：*Freddy*

drank the lukewarm coffee. 弗雷迪喝了那杯温暾的咖啡。

lullaby /ˈlʌləbaɪ/ *countable noun* 可数名词 (lullabies)
a quiet song that you sing to a baby to help it to go to sleep 摇篮曲；催眠曲

lump /lʌmp/ *countable noun* 可数名词
1 a solid piece of something 块：*a lump of coal* 一块煤
2 a small, hard part on or in your body 肿块：*I've got a painful lump in my mouth.* 我嘴里有个肿块很疼。

lumpy /ˈlʌmpi/ *adjective* 形容词 (lumpier, lumpiest)
containing lumps or covered with lumps 有块状物的；为块状物所覆盖的：*I lay on the lumpy bed and listened to the noise of traffic outside.* 我躺在高低不平的床上，听着外面车辆的喧闹声。

lunch /lʌntʃ/ *noun* 名词 (lunches)
the meal that you have in the middle of the day 午饭；午餐：*Are you free for lunch?* 你有空儿吃个午饭吗？ ◻ *Dad doesn't enjoy business lunches.* 爸爸不喜欢商务午餐。

lunchtime /ˈlʌntʃtaɪm/ *uncountable noun* 不可数名词
the time of the day when people have their lunch 午餐时间：*Could we meet at lunchtime?* 我们能在午餐时间见个面吗？

lung /lʌŋ/ *countable noun* 可数名词
one of the two large organs inside your chest that you use for breathing 肺：*Her father died of lung cancer last year.* 她父亲去年死于肺癌。

lush /lʌʃ/ *adjective* 形容词 (lusher, lushest)
having a lot of very healthy grass or plants 茂盛的；茂密的；草木繁茂的：*The lawn was lush and green.* 草坪郁郁葱葱。

luxurious /lʌɡˈʒʊəriəs/ *adjective* 形容词
very comfortable and expensive 奢华的；豪华的：*My aunt and uncle stayed in a luxurious hotel in Paris.* 我叔叔婶婶住在巴黎一家豪华酒店里。

luxury /ˈlʌkʃəri/ *noun* 名词 (luxuries)
1 *uncountable* 不可数 when you are able to buy all the beautiful and expensive things that you want 奢侈；奢华：*He leads a life of luxury.* 他过着奢华的生活。
2 *countable* 可数 something pleasant and expensive that people want but do not really need 奢侈品：*Having a holiday is a luxury they can no longer afford.* 度假是他们再也负担不起的奢侈品。

lying /ˈlaɪɪŋ/
→ see 见 **lie**

lyrics /ˈlɪrɪks/ *plural noun* 复数名词
the words of a song 歌词：*The music is great, and the lyrics are so funny.* 音乐很棒，歌词也很有趣。

Mm

macaroni /ˌmækəˈrəʊni/ *uncountable noun* 不可数名词
a type of pasta made in the shape of short, hollow tubes 通心面；通心粉

machine /məˈʃiːn/ *countable noun* 可数名词
a piece of equipment that uses electricity or an engine to do a particular job 机器；机械: *I put the coin in the coffee machine.* 我把硬币投进咖啡机里。

machinery /məˈʃiːnəri/ *uncountable noun* 不可数名词
large pieces electrical equipment that do a particular job 机械；大型机器: *We need to invest in new machinery for our factories.* 我们得投资给工厂添置新机械设备。

mad /mæd/ *adjective* 形容词 (**madder, maddest**)
1 having a medical condition that makes you behave in a strange way (*informal* 非正式) 疯的；精神错乱的: *She was afraid of going mad.* 她怕自己会疯掉。
2 very stupid (*informal* 非正式) 非常愚蠢的: *You're going to swim in that water? You must be mad!* 你要在那样的水里游泳？你疯了吧！
3 not controlled 失控的；狂乱的: *There was a mad rush to get out of the building.* 人们疯了般冲出大楼。
▸ **madly** /ˈmædli/ *adverb* 副词: *People on the streets were waving madly.* 街上的人们疯狂地挥手。
be mad about something/someone to like something or someone very much (*informal* 非正式) 迷恋某事物 / 某人: *I'm mad about sports.* 我痴迷体育。 □ *He's mad about you.* 他很迷恋你。
drive someone mad to make someone very angry (*informal* 非正式) 令某人狂怒: *Stop asking questions! You're driving me mad!* 别再问了！你要把我逼疯了！
go mad to become very angry (*informal* 非正式) 大发雷霆: *My mum went mad when I told her about the vase.* 我把花瓶的事儿告诉了妈妈，她听后火冒三丈。

madam /ˈmædəm/ *also 亦作* **Madam** *noun* 名词
1 a polite way of talking to a woman (尊称) 女士，夫人: *Good morning, madam.* 早上好，夫人。
2 a word that you use at the beginning of a formal letter to a woman (正式信函抬头用语) 女士: *Dear Madam ...* 尊敬的女士……

made¹ /meɪd/
→ see 见 **make**

made² /meɪd/ *adjective* 形容词
made of something used for describing the substance that was used to make something 用某物做成的: *The top of the table is made of glass.* 桌面是玻璃材质。

madly /ˈmædli/ *adverb* 副词
1 very much 非常；十分: *She is madly in love with him.* 她爱他爱得死去活来。
2 in a wild way 疯狂地；发疯似的: *The crowd was cheering madly.* 众人疯狂地欢呼。

magazine /ˌmæɡəˈziːn/ *countable noun* 可数名词
a thin book with stories and pictures that you can buy every week or every month 杂志；期刊: *a fashion magazine* 时尚杂志

magic /ˈmædʒɪk/ *uncountable noun* 不可数名词
1 a special power that seems to make impossible things happen 魔法；法术: *Most children believe in magic.* 大多数孩子相信魔法。
2 tricks that a person performs in order to entertain people 魔术；戏法: *His stage act combines magic, music and humour.* 他的舞台表演融合了魔术、音乐和幽默。

magical /ˈmædʒɪkəl/ *adjective* 形容词
seeming to use magic 有魔力的；有神奇力量的: *I loved the story of a little boy who has magical powers.* 我喜欢那个讲一个小男孩有魔法的故事。

magician /məˈdʒɪʃən/ *countable noun* 可数名词
a person who entertains people by doing magic tricks 魔术师

magnet /ˈmæɡnɪt/ *countable noun* 可数名词
a piece of special metal that attracts iron towards it 磁体；磁铁: *The children used a magnet to find objects made of iron.* 孩子们用一块磁铁寻找铁质物件。

magnet 磁铁

magnetic /mæɡˈnetɪk/ *adjective* 形容词
1 acting like a magnet 有磁性的；磁铁似的: *Because steel is made from iron, it is magnetic.* 由于钢是铁炼成的，所以它有磁性。
2 describing objects that use a magnetic substance to hold information that can be read by computers (机读信息存储器件) 使用磁性材料的: *The bank sent him an ID card with a magnetic strip.* 银行寄给他一张磁条 ID 卡。

magnificent /mæɡˈnɪfɪsənt/ *adjective* 形容词
extremely good or beautiful 极好的；极美的: *They bought a magnificent country house.* 他们买了一幢乡间豪宅。

magnify /ˈmæɡnɪfaɪ/ *verb* 动词 (**magnifies, magnifying, magnified**)
to make something look larger than it really is 放大；扩大: *This telescope magnifies objects 11 times.* 这架望远镜可以将物体放大 11 倍。

magnifying glass *countable noun* 可数名词 (**magnifying glasses**)
a piece of glass that makes objects seem to be bigger than they really are 放大镜

maid /meɪd/ *countable noun* 可数名词
a woman whose job is to clean rooms in a hotel or private house (宾馆的)女服务员，女佣洁员；(私宅的)女佣，保姆: *A maid comes every morning to clean the hotel room.* 一个女保洁员每天早上来打扫房间。

mail¹ /meɪl/ *uncountable noun* 不可数名词
the letters and packages or email that you receive 邮件: *There was no mail this morning.* 今天早上没有邮件。 □ *With web-based email, you can check your mail from anywhere.* 有了网络电邮，你可以随处查看邮件。

mail² /meɪl/ *verb* 动词 (**mails, mailing, mailed**) (*American* 美国英语)
→ see 见 **post**: *I'll mail it to you on Friday.* 周五我会给你寄过去。

mailbox /ˈmeɪlbɒks/ *countable noun* 可数名词 (**mailboxes**)
1 (*American* 美国英语) → see 见 **letter box**
2 (*American* 美国英语) → see 见 **postbox**
3 the file on a computer where your email is stored (计算机上存储电子邮件的)电子邮箱: *There were 30 new messages in his mailbox.* 他邮箱里有 30 条新信息。

mail order *uncountable noun* 不可数名词
a system of buying goods, in which you order things from a website or a special book (called a catalogue), and the company sends them to you by post 邮购: *The toys are available by mail order.* 这些玩具可以邮购。

main /meɪn/ *adjective* 形容词
most important 主要的；最重要的: *The main reason I came today was to say sorry.* 我今天来主要是为了赔个不是。

main clause *countable noun* 可数名词
a part of a sentence that can stand alone as a complete sentence 主句

mainland /ˈmeɪnlænd/ *singular noun* 单数名词
the largest piece of land in a country, not including any smaller islands (国家的)大陆，本土: *The island's teenagers go to school on the mainland.* 岛上青少年到本土上学。

mainly /ˈmeɪnli/ *adverb* 副词
used for saying that a statement is mostly true 主要；大部分: *The African people living here are mainly from Senegal.* 在这儿生活的非洲人大多来自塞内加尔。

maintain /meɪnˈteɪn/ *verb* 动词 (**maintains, maintaining, maintained**)
1 to make something continue at the same level 维持；保持: *The army is trying to maintain order in the country.* 军队力图维护国家秩序。
2 to keep a road, building, vehicle or machine in good condition 维修；保养: *The house costs a lot to maintain.* 房子维修花销不菲。

maintenance /ˈmeɪntɪnəns/ *uncountable noun* 不可数名词
the process of keeping something in good condition 维护；维修；保养: *Maintenance*

majestic – malaria

work on the building starts next week. 大楼维修工作下周启动。

majestic /məˈdʒestɪk/ *adjective* 形容词
very beautiful and grand 壮丽的；壮美的：*We will miss the majestic mountains and the emerald green sea.* 我们会怀念这壮丽的群山和翠绿的大海。

majesty /ˈmædʒɪsti/ *uncountable noun* 不可数名词
the quality of being beautiful and grand 壮丽；壮美：*The poem describes the majesty of the mountains.* 这首诗描绘了山的壮丽。
Your/His/Her Majesty used when you are talking to or about a king or a queen 陛下（对国王或女王的尊称）：*His Majesty would like to see you now.* 陛下现在要召见你。

major¹ /ˈmeɪdʒə/ *adjective* 形容词
1 more important than other things 主要的；重大的：*Homelessness is a major problem in some cities.* 无家可归问题是一些城市的一大难题。
2 used for talking about a scale (= a series of musical notes) with half steps in sound between the third and fourth and the seventh and eighth notes. Compare with **minor**. 大调的（比较 minor）：*A C major scale uses only the white keys on a piano.* *C 大调音阶只用到钢琴上的白键。

major² /ˈmeɪdʒə/ *countable noun* 可数名词
an officer of high rank in the army 少校：*He was a major in the war.* 他在那场战争中是个少校。

majority /məˈdʒɒrɪti/ *singular noun* 单数名词
more than half of the people or things in a group 多数；过半数：*The majority of my patients are women.* 我的患者半数以上是女性。

make¹ /meɪk/ *verb* 动词 (**makes, making, made**)
1 to produce, build or create something 制造；建造；创造：*She makes all her own clothes.* 她的衣服都是自己做的。 □ *We make solid wood furniture.* 我们制作实木家具。
2 used with nouns to show that someone does or says something（与名词连用）出，作出：*I'd just like to make a comment.* 我只想说几句。 □ *I made a few phone calls.* 我打了几个电话。
3 to cause someone to do or feel something 使；致使；引起：*The smoke made him cough.* 烟呛得他咳嗽。 □ *My boss's behaviour makes me so angry!* 上司的做派让我非常生气！
4 to force someone to do something 迫使；强迫：*Mum made me apologize to him.* 妈妈让我向他道歉。
5 to earn money 赚，挣（钱）：*He's good-looking, smart and makes lots of money.* 他长得帅，脑子灵，挣钱多。
6 used for saying what two numbers add up to 等于；合计为：*Four twos make eight.* *4 个 2 加起来等于 8。
make something into something to change something so that it becomes a different thing 使一物变为另一物：*They made their flat into a beautiful home.* 他们将公寓变成了美丽的家。
make something/someone out to be able to see, hear or understand something 分辨出（或弄清楚）某物/某人：*I could just make out a tall figure of a man.* 我只看见一个高大男子的身影。 □ *I couldn't make out what he was saying.* 我搞不懂他的话。
make something up to invent something such as a story or excuse 编造（故事、借口等）：*It was all lies. I made it all up.* 那都是瞎话。我编的。
make up to become friends again after an argument 和好；言归于好：*You two are always fighting and then making up again.* 你们俩总是斗来斗去，然后又言归于好。

make² /meɪk/ *countable noun* 可数名词
the name of the company that made something 品牌；牌子：*What make of car do you drive?* 你开什么牌子的车？

maker /ˈmeɪkə/ *countable noun* 可数名词
the person or company that makes something 生产者；制造者：*Japan's two largest car makers reported increased sales last month.* 日本两大汽车生产商上月公布销售额实现增长。

make-up also 亦作 **makeup** *uncountable noun* 不可数名词
the creams and powders that people put on their face to make themselves look more attractive. Actors also wear make-up. 化妆品：*She doesn't usually wear much make-up.* 她平常不怎么化妆。

malaria /məˈleəriə/ *uncountable noun* 不可数名词
a serious disease that small flying insects (= mosquitoes) carry 疟疾

male /meɪl/ ***countable noun*** 可数名词
1 a person or an animal that belongs to the sex that does not have babies 男性；雄性：*Two 17-year-old males were arrested at their school on Tuesday.* 星期二两名17岁男性在学校被捕。● **male** *adjective* 形容词：*Two male cats were fighting in the street.* 两只公猫在街上打架。
2 a man or a boy 男人；男孩：*This disease affects males more than females.* 这种疾病对于男性的影响大于女性。● **male** *adjective* 形容词：*The rate of male unemployment has gone up.* 男性失业率上升。

mall /mɔːl, mæl/ ***countable noun*** 可数名词 (*American* 美国英语)
→ see 见 **shopping centre**

mammal /ˈmæməl/ ***countable noun*** 可数名词
an animal that feeds its babies with milk 哺乳动物

man /mæn/ *noun* 名词 (**men**)
1 *countable* 可数 an adult male human 男人；成年男子：*A handsome man walked into the room.* 一位英俊的男士走进屋里。 □ *Both men and women will enjoy this film.* 男人和女人都会喜欢这部影片。
2 used for talking about all humans, including both males and females. Some people dislike this use, and prefer to say **human beings** or **people**. 人，人类 (有人反感此用法，倾向于用 human beings 或 people)：*Man first arrived in the Americas thousands of years ago.* 人类数千年前首次抵达美洲。

manage /ˈmænɪdʒ/ *verb* 动词 (**manages, managing, managed**)
1 to control a business 管理 (企业)：*Two years after starting the job, he was managing the shop.* 入职两年后他当上了店铺主管。
2 to succeed in doing something, especially something difficult 成功做到 (尤指难事)：*Three girls managed to escape the fire.* *3 个女孩设法逃出了火场。

management /ˈmænɪdʒmənt/ *noun* 名词
1 *uncountable* 不可数 the control of a business or other organization 经营；管理：*The zoo needed better management, not more money.* 动物园需要的是加强管理，而不是更多资金。
2 the people who control a business or other organization 经营者；管理层：*The management is trying hard to keep employees happy.* 管理层想方设法保持员工的幸福感。

manager /ˈmænɪdʒə/ ***countable noun*** 可数名词
a person who controls all or part of a business or organization (企业或其他组织的) 管理者，经理：*Each department manager is responsible for staff training.* 各部门经理负责员工培训。

mane /meɪn/ ***countable noun*** 可数名词
the long, thick hair that grows from the neck of some animals 鬃毛；鬣：*You can wash the horse's mane at the same time as its body.* 你可以同时清洗马身和马鬃。

manga /ˈmæŋɡə/ ***uncountable noun*** 不可数名词
a type of Japanese comic book (日本) 漫画：*He looks like a character from a manga comic.* 他长得像一个日本漫画人物。

mango /ˈmæŋɡəʊ/ *noun* 名词 (**mangoes** or 或 **mangos**)
a large, sweet, yellow or red fruit that grows on trees in hot countries 杧果；芒果

manicure /ˈmænɪˌkjʊə/ *verb* 动词 (**manicures, manicuring, manicured**)
to care for your hands or nails by rubbing cream into your skin and cleaning and cutting your nails 护理 (手)；修剪 (指甲)：*She carefully manicured her long nails.* 她精心修剪长长的指甲。● **manicure** *countable noun* 可数名词：*I have an appointment for a manicure this afternoon.* 我今天下午约了美甲。

manipulate /məˈnɪpjʊˌleɪt/ *verb* 动词 (**manipulates, manipulating, manipulated**)
to control people or events for your own benefit (为私利而) 操纵，控制 (人或事件)：*The government is trying to manipulate public opinion.* 政府想操控舆论。

mankind /ˌmænˈkaɪnd/ ***uncountable noun*** 不可数名词
used for talking about all humans when you are considering them as a group. Some people dislike this use. 人类 (有人反感此用法)：*We hope for a better future for all mankind.* 我们希望全人类拥有更加美好的未来。

man-ˈmade also 亦作 **manmade** *adjective* 形容词
made by people 人工的；人造的；人为的：

Some of the world's problems are man-made. 有些世界问题是人为的。▫ When the dam was built, three man-made lakes were created. 大坝建成后，造出了 3 座人工湖。

manner /ˈmænə/ **noun** 名词
1 singular 单数 the way that you do something 方式；做法：She smiled in a friendly manner. 她友好地微笑。
2 [manners] plural 复数 how polite you are when you are with other people 礼貌：He dressed well and had perfect manners. 他衣冠楚楚，彬彬有礼。▫ Is it bad manners to talk on a mobile phone on the train? 在火车上打手机是不礼貌的吗？

manoeuvre /məˈnuːvə/ **verb** 动词 (**manoeuvres, manoeuvring, manoeuvred**)
to skilfully move something into or out of a difficult position（在进出不便的地方）熟练移动（物体）：He manoeuvred the car through the narrow gate. 他熟练地驾车穿过了窄窄的大门。● **manoeuvre noun** 名词：The aeroplanes performed some difficult manoeuvres. 飞机表演了一些高难度的机动动作。

mansion /ˈmænʃən/ **countable noun** 可数名词
a very large, expensive house 宅第；大宅：He bought an eighteenth-century mansion in Berkshire. 他买下了伯克郡一座 18 世纪的大宅。

mantelpiece /ˈmæntəlˌpiːs/ **countable noun** 可数名词
a shelf above the place where a fire is in a room 壁炉架；壁炉台

manual[1] /ˈmænjuəl/ **adjective** 形容词
1 used for describing work in which you use your hands or your physical strength 体力的；手工的：He began his career as a manual worker. 他初入职场干的是体力活儿。
2 operated by hand, rather than by electricity or a motor 手动的；人工的：We used a manual pump to get the water out of the hole. 我们用一台手摇泵排出坑里的水。

manual[2] /ˈmænjuəl/ **countable noun** 可数名词
a book that tells you how to do something 手册；说明书：He advised me to read the instruction manual first. 他建议我先看一下操作手册。

manufacture /ˌmænjuˈfæktʃə/ **verb** 动词 (**manufactures, manufacturing, manufactured**)
to make something in a factory 制造；生产：The company manufactures plastics. 该公司生产塑料。● **manufacture uncountable noun** 不可数名词：Coal is used in the manufacture of steel. 煤炭用于炼钢。

manufacturer /ˌmænjuˈfæktʃərə/ **countable noun** 可数名词
a company that makes large amounts of things 制造商；生产商：He works for the world's largest doll manufacturer. 他在世界最大的玩偶厂家工作。

manufacturing /ˌmænjuˈfæktʃərɪŋ/ **uncountable noun** 不可数名词
the business of making things in factories 制造；生产：During the 1980s, 300,000 workers in the manufacturing industry lost their jobs. 20 世纪 80 年代，30 万制造业工人丢了饭碗。

many /ˈmeni/ **adjective** 形容词，**adverb** 副词
1 used for talking about a large number of people or things 很多；许多；众多：Many people would disagree with that opinion. 很多人会不赞同那个看法。▫ Not many shops are open on Sunday. 星期天开门的店铺不多。● **many pronoun** 代词：He made a list of his friends. There weren't many. 他罗列了一下朋友的名字。人不多。
2 used when you are asking or replying to questions about numbers of things or people（用于提问或回答数量）多少，多：'How many of their songs were hits?' — 'Not very many.' "他们的歌火起来的有多少？" —— "不太多。"

many of used for talking about a large number of people or things 很多；许多：Why do many of us feel that we need to get married? 为什么我们很多人觉得得结婚呢？

LANGUAGE HELP 语言提示
Many or **much**? 用 many 还是 much？You use **many** with countable nouns. many 后接可数名词：There are many books on the subject. 有很多书讲这个话题。
You use **much** if you want to talk about a large amount of something. much 表示某物数量很大：There's too much sugar in my tea. 我茶里放的糖太多了。

map /mæp/ *countable noun* 可数名词
a drawing of a particular area such as a city or a country, that shows things like mountains, rivers and roads 地图：*The detailed map helps tourists find their way around the city.* 详细的地图帮助游客在城中找到他们的路线。
→ Look at picture on P9 参见彩插第 9 页

map 地图

marathon /ˈmærəθən/ *countable noun* 可数名词
a race in which people run a distance of 26 miles (= about 42 km) 马拉松：*He is running in his first marathon next weekend.* 他下周要跑自己的第一个马拉松。

marble /ˈmɑːbəl/ *noun* 名词
1 *uncountable* 不可数 a type of very hard rock that people use to make parts of buildings or statues (= models of people) 大理石
2 [**marbles**] *plural* 复数 a children's game that you play with small balls made of coloured glass (called marbles) 弹玻璃球游戏：*Two boys were playing marbles.* 两个男孩儿在弹玻璃球。

march /mɑːtʃ/ *verb* 动词 (**marches, marching, marched**)
1 to walk somewhere with regular steps, as a group 列队行进：*Some soldiers were marching down the street.* 一些士兵在街上列队行进。● **march** *countable noun* 可数名词 (**marches**)：*After a short march, the soldiers entered the village.* 短暂行军之后，士兵们进入了村子。
2 to walk through the streets in a large group of people in order to show that you disagree with something（表示抗议的）游行：*Thousands of people marched through the city to protest against the war.* 数千人在市内游行抗议这场战争。● **march** *countable noun* 可数名词 (**marches**)：*Organizers expect 300,000 protesters to join the march.* 组织者预计会有 30 万抗议者加入这场游行。
3 to walk somewhere quickly, often because you are angry（常因生气而）快步走：*He marched into the kitchen without knocking.* 他没敲门就闯进了厨房。

March /mɑːtʃ/ *noun* 名词
the third month of the year 三月：*I flew to Milwaukee in March.* 我 3 月飞到了密尔沃基。□ *She was born on 6th March, 1920.* 她出生于 1920 年 3 月 6 日。

margarine /ˌmɑːdʒəˈriːn/ *noun* 名词
a yellow substance that is made from vegetable oil, and is similar to butter 人造黄油；人造奶油

margin /ˈmɑːdʒɪn/ *countable noun* 可数名词
1 the difference between two amounts 差额：*The team won with a 5-point margin.* 该队以 5 分优势获胜。
2 the empty space down the side of a page 页边空白：*She wrote comments in the margin.* 她在页边空白处写了评注。

marine /məˈriːn/ *adjective* 形容词
relating to the sea 海洋的：*The film shows the colourful marine life in the Indian Ocean.* 影片呈现了印度洋丰富多彩的海洋生物。

marital /ˈmærɪtəl/ *adjective* 形容词
relating to marriage 婚姻的：*When I was thirteen, my parents started having marital problems.* 我 13 岁那年，父母的婚姻开始出现问题。

mark¹ /mɑːk/ *countable noun* 可数名词
1 a small area of something such as dirt that has accidentally got onto a surface or piece of clothing 斑点；污迹；痕迹：*There was a red paint mark on the wall.* 墙上有一个红漆点子。
2 a written or printed symbol 记号；标记：*a question mark* 问号

mark² /mɑːk/ *verb* 动词 (**marks, marking, marked**)
1 to write a particular word on something 标记；在…上做记号：*She marked the bill 'paid'.* 她在账单上标了"已付"。
2 to write a number or letter on a student's work to show how good it is 批改；给…打分：*The teacher was marking essays after class.* 老师课后在批改作文。
3 to show where a particular thing is 表明，

显示（位置）: *A big hole in the road marks the place where the bomb landed.* 公路上的一个大坑显示了炸弹落下的地方。

market¹ /ˈmɑːkɪt/ ***countable noun*** 可数名词
1 a place where people buy and sell products 市场；集市: *They usually buy their fruit and vegetables at the market.* 他们一般去市场买水果和蔬菜。
2 the people who want to buy a particular product 市场（指有购买意愿的人群）: *The market for organic wines is growing.* 有机葡萄酒的市场在增长。

market² /ˈmɑːkɪt/ ***verb*** 动词 (**markets, marketing, marketed**)
to advertise and sell a product 营销；推销；推广: *The products were marketed under a different brand name in Europe.* 这些产品换了个牌子在欧洲推广。

▶ **marketing** /ˈmɑːkɪtɪŋ/ ***uncountable noun*** 不可数名词: *She works in the marketing department of a large company.* 她供职于一家大公司的营销部。

marmalade /ˈmɑːməleɪd/ ***uncountable noun*** 不可数名词
a food like jam that is usually made from oranges 橘子酱；马茉兰果酱

marriage /ˈmærɪdʒ/ ***noun*** 名词
1 *countable* 可数 the relationship between two people who are married 婚姻: *After fifteen years together, they still have a happy marriage.* 他们在一起15年了，婚姻仍然美满。
2 the time when two people get married 结婚: *a marriage ceremony* 婚礼

married /ˈmærɪd/ ***adjective*** 形容词
having a husband or wife 结婚的；已婚的: *We have been married for 14 years.* 我们结婚14年了。 □ *She is married to an Englishman.* 她嫁给了一个英格兰人。

marry /ˈmæri/ ***verb*** 动词 (**marries, marrying, married**)
to legally become partners in a special ceremony 结婚；娶；嫁: *I thought he would change after we got married.* 我以为我们婚后他会改变的。 □ *They married a month after they met.* 他们认识一个月后就结婚了。 □ *He wants to marry her.* 他想娶她。

marsh /mɑːʃ/ ***noun*** 名词 (**marshes**)
a soft, wet area of land 沼泽；草本沼泽

marshmallow /ˈmɑːʃmæləʊ/ ***countable noun*** 可数名词

a soft pink or white sweet 棉花软糖

marvellous /ˈmɑːvələs/ ***adjective*** 形容词
very good 非常好的；非凡的: *It's a marvellous piece of music.* 这是一支令人叫绝的乐曲。

masculine /ˈmæskjʊlɪn/ ***adjective*** 形容词
1 typical of men 男性的；阳刚的: *She has a deep, rather masculine voice.* 她有一副低沉、相当男性化的嗓子。
2 used for describing a noun, pronoun or adjective that has a different form from other forms (such as 'feminine' forms) in some languages. Compare with **feminine**. （名词、代词或形容词）阳性的（比较 **feminine**）

mash /mæʃ/ ***verb*** 动词 (**mashes, mashing, mashed**)
to press food to make it soft 捣烂（食物）；把…捣成糊: *Mash the bananas with a fork.* 用叉子把香蕉捣成糊。

mask /mɑːsk/ ***countable noun*** 可数名词
something that you wear over your face to protect it or to hide it 面具；面罩: *A man wearing a mask entered the restaurant at about 1.40 p.m. and took out a gun.* 下午1点40分左右，一名蒙面男子进入饭店后掏出一把枪。 □ *Wear a mask to protect yourself from the smoke.* 戴上面罩，防止吸入烟雾。

masked /mɑːskt/ ***adjective*** 形容词
wearing a mask 蒙面的；戴面具（或面罩）的: *Two masked men came through the doors carrying guns.* 两名蒙面男子持枪进门。

mass /mæs/ ***noun*** 名词 (**masses**)
1 *singular* 单数 a large amount of something 大量；许多: *She had a mass of black hair.* 她有一头浓密的黑发。
2 (also 亦作 **Mass**) a Christian church ceremony, especially in a Roman Catholic church（尤指天主教的）弥撒: *She went to Mass each day.* 她每天做弥撒。
3 the amount of physical matter that something contains 质量: *Pluto and Triton have nearly the same size, mass and density.* 冥王星和海卫一的体积、质量和密度几乎相同。

masses of something a large amount of something (*informal* 非正式) 大量某物；许多某物: *I have masses of work to do.* 我有一大堆的工作要做。

massacre /ˈmæsəkə/ ***noun*** 名词
an occasion when a large number of

people are killed at the same time in a violent and cruel way 屠杀: *Her mother died in the massacre.* 她母亲死于这场大屠杀。● **massacre** *verb* 动词 (**massacres, massacring, massacred**): *Three hundred people were massacred by the soldiers.* *300 人遭到士兵们的屠杀。

massage /ˈmæsɑːʒ/ *noun* 名词
the activity of rubbing someone's body to make them relax or to reduce their pain 按摩; 推拿: *Alex asked me if I wanted a massage.* 亚历克斯问我要不要按摩。● **massage** *verb* 动词 (**massages, massaging, massaged**): *She was massaging her right foot.* 她在按摩自己的右脚。

massive /ˈmæsɪv/ *adjective* 形容词
very large 巨大的; 庞大的: *They borrowed massive amounts of money.* 他们大量举债。

mast /mɑːst/ *countable noun* 可数名词
one of the tall poles that support the sails of a boat 桅; 桅杆

master¹ /ˈmɑːstə/ *countable noun* 可数名词
1 the person who controls another person or an animal 主人: *The dog was listening to its master's voice.* 这条狗在听主人的声音
2 someone who is extremely skilled at a particular activity 大师; 高手: *She was a master of the English language.* 她是英语高手。

master² /ˈmɑːstə/ *verb* 动词 (**masters, mastering, mastered**)
to learn how to do something well 掌握; 精通: *David soon mastered the skills of baseball.* 戴维很快掌握了棒球技术。

masterpiece /ˈmɑːstəˌpiːs/ *countable noun* 可数名词
an extremely good painting, novel, film or other work of art 杰作; 佳作; 精品: *His book is a masterpiece.* 他的书是一部精品。

master's deˌgree *countable noun* 可数名词
a university qualification that is of a higher level than an ordinary degree 硕士学位

mat /mæt/ *countable noun* 可数名词
1 a small piece of cloth, wood or plastic that you put on a table to protect it (保护桌面用的)小垫: *a set of red and white checked place mats* 一套红白格子餐具垫
2 a small piece of thick material that you put on the floor 地垫: *There was a letter on the door mat.* 门垫上有一封信。

match¹ /mætʃ/ *countable noun* 可数名词 (**matches**)
1 a small wooden or paper stick that produces a flame when you move it along a rough surface 火柴: *Kate lit a match and held it up to the candle.* 凯特划着一根火柴伸到蜡烛上。

match 火柴

2 a sports game between two people or teams (体育)比赛, 竞赛: *He was watching a tennis match.* 他正在看一场网球赛。
□ *Are you playing in the football match tomorrow?* 明天的足球赛你上场吗？

match² /mætʃ/ *verb* 动词 (**matches, matching, matched**)
to have the same colour or design as another thing, or to look good with it (颜色、样式等)与…相配: *Do these shoes match my dress?* 这双鞋配我的连衣裙吗？
▶ **matching** /ˈmætʃɪŋ/ *adjective* 形容词: *She wore a hat and a matching scarf.* 她戴了顶帽子, 搭了条相配的围巾。

mate¹ /meɪt/ *countable noun* 可数名词
1 the sexual partner of an animal 配偶: *The male bird shows its brightly coloured feathers to attract a mate.* 雄鸟展示自己鲜艳的羽毛来求偶。
2 a friend (*informal* 非正式) 朋友: *A mate of mine used to play football for Liverpool.* 我的一个哥们儿以前在利物浦队踢球。

mate² /meɪt/ *verb* 动词 (**mates, mating, mated**)
when male and female animals mate, they have sex in order to produce babies (动物)交配: *After mating, the female does not eat.* 交配后, 雌性不进食。

material /məˈtɪəriəl/ *noun* 名词
1 cloth 布料: *The thick material of her skirt was too warm for summer.* 她的裙子布料厚, 夏天穿太热。
2 [**materials**] *plural* 复数 the things that you need for a particular activity 材料; 原料: *building materials* 建筑材料

maternal /məˈtɜːnəl/ *adjective* 形容词
typical of a mother towards her child 母亲般慈爱的; 母亲的: *No love is stronger than maternal love.* 什么爱也强不过母爱。

mathematical - mayor

mathematical /ˌmæθəˈmætɪkəl/ *adjective* 形容词
involving numbers and calculating 数学的: *He made some quick mathematical calculations.* 他做了一些数学速算。

mathematics /ˌmæθəˈmætɪks/ *uncountable noun* 不可数名词
the study of numbers, quantities or shapes 数学: *Dr Lewis is a lecturer in mathematics at the University of Leeds.* 刘易斯博士是利兹大学数学讲师。
→ Look at picture on P2 参见彩插第 2 页

maths /mæθs/ *uncountable noun* 不可数名词
→ see 见 **mathematics**

matinee /ˈmætɪneɪ/ *countable noun* 可数名词
a performance of a play or a showing of a film in the afternoon（戏剧、电影的）下午场

matter¹ /ˈmætə/ *noun* 名词
1 *countable* 可数 something that you must talk about or do 事情；问题: *She wanted to discuss a private matter with me.* 她想和我谈一件私事。
2 [**matters**] *plural* 复数 a situation that someone is involved in 事态；情况: *If it would make matters easier, I will come to New York.* 如果这样能减少问题，我愿意来纽约。
3 *uncountable* 不可数 a type of substance 物质: *There was a strong smell of rotting vegetable matter.* 有一股刺鼻的腐烂蔬菜的味儿。
● **what's the matter?** used when you think that someone has a problem and you want to know what it is 怎么了？出什么事儿了？: *Carol, what's the matter? You don't seem happy.* 卡萝尔，怎么了？你好像不开心。

matter² /ˈmætə/ *verb* 动词 (**matters, mattering, mattered**)
to be important to someone 要紧；有重要意义: *A lot of the food goes on the floor but that doesn't matter.* 好多食物掉在了地板上，不过没有关系。

mattress /ˈmætrəs/ *countable noun* 可数名词 (**mattresses**)
the thick, soft part of a bed that you lie on 床垫

mature¹ /məˈtjʊə/ *adjective* 形容词 (**maturer, maturest**)
1 fully grown 长成的；长大的；成熟的
2 behaving in a responsible and sensible way 老成的；表现成熟的: *Fiona was mature for her age.* 以菲奥娜的年纪而言，她算成熟的了。

▶ **maturity** /məˈtjʊərɪti/ *uncountable noun* 不可数名词: *Her speech showed great maturity.* 她的讲话显得很成熟。

mature² /məˈtjʊə/ *verb* 动词 (**matures, maturing, matured**)
to become an adult 长成；长大；成熟: *The children will face many challenges as they mature into adulthood.* 孩子们长大成人后会面临许多挑战。

maximum /ˈmæksɪməm/ *adjective* 形容词
used for describing the largest amount possible（数量）最大的，极大的: *Today's maximum temperature in the city will be 80 degrees.* 今天市内最高气温可达 80 度。
● **maximum** *singular noun* 单数名词: *Brett faces a maximum of two years in prison.* 布雷特面临最高两年刑期。

may /meɪ/ *modal verb* 情态动词
1 used for showing that there is a possibility that something will happen or is true（表示可能性）可能，也许: *We may have some rain today.* 我们这儿今天可能会下点儿雨。 ▫ *I may be back next year.* 我明年也许会回来。
2 used for saying that someone is allowed to do something（表示许可）可以，能: *You may send a cheque or pay by credit card.* 你可以寄张支票，也可以刷信用卡。 ▫ *May we come in?* 我们能进屋吗？

May /meɪ/ *noun* 名词
the fifth month of the year 五月: *We went on holiday in May.* 我们5月去度了个假。

maybe /ˈmeɪbi/ *adverb* 副词
1 used when you are uncertain about something（表示不确定）也许，可能，大概: *Maybe she is in love.* 兴许她恋爱了。 ▫ *I do think about having children, maybe when I'm 40.* 我确实考虑过要孩子，也许等到我 40 岁吧。
2 used when you are making suggestions or giving advice（表示建议、忠告）或许，也许: *Maybe we can go to the cinema or something.* 或许我们可以看场电影什么的。 ▫ *Maybe you should see a doctor.* 也许你得找大夫看看。

mayonnaise /ˌmeɪəˈneɪz/ *uncountable noun* 不可数名词
a cold, thick sauce made from eggs and oil 蛋黄酱

mayor /meə/ *countable noun* 可数名词
the person who is responsible for the government of a city or a town 市长；镇长

The mayor of New York made a speech. 纽约市长讲了话.
→ Look at picture on P10 参见彩插第 10 页

maze /meɪz/ **countable noun** 可数名词
a place that is difficult to find your way through 迷宫；迷阵；迷宫般的地方：Only the local people know their way through the town's maze of streets. 只有当地人知道怎么穿过该城迷宫般的街道。

me /mi, STRONG 强读 mi:/ **pronoun** 代词
used when you are talking about yourself （宾格）我：He asked me to go to California with him. 他要我跟他去加利福尼亚。

meadow /ˈmedəʊ/ **countable noun** 可数名词
a field that has grass and flowers growing in it 草甸；草场；草地

meal /mi:l/ **countable noun** 可数名词
1 an occasion when people sit down and eat 一餐；一顿饭：She sat next to him during the meal. 用餐时她挨着他坐。
2 the food you eat during a meal 一餐所吃的食物：Logan finished his meal in silence. 洛根默默地吃完了饭。

mean¹ /mi:n/ **verb** 动词 (means, meaning, meant)
1 to have a particular meaning 表示；意思是：'Unable' means 'not able'. *unable 表示"不能的"。□ What does 'software' mean? *software 是什么意思？
2 used for saying that a second thing will happen because of a first thing 意味着：The new factory means more jobs for people. 新厂意味着更多人就业。
3 to be serious about what you are saying 对…当真：He said he loves her, and I think he meant it. 他说爱她，我觉得他是认真的。
mean a lot to someone to be very important to someone 对某人来说非常重要：Be careful with the photos. They mean a lot to me. 一定要小心对待那些照片。它们对我意义重大。
mean to do something to do something deliberately 有意做某事：I'm so sorry. I didn't mean to hurt you. 抱歉。我无意伤害你。

mean² /mi:n/ **adjective** 形容词 (meaner, meanest)
unkind or cruel 刻薄的；残忍的：Don't be mean to your brother! 别对弟弟那么苛刻！

mean³ /mi:n/ **singular noun** 单数名词
the amount that you get if you add a set of numbers together and divide them by the number of things that you originally added together. For example, the mean of 1, 3, 5 and 7 is 4 (1+3+5+7=16; 16 ÷ 4=4). 平均数；均值

meaning /ˈmi:nɪŋ/ **noun** 名词
the idea that a word or an expression represents 意思；意义；含义：Do you know the meaning of the words you're singing? 你明白你唱的那些词儿是什么意思吗？

meaningless /ˈmi:nɪŋləs/ **adjective** 形容词
having no meaning or purpose 无意义的；无目的的：After her death, he felt that his life was meaningless. 她死后，他自觉生活没了意义。

means /mi:nz/ **countable noun** 可数名词
a means of doing something a way to do something 做某事的方法：He searched for a door or some other means of escape. 他寻找门或其他什么逃生途径。

meant¹ /ment/
→ see 见 **mean**

meant² /ment/ **verb** 动词
meant to intended to be or do a particular thing 本应…的；本打算…的：I can't say any more, it's meant to be a big secret. 我不能多说了，这本来是重大机密。□ He was meant to arrive an hour ago. 他本应一小时之前抵达。

meantime /ˈmi:ntaɪm/ **noun** 名词
in the meantime used for talking about the period of time between two events 其间；同时：Elizabeth wants to go to college but in the meantime she has to work. 伊丽莎白想上大学，可同时又得上班。

meanwhile /ˈmi:nwaɪl/ **adverb** 副词
used for talking about the period of time between two events or what happens while another thing is happening 其间；同时：I'll be ready to meet them tomorrow. Meanwhile, I'm going to talk to Karen. 明天我会准备好会见他们。同时，我打算跟卡伦谈谈。□ We stayed up late into the night. Meanwhile, the snow was still falling outside. 我们熬到了深夜。其间，外面的雪还在下。

measles /ˈmi:zəlz/ **uncountable noun** 不可数名词
an illness that gives you a high fever and red spots on your skin 麻疹

measure¹ /ˈmeʒə/ **verb** 动词 (measures, measuring, measured)
1 to find out the size of something 测量（物体尺寸）：Measure the length of the table. 测一下桌子的长度。

measure – medium

2 used for describing the size of something as a particular length or amount（长度、数量等）量度为: *The football pitch measures 400 feet.* 这个足球场长 400 英尺。

measure² /ˈmeʒə/ *countable noun* 可数名词
a way of trying to achieve something (*formal* 正式) 措施；举措；行动: *The police are taking measures to deal with the problem.* 警方正在采取措施应对这一问题。

measurement /ˈmeʒəmənt/ *countable noun* 可数名词
the number that you get when you measure something 测量结果: *You'll need to take the measurements of the room when you go to buy the furniture.* 去买家具时你得带上测得的房间尺寸。

meat /miːt/ *noun* 名词
the part of an animal that people cook and eat（食用的）肉: *I don't eat meat or fish.* 我不吃肉，也不吃鱼。
→ Look at picture on P5 参见彩插第 5 页

mechanic /mɪˈkænɪk/ *countable noun* 可数名词
a person whose job is to repair machines and engines, especially car engines（尤指修理汽车发动机的）机械师，机械修理工: *Your mechanic should check the brakes on your car at least once a year.* 维修师傅每年至少得检查一次你座驾的刹车。
→ Look at picture on P16 参见彩插第 16 页

mechanical /mɪˈkænɪkəl/ *adjective* 形容词
used for describing an object that has parts that move when it is working（物件）机械的: *a mechanical clock* 机械时钟

mechanism /ˈmekənɪzəm/ *countable noun* 可数名词
a part of a machine（机械的）机件，构件: *The locking mechanism on the car door was broken.* 车门闭锁机构坏了。

medal /ˈmedəl/ *countable noun* 可数名词
a small metal disc that you receive as a prize for doing something very good 奖牌；奖章；勋章: *He won the long jump gold medal.* 他获得了跳远金牌。

medal 奖牌

media¹ /ˈmiːdiə/ *singular noun* 单数名词
television, radio, newspapers and magazines 媒体: *A lot of people in the media have asked me that question.* 媒体圈很多人问过我那个问题。 □ *They told their story to the news media.* 他们把自己的故事讲给了新闻媒体。

media² /ˈmiːdiə/
a plural of **medium**（medium 的复数形式之一）

median /ˈmiːdiən/ *countable noun* 可数名词
the number that is in the middle of a set of numbers when they are arranged in order. For example, in the numbers 1, 2, 3, 4, 5, the median is 3. 中位数

medical /ˈmedɪkəl/ *adjective* 形容词
relating to illness and injuries and how to treat or prevent them 医学的；医疗的；医药的: *Several police officers received medical treatment for their injuries.* 几名警察的伤得到了医治。

medication /ˌmedɪˈkeɪʃən/ *uncountable noun* 不可数名词
medicine that is used for treating and curing illness 药；药物: *Are you taking any medication?* 你在服用什么药吗？

medicine /ˈmedsən/ *noun* 名词
1 *uncountable* 不可数 the treatment of illness and injuries by doctors and nurses 医学: *He decided on a career in medicine.* 他决定从医。
2 a substance that you use to treat or cure an illness 药；药物: *The medicine saved his life.* 这种药救了他的命。

medieval /ˌmediˈiːvəl/ *adjective* 形容词
relating to the period of European history between A.D. 476 and about A.D. 1500 中世纪的（指欧洲历史上公元 476 年至约公元 1500 年这段时期）: *On our trip we visited a medieval castle.* 旅途中我们参观了一座中世纪城堡。

medium¹ /ˈmiːdiəm/ *adjective* 形容词
neither large nor small 中等的；中号的: *Mix the cream and eggs in a medium bowl.* 把奶油和鸡蛋放在中号碗里搅打。 □ *For this recipe, you will need one medium-sized onion.* 做这道菜需要一个中等大小的洋葱。

medium² /ˈmiːdiəm/ *countable noun* 可数名词 (**mediums** or 或 **media**)
a substance or material such as paint, wood or stone that an artist uses（艺术家采用的）载体，材料: *Hyatt uses the medium*

of oil paint. 海厄特使用油画颜料这种介质。

meet /miːt/ *verb* 动词 (**meets, meeting, met**)
1 to see someone who you know by chance and speak to them 遇见；碰到：*I met Shona in town today.* 我今天在城里碰到了肖纳。
2 to see someone who you do not know and speak to them for the first time 结识；认识：*I have just met an amazing man.* 我刚认识了一个奇人。
3 to go somewhere with someone because you have planned to be there together（如约）会面，碰面：*We could meet for a game of tennis after work.* 咱们可以下班后见个面打场网球。
4 to go to a place and wait for someone to arrive 接；迎接：*Mum met me at the station.* 妈妈在车站接我。
5 to join together 相交；交汇：*This is the point where the two rivers meet.* 这里是两条河的交汇处。

meeting /ˈmiːtɪŋ/ *countable noun* 可数名词
an event in which a group of people come together to discuss things or make decisions 会议：*Can we have a meeting to discuss that?* 咱们开个会讨论一下那件事？

megabyte /ˈmeɡəˌbaɪt/ *countable noun* 可数名词
a unit for measuring information in computing. There are one million bytes in a megabyte. 兆字节，百万字节（计算机信息量单位）：*The hard drive has 256 megabytes of memory.* 硬盘有 256 兆字节的存储空间。

melody /ˈmelədi/ *countable noun* 可数名词 (**melodies**)
a group of musical notes that sound pleasant together 旋律；曲调：*He could sing a melody before he could talk.* 他会说话之前就会哼曲子了。

melon /ˈmelən/ *noun* 名词
a large fruit with soft, sweet flesh and a hard green or yellow skin 瓜；甜瓜：*For dessert, there were grapes and juicy slices of melon.* 餐后甜点有葡萄和多汁的甜瓜片。

melt /melt/ *verb* 动词 (**melts, melting, melted**)
to change from a solid substance to a liquid because of heat（使）融化；（使）熔化：*The snow melted.* 雪化了。☐ *Melt the chocolate in a bowl.* 把巧克力放在碗里化开。
→ Look at picture on P6 参见彩插第 6 页

melting point *countable noun* 可数名词
the temperature at which a substance melts when you heat it. 熔点

member /ˈmembə/ *countable noun* 可数名词
someone or something that belongs to a group or an organization 成员；会员：*Joe is a member of the Democratic Party.* 乔是民主党党员。☐ *A member of the team saw the accident.* 一名队员目睹了这起事故。

Member of Parliament *countable noun* 可数名词
a person who has been chosen by the people in a particular area to represent them in a country's parliament. The short form 'MP' is also used. 议员（缩写形式为 MP）

membership /ˈmembəʃɪp/ *noun* 名词
1 *uncountable* 不可数 being a member of an organization 成员资格；会员身份：*Employees have free membership at the gym.* 员工免费成为体育馆会员。
2 the people who belong to an organization 全体成员（或会员）：*The organization had a membership of 409,000.* 该组织有 40.9 万名会员。

memo /ˈmeməʊ/ *countable noun* 可数名词
a short note that you send to a person who works with you（留给同事的）备忘录，便条，便笺：*He sent a memo to everyone in his department.* 他给部门里每个人都发送了一份备忘录。

memorable /ˈmemərəbəl/ *adjective* 形容词
easy to remember because of being special or very enjoyable 难忘的：*Our wedding was a very memorable day.* 我们的婚礼是个非常难忘的日子。

memorize /ˈmeməˌraɪz/ *verb* 动词 (**memorizes, memorizing, memorized**)
to learn something so that you can remember it exactly 记住；记忆：*He tried to memorize the way to Rose's street.* 他想记住去罗丝家那条街怎么走。

memory /ˈmeməri/ *noun* 名词 (**memories**)
1 your ability to remember things 记性；记忆力：*All the details of the meeting are clear in my memory.* 我对会议所有细节都记忆犹新。☐ *He has a good memory for faces.* 他对别人的长相过目不忘。
2 *countable* 可数 something that you remember from the past 记忆；回忆：*She has happy memories of her childhood.* 她有幸福的童年回忆。

3 *countable* 可数 the part of a computer where it stores information 存储器: *The data is stored in the computer's memory.* 数据存储在计算机存储器里。

memory card *countable noun* 可数名词
a small part that stores information inside a piece of electronic equipment such as a camera 存储卡

memory stick *countable noun* 可数名词
a small object for storing computer information that you can carry with you and use in different computers 优盘
→ Look at picture on P11 参见彩插第 11 页

men /men/
the plural of **man**（man 的复数形式）

mend /mend/ *verb* 动词 (**mends, mending, mended**)
to repair something 修理; 修补: *He earns money by mending bicycles.* 他靠修自行车挣钱。

menswear /'menzweə/ *uncountable noun* 不可数名词
clothing for men 男装: *Charlton bought the menswear shop five years ago.* 查尔顿 5 年前买下了这家男装店。

mental /'mentəl/ *adjective* 形容词
relating to the mind 心理的: *mental illness* 心理疾病
▶ **mentally** /'mentəli/ *adverb* 副词: *The exam made him mentally tired.* 考试让他心累。

mention /'menʃən/ *verb* 动词 (**mentions, mentioning, mentioned**)
to say something about someone or something, without giving much information 提起; 谈及; 说到: *She mentioned her mother but not her father.* 她提到了妈妈，但没提爸爸。 □ *I mentioned that I didn't really like pop music.* 我说过我不是特别喜欢流行乐。

menu /'menju:/ *countable noun* 可数名词
1 a list of the food and drink that you can have in a restaurant（饭店的）菜单: *A waiter offered him the menu.* 一位服务员把菜单递给了他。
2 a list of choices on a computer screen, showing things that you can do using a particular program（计算机屏幕上的）选单，菜单: *Press F7 to show the print menu.* 按 F7 显示打印菜单。

merchandise /'mɜːtʃəndaɪz, -daɪs/ *uncountable noun* 不可数名词
products that you can buy (*formal* 正式) 商品: *The company's annual football merchandise sales are about £1.5 billion.* 公司足球商品年销售额约为 15 亿英镑。

mercury /'mɜːkjʊri/ *uncountable noun* 不可数名词
a silver-coloured liquid metal that is used in thermometers 汞; 水银

mercy /'mɜːsi/ *uncountable noun* 不可数名词
when someone chooses not to harm or punish someone 仁慈; 怜悯; 宽恕: *His life was now at the mercy of a judge.* 他的命现在掌握在法官手里。

mere /mɪə/ *adjective* 形容词 (**merest**)
used for saying that something is small or not important 区区的; 仅仅的: *A mere five per cent of school headteachers are women.* 只有 5% 的学校校长是女性。

merely /'mɪəli/ *adverb* 副词
only 仅仅; 只是: *She said this was merely her own opinion.* 她说这只是她个人的看法。 □ *Dieter merely looked at him, saying nothing.* 迪特尔只是看着他，一言不发。

merge /mɜːdʒ/ *verb* 动词 (**merges, merging, merged**)
to join together to make one new thing 合并; 归并: *His company has merged with the advertising firm Saatchi & Saatchi.* 他的公司已经同萨奇广告公司合并了。

merit /'merɪt/ *noun* 名词
1 *uncountable* 不可数 good qualities 好品质; 价值: *The drawings have great artistic merit.* 这些绘画有很高的艺术价值。
2 [**merits**] *plural* 复数 the good points of something 优点; 长处: *We will consider the merits of all candidates before making our decision.* 我们会在考量所有应聘者的优点后再作决定。

mermaid /'mɜːmeɪd/ *countable noun* 可数名词
a woman in stories who has a fish's tail and lives in the sea（童话中的）美人鱼

merry /'meri/ *adjective* 形容词 (**merrier, merriest**)
happy and cheerful 欢快的; 愉快的; 兴高采烈的: *She sang a merry little tune.* 她唱了一支欢快的小曲儿。 □ *Merry Christmas, everyone!* 祝大家圣诞快乐!

mess[1] /mes/ *noun* 名词
1 *singular* 单数 when a place is not tidy 杂乱; 不整洁: *After the party, the house was a mess.* 派对结束后，房子里一片狼藉。

2 a situation that is full of problems 困境；混乱：*I've made such a mess of my life.* 我把自己的生活搞得一团糟。□ *Those are the reasons why the economy is in such a mess.* 那些便是经济一团糟的原因所在。

mess² /mes/ *verb* 动词 (**messes, messing, messed**)
mess about or **mess around** to spend time doing things for fun, or for no particular reason 瞎玩；闲混：*We were just messing around playing with paint.* 我们只是玩玩颜料打发时间。
mess something up
1 to make something go wrong (*informal* 非正式) 把某事物搞糟；扰乱某事物：*This has messed up our plans.* 这打乱了我们的计划。
2 to make a place or a thing dirty or not tidy (*informal* 非正式) 弄脏某物；弄乱某物：*He didn't want to mess up his tidy hair.* 他不想弄乱自己整洁的头发。

message /ˈmesɪdʒ/ *countable noun* 可数名词
a piece of information that you send to someone 消息；信息：*I'm getting emails and messages from friends all over the world.* 我不断收到来自世界各地朋友们的电邮和信息。

ˈmessage ˌboard *countable noun* 可数名词
a system that allows users to send and receive messages on the Internet（因特网上的）消息公告板，留言板

messy /ˈmesi/ *adjective* 形容词 (**messier, messiest**)
1 not tidy 脏乱的；凌乱的：*His writing is rather messy.* 他的字写得乱糟糟的。
2 making things dirty or not tidy 邋遢的；不爱整洁的：*She's a terribly messy cook.* 她做饭时现场会一片狼藉。

messy 邋遢的

She's a terribly messy cook. 她做饭时现场会一片狼藉。

met /met/
→ see 见 **meet**

metal /ˈmetəl/ *noun* 名词
a hard substance such as iron, steel or gold 金属：*All of the houses had metal roofs.* 所有房屋都是金属屋顶。

metaphor /ˈmetəfɔː/ *noun* 名词
a way of describing someone or something by showing their similarity with something else. For example, the metaphor 'a shining light' describes a person who is very skilful or intelligent. 隐喻：*She uses a lot of religious metaphors in her writing.* 她在写作中大量使用宗教隐喻。

meteor /ˈmiːtiə/ *countable noun* 可数名词
a piece of rock from space that burns very brightly when it falls to Earth 流星

meter /ˈmiːtə/ *countable noun* 可数名词
1 an instrument that measures and records something 计；仪；表：*A man came to read the electricity meter.* 一名男子来抄电表。
2 (*American* 美国英语) → see 见 **metre**

method /ˈmeθəd/ *countable noun* 可数名词
a way of doing something 方法；办法：*Teachers are allowed to try out different teaching methods.* 教师可以尝试不同的教学法。

metre /ˈmiːtə/ *countable noun* 可数名词
(*American* 美国英语：**meter**)
a unit for measuring length. There are 100 centimetres in a metre. 米（长度单位，1 米 = 100 厘米）：*She's running the 1,500 metre race.* 她将参加 1,500 米赛跑。
→ Look at picture on P2 参见彩插第 2 页

metric /ˈmetrɪk/ *adjective* 形容词
expressed in metres, grams or litres 公制的；米制的：*A gram is a unit of weight in the metric system.* 克是公制重量单位。

ˌmetric ˈton *countable noun* 可数名词
1,000 kilograms 公吨（1 公吨 = 1,000 千克）：*The Wall Street Journal uses 220,000 metric tons of paper each year.*《华尔街日报》每年用掉 22 万公吨纸张。

mg
short for (缩写 =) **milligram** or **milligrams**

miaow /miˈaʊ/ *countable noun* 可数名词
the sound that a cat makes 喵（猫叫声）：*We could hear the miaow of a cat.* 我们能听见有只猫在喵喵叫。● **miaow** *verb* 动词 (**miaows, miaowing, miaowed**)：*I could*

hear a cat miaowing outside. 我能听见外面有只猫在喵喵叫。

mice /maɪs/
the plural of **mouse** (mouse 的复数形式)

microbe /ˈmaɪkrəʊb/ ***countable noun*** 可数名词
a very small living thing that you cannot see without special equipment 微生物: *We have to kill the microbes that cause food poisoning.* 我们必须杀灭造成食物中毒的微生物。

microchip /ˈmaɪkrəʊˌtʃɪp/ ***countable noun*** 可数名词
a very small part inside a computer that makes it work 微型芯片

microphone /ˈmaɪkrəˌfəʊn/ ***countable noun*** 可数名词
a piece of electronic equipment that you use to make sounds louder or to record them onto a machine 传声器;话筒;麦克风

microphone 话筒

microscope /ˈmaɪkrəˌskəʊp/ ***countable noun*** 可数名词
a scientific instrument that makes very small objects look bigger 显微镜

microwave /ˈmaɪkrəʊˌweɪv/ ***countable noun*** 可数名词
(also 亦作 **microwave oven**) an oven that cooks food very quickly using electric waves 微波炉

midday /ˌmɪdˈdeɪ/ ***uncountable noun*** 不可数名词
twelve o'clock in the middle of the day 中午;正午: *At midday everyone had lunch.* 中午大家都吃了午饭。

middle[1] /ˈmɪdəl/ ***noun*** 名词
1 countable 可数 the part of something that is furthest from the edges 中部;中央;中间: *Howard stood in the middle of the room.* 霍华德站在屋子中央。
2 singular 单数 the part between the beginning and the end of a period of time (时间段的)中段,中间: *I woke up in the middle of the night and heard a noise outside.* 我半夜醒来,听见外面有动静。
in the middle of doing something busy doing something 忙于做某事: *I'm in the middle of cooking dinner.* 我正忙着做晚饭。

middle[2] /ˈmɪdəl/ ***adjective*** 形容词
having an equal number of objects on each side 正中的;中间的;当中的: *The middle button of his uniform jacket was missing.* 他制服短上衣中间的扣子掉了。

ˌmiddle ˈage ***uncountable noun*** 不可数名词
the time in your life when you are between the ages of about 40 and 65 中年: *Men often gain weight in middle age.* 男性往往中年发福。

ˌmiddle-ˈaged ***adjective*** 形容词
between the ages of about 40 and 65 中年的: *Most of the men were middle-aged married businessmen.* 这些男士大多是中年已婚生意人。

ˌMiddle ˈAges ***plural noun*** 复数名词
the period of time in European history between the end of the Roman Empire in 476 AD and about 1500 AD 中世纪(指欧洲历史上自公元 476 年罗马帝国灭亡至约公元 1500 年这段时期)

ˌmiddle ˈclass ***countable noun*** 可数名词 (**middle classes**)
(also 亦作 **middle classes**) the people in a society who are not very rich and not very poor, for example business people, doctors and teachers 中产阶级;中产阶层: *Most writers come from the middle class.* 大多数作家出身中产阶级。● **middle class** ***adjective*** 形容词: *They live in a very middle class area.* 他们生活在一个典型的中产阶层居住区。

midnight /ˈmɪdnaɪt/ ***uncountable noun*** 不可数名词
twelve o'clock in the middle of the night 子夜;午夜;半夜: *It was well after midnight.* 时间早就过了午夜。

midway /ˌmɪdˈweɪ/ ***adverb*** 副词
at the same distance from each of two places 在中途;在半路;在中间: *The studio is midway between his office and his home.* 工作室在他办公室和家中间。

might[1] /maɪt/ ***modal verb*** 情态动词
used when something is possible 可能;也许: *I might go to study in England.* 我也许去英格兰念书。 □ *They still hope that he might be alive.* 他们仍然怀着他可能还活着的希望。

might[2] /maɪt/ ***uncountable noun*** 不可数名词
power or strength 力气;力量: *I pulled with all my might.* 我用全力拉。

mightn't /ˈmaɪtənt/
short for (缩写 =) 'might not'

might've /ˈmaɪtəv/
short for (缩写 =) 'might have'

mighty /ˈmaɪti/ *adjective* 形容词 (**mightier, mightiest**)
very large or powerful 巨大的；强大的：*There was a mighty roar from the crowd as the band came on stage.* 乐队登台时，观众一片山呼海啸。

migraine /ˈmiːɡreɪn/ *noun* 名词
a severe pain in your head that makes you feel very ill 偏头痛：*Her mother suffered from migraines.* 她妈妈患有偏头痛。

migrant /ˈmaɪɡrənt/ *countable noun* 可数名词
a person who moves from one place to another, especially in order to find work（尤指寻求就业岗位的）移民，移居者：*Most of his workers were migrants from the South.* 他的工人大多是南方来的移民。

migrate /maɪˈɡreɪt/ *verb* 动词 (**migrates, migrating, migrated**)
1 to move from one place to another, usually in order to find work（通常为寻求就业岗位而）移居，迁徙：*People migrate to cities like Jakarta searching for work.* 人们流入雅加达这样的城市找工作。
▶ **migration** /maɪˈɡreɪʃən/ *uncountable noun* 不可数名词：*There was a large migration of people to the city.* 人口大量流入该市。
2 to move from one part of the world to another at the same time every year（动物）迁徙：*Most birds have to fly long distances to migrate.* 大多数鸟迁徙都要长途飞行。
▶ **migration** /maɪˈɡreɪʃən/ *uncountable noun* 不可数名词：*Scientists are tracking the migration of bears.* 科学家正在追踪熊的迁徙。

mild /maɪld/ *adjective* 形容词 (**milder, mildest**)
1 not very strong 柔和的；温和的；不太强烈的：*This cheese has a soft, mild flavour.* 这种干酪味道清淡柔和。
2 not too hot and not too cold 暖和的；不热不冷的：*We like the area because it has very mild winters.* 我们喜欢这个地方，因为这里的冬天非常暖和。

mile /maɪl/ *countable noun* 可数名词
a unit for measuring distance. A mile is equal to about 1.6 kilometres. There are 5,280 feet in a mile. 英里（长度单位，1 英里 ≈ 1.6 千米）：*They drove 600 miles across the desert.* 他们驾车 600 英里穿越沙漠。

mileage /ˈmaɪlɪdʒ/ *noun* 名词
the distance that a vehicle has travelled, measured in miles 英里里程：*The car has a low mileage.* 这辆车跑的里程不多。

military /ˈmɪlɪtri/ *adjective* 形容词
relating to the armed forces of a country 军事的；军队的；军用的：*Military action may become necessary.* 军事行动可能不可避免。
□ *The president attended a meeting of military leaders.* 总统出席了军方领导人会议。

milk[1] /mɪlk/ *uncountable noun* 不可数名词
1 the white liquid that cows and some other animals produce, which people drink（饮用的）奶：*He went out to buy a pint of milk.* 他出去买了一品脱奶。
2 the white liquid that a mother makes in her body to feed her baby 母乳：*Milk from the mother's breast is a perfect food for the human baby.* 母乳是婴儿的最佳食物。
→ Look at picture on P5 参见彩插第 5 页

milk[2] /mɪlk/ *verb* 动词 (**milks, milking, milked**)
to take milk from a cow or another animal 给（牛等动物）挤奶：*Farm workers milks the cows in the morning.* 农场工人早晨挤牛奶。

milky /ˈmɪlki/ *adjective* 形容词 (**milkier, milkiest**)
containing a lot of milk 含奶多的：*I want a big cup of milky coffee.* 我想要一大杯牛奶咖啡。

mill /mɪl/ *countable noun* 可数名词
1 a building in which flour is made from grain 磨坊；面粉厂：*The old mill is now a restaurant.* 老磨坊现在成了一家饭店。
2 a factory where materials such as steel, wool or cotton are made（从事炼钢、毛纺、棉纺等的）工厂：*He started work in a cotton mill at the age of ten.* 他 10 岁开始在一家棉纺厂工作。

milligram /ˈmɪlɪˌɡræm/ also 亦作 **milligramme** *countable noun* 可数名词
a unit for measuring weight. There are one thousand milligrams in a gram. 毫克（重量单位，1,000 毫克 = 1 克）：*He added 0.5 milligrams of sodium.* 他加了 0.5 毫克钠。

millilitre /ˈmɪlɪˌliːtə/ *countable noun* 可数名词
a unit for measuring volume for liquids

millimetre - mind

and gases. There are one thousand millilitres in a litre. 毫升（液体、气体容量单位，1,000 毫升 = 1 升）: *The nurse measured 100 millilitres of blood.* 护士量取了 100 毫升血。
→ Look at picture on P2 参见彩插第 2 页

millimetre /ˈmɪlɪˌmiːtə/ *countable noun* 可数名词
a unit for measuring length. There are ten millimetres in a centimetre. 毫米（长度单位，10 毫米 = 1 厘米）: *The creature is tiny, just 10 millimetres long.* 这种生物很小，只有 10 毫米长。
→ Look at picture on P2 参见彩插第 2 页

million /ˈmɪljən/

> **LANGUAGE HELP** 语言提示
> The plural form is **million** after a number. 用在数字后，复数形式为 million。

the number 1,000,000 一百万: *A million people visit the county each year.* 每年有百万人到访该郡。
millions of a very large number of people or things 亿万的；许许多多的: *The programme was watched on television in millions of homes.* 亿万家庭守在电视机前观看了这个节目。

millionaire /ˌmɪljəˈneə/ *countable noun* 可数名词
a person who has more than a million pounds 百万富翁: *By the time he died, he was a millionaire.* 他去世时身家百万。

mime¹ /maɪm/ *noun* 名词
a way of telling a story using your face, hands and body, but without using speech 哑剧: *The story is told through music and mime.* 这个故事是以音乐配哑剧的形式讲述的。

mime² /maɪm/ *verb* 动词 (**mimes, miming, mimed**)
to describe something using movements rather than speech 以动作表现: *He mimed the act of hammering a nail into a piece of wood.* 他做了个往木头上钉钉子的动作。

mimic /ˈmɪmɪk/ *verb* 动词 (**mimics, mimicking, mimicked**)
to copy someone in an amusing way（为逗乐）模仿，学…的样子: *He could mimic anybody, and often made Olivia laugh.* 他可以模仿任何人，经常逗得奥利维娅哈哈大笑。

mince /mɪns/ *uncountable noun* 不可数名词
meat that has been cut into very small pieces using a machine 绞碎的肉；肉馅: *Fry the mince in a frying pan.* 把绞碎的肉放在煎锅里煎一下。

mind¹ /maɪnd/ *countable noun* 可数名词
all your thoughts and the way that you think about things 心思；头脑；心理: *She is a bit deaf, but her mind is still sharp.* 她耳朵有点儿背，不过脑子还是很灵光。
change your mind to change a decision or an opinion 变卦；改变主意: *I was going to vote for him, but I changed my mind.* 我本打算把票投给他，但我改主意了。
make up your mind to decide something 拿定主意；下定决心: *He made up his mind to call Kathy.* 他决定打电话给凯茜。
on your mind used for describing something that you are worried about and think about a lot 牵挂于心；惦念: *I don't sleep well. I've got a lot on my mind.* 我睡不好。我有很多心事。
out of your mind crazy (*informal* 非正式) 疯狂的；精神失常的: *What are you doing? Are you out of your mind?* 你这是干什么？你疯了吗？
take your mind off something to help you to stop thinking about a problem for a while 使心里暂时放下某事物: *A film might take your mind off your problems.* 看场电影也许能让你暂时放下烦恼。

mind² /maɪnd/ *verb* 动词 (**minds, minding, minded**)
to feel annoyed or angry about something 介意；在乎；反感: *Mr Hernandez, would you mind waiting here a moment?* 埃尔南德斯先生，麻烦您在这里等一会儿行吗？ □ *It was hard work but she didn't mind.* 活儿很重，可她不在乎。
I don't mind used when you are happy to do or have either of two choices 随便；都可以；无所谓: '*Would you rather play tennis or baseball?*' — '*I don't mind.*' "你想打网球还是棒球？" —— "都行。"
I wouldn't mind something/I wouldn't mind doing something used for saying that someone would like something 我想要某物 / 我想做某事: *I wouldn't mind a cup of coffee.* 我想来杯咖啡。
mind out! used for telling someone to be careful 小心！当心！
never mind used when something is not important 没关系；不要紧: '*He's not

coming.' — 'Oh, never mind, we'll start eating without him.' "他不来了。"——"哦，没关系，咱们自己吃吧。"

mine¹ /maɪn/ **pronoun** 代词
something that belongs to me 我的（东西）: *Her right hand was close to mine.* 她右手离我的手很近。□ *That isn't your bag, it's mine.* 那个不是你的包，是我的。

mine² /maɪn/ **countable noun** 可数名词
1 a deep hole in the ground from which people dig coal, diamonds or gold 矿；矿井: *The company owns gold and silver mines.* 公司拥有金银矿。
2 a bomb that is hidden under the ground 雷；地雷

mine³ /maɪn/ **verb** 动词 (**mines, mining, mined**)
to dig deep holes and tunnels into the ground to remove coal, diamonds or gold 开采；采掘: *Diamonds are mined in South Africa.* 南非有钻石矿在开采。
▶ **miner** /ˈmaɪnə/ **countable noun** 可数名词: *My father was a miner.* 我父亲是个矿工。

mineral /ˈmɪnərəl/ **countable noun** 可数名词
a natural substance such as gold, salt or coal that comes from the ground 矿物

ˈmineral ˌwater **uncountable noun** 不可数名词
water that comes from the ground that contains substances that are good for your health 矿泉水

miniature /ˈmɪnɪtʃə/ **adjective** 形容词
very small, or much smaller than usual 微小的；微型的；缩微的: *The toy house was filled with miniature chairs and tables.* 玩具屋里摆满了微型桌椅。

minimal /ˈmɪnɪməl/ **adjective** 形容词
very small 非常小的；极小的: *The health risk is minimal, so there's no need to worry.* 健康风险很低，用不着担心。

minimize /ˈmɪnɪmaɪz/ **verb** 动词 (**minimizes, minimizing, minimized**)
to make something as small as possible 使最小化；将⋯降到最低: *We have done everything possible to minimize the risk of accidents.* 我们已竭尽所能最大限度地降低事故风险。

minimum /ˈmɪnɪməm/ **adjective** 形容词
used for talking about the smallest amount that is possible 最小的；最低限度的: *Pupils remain at school at least until the minimum age of 16.* 学生在学校至少要上到 16 岁，这是最低年龄要求。□ *Many people in the country are still working for less than the minimum wage.* 该国很多人的薪酬仍然低于最低工资水平。● **minimum** **singular noun** 单数名词: *Dr Rayman runs a minimum of three miles every day.* 赖曼博士每天至少跑 3 英里。

minister /ˈmɪnɪstə/ **countable noun** 可数名词
1 a religious leader in some types of church（某些教会的）牧师: *Thirty priests, ministers and rabbis attended the meeting.* *30 位司祭、牧师和拉比出席了会议。
2 a senior person in a government in some countries（政府的）部长，大臣: *When the government came to power, he was named finance minister.* 该届政府上台后，他被任命为财政大臣。

ministry /ˈmɪnɪstri/ **countable noun** 可数名词 (**ministries**)
a government department that deals with one particular thing（政府的）部: *He has worked for both the ministry of education and the ministry of the interior.* 他在教育部和内政部都工作过。

minor /ˈmaɪnə/ **adjective** 形容词
1 not very important or serious 次要的；不太重要的；不太严重的: *The soldier suffered only minor injuries.* 这位战士只是受了点小伤。□ *They both have minor roles in the film.* 他们两个在影片中都是小角色。
2 used in music for talking about a scale (= a series of musical notes) in which the third note is one half step lower than the related major scale. Compare with **major**.（音乐）小调的（比较 major）: *an A minor scale* *A 小调音阶

minority /mɪˈnɒrɪti/ **singular noun** 单数名词
fewer than half the amount of people or things 少数: *Only a minority of mothers in this neighbourhood go out to work.* 这个街区只有少数妈妈出去工作。

mint /mɪnt/ **noun** 名词
1 uncountable 不可数 a plant that has leaves with a fresh, strong taste and smell 薄荷: *The waiter brought us two glasses of mint tea.* 服务员给我们端来两杯薄荷茶。
2 countable 可数 a sweet with this flavour 薄荷糖: *Sam offered me a mint.* 萨姆给了我一块薄荷糖。

minus¹ /ˈmaɪnəs/ **conjunction** 连词
used when you are taking one number away from another number 减；减去: *One*

minus one is zero. *1 减 1 等于 0。
→ Look at picture on P2 参见彩插第 2 页

minus² /ˈmaɪnəs/ *adjective* 形容词
used before a number or an amount to show that it is less than zero 负的；零下的： *The temperature dropped to minus 20 degrees F.* 温度降到了零下 20 华氏度。

minute¹ /ˈmɪnɪt/ *countable noun* 可数名词
a unit for measuring time. There are sixty seconds in one minute, and there are sixty minutes in one hour. 分；分钟： *The pizza will take twenty minutes to cook.* 比萨饼需要 20 分钟才能做好。
in a minute very soon 一会儿；很快： *The doctor will be with you in a minute.* 大夫一会儿就来。
just a minute or **wait a minute** said when you want someone to wait for a short period of time 稍等；等一下： *Wait a minute, something is wrong here.* 等一下，这里有点儿不对劲儿。
this minute immediately 立即；马上： *You come back here this minute!* 你马上给我回来！

minute² /maɪˈnjuːt/ *adjective* 形容词
very small 非常小的；微小的： *You only need to use a minute amount of glue.* 你只需要用一丁点儿胶水。

miracle /ˈmɪrəkəl/ *countable noun* 可数名词
a surprising and lucky event that you cannot explain 奇迹： *It's a miracle that Chris survived the accident.* 克里斯大难不死，真是个奇迹。

mirror /ˈmɪrə/ *countable noun* 可数名词
a flat piece of special glass that you can see yourself in 镜子

mirror 镜子

Dan looked at himself in the mirror.
丹照了照镜子。

misbehaviour /ˌmɪsbɪˈheɪvjə/ *uncountable noun* 不可数名词

bad behaviour (*formal* 正式) 不良行为： *Our teachers will not tolerate misbehaviour.* 我们老师不会容许不端行为。

mischief /ˈmɪstʃɪf/ *uncountable noun* 不可数名词
bad or silly behaviour that is annoying but not too serious 淘气；捣蛋；恶作剧： *Jacob's a typical little boy — full of mischief.* 雅各布是个典型的小男孩儿——就爱调皮捣蛋。

mischievous /ˈmɪstʃɪvəs/ *adjective* 形容词
liking to play tricks on people and behaving in a silly, but not very bad way 淘气的；调皮的；爱捣蛋的： *Megan gave me a mischievous smile.* 梅甘调皮地冲我笑了一下。
▶ **mischievously** /ˈmɪstʃɪvəsli/ *adverb* 副词： *Thomas grinned mischievously at Anna.* 托马斯冲安娜调皮地咧嘴笑了。

miserable /ˈmɪzərəbəl/ *adjective* 形容词
1 very unhappy 痛苦的；非常不悦的： *My job was making me miserable.* 我的工作让我非常不开心。
▶ **miserably** /ˈmɪzərəbli/ *adverb* 副词： *'I feel so guilty,' Diane said miserably.* "我很内疚。"黛安娜痛苦地说。
2 making you feel unhappy 令人苦恼的： *It was a grey, wet, miserable day.* 那是一个阴沉灰暗的雨天。

misery /ˈmɪzəri/ *noun* 名词 (**miseries**)
great unhappiness 痛苦；苦难： *People never forget the misery of war.* 人们永远忘不了战争的苦痛。

misfortune /ˌmɪsˈfɔːtʃuːn/ *noun* 名词
something unpleasant or unlucky that happens to you 不幸；灾祸： *She seems to enjoy other people's misfortunes.* 她似乎喜欢幸灾乐祸。

mislead /ˌmɪsˈliːd/ *verb* 动词 (**misleads, misleading, misled**)
to make someone believe something that is not true 误导；使误信： *The administration has misled the public about this issue.* 政府在这件事上误导了公众。

misleading /ˌmɪsˈliːdɪŋ/ *adjective* 形容词
making you believe something that is not true 误导性的： *Companies must make sure that their advertisements are not misleading.* 公司必须确保自己的广告不会误导人。

misled /ˌmɪsˈled/
→ see 见 **mislead**

miss /mɪs/ *verb* 动词 (misses, missing, missed)
1 to not manage to hit or catch something 未击中；未抓住：*His first shot missed the goal completely.* 他第一次射门偏出球门老远。□ *Morrison just missed the ball.* 莫里森硬是没拿到球。
2 to not notice something 未注意到：*What did he say? I missed it.* 他说什么？我没听见。
3 to feel sad that someone is not there 思念，想念（不在身边的人）：*I miss my family terribly.* 我特别想念家人。
4 to feel sad because you no longer have something 怀念（失去之物）：*I love my flat, but I miss my garden.* 我喜欢我的公寓，但我怀念我的花园。
5 to arrive too late to get on an aeroplane or a train 错过，没赶上（飞机、火车等）：*He missed the last bus home.* 他错过了回家的末班车。
6 to not take part in a meeting or an activity 未参加（会议、活动等）：*He missed the party because he had to work.* 他错过了聚会，因为他得上班。
miss out on something to not have the chance take part in something 错过某事；没机会参加某事：*You missed out on all the fun yesterday.* 昨天的乐事你一件也没赶上。

Miss /mɪs/ *noun* 名词 (**Misses**)
used in front of the name of a girl or a woman who is not married (*formal* 正式) 小姐（用于女孩或未婚女子的姓名前）：*It was nice talking to you, Miss Ellis.* 和您聊天真开心，埃利斯小姐。

missile /ˈmɪsaɪl/ *countable noun* 可数名词
1 a weapon that flies through the air and explodes when it hits something 导弹：*The army fired missiles at the building.* 军队向大楼发射了导弹。
2 anything that you can throw as a weapon（作为武器的）投掷物，投射物：*The youths were throwing missiles at the police.* 年轻人在朝警察扔东西。

missing /ˈmɪsɪŋ/ *adjective* 形容词
used for describing someone or something that is not in its usual place, and that you cannot find 找不着的；失踪的；丢失的：*I discovered that my mobile phone was missing.* 我发现手机不见了。□ *Police are hunting for the missing girl.* 警方正在搜寻失踪的女孩。

mission /ˈmɪʃən/ *countable noun* 可数名词
an important job that someone has to do, especially one that involves travelling（尤指需要出行的）使命，重要任务：*His government sent him on a mission to North America.* 政府派他前往北美执行任务。

misspell /ˌmɪsˈspel/ *verb* 动词 (misspells, misspelling, misspelled)
to not spell a word correctly 拼错（词语）：*Sorry I misspelled your last name.* 抱歉，我把您的姓拼错了。

mist /mɪst/ *uncountable noun* 不可数名词
a lot of tiny drops of water in the air, that make it difficult to see 薄雾；霭：*The mist did not lift until midday.* 雾霭直到中午才消散。
▶ **misty** /ˈmɪsti/ *adjective* 形容词：*Charlie looked across the misty valley.* 查利眺望雾蒙蒙的山谷对面。

mistake[1] /mɪˈsteɪk/ *countable noun* 可数名词
something that is not correct 错；错误：*Tony made three spelling mistakes in the letter.* 托尼信里有 3 处拼写错误。
by mistake accidentally 意外地；无意中；错误地：*I was in a hurry and called the wrong number by mistake.* 我匆忙中无意拨错了号码。

mistake[2] /mɪˈsteɪk/ *verb* 动词 (**mistakes, mistaking, mistook, mistaken**)
to wrongly think that one person is another person 认错（人）：*People are always mistaking Lauren for her sister because they are so alike.* 人们总是把劳伦错当成她姐姐，因为她俩长得太像了。

mistaken[1] /mɪˈsteɪkən/
→ see 见 **mistake**

mistaken[2] /mɪˈsteɪkən/ *adjective* 形容词
wrong about something 搞错的；弄错的：*I think that you must be mistaken — Jackie wouldn't do a thing like that.* 我觉得你一定是弄错了——杰基不会做那种事。
▶ **mistakenly** /mɪˈsteɪkənli/ *adverb* 副词：*The thieves mistakenly believed there was no one in the house.* 窃贼们误以为房子里没人。

mistook /mɪˈstʊk/
→ see 见 **mistake**

mistrust /ˌmɪsˈtrʌst/ *verb* 动词 (mistrusts, mistrusting, mistrusted)
to not trust someone 不信任；不相信：*He mistrusts all journalists.* 他不相信任何记者。● **mistrust** *countable noun* 可数名词：*There is a deep mistrust of the police*

around here. 这地方的人非常不信任警察。

misunderstand /ˌmɪsʌndəˈstænd/ *verb* 动词 (**misunderstands, misunderstanding, misunderstood**)
to not understand someone or something correctly 误解；误会：*I think you've misunderstood me.* 我觉得你误会我了。

misunderstanding /ˌmɪsʌndəˈstændɪŋ/ *noun* 名词
a situation where someone does not understand something correctly 误解；误会：*Make your plans clear to avoid misunderstandings.* 把你的方案说清楚，免得产生误会。

misunderstood /ˌmɪsʌndəˈstʊd/
→ see 见 **misunderstand**

mitten /ˈmɪtən/ *countable noun* 可数名词
a glove that has one part that covers your thumb and another part that covers your four fingers together 连指手套：*a pair of mittens* 一副连指手套

mix /mɪks/ *verb* 动词 (**mixes, mixing, mixed**)
1 to put different things together so that they make something new 混合；掺和：*Mix the sugar with the butter.* 把糖跟黄油混合起来。

mix 混合

2 to join together and make something new 溶合；融合；熔合：*Oil and water don't mix.* 油水不相融。

mix someone/something up to think that one of two things or people is the other one 将某人／某事物搞混：*People often mix me up with my brother.* 人们经常把我跟弟弟搞混。 □ *Children often mix up their words.* 儿童经常前言不搭后语。

mixed /mɪkst/ *adjective* 形容词
including different types of things or people 混合的；混杂的：*There was a very mixed group of people at the party.* 聚会上来了形形色色的人。□ *For lunch we had pasta and a mixed salad.* 午餐我们吃了意大利面和什锦沙拉。

mixer /ˈmɪksə/ *countable noun* 可数名词
a machine that you use for mixing things together 搅拌机；搅拌器：*Beat the egg yolks and sugar with an electric mixer.* 用电动搅拌器搅拌蛋黄和糖。

mixture /ˈmɪkstʃə/ *countable noun* 可数名词
a substance that you make by mixing different substances together 混合物：*The sauce is a mixture of chocolate and cream.* 酱汁由巧克力和奶油混合而成。

ml
short for (缩写 =) **millilitre** or **millilitres**

mm
short for (缩写 =) **millimetre** or **millimetres**

moan /məʊn/ *verb* 动词 (**moans, moaning, moaned**)
1 to make a low sound because you are unhappy or in pain 呻吟：*The wounded soldier was moaning in pain.* 那个受伤的士兵在痛苦地呻吟。 ● **moan** *countable noun* 可数名词：*She gave a soft moan of discomfort.* 她轻轻发出了一声难受的呻吟。
2 to complain, or speak in a way which shows that you are unhappy 抱怨；发牢骚：*They're always moaning about the weather.* 他们老是抱怨天气。

mobile¹ /ˈməʊbaɪl/ *adjective* 形容词
that can easily move or be moved from place to place 移动的；活动的：*The family live in a three-bedroom mobile home near Las Cruces in New Mexico.* 这家人住在新墨西哥州拉斯克鲁塞斯市附近的一座三居室活动房里。□ *Grandpa's eighty but he's still very mobile.* 爷爷 80 岁了，可他行动还是很麻利。

mobile² /ˈməʊbaɪl/ *countable noun* 可数名词
→ see 见 **mobile phone**

ˌmobile ˈphone *countable noun* 可数名词
(*American* 美国英语：**cellphone**)
(also 亦作 **mobile**) a telephone that you can carry wherever you go 手机；移动电话：*The woman called the police on her mobile phone.* 女子用手机报了警。
→ Look at picture on P11 参见彩插第 11 页

mock /mɒk/ *verb* 动词 (**mocks, mocking, mocked**)
to laugh at someone and try to make them feel foolish 嘲笑；讥笑：*My friends mocked*

me because I didn't have a girlfriend. 朋友们嘲笑我，因为我没有女朋友。

modal /ˈməʊdəl/ *countable noun* 可数名词
(also 亦作 **modal auxiliary**) used in grammar to talk about a word such as 'can' or 'would' which is used with another verb to say that something is possible or necessary 情态动词

model¹ /ˈmɒdəl/ *countable noun* 可数名词
1 a small copy of something 模型: *At school, the children are making a model of the solar system.* 学校里，孩子们正在做太阳系模型。□ *I made the model using paper and glue.* 我用纸和胶水做了这个模型。
● **model** *adjective* 形容词: *I spent my childhood building model aircraft.* 我童年是在做飞机模型中度过的。
2 a particular design of a vehicle or a machine (车辆或机器的) 型号: *You don't need an expensive computer, just a basic model.* 你不需要太贵的电脑，基本款就行。
3 a person who sits or stands in front of an artist so that they can draw or paint them (艺术家的) 模特儿: *The model for his painting was his sister.* 他作画用的模特儿是他妹妹。
4 a person whose job is to wear and show new clothes in photographs and at fashion shows, so that people can see them and buy them (时装) 模特儿: *Kim dreams of becoming a fashion model.* 金梦想成为时装模特儿。

model² /ˈmɒdəl/ *verb* 动词 (**models, modelling, modelled**)
to wear clothes as a model 做时装模特儿: *Nicole began modelling at age 15.* 妮科尔15岁入行做时装模特儿。

modem /ˈməʊdem/ *countable noun* 可数名词
a piece of equipment that uses a telephone line to connect computers 调制解调器: *a mobile phone with a built-in modem* 一部内置调制解调器的手机

moderate /ˈmɒdərət/ *adjective* 形容词
not too much or too little 适中的；适量的；适度的: *Temperatures are moderate between October and March.* *10月至来年3月气温不冷不热。
▶ **moderately** /ˈmɒdərətli/ *adverb* 副词: *Heat the oil until it is moderately hot.* 把油加热到温热。

modern /ˈmɒdən/ *adjective* 形容词
new, or relating to the present time 现代的；新式的: *I like antiques, but my husband prefers modern furniture.* 我喜欢古式家具，可我丈夫喜欢现代家具。□ *modern society* 现代社会

modernize /ˈmɒdəˌnaɪz/ *verb* 动词 (**modernizes, modernizing, modernized**)
to change something such as a system or a factory by introducing new equipment, methods or ideas 使现代化；对…进行现代化改造: *We need to modernize our schools.* 我们需要对学校进行现代化改造。

modest /ˈmɒdɪst/ *adjective* 形容词
not talking much about your abilities, skills or successes 谦虚的；谦逊的: *He's modest, as well as being a great player.* 他是一位谦虚而伟大的运动员。
▶ **modestly** /ˈmɒdɪstli/ *adverb* 副词: *'I was just lucky,' Hughes said modestly.* "我只是幸运而已。"休斯谦逊地说。

modesty /ˈmɒdɪsti/ *uncountable noun* 不可数名词
the quality of not talking much about your abilities, skills or successes 谦虚；谦逊: *His humour and gentle modesty won affection and friendships everywhere.* 他幽默风趣、温和谦逊，到哪儿都招人喜欢，都能交上朋友。

modify /ˈmɒdɪfaɪ/ *verb* 动词 (**modifies, modifying, modified**)
to change something slightly, usually in order to improve it (通常为改进而) 微调，略微改动: *Helen and her husband modified the design of the house to suit their family's needs.* 海伦和丈夫微调了一下房屋设计，以适应他们家庭的需要。
▶ **modification** /ˌmɒdɪfɪˈkeɪʃən/ *noun* 名词: *They made a few small modifications to the plan.* 他们对方案做了一些微调。

moist /mɔɪst/ *adjective* 形容词 (**moister, moistest**)
slightly wet 微湿的；潮湿的: *The soil was moist after the rain.* 雨后土壤湿润。

moisture /ˈmɔɪstʃə/ *uncountable noun* 不可数名词
small drops of water in the air, on a surface, or in the ground 水分；湿气；潮气: *Keep the food covered so that it doesn't lose moisture.* 把饭菜盖上，免得水分流失。

mole /məʊl/ *countable noun* 可数名词
1 a natural dark spot on your skin 痣: *Rebecca has a mole on the side of her nose.* 丽贝卡鼻侧有颗痣。

2 a small animal with black fur that lives under the ground 鼹鼠

mole 鼹鼠

molecule /ˈmɒlɪˌkjuːl/ *countable noun* 可数名词
the smallest amount of a chemical substance that can exist by itself 分子: *These combinations of atoms are called molecule.* 原子的这些组合称为分子。

mom /mɒm/ *countable noun* 可数名词
（*American* 美国英语，*informal* 非正式）
→ see 见 **mum**

moment /ˈməʊmənt/ *countable noun* 可数名词
1 a very short period of time 片刻；瞬间: *In a moment he was gone.* 一转眼他就不见了。
2 the time when something happens 时刻；时候: *At that moment a car stopped at the house.* 就在那时，一辆汽车在房前停了下来。
at the moment or **at this moment** at or around the time when you are speaking 此刻；此时；眼下: *At the moment, the team is playing very well.* 眼下，球队打得非常好。
for the moment now, but not in the future 现在；目前；暂时: *For the moment, everything is fine.* 目前，一切都好。
in a moment very soon 马上；很快；一会儿: *'Please take a seat. Mr Garcia will see you in a moment.'* "请坐。加西亚先生一会儿就来见你。"

monarchy /ˈmɒnəki/ *noun* 名词 (**monarchies**)
a system in which a country has a king or queen 君主制；君主政体: *Greece abolished the monarchy in 1974.* 希腊于1974年废除君主制。

Monday /ˈmʌndeɪ, -di/ *noun* 名词
the day after Sunday and before Tuesday 星期一: *I went back to work on Monday.* 我星期一回去上班。□ *The first meeting was last Monday.* 第一次会面是在上周一。

money /ˈmʌni/ *uncountable noun* 不可数名词

the coins or notes that you use to buy things 钱；金钱: *Cars cost a lot of money.* 汽车很贵。□ *She spends too much money on clothes and shoes.* 她在衣服和鞋子上花钱太多。

monitor /ˈmɒnɪtə/ *verb* 动词 (**monitors, monitoring, monitored**)
to watch how something develops or progresses over a period of time 监视；监控；监测: *Doctors closely monitored her progress.* 医生们密切关注着她的病情进展。

monk /mʌŋk/ *countable noun* 可数名词
a member of a group of religious men who live together in a special building 僧侣；修道士

monkey /ˈmʌŋki/ *countable noun* 可数名词
an animal that has a long tail and can climb trees 猴子

monopoly /məˈnɒpəli/ *noun* 名词
1 a situation where a company or a person has complete control over something 垄断，独占: *The East India Company had a monopoly on all trade to Britain from the East.* 东印度公司垄断了东方国家至英国的全部贸易。
2 *countable* 可数 the only company that provides a particular product 垄断企业；专卖公司: *The company is a state-owned monopoly.* 该公司是国有垄断企业。

monotonous /məˈnɒtənəs/ *adjective* 形容词
very boring; never changing 单调的；枯燥的: *It's monotonous work, like most factory jobs.* 像大多数工厂岗位一样，这份工作单调乏味。

monsoon /mɒnˈsuːn/ *countable noun* 可数名词
the season in Southern Asia when there is a lot of very heavy rain (南亚的)季风季节，雨季: *The monsoon season lasts for about four months each year.* 季风季节每年大约持续4个月。

monster /ˈmɒnstə/ *countable noun* 可数名词
a big, ugly and frightening creature in stories 怪物；怪兽: *The film is about a monster in the wardrobe.* 影片刻画了一只衣橱怪兽。

month /mʌnθ/ *countable noun* 可数名词
one of the twelve parts that a year is divided into 月；月份: *September is the ninth month of the year.* 9月是一年中第9个月。□ *We go on holiday next month.* 我们下个月去度假。

monthly /ˈmʌnθli/ *adjective* 形容词, *adverb* 副词
happening every month 每月(的); 按月(的): *The monthly rent for his flat is £1,000.* 他的公寓月租为 1,000 英镑.
□ *The magazine is published monthly.* 这份杂志是月刊.

monument /ˈmɒnjumənt/ *countable noun* 可数名词
something that you build to help people remember an important event or person 纪念性建筑; 纪念碑: *This monument was built in memory of the soldiers who died in the war.* 这座纪念碑是为纪念阵亡将士而建.

moo /muː/ *verb* 动词 (moos, mooing, mooed)
to make the long, low sound of a cow (牛)哞哞叫: *We could hear the cows mooing.* 我们能听见牛在哞哞地叫.

mood /muːd/ *countable noun* 可数名词
the way you are feeling at a particular time 心境; 心情; 情绪: *Dad is in a very good mood today.* 爸爸今天心情特别好. □ *I had an argument with my girlfriend, so I was in a bad mood.* 我跟女朋友拌了嘴, 心情不好.

moody /ˈmuːdi/ *adjective* 形容词 (moodier, moodiest)
often becoming sad or angry without any warning 情绪化的; 喜怒无常的: *David's mother is very moody.* 戴维的妈妈很情绪化.

moon /muːn/ *singular noun* 单数名词
the large object that shines in the sky at night 月亮; 月球: *The first man on the moon was an American, Neil Armstrong.* 登月第一人是一名美国人, 叫尼尔·阿姆斯特朗.

moonlight /ˈmuːnlaɪt/ *uncountable noun* 不可数名词
the light that comes from the moon at night 月光: *They walked along the road in the moonlight.* 他们在月光下沿路散步.

moose /muːs/ *countable noun* 可数名词 (moose)
the largest member of the deer family 驼鹿: *In the autumn, they hunt moose.* 秋天, 他们捕猎驼鹿.

mop /mɒp/ *countable noun* 可数名词
a long stick with a lot of thick pieces of string at one end. You use it for washing floors. 拖把; 墩布 ● **mop** *verb* 动词 (mops, mopping, mopped): *I could see a woman mopping the stairs.* 我能看到一个女人在拖楼梯.

mop 拖地

moral¹ /ˈmɒrəl/ *noun* 名词
1 [morals] *plural* 复数 your ideas and beliefs about right and wrong behaviour 道德; 道义; 品德: *Amy has strong morals and high standards.* 埃米道德观念强, 道德水准高.
2 *countable* 可数 what you learn from a story or event about how you should or should not behave 寓意; 教益: *The moral of this sad story is 'do not trust anyone'.* 这个悲惨故事的寓意是"不要相信任何人".

moral² /ˈmɒrəl/ *adjective* 形容词
relating to people's beliefs about what is right or wrong 道德的; 道义的: *We all have a moral duty to stop racism.* 我们都有制止种族歧视的道义责任.
▶ **morally** /ˈmɒrəli/ *adverb* 副词: *It is morally wrong to kill a person.* 杀人是不道德的.

more /mɔː/ *adjective* 形容词, *adverb* 副词
1 used for talking about a greater amount of something 更多的; 较多的: *More people are surviving heart attacks than ever before.* 现在心脏病患者的存活率以往任何时候都高. □ *I need more time to think about what to do.* 我需要多一点时间考虑怎么办. ● **more** *pronoun* 代词: *As they worked harder, they ate more.* 他们干活儿更卖力了, 饭量也就大了起来. □ *We should do more to help these people.* 我们应该加大力度帮助这些人.
2 used for showing that something continues to happen 继续; 再; 多: *You should talk about your problems more.* 你应该多谈谈自己的问题.

more and more used for showing that something is becoming greater all the time 越来越: *She began eating more and more.* 她开始吃得越来越多.

more of something a greater amount of something than before, or than usual 更多某事物：*They're doing more of their own work.* 他们担负起自己更多的工作。
more than something used for talking about a greater amount of something than the amount mentioned 超过某事物：*The airport had been closed for more than a year.* 机场已经关闭了一年多。

moreover /mɔː'rəʊvə/ *adverb* 副词
used when you are adding more information about something (*formal* 正式) 再者；而且；此外：*She saw that there was a man behind her. Moreover, he was staring at her.* 她看见自己身后有个男人，而且，他在盯着自己看。

morning /'mɔːnɪŋ/ *noun* 名词
the part of each day between the time that people usually wake up and noon 早晨；上午：*Tomorrow morning we will take a walk around the city.* 明早我们会在城里走一走。 □ *On Sunday morning the telephone woke Bill.* 星期天早晨电话吵醒了比尔。
in the morning during the morning of the following day 次日早晨；明天早上：*I'm flying to St. Louis in the morning.* 明早我要飞往圣路易斯。

mortgage /'mɔːgɪdʒ/ *countable noun* 可数名词
a loan of money that you get from a bank in order to buy a house 房屋抵押贷款；房屋按揭贷款：*I had to sell my home because I couldn't afford the mortgage payments.* 我只要卖掉房子，因为我付不起按揭贷款了。

mosaic /məʊ'zeɪɪk/ *noun* 名词
a surface that is made of small pieces of coloured glass or stone 镶嵌图案；马赛克：*a Roman house with a beautiful mosaic floor* 地板镶嵌着漂亮马赛克的罗马房子
→ Look at picture on P10 and P13 参见彩插第 10 页和第 13 页

Moslem /'mɒzləm, 'mʊzlɪm/ *countable noun* 可数名词
→ see 见 **Muslim**

mosque /mɒsk/ *countable noun* 可数名词
a building where Muslims go to pray 清真寺

mosquito /mɒ'skiːtəʊ/ *countable noun* 可数名词 (**mosquitoes** or 或 **mosquitos**)
a small flying insect that bites people and animals 蚊子

moss /mɒs/ *noun* 名词 (**mosses**)
a very small, soft, green plant that grows on wet soil, or on wood or stone 藓类（植物）：*The ground was covered with moss.* 地面上长满了苔藓。

most /məʊst/ *adjective* 形容词, *adverb* 副词
1 used for talking about the largest amount of people or things 大部分的；大多数的：*Most people think he is a great actor.* 大多数人觉得他是个伟大的演员。
● **most** *pronoun* 代词：*Seventeen people were hurt. Most were students.* 17 人受伤，大多数是学生。
2 used for showing that something is true or happens more than anything else 最；最为：*What do you like most about your job?* 对于你的工作，你最喜欢哪一点？
make the most of something to use something in the best possible way 充分利用某事物：*You should make the most of what you have if you want to be happy.* 想要幸福，就要充分享受你所拥有的一切。
most of used for talking about the largest quantity of people or things 大部分的；大多数的：*Most of the houses here are very old.* 这里大部分房子都很老。 □ *I was away from home most of the time.* 我大多数时间出门在外。

mostly /'məʊstli/ *adverb* 副词
almost always 基本上；大部分；几乎总是：*My friends are mostly students.* 我的朋友基本上都是学生。 □ *Cars are made mostly of metal.* 汽车主要由金属制成。

motel /məʊ'tel/ *countable noun* 可数名词
a hotel for people who are travelling by car 汽车旅馆

moth /mɒθ/ *countable noun* 可数名词
an insect that has large wings and is attracted by lights at night 蛾

mother /'mʌðə/ *countable noun* 可数名词
your female parent 母亲；妈妈：*She's a mother of two children.* 她是两个孩子的母亲。

motherhood /'mʌðəˌhʊd/ *uncountable noun* 不可数名词
the state of being a mother 母亲身份：*I love motherhood. It's just the most extraordinary thing.* 我喜欢做母亲。这实在是最了不起的事儿。

'mother-in-ˌlaw *countable noun* 可数名词 (**mothers-in-law**)
the mother of your husband or wife 婆婆；

岳母

motion /ˈməʊʃn/ *uncountable noun* 不可数名词
movement 运动；运行：*The doors will not open when the lift is in motion.* 电梯运行时门不会打开。

motionless /ˈməʊʃnləs/ *adjective* 形容词
not moving at all 不动的；静止的：*They stood motionless, staring at each other.* 他们一动不动地站着，四目相视。

motivate /ˈməʊtɪˌveɪt/ *verb* 动词 (**motivates, motivating, motivated**)
to make someone feel determined to do something 激励；激发：*How do you motivate people to work hard?* 你怎么激励人们努力工作？
▶ **motivated** /ˈməʊtɪˌveɪtɪd/ *adjective* 形容词：*We are looking for a highly motivated and hard-working professional.* 我们正在物色一个积极性高、吃苦耐劳的专业技术人才。
▶ **motivation** /ˌməʊtɪˈveɪʃn/ *uncountable noun* 不可数名词：*His poor performance is caused by lack of motivation.* 他表现欠佳是因为动力不足。

motive /ˈməʊtɪv/ *countable noun* 可数名词
your reason for doing something 动机：*Police do not think robbery was a motive for the killing.* 警方认为杀人不是为了劫财。

motor /ˈməʊtə/ *countable noun* 可数名词
the part of a machine that makes it move or work 发动机；电动机；马达：*She got in the boat and started the motor.* 她上船发动了马达。

motorbike /ˈməʊtəˌbaɪk/ *countable noun* 可数名词
a vehicle with two wheels and an engine 摩托车

motorist /ˈməʊtərɪst/ *countable noun* 可数名词
a person who drives a car 汽车司机；汽车驾驶员：*Motorists should take extra care on the roads when it is raining.* 雨天司机要格外小心路况。

motorway /ˈməʊtəˌweɪ/ *noun* 名词
a wide road that allows cars to travel very fast over a long distance 高速公路：*the M1 motorway* M1 高速公路

motto /ˈmɒtəʊ/ *countable noun* 可数名词 (**mottoes** 或 **mottos**)
a short sentence or phrase that gives a rule for sensible behaviour 格言；箴言；座右铭：*My motto is 'Don't start what you can't finish'.* 我的座右铭是"不做有始无终的事"。

mould¹ /məʊld/ *noun* 名词
1 *countable* 可数 a hollow container that you pour liquid into. When the liquid becomes solid, it takes the same shape as the mould. 模具；模子：*Pour the mixture into moulds and place them in the fridge.* 把混合物倒入模具，然后放进冰箱里。
2 *uncountable* 不可数 a soft grey, green or blue substance that grows on old food or on damp surfaces 霉菌：*Hannah discovered mould growing in her bedroom cupboard.* 汉娜发现自己卧室的壁橱生霉菌了。

mould² /məʊld/ *verb* 动词 (**moulds, moulding, moulded**)
to make a soft substance into a particular shape 模塑；使（软材料）成模型：*The mixture is heated then moulded.* 混合物加热后模塑成型。

mound /maʊnd/ *countable noun* 可数名词
a large, round pile of something 墩；丘；堆：*huge mounds of soil* 大堆大堆的泥土

mountain /ˈmaʊntɪn/ *countable noun* 可数名词
a very high area of land with steep sides 山：*Mt. McKinley is the highest mountain in North America.* 麦金利山是北美洲第一高山。
→ Look at picture on P7 参见彩插第 7 页
a mountain of something 或 **mountains of something** a very large amount of something (*informal* 非正式) 大堆（或堆积如山）的某物：*He has a mountain of homework.* 他有一大堆家庭作业。

ˈmountain ˌbike *countable noun* 可数名词
a bicycle with a strong frame and thick tyres 山地自行车

mountaineer /ˌmaʊntɪˈnɪə/ *countable noun* 可数名词
a person who is skilful at climbing the steep sides of mountains 登山家；登山运动员

mountainous /ˈmaʊntɪnəs/ *adjective* 形容词
having a lot of mountains 多山的：*There were some beautiful photos of the country's mountainous landscape.* 有一些该国山景的漂亮照片。

mourn /mɔːn/ *verb* 动词 (**mourns, mourning, mourned**)
to show your deep sadness about someone who has died in the way that

you behave 哀悼；悼念；伤悼: *He mourned for his dead son.* 他伤悼死去的儿子。
▶ **mourning** /ˈmɔːnɪŋ/ ***uncountable noun*** 不可数名词: *He is still in mourning for his parents.* 他还在哀悼双亲。

mourner /ˈmɔːnə/ ***countable noun*** 可数名词
a person who goes to a funeral 哀悼者；吊丧者；吊唁者: *Crowds of mourners gathered outside the church.* 成群的吊唁者聚集在教堂外。

mouse /maʊs/ ***countable noun*** 可数名词 (**mice**)
1 a small animal with a long tail 老鼠；耗子
2 an object that you use to do things on a computer without using the keyboard 鼠标: *I clicked the mouse and the message appeared on the screen.* 我点击鼠标，消息出现在了屏幕上。
→ Look at picture on P11 参见彩插第 11 页

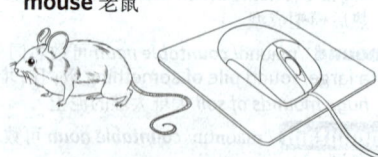
mouse 鼠标
mouse 老鼠

'mouse ˌmat ***countable noun*** 可数名词
a flat piece of soft material that you move the mouse on when you use a computer 鼠标垫
→ Look at picture on P11 参见彩插第 11 页

mousse /muːs/ ***uncountable noun*** 不可数名词
a sweet, light food made from eggs and cream 慕斯，奶油冻 (用鸡蛋、奶油制成): *His favourite dessert is chocolate mousse.* 他最爱吃的甜点是巧克力慕斯。

moustache /məˈstɑːʃ/ ***countable noun*** 可数名词
the hair that grows on a man's upper lip 髭；唇上须: *He was short and bald, and he had a moustache.* 他又矮又秃，上唇蓄着胡子。

mouth /maʊθ/ ***countable noun*** 可数名词
1 the part of your face that you use for eating or speaking 嘴；口: *When you cough, please cover your mouth.* 咳嗽时请捂住嘴。
→ Look at picture on P4 参见彩插第 4 页
2 the entrance or opening of a cave or a bottle (洞、瓶之) 口: *He stopped at the mouth of the tunnel.* 他在隧道口停了下来。

3 the place where a river goes into the sea 河口；入海口

mouthful /ˈmaʊθfʊl/ ***countable noun*** 可数名词
the amount of drink or food that you can put in your mouth at one time (饮料或食物的) 一口: *She drank a mouthful of coffee.* 她喝了一口咖啡。

move¹ /muːv/ ***verb*** 动词 (**moves, moving, moved**)
1 to put something in a different place 移动，挪动 (物体): *A police officer asked him to move his car.* 一名警察要他挪一下车。
2 to change position or go to a different place (人或物体) 移动，活动，动弹: *The train began to move.* 火车开动了。 □ *She waited for him to get up, but he didn't move.* 她等他起来，可他动也不动。
3 to go to live in a different place 搬家；搬迁: *She's moving to Cornwall next month.* 她下个月要搬到康沃尔去。
4 to make someone have strong feelings, especially of sadness, pity or sympathy 感动；打动: *The story surprised and moved me.* 这个故事让我既惊讶又感动。
▶ **moved** /muːvd/ ***adjective*** 形容词: *We felt quite moved when we heard his story.* 听了他的故事，我们十分感动。
move in to begin to live somewhere 搬来；迁入: *A new family has moved in next door.* 隔壁新搬来一家人。
move out to stop living in a particular place 搬走；迁出: *I wasn't happy living there, so I decided to move out.* 我住在那儿不开心，于是决定搬走。

move² /muːv/ ***countable noun*** 可数名词
1 when you change position or go to a different place 动作；行动: *The doctor made a move towards the door.* 医生朝门口挪了一步。
2 when you go to live in a different place 搬家；搬迁: *After his move to Liverpool, he got a job as an actor.* 搬到利物浦后，他谋到了一份演员的工作。
3 something you do in order to achieve something 举动；举措: *Leaving my job was a good move.* 离职是明智之举。

movement /ˈmuːvmənt/ ***noun*** 名词
1 when you change position, or go from one place to another 移动；活动: *Brian was injured and now has limited movement in his left arm.* 布赖恩受伤了，目前左臂活

动受限。
2 *countable* 可数 a group of people who have the same beliefs or ideas 运动（团体）: *It was one of the biggest political movements in the country.* 这是该国规模最大的政治运动之一。

mover /ˈmuːvə/ *countable noun* 可数名词
a person whose job is to move furniture or equipment from one building to another 搬家工人: *furniture movers* 家具搬家工人

movie /ˈmuːvi/ *countable noun* 可数名词
(*American* 美国英语)
→ see 见 **film**
the movies (*American* 美国英语) → see 见 **the cinema**

moving /ˈmuːvɪŋ/ *adjective* 形容词
making you feel a strong emotion such as sadness, pity or sympathy 感人的；动人的: *This is a moving story of the love between a master and his loyal dog.* 这是一个动人的故事，讲述了主人和他的忠犬之间的爱。

mow /məʊ/ *verb* 动词 (**mows, mowing, mowed, mown**)
to cut an area of grass using a machine (called a mower) 用割草机割（或修剪）: *Connor was in the garden, mowing the lawn.* 康纳在花园里修剪草坪。

mown /məʊn/
→ see 见 **mow**

mozzarella /ˌmɒtsəˈrelə/ *uncountable noun* 不可数名词
a type of white Italian cheese 莫泽雷勒干酪（一种意大利白色干酪）: *Maria made a delicious pizza topped with tomato and mozzarella.* 玛丽亚做了一个美味的比萨，上面放了番茄和莫泽雷勒干酪。

MP /ˌem ˈpiː/ *countable noun* 可数名词 (**MPs**)
In Britain, a person who has been elected to represent the people from a particular area in the government. **MP** is short for (缩写 =) 'Member of Parliament'. (英国)下院议员

MP3 /ˌem piː ˈθriː/ *countable noun* 可数名词 (**MP3s**)
a type of computer file that contains music *MP3 文件

MP3 player *countable noun* 可数名词
a small machine for listening to music that is stored on computer files *MP3 播放器
→ Look at picture on P11 参见彩插第 11 页

mph also 亦作 **m.p.h.**

used for showing the speed of a vehicle. **Mph** is short for (缩写 =) 'miles per hour'. 英里／小时

Mr /ˈmɪstə/ *noun* 名词
used before a man's name when you want to be polite or formal 先生（礼貌或正式用语，用于男子姓名前）: *Could I please speak to Mr Johnson?* 请找一下约翰逊先生好吗？ □ *Our teacher this term is called Mr Becker.* 本学期教我们的老师叫贝克尔先生。

Mrs /ˈmɪsɪz/ *noun* 名词
used before the name of a married woman when you want to be polite or formal 夫人，太太（礼貌或正式用语，用于已婚女子姓名前）: *Hello, Mrs Morley. How are you?* 你好，莫利夫人。近来可好？ □ *Excuse me, does Mrs Anne Pritchard live here?* 借问一下，安妮·普里查德夫人住这里吗？

Ms /məz, mɪz/ *noun* 名词
used, especially in written English, before a woman's name, instead of **Mrs** or **Miss** 女士（用于女子姓名前，代替 Mrs 或 Miss，尤用于书面语）: *Ms Kennedy refused to speak to reporters after the meeting.* 肯尼迪女士会后拒绝接受记者采访。

much /mʌtʃ/ *adjective* 形容词, *adverb* 副词
1 used for talking about the large amount of something 许多的；大量的: *I ate too much food.* 我吃得太多了。 □ *These plants do not need much water.* 这些植物不怎么需要水。 □ *I don't have much free time these days.* 我近来没什么空儿。● **much** *pronoun* 代词: *I ate too much.* 我吃得太多了。
2 a lot 很；非常；…得多: *His car is much bigger than mine.* 他的车比我的大多了。 □ *Thank you very much.* 非常感谢。 □ *He doesn't like jazz much.* 他不太喜欢爵士乐。
how much used to ask questions about amounts (用于询问数量)多少: *How much money can I spend?* 我能花多少钱？
not...much not very often 不太经常: *Gwen did not see her father very much.* 格温不怎么见她父亲。

LANGUAGE HELP 语言提示
See note at **many**. 见 **many** 的语言提示。

mud /mʌd/ *uncountable noun* 不可数名词
a sticky mixture of earth and water 泥；泥巴: *Andy's clothes were covered with mud.* 安迪衣服上都是泥。

muddle[1] /ˈmʌdəl/ *noun* 名词
in a muddle confused 糊涂的；困惑的；混

乱的：*My thoughts are all in a muddle.* 我心里一团乱麻。

muddle² /ˈmʌdəl/ *verb* 动词 (**muddles, muddling, muddled**)
(*also 亦作* **muddle someone / something up**) to think that someone or something is another person or thing 弄混；混淆；将…混为一谈：*People often muddle up the two names.* 人们经常把这两个名字弄混。

muddled /ˈmʌdəld/ *adjective* 形容词 confused 糊涂的；困惑的；混乱的：*I'm a bit muddled. I'm not sure where to begin.* 我有点儿糊涂，不知道从哪儿下手。

muddy /ˈmʌdi/ *adjective* 形容词 (**muddier, muddiest**)
covered with mud 满是泥的；泥泞的：*Philip left his muddy boots at the kitchen door.* 菲利普把满是泥的靴子丢在了厨房门口。

muffin /ˈmʌfɪn/ *countable noun* 可数名词 a small, round, sweet cake that often has fruit inside 松糕；松饼：*a blueberry muffin* 蓝莓松糕

mug¹ /mʌɡ/ *countable noun* 可数名词 a deep cup with straight sides 马克杯：*He poured tea into the mugs.* 他把茶倒进几个马克杯里。

mugs 马克杯

mug² /mʌɡ/ *verb* 动词 (**mugs, mugging, mugged**)
to attack someone and steal their money 抢劫；打劫：*I was walking to my car when this guy tried to mug me.* 我正朝我车那边走，这个家伙动手想抢劫我。

▶ **mugger** /ˈmʌɡə/ *countable noun* 可数名词：*When the mugger grabbed her handbag, Ms Jones fell to the ground.* 劫匪抢了琼斯女士的手提包，她摔倒在地。

multicoloured /ˌmʌltiˈkʌləd/ *adjective* 形容词
having many different colours 多彩的；色彩缤纷的：*Diego was wearing a new, multicoloured shirt.* 迭戈穿了件色彩斑斓的新衬衣。

multimedia /ˌmʌltiˈmiːdiə/ *uncountable noun* 不可数名词
used for describing computer programs that have sound, pictures and film, as well as text 多媒体：*Most of his teachers use multimedia in the classroom.* 他的大多数老师课上都使用多媒体。

multinational /ˌmʌltiˈnæʃənəl/ *adjective* 形容词
1 having offices or businesses in many different countries（公司等）跨国的：*multinational companies* 跨国公司
● **multinational** *countable noun* 可数名词：*Large multinationals control the industry.* 大型跨国公司控制着这个产业。
2 involving people from several different countries 多国的；人员来自多国的：*The U.S. troops would be part of a multinational force.* 美军将是多国部队的一个组成部分。

multiple /ˈmʌltɪpəl/ *adjective* 形容词
consisting of many parts, involving many people or having many uses 多部分的；多人的；多用途的：*He died of multiple injuries.* 他身体多处受伤而亡。

multiply /ˈmʌltɪplaɪ/ *verb* 动词 (**multiplies, multiplying, multiplied**)
to add a number to itself a certain number of times 乘：*What do you get if you multiply six by nine?* 6 乘 9 等于多少？
▶ **multiplication** /ˌmʌltɪplɪˈkeɪʃən/ *uncountable noun* 不可数名词：*a multiplication sum* 乘法运算
→ Look at picture on P2 参见彩插第 2 页

multistorey /ˌmʌltiˈstɔːri/ *adjective* 形容词
with several floors at different levels above the ground（建筑物）多层的：*The shop is in a big multistorey building.* 这家店在一座大型多层建筑里。

mum /mʌm/ *countable noun* 可数名词
(*American 美国英语*: **mom**)
your mother (*informal 非正式*) 妈妈：*We waited for my mum and dad to get home.* 我们等爸爸妈妈回家。 □ *Bye, Mum. Love you.* 拜拜，妈妈。爱你。

mumble /ˈmʌmbəl/ *verb* 动词 (**mumbles, mumbling, mumbled**)
to speak quietly and not clearly 咕哝；嘟哝；小声含混地说：*The boy blushed and mumbled a few words.* 男孩儿脸红了，咕哝了几句。

mummy /ˈmʌmi/ *countable noun* 可数名词 (**mummies**)
1 a young child's word for their mother (*informal 非正式*) 妈咪（儿语）：*Please can I have a biscuit, Mummy?* 妈咪，我能吃一块饼干吗？ □ *I want my mummy.* 我要妈咪。

2 a dead body that was preserved long ago by being rubbed with special oils and wrapped in cloth 木乃伊: *an ancient Egyptian mummy* 一具古埃及木乃伊

murder¹ /ˈmɜːdə/ ***noun*** 名词
the crime of deliberately killing a person 谋杀(罪): *The jury found him guilty of murder.* 陪审团裁定他犯有谋杀罪。□ *The detective has worked on hundreds of murder cases.* 这位侦探已经经手过数百件谋杀案。

murder² /ˈmɜːdə/ ***verb*** 动词 (**murders, murdering, murdered**)
to commit the crime of killing someone deliberately 谋杀; 蓄意杀害: *The film is about a woman who murders her husband.* 影片讲述了一个谋害丈夫的女子的故事。
▶ **murderer** /ˈmɜːdərə/ ***countable noun*** 可数名词: *One of these men is the murderer.* 这些男子中有一个就是凶手。

murmur /ˈmɜːmə/ ***verb*** 动词 (**murmurs, murmuring, murmured**)
to say something very quietly 低语; 咕哝: *He turned and murmured something to Karen.* 他转身跟卡伦咕哝了些什么。□ *'It's lovely,' she murmured.* "好可爱。"她低声道。● **murmur** ***countable noun*** 可数名词: *They spoke in low murmurs.* 他们悄声低语。

muscle /ˈmʌsəl/ ***noun*** 名词
one of the parts inside your body that connect your bones, and that help you to move 肌肉: *Exercise helps to keep your muscles strong.* 锻炼有助于保持肌肉强健。
→ Look at picture on P5 参见彩插第 5 页

muscular /ˈmʌskjʊlə/ ***adjective*** 形容词
having strong, firm muscles 肌肉发达的: *Jordan was tall and muscular.* 乔丹身材高大, 肌肉发达。

museum /mjuːˈziːəm/ ***countable noun*** 可数名词
a building where you can look at interesting and valuable objects 博物馆; 博物院: *Hundreds of people came to the museum to see the exhibition.* 数百人来博物馆看这个展览。

mushroom /ˈmʌʃruːm/ ***noun*** 名词
a plant with a short stem and a round top that you can eat 蘑菇: *There are many types of wild mushroom, and some of them are poisonous.* 野生蘑菇有很多种, 其中一些有毒。

mushroom 蘑菇

music /ˈmjuːzɪk/ ***uncountable noun*** 不可数名词
1 the pleasant sound that you make when you sing or play instruments 音乐; 乐曲: *Diane is studying classical music.* 黛安娜在学习古典乐。□ *What's your favourite type of music?* 你最喜欢什么类型的音乐?
2 the symbols that you write on paper to tell people what to sing or play 乐谱: *He can't read music.* 他不识谱。
→ Look at picture on P12 参见彩插第 12 页

musical¹ /ˈmjuːzɪkəl/ ***adjective*** 形容词
1 relating to playing or studying music 音乐的: *Many of the kids have real musical talent.* 这些孩子很多都有非常高的音乐天分。
2 having a natural ability and interest in music 有音乐天赋的; 喜爱音乐的: *I come from a musical family.* 我来自音乐世家。

musical² /ˈmjuːzɪkəl/ ***countable noun*** 可数名词
a play or a film that uses singing and dancing in the story 音乐剧; 歌舞片: *Have you seen the musical, 'Miss Saigon'?* 你看过音乐剧《西贡小姐》吗?

musical instrument ***countable noun*** 可数名词
an object such as a piano, guitar or violin that you play in order to produce music 乐器: *The drum is one of the oldest musical instruments.* 鼓是最古老的乐器之一。
→ Look at pictures on P12 参见彩插第 12 页

musician /mjuːˈzɪʃən/ ***countable noun*** 可数名词
a person who plays a musical instrument as their job or hobby 音乐家; 乐师; 乐手: *Michael is a brilliant musician.* 迈克尔是位才华横溢的音乐家。

Muslim /ˈmʊzlɪm/ ***countable noun*** 可数名词
someone who believes in the religion of Islam and lives according to its rules 穆斯林; 伊斯兰教信徒 ● **Muslim** ***adjective*** 形容词: *an ancient Muslim mosque* 一座古清

真寺

must /məst, STRONG 强读 mʌst/ *modal verb* 情态动词
1 used for showing that you think something is very important or necessary 必须；一定要：*Your clothes must fit well.* 衣服必须穿得非常合身才行。▫ *You must tell me everything you know.* 你一定要把你知道的都告诉我。
2 used for showing that you are almost sure that something is true 肯定；一定：*Claire's car isn't there, so she must be at work.* 克莱尔的车不在，她一定是在工作。

mustard /ˈmʌstəd/ *noun* 名词
a spicy yellow or brown sauce that you eat with meat 芥末酱：*I had a chicken and mustard sandwich for lunch.* 我午饭吃了芥末鸡肉三明治。

mustn't /ˈmʌsnt/
short for (缩写 =) 'must not'

must've /ˈmʌstəv/
short for (缩写 =) 'must have'

mutter /ˈmʌtə/ *verb* 动词 (**mutters, muttering, muttered**)
to speak in a very quiet voice that is difficult to hear, often when you are angry about something (伴有怒气地) 嘟囔，嘟哝：*'He's crazy,' she muttered.* "他疯了。"她嘟囔道。

mutual /ˈmjuːtʃuəl/ *adjective* 形容词
felt or done by two people or groups 二者共同的；相互的：*It was a mutual decision by Dean and me.* 这是我和迪安的共同决定。▫ *Nick didn't like me, and the feeling was mutual.* 尼克不喜欢我，我也不喜欢他。

my /maɪ/ *adjective* 形容词
belonging or relating to yourself 我的：*We can eat at my house tonight.* 今晚我们可以在我家吃饭。

myself /maɪˈself/ *pronoun* 代词
1 used when the person speaking or writing is both the subject and the object of the verb 我自己；我本人：*I asked myself what I should do.* 我问自己该怎么办。
2 used for saying that you do something alone without help from anyone else 自己；独自；我一个人：*'Where did you get that dress?' — 'I made it myself.'* "你那条连衣裙在哪儿买的？" —— "我自己做的。"

mysterious /mɪˈstɪəriəs/ *adjective* 形容词
strange, and not known about or understood 神秘的；离奇的：*A mysterious illness made him sick.* 他得了一种怪病。
▶ **mysteriously** /mɪˈstɪəriəsli/ *adverb* 副词：*The evidence mysteriously disappeared.* 证据离奇地消失了。

mystery /ˈmɪstəri/ *countable noun* 可数名词 (**mysteries**)
1 something that you cannot explain or understand 谜；奥秘；怪事；神秘事物：*Why he behaved in this way is a mystery.* 他为什么这样做是个谜。
2 a story or a film about a crime or strange events that are only explained at the end 悬疑故事；悬疑片：*I was alone at home watching a murder mystery on TV.* 我一个人在家看电视上的一部凶杀悬疑片。

myth /mɪθ/ *noun* 名词
1 an ancient story about gods and magic 神话：*the famous Greek myth of Medusa, the snake-haired monster* 有关蛇发女妖美杜莎的著名希腊神话
2 a belief or an explanation that is not true 错误信念；误解：*This story is a myth.* 这个说法是个误会。

Nn

nag /næg/ *verb* 动词 (**nags, nagging, nagged**)
to keep asking someone to do something 絮叨；唠叨: *My mum's always nagging me about getting a good job.* 我妈妈总是唠叨着让我找份好工作。

nail¹ /neɪl/ *countable noun* 可数名词
1 a thin piece of metal with one pointed end and one flat end that you hit with a hammer in order to fix things together 钉子: *A mirror hung on a nail above the sink.* 水槽上方用钉子挂着一面镜子。
2 the thin hard part that grows at the end of each of your fingers and toes 指甲；趾甲: *Try to keep your nails short.* 要常剪指甲。

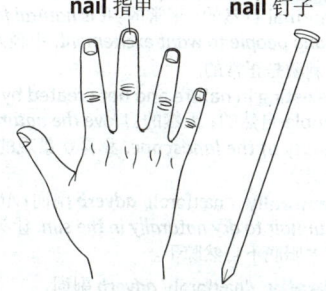

nail 指甲   nail 钉子

nail² /neɪl/ *verb* 动词 (**nails, nailing, nailed**)
1 to fasten something in a particular position using one or more nails (用钉子) 固定，钉牢: *The sign was nailed to a tree.* 标语被钉在了树上。
2 to do something very well or successfully (*informal* 非正式) 做好；成功完成: *Well done! You nailed it!* 干得好！你成功了！

naive /naɪˈiːv/ *also* 亦作 **naïve** *adjective* 形容词
without much experience of life; expecting things to be easy 天真的；幼稚的: *I was naive to think they would agree.* 我天真地以为他们会同意。

naked /ˈneɪkɪd/ *adjective* 形容词
not wearing any clothes 赤身裸体的: *She held the naked baby in her arms.* 她把赤裸的婴儿抱在怀里。

name¹ /neɪm/ *countable noun* 可数名词
1 the word or words that you use to talk to a particular person, or to talk about them (人的)名字，姓名: '*What's his name?*' — '*Peter.*' "他叫什么名字？" —— "彼得。"
2 the word or words that you use to talk about a particular place or thing (地方、物体的)名称: *What is the name of this street?* 这条街叫什么名字？ □ *Can you tell me the name of this plant?* 你能告诉我这种植物的名称吗？

name² /neɪm/ *verb* 动词 (**names, naming, named**)
to give someone or something a name 给…取名；给…命名: *He named his first child Christopher after his brother.* 他以哥哥的名字给他的第一个孩子取名为克里斯托弗。
call someone names to say unpleasant things to someone 谩骂某人: *It's cruel to call people names.* 谩骂别人很刻毒。

nanny /ˈnæni/ *countable noun* 可数名词 (**nannies**)
a person whose job is to take care of children in a family (照看小孩的)保姆

nap /næp/ *countable noun* 可数名词
a short sleep, usually during the day (通常指在白天的)打盹儿，小睡: *We had a nap after lunch.* 午餐后，我们打了个盹儿。

napkin /ˈnæpkɪn/ *countable noun* 可数名词
a square of cloth or paper that you use when you are eating to protect your clothes, or to wipe your mouth or hands 餐巾；餐巾纸

nappy /ˈnæpi/ *countable noun* 可数名词 (**nappies**) (*American* 美国英语: **diaper**)
a piece of cloth or strong paper that a baby wears around its bottom and between its legs 尿布: *I need to change the baby's nappy.* 我需要给宝宝换尿布。

narrator /nəˈreɪtə/ *countable noun* 可数名词
the person who tells the story in a book or

a film（书中或电影中的）叙述者，讲述者：*The story's narrator is a famous actress.* 故事的讲述者是一位著名女演员。

narrow /ˈnærəʊ/ *adjective* 形容词
(**narrower, narrowest**)
small in distance from one side to the other 狭窄的：*We walked through the town's narrow streets.* 我们穿过镇上狭窄的街道。

nasty /ˈnɑːsti/ *adjective* 形容词 (**nastier, nastiest**)
1 very unpleasant 令人十分不快的；令人厌恶的：*This medicine has a very nasty taste.* 这药太难吃了。□ *The tax increase was a nasty surprise for businesses.* 加税对企业来说可谓飞来横祸。
2 unkind 不友善的；恶毒的：*If anyone is nasty to you, you should tell the teacher.* 如果有人对你有恶意，你应该告诉老师。

nation /ˈneɪʃən/ *countable noun* 可数名词
an individual country, its people and its social and political structures 国家：*the United States and other nations* 美国和其他国家

national /ˈnæʃənəl/ *adjective* 形容词
1 relating to the whole of a country or nation 全国的；国家的：*He's the manager of the French national football team.* 他是法国国家足球队主教练。□ *The ad appeared in the national newspapers.* 这则广告刊登在全国性报纸上。
2 typical of the people or traditions of a particular country or nation 国民的；民族的：*When you travel abroad, you must respect national traditions.* 出国旅行时，必须尊重当地的民族传统。□ *The national dress of Scotland is the kilt.* 苏格兰的民族服装是短褶裙。

national anthem /ˌnæʃənəl ˈænθəm/ *countable noun* 可数名词
the official song of a country 国歌：*The national anthem was played while the winners received their medals.* 获胜者领奖牌时奏响了国歌。

nationality /ˌnæʃəˈnæləti/ *noun* 名词 (**nationalities**)
the state of being a legal citizen of a particular country 国籍：*I'm not sure of her nationality, but I think she's Canadian.* 我不清楚她的国籍，但是我觉得她是加拿大人。

nationwide /ˌneɪʃənˈwaɪd/ *adjective* 形容词, *adverb* 副词

happening or existing in all parts of a country 全国性的；在全国范围：*Car crime is a nationwide problem.* 汽车犯罪是个全国性问题。□ *Unemployment fell nationwide last month.* 上个月全国范围内的失业率都下降了。

native¹ /ˈneɪtɪv/ *adjective* 形容词
relating to the particular country, region or town where you were born 出生地的；原产地的：*It was his first visit to his native country since 1948.* 这是他自1948年以来第一次到访他的祖国。□ *The garden features Australian native plants.* 这个花园里以澳大利亚的本土植物为主。

native language the first language that you learned to speak when you were a child 母语：*Her native language was Swedish.* 她的母语是瑞典语。

native² /ˈneɪtɪv/ *countable noun* 可数名词
someone who was born in a particular country, region or town 出生于某国（或某地）的人：*The owner of the restaurant is a native of Hong Kong.* 饭店老板是香港人。

natural /ˈnætʃərəl/ *adjective* 形容词
1 normal 自然的；正常的：*It is natural for young people to want excitement.* 年轻人追求刺激是正常的。
2 existing in nature and not created by people 自然的；天然的：*I love the natural beauty of the landscape.* 我喜欢景观的自然美。
▶ **naturally** /ˈnætʃərəli/ *adverb* 副词：*Allow your hair to dry naturally in the sun.* 让头发在太阳底下自然晾干。

naturally /ˈnætʃərəli/ *adverb* 副词
used for showing that something is very obvious and not surprising 当然地；自然地：*When things go wrong, we naturally feel disappointed.* 事情出错时，我们当然会感到失望。

nature /ˈneɪtʃə/ *noun* 名词
1 *uncountable* 不可数 all the animals, plants and things that happen in the world that are not made or caused by people 大自然；自然界：*The essay discusses the relationship between humans and nature.* 这篇文章讨论了人与自然的关系。

> **LANGUAGE HELP** 语言提示
> See note at **countryside**. 见 countryside 的语言提示。

2 *singular* 单数 a person's character,

which they show by the way they behave 个性；天性: *People called her 'Sunny' because of her friendly nature.* 她天性友善，所以人们都叫她"阳光"。

naughty /ˈnɔːti/ *adjective* 形容词 (**naughtier, naughtiest**)
badly behaved; not doing what someone tells you to do 顽皮的；不听话的: *When I'm very naughty, my mum sends me to bed early.* 我调皮过火的时候，妈妈就打发我早点上床睡觉。

nausea /ˈnɔːziə/ *uncountable noun* 不可数名词
a feeling that you are going to vomit 恶心: *The symptoms include headaches and nausea.* 症状包括头疼、恶心。

naval /ˈneɪvəl/ *adjective* 形容词
relating to a country's navy 海军的: *He was a senior naval officer.* 他是海军高级军官。

navigate /ˈnævɪɡeɪt/ *verb* 动词 (**navigates, navigating, navigated**)
1 to find the direction that you need to travel in, using a map or the sun, for example 导航；确定方向: *We navigated using the sun by day and the stars by night.* 我们白天靠太阳、晚上靠星星来确定方向。
2 to find the information that you need in a website by clicking on particular words or images (= links) that take you from one web page to another 在（网站）中导航: *A home page gives users information and helps them to navigate the site.* 主页为用户提供信息，并为他们提供网站导航。
▶ **navigation** /ˌnævɪˈɡeɪʃən/ *uncountable noun* 不可数名词: *Navigation through the site is simple and quick.* 网站导航简单又快捷。

navy /ˈneɪvi/ *noun* 名词 (**navies**)
a country's warships and the people who work in them 海军: *Her son is in the navy.* 她儿子在海军服役。

ˌnavy ˈblue *adjective* 形容词
very dark blue in colour 海军蓝的；藏青色的: *I wore navy blue trousers and a white shirt.* 我穿了藏青色的裤子和白色的衬衫。
● **navy blue** *noun* 名词: *She was dressed in navy blue.* 她穿了一身藏青色的衣服。

near /nɪə/ *preposition* 介词
only a short distance away; close to someone or something 在…附近；靠近: *Don't come near me!* 不要靠近我! □ *The café is near the station in Edmonton.* 咖啡馆在埃德蒙顿车站附近。● **near** *adjective* 形容词 (**nearer, nearest**): *Excuse me, where's the nearest post office?* 打扰一下，请问最近的邮局怎么走？
in the near future very soon 在不久的将来: *I hope I'll be able to meet her in the near future.* 我希望不久之后就能见到她。

nearby /ˌnɪəˈbaɪ/ *adjective* 形容词, *adverb* 副词
only a short distance away; close 附近的；在近处: *He sat at a nearby table.* 他坐在邻桌。□ *Her sister lives nearby.* 她妹妹住在附近。

nearly /ˈnɪəli/ *adverb* 副词
1 almost a particular amount（数量上）几乎，将近: *He has worked for the company for nearly 20 years.* 他在这家公司工作了近20年。
2 almost a particular time or state（时间或状态上）即将，就要: *'What time is it?' — 'Nearly five o'clock.'* "几点了？"——"快5点了。" □ *I've nearly finished.* 我就要完成了。

neat /niːt/ *adjective* 形容词 (**neater, neatest**)
with everything in the correct place 整洁的；整齐的: *She's got very neat handwriting.* 她的字迹非常工整。
▶ **neatly** /ˈniːtli/ *adverb* 副词: *He folded his newspaper neatly and put it in his bag.* 他把报纸整齐地叠起来装进了包里。

necessary /ˈnesɪsəri/ *adjective* 形容词
needed in order to do something, have something or make something happen 必要的；必需的: *Exercise is necessary if you want to lose weight.* 想要减肥，锻炼必不可少。□ *I'm sure I've got the necessary skills for this job.* 我确信自己已经掌握了这份工作所需的技能。

necessity /nɪˈsesɪti/ *countable noun* 可数名词 (**necessities**)
something that you must have to live 必需品: *The price of food and other necessities has increased.* 食品和其他必需品都涨价了。

neck /nek/ *countable noun* 可数名词
1 the part of your body between your head and the rest of your body 颈；脖子: *He was wearing a red scarf around his neck.* 他脖子上围着一条红围巾。
→ Look at picture on P4 参见彩插第 4 页
2 the part of a shirt or dress that surrounds your neck 衣领: *She wore a dress with a high neck.* 她穿了一条高领连衣裙。

necklace - negligence

necklace /ˈnekləs/ *countable noun* 可数名词
a piece of jewellery that you wear around your neck 项链：*She was wearing a diamond necklace.* 她戴了一条钻石项链。

necklace 项链

nectarine /ˈnektəriːn, -rɪn/ *countable noun* 可数名词
a red-and-yellow fruit with a smooth skin 油桃

need¹ /niːd/ *verb* 动词 (**needs, needing, needed**)
1 to require something 需要（某物）：*He desperately needed money.* 他急需钱。
2 to have to do something because it is necessary 必须，得（做某事）：*I need to make a phone call.* 我得打个电话。

need² /niːd/ *noun* 名词
1 singular 单数 a situation in which you must have or do something 需要；需求：*There is a need for more schools in the area.* 这个地区需要增建学校。□ *There is a need to recruit more doctors and nurses in this country.* 这个国家需要扩招医护人员。
2 [needs] plural 复数 things that you want or must have 需求品；必需品：*Parents have to look after their child's physical and emotional needs.* 父母必须照顾到孩子的生理和情感需求。

needle /ˈniːdəl/ *countable noun* 可数名词
1 a small, thin metal tool with a sharp point that you use for sewing 缝衣针：*If you get me a needle and thread, I'll sew the button on.* 给我针线，我能把扣子缝上。
2 a thin hollow metal tube with a sharp point that is used for putting a drug into someone's body 注射针：*Dirty needles spread disease.* 不洁针头会传播疾病。
3 the long strip of metal or plastic on an instrument that shows a measurement of, for example, speed or weight（仪器上的）指针：*The needle on the boiler is pointing to 200 degrees.* 锅炉上的指针指着 200 度。
4 one of the thin, hard, pointed parts of some trees that stay green all year 针叶：*There was a thick layer of pine needles on the ground.* 地上有一层厚厚的松针。

needless /ˈniːdləs/ *adjective* 形容词
not necessary; able to be avoided 不必要的；可避免的：*His death was so needless.* 他的死太没有必要了。
▶ **needlessly** /ˈniːdləsli/ *adverb* 副词：*Children are dying needlessly.* 孩子们在白白死去。

needn't /ˈniːdənt/
short for (缩写 =) 'need not'

needy /ˈniːdi/ *adjective* 形容词 (**needier, neediest**)
without enough food, medicine or clothing 贫苦的；穷困的：*They provide housing for needy families.* 他们为贫困家庭提供住房。

negative¹ /ˈnegətɪv/ *adjective* 形容词
1 unpleasant or harmful 令人不悦的；有害的：*Patients talked about their negative childhood experiences.* 患者们谈论了痛苦的童年经历。
2 considering only the bad aspects of a situation 消极的；负面的：*When someone asks for your opinion, don't be negative.* 有人询问你的意见时，不要流露出消极情绪。
▶ **negatively** /ˈnegətɪvli/ *adverb* 副词：*Why do so many people think negatively?* 为什么这么多人思想都很消极？
3 saying or meaning 'no' 否定的：*Dr Robertson gave a negative response.* 罗伯逊博士给了否定回应。
▶ **negatively** /ˈnegətɪvli/ *adverb* 副词：*Sixty percent of people answered negatively.* 60% 的人给了否定回答。
4 less than zero. Compare with **positive**.（数字）负的（比较 positive）：*a negative number such as minus 5* 负数，如 –5

negative² /ˈnegətɪv/ *countable noun* 可数名词
in grammar, a form that is used for saying 'no' or 'not', such as 'don't' and 'haven't'（语法中的）否定式

neglect /nɪˈglekt/ *verb* 动词 (**neglects, neglecting, neglected**)
to not take care of someone or something 忽视；疏于照料：*The neighbours claim that she is neglecting her children.* 邻居们称她疏于照看孩子。● **neglect** *uncountable noun* 不可数名词：*The house is being repaired after years of neglect.* 这座房子失修多年，目前正在修缮。
▶ **neglected** /nɪˈglektɪd/ *adjective* 形容词：*a neglected child* 疏于照管的孩子

negligence /ˈneglɪdʒəns/ *uncountable noun* 不可数名词
when someone does not do something

that they should do 失职；疏忽：*His negligence caused the accident.* 他的失职导致了这场事故。
▶**negligent** /ˈneglɪdʒənt/ *adjective* 形容词：*The jury decided that the airline was negligent.* 陪审团裁定航空公司存在疏漏。
▶**negligently** /ˈneglɪdʒəntli/ *adverb* 副词：*I believe that the doctor acted negligently.* 我认为这个医生疏于职守。

negotiate /nɪˈɡəʊʃieɪt/ *verb* 动词 (negotiates, negotiating, negotiated) to talk about a problem or a situation in order to reach an agreement 谈判；协商；磋商：*The unions are negotiating with the Japanese car firm.* 工会正在与这家日本汽车公司谈判。

negotiations /nɪˌɡəʊʃiˈeɪʃənz/ *plural noun* 复数名词 discussions between people, during which they try to reach an agreement 谈判；协商；磋商：*The negotiations were successful.* 谈判成功了。

neigh /neɪ/ *verb* 动词 (neighs, neighing, neighed) when a horse neighs, it makes its typical loud sound (马)嘶鸣：*The horse neighed and disappeared amongst the trees.* 马儿一声嘶鸣，随后消失在树林里。● **neigh** *countable noun* 可数名词：*The horse gave a loud neigh.* 马儿发出一声嘹亮的嘶鸣。

neighbour /ˈneɪbə/ *countable noun* 可数名词 someone who lives near you 邻居：*Sometimes we invite the neighbours over for dinner.* 有时我们会邀请邻居过来共进晚餐。

neighbourhood /ˈneɪbəhʊd/ *countable noun* 可数名词 one of the parts of a town where people live (城镇的)街区，邻里：*Their house is in a quiet, residential neighbourhood.* 他们的房子在一个安静的住宅区。

neither /ˈnaɪðə, ˈniːðə/ *adjective* 形容词, *adverb* 副词
1 not one or the other 两者都不(的)；两者中无一(的)：*At first, neither man could speak.* 起初，两个人都说不出话。▢ *Neither of us felt like going out.* 我俩都不想出去。
2 also not 也不；都不：*I never learned to swim and neither did they.* 我从没学过游泳，他们也没有。
neither ... nor used when you are talking about two or more things that are not true

or do not happen 既不⋯也不⋯：*Professor Hisamatsu spoke neither English nor German.* 久松教授既不说英语也不说德语。

neon /ˈniːɒn/ *adjective* 形容词 filled with a special gas (= neon) that produces a bright electric light 霓虹的；充氖气的：*In the city streets the neon lights flashed.* 城市的街道上，霓虹灯闪烁着。

nephew /ˈnefjuː, ˈnev-/ *countable noun* 可数名词 the son of your sister or brother 侄子；外甥：*I am planning a birthday party for my nephew.* 我在为侄子筹划一场生日聚会。

nerve /nɜːv/ *noun* 名词
1 *countable* 可数 one of the long thin threads in your body that send messages between your brain and other parts of your body 神经：*pain from a damaged nerve* 受损神经产生的痛
→ Look at picture on P5 参见彩插第 5 页
2 *uncountable* 不可数 the courage that you need to do something difficult or dangerous 勇气；胆量：*I don't know why he lost his nerve.* 我不知道他为什么没了勇气。
get on someone's nerves to annoy someone (*informal* 非正式) 使某人烦恼：*The children's noisy games were getting on his nerves.* 孩子们闹哄哄地做着游戏，这让他心烦意乱。

nerves /nɜːvz/ *plural noun* 复数名词 feelings of worry or fear 忧虑；紧张；忧惧：*He plays the piano to calm his nerves and relax.* 他弹钢琴来安抚自己的紧张情绪，让自己放松下来。
→ Look at picture on P5 参见彩插第 5 页

nervous /ˈnɜːvəs/ *adjective* 形容词 frightened or worried 忧虑的；紧张的；忧惧的：*I was very nervous during the job interview.* 求职面试中我很紧张。
▶**nervously** /ˈnɜːvəsli/ *adverb* 副词：*Beth stood up nervously when the teacher came into the room.* 老师进屋时，贝丝紧张地站了起来。
▶**nervousness** /ˈnɜːvəsnəs/ *uncountable noun* 不可数名词：*I smiled warmly so he wouldn't see my nervousness.* 我热情地笑起来，这样他就看不出我紧张了。

nest[1] /nest/ *countable noun* 可数名词 the place where a bird, a small animal or an insect keeps its eggs or its babies 巢；窝：*The cuckoo leaves its eggs in the nests of other birds.* 布谷鸟把蛋下在其他鸟的巢中。

nest² /nest/ verb 动词 (nests, nesting, nested)
to build a nest and lay eggs there 筑巢；搭窝：*There are birds nesting on the cliffs.* 有的鸟会将巢筑在悬崖上。

net /net/ noun 名词
1 uncountable 不可数 a material made of threads or wire with spaces in between 网：*There were net curtains in the windows.* 窗户上有纱帘。
2 countable 可数 a piece of net that you use for a particular purpose, often in sports（常用于运动中的）网：*a fishing net* 渔网 ▫ *Torres headed the ball into the net.* 托雷斯把球顶进了网。

the 'Net singular noun 单数名词
→ see 见 **Internet**：*The study looked at doing business on the Net.* 这项研究着眼于网络商务。

netball /ˈnetbɔːl/ uncountable noun 不可数名词
a game where two teams of seven players, usually women, try to score goals by throwing a ball through a high net（女子）无挡板篮球

network /ˈnetwɜːk/ countable noun 可数名词
a large number of people or things that have a connection with each other and that work together 网络；人际关系网：*She has a strong network of friends and family to help her.* 她有强大的亲友关系网来帮她。▫ *Their computers are connected on a wireless network.* 他们的电脑连着无线网。

neutral /ˈnjuːtrəl/ adjective 形容词
1 not supporting either side in an argument or a war 中立的：*Switzerland remained neutral during World War II.* 二战期间，瑞士保持中立。
2 not showing what you are thinking or feeling 不露声色的：*Isabel said in a neutral voice, 'You're very late, darling.'* 伊莎贝尔平静地说：“你来得太晚了，亲爱的。”

never /ˈnevə/ adverb 副词
at no time in the past, the present or the future 从不；永不：*I have never been abroad.* 我从未出过国。▫ *That was a mistake. I'll never do it again.* 那是个错误。我再也不会那样做了。▫ *Never look directly at the sun.* 绝对不要直视太阳。

nevertheless /ˌnevəðəˈles/ adverb 副词
however; in spite of that (formal 正式) 然而；尽管如此：*Leon had problems, but nevertheless managed to finish his most famous painting.* 莱昂遇到了一些问题，但尽管如此他还是设法完成了他最著名的那幅画。

new /njuː/ adjective 形容词 (newer, newest)
1 recently created or invented 新的；新做的：*They've just opened a new hotel.* 他们刚刚开了一家新酒店。▫ *These ideas are not new.* 这些想法并不新鲜。
2 not used or owned by anyone before you 崭新的；未使用过的：*That afternoon she went out and bought a new dress.* 那天下午她出去买了一条新连衣裙。▫ *There are many boats, new and used, for sale.* 有许多船只在出售，有新的也有旧的。
3 different from before 新的；与过去不同的：*I had to find somewhere new to live.* 我不得不找一个新地方居住。▫ *Rachel has a new boyfriend.* 蕾切尔有了一个新男友。

newborn /ˈnjuːbɔːn/ adjective 形容词
having just been born 新生的；初生的：*a mother and her newborn child* 妈妈和她的新生儿

newcomer /ˈnjuːkʌmə/ countable noun 可数名词
a person who has recently arrived in a place 新来者：*She's a newcomer to London.* 她初来伦敦。

newly /ˈnjuːli/ adverb 副词
used for showing that an action or a situation is very recent 新近；最近：*She was young at the time, and newly married.* 那时她年轻，刚结婚。

news /njuːz/ uncountable noun 不可数名词
1 information about recent events 消息：*We waited and waited for news of him.* 我们左等右等，盼着他的消息。▫ *I've just had some bad news — I failed my exam.* 我刚刚得知一个坏消息——我考试没及格。
2 information about recent events that is reported in newspapers, or on the radio, television or Internet 新闻：*Here are some of the top stories in the news.* 这是一些新闻头条。
3 a television or radio programme that gives information about recent events（广播电视的）新闻节目：*I heard all about the bombs on the news.* 我从新闻广播里得知了有关炸弹的消息。

LANGUAGE HELP 语言提示
News is an uncountable noun. When you are talking about a particular fact or

message, you can say a **piece of news**. You call an individual story or report a **news item**. *news 是不可数名词。表示一则新闻或消息用 a piece of news，一篇新闻报道用 a news item。

newsagent /ˈnjuːzeɪdʒənt/ *countable noun* 可数名词
1 a person who sells things like newspapers, cigarettes and sweets 报刊零售商（也卖香烟、糖果等）
2 (also 亦作 **newsagent's**) a shop that sells things like newspapers, cigarettes and sweets 报刊经销店；书报亭

newsletter /ˈnjuːzletə/ *countable noun* 可数名词
a report giving information about an organization that is sent regularly to its members（组织定期发送给成员的）内部通讯，简讯: *All members receive a free monthly newsletter.* 所有会员都会收到免费的每月通讯。

newspaper /ˈnjuːspeɪpə/ *countable noun* 可数名词
a number of large sheets of folded paper, with news, advertisements and other information printed on them 报纸: *They read about it in the newspaper.* 他们在报纸上看到了这个。

New Year's Day *uncountable noun* 不可数名词
1st January, the time when people celebrate the start of a year 元旦；新年

next /nekst/ *adjective* 形容词, *adverb* 副词
1 coming immediately after this one or after the previous one 紧接着的；接下来的: *I got up early the next morning.* 第二天早上我早早地起了床。 □ *I took the next available flight.* 我乘坐下一班可搭乘的飞机。 □ *Who will be the next mayor?* 谁会出任下一任市长？
2 used for talking about the first day, week or year that comes after this one or the previous one（时间）紧接着的，下一个的: *Let's go to see a film next week.* 我们下周去看电影吧。 □ *He retires next January.* 他明年1月份退休。
3 nearest 离得最近的；紧邻的: *There was a party going on in the next room.* 隔壁房间正在举行一个聚会。 □ *He married a girl from the next village.* 他娶了邻村的一个姑娘。
4 immediately after this time or a time in the past 接下来；随后: *I don't know what to do next.* 我不知道接下来做什么。 □ *What happened next?* 之后发生了什么？
next to someone/something beside 在某人/某物近旁: *She sat down next to him on the sofa.* 她挨着他在沙发上坐下。

nibble /ˈnɪbəl/ *verb* 动词 (**nibbles, nibbling, nibbled**)
to eat something by biting very small pieces of it 啃；啃咬；小口吃: *He was nibbling a biscuit.* 他在啃饼干。 □ *She nibbled at a piece of bread.* 她在一小口一小口地吃一片面包。

nice /naɪs/ *adjective* 形容词 (**nicer, nicest**)
1 attractive, pleasant or enjoyable 吸引人的；美好的；令人愉快的: *The chocolate cake was very nice.* 巧克力蛋糕非常美味。 □ *It's nice to be here together again.* 又在这儿相聚了，太好了。
▶ **nicely** /ˈnaɪsli/ *adverb* 副词: *The book is nicely illustrated.* 这本书插图精美。
2 friendly and pleasant 友好的；和善的: *I've met your father and he's very nice.* 我见过你父亲，他很和善。 □ *They were extremely nice to me.* 他们对我极好。
▶ **nicely** /ˈnaɪsli/ *adverb* 副词: *He treated you nicely.* 他对你很好。

nickname /ˈnɪkneɪm/ *countable noun* 可数名词
an informal name for someone or something 绰号；外号: *His nickname is 'Red' because of his red hair.* 他的外号叫"红毛"，因为他的头发是红色的。
● **nickname** *verb* 动词 (**nicknames, nicknaming, nicknamed**): *The children nicknamed him 'The Giraffe' because he was so tall.* 孩子们给他起了个外号叫"长颈鹿"，因为他长得太高了。

niece /niːs/ *countable noun* 可数名词
the daughter of your sister or brother 侄女；外甥女: *He bought a present for his niece.* 他给侄女买了一件礼物。

night /naɪt/ *noun* 名词
1 the time when it is dark outside, and most people sleep 夜；夜晚: *The rain continued all night.* 雨下了一整夜。 □ *It was a dark, cold night.* 那是一个黑暗而寒冷的夜晚。 □ *It's eleven o'clock at night in Moscow.* 现在是莫斯科晚上11点。
2 *countable* 可数 the period of time between the end of the afternoon and the time that you go to bed 晚间，晚上（指傍

nightclub - noise

晚至入睡前的一段时间）: *Did you go to Kelly's party last night?* 昨晚你去参加凯莉的聚会了吗？

nightclub /ˈnaɪtklʌb/ *countable noun* 可数名词
a place where people go late in the evening to drink and dance 夜总会；夜店

nightdress /ˈnaɪtdres/ *countable noun* 可数名词 (**nightdresses**)
a loose dress that a woman or girl wears in bed 女式睡袍

nightly /ˈnaɪtli/ *adjective* 形容词, *adverb* 副词
happening every night 每夜（的）；每晚（的）: *We watched the nightly news.* 我们看了晚间新闻。 □ *She appears nightly on the television news.* 她每晚都会出现在电视新闻中。

nightmare /ˈnaɪtmeə/ *countable noun* 可数名词
1 a very frightening dream 噩梦；梦魇: *She had nightmares for weeks after seeing that film.* 看了那部电影之后，她做了好几周噩梦。
2 something that is very unpleasant 令人十分不快的事物: *New York traffic is a nightmare.* 纽约的交通简直是噩梦。

ˈnight-ˌtime *singular noun* 单数名词
the period of time between the time when it gets dark and the time when it gets light 夜间: *The pain is often worse at night-time.* 夜间疼痛往往会加剧。

nil /nɪl/
zero; often used in scores of sports games 零（常用于表示体育比赛得分）: *They lost two nil to Italy.* 他们 0 比 2 输给了意大利队。

nine /naɪn/
the number 9 九

nineteen /ˌnaɪnˈtiːn/
the number 19 十九

ninety /ˈnaɪnti/
the number 90 九十

ninth¹ /naɪnθ/ *adjective* 形容词, *adverb* 副词
counted as number nine in a series 第九: *January the ninth* 1月9号 □ *He came ninth in the race.* 比赛中他得了第 9 名。

ninth² /naɪnθ/ *noun* 名词
one of nine equal parts of something (1/9) 九分之一: *The area covers one ninth of the Earth's surface.* 这块区域占了地球表面的九分之一。

no¹ /nəʊ/ *exclamation* 感叹词
1 used for giving a negative response to a question（用于给出否定回答）不，没有: *'Are you having any problems?' — 'No, I'm OK.'* "你有什么问题吗？" —— "没有，我挺好的。" □ *'Would you like a coffee?' — 'No, thank you, I've had one already.'* "你要喝杯咖啡吗？" —— "不，谢谢，我已经喝了一杯了。" □ *'Can I have another biscuit, mum?' — 'No, you've had enough.'* "妈妈，我能再吃块饼干吗？" —— "不行，你已经吃得够多了。"
2 used when you are shocked or disappointed about something（表示震惊或失望）不会吧: *Oh no! I've forgotten to do my maths homework.* 噢，不会吧！我忘了做数学作业。

no² /nəʊ/ *adjective* 形容词
1 not any or not one person or thing 没有；无: *I have no idea what you are talking about.* 你在讲什么，我一点儿也不懂。 □ *In this game, there are no rules.* 这场游戏没有规则。
2 used in notices to say that something is not allowed 禁止…的；不得…的: *No parking.* 禁止停车。 □ *NO ENTRY.* 请勿入内。

No. (**Nos**)
short for (缩写 =) **number**

nobody /ˈnəʊbɒdi/ *pronoun* 代词
not a single person 没有人；无人: *For a long time nobody spoke.* 很长一段时间里没有人讲话。

nod /nɒd/ *verb* 动词 (**nods, nodding, nodded**)
to move your head downwards and upwards to show that you are answering 'yes' to a question, or to show that you agree with something 点头（表示肯定回答或赞同）: *'Are you okay?' I asked. She nodded and smiled.* "你还好吗？"我问道。她点点头，笑了笑。 ● **nod** *countable noun* 可数名词: *She gave a nod and said, 'I see.'* 她点了一下头说："我明白了。"

noise /nɔɪz/ *noun* 名词
1 *uncountable* 不可数 a loud or unpleasant sound 噪音；喧闹声: *Don't make so much noise!* 不要制造这么多噪音！ □ *I'll never forget the noise from the crowd at the end of the game.* 我永远忘不了比赛结束时人群的喧闹声。
2 *countable* 可数 a sound that someone or something makes 响声；声音: *Suddenly*

there was a noise like thunder. 突然雷鸣般一声响。

noisy /'nɔɪzi/ *adjective* 形容词 (**noisier, noisiest**)
1 making a lot of loud or unpleasant noise 喧闹的；有噪音的: *It was a car with a particularly noisy engine.* 这辆车的引擎噪音特别大。
▶ **noisily** /'nɔɪzɪli/ *adverb* 副词: *The students cheered noisily.* 学生们大声欢呼起来。
2 full of a lot of loud or unpleasant noise 充满噪音的；嘈杂的: *The airport was crowded and noisy.* 机场拥挤、嘈杂。

nominate /'nɒmɪˌneɪt/ *verb* 动词 (**nominates, nominating, nominated**)
to formally suggest someone's name for a job, a position or a prize 提名；推荐: *The Australian actor was nominated for an Oscar.* 这位澳大利亚演员获得了奥斯卡提名。
▶ **nomination** /ˌnɒmɪ'neɪʃən/ *countable noun* 可数名词: *He'll probably get a nomination for best actor.* 他可能会获得最佳男演员的提名。

none /nʌn/ *pronoun* 代词
not one or not any of a group of people or things 没有一个；全无: *None of us knew her.* 我们当中没有人认识她。

nonetheless /ˌnʌnðə'les/ *adverb* 副词
however; in spite of this (*formal* 正式) 然而；但是: *There is still a long way to go. Nonetheless, some progress has been made.* 路还很长，不过已经取得了一些进展。

nonfiction /ˌnɒn'fɪkʃən/ *uncountable noun* 不可数名词
writing that is about real people and events rather than imaginary ones 纪实文学；非虚构类作品: *The school library contains both fiction and nonfiction.* 学校图书馆里既有小说也有纪实作品。

nonsense /'nɒnsəns/ *uncountable noun* 不可数名词
something that is not true or that is silly 胡说；蠢话: *Most doctors say that this idea is complete nonsense.* 大部分医生都说这种观点完全是胡说八道。 □ *Peter said I was talking nonsense.* 彼得说我在说胡话。

non-stop /ˌnɒn'stɒp/ *adjective* 形容词, *adverb* 副词
continuing without stopping 不停(的)；不间断(的): *A non-stop flight from London takes you straight to Antigua.* 从伦敦到安提瓜可乘坐直达航班。 □ *We drove non-stop from New York to Miami.* 我们从纽约直接开到迈阿密。

noodles /'nuːdəlz/
plural noun 复数名词
long, thin strips of pasta (= a type of food made from eggs, flour and water) used especially in Chinese and Italian cooking 面条

noodles 面条

noon /nuːn/ *uncountable noun* 不可数名词
twelve o'clock in the middle of the day 正午；中午: *The meeting started at noon.* 会议中午开始。

no one *pronoun* 代词
not a single person, or not a single member of a particular group or set 没有人: *We asked everyone in the room, but no one wanted to help.* 我们求助于屋里所有的人，但是没有人想帮忙。

nor /nɔː/ *conjunction* 连词
used after 'neither' to introduce the second of two negative things（用于 neither 之后引出第二个否定项）也不，也没有: *Neither his friends nor his family knew how old he was.* 他的朋友和家人都不知道他多大。

the norm /ðə 'nɔːm/ *singular noun* 单数名词
the usual, expected situation 常态；通常情况: *Families of six or seven are the norm here.* 这里一家通常六七口人。

normal /'nɔːməl/ *adjective* 形容词
usual and ordinary 正常的；平常的: *Her height and weight are normal for her age.* 她的身高和体重在她这个年龄是正常的。

normally /'nɔːməli/ *adverb* 副词
1 used for saying what usually happens 通常；平常: *Normally the bill is less than £30 a month.* 通常，每个月的账单不超过 30 英镑。 □ *I normally get up at 7 a.m. for work.* 我通常早上 7 点起床工作。
2 in the usual or ordinary way 正常地: *She's getting better and beginning to eat normally again.* 她好多了，又开始正常吃饭了。

north /nɔːθ/ *also* 亦作 **North** *uncountable noun* 不可数名词
the direction that is on your left when you are looking at the sun in the morning 北；北方: *In the north, snow and ice cover the ground.* 在北方，冰雪覆盖大地。 □ *He lives in the north of Canada.* 他住在加拿大北部。

north-east – nothing

- **north** *adjective* 形容词, *adverb* 副词: *North America* 北美洲 □ *A cold north wind was blowing.* 寒冷的北风呼啸。□ *Anita drove north up the M1 motorway.* 安妮塔向北驶入 M1 高速公路。
→ Look at picture on P9 参见彩插第 9 页
▶ **northern** /ˈnɔːðən/ *adjective* 形容词: *Northern Ireland* 北爱尔兰

north-east /ˌnɔːθˈiːst/ *uncountable noun* 不可数名词
the direction that is between north and east 东北；东北方: *They live in Jerusalem, more than 250 miles to the north-east.* 他们住在耶路撒冷，距离东北部 250 多英里。
- **north-east** *adjective* 形容词: *northeast Louisiana* 路易斯安那州东北部
→ Look at picture on P9 参见彩插第 9 页
▶ **north-eastern** /ˌnɔːθˈiːstən/ *adjective* 形容词: *Ian comes from northeastern Canada.* 伊恩来自加拿大东北部。

northerly /ˈnɔːðəli/ *adjective* 形容词
1 moving to the north or towards the north 向北的: *The storm is moving in a northerly direction.* 风暴正在向北移动。
2 coming from the north 来自北方的: *a cold northerly wind* 寒冷的北风

north-west /ˌnɔːθˈwest/ *uncountable noun* 不可数名词
the direction that is between north and west 西北；西北方: *My home town is in the north-west.* 我的家乡在西北地区。
- **north-west** *adjective* 形容词: *I live in north-west London.* 我住在伦敦西北部。
→ Look at picture on P9 参见彩插第 9 页
▶ **north-western** /ˌnɔːθˈwestən/ *adjective* 形容词: *We visited a resort in north-western Australia.* 我们参观了澳大利亚西北部的一处景点。

nose /nəʊz/ *countable noun* 可数名词
the part of your face above your mouth, that you use for smelling and breathing 鼻子: *She wiped her nose with a tissue.* 她用纸巾擦了擦鼻子。
→ Look at picture on P4 参见彩插第 4 页

nostril /ˈnɒstrɪl/ *countable noun* 可数名词
one of the two holes at the end of your nose 鼻孔: *Keeping your mouth closed, breathe in through your nostrils.* 闭着嘴，用鼻孔吸气。

not /nɒt/ *adverb* 副词

> **LANGUAGE HELP** 语言提示
> Use the short form **n't** when you are speaking English. For example, 'didn't' is short for 'did not'. 口语中，用缩写形式 n't，如 did not 缩作 didn't。

used for forming negative sentences (用于构成否定句) 不，没有: *Their plan was not working.* 他们的计划没起作用。
not at all used as a strong way of saying 'No' or of agreeing that the answer to a question is 'No'（用于强调）一点儿也不: *'Sorry, am I bothering you?' — 'No. Not at all.'* "对不起，我打扰到您了吗？" —— "没有，完全没有。"

note¹ /nəʊt/ *countable noun* 可数名词
1 a short letter 便条；便笺: *Steven wrote her a note and left it on the table.* 史蒂文给她写了张便条，留在了桌子上。
2 something that you write down to remind yourself of something 记录；笔记: *She didn't take notes on the lecture.* 她没有在讲座上记笔记。
3 a short piece of extra information in a book or an article 注释；说明: *See Note 16 on p.223.* 参阅第 223 页注释 16。
4 a piece of paper money 纸币；钞票: *He paid the taxi driver with a £20 note.* 他给了出租车司机一张 20 英镑的纸币。
5 one particular sound, or a symbol that represents this sound 音；音符: *She has a deep voice and can't sing high notes.* 她嗓音低沉，唱不了高音。

note² /nəʊt/ *verb* 动词 (**notes, noting, noted**)
(also 亦作 **note something down**) to write something down 记录；记下: *The police officer noted the number.* 警察记录下了号码。□ *She noted down his phone number.* 她记下了他的电话号码。

notebook /ˈnəʊtbʊk/ *countable noun* 可数名词
1 a small book for writing notes in 笔记本: *He took a notebook and pen from his pocket.* 他从口袋里拿出了笔记本和笔。
2 a small personal computer that you carry with you 笔记本电脑: *She watched the DVD on her notebook.* 她在笔记本电脑上看 DVD。

notepaper /ˈnəʊtpeɪpə/ *uncountable noun* 不可数名词
paper that you use for writing letters on 信纸；信笺

nothing /ˈnʌθɪŋ/ *pronoun* 代词
not a single thing, or not a single part of

something 没有什么；没有一点儿: *There is nothing wrong with the car.* 这辆车一点儿问题也没有。□ *There was nothing in the fridge except some butter.* 冰箱里除了黄油什么都没有。

for nothing
1 without a successful result 徒劳地；毫无结果地: *I've done all this work for nothing!* 我这些工作都白做了！
2 for no money; free 不要钱地；免费地: *I'm giving all my DVDs away for nothing.* 我免费赠送我所有的 DVD。

nothing like not at all like 一点儿也不像: *You're nothing like your brother.* 你和你哥哥一点儿也不像。

notice¹ /ˈnəʊtɪs/ *verb* 动词 (**notices, noticing, noticed**)
to become aware of someone or something 觉察到；注意到: *Did you notice anything unusual about him?* 你注意到他有什么不正常的地方了吗？□ *She noticed he was acting strangely.* 她注意到他举止怪异。

notice² /ˈnəʊtɪs/ *noun* 名词
1 countable 可数 a piece of writing in a place where everyone can read it 通告；布告；通知: *The notice said 'Please close the door'.* 告示上写着"请关门"。
2 uncountable 不可数 a warning in advance that something is going to happen 警告；预告: *They moved her to a different office without notice.* 他们没有事先通知就让她搬到了另一个办公室。□ *You must give 30 days' notice if you want to cancel the contract.* 如果你想取消合同，须提前 30 天通知。

take no notice or **not take any notice** to pay no attention to someone or something 不理会；不注意: *I tried to warn them, but they didn't take any notice.* 我试图警告他们，但是他们根本没有理会。

noticeable /ˈnəʊtɪsəbl/ *adjective* 形容词
easy to see, hear or recognize 容易注意到的；显著的: *The improvement in the quality of the food here is noticeable.* 这里食品质量的改善很明显。

noticeboard /ˈnəʊtɪsˌbɔːd/ *countable noun* 可数名词
a board on a wall for notices giving information 布告牌；告示板: *Her telephone number was pinned to the noticeboard.* 她的电话号码钉在布告牌上。
→ Look at picture on P1 参见彩插第 1 页

notification /ˌnəʊtɪfɪˈkeɪʃən/ *countable noun* 可数名词
a message, sound or symbol on your phone or computer telling you that someone has sent you a message or put something new for you to look at on a website 消息提示: *We are constantly interrupted by notifications that we don't need.* 我们总是被一些不需要的消息提示所打断。

notify /ˈnəʊtɪfaɪ/ *verb* 动词 (**notifies, notifying, notified**)
to officially tell someone about something (*formal* 正式) 通报；通知: *We have notified the police.* 我们已经通知了警方。

nought /nɔːt/
the number 0 零

noun /naʊn/ *countable noun* 可数名词
a word such as 'car', 'love' or 'Anne' that is used for talking about a person or a thing 名词

nourish /ˈnʌrɪʃ/ *verb* 动词 (**nourishes, nourishing, nourished**)
to give a person, an animal or a plant the food that they need to live, grow and be healthy 给…提供营养；滋养: *The food you eat nourishes both you and your baby.* 你吃的食物给你和宝宝都提供了营养。
▶ **nourishing** /ˈnʌrɪʃɪŋ/ *adjective* 形容词: *nourishing home-cooked food* 有营养的自制食品
▶ **nourishment** /ˈnʌrɪʃmənt/ *uncountable noun* 不可数名词: *These drinks will provide sick children with the nourishment they need to recover.* 这些饮品将为患病儿童提供康复所需要的营养。

novel¹ /ˈnɒvəl/ *countable noun* 可数名词
a long written story about imaginary people and events（长篇）小说: *He's reading a novel by Herman Hesse.* 他在看一本赫尔曼·黑塞写的长篇小说。
→ Look at picture on P3 参见彩插第 3 页

novel² /ˈnɒvəl/ *adjective* 形容词
new or different from anything else 新的；新颖的: *Here's a novel way to entertain a group of friends.* 这是招待一群朋友的新法子。

novelist /ˈnɒvəlɪst/ *countable noun* 可数名词
a person who writes novels (= long written stories about imaginary people and events) 小说家: *Archer was a best-selling novelist.* 阿彻是畅销小说家。

novelty /ˈnɒvəlti/ *countable noun* 可数名词 (**novelties**)
something that is new and interesting 新颖的事物；新奇的事物：*Tourists are still a novelty on the island.* 游客鲜少造访这座岛。

November /nəʊˈvembə/ *noun* 名词
the eleventh month of the year 十一月：*He came to New York in November 1939.* 他1939 年 11 月来到了纽约。

now¹ /naʊ/ *adverb* 副词
used for talking about the present time 现在；目前：*I must go now.* 我现在必须走了。□ *She should know that by now.* 现在她应该知道这件事。● **now** *pronoun* 代词：*Now is your chance to talk to him.* 现在你有机会去跟他谈了。
now and then sometimes but not very often or regularly 有时；偶尔：*Now and then they heard the sound of traffic outside.* 他们偶尔听到外面的车辆声。□ *My daughter comes home to visit every now and again.* 我女儿偶尔会回家看看。

now² /naʊ/ *conjunction* 连词
used for showing that something has happened, and as a result something else will happen 既然；由于：*Now that our children are older, I am returning to full-time work.* 既然孩子们大些了，我要重返全职工作了。

nowadays /ˈnaʊəˌdeɪz/ *adverb* 副词
now generally, and not in the past 如今：*Nowadays almost all children spend some time playing electronic and computer games.* 如今，几乎所有的孩子都会花一些时间玩电子游戏和电脑游戏。

nowhere /ˈnəʊweə/ *adverb* 副词
not in any place, or not to any place 任何地方都不；无处：*I have nowhere else to go.* 我没有别的地方可以去。

nuclear /ˈnjuːkliə/ *adjective* 形容词
1 relating to the energy that is released when the central parts (= nuclei) of atoms are split or combined 核能的：*We're building a nuclear power station.* 我们在建一座核电站。□ *They don't have any nuclear weapons.* 他们没有任何核武器。
2 used for describing the central part of an atom or cell (= nucleus) 原子核的：*He is studying nuclear physics.* 他正在学习核物理。

nucleus /ˈnjuːkliəs/ *countable noun* 可数名词 (**nuclei** /ˈnjuːkliˌaɪ/)
the central part of an atom or a cell 原子核；细胞核

nude¹ /njuːd/ *adjective* 形容词
not wearing any clothes 赤裸的；裸体的：*She came into the room, almost completely nude.* 她进屋时近乎全裸。

nude² /njuːd/ *countable noun* 可数名词
a painting or a piece of art that shows someone who is not wearing any clothes 裸体画；裸体雕像；裸体人像

nudge /nʌdʒ/ *verb* 动词 (**nudges, nudging, nudged**)
to push someone gently, usually with your elbow (用肘)轻推：*I nudged Stan and pointed again.* 我用胳膊肘碰了碰斯坦，又指了一下。● **nudge** *countable noun* 可数名词：*She gave him a nudge.* 她轻轻推了他一下。

nuisance /ˈnjuːsəns/ *countable noun* 可数名词
someone or something that annoys you 讨厌的人；麻烦的事物：*He can be a bit of a nuisance sometimes.* 有时候他有些烦人。

numb /nʌm/ *adjective* 形容词 (**number, numbest**)
unable to feel anything 麻木的；失去知觉的：*It was so cold that his fingers were numb.* 太冷了，他的手指都没知觉了。

number¹ /ˈnʌmbə/ *countable noun* 可数名词
1 a word such as 'two', 'nine' or 'twelve' or a symbol such as 1, 3 or 47 that is used in counting 数；数字：*I don't know my room number.* 我不知道我的房间号。□ *What's your phone number?* 你的电话号码是什么？
2 used with words such as 'large' or 'small' to say approximately how many things or people there are (与 large 或 small 连用，表示约数)数量，数目：*I received a large number of emails on the subject.* 我收到了许多有关这一主题的邮件。

number² /ˈnʌmbə/ *verb* 动词 (**numbers, numbering, numbered**)
to mark something with a number, usually starting at 1 把…编号；给…标号：*He cut the paper up into tiny squares, and he numbered each one.* 他把纸剪成了一些正方形小纸片，并给每一张纸片标了号。

ˈnumber ˌplate *countable noun* 可数名词
a metal sign on the back and front of a vehicle, with numbers and letters on it 车牌：*a car with foreign number plates* 一辆挂着外国车牌的车

numeral /ˈnjuːmərəl/ *countable noun* 可数名词
a written symbol that represents a number 数字: *The Roman numeral for 7 is VII.* 在罗马数字中 7 是 VII。

numerous /ˈnjuːmərəs/ *adjective* 形容词
many 许多的: *He made numerous attempts to lose weight.* 他曾多次尝试减肥。

nun /nʌn/ *countable noun* 可数名词
a member of a group of religious women who often live together in a special building 修女；尼姑: *When I was seventeen, I decided to become a nun.* *17 岁那年我决定当修女。

nurse /nɜːs/ *countable noun* 可数名词
a person whose job is to care for people who are ill or injured 护士: *She thanked the nurses who cared for her.* 她感谢了照顾她的护士。 • **nurse** *verb* 动词 (**nurses, nursing, nursed**): *My mother has nursed him for the last ten years.* *10 年来我妈妈一直照顾他。
→ Look at picture on P16 参见彩插第 16 页

nursery /ˈnɜːsəri/ *countable noun* 可数名词 (**nurseries**)
1 a place where small children and babies are cared for while their parents are at work 托儿所: *My daughter goes to nursery in the mornings.* 我女儿上午去托儿所。
2 a room in a family home in which the young children of the family sleep or play 育儿室；儿童房: *We painted bright pictures on the walls in the children's nursery.* 我们在育儿室墙上涂了色彩鲜艳的画。
3 a place where people grow and sell plants 苗圃: *Buy your plants at the local nursery.* 到本地苗圃购买花草。

ˈnursery ˌrhyme *countable noun* 可数名词
a poem or a song for young children 儿歌；童谣

ˈnursing ˌhome *countable noun* 可数名词
a residence for old or ill people 养老院；疗养院: *He died in a nursing home in Florida at the age of 87.* 他在佛罗里达一家养老院去世，享年 87 岁。

nut /nʌt/ *countable noun* 可数名词
1 a dry fruit with a hard shell 坚果: *Nuts and seeds are very good for you.* 坚果和种子对你非常有好处。
2 a thick metal ring that you put onto a bolt (= a long piece of metal), that is used for holding heavy things together 螺母: *If you want to repair the wheels, you must remove the four nuts.* 想修理轮子，必须卸掉那 4 个螺母。

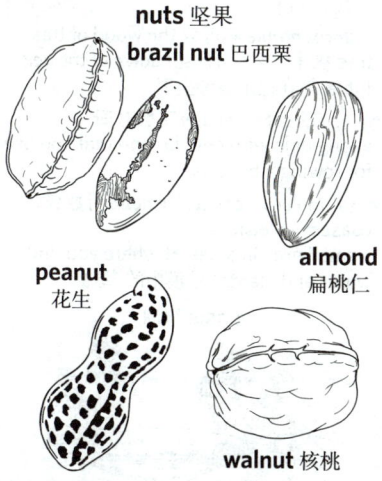

nuts 坚果
brazil nut 巴西栗
peanut 花生
almond 扁桃仁
walnut 核桃

nutrient /ˈnjuːtriənt/ *countable noun* 可数名词
a substance that helps plants and animals to grow and stay healthy 养分；营养物质: *The juice contains vitamins, minerals and other essential nutrients.* 这种果汁含有维生素、矿物质以及其他必需的营养物质。

nutritious /njuːˈtrɪʃəs/ *adjective* 形容词
containing things that help your body to be healthy 有营养的；营养价值高的: *It is important to eat nutritious foods.* 吃东西一定要有营养。

nylon /ˈnaɪlɒn/ *uncountable noun* 不可数名词
a strong, artificial substance that is used for making cloth and plastic 尼龙: *I packed a sleeping bag, a pocket knife and some strong nylon rope.* 我装上一个睡袋、一把折刀和一些结实的尼龙绳。

Oo

oak /əʊk/ *noun* 名词
1 (also 亦作 **oak tree**) a type of large tree 栎树；橡树
2 **uncountable** 不可数 the wood of this tree 栎木；橡木：*He sat down at the oak table.* 他在橡木桌旁坐下。

oar /ɔː/ *countable noun* 可数名词
a long pole with one flat end that you use for rowing a boat 桨

oasis /əʊˈeɪsɪs/ *countable noun* 可数名词 (**oases** /əʊˈeɪsiːz/)
a small area in a desert where you find water and plants（沙漠中的）绿洲

oasis 绿洲

oatmeal /ˈəʊtmiːl/ *uncountable noun* 不可数名词
a hot, thick food that people eat for breakfast. It is made from oats cooked in water or milk. 燕麦片粥

oats /əʊts/ *plural noun* 复数名词
a type of grain that is used in foods 燕麦

obedient /əʊˈbiːdiənt/ *adjective* 形容词
doing what you are told to do 服从的；顺从的：*As a child, Charlotte was an obedient daughter.* 夏洛特小时候是个听话的女儿。
▶ **obedience** /əʊˈbiːdiəns/ *uncountable noun* 不可数名词：*He expected complete obedience from his sons.* 他想要儿子完全服从自己。
▶ **obediently** /əʊˈbiːdiəntli/ *adverb* 副词：*The dog sat beside him obediently.* 狗温顺地坐在他身边。

obese /əʊˈbiːs/ *adjective* 形容词
very fat, in a way that is not healthy 肥胖的：*Obese people often have more health problems than thinner people.* 肥胖的人往往比瘦的人有更多健康问题。

obey /əʊˈbeɪ/ *verb* 动词 (**obeys, obeying, obeyed**)
to do what you are told to do 服从；遵守：*Most people obey the law.* 大多数人都遵守法律。

object¹ /ˈɒbdʒɪkt/ *countable noun* 可数名词
1 a thing that has a shape, and that is not alive 物体；东西：*I have to wear glasses because I can't see distant objects clearly.* 我必须戴眼镜，因为我看不清远处的东西。□ *We could hear someone throwing small, hard objects on to the roof.* 我们听到有人往屋顶上扔坚硬的小东西。
2 the purpose of what someone is doing 目的；目标；宗旨：*The object of the event is to raise money.* 这场活动旨在筹款。
3 the person or thing that is affected by the action of a verb 宾语

object² /əbˈdʒekt/ *verb* 动词 (**objects, objecting, objected**)
to say that you do not agree with something, or that you do not like it 反对；不喜欢：*A lot of people objected to the book.* 许多人都不喜欢这本书。

objection /əbˈdʒekʃən/ *noun* 名词
a reason for not liking or agreeing with something 反对的理由；异议：*I don't have any objection to people making money.* 我没有理由反对人们赚钱。

objective /əbˈdʒektɪv/ *countable noun* 可数名词
the thing that you are trying to achieve 目标；目的：*Our main objective was to find the child.* 我们的主要目标是找到这个孩子。

obligation /ˌɒblɪˈɡeɪʃən/ *noun* 名词
something that you should do 义务；责任：*The judge has an obligation to find out the truth.* 法官有义务查明真相。

obligatory /əˈblɪɡətri/ *adjective* 形容词
something that you must do because of a rule or a law (按照规定或法律) 强制性的，必须履行的：*These medical tests are not obligatory.* 这些医学检查不是强制性的。

oblige /əˈblaɪdʒ/ *verb* 动词 (**obliges, obliging, obliged**)
be obliged to do something to have to do something because a situation or a law makes it necessary for you to do it (因形势或法律而) 被迫做某事：*My family needed the money so I was obliged to work.* 我家里需要这份钱，所以我不得不工作。

oblong /ˈɒblɒŋ/ *countable noun* 可数名词
a shape that has two long sides and two short sides 矩形；长方形：*a pattern of oblongs* 长方形图案 ◻ *'What do you call this shape?' — 'It's an oblong.'* "这种形状叫什么？"——"长方形。" ● **oblong** *adjective* 形容词：*Ten people sat around a large oblong table.* 10 个人围坐在一张大的长方形桌子边。

oboe /ˈəʊbəʊ/ *noun* 名词
a musical instrument that you blow. It is a long black wooden tube with keys on it that you press, and a double reed (= small flat part that moves and makes a sound when you blow). 双簧管
→ Look at picture on P12 参见彩插第 12 页

obscene /əbˈsiːn/ *adjective* 形容词
relating to sex or violence in an unpleasant and shocking way 淫秽的；暴力的：*obscene photographs* 淫秽照片

observe /əbˈzɜːv/ *verb* 动词 (**observes, observing, observed**)
to watch people or things carefully in order to learn something about them 观察；观测：*Olson observed the behaviour of babies.* 奥尔森观察了婴儿的行为。

obsession /əbˈseʃən/ *noun* 名词
a person or thing that someone spends too much time thinking about (对人或事物的) 痴迷，迷恋：*She tried to forget her obsession with Christopher.* 她努力忘记对克里斯托弗的迷恋。

obstacle /ˈɒbstəkəl/ *countable noun* 可数名词
something that makes it difficult for you to do what you want to do 障碍；阻碍：*We had to overcome two major obstacles.* 我们必须克服两大障碍。

obstinate /ˈɒbstɪnət/ *adjective* 形容词
determined to do what you want to do 固执的；倔强的：*When she says 'no', nothing can make her change her mind, and she can be very obstinate.* 她要是说"不"，什么也改变不了她的主意，她会非常固执。

obstruct /əbˈstrʌkt/ *verb* 动词 (**obstructs, obstructing, obstructed**)
to stop someone from passing 阻塞；妨碍：*A group of cars obstructed the road.* 一队汽车阻塞了道路。

obstruction /əbˈstrʌkʃən/ *countable noun* 可数名词
something that blocks a road or a path 路障；障碍物：*The cars outside his house were causing an obstruction.* 他家外面的汽车造成了堵塞。

obtain /əbˈteɪn/ *verb* 动词 (**obtains, obtaining, obtained**)
to get something (*formal* 正式) 获得；得到：*Evans tried to obtain a false passport.* 埃文斯试图弄到一本假护照。

obvious /ˈɒbviəs/ *adjective* 形容词
easy to see or understand 明显的；浅显的：*It's obvious that he's worried about us.* 很明显，他担心我们。

obviously /ˈɒbviəsli/ *adverb* 副词
used for saying that something is easily noticed, seen or recognized 显然；明显：*He obviously likes you very much.* 他显然很喜欢你。

occasion /əˈkeɪʒən/ *countable noun* 可数名词
1 a time when something happens (某事发生的) 时刻；次：*I gave her money on several occasions.* 我给了她几次钱。
2 an important event, ceremony or celebration 重大活动；仪式；庆典：*The wedding was a happy occasion.* 婚礼是个喜庆的场合。

occasional /əˈkeɪʒənəl/ *adjective* 形容词
happening sometimes, but not often 偶尔的：*I get occasional headaches.* 我偶尔会头疼。
▶ **occasionally** /əˈkeɪʒənəli/ *adverb* 副词：*He misbehaves occasionally.* 他偶尔会不守规矩。

occupant /ˈɒkjupənt/ *countable noun* 可数名词
the person who lives or works in a building or a room (建筑物或房间的) 居住者，占用者：*Most of the occupants left the building before the fire spread.* 大部分住户在火势蔓延前离开了这栋楼。

occupation /ˌɒkjʊˈpeɪʃn/ *noun* 名词
1 *countable* 可数 someone's job 职业；工作：*Please write down your name and occupation.* 请写下你的姓名和职业。
2 *countable* 可数 something that you spend time doing, either for fun or because it needs to be done 消遣；须做的事：*Cooking was his favourite occupation.* 烹饪是他最喜欢的消遣。
3 *uncountable* 不可数 when a foreign army enters and controls a country 占领；占据：*She lived in France during Nazi Germany's occupation.* 她生活在纳粹德国占领下的法国。

occupied /ˈɒkjʊpaɪd/ *adjective* 形容词
1 being used 被占用的：*The chair was occupied by his wife.* 这把椅子让他老婆占用了。
2 busy 忙着（做…）的：*Don't get bored. Keep your brain occupied.* 别厌倦。保持大脑全神贯注。

occupy /ˈɒkjʊpaɪ/ *verb* 动词 (**occupies, occupying, occupied**)
1 to live or work in a place 占有，使用（某地）：*The company occupies the top floor of the building.* 这家公司占用着这栋楼的顶层。
2 to move into a place and use force to control it 占领；侵占：*U.S. forces occupy a part of the country.* 美军占领了该国一部分领土。
3 to be busy doing something or thinking about it 使忙碌；占用（时间）；使全神贯注：*Her career occupies all of her time.* 事业占据了她所有的时间。

occur /əˈkɜː/ *verb* 动词 (**occurs, occurring, occurred**)
to happen 发生：*The car crash occurred at night.* 车祸发生在夜里。
occur to someone to suddenly come into somebody's mind 某人突然想起：*Suddenly it occurred to her that the door might be open.* 她突然想起来门可能没关。

occurrence /əˈkʌrəns/ *countable noun* 可数名词
something that happens (*formal* 正式) 发生的事；事件：*Complaints against the company were an everyday occurrence.* 对这家公司的投诉是家常便饭。

ocean /ˈəʊʃn/ *countable noun* 可数名词
one of the five very large areas of salt water on the Earth's surface 洋；海洋：*the Pacific Ocean* 太平洋

→ Look at picture on P9 参见彩插第 9 页

o'clock /əˈklɒk/ *adverb* 副词
used after numbers from one to twelve to say what time it is *…点钟：*I went to bed at ten o'clock last night.* 我昨晚 10 点钟上床睡觉。

octave /ˈɒktɪv/ *countable noun* 可数名词
a series of eight notes in music, or the difference between the first and last notes in the series 八度；八度音程

October /ɒkˈtəʊbə/ *noun* 名词
the tenth month of the year 十月：*We went away in early October.* 我们 10 月初离家。□ *They left on October 2.* 他们 10 月 2 号离开的。

octopus /ˈɒktəpəs/ *noun* 名词 (**octopuses**)
a soft sea animal with eight long arms 章鱼；八爪鱼

octopus 章鱼

odd /ɒd/ *adjective* 形容词 (**odder, oddest**)
1 strange or unusual 奇怪的；异常的：*His behaviour was odd.* 他行为异常。
▶ **oddly** /ˈɒdli/ *adverb* 副词：*He dresses rather oddly.* 他穿得很奇怪。
2 used for describing numbers such as 3 and 17, that cannot be divided exactly by the number two 奇数的
3 not belonging to the same set or pair 不成套的；不成对的；单个的：*I'm wearing odd socks.* 我穿的袜子不成对。

odds /ɒdz/ *plural noun* 复数名词
how likely it is that something will happen（某事发生的）可能性，概率：*What are the odds of finding a parking space right outside the door?* 找到一个就在门口的停车位的可能性有多大？

odour /ˈəʊdə/ *noun* 名词
a smell 气味：*A bad egg will have an unpleasant odour when you break open the shell.* 把坏鸡蛋的壳磕破，你会闻到一股臭味。

of /əv, STRONG 强读 ɒv/ *preposition* 介词
1 used for saying what someone or something is connected with（用于表示人

或事物与…有关联）: *Police searched the homes of the criminals.* 警察搜查了这些罪犯的家。▫ *the mayor of Los Angeles* 洛杉矶市市长
2 used for saying what something relates to（用于说明某事物与…相关）: *He was trying to hide his feelings of anger.* 他在努力掩饰自己的愤怒。
3 used for talking about someone or something else who is involved in an action（用于谈论涉及的人或事物）: *He was dreaming of her.* 他梦到了她。
4 used for showing that someone or something is part of a larger group（用于表示作为一组人或事物的一部分）: *She is the youngest child of three.* 她是 3 个孩子中最小的。
5 used for talking about amounts or contents（用于表示数量或内容）: *The boy was drinking a glass of milk.* 男孩在喝一杯奶。
6 used for saying what caused a person's or an animal's death（用于表示人或动物的死因）: *He died of a heart attack.* 他死于心脏病。
7 used for describing someone's behaviour（用于形容人的行为）: *It's very kind of you to help.* 你能帮忙真的太好了。▫ *It was rude of him to interrupt you.* 他打断了你的话，这很无礼。

of course *adverb* 副词
1 used for suggesting that something is not surprising 当然；自然: *Of course there were lots of interesting things to see.* 当然有很多有趣的东西可看。
2 used as a polite way of giving permission（用于礼貌地表示许可）当然: *'Can I ask you something?' — 'Yes, of course.'* "我能问您一些事儿吗？" —— "当然可以。"

off¹ /ɒf/ *preposition* 介词
1 used for saying that something is no longer on another thing 从…移开；从…脱离: *He took his feet off the desk.* 他把脚从桌上移开。● **off** *adverb* 副词: *I broke off a piece of chocolate and ate it.* 我掰下一块巧克力吃掉了。
2 out of a bus, a train or a plane 从（公交车、火车或飞机上）下来: *Don't get off a moving train!* 火车运行时不要下车！● **off** *adverb* 副词: *At the next station, the man got off.* 那个男人在下一站下了车。
3 away from a place 远离（某地）: *The police told visitors to keep off the beach.* 警方告诫游客不要去海滩。

off² /ɒf/ *adverb* 副词
1 away 离开: *He was just about to drive off.* 他正打算驾车离开。
2 away from work or school 休息；不工作；不上学: *She took the day off.* 她休了一天假。
3 away in time（时间上）离，距: *An agreement is still a long way off.* 要达成协议还遥遥无期。
4 not being used 关着；不在使用中: *Her bedroom light was off.* 她卧室的灯关着。

offence /əˈfens/ *noun* 名词
1 *countable* 可数 a crime that breaks a law 罪行；违法行为: *There is a fine of $1,000 for a first offence.* 初犯罚款 1,000 美元。
2 *uncountable* 不可数 when someone is upset by another person's behaviour 冒犯；得罪: *He didn't mean to cause offence.* 他无意得罪谁。
take offence to be upset by something that someone says or does（对某事）生气，动怒: *Many people took offence at his sexist jokes.* 许多人被他的黄色笑话惹恼。

offend /əˈfend/ *verb* 动词 (**offends, offending, offended**)
to say or do something that upsets someone 冒犯；得罪: *I'm sorry if I offended you.* 如果我冒犯了你，我感到抱歉。

offensive /əˈfensɪv/ *adjective* 形容词
rude or insulting; upsetting people 无礼的；冒犯性的；得罪人的: *an offensive remark* 冒犯的言语

offer¹ /ˈɒfə/ *verb* 动词 (**offers, offering, offered**)
1 to ask someone if they would like to have something 提供；给予: *He offered his seat to the young woman.* 他把座位让给了那名年轻女子。▫ *She offered him a cup of coffee.* 她给了他一杯咖啡。
2 to say that you are willing to do something 主动提议（做某事）: *Peter offered to teach me to drive.* 彼得主动提出教我开车。

offer² /ˈɒfə/ *countable noun* 可数名词
something that someone says they will give you or do for you 提供物；主动提议: *I hope you will accept my offer of help.* 我希望你能接受我提供的帮助。

office /ˈɒfɪs/ *noun* 名词
1 *countable* 可数 a place where people

work sitting at a desk 办公室: *I work in an office with about 25 people.* 我在一间约有 25 人的办公室工作。
2 *countable* 可数 a department of an organization, especially the government (尤指政府的)部，厅，处: *the Foreign Office* 外交部
3 *countable* 可数 a small building or room where people can go for information or tickets (提供问询、售票服务的)处，所: *a tourist office* 游客问询处
4 *uncountable* 不可数 an important job in a government (政府的)要职: *The events marked the president's four years in office.* 这些活动庆祝总统就职 4 周年。

officer /ˈɒfɪsə/ *countable noun* 可数名词
1 a person who is in charge of other people in the armed forces 军官: *Her son is an officer in the army.* 她儿子是陆军军官。
2 a member of the police force 警察；警官: *The officer saw no sign of a robbery.* 警察没有看出抢劫的迹象。 ▫ *Officer Montoya was the first on the scene.* 蒙托亚警官第一个赶到现场。
3 a person who has a responsible position in an organization (机构的)管理人员，官员: *She's the chief executive officer of the company.* 她是公司的首席执行官。

official¹ /əˈfɪʃəl/ *adjective* 形容词
1 approved by the government or by someone in power 官方的；正式的: *They destroyed all the official documents.* 他们销毁了所有官方文件。
▶ **officially** /əˈfɪʃəli/ *adverb* 副词: *The results have not been officially announced.* 结果尚未正式公布。
2 carried out by a person in power as part of their job 公务的；公职的: *The president is in Brazil for an official visit.* 总统正在巴西进行正式访问。

official² /əˈfɪʃəl/ *countable noun* 可数名词 a person who holds a position of power in an organization (机构的)官员；高级职员: *Government officials said that they discussed the matter this morning.* 政府官员说他们今早讨论了此事。

offline /ˌɒfˈlaɪn/ *adjective* 形容词, *adverb* 副词
not connected to the Internet. Compare with **online**. 脱机(的)，离线(的)(比较 online): *Test your website offline before you put it on the Web.* 网站上线之前，先进行离线测试。 ▫ *Your computer is currently offline.* 你的电脑目前处于脱机状态。

often /ˈɒfən/ *adverb* 副词
happening many times or much of the time 常常；经常: *They often spend the weekend together.* 他们经常一起过周末。 ▫ *That doesn't happen very often.* 这不经常发生。
every so often happening sometimes, but not very often 有时；偶尔: *She visited her aunt in Scotland every so often.* 她有时会去看望苏格兰的姑姑。
how often? used for asking questions about frequency (用于询问频率)每隔多久？: *How often do you brush your teeth?* 你多久刷一次牙？

> **LANGUAGE HELP** 语言提示
> If you want to talk about something that happens several times within a short period of time, you say, for example, *I phoned her several times yesterday.* 表示某事在短时间内发生数次，可用 I phoned her several times yesterday (我昨天给她打了几次电话)这类说法。

oh /əʊ/ *exclamation* 感叹词
used for expressing a feeling such as surprise, pain, annoyance or happiness (表示惊讶、痛苦、恼怒、喜悦等情绪)哦，噢: *'Oh!' Kenny said. 'Has everyone gone?'* "哦！"肯尼说，"大家都走了吗？"

oil¹ /ɔɪl/ *noun* 名词
1 a smooth, thick liquid that is used for making machines work. Oil is found underground. 石油；燃油: *The company buys and sells 600,000 barrels of oil a day.* 这家公司一天买卖 60 万桶石油。
2 a smooth, thick liquid made from plants, that is often used for cooking 植物油；食用油: *olive oil* 橄榄油

oil² /ɔɪl/ *verb* 动词 (**oils, oiling, oiled**)
to put oil onto or into something to make it work smoothly or to protect it 给…加润滑油；给…上油: *He oiled the lock on the door.* 他给门锁上了油。

oil painting *countable noun* 可数名词
a picture that is painted using oil paints 油画

oily /ˈɔɪli/ *adjective* 形容词 (**oilier, oiliest**)
looking, feeling or tasting like oil 油状的；似油的；有油味的: *He wiped his hands on an oily rag.* 他用一块沾满油污的破布擦了

手。▫ Paul thought the sauce was too oily. 保罗觉得这酱汁太油了。

ointment /ˈɔɪntmənt/ *noun* 名词
a smooth, thick substance that you put on sore or damaged skin 软膏；油膏；药膏：*Ointments are available for the treatment of skin problems.* 治疗皮肤病症有软膏可用。

okay /ˌəʊˈkeɪ/ *also* 亦作 **OK** or 或 **O.K.** or 或 **ok** *adjective* 形容词
1 acceptable (*informal* 非正式) 可以的；可接受的：*Is it okay if I go by myself?* 我可以自己去吗？
2 safe and well (*informal* 非正式) 安好的：*Check that the baby's okay.* 看看宝宝是不是一切正常。
3 used for showing that you agree to something (*informal* 非正式)（表示同意）行，好：*'Just tell him I would like to talk to him.' — 'OK.'* "就告诉他我想和他谈谈。" —— "好的。"
4 used for checking whether the person you are talking to understands what you have said and accepts it (*informal* 非正式)（用于询问对方是否领会并接受）可以吗，行吗：*We'll meet next week, OK?* 那我们就下周见？

old /əʊld/ *adjective* 形容词 (**older, oldest**)
1 having lived for many years; not young 年老的；上年纪的：*Mr Kaufmann was a small old man with a beard.* 考夫曼先生是个蓄着络腮胡子的小老头。
2 used for talking or asking about the age of someone or something *…岁的；存在…时间的：*He is three months old.* 他 3 个月大。 ▫ *Her car is less than three years old.* 她的车买了不到 3 年。
3 having existed for a long time 存在已久的：*We live in a beautiful old house.* 我们住在一座漂亮的老房子里。 ▫ *These books look very old.* 这些书看上去很有年头了。
4 used for talking about something that used to be part of your life 原先的；原来的：*I still remember my old school.* 我还记得我以前的学校。
5 an old friend is someone who has been your friend for a long time（朋友）旧交的，结交已久的：*I called my old friend John Horner.* 我给老朋友约翰·霍纳打了电话。

old age *uncountable noun* 不可数名词
the part of your life when you are old 老年；晚年：*They didn't have much money in their old age.* 他们晚年没有多少钱。

old-fashioned *adjective* 形容词
no longer used, done or believed by most people 过时的；老式的：*The kitchen was old-fashioned and in bad condition.* 厨房是老式的，破旧不堪。

olive /ˈɒlɪv/ *noun* 名词
a small green or black fruit with a bitter taste 橄榄

olive oil *uncountable noun* 不可数名词
a type of oil that is used in cooking 橄榄油

the Olympic Games /ði əˌlɪmpɪk ˈgeɪmz/ *noun* 名词
an international sports competition that takes place every four years, each time in a different country (*trademark* 商标) 奥林匹克运动会；奥运会

omelette /ˈɒmlət/ *also* 亦作 **omelet** *countable noun* 可数名词
a type of food made by beating eggs and cooking them in a frying pan 煎蛋饼；摊鸡蛋：*She made a cheese omelette.* 她做了奶酪蛋饼。

omit /əˈmɪt/ *verb* 动词 (**omits, omitting, omitted**)
to not include something 省略；删去：*Omit the salt in this recipe.* 这个食谱不要放盐。

omnivore /ˈɒmnɪvɔː/ *countable noun* 可数名词
an animal that eats both meat and plants. Compare with **carnivore** and **herbivore**. 杂食动物（比较 carnivore 和 herbivore）

on¹ /ɒn/ *preposition* 介词
1 supported by or touching a surface（表示支撑或接触）在…上：*He was sitting on the sofa.* 他坐在沙发上。 ▫ *There was a large box on the table.* 桌子上有一个大盒子。
2 attached to a surface（表示附着）在…上：*We hung some paintings on the walls.* 我们在墙上挂了几幅画。 ▫ *You've got dirt on your face.* 你脸上有脏东西。
3 in a bus, train or plane 上（公共汽车、火车或飞机）：*We got on the plane.* 我们上了飞机。
4 travelling in a bus, train or plane（表示乘坐公共汽车、火车或飞机）在…上：*I'm on the train at the moment.* 我现在在火车上。
5 used for showing the instrument or equipment that is used to do something 用（乐器或设备）：*I played these songs on the piano.* 我用钢琴弹奏了这些歌。 ▫ *She*

spends most of the day on the computer. 她白天大部分时间都对着电脑。
6 being broadcast 在(广播电视)上：What's on TV tonight? 今晚有什么电视节目？
7 used for showing a day or a date (表示日期)在，于：This year's event will be on June 19th. 今年的活动将于 6 月 19 日举行。□ We'll see you on Tuesday. 我们周二去看你。
8 used for saying what something is about 关于：He wrote a book on the history of Russian ballet. 他写了一本讲述俄罗斯芭蕾舞史的书。

on² /ɒn/ *adverb* 副词
1 used for showing that someone is wearing a piece of clothing 穿上；戴上：He put his coat on. 他穿上了外套。□ I can't go out. I don't have any shoes on. 我出不了门。我没穿鞋。
2 used for saying that someone is continuing to do something 继续：They walked on for a while. 他们继续走了一会儿。
3 being used 使用中；开着：The lights were on, but nobody was at home. 灯开着，但是家里没有人。

once¹ /wʌns/ *adverb* 副词
1 happening one time only 一次；一回：I met Miquela once, at a party. 我见过米克拉一次，在一个聚会上。□ The baby hasn't once slept through the night. 宝宝整晚都没睡。
2 true at some time in the past, but no longer true 曾经；一度：Her parents once owned a shop. 她父母曾开过一家店。
at once immediately 立即；马上：I have to go at once. 我必须马上走。
for once happening on this particular occasion only 就这么一次；只这么一回：For once, Dad is not complaining. 就这么一次，爸爸没有发牢骚。

once² /wʌns/ *conjunction* 连词
happening immediately after another thing has happened 一旦；——(就…)：The decision was easy once he read the letter. 他一旦看了这封信，就好作决定了。

one¹ /wʌn/ *pronoun* 代词
1 used instead of the name of a person or a thing (用于替代人或事物的名称)：'Which dress do you prefer?' — 'I like the red one.' "你喜欢哪一条裙子？" — "红色那条。" □ Cut up the large potatoes, but leave the small ones, please. 请把大土豆切成小块，把小土豆留下。
2 people in general (*formal* 正式)(泛指)人：One can get very tired on these long flights. 在这些长途飞行中，人会非常疲劳。
one or two a few 一两个；几个：We made one or two changes. 我们做了一两处改动。

one² /wʌn/
the number 1 一：They have one daughter. 他们有一个女儿。

one³ /wʌn/ *adjective* 形容词
used for talking about a time in the past or in the future (过去或未来的)某一(时间)：Would you like to go out one night? 你想找个晚上出去吗？□ One day, she called me at my office. 有一天，她打电话到我的办公室。

one's¹ /wʌnz/ *adjective* 形容词
used for showing that something belongs to or relates to people in general (*formal* 正式)(泛指)人的；自己的：It is natural to want to care for one's family and children. 想照顾自己家人孩子是人之常情。

one's² /wʌnz/
a spoken form of 'one is' or 'one has' (one is 或 one has 的一种口语形式)：No one's going to hurt you. 没人会伤害你。□ This one's been broken too. 这个也已经破了。

oneself /wʌn'self/ *pronoun* 代词
used by speakers or writers to make statements about themselves and people in general (*formal* 正式)自己；自身：To think, one must have time to oneself. 人要思考就必须有属于自己的时间。
by oneself alone (*formal* 正式)独自：Travelling by oneself can be an enjoyable experience. 独自旅行会是一种非常愉快的经历。

one-ˈway *adjective* 形容词
1 with traffic moving in one direction 单向的；单行的
2 from one place to another, but not back again 单程的：She used the money to buy a one-way ticket to New Zealand. 她用这些钱买了去新西兰的单程票。

onion /ˈʌnjən/ *noun* 名词
a round vegetable with many layers. It has a strong, sharp smell and taste. 洋葱

online /ˌɒnˈlaɪn/ *adjective* 形容词, *adverb* 副词
1 using the Internet to sell goods 在线业务的；网上的：an online bookshop 网上书店

2 connected to the Internet. Compare with **offline**. 联机（的），在线（的）（比较 offline）: *You can chat to other people who are online.* 你可以和其他在线的人聊天。 ▫ *I buy most of my clothes online.* 我大多数衣服都是在网上买的。

onlooker /ˈɒnlʊkə/ *countable noun* 可数名词 someone who watches an event but does not take part in it 旁观者: *A group of onlookers stood and watched the fight.* 一群旁观者站在那里看着这场打斗。

only¹ /ˈəʊnli/ *adjective* 形容词, *adverb* 副词
1 involving no other person or thing 仅仅; 只有: *Only one person knew the answer.* 只有一个人知道答案。 ▫ *We have only twelve students in our class.* 我们班只有 12 名学生。
2 one person or thing of a particular type 仅有的; 唯一的: *She's the only girl in the class.* 她是班上唯一的女孩。
3 used for describing a child who has no brothers or sisters（子女）独生的: *I'm an only child, and I like it.* 我是家里的独生子，我喜欢这感觉。
4 used for saying how small or short something is（表示小或少）仅仅, 才: *Their house is only a few miles from here.* 他们家离这儿只有几英里远。
only just used for saying that something happened a very short time ago 刚才; 刚刚: *She's only just arrived.* 她刚到。

only² /ˈəʊnli/ *conjunction* 连词 but (*informal* 非正式): 只不过; 只是: *It's like my house, only it's nicer.* 这和我的房子很像，只不过更漂亮。

onto /ˈɒntuː/ *preposition* 介词
1 to a position on a surface 到⋯的上面: *The cat climbed onto her lap.* 猫爬到了她腿上。
2 into a bus, train or plane 到（公共汽车、火车或飞机）上: *He got onto the plane.* 他上了飞机。

ooh /uː/ also 亦作 **oo** *exclamation* 感叹词 used for showing that you are surprised or excited, or when you think something is pleasant or unpleasant (*informal* 非正式) 嗬; 哇; 呀: *Ooh, that hurts.* 嗬, 好疼。

oops /ʊps/ *exclamation* 感叹词 used when a small mistake or accident has happened（用于出了小错误或意外时）哎呀, 啊呀: *Oops! Sorry. Are you all right?* 哎呀！对不起。你还好吗？

ooze /uːz/ *verb* 动词 (**oozes**, **oozing**, **oozed**) to flow out of something slowly and in small amounts 渗出: *They drank the liquid that oozed from the fruit.* 他们喝了水果中渗出的汁液。

open¹ /ˈəʊpən/ *verb* 动词 (**opens**, **opening**, **opened**)
1 to move something so that it is no longer covered or closed 打开: *He opened the window.* 他打开了窗户。 ▫ *After a few seconds, I opened my eyes.* 几秒之后，我睁开了眼。 ● **open** *adjective* 形容词: *His eyes were open and he was smiling.* 他睁着眼睛，微笑着。

open 打开

He opened the window. 他打开了窗户。

2 to remove part of a container so that you can take out what is inside 将⋯开封; 拆开: *Nicole opened the silver box on the table.* 妮科尔打开了桌上的银盒子。
3 to move the covers of a book so that you can see the pages inside 翻开（书）: *He opened the book and started to read.* 他翻开书开始阅读。
4 to give a computer an instruction to show a file on the screen 打开（计算机文件）: *To open a file, go to the File menu.* 要打开文件, 就进入"文件"菜单。
5 when a shop, office or public building opens, people can go into it 开门; 营业: *The banks will open again on Monday morning.* 银行要到周一早上才开门。 ● **open** *adjective* 形容词: *The shop is open Monday to Friday, 9 a.m. to 6 p.m.* 这家商店周一至周五每天早上 9 点到下午 6 点营业。

open² /ˈəʊpən/ *adjective* 形容词
1 honest about your thoughts and feelings 坦诚的; 坦率的: *He was always open with her.* 他对她一直都很坦诚。
2 ready and willing to consider or accept suggestions or ideas 开放的; 愿意考虑（或

open-air – oppose

接受)的：*We are always open to suggestions.* 我们一直都乐于接受建议。

open-air *adjective* 形容词
outside; not in a building 户外的；露天的：*an open-air concert* 露天音乐会

opener /'əʊpənə/ *countable noun* 可数名词
a tool that is used for opening cans or bottles (罐或瓶的)开启工具：*a tin opener* 开罐器

opening¹ /'əʊpənɪŋ/ *adjective* 形容词
used for describing the first one in a series of events, days or weeks 开始的；开端的：*The team lost the opening game.* 这支队伍在揭幕战中失利了。

opening² /'əʊpənɪŋ/ *countable noun* 可数名词
a hole or an empty space that things or people can pass through 孔；洞；缺口：*He managed to get through a narrow opening in the fence.* 他成功地从围栏上一个狭窄的缺口钻了过去。

open-minded *adjective* 形容词
willing to listen to other people's ideas 思想开明的；豁达的：*He says that he is open-minded about tomorrow's talks.* 他说他对于明天的会谈持开放态度。

opera /'ɒprə/ *noun* 名词
a play with music in which all the words are sung 歌剧：*an opera singer* 歌剧演员
▶ **operatic** /ˌɒpə'rætɪk/ *adjective* 形容词：*He was famous for his operatic voice.* 他以歌剧嗓音闻名。

operate /'ɒpəˌreɪt/ *verb* 动词 (**operates, operating, operated**)
1 when an organization operates, it does the work it is supposed to 经营；运营：*The organization has been operating in the area for some time.* 这家机构已经在此地运营一段时间了。
2 to make a machine work 操作(机器)：*Weston showed him how to operate the machine.* 韦斯顿向他展示了如何操作这台机器。
3 to cut open a patient's body in order to remove or repair a part (医生)做手术：*Surgeons operated on Max to remove a brain tumour.* 医生们给马克斯动了手术，切除了脑瘤。

operating system *countable noun* 可数名词
the main program of a computer that controls all the other programs 操作系统：*Which operating system do you use?* 你用的是什么操作系统？

operation /ˌɒpə'reɪʃn/ *countable noun* 可数名词
1 an organized activity that involves many people doing different things (参与者众多、有组织的)行动：*The rescue operation began on Friday.* 救援行动于周五开始。
2 when a doctor cuts open a patient's body in order to remove, replace or repair a part 手术：*Charles had an operation on his arm.* 查尔斯的胳膊动了一次手术。

operator /'ɒpəˌreɪtə/ *countable noun* 可数名词
1 a person who connects telephone calls in a place such as an office or a hotel 话务员；电话接线员：*He called the operator.* 他呼叫了接线员。
2 a person whose job is to operate or control a machine (机器)操作员：*a crane operator* 起重机操作员
3 a person or a company that operates a business 经营者；运营商：*Several tour operators offer day trips to lakes and castles around the city.* 有几家旅行社提供城市周边湖泊、城堡一日游。

opinion /ə'pɪnjən/ *noun* 名词
1 *countable* 可数 what someone thinks about something 意见；见解；主张：*I didn't ask for your opinion.* 我没有问你的意见。
2 *singular* 单数 what you think about someone's character or ability (对某人的)评价，印象：*I don't have a very high opinion of Thomas.* 我对托马斯评价不是很高。

opponent /ə'pəʊnənt/ *countable noun* 可数名词
the person who is against you in a sports competition (体育比赛中的)对手：*She'll face six opponents in today's race.* 今天的比赛中她将面对6位对手。

opportunity /ˌɒpə'tjuːnɪti/ *noun* 名词 (**opportunities**)
a situation in which it is possible for you to do something that you want to do 机会；时机：*I had an opportunity to go to New York and study.* 我有一个去纽约学习的机会。

oppose /ə'pəʊz/ *verb* 动词 (**opposes, opposing, opposed**)
to disagree with what someone wants to do, and to try to stop them from doing it 反对；抵制：*He said that he would oppose*

any tax increase. 他说任何增税他都反对。

opposed /əˈpəʊzd/ *adjective* 形容词
disagreeing with something 反对的；抵制的：*I am opposed to any form of terrorism.* 我反对任何形式的恐怖主义。

opposite¹ /ˈɒpəzɪt/ *preposition* 介词
across from 在…的对面：*Jennie sat opposite Sam at breakfast.* 珍妮吃早餐时坐在萨姆对面。● **opposite** *adverb* 副词：*He looked at the buildings opposite.* 他看着对面的建筑物。

opposite² /ˈɒpəzɪt/ *adjective* 形容词
used for describing similar things that are completely different in a particular way（同类事物在特定方面）截然相反的，全然不同的：*We watched the cars driving in the opposite direction.* 我们看着车辆往相反方向驶去。● **opposite** *countable noun* 可数名词：*Whatever he says, he's probably thinking the opposite.* 不管他嘴上说什么，他心里想的可能是另一套。

opposition /ˌɒpəˈzɪʃən/ *uncountable noun* 不可数名词
strong disagreement（强烈的）反对，抵制：*There is strong opposition to the plan from local people.* 该计划遭到当地人强烈反对。

optician /ɒpˈtɪʃən/ *countable noun* 可数名词
a person whose job is to make and sell glasses 眼镜师；眼镜商

optimism /ˈɒptɪˌmɪzəm/ *uncountable noun* 不可数名词
a feeling of hope about the success of something 乐观：*There is optimism about the possibility of peace.* 人们对和平前景表示乐观。
▶ **optimist** /ˈɒptɪmɪst/ *countable noun* 可数名词：*He is an optimist about the country's future.* 他对于国家的未来很乐观。

optimistic /ˌɒptɪˈmɪstɪk/ *adjective* 形容词
hopeful about the success of something 乐观的：*She is optimistic that they can reach an agreement.* 她对他们达成协议持乐观态度。

option /ˈɒpʃən/ *countable noun* 可数名词
a choice between two or more things 选项；选择：*We will consider all options before making a decision.* 作决定之前我们会考虑所有选项。

optional /ˈɒpʃənəl/ *adjective* 形容词
if something is optional, you can choose whether or not you do it or have it 可选择的；非强制的：*All students have to study maths, but history and geography are optional.* 所有学生都必须学数学，但是历史和地理可以选修。

or /ə, STRONG ɔː/ *conjunction* 连词
1 used for showing choices or possibilities 或者；要么：*'Do you want tea or coffee?' John asked.* "你想喝茶还是咖啡？"约翰问。□ *Either you change your behaviour, or you will have to leave.* 要么改变自己的行为，要么就得离开。
2 used between two numbers to show that you are giving an approximate amount（用于两个数字之间表示概数）或，大约：*You should only drink one or two cups of coffee a day.* 你一天应该只喝一两杯咖啡。
3 used for introducing a warning that something bad could happen（用于警告）否则，要不然：*She has to have the operation, or she will die.* 她必须做手术，不然她会死的。

oral /ˈɔːrəl/ *adjective* 形容词
1 spoken rather than written 口头的：*The English test includes written and oral examinations.* 英语测试包括笔试和口试。
2 relating to your mouth 口的；口腔的：*good oral hygiene* 良好的口腔卫生

orange¹ /ˈɒrɪndʒ/ *adjective* 形容词
of a colour between red and yellow 橙色的；橘色的
→ Look at picture on P13 参见彩插第 13 页

orange² /ˈɒrɪndʒ/ *noun* 名词
1 a round, juicy fruit with a thick, orange-coloured skin 橙子
2 a colour between red and yellow 橙色；橘色：*His supporters were dressed in orange.* 他的支持者身着橘色衣服。

orbit /ˈɔːbɪt/ *countable noun* 可数名词
the curved path of an object that goes around a planet, a moon or the sun（天体等的）轨道：*The Earth has an orbit that changes.* 地球运行的轨道是变化的。
● **orbit** *verb* 动词 (**orbits**, **orbiting**, **orbited**)：*The moon orbits the Earth.* 月球绕着地球转。

orbit 轨道

orchard /ˈɔːtʃəd/ *countable noun* 可数名词
an area of land where fruit trees grow 果园

orchestra /ˈɔːkɪstrə/ *countable noun* 可数名词
a large group of musicians who play different instruments together 管弦乐队; 管弦乐团: *The orchestra began to play.* 管弦乐队开始演奏了。

ordeal /ɔːˈdiːl/ *countable noun* 可数名词
a difficult and very unpleasant experience 煎熬; 折磨: *The attack was a terrifying ordeal for both victims.* 这场袭击对于两位受害者来说是一场可怕的梦魇。

order[1] /ˈɔːdə/ *verb* 动词 (**orders, ordering, ordered**)
1 to tell someone to do something 命令; 指示: *Williams ordered him to leave.* 威廉斯命令他离开。
2 to ask for something to be sent to you from a company 订; 订购: *They ordered a new washing machine on the Internet.* 他们在网上订购了一台新洗衣机。
3 to ask for food and drinks to be brought to you in a restaurant 点餐: *The waitress asked, 'Are you ready to order?'* 女服务员问: "您准备点餐了吗?"

order[2] /ˈɔːdə/ *noun* 名词
1 *countable* 可数 the words that someone says when they tell you to do something 命令; 指示: *The commander gave his men orders to move out of the camp.* 指挥官命令手下撤离营地。
2 *countable* 可数 the thing that someone has asked for 所订货物; 所点餐品: *He's just placed an order for a new car.* 他刚刚订购了一辆新车。 □ *The waiter returned with their order.* 服务员端着他们点的餐回来了。
3 *uncountable* 不可数 an arrangement where one thing is first, another thing is second, another thing is third, and so on 顺序; 次序: *The books are all arranged in alphabetical order.* 这些书全按字母顺序排列。
4 *uncountable* 不可数 the situation that exists when everything is in the correct place, or happens at the correct time 整齐; 有条理: *Everything on the desk is in order.* 桌子上所有东西都摆放得整齐有序。
5 *uncountable* 不可数 the situation that exists when people obey the law and do not fight 秩序; 治安: *The army went to the islands to restore order.* 军队前往岛屿恢复治安。
in order to so that you can achieve something 为了⋯: *The operation was necessary in order to save the baby's life.* 要拯救宝宝的性命, 就必须手术。
in working order working properly 运转良好; 状况良好: *His old car is still in perfect working order.* 他那辆旧车状态依然好得很。
out of order not working properly 发生故障; 失灵: *Their phone's out of order.* 他们的电话出问题了。

ordinary /ˈɔːdɪnri/ *adjective* 形容词
normal and not special or different 平常的; 普通的: *These are just ordinary people living ordinary lives.* 这些人就是普通人, 过着平凡的生活。
out of the ordinary unusual or different 不寻常; 异常: *The police asked people to report anything out of the ordinary.* 警察要求人们报告任何不寻常之处。

organ /ˈɔːɡən/ *countable noun* 可数名词
1 a part of your body that has a particular purpose 器官: *The brain is the most powerful organ in the body.* 大脑是人体中最强大的器官。
2 a large musical instrument that is like a piano 管风琴: *a church organ* 教堂管风琴

organic /ɔːˈɡænɪk/ *adjective* 形容词
grown without using chemicals 有机的; 无公害的: *We buy only organic fruit and vegetables.* 我们只买有机果蔬。

organism /ˈɔːɡəˌnɪzəm/ *countable noun* 可数名词
a living thing 生物; 有机体: *We study very small organisms such as bacteria.* 我们研究细菌这样的微生物。

organization /ˌɔːɡənaɪˈzeɪʃən/ *noun* 名词
1 *countable* 可数 an official group of people such as a business or a club 组织; 机构: *She worked for the same organization for six years.* 她在同一家机构工作了6年。
2 *uncountable* 不可数 when you plan or arrange an activity (活动的) 组织, 安排: *I helped in the organization of the concert.* 我参与组织了这场音乐会。

organize /ˈɔːɡəˌnaɪz/ *verb* 动词 (**organizes, organizing, organized**)
1 to plan or arrange something 组织; 筹划; 安排: *We decided to organize a concert.* 我们决定组织一场音乐会。
▶ **organizer** /ˈɔːɡəˌnaɪzə/ *countable noun* 可数名词: *Organizers are hoping to raise £65,000 from the concert.* 组织者希望通过

这场音乐会筹集 6.5 万英镑。
2 to plan or arrange things in a tidy and effective way 整理；使有条理：*He began to organize his papers.* 他开始整理自己的文件。

organized /ˈɔːɡəˌnaɪzd/ *adjective* 形容词
planning your work and activities carefully 有序的；有条理的：*Managers need to be very organized.* 管理者需要非常有条理。

oriental /ˌɔːriˈentəl/ *adjective* 形容词
used for talking about things that come from places in eastern Asia. Do not use **oriental** for talking about people. 东方的（不要用 oriental 指东方人）：*He was an expert in oriental art.* 他是研究东方艺术的专家。

origin /ˈɒrɪdʒɪn/ *countable noun* 可数名词
1 the way something started 起源；来源：*Scientists study the origin of life on Earth.* 科学家们研究地球上生命的起源。
2 the country, race, or class of someone's parents or ancestors 族裔；血统；出身：*Americans of Hispanic origin* 西班牙裔美国人

original¹ /əˈrɪdʒənəl/ *adjective* 形容词
1 used for talking about something that existed at the beginning 最初的；原来的：*The original plan was to go by bus.* 原计划是乘公共汽车前往。
▶ **originally** /əˈrɪdʒənəli/ *adverb* 副词：*Wright lives in London but he is originally from Melbourne.* 赖特住在伦敦，但他原籍是墨尔本。
2 showing that the person who did something has imagination and new ideas 独创的；新颖的：*He is the most original painter of the past 100 years.* 他是过去 100 年来最具独创性的画家。

original² /əˈrɪdʒənəl/ *countable noun* 可数名词
something that is not a copy 原件；原作：*Make a copy of the document and send the original to your employer.* 将文件复印一份，然后将原件寄给雇主。

ornament /ˈɔːnəmənt/ *countable noun* 可数名词
an attractive object that you use to decorate your home（家中的）装饰品，点缀品：*There were a few ornaments on the shelf.* 架子上有一些装饰品。

orphan /ˈɔːfən/ *countable noun* 可数名词
a child whose parents are dead 孤儿

orphanage /ˈɔːfənɪdʒ/ *countable noun* 可数名词
a place where orphans live 孤儿院

OS /ˌəʊ ˈes/ *countable noun* 可数名词 (**OS's**)
short for（缩写 =) **operating system**

ostrich /ˈɒstrɪtʃ/ *countable noun* 可数名词 (**ostriches**)
a very large bird that cannot fly 鸵鸟

ostrich 鸵鸟

other /ˈʌðə/ *adjective* 形容词
1 used for talking about more things or people that are like the thing or the person you have mentioned（表示与已提及的物或人同类）其余的：*Mr Johnson and the other teachers are very worried.* 约翰逊先生和其他老师都非常担心。● **other** *pronoun* 代词：*He had a pen in one hand and a book in the other.* 他一手持笔，一手拿书。
2 used for talking about a thing or a person that is different from the thing or the person you have mentioned（表示与已提及的物或人不同）别的，其他的：*He will have to accept it; there is no other way.* 对此他只能接受，别无选择。
3 used for talking about the second of two things or people（两者中）另一的：*William was at the other end of the room.* 威廉在房间另一头。
the other day used for talking about a day in the recent past 前几天；前不久：*I called her the other day.* 我前不久给她打了电话。

otherwise /ˈʌðəˌwaɪz/ *adverb* 副词
1 used for saying what the result would be if the situation was different 否则；不然：*I really enjoy this job, otherwise I would not be here.* 我真的很喜欢这份工作，不然我不会在这里。
2 used when you mention a different condition or way 除此之外；在其他方面：*He was very tired but otherwise happy.* 他很累，除此之外，他很幸福。□ *Take one pill three times a day, unless you are told otherwise by a doctor.* 每次 1 片，每日 3 次，或遵医嘱。

ouch /aʊtʃ/ *exclamation* 感叹词
used when you suddenly feel pain（表示突然觉得疼痛）哎哟：*The stones cut her feet. 'Ouch, ouch!' she cried.* 石头划伤了她的脚。

"哎哟，哎哟！"她叫道。

oughtn't /ˈɔːtnt/
short for (缩写 =) 'ought not'

ought to /ˈɔːt tə/ *modal verb* 情态动词
1 used for saying that something is the right thing to do 应当; 应该: *You ought to read this book.* 你应该读一读这本书。
2 used for saying that you think something will be true or will happen (表示认为某事可能成真或会发生) 应该: *'This party ought to be fun,' he told Alex.* "这次聚会应该很有趣。"他对亚历克斯说。

ounce /aʊns/ *countable noun* 可数名词
a unit for measuring weight. There are sixteen ounces in a pound and one ounce is equal to around 28.35 grams. 盎司 (重量单位, 1 磅 = 16 盎司, 1 盎司 ≈ 28.35 克)

our /aʊə/ *adjective* 形容词
belonging or relating both to you and to one or more other people 我们的: *We're expecting our first baby.* 我们即将迎来第一个宝宝。

ours /aʊəz/ *pronoun* 代词
used when you are talking about something that belongs to you and one or more other people 我们的: *That car is ours.* 那辆车是我们的。

ourselves /ˌaʊəˈselvz/ *pronoun* 代词
1 used when you are talking about yourself and one or more other people 我们自己: *We sat by the fire to keep ourselves warm.* 我们坐在火边取暖。
2 used for showing that you and one or more other people did something, rather than anyone else 我们自己; 我们亲自: *We built the house ourselves.* 这座房子是我们自己建造的。

out /aʊt/ *adjective* 形容词, *adverb* 副词
1 away from a place (从某处) 出来: *He took out his notebook.* 他掏出了笔记本。
2 not at home 外出; 不在家: *I called you yesterday, but you were out.* 我昨天给你打电话, 但你不在家。
3 no longer shining (灯) 熄灭的, 关着的: *All the lights were out in the house.* 房子里的灯全都灭了。
4 no longer burning (火) 熄灭的: *Please don't let the fire go out.* 请不要让火熄灭。
5 published and for sale 出版的; 上市的: *Their new CD is out now.* 他们的新 CD 现已上市。• **out** *adverb* 副词: *The book came out in June.* 这本书于 6 月出版。

6 outside the area of play in games such as tennis and basketball. Compare with **in**. (网球、篮球等运动中) 界外的 (比较 in): *The referee agreed that the ball was out.* 裁判也认同这球出界了。
7 If you go out of a place, you leave it (从某处) 出去: *She ran out of the house.* 她从房子里跑了出来。
8 If you take something out of a container, you remove it (拿) 出; (取) 出: *I took the key out of my handbag.* 我从手提包里掏出了钥匙。

out of used for talking about a smaller group that is part of a larger group (表示比例) 每⋯中: *Three out of four people say there's too much violence on TV.* 四分之三的人认为电视上的暴力场景太多了。

out of something
1 used for showing that something has all been used 用尽某物的; 用完某物的: *We're out of milk. Can you get some at the supermarket?* 我们没有牛奶了。你可以去超市买一些吗？
2 used for saying what something has been produced from 用某物 (制成或建成) 的: *The house is made out of wood.* 这房子是用木头建成的。

outbox /ˈaʊtbɒks/ *countable noun* 可数名词
the place that your computer stores emails that have not yet been sent (计算机中储存未发送邮件的) 发件箱: *I had dozens of unsent messages in my outbox.* 我的发件箱里有几十封未发送邮件。

outbreak /ˈaʊtbreɪk/ *countable noun* 可数名词
a sudden start of something bad (坏事的) 暴发: *This is the worst ever outbreak of the disease.* 这是有史以来该病最严重的一次暴发。

outcome /ˈaʊtkʌm/ *countable noun* 可数名词
the situation that exists at the end of an activity 结果; 结局: *It's too early to know the outcome of the election.* 现在想知道选举结果还为时过早。

outdoor /ˌaʊtˈdɔː/ *adjective* 形容词
happening outside and not in a building 户外的; 露天的: *If you enjoy outdoor activities, you should try rock climbing.* 你要是喜欢户外活动, 应该试试攀岩。

outdoors /ˌaʊtˈdɔːz/ *adverb* 副词
happening outside rather than in a building 在户外; 在室外: *It was warm*

enough to play outdoors all afternoon. 天气暖和，整个下午都可以在户外玩耍。

outer /ˈaʊtə/ *adjective* 形容词
on the outside of something 外部的；外面的：*This material forms the hard outer surface of the tooth.* 这种物质形成了牙齿坚硬的外表面。

outfit /ˈaʊtfɪt/ *countable noun* 可数名词
a set of clothes 成套服装：*I need a new outfit for the wedding.* 我需要一套新衣服参加婚礼。

outing /ˈaʊtɪŋ/ *countable noun* 可数名词
a short trip, usually with a group of people（通常指一群人的）短途游，外出游玩：*We went on an outing to the local cinema.* 我们一起去了当地的影院。

outline¹ /ˈaʊtlaɪn/ *countable noun* 可数名词
outline 轮廓
1 a general explanation or description of something 概要；概述：*We are sending you an outline of the plan.* 我们会给你发一份计划概要。
2 the general shape of an object or a person 轮廓；外形：*He could only see the dark outline of the man.* 他只能看见那个男人黑影的轮廓。

outline² /ˈaʊtlaɪn/ *verb* 动词 (outlines, outlining, outlined)
to give a general explanation or description of something 概述；概括：*The report outlined some possible changes to the rules.* 这份报告概述了可能会对规则做的一些修改。

outlook /ˈaʊtlʊk/ *noun* 名词
1 *singular* 单数 what will probably happen 前景；展望：*The economic outlook is not good.* 经济前景不好。
2 *countable* 可数 your general feeling about life（对人生的）看法，观点：*He had a positive outlook on life.* 他有着积极的人生观。

out of ˈdate also 亦作 **out-of-date** *adjective* 形容词
old-fashioned and no longer useful 过时的；陈旧的；老式的：*The rules are out of date.* 这些规则过时了。 □ *They were using an out-of-date map.* 他们用的是一张过时的地图。

output /ˈaʊtpʊt/ *uncountable noun* 不可数名词
the amount that a person or a thing produces 产量；产出：*There has been a large fall in industrial output.* 工业产量大幅滑坡。

outrage¹ /ˈaʊtreɪdʒ/ *verb* 动词 (outrages, outraging, outraged)
to shock someone or make them very angry 使震惊；激怒；使震怒：*Many people were outraged by his comments.* 他的评论激怒了很多人。

outrage² /ˈaʊtreɪdʒ/ *uncountable noun* 不可数名词
an intense feeling of anger and shock 震怒；愤慨；义愤：*Several teachers wrote to the newspapers to express their outrage.* 几位老师给报社写信表达他们的愤怒。

outrageous /aʊtˈreɪdʒəs/ *adjective* 形容词
shocking someone or making them very angry 骇人的；令人愤慨的：*It was outrageous behaviour.* 这种行为是骇人听闻的。

outside¹ /ˌaʊtˈsaɪd/ *adverb* 副词
not in a building, but very close to it 在外面（指在建筑物外面不远处）：*She went outside to look for Sam.* 她去外面找萨姆。
● **outside** *preposition* 介词：*She found him standing outside the classroom.* 她发现他站在教室外面。

outside² /ˌaʊtˈsaɪd/ *countable noun* 可数名词
the part of something that surrounds or covers the rest of it 外表；外部：*The outside of the building was recently painted.* 这栋建筑物的外墙最近刚粉刷过。
● **outside** /ˌaʊtˈsaɪd/ *adjective* 形容词：*The outside wall is painted white.* 外墙刷成了白色。

outskirts /ˈaʊtskɜːts/ *plural noun* 复数名词
the parts of a town or a city that are furthest away from its centre 城郊；郊区：*I live on the outskirts of the city.* 我住在城郊。

outstanding /aʊtˈstændɪŋ/ *adjective* 形容词
much better than other people or things of a similar type 出众的；杰出的：*She is an outstanding athlete.* 她是一名杰出的运动员。

oval /ˈəʊvəl/ *adjective* 形容词
having a shape like an egg 椭圆形的；卵形的：*She had an oval face with large, dark eyes.* 她长着一张鹅蛋脸、一双乌黑的大眼睛。 ● **oval** *countable noun* 可数名词：*Draw an oval with two eyes, a nose and a mouth.* 画一个椭圆，再画两只眼睛、一个鼻子和一

oven – overheat

张嘴。
→ Look at picture on P2 参见彩插第 2 页

oven /ˈʌvən/ *countable noun* 可数名词
a piece of equipment for cooking that is like a large metal box with a door 烤炉；烤箱

over¹ /ˈəʊvə/ *preposition* 介词
1 directly above or higher than another thing 在…正上方；在…上面；在…上空：*There was a gold mirror over the fireplace.* 壁炉上方有一面金色的镜子。◇ *I heard some planes flying over the house.* 我听到有几架飞机从房子上空飞过。
2 covering part or all of something（部分或全部覆盖）在…上面：*He lay down and pulled the blanket over himself.* 他躺下把毯子盖在身上。◇ *Pour the sauce over the mushrooms.* 将酱汁倒在蘑菇上。
3 across to the other side of something 从…一边到另一边：*They jumped over the wall.* 他们跳过墙去。
4 more than a particular amount 超出（特定数量）：*The house cost over £1 million.* 这栋房子花了 100 多万英镑。

over² /ˈəʊvə/ *adjective* 形容词，*adverb* 副词
1 used for talking about a short distance（表示距离近）在那边；在近旁：*Come over here!* 过来呀！◇ *The café is just over there.* 咖啡馆就在那边。
2 in a different position so that the part that was facing up is now facing down 翻转地：*His car rolled over on an icy road.* 他的车在结冰的路上翻了个底儿朝天。
3 completely finished 结束的；完结的：*The war is over.* 战争结束了。◇ *I am glad it's all over.* 彻底结束了，我很开心。

overcame /ˌəʊvəˈkeɪm/
→ see 见 **overcome**

overcast /ˈəʊvəkɑːst/ *adjective* 形容词
completely covered with cloud 阴天的：*He looked up at the grey, overcast sky.* 他抬头望着灰蒙蒙、阴沉的天空。

overcome /ˌəʊvəˈkʌm/ *verb* 动词
(**overcomes, overcoming, overcame, overcome**)
1 to successfully deal with or control a problem or a feeling 克服；控制：*Molly finally overcame her fear of flying.* 莫莉最终克服了对坐飞机的恐惧。
2 if you are overcome by a feeling, you feel it very strongly（感情）压倒，极大影响：*The night before the test I was overcome by*

fear. 考试前夜，恐惧吞噬了我。

overcrowded /ˌəʊvəˈkraʊdɪd/ *adjective* 形容词
with too many people 过度拥挤的：*We sat on the overcrowded beach.* 我们坐在人满为患的沙滩上。

overdue /ˌəʊvəˈdjuː/ *adjective* 形容词
late or delayed 逾期的；延误的：*Your tax payment is overdue.* 你未按时缴纳税款。◇ *Mr Giuliano said the changes were long overdue.* 朱利亚诺先生表示早该改变了。

overflow /ˌəʊvəˈfləʊ/ *verb* 动词 (**overflows, overflowing, overflowed**)
1 to have liquid flowing over the edges（容器等）溢水，溢出液体：*The sink overflowed.* 水槽溢水了。
2 to flow over the edges（液体）漫出；（河流）泛滥：*During the heavy rains, the river overflowed.* 暴雨期间，河水泛滥。

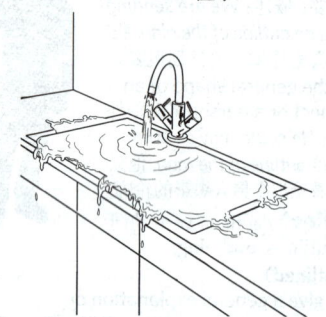

overflow 溢水

overhead *adjective* 形容词，*adverb* 副词

> **PRONUNCIATION HELP** 发音提示
> adjective /ˈəʊvəhed/, adverb /ˌəʊvəˈhed/.
> 形容词读作 /ˈəʊvəhed/，副词读作 /ˌəʊvəˈhed/。

above you 在头顶上方（的）：*She turned on the overhead light.* 她打开头顶上方的灯。◇ *Planes passed overhead.* 飞机从头顶上空飞过。

overhear /ˌəʊvəˈhɪə/ *verb* 动词 (**overhears, overhearing, overheard**)
to hear what someone says when they are not talking to you 偶然听到；无意中听到：*I overheard two doctors discussing me.* 我偶然间听到两位医生在谈论我。

overheat /ˌəʊvəˈhiːt/ *verb* 动词 (**overheats, overheating, overheated**)
to become too hot 变得过热；使过热：*The*

car's engine was overheating. 汽车发动机过热。

overlap /ˌəʊvəˈlæp/ *verb* 动词 (**overlaps, overlapping, overlapped**)
to cover a part of another thing 交叠；部分重叠：*The two circles overlap.* 两个圆部分重叠。

overlook /ˌəʊvəˈlʊk/ *verb* 动词 (**overlooks, overlooking, overlooked**)
1 to not notice something 忽视；忽略：*We cannot overlook this important fact.* 我们不能忽略掉这个重要的事实。
2 if a building or window overlooks a place, you can see the place clearly from the building or window (建筑物或窗户) 俯瞰, 俯视：*The hotel's rooms overlook a beautiful garden.* 酒店房间俯瞰着一座漂亮的花园。

overnight /ˌəʊvəˈnaɪt/ *adjective* 形容词
happening through the whole night or at some point during the night 夜间的；晚上的：*He decided to take an overnight fishing trip.* 他决定来一次夜钓。● **overnight** /ˌəʊvəˈnaɪt/ *adverb* 副词：*The decision was made overnight.* 这个决定是在夜里作出的。

overseas /ˌəʊvəˈsiːz/ *adjective* 形容词, *adverb* 副词
used for describing things or people that are in or that come from foreign countries 海外的；在国外：*He enjoyed his overseas trip.* 他这次海外之行很愉快。□ *He's now working overseas.* 他现在在国外工作。

oversleep /ˌəʊvəˈsliːp/ *verb* 动词 (**oversleeps, oversleeping, overslept**)
to sleep longer than you should 睡过头；睡得过久：*I forgot to set my alarm and I overslept.* 我忘了定闹钟，睡过了头。

overtake /ˌəʊvəˈteɪk/ *verb* 动词 (**overtakes, overtaking, overtook, overtaken**)
to pass another car or person that is going in the same direction 超过；超越：*You should never overtake on a bend.* 绝不要在弯道超车。

overtaken /ˌəʊvəˈteɪkən/
→ see 见 **overtake**

overtime /ˈəʊvətaɪm/ *uncountable noun* 不可数名词
extra time that you spend doing your job 加时；加点；加班时间：*He worked overtime to finish the job.* 他加班完成工作。

overtook /ˌəʊvəˈtʊk/
→ see 见 **overtake**

overweight /ˌəʊvəˈweɪt/ *adjective* 形容词
weighing more than is considered healthy or attractive (人) 超重的

overwhelming /ˌəʊvəˈwelmɪŋ/ *adjective* 形容词
affecting you very strongly 极其强烈的；难以抗拒的：*She had an overwhelming feeling of guilt.* 她愧疚得不能自已。

owe /əʊ/ *verb* 动词 (**owes, owing, owed**)
1 to have to pay money to someone 欠（债）；欠（…钱）：*The company owes money to more than 60 banks.* 这家公司欠60多家银行的债。□ *Blake owed him £50.* 布莱克欠他50英镑。
2 to want to do something for someone because you are grateful to them 亏欠（…人情）：*She thought Will owed her a favour.* 她觉得威尔欠她一个人情。

owl /aʊl/ *countable noun* 可数名词
a bird with large eyes that is active at night 猫头鹰；鸮

own¹ /əʊn/ *adjective* 形容词
1 used for saying that something belongs to or is done by a particular person or thing 自己的；本人的：*I wanted to have my own business.* 我想拥有自己的生意。□ *They prefer to make their own decisions.* 他们喜欢自己拿主意。● **own** *pronoun* 代词：*The man's face was a few inches from my own.* 那男人的脸和我的脸隔了几英寸。
2 used for saying that something is used by only one person or thing 自己专用的；自己特有的：*Jennifer wanted her own room.* 珍妮弗想要自己的房间。
on your own
1 alone 单独；独自：*He lives on his own.* 他独自生活。
2 without any help 独立；依靠自己：*I work best on my own.* 我独立工作时效果最好。

own² /əʊn/ *verb* 动词 (**owns, owning, owned**)
to have something that belongs to you 有；拥有：*His father owns a local computer shop.* 他父亲在当地有一家电脑店。

owner /ˈəʊnə/ *countable noun* 可数名词
the person that something belongs to 物主；主人；所有者：*My brother is the owner of the shop.* 我哥哥是这家商店的店主。

ownership /ˈəʊnəʃɪp/ *uncountable noun* 不可数名词
when you own something 所有权：*There has been an increase in home ownership.* 拥

oxygen /ˈɒksɪdʒən/ ***uncountable noun*** 不可数名词
a gas in the air that is needed by all plants and animals 氧；氧气

oyster /ˈɔɪstə/ ***countable noun*** 可数名词
a small flat sea animal that has a hard shell and is eaten as food. Oysters can produce pearls (= small round white objects used for making jewellery). 牡蛎；蚝

oz.
short for (缩写 =) ounce

the ozone layer /ði ˈəʊzəʊnˌleɪə/ ***singular noun*** 单数名词
the area high above the Earth's surface that protects living things from the harmful effects of the sun 臭氧层: *Scientists discovered another hole in the ozone layer last month.* 科学家上个月又发现了一处臭氧层空洞。

Pp

pace¹ /peɪs/ *noun* 名词
1 *singular* 单数 the speed at which something happens 速度；节奏：*Since her illness, she is taking life at a slower pace.* 她生病后开始放慢生活节奏。
2 *countable* 可数 the distance that you move when you take one step 步幅：*Peter walked a few paces behind me.* 彼得走在我后面，离我几步远。

pace² /peɪs/ *verb* 动词 (**paces, pacing, paced**) to keep walking around in a small area because you are worried (因焦虑) 在…走来走去，来回踱步于：*As they waited, Kravis paced the room nervously.* 他们等待的时候，克拉维斯在屋里不安地踱来踱去。

pack¹ /pæk/ *verb* 动词 (**packs, packing, packed**) to put clothes and other things into a bag, because you are going away 收拾（行李）；装箱；打包：*When I was 17, I packed my bags and left home.* 17岁时，我收拾行囊离开了家。▫ *I began to pack for the trip.* 我开始为这次旅行整理行装。

pack 收拾（行李）

pack² /pæk/ *countable noun* 可数名词
1 a collection of things that are kept together 一套；一包：*The club will send you an information pack.* 俱乐部会给你寄一个资料包。
2 a group of wild dogs or similar animals (野狗或类似动物的) 一群
3 a set of 52 playing cards (纸牌的) 一副：

a pack of playing cards 一副纸牌

package /ˈpækɪdʒ/ *countable noun* 可数名词 something that is wrapped in paper, or in a box or an envelope 包裹：*I tore open the package.* 我撕开那个包裹。

packaging /ˈpækɪdʒɪŋ/ *uncountable noun* 不可数名词
the paper or plastic that something is in when you buy it 外包装：*Avoid buying food with plastic packaging.* 避免购买塑料包装的食品。

packed /pækt/ *adjective* 形容词
very full of people 非常拥挤的；挤满人的：*The shop was packed.* 这家商店挤满了人。

ˌpacked ˈlunch *countable noun* 可数名词 (**packed lunches**)
food that you take to work or school, and eat as your lunch (带去上班或上学的) 自备午餐

packet /ˈpækɪt/ *countable noun* 可数名词 a small box, bag or envelope in which an amount of something is sold (商品的) 小盒，小包，小袋：*He bought a packet of biscuits.* 他买了一盒饼干。

pad /pæd/ *countable noun* 可数名词
1 a thick, flat piece of soft material, used for cleaning things or for protection 垫子；衬垫；护垫：*Please wear a helmet and elbow pads.* 请戴上头盔和护肘。▫ *Have you tried using an oven-cleaning pad?* 你试过烤箱清洁布吗？
2 a number of pieces of paper attached together along one side 便笺本；拍纸簿：*Have a pad ready and write down the information.* 准备好便笺簿，把信息记录下来。

padded /ˈpædɪd/ *adjective* 形容词
containing soft material that makes something softer or warmer, or that protects it 有衬垫的：*a padded jacket* 棉夹克 ▫ *a padded envelope* 气泡信封

padding /ˈpædɪŋ/ *uncountable noun* 不可数名词
soft material in something that makes it

softer or warmer, or that protects it 垫料；衬料：*These headphones have foam rubber padding.* 这副头戴式耳机衬有泡沫橡胶垫料。▫ *Players must wear padding to protect them from injury.* 运动员必须戴防护垫以免受伤。

paddle[1] /ˈpædəl/ *countable noun* 可数名词
a short pole with a wide flat part at the end, that you use to move a small boat through water 桨；船桨

paddle[2] /ˈpædəl/ *verb* 动词 (**paddles, paddling, paddled**)
1 to walk or stand in shallow water, for example at the edge of the sea, for pleasure 玩水；戏水：*There is a lovely little stream that you can paddle in.* 有一条美丽的小溪，可以在其中戏水。● **paddle** *countable noun* 可数名词：*Let's go for a paddle in the sea.* 咱们去海里玩水吧。
2 to move a small boat through water using a paddle 用桨划（船）：*He paddled a canoe across the Congo river.* 他划着独木舟穿过刚果河。

padlock /ˈpædlɒk/ *countable noun* 可数名词
a metal lock that is used for fastening two things together 挂锁；扣锁：*They put a padlock on the door of his house.* 他们给他房子的大门上了把挂锁。

page /peɪdʒ/ *countable noun* 可数名词
one side of a piece of paper in a book, a magazine or a newspaper（书籍的）页；（报刊的）版：*Turn to page 4.* 翻到第 4 页。▫ *The story was on the front page of The Times.* 这篇报道刊登在《泰晤士报》的头版。

paid /peɪd/
→ see 见 **pay**

pain /peɪn/ *noun* 名词
1 the feeling that you have in a part of your body, because of illness or an injury 疼；痛：*I felt a sharp pain in my lower back.* 我感觉到后腰一阵剧痛。▫ *My legs are sore and I'm in pain all the time.* 我的腿很疼，疼得我一刻不得消停。
2 *uncountable* 不可数 the sadness that you feel when something upsets you 痛苦；悲痛：*I could see that my words caused him great pain.* 我可以看出，我的话让他很痛苦。
a pain or **a pain in the neck** very annoying (*informal* 非正式) 讨厌鬼；烦心事：*I like her work, but she can be a pain in the neck.* 她活儿做得不错，可她这个人有时很讨

人厌。

painful /ˈpeɪnfʊl/ *adjective* 形容词
1 hurting 疼痛的：*Her toe was swollen and painful.* 她的脚趾又肿又痛。
▶ **painfully** /ˈpeɪnfʊli/ *adverb* 副词：*Matt banged his head painfully as he climbed out of the window.* 马特从窗户爬出来时撞疼了头。
2 making you feel sad and upset 令人痛苦的：*His unkind remarks brought back painful memories.* 他这些刻薄的话勾起了痛苦的回忆。

painkiller /ˈpeɪnkɪlə/ *countable noun* 可数名词
a drug that reduces or stops physical pain 止痛药

painless /ˈpeɪnləs/ *adjective* 形容词
causing no physical pain 无痛的：*The operation is a quick, painless procedure.* 手术过程很快且无痛苦。

paint[1] /peɪnt/ *uncountable noun* 不可数名词
a coloured liquid that you put onto a surface with a brush 油漆；颜料：*We'll need about three cans of red paint.* 我们需要大概 3 罐红色颜料。
→ Look at picture on P13 参见彩插第 13 页

paint[2] /peɪnt/ *verb* 动词 (**paints, painting, painted**)
1 to cover a wall or an object with paint 给…刷油漆：*They started to paint the walls.* 他们开始给墙刷漆。

paint 给…刷油漆

They started to paint the walls.
他们开始给墙刷漆。

2 to produce a picture of something using paint 用颜料画：*He is very good at painting flowers.* 他很擅长画花卉。▫ *Monet painted hundreds of pictures of water lilies.* 莫奈画了几百幅睡莲。

School and Study 学校与学习

Mathematics 数学

6-3=3
six minus three
equals three
六减三等于三

6÷2=3
six divided by two
equals three
六除以二等于三

3+3=6
three plus three
equals six
三加三等于六

2.5
two point five
二点五

3x2=6
three times two equals six
三乘以二等于六

50%
fifty per cent
百分之五十

a half (1/2)
二分之一

a quarter (1/4)
四分之一

a third (1/3)
三分之一

three quarters (3/4)
四分之三

Shapes 形状

triangle 三角形

square 正方形

circle 圆

hexagon 六边形

oval 椭圆

rectangle
长方形；矩形

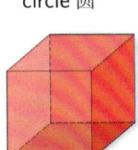
cube 立方体

cylinder 圆柱

Measurements 度量衡

length 长度

weight 重量

volume 容积；容量

10 millimetres (mm) 毫米 = 1 centimetre (cm) 厘米
100 centimetres (cm) 厘米 = 1 metre (m) 米
1000 metres (m) 米 = 1 kilometre (km) 千米

1000 grams (g) 克
= 1 kilogram (kg) 千克

1000 millilitres (ml)
毫升 = 1 litre (l) 升

For telling the time, see page xxvi.
时刻表示法见第 xxvi 页。

Language 语言

Skills 技能

reading 读　　writing 写　　listening 听　　speaking 说

Writing 写

- small letter 小写字母
- capital letter 大写字母
- word 单词
- sentence 句子
- title 标题
- introduction 引言
- paragraph 段落
- conclusion 结尾
- essay 短文

Reading 读

poem 诗歌

novel 小说

play 戏剧

dictionary 词典

For grammatical labels, see pages x–xii. For punctuation, see pages xxi–xxiii.
语法标签见第 x—xii 页。 标点符号用法见第 xxi—xxiii 页。

Science 科学

The body 人体

Inside the body 人体内部

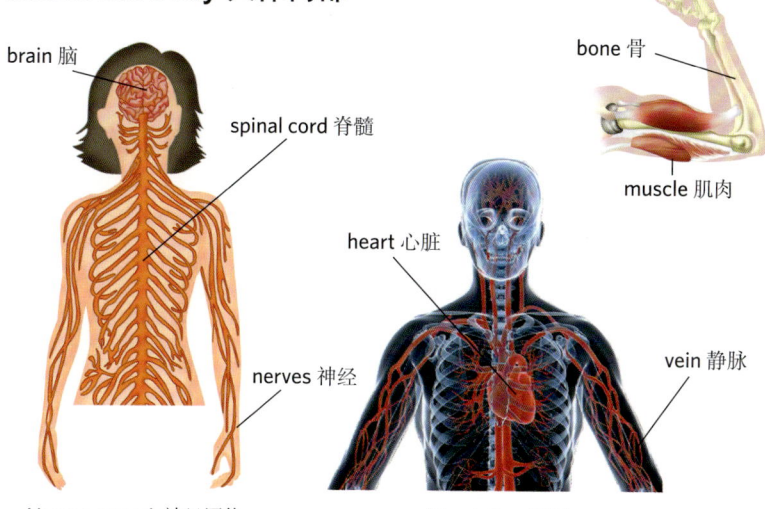

Nerve network 神经网络

Circulation 循环

A healthy diet 健康膳食

meat 肉　　fish 鱼　　egg 蛋　　milk 奶　　cheese 干酪

pasta 意大利面　　bread 面包　　rice 米饭　　potato 土豆　　cereal 麦片粥

apple 苹果　　banana 香蕉　　broccoli 西蓝花　　cabbage 卷心菜　　carrot 胡萝卜

Science 科学

Materials and their properties 材料及其属性

solid 固体

liquid 液体

gas 气体

melt 融化

evaporate 蒸发
boil 沸腾

freeze 冻结

Electricity 电

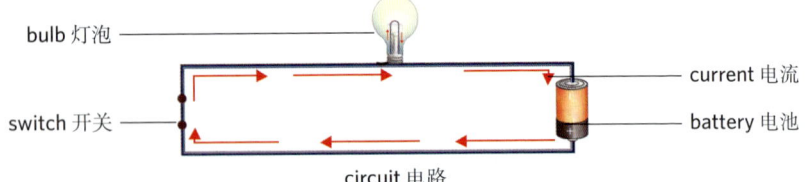

bulb 灯泡
switch 开关
current 电流
battery 电池
circuit 电路

Forces and motion 力与运动

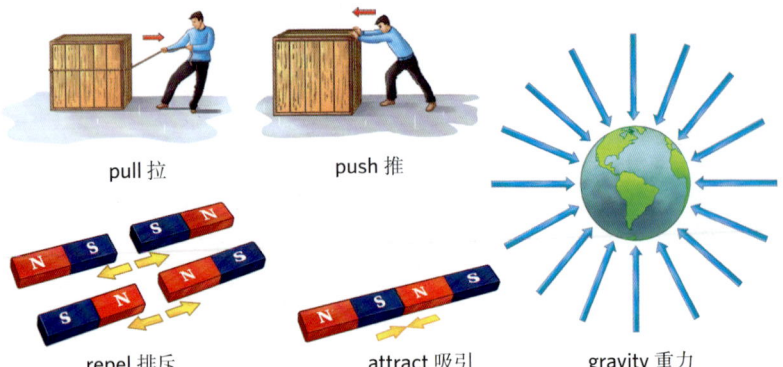

pull 拉
push 推
repel 排斥
attract 吸引
gravity 重力

Geography 地理

The natural world 自然界

cliff 悬崖
beach 海滩
sea 海

lake 湖 | mountain 山

forest 森林

glacier 冰川

island 岛屿

cave 洞穴

river 河流

waterfall 瀑布

Geography 地理

Weather 天气

It's rainy 下雨

It's sunny 晴天

It's cloudy 多云

It's windy 刮风

It's foggy 雾天

It's snowy 雪天

It's stormy 风暴天

It's icy 冰冻天

flood 洪水

lightning 闪电

rainbow 彩虹

Seasons 季节

spring 春

summer 夏

autumn 秋

winter 冬

Equipment 装备

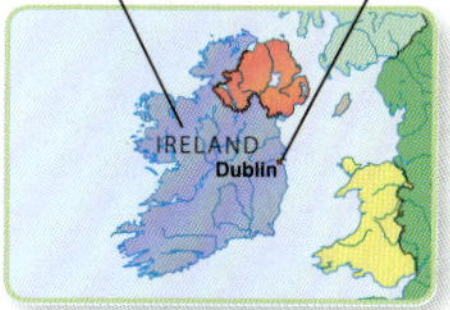

country 国家
capital 首都
IRELAND
Dublin

map 地图

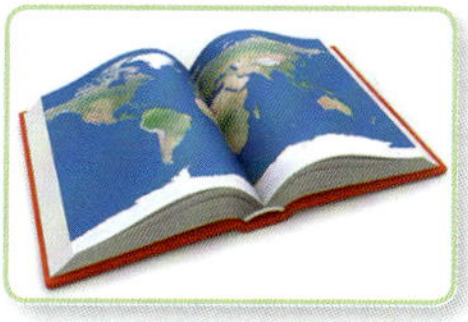

atlas 地图集

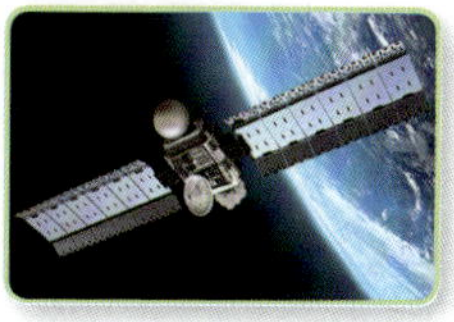

satellite 卫星

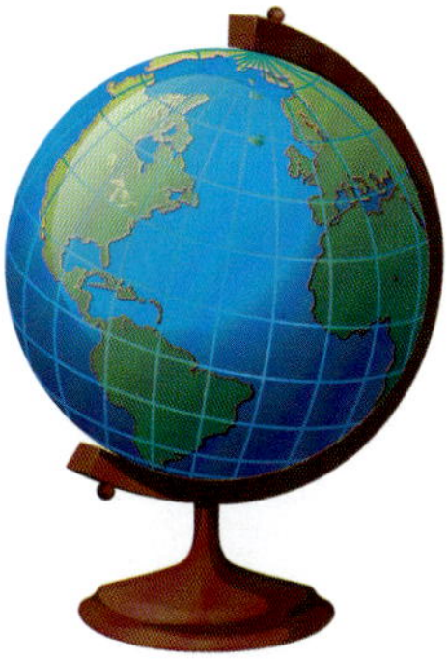

globe 地球仪

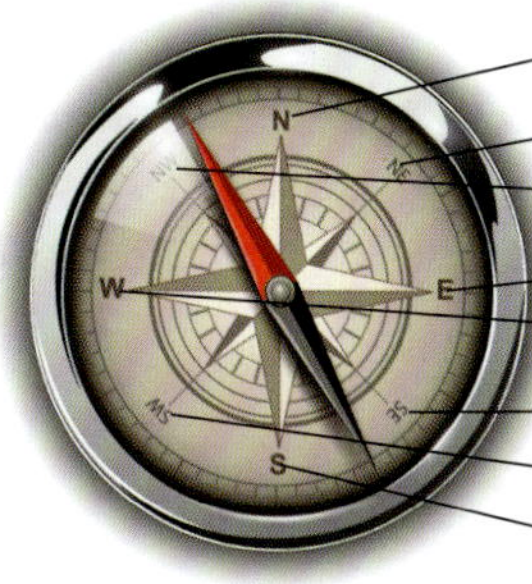

N
W
E
S
north 北
north-east 东北
north-west 西北
east 东
west 西
south-east 东南
south-west 西南
south 南

compass 罗盘

Reading maps 看地图

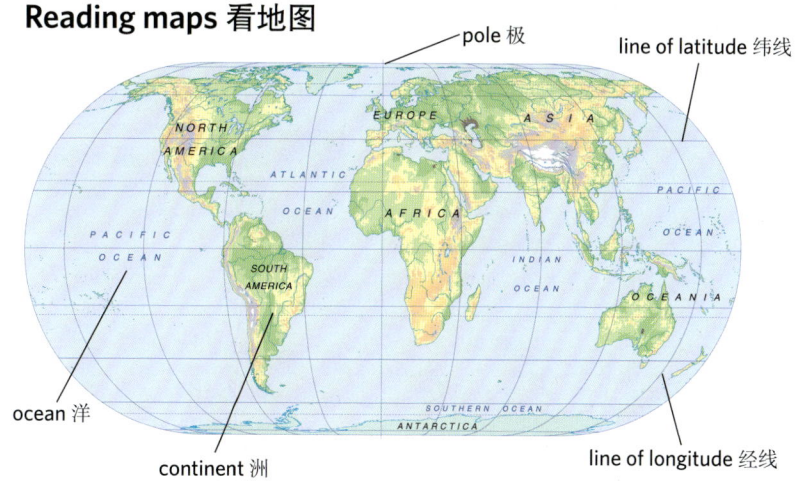

pole 极
line of latitude 纬线
NORTH AMERICA
EUROPE
ASIA
ATLANTIC OCEAN
AFRICA
PACIFIC OCEAN
SOUTH AMERICA
INDIAN OCEAN
OCEANIA
SOUTHERN OCEAN
ANTARCTICA
ocean 洋
continent 洲
line of longitude 经线

History and Social Studies
历史与社会科学

Historical figures 历史人物

king 国王

queen 女王

knight 骑士

soldier 士兵

prime minister 首相 / president 总统

mayor 市长

archaeologist 考古工作者

Historical objects 历史物件

cave 洞穴

spear 矛

axe 斧

shield 盾

coin 硬币

jewellery 首饰

mosaic 马赛克

cooking pot 炖煮罐

tools 工具

chariot 战车

castle 城堡

statue 雕像

Technology 技术

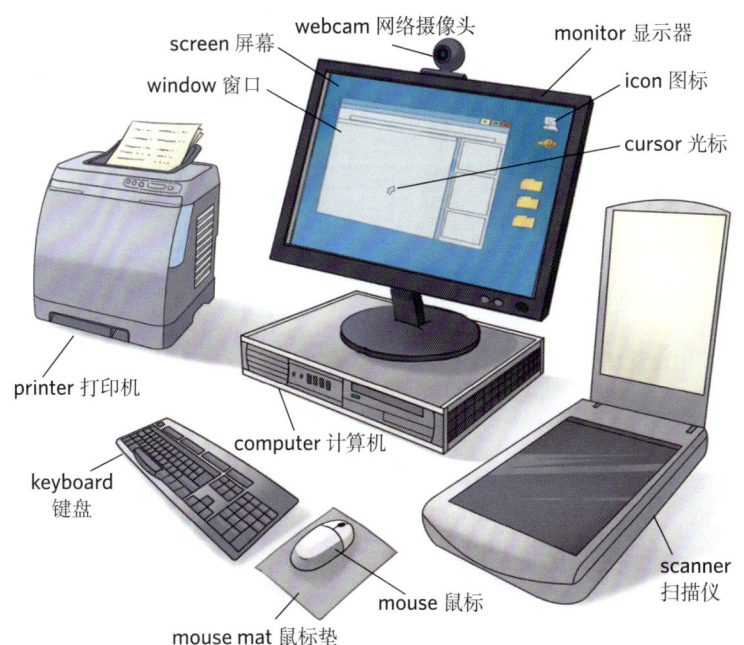

- webcam 网络摄像头
- screen 屏幕
- window 窗口
- monitor 显示器
- icon 图标
- cursor 光标
- printer 打印机
- computer 计算机
- keyboard 键盘
- mouse 鼠标
- mouse mat 鼠标垫
- scanner 扫描仪

mobile phone 手机

tablet 平板电脑

DVD player and DVD
数字光碟播放机及数字光碟

CD player and CD
光碟播放器及光碟

MP3 player
MP3 播放器

laptop
笔记本电脑

memory stick
优盘

game console
游戏机

satellite dish
碟形卫星电视天线

email
电子邮件

text message
短信

satnav
卫星导航仪

Music 音乐

String instruments 弦乐器

harp 竖琴   guitar 吉他   violin 小提琴   viola 中提琴   cello 大提琴   double bass 低音提琴

Brass instruments 铜管乐器

  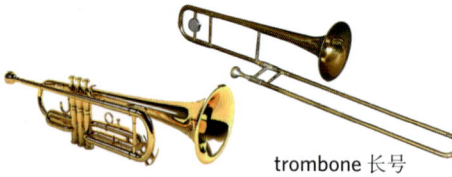 

French horn 法国号   trumpet 小号   trombone 长号   tuba 大号

Woodwind instruments 木管乐器

clarinet 单簧管   oboe 双簧管   recorder 竖笛   flute 长笛   bassoon 大管   saxophone 萨克斯管

Percussion and Keyboard instruments 打击乐器和键盘乐器

cymbals 钹   xylophone 木琴   tambourine 铃鼓   drum 鼓   piano 钢琴

Art and Design 美术与设计

Colours 颜色

 beige 米色
 black 黑色
 blue 蓝色
 brown 褐色
 green 绿色
 grey 灰色

 orange 橙色
 pink 粉色
 purple 紫色
 red 红色
 white 白色
 yellow 黄色

Styles 类型

 painting 绘画
 portrait 肖像
 drawing 素描
 sketch 速写

 photograph 照片
 sculpture 雕塑
 pottery 陶器
 mosaic 马赛克

Materials 材料

 paint 颜料
 paintbrush 画笔
 pencil 铅笔
 canvas 画布

 easel and paper 画架和纸
 chalk 粉笔
 charcoal 炭条
 clay 黏土

Sports
体育

rugby 英式橄榄球

football/soccer 足球

basketball 篮球

hockey 曲棍球

cycling 自行车运动

skiing 滑雪

swimming 游泳

tennis 网球

gymnastics 体操

jogging 健身跑

horse riding 马术

hiking 徒步游

Personal, Social and Health Education
个人、社会与健康教育

angry 生气

bored 厌烦

happy 高兴

frightened 害怕

excited 兴奋

sad 悲伤

surprised 惊讶

tired 疲倦

shocked 震惊

confused 困惑

Jobs 职业

 actor/actress 演员

 builder 建筑工人

 businessman/businesswoman 商人

 carpenter 木匠

 chef 厨师

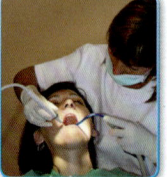 dentist 牙医

 doctor 医生

 electrician 电工

 farmer 农民

 firefighter 消防员

 hairdresser 美发师

 mechanic 机修工

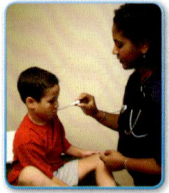 nurse 护工

 pilot 飞行员

 plumber 水暖工

 police officer 警察

 shop assistant 店员

 teacher 教师

 vet 兽医

 waiter/waitress 服务员

paintbrush /ˈpeɪntbrʌʃ/ *countable noun* 可数名词 (**paintbrushes**)
a brush that you use for painting 画笔；油漆刷
→ Look at picture on P13 参见彩插第 13 页

painter /ˈpeɪntə/ *countable noun* 可数名词
1 an artist who paints pictures 画家: *The film is about the Dutch painter, Vincent van Gogh.* 这部电影是关于荷兰画家文森特·凡高的。
2 a person whose job is to paint walls, doors or other parts of buildings 油漆工: *I worked as a house painter for about five years.* 我做了大概 5 年的房屋油漆工。

painting /ˈpeɪntɪŋ/ *noun* 名词
1 *countable* 可数 a picture that someone has painted 画；画作: *She hung a large painting on the wall.* 她在墙上挂了一幅特别大的画。
→ Look at picture on P13 参见彩插第 13 页
2 *uncountable* 不可数 the activity of painting pictures or covering surfaces with paint 绘画: *I really enjoy painting and gardening.* 我特别喜欢画画和园艺。

pair /peə/ *countable noun* 可数名词
1 two things of the same size and shape that are used together 一双；一对；一副: *She wore a pair of plain black shoes.* 她穿了一双样式简单的黑鞋子。 □ *a pair of earrings* 一副耳环
2 an object that has two main parts of the same size and shape 一条，一把，一套（成对的东西）: *He was wearing a pair of old jeans.* 他穿着一条旧牛仔裤。 □ *She took a pair of scissors out of her bag.* 她从包里拿出一把剪刀。
3 two people who are doing something together（人的）一对，一组: *a pair of teenage boys* 两个 10 多岁的男孩 □ *The eight children are working in pairs.* 8 个孩子两两合作。

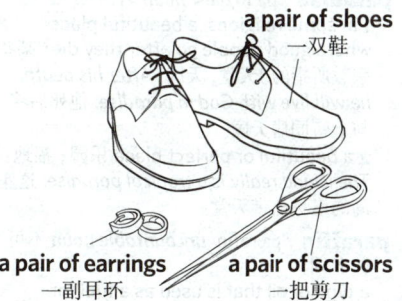

a pair of shoes 一双鞋
a pair of earrings 一副耳环
a pair of scissors 一把剪刀

pal /pæl/ *countable noun* 可数名词
a friend (*informal* 非正式) 朋友: *They talked like old pals.* 他们像老朋友一样交谈。

palace /ˈpælɪs/ *countable noun* 可数名词
a very large impressive house where a king, a queen, or a president lives 王宫；宫殿: *We visited Buckingham Palace.* 我们参观了白金汉宫。

pale /peɪl/ *adjective* 形容词 (**paler**, **palest**)
1 not strong or bright in colour（颜色）浅的，淡的: *She's wearing a pale blue dress.* 她穿着一条浅蓝色连衣裙。
2 with a face that is a lighter colour than usual（脸色）苍白的，无血色的: *She looked pale and tired.* 她脸色苍白，疲惫不堪。

palm /pɑːm/ *noun* 名词
1 (also 亦作 **palm tree**) a tree that grows in hot countries, with long leaves at the top, and no branches 棕榈树: *white sand and palm trees* 白沙滩和棕榈树
2 *countable* 可数 the inside part of your hand, between your fingers and your wrist 手掌: *Danny hit the table with the palm of his hand.* 丹尼用手掌拍桌子。

pamphlet /ˈpæmflət/ *countable noun* 可数名词
a very thin book with a paper cover that gives information about something 小册子；手册: *They gave me a pamphlet about parenting.* 他们给了我一本育儿手册。

pan /pæn/ *countable noun* 可数名词
a round metal container with a long handle, that you use for cooking things in 平底锅: *Heat the butter and oil in a large pan.* 把黄油和食用油放在大平底锅里加热。

pancake /ˈpænkeɪk/ *countable noun* 可数名词
a thin, round food made from milk, flour and eggs, cooked in a frying pan 烙饼；薄饼

panda /ˈpændə/ *countable noun* 可数名词
a large animal from China with black and white fur 大熊猫

pane /peɪn/ *countable noun* 可数名词
a flat sheet of glass in a window or a door（窗户或门上的）一块玻璃: *Her mother had replaced the broken pane of glass.* 她妈妈换掉了那块碎玻璃。

panel /ˈpænəl/ *countable noun* 可数名词
1 a flat piece of wood or other material that forms part of a larger object such as a door（门等的）镶板，嵌板: *There was a*

glass panel in the centre of the door. 门中间镶嵌着玻璃板。
2 a board with switches and controls on it 仪表板；控制板：*You can switch the lights on or off using a control panel.* 可以用控制面板开关电灯。
3 a small group of people who discuss something in public or who make a decision 专题讨论小组；决策小组：*The government will take advice from a panel of experts.* 政府将咨询专家小组的意见。

panic /ˈpænɪk/ *uncountable noun* 不可数名词
a strong feeling of worry or fear that makes you act without thinking carefully 恐慌；惊慌失措：*An earthquake caused panic among the population.* 地震引发了民众恐慌。● **panic** *verb* 动词 (**panics, panicking, panicked**)：*Guests panicked and screamed when the bomb exploded.* 炸弹爆炸时，客人们惊慌失措，失声尖叫。

panini /pæˈniːni/ *noun* 名词 (**panini** or 或 **paninis**)
a type of Italian bread that is made into a sandwich and then heated 帕尼尼（意大利一种三明治）

pant /pænt/ *verb* 动词 (**pants, panting, panted**)
to breathe quickly and loudly, because you have been running or because you are very hot 喘气；喘息：*Dogs lose body heat by panting and sweating.* 狗通过喘气和流汗散发身体热量。

pants /pænts/ *plural noun* 复数名词
1 a piece of underwear that covers the area between your waist and your legs 内裤
2 (*American* 美国英语)→ see 见 **trousers**：*He wore brown corduroy pants and a white cotton shirt.* 他穿着一条棕色灯芯绒裤子和一件白色棉质衬衫。

paper /ˈpeɪpə/ *noun* 名词
1 *uncountable* 不可数 a material that you write on or wrap things with 纸：*He wrote his name down on a piece of paper.* 他在一张纸上写下自己的名字。□ *He carried the groceries in a paper bag.* 他把食品杂货装在纸袋里拿着。
→ Look at pictures on P1 and P13 参见彩插第 1 页和第 13 页
2 *countable* 可数 a newspaper 报纸：*I might get a paper when I go into town.* 我进城时可以买张报纸。
3 [**papers**] *plural* 复数 sheets of paper with information on them 文件；材料：*The briefcase contained important official papers.* 公文包里放着重要的官方文件。

paperback /ˈpeɪpəˌbæk/ *countable noun* 可数名词
a book with a thin cardboard or paper cover 平装书；简装书：*I'll buy the book when it comes out in paperback.* 这书出平装本时我会买一本。

paperboy /ˈpeɪpəˌbɔɪ/ *countable noun* 可数名词
a boy who delivers newspapers to people's homes 报童

ˈpaper clip *countable noun* 可数名词
a small piece of metal that is used for holding pieces of paper together 回形针；曲别针
→ Look at picture on P1 参见彩插第 1 页

paperwork /ˈpeɪpəˌwɜːk/ *uncountable noun* 不可数名词
work that involves dealing with letters, reports and records 文书工作：*There will be paperwork — forms to fill in, letters to write.* 会有填表、写信之类的文书工作。

parachute /ˈpærəˌʃuːt/ *countable noun* 可数名词
a large piece of thin material that a person attaches to their body when they jump from an aircraft to help them float safely to the ground 降落伞：*They fell 41,000 feet before opening their parachutes.* 他们下降 41,000 英尺之后打开降落伞。

parade /pəˈreɪd/ *countable noun* 可数名词
a line of people or vehicles moving through a public place in order to celebrate an important event（为庆祝重大事件的）游行，列队行进：*A military parade marched down Pennsylvania Avenue.* 阅兵队列沿宾夕法尼亚大道行进。

paradise /ˈpærəˌdaɪs/ *noun* 名词
1 in some religions, a beautiful place where good people go after they die（某些宗教所指的）天堂，天国：*After his death, he will live with God in paradise.* 他死后将与上帝同居天国。
2 a beautiful or perfect place 乐园；福地：*The island really is a tropical paradise.* 这座岛屿堪称热带天堂。

paraffin /ˈpærəfɪn/ *uncountable noun* 不可数名词
a type of oil that is used as a fuel for

heating and lights 煤油

paragraph /ˈpærəɡrɑːf/ ***countable noun*** 可数名词
a section of a piece of writing that begins on a new line and contains more than one sentence(文章的)段，段落: *The essay begins with a short introductory paragraph.* 文章开头是一段简短的介绍。
→ Look at picture on P3 参见彩插第 3 页

parallel /ˈpærəlel/ ***adjective*** 形容词
used for describing two lines that are the same distance apart along their whole length 平行的: *Remsen Street is parallel with Montague Street.* 雷姆森大街与蒙塔古大街平行。

paralyse /ˈpærəˌlaɪz/ ***verb*** 动词 (**paralyses, paralysing, paralysed**)
to cause someone to be unable to move all or part of their body because of an accident or an illness 使瘫痪；使麻痹: *She is paralysed from the waist down.* 她自腰以下瘫痪。

parcel /ˈpɑːsəl/ ***countable noun*** 可数名词
something that is wrapped in paper so that it can be sent by post 包裹；邮包: *They sent parcels of food and clothing.* 他们寄送了装有食品和衣物的包裹。

pardon /ˈpɑːdən/ ***exclamation*** 感叹词
I beg your pardon used as a way of apologizing for making a small mistake 抱歉；请原谅: *I beg your pardon. I thought you were someone else.* 抱歉，我把你错认成其他人了。
Pardon? or **I beg your pardon?** used when you want someone to repeat what they have just said 能再说一遍吗？: '*Will you let me open it?*' — '*Pardon?*' — '*Can I open it?*' "我能打开它吗？" —— "能再说一遍吗？" —— "我能打开它吗？"

parent /ˈpeərənt/ ***countable noun*** 可数名词
your mother or your father 父亲；母亲: *Children need their parents.* 孩子需要父母。

parenthood /ˈpeərəntˌhʊd/ ***uncountable noun*** 不可数名词
the state of being a parent 父母的身份: *They had to deal with the responsibilities of parenthood.* 他们须肩负起为人父母的责任。

park¹ /pɑːk/ ***countable noun*** 可数名词
a public area of land with grass and trees, usually in a town, where people go to relax and enjoy themselves 公园: *Hyde Park* 海德公园 ▫ *I took a walk with the dog around the park.* 我带着狗绕公园散步。

park² /pɑːk/ ***verb*** 动词 (**parks, parking, parked**)
to stop a vehicle and leave it somewhere 停车；泊车: *They parked in the street outside the house.* 他们将车停在屋外的街道上。▫ *He found a place to park the car.* 他找到了一个停车位。
▶ **parking** /ˈpɑːkɪŋ/ ***uncountable noun*** 不可数名词: *Parking is allowed only on one side of the street.* 这条街道只能在一侧停车。

parliament /ˈpɑːləmənt/ ***also*** 亦作 **Parliament** ***countable noun*** 可数名词
the group of people who make or change the laws of some countries 议会；国会: *The German Parliament today approved the policy.* 德国议会今天批准了这项政策。

parody /ˈpærədi/ ***noun*** 名词 (**parodies**)
a piece of writing, drama or music that copies something in an amusing way 滑稽模仿作品: *The school show was a parody of the 'Star Wars' films.* 学校的这场演出戏仿了《星球大战》系列电影。

parrot /ˈpærət/ ***countable noun*** 可数名词
a tropical bird with a curved beak and very bright or grey feathers 鹦鹉

parsley /ˈpɑːsli/ ***uncountable noun*** 不可数名词
a type of plant (= a herb) with small green leaves that you use in cooking 欧芹

part¹ /pɑːt/ ***noun*** 名词
1 a piece of something 部分: *This was a part of Paris he loved.* 这是他热爱的巴黎的一部分。▫ *Perry spent part of his childhood in Canada.* 佩里在加拿大度过了一段童年时光。
2 countable 可数 a piece of a machine 零件；部件: *The company makes small parts for planes.* 这家公司生产飞机零部件。
3 countable 可数 one character's words and actions in a play or film(戏剧或电影中的)角色: *He played the part of Hamlet.* 他扮演哈姆莱特。
take part in something to do an activity together with other people 参与某事: *Thousands of students took part in the demonstrations.* 成千上万的学生参加了示威游行。

part² /pɑːt/ ***verb*** 动词 (**parts, parting, parted**)
part with something to give or sell something that you would prefer to keep 放弃，交出，卖掉(难舍之物): *Think*

carefully before parting with money. 考虑清楚了再交钱。

partial /ˈpɑːʃəl/ *adjective* 形容词
not complete 部分的；不完全的: *These plants prefer to grow in partial shade.* 这些植物更喜欢半阴的环境。
▸ **partially** /ˈpɑːʃəli/ *adverb* 副词: *Lisa is partially blind.* 莉萨丧失了一部分视力。

participant /pɑːˈtɪsɪpənt/ *countable noun* 可数名词
a person who takes part in an activity 参与者；参加者: *Participants in the course will learn techniques to improve their memory.* 修习这门课程者将学会提升记忆力的方法。

participate /pɑːˈtɪsɪpeɪt/ *verb* 动词
(**participates, participating, participated**)
to take part in an activity 参与；参加: *Some of the children participated in sports or other physical activities.* 这些孩子中有一部分人参加了体育运动或其他体力活动。
▸ **participation** /pɑːˌtɪsɪˈpeɪʃən/ *uncountable noun* 不可数名词: *Doctors recommend exercise or participation in sport at least two times a week.* 医生建议一周至少锻炼或参加体育运动两次。

participle /ˈpɑːtɪsɪpəl/ *countable noun* 可数名词
a form of the verb that usually ends in '-ed' or '-ing' 分词（指过去分词或现在分词）

particular /pəˈtɪkjʊlə/ *adjective* 形容词
1 used for showing that you are talking about one thing or one type of thing rather than other similar ones 特定的；特指的: *Where did you hear that particular story?* 那个故事你是从哪儿听到的？ ▫ *I have to know exactly why I'm doing a particular job.* 我得弄清楚自己为什么要做某项工作。
2 greater or stronger than usual 格外的；特别的: *We place particular importance on language training.* 我们特别重视语言培训。
3 choosing and doing things very carefully 挑剔的；讲究的: *Ted is very particular about the clothes he wears.* 特德在着装方面很讲究。
in particular especially; more than others 尤其；特别: *Why did he notice her car in particular?* 他为什么会特别注意到她的车？

particularly /pəˈtɪkjʊləli/ *adverb* 副词
more than usual or more than others 特别；尤其: *Keep your office space looking good,*
particularly your desk. 保持办公环境整洁，尤其是办公桌。 ▫ *I particularly liked the wooden chairs.* 我格外喜欢木制椅子。

partly /ˈpɑːtli/ *adverb* 副词
not completely, but a little 部分地；某种程度上: *It's partly my fault.* 这在一定程度上是我的错。

partner /ˈpɑːtnə/ *countable noun* 可数名词
1 your husband or wife, or your boyfriend or girlfriend 配偶；伴侣: *Len's partner died four years ago.* 莱恩的爱人4年前去世了。
2 the person you are playing or dancing with 同伴；搭档: *She needed a new partner for the doubles game.* 她需要一个新搭档一起参加双打比赛。
3 one of the people who own a firm or a business 合伙人: *He's a partner in a Chicago law firm.* 他是芝加哥一家律师事务所的合伙人。

partnership /ˈpɑːtnəʃɪp/ *noun* 名词
a relationship in which two or more people or groups work together 伙伴关系；合作关系: *We want to develop a closer partnership between the government and the car industry.* 我们想要在政府和汽车行业间建立起更亲密的合作关系。

part of ˈspeech *countable noun* 可数名词
(**parts of speech**)
a particular class of word such as noun, adjective or verb 词类，词性（如名词、形容词、动词等）

ˌpart-ˈtime *adjective* 形容词, *adverb* 副词
LANGUAGE HELP 语言提示
The adverb is spelled **part time**. 副词拼作 part time。

working for only part of each day or week 在部分时间工作（的）；以兼职方式（的）: *She is trying to get a part-time job in an office.* 她想找个坐办公室的兼职工作。 ▫ *I want to work part time.* 我想干兼职。

party /ˈpɑːti/ *countable noun* 可数名词
(**parties**)
1 a social event at which people enjoy themselves doing things like eating or dancing 聚会；派对: *The couple met at a party.* 那对情侣是在一个派对上认识的。 ▫ *We organized a huge birthday party.* 我们举办了盛大的生日聚会。
2 a political organization whose members have similar aims and beliefs 政党；党派: *He is a member of the Republican Party.* 他

是共和党党员。
3 a group of people doing something together（一起做某事的）团体，团队: *We passed by a party of tourists.* 我们经过一队游客。

pass¹ /pɑːs/ *verb* 动词 (**passes, passing, passed**)
1 to go past someone or something 经过；走过: *When she passed the library door, the telephone began to ring.* 她经过图书馆门口时，电话响了。□ *Jane stood aside to let her pass.* 简站到一边让她过去。
2 to move in a particular direction（朝特定方向）行进: *He passed through the doorway into the kitchen.* 他穿过门道走进厨房。□ *A helicopter passed overhead.* 一架直升机从头顶上空飞过。
3 to give an object to someone 递；传递: *Pam passed the books to Dr Wong.* 帕姆把那些书递给黄博士。
4 to kick or throw a ball to someone 传（球）: *Hawkins passed the ball to Payton.* 霍金斯把球传给佩顿。
5 to go by 消逝；过去: *Time passes quickly when you are enjoying yourself.* 快乐的时光总是过得很快。
6 to spend time in a particular way 度过，消磨，打发（时间）: *The children passed the time watching TV.* 孩子们看电视打发时间。
7 to succeed in an examination 通过（考试）: *Tina passed her driving test last week.* 蒂娜上周通过了驾照考试。
8 to formally agree to a new law 通过，批准（法律）: *The government passed a law that allowed banks to sell insurance.* 政府通过一项法律，准许银行销售保险。
pass away to die 去世；逝世: *She passed away last year.* 她去年过世了。
pass out to suddenly become unconscious 失去知觉；昏迷: *He felt sick and then passed out.* 他感到恶心，之后昏了过去。
pass something on to give someone some information 传递（某信息）: *Mary Hayes passed on the news to McEvoy.* 玛丽·海斯将消息传递给麦克伊伊。

pass² /pɑːs/ *countable noun* 可数名词 (**passes**)
1 a document that allows you to do something 许可证；通行证: *He used his journalist's pass to enter the White House.* 他凭记者通行证进入了白宫。
2 an act of throwing or kicking a ball to someone on your team 传球: *Bryan*

Randall threw a short pass to Ernest Wilford. 布赖恩·兰德尔一记短传，球到了欧内斯特·威尔福德手中。

passage /ˈpæsɪdʒ/ *countable noun* 可数名词
1 a long narrow space that connects one place or room with another 通道；走廊: *A dark narrow passage led to the kitchen.* 穿过一条昏暗狭窄的通道，就到了厨房。
2 a short part of a book 段落；章节: *He read a passage to her from one of Max's books.* 他给她读了马克斯一本书中的一个段落。

passenger /ˈpæsɪndʒə/ *countable noun* 可数名词
a person who is travelling in a vehicle such as a bus, a boat or a plane, but who is not driving it 乘客；旅客: *Mr Smith was a passenger in the car when it crashed.* 车祸发生时，史密斯先生正在那辆车上。

passion /ˈpæʃən/ *noun* 名词
1 *uncountable* 不可数 a very strong feeling about something or a strong belief in something 热情，激情: *He spoke with great passion.* 他热情洋溢地讲着话。
2 *countable* 可数 a very strong interest in something that you like very much 强烈的爱好，酷爱: *She has a passion for music.* 她酷爱音乐。

passionate /ˈpæʃənət/ *adjective* 形容词
having very strong feelings about something or a strong belief in it 热情的；狂热的: *He is very passionate about the project.* 他对那个项目很有热情。

passive¹ /ˈpæsɪv/ *adjective* 形容词
allowing things to happen without taking action 被动的；消极的: *I disliked his passive attitude.* 我讨厌他消极的态度。
▶ **passively** /ˈpæsɪvli/ *adverb* 副词: *He sat there passively, waiting for me to say something.* 他消极地坐在那里，等我开口说话。

passive² /ˈpæsɪv/ *singular noun* 单数名词
the form of a verb that you use to show that the subject does not perform the action but is affected by it. For example, in 'He's been murdered', the verb **murder** is in the passive. Compare with **active**.（动词的）被动式（比较 active）

passport /ˈpɑːspɔːt/ *countable noun* 可数名词
an official document that you have to show when you enter or leave a country

护照: *You should take your passport with you when you change your money.* 兑换货币时要带上护照。

password /ˈpɑːswɜːd/ *countable noun* 可数名词
a secret word or phrase that allows you to enter a place or to use a computer system 密码; 口令: *Please contact us for a username and password.* 请联系我们获取用户名和密码。

past¹ /pɑːst/ *singular noun* 单数名词
the time before the present, and the things that happened then 过去; 往昔: *In the past, most babies with the disease died.* 过去, 患这种病的婴儿大部分都夭折了。

past² /pɑːst/ *preposition* 介词
1 used for talking about a time that is thirty minutes or less after a particular hour (表示时间过整点但不超过30分钟) 过: *It's ten past eleven.* 现在是 11 点 10 分。
2 from one side to the other of someone or something 经过: *I walked past her.* 我从她身边走过。 ● **past** *adverb* 副词: *An ambulance drove past.* 一辆救护车开过。

past 经过

I walked past her. 我从她身边走过。

pasta /ˈpæstə/ *noun* 名词
a type of food made from a mixture of flour, eggs and water that is made into different shapes and then boiled 意大利面食: *Italian pizzas and pasta are the restaurant's specialities.* 这家饭店的特色是意大利风味的比萨饼和面食。
→ Look at picture on P5 参见彩插第 5 页

paste /peɪst/ *verb* 动词 (**pastes, pasting, pasted**)
1 to put glue onto a surface and stick something onto it (用胶水) 粘贴, 黏合: *He pasted labels onto the bottles.* 他把标签贴在瓶子上。
2 to copy or move text or images into a computer document from another part of the document, or from another document (在计算机上) 粘贴(文本或图片): *The text can be copied and pasted into your email program.* 文本可复制粘贴至电子邮件里。

pastel¹ /ˈpæstəl/ *adjective* 形容词
pale rather than dark or bright in colour (色彩)淡的, 柔和的: *Mother always chooses clothes in delicate pastel shades.* 妈妈总是挑选颜色淡雅柔和的衣服。
□ *pastel pink, blue and green* 淡粉色、蓝色和绿色

pastel² /ˈpæstəl/ *countable noun* 可数名词
a stick of colour made of a substance like chalk, and used by artists for drawing 彩色粉笔: *This paper is ideal for use with paints, crayons and pastels.* 这种纸非常适合用颜料、蜡笔和彩色粉笔作画。

pastry /ˈpeɪstri/ *noun* 名词 (**pastries**)
1 *uncountable* 不可数 a food made from flour, fat and water that is often used for making pies (= dishes of meat, vegetables or fruit with a cover made of pastry) 油酥面团; 油酥面皮
2 *countable* 可数 a small cake 油酥点心: *The bakery sells delicious cakes and pastries.* 这家面包房出售美味的蛋糕和油酥点心。

past tense *countable noun* 可数名词
the form of a verb that is used for talking about the time that came before the present. For example, the past tense of the verb 'see' is 'saw'. (动词)过去式

pat /pæt/ *verb* 动词 (**pats, patting, patted**)
to touch something or someone lightly with your flat hand 轻拍: *'Don't you worry,' she said, patting me on the knee.* "别担心。"她轻拍着我的膝盖说。 □ *The lady patted her hair nervously.* 那位女士焦虑地拍着自己的头发。 ● **pat** *countable noun* 可数名词: *He gave her a friendly pat on the shoulder.* 他友好地轻拍了一下她的肩膀。

patch /pætʃ/ *countable noun* 可数名词 (**patches**)
1 a part of a surface that is different in appearance from the area around it (与周围不同的)小块, 小片: *She noticed the bald patch on the top of his head.* 她注意到他头顶秃了一块。 □ *There was a small patch of blue in the grey clouds.* 灰色的云团中透出一小片蓝天。
2 a piece of material that you use to cover

a hole in a piece of clothing 补丁；补片：
Brad was wearing an old jacket with leather patches on the elbows. 布拉德穿着一件旧夹克，肘部打着皮革补丁。

path /pɑːθ/ *countable noun* 可数名词
a long, narrow piece of ground that people walk along 小路；小径：*We followed the path along the cliff.* 我们沿悬崖边的小路前行。

pathetic /pəˈθetɪk/ *adjective* 形容词
weak or not very good 拙劣的；差劲的：*What a pathetic attempt to hide the truth.* 这一企图隐瞒事实的做法真差劲。

patience /ˈpeɪʃəns/ *uncountable noun* 不可数名词
the ability to stay calm and not get annoyed, for example, when something takes a long time 耐心；耐性：*He doesn't have the patience to wait.* 他没有耐心等待。

patient¹ /ˈpeɪʃənt/ *countable noun* 可数名词
a person who receives medical treatment from a doctor 病人；患者：*The patient was suffering from heart problems.* 这位病人患有心脏病。

patient² /ˈpeɪʃənt/ *adjective* 形容词
able to stay calm and not get annoyed, for example, when something takes a long time 耐心的；有耐性的：*Please be patient — your cheque will arrive soon.* 请耐心等待——您的支票很快就到。
▶ **patiently** /ˈpeɪʃəntli/ *adverb* 副词：*She waited patiently for Frances to finish talking.* 她耐心地等弗朗西丝把话讲完。

patio /ˈpætiəʊ/ *countable noun* 可数名词
a flat area next to a house, where people can sit and relax or eat（与房屋相连的）露台，平台

patriotic /ˌpætriˈɒtɪk, ˌpeɪt-/ *adjective* 形容词
loving your country and feeling very loyal towards it 爱国的：*They are very patriotic men who give everything for their country.* 他们非常爱国，将自己的一切都献给了他们的国家。

patrol¹ /pəˈtrəʊl/ *verb* 动词 (**patrols, patrolling, patrolled**)
to move around an area to make sure that there is no trouble there 巡逻；巡查：*Prison officers continued to patrol the grounds.* 狱警继续巡视场地。

patrol² /pəˈtrəʊl/ *countable noun* 可数名词
1 when someone moves around an area to make sure that there is no trouble there 巡逻；巡查：*The army is now on patrol.* 目前部队正在巡逻。
2 a group of soldiers or vehicles that move around an area in order to make sure that there is no trouble there 巡逻队；巡逻车队：*The three men attacked a border patrol last night.* 昨晚3名男子袭击了边境巡逻队。

pattern /ˈpætən/ *countable noun* 可数名词
1 the repeated or regular way in which something happens or is done 模式；方式：*All three attacks followed the same pattern.* *3次袭击模式相同。
2 an arrangement of lines or shapes that form a design 图案；花样：*The carpet had a pattern of light and dark stripes.* 地毯有深浅条纹相间的图样。

pattern 图案

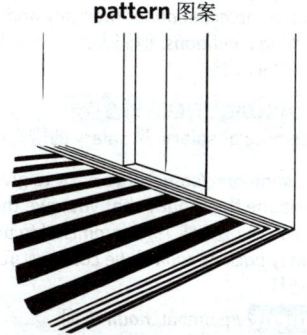

pause /pɔːz/ *verb* 动词 (**pauses, pausing, paused**)
to stop for a short time while you are doing something, and then continue 停顿；暂停：*'It's rather embarrassing,' he began, and paused.* "非常令人难堪。"他开口道，然后停顿了一下。□ *She started speaking when I paused for breath.* 我停下来喘气时她开口说起话来。● **pause** *countable noun* 可数名词：*After a pause Al said: 'I'm sorry if I upset you.'* 阿尔稍停片刻之后说道："要是让你不高兴了，我很抱歉。"

pavement /ˈpeɪvmənt/ *countable noun* 可数名词 (*American* 美国英语：**sidewalk**)
a path with a hard surface, usually by the side of a road 人行道：*He was hurrying along the pavement.* 他沿人行道匆匆前行。

paw /pɔː/ *countable noun* 可数名词
the foot of an animal such as a cat, dog or bear（猫、狗、熊等的）爪：*The kitten was black with white front paws.* 这是一只黑色的小猫，前爪是白色的。

pay /peɪ/ *verb* 动词 (**pays, paying, paid**)
1 to give someone an amount of money for something that you are buying 付钱：*Can I pay for my ticket with a credit card?* 我能用信用卡付款买票吗？
2 to give someone an amount of money for something such as a bill or a debt 支付（账单）；偿还（欠债）：*She paid the hotel bill before she left.* 她离开之前付了酒店账单。 □ *The company was fined and ordered to pay court costs.* 这家公司被处以罚款，并被勒令支付诉讼费用。
3 to give someone money for the work that they do 给⋯付工资；给⋯付酬劳：*The lawyer was paid a huge salary.* 这位律师薪酬很高。□ *I get paid monthly.* 我按月领工资。● **pay** *uncountable noun* 不可数名词：*They complained about their pay and working conditions.* 他们表达了对薪水和工作条件的不满。

> **LANGUAGE HELP 语言提示**
> See note at **salary**. 见 salary 的语言提示。

pay someone/something back to give someone the money that you owe them 还某人钱 / 还（钱）：*He promised to pay the money back as soon as he could.* 他承诺尽快还钱。

payment /ˈpeɪmənt/ *noun* 名词
1 *countable* 可数 an amount of money that is paid to someone 支付的款项；付款额：*You will receive 13 monthly payments.* 你会拿到 13 个月的薪水。
2 *uncountable* 不可数 the act of paying money or of being paid 付款；收款：*Players now expect payment for interviews.* 如今运动员希望接受采访能有报酬。

PC /ˌpiːˈsiː/ *countable noun* 可数名词 (**PCs**)
a computer that people use at school, at home or in an office. **PC** is short for (缩写 =) **personal computer**. 个人计算机

PDF /ˌpiː diː ˈef/ *countable noun* 可数名词 (**PDFs**)
a computer document that looks exactly like the original document. **PDF** is short for (缩写 =) 'Portable Document Format'. 可移植文档格式；PDF 格式

PE /ˌpiː ˈiː/ *uncountable noun* 不可数名词
the school subject in which students do physical exercises or take part in physical games and sports. **PE** is short for (缩写 =) **physical education**. 体育（课）

pea /piː/ *countable noun* 可数名词
a very small, round, green vegetable 豌豆

peace /piːs/ *uncountable noun* 不可数名词
1 a situation where there is not a war 和平；太平：*The new rulers brought peace to the country.* 新的统治者给这个国家带来了和平。□ *The two countries signed a peace agreement.* 两国签署了和平协议。
2 the state of being quiet and calm 安静；宁静；平静：*I just want some peace and quiet.* 我就想清净一下。

peaceful /ˈpiːsfʊl/ *adjective* 形容词
1 not involving war or violence 和平的：*He has attempted to find a peaceful solution to the conflict.* 他试图寻求和平解决这次冲突的方案。
▶ **peacefully** /ˈpiːsfʊli/ *adverb* 副词：*The governor asked the protestors to leave peacefully.* 州长要求抗议者和平解散。
2 quiet and calm 宁静的；平静的：*The garden looked so peaceful.* 花园看上去很宁静。

peach¹ /piːtʃ/ *noun* 名词 (**peaches**)
1 *countable* 可数 a round fruit with a soft red and orange skin 桃子
2 a pale colour between pink and orange 桃红色；粉红色：*The room was decorated in peach.* 这个房间粉刷成桃红色。

peach² /piːtʃ/ *adjective* 形容词
of a pale colour between pink and orange 桃红色的；粉红色的：*a peach silk blouse* 桃红色的丝绸衬衫

peak /piːk/ *countable noun* 可数名词
1 the point at which a process or an activity is at its strongest 顶点；顶峰：*His career was at its peak when he died.* 他去世时职业生涯正值顶峰。
2 a mountain or the top of a mountain 山峰；山顶：*They could see the snowy peaks of the Canadian Rockies.* 他们能看到加拿大落基山脉白雪皑皑的顶峰。

peanut /ˈpiːnʌt/ *countable noun* 可数名词
a small nut that you can eat 花生

pear /peə/ *countable noun* 可数名词
a juicy fruit that is narrow at the top and wider at the bottom. Pears have white flesh and green, yellow or brown skin. 梨

pearl /pɜːl/ *countable noun* 可数名词
a hard, white, shiny round object that grows inside the shell of an oyster (= a water creature). Pearls are used for making jewellery. 珍珠：*She wore a string*

of pearls. 她戴着一串珍珠。

peasant /ˈpezənt/ *countable noun* 可数名词
a poor farmer or farm worker in a poor country 农民：*The film describes the customs and habits of peasants in Peru.* 这部影片讲述了秘鲁农民的风俗习惯。

pebble /ˈpebəl/ *countable noun* 可数名词
a small, smooth stone 卵石

peculiar /pɪˈkjuːliə/ *adjective* 形容词
strange or unusual 奇怪的；不寻常的：*Mr Kennet has a rather peculiar sense of humour.* 肯尼特先生有种很不寻常的幽默感。

pedal[1] /ˈpedəl/ *countable noun* 可数名词
1 one of the two parts that you push with your feet to make a bicycle move（自行车的）脚蹬
2 a part that you press with your foot in order to control a car or a machine（汽车或机器的）踏板：*the brake pedal* 刹车踏板

pedal 脚蹬

pedal[2] /ˈpedəl/ *verb* 动词 (**pedals, pedalling, pedalled**)
to push the pedals of a bicycle around with your feet to make it move 蹬自行车：*We pedalled slowly through the city streets.* 我们骑着自行车慢慢地穿过城市的街道。

pedestrian /pɪˈdestriən/ *countable noun* 可数名词
a person who is walking, especially in a town or city（尤指城镇的）步行者，行人：*The city's pavements were busy with pedestrians.* 城市的人行道上行人往来不绝。

pe,destrian ˈcrossing *countable noun* 可数名词 (*American* 美国英语：**crosswalk**)
a place where drivers must stop to let people cross a street 人行横道

peek /piːk/ *verb* 动词 (**peeks, peeking, peeked**)
to look at something or someone quickly and often secretly 瞥；偷看；窥视：*She peeked at him through a crack in the wall.* 她透过墙缝窥视他。● **peek** *countable noun* 可数名词：*I had a peek at his computer screen.* 我瞥了一眼他的电脑屏幕。

peel[1] /piːl/ *noun* 名词
the skin of a fruit such as a lemon or an apple（柠檬、苹果等的）外皮；果皮：*Add in the grated lemon peel.* 加上擦碎的柠檬皮。

peel[2] /piːl/ *verb* 动词 (**peels, peeling, peeled**)
1 to remove the skin of fruit or vegetables 给（果蔬）去皮：*She began peeling potatoes.* 她开始削土豆皮。
2 to come away or remove from a surface 剥落；剥掉；揭下：*Paint was peeling off the walls.* 墙上的涂料开始剥落。▫ *It took me two days to peel off the labels.* 我花了两天时间把这些标签揭下来。

peep /piːp/ *verb* 动词 (**peeps, peeping, peeped**)
to take a quick, often secret, look at something 偷看；窥视：*A small child was peeping through the window at him.* 一个小孩子透过窗户偷看他。● **peep** *singular noun* 单数名词：*She lifted the lid and took a quick peep inside.* 她打开盖子，很快地扫了里面一眼。

peer /pɪə/ *verb* 动词 (**peers, peering, peered**)
to look at something very closely, usually because it is difficult to see clearly 仔细看；端详：*He found her peering at a computer print-out.* 他看到她正盯着一份计算机打印稿看。

peg /peg/ *countable noun* 可数名词
1 a small piece of wood or metal that you use for attaching one thing to another thing（木头或金属的）钉子，楔子，橛子：*He builds furniture using wooden pegs instead of nails.* 他做家具用楔子，不用钉子。

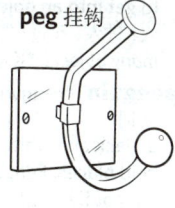

peg 挂钩

2 a small hook on a wall that you hang things on 挂钩：*His jacket hung on the peg in the kitchen.* 他的夹克衫挂在厨房的挂钩上。

pelvis /ˈpelvɪs/ *countable noun* 可数名词 (**pelvises**)
the wide, curved group of bones between your back and your legs 骨盆

pen /pen/ *countable noun* 可数名词
a long thin object that you use for writing

with ink (= coloured liquid) 笔；钢笔
→ Look at picture on P1 参见彩插第 1 页

penalty /ˈpenəlti/ ***countable noun*** 可数名词 (**penalties**)
1 a punishment for doing something that is against a law or rule 惩罚；处罚：*The maximum penalty for dangerous driving is five years in prison.* 危险驾驶的最高处罚是 5 年监禁。
2 a punishment for the team that breaks a rule in sports such as football and hockey, and an advantage for the other team（体育比赛中的）判罚，点球：*The referee awarded a penalty.* 裁判判了点球。

pence /pens/
a plural of **penny**（penny 的复数形式之一）

pencil /ˈpensəl/ ***countable noun*** 可数名词
a thin piece of wood with a black or coloured substance through the middle that you use to write or draw with 铅笔：*She used a pencil and some blank paper to draw the picture.* 她用一支铅笔和几张白纸画画。
→ Look at pictures on P1 and P13 参见彩插第 1 页和第 13 页

pencil sharpener /ˈpensəl ˌʃɑːpənə/ ***countable noun*** 可数名词
an object with a blade inside, used for making pencils sharper 卷笔刀；削笔器
→ Look at picture on P1 参见彩插第 1 页

penetrate /ˈpenɪˌtreɪt/ ***verb*** 动词 (**penetrates, penetrating, penetrated**)
to get into an object or pass through it 渗入；进入；穿过；穿透：*X-rays can penetrate many objects.* *X 射线能够穿透很多物体。

penguin /ˈpeŋɡwɪn/ ***countable noun*** 可数名词
a black and white bird that lives in very cold places. Penguins can swim but they cannot fly. 企鹅

peninsula /pəˈnɪnsjʊlə/ ***countable noun*** 可数名词
a long narrow piece of land that sticks out from a larger piece of land and is almost completely surrounded by water 半岛：*the Alaskan peninsula* 阿拉斯加半岛

penis /ˈpiːnɪs/ ***countable noun*** 可数名词 (**penises**)
the part of a man's body that he uses when he gets rid of waste liquid (= urine) and when he has sex 阴茎

penknife /ˈpennaɪf/ ***countable noun*** 可数名词 (**penknives** /ˈpennaɪvz/)
a small knife with a blade that folds back into the handle 小折刀

penny /ˈpeni/ ***countable noun*** 可数名词 (**pennies** or 或 **pence**)
a small British coin. There are one hundred pennies in a pound. 便士（英国硬币，100 便士 = 1 英镑）：*The price of petrol rose by more than a penny a litre.* 汽油价格每升涨了 1 个多便士。

pension /ˈpenʃən/ ***countable noun*** 可数名词
money that you regularly receive from a business or the government after you stop working because of your age 退休金；养老金：*He gets a £35,000-a-year pension.* 他的退休金为每年 35,000 英镑。
▶ **pensioner** /ˈpenʃənə/ ***countable noun*** 可数名词：*She's an 83-year-old pensioner who still enjoys cycling.* 她已是领取养老金的 83 岁老人了，但还是喜欢骑自行车。

pentagon /ˈpentəɡɒn/ ***countable noun*** 可数名词
a shape with five straight sides 五边形

people /ˈpiːpəl/ ***plural noun*** 复数名词
men, women and children 人；人们：*Millions of people have lost their homes.* 数百万人失去了家园。□ *He's reading a book about the people of Angola.* 他在读一本讲安哥拉人的书。

pepper /ˈpepə/ ***noun*** 名词
1 ***uncountable*** 不可数 a spice with a hot taste that you put on food 胡椒粉：*Season with salt and pepper.* 用盐和胡椒粉调味。
2 ***countable*** 可数 a hollow green, red or yellow vegetable with seeds inside it 甜椒；灯笼椒；柿子椒：*Thinly slice two red or green peppers.* 把两个红甜椒或青椒切成细丝。

peppermint /ˈpepəˌmɪnt/ ***noun*** 名词
1 ***uncountable*** 不可数 oil from the peppermint plant with a strong, sharp flavour 薄荷油
2 ***countable*** 可数 a sweet with a peppermint flavour 薄荷糖

per /pɜː/ ***preposition*** 介词
for each or in each. For example, if a vehicle is travelling at 40 miles per hour, it travels 40 miles in each hour. 每；每一：*They spend £200 per week on groceries.* 他们每周花 200 英镑买食品杂货。

per annum /pər ˈænəm/ *adverb* 副词
each year 每年: *They must pay a fee of £3,000 per annum.* 他们每年要付 3,000 英镑的费用。

perceive /pəˈsiːv/ *verb* 动词 (**perceives, perceiving, perceived**)
1 to notice or realize something, especially when it is not obvious 注意到；觉察到: *A great artist teaches us to perceive reality in a different way.* 一位伟大的艺术家教会我们以不同的方式感知现实世界。
2 to think of something in a particular way 认为；将…视为: *Stress is widely perceived as a cause of heart disease.* 人们普遍认为压力是导致心脏病的一个因素。

per cent /pə ˈsent/ *countable noun* 可数名词 (**per cent**)
used for talking about amounts as parts of a hundred. One hundred per cent (100%) is all of something, and 50 per cent (50%) is half. 百分之…: *Only ten per cent of our customers live in this city.* 我们的客户中仅有 10% 居住在这个城市。
→ Look at picture on P2 参见彩插第 2 页

percentage /pəˈsentɪdʒ/ *countable noun* 可数名词
an amount of something 百分比；百分率: *He regularly eats foods with a high percentage of protein.* 他定期吃高蛋白食品。

perch /pɜːtʃ/ *verb* 动词 (**perches, perching, perched**)
1 to sit on the edge of something 坐在…边缘: *He perched on the corner of the desk.* 他坐在桌子角上。
2 to land on a branch or a wall and stand there 栖息；停留: *Two birds perched on a nearby fence.* 两只鸟停在近旁的栅栏上。

percussion /pəˈkʌʃən/ *uncountable noun* 不可数名词
musical instruments that you hit, such as drums 打击乐器
→ Look at picture on P12 参见彩插第 12 页

perfect /ˈpɜːfɪkt/ *adjective* 形容词
as good as it could possibly be 完美的；最佳的: *He spoke perfect English.* 他英语说得棒极了。 □ *Nobody is perfect.* 人无完人。
▶ **perfectly** /ˈpɜːfɪktli/ *adverb* 副词: *The system worked perfectly.* 该系统运行顺畅。

perfection /pəˈfekʃən/ *uncountable noun* 不可数名词
the quality of being as good as possible 完美；最佳: *The meat was cooked to perfection.* 这肉烹饪得美味无比。

'perfect tense *countable noun* 可数名词
the form of a verb that is made with 'has' or 'had' and the past participle. For example, in the sentence 'I have seen that film', the verb 'see' is in the perfect tense. (动词的)完成式(包括现在完成式和过去完成式)

perform /pəˈfɔːm/ *verb* 动词 (**performs, performing, performed**)
1 to do a task or an action 做；履行；执行: *You must perform this exercise correctly to avoid back pain.* 做这项锻炼姿势要正确，否则会背痛。 □ *The surgeon performed an operation on his leg.* 外科医生给他的腿做了手术。
2 to do a play, a piece of music or a dance in front of an audience 表演；演出: *They will be performing works by Bach and Scarlatti.* 他们将演奏巴赫和斯卡拉蒂的作品。
▶ **performer** /pəˈfɔːmə/ *countable noun* 可数名词: *She was one of the top jazz performers in New York City.* 她是纽约市顶尖爵士乐演奏者之一。
3 to do something well or badly 表现: *He performed well in his exams.* 他这次考试考得不错。 □ *The industry has performed poorly this year.* 这个行业今年不景气。

performance /pəˈfɔːməns/ *noun* 名词
1 *countable* 可数 when you entertain an audience by singing, dancing or acting 表演；演出: *They were giving a performance of Bizet's 'Carmen'.* 他们正在表演比才的作品《卡门》。
2 how successful someone or something is or how well they do something 表现；业绩；性能: *The study looked at the performance of 18 surgeons.* 这项研究调查了 18 名外科医生的工作表现。 □ *He spoke about the poor performance of the economy.* 他谈及经济的不景气。

perfume /ˈpɜːfjuːm/ *noun* 名词
a liquid with a pleasant smell that you put on your skin 香水: *The hall smelled of her mother's perfume.* 大厅里弥漫着她母亲身上的香水味。

perhaps /pəˈhæps, præps/ *adverb* 副词
used for showing that you are not sure whether something is true, possible or likely 可能；大概；也许: *In the end they lost millions, perhaps billions.* 最后他们损

失掉几百万，或许是几十亿。▫ *Perhaps, in time, they will understand.* 或许他们最终会明白的。

perimeter /pəˈrɪmɪtə/ ***countable noun*** 可数名词
the total distance around the edge of a flat shape（平面图形的）周长：*To work out the perimeter of a rectangle, you need to know its length and width.* 要想算出长方形的周长，需要知道其长和宽。

period /ˈpɪəriəd/ ***countable noun*** 可数名词
1 a length of time 一段时间；时期：*He couldn't work for a long period of time.* 他不能长时间工作。
2 (*American* 美国英语)→ see 见 **full stop**
3 the time when a woman loses blood from her body each month 月经；经期

permanent /ˈpɜːmənənt/ ***adjective*** 形容词
continuing forever or for a very long time 永久的；长期不变的：*Some ear infections can cause permanent damage.* 一些耳部感染能造成永久性损伤。▫ *He's never had a permanent job.* 他从没有过稳定的工作。
▶ **permanently** /ˈpɜːmənəntli/ ***adverb*** 副词：*His confidence has been permanently affected.* 他的信心一蹶不振。

permission /pəˈmɪʃən/ ***uncountable noun*** 不可数名词
when you are allowed to do something 准许；许可：*He asked permission to leave the room.* 他请求批准离开房间。▫ *They cannot leave the country without permission.* 他们不能擅自离开该国。

permit[1] /pəˈmɪt/ ***verb*** 动词 (**permits, permitting, permitted**)
to allow someone to do something (*formal* 正式) 允许；准许：*The guards permitted me to bring my camera.* 门卫允许我带照相机。

permit[2] /ˈpɜːmɪt/ ***countable noun*** 可数名词
an official document that allows you to do something 许可证：*She hasn't got a work permit.* 她没有工作许可证。

persevere /ˌpɜːsɪˈvɪə/ ***verb*** 动词 (**perseveres, persevering, persevered**)
to continue to do something difficult 坚持：*Berman ignored their criticisms, and persevered with his plan.* 伯曼无视他们的批评，坚持自己的计划。

person /ˈpɜːsən/ ***countable noun*** 可数名词 (**people**)
a man, a woman or a child 人：*At least one person died and several others were injured.* 至少一人死亡，还有数人受伤。▫ *They were both lovely, friendly people.* 他们俩都很友好和善。
in person in the same place as someone, and not speaking to them on the telephone or writing to them 本人，当面（而非在电话或信件中）：*She saw him in person for the first time last night.* 她昨晚第一次看到了他本人。

personal /ˈpɜːsənəl/ ***adjective*** 形容词
1 relating to a particular person 个人的；某人的：*The story is based on his own personal experience.* 这个故事基于他的亲身经历。▫ *That's just my personal opinion.* 这只是我个人的观点。
2 relating to your feelings, relationships and health（感情、关系、健康方面）个人的，私人的：*Did he mention that he has any personal problems?* 他有没有提过个人有什么困难？

ˌpersonal comˈputer ***countable noun*** 可数名词
a computer that you use at work, school or home. The short form **PC** is also used. 个人计算机，个人电脑（缩写形式为 **PC**）

personality /ˌpɜːsəˈnælɪti/ ***noun*** 名词 (**personalities**)
the qualities that make you different from other people 性格；个性：*She has such a kind, friendly personality.* 她性格非常善良友好。

personally /ˈpɜːsənəli/ ***adverb*** 副词
1 used for showing that you are giving your own opinion 在个人看来；就本人而言：*Personally I think it's a waste of time.* 我个人认为这是在浪费时间。
2 used for showing that you do something yourself rather than letting someone else do it 亲自：*He wrote to them personally to explain the situation.* 他亲自给他们写信解释这一情况。

personnel /ˌpɜːsəˈnel/ ***plural noun*** 复数名词
the people who work for an organization（机构的）人员，职员：*The president will give a speech to military personnel at the army base.* 总统将向军事基地中的军职人员发表讲话。

perspective /pəˈspektɪv/ ***noun*** 名词
1 ***countable*** 可数 a particular way of thinking about something 视角；思考方式：*The death of his father has given him a new*

perspective on life. 父亲的死让他对人生有了新的思考。
2 *uncountable* 不可数 a way, in art, of making some objects or people in a picture seem further away from others（艺术中的）透视法

perspiration /ˌpɜːspɪˈreɪʃən/ *uncountable noun* 不可数名词
the liquid that appears on your skin when you are hot (*formal* 正式) 汗；汗珠：*His hands were wet with perspiration.* 他手上全是汗。

persuade /pəˈsweɪd/ *verb* 动词 (**persuades, persuading, persuaded**)
to make someone do something by talking to them 劝说；说服：*My husband persuaded me to come.* 我丈夫说服我前来。

persuasion /pəˈsweɪʒən/ *uncountable noun* 不可数名词
the process of making someone do or think something 说服；劝说：*After much persuasion from Ellis, she agreed to perform.* 经埃利斯一番劝说，她答应表演。

pessimism /ˈpesɪˌmɪzəm/ *uncountable noun* 不可数名词
the belief that bad things are going to happen 悲观；悲观主义：*There was a general pessimism about the economy.* 对经济普遍存在着悲观态度。
▶ **pessimist** /ˈpesɪmɪst/ *countable noun* 可数名词：*I'm a natural pessimist, so I usually expect the worst.* 我是天生的悲观主义者，总是想到最坏的情况。
▶ **pessimistic** /ˌpesɪˈmɪstɪk/ *adjective* 形容词：*She is so pessimistic about the future.* 她对未来非常悲观。

pest /pest/ *countable noun* 可数名词
1 an insect or a small animal that damages crops or food 害虫；有害动物：*They use chemicals to fight pests and diseases.* 他们用化学品防治病虫害。
2 someone, especially a child, who is annoying you (*informal* 非正式) 讨厌鬼（尤指小孩）：*He climbed on the table, pulled my hair, and was generally a pest.* 他爬到桌子上，揪我的头发，总之是个讨厌鬼。

pet /pet/ *countable noun* 可数名词
an animal that you keep in your home 宠物：*Do you have any pets?* 你养宠物吗？

petal /ˈpetəl/ *countable noun* 可数名词
the thin coloured parts of a plant that form the flower 花瓣：*rose petals* 玫瑰花瓣

petition /pəˈtɪʃən/ *countable noun* 可数名词
a document that contains the signatures of a group of people who are asking a government or other official group to do a particular thing 请愿书：*The government received a petition signed by 4,500 people.* 政府收到一份有 4,500 人签名的请愿书。

petrol /ˈpetrəl/ *uncountable noun* 不可数名词 (*American* 美国英语：**gasoline**)
the fuel which you use in cars and some other vehicles to make the engine go 汽油

ˈpetrol ˌstation *countable noun* 可数名词
a place where you buy fuel for your car 加油站

pharmacist /ˈfɑːməsɪst/ *countable noun* 可数名词
a person whose job is to prepare and sell medicines 药剂师：*Ask your pharmacist for advice.* 征求药剂师的意见。

pharmacy /ˈfɑːməsi/ *countable noun* 可数名词 (**pharmacies**)
a place where you can buy medicines 药店；药房：*Pick up the medicine from the pharmacy.* 去药房拿药。

phase /feɪz/ *countable noun* 可数名词
a particular stage in a process 阶段；时期：*6,000 women will take part in the first phase of the project.* 该项目第一阶段将有 6,000 名女性参加。

philosopher /fɪˈlɒsəfə/ *countable noun* 可数名词
a person who studies or writes about philosophy 哲学家：*He admired the Greek philosopher Plato.* 他很崇拜希腊哲学家柏拉图。

philosophy /fɪˈlɒsəfi/ *noun* 名词 (**philosophies**)
1 *uncountable* 不可数 the study of ideas about the meaning of life 哲学：*She is studying traditional Chinese philosophy.* 她在研究中国传统哲学。
▶ **philosophical** /ˌfɪləˈsɒfɪkəl/ *adjective* 形容词：*They often had philosophical discussions.* 他们经常讨论哲学问题。
2 *countable* 可数 a particular theory or belief 人生哲学；生活信条：*The best philosophy is to change to a low-sugar diet.* 最好的生活方式是吃低糖食品。

phone[1] /fəʊn/ *countable noun* 可数名词
a piece of equipment that you use to talk to someone else in another place 电话：*Two minutes later the phone rang.* 两分钟

phone - physics

后电话响了。

phone² /fəʊn/ *verb* 动词 (phones, phoning, phoned)
to contact someone and speak to them by telephone 给…打电话: *He phoned Laura to see if she was better.* 他给劳拉打电话问她是否好点了。□ *'Did anybody phone?' asked Alberg.* "有人打电话了吗？"阿尔伯格问道。
on the phone speaking to someone by telephone 在打电话: *She's always on the phone.* 她总是在打电话。

'phone book *countable noun* 可数名词
a book that contains a list of the names, addresses, and telephone numbers of the people in a town or area 电话号码簿

'phone call *countable noun* 可数名词
when you use a telephone to speak to someone who is in another place 打电话；通话: *I have to make a phone call.* 我得打个电话。

'phone number *countable noun* 可数名词
the number of a particular phone 电话号码: *What's your phone number?* 你电话号码是多少？

photo /'fəʊtəʊ/ *countable noun* 可数名词
→ see 见 **photograph**

photocopier /'fəʊtəʊˌkɒpiə/ *countable noun* 可数名词
a machine that copies documents by photographing them 复印机

photocopy /'fəʊtəʊˌkɒpi/ *countable noun* 可数名词 (**photocopies**)
a copy of a document that you make using a special machine (= a photocopier) 复印件: *He gave me a photocopy of the letter.* 他给了我一份这封信的复印件。
● **photocopy** *verb* 动词 (**photocopies, photocopying, photocopied**): *He photocopied the documents before sending them off.* 他把文件复印之后寄了出去。

photograph /'fəʊtəɡrɑːf/ *countable noun* 可数名词
a picture that you take with a camera 照片；相片: *He wants to take some photographs of the house.* 他想给这幢房子拍一些照片。● **photograph** *verb* 动词 (**photographs, photographing, photographed**) (*formal* 正式): *She photographed the children.* 她给孩子们拍了照。
→ Look at picture on P13 参见彩插第 13 页

photographer /fə'tɒɡrəfə/ *countable noun*
可数名词
someone who takes photographs as a job or a hobby 摄影师；摄影爱好者: *He's a professional photographer.* 他是个职业摄影师。

photography /fə'tɒɡrəfi/ *uncountable noun* 不可数名词
the skill or process of producing photographs 摄影(术): *Photography is one of her hobbies.* 摄影是她的爱好之一。

photosynthesis /ˌfəʊtəʊ'sɪnθəsɪs/ *uncountable noun* 不可数名词
the way that green plants make their food using the light of the sun 光合作用

phrasal verb /ˌfreɪzəl 'vɜːb/ *countable noun* 可数名词
a combination of a verb and an adverb or preposition, for example, 'get over' or 'give up', which together have a particular meaning 短语动词

phrase /freɪz/ *countable noun* 可数名词
a group of words that you use together as part of a sentence, for example, 'in the morning' 短语: *At the end of the book, there is a glossary of useful words and phrases.* 书末附有实用单词和短语词表。

physical /'fɪzɪkəl/ *adjective* 形容词
connected with a person's body, rather than with their mind 身体的；肉体的: *Physical activity promotes good health.* 体育锻炼可增强体质。
▶ **physically** /'fɪzɪkəli/ *adverb* 副词: *Kerry is physically active and in excellent health.* 克里积极参与运动，身体非常棒。

physical edu'cation *uncountable noun* 不可数名词
the school subject in which students do physical exercises or take part in physical games and sports 体育(课)

physicist /'fɪzɪsɪst/ *countable noun* 可数名词
a person who studies physics 物理学家: *He was one of the best nuclear physicists in the country.* 他是该国最杰出的核物理学家之一。

physics /'fɪzɪks/ *uncountable noun* 不可数名词
the scientific study of things such as heat, light and sound 物理学: *His favourite school subjects were chemistry and physics.* 他在学校最喜欢的课是化学和物理。

pianist /ˈpiːənɪst/ *countable noun* 可数名词
a person who plays the piano 钢琴家；钢琴演奏者：*She wants to be a concert pianist.* 她想成为一名音乐会的钢琴演奏家。

piano /piˈænəʊ/ *noun* 名词
a large musical instrument that you play by pressing black and white bars (= keys) 钢琴：*I taught myself how to play the piano.* 我自学了弹钢琴。
→ Look at picture on P12 参见彩插第 12 页

piccolo /ˈpɪkələʊ/ *noun* 名词
a musical instrument that is like a small flute (= a pipe that you put across your lips and blow) 短笛

pick /pɪk/ *verb* 动词 (**picks, picking, picked**)
1 to choose a particular person or thing 挑选；选择：*Mr Nowell picked ten people to interview.* 诺埃尔先生选了 10 个人面试。
2 to take flowers, fruit or leaves from a plant or tree 采；摘：*I've picked some flowers from the garden.* 我从花园里采了些花。

pick on someone to repeatedly criticize someone or treat them unkindly (*informal* 非正式) 找某人的碴儿；故意刁难某人：*Bullies often pick on younger children.* 霸凌者经常欺负年龄更小的孩子。

pick someone/something out
1 to recognize someone or something when it is difficult to see them 辨认出某人 / 某物；分辨出某人 / 某物：*I had trouble picking out the words, even with my glasses on.* 即使戴上眼镜，我也很难辨认出这些字。
2 to choose someone or something from a group of people or things 挑选出某人 / 某物：*They picked me out to represent the whole team.* 他们选我当队代表。

pick someone/something up to collect someone or something from a place, often in a car (常指开车) 接载某人 / 取走某物：*Please could you pick me up at 5pm?* 你下午 5 点开车接我好吗？ □ *She went to her parents' house to pick up some clean clothes.* 她去父母家取些干净衣服。

pick something up
1 to lift something up 捡起某物：*He picked his cap up from the floor.* 他从地板上捡起帽子。
2 to learn a skill or an idea over a period of time without really trying (*informal* 非正式)（不费力地）学会…，获得…：*Her*

children have picked up English really quickly. 她的几个孩子很快就学会了英语。

pickle /ˈpɪkəl/ *noun* 名词
1 *uncountable* 不可数 a cold, spicy sauce with pieces of vegetable and fruit in it 菜酱：*a cheese and pickle sandwich* 奶酪菜酱三明治
2 [**pickles**] *plural* 复数 a vegetable that has been kept in vinegar (= a strong, sharp liquid) for a long time 泡菜；腌菜：*He had a hamburger with pickles.* 他吃了一个夹有泡菜的汉堡。

picnic /ˈpɪknɪk/ *countable noun* 可数名词
when you eat a meal outdoors, usually in a park or a forest, or at the beach 野餐：*We're going on a picnic tomorrow.* 我们明天要去野餐。● **picnic** *verb* 动词 (**picnics, picnicking, picnicked**)：*Afterwards, we picnicked by the river.* 之后，我们在河边野餐。

picture¹ /ˈpɪktʃə/ *countable noun* 可数名词
1 a drawing or painting 画；图画：*She drew a picture with coloured chalk.* 她用彩色粉笔画了一幅画。
2 a photograph 照片：*I love taking pictures of animals.* 我喜欢拍摄动物。

picture² /ˈpɪktʃə/ *verb* 动词 (**pictures, picturing, pictured**)
to think of something and see it in your mind 想象；设想：*He pictured her with long black hair.* 他想象她留着黑色长发的样子。

pie /paɪ/ *noun* 名词
a dish of fruit, meat or vegetables that is covered with pastry (= a mixture of flour, butter and water) and baked 馅饼，派（内有蔬菜或肉的点心）：*We each had a slice of apple pie.* 我们每人吃了一块苹果派。

piece /piːs/ *countable noun* 可数名词
1 a part of something（表示一部分）块，片，件：*You must only take one piece of cake.* 你只能吃一块蛋糕。□ *Cut the chicken into pieces.* 把鸡肉切块。
2 an amount of something（表示数量）件，条，首：*That's an interesting piece of information.* 那则消息很有趣。□ *This is his finest piece of work yet.* 这是他目前为止最棒的作品。□ *He has composed 1,500 pieces of music for TV.* 他已创作了 1,500 首电视配乐。

in pieces broken 碎成片的：*The china vase was in pieces on the floor.* 瓷花瓶在地板上摔成了碎片。

pierce /pɪəs/ *verb* 动词 (**pierces, piercing, pierced**)
1 to make a hole in something with a sharp object 扎穿；刺破: *Pierce the chicken with a sharp knife to check that it is cooked.* 用锋利的小刀扎一下鸡肉，看有没有熟。
2 to make small holes through someone's ears so that they can wear earrings (= jewellery for the ears) in them 给（耳朵）打洞: *I'm having my ears pierced on Saturday.* 我周六要去扎耳洞。

piercing /ˈpɪəsɪŋ/ *adjective* 形容词
used for describing a sound that is high and clear in a sharp and unpleasant way 刺耳的；尖厉的: *She let out a piercing scream.* 她发出刺耳的尖叫声。

pig /pɪɡ/ *countable noun* 可数名词
1 a farm animal with a fat body and short legs, that is kept for its meat 猪: *Children can help feed the pigs.* 孩子们能帮着喂猪。
2 used as a rude way of talking about someone who is unkind or who eats too much (*informal* 非正式) 猪猡；讨厌鬼；贪吃鬼: *You've eaten my toast, you greedy pig!* 你把我的吐司给吃了，你这头贪吃的猪！

pigeon /ˈpɪdʒɪn/ *countable noun* 可数名词
a large grey bird that is often seen in cities 鸽子

pigtail /ˈpɪɡteɪl/ *countable noun* 可数名词
a length of hair hanging loose in a bunch, or twisted and tied at the end 辫子；马尾辫；麻花辫: *Her hair was tied back in pigtails.* 她的头发在脑后梳成马尾。

pile¹ /paɪl/ *countable noun* 可数名词
several things lying on top of each other 堆；摞: *We searched through the pile of boxes.* 我们在那堆盒子里搜寻。 □ *There was a huge pile of shoes by the door.* 门边有一大堆鞋子。

pile² /paɪl/ *verb* 动词 (**piles, piling, piled**)
to put things somewhere so that they form a pile 堆放；摞起: *He was piling clothes into the suitcase.* 他正往手提箱里叠放衣服。
pile something up to put one thing on top of another to form a pile 堆放某物；摞起某物: *They piled up rocks to build a wall.* 他们用石块垒墙。

pill /pɪl/ *countable noun* 可数名词
a small, solid, round piece of medicine that you swallow 药丸；药片: *Why do I have to take all these pills?* 我为什么要把这些药片都吃下去？

pillar /ˈpɪlə/ *countable noun* 可数名词
a tall, solid structure that usually supports part of a building 柱子；支柱: *There were eight huge pillars supporting the roof.* *8 根巨柱撑起屋顶。

pillow /ˈpɪləʊ/ *countable noun* 可数名词
a soft object that you rest your head on when you are in bed 枕头

pillowcase /ˈpɪləʊˌkeɪs/ *countable noun* 可数名词
a cloth cover for a pillow 枕套

pilot /ˈpaɪlət/ *countable noun* 可数名词
a person who controls an aircraft 飞行员: *He spent seventeen years as an airline pilot.* 他当过 17 年航空公司飞行员。
→ Look at picture on P16 参见彩插第 16 页

pin¹ /pɪn/ *countable noun* 可数名词
a very small, thin piece of metal with a point at one end, used for fastening things together 大头针: *She looked in her box of needles and pins.* 她在装缝衣针和大头针的盒子里翻了翻。

pin² /pɪn/ *verb* 动词 (**pins, pinning, pinned**)
1 to fix something somewhere with a pin （用大头针）钉住: *They pinned a notice to the door.* 他们把通知钉到门上。
2 to press someone against a surface so that they cannot move 按住；压住: *I pinned him down until the police arrived.* 我按住他，直到警察赶到。

pinch¹ /pɪntʃ/ *verb* 动词 (**pinches, pinching, pinched**)
1 to press someone's skin between your thumb and first finger 捏；拧；掐: *She pinched his arm as hard as she could.* 她使出浑身力气拧他的胳膊。
2 to steal something (*informal* 非正式) 偷: *Alex has pinched my book.* 亚历克斯偷了我的书。

pinch² /pɪntʃ/ *countable noun* 可数名词 (**pinches**)
1 when you press someone's skin between your thumb and first finger 捏；拧；掐: *She gave him a little pinch.* 她轻轻拧了他一下。
2 the amount of salt, pepper or other powder that you can hold between your thumb and your first finger 一撮；少量: *Add a pinch of cinnamon to the apples.* 往苹果上放一撮肉桂粉。

pine /paɪn/ *noun* 名词
1 (also 亦作 **pine tree**) a tall tree with long, thin leaves that it keeps all year 松树: *The high mountains are covered in pine trees.* 高山上长满了松树。
2 *uncountable* 不可数 the wood of this tree 松木: *There's a big pine table in the kitchen.* 厨房里有一张大松木桌子。

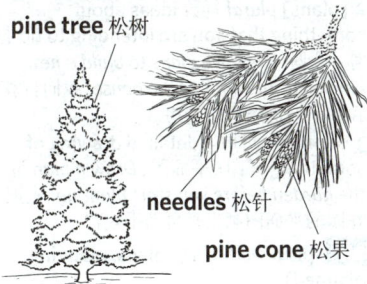
pine tree 松树 / needles 松针 / pine cone 松果

pineapple /ˈpaɪnæpəl/ *noun* 名词
a large fruit with sweet, yellow flesh and thick, brown skin 菠萝; 凤梨

pink /pɪŋk/ *adjective* 形容词 (**pinker, pinkest**)
of the colour between red and white 粉红色的: *She wore pink lipstick.* 她涂着粉红色唇膏。● **pink** *noun* 名词: *I prefer pale pinks and blues.* 我喜欢淡粉色和淡蓝色。
→ Look at picture on P13 参见彩插第 13 页

pint /paɪnt/ *countable noun* 可数名词
a unit for measuring liquids that is equal to around 0.57 litres in Britain, and around 0.47 liters in America 品脱(液量单位，1 英制品脱≈0.57 升, 1 美制品脱≈0.47 升): *Each carton contains a pint of milk.* 每个纸盒装有一品脱牛奶。 □ *Drink half a pint of water before meals.* 饭前喝半品脱水。

pioneer /ˌpaɪəˈnɪə/ *countable noun* 可数名词
one of the first people to be involved in a particular activity 先锋; 先驱: *He was one of the leading pioneers of the Internet.* 他是因特网领域的领军人物之一。

pip /pɪp/ *countable noun* 可数名词
one of the small, hard seeds in a fruit such as an apple or an orange (苹果、橘子等水果的)核, 籽, 种子

pipe /paɪp/ *countable noun* 可数名词
1 a long tube that a liquid or a gas can flow through 管道; 管子: *They are going to replace the old water pipes.* 他们要更换旧水管。

2 an object that is used for smoking tobacco (= dried leaves that are used for making cigarettes) 烟斗: *Do you smoke a pipe?* 你抽烟斗吗？

pirate /ˈpaɪrət/ *countable noun* 可数名词
a person who attacks ships and steals property from them 海盗: *The hero must find the pirates and the hidden gold.* 男主角须找到海盗和被藏起的黄金。

pistol /ˈpɪstəl/ *countable noun* 可数名词
a small gun 手枪

pit /pɪt/ *countable noun* 可数名词
1 a large hole that is dug in the ground (地面的)洞, 坑, 井: *Eric fell into the pit.* 埃里克掉进洞里。
2 the part of a coal mine that is under the ground 煤矿井

pitch /pɪtʃ/ *noun* 名词 (**pitches**)
1 *countable* 可数 an area of ground that is used for playing a game such as football 球场: *a cricket pitch* 板球场
2 *uncountable* 不可数 how high or low a sound is 音高: *The pitch of a voice falls at the end of a sentence.* 句末音调下降。

pity¹ /ˈpɪti/ *verb* 动词 (**pities, pitying, pitied**)
to feel very sorry for someone 可怜; 同情; 怜悯: *I don't know whether to hate or pity him.* 我不知道该恨他还是同情他。

pity² /ˈpɪti/ *uncountable noun* 不可数名词
when you feel very sorry for someone 同情; 怜悯: *He felt a sudden tender pity for her.* 他突然对她涌起怜惜之情。
a pity used for saying that you feel disappointed 可惜的事; 遗憾的事: *It's a pity you arrived so late.* 你到得太晚了，真遗憾。

pizza /ˈpiːtsə/ *noun* 名词
a flat, round piece of bread that is covered with tomatoes, cheese and sometimes other foods, and then baked in an oven 比萨饼: *I ordered a thin-crust pizza.* 我订了一个薄脆比萨饼。

place¹ /pleɪs/ *countable noun* 可数名词
1 a particular building, area, town or country 地方; 地点; 地区: *Keep your dog on a lead in public places.* 在公共场所狗要系上牵狗绳。 □ *Please state your time and place of birth.* 请告知您的出生日期和地点。
2 the right or usual position for something 应在位置; 所属位置: *He returned the photo to its place on the shelf.* 他把照片放

回架子原处。

3 a seat for one person 座位；位子：*This girl was sitting in my place.* 这个女孩坐在我的位子上。

4 someone's position in a race or competition（速度比赛或竞赛的）名次，位次：*Victoria is in third place with 22 points.* 维多利亚得了 22 分，位居第三。

5 your home (*informal* 非正式) 家；住所：*Let's all go back to my place!* 都回我那儿吧！

in place in the correct position 归位；在正确位置：*A wide band held her hair in place.* 她的头发用宽发带扎了起来。

in place of something/someone instead of something or someone 代替某物／某人：*Try using herbs and spices in place of salt.* 试试用香草和调味料代替盐。

take place to happen 发生：*The discussions took place in Paris.* 会谈在巴黎举行。

place² /pleɪs/ ***verb*** 动词 (**places, placing, placed**)
to put something somewhere 放置；安放：*Brand placed the letter in his pocket.* 布兰德把信放进口袋。

plain¹ /pleɪn/ ***adjective*** 形容词 (**plainer, plainest**)
1 all one colour, without any pattern or writing 单色的；素色的：*A plain carpet makes a room look bigger.* 房间铺素色地毯会显得大一些。 □ *He placed the paper in a plain envelope.* 他把纸放进一个素色信封里。

2 very simple in style 朴素的；简朴的：*It was a plain, grey stone house.* 这是一栋朴素的灰色石头房子。

3 easy to recognize or understand 明显的；清楚的：*It was plain to him what he had to do.* 他很清楚自己得做什么。

4 ordinary and not at all beautiful 长相一般的；相貌平平的：*She was a shy, rather plain girl.* 她是个相貌平平、害羞的女孩。

plain² /pleɪn/ ***countable noun*** 可数名词
a large flat area of land with very few trees on it 平原：*She stood alone on the grassy plain.* 她独自站在百草丰茂的平原上。

plait /plæt/ ***verb*** 动词 (**plaits, plaiting, plaited**)
to put three pieces of hair or rope over and under each other to make one thick piece 把（头发或绳子）编成辫状：*Joanna plaited her hair.* 乔安娜把头发编成辫子。

● **plait** ***countable noun*** 可数名词：*Her hair was tied in a long plait.* 她的头发编成了一条长辫子。

plan¹ /plæn/ ***noun*** 名词
1 ***countable*** 可数 a method for doing something that you think about in advance 计划；方案：*They are meeting to discuss the peace plan.* 他们将会面商讨和平方案。 □ *She says that everything is going according to plan.* 她说一切都在按计划进行。

2 [**plans**] ***plural*** 复数 ideas about something that you are intending to do 打算；计划：*We have plans to build a new kitchen at the back of the house.* 我们打算在房子后面新建个厨房。

3 ***countable*** 可数 a detailed drawing of something 详图；平面图：*Draw a plan of the garden before you start planting.* 先把花园的平面图画出来再动手栽种。

plan² /plæn/ ***verb*** 动词 (**plans, planning, planned**)
to decide in detail what you are going to do 计划；筹划：*Plan what you're going to eat.* 计划一下要吃什么。 □ *He plans to leave Baghdad on Monday.* 他计划周一离开巴格达。 □ *They came together to plan for the future.* 他们齐聚一堂筹划未来。

▶ **planning** /ˈplænɪŋ/ ***uncountable noun*** 不可数名词：*The trip needs careful planning.* 此行需要周密计划。

plane /pleɪn/ ***countable noun*** 可数名词
a vehicle with wings and engines that can fly 飞机：*He had plenty of time to catch his plane.* 他有充裕的时间赶飞机。

planet /ˈplænɪt/ ***countable noun*** 可数名词
a large, round object in space that moves around a star. The Earth is a planet. 行星：*We study the planets in the solar system.* 我们研究太阳系中的行星。

plant¹ /plɑːnt/ ***countable noun*** 可数名词
1 a living thing that grows in the earth and has a stem, leaves and roots 植物：*Water each plant daily.* 每天每株植物都浇浇水。

2 a factory, or a place where power is produced 工厂；发电厂：*We visited one of Ford's car*

plant 植物
— **flower** 花
— **petal** 花瓣
— **bud** 花蕾
— **leaf** 叶
— **stalk** 柄
— **stem** 茎
— **root** 根

assembly plants. 我们参观了福特的一家汽车装配厂。

plant² /plɑːnt/ *verb* 动词 (**plants, planting, planted**)
to put something into the ground so that it will grow 种植；栽种: *He plans to plant fruit trees.* 他计划种些果树。

plasma screen /ˈplæzmə ˌskriːn/ or 或 **plasma display** /ˈplæzmə ˌdɪspleɪ/ *countable noun* 可数名词
a type of thin television screen or computer screen with good quality images（电视或计算机的）等离子屏

plaster¹ /ˈplɑːstə/ *noun* 名词
1 (*American* 美国英语: **Band-Aid**) *countable* 可数 a small piece of sticky material used for covering small cuts on your body 创可贴: *He had cuts on his face and a plaster on his right hand.* 他脸上有伤口，右手贴着创可贴。
2 *uncountable* 不可数 a substance that is used for making a smooth surface on the inside of walls and ceilings 石膏；灰泥；灰浆: *There were huge cracks in the plaster.* 灰泥上出现了多条大裂缝。
in plaster with a hard white cover around your leg or arm to protect a broken bone 打着石膏: *I had my arm in plaster for two months.* 我胳膊打了两个月石膏。

plaster² /ˈplɑːstə/ *verb* 动词 (**plasters, plastering, plastered**)
to cover a wall or a ceiling with a layer of plaster 涂石膏（或灰泥）于；在…上抹灰浆: *He has just plastered the ceiling.* 他刚给天花板抹上灰浆。

plastic /ˈplæstɪk/ *noun* 名词
a light but strong material that is produced by a chemical process 塑料: *The windows are made from sheets of plastic.* 这些窗户由塑料板制成。□ *a plastic bottle* 塑料瓶 □ *a plastic bag* 塑料袋

plastic ˈsurgery *uncountable noun* 不可数名词
an operation to repair damaged skin, or to change someone's appearance 整形手术；整形外科: *She had plastic surgery to change the shape of her nose.* 她做了鼻子整形手术。

plate /pleɪt/ *countable noun* 可数名词
a flat dish that is used for holding food 盘子；碟: *Anita pushed her plate away.* 安妮塔把盘子推开。□ *He ate a huge plate of spaghetti.* 他吃了一大盘意大利面。

plateau /ˈplætəʊ/ *countable noun* 可数名词 (**plateaus** or 或 **plateaux** /ˈplætəʊz/)
a large area of high and fairly flat land 高原: *The house is on a wide grassy plateau.* 房子位于宽阔的草地高原上。

platform /ˈplætfɔːm/ *countable noun* 可数名词
1 a flat, raised structure on which someone or something can stand 平台；讲台；舞台: *He walked towards the platform to begin his speech.* 他走向讲台开始讲话。
2 the area in a train station where you wait for a train（火车站的）站台，月台: *a railway platform* 火车站站台

play¹ /pleɪ/ *verb* 动词 (**plays, playing, played**)
1 to spend time using toys and taking part in games 玩；玩耍: *Polly was playing with her dolls.* 波莉正在玩她的洋娃娃。
2 to take part in a game or a sport 参加（比赛或体育项目）: *The twins played cards.* 那对双胞胎打了牌。□ *I used to play basketball.* 我过去常打篮球。
3 to compete against another person or team in a sport or a game 和…比赛: *Manchester United will play Liverpool today.* 曼联队今天将迎战利物浦队。
4 to perform the part of a particular character in a play or film 扮演，饰演（角色）: *He played Mr Hyde in the film.* 他在片中饰演海德先生。
5 to produce music from a musical instrument 弹奏，演奏（乐器）: *Nina was playing the piano.* 尼娜在弹钢琴。□ *He played for me.* 他为我弹奏。
6 to put a CD into a machine and listen to it 播放（光碟）: *She played her music too loudly.* 她的音乐声开得太大了。
play a joke/trick on someone to deceive someone or give them a surprise for fun 和某人开玩笑/捉弄某人: *She wanted to play a trick on her friends.* 她想捉弄一下朋友们。

play² /pleɪ/ *noun* 名词
1 *uncountable* 不可数 when someone spends time using toys and taking part in games 玩；玩耍: *Children learn mainly through play.* 孩子们主要在玩中学。
2 *countable* 可数 a piece of writing performed in a theatre, on the radio or on television 戏剧；剧本: *'Hamlet' is my*

favourite play. 《哈姆莱特》是我最喜欢的戏剧。
→ Look at picture on P3 参见彩插第 3 页

player /ˈpleɪə/ *countable noun* 可数名词
1 a person who takes part in a sport or game 运动员；选手；游戏者: *She was a good tennis player.* 她网球打得很好。
▫ *The game is for three players.* 这个游戏要 3 个人玩。
2 a musician 演奏者: *He's a professional trumpet player.* 他是个职业小号手。

playful /ˈpleɪfʊl/ *adjective* 形容词
not very serious 闹着玩的；不当真的: *She gave him a playful kiss.* 她顽皮地吻了他一下。

playground /ˈpleɪɡraʊnd/ *countable noun* 可数名词
a piece of land where children can play 儿童游戏场；操场: *The park has playground equipment made of wood.* 这个公园有木制的儿童游乐设施。

playgroup /ˈpleɪɡruːp/ also 亦作 **play group** *countable noun* 可数名词
an informal school for very young children 幼儿游戏班

¹playing card *countable noun* 可数名词
a thin piece of cardboard with numbers or pictures printed on it that is used for playing games 纸牌；扑克牌: *He started to shuffle a pack of playing cards.* 他开始洗一副牌。

¹playing field *countable noun* 可数名词
a large area of grass where people play sports 运动场: *The town has three grass playing fields and 18 football teams.* 这个城镇有 3 块草皮运动场、18 支足球队。

playtime /ˈpleɪtaɪm/ *countable noun* 可数名词
the period of time between lessons at school when children can play outside (学校的)课间休息: *Friends in different classes can meet up at playtime.* 不在一个班的朋友可以在课间休息时见面。

playwright /ˈpleɪraɪt/ *countable noun* 可数名词
a person who writes plays 剧作家；编剧

plea /pliː/ *countable noun* 可数名词
an emotional request for something 恳求；请求: *Their president made a desperate plea for international help.* 他们的总统急切地恳求国际援助。 ▫ *It was an emotional plea for help.* 这请求助恳切动人。

plead /pliːd/ *verb* 动词 (**pleads, pleading, pleaded**)
to ask someone in an emotional way to do something 恳求；求求: *The lady pleaded with her daughter to come back home.* 这位女士恳求她的女儿回家。

plead guilty/not guilty to officially say in a court of law that you are guilty or not guilty of a crime 认罪 / 不认罪: *Morris pleaded guilty to robbery.* 莫里斯承认犯有抢劫罪。

pleasant /ˈplezənt/ *adjective* 形容词 (**pleasanter, pleasantest**)
1 enjoyable or attractive 宜人的；令人愉快的: *It was a very pleasant surprise to receive a free ticket.* 得到一张免费票真是喜从天降。 ▫ *I have many pleasant memories of this place.* 我对这个地方有很多美好的回忆。
2 nice and friendly 友好的；友善的: *The doctor was a handsome, pleasant young man.* 医生是一位英俊友善的年轻男子。

please¹ /pliːz/ *adverb* 副词
1 used when you are politely asking someone to do something (用于礼貌地请求)请，请问: *Can you help us, please?* 请问您能帮帮我们吗？ ▫ *Please come in.* 请进。 ▫ *Can we have the bill, please?* 劳驾，买单。
2 used when you are accepting something politely (用于客气地接受)好的，谢谢: *'Tea?' — 'Yes, please.'* "茶？" —— "好的，谢谢。"

please² /pliːz/ *verb* 动词 (**pleases, pleasing, pleased**)
to make someone feel happy and satisfied 使高兴；使满意: *I just want to please you.* 我只是想让你高兴。 ▫ *He always tried to please her.* 他总是设法取悦她。

pleased /pliːzd/ *adjective* 形容词
happy about something or satisfied with something 高兴的；满意的: *I'm so pleased that we solved the problem.* 我们解决了那个问题，我特别高兴。 ▫ *I am very pleased with your work.* 我对你的工作很满意。

pleased to meet you a polite way of saying hello to someone that you are meeting for the first time (初次见面时的礼貌问候语) 很高兴认识你

pleasing /ˈpliːzɪŋ/ *adjective* 形容词
giving you pleasure and satisfaction 令人愉悦的；使人满意的: *The pleasing smell of fresh coffee came from the kitchen.* 从厨房飘来新煮咖啡的香味。

pleasure /ˈpleʒə/ *noun* 名词
1 uncountable 不可数 a feeling of

happiness and satisfaction 快乐；满足：*Watching sports gave him great pleasure.* 观看体育比赛给他以极大的快乐。□ *Everybody takes pleasure in eating.* 每个人都能从吃东西中得到满足。

2 *countable* 可数 an activity or an experience that you find enjoyable 乐事；乐趣：*Watching TV is our only pleasure.* 看电视是我们唯一的乐趣。□ *It was a pleasure to see her smiling face.* 很高兴看到她的笑容。

It's a pleasure or **It's my pleasure** a polite way of answering someone who thanks you for doing something（回应对方答谢的礼貌用语）不客气，不用谢：*'Thanks very much for waiting for me.' — 'It's a pleasure.'* "非常感谢你等我。"——"别客气。"

plectrum /ˈplektrʌm/ *countable noun* 可数名词
a small piece of plastic that you use for playing the strings of a guitar（吉他的）拨子，拨片

plenty /ˈplenti/ *pronoun* 代词
a large amount 大量；许多：*I don't like long interviews. Fifteen minutes is plenty.* 我不喜欢太长时间的访谈。15分钟够长的了。
plenty of something a large amount of something 大量事物：*Don't worry. There's still plenty of time.* 别担心。时间还很充裕。□ *Most businesses face plenty of competition.* 大多数企业面临着巨大的竞争压力。

pliers /ˈplaɪəz/ *plural noun* 复数名词
a tool with two handles at one end and two hard, flat, metal parts at the other that is used for holding or pulling things 钳子：*Hold the nail at its base with pliers.* 用钳子夹住钉子底部。

pliers 钳子

plop /plɒp/ *countable noun* 可数名词
the soft sound of something dropping into water（物体落水的）啪嗒声，扑通声：*Another drop of water fell with a soft plop.* 又一滴水啪嗒一声轻轻落下。● **plop** *verb* 动词 (**plops, plopping, plopped**)：*The ice cream plopped to the ground.* 冰激凌啪嗒一声掉在地上。

plot¹ /plɒt/ *verb* 动词 (**plots, plotting, plotted**)

to plan secretly to do something 密谋；图谋：*They plotted to overthrow the government.* 他们密谋推翻政府。

plot² /plɒt/ *noun* 名词
1 *countable* 可数 a secret plan to do something 阴谋：*We have uncovered a plot to kill the president.* 我们侦破了一起刺杀总统的阴谋。

2 a series of events that make up the story of a film or a book（电影或书籍中的）情节：*He told me the plot of his new book.* 他给我讲述了他新书的情节。

3 *countable* 可数 a small piece of land, especially one that is intended for a particular purpose（尤指有特殊用途的）小块土地：*I bought a small plot of land and built a house on it.* 我买了一小块地，在上面盖了一栋房子。

plough /plaʊ/ *countable noun* 可数名词
a large farming tool that is pulled across the soil to turn it over, usually before seeds are planted 犁 ● **plough** *verb* 动词 (**ploughs, ploughing, ploughed**)：*They were using horses to plough their fields.* 他们当时用马犁地。

pluck /plʌk/ *verb* 动词 (**plucks, plucking, plucked**)
to pull the strings of a musical instrument with your fingers, so that they make a sound 弹，拨（弦乐器）：*Nell was plucking a harp.* 内尔在弹奏竖琴。

plug¹ /plʌg/ *countable noun* 可数名词
1 the plastic object with metal pins that connects a piece of electrical equipment to the electricity supply 插头：*Remove the power plug when you have finished.* 你弄完之后要拔掉电源插头。

2 a round object that you use to block the hole in a bath or a sink（浴缸或水池的）塞子：*She put in the plug and filled the sink with cold water.* 她塞上塞子，给水池注满凉水。

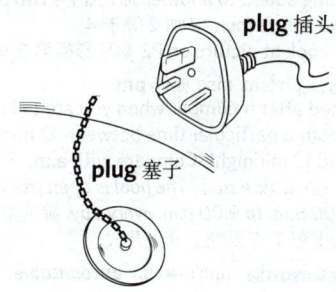

plug 插头

plug 塞子

plug² /plʌɡ/ ***verb*** 动词 (**plugs, plugging, plugged**)
to block a hole with something 堵；塞：*We are working to plug a major oil leak.* 我们正在设法堵住主要的漏油点。
plug something in to connect a piece of electrical equipment to the electricity supply 给(电器)接通电源：*I had a TV, but there was no place to plug it in.* 我有电视，但没地方接电源。

plum /plʌm/ ***countable noun*** 可数名词
a small, sweet fruit with a smooth purple, red or yellow skin and a large seed (= a stone) in the middle 李子；梅子

plumber /ˈplʌmə/ ***countable noun*** 可数名词
a person whose job is to put in and repair things like water and gas pipes, toilets and baths 水暖工；管子工
→ Look at picture on P16 参见彩插第 16 页

plump /plʌmp/ ***adjective*** 形容词 (**plumper, plumpest**)
round and rather heavy 丰满的；胖乎乎的：*Maria was small and plump.* 玛丽亚身材娇小丰满。

plunge /plʌndʒ/ ***verb*** 动词 (**plunges, plunging, plunged**)
1 to fall or jump into water (向水中)坠落，跳：*The bus plunged into a river.* 那辆公共汽车栽进了河里。
2 to push an object violently into something 猛插；猛刺：*He plunged a fork into his dinner.* 他把叉子插进晚餐。

plural /ˈplʊərəl/ ***countable noun*** 可数名词
the form of a noun that is used for talking about more than one person or thing 复数形式：*'People' is the plural of 'person'.*
*people 是 person 的复数形式。● **plural adjective*** 形容词：*'Men' is the plural form of 'man'.* *men 是 man 的复数形式。

plus /plʌs/ ***conjunction*** 连词
used for showing that one number is being added to another 加；加上：*Two plus two equals four.* *2 加 2 等于 4。
→ Look at picture on P2 参见彩插第 2 页

p.m. /ˌpiː ˈem/ also 亦作 **pm**
used after a number when you are talking about a particular time between 12 noon and 12 midnight. Compare with **a.m.** 下午，午后（比较 a.m.）：*The pool is open from 7.00 a.m. to 9.00 p.m. every day.* 游泳池每天上午 7 点至晚上 9 点开放。

pneumonia /njuːˈməʊniə/ ***uncountable noun*** 不可数名词
a serious disease that affects the lungs 肺炎：*She nearly died of pneumonia.* 她差点儿死于肺炎。

pocket¹ /ˈpɒkɪt/ ***countable noun*** 可数名词
a part of a piece of clothing that you can put things in 衣兜；衣袋；口袋：*He put the key in his jacket pocket.* 他把钥匙放进夹克口袋里。

pocket² /ˈpɒkɪt/ ***adjective*** 形容词
used for describing something that is small enough to fit into a pocket 可装入衣袋的；便携式的；袖珍的：*a pocket calculator* 便携计算器

pocket money ***uncountable noun*** 不可数名词
money that parents give to their children, usually every week (家长给孩子的)零花钱，零用钱：*Her parents gave her £6 pocket money a week.* 她父母每星期给她 6 英镑零花钱。

pod /pɒd/ ***countable noun*** 可数名词
a seed container that grows on some plants 荚；豆荚：*We bought fresh peas in their pods.* 我们买了带豆荚的新鲜豌豆。

podcast /ˈpɒdkɑːst/ ***countable noun*** 可数名词
a file containing a radio show or something similar, that you can listen to on a computer or an MP3 player (= a small piece of electrical equipment for listening to music) 播客（一种可在电脑和 MP3 上播放的音频文件）：*There are thousands of new podcasts available every day.* 每天有成千上万的新播客。

poem /ˈpəʊɪm/ ***countable noun*** 可数名词
a piece of writing in which the words are chosen for their beauty and sound, and are arranged in short lines 诗；韵文：*He read to her from a book of love poems.* 他读一本爱情诗集给她听。
→ Look at picture on P3 参见彩插第 3 页

poet /ˈpəʊɪt/ ***countable noun*** 可数名词
a person who writes poems 诗人：*He was a painter and a poet.* 他既是画家，又是诗人。

poetry /ˈpəʊɪtri/ ***uncountable noun*** 不可数名词
the form of literature that consists of poems (作为文学形式的)诗，诗歌：*We studied Russian poetry last term.* 上学期我们学习了俄罗斯诗歌。

point – poke

point¹ /pɔɪnt/ *noun* 名词
1 *countable* 可数 an idea or a fact 观点；看法：*We disagreed with every point she made.* 她提出的观点我们一个都不同意。
2 *singular* 单数 the purpose of something 目的；意图：*What is the point of worrying?* 担心有什么用呢？ □ *There's no point in fighting.* 争吵没有意义。
3 *countable* 可数 a particular position or time（特定的）位置，时间：*We're all going to die at some point.* 我们都将在某个时间死去。
4 *countable* 可数 the thin, sharp end of an object, such as a knife or a needle 尖头；尖端：*Greg felt the cold point of a knife against his neck.* 格雷格感觉到冰冷的刀尖抵在脖子上。
5 *countable* 可数 the small dot that separates whole numbers from parts of numbers 小数点：*The highest temperature today was 98.5°F (ninety-eight point five degrees).* 今天最高气温为华氏 98.5 度。
6 *countable* 可数 a mark that you win in a game or a sport（游戏或体育运动中的）点，分：*Chamberlain scored 50 points.* 张伯伦得了 50 分。
on the point of something about to do something 正要做某事：*He was on the point of answering when the phone rang.* 他正要回答，这时电话铃响了。
point of view your opinion about something 观点；看法；态度：*We would like to hear your point of view.* 我们想听听你的观点。

point² /pɔɪnt/ *verb* 动词 (**points, pointing, pointed**)
1 to use your finger to show where someone or something is（用手指）指：*I pointed at the boy sitting near me.* 我指着坐在我旁边的男孩。

point（用手指）指

I pointed at the boy sitting near me. 我指着坐在我旁边的男孩。

2 to hold something towards someone or something 把（某物）指向；将（某物）对准：*She smiled when Laura pointed a camera at her.* 劳拉用相机对准她时，她露出了笑容。
point something out to tell someone about a fact or show it to them 指出某事物：*He pointed out the errors in the book.* 他指出了这本书中的错误。

pointed /'pɔɪntɪd/ *adjective* 形容词
with a point at one end 尖的；有尖头的：*William was uncomfortable in his new pointed shoes.* 威廉穿着他那双新尖头鞋，感觉不舒服。

pointless /'pɔɪntləs/ *adjective* 形容词
with no sense or purpose 无意义的；无目的的：*Without an audience, the performance is pointless.* 没有观众，表演就没有意义。

poison¹ /'pɔɪzən/ *noun* 名词
a substance that harms or kills people or animals if they swallow or touch it 毒药；毒物；毒素：*Poison from the factory is causing the fish to die.* 工厂排出的有毒物质在导致鱼类不断死亡。

poison² /'pɔɪzən/ *verb* 动词 (**poisons, poisoning, poisoned**)
to harm someone or something by giving them poison 毒害；毒死：*They say that she poisoned her father.* 他们说她毒死了自己的父亲。

poisonous /'pɔɪzənəs/ *adjective* 形容词
1 containing poison 有毒的：*All parts of this tree are poisonous.* 这棵树各个部分都有毒。
2 used for describing an animal that produces a substance that will kill you or make you ill if the animal bites you（动物）带毒的，分泌毒物的：*The zoo keeps a selection of poisonous spiders and snakes.* 这家动物园有许多种毒蜘蛛和毒蛇。

poke /pəʊk/ *verb* 动词 (**pokes, poking, poked**)
1 to quickly push someone or something with your finger or with a sharp object 戳；捅：*Lindy poked him in the arm.* 林迪戳了戳他的胳膊。● **poke** *countable noun* 可数名词：*John gave Richard a playful poke.* 约翰开玩笑地捅了理查德一下。
2 to push one thing into another 把（某物）插入；把（某物）戳进：*He poked the stick into the hole.* 他把棍子插入洞里。

poker /ˈpəʊkə/ *uncountable noun* 不可数名词
a card game that is usually played in order to win money 扑克牌游戏：*Len and I play poker every week.* 我和莱恩每周都打扑克。

pole /pəʊl/ *countable noun* 可数名词
1 a long thin piece of wood or metal, used especially for supporting things（尤用于支撑的）杆，柱：*The car went off the road, knocking down a telephone pole.* 汽车冲出马路，撞倒了电话线杆。
2 the two opposite ends of the Earth, which are its most northern and southern points 极；地极：*For six months of the year, there is very little light at the poles.* 南北两极一年中有 6 个月光照极少。
→ Look at picture on P9 参见彩插第 9 页

police /pəˈliːs/ *plural noun* 复数名词
1 the organization that is responsible for making sure that people obey the law 警察部门；警察机关：*The police are looking for the car.* 警方正在寻找那辆车。□ *Police say they have arrested twenty people.* 警方说他们已逮捕了 20 人。
2 men and women who are members of the police 警察；警员：*More than one hundred police are in the area.* 这一地区有 100 多名警察。

poˈlice ˌcar *countable noun* 可数名词
a vehicle used by the police 警车

poˈlice ˌforce *countable noun* 可数名词
an organization that is responsible for making sure that people obey the law 警察部门；警察机关：*I want to join the police force.* 我想当警察。

policeman /pəˈliːsmən/ *countable noun* 可数名词 (**policemen** /pəˈliːsmen/)
a man who is a member of the police force 男警察

poˈlice ˌofficer *countable noun* 可数名词
a member of the police force 警察；警官：*a senior police officer* 高级警官
→ Look at picture on P16 参见彩插第 16 页

poˈlice ˌstation *countable noun* 可数名词
the local office of the police in a particular area 警察局；派出所：*Two police officers arrested him and took him to the police station.* 两名警察逮捕了他，并将他带到警察局。

policewoman /pəˈliːswʊmən/ *countable noun* 可数名词 (**policewomen** /pəˈliːswɪmɪn/)
a woman who is a member of the police force 女警察

policy /ˈpɒlɪsi/ *noun* 名词 (**policies**)
a set of ideas or plans about a particular subject, especially in politics, economics or business（尤指政治、经济或商业方面的）政策，方针：*There will be some important changes in foreign policy.* 外交政策将会有重大改变。

polish¹ /ˈpɒlɪʃ/ *noun* 名词 (**polishes**)
a substance that you put on a surface in order to clean it and make it shine 上光剂；亮光剂：*Furniture polish will clean and protect your table.* 家具上光剂能清洁并保护桌子。

polish² /ˈpɒlɪʃ/ *verb* 动词 (**polishes, polishing, polished**)
to rub something to make it shine 擦亮；磨光：*He polished his shoes.* 他擦亮鞋子。

He polished his shoes. 他擦亮鞋子。

polite /pəˈlaɪt/ *adjective* 形容词 (**politer, politest**)
behaving with respect towards other people 有礼貌的；客气的：*He seemed a quiet and very polite young man.* 他似乎是个言语不多、非常有礼貌的年轻人。
▶ **politely** /pəˈlaɪtli/ *adverb* 副词：*'Your home is beautiful,' I said politely.* 我客气地说：“你家真漂亮。”
▶ **politeness** /pəˈlaɪtnəs/ *uncountable noun* 不可数名词：*She listened to him, but only out of politeness.* 她只是出于礼貌才听他讲话。

political /pəˈlɪtɪkəl/ *adjective* 形容词
relating to politics or the government 政治的；政府的：*I am not a member of any political party.* 我并非任何政党的党员。
▶ **politically** /pəˈlɪtɪkli/ *adverb* 副词：*Politically, this is a very risky move.* 从政治角度来看，这是非常冒险的举动。

poˌlitical ˈparty *noun* 名词 (**political parties**)
an organization whose members share

politician /ˌpɒlɪˈtɪʃən/ *countable noun* 可数名词
a person who works in politics, especially a member of a government 政治家；从政者；(尤指)政府人员：*They have arrested a number of politicians.* 他们逮捕了好几个从政者。

politics /ˈpɒlɪtɪks/ *noun* 名词
1 *uncountable* 不可数 the activities and ideas that are concerned with government 政治活动；政治事务：*He was involved in local politics.* 他卷入了当地政治事务之中。
2 *plural* 复数 your beliefs about what a government should do 政治主张；政治信仰：*His politics are extreme and often confused.* 他的政治主张既极端又混乱。

poll /pəʊl/ *countable noun* 可数名词
a way of discovering what people think about something by asking them questions 民意调查；民意测验：*The polls are showing that women are very involved in this campaign.* 民意调查显示女性正积极参与这场运动。

pollen /ˈpɒlən/ *noun* 名词
a powder that is produced by flowers 花粉：*The male bee carries the pollen from one flower to another.* 雄蜂将花粉从一朵花传播到另一朵花上。

pollute /pəˈluːt/ *verb* 动词 (**pollutes, polluting, polluted**)
to make water, air or land dirty 污染：*Industry pollutes our rivers with chemicals.* 工业排放的化学物质会污染我们的河流。
▶ **polluted** /pəˈluːtɪd/ *adjective* 形容词：*Fish are dying in the polluted rivers.* 遭到污染的河流中鱼类在不断死亡。

pollution /pəˈluːʃən/ *uncountable noun* 不可数名词
1 the process of making water, air or land dirty and dangerous 污染：*The government announced plans for reducing pollution of the air, sea, rivers and soil.* 政府公布了降低空气污染、海洋污染、河流污染和土壤污染的方案。
2 poisonous substances that pollute water, air or land 污染物：*The level of pollution in the river was falling.* 河水的污染程度在下降。

polyester /ˌpɒliˈestə/ *uncountable noun* 不可数名词
a type of artificial material that is mainly used for making clothes (主要用作衣料的)聚酯纤维，涤纶：*He wore a shirt made of green polyester.* 他身穿一件绿色涤纶衬衫。

pond /pɒnd/ *countable noun* 可数名词
a small area of water 池塘；水塘：*We sat on a bench beside the duck pond.* 我们坐在鸭塘边的一张长椅上。

pony /ˈpəʊni/ *countable noun* 可数名词 (**ponies**)
a small or young horse 小马；幼马

ponytail /ˈpəʊniˌteɪl/ *countable noun* 可数名词
a hairstyle in which your hair is tied up at the back of your head and hangs down like a horse's tail 马尾辫：*Her long, fine hair was tied back in a ponytail.* 她长而纤细的头发在脑后扎成一个马尾辫。

pool /puːl/ *noun* 名词
1 *countable* 可数 → see 见 **swimming pool**：*Does the hotel have a heated indoor pool?* 这家宾馆有室内温水游泳池吗？
2 *countable* 可数 a small area of liquid (液体的)一摊，一小片：*a pool of blood* 一摊血
3 *uncountable* 不可数 a game that is played on a special table. Players use a long stick to hit a white ball so that it knocks numbered coloured balls into six holes around the edge of the table. 落袋台球；普尔台球

poor /pʊə/ *adjective* 形容词 (**poorer, poorest**)
1 having very little money and few possessions 贫穷的；贫困的：*'We were very poor in those days,' he says.* "那时候我们很穷。"他说。
2 used for showing that you are sorry for someone (用于表示同情)可怜的，不幸的：*I feel sorry for that poor child.* 我为那个可怜的孩子感到难过。□ *Poor Mike. Does he feel better now?* 可怜的迈克。他现在好些了吗？
3 bad 糟糕的；不好的：*The illegal copies are of very poor quality.* 盗版产品质量很差。□ *The actors gave a poor performance.* 演员们演得很差劲。
▶ **poorly** /ˈpʊəli/ *adverb* 副词：*'We played poorly in the first game,' Mendez said.* "第一场比赛我们踢得很糟糕。"门德斯说。

the poor people who are poor 穷人；贫民：*There are huge differences between the rich* and the poor. 贫富差异巨大。

pop¹ /pɒp/ *noun* 名词
1 *uncountable* 不可数 modern music that usually has a strong rhythm and uses electronic equipment 流行音乐: *Their music is a combination of Caribbean rhythms and European pop.* 他们的音乐融合了加勒比海韵律和欧洲流行音乐。□ *Her room is covered with posters of pop stars.* 她房间里贴满了流行歌星的海报。
2 *countable* 可数 a short, sharp sound 砰的一声; 啪的一声: *Each piece of corn will make a loud pop when it is cooked.* 烹调时，每粒玉米都会发出响亮的啪的一声。

pop² /pɒp/ *verb* 动词 (**pops, popping, popped**)
1 to make a short, sharp sound 发出砰的一声; 发出啪的一声: *He heard a balloon pop behind his head.* 他听到气球在他脑后砰的一声爆了。
2 to put something somewhere quickly (*informal* 非正式) 迅速放（某物）: *He popped some gum in his mouth.* 他迅速将口香糖塞进嘴里。
3 to go somewhere quickly 匆匆地去; 快速地来: *Their mum popped out to post a letter.* 他们的妈妈匆匆出去邮信。

pop in to go to someone's house for a short time 短暂到访: *Wendy popped in for coffee.* 温迪来喝了杯咖啡。

popcorn /ˈpɒpkɔːn/ *uncountable noun* 不可数名词
a type of food that consists of grains of corn that have been heated until they have burst and become large and light 爆米花

pope /pəʊp/ *countable noun* 可数名词
the leader of the Roman Catholic Church (天主教的) 教皇: *The pope prayed for peace.* 教皇祈祷和平。

popular /ˈpɒpjʊlə/ *adjective* 形容词
1 liked by a lot of people 受欢迎的; 受喜爱的: *He was the most popular politician in Scotland.* 他是苏格兰最受人爱戴的政治家。□ *Chocolate sauce is always popular with kids.* 巧克力酱总是深受孩子们喜爱。
▶ **popularity** /ˌpɒpjʊˈlærɪti/ *uncountable noun* 不可数名词: *The singer's popularity grew with his successful tour.* 随着巡回演出的成功，这位歌手的人气也越来越高。
2 believed or thought by most people 普遍的; 大众化的: *There is a popular belief that unemployment causes crime.* 人们普遍认为失业会导致犯罪。

population /ˌpɒpjʊˈleɪʃən/ *countable noun* 可数名词
all the people who live in a country or an area 人口: *Bangladesh now has a population of about 150 million.* 孟加拉国现有大约 1.5 亿人口。

porch /pɔːtʃ/ *countable noun* 可数名词 (**porches**)
a covered area with a roof and sometimes walls at the entrance to a building 门廊; 门厅: *I was standing in the porch because it was raining.* 我站在门廊里避雨。

pore /pɔː/ *countable noun* 可数名词
one of the very small holes in your skin (皮肤的) 毛孔: *Use hot water to clear blocked pores.* 用热水清洗堵塞的毛孔。

pork /pɔːk/ *uncountable noun* 不可数名词
meat from a pig 猪肉: *He said he didn't eat pork.* 他说他不吃猪肉。

porridge /ˈpɒrɪdʒ/ *uncountable noun* 不可数名词
a thick food made by cooking oats (= a type of grain) in water or milk 麦片粥

port /pɔːt/ *countable noun* 可数名词
1 a town by the sea where ships arrive and leave 港口城市; 港市: *We stopped at the Mediterranean port of Marseilles.* 我们在地中海港口城市马赛停了一下来。
2 a place on a computer where you can attach another piece of equipment (计算机的) 端口: *The scanner plugs into the printer port of your computer.* 扫描仪可连接到计算机的打印机端口。

portable /ˈpɔːtəbəl/ *adjective* 形容词
designed to be carried or moved around 便携式的; 轻便的: *The iPod can be used as a portable storage device for all types of file.* *iPod 可以用作各种文件的便携式储存设备。

porter /ˈpɔːtə/ *countable noun* 可数名词
a person whose job is to carry things, for example, people's luggage 搬运工; 行李工: *Our taxi arrived at the station and a porter came to the door.* 我们的出租车抵达车站后，一名行李工来到门口。

portion /ˈpɔːʃən/ *countable noun* 可数名词
1 a part of something 部分: *Only a small portion of the castle was damaged.* 城堡仅有一小部分受损。□ *I have spent a large portion of my life here.* 我在这里度过了生

命中很长的一段时光。
2 the amount of food that is given to one person at a meal (食物的)一份: *The portions were huge.* 每份餐都是超大份儿。

portrait /ˈpɔːtrət/ *countable noun* 可数名词
a painting, drawing or photograph of a particular person 肖像；画像: *The wall was covered with family portraits.* 墙上挂满了家庭成员的画像。
→ Look at picture on P13 参见彩插第 13 页

pose¹ /pəʊz/ *verb* 动词 (**poses, posing, posed**)
1 to stay in one position so that someone can photograph you or paint you 摆姿势；摆造型: *The six foreign ministers posed for photographs.* 6 位外交部长摆好姿势合影。
2 to ask a question (*formal* 正式) 提出(问题): *I finally posed the question, 'Why?'* 我最后问道: "为什么?"

pose² /pəʊz/ *countable noun* 可数名词
a position that you stay in when someone is photographing you or painting you (供人拍照或作画的)姿势，造型: *We tried various poses.* 我们试摆了各种造型。

posh /pɒʃ/ *adjective* 形容词 (**posher, poshest**)
fashionable and expensive (*informal* 非正式) 时髦的；豪华的: *We stayed one night in a posh hotel.* 我们在豪华酒店住了一晚。

position /pəˈzɪʃən/ *countable noun* 可数名词
1 the place where someone or something is 位置；方位: *Measure and mark the position of the handle on the door.* 测量并标出把手在门上的位置。
2 the way you are sitting, lying or standing 姿势；姿态: *Mr Horwood raised himself to a sitting position.* 霍伍德先生坐起身来。
3 a job in a company or an organization (*formal* 正式) 职位；职务: *He left a career in teaching to take a position with IBM.* 他辞去教学工作到 IBM 任职。
4 the situation you are in at a particular time 处境；状况；形势: *He's going to be in a very difficult position if things go badly.* 如果事情进展不顺，他将陷入十分艰难的境地。□ *The club's financial position is still uncertain.* 这家俱乐部的财政状况尚不明确。

positive /ˈpɒzətɪv/ *adjective* 形容词
1 hopeful and confident 积极的；乐观的: *Be positive about your future.* 要对自己的未来充满信心。
▶ **positively** /ˈpɒzətɪvli/ *adverb* 副词: *You really must try to start thinking positively.* 你真该努力以积极的心态去思考问题了。
2 pleasant and helpful 愉悦的；有益的: *I want to have a positive effect on my children's lives.* 我希望能给孩子们的生活带来积极影响。
3 completely sure about something 确信的；肯定的: *'Judith's never late. Are you sure she said eight?' — 'Positive.'* "朱迪丝从不迟到。你确定她说的是 8 点到?" —— "我确定。"
4 showing that something has happened or is present in a medical or scientific test (化验或试验结果)阳性的: *If the test is positive, treatment will start immediately.* 如果化验结果呈阳性，将立即开始治疗。
5 higher than zero. Compare with **negative**. (数字)正的(比较 **negative**)

possess /pəˈzes/ *verb* 动词 (**possesses, possessing, possessed**)
to have or own something 拥有；占有: *They sold everything they possessed to raise the money.* 他们卖掉所拥有的一切来筹这笔钱。

possession /pəˈzeʃən/ *noun* 名词
1 *uncountable* 不可数 the state of having or owning something (*formal* 正式) 拥有；占有: *He was found in possession of stolen goods.* 他被发现持有偷盗的赃物。
2 [**possessions**] *plural* 复数 the things that you own or have with you at a particular time 财产；财物: *People have lost their homes and all their possessions.* 人们失去了自己的家园和所有财产。

possessive /pəˈzesɪv/ *adjective* 形容词
used for describing a word such as 'my' or 'his' that shows who or what something belongs to 所有格的

possibility /ˌpɒsɪˈbɪlɪti/ *countable noun* 可数名词 (**possibilities**)
a situation when something might happen 可能；可能性: *There is a possibility that they jailed the wrong man.* 他们有可能拘留错了人。

possible /ˈpɒsɪbəl/ *adjective* 形容词
1 able to be done 做得到的；能实现的: *If it is possible to find out where your brother is, we will.* 如果能找出你兄弟在哪儿，我们就会去找。□ *Anything is possible if you want it enough.* 只要有足够的信念，任何事情都是有可能的。
2 used for describing a situation where

something might be true, although you do not know for sure 可能的；也许的: *It is possible that he's telling the truth.* 他说的可能是实情。
as soon as possible as soon as you can 尽快: *Please make your decision as soon as possible.* 请尽快作决定。

possibly /ˈpɒsɪbli/ *adverb* 副词
1 used when you are not sure if something is true or if it will happen 可能；也许: *Exercise will possibly protect against heart attacks.* 锻炼或许能预防心脏病。
2 used for saying that something is possible 尽量；尽可能: *They've done everything they can possibly think of.* 凡是能想到的，他们都去做了。 *I can't possibly answer that!* 我无论如何也回答不了那个问题！

post¹ /pəʊst/ *verb* 动词 (**posts, posting, posted**)
1 (*American* 美国英语: **mail**) to send a letter or a parcel somewhere by post 邮寄；寄出: *I posted a letter to Stanley.* 我给斯坦利寄了一封信。 *I'm posting you a cheque.* 我会给你寄一张支票。
2 to put something on a wall so that everyone can see it 张贴；贴出: *Officials began posting warning notices.* 官员们开始张贴警示公告。
3 to put information on a website so that other people can see it (在网站上) 公布，发布: *The statement was posted on the Internet.* 那则声明发布在网上了。

post² /pəʊst/ *noun* 名词
1 (*American* 美国英语: **mail**) *singular* 单数 the system that collects and delivers letters and packages 邮政；邮寄；邮递: *The cheque is in the post.* 支票已寄出。 *The winner will be informed by post.* 获胜者将以邮件形式通知。
2 (*American* 美国英语: **mail**) *uncountable* 不可数 letters and packages that you send or receive 邮件；邮包: *There has been no post for three weeks.* 已经3周没有邮件了。
3 *countable* 可数 an important job in an organization (*formal* 正式) 要职: *She accepted the post of the director's assistant.* 她接受了经理助理的职位。
4 *countable* 可数 a strong piece of wood or metal that is set into the ground 柱；杆；桩: *The car went through a red light and hit a fence post.* 那辆车闯红灯，撞到了栅栏桩上。

5 *countable* 可数 something such as a message or picture that you put on a website so that other people can see it (网站上的) 帖子: *He apologized in a Facebook post.* 他在脸书上发贴子道歉。

postage /ˈpəʊstɪdʒ/ *uncountable noun* 不可数名词
the money that you pay for sending post 邮资；邮费: *All prices include postage.* 全部价格均含邮费。

postbox /ˈpəʊstbɒks/ also 亦作 **post box** *countable noun* 可数名词 (**postboxes**) (*American* 美国英语: **mailbox**)
a box in the street where you put letters that you want to send 邮箱；邮筒

postcard /ˈpəʊstkɑːd/ also 亦作 **post card** *countable noun* 可数名词
a thin card, often with a picture on one side, that you can write on and post to someone without using an envelope 明信片

postcode /ˈpəʊstkəʊd/ also 亦作 **post code** *countable noun* 可数名词 (*American* 美国英语: **zip code**)
a short series of numbers and letters at the end of an address 邮政编码；邮编

poster /ˈpəʊstə/ *countable noun* 可数名词
a large notice or picture that you stick on a wall 海报；招贴画: *I saw a poster for the jazz festival in Monterey.* 我看到了蒙特雷爵士音乐节的海报。

postman /ˈpəʊstmən/ *countable noun* 可数名词 (**postmen** /ˈpəʊstmən/)
a man who collects and delivers letters and packages 邮递员；邮差

ˈpost ˌoffice *countable noun* 可数名词
a building where you can buy stamps and send post 邮局: *She needed to get to the post office before it closed.* 她得在邮局关门前到达。

postpone /pəʊsˈpəʊn/ *verb* 动词 (**postpones, postponing, postponed**)
to arrange for an event to happen at a later time 推迟；推延: *He decided to postpone the trip until the following day.* 他决定将出行推延至第二天。

pot /pɒt/ *noun* 名词
1 *countable* 可数 a deep round container used for cooking food 锅: *The shelf is full of metal cooking pots.* 搁板上摆满了烹饪用的金属锅。
2 a round container that is used for a

particular purpose 壶；罐；桶：*She asked him to pass the coffee pot.* 她让他把咖啡壶递过来。 □ *a pot of paint* 一桶油漆

potato /pəˈteɪtəʊ/ *noun* 名词 (**potatoes**)
a hard, round, white vegetable with brown or red skin. Potatoes grow under the ground. 马铃薯；土豆
→ Look at picture on P5 参见彩插第 5 页

poˈtato ˌchip *countable noun* 可数名词 (*American* 美国英语)
→ see 见 **crisp**

potential¹ /pəˈtenʃəl/ *adjective* 形容词
used for saying that someone or something could become a particular type of person or thing 潜在的；可能的：*The company has identified 60 potential customers.* 这家公司找到了 60 位潜在客户。 □ *We are aware of the potential problems.* 我们意识到了潜在的问题。
▶ **potentially** /pəˈtenʃəli/ *adverb* 副词：*This is a potentially dangerous situation.* 这一局势存在潜在的危险。

potential² /pəˈtenʃəl/ *uncountable noun* 不可数名词
the possibility that someone or something could become successful or useful in the future 潜能；潜力；潜质：*The boy has great potential.* 这个男孩非常有潜质。

pottery /ˈpɒtəri/ *uncountable noun* 不可数名词
pots, dishes and other objects made from a special type of earth (= clay) 陶器：*The shop sells a fine range of pottery.* 这家商店出售各种上等陶器。
→ Look at picture on P13 参见彩插第 13 页

poultry /ˈpəʊltri/ *plural noun* 复数名词
birds that people keep for their eggs and meat, such as chickens 家禽

pounce /paʊns/ *verb* 动词 (**pounces, pouncing, pounced**)
to suddenly jump on someone or something 猛扑；突袭：*He pounced on the photographer and knocked him to the ground.* 他猛地扑向摄影师，将其打倒在地。

pound /paʊnd/ *countable noun* 可数名词
1 a unit of weight that is used in the U.S., Britain and some other countries. One pound is equal to around 0.454 kilograms. 磅（美国、英国等国重量单位，1 磅 ≈ 0.454 千克）：*Her weight was under ninety pounds.* 她的体重不足 90 磅。 □ *a pound of cheese* *1 磅干酪

2 the unit of money (£) that is used in the U.K. 英镑（英国货币单位，符号为 £）

pour /pɔː/ *verb* 动词 (**pours, pouring, poured**)
1 to make a liquid or other substance flow out of a container 倾倒；倒出：*She poured some water into a bowl.* 她往碗里倒了些水。 □ *She asked Tillie to pour her a cup of coffee.* 她让蒂莉给她倒杯咖啡。

pour 倒出

2 to flow somewhere quickly and in large amounts 涌流：*Blood was pouring from his broken nose.* 血从他受伤的鼻子里涌了出来。 □ *Tears poured down our faces.* 我们泪流满面。
3 to rain very heavily （雨）倾泻，倾盆而下：*It was still pouring outside.* 外面依然下着大雨。

poverty /ˈpɒvəti/ *uncountable noun* 不可数名词
the state of being very poor 贫穷；贫困：*Many of these people are living in poverty.* 这些人中有不少还生活在贫困之中。

powder /ˈpaʊdə/ *uncountable noun* 不可数名词
a fine dry dust 粉末：*Put a small amount of the powder into a container and mix with water.* 将少许粉末放入容器，加水混合。 □ *cocoa powder* 可可粉

power /ˈpaʊə/ *noun* 名词
1 *uncountable* 不可数 control over people 控制力；影响力：*When children are young, parents still have a lot of power.* 孩子年幼时，父母仍在很多方面说了算。
2 *uncountable* 不可数 your ability to do something 能力；本领：*She has the power to charm anyone.* 她能迷住任何人。
3 *countable* 可数 the legal right to do something 权力；职权：*The police have the power to arrest people who carry knives.* 警方有权拘捕持刀者。

4 *uncountable* 不可数 the physical strength of something, or the ability that it has to affect things 力量；威力：*This vehicle has more power and better brakes.* 这辆车动力更足、刹车更好。
5 *uncountable* 不可数 energy that can be used for making electricity or for making machines work 能源；能量：*Nuclear power is cleaner than coal.* 核能比煤清洁。□ *The storm left a million homes without electrical power.* 那场风暴造成 100 万户家庭断电。
6 *countable* 可数 used in maths for talking about the number of times that you multiply a number by itself. For example, '5 to the power of 5' means '5x5x5x5x5'. （数学中的）幂，乘方
in power in charge of a country or an organization 执政的；掌权的：*Amin was in power for eight years.* 阿明曾经执政 8 年。

powerful /ˈpaʊəfʊl/ *adjective* 形容词
1 able to control people and events 有控制力的；有影响力的：*You're a powerful man — people will listen to you.* 你是有影响力的人——大家会听你的。□ *Russia and India are two large, powerful countries.* 俄罗斯和印度是两个强大的大国。
2 physically strong 强壮的；强健的：*He lifts weights to maintain his powerful muscles.* 他通过举重保持肌肉强健。
3 very strong or having a strong effect 强烈的；强效的：*We need more and more powerful computer systems.* 我们需要功能日益强大的计算机系统。□ *There was a powerful smell of petrol in the car.* 汽车里有股浓浓的汽油味。
4 loud 响亮的；洪亮的：*Mrs Jones's powerful voice interrupted them.* 琼斯夫人洪亮的嗓音打断了他们。

powerless /ˈpaʊələs/ *adjective* 形容词
unable to do anything to control a situation 无控制力的；无影响力的：*If you don't have money, you're powerless.* 没钱寸步难行。□ *Security guards were powerless to stop the crowd.* 保安无力阻止人群。

'power line *countable noun* 可数名词
a cable, especially above ground, along which electricity travels to an area or building（尤指地面之上的）电力线，输电线

practical /ˈpræktɪkəl/ *adjective* 形容词
1 involving real situations and events, rather than ideas and theories 实际的；实践的：*Our system is the most practical way of preventing crime.* 我们的系统是预防犯罪最切实可行的方式。
2 sensible and able to deal effectively with problems 明智的；务实的：*We need a practical person to take care of the details.* 我们需要一个务实之人来处理细枝末节。□ *You were always so practical, Maria.* 玛丽亚，你以前一向很注重实效。
3 useful rather than just being fashionable or attractive 实用的：*We'll need plenty of lightweight, practical clothes.* 我们将需要大量轻便实用的衣服。

practically /ˈpræktɪkəli/ *adverb* 副词
almost 几乎；简直：*He's known the old man practically all his life.* 他几乎打记事起就认识这个老人。

practice /ˈpræktɪs/ *noun* 名词
1 *countable* 可数 something that people do regularly 惯例；常规：*They campaign against the practice of using animals for experiments.* 他们发起运动抗议用动物做实验的惯例。
2 *uncountable* 不可数 the act of doing something regularly in order to be able to do it better 练习；训练：*It takes a lot of practice to become a good musician.* 多下功夫练习才能成为一名优秀的音乐家。

practise /ˈpræktɪs/ *verb* 动词 (**practises, practising, practised**)
to do something regularly in order to do it better 练习；训练：*She practised the piano in the school basement.* 她在学校的地下室里练习钢琴。□ *Keep practising, and maybe next time you'll do better.* 坚持练习，也许下次你就能做得更好。

praise /preɪz/ *verb* 动词 (**praises, praising, praised**)
to say that you admire or respect someone or something for something they have done 表扬；称赞；赞扬：*The passengers praised John for saving their lives.* 乘客们赞扬约翰救了他们的性命。
● **praise** *uncountable noun* 不可数名词：*The ladies are full of praise for the staff.* 女士们高度赞扬工作人员。

pram /præm/ *countable noun* 可数名词
a small bed with four wheels, used for pushing a baby around when you go out 婴儿车

prawn /prɔːn/ *countable noun* 可数名词
(*American* 美国英语：**shrimp**)
a small sea animal with ten legs which

becomes pink when you cook it 对虾；明虾

pray /preɪ/ *verb* 动词 (**prays, praying, prayed**)
1 to speak to God or a god 祈祷；祷告：*We pray that Billy's family will now find peace.* 我们祈祷比利的家人现在能找到安宁。
2 to hope very much that something will happen 祈求；祈望：*I'm praying for good weather.* 我祈求有个好天气。□ *I'm praying that someone will do something before it's too late.* 我祈求有人能在还来得及的时候做点什么。

prayer /preə/ *noun* 名词
1 *countable* 可数 the words that a person says when they speak to God or a god 祷词；祷文：*They should say a prayer for the people on both sides.* 他们应该为双方人民祈祷。
2 *uncountable* 不可数 the activity of speaking to God or a god 祈祷；祷告：*The monks give their lives to prayer.* 僧侣们终其一生，坚持祷告。

precaution /prɪˈkɔːʃən/ *countable noun* 可数名词
an action that is intended to prevent something bad from happening 预防措施：*Just as a precaution, he should move to a safe place.* 为了以防万一，他应该搬到安全的地方。

precede /prɪˈsiːd/ *verb* 动词 (**precedes, preceding, preceded**)
to happen before something else (*formal* 正式) 发生在…之前；先于：*In English, adjectives usually precede the noun they describe.* 在英语中，形容词通常放在所修饰的名词之前。

precious /ˈpreʃəs/ *adjective* 形容词
1 rare and worth a lot of money 珍贵的；宝贵的：*The company mines precious metals throughout North America.* 这家公司在整个北美洲开采贵重金属。
2 important to you; that you do not want to lose 珍爱的；珍视的：*Her family's support is particularly precious to Josie.* 家人的支持对乔茜来说尤为可贵。

precise /prɪˈsaɪs/ *adjective* 形容词
exact and accurate in all details 精确的；准确的：*I can remember the precise moment when I heard the news.* 我能清楚地记得我听到消息时的那一刻。

precisely /prɪˈsaɪsli/ *adverb* 副词
accurately and exactly 准确地；精确地：

Nobody knows precisely how many people are still living there. 没有人确切知道还有多少人住在那里。

precision /prɪˈsɪʒən/ *uncountable noun* 不可数名词
when someone does something exactly as it should be done 准确；精确：*He hits the ball with precision.* 他击球精准。

predator /ˈpredətə/ *countable noun* 可数名词
an animal that kills and eats other animals 捕食者；捕食性动物：*With no natural predators on the island, the animals lived happily.* 岛上没有天敌，动物们快乐地生活着。

predict /prɪˈdɪkt/ *verb* 动词 (**predicts, predicting, predicted**)
to say that an event will happen 预言；预测：*The old man correctly predicted the results of fifteen matches.* 老人准确预言了 15 场比赛的结果。
▶ **prediction** /prɪˈdɪkʃən/ *noun* 名词：*My prediction is that the process will take about 5 years.* 我预测这个过程将需要 5 年左右的时间。

predictable /prɪˈdɪktəbəl/ *adjective* 形容词
that can be predicted 可预测的；可预见的：*This was a predictable reaction.* 这个反应在意料之中。

preface /ˈprefɪs/ *countable noun* 可数名词
an introduction at the beginning of a book（图书的）序言：*Have you read the preface to Kelman's novel?* 你看过克尔曼那本小说的序言吗？

prefer /prɪˈfɜː/ *verb* 动词 (**prefers, preferring, preferred**)
to like someone or something better than another person or thing 偏爱；更喜欢：*Does he prefer a particular type of music?* 他偏爱某一种音乐吗？ □ *I preferred books to TV.* 我更喜欢读书而不是看电视。□ *He would prefer to be in Philadelphia.* 他更喜欢待在费城。

LANGUAGE HELP 语言提示
Expressions such as **like...better** and **would rather** are used more often than **prefer**. *like...better 和 would rather 这类表述比 prefer 更常用。Instead of saying 不说 *I prefer football to tennis*, you can say 而说：*I like football better than tennis.*（比起网球，我更喜欢足球。）Instead of saying 不说 *I'd prefer an apple*,

you can say 而说: *I'd rather have an apple.*（我更想吃个苹果。）Instead of saying 不说 *I'd prefer to walk,* you can say 而说: *I'd rather walk.*（我更愿意步行。）

preferable /ˈprefrəbəl/ *adjective* 形容词
better or more suitable than something else 更好的；更合适的；更可取的: *For me, a trip to the supermarket is preferable to buying food on the Internet.* 对我来说，在网上买食品不如去超市。
▶ **preferably** /ˈprefrəbli/ *adverb* 副词: *Get exercise, preferably in the fresh air.* 做运动，最好在空气清新的地方。

preference /ˈprefərəns/ *noun* 名词
a feeling that you would like to have or do one thing rather than something else 偏爱；喜好: *Customers have shown a preference for salty snacks.* 顾客们表现出了对咸味小吃的偏爱。

prefix /ˈpriːfɪks/ *countable noun* 可数名词 (**prefixes**)
a letter or group of letters that is added to the beginning of a word in order to form a different word. For example, the prefix 'un-' is added to 'happy' to form 'unhappy'. Compare with **suffix**. 前缀（比较 suffix）

pregnant /ˈpregnənt/ *adjective* 形容词
having a baby or babies developing in your body 怀孕的；妊娠的: *I'm seven months pregnant.* 我怀孕 7 个月了。
▶ **pregnancy** /ˈpregnənsi/ *noun* 名词 (**pregnancies**): *We keep a record of your weight gain during pregnancy.* 我们记录你怀孕期间的增重情况。

prejudice /ˈpredʒʊdɪs/ *noun* 名词
an unreasonable dislike of a particular group of people or things 偏见: *These people have always suffered from racial prejudice.* 这些人一直遭受着种族偏见。
□ *There seems to be some prejudice against workers over 45.* *45 岁以上的工人似乎遭受着一些偏见。

prejudiced /ˈpredʒʊdɪst/ *adjective* 形容词
having an unreasonable dislike of someone from a different group 有偏见的: *They complained that the police were racially prejudiced.* 他们投诉警方存在种族偏见。

preliminary /prɪˈlɪmɪnri/ *adjective* 形容词
taking place at the beginning of an event, often as a form of preparation 初步的；预

备的: *Preliminary results show the Republican Party with 11 per cent of the vote.* 初步结果显示共和党得票率为 11%。

premature /ˌpreməˈtʃʊə/ *adjective* 形容词
1 happening earlier than people expect 过早的；超前的；提前的: *Heart disease is a common cause of premature death.* 心脏病是早逝的一个常见原因。
2 born before the expected date 早产的: *Even very young premature babies respond to their mother's presence.* 甚至连非常小的早产儿都对母亲的存在有反应。

preparation /ˌprepəˈreɪʃən/ *noun* 名词
1 *uncountable* 不可数 the process of getting something ready for use 准备；预备: *Todd put the papers in his briefcase in preparation for the meeting.* 托德把文件放进公文包，准备赴会。
2 [**preparations**] *plural* 复数 all the arrangements that are made for a future event 准备工作；筹备工作: *We were making preparations for our wedding.* 我们在筹备婚礼。

prepare /prɪˈpeə/ *verb* 动词 (**prepares, preparing, prepared**)
1 to make something ready 把…准备好；把…预备好: *We will need several weeks to prepare the report for publication.* 我们将需要数周的时间把要发布的报告准备好。
2 to get ready for an event 筹备；(为…)做准备: *You should begin to prepare for the cost of your child's education.* 你们应该开始准备孩子的教育费用了。
3 to get food ready 准备（食物）；做（饭菜）: *She started preparing dinner.* 她开始准备晚餐。

prepared /prɪˈpeəd/ *adjective* 形容词
1 willing to do something if necessary（如有必要）愿意的: *Are you prepared to help if we need you?* 我们需要你的话你愿意帮忙吗？
2 ready for something that you think is going to happen 准备好的；有准备的: *Police are prepared for large crowds.* 警方为大规模人群聚集做好了准备。

preposition /ˌprepəˈzɪʃən/ *countable noun* 可数名词
a word such as 'by', 'for', 'into' or 'with' that usually comes before a noun 介词

prescribe /prɪˈskraɪb/ *verb* 动词 (**prescribes, prescribing, prescribed**)
to tell someone what medicine or

prepositions 介词

across 横过

She is walking across the road.
她正穿过公路。

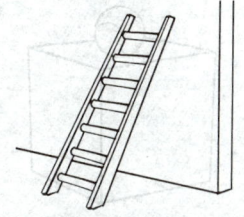

against 倚靠

The ladder is leaning against the wall. 梯子倚在墙上。

along 沿着

He is walking along the road.
他正沿着路走。

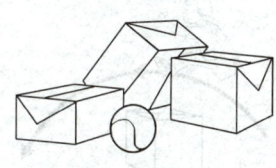

among 在…中间

The ball is among the boxes.
球在几个箱子中间。

behind 在…后面

The boy is behind the box.
男孩儿在箱子后面。

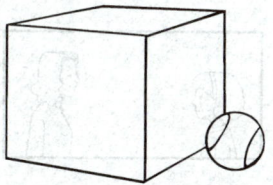

beside 在…旁边

The ball is beside the box.
球在箱子旁边。

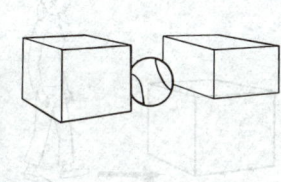

between 在(两者)之间

The ball is between the boxes.
球在两个箱子中间。

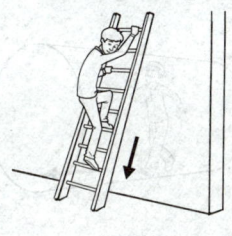

down 从…上下来

He is climbing down the ladder.
他正从梯子上下来。

near 靠近 **far away** 远离

He is near the road.
他在路旁边。
She is far away from him.
她离他很远。

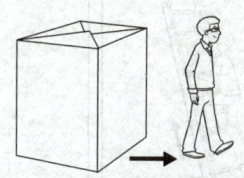

from 从…起始

He is walking away from the box. 他从箱子边走开。

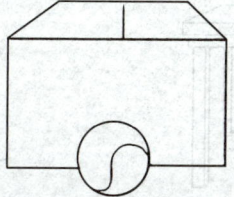

in front of 在…前面

The ball is in front of the box.
球在箱子前面。

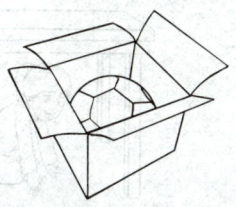

inside 在…里面

The ball is inside the box.
球在箱子里面。

prepositions

prepositions 介词

into 到…里面

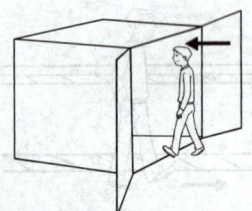

He is walking into the box.
他正往箱子里走。

on 在…上面

The ball is on the box.
球在箱子上面。

on top of 在…顶上

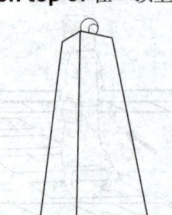

The ball is on top of the box.
球在箱子顶上。

opposite 在…对面

They are opposite each other.
她俩面对面。

out of 从…中出来

She is jumping out of the box.
她正跳出箱子。

over 越过

He is jumping over the box.
他正跳过箱子。

round 绕着

She is running round the box.
她正绕着箱子跑。

through 穿过

He is walking through the tunnel. 他正穿行在隧道之中。

towards 向;朝

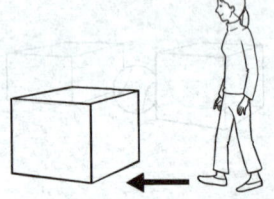

She is walking towards the box. 她正朝箱子走去。

under 在…下面

She is under the table.
她在桌子下面。

up 沿…向上

He is climbing up the ladder.
他正在爬梯子。

treatment to have 开(药、处方): *The doctor examines the patient and prescribes medication.* 大夫检查患者后开药。

prescription /prɪˈskrɪpʃən/ *countable noun* 可数名词
a piece of paper on which a doctor writes an order for medicine 处方；药方: *He gave me a prescription for some cream.* 他给我开了些药膏。

presence /ˈprezəns/ *singular noun* 单数名词
the fact that someone is in a place 在场；出席: *His presence always causes trouble.* 他的出现总会惹出事端。
in someone's presence in the same place as someone 当着某人的面；在某人在场的情况下: *Children should do their homework in the presence of their parents.* 孩子做家庭作业时应有家长在场。

present¹ /ˈprezənt/ *adjective* 形容词
1 at an event or in a place 在场的；出席的: *Nine people were present at the meeting.* 9人出席了会议。
2 existing now 现存的；现有的；目前的: *The present situation is very difficult for us.* 当前局势对我们非常不利。
at present now 目前；现在: *At present, we do not know the cause of the disease.* 眼下，我们不清楚病因。

present² /ˈprezənt/ *countable noun* 可数名词
something that you give to someone, for example, on their birthday 礼物；礼品: *She bought a birthday present for her mother.* 她给母亲买了一份生日礼物。

present³ /prɪˈzent/ *verb* 动词 (**presents, presenting, presented**)
to formally give something to someone 颁发；授予；呈递: *The mayor presented him with a gold medal.* 市长授予他一枚金质奖章。 □ *Betty will present the prizes to the winners.* 贝蒂将为优胜者颁奖。

presentation /ˌprezənˈteɪʃən/ *noun* 名词
1 *countable* 可数 an event at which someone is given an award 颁奖仪式；颁奖典礼: *He received his award at a presentation in Oxford.* 他在牛津的颁奖典礼上领了奖。
2 *countable* 可数 an occasion when someone shows or explains something to a group of people 展示；演示；报告: *Philip and I gave a short presentation.* 我和菲利普做了简短的展示。
3 *uncountable* 不可数 when an award is formally given to someone 颁发；授予: *The evening began with the presentation of awards.* 当晚先是颁发了各个奖项。

present continuous *singular noun* 单数名词
the structure that uses 'be' and the '-ing' form of a verb. An example of the present continuous is 'He is walking down the road'. (动词的)现在进行时

present perfect *singular noun* 单数名词
the form of a verb that you use to talk about things that began in the past and are still happening or still important in the present. The present perfect is formed with the verb 'have' and a past participle (= a verb form that ends in '-ed' for regular verbs). An example of the present perfect is 'She has promised to come'. (动词的)现在完成式

present tense *countable noun* 可数名词
the form of a verb that is used for talking about things that exist, things that are happening now or things that happen regularly (动词的)一般现在式

preservative /prɪˈzɜːvətɪv/ *noun* 名词
a chemical that keeps something in good condition 防腐剂: *The list shows all the preservatives used in food processing.* 清单列明了食品加工过程中使用的所有防腐剂。

preserve /prɪˈzɜːv/ *verb* 动词 (**preserves, preserving, preserved**)
1 to take action to save something or protect it 保护；维护: *We need to preserve the forest.* 我们得保护森林。
▶ **preservation** /ˌprezəˈveɪʃən/ *uncountable noun* 不可数名词: *We're collecting money for the preservation of our historic buildings.* 我们在筹钱保护历史建筑。
2 to treat food in order to make it last longer 保存(食物): *Use only enough sugar to preserve the plums.* 用足量的糖保存李子就够了。

preside /prɪˈzaɪd/ *verb* 动词 (**presides, presiding, presided**)
to be in charge of a meeting 主持(会议): *He presided over the weekly meetings of the organization.* 他主持了该组织的每周例会。

presidency /ˈprezɪdənsi/ *countable noun* 可数名词 (**presidencies**)
the position of being the president of a country or an organization 总统(或主席)

president – prevent

职位；总裁职位：*He was offered the presidency of the University of Saskatchewan.* 他被邀请担任萨斯喀彻温大学校长一职。

president /ˈprezɪdənt/ *noun* 名词
1 the person who is in charge of a country that has no king or queen 总统；主席：*The president must act quickly.* 总统必须从速行动。
→ Look at picture on P10 参见彩插第 10 页
2 *countable* 可数 the person who has the highest position in an organization（组织的）总裁，负责人：*He is the national president of the Screen Actors Guild.* 他是美国演员工会主席。
▶ **presidential** /ˌprezɪˈdenʃəl/ *adjective* 形容词：*He is reporting on Peru's presidential election.* 他在报道秘鲁总统大选。

press¹ /pres/ *verb* 动词 (**presses, pressing, pressed**)
1 to push something firmly against something else 压；挤；按；捺：*He pressed his back against the door.* 他后背抵在门上。
2 to push a button or a switch with your finger in order to make a machine work 按（按钮或开关）：*David pressed a button and the door closed.* 戴维按了个按钮，门关上了。
3 to push hard against something with your foot or hand 踩；用力按：*He pressed the accelerator hard.* 他狠踩了油门。
4 to iron clothes 熨烫（衣服）：*Vera pressed his shirt.* 薇拉把他的衬衫熨了。

press² /pres/ *uncountable noun* 不可数名词 newspapers and magazines, and the people who write for them 报刊；报界；新闻界：*She gave several interviews to the local press.* 她接受了当地报刊的几次采访。

pressure /ˈpreʃə/ *uncountable noun* 不可数名词
1 force that you produce when you press hard on something 压力：*The pressure of his fingers on her arm relaxed.* 他手指按在她胳膊上的力度减轻了。
2 force produced by the gas or liquid in a place or a container（气体、液体的）压力，压强：*If the pressure falls in the cabin, an oxygen mask will drop in front of you.* 舱内气压下降的话，氧气面罩会垂至你面前。
3 a situation where you feel that you must do a lot of things or make an important decision in very little time（时间紧张造成的）压力：*Can you work under pressure?* 你能在压力下工作吗？

presumably /prɪˈzjuːməbli/ *adverb* 副词 probably 大概；很可能：*He's not going this year, presumably because of his age.* 他今年不去，大概是因为年纪。

presume /prɪˈzjuːm/ *verb* 动词 (**presumes, presuming, presumed**) to think that something is true, although you are not sure 觉得；猜测；推测：*I presume that you're here on business.* 我觉得你是来这里出差。 □ *'Has he been home all week?' — 'I presume so.'* "他一周都待在家里？" ——"我猜是吧。"

pretend /prɪˈtend/ *verb* 动词 (**pretends, pretending, pretended**)
1 to try to make people believe that something is true, although in fact it is not 假装；伪装；装作：*I pretend that things are really okay when they're not.* 情况不好时我假装一点事儿也没有。 □ *He pretended to be asleep.* 他假装睡着了。
2 to imagine that you are doing something, for example, as part of a game 想象；设想；假装：*She can sunbathe and pretend she's in Cancun.* 她会晒晒太阳，想象自己在坎昆。

pretty /ˈprɪti/ *adjective* 形容词, *adverb* 副词 (**prettier, prettiest**)
1 attractive and pleasant 美丽的；漂亮的：*She's a very charming and pretty girl.* 她是个非常迷人的漂亮女孩。 □ *We stayed in a very pretty little town.* 我们待在一个非常漂亮的小城。

LANGUAGE HELP 语言提示
See note at **beautiful**. 见 beautiful 的语言提示。

2 used before an adjective or adverb to mean 'fairly' (*informal* 非正式)（用于形容词或副词前）颇，很，相当：*I had a pretty good idea what she was going to do.* 我很清楚她会怎么做。

prevent /prɪˈvent/ *verb* 动词 (**prevents, preventing, prevented**) to make sure that something does not happen 阻止；防止；妨碍；预防：*The best way to prevent injury is to wear a seat belt.* 防止受伤的最好办法是系好安全带。 □ *The disease can prevent you from walking properly.* 这种病会妨碍正常行走。
▶ **prevention** /prɪˈvenʃən/ *uncountable noun* 不可数名词：*Scientists are still learning about the prevention of heart disease.* 科学

家仍在研究预防心脏病的方法。

previous /ˈpriːviəs/ *adjective* 形容词
used for describing something that happened or existed before something else 先前的；以前的；早先的：She has a teenage daughter from a previous marriage. 她和前夫有一个十几岁的女儿。
▶ **previously** /ˈpriːviəsli/ *adverb* 副词：The railways were previously owned by private companies. 铁路先前归属私有公司。

prey /preɪ/ *uncountable noun* 不可数名词
the birds or other animals that an animal hunts and eats in order to live 猎物；被食者；捕获物：These animals can hunt prey in the water or in trees. 这些动物可以入水或上树捕食猎物。

price /praɪs/ *countable noun* 可数名词
the amount of money that you have to pay in order to buy something 价格；价钱：We have seen huge changes in the price of gas. 我们经历了燃气价格天翻地覆的变化。
☐ They expect house prices to rise. 他们预计房价会上涨。

priceless /ˈpraɪsləs/ *adjective* 形容词
1 worth a very large amount of money 无价的；极贵重的：Several priceless treasures were stolen from the museum last night. 昨夜博物馆有数件无价珍宝失窃。
2 extremely useful or valuable 极有用的；极有价值的：Our national parks are priceless treasures. 我们的国家公园是无价之宝。

prick /prɪk/ *verb* 动词 (pricks, pricking, pricked)
1 to make small holes in something with a sharp object 刺；戳；扎：Prick the potatoes and rub the skins with salt. 把土豆扎几下，用盐揉搓土豆皮。
2 to press into someone's skin and hurt them 刺，扎(人的皮肤)：It felt like a needle pricking me in the foot. 我觉得有个针头在扎我的脚。

pride /praɪd/ *uncountable noun* 不可数名词
1 a feeling of satisfaction that you have because you have done something well (因成就而产生的)自豪，得意，骄傲：We all felt the sense of pride when we finished early. 我们提前完成时，大家都觉得自豪。
☐ We take pride in offering you the highest standards. 我们为向您提供最高水准的服务而感到自豪。
2 a sense of dignity and self-respect 自尊：

His pride wouldn't allow him to ask for help. 他的自尊不允许他求助。

priest /priːst/ *countable noun* 可数名词
a person who has religious duties in a place where people worship 牧师；司祭；神父；司铎；教士：He trained to be a Catholic priest. 他受训成了天主教神父。

primarily /ˈpraɪmərɪli/ *adverb* 副词
mainly 主要地；根本地：These reports come primarily from passengers on the plane. 这些报告主要来自机上乘客。

primary /ˈpraɪməri/ *adjective* 形容词
1 most important (*formal* 正式) 首要的；主要的；最重要的：Language difficulties were the primary cause of his problems. 语言困难是他遭遇问题的主因。
2 relating to the first few years of formal education for children (教育)初等的，基础的，小学的：Most primary students now have experience with computers. 现在大多数小学生都有计算机操作经验。

primary colour *countable noun* 可数名词
one of the three colours (red, yellow and blue) that can be mixed together to produce other colours 原色(指红、黄、蓝三种基本颜色之一)：The toys come in bright primary colours that kids will love. 这些玩具使用的都是孩子们会喜欢的亮丽原色。

primary school *countable noun* 可数名词
a school for children between the ages of 4 or 5 and 11 小学：She's in her third year at Greenside Primary School. 她在格林塞德小学上3年级。

prime minister /ˌpraɪm ˈmɪnɪstə/ *countable noun* 可数名词
the leader of the government in some countries 首相；总理
→ Look at picture on P10 参见彩插第 10 页

primitive /ˈprɪmɪtɪv/ *adjective* 形容词
1 belonging to a society in which people live in a very simple way, usually without industries or a writing system (社会等)原始的，未开化的：He has travelled the world, visiting many primitive societies. 他周游世界，造访过许多原始社会。
2 belonging to a very early period in the development of an animal or a plant (动植物)原始的：primitive man 原始人
3 very simple in style 简陋的；非常简朴的：The conditions in the camp are primitive. 营内条件很简陋。

prince /prɪns/ *noun* 名词
a male member of a royal family, especially the son of the king or queen 王子（指王室男性成员，尤指国王或女王之子）

princess /ˌprɪnˈses, ˈprɪnses/ *noun* 名词 (**princesses**)
a female member of a royal family, usually the daughter of a king or queen or the wife of a prince 公主（指王室女性成员，通常指国王或女王之女）；王妃

principal¹ /ˈprɪnsəpəl/ *adjective* 形容词
first in order of importance 首要的；最重要的：*Money was not the principal reason for his action.* 钱不是他那么做的首要原因。□ *Newspapers were the principal source of information.* 报纸是最重要的信息源。

principal² /ˈprɪnsəpəl/ *countable noun* 可数名词
the person in charge of a school, college or university 校长：*Donald King is the principal of Dartmouth High School.* 唐纳德·金是达特茅斯高中的校长。

principle /ˈprɪnsəpəl/ *noun* 名词
1 [**principles**] *plural* 复数 rules or ideas that you have about how you should behave（个人的）行为准则，道德原则：*It's against my principles to be dishonest.* 骗人有违我的做人原则。
2 *countable* 可数 a rule about how something works or happens（某事物运行或发生的）原则，原理：*The first principle of democracy is that people should have the right to vote.* 民主的第一条原则就是人民应有选举权。

print¹ /prɪnt/ *verb* 动词 (**prints, printing, printed**)
1 to use a machine to put words or pictures on paper 打印；印刷：*The publishers have printed 40,000 copies of the novel.* 这部小说出版商已经印刷了4万册。
2 to write in letters that are not joined together 用印刷体书写（笔画之间无连笔）：*Please sign here, then print your name and address.* 请在这里签名，然后用印刷体写上您的姓名、地址。

print something out to use a machine to produce a copy of a computer file on paper 打印（计算机文件）：*I printed out a copy of the letter and put it on Mr Miller's desk.* 我把信打印了一份，放到了米勒先生的案头。

print² /prɪnt/ *uncountable noun* 不可数名词
all the letters and numbers in a printed document 印刷字体；印出的字：*I can't read this — the print is too small.* 我看不了这个——字太小了。

printer /ˈprɪntə/ *countable noun* 可数名词
1 a machine for printing copies of computer documents on paper 打印机
→ Look at picture on P11 参见彩插第11页
2 a person or a company whose job is printing things such as books 印刷工；印刷厂；印刷公司：*Franklin was a printer, a publisher and a diplomat.* 富兰克林是印刷工、出版商和外交家。

printout /ˈprɪntaʊt/ *also* 亦作 **print-out** *countable noun* 可数名词
a piece of paper with information from a computer printed on it（计算机）打印件：*Maria gave me a printout of the email.* 玛丽亚给了我一份电子邮件打印件。

prior /ˈpraɪə/ *adjective* 形容词
prior to something happening before a particular time or event (*formal* 正式) 在（特定时间或事件）之前：*Prior to his trip to Japan, Steven was in New York.* 日本之行之前，史蒂文身在纽约。

priority /praɪˈɒrɪti/ *countable noun* 可数名词 (**priorities**)
the most important thing, that you have to deal with before everything else 优先事项；最重要的事：*Her children are her first priority.* 孩子是她的头等大事。□ *The government's priority is to build more schools.* 政府的当务之急是增建学校。

give priority to someone/something to treat someone or something as more important than anyone or anything else 优先考虑某人/某事物；给予某人/某事物优先权：*The government should give priority to environmental issues.* 政府应该优先考虑环境问题。

take priority or **have priority** to be more important than other things 优先：*The needs of the poor must take priority over the desires of the rich.* 穷人的需求必须优先于富人的欲望。

prison /ˈprɪzən/ *noun* 名词
a building where criminals are kept as punishment 监狱；监牢：*He was sent to prison for five years.* 他被关押了5年。

prisoner /ˈprɪzənə/ *countable noun* 可数名词
a person who is not free, usually because

they are in prison 囚犯；犯人；战俘：*A prisoner escaped from Holloway Prison early on Monday.* 星期一早上有一名犯人从霍洛韦监狱逃走。□ *More than 30,000 Australians were taken prisoner in World War II.* 二战中 3 万多名澳大利亚人沦为战俘。

privacy /ˈprɪvəsi/ *uncountable noun* 不可数名词
the freedom to do things without people knowing what you are doing 隐私：*We have changed the names to protect the privacy of the people involved.* 我们使用了化名，以保护当事人隐私。

private /ˈpraɪvɪt/ *adjective* 形容词
1 not owned by the government 私有的；私营的；私立的；民办的：*a private hospital* 私人医院 □ *Their children go to a private school.* 他们的子女就读于一所私立学校。
2 only for one particular person or group, and not for everyone 私密的；私下的：*It was a private conversation, so I'm not going to talk about it to anyone else.* 这是私密谈话，所以我不会跟其他任何人谈起。
▶ **privately** /ˈpraɪvɪtli/ *adverb* 副词：*We need to talk privately.* 我们需要私下聊聊。
3 concerning your personal relationships and activities, and not your job 个人的；私人的：*I've always kept my private and professional life separate.* 我始终把私生活和工作分开。
4 quiet, where you can be alone without being disturbed 僻静的；无人打扰的：*It was the only private place they could find.* 这是他们找得到的唯一一个僻静场所。
in private without other people being there 私下里：*Mark asked to talk to his boss in private.* 马克要求和老板私下谈。

privilege /ˈprɪvɪlɪdʒ/ *countable noun* 可数名词
a special advantage that only one person or group has 特殊待遇；特权：*We are not asking for special privileges, we simply want equal opportunity.* 我们不要特权，只想要平等机会。

privileged /ˈprɪvɪlɪdʒd/ *adjective* 形容词
having an advantage that most other people do not have, often because you are rich（常因富有而）享受特殊待遇的，有特权的：*They had a privileged childhood.* 他们的童年过着锦衣玉食的生活。

prize /praɪz/ *countable noun* 可数名词
money or a special object that you give to the person who wins a game, a race or a competition 奖金；奖品；奖赏：*He won first prize in the golf tournament.* 他获得了高尔夫球锦标赛的一等奖。

probability /ˌprɒbəˈbɪlɪti/ *noun* 名词 (**probabilities**)
how likely something is to happen 概率；可能性：*We believe there is a high probability of success.* 我们相信成功的概率很高。

probable /ˈprɒbəbəl/ *adjective* 形容词
likely to be true or likely to happen 可能的；也许的：*Jess is a great player, and it's highly probable that she will win.* 杰丝是个伟大的选手，她极可能会赢。

probably /ˈprɒbəbli/ *adverb* 副词
likely to be true or to happen, although you are not sure 可能；也许；大概：*I will probably go home on Tuesday.* 我周二可能会回家。□ *Van Gogh is probably the best-known painter in the world.* 凡高可能是世界上最著名的画家。

problem /ˈprɒbləm/ *countable noun* 可数名词
1 something or someone that causes difficulties, or that makes you worry 问题；难题；麻烦：*Pollution is a problem in this city.* 污染是这个城市的一个问题。□ *The government has failed to solve the problem of unemployment.* 政府未能解决失业问题。
2 a special type of question that you have to think hard about in order to answer（须认真思考作答的）题，问题：*a maths problem* 数学题

procedure /prəˈsiːdʒə/ *noun* 名词
the usual or correct way of doing something 步骤；规程；程序；做法：*If your car is stolen, the correct procedure is to report the theft to the local police.* 汽车被盗后，正确做法是向当地警方报案。

proceed /prəˈsiːd/ *verb* 动词 (**proceeds, proceeding, proceeded**)
1 to do something after doing something else 接着做；接下来做：*He picked up a book, which he proceeded to read.* 他拿起一本书，接着读了起来。
2 to continue (*formal* 正式) 继续做；继续进行：*The building work is proceeding very slowly.* 建造工作进展非常缓慢。

process /ˈprəʊses/ *countable noun* 可数名词 (**processes**)
a series of actions that have a particular

result 过程；进程：*After the war, the population began the long process of returning to normal life.* 战后，人们开始了回归正常生活的漫长历程。

procession /prəˈseʃən/ *countable noun* 可数名词
a line of people or vehicles that follow one another as part of a ceremony（人或车辆的）队列，队伍：*Sam watched the procession pass him slowly on its way to the palace.* 萨姆看着队伍缓缓从他身旁经过走向王宫。

processor /ˈprəʊsesə/ *countable noun* 可数名词
the part of a computer that performs the tasks that the user has requested（计算机的）处理器

produce[1] /prəˈdjuːs/ *verb* 动词 (**produces, producing, produced**)
1 to make or grow something 生产；产出：*The company produces about 2.3 million tons of steel a year.* 公司每年产钢约 230 万吨。
▶ **producer** /prəˈdjuːsə/ *countable noun* 可数名词：*It is clear which country is the world's leading oil producer.* 人们都清楚谁是世界头号产油国。
2 to cause something to happen 引起；造成；产生：*The talks failed to produce results.* 会谈未能谈出结果。
3 to organize a play or a film, and decide how it should be made 制作（戏剧或电影）：*The film was produced and directed by Johnny White.* 本片由约翰尼·怀特制作并执导。
▶ **producer** /prəˈdjuːsə/ *countable noun* 可数名词：*The film was created by producer Alison Millar.* 该影片由制片人艾利森·米勒制作。

produce[2] /ˈprɒdjuːs/ *uncountable noun* 不可数名词
food that you grow on a farm to sell 农产品：*The restaurant uses as much local produce as possible.* 饭店尽可能使用本地农产品。

product /ˈprɒdʌkt/ *countable noun* 可数名词
something that you make or grow in order to sell it 产品；制品：*This mobile phone is one of the company's most successful products.* 这款手机是公司最成功的产品之一。

production /prəˈdʌkʃən/ *noun* 名词
1 *uncountable* 不可数 the process of making or growing something in large amounts, or the amount of goods that you make or grow 生产；产量：*This car went into production last year.* 这款汽车去年投入生产。□ *The factory needs to increase production.* 工厂需要提高产量。
2 *countable* 可数 a play or other show that is performed in a theatre（剧院上演的）戏剧，节目：*Tonight our class is going to see a production of 'Othello'.* 今晚我们班要去看剧目《奥赛罗》。

productive /prəˈdʌktɪv/ *adjective* 形容词
producing or doing a lot 多产的；高产的：*Training makes workers more productive.* 培训能提高工人的生产力。

profession /prəˈfeʃən/ *countable noun* 可数名词
a type of job for which you need special education or training（需要专门教育或培训的）职业：*Ava was a doctor by profession.* 阿娃的职业是医生。

professional[1] /prəˈfeʃənəl/ *adjective* 形容词
1 relating to a person's work, especially work that requires special training 职业的；专业的：*Get professional advice from your accountant first.* 先听取一下会计师的专业意见。
2 doing a particular activity as a job rather than just for enjoyment 职业性的；专业的；非业余的：*My parents were professional musicians.* 我父母是职业音乐人。
▶ **professionally** /prəˈfeʃənəli/ *adverb* 副词：*I've been singing professionally for 10 years.* 我当职业歌手已经 10 年了。

professional[2] /prəˈfeʃənəl/ *countable noun* 可数名词
someone who does an activity as a job, rather than just for enjoyment 职业人士；非业余人士：*The competition is open to both professionals and amateurs.* 此次比赛职业人士、业余人员均可参加。

professor /prəˈfesə/ *countable noun* 可数名词
a senior teacher at a university 教授：*Kate is a professor of history at Oxford University.* 凯特是牛津大学历史学教授。

profile /ˈprəʊfaɪl/ *countable noun* 可数名词
1 the shape of your face when people see it from the side 侧面像；侧脸轮廓：*He was slim, with black hair and a handsome profile.* 他身材瘦长，黑头发，侧脸帅气。
2 a part of a social media website where

someone posts their name, picture, and personal information (社交媒体上的)人物简介: *It says on her profile that she likes travelling.* 她简介里说自己喜欢旅行。

profit /ˈprɒfɪt/ *noun* 名词
the amount of money that you gain when you sell something for more than you paid for it 利润; 盈利: *When he sold the house, Chris made a profit of about £50,000.* 克里斯卖掉房子后获利约5万英镑。

profitable /ˈprɒfɪtəbəl/ *adjective* 形容词
making a profit 赢利的; 有利润的: *The business started to be profitable in its second year.* 企业第二年开始赢利。

program¹ /ˈprəʊɡræm/ *countable noun* 可数名词
a set of instructions that a computer uses to do a particular task (计算机的)程序: *Ada Lovelace wrote the world's first computer program in 1842.* 1842年，埃达·洛夫莱斯编写了世界上第一款计算机程序。

program² /ˈprəʊɡræm/ *verb* 动词 (programs, programming, programmed)
to give a computer or a machine a set of instructions so that it can do a particular task 给(计算机等)编写程序: *They can teach you how to program a computer in two weeks.* 他们能在两周内教会你怎么给计算机编程。

▶ **programming** /ˈprəʊɡræmɪŋ/ *uncountable noun* 不可数名词: *Java is a popular programming language.* *Java是一种流行的编程语言。

▶ **programmer** /ˈprəʊɡræmə/ *countable noun* 可数名词: *Greg works as a computer programmer.* 格雷格是计算机程序员。

programme /ˈprəʊɡræm/ *countable noun* 可数名词
1 a plan of things to do 计划; 规划; 方案: *The art gallery's education programme includes art classes for all ages.* 该美术馆的教育规划包括针对各年龄段的美术课程。
2 a television or radio show (电视或广播)节目: *a network television programme* 网络电视节目
3 a small book or sheet of paper that tells you about a play or concert (戏剧或音乐会的)节目单: *When you go to concerts, it's helpful to read the programme.* 去听音乐会时，不妨看一下节目单。

progress¹ /ˈprəʊɡres/ *uncountable noun* 不可数名词

the process of gradually improving or getting nearer to achieving something 进步; 进展: *We are making progress in the fight against cancer.* 我们在抗癌斗争中不断进步。

progress² /prəˈɡres/ *verb* 动词 (progresses, progressing, progressed)
1 to improve or become more advanced or successful 进步; 提高; 取得进展: *All our students are progressing well.* 我们所有学生都逐渐取得不错的进步。
2 to continue to happen over a period of time 继续进行: *As the evening progressed, Leila grew tired.* 夜色渐深，利拉渐渐生倦意。
in progress having started and still happening 在进行中: *The game was already in progress when we arrived.* 我们到场时，比赛已经开始了。

prohibit /prəˈhɪbɪt/ *verb* 动词 (prohibits, prohibiting, prohibited)
to officially say that something is illegal (*formal* 正式) 禁止: *Smoking is prohibited here.* 此处禁止吸烟。

project¹ /ˈprɒdʒekt/ *countable noun* 可数名词
1 a plan that takes a lot of time and effort 项目; 工程; 计划: *The charity is funding a housing project in India.* 该慈善机构正在资助印度的一个住房项目。
2 a piece of work that involves a student finding out a lot of information about a subject and then writing about it (学生的)课题, 研究项目: *Our class has just finished a project on ancient Greece.* 我们班刚刚完成了一个古希腊课题。

projector /prəˈdʒektə/ *countable noun* 可数名词
a machine that shows films or pictures on a screen or a wall 投影仪
→ Look at picture on P1 参见彩插第1页

prologue /ˈprəʊlɒɡ/ *countable noun* 可数名词
a part of a play, book or film that introduces the story 序言; 序幕; 开场白: *She first appears in the prologue to the novel.* 她第一次出现是在小说序言中。

prolong /prəˈlɒŋ/ *verb* 动词 (prolongs, prolonging, prolonged)
to make something last longer 延长; 拖长; 拉长: *I did not wish to prolong the conversation.* 我不想拖长谈话。

prominent /ˈprɒmɪnənt/ *adjective* 形容词
1 important and well-known 显要的; 卓越的; 杰出的: *Michelle is married to a*

prominent lawyer in Portland. 米歇尔嫁给了波特兰一位赫赫有名的律师。
2 big; that can be seen very easily 大的；显眼的；显著的: *a prominent nose* 大鼻子

promise /ˈprɒmɪs/ *verb* 动词 (**promises, promising, promised**)
to say that you will certainly do something 承诺；许诺；保证；答应: *She promised to write to me soon.* 她答应很快就给我写信。 □ *I promise that I'll help you all I can.* 我答应尽力帮你。 □ *Promise me you'll come to the party.* 答应我来参加聚会。 ● **promise** *countable noun* 可数名词: *If you make a promise, you should keep it.* 许了诺，就要信守。 □ *James broke every promise he made.* 詹姆斯说话从来就不算话。

promote /prəˈməʊt/ *verb* 动词 (**promotes, promoting, promoted**)
1 to help to make something successful 促进；推动；推广: *There will be a new TV campaign to promote the products.* 为了推广产品，会有新一轮电视宣传。
2 to give someone a more important job in the same organization 晋升；提拔；擢升: *Richard has just been promoted to general manager.* 理查德刚刚被提拔为总经理。
▶ **promotion** /prəˈməʊʃn/ *noun* 名词: *We went out for dinner to celebrate Dad's promotion.* 我们下馆子庆祝爸爸升职。

prompt /prɒmpt/ *adjective* 形容词
done quickly 即刻的；立即的；迅速的: *These questions require prompt answers from the government.* 这些问题需要政府马上解决。

promptly /ˈprɒmptli/ *adverb* 副词
1 immediately 立即；马上；即刻: *Grandma sat down, and promptly fell asleep.* 奶奶坐下后马上就睡着了。
2 at exactly a particular time 正好；准时: *Promptly at seven o'clock, we left the hotel.* 7 点整，我们离开宾馆。

pronoun /ˈprəʊnaʊn/ *countable noun* 可数名词
a word that you use instead of a noun when you are talking about someone or something. 'It', 'she', 'something' and 'myself' are pronouns. 代词

pronounce /prəˈnaʊns/ *verb* 动词 (**pronounces, pronouncing, pronounced**)
to make the sound of a word 发出（单词）的音；读；念: *Have I pronounced your name correctly?* 你的名字我念对了吗？

pronunciation /prəˌnʌnsiˈeɪʃn/ *noun* 名词

the way that you say a word 发音；读法: *We are learning about the differences between Canadian and American pronunciation.* 我们正在学习加拿大人和美国人在发音上的差异。

proof /pruːf/ *uncountable noun* 不可数名词
something that shows that something else is true or exists 证明；证据: *The scientists hope to find proof that there is water on Mars.* 科学家希望找到火星上有水的证据。

propaganda /ˌprɒpəˈɡændə/ *uncountable noun* 不可数名词
information that a political organization uses in order to influence people（政治组织的）宣传: *The media began a huge propaganda campaign.* 媒体发起了一场声势浩大的宣传攻势。

propeller /prəˈpelə/ *countable noun* 可数名词
a part of a boat or an aircraft that turns around very fast and makes the boat or the aircraft move（船或航空器的）推进器；螺旋桨: *One of the ship's propellers was damaged in the accident.* 这艘船有一个螺旋桨在事故中损坏了。

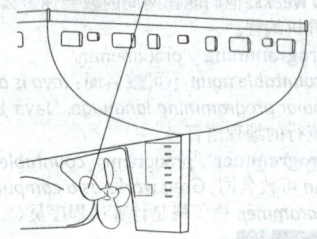

propeller 螺旋桨

proper /ˈprɒpə/ *adjective* 形容词
1 real (*informal* 非正式) 真正的；正当的；正经的: *He hasn't got a proper job.* 他没有正经工作。
2 correct or most suitable 正确的；最合适的: *The book is intended as a guide to proper behaviour.* 这本书意在指导人如何做到举止得体。

proper noun *countable noun* 可数名词
(also 亦作 **proper name**) the name of a particular person, place, organization or thing. Proper nouns begin with a capital letter. 专有名词

property /ˈprɒpəti/ *noun* 名词 (**properties**)
1 *uncountable* 不可数 anything that

belongs to you (*formal* 正式) 所有物；财物：*'That's my property. You can't just take it.'* "那是我的财物。你不能随便拿走。"
2 a building and the land around it (*formal* 正式) 物业；房地产：*Get out of here — this is a private property!* 出去——这里是私人物业！

proportion /prəˈpɔːʃən/ *noun* 名词
1 *countable* 可数 a part of an amount (*formal* 正式)（数量的）部分：*A large proportion of the fish in that area have died.* 那片水域的鱼有一大部分死了。
2 *countable* 可数 the number of one type of person or thing in a group compared to the total number of people or things in the group 比例：*The proportion of the population using mobile phones is 90-95%.* 手机用户在人口中的比例为 90% 至 95%。
3 *uncountable* 不可数 the correct relationship between the size of objects in a piece of art（艺术作品中物体的）匀称，均衡：*the symmetry and proportion of classical Greek and Roman architecture* 古希腊和古罗马建筑的对称和均衡

proposal /prəˈpəʊzəl/ *countable noun* 可数名词
1 a suggestion or a plan 提议；建议；方案：*The president has announced new proposals for a peace agreement.* 总统已经宣布了新的和平协议方案。
2 the act of asking someone to marry you 求婚：*Pam accepted Matt's proposal of marriage.* 帕姆答应了马特的求婚。

propose /prəˈpəʊz/ *verb* 动词 (**proposes, proposing, proposed**)
1 to suggest a plan or an idea 提议；建议；提出：*The minister has proposed a change in the law.* 部长提议修改法律。
2 to ask someone to marry you 求婚：*David proposed to his girlfriend when they were on holiday in Paris.* 戴维和女友在巴黎度假时向她求了婚。

prose /prəʊz/ *uncountable noun* 不可数名词 ordinary written language, not poetry 散文（与诗相对）：*Hannah writes both poetry and prose.* 汉娜既作诗，也写散文。

prosecute /ˈprɒsɪˌkjuːt/ *verb* 动词 (**prosecutes, prosecuting, prosecuted**)
to say formally in a law court that a person has committed a crime 起诉；控诉；对…提起公诉：*The man was prosecuted for a killing at a petrol station in Birmingham.* 这名男子被控在伯明翰一加油站杀死一人。
▶**prosecution** /ˌprɒsɪˈkjuːʃən/ *noun* 名词：*This evidence led to the prosecution of the former leader.* 这项证据导致前任领导人被起诉。

protect /prəˈtekt/ *verb* 动词 (**protects, protecting, protected**)
to keep someone or something safe from harm or damage 保护；防护：*Make sure you protect your children from the sun's harmful rays.* 务必做好防护，让孩子们免受太阳有害射线伤害。

protection /prəˈtekʃən/ *noun* 名词
something that stops you from being harmed or damaged by something unpleasant 保护；防护：*Long-sleeved T-shirts offer greater protection against the sun.* 长袖 T 恤遮阳效果更佳。

protective /prəˈtektɪv/ *adjective* 形容词
1 intended to protect you from injury or harm 保护的；防护的：*You should wear protective gloves when you are gardening.* 做园艺时应该戴上防护手套。
2 looking after someone and trying to keep them safe 呵护的；有保护欲的：*Ben is very protective toward his mother.* 本对母亲呵护备至。

protein /ˈprəʊtiːn/ *noun* 名词
a substance that the body needs which is found in meat, eggs, fish and milk 蛋白质：*Fish is a major source of protein.* 鱼肉是主要的蛋白质来源。

protest[1] /prəˈtest/ *verb* 动词 (**protests, protesting, protested**)
to say or show publicly that you do not approve of something 抗议；公开反对：*The students were protesting against the arrest of one of their teachers.* 学生们抗议他们有位老师被捕。
▶**protester** /prəˈtestə/ *countable noun* 可数名词：*The protesters say that the government is corrupt.* 抗议者称政府腐败。

protest[2] /ˈprəʊtest/ *noun* 名词
the act of showing publicly that you do not approve of something 抗议：*I took part in a protest against the war.* 我参加了一场反战抗议活动。

Protestant /ˈprɒtɪstənt/ *countable noun* 可数名词
a Christian (= a person who believes that Jesus Christ is the son of God) who is not a Catholic (= a member of the part of the

Christian church whose leader is known as the Pope) 新教教徒

protractor /prə'træktə/ *countable noun* 可数名词
a flat piece of plastic or metal in the shape of a half-circle, used for measuring angles 量角器；角度尺；分度器
→ Look at picture on P1 参见彩插第 1 页

proud /praʊd/ *adjective* 形容词 (**prouder, proudest**)
1 pleased and satisfied about something good that you or other people close to you have done 引以为荣的；自豪的：*His dad was very proud of him.* 他爸爸为他感到非常骄傲。
▶ **proudly** /'praʊdli/ *adverb* 副词：*Nick wears his police uniform proudly.* 尼克骄傲地穿着警服。
2 thinking that you are better or more important than other people 自大的；骄傲的；傲慢的：*He described his boss as 'proud and selfish'.* 他说自己老板"自负又自私"。

prove /pruːv/ *verb* 动词 (**proves, proving, proved**)
to show that something is true 证明；证实：*These results prove that we were right.* 这些结果证明我们是对的。

proverb /'prɒvɜːb/ *countable noun* 可数名词
a short sentence that people often say, because it gives advice or tells you something about life 谚语：*An old Arab proverb says, 'The enemy of my enemy is my friend.'* 一则古老的阿拉伯谚语说："敌人的敌人是朋友。"

provide /prə'vaɪd/ *verb* 动词 (**provides, providing, provided**)
to give something to someone that they need or want 提供；供给；给予：*The company's website provides lots of useful information.* 公司网站提供大量有用信息。 ▫ *The refugees were provided with food and accommodation.* 难民得到了食宿供应。

provided /prə'vaɪdɪd/ *conjunction* 连词
used for saying that something will happen only if a second thing also happens 如果；假如；只要：*He can go running at his age, provided that he is sensible.* 他这个年纪可以跑步，只要能量力而为。

providing /prə'vaɪdɪŋ/ *conjunction* 连词
→ see 见 **provided**

province /'prɒvɪns/ *countable noun* 可数名词
a large part of a country that has its own local government 省；省份：*the Canadian province of British Columbia* 加拿大不列颠哥伦比亚省

provision /prə'vɪʒən/ *uncountable noun* 不可数名词
the act of giving something to people who need or want it 提供；供应；供给：*This department is responsible for the provision of legal services.* 这个部门负责提供法律服务。

provisional /prə'vɪʒənəl/ *adjective* 形容词
used for describing something that has been arranged or exists now, but that may be changed in the future 临时的；暂时的：*Your provisional driving licence is valid for 18 months.* 你的临时驾照有效期是 18 个月。
▶ **provisionally** /prə'vɪʒənəli/ *adverb* 副词：*She provisionally accepted the job offer.* 她暂时接受了这个岗位。

provoke /prə'vəʊk/ *verb* 动词 (**provokes, provoking, provoked**)
to deliberately annoy someone and try to make them angry 挑衅；挑拨；刺激：*The demonstrators did not provoke the police and everyone remained calm.* 示威者没有挑衅警察，大家都很克制。

prune /pruːn/ *countable noun* 可数名词
a dried plum 洋李脯；梅干

P.S. /ˌpiː 'es/ also 亦作 **PS**
written when you add something at the end of a letter after you have signed it (用于信末签名后) 附言，又及：*P.S. Please show your friends this letter.* 又及：请以此信示汝诸友。

psychiatrist /saɪ'kaɪətrɪst/ *countable noun* 可数名词
a doctor who takes care of people who have illnesses of the mind 精神病医师：*When Sarah was 16, a psychiatrist treated her for depression.* 萨拉 16 岁那年，有位精神病医师给她看过抑郁症。

psychological /ˌsaɪkə'lɒdʒɪkəl/ *adjective* 形容词
concerned with a person's mind and thoughts 心理的：*Guilt can lead to psychological illness.* 内疚可以导致心理疾病。

psychology /saɪ'kɒlədʒi/ *uncountable noun* 不可数名词
the study of the human mind and the

reasons for people's behaviour 心理学: Scott is a professor of educational psychology at Sussex University. 斯科特是萨塞克斯大学教育心理学教授。
▶ **psychologist** /saɪˈkɒlədʒɪst/ *countable noun* 可数名词: Amy is seeing a psychologist. 埃米正在接受心理咨询。

pub /pʌb/ *countable noun* 可数名词
a building where people can buy and drink alcoholic drinks 酒吧；酒馆

public[1] /ˈpʌblɪk/ *noun* 名词
the public people in general, or everyone 公众；大众；民众: The exhibition is open to the public from tomorrow. 此次展览自明日起向公众开放。
in public when other people are there 当众；公开: He hasn't performed in public in more than 40 years. 他有 40 多年没公开演出了。

public[2] /ˈpʌblɪk/ *adjective* 形容词
1 relating to all the people in a country or a community 公众的；大众的；民众的: The government's policies still have strong public support. 政府政策仍得到公众大力支持。
2 for everyone to use 公共的；公用的: The city's public library was built in 1911. 该市的公共图书馆建于 1911 年。 ▫ The government has promised to improve public services such as schools and post offices. 政府承诺改善学校、邮局等公共服务。▫ public transport 公共交通

publication /ˌpʌblɪˈkeɪʃən/ *noun* 名词
1 *uncountable* 不可数 the act of printing a book or a magazine and sending it to shops to be sold 出版: The shop stayed open late to celebrate the book's publication. 该店营业至深夜，以庆祝此书出版。
2 *countable* 可数 a book or a magazine 出版物；书刊: My uncle has written for several publications. 我叔叔给几家杂志写过稿。

publicity /pʌˈblɪsɪti/ *uncountable noun* 不可数名词
when people are provided with information about a person or a product 宣传；报道: A lot of publicity was given to the talks. 这次会谈得到了广泛报道。

publicize /ˈpʌblɪsaɪz/ *verb* 动词
(**publicizes**, **publicizing**, **publicized**)
to let people know about something 宣传；报道: The author appeared on television to publicize her latest book. 作者上电视宣传她的新书。

ˌpublic ˈschool *countable noun* 可数名词
in Britain, a school for students aged between 13 and 18 which parents have to pay for. The students often live at the school while they are studying.（英国的）公学，私立寄宿制中学

publish /ˈpʌblɪʃ/ *verb* 动词 (**publishes**, **publishing**, **published**)
to prepare and print copies of a book, a magazine or a newspaper 出版: HarperCollins will publish his new novel on March 4. 哈珀·柯林斯公司将于 3 月 4 日出版他的新小说。

publisher /ˈpʌblɪʃə/ *countable noun* 可数名词
a person or a company that publishes books, newspapers or magazines 出版商；出版社；出版人: She sent the book to a publisher and got a positive response. 她把书稿寄给一家出版社，得到了积极回应。

pudding /ˈpʊdɪŋ/ *noun* 名词
1 a sweet dish that you eat at the end of a meal（餐后）甜点: There's fruit salad and ice cream for pudding. 甜点有水果沙拉和冰激凌。
2 a cooked sweet food like a warm cake, made with flour, fat and eggs 布丁: a Christmas pudding 圣诞布丁

puddle /ˈpʌdəl/ *countable noun* 可数名词
a small pool of water on the ground 小水坑；水洼: Young children love splashing in puddles. 小孩子喜欢在水洼里踩水。

puddle 水洼

puff[1] /pʌf/ *countable noun* 可数名词
a small amount of air or smoke that is blown from somewhere（气或烟的）缕，小股: Puffs of steam rose into the air and

vanished. 缕缕蒸汽升腾到空中消散了。

puff[2] /pʌf/ *verb* 动词 (**puffs, puffing, puffed**)
to breathe loudly and quickly, usually because you have been running（通常因奔跑而）气喘吁吁: *He puffs and pants if he has to walk up the stairs.* 如果他必须爬楼梯的话，会呼哧呼哧直喘。

pull /pʊl/ *verb* 动词 (**pulls, pulling, pulled**)
to hold something firmly and use force to move it 拉；拔；拖；拽: *The dentist had to pull out all Grandpa's teeth.* 牙医只好拔光了爷爷的牙。 □ *I helped to pull the boy out of the water.* 我帮忙把男孩儿从水里拉上来。 □ *Someone pulled her hair.* 有人揪她头发。
→ Look at picture on P6 参见彩插第 6 页
● **pull** *countable noun* 可数名词: *He felt a pull on the fishing line.* 他感到钓丝被扯了一下。

pull away when a vehicle pulls away, it starts moving forwards（车辆）启动，开始驶离: *I watched the car pull away.* 我看着汽车开走。

pull in to stop a vehicle somewhere 停车: *The bus pulled in at the side of the road.* 公共汽车在路边停了下来。

pull into something to move a vehicle into a place and stop there 驶入某地停下: *David pulled into the driveway in front of her garage.* 戴维驶上车道停在了她家车库前面。

pull out to move a vehicle out into the road or nearer the centre of the road 开车上路；驶向路中央: *I looked in the rear mirror, and pulled out into the street.* 我看着后视镜，驶上街道。

pull over to move a vehicle closer to the side of the road and stop there 靠路边停车: *I pulled over to let the police car pass.* 我靠路边停下，让警车过去。

pull something down to deliberately destroy a building 拆掉，拆毁（建筑物）: *They pulled the offices down, leaving a large open space.* 他们拆掉办公室，腾出了一大块空地。

pull up to slow down a vehicle and stop 减速停车: *The taxi pulled up and the driver jumped out.* 出租车减速停了下来，司机跳出车外。

pull yourself together to control your feelings and be calm again 平静下来: '*Now stop crying and pull yourself together!*' "好了，别哭了，平静一下！"

pullover /ˈpʊləʊvə/ *countable noun* 可数名词
a warm piece of clothing that covers the upper part of your body and your arms 套衫；套头毛衣

pulse /pʌls/ *countable noun* 可数名词
the regular beat of your heart that you can feel when you touch your wrist and other parts of your body 脉搏: *Dr Garcia checked her pulse and breathing.* 加西亚大夫检查了她的脉搏和呼吸。

pump[1] /pʌmp/ *countable noun* 可数名词
a machine that makes a liquid or a gas flow in a particular direction 泵；气筒: *A pump brings water directly from the well.* 一台水泵直接从井里抽水。 □ *There are three water pumps in the village.* 村里有 3 台水泵。

pump[2] /pʌmp/ *verb* 动词 (**pumps, pumping, pumped**)
to make a liquid or a gas flow in a particular direction 泵；泵送；抽运: *The heart pumps blood around the body.* 心脏向全身泵血。

pump something up to fill something such as a tyre with air 给某物打气: *Pump all the tyres up well.* 把所有轮胎都打好气。

pumpkin /ˈpʌmpkɪn/ *noun* 名词
a large, round, orange vegetable with a thick skin 南瓜: *pumpkin pie* 南瓜馅饼

pun /pʌn/ *countable noun* 可数名词
a clever and amusing use of a word or phrase that has two meanings 双关

punch /pʌntʃ/ *verb* 动词 (**punches, punching, punched**)
1 to hit someone or something hard with your fist (= your hand, when your fingers are all closed tightly) 挥拳猛打: *During a concert, the singer punched a photographer.* 音乐会上，歌手挥拳打了一名摄影师。 ● **punch** *countable noun* 可数名词 (**punches**): *My brother gave me a punch in the nose.* 我弟弟一拳打在我鼻子上。
2 to make holes in something by pushing or pressing it with something sharp 穿，捅，戳（孔）: *I took a pen and punched a hole in the box.* 我拿笔在箱子上戳了个洞。

punctual /ˈpʌŋktʃuəl/ *adjective* 形容词
arriving somewhere at the right time 准时的；守时的: *He's always very punctual.* 他一向非常守时。
▶ **punctually** /ˈpʌŋktʃuəli/ *adverb* 副词:

The guests all arrived punctually, at eight o'clock. *8点客人都准时到场。

punctuation /ˌpʌŋktʃuˈeɪʃn/ *uncountable noun* 不可数名词
signs such as ( ), ! or ? that you use to divide writing into sentences and phrases 标点: You have to give more attention to punctuation and grammar. 你得在标点和语法上再上点心。

ˌpunctuˈation ˌmark *countable noun* 可数名词
a symbol such as ( ), ! or ? 标点符号

puncture /ˈpʌŋktʃə/ *countable noun* 可数名词
a small hole that has been made by a sharp object (利器造成的) 刺孔, 破洞: I repaired the puncture in my front tyre. 我补好了前胎的破洞。● **puncture** *verb* 动词 (**punctures, puncturing, punctured**): The bullet punctured his left lung. 子弹打穿了他的左肺。

puncture 破洞

punish /ˈpʌnɪʃ/ *verb* 动词 (**punishes, punishing, punished**)
to make someone suffer in some way because they have done something wrong 惩罚, 处罚 (犯错者): His parents punished him for being rude. 他父母因为他言行粗鲁惩罚了他。

punishment /ˈpʌnɪʃmənt/ *noun* 名词
a particular way of punishing someone 惩罚; 处罚: There will be tougher punishments for violent crimes. 对暴力犯罪将加重处罚力度。

pup /pʌp/ *countable noun* 可数名词
1 a young dog 狗崽; 小狗: We've had Pongo since he was a pup. 蓬戈还是狗崽的时候我们就养着了。
2 a baby of some other animals (其他某些动物的) 幼崽: grey seal pups 灰海豹幼崽

pupil /ˈpjuːpɪl/ *countable noun* 可数名词
1 one of the children who go to a school (小) 学生: Around 270 pupils attend this school. 约 270 名学生在该校就读。
→ Look at picture on P1 参见彩插第 1 页
2 the small, round, black hole in the centre of your eye 瞳孔: In low light the pupils are wide open to allow light into the eye. 光线微弱时, 瞳孔放大让光线进入眼睛。

puppet /ˈpʌpɪt/ *countable noun* 可数名词
a small model of a person or animal that you can move 木偶; 傀儡

puppy /ˈpʌpi/ *countable noun* 可数名词 (**puppies**)
a young dog 狗崽; 小狗

purchase¹ /ˈpɜːtʃɪs/ *verb* 动词 (**purchases, purchasing, purchased**)
to buy something (*formal* 正式) 购; 购买; 采购: He purchased a ticket for the concert. 他买了那场音乐会的门票。

purchase² /ˈpɜːtʃɪs/ *noun* 名词
1 *uncountable* 不可数 the act of buying something (*formal* 正式) 购; 购买; 采购: The Canadian company announced the purchase of 1,663 shops in the U.S. 这家加拿大公司宣布在美国收购 1,663 家零售店。
2 *countable* 可数 something that you buy (*formal* 正式) 购置物; 购入物: Her latest purchase is a shiny, black motorcycle. 她最近购买了一辆闪亮的黑色摩托。

pure /pjʊə/ *adjective* 形容词 (**purer, purest**)
1 not mixed with anything else 纯的; 纯粹的: I bought a carton of pure orange juice. 我买了一盒纯橙汁。
2 clean and not containing any harmful substances 纯净的; 洁净的; 不含有害物质的: The water is so pure that we drink it from the stream. 水特别干净, 我们直接喝了溪水。
3 complete and total 完全的; 全然的: There was a look of pure surprise on his face. 他一脸诧异。

purely /ˈpjʊəli/ *adverb* 副词
only or completely 纯粹; 完全: This car is designed purely for speed. 这款汽车完全是为追求速度设计的。

purple /ˈpɜːpəl/ *adjective* 形容词
a red-blue colour 紫色的: She wore a purple dress. 她穿了一条紫色连衣裙。
● **purple** *noun* 名词: I love the purples and greys of the Scottish mountains. 我喜欢苏

格兰山地深深浅浅的紫和浓淡不一的灰。
→ Look at picture on P13 参见彩插第 13 页

purpose /ˈpɜːpəs/ *countable noun* 可数名词
the reason why you do something 目的；意图：*The purpose of the occasion was to raise money for charity.* 本次活动的目的是募集善款。
on purpose not by accident 故意地；蓄意地；有意地：*I'm sure that Pedro hit me on purpose.* 我确信佩德罗是存心打我。

purr /pɜː/ *verb* 动词 (**purrs, purring, purred**)
when a cat purrs, it makes a low sound with its throat（猫）发出喵音，发出呼噜声：*The little black kitten purred and rubbed against my leg.* 小黑猫发出呼噜声，蹭了蹭我的腿。

purse /pɜːs/ *countable noun* 可数名词
1 a very small bag used for carrying money, especially by women（尤指女式）钱包，钱夹子：*a brown leather purse* 棕色皮夹子
2 (*American* 美国英语) → see 见 **handbag**

pursue /pəˈsjuː/ *verb* 动词 (**pursues, pursuing, pursued**)
to follow someone or something because you want to catch them (*formal* 正式) 追捕；追赶；追逐：*Police pursued the driver for two miles.* 警方追了那名司机两英里。

pursuit /pəˈsjuːt/ *uncountable noun* 不可数名词
when you are trying to get something 追求；追寻：*He has travelled the world in pursuit of his dream.* 他走遍世界追寻梦想。

push /pʊʃ/ *verb* 动词 (**pushes, pushing, pushed**)
1 to use force to make something move forward or away from you 推：*I pushed back my chair and stood up.* 我把椅子往后一推，站起身来。 □ *The men pushed him into the car and locked the door.* 几名男子把他推进汽车，锁上了车门。 □ *Justin put both hands on the door and pushed hard.* 贾斯廷双手放在门上使劲推。 ● **push** *countable noun* 可数名词 (**pushes**)：*Laura gave me a sharp push and I fell to the ground.* 劳拉猛推了我一下，我摔倒在地。
→ Look at picture on P6 参见彩插第 6 页
2 to press a button on a machine with your finger 按（按钮）：*Christina got inside the lift and pushed the button for the third floor.* 克里斯蒂娜走进电梯，按了四楼。

push 推

Justin put both hands on the door and pushed hard. 贾斯廷双手放在门上使劲推。

pushchair /ˈpʊʃtʃeə/ *countable noun* 可数名词
a small chair on wheels used for moving a young child around 婴儿推车

put /pʊt/ *verb* 动词 (**puts, putting, put**)
1 to move something into a particular place or position 放置：*Steven put the photograph on the desk.* 史蒂文把照片放到桌上。 □ *She put her hand on Grace's arm.* 她把手搭在格雷丝的胳膊上。 □ *Now, where did I put my purse?* 唉，我把钱包放哪儿了呢？
2 to cause someone or something to be in a particular state or situation 使处于特定状态（或境地）：*Your carelessness put the children in danger.* 你的疏忽陷孩子们于险境。
put someone through to connect someone on the telephone to the person they want to speak to 为某人接通电话：*Hold on, please. I'll just put you through.* 请稍等。我这就给您接通。
put something away to put something back in the place where it is usually kept 把某物放回原位；收起某物：*Kyle put the milk away in the fridge.* 凯尔把牛奶放回冰箱。
put something down to stop holding something and place it on a surface 放下某物：*The woman put down her newspaper and looked at me.* 那个女人放下报纸看着我。
put something off to delay doing something 推迟某事；拖延某事：*Tony always puts off making difficult decisions.* 遇到不好拿的主意，托尼总是放放再说。
put something on
1 to place clothing or make-up on your

body in order to wear it 穿上（衣服）；涂抹上（化妆品）：*Grandma put her coat on and went out.* 奶奶穿上大衣出去了。▫ *She put on lipstick and combed her hair.* 她涂上口红，梳了梳头。
2 to make a piece of electrical equipment start working 打开（电气设备）：*Maria sat up in bed and put on the light.* 玛丽亚从床上坐起来，打开灯。
3 to place a CD in a CD player and listen to it 播放（光碟）
put something out to make a fire stop burning 扑灭，熄灭（火）：*All day, firefighters have been trying to put out the blaze.* 整整一天，消防员一直在努力灭火。
put something up
1 to build a wall or a building 建造（墙或建筑物）：*The Smiths have put up electric fences on their farm.* 史密斯一家已经给农场架设了电围栏。
2 to attach a poster or a notice to a wall or board 张贴，张挂（海报、告示等）：*They're putting new street signs up.* 他们正在张贴新的街道标识。
put up with something to accept someone or something unpleasant without complaining 忍受某事物；容忍某事物：*I won't put up with your bad behaviour any longer.* 我不会再容忍你胡作非为了。▫ *It was a very bad injury, and he's put up with a lot of pain.* 伤势很重，他忍受了巨大的痛苦。

puzzle[1] /ˈpʌzəl/ ***verb*** 动词 (**puzzles, puzzling, puzzled**)
to leave you feeling confused because you do not understand something 使迷惑；使困惑：*My sister's behaviour puzzles me.* 妹妹的举动让我困惑不解。
▸ **puzzled** /ˈpʌzəld/ ***adjective*** 形容词：*Joshua was puzzled by her reaction to the news.* 她得知消息后的反应把乔舒亚搞糊涂了。
▸ **puzzling** /ˈpʌzəlɪŋ/ ***adjective*** 形容词：*Michael's comments are very puzzling.* 迈克尔的言论让人一头雾水。

puzzle[2] /ˈpʌzəl/ ***noun*** 名词
1 *countable* 可数 a question that is difficult to answer correctly, or a game or a toy that is difficult to put together properly 谜；难题；益智游戏；智力玩具：*Mum loves doing word puzzles.* 妈妈喜欢猜字谜。
2 *singular* 单数 someone or something that is hard to understand 谜一般的人（或事物）；令人费解的人（或事物）：*The rise in the number of accidents on the motorway remains a puzzle.* 高速公路事故数量上升仍然是个谜。

pyjamas /pəˈdʒɑːməz/ ***plural noun*** 复数名词
loose trousers and a top that people wear in bed 睡衣：*I don't usually get out of my pyjamas on Saturday mornings.* 星期六早晨我一般都不换下睡衣。

pyramid /ˈpɪrəmɪd/ ***countable noun*** 可数名词
a solid shape with a flat base and flat sides that form a point where they meet at the top 金字塔：*the Egyptian Pyramids* 埃及金字塔

python /ˈpaɪθən/ ***countable noun*** 可数名词
a type of large snake 蟒蛇

Qq

quack /kwæk/ *countable noun* 可数名词
the sound that a duck makes（鸭子的）嘎嘎声，呱呱声：*the quack of a duck* 鸭子的嘎嘎声 ● **quack** *verb* 动词 (**quacks, quacking, quacked**)：*There were ducks quacking on the lawn.* 草坪上有鸭子在嘎嘎叫。

qualification /ˌkwɒlɪfɪˈkeɪʃən/ *countable noun* 可数名词
an examination result or a skill that you need to be able to do something 资格；资历：*I believe I have all the qualifications to be a good teacher.* 我相信我具备成为一名好教师的所有条件。口 *All our workers have professional qualifications in engineering.* 我们所有人员都具有工程方面的专业资格。

qualified /ˈkwɒlɪfaɪd/ *adjective* 形容词
having the right skills or special training in a particular subject 具备相关资历的；合格的：*Blake is a qualified teacher.* 布莱克是一位有资历的教师。

qualify /ˈkwɒlɪfaɪ/ *verb* 动词 (**qualifies, qualifying, qualified**)
1 to be successful in one part of a competition so that you can go on to the next stage 取得（下一轮）比赛资格：*We qualified for the final by beating Stanford.* 我们打败了斯坦福大学，取得决赛资格。
2 to have the right to do or have something 使合格；使具备资格：*This course does not qualify you for a job in sales.* 修读本课程并不表示就有资格从事销售工作。
3 to finish your training for a particular job 具备资格；合格：*I qualified, and started teaching last year.* 我取得了资格，去年开始教书。

quality /ˈkwɒlɪti/ *noun* 名词 (**qualities**)
1 *uncountable* 不可数 how good or bad something is 质量；品质：*The quality of the food here is excellent.* 这里的食物质量很好。
2 *countable* 可数 a particular characteristic of a person or thing 特征；特质；特色：*He has a childlike quality.* 他有

一种孩子气。

quantity /ˈkwɒntɪti/ *noun* 名词 (**quantities**)
an amount 数量：*Pour a small quantity of water into a pan.* 向平底锅中倒入少量水。

quarrel /ˈkwɒrəl/ *countable noun* 可数名词
an angry argument between two or more people 争吵；吵架；口角：*I had a terrible quarrel with my brother.* 我和弟弟大吵了一架。 ● **quarrel** *verb* 动词 (**quarrels, quarrelling, quarrelled**)：*Yes, we quarrelled over something silly.* 是的，我们为了一些愚蠢的事情争吵。

quarry /ˈkwɒri/ *countable noun* 可数名词 (**quarries**)
a place where stone or minerals are dug out of the ground 采石场

quarter /ˈkwɔːtə/ *countable noun* 可数名词
1 one of four equal parts of something 四分之一：*A quarter of the residents are over 55 years old.* 四分之一的居民年龄在55岁以上。口 *I'll be with you in a quarter of an hour.* 我一刻钟后来找你。
→ Look at picture on P2 参见彩插第2页
2 a fixed period of three months 三个月；季度；季：*We will send you a bill every quarter.* 我们会每季度给你寄一张账单。
(a) quarter to/(a) quarter past used when you are telling the time to talk about the fifteen minutes before or after an hour （整点之前）差15分钟，差一刻/（整点之后）过15分钟，过一刻：*We arrived at quarter to nine that night.* 我们那天晚上9点差一刻到的。

quarter 四分之一

quartet /kwɔːˈtet/ *countable noun* 可数名词
1 a group of four people who play musical instruments or sing together 四重奏乐团；四重唱组合：*a string quartet* 弦乐四重奏乐团
2 a piece of music for four instruments or

four singers 四重奏曲；四重唱曲

quay /kiː/ *countable noun* 可数名词
a long structure built next to water where boats can stop 码头

queen /kwiːn/ *noun* 名词
1 a woman from a royal family who rules a country 女王：*Queen Elizabeth* 伊丽莎白女王
2 the wife of a king 王后
→ Look at picture on P10 参见彩插第 10 页

query /ˈkwɪəri/ *countable noun* 可数名词 (**queries**)
a question 疑问；问题：*If you have any queries, please do not hesitate to contact us.* 如果您有任何疑问，请随时与我们联系。

question[1] /ˈkwestʃən/ *noun* 名词
1 *countable* 可数 something that you say or write in order to ask a person about something 问题：*They asked a lot of questions about her health.* 他们问了很多关于她健康状况的问题。
2 *singular* 单数 doubt about something 怀疑；疑问：*There's no question about their success.* 他们的成功毫无疑问。
3 *countable* 可数 a problem or a subject that needs to be considered（待处理的）问题，议题：*The question of nuclear energy is complex.* 核energy问题错综复杂。
4 *countable* 可数 a problem in an examination that tests your knowledge 考题；试题：*Please answer all six questions.* 请回答所有 6 个问题。
out of the question completely impossible 完全不可能的：*An expensive holiday is out of the question for him.* 花大钱去度假对他来说绝无可能。

question[2] /ˈkwestʃən/ *verb* 动词
(**questions, questioning, questioned**)
1 to ask someone a lot of questions about something 问；提问：*The doctor questioned Jim about his parents.* 医生向吉姆询问了他父母的情况。
▶ **questioning** /ˈkwestʃənɪŋ/ *uncountable noun* 不可数名词：*The police want thirty-two people for questioning.* 警方想询问 32 人。
2 to express doubts about something 怀疑；质疑：*They never question the doctor's decisions.* 他们从不质疑医生的决定。

question mark *countable noun* 可数名词
the mark (?) that is used in writing at the end of a question 问号

questionnaire /ˌkwestʃəˈneə/ *countable noun* 可数名词
a list of questions that a lot of people answer in order to provide information for a person or an organization 问卷；调查表：*Each person will fill out a five-minute questionnaire.* 每人将填写一份 5 分钟的问卷。

queue /kjuː/ *countable noun* 可数名词
(*American* 美国英语：**line**)
a line of people or vehicles that are waiting for something 等候队列；*She waited in the bus queue.* 她排队等公交车。
● **queue** *verb* 动词 (**queues, queuing** or 或 **queueing, queued**) (also 亦作 **queue up**)：*I had to queue for quite a while.* 我不得不排了好一会儿队。□ *We all had to queue up to get our tickets.* 我们都不得不排队取票。

quick /kwɪk/ *adjective* 形容词 (**quicker, quickest**)
1 moving or doing things with great speed 快的；迅速的：*You'll have to be quick.* 你得快点儿。
▶ **quickly** /ˈkwɪkli/ *adverb* 副词：*Cussane worked quickly.* 库塞因干活儿很利索。
2 taking or lasting only a short time 短暂的：*He took a quick look around the room.* 他迅速环视了一下房间。
▶ **quickly** /ˈkwɪkli/ *adverb* 副词：*You can get fit quite quickly if you exercise.* 只要你锻炼，很快就会健康起来。
3 happening with very little delay 迅速的；毫不耽搁的：*We are hoping for a quick end to the strike.* 我们希望罢工能很快结束。
▶ **quickly** /ˈkwɪkli/ *adverb* 副词：*We need to get the money back as quickly as possible.* 我们需要尽快把钱拿回来。

quiet /ˈkwaɪət/ *adjective* 形容词 (**quieter, quietest**)
1 making only a small amount of noise 安静的；轻声的：*The car has an extremely quiet engine.* 这辆汽车的发动机非常安静。
▶ **quietly** /ˈkwaɪətli/ *adverb* 副词：*She spoke so quietly that we couldn't understand what she said.* 她说话那么轻，我们听不懂她说什么。
2 with no activity or trouble 平静的；清净的；宁静的：*It's a quiet little village.* 这是一个安静的小村庄。
3 not saying anything 不出声的；一言不发的：*Be quiet and go to sleep.* 安静点儿，睡觉去。

quilt – the Qu'ran

▶**quietly** /ˈkwaɪətli/ *adverb* 副词：*Amy stood quietly in the doorway.* 埃米静静地站在门口。

quilt /kwɪlt/ *countable noun* 可数名词
a bed cover filled with soft, warm material 被子

quit /kwɪt/ *verb* 动词 (**quits, quitting, quit**)
to choose to stop doing an activity (*informal* 非正式) 停止；戒掉；辞去：*Christina quit her job last year.* 克里斯蒂娜去年辞职了。□ *That's enough! I quit!* 够了！我不干了！

quite /kwaɪt/ *adverb* 副词
1 a little or a lot, but not extremely 颇；相当：*I felt quite bad about it at the time.* 当时我对此感到很难过。□ *I knew her mother quite well.* 我很了解她母亲。□ *Our house is quite a long way from the city.* 我们家离市区很远。
2 completely 完全；彻底：*I haven't quite finished my project.* 我还没有彻底完成我的项目。□ *My position is quite different.* 我的立场完全不同。

quite a/an used before a noun to say that a person or thing is very impressive or unusual (用于名词前，强调很突出或不寻常)：*He's quite a character.* 他很有个性。

quiz /kwɪz/ *countable noun* 可数名词 (**quizzes**)
a game or a competition in which someone tests your knowledge by asking you questions 知识问答：*We'll have a quiz after our visit to the museum.* 参观完博物馆，我们将举行一场知识竞答。

quotation /kwəʊˈteɪʃən/ *countable noun* 可数名词
a sentence or a phrase from a book, a poem, a speech or a play 引语；引文：*He used quotations from Martin Luther King Jr. in his lecture.* 他在演讲中引用了小马丁·路德·金的话。

quoˈtation marks *plural noun* 复数名词
marks that are used in writing to show where speech begins and ends. Quotation marks are usually written or printed as "..." or '...'. 引号

quote[1] /kwəʊt/ *verb* 动词 (**quotes, quoting, quoted**)
to repeat what someone has written or said 引用；引述：*She quoted a line from a book.* 她引用了一本书中的一句话。

quote[2] /kwəʊt/ *noun* 名词
1 countable 可数 a section from a book, poem, play or speech 引语；引文：*He finished with a quote from one of his favourite poems.* 他最后引用了他最喜欢的一首诗中的一句话。
2 [**quotes**] *plural* 复数 (*informal* 非正式)
→ see 见 **quotation marks**：*The word 'remembered' is in quotes here.* *remembered 这个词在这里用了引号。

the Qu'ran /ðə kʊˈrɑːn/ *noun* 名词
→ see 见 **the Koran**

rabbi /ˈræbaɪ/ *countable noun* 可数名词
a Jewish religious leader 拉比（犹太教领袖）

rabbit /ˈræbɪt/ *countable noun* 可数名词
a small animal that has long ears and lives in a hole in the ground 兔子

race[1] /reɪs/ *noun* 名词
1 *countable* 可数 a competition to see who is the fastest 赛跑；竞速赛: *Mark easily won the race.* 马克轻松赢得比赛。□ *a horse race* 赛马比赛
2 one of the groups that humans can be divided into because they look similar, for example with the same skin colour 种族；人种: *The college welcomes students of all races.* 学院欢迎各种族学生。

race[2] /reɪs/ *verb* 动词 (**races, racing, raced**)
1 to take part in a race 参加竞速比赛: *Leo started racing in the early 1950s.* 利奥在20世纪50年代初开始参加比赛。□ *We raced them to the top of the hill.* 我们和他们比赛看谁先到山顶。
2 to go somewhere as quickly as possible 全速移动: *He raced across town to the hospital.* 他迅速穿过小镇去医院。

racecourse /ˈreɪskɔːs/ *also* 亦作 **race course** *countable noun* 可数名词
a place where horses race 赛马场；跑马场

racial /ˈreɪʃəl/ *adjective* 形容词
relating to people's race 种族的；人种的: *The new law promotes racial equality.* 新法促进种族平等。
▶ **racially** /ˈreɪʃəli/ *adverb* 副词: *a racially-mixed school* 种族混合学校

racing /ˈreɪsɪŋ/ *uncountable noun* 不可数名词
the sport of competing in races 竞速；赛跑；赛车；赛马: *a racing car* 一辆赛车

racism /ˈreɪsɪzəm/ *uncountable noun* 不可数名词
the belief that people of some races are not as good as others 种族主义；种族歧视: *Many of these children experienced racism in their daily lives.* 这些儿童中有许多在日常生活中遭遇过种族歧视。□ *The level of racism is increasing.* 种族歧视程度日益加剧。

racist[1] /ˈreɪsɪst/ *adjective* 形容词
influenced by the belief that some people are better than others because they belong to a particular race 种族主义的；种族歧视的: *We live in a racist society.* 我们生活在一个种族主义社会。

racist[2] /ˈreɪsɪst/ *countable noun* 可数名词
someone who is racist 种族主义者: *He was attacked by a gang of white racists.* 他遭到一伙白人种族主义者攻击。

rack /ræk/ *countable noun* 可数名词
a frame or a shelf, usually with bars, that is used for holding things 支架；架子: *Put all your bags in the luggage rack.* 把你所有的包都放到行李架上。

racket /ˈrækɪt/ *noun* 名词
1 *countable* 可数 (*also* 亦作 **racquet**) a thing that is used for hitting the ball in some games 球拍: *I got a tennis racket for my birthday.* 我生日得到了一支网球拍。
2 *singular* 单数 a loud, unpleasant noise 喧哗；吵闹: *The children are making a racket upstairs.* 孩子们在楼上吵闹。

racket 球拍

radar /ˈreɪdɑː/ *noun* 名词
a way of discovering the position of objects when they cannot be seen, by using radio signals 雷达: *They saw the submarine on the ship's radar screen.* 他们在船载雷达屏幕上看到了潜艇。

radiation /ˌreɪdiˈeɪʃən/ *uncountable noun* 不可数名词
a type of energy that comes from some substances. Too much radiation is harmful to living things. 辐射: *The gas protects the Earth against radiation from the sun.* 这种

radiator - rainbow

气体保护地球免受太阳辐射。

radiator /ˈreɪdiˌeɪtə/ *countable noun* 可数名词
1 a metal object that is full of hot water or steam, and is used for heating a room 散热器；暖气片
2 the part of the engine of a car that is filled with water in order to cool the engine（汽车发动机的）散热器，冷却水箱

radio /ˈreɪdiəʊ/ *noun* 名词
1 *countable* 可数 a piece of equipment that you use in order to listen to radio programmes 收音机：*He turned on the radio.* 他打开了收音机。
2 *uncountable* 不可数 a system of sending and receiving sound using electronic signals 无线电通话：*They are in radio contact with the leader.* 他们用无线电与领导保持联系。
3 *countable* 可数 a piece of equipment that is used for sending and receiving spoken messages 无线电通话设备：*The police officer called for extra help on his radio.* 那名警察用无线对讲机请求支援。
• **radio** *verb* 动词 (**radios, radioing, radioed**)：*The officer radioed for advice.* 警察用无线电请求指示。

ˈradio ˌwave *countable noun* 可数名词 the form in which radio signals travel 无线电波

radius /ˈreɪdiəs/ *countable noun* 可数名词 (**radii** /ˈreɪdiaɪ/) the distance from the centre of a circle to its outside edge 半径：*We offer free delivery within a 5-mile radius of our shop.* 我们店方圆5英里内免费送货。

raffle /ˈræfəl/ *countable noun* 可数名词 a competition in which you buy tickets with numbers on them. If your number is chosen, you win a prize. 抽彩；抽奖：*raffle tickets* 彩票

raft /rɑːft/ *countable noun* 可数名词 a flat boat that is made from large pieces of wood that are tied together 筏；木排

rag /ræɡ/ *noun* 名词
1 a piece of old cloth 旧布；破布：*He was wiping his hands on an oily rag.* 他正在用一块满是油污的破布擦手。
2 **[rags]** *plural* 复数 old torn clothes 破旧衣服：*The streets were full of children dressed in rags.* 街上满是衣衫褴褛的孩子。

rage /reɪdʒ/ *noun* 名词 strong anger that is difficult to control 暴怒；狂怒：*His face was red with rage.* 他气得脸都红了。

ragged /ˈræɡɪd/ *adjective* 形容词
1 wearing clothes that are old and torn 衣衫褴褛的；破衣烂衫的：*A thin ragged man sat on the park bench.* 公园长椅上坐着一个衣衫褴褛的瘦子。
2 old and torn 破旧的；褴褛的：*children in ragged clothes* 衣衫褴褛的孩子们

raid /reɪd/ *verb* 动词 (**raids, raiding, raided**) to enter a building suddenly in order to look for someone or something 突击搜捕；突然搜查：*Police raided the company's offices.* 警方突击搜查了这家公司的办公室。 • **raid** *countable noun* 可数名词：*They were arrested after a raid on a house by police.* 他们在警方突袭一所房子后被捕。

rail /reɪl/ *countable noun* 可数名词
1 a horizontal bar that you hold for support 栏杆；扶手：*She held the hand rail tightly.* 她紧紧抓住扶手。
2 a horizontal bar that you hang things on（挂物件的）横杆：*a curtain rail* 窗帘杆
3 one of the metal bars that trains run on 铁轨；轨道：*The train left the rails.* 火车出轨了。
by rail on a train 乘火车：*The president arrived by rail.* 总统乘火车到达。

railing /ˈreɪlɪŋ/ *countable noun* 可数名词 a fence that is made from metal bars 金属围栏：*He jumped over the railing to shake hands with the fans.* 他跳过金属栏杆去和粉丝握手。

railway /ˈreɪlweɪ/ *countable noun* 可数名词 a metal track between two places that trains travel along 铁路；铁道：*The road ran beside a railway.* 这条路在一条铁路旁边。

ˈrailway ˌstation *countable noun* 可数名词 a place where trains stop so that people can get on or off 火车站

rain /reɪn/ *uncountable noun* 不可数名词 water that falls from the clouds in small drops 雨；雨水：*We got very wet in the rain.* 我们在雨中淋透了。 • **rain** *verb* 动词 (**rains, raining, rained**)：*It was raining hard.* 雨下得很大。

rainbow /ˈreɪnbəʊ/ *countable noun* 可数名词 a half circle of different colours that you can sometimes see in the sky when it rains 虹；彩虹

→ Look at picture on P8 参见彩插第 8 页

raincoat /ˈreɪnkəʊt/ *countable noun* 可数名词
a coat that you can wear to keep dry when it rains 雨衣

raindrop /ˈreɪndrɒp/ *countable noun* 可数名词
a single drop of rain 雨点；雨滴

rainfall /ˈreɪnfɔːl/ *uncountable noun* 不可数名词
the amount of rain that falls in a place during a particular period 雨量: *This month we have recorded below-average rainfall.* 这个月我们记录的雨量低于平均水平。

rainforest /ˈreɪnfɒrɪst/ *noun* 名词
a thick forest of tall trees that grows in tropical areas where there is a lot of rain (热带)雨林: *We watched a programme about the destruction of the Amazon Rainforest.* 我们看了一个讲亚马孙雨林遭到破坏的节目。

rainy /ˈreɪni/ *adjective* 形容词 (**rainier, rainiest**)
raining a lot 下雨的；多雨的: *Here are some fun things to do on a rainy day.* 这是雨天可以做的一些趣事。
→ Look at picture on P8 参见彩插第 8 页

raise /reɪz/ *verb* 动词 (**raises, raising, raised**)
1 to move something upwards 举起；抬起: *He raised his hand to wave.* 他举起手来挥动。 □ *Milton raised the glass to his lips.* 米尔顿把杯子举到嘴边。
2 to increase the rate or level of something 增加；提高: *Many shops have raised their prices.* 许多商店提高了价格。 □ *Keep calm, and don't raise your voice.* 保持冷静，不要提高嗓门。
3 to ask people for money for a particular purpose 募集，筹措(资金): *The event is to raise money for the school.* 这场活动是为学校筹款。
4 to start to talk about a subject 提起，提出(话题): *The matter will be raised at our annual meeting.* 这个问题将在我们的年会上提出。
5 to take care of children until they are grown up 抚养，养育(子女): *She raised four children on her own.* 她独自抚养了 4 个孩子。

LANGUAGE HELP 语言提示
See note at **rise**. 见 **rise** 的语言提示。

raisin /ˈreɪzən/ *countable noun* 可数名词
a dried grape (= a small green or purple fruit) 葡萄干

rake /reɪk/ *countable noun* 可数名词
a garden tool with a long handle, used for collecting loose grass or leaves 耙子
● **rake** *verb* 动词 (**rakes, raking, raked**): *We raked the leaves into a pile.* 我们把树叶耙成一堆。

rake 耙子

rally /ˈræli/ *countable noun* 可数名词 (**rallies**)
a large public meeting that is held in order to show support for something 公众集会；群众大会: *They organized a rally to demand better working conditions.* 他们组织了一场集会，要求改善工作条件。

ram /ræm/ *countable noun* 可数名词
an adult male sheep 成年公羊

RAM /ræm/ *uncountable noun* 不可数名词
the part of a computer where information is stored while you are using it. **RAM** is short for (缩写 =) 'Random Access Memory'. 随机存储器；内存

ramp /ræmp/ *countable noun* 可数名词
a surface with a slope between two places that are at different levels 坡道；斜坡: *There's a wheelchair ramp at the front entrance of the school.* 学校前门有轮椅坡道。

ran /ræn/
→ see 见 **run**

ranch /rɑːntʃ/ *countable noun* 可数名词 (**ranches**)
a large farm used for keeping animals 牧场: *He owns a cattle ranch in Texas.* 他在得克萨斯有一个养牛场。

random /ˈrændəm/ *adjective* 形容词
1 used for describing a process in which all the people or things involved have an equal chance of being chosen 随机的: *The*

survey used a random sample of two thousand people. 这项调查随机抽取了 2,000 人作为样本。
2 not following a plan or pattern 随意的；任意的：*We have seen random violence against innocent victims.* 我们目睹了对无辜受害者的无端暴行。
at random happening without a plan or a pattern 随意地；随机地；胡乱地：*The gunman fired at random.* 枪手胡乱开枪。

rang /ræŋ/
→ see 见 **ring**

range¹ /reɪndʒ/ *countable noun* 可数名词
1 a number of different things of the same type（同类物品的）一系列：*These products come in a wide range of colours.* 这些产品有各种各样的颜色。
2 the complete group that is included between two points on a scale 范围：*The age range is between 35 and 55.* 年龄范围在 35 岁至 55 岁之间。
3 how far something can reach 可以达到的距离：*This electric car has a range of 100 miles.* 这辆电动汽车的续驶里程为 100 英里。
4 a group of mountains or hills 山脉：*snowy mountain ranges* 白雪皑皑的山脉

range² /reɪndʒ/ *verb* 动词 (**ranges, ranging, ranged**)
to be between two fixed points on a scale 在…之间变动：*The children range in age from five to fourteen.* 这些孩子的年龄从 5 岁到 14 岁不等。

rank /ræŋk/ *noun* 名词
the position that someone has in an organization 级别；职级：*He holds the rank of colonel in the British Army.* 他有英国陆军上校军衔。

ransom /ˈrænsəm/ *noun* 名词
the money that has to be paid to someone so that they will set a person free 赎金：*Her kidnapper asked for a £250,000 ransom.* 绑架她的人索要 25 万英镑赎金。

rap¹ /ræp/ *uncountable noun* 不可数名词
a type of modern music in which the words are spoken 说唱乐；饶舌音乐：*He performs with a rap group.* 他和一个说唱乐队一起表演。
▶ **rapper** /ˈræpə/ *countable noun* 可数名词：*He's a singer and a talented rapper.* 他是个歌手，也是个有天赋的说唱歌手。

rap² /ræp/ *verb* 动词 (**raps, rapping, rapped**)
to perform rap music 表演说唱乐；唱饶舌歌：*The kids rap and also sing.* 孩子们说唱，也唱歌。

rapid /ˈræpɪd/ *adjective* 形容词
1 happening very quickly（事件的发生）迅速的，快速的：*This is the end of the country's rapid economic growth.* 这是该国经济快速增长的终结。
▶ **rapidly** /ˈræpɪdli/ *adverb* 副词：*The firm continues to grow rapidly.* 这家公司继续迅速发展。
2 moving very fast（移动）快速的：*He walked at a rapid pace.* 他走得很快。
▶ **rapidly** /ˈræpɪdli/ *adverb* 副词：*He was moving rapidly around the room.* 他在房间里快速地转来转去。

rare /reə/ *adjective* 形容词 (**rarer, rarest**)
1 not seen or heard very often 稀罕的；珍贵的：*This is one of the rarest birds in the world.* 这是世界上最稀有的鸟类之一。
2 not happening very often 难得的；罕见的；不常发生的：*They have dinner together on the rare occasions when they are both at home.* 他俩难得都在家的时候会一起吃晚饭。
▶ **rarely** /ˈreəli/ *adverb* 副词：*I rarely take taxis.* 我很少坐出租车。
3 used for describing meat that is cooked very lightly so that the inside is still red（肉）一分熟的：*freshly-cooked rare steak* 新煎的一分熟牛排

rash¹ /ræʃ/ *adjective* 形容词
acting without thinking carefully first 轻率的；鲁莽的：*Don't make any rash decisions.* 不要草率做决定。

rash² /ræʃ/ *countable noun* 可数名词 (**rashes**)
an area of red spots that appears on your skin 疹；皮疹：*I always get a rash when I eat nuts.* 我一吃坚果就起疹子。

raspberry /ˈrɑːzbri/ *countable noun* 可数名词 (**raspberries**)
a small, soft, red fruit that grows on bushes 树莓；木莓；覆盆子

rat /ræt/ *countable noun* 可数名词
an animal that has a long tail and looks like a large mouse 老鼠；耗子

rate /reɪt/ *countable noun* 可数名词
1 how fast or how often something happens 速度；频率；比率：*An adult's heart rate is about 72 beats per minute.* 成

年人的心率大约是每分钟 72 次。☐ *Spain has a very low birth rate.* 西班牙人口出生率非常低。
2 the amount of money that goods or services cost 价格；费用：*The hotel offers a special weekend rate.* 这家旅馆周末有特价。
at any rate anyway 反正；至少：*His friends liked her — well, most of them at any rate.* 他的朋友们喜欢她——哦，反正大部分都喜欢。

rather /ˈrɑːðə/ *adverb* 副词
more than a little 颇；相当：*I thought the film was rather boring.* 我觉得这部电影比较无聊。
rather than instead of, in place of 而不是：*I use the bike when I can, rather than the car.* 我能骑自行车就不开车。
would rather do something would prefer to do something 更喜欢做某事：*Kids would rather play than study.* 比起学习，孩子们更喜欢玩。

ratio /ˈreɪʃiəʊ/ *countable noun* 可数名词
a relationship between two things when it is expressed in numbers or amounts 比；比率：*The adult to child ratio is one to six.* 成人与儿童的比率是1比6。

ration¹ /ˈræʃən/ *noun* 名词
1 countable 可数 a small amount of something that you are allowed to have when there is not much of it（供应有限时的）配给量：*The meat ration was 250 grams per month during the war.* 战争期间肉类配给量是每月 250 克。
2 [rations] plural 复数 the food that is given to soldiers or to people who do not have enough food（给战士或食品短缺者的）定量口粮

ration² /ˈræʃən/ *verb* 动词 (rations, rationing, rationed)
to only allow someone to have a small amount of something 定量配给；限量供给：*Food such as bread and rice was rationed.* 面包和大米这样的食物是定量配给的。

rational /ˈræʃənəl/ *adjective* 形容词
based on reason rather than on emotion 理性的；合理的：*They discussed it in a rational manner.* 他们理性地讨论了这件事。
▶ **rationally** /ˈræʃənəli/ *adverb* 副词：*It is difficult to think rationally when you're worried.* 心存忧虑时很难理性思考。

rattle¹ /ˈrætəl/ *verb* 动词 (rattles, rattling, rattled)
to hit against something hard and make short, sharp, knocking sounds 哗啦响；咔嗒响：*The windows rattled in the wind.* 窗户在风中哐啷作响。

rattle² /ˈrætəl/ *countable noun* 可数名词
a baby's toy with small, loose objects inside that make a noise when the baby shakes it 摇铃

rave /reɪv/ *verb* 动词 (raves, raving, raved)
to speak or write about something with great enthusiasm 热情洋溢地谈论（或书写）；极力夸赞：*Rachel raved about the film.* 蕾切尔对这部电影赞不绝口。

raw /rɔː/ *adjective* 形容词 (rawer, rawest)
1 used for describing materials or substances that are in their natural state 自然状态的；未经加工的：*raw sugar* 粗糖
2 not cooked 生的；未做熟的：*This is a Japanese dish made of raw fish.* 这是一道用生鱼做的日本菜。

ray /reɪ/ *countable noun* 可数名词
a narrow line of light 光线：*Protect your eyes against the sun's rays.* 保护你的眼睛不受阳光伤害。

razor /ˈreɪzə/ *countable noun* 可数名词
a tool that people use for shaving 剃须刀

razor 剃须刀

reach /riːtʃ/ *verb* 动词 (reaches, reaching, reached)
1 to arrive at a place 到达；抵达：*He did not stop until he reached the door.* 他一直走到门口才停下来。
2 to be at a certain level or amount 达到（某一水平或数量）：*The number of unemployed could reach 3 million next year.* 明年失业人数可能达到 300 万。
3 to move your arm and hand to take or touch something 伸手够（某物）：*She tried to reach the cake on the counter.* 她想够到厨房操作台上的蛋糕。
4 to be able to touch something by stretching out your arm or leg 够得着：*Can you reach your toes with your fingertips?* 你能用指尖够到脚趾吗？
5 to contact someone, usually by telephone（通常指用电话）联系，与…取得联系：*You can reach me at this phone*

number. 你可以打这个电话号码联系我。

reach 伸手够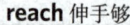

She tried to reach the cake on the counter. 她想够到厨房操作台上的蛋糕。

react /riˈækt/ *verb* 动词 (**reacts, reacting, reacted**)
1 to behave in a particular way because of something that has happened 作出反应；回应：*They reacted violently to the news.* 他们对这则消息反应强烈。
2 to combine chemically to form another substance 起化学反应：*Calcium reacts with water.* 钙和水会起化学反应。

reaction /riˈækʃən/ *noun* 名词
1 what you feel, say or do because of something 反应；回应：*He showed no reaction when I told him the result.* 我告诉他结果时，他毫无反应。
2 *countable* 可数 a process in which two substances combine together chemically to form another substance 化学反应：*a chemical reaction between oxygen and hydrogen* 氢氧之间的化学反应

read *verb* 动词 (**reads, reading, read**)

> **PRONUNCIATION HELP** 发音提示
> When it is the present tense, **read** is pronounced /riːd/ ; **read** is also the past tense and past participle, when it is pronounced /red/ . *read 用作现在式时读作 /riːd/，用作过去式、过去分词时读作 /red/。

1 to look at written words and understand them 阅读：*Have you read this book?* 你读过这本书吗？ □ *I read about it in the paper.* 我在报纸上看到过此事。□ *She spends all her time reading.* 她所有时间都花在阅读上。
2 to say words that you can see 念；朗读；诵读：*Kevin always read a story to the twins when he got home.* 凯文回家后总是给双胞胎读个故事。

read someone's mind/thoughts to know exactly what someone is thinking 读懂某人的心思

read something out to read something to other people (向别人) 朗读某事物，宣读某事物：*She asked us to read out the answers to the exercise.* 她让我们把练习题答案念出来。

reader /ˈriːdə/ *countable noun* 可数名词
a person who reads a newspaper, a magazine or a book 读者：*The article gives readers an interesting view of life in Spain.* 这篇文章为读者了解西班牙的生活提供了一个有趣的视角。

readily /ˈredɪli/ *adverb* 副词
in a way that shows that you are very willing to do something 欣然地；乐意地：*I asked her to help, and she readily agreed.* 我请她帮忙，她欣然同意。

reading /ˈriːdɪŋ/ *uncountable noun* 不可数名词
the activity of reading books 阅读；读书：*I love reading.* 我爱读书。
→ Look at picture on P3 参见彩插第 3 页

ready /ˈredi/ *adjective* 形容词 (**readier, readiest**)
1 completely prepared for something (人) 准备好的，准备妥当的：*It takes her a long time to get ready for school.* 她花了很长时间为上学做准备。
2 prepared so that you can use it 做好可用的：*Go and tell your sister that lunch is ready.* 去告诉你妹妹午饭做好了。
3 willing to do something 乐意的；愿意的：*They were ready to help.* 他们乐意帮忙。

real /riːl/ *adjective* 形容词
1 actually existing 真实的；非虚构的：*No, it wasn't a dream. It was real.* 不，那不是梦，是真的。
2 natural, and not a copy 天然的；非仿制的：*I love the smell of real leather.* 我喜欢真皮的味道。
3 true 真正的：*This was the real reason for her call.* 这是她打电话的真正原因。

realistic /ˌriːəˈlɪstɪk/ *adjective* 形容词
1 recognizing and accepting the true nature of a situation 现实的；务实的；实事求是的：*Police must be realistic about violent crime.* 警察必须对暴力犯罪采取实事求是的态度。
2 when the people and things in a picture,

a story or a film are like people and things in real life 逼真的；栩栩如生的

reality /riˈælɪti/ *noun* 名词 (**realities**)
1 *uncountable* 不可数 used for talking about real things rather than imagined or invented ideas 现实：*Her dream ended and she had to return to reality.* 梦结束了，她不得不回到现实。
2 *countable* 可数 the truth about a situation, especially when it is unpleasant（尤指不如意的）实际情况：*Politicians do not understand the realities of war.* 政客们不懂战争的实际情况。

realize /ˈriːəˌlaɪz/ *verb* 动词 (**realizes, realizing, realized**)
to become aware that something is true or to understand it 理解；认识到；意识到：*As soon as we realized that something was wrong, we rushed to help.* 我们一意识到不对劲儿，就赶紧去帮忙。 □ *People don't realize how serious the situation is.* 人们没有意识到情况有多严重。
▶ **realization** /ˌriːəlaɪˈzeɪʃən/ *uncountable noun* 不可数名词: *A terrible realization struck him.* 他突然意识到一件可怕的事。

really /ˈriːəli/ *adverb* 副词
1 used for giving a sentence a stronger meaning 确实；的确：*I'm very sorry. I really am.* 我很抱歉，真的。
2 used when you are discussing the real facts about something 真正地；真实地：*You're not really leaving, are you?* 你不是真心要走，对吧。
really? used for expressing surprise at what someone has said（表示惊讶）真的吗？：*'I once met the president.'—'Really?'* "我曾经见过总统。"——"真的吗？"

reappear /ˌriːəˈpɪə/ *verb* 动词 (**reappears, reappearing, reappeared**)
to return again after having been away or out of sight 再现；重现

rear[1] /rɪə/ *singular noun* 单数名词
the back part of something 后部：*Mr Forbes was sitting in the rear of the vehicle.* 福布斯先生坐在车子的后面。 □ *The car hit the rear of the lorry.* 汽车撞上了卡车车尾。
● **rear** *adjective* 形容词: *You must fasten all rear seat belts.* 必须系好后排所有座椅的安全带。

rear[2] /rɪə/ *verb* 动词 (**rears, rearing, reared**)
1 to take care of children until they are old enough to take care of themselves 抚养；

养育（孩子）：*I was reared in Texas.* 我在得克萨斯长大。
2 to keep and take care of a young animal until it is old enough to be used for work or food 饲养（幼崽）：*She spends a lot of time rearing animals.* 她花很多时间饲养动物。
3 used for saying that a horse moves the front part of its body upwards, so that it is standing on its back legs（马）用后腿直立：*The horse reared and threw off its rider.* 那匹马来了个后腿直立，把骑手摔了下来。

rearrange /ˌriːəˈreɪndʒ/ *verb* 动词 (**rearranges, rearranging, rearranged**)
to change the way that things are organized 重新排列：*Malcolm rearranged all the furniture.* 马尔科姆重新布置了所有家具。

reason /ˈriːzən/ *noun* 名词
1 *countable* 可数 a fact or situation that explains why something happens 原因；理由：*There is a reason for every important thing that happens.* 每一件重要事情的发生都是有原因的。
2 *uncountable* 不可数 the ability that people have to think and to make sensible judgements 推理能力；理性：*He was more interested in emotion than reason.* 他对情感比对理智更感兴趣。

reasonable /ˈriːzənəbəl/ *adjective* 形容词
1 fair and sensible 讲理的；明事理的：*She seems to be a reasonable person.* 她似乎是个通情达理的人。 □ *That's a perfectly reasonable decision.* 这是一个非常合理的决定。
2 fairly good, but not very good 不错的；还算好的；过得去的：*The boy spoke reasonable French.* 那男孩法语讲得还可以。
▶ **reasonably** /ˈriːzənəbli/ *adverb* 副词: *I can dance reasonably well.* 我舞跳得还不错。

reassure /ˌriːəˈʃʊə/ *verb* 动词 (**reassures, reassuring, reassured**)
to say or do things to make someone stop worrying about something 使安心；消除…的顾虑
▶ **reassurance** /ˌriːəˈʃʊərəns/ *uncountable noun* 不可数名词: *He needed reassurance that she loved him.* 她保证爱他，他心里才踏实。

reassuring /ˌriːəˈʃʊərɪŋ/ *adjective* 形容词
making you feel less worried about something 令人安心的；使人放心的：*It*

was reassuring to hear Jane's voice. 听到简的声音让人安心。

rebel¹ /ˈrebəl/ *countable noun* 可数名词
a person who is fighting against the people who are in charge somewhere, for example the government 叛乱分子；造反者；反政府的人: *There is still heavy fighting between rebels and government forces.* 叛军和政府军之间仍有激战。

rebel² /rɪˈbel/ *verb* 动词 (**rebels, rebelling, rebelled**)
to fight against the people who are in charge 造反；反抗；反叛: *Teenagers often rebel against their parents.* 青少年经常与父母对着干。

rebellion /rɪˈbeliən/ *noun* 名词
when a large group of people fight against the people who are in charge, for example, the government 叛乱；造反: *We are awaiting the government's response to the rebellion.* 我们正在等待政府回应叛乱。

reboot /ˌriːˈbuːt/ *verb* 动词 (**reboots, rebooting, rebooted**)
to turn off a computer and start it again 重新启动（计算机）: *When you reboot your computer, the software is ready to use.* 重新启动电脑，软件就可以使用了。

recall /rɪˈkɔːl/ *verb* 动词 (**recalls, recalling, recalled**)
to remember something 记起；回忆起: *He recalled meeting Pollard during a business trip.* 他回忆起有一次出差时见到波拉德的情景。

receipt /rɪˈsiːt/ *countable noun* 可数名词
a piece of paper that shows that you have received goods or money from someone 收据；收条: *I gave her a receipt for the money.* 我收到钱后给了她一张收据。

receive /rɪˈsiːv/ *verb* 动词 (**receives, receiving, received**)
to get something after someone gives it to you or sends it to you 接到；收到: *They received their awards at a ceremony in San Francisco.* 他们在旧金山的一个典礼上领了奖。

receiver /rɪˈsiːvə/ *countable noun* 可数名词
the part of a telephone that you hold near to your ear and speak into（电话的）听筒，受话器: *She picked up the receiver and started to dial.* 她拿起听筒开始拨号。

recent /ˈriːsənt/ *adjective* 形容词
that happened only a short time ago 近来的；最近的: *Brad broke his leg on a recent trip to Dorset.* 布拉德最近去多塞特旅行时摔断了腿。

recently /ˈriːsəntli/ *adverb* 副词
only a short time ago 最近；不久前: *The bank recently opened a branch in Manchester.* 这家银行最近在曼彻斯特开了一家分行。

reception /rɪˈsepʃən/ *noun* 名词
1 *countable* 可数 a formal party that is given to welcome someone, or to celebrate a special event 招待会；宴会: *We were invited to their wedding reception.* 我们受邀参加他们的婚宴。
2 *uncountable* 不可数 the desk in a hotel or a large building that you go to when you first arrive（旅馆或大楼的）前台，服务台，接待处: *She was waiting at reception.* 她在前台等着。

receptionist /rɪˈsepʃənɪst/ *countable noun* 可数名词
a person in a hotel or a large building whose job is to answer the telephone and deal with visitors 前台接待员

recession /rɪˈseʃən/ *noun* 名词
a period when the economy of a country is not growing（经济的）衰退，萧条: *The oil price increases sent Europe into recession.* 油价上涨使欧洲陷入衰退。

recipe /ˈresɪpi/ *countable noun* 可数名词
a list of food and a set of instructions telling you how to cook something 食谱: *Do you have a recipe for chocolate cake?* 你有巧克力蛋糕的食谱吗？

recite /rɪˈsaɪt/ *verb* 动词 (**recites, reciting, recited**)
to say a poem or other piece of writing to other people after you have learned it 背诵；吟诵；朗诵: *We each had to recite a poem in front of the class.* 我们每个人都必须在全班同学面前背诵一首诗。

reckless /ˈrekləs/ *adjective* 形容词
not caring about danger, or the results of your actions 鲁莽的；不顾后果的: *He was stopped for reckless driving.* 他因危险驾驶被拦下。

reckon /ˈrekən/ *verb* 动词 (**reckons, reckoning, reckoned**)
to think that something is probably true (*informal* 非正式) 料想；估计: *I reckon it's about three o'clock.* 我估计大约是3点钟。

recognition /ˌrekəɡˈnɪʃən/ *uncountable noun* 不可数名词
the act of knowing who a person is or what something is when you see them 认出；识别: *There was no sign of recognition on her face.* 她似乎没有认出来。

recognize /ˈrekəɡˌnaɪz/ *verb* 动词 (**recognizes, recognizing, recognized**)
to know someone or something because you have seen or heard them before 认出；辨认出: *She recognized him immediately.* 她立刻认出了他。

recollection /ˌrekəˈlekʃən/ *noun* 名词
a memory 回忆；记忆: *Pat has few recollections of the trip.* 帕特对那次旅行没什么记忆。

recommend /ˌrekəˈmend/ *verb* 动词 (**recommends, recommending, recommended**)
1 to suggest that someone would find a particular person or thing good or useful 推荐；举荐: *I recommend Barbados as a place for a holiday.* 我推荐去巴巴多斯度假。 □ *I'll recommend you for the job.* 我将推荐你做这项工作。
2 to suggest that something should be done 建议；劝告: *The doctor recommended that I lose some weight.* 医生建议我减肥。
▶ **recommendation** /ˌrekəmenˈdeɪʃən/ *countable noun* 可数名词: *We listened to the committee's recommendations.* 我们听取了委员会的建议。

record¹ /ˈrekɔːd/ *countable noun* 可数名词
1 a written account or photographs of something that can be looked at later 记录；记载: *Keep a record of all the payments.* 记下所有支付款项。
2 a round, flat piece of black plastic on which sound, especially music, is stored, that can be played on a record player (= machine for playing records) 唱片
3 the best result ever in a particular sport or activity (体育运动或活动的) 纪录，最佳成绩: *He set the world record of 12.92 seconds.* 他创造了 12.92 秒的世界纪录。

record² /rɪˈkɔːd/ *verb* 动词 (**records, recording, recorded**)
1 to write down or photograph a piece of information or an event so that in the future people can look at it 记录；记载: *Her letters record the details of her life in China.* 她的信记录了她在中国生活的细节。
2 to store something such as a speech or a performance in a computer file or on a disk so that it can be heard or seen again later 录制；录(音)；录(像): *Viewers can record the films.* 观众可以把电影录下来。

recorder /rɪˈkɔːdə/ *noun* 名词
a wooden or plastic musical instrument in the shape of a pipe. You play it by blowing down one end and covering holes with your fingers. 竖笛
→ Look at picture on P12 参见彩插第 12 页

recording /rɪˈkɔːdɪŋ/ *noun* 名词
1 *countable* 可数 a computer file or a disk on which moving pictures and sounds are stored 录音；录像: *There is a recording of his police interview.* 有一段他接受警方问讯的录音。
2 *uncountable* 不可数 the process of storing moving pictures and sounds on computer files or disks 录制: *This has been a bad time for the recording industry.* 对唱片业来说，这个时期很艰难。

recount /rɪˈkaʊnt/ *verb* 动词 (**recounts, recounting, recounted**)
to tell or describe a story or an event to people (*formal* 正式) 讲述；叙述: *He recounted the story of his first day at work.* 他讲述了他第一天上班的经过。

recover /rɪˈkʌvə/ *verb* 动词 (**recovers, recovering, recovered**)
1 to become well again after an illness or an injury 康复；痊愈；复原: *He is recovering from a knee injury.* 他膝盖受伤，正在康复中。
2 to find or get back something that has been lost or stolen 找回；寻回: *Police searched houses and recovered stolen goods.* 警察搜查了房屋，起获了赃物。

> **LANGUAGE HELP** 语言提示
> **Recover** is a fairly formal word. In conversation, you usually say that someone **gets better**. *recover 较正式，会话中通常用 get better。

recovery /rɪˈkʌvəri/ *noun* 名词 (**recoveries**)
when an ill person becomes well again 恢复；康复；痊愈: *Natalie is making an excellent recovery from a serious knee injury.* 纳塔莉膝盖受了重伤，现在恢复得很好。

recreation /ˌrekriˈeɪʃən/ *uncountable noun* 不可数名词
things that you do in your spare time to

relax 娱乐；消遣：*Saturday afternoon is for recreation.* 星期六下午是娱乐时间。

recruit¹ /rɪˈkruːt/ *verb* 动词 (recruits, recruiting, recruited)
to ask people to join an organization 招募；征召；招聘：*We need to recruit and train more teachers.* 我们需要招聘并培训更多教师。
▶ **recruitment** /rɪˈkruːtmənt/ *uncountable noun* 不可数名词：*There has been a drop in the recruitment of soldiers.* 征兵人数有所下降。

recruit² /rɪˈkruːt/ *countable noun* 可数名词
a person who has recently joined an organization or an army 新成员；新兵：*He's a new recruit to the police force.* 他是名新警员。

rectangle /ˈrektæŋɡəl/ *countable noun* 可数名词
a shape with four straight sides and four 90° angles 长方形；矩形
→ Look at picture on P2 参见彩插第 2 页
▶ **rectangular** /rekˈtæŋɡjʊlə/ *adjective* 形容词：*The room contains a rectangular table.* 房间里有一张长方形桌子。

recur /rɪˈkɜː/ *verb* 动词 (recurs, recurring, recurred)
to happen more than once 不止一次发生；反复出现：*I have a recurring dream about being late for an important meeting.* 我反复梦见自己开重要会议时迟到。

recycle /riːˈsaɪkəl/ *verb* 动词 (recycles, recycling, recycled)
to put things such as paper or bottles that have already been used through a process so that they can be used again 再利用；回收利用
▶ **recycled** /riːˈsaɪkəld/ *adjective* 形容词：*recycled plastic* 再生塑料

red¹ /red/ *adjective* 形容词 (redder, reddest)
1 having the colour of blood or of a tomato 红的；红色的：*a bunch of red roses* 一束红玫瑰
→ Look at picture on P13 参见彩插第 13 页
2 used for describing hair that is between red and brown in colour（毛发）红褐色的

red² /red/ *noun* 名词
the colour of blood or a tomato 红色：*She was dressed in red.* 她一身红色装束。
→ Look at picture on P13 参见彩插第 13 页

reduce /rɪˈdjuːs/ *verb* 动词 (reduces, reducing, reduced)
to make something smaller or less 缩小；减少：*Exercise reduces the risks of heart disease.* 锻炼可以降低患心脏病的风险。□ *The dress was reduced from £35 to £20.* 这条连衣裙从 35 英镑降到了 20 英镑。

reduction /rɪˈdʌkʃən/ *noun* 名词
when something is made smaller or less 缩小；减少：*We have noticed a sudden reduction in prices.* 我们注意到价格突然下降。

redundant /rɪˈdʌndənt/ *adjective* 形容词
without a job because there is not enough work or money to keep you 被裁减的；被裁退的：*My husband was made redundant last year.* 我丈夫去年被裁掉了。

reed /riːd/ *countable noun* 可数名词
a tall plant that grows in large groups in shallow water or on wet ground 芦苇

refer /rɪˈfɜː/ *verb* 动词 (refers, referring, referred)
refer to something
1 to describe a particular thing 意指某事物；指涉某事物：*The word 'man' refers to an adult male.* *man* 一词指的是成年男性。
2 to look in a book or on the Internet for information 查阅某物；参考某物：*He referred briefly to his notebook.* 他略略地看了看笔记本。
▶ **reference** /ˈrefərəns/ *uncountable noun* 不可数名词：*Keep this book in a safe place for reference.* 把这本书放到安全的地方以备查阅。
refer to something/someone to mention a particular subject or person 提到某事物／某人：*He referred to his trip to Canada.* 他提到了他的加拿大之行。
▶ **reference** /ˈrefərəns/ *noun* 名词：*He made no reference to any agreement.* 他没有提到任何协议。
with reference to something or **in reference to something** used for saying what something is about 关于某事物：*I am writing in reference to your advertisement for a personal assistant.* 我写此信是为了应聘贵公司招聘的私人助理一职。

referee /ˌrefəˈriː/ *countable noun* 可数名词
the person who controls a sports event such as a football game or a boxing match（足球、拳击等比赛的）裁判 ● **referee** *verb*

动词 (**referees, refereeing, refereed**)：*Vautrot refereed in two football games.* 沃特罗执法了两场足球比赛。

reference[1] /ˈrefərəns/ *adjective* 形容词
used for describing books that you look at when you need information or facts about a subject（书）供参考的

reference[2] /ˈrefərəns/ *countable noun* 可数名词
a letter that is written by someone who knows you, describing your character and your abilities 推荐信；介绍信：*My boss gave me a good reference.* 我老板给我写了封很好的推荐信。

reflect /rɪˈflekt/ *verb* 动词 (**reflects, reflecting, reflected**)
1 to show that an opinion or a situation exists 反映；显示；表明：*The report reflects the views of both students and teachers.* 这份报告反映了师生双方的观点。
2 used for saying that light or heat is sent back from a surface 反射（光或热）：*The sun reflected off the snow-covered mountains.* 白雪覆盖的群山反射着阳光。
3 to show the image of something in a mirror or in water 反映，映出（影像）：*His face was reflected in the mirror.* 他的脸映在镜子里。

reflection /rɪˈflekʃən/ *countable noun* 可数名词
1 an image that you can see in a mirror or in glass or water 映像，倒影：*Meg stared at her reflection in the mirror.* 梅格凝视着镜子中的自己。
2 something that shows what someone or something is like 反映；表现：*His drawings are a reflection of his own unhappiness.* 他的画作是自身不幸的反映。

reflexive pronoun /rɪˌfleksɪv ˈprəʊnaʊn/ *countable noun* 可数名词
a word such as 'myself' that you use to talk about the subject of a sentence 反身代词

reflexive verb /rɪˌfleksɪv ˈvɜːb/ *countable noun* 可数名词
a verb whose subject and object always refer to the same person or thing. An example is 'to enjoy yourself'. 反身动词

reform[1] /rɪˈfɔːm/ *noun* 名词
1 *uncountable* 不可数 changes and improvements to a law or a social system 改革；变革：*We will introduce a programme of economic reform.* 我们将提出一项经济改革方案。
2 a change that is intended to be an improvement 改良；改善：*The government promised tax reforms.* 政府承诺进行税制改革。

reform[2] /rɪˈfɔːm/ *verb* 动词 (**reforms, reforming, reformed**)
1 to change or improve something such as a law or a social system 改革；改进；改良：*He has plans to reform the country's economy.* 他计划改革国家经济。
2 to start behaving well 改正；改过自新：*After his time in prison, James promised to reform.* 服刑后，詹姆斯承诺改过自新。

refresh /rɪˈfreʃ/ *verb* 动词 (**refreshes, refreshing, refreshed**)
to make you feel better when you are hot, tired or thirsty 使恢复精力；使精神振奋：*The water refreshed them.* 他们喝了水之后精神一振。
▶ **refreshed** /rɪˈfreʃt/ *adjective* 形容词：*He awoke feeling completely refreshed.* 他醒来时感到神清气爽。

refreshing /rɪˈfreʃɪŋ/ *adjective* 形容词
1 making you feel less hot, tired or thirsty 提神的；使人精力充沛的；使人精神振奋的：*They serve refreshing drinks at the poolside.* 他们在池边端送提神饮料。
2 unusual in a pleasant way 令人耳目一新的；别具一格的：*It's refreshing to hear someone speaking so honestly.* 听到有人如此坦率直言让人感觉很新鲜。

refreshments /rɪˈfreʃmənts/ *plural noun* 复数名词
drinks and small amounts of food that are provided, for example, during a meeting or a trip（会议或旅行期间供应的）茶点，小食：*Refreshments will be provided.* 届时会有茶点。

refrigerator /rɪˈfrɪdʒəˌreɪtə/ *countable noun* 可数名词（*formal* 正式）
→ see 见 **fridge**

refuge /ˈrefjuːdʒ/ *countable noun* 可数名词
a place where you go for safety and protection 收容所；避难所：*He works in a refuge for homeless people.* 他在一家无家可归者收容所工作。
take refuge to go somewhere to try to protect yourself from harm 避难：*They took refuge in a shelter.* 他们在一个避难所避难。

refugee /ˌrefjuːˈdʒiː/ *countable noun* 可数名词
a person who has been forced to leave their home or their country, because it is too dangerous for them there 难民: *She grew up in a refugee camp in Pakistan.* 她在巴基斯坦的一个难民营长大。

refund[1] /ˈriːfʌnd/ *countable noun* 可数名词
money that is returned to you because you have paid too much, or because you have returned goods to a shop 退款；返还款: *He took the boots back to the shop and asked for a refund.* 他把靴子拿回商店要求退款。

refund[2] /rɪˈfʌnd/ *verb* 动词 (**refunds, refunding, refunded**)
to return the money that someone has paid for something 退还（钱款）；退（款）: *We will refund your delivery costs if the items arrive later than 12 noon.* 货物中午12点前未送达，我们将退还您的运费。

refusal /rɪˈfjuːzəl/ *noun* 名词
when someone says that they will not do, allow or accept something 拒绝；回绝: *The workers have repeated their refusal to take part in the programme.* 工人们一再拒绝参与这个计划。

refuse /rɪˈfjuːz/ *verb* 动词 (**refuses, refusing, refused**)
1 to say that you will not do something 拒绝做: *He refused to comment.* 他拒绝发表评论。
2 to say that you will not give something to someone 拒绝给: *The United States has refused him a visa.* 美国拒绝给他签证。
3 to not accept something that is offered to you 拒绝接受: *The patient has the right to refuse treatment.* 病人有权拒绝治疗。

regard[1] /rɪˈɡɑːd/ *verb* 动词 (**regards, regarding, regarded**)
to believe that someone or something is a particular thing 将…视为；将…看作: *He was regarded as the most successful president of modern times.* 他被视为现代最成功的总统。

regard[2] /rɪˈɡɑːd/ *noun* 名词
1 *uncountable* 不可数 a feeling of respect for someone or something 敬佩；尊敬: *I have a very high regard for him and his achievements.* 我非常敬佩他的为人和他的成就。
2 [**regards**] *plural* 复数 used as a way of expressing friendly feelings toward someone 致意；问候: *Give my regards to your family.* 代我向你的家人问好。
with regard to something or **in regard to something** used for showing which subject is being talked about 至于某事物；关于某事物: *How happy are you with regard to your work?* 你对你的工作满意度如何？

regarding /rɪˈɡɑːdɪŋ/ *preposition* 介词
about someone or something 关于；有关: *He refused to give any information regarding the man's financial situation.* 他拒绝提供任何有关此人经济状况的信息。

regardless /rɪˈɡɑːdləs/ *adverb* 副词
regardless of something used for saying that a first thing is not affected or influenced at all by a second thing 不管某事物；不顾某事物；不理会某事物: *The organization helps anyone regardless of their age.* 这个组织帮助任何年龄段的人。

reggae /ˈreɡeɪ/ *uncountable noun* 不可数名词
a type of West Indian popular music with a very strong beat 雷格（一种节奏强劲的西印度群岛流行音乐）

regiment /ˈredʒɪmənt/ *countable noun* 可数名词
a part of an army（军队的）团

region /ˈriːdʒən/ *countable noun* 可数名词
an area of a country or of the world 地区；区域: *Do you have a map of the coastal region of Brazil?* 你有巴西沿海地区的地图吗？
▶ **regional** /ˈriːdʒənəl/ *adjective* 形容词: *French regional cooking* 法国地方菜

register[1] /ˈredʒɪstə/ *countable noun* 可数名词
an official list of people or things 名册；登记表；注册簿: *We'll check the register of births, deaths and marriages.* 我们要核对出生、死亡和婚姻登记簿。

register[2] /ˈredʒɪstə/ *verb* 动词 (**registers, registering, registered**)
1 to put your name on an official list, in order to be able to do a particular thing 登记；注册: *Thousands of people registered to vote.* 成千上万人登记投票。
▶ **registration** /ˌredʒɪˈstreɪʃən/ *uncountable noun* 不可数名词: *The website is free, but it asks for registration from users.* 该网站是免费的，但要求用户注册。

2 to show a particular value on a scale or a measuring instrument 显示(读数): *The earthquake registered 5.7 on the Richter scale.* 这次地震的震级为里氏 5.7 级。

regi'stration ˌnumber *countable noun* 可数名词
the numbers and letters on the front and back of a car or other road vehicle (车辆的)牌照号码

regret¹ /rɪˈɡret/ *verb* 动词 (**regrets, regretting, regretted**)
to feel sorry that you did something 后悔；对…感到遗憾: *I regret my decision to leave my job.* 我后悔作了离职的决定。 □ *I regret breaking up with my boyfriend.* 我后悔和男朋友分手。

regret² /rɪˈɡret/ *noun* 名词
a feeling of sadness or disappointment, caused by something that you have done or not done 后悔；遗憾: *He had no regrets about leaving.* 他并不后悔离开。

regular /ˈreɡjʊlə/ *adjective* 形容词
1 used for describing events that have equal amounts of time between them, so that they happen, for example, at the same time each day or each week 有规律的；定期的: *Get regular exercise.* 要定期锻炼。
2 happening often 频繁的；经常(发生)的: *We meet on a regular basis.* 我们经常见面。
▶ **regularly** /ˈreɡjʊləli/ *adverb* 副词: *He writes regularly for the magazine.* 他定期为杂志撰稿。
3 going to a place or a shop often 常去某地的；经常光顾的: *She was a regular visitor to the museum.* 她是博物馆的常客。
4 normal or usual 通常的；平常的: *He sat at his regular table by the windows.* 他照例坐在那张靠窗的桌子旁。
5 used for describing a shape with straight or smooth edges, or where both halves are the same 均匀的；端正的；齐整的: *He's a man of average height with regular features.* 他中等身材，五官端正。
6 used for describing a noun or a verb that follows the usual rules of grammar. For example, 'work' is a regular verb, because the past is formed with '-ed'. Compare with **irregular**. (名词、动词等)规则的，规则变化的(比较 **irregular**): *The past tense of English regular verbs ends in -ed.* 英语规则动词的过去式以 -ed 结尾。

regulation /ˌreɡjʊˈleɪʃən/ *countable noun* 可数名词
a rule for controlling the way people behave or do things 规章；规则；条例: *Here are the new safety regulations.* 这是新的安全规定。

rehearsal /rɪˈhɜːsəl/ *noun* 名词
a practice of a performance 排练；排演: *Tomorrow we start rehearsals for the concert.* 我们明天开始为音乐会排练。

rehearse /rɪˈhɜːs/ *verb* 动词 (**rehearses, rehearsing, rehearsed**)
to practise a play, a dance or a piece of music 排练；排演: *The actors are rehearsing a play.* 演员们正在排练一出戏。 □ *Thousands of people are rehearsing for the ceremony.* 成千上万人在为典礼排练。

reign /reɪn/ *verb* 动词 (**reigns, reigning, reigned**)
to rule a country as king or queen (国王或女王)统治，当政: *Henry II reigned in England from 1154 to 1189.* 亨利二世于 1154 年至 1189 年统治英格兰。 ● **reign** *countable noun* 可数名词: *Queen Victoria's reign* 维多利亚女王统治时期

reindeer /ˈreɪndɪə/ *countable noun* 可数名词 (**reindeer**)
a big animal with large horns that lives in northern areas of Europe, Asia and America 驯鹿

reins /reɪnz/ *plural noun* 复数名词
the long thin pieces of leather that fit around a horse's neck, and that are used for controlling the horse (马的)缰绳: *She held the reins while the horse pulled.* 马拉动时她拉着缰绳。

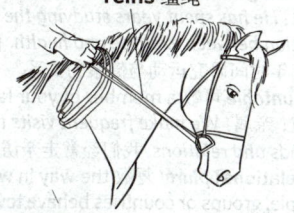

reins 缰绳

reject /rɪˈdʒekt/ *verb* 动词 (**rejects, rejecting, rejected**)
1 to not accept or agree to something 拒绝接受；不同意: *The president rejected the offer.* 总统拒绝了这一提议。
2 to not offer a job or a course of study to someone 拒收；不录用: *He was rejected*

by several universities. 他被几所大学拒绝录取。

▶ **rejection** /rɪˈdʒekʃən/ *countable noun* 可数名词: *Be prepared for lots of rejections before you get a job.* 在得到一份工作之前，要做好多次被拒的准备。

rejoice /rɪˈdʒɔɪs/ *verb* 动词 (**rejoices, rejoicing, rejoiced**)
to be very happy about something and show this in the way that you behave 感到欣喜: *We rejoiced in the victory.* 我们为胜利欣喜若狂。

▶ **rejoicing** /rɪˈdʒɔɪsɪŋ/ *uncountable noun* 不可数名词: *There was much rejoicing at the news.* 听到这个消息，大家喜出望外。

relate /rɪˈleɪt/ *verb* 动词 (**relates, relating, related**)
1 to be about a particular subject 涉及；与…相关: *We are collecting all the information relating to the crime.* 我们正在收集与此案有关的所有资料。
2 used for describing the connection that exists between two things 联系: *There is new thinking about how the two sciences relate.* 关于这两门科学之间的联系有了新见解。

related /rɪˈleɪtɪd/ *adjective* 形容词
1 connected in some way 相关的: *Crime and poverty are closely related.* 犯罪和贫穷密切相关。
2 belonging to the same family 同属一家的；有亲属关系的: *The boys have the same last name but they are not related.* 几个男孩的姓相同，但他们没有亲属关系。

relation /rɪˈleɪʃən/ *noun* 名词
1 *countable* 可数 the connection between two things (两个事物之间的)关系，联系，关联: *He has spent years studying the relation between exercise and health.* 他花了几年时间研究运动与健康的关系。
2 *countable* 可数 a member of your family 亲戚；亲属: *We make frequent visits to friends and relations.* 我们经常走亲访友。
3 [**relations**] *plural* 复数 the way in which people, groups or countries behave towards each other (人、团体、国家之间的)关系，联系: *The country has good relations with Israel.* 该国与以色列关系良好。

relationship /rɪˈleɪʃənʃɪp/ *countable noun* 可数名词
1 the way in which two people or groups feel and behave towards each other (两个人、团体等之间的)关系，联系: *The ministers want to maintain the friendly relationship between the two countries.* 部长们希望维持两国之间的友好关系。
2 a close friendship between two people, especially involving romantic or sexual feelings 亲密关系；(尤指)情爱关系，性爱关系: *She could not accept that their relationship was over.* 她无法接受他们的恋情结束了。
3 the way in which two things are connected (两事物之间的)关系，联系，关系: *Is there a relationship between diet and cancer?* 饮食和癌症之间有关系吗？

relative /ˈrelətɪv/ *countable noun* 可数名词
a member of your family 亲戚；亲属: *Ask a relative to look after the children.* 找个亲戚照看孩子。

relax /rɪˈlæks/ *verb* 动词 (**relaxes, relaxing, relaxed**)
1 to feel more calm and less worried 放松；镇定；冷静: *You should relax and stop worrying.* 你应该放松，不要担心。

▶ **relaxation** /ˌriːlækˈseɪʃən/ *uncountable noun* 不可数名词: *Try learning some relaxation techniques.* 试着学习一些放松的技巧。

▶ **relaxed** /rɪˈlækst/ *adjective* 形容词: *The atmosphere at lunch was relaxed.* 午餐的气氛很轻松。

▶ **relaxing** /rɪˈlæksɪŋ/ *adjective* 形容词: *I find cooking very relaxing.* 我觉得做饭让人非常放松。
2 to make a part of your body become less stiff or tight 使放松；使松弛: *Have a massage to relax your muscles.* 按摩一下，放松放松肌肉。

relay /ˈriːleɪ/ *countable noun* 可数名词
(also 亦作 **relay race**) a race between two or more teams in which each member of the team runs or swims one section of the race 接力赛: *Britain's chances of winning the relay are good.* 英国赢得接力赛的机会很大。

release¹ /rɪˈliːs/ *verb* 动词 (**releases, releasing, released**)
1 to allow a person or an animal to go free 释放；使自由: *He was released from prison the next day.* 第二天他获释出狱。
2 to stop holding someone or something (*formal* 正式) 放开；松开: *He released her hand.* 他松开了她的手。
3 to make a new CD, DVD or film available so that people can buy it or see it 发行，推出(激光唱片、数字光碟或电影): *He is*

releasing a CD of love songs. 他即将推出一张情歌唱片。

release² /rɪˈliːs/ *countable noun* 可数名词
a CD, DVD or film that has just become available for people to buy or see 新激光唱片；新数字光碟；新电影：*a new release* 新发行的产品

relevant /ˈreləvənt/ *adjective* 形容词
important in a situation or to a person 相关的；切题的；重要的：*They are trying to make politics more relevant to younger people.* 他们正努力使政治更贴近年轻人。

reliable /rɪˈlaɪəbəl/ *adjective* 形容词
1 that you can trust to work well 可信赖的；可依靠的：*She was efficient and reliable.* 她办事效率高，为人可靠。
2 probably correct 可信度高的；可靠的：*There is no reliable information about how many people have died.* 目前没有关于死亡人数的可靠信息。
▶ **reliably** /rɪˈlaɪəbli/ *adverb* 副词：*We are reliably informed that he is here.* 我们得到可靠消息说他在这里。
▶ **reliability** /rɪˌlaɪəˈbɪləti/ *uncountable noun* 不可数名词：*We have serious doubts about the reliability of this information.* 我们对这一信息的可靠性深表怀疑。

relief /rɪˈliːf/ *uncountable noun* 不可数名词
1 when you feel happy because something unpleasant has not happened or is no longer happening 宽慰；轻松；解脱：*I breathed a sigh of relief.* 我如释重负地舒了一口气。
2 when pain or worry stops (痛楚或忧虑的) 解除，消除，缓和：*These drugs will give relief from pain.* 这些药可以镇痛。
3 money, food or clothing that is provided for people who suddenly need it 救济金：*Relief agencies are hoping to provide food and shelter in the flooded area.* 救援机构希望在洪水受灾地区提供食品和避难所。

relieved /rɪˈliːvd/ *adjective* 形容词
feeling happy because something unpleasant has not happened or is no longer happening 感到宽慰的；放心的；如释重负的：*We are relieved to be back home.* 回到家我们感到如释重负。

religion /rɪˈlɪdʒən/ *noun* 名词
1 *uncountable* 不可数 belief in a god or gods and the activities that are connected with this belief 宗教信仰：*There's little interest in organized religion.* 人们对有组织的宗教信仰没什么兴趣。
2 *countable* 可数 a particular system of belief in a god or gods and the activities that are connected with this system 宗教：*the Christian religion* 基督教

religious /rɪˈlɪdʒəs/ *adjective* 形容词
1 connected with religion 宗教的：*Religious groups are able to meet quite freely.* 宗教团体可以相当自由地集会。
2 having a strong belief in a god or gods 笃信宗教的；虔诚的

reluctant /rɪˈlʌktənt/ *adjective* 形容词
unwilling to do something 不情愿的；勉强的：*Mr Phillips was reluctant to ask for help.* 菲利普斯先生不愿寻求帮助。
▶ **reluctantly** /rɪˈlʌktəntli/ *adverb* 副词：*We reluctantly agreed to let him go.* 我们勉强同意让他走。
▶ **reluctance** /rɪˈlʌktəns/ *uncountable noun* 不可数名词：*Frank boarded his train with great reluctance.* 弗兰克极不情愿地上了火车。

rely /rɪˈlaɪ/ *verb* 动词 (relies, relying, relied)
rely on someone/something
1 to need someone or something in order to live or work properly 依靠 (或依赖) 某人/某事物：*They relied heavily on our advice.* 他们非常依赖我们的建议。
2 to be able to trust someone to do something 信任某人；信赖某人：*I know I can rely on you to deal with the problem.* 我知道我可以依靠你来处理这个问题。

remain /rɪˈmeɪn/ *verb* 动词 (remains, remaining, remained)
1 to stay in a particular state or condition 仍然是；保持：*The men remained silent.* 男人们保持沉默。 □ *The government remained in control.* 政府仍在控制之中。
2 to stay in a place and not move away 留；逗留：*Police asked people to remain in their homes.* 警方要求人们待在家中。

remainder /rɪˈmeɪndə/ *uncountable noun* 不可数名词
the remainder the part of something that is still there after the first part has gone 剩余物；残余部分：*He drank the remainder of his coffee.* 他喝完了剩下的咖啡。

remaining /rɪˈmeɪnɪŋ/ *adjective* 形容词
relating to the things or people out of a group that still exist, or that are still present 剩的；余下的：*He spoke to his few remaining supporters.* 他对所剩无几的

支持者发表了讲话。

remains /rɪˈmeɪnz/ *plural noun* 复数名词
the parts of something that are left after most of it has been taken away or destroyed 剩余物；残留物；遗迹：*They were cleaning up the remains of their picnic.* 他们正在清理野餐剩下的东西。

remark[1] /rɪˈmɑːk/ *verb* 动词 (**remarks, remarking, remarked**)
to say something 说；谈论；评论：*He remarked that it was very cold.* 他说天气很冷。 □ *She remarked on how tired I looked.* 她说我显得特别累。

remark[2] /rɪˈmɑːk/ *countable noun* 可数名词
something that you say 言论；话语：*She made rude remarks about his weight.* 她粗鲁地评论他的体重。

remarkable /rɪˈmɑːkəbəl/ *adjective* 形容词
very unusual or surprising in a good way 了不起的；非凡的：*He was a remarkable man.* 他是个了不起的人。
▶ **remarkably** /rɪˈmɑːkəbli/ *adverb* 副词：*The book was remarkably successful.* 这本书非常成功。

remedy /ˈremədi/ *countable noun* 可数名词 (**remedies**)
1 something that stops a problem or a bad situation 解决办法；补救措施：*The government's remedy involved tax increases.* 政府的补救措施包括增加税收。
2 something that makes you feel better when you are ill 疗法；药物：*natural remedies for infections* 天然的抗感染药物

remember /rɪˈmembə/ *verb* 动词 (**remembers, remembering, remembered**)
1 to still have an idea of people or events from the past in your mind 记得：*I remember the first time I met him.* 我记得第一次见他时的样子。 □ *I remember that we went to his wedding.* 我记得我们去参加了他的婚礼。 □ *The weather was terrible; do you remember?* 天气糟透了，你还记得吗？
2 to become aware of something again after a time when you did not think about it 想起；记起：*She remembered that she was going to the club that evening.* 她想起来那天晚上要去俱乐部。
3 to not forget to do something 记住：*Please remember to post the letter.* 请记住寄这封信。

remind /rɪˈmaɪnd/ *verb* 动词 (**reminds, reminding, reminded**)

1 to say something that makes someone think about a fact or an event that they already know about 使想起；唤起…的记忆：*She reminded Tim of the last time they met.* 她使蒂姆想起他们上次见面时的情景。
2 to say something that makes someone remember to do something 提醒：*Can you remind me to buy some milk?* 你能提醒我买些牛奶吗？
3 to be similar to another person or thing and make someone think about them 使想起（类似的人或事物）：*She reminds me of your sister.* 她使我想起了你妹妹。

reminder /rɪˈmaɪndə/ *countable noun* 可数名词
something that makes you think about something again 提醒物；引起回忆物：*The scar on her hand was a constant reminder of the accident.* 她手上的伤疤令人不断回想起那次事故。

remorse /rɪˈmɔːs/ *uncountable noun* 不可数名词
a strong feeling of sadness and regret about something wrong that you have done 懊悔；自责：*He was filled with remorse.* 他深感懊悔。

remote /rɪˈməʊt/ *adjective* 形容词 (**remoter, remotest**)
far away from cities and places where most people live 偏僻的；偏远的：*They came from distant villages in remote areas.* 他们来自偏僻地区的遥远村庄。

re͵mote conˈtrol *countable noun* 可数名词
the piece of equipment that you use to control a television or other piece of equipment from a distance 遥控器；遥控设备：*Rachel picked up the remote control and turned on the television.* 蕾切尔拿起遥控器打开电视。

remotely /rɪˈməʊtli/ *adverb* 副词
used with a negative to mean 'in any way'（与否定词连用）完全，一点儿也：*He wasn't remotely interested in her.* 他对她一点儿也不感兴趣。

removal /rɪˈmuːvəl/ *uncountable noun* 不可数名词
the act of removing something 移除；去除；挪走：*She had surgery for the removal of a tumour.* 她做了肿瘤切除手术。

remove /rɪˈmuːv/ *verb* 动词 (**removes, removing, removed**)
1 to take something away from a place

(formal 正式) 移除；移走：*Remove the cake from the oven when it is cooked.* 蛋糕烤好后从烤箱里拿出来。
2 to take off clothing (formal 正式) 脱下（衣服）：*He removed his jacket.* 他脱下夹克衫。

renew /rɪˈnjuː/ *verb* 动词 (**renews, renewing, renewed**)
to get something new to replace something old, or to arrange for the old thing to continue 更新；更换；延续：*Larry's landlord refused to renew his lease.* 拉里的房东拒绝续租。

renewable /rɪˈnjuːəbl/ *adjective* 形容词
used for describing resources that are natural and always available, such as wind, water and sunlight（风、水、太阳能等）可再生的：*renewable energy sources* 可再生能源

rent /rent/ *verb* 动词 (**rents, renting, rented**)
1 to pay the owner of something in order to be able to use it yourself 租用；租借：*She rents a house with three other women.* 她和另外3个女人合租了一所房子。● **rent** *noun* 名词：*She worked hard to pay the rent on the flat.* 她努力工作以支付公寓的租金。
2 (also 亦作 **rent something out**) to let someone have and use something in exchange for money 出租：*She rented rooms to university students.* 她把房间租给大学生。□ *Last summer Brian rented out his house and went camping.* 去年夏天布赖恩将房子出租，去露营了。

repaid /rɪˈpeɪd/
→ see 见 **repay**

repair /rɪˈpeə/ *verb* 动词 (**repairs, repairing, repaired**)
to fix something that has been damaged or is not working properly 修理；修补；修缮：*He has repaired the roof.* 他修理了屋顶。
● **repair** *countable noun* 可数名词：*Repairs were made to the roof.* 屋顶修理过了。

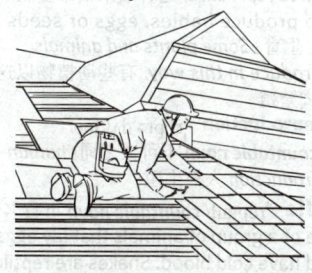

repair 修理

He has repaired the roof. 他修理了屋顶。

repay /rɪˈpeɪ/ *verb* 动词 (**repays, repaying, repaid**)
to pay back money that you borrowed from someone 还（钱）；偿还：*They will have to repay the debt with interest.* 他们将不得不还债付息。

repayment /rɪˈpeɪmənt/ *noun* 名词
1 *uncountable* 不可数 the act or process of paying money back to the person you borrowed it from 还款；偿还；清偿：*The bank will expect the repayment of the £114 million loan.* 银行将要求清偿1.14亿英镑的贷款。
2 *countable* 可数 money that you pay back to the person you borrowed it from 还款（款项）：*He took out a loan with small, frequent repayments.* 他借了一笔频繁小额还款的贷款。

repeat¹ /rɪˈpiːt/ *verb* 动词 (**repeats, repeating, repeated**)
1 to say or write something again 重复；重说；重写：*She repeated her request for more money.* 她重复了她要更多钱的要求。□ *He repeated that he was innocent.* 他再次说他是无辜的。
2 to say or write the same thing that someone else has said or written 复述；重复；转述：*She had a habit of repeating everything I said to her.* 她有重复我对她说的每句话的习惯。
3 to do an action again 重复做：*Repeat this exercise five times a week.* 每周重复这个练习5次。

repeat² /rɪˈpiːt/ *countable noun* 可数名词
a television or radio programme that has been shown before（广播电视的）重播节目

repeated /rɪˈpiːtɪd/ *adjective* 形容词
happening many times 重复的；反复发生的：*He did not return the money, despite repeated reminders.* 尽管再三发出催讨通知单，他还是没有还钱。
▶ **repeatedly** /rɪˈpiːtɪdli/ *adverb* 副词：*I asked him repeatedly to help me.* 我一再请求他帮助我。

repetition /ˌrepɪˈtɪʃən/ *noun* 名词
an occasion when something happens again 重复；重演：*The city government wants to prevent a repetition of last year's violence.* 市政府想防止去年的暴力事件重演。

repetitive /rɪˈpetɪtɪv/ *adjective* 形容词
boring because it involves repeating an

action many times 重复性的；重复乏味的：*They are factory workers who do repetitive jobs.* 他们是做重复性工作的工厂工人。

replace /rɪ'pleɪs/ *verb* 动词 (**replaces, replacing, replaced**)
1 to do the job of another person or thing 代替；取代：*During the war, many women replaced male workers.* 战争期间，许多女性做了男工人的工作。
2 to get something new in the place of something that is damaged or lost 更换；替换：*The shower broke so we have to replace it.* 淋浴器坏了，我们必须更换。
3 to put something back where it was before 将…放回原处：*Replace the caps on the bottles.* 把瓶盖盖好。

replacement /rɪ'pleɪsmənt/ *countable noun* 可数名词
a person or a thing that replaces another 接替者；替代品：*It won't be easy to find a replacement for Grace.* 找个接替格雷丝的人可不容易。

replay /'riːpleɪ/ *countable noun* 可数名词
1 an occasion when an action on television is broadcast again（电视节目中的）重放，重演，重播：*We watched the replay of the incident.* 我们观看了事件的重播。
2 a game which two teams play again because nobody won the first time（因未决出胜负而进行的）重赛

reply /rɪ'plaɪ/ *verb* 动词 (**replies, replying, replied**)
to say or write an answer to something that someone says or writes to you 回答；答复：*'That's a nice dress,' said Michael. 'Thanks,' she replied.* "这条连衣裙真漂亮。"迈克尔说。"谢谢。"她答道。▫ *He replied that this was impossible.* 他回答说这是不可能的。▫ *He never replied to my letters.* 他从不回我的信。● **reply** *countable noun* 可数名词 (**replies**)：*I called his name, but there was no reply.* 我叫他的名字，但没人应答。

report[1] /rɪ'pɔːt/ *verb* 动词 (**reports, reporting, reported**)
1 to tell people about something that happened 汇报；报告；通报：*I reported the crime to the police.* 我向警察报了案。▫ *Officials reported that four people were killed.* 官方报道有 4 人被害。
2 to tell an official person or organization about something wrong that someone has done 举报；告发：*His boss reported him to the police.* 他的老板向警方告发了他。

report[2] /rɪ'pɔːt/ *countable noun* 可数名词
1 a newspaper article or a broadcast that gives information about something that happened 报道：*According to a newspaper report, they are getting married next month.* 据报纸报道，他们下个月结婚。
2 a piece of work that a student writes on a particular subject 研究报告：*We had to do a book report on 'Huckleberry Finn'.* 我们得写一篇关于《哈克贝利·费恩历险记》的读书报告。
3 a document that a teacher writes to tell parents about their children's work and progress（学生的）成绩报告单

reporter /rɪ'pɔːtə/ *countable noun* 可数名词
someone who writes newspaper articles or broadcasts the news 记者；通讯员：*My dad is a TV reporter.* 我爸爸是一名电视记者。

represent /ˌreprɪ'zent/ *verb* 动词 (**represents, representing, represented**)
1 to act or make decisions for a person or a group 代表：*We vote for politicians to represent us.* 我们投票选举政治家来代表我们。
2 to mean something or be a sign of something 表示；象征：*The red line on the map represents a wall.* 地图上的红线代表一堵墙。

representative /ˌreprɪ'zentətɪv/ *countable noun* 可数名词
a person who acts or makes decisions for another person or group 代表：*Michael is our class representative.* 迈克尔是我们班的代表。

reproduce /ˌriːprə'djuːs/ *verb* 动词 (**reproduces, reproducing, reproduced**)
1 to copy something 复制：*The effect was hard to reproduce.* 这种效果很难复制。
2 to produce babies, eggs or seeds 繁殖；生育：*Some plants and animals reproduce in this way.* 有些动植物以这种方式繁殖。
▶ **reproduction** /ˌriːprə'dʌkʃən/ *uncountable noun* 不可数名词：*human reproduction* 人类生殖

reptile /'reptaɪl/ *countable noun* 可数名词
one of a group of animals that lay eggs and have cold blood. Snakes are reptiles. 爬行动物

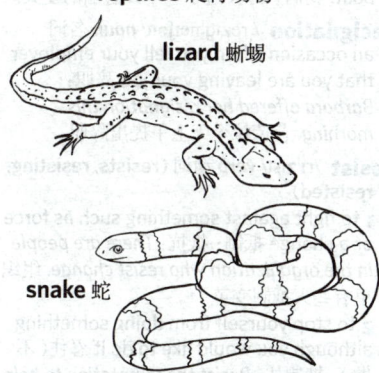

reptiles 爬行动物
lizard 蜥蜴
snake 蛇

republic /rɪˈpʌblɪk/ *countable noun* 可数名词
a country with no king or queen where the people choose their government 共和国：*In 1918, Austria became a republic.* 1918 年，奥地利成为共和国。

repulsive /rɪˈpʌlsɪv/ *adjective* 形容词
used for describing a person or a thing that is so unpleasant that people do not want to see them 令人厌恶的；令人反感的：*Some people found the film repulsive.* 有些人觉得这部电影令人反感。

reputation /ˌrepjuˈteɪʃən/ *countable noun* 可数名词
the opinion that people have about someone or something 名声；名誉：*This college has a good reputation.* 这所大学声誉很好。 □ *He has a reputation for honesty.* 他的诚实出了名。

request /rɪˈkwest/ *verb* 动词 (requests, requesting, requested)
to ask for something politely or formally (*formal* 正式) 请求；要求：*To request more information, please tick this box.* 如欲获取更多资料，请勾选此框。● **request** *countable noun* 可数名词：*They agreed to his request for more money.* 他们同意了他要更多钱的要求。

require /rɪˈkwaɪə/ *verb* 动词 (requires, requiring, required)
1 to need something (*formal* 正式) 需求；需要：*If you require more information, please write to this address.* 如果你需要更多信息，请写信到这个地址。
2 to demand that someone does something or has something (*formal* 正式) 要求：*The rules require employers to provide safety training.* 这些规定要求雇主提供安全培训。

requirement /rɪˈkwaɪəmənt/ *countable noun* 可数名词
something that you must have 必备物；要求：*Our products meet all legal requirements.* 我们的产品符合所有法律要求。

rescue¹ /ˈreskju/ *verb* 动词 (rescues, rescuing, rescued)
to save someone from a dangerous situation 营救；救援：*They rescued 20 people from the roof of the building.* 他们从楼顶救出 20 人。

rescue² /ˈreskju/ *noun* 名词
an attempt to save someone from a dangerous situation 营救；救援：*He helped in the rescue of a bus driver from the river.* 他帮忙从河里救出一名公交车司机。 □ *a big rescue operation* 大型救援行动
come to someone's rescue to help someone when they are in danger 营救某人：*A neighbour came to her rescue.* 一位邻居来救她。

research /rɪˈsɜːtʃ/ *uncountable noun* 不可数名词
when someone studies something and tries to discover facts about it 研究；调查：*My brother does scientific research.* 我哥哥做科学研究。● **research** *verb* 动词 (researches, researching, researched)：*She spent two years researching the subject.* 她花了两年时间研究这个课题。

resemblance /rɪˈzembləns/ *noun* 名词
when two people or things are similar to each other 相似；相像：*There was a strong resemblance between the two girls.* 这两个女孩长得很像。

resemble /rɪˈzembəl/ *verb* 动词 (resembles, resembling, resembled)
to look similar to another person or thing 和…相似；像：*She resembles her mother.* 她像她母亲。

resent /rɪˈzent/ *verb* 动词 (resents, resenting, resented)
to feel angry about something because you think it is not fair (觉得不公平而)愤恨，感到气愤，愤愤不平：*Certain people resented my success.* 有些人忌恨我的成功。

resentment /rɪˈzentmənt/ *noun* 名词
anger that someone feels about something because they think it is not fair 愤恨；怨恨：*Too many rules can cause resentment.* 太多规则会引起怨恨。

reservation /ˌrezəˈveɪʃən/ **countable noun** 可数名词
a room or a seat that a hotel, a transport company or a restaurant keeps ready for you 预订；预约：*Have you cancelled our reservation?* 你取消我们的预订了吗？

reserve[1] /rɪˈzɜːv/ **verb** 动词 (**reserves, reserving, reserved**)
to keep something for a particular person or purpose 预留；保留：*A room was reserved for him.* 为他预留了一个房间。

reserve[2] /rɪˈzɜːv/ **countable noun** 可数名词
a supply of something that you can use when you need it 储备；贮存物：*Which country has the world's largest oil reserves?* 哪个国家的石油储量位居世界第一？
in reserve for using when you need it 储备；备用：*I always try to keep a little money in reserve.* 我总是设法储备一点儿钱。

reserved /rɪˈzɜːvd/ **adjective** 形容词
hiding your feelings 内向的；内敛的；矜持的：*He was quiet and reserved.* 他沉默内敛。

reservoir /ˈrezəˌvwɑː/ **countable noun** 可数名词
a lake that is used for storing water before people use it 水库：*The reservoir provides drinking water for the city of Oxford.* 这座水库为牛津市提供饮用水。

residence /ˈrezɪdəns/ **countable noun** 可数名词
a large house where an important person lives (*formal* 正式) 宅第；府邸：*the president's official residence* 总统官邸

resident /ˈrezɪdənt/ **countable noun** 可数名词
a person who lives in a house or an area 居民：*Local residents complained that the road was dangerous.* 当地居民抱怨这条路很危险。

residential /ˌrezɪˈdenʃəl/ **adjective** 形容词
containing houses rather than offices or shops 住宅的；居住性的：*We drove through a residential area of Birmingham.* 我们开车经过伯明翰一个居民区。

resign /rɪˈzaɪn/ **verb** 动词 (**resigns, resigning, resigned**)
to tell your employer that you are leaving a job 辞职：*He was forced to resign.* 他被迫辞职。
resign yourself to something to accept an unpleasant situation because you cannot change it 无奈地接受某事物：*We resigned ourselves to another summer without a boat.* 我们只好又过了一个没有船的夏天。

resignation /ˌrezɪɡˈneɪʃən/ **noun** 名词
an occasion when you tell your employer that you are leaving your job 辞职：*Barbara offered her resignation this morning.* 芭芭拉今天上午提出辞职。

resist /rɪˈzɪst/ **verb** 动词 (**resists, resisting, resisted**)
1 to fight against something such as force or a change 抵制；抵抗：*There are people in the organization who resist change.* 组织里有些人抵制变革。
2 to stop yourself from doing something although you would like to do it 忍住（不做）；抑制住：*Resist the temptation to help your child too much.* 坚持住，不要过多帮助孩子。

resistance /rɪˈzɪstəns/ **uncountable noun** 不可数名词
when you fight against something such as force or a change 抵制；抵抗；反抗：*I am aware of his resistance to anything new.* 我知道他对任何新事物都有抵触。□ *The soldiers are facing strong resistance.* 士兵们面临着顽强的抵抗。

resolution /ˌrezəˈluːʃən/ **countable noun** 可数名词
when you decide to try very hard to do something 决心；决定：*They made a resolution to get more exercise.* 他们决心多锻炼。

resolve /rɪˈzɒlv/ **verb** 动词 (**resolves, resolving, resolved**)
1 to find a solution to a problem, an argument or a difficulty (*formal* 正式) 解决（问题、争论或困难）：*We must resolve these problems.* 我们必须解决这些问题。
2 to make a decision to do something (*formal* 正式) 决心；决定：*Judy resolved to be a better friend.* 朱迪决心做一个更好的朋友。

resort /rɪˈzɔːt/ **countable noun** 可数名词
a place that provides activities for people who stay there during their holiday 旅游胜地；度假胜地：*The ski resorts are busy.* 滑雪胜地很热闹。
as a last resort because you can find no other solution to a problem 作为最后手段，万般无奈下：*As a last resort, we hired an expert.* 迫不得已，我们聘请了一位专家。

resources /rɪˈzɔːsɪz/ **plural noun** 复数名词
money and other things that a country, an

organization or a person has and can use 资源: *We must protect the country's natural resources, including water.* 我们必须保护国家的自然资源，包括水资源。

respect¹ /rɪˈspekt/ *verb* 动词 (**respects, respecting, respected**)
to have a good opinion of someone 尊敬；敬重: *I want people to respect me for my work.* 我希望人们尊重我的工作。

respect² /rɪˈspekt/ *uncountable noun* 不可数名词
when you have a good opinion of someone or something, and consider them to be important 尊敬；敬意: *I have great respect for Tom.* 我非常尊敬汤姆。 □ *You should show respect for people's rights.* 你应该尊重人们的权利。

respectable /rɪˈspektəbəl/ *adjective* 形容词
used for describing someone or something that people have a good opinion of, and think is morally correct 可敬的；值得尊敬的: *He comes from a respectable family.* 他出身名门。

respectful /rɪˈspektfʊl/ *adjective* 形容词
polite to people 恭敬有礼的；尊敬人的: *The children were always respectful to older people.* 孩子们一直尊敬长者。

respiration /ˌrespəˈreɪʃən/ *uncountable noun* 不可数名词
the process of breathing 呼吸

respond /rɪˈspɒnd/ *verb* 动词 (**responds, responding, responded**)
to react to something that someone does or says by doing or saying something 回应；回答: *They responded to the president's request for financial help.* 他们响应了总统的经济援助要求。 □ *The army responded with bombs.* 军队以炸弹还击。

response /rɪˈspɒns/ *countable noun* 可数名词
a reply or a reaction to something that someone does or says 回应；回答: *There was no response to his remarks.* 他的言论无人响应。

responsibility /rɪˌspɒnsɪˈbɪlɪti/ *noun* 名词
1 *uncountable* 不可数 to have the job of dealing with something or someone 责任；负责: *Each manager had responsibility for ten people.* 每个经理负责10个人。
2 *uncountable* 不可数 when you agree that something bad that happened was your fault（坏事）责任: *No one admitted* responsibility for the attacks. 没有人承认对袭击事件负责。
3 [**responsibilities**] *plural* 复数 duties 职责；义务: *He is busy with work and family responsibilities.* 他工作、家庭两头忙。

responsible /rɪˈspɒnsɪbəl/ *adjective* 形容词
1 having the job or duty to deal with something 有责任的；负责的: *I met the people who are responsible for sales and advertising.* 我见了负责销售和广告的人。
2 used for saying that a particular event or situation is someone's fault（对特定事件或形势）负有责任的: *He still felt responsible for her death.* 他仍然觉得对她的死负有责任。
3 behaving in a proper and sensible way 负责任的；有责任心的: *She's a responsible child who often helps around the house.* 她是个有责任感的孩子，经常帮忙做家务。

rest¹ /rest/ *verb* 动词 (**rests, resting, rested**)
1 to spend some time relaxing after doing something tiring 休息；歇息: *He's tired, and the doctor advised him to rest.* 他累了，医生建议他休息。
2 to put one thing on another thing 放置；使倚靠: *He rested his arms on the table.* 他把胳膊搁在桌子上。

rest² /rest/ *noun* 名词
when you spend some time relaxing after doing something tiring 休息；歇息: *You're exhausted — go home and get some rest.* 你累坏了——回家休息一下吧。
the rest the parts of something that are left 剩余部分: *It was an experience I will remember for the rest of my life.* 这段经历我会铭记余生。 □ *I ate two cakes and saved the rest.* 我吃了两块蛋糕，剩下的留了下来。

restaurant /ˈrestərɒnt/ *countable noun* 可数名词
a place where you can buy and eat a meal 饭店；餐馆；饭馆: *We ate at an Italian restaurant.* 我们在一家意大利餐馆吃了饭。

restless /ˈrestləs/ *adjective* 形容词
bored or nervous, and wanting to move around 坐立不安的；不耐烦的: *I got restless and moved to San Francisco.* 我变得焦躁不安，搬到了旧金山。 □ *My father seemed very restless and excited.* 我父亲看上去坐立不安，非常兴奋。

restore /rɪˈstɔː/ *verb* 动词 (**restores, restoring, restored**)
to make something or someone good or

well again 恢复；修复：*We will restore her to health.* 我们会让她恢复健康。▫ *They are experts in restoring old buildings.* 他们是修复旧建筑的专家。

restrain /rɪˈstreɪn/ *verb* 动词 (**restrains, restraining, restrained**)
1 to use force to stop someone from doing something（用武力）制止，阻止，管制：*Wally held my arm to restrain me.* 沃利抓住我的胳膊想拦住我。
2 to stop yourself from showing an emotion 克制；控制；忍住：*She was unable to restrain her anger.* 她抑制不住自己的愤怒。

restrict /rɪˈstrɪkt/ *verb* 动词 (**restricts, restricting, restricted**)
1 to limit something 限制，限定：*The school is restricting the number of students it accepts this year.* 学校正在限制今年的招生人数。
2 to prevent someone or something from acting freely 束缚；妨碍；阻碍：*The bandage restricts the movement in my right arm.* 绷带使我右臂活动不便。
▸ **restriction** /rɪˈstrɪkʃən/ *noun* 名词：*Are there any parking restrictions in this street?* 这条街上有停车限制吗？

restroom /ˈrestrʊm/ also 亦作 **rest room** *countable noun* 可数名词 (*American* 美国英语)
→ see 见 **toilet**

result¹ /rɪˈzʌlt/ *countable noun* 可数名词
1 something that happens or exists because something else has happened 结果；后果：*People developed the disease as a direct result of their work.* 人们得这种病的直接原因是他们的工作。
2 facts such as a score that you get at the end of a competition or a test（比赛）得分；（考试）成绩；结果：*Are you happy with the election results?* 你对选举结果满意吗？

result² /rɪˈzʌlt/ *verb* 动词 (**results, resulting, resulted**)
result from something to be caused by a particular event or action 因某事物发生；随某事物产生：*Many health problems result from a poor diet.* 许多健康问题是不良饮食引起的。
result in something to cause a particular situation or event 造成某事；导致某事：*Half of all road accidents result in head injuries.* 一半的交通事故导致头部受伤。

resume /rɪˈzjuːm/ *verb* 动词 (**resumes, resuming, resumed**)
to begin an activity again (*formal* 正式)（中断后）恢复，继续：*After the war he resumed his job at Wellesley College.* 战后，他在韦尔斯利学院恢复了职位。▫ *The talks will resume on Tuesday.* 会谈将于周二继续。

résumé /ˈrezjʊmeɪ/ also 亦作 **resume** *countable noun* 可数名词 (*American* 美国英语)
→ see 见 **CV**

retail /ˈriːteɪl/ *uncountable noun* 不可数名词
when a business sells goods directly to the public 零售：*My sister works in retail, in a clothing shop.* 我姐姐在一家服装店做零售工作。

retailer /ˈriːteɪlə/ *countable noun* 可数名词
a business that sells goods directly to the public 零售商；零售店：*a furniture retailer* 家具零售商

retain /rɪˈteɪn/ *verb* 动词 (**retains, retaining, retained**)
to continue to have something (*formal* 正式) 保持：*He was looking for a way to retain control of his company.* 他在寻找一种方法来保持他对公司的控制。

rethink /riːˈθɪŋk/ *verb* 动词 (**rethinks, rethinking, rethought**)
to think about something such as a problem or a plan again and change it 重新考虑：*Both political parties are rethinking their policies.* 两个政党都在重新考虑他们的政策。

retire /rɪˈtaɪə/ *verb* 动词 (**retires, retiring, retired**)
to leave your job and usually stop working completely 退休：*He planned to retire at 65.* 他计划 65 岁退休。
▸ **retired** /rɪˈtaɪəd/ *adjective* 形容词：*I am a retired teacher.* 我是一名退休教师。

retirement /rɪˈtaɪəmənt/ *uncountable noun* 不可数名词
the period in someone's life after they retire 退休（生活）：*What do you plan to do during retirement?* 你退休后打算做什么？

retreat /rɪˈtriːt/ *verb* 动词 (**retreats, retreating, retreated**)
to move away from something or someone 撤退；退却：*I retreated from the room.* 我从房间里退了出来。▫ *The French soldiers were forced to retreat.* 法国士兵被

return¹ /rɪˈtɜːn/ *verb* 动词 (**returns, returning, returned**)
1 to go back to a place 返回；回来；回去：*He will return to Moscow tomorrow.* 他明天将返回莫斯科。
2 to give back or put back something that you borrowed or took 归还；带回；放回：*They will return the money later.* 他们以后会还钱的。

return² /rɪˈtɜːn/ *noun* 名词
1 *singular* 单数 when someone arrives back at a place where they were before 返回；回来；归来：*Kenny explained the reason for his return to London.* 肯尼解释了他返回伦敦的原因。
2 *countable* 可数 (also 亦作 **return ticket**) a ticket for a journey to a place and back again 往返票
in return done because someone did something for you 作为回报：*He smiled at Alison and she smiled in return.* 他对艾莉森微笑，她也对他微笑。

reunion /riːˈjuːniən/ *noun* 名词
a meeting between people who have not seen each other for a long time 团聚；重逢：*I am planning a family reunion.* 我正在计划一次家庭聚会。

reunite /ˌriːjuːˈnaɪt/ *verb* 动词 (**reunites, reuniting, reunited**)
to see each other again after a long time 团聚；重逢：*She was finally reunited with her family.* 她终于和家人团聚了。

reveal /rɪˈviːl/ *verb* 动词 (**reveals, revealing, revealed**)
1 to tell people something that they do not know already 透露；揭露；揭示：*She has refused to reveal any more details.* 她拒绝透露更多细节。
2 to show something by removing the thing that was covering it 显出；露出；展示：*She smiled, revealing small white teeth.* 她笑了，露出细小洁白的牙齿。

revenge /rɪˈvendʒ/ *uncountable noun* 不可数名词
something bad you do to someone who has hurt or harmed you 报复；报仇：*He wanted revenge for the way they treated his mother.* 他们那样对待他的母亲，他想报仇。

revenue /ˈrevənjuː/ *noun* 名词
money that a company, organization or government receives from people 收益；财政收入；税收收入：*The company gets 98% of its revenue from Internet advertising.* 该公司 98% 的收入来自网络广告。

Reverend /ˈrevərənd/ *noun* 名词
a title used before the name of a Christian church leader（对基督教会中圣职的尊称）牧师，神父：*The Reverend Jim Simons led the service.* 吉姆·西蒙斯牧师主持了礼拜仪式。

reverse¹ /rɪˈvɜːs/ *verb* 动词 (**reverses, reversing, reversed**)
1 to change a decision or a situation to the opposite decision or situation 颠倒；彻底转变；使完全相反：*They will not reverse the decision to increase prices.* 他们不会改变涨价的决定。
2 to arrange a group of things in the opposite order 使次序颠倒；使反转：*You've made a spelling mistake. You need to reverse the 'i' and the 'e'.* 你犯了一个拼写错误，i 和 e 的顺序要反过来。
3 to drive backwards in a vehicle 倒车：*A car reversed out of the driveway.* 一辆车倒出车道。

reverse² /rɪˈvɜːs/ *uncountable noun* 不可数名词
the control that makes a car ready to drive backwards（汽车的）倒挡：*I put the car in reverse.* 我给汽车挂上倒挡。

review¹ /rɪˈvjuː/ *countable noun* 可数名词
1 an occasion when you examine something to see if it needs changes 重新审视；检讨：*The president ordered a review of the situation.* 总统命令对该情况进行审查。
2 a report that gives an opinion about something such as a book or a film（书、电影等的）评论：*The film got a good review in the magazine.* 该影片在这本杂志上得到好评。

review² /rɪˈvjuː/ *verb* 动词 (**reviews, reviewing, reviewed**)
1 to consider something carefully to see if it needs changes 复查；重新审视；检讨：*The new plan will be reviewed by the city council.* 市议会将对新计划进行审查。
2 to write a report that gives your opinion of something such as a book or a film 评论（书、电影等）：*She reviews all the new DVDs.* 她对所有新出的 DVD 作了评论。

▶ **reviewer** /rɪˈvjuːə/ *countable noun* 可数

名词: He's a reviewer for The New York Times. 他是《纽约时报》的评论员。

revise /rɪ'vaɪz/ *verb* 动词 (revises, revising, revised)
1 to change something in order to make it better or more correct 修改；修订: *Ask a friend to revise a paragraph that you have written.* 请朋友修改你写的一个段落。 □ *We are revising the rules.* 我们正在修改规则。
2 to study something again in order to prepare for an exam（考试前）复习，温习: *I have to revise for my maths exam.* 我得复习准备数学考试。
▶ **revision** /rɪ'vɪʒən/ *uncountable noun* 不可数名词: *exam revision* 考试复习

revive /rɪ'vaɪv/ *verb* 动词 (revives, reviving, revived)
to become conscious again or to make someone conscious again（使）复苏；（使）复活: *A doctor revived the patient.* 一名医生使病人苏醒过来。

revolt /rɪ'vəʊlt/ *noun* 名词
an occasion when a group of people fight against a person or an organization that has control 反抗；反叛；起义: *It was a revolt by ordinary people against their leaders.* 这是普通民众对领导人的反抗。
● **revolt** *verb* 动词 (revolts, revolting, revolted): *California citizens revolted against higher taxes.* 加州市民反对增税。

revolting /rɪ'vəʊltɪŋ/ *adjective* 形容词
extremely unpleasant 令人极其反感的；令人作呕的: *The smell was revolting.* 那气味令人作呕。

revolution /ˌrevə'luːʃən/ *countable noun* 可数名词
1 an attempt by a group of people to change their country's government by using force 革命: *The period since the revolution has been peaceful.* 革命以来的这段时期是和平的。
2 an important change in a particular area of activity 巨变；变革: *There was a revolution in ship design in the nineteenth century.* 19世纪船舶设计发生了一场革命。

revolutionary /ˌrevə'luːʃənri/ *adjective* 形容词
1 trying to cause a revolution 革命的: *Do you know anything about the revolutionary movement?* 你了解这场革命运动吗？
2 changing the way that something is done or made 产生巨变的；革新的: *It is a revolutionary new product.* 这是一种革命性的新产品。

revolve /rɪ'vɒlv/ *verb* 动词 (revolves, revolving, revolved)
to move or turn in a circle 旋转；环绕: *The Earth revolves around the sun.* 地球绕着太阳转。
revolve around something to have something as the most important part 围绕某事物；以某事物为中心: *Her life has revolved around sports.* 她的生活一直以体育运动为中心。

revolver /rɪ'vɒlvə/ *countable noun* 可数名词
a type of small gun 左轮手枪

reward /rɪ'wɔːd/ *countable noun* 可数名词
something that someone gives you because you have done something good 奖励；报酬: *The school gives rewards for good behaviour.* 学校奖励表现好的同学。
● **reward** *verb* 动词 (rewards, rewarding, rewarded): *She was rewarded for her years of hard work.* 她多年的辛勤工作得到了回报。

rewarding /rɪ'wɔːdɪŋ/ *adjective* 形容词
giving you satisfaction or bringing you benefits 值得做的；有益的: *I have a job that is very rewarding.* 我有一份非常有意义的工作。

rewrite /ˌriː'raɪt/ *verb* 动词 (rewrites, rewriting, rewrote, rewritten)
to write something in a different way in order to improve it 重写；改写: *She decided to rewrite her article.* 她决定重写文章。

rhinoceros /raɪ'nɒsərəs/ *countable noun* 可数名词 (rhinoceroses)
a large animal from Asia or Africa with a horn on its nose 犀牛

rhyme[1] /raɪm/ *verb* 动词 (rhymes, rhyming, rhymed)
to end with a very similar sound to another word（字词）押韵: *'June' rhymes with 'moon'.* *June 和 moon 押韵。 □ *'June' and 'moon' rhyme.* *June 和 moon 押韵。

rhyme[2] /raɪm/ *countable noun* 可数名词
a poem that has words that rhyme at the ends of its lines 押韵诗: *He was teaching Helen a rhyme.* 他在教海伦一首押韵诗。

rhythm /'rɪðəm/ *noun* 名词
a regular pattern of sounds or movements 节奏；韵律: *Listen to the rhythms of jazz.*

听爵士乐的节奏。

rhythmic /ˈrɪðmɪk/ or 或 **rhythmical** /ˈrɪðmɪkəl/ *adjective* 形容词
repeated in a regular pattern 有节奏（或规律）的；节奏分明的: *Good breathing is slow and rhythmic.* 正确的呼吸方式应是缓慢而有节奏的。

rib /rɪb/ *countable noun* 可数名词
one of the 12 pairs of curved bones that surround your chest 肋骨: *Her heart was beating hard against her ribs.* 她的心剧烈地跳动着，撞击着她的胸膛。

ribbon /ˈrɪbən/ *noun* 名词
a long, narrow piece of cloth that you use to tie things together, or as a decoration 丝带；带子: *She tied her hair with a ribbon.* 她用丝带扎着头发。

ribbon 丝带

ˈrib cage *countable noun* 可数名词
the structure of bones in your chest that protects your lungs and other organs 胸廓

rice /raɪs/ *uncountable noun* 不可数名词
white or brown grains from a plant that grows in wet areas 稻米；大米: *The meal consisted of chicken, rice and vegetables.* 这顿饭包括鸡肉、米饭和蔬菜。
→ Look at picture on P5 参见彩插第 5 页

rich /rɪtʃ/ *adjective* 形容词 (**richer, richest**)
having a lot of money or valuable possessions 富裕的；富有的: *He was a very rich man.* 他是一个非常富有的人。
the rich rich people 富人；有钱人: *Only the rich can afford to live there.* 只有富人才住得起那里。

rid /rɪd/ *adjective* 形容词
get rid of something/someone to remove something or someone completely or make them leave 除掉（或清除）某事物 / 摆脱某人: *We had to get rid of our old car because it was too small.* 我们不得不把旧车处理掉，它太小了。

ridden /ˈrɪdən/
→ see 见 **ride**

riddle /ˈrɪdəl/ *countable noun* 可数名词
a question that seems to be nonsense, but that has a clever answer 谜语

ride¹ /raɪd/ *verb* 动词 (**rides, riding, rode, ridden**)
1 to sit on a bicycle or a horse, control it and travel on it 骑（自行车或马）: *Riding a bike is great exercise.* 骑自行车是很好的锻炼。□ *We passed three men riding on motorcycles.* 我们经过 3 个骑摩托车的人。
2 to travel in a vehicle 乘坐（交通工具）: *He rode in the bus to the hotel.* 他坐公共汽车去酒店。

ride² /raɪd/ *countable noun* 可数名词
a trip on a horse or a bicycle, or in a vehicle（骑马、骑车、乘车等的）旅程: *She took some friends for a ride in the car.* 她带了一些朋友去开车兜风。

rider /ˈraɪdə/ *countable noun* 可数名词
someone who rides a horse, a bicycle or a motorcycle 骑手；骑马（或自行车、摩托车）的人

ridge /rɪdʒ/ *countable noun* 可数名词
a long, narrow part of something that is higher than the rest 脊；隆起: *It's a high road along a mountain ridge.* 这是一条沿着山脊而上的公路。

ridiculous /rɪˈdɪkjʊləs/ *adjective* 形容词
very silly or not serious 荒谬的；可笑的: *They thought it was a ridiculous idea.* 他们认为这个想法很可笑。

riding /ˈraɪdɪŋ/ *uncountable noun* 不可数名词
the activity or sport of riding horses 骑马（运动）: *The next morning we went riding.* 第二天早上我们去骑马了。

rifle /ˈraɪfəl/ *countable noun* 可数名词
a long gun 步枪；来复枪: *They shot him with a rifle.* 他们用步枪向他射击。

right¹ /raɪt/ *adjective* 形容词, *adverb* 副词
1 correct or in a correct way 正确的（地）: *Ron was right about the result of the election.* 关于选举结果，罗恩是对的。□ *'C' is the right answer.* "C"是正确答案。□ *If I'm going to do something, I want to do it right.* 如果我要做某件事，我想把它做好。
2 best 最好的；最合适的: *You made the right choice in moving to New York.* 你搬到纽约是正确的选择。
3 morally good and acceptable 正当的；妥当的: *It's not right to leave the children here alone.* 把孩子们单独留在这儿是不对的。
4 to the side that is towards the east when you look north 往右边；向右边: *Turn right into the street.* 向右拐到大街上。
5 on the right side of your body 右边的: *He held his right arm out in front of him.* 他把右臂伸到前面。

6 used for saying that something happens exactly in a particular place or at a particular time 正好；恰好：*A car appeared right in front of him.* 一辆汽车出现在他的正前方。□ *Liz arrived right on time.* 利兹准时到达。

be right back to get back to a place in a very short time 马上回来：*I'm going to get some water. I'll be right back.* 我去弄点水，马上回来。

right away immediately (*informal* 非正式) 立即；马上：*He wants to see you right away.* 他要马上见你。

right² /raɪt/ *noun* 名词
1 uncountable 不可数 used for talking about actions that are morally good and acceptable 正当；公正；正确：*He knew right from wrong.* 他明辨是非。
2 singular 单数 the side that is towards the east when you look north 右方；右边：*On the right is a vegetable garden.* 右边是一个菜园。
3 something that you are allowed to do morally, or by law 权利：*We have the right to protest.* 我们有权抗议。□ *Make sure you know your rights.* 确保你知晓自己的权利。

right³ /raɪt/ *exclamation* 感叹词
used for checking whether you are correct （用于确认）对吗，是吧：*'You're coming to the party, right?'* "你要来参加聚会，对吗？"

right angle *countable noun* 可数名词
an angle that looks like a letter 'L' and equals 90 degrees 直角

right-hand *adjective* 形容词
on or near the right side of something 右边的；右面的：*There's a church on the right-hand side of the road.* 路的右边有一座教堂。

right-handed *adjective* 形容词
using your right hand rather than your left hand for activities such as writing and sports 惯用右手的

right-wing *adjective* 形容词
supporting the ideas of the political right 右翼的；右派的：*a right-wing politician* 右翼政客

rigid /ˈrɪdʒɪd/ *adjective* 形容词
1 that cannot be changed 死板的；一成不变的：*We have rigid rules about student behaviour.* 我们对学生的行为有严格规定。
2 stiff and not bending, stretching or twisting easily 坚硬的；不易弯曲的：*Use rigid plastic containers.* 使用硬质塑料容器。

rim /rɪm/ *countable noun* 可数名词
the edge of a curved object（弯曲之物的）边缘，边沿：*She looked at him over the rim of her glass.* 她越过玻璃杯口边沿看着他。

rind /raɪnd/ *noun* 名词
1 the thick outside skin of a fruit such as a lemon or an orange（柠檬、橙子等的）果皮
2 the hard outside edge of cheese that you do not eat（干酪的）外皮

ring¹ /rɪŋ/ *verb* 动词 (rings, ringing, rang, rung)
1 to make the sound of a bell 使（铃）鸣响，按（铃）；（铃）发出声响：*The school bell rang.* 学校的铃响了。□ *They rang the bell but nobody came to the door.* 他们按了门铃，但没人来开门。
2 (also 亦作 **ring someone up**) to telephone someone 给⋯打电话：*He rang me at my mother's.* 他打电话到我妈妈家找我。

ring someone back to phone someone again 给某人回电话：*Tell her I'll ring her back in a few minutes.* 告诉她我几分钟后再打过去。

ring someone up to phone someone 给某人打电话：*You can ring us up any time.* 你可以随时给我们打电话。

ring² /rɪŋ/ *countable noun* 可数名词
1 the sound of a bell 铃声；钟声：*There was a ring at the door.* 门铃响了。
2 a small circle of metal that you wear on your finger 戒指；指环：*She was wearing a gold wedding ring.* 她戴着一枚黄金婚戒。
3 something in the shape of a circle 圆；环：*They built the fire in a ring of stones.* 他们在一圈石头中生起火。

to give someone a ring to make a telephone call to somebody (*informal* 非正式) 给某人打电话：*We'll give him a ring later.* 我们一会儿给他打电话。

ringtone /ˈrɪŋtəʊn/ *countable noun* 可数名词
the sound that your mobile phone makes when someone calls you 手机铃声

rink /rɪŋk/ *countable noun* 可数名词
a large area of ice where people go to ice-skate (= move over ice in special boots) 溜冰场：*There were hundreds of skaters on the rink.* 溜冰场上有数百名溜冰者。

rinse /rɪns/ *verb* 动词 (**rinses, rinsing, rinsed**) to wash something in order to remove dirt or soap from it 冲洗；洗刷：*Make sure you rinse all the shampoo out of your hair.* 一定要把头发上的洗发水彻底冲洗干净。

riot /'raɪət/ *countable noun* 可数名词 an occasion when a group of people behave violently in a public place 暴乱；骚乱：*Twelve people were injured during a riot at the prison.* 在一场监狱暴乱中有 12 人受伤。● **riot** *verb* 动词 (**riots, rioting, rioted**)：*They rioted against the government.* 他们发动暴乱反对政府。

rip /rɪp/ *verb* 动词 (**rips, ripping, ripped**) to tear something quickly 猛地撕开；扯破：*I ripped my trousers when I fell.* 我跌倒时把裤子扯破了。
rip something up to tear something into small pieces 把某物撕碎：*He ripped up the letter and threw it in the fire.* 他把信撕碎扔进火里。

ripe /raɪp/ *adjective* 形容词 (**riper, ripest**) used for describing fruit or vegetables that are ready to eat（水果或蔬菜）成熟的：*Choose firm but ripe fruit.* 选择硬实但成熟的水果。

ripple /'rɪpəl/ *countable noun* 可数名词 a little wave on the surface of water 波纹；水波；涟漪 ● **ripple** *verb* 动词 (**ripples, rippling, rippled**)：*If you throw a stone in a pool, the water ripples.* 往池塘里扔块石头，水面就会泛起涟漪。

rise /raɪz/ *verb* 动词 (**rises, rising, rose, risen**)
1 to move upwards 上升；攀升：*We could see black smoke rising from the chimney.* 我们可以看见黑烟从烟囱里升起。
2 to stand up (*formal* 正式) 站起来：*He rose slowly from the chair.* 他慢慢地从椅子上站起来。
3 to get out of bed (*formal* 正式) 起床：*Tony rose early.* 托尼起得很早。
4 when the sun or the moon rises, it appears in the sky（太阳或月亮）升起
5 to increase 上升；上涨；提高：*His income rose by £5,000.* 他的收入增加了 5,000 英镑。● **rise** *countable noun* 可数名词：*a pay rise* 涨工资

LANGUAGE HELP 语言提示
Rise or raise? 用 rise 还是 raise？
Rise does not have an object. *rise 后不接宾语：*House prices are likely to rise.* 房价可能会涨。
Raise has an object. *raise 后接宾语：*The government has decided to raise taxes.* 政府决定加税。

risen /'rɪzən/
→ see 见 **rise**

risk¹ /rɪsk/ *noun* 名词
1 a possibility that something bad will happen 风险；危险：*There is a small risk of damage.* 有些许损坏的风险。
2 *countable* 可数 something or someone that is likely to harm you 隐患；危险人物；威胁：*Being very fat is a health risk.* 过于肥胖有健康隐患。
at risk in a situation where something bad might happen 处于危险中：*Our nation is at risk from an attack.* 我们国家面临着遭到攻击的危险。
take a risk to do something that might have bad results 冒险：*You're taking a big risk by leaving your job.* 你离职是在冒很大的风险。

risk² /rɪsk/ *verb* 动词 (**risks, risking, risked**)
1 to do something knowing that something bad might happen as a result 冒…的风险：*He risked breaking his leg when he jumped.* 他跳的时候冒着摔断腿的危险。
2 to behave in a way that might result in something important being lost or harmed 使面临危险；使冒险：*She risked her own life to help him.* 她冒着生命危险去帮助他。

risky /'rɪski/ *adjective* 形容词 (**riskier, riskiest**) dangerous or likely to fail 冒险的；有风险的：*They encourage young people to avoid risky behaviour.* 他们鼓励年轻人避免危险行为。

ritual /'rɪtʃuəl/ *noun* 名词 a series of actions that people perform in a particular order 典礼；仪式：*Every religion has holy days and rituals such as praying.* 每个宗教都有宗教节日和仪式，比如祈祷。

rival /'raɪvəl/ *countable noun* 可数名词 someone who competes against someone else 竞争对手：*He was accused of spying on his political rivals.* 他被指控暗中监视他的政治对手。

river /'rɪvə/ *countable noun* 可数名词 a long line of water that flows into a sea 河；江
→ Look at picture on P7 参见彩插第 7 页

road /rəʊd/ *countable noun* 可数名词
a long piece of hard ground that vehicles travel on 路；道路；公路：*There was very little traffic on the roads.* 路上的车辆很少。

roam /rəʊm/ *verb* 动词 (**roams, roaming, roamed**)
to move around an area without planning where exactly you are going 闲逛；游荡：*Children roamed the streets in groups.* 孩子们成群地在街上游荡。

roar /rɔː/ *verb* 动词 (**roars, roaring, roared**)
to make a very loud noise 吼叫；咆哮；轰鸣：*The engine roared, and the vehicle moved forward.* 发动机发出轰鸣声，车辆向前行驶。● **roar** *countable noun* 可数名词：*When did you first hear the roar of a lion?* 你第一次听到狮子的吼声是什么时候？

roast /rəʊst/ *verb* 动词 (**roasts, roasting, roasted**)
to cook meat or other food in an oven or over a fire 烤；炙：*He roasted the chicken.* 他烤了鸡肉。● **roast** *adjective* 形容词：*We had roast potatoes.* 我们吃了烤土豆。

rob /rɒb/ *verb* 动词 (**robs, robbing, robbed**)
to steal money or property from someone 抢劫；掠夺：*She was robbed of her watch.* 她的手表被抢了。
▶ **robber** /'rɒbə/ *countable noun* 可数名词：*a bank robber* 银行劫匪

robbery /'rɒbəri/ *noun* 名词 (**robberies**)
an occasion when a person steals money or property from a place 抢劫：*There have been several robberies in the area.* 该地区发生了几起抢劫案。

robe /rəʊb/ *countable noun* 可数名词
a special piece of clothing that an important person wears during a ceremony (*formal* 正式) 袍服；礼袍：*The judge was wearing a black robe.* 法官穿着一件黑色长袍。

robin /'rɒbɪn/ *countable noun* 可数名词
a brown bird with a red chest 欧亚鸲；知更鸟

robot /'rəʊbɒt/ *countable noun* 可数名词
a machine that can move and perform tasks automatically 机器人：*We have robots that we could send to the moon.* 我们有可以送去月球的机器人。

rock[1] /rɒk/ *noun* 名词
1 *uncountable* 不可数 the hard substance that is in the ground and in mountains 岩石：*We tried to dig, but the ground was solid rock.* 我们试图挖掘，但地面是坚硬的岩石。
2 *countable* 可数 a large piece of rock 巨石；岩块：*She sat on a rock and looked out across the sea.* 她坐在一块岩石上眺望大海。
3 *uncountable* 不可数 (*also* 亦作 **rock music**) loud music with a strong beat that you play on electric instruments 摇滚乐：*We went to a rock concert.* 我们去听摇滚音乐会。

rock[2] /rɒk/ *verb* 动词 (**rocks, rocking, rocked**)
1 to move slowly backwards and forwards 摇晃；晃动：*His body rocked gently in the chair.* 他的身体在椅子上轻轻地摇晃。
2 to make something move slowly backwards and forwards 使摇晃；使晃动：*She rocked the baby in her arms.* 她摇晃着怀里的婴儿。

ˌrock and ˈroll *also* 亦作 **rock'n'roll** *uncountable noun* 不可数名词
a type of music that was popular in the 1950s 摇滚乐：*Elvis Presley was known as the King of Rock and Roll.* 埃尔维斯·普雷斯利被称为摇滚乐之王。

rocket /'rɒkɪt/ *countable noun* 可数名词
1 a vehicle that people use to travel into outer space 火箭：*This is the rocket that took them to the moon.* 这是把他们带到月球的火箭。
2 a missile which contains a substance that can cause an explosion 火箭弹：*There was another rocket attack on the city.* 这座城市又遭到火箭弹袭击。

rocky /'rɒki/ *adjective* 形容词 (**rockier, rockiest**)
having a lot of rocks in it 多岩石的；嶙峋的：*The paths are very rocky.* 小路上布满岩石。

rod /rɒd/ *countable noun* 可数名词
a long, thin, metal or wooden bar (细长的) 杆，竿，棒：*The roof was supported with steel rods.* 屋顶由钢条支撑着。

rode /rəʊd/
→ see 见 **ride**

rodent /'rəʊdənt/ *countable noun* 可数名词
a small animal such as a mouse, with sharp front teeth 啮齿动物 (如老鼠)

role /rəʊl/ *countable noun* 可数名词
1 what someone or something should do

in a situation 职能；角色：*We discussed the role of parents in raising their children.* 我们讨论了父母在抚养孩子过程中扮演的角色。
2 the character that an actor plays in a film or a play（演员的）角色：*Who plays the role of the doctor?* 谁扮演医生的角色？

roll¹ /rəʊl/ *verb* 动词 (rolls, rolling, rolled)
1 to move along a surface, turning over many times（使）滚动；（使）翻滚：*The pencil rolled off the desk.* 铅笔从书桌上滚落下来。□ *I rolled a ball to the baby.* 我把球滚给小宝宝。
2 to move quickly down a surface 滚落；滑落：*Tears rolled down her cheeks.* 眼泪顺着她的脸颊滚落下来。
roll something up to form something into the shape of a ball or a tube 把某物卷成球形（或筒状）：*Steve rolled up the paper bag.* 史蒂夫把纸袋卷起来。

roll² /rəʊl/ *countable noun* 可数名词
1 a long piece of something such as paper that you form into the shape of a tube 卷；卷状物：*There are twelve rolls of cloth here.* 这儿有 12 卷布。
2 a small piece of bread that is round or long 小圆面包；小面包条：*He spread some butter on a roll.* 他在小面包条上涂了一些黄油。

Rollerblade /ˈrəʊləˌbleɪd/ *countable noun* 可数名词
a type of roller-skate with a single line of wheels along the bottom (*trademark* 商标) 罗勒布雷德直排轮滑鞋
▶ **rollerblading** /ˈrəʊləˌbleɪdɪŋ/ *uncountable noun* 不可数名词 (*trademark* 商标)：*Rollerblading is great fun for everyone.* 玩直排轮滑对每个人来说都很有趣。

roller-skate /ˈrəʊləˌskeɪt/ *countable noun* 可数名词
a boot with small wheels on the bottom 旱冰鞋；滚轴溜冰鞋：*a pair of roller skates* 一双旱冰鞋
▶ **roller-skating** /ˈrəʊləˌskeɪtɪŋ/ *uncountable noun* 不可数名词：*Roller-skating and swimming are my favourite hobbies.* 滑旱冰和游泳是我最大的爱好。

Roman Catholic /ˌrəʊmən ˈkæθlɪk/ *adjective* 形容词
(*also* 亦作 **Catholic**) belonging to a section of the Christian Church that has the Pope as its leader 天主教的：*I am a Roman Catholic priest.* 我是一名天主教神父。● **Roman Catholic** *countable noun* 可数名词：*Maria was a Roman Catholic.* 玛丽亚是天主教徒。

romance /rəˈmæns, ˈrəʊmæns/ *countable noun* 可数名词
1 a relationship between two people who love each other but who are not married 恋爱关系；风流韵事：*After a short romance they got married.* 短暂恋爱之后，他们结婚了。
2 a book or a film about a romantic relationship 爱情小说；爱情电影：*Claire writes romances and young adult fiction.* 克莱尔写言情和青春小说。

romantic /rəʊˈmæntɪk/ *adjective* 形容词
used when you are talking about love and romance 爱情的；浪漫的：*He was not interested in a romantic relationship with me.* 他对和我谈恋爱不感兴趣。□ *It is a lovely romantic film.* 这是一部温馨的爱情电影。

roof /ruːf/ *countable noun* 可数名词
1 the top surface that covers a building 屋顶：*The house has a red roof.* 这房子的屋顶是红色的。
2 the top of a vehicle 车顶：*He listened to the rain on the roof of the car.* 他听着雨拍打车顶的声音。

room /ruːm, rʊm/ *noun* 名词
1 *countable* 可数 a separate area inside a building that has its own walls 房间；室：*A minute later he left the room.* *1* 分钟后他离开了房间。
2 *uncountable* 不可数 enough empty space 空间：*There is room for 80 guests.* 有容纳 80 位客人的空间。

root /ruːt/ *countable noun* 可数名词
the part of a plant that grows under the ground（植物的）根，根茎：*She dug a hole near the roots of an apple tree.* 她在一棵苹果树的根部附近挖了一个洞。

rope /rəʊp/ *noun* 名词
a type of very thick string that is made by twisting together several strings or wires 绳子；绳索：*He tied the rope around his waist.* 他把绳子系在腰间。

rose¹ /rəʊz/
→ see 见 **rise**

rose² /rəʊz/ *countable noun* 可数名词
a flower with a pleasant smell and sharp

points (= thorns) on its stems 玫瑰；蔷薇

rot /rɒt/ **verb** 动词 (**rots, rotting, rotted**)
to get old and become softer, and sometimes smell bad 腐烂；腐败: *The grain will start to rot after the rain.* 雨后谷物将开始腐烂。

rotate /rəʊˈteɪt/ **verb** 动词 (**rotates, rotating, rotated**)
to turn in a circle around a central line or point 旋转；转动: *The Earth rotates every 24 hours.* 地球每 24 小时自转一周。
▶ **rotation** /rəʊˈteɪʃn/ **noun** 名词: *We learned about the daily rotation of the Earth.* 我们了解了地球每天的自转。

rotten /ˈrɒtn/ **adjective** 形容词
1 old and soft, and sometimes smelling bad 腐烂的；腐败的: *The smell was very strong — like rotten eggs.* 气味很浓——像臭鸡蛋。
2 very unpleasant or bad (*informal* 非正式) 糟糕的；恶劣的: *I think it's a rotten idea.* 我认为这是个烂主意。

rough /rʌf/ **adjective** 形容词 (**rougher, roughest**)
1 not smooth or even 粗糙的；凹凸不平的: *His hands were rough.* 他的手很粗糙。
2 using too much force 粗暴的；粗野的；猛烈的: *Football's a rough game.* 足球是一项剧烈运动。
▶ **roughly** /ˈrʌfli/ **adverb** 副词: *They roughly pushed past him.* 他们粗暴地从他身边挤过去。
3 not exact or complete 粗略的；大致的: *This is a rough guess of how much petrol we need.* 这是对我们所需汽油的粗略估计。
▶ **roughly** /ˈrʌfli/ **adverb** 副词: *Cancer kills roughly half a million people a year.* 每年大约有 50 万人死于癌症。

round¹ /raʊnd/ **adjective** 形容词 (**rounder, roundest**)
shaped like a circle or a ball 圆形的；球形的: *She has a round face.* 她有一张圆脸。

round² /raʊnd/ **countable noun** 可数名词
one game or a part of a competition (游戏或比赛的) 轮，次，局，场: *The team went through to the fifth round of the competition.* 这个队进入了比赛的第 5 轮。
□ *On Sundays, he has a round of golf at the club.* 星期天他都会在俱乐部打一场高尔夫球。

roundabout /ˈraʊndəˌbaʊt/ **countable noun** 可数名词

1 a circle in the road where several roads meet, that vehicles must drive round until they reach the road they need (道路汇合处的) 环行交叉；交通环岛
2 a round structure in a park, that children can sit on and turn around and around 旋转平台 (儿童游乐设施)

rounded /ˈraʊndɪd/ **adjective** 形容词
curved in shape, without any points or sharp edges 圆形的: *We came to a low, rounded hill.* 我们来到一座低矮的圆形小山旁。

route /ruːt/ **countable noun** 可数名词
a way from one place to another 路线；路径: *Which is the most direct route to the centre of the town?* 到市中心最直接的路线是哪一条？

routine /ruːˈtiːn/ **noun** 名词
the usual activities that you do every day 常规；例行公事: *The players changed their daily routine.* 球员们改变了他们的日常习惯。

row¹ /rəʊ/ **countable noun** 可数名词
a line of things or people 排；列；行: *They drove past a row of pretty little houses.* 他们开车经过一排漂亮的小房子。

row² /rəʊ/ **verb** 动词 (**rows, rowing, rowed**)
to make a boat move through the water by using oars (= long pieces of wood with flat ends) 划 (船): *I rowed across the lake.* 我划船过了湖。

row 划船

I rowed across the lake.
我划船过了湖。

row³ /raʊ/ **countable noun** 可数名词
an argument 吵架；争吵: *She was having a row with her sister.* 她那时正在和姐姐吵架。

royal /ˈrɔɪəl/ **adjective** 形容词
relating to a king or a queen 皇家的；王室的；国王的；女王的: *We have an invitation to a royal garden party.* 我们接到了参加皇家花园派对的邀请。

royalty /ˈrɔɪəlti/ **uncountable noun** 不可数名词
used when you are talking about the members of royal families 皇家成员；王室

成员：*He met royalty and government leaders from around the world.* 他会见了来自世界各地的皇室成员和政府领导人。

rub /rʌb/ *verb* 动词 (**rubs, rubbing, rubbed**)
1 to move a cloth or your fingers backwards and forwards over something（用布或手指）擦，搓：*He rubbed his stiff legs.* 他揉搓着僵硬的双腿。❑ *She took off her glasses and rubbed them with a soft cloth.* 她摘下眼镜，用一块软布擦了擦。
2 to spread a substance over the surface using your hand（用手）涂，抹，搽：*He rubbed oil into my back.* 他往我背上擦油。
rub something out to use a rubber to remove something you have written on paper 用橡皮擦掉（字迹等）

rubber /'rʌbə/ *noun* 名词
1 *uncountable* 不可数 a strong substance used for making tyres, boots and other products 橡胶：*I can smell burning rubber.* 我能闻到橡胶烧灼的味道。
2 (*American* 美国英语：**eraser**) *countable* 可数 a small piece of rubber that you use for removing marks you have made with a pencil 橡皮
→ Look at picture on P1 参见彩插第 1 页

rubber band *countable noun* 可数名词 a thin circle of rubber that you put around things such as papers in order to keep them together 橡皮筋；橡皮圈：*Her blonde hair was tied back with a rubber band.* 她的金发用橡皮筋扎在脑后。

rubbish /'rʌbɪʃ/ *uncountable noun* 不可数名词 (*American* 美国英语：**garbage**)
1 things you do not want any more 垃圾；废弃物：*I thought her note was just a bit of rubbish.* 我以为她的便条只是一张废纸。
2 something that is very poor quality 劣质的东西：*He thought her book was rubbish.* 他认为她的书很差劲。

ruby /'ru:bi/ *countable noun* 可数名词 (**rubies**)
a dark-red stone that is used in jewellery 红宝石：*I want a ruby ring.* 我想要一个红宝石戒指。

rucksack /'rʌksæk/ *countable noun* 可数名词
a bag that you carry on your back 背包

rude /ru:d/ *adjective* 形容词 (**ruder, rudest**)
1 not polite 无理的；粗鲁的：*He's so rude to her friends.* 他对她的朋友太粗鲁了。
▶ **rudely** /'ru:dli/ *adverb* 副词：*Some hotel guests treat our employees rudely.* 有些旅馆住客对我们的雇员很粗鲁。
▶ **rudeness** /'ru:dnəs/ *uncountable noun* 不可数名词：*Mum was annoyed at Cathy's rudeness.* 妈妈对凯茜的粗鲁很生气。
2 likely to embarrass or offend people 庸俗的；下流的：*Fred keeps telling rude jokes.* 弗雷德一直在讲下流的笑话。

rug /rʌɡ/ *countable noun* 可数名词 a piece of thick cloth that you put on a small area of a floor 小地毯：*There was a beautiful red rug on the floor.* 地板上有一块漂亮的红色小地毯。

rugby /'rʌɡbi/ *uncountable noun* 不可数名词 a game that is played by two teams who try to get a ball past a line at the end of the pitch 英式橄榄球运动
→ Look at picture on P14 参见彩插第 14 页

ruin /'ru:ɪn/ *verb* 动词 (**ruins, ruining, ruined**)
to completely harm, damage or spoil something 毁坏；破坏；糟蹋：*My wife was ruining her health.* 我妻子正在毁掉自己的健康。

ruins /'ru:ɪnz/ *plural noun* 复数名词 the parts of a building that remain after something destroys the rest 废墟；残垣断壁：*Police found two bodies in the ruins of the house.* 警方在房子的废墟中发现了两具尸体。
in ruins with only some parts remaining 严重受损的；遭毁灭的：*The church was in ruins.* 教堂成了废墟。

rule¹ /ru:l/ *countable noun* 可数名词 something that tells you what you must do or must not do 规则；规矩；规定：*I need a book that explains the rules of basketball.* 我需要一本解释篮球规则的书。

rule² /ru:l/ *verb* 动词 (**rules, ruling, ruled**)
to control the affairs of a country 统治，治理（国家）：*King Hussein ruled for 46 years.* 侯赛因国王统治了 46 年。
rule something out to decide that a course of action, an idea or a solution is impossible or not practical 把某事物排除在外；认为某事物不合适

ruler /'ru:lə/ *countable noun* 可数名词
1 the person who rules a country 统治者：*He was the ruler of France at that time.* 他当时是法国的统治者。
2 a long, flat object that you use for measuring things and for drawing straight

lines 直尺；尺子
→ Look at picture on P1 参见彩插第1页

rumble /ˈrʌmbəl/ *countable noun* 可数名词
a low, continuous noise 隆隆声: *We could hear the distant rumble of traffic.* 我们能听到远处车辆的隆隆声。●**rumble** *verb* 动词 (**rumbles, rumbling, rumbled**): *Her stomach was rumbling because she did not eat breakfast.* 她的肚子咕噜咕噜直叫，因为她没吃早饭。

rumour /ˈruːmə/ *noun* 名词
information that people talk about, that may not be true 谣言；流言: *There's a rumour that you're leaving.* 有传言说你要走了。

run[1] /rʌn/ *verb* 动词 (**runs, running, ran, run**)
1 to move very quickly on your legs 跑；奔跑: *It's very dangerous to run across the road.* 跑着过马路是很危险的。
▸**running** /ˈrʌnɪŋ/ *uncountable noun* 不可数名词: *He goes running every morning.* 他每天早上去跑步。
2 to go in a particular direction 伸展；延伸: *The road runs east from Oxford to Cowley.* 这条路从牛津向东延伸到考利。
3 to be in charge of a business or an activity 管理；经营: *She runs a restaurant in San Francisco.* 她在旧金山经营一家餐馆。
4 to be switched on and working 运行；运转: *Sam waited in the car, with the engine running.* 萨姆在车里等着，没有熄火。
5 to take passengers between two places（按某路线）行驶: *A bus runs between the station and the town centre.* 车站和市中心之间有公共汽车往返。
6 to flow in a particular direction 流动；流淌: *Tears were running down her cheeks.* 眼泪顺着她的脸颊流下来。

run away to leave a place because you are unhappy or afraid there 逃走；逃离: *The girl turned and ran away.* 女孩转身跑开了。

run into someone to meet someone unexpectedly 偶然遇见某人: *He ran into William in the supermarket.* 他在超市碰到了威廉。

run into someone/something to hit someone or something with a vehicle（开车）撞上某人／某物: *The driver was going too fast and ran into a tree.* 司机开得太快，撞上了一棵树。

run off to go away from a place when you should stay there 跑掉；跑开: *Our dog is always running off.* 我们的狗总是乱跑。

□ *The thief ran off when he saw her.* 小偷看见她就跑掉了。

run out of something to have no more of something left 用完某物；耗尽某物: *We ran out of milk this morning.* 我们今天早上没有牛奶了。

run someone over to hit someone with a vehicle so that they fall to the ground（汽车等）撞倒某人，碾过某人: *A police car ran her over.* 一辆警车从她身上碾过。

run[2] /rʌn/ *noun* 名词
1 when you move very quickly on your legs 跑；跑步: *After a six-mile run, Jackie went home for breakfast.* 跑了6英里后，杰基回家吃早饭。
2 *countable* 可数 one point in the game of cricket or baseball（板球或棒球的）一分: *The Blue Jays have scored 173 runs in their past 24 games.* 蓝鸟队在过去的24场比赛中得到173分。

in the long run used for saying what you think will happen over a long period of time in the future 从长远来看: *Spending more on education now will save money in the long run.* 现在在教育上多花钱从长远来看会省钱。

run-ˈdown *adjective* 形容词
1 tired or slightly ill (*informal* 非正式) 疲惫的；略感不适的
2 in very bad condition 破败的；失修的: *He promised financial help for run-down areas.* 他承诺对破败的地区提供财政援助。

rung[1] /rʌŋ/
→ see 见 **ring**

rung[2] /rʌŋ/ *countable noun* 可数名词   rung 梯级
one of the steps that you climb up on a ladder（梯子的）横档，梯级

runner /ˈrʌnə/ *countable noun* 可数名词
a person who runs, or who is running 奔跑的人；赛跑选手: *He is the oldest runner in the race.* 他是比赛中最年长的赛跑选手。

runner-ˈup *countable noun* 可数名词 (**runners-up**)
the person who is in second place in a race or competition 第二名；亚军: *The runner-up will receive £500.* 亚军将获得500英镑。

runny /ˈrʌni/ *adjective* 形容词 (**runnier, runniest**)
having more liquid than usual 稀软的；呈流质状的: *Warm the jelly until it is runny.* 把果冻加热，直到它变稀软。
a runny nose when a thick liquid flows from your nose, for example because you have a cold 流鼻涕

runway /ˈrʌnweɪ/ *countable noun* 可数名词
a long road that an aircraft travels on before it starts flying（飞机）跑道

rural /ˈrʊərəl/ *adjective* 形容词
not near cities or large towns 乡村的；农村的: *The service is ideal for people who live in rural areas.* 这项服务很适合生活在农村地区的人。

rush[1] /rʌʃ/ *verb* 动词 (**rushes, rushing, rushed**)
1 to go somewhere quickly 迅速移动；冲: *Emma rushed into the room.* 埃玛冲进房间。
2 to do something quickly 匆忙做: *Foreign banks rushed to buy as many dollars as they could.* 外国银行争相购买尽可能多的美元。
3 to take someone to a place quickly 将⋯迅速送到（某处）: *They rushed him to a hospital.* 他们赶紧把他送到医院。

rush[2] /rʌʃ/ *noun* 名词
in a rush quickly 很快地；匆忙地: *The men left in a rush.* 那些人匆忙离开了。

rush hour *countable noun* 可数名词
a period of the day when most people are travelling to or from their job（上下班时间）交通高峰时段: *Try to avoid travelling during the evening rush hour.* 尽量避免在傍晚高峰时间出行。

rust /rʌst/ *uncountable noun* 不可数名词
a red-brown substance that forms on iron or steel when it is wet 锈；铁锈: *The old car was red with rust.* 那辆旧汽车锈得发红。 ● **rust** *verb* 动词 (**rusts, rusting, rusted**): *Iron rusts if you do not keep it dry.* 铁如果不保持干燥就会生锈。

rustle /ˈrʌsəl/ *verb* 动词 (**rustles, rustling, rustled**)
to make soft sounds while moving 发出轻轻的摩擦声；发出沙沙声: *The leaves rustled in the wind.* 树叶在风中沙沙作响。
● **rustle** *countable noun* 可数名词: *We listened to the rustle of leaves outside.* 我们听着外面树叶的沙沙声。

rusty /ˈrʌsti/ *adjective* 形容词 (**rustier, rustiest**)
having some rust on it 生锈的: *The house has a rusty iron gate.* 这所房子有一扇生锈的铁门。

rut /rʌt/ *countable noun* 可数名词
a deep, narrow mark that the wheels of a vehicle make in the ground 车辙: *He drove slowly over the ruts in the road.* 他慢慢驶过路上的车辙。
in a rut having a particular way of doing things that is difficult to change 单调乏味的: *I don't like being in a rut.* 我不喜欢一成不变的生活。

ruthless /ˈruːθləs/ *adjective* 形容词
cruel and not caring if your actions harm other people 残酷无情的；残忍的: *a ruthless dictator* 残酷无情的独裁者

Ss

sack[1] /sæk/ **countable noun** 可数名词
a large bag made of thick paper or rough material 厚纸袋；麻布袋：*a sack of potatoes* 一麻袋土豆
get the sack to be told that you must leave your job 解雇；被开除

sack[2] /sæk/ **verb** 动词 (**sacks, sacking, sacked**)
to tell someone to leave their job 解雇；开除：*He was sacked for stealing from the company.* 他因在公司行窃被开除。

sacred /ˈseɪkrɪd/ **adjective** 形容词
having a special religious meaning 神圣的：*The eagle is sacred to Native Americans.* 对于美洲印第安人而言，雕是神圣之物。

sacrifice /ˈsækrɪˌfaɪs/ **verb** 动词 (**sacrifices, sacrificing, sacrificed**)
1 to give up something valuable or important in order to get something else for yourself or for other people 牺牲；献出：*She sacrificed family life for her career.* 她为了事业舍弃了家庭。 ● **sacrifice** noun 名词：*The family made many sacrifices so that they could send the children to a good school.* 为了能让孩子们上好学校，这家人付出了很多牺牲。
2 to kill an animal in a special religious ceremony in order to say thank you to a god 以（动物）作祭献：*The village elders sacrificed a chicken.* 村子里的长者以一只鸡作祭品。

sad /sæd/ **adjective** 形容词 (**sadder, saddest**)
1 unhappy 悲伤的；伤心的：*I'm sad that Jason's leaving.* 贾森要走了，我感到很难过。
▶ **sadly** /ˈsædli/ **adverb** 副词：*'My girlfriend is moving away,' he said sadly.* "我女朋友要搬走了。"他伤心地说。
→ Look at picture on P15 参见彩插第 15 页
▶ **sadness** /ˈsædnəs/ **uncountable noun** 不可数名词：*I left with a mixture of sadness and joy.* 我怀着悲喜交加的心情离开了。
2 making you feel unhappy 令人难过的：*It was a sad ending to a great story.* 这个故事很精彩，但结局让人难过。 ▫ *I have some sad news for you.* 我有个坏消息要告诉你。

saddle /ˈsædəl/ **countable noun** 可数名词 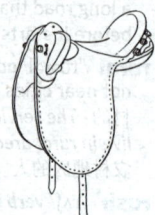 saddle 马鞍
1 a leather seat that you put on the back of an animal 鞍子；马鞍：*He put a saddle on the horse.* 他给马装好马鞍。
2 a seat on a bicycle or a motorcycle（自行车或摩托车的）车座

safari /səˈfɑːri/ **countable noun** 可数名词
a trip to look at or hunt wild animals 观兽旅行；游猎：*She went on a seven-day African safari.* 她踏上了为期 7 天的非洲观兽之旅。

safe[1] /seɪf/ **adjective** 形容词 (**safer, safest**)
1 not dangerous 安全的；不构成危险的：*We must try to make our roads safer.* 我们必须尽力使我们的道路更安全。
2 not in danger 平安的；处境安全的：*Where's Sophie? Is she safe?* 索菲在哪儿？她安全吗？
▶ **safely** /ˈseɪfli/ **adverb** 副词：*'Drive safely,' he said, waving goodbye.* "小心开车。"他边说边挥手告别。

safe[2] /seɪf/ **countable noun** 可数名词
a strong metal box with a lock, where you keep money or other valuable things 保险柜：*Who has the key to the safe?* 谁有保险柜的钥匙？

safety[1] /ˈseɪfti/ **uncountable noun** 不可数名词
the state of not being in danger 安全；平安：*We need to improve safety on our roads.* 我们需要改善道路的交通安全。

safety[2] /ˈseɪfti/ **adjective** 形容词
intended to make something less dangerous 保障安全的：*There are child safety locks on all the gates.* 所有门都装上了儿童安全锁。

sag /sæg/ **verb** 动词 (**sags, sagging, sagged**)
to hang down loosely or to have a fold in the middle 松垂；下垂；下凹：*The dress*

won't sag or lose its shape after washing. 这条连衣裙洗后依然挺括，不会变形。

said /sed/
→ see 见 **say**

sail¹ /seɪl/ *countable noun* 可数名词
a large piece of cloth on a boat, that catches the wind and moves the boat along 帆

sail² /seɪl/ *verb* 动词 (**sails, sailing, sailed**)
1 a boat sails when it moves over water (船)航行，行驶: *The ferry sails between Seattle and Bremerton.* 渡轮在西雅图和布雷默顿之间航行。
2 to use a boat's sails to move it across water 使扬帆行驶；驾驶(船只): *I'd like to buy a big boat and sail it around the world.* 我想买一艘大船，然后开着它环游世界。

sailing /'seɪlɪŋ/ *uncountable noun* 不可数名词
the activity or sport of sailing boats 帆船驾驶；帆船运动: *There was swimming and sailing on the lake.* 湖里有人游泳有人玩帆船。

sailor /'seɪlə/ *countable noun* 可数名词
someone who works on a ship or who sails a boat 水手；船员；海员

saint /seɪnt/ *countable noun* 可数名词
in certain religions, someone who has died, and whose life was a perfect example of the way people should live 圣徒；圣人: *Every church here was named after a saint.* 这里的每座教堂都以一位圣徒的名字命名。

sake /seɪk/ *noun* 名词
for something's/someone's sake or **for the sake of something/someone** to help something or someone, or because of something or someone 因为某事物／某人的缘故: *For safety's sake never stand directly behind a horse.* 为安全起见，千万别站在马的正后方。□ *Please do a good job, for Stan's sake.* 看在斯坦的份上，请好好干。□ *For the sake of peace, I am willing to forgive them.* 为维持和睦，我愿意原谅他们。□ *They stayed together for the sake of the children.* 他们因为孩子还在一起。

salad /'sæləd/ *noun* 名词
a mixture of foods, especially vegetables, that you usually serve cold 沙拉: *She ordered a pasta and a green salad.* 她点了意大利面和蔬菜沙拉。

salary /'sæləri/ *noun* 名词 (**salaries**)
the money that you earn from your employer 薪资；薪金；薪酬；薪水: *The lawyer was paid a huge salary.* 那名律师薪水极高。

LANGUAGE HELP 语言提示

Pay, salary, or **wages**? 用 pay、salary 还是 wages？
Use the noun **pay** to talk in general about the money people get from their employer for doing their job. 泛指薪酬时用 pay。
Professional people and office workers receive a **salary**, which is paid every month. 表示专业技术人才或办公室职员按月领取的薪酬用 salary。
People who do physical work, for example in a factory, receive **wages**, or **a wage**. 工厂工人等体力劳动者领取的薪酬用 wages 或 a wage。

sale /seɪl/ *noun* 名词
1 *singular* 单数 when you sell something for money 卖；销售: *He made a lot of money from the sale of the business.* 他把公司卖掉得了一大笔钱。
2 *countable* 可数 a time when a shop sells things at less than their normal price (商店的)清仓季，打折活动: *Did you know the bookshop was having a sale?* 你当时知不知道书店正打折呢？
for sale available for people to buy 待售: *The house had a 'For Sale' sign in the garden.* 这房子的花园里竖着"待售"的牌子。
on sale available for less than the normal price 打折出售: *She bought the coat on sale at a department store.* 她在百货商店买了这件打折的大衣。

salesman /'seɪlzmən/ *countable noun* 可数名词 (**salesmen** /'seɪlzmen/)
a man whose job is to sell things 男店员；男售货员；男推销员: *He's an insurance salesman.* 他是名保险推销员。

salesperson /'seɪlzpɜːsən/ *countable noun* 可数名词 (**salespeople** /'seɪlzpiːpəl/ or 或 **salespersons**)
a person whose job is to sell things 店员；售货员；推销员: *Be sure to ask the salesperson for help.* 一定要求助于售货员。

saleswoman /'seɪlzwʊmən/ *countable noun* 可数名词 (**saleswomen** /'seɪlzwɪmɪn/)
a woman whose job is to sell things 女店员；女售货员；女推销员: *She spent three years as a saleswoman.* 她做了3年的推

销员。

saliva /səˈlaɪvə/ *uncountable noun* 不可数名词
the liquid in your mouth that helps you to swallow food 唾液: *They tested his saliva.* 他们化验了他的唾液。

salmon /ˈsæmən/ *noun* 名词 (**salmon**)
1 *countable* 可数 a large fish with silver skin 鲑(鱼); 大麻哈鱼
2 *uncountable* 不可数 the pink flesh of this fish that you can eat 鲑鱼肉; 大麻哈鱼肉: *He gave them a plate of salmon.* 他给他们一盘鲑鱼肉。

salon /ˈsælɒn/ *countable noun* 可数名词
a place where you go to have your hair cut, or to have beauty treatments 美发厅; 美容院; 发廊: *The club has a beauty salon and two swimming pools.* 这家俱乐部有一个美容院和两个游泳池。

salt /sɔːlt/ *uncountable noun* 不可数名词
a white substance that you use to improve the flavour of food 盐; 食盐: *Now add salt and pepper.* 现在加入盐和胡椒粉。

salty /ˈsɔːlti/ *adjective* 形容词 (**saltier, saltiest**)
containing salt or tasting of salt 含盐的; 咸的: *He eats too many crisps and salty snacks.* 他吃了太多薯片和咸味小吃。

salute /səˈluːt/ *verb* 动词 (**salutes, saluting, saluted**)
to make a special sign to show your respect for someone, for example by raising your right hand to your head, like a soldier 敬礼; 向⋯致敬: *The sailors saluted as the captain entered the room.* 舰长走进房间时，水手们敬礼。 □ *The two guards saluted the major.* 两名警卫向少校敬礼。

salute 敬礼

same /seɪm/ *adjective* 形容词
1 very similar 相同的; 同样的: *The houses are all the same.* 这些房子全都一样。
2 used to show that you are talking about only one thing, and not two different ones 同一的: *Jason works at the same office as Gabrielle.* 贾森和加布丽埃勒在同一个办公室工作。 □ *He gets up at the same time every day.* 他每天在同一时间起床。

sample /ˈsɑːmpəl/ *countable noun* 可数名词
a small amount of something that shows you what the rest of it is like 样品; 样本: *We're giving away 2,000 free samples of the perfume.* 我们正在免费发放 2,000 份香水试用样品。 □ *The doctor took a blood sample.* 医生拿走了一份血样。

sand /sænd/ *uncountable noun* 不可数名词
a powder made of very small pieces of stone that you find in some deserts and on most beaches 沙; 沙子: *They walked across the sand to the water's edge.* 他们走过沙地来到水边。

sandal /ˈsændəl/ *countable noun* 可数名词
a light shoe that you wear in warm weather 凉鞋: *He put on a pair of old sandals.* 他穿上了一双旧凉鞋。

sandwich /ˈsænwɪdʒ/ *countable noun* 可数名词
two slices of bread with another food such as cheese or meat between them 三明治: *She ordered an egg sandwich.* 她点了一份鸡蛋三明治。

sandy /ˈsændi/ *adjective* 形容词 (**sandier, sandiest**)
covered with sand 铺满沙子的: *The island has long, sandy beaches.* 这个岛有长长的沙滩。

sane /seɪn/ *adjective* 形容词 (**saner, sanest**)
thinking and behaving normally and reasonably; not mad 心智健全的; 神志正常的: *He seemed perfectly sane.* 他看上去神志十分正常。

sang /sæŋ/
→ see 见 **sing**

sank /sæŋk/
→ see 见 **sink**

sarcasm /ˈsɑːkæzəm/ *uncountable noun* 不可数名词
the use of words or phrases that are the opposite of what you really mean in order to be rude to someone 讽刺; 嘲笑; 挖苦: *'How nice of you to join us,' he said with heavy sarcasm.* "你能加入我们可真是太好了。"他狠狠挖苦道。

sarcastic /sɑːˈkæstɪk/ *adjective* 形容词
saying the opposite of what you really

mean in order to be rude to someone 讽刺的；嘲笑的；挖苦的: He made some very sarcastic comments. 他冷嘲热讽地点评了几句。

sardine /sɑːˈdiːn/ **countable noun** 可数名词
a small sea fish that you can eat 沙丁鱼: They opened a can of sardines. 他们打开了一罐沙丁鱼。

sat /sæt/
→ see 见 **sit**

satellite /ˈsætəˌlaɪt/ **countable noun** 可数名词
a piece of electronic equipment that is sent into space in order to receive and send back information 人造卫星: The rocket carried two communications satellites. 火箭搭载了两颗通信卫星。
→ Look at picture on P9 参见彩插第 9 页

ˈsatelliteˌdish countable noun 可数名词
a piece of equipment that people put on their house in order to receive television signals from a satellite 碟形卫星电视天线
→ Look at picture on P11 参见彩插第 11 页

ˌsatelliteˈnaviˌgation uncountable noun 不可数名词
a system that uses information from a satellite (= an object that moves around the Earth in space) to help you to find your way 卫星导航: Many of the boats have satellite navigation. 这些船很多都装了卫星导航。

ˌsatelliteˈtelevision uncountable noun 不可数名词
a system of broadcasting television programs that are sent to your television from a satellite (= an object that moves around the Earth in space) 卫星电视: We have access to 49 satellite television channels. 我们能收到 49 个卫星电视频道。

satin /ˈsætɪn/ **noun** 名词
a smooth, shiny type of cloth 缎子: She's wearing a satin dress. 她穿着一条缎面连衣裙。

satire /ˈsætaɪə/ **noun** 名词
1 uncountable 不可数 the use of humour to criticize people's behaviour or ideas 讽刺；讥讽: He loved the book's humour and satire. 他喜欢这本书的诙谐和讽刺。
2 countable 可数 a play, a film or a piece of writing that uses humour to criticize people's behaviour or ideas 讽刺作品: The film is a satire on American politics. 这部电影讽刺了美国政治。

satisfaction /ˌsætɪsˈfækʃən/ **uncountable noun** 不可数名词
the feeling of being pleased to do or to get something 满意；满足: It gives me a real sense of satisfaction when I help someone. 帮助他人时让我有种真正的满足感。

satisfactory /ˌsætɪsˈfæktəri/ **adjective** 形容词
good enough for a particular purpose 令人满意的；够好的: I never got a satisfactory answer. 我从未得到一个令人满意的答复。

satisfied /ˈsætɪsˌfaɪd/ **adjective** 形容词
happy because you have what you wanted 满意的；满足的: Doctors are satisfied with his condition. 医生们对他的状况很满意。

satisfy /ˈsætɪsfaɪ/ **verb** 动词 (**satisfies, satisfying, satisfied**)
to give someone enough of what they want or need 使满意；使满足: Milk alone should satisfy your baby's hunger. 奶就足以喂饱你的宝宝了。

satisfying /ˈsætɪsˌfaɪɪŋ/ **adjective** 形容词
making you feel happy because you have what you want, or you are doing what you want 令人满意的；令人满足的: Taking care of children can be very satisfying. 照顾小孩子能给人极大的满足感。

satnav /ˈsætˌnæv/ **noun** 名词
a piece of equipment in a car that tells you the best way of getting to a place (车载)卫星导航仪: We didn't have a satnav, so we had to use a map. 我们没有安装卫星导航，所以只好看地图。
→ Look at picture on P11 参见彩插第 11 页

Saturday /ˈsætədeɪ, -di/ **noun** 名词
the day after Friday and before Sunday 星期六: He called her on Saturday morning. 他周六早上给她打了电话。□ Every Saturday, Dad made soup. 爸爸每周六都做汤。

sauce /sɔːs/ **noun** 名词
a thick liquid that you eat with other food 调味汁；酱: The pasta is cooked in a garlic and tomato sauce. 这份意大利面拌入了蒜蓉番茄酱。

saucepan /ˈsɔːspən/ **countable noun** 可数名词
a deep metal cooking pot, usually with a long handle and a lid (长柄的)炖锅，深平底锅: Place the potatoes in a saucepan and

boil them. 把土豆放入炖锅中煮。

saucepan
炖锅

saucer /ˈsɔːsə/ *countable noun* 可数名词
a small curved plate that you put under a cup 茶碟；茶托

sauna /ˈsɔːnə/ *countable noun* 可数名词
a very hot room that is filled with steam, where people relax 桑拿浴室；蒸汽浴室：*The hotel has a sauna and a swimming pool.* 这家酒店有一个桑拿浴室和一个游泳池。

sausage /ˈsɒsɪdʒ/ *noun* 名词
a mixture of very small pieces of meat, spices and other foods, inside a long thin skin 香肠；腊肠：*They ate sausages for breakfast.* 他们早饭吃了香肠。

savage /ˈsævɪdʒ/ *adjective* 形容词
very cruel or violent 凶残的；残暴的：*This was a savage attack on a young girl.* 这是对一个年轻女孩的野蛮袭击。

save¹ /seɪv/ *verb* 动词 (**saves, saving, saved**)
1 to help someone to escape from a dangerous or a bad situation 拯救；救助：*We must save these children from disease and death.* 我们必须救助这些孩子，让他们远离疾病和死亡。
2 (also 亦作 **save up**) to gradually collect money by spending less than you get 攒（钱）；存（钱）：*Tim and Barbara are now saving for a house.* 蒂姆和芭芭拉正在攒钱买房子。 ▫ *I was saving money to go to college.* 我一直为上大学攒钱。 ▫ *Taylor was saving up for something special.* 泰勒一直攒钱以备特殊之用。
3 to use less of something 节省；节约：*Going through the city by bike saves time.* 骑自行车在这座城市中穿行很省时间。 ▫ *We're trying to save water.* 我们尽量节约用水。
4 to keep something because you will need it later 保留；留下：*Save the vegetable water for making the sauce.* 留下煮菜的汤做调味汁。
5 to give a computer an instruction to store some information 保存；存盘：*It's important to save frequently when you are working on a document.* 编辑文档时随时保存很重要。

save² /seɪv/ *countable noun* 可数名词
the act of stopping someone from scoring a goal in a sports game（体育比赛中的）救球：*The goalkeeper made some great saves.* 守门员有几次精彩救球。

savings /ˈseɪvɪŋz/ *plural noun* 复数名词
all the money that you have saved, especially in a bank 存款；积蓄：*Her savings were in the First National Bank.* 她的钱存在第一国民银行里。

savoury /ˈseɪvəri/ *adjective* 形容词
having a salty flavour rather than a sweet one 咸味的：*We had all sorts of sweet and savoury snacks at the party.* 我们为聚会准备了各种甜咸小吃。

saw¹ /sɔː/
→ see 见 **see**

saw² /sɔː/ *countable noun* 可数名词
a metal tool for cutting wood 锯 ● **saw** *verb* 动词 (**saws, sawing, sawed, sawn**)：*He escaped by sawing through the bars of his jail cell.* 他锯断牢房的窗栅栏逃跑了。 ▫ *I sawed the dead branches off the tree.* 我锯掉树上的枯枝。

sawn /sɔːn/
→ see 见 **saw**

saxophone /ˈsæksəˌfəʊn/ *noun* 名词
a musical instrument made of metal that you play by blowing into it 萨克斯管
→ Look at picture on P12 参见彩插第 12 页

say¹ /seɪ/ *verb* 动词 (**says, saying, said**)
1 to speak words 说；讲：*She said that they were very pleased.* 她说他们很高兴。 ▫ *I packed and said goodbye to Charlie.* 我收拾好行李和查利道别。

> **LANGUAGE HELP** 语言提示
> **Say** or **tell**? 用 say 还是 tell？
> Use **say** with the actual words that someone speaks, or before **that** with reported speech. *say 后接实际话语，或 that 引导的间接引语：*He said 'I don't feel well.'* 他说："我不太舒服。" ▫ *He said that he didn't feel well.* 他说他不太舒服。
> Remember: You **say something to someone**. 注意：跟某人说某事要用 say something to someone：*What did she say to you?* 她跟你说了什么？
> You **tell someone something**. 告诉某人某事则要用 tell someone something：*He*

told Alison the news. 他把这则消息告诉了艾莉森。
2 to give information in writing or in numbers 表明；指示：*The clock said four minutes past eleven.* 时钟显示时间是 11 点 4 分。

say² /seɪ/ *noun* 名词
have your say in something to have the right to give your opinion about something 对某事物有发言权：*He should have a say in the decisions that affect his life.* 对影响到自己生活的决定，他应该有权发表意见。

saying /ˈseɪɪŋ/ *countable noun* 可数名词
something that people often say, that gives advice about life 谚语；格言；警句：*Remember that old saying: 'Forgive and forget.'* 记住那句老话：既往不咎。

scab /skæb/ *countable noun* 可数名词
a hard, dry cover that forms over the surface of a wound 痂：*After a few days, the spots become dry and form scabs.* 几天之后，这些小疱干瘪，结了痂。

scaffolding /ˈskæfəldɪŋ/ *uncountable noun* 不可数名词
a frame of metal bars that people can stand on when they are working on the outside of a building (用于室外施工的) 脚手架：*Builders have put up scaffolding around the tower.* 建筑工人已经在塔周围搭好了脚手架。

scald /skɔːld/ *verb* 动词 (**scalds, scalding, scalded**)
to burn yourself with very hot liquid or steam 烫伤：*A patient scalded herself in the bath.* 一名病人在洗澡时烫伤了自己。

scale /skeɪl/ *noun* 名词
1 *countable* 可数 a set of levels or numbers that you use to measure things 等级；级别：*The earthquake measured 5.5 on the Richter scale.* 这场地震为里氏 5.5 级。
2 *countable* 可数 one of the small, flat pieces of hard skin that cover the body of animals like fish and snakes 鳞；鳞片
3 *singular* 单数 the size or level of something 规模；范围；程度：*He doesn't realize the scale of the problem.* 他没有意识到问题的严重性。
4 *countable* 可数 a set of musical notes that are played in a fixed order 音阶：*the scale of F major* *F 大调音阶 ▫ *Celia was practising her scales on the piano.* 西莉亚在钢琴上练习音阶。

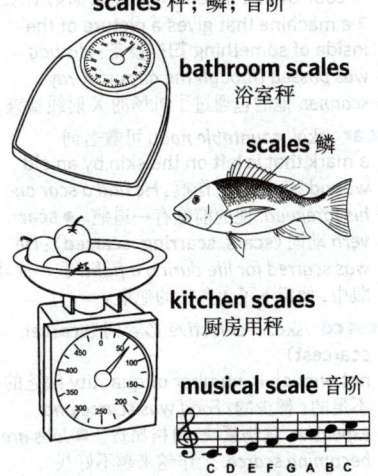

scales 秤；鳞；音阶
bathroom scales 浴室秤
scales 鳞
kitchen scales 厨房用秤
musical scale 音阶
C D E F G A B C

scales /skeɪlz/ *plural noun* 复数名词
a machine that you use for weighing people or things 秤；磅秤；天平：*He weighed himself on the bathroom scales.* 他上浴室秤称体重。

scalp /skælp/ *countable noun* 可数名词
the skin under the hair on your head 头皮：*Try this treatment for beautiful thick hair and a healthy scalp.* 本疗法可以让您拥有浓密的秀发和健康的头皮。

scan /skæn/ *verb* 动词 (**scans, scanning, scanned**)
1 to look through a piece of writing quickly to find important or interesting information 浏览；粗略地看：*She scanned the front page of the newspaper.* 她浏览了报纸的头版。
2 to make an electronic copy of a picture or a document using a special piece of equipment (= a scanner) 扫描 (图片或文件)：*She scanned the images into her computer.* 她把图像扫描进自己的电脑里。

scandal /ˈskændəl/ *countable noun* 可数名词
a situation or an event that people think is shocking 丑闻：*It was a financial scandal.* 这是一起金融丑闻。

scanner /ˈskænə/ *countable noun* 可数名词
1 a machine that you use to make an electronic copy of something, such as a picture or a document 扫描仪：*Scan your photos using any desktop scanner.* 找台台式扫描仪把你的照片扫描一下。

→ Look at picture on P11 参见彩插第 11 页
2 a machine that gives a picture of the inside of something 扫描设备: *His bag was passed through the airport X-ray scanner.* 他的包通过了机场的 X 射线检查。

scar /skɑː/ *countable noun* 可数名词
a mark that is left on the skin by an old wound 疤；伤疤；伤痕: *He had a scar on his forehead.* 他的前额有一道疤。● **scar** *verb* 动词 (**scars, scarring, scarred**): *He was scarred for life during a fight.* 在一次斗殴中，他留下了永久性的疤痕。

scarce /skeəs/ *adjective* 形容词 (**scarcer, scarcest**)
not enough in number or quantity 缺乏的；不足的；稀少的: *Food was scarce and expensive.* 食物紧缺，价格昂贵。□ *Jobs are becoming scarce.* 工作越来越不好找。

scarcely /'skeəsli/ *adverb* 副词
used for emphasizing that something is only just true 刚刚；勉强: *He could scarcely breathe.* 他几乎喘不过气来。

scare¹ /skeə/ *verb* 动词 (**scares, scaring, scared**)
to frighten or worry someone 使惊恐；使担忧: *The thought of failure scares me.* 一想到失败我就感到害怕。

scare² /skeə/ *noun* 名词
1 *singular* 单数 when someone or something frightens or worries you 惊恐；惊吓: *You gave us a terrible scare!* 你吓了我们一大跳！
2 *countable* 可数 a situation where many people are afraid or worried about something 恐惧；恐慌: *The new drug was the subject of a recent health scare.* 这种新药是最近一场健康恐慌的话题。

scared /skeəd/ *adjective* 形容词
frightened or worried 惊恐的；担忧的: *I'm not scared of him.* 我不怕他。

scarf /skɑːf/ *countable noun* 可数名词 (**scarves** /skɑːvz/)
a piece of cloth that you wear around your neck or head 围巾；头巾: *He loosened the scarf around his neck.* 他松了松脖子上的围巾。

scary /'skeəri/ *adjective* 形容词 (**scarier, scariest**)
frightening (*informal* 非正式) 引起恐慌的；骇人的: *The film is too scary for children.* 这部电影太吓人，不适合儿童观看。

scatter /'skætə/ *verb* 动词 (**scatters, scattering, scattered**)
to throw or drop things over an area so that they spread over it 撒: *She scattered the flowers over the grave.* 她把花撒在坟墓上。

scene /siːn/ *countable noun* 可数名词
1 a part of a play, a film or a book that happens in the same place（戏剧或书的）场面，片段；（电影的）镜头: *This is the opening scene of 'The Adventures of Tom Sawyer'.* 这是《汤姆·索亚历险记》的开篇场景。
2 a place when you are describing what is there 场景；场面: *The photographs show scenes of everyday life in the village.* 这些照片展现了村子的日常生活情景。□ *It's a scene of complete horror.* 那是一个十分恐怖的场面。
3 the place where an event happened 现场；发生地: *Firefighters rushed to the scene of the car accident.* 消防员匆匆赶往车祸现场。

scenery /'siːnəri/ *uncountable noun* 不可数名词
1 the land, water or plants that you can see around you in a country area 风景；景色；风光: *Most visitors come for the island's beautiful scenery.* 大部分游客为了欣赏小岛的美丽风景而来。
2 the objects or the backgrounds in a theatre that show where the action in the play is happening（舞台）布景: *The actors will move the scenery themselves.* 演员会自己移动布景。

scent /sent/ *countable noun* 可数名词
the pleasant smell that something has 香味: *This perfume gives off a heavy scent of roses.* 这款香水散发出浓浓的玫瑰花香。
▶ **scented** /'sentɪd/ *adjective* 形容词: *scented soap* 香皂

schedule /'ʃedjuːl/ *countable noun* 可数名词
a plan that gives a list of the times when things will happen 日程安排: *For best results, plan a training schedule.* 要得到最满意的结果，就得制订一份训练计划表。
behind schedule after the planned time 落后于预定时间: *The project is about three months behind schedule.* 该项目比预计时间晚了约 3 个月。

scheme /skiːm/ *verb* 动词 (**schemes, scheming, schemed**)
to make secret plans to do something 密

谋；图谋：*The family was scheming to stop the wedding.* 这家人在密谋阻止婚礼。
☐ *She thinks that everyone is scheming against her.* 她觉得所有人都在算计她。

scholar /ˈskɒlə/ *countable noun* 可数名词
a person who studies an academic subject and who knows a lot about it (*formal* 正式) 学者：*The library is full of scholars and researchers.* 图书馆里全是学者和研究员。

scholarship /ˈskɒləʃɪp/ *countable noun* 可数名词
money to help you to continue studying 奖学金：*He won a scholarship to the Pratt Institute of Art.* 他获得了普拉特艺术学院的奖学金。

school /skuːl/ *noun* 名词
1 a place where people go to learn（中、小）学校：*The school was built in the 1960s.* 这所学校建于 20 世纪 60 年代。
→ Look at picture on P1 参见彩插第 1 页
2 *uncountable* 不可数 your time in school or college 上学；上学阶段：*Parents want their kids to do well in school.* 家长希望自己的孩子在学校表现出色。☐ *Jack graduated from school in May.* 杰克 5 月份从学校毕业。

schoolteacher /ˈskuːltiːtʃə/ *countable noun* 可数名词
a teacher in a school（中小学）教师

science /ˈsaɪəns/ *uncountable noun* 不可数名词
the study of natural things 科学：*He studied plant science at university.* 他在大学读植物学专业。
→ Look at pictures on PP4-6 参见彩插第 4 页至第 6 页

science fiction *uncountable noun* 不可数名词
stories in books, magazines and films about things that happen in the future or in other parts of the universe. The short form **sci-fi** is often used. 科幻小说，科幻（缩写形式为 sci-fi）

scientific /ˌsaɪənˈtɪfɪk/ *adjective* 形容词
relating to science 科学的：*He spends a lot of time conducting scientific research.* 他投入大量时间做科学研究。

scientist /ˈsaɪəntɪst/ *countable noun* 可数名词
someone whose job is to teach or do research in science 科学家：*Scientists have discovered a new gene.* 科学家发现了一种

scholar - score

新型基因。

sci-fi /ˈsaɪˌfaɪ/ *uncountable noun* 不可数名词
short for（缩写 =）**science fiction**（*informal* 非正式）

scissors /ˈsɪzəz/ *plural noun* 复数名词
scissors 剪刀
a small tool for cutting with two sharp parts that are joined together 剪刀；剪子：*Cut the card using scissors.* 用剪刀剪卡片。
→ Look at picture on P1 参见彩插第 1 页

scoop /skuːp/ *verb* 动词（scoops, scooping, scooped）
to remove something from a container with your hand or with a spoon 舀；盛：*He was scooping dog food out of a can.* 他正从罐头里往外盛狗粮。
scoop something up to put your hands under something and lift it 掬起某物；捧起某物：*Use both hands to scoop up the leaves.* 用双手捧起叶子。

scooter /ˈskuːtə/ *countable noun* 可数名词
1 a small light motorcycle with a low seat 小型摩托车
2 a child's vehicle with a long handle and two wheels joined by a long board（儿童）滑板车

scorch /skɔːtʃ/ *verb* 动词（scorches, scorching, scorched）
to burn something slightly 使烧糊；使烤焦：*Many of my plants were scorched by the sun.* 我种的许多植物被太阳晒伤了。

score[1] /skɔː/ *verb* 动词（scores, scoring, scored）
1 to get a goal or a point in a sport or a game（比赛中）得（分），进（球）：*Patten scored his second goal of the game.* 帕滕打进本场比赛的第 2 粒进球。
2 to achieve a particular amount on a test（考试中）得（分）：*Kelly scored 88 on the test.* 凯利考了 88 分。

score[2] /skɔː/ *countable noun* 可数名词
1 the number of points that someone has won in a game or a test（比赛的）得分；（考试的）分数，成绩：*Hogan won, with a score of 287.* 霍根以 287 分赢得了比赛。
2 the result of a game（比赛的）比分，结果：*The final score was 4-1.* 最终比分是 4

比 1。

scorn /skɔːn/ **uncountable noun** 不可数名词
a strong feeling of not liking or respecting someone or something 轻蔑；鄙视：*Her words attracted scorn and anger.* 她的话遭到鄙视，让人听了愤怒。

scornful /ˈskɔːnfʊl/ **adjective** 形容词
showing that you do not like or respect someone or something 鄙夷的；轻蔑的：*He is deeply scornful of politicians.* 他极其鄙视政客。

▶ **scornfully** /ˈskɔːnfʊli/ **adverb** 副词：*They laughed scornfully.* 他们轻蔑地大笑。

scout /skaʊt/ **verb** 动词 (**scouts, scouting, scouted**)
to go around an area in order to search for something 侦察；搜寻：*She's scouting for locations to open a restaurant.* 她在物色开餐馆的地点。

Scout /skaʊt/ **countable noun** 可数名词
a member of the Scouts (= an organization that teaches boys practical skills, and encourages them to help other people) 童子军队员

scowl /skaʊl/ **verb** 动词 (**scowls, scowling, scowled**)
to make an angry face 沉下脸；绷着脸：*He scowled, and slammed the door.* 他怒气冲冲地把门砰地关上了。

scramble /ˈskræmbəl/ **verb** 动词 (**scrambles, scrambling, scrambled**)
to move quickly over rocks or up a hill, using your hands to help you（快速地）爬，攀登：*We scrambled over the rocks to the beach.* 我们爬过岩石来到海滩。

scrap¹ /skræp/ **countable noun** 可数名词
a very small piece or amount of something 小块；一丁点儿：*A scrap of red paper was found in her handbag.* 在她的手提包里发现了一小块红纸片。

scrap² /skræp/ **verb** 动词 (**scraps, scrapping, scrapped**)
to get rid of something or cancel it 摆脱；废除：*The government has scrapped plans to build a new airport.* 政府已经取消了修建新机场的计划。

scrape /skreɪp/ **verb** 动词 (**scrapes, scraping, scraped**)
1 to accidentally rub a part of your body against something hard and rough, and damage it slightly 擦伤，刮破（身体部位）：*She fell, scraping her hands and knees.* 她摔倒了，双手和膝盖都蹭破了。
2 to remove something from a surface by moving a sharp object over it（用锋利物）刮落，削掉：*She scraped the frost off the car windows.* 她把车窗上的霜刮掉。

scratch¹ /skrætʃ/ **verb** 动词 (**scratches, scratching, scratched**)
1 to rub your fingernails against the skin on a part of your body 挠；搔：*He scratched his head thoughtfully.* 他若有所思地挠了挠头。 □ *My arms are very itchy and I can't stop scratching.* 我胳膊特别痒，我忍不住不停地挠。
2 to make small cuts on someone's skin or on the surface of something 划伤（皮肤）；划损（物体表面）：*The branches scratched my face.* 树枝划伤了我的脸。

scratch² /skrætʃ/ **countable noun** 可数名词 (**scratches**)
a small cut made by a sharp object 划伤；划痕：*He had scratches on his face and neck.* 他的脸部和颈部都有划伤。

scream /skriːm/ **verb** 动词 (**screams, screaming, screamed**)
to give a loud, high cry because you are hurt or frightened 尖叫；惊呼：*Women were screaming in the houses nearest the fire.* 离大火最近的几所房子里传来女人们的尖叫。 ● **scream countable noun** 可数名词：*Rose gave a loud scream.* 罗丝发出一声尖叫。

screech /skriːtʃ/ **verb** 动词 (**screeches, screeching, screeched**)
to make an unpleasant high sound 发出刺耳声：*Two police cars screeched into the car park.* 两辆警车冲进停车场，发出了刺耳的声音。

screen /skriːn/ **countable noun** 可数名词
1 a flat surface on a piece of electronic equipment, such as a television or a computer, where you see pictures or words（电视、计算机等的）屏幕
→ Look at picture on P11 参见彩图第 11 页
2 the flat area on the wall of a cinema, where you see the film（电影）银幕：*The cinema has 20 screens.* 这家电影院有 20 块银幕。

screensaver /ˈskriːnseɪvə/ **countable noun** 可数名词
a moving picture that appears on a computer screen when the computer is not being used（计算机的）屏幕保护程序，

屏保

screw[1] /skruː/ *countable noun* 可数名词
a small metal object with a sharp end, that you use to join things together 螺（丝）钉；螺丝: *Each shelf is attached to the wall with screws.* 每个架子都用螺钉固定在了墙上。

screw[2] /skruː/ *verb* 动词 (**screws, screwing, screwed**)
1 to join one thing to another thing using a screw 用螺钉固定: *I screwed the shelf on the wall myself.* 我自己用螺钉把架子固定在了墙上。
2 to turn something in order to attach it to something else 旋紧；拧紧: *Make sure you screw the lid on tightly.* 一定要拧紧盖子。

screwdriver /'skruːdraɪvə/ *countable noun* 可数名词
a tool that you use for turning screws 螺丝刀

screwdriver 螺丝刀

scribble /'skrɪbəl/ *verb* 动词 (**scribbles, scribbling, scribbled**)
to write or draw something quickly and roughly 匆匆地写；草草地画: *She scribbled a note to her mother.* 她草草地给妈妈写了张便条。

script /skrɪpt/ *countable noun* 可数名词
the written words that actors speak in a play, a film or a television programme 剧本；脚本: *Jenny's writing a film script.* 珍妮正在写一部电影剧本。

scroll /skrəʊl/ *verb* 动词 (**scrolls, scrolling, scrolled**)
to move the text on a computer screen up or down to find the information that you need（在计算机屏幕上）滚动文档: *I scrolled down to find 'United States of America'.* 我向下滚动文档搜索"美利坚合众国"。

scrub /skrʌb/ *verb* 动词 (**scrubs, scrubbing, scrubbed**)
to rub something hard in order to clean it 擦洗；刷洗: *Surgeons must scrub their hands and arms with soap and water.* 外科医生必须用肥皂和水刷洗双手和胳膊。

scruffy /'skrʌfi/ *adjective* 形容词 (**scruffier, scruffiest**)
dirty and messy 脏乱的；邋遢的: *The man was pale, scruffy and unshaven.* 那名男子面色苍白，邋邋遢遢，胡子拉碴。

sculptor /'skʌlptə/ *countable noun* 可数名词
an artist who makes solid works of art out of stone, metal or wood 雕刻家；雕塑家: *The sculptor carved the swan from a solid block of ice.* 雕刻家用一个冰块雕出了天鹅。

sculpture /'skʌlptʃə/ *noun* 名词
1 a piece of art that is made into a shape from a material like stone or wood 雕刻品；雕塑品；雕像: *There were stone sculptures of different animals.* 有各种动物的石雕。
→ Look at picture on P13 参见彩插第 13 页
2 *uncountable* 不可数 the art of creating objects (= sculptures) from a substance like stone or wood 雕刻艺术；雕塑艺术: *Both of them studied sculpture.* 他们二人都学习雕刻。

sea /siː/ *countable noun* 可数名词
a large area of salty water that is part of an ocean or is surrounded by land 海；海洋: *They swam in the warm Caribbean Sea.* 他们在温暖的加勒比海游泳。
→ Look at picture on P7 参见彩插第 7 页

seafood /'siːfuːd/ *noun* 名词
fish and other small animals from the sea that you can eat 海鲜；海产品: *Let's find a seafood restaurant.* 咱们找家海鲜饭店吧。

seagull /'siːɡʌl/ *countable noun* 可数名词
a common type of bird with white or grey feathers that lives near the sea 海鸥

seal[1] /siːl/ *verb* 动词 (**seals, sealing, sealed**)
to close an envelope by folding part of it and sticking it down 封上（信封）: *He sealed the envelope and put on a stamp.* 他把信封封好，贴了张邮票。

seal[2] /siːl/ *countable noun* 可数名词
a large animal with a rounded body and short fur that eats fish and lives near the sea 海豹

seam /siːm/ *countable noun* 可数名词
a line where two pieces of cloth are joined together（缝合两块布的）线缝，接缝

search[1] /sɜːtʃ/ *verb* 动词 (**searches, searching, searched**)
1 to look carefully for something or someone 搜寻；搜索: *Police are already searching for the men.* 警方已在搜寻那些人。
2 to look carefully in a place for something or someone 搜查（某地）: *The police are searching the town for the missing men.* 警方为寻找失踪人员正在搜查该镇。

search² /sɜːtʃ/ countable noun 可数名词 (searches)
an attempt to find something or someone by looking for them carefully 搜寻；搜索：*The search was stopped because of the heavy snow.* 搜索因大雪而中断。

'search ,engine countable noun 可数名词
a computer program that you use to search for information on the Internet（因特网的）搜索引擎

seaside /ˈsiːsaɪd/ singular noun 单数名词
an area that is close to the sea, especially where people go for their holidays（尤指作为度假地的）海边，海滨

season /ˈsiːzən/ countable noun 可数名词
1 one of the four parts of a year that each have their own typical weather conditions 季节：*Autumn is my favourite season.* 秋天是我最喜欢的季节。
→ Look at picture on P8 参见彩插第8页
2 a time each year when something happens（一年中发生某事的）旺季，季节：*The football season begins again soon.* 足球赛季马上又要开始了。

seat /siːt/ countable noun 可数名词
something that you can sit on 座位；座椅：*We had front-row seats at the concert.* 我们坐在音乐会的前排位置。□ *The car has comfortable leather seats.* 这辆车配有舒适的皮座椅。
take a seat to sit down (*formal* 正式)坐下；入座：*'Take a seat,' he said.* "请坐。"他说。

'seat ,belt countable noun 可数名词
a long belt that you fasten around your body in a vehicle to keep you safe 安全带：*Please fasten your seat belts.* 请系好安全带。

seaweed /ˈsiːwiːd/ uncountable noun 不可数名词
a plant that grows in the sea 海草；海藻

second¹ /ˈsekənd/ countable noun 可数名词
a measurement of time. There are sixty seconds in one minute. 秒：*For a few seconds nobody spoke.* 有几秒钟大家都沉默不语。

second² /ˈsekənd/ adjective 形容词
the person or thing that you count as number two in a series 第二的；第二个的：*It was the second day of his visit to Florida.* 那是他到佛罗里达的第2天。● **second** *adverb* 副词：*Emma came in second in the race.* 埃玛在赛跑中获得第2名。

secondary /ˈsekəndri/ adjective 形容词
less important than something else 第二位的；次要的；从属的：*Money is of secondary importance to them. Happiness comes first.* 金钱对他们来说是次要的，幸福最重要。

'secondary ,school countable noun 可数名词
a school for students between the ages of 11 and 18 * 中学：*They take examinations after five years of secondary school.* 他们成5年中学学习后参加考试。

'second-,hand adjective 形容词
already used by another person; not new 二手的；用过的：*They could just afford a second-hand car.* 他们只买得起二手车。

secondly /ˈsekəndli/ adverb 副词
used when you want to talk about a second thing, or give a second reason for something 第二；其次：*Firstly, involve your children in planning the holiday, and secondly, ask your travel agent for family-friendly suggestions.* 首先，让孩子们参与策划假期活动；其次，向旅行代办人咨询适合家庭出行的建议。

secrecy /ˈsiːkrəsi/ uncountable noun 不可数名词
a situation in which you do not tell anyone about something 保密；秘密：*They met in complete secrecy.* 他们在完全保密的情况下见了面。

secret¹ /ˈsiːkrɪt/ adjective 形容词
with only a small number of people knowing about something, and not telling anyone else about it 秘密的；保密的：*They tried to keep their marriage secret.* 他们试图隐婚。

secret² /ˈsiːkrɪt/ countable noun 可数名词
something that only a small number of people know and that they do not tell anyone else about 秘密：*Can you keep a secret?* 你能保守秘密吗？

secretarial /ˌsekrəˈteəriəl/ adjective 形容词
relating to typing letters, answering the telephone and other work done in an office 秘书工作的：*I was doing temporary secretarial work.* 我暂时做秘书工作。

secretary /ˈsekrətri/ countable noun 可数名词 (secretaries)
1 a person whose job is to type letters, answer the telephone, and do other office work 秘书

2 a person with an important position in the government 部长；大臣：*The Foreign Secretary will meet with the president tomorrow.* 外交部长明天将同总统见面。

secretive /ˈsiːkrətɪv/ *adjective* 形容词
not sharing your knowledge, feelings or intentions 不外露的；讳莫如深的：*She's very secretive about how much money she has.* 她对自己有多少钱讳莫如深。

section /ˈsekʃən/ *countable noun* 可数名词
a particular part of something 部分：*It is wrong to blame one section of society for all these problems.* 将所有这些问题归咎于社会的某一个部分是不对的。□ *He works in the research section of the company.* 他任职于公司的研发部门。

secure /sɪˈkjʊə/ *adjective* 形容词
1 well protected, so that people cannot enter or leave 安全的；防守严密的：*We'll make our home as secure as possible.* 我们将尽可能保证家里安全。
▶ **securely** /sɪˈkjʊəli/ *adverb* 副词：*He locked the heavy door securely.* 他锁紧那扇厚重的门。
2 properly fixed in position 牢固的；稳固的：*The farmer made sure that the fence was always secure.* 农民要确保栅栏始终牢固。
▶ **securely** /sɪˈkjʊəli/ *adverb* 副词：*He fastened his belt securely.* 他系好安全带。
3 a secure job will not end soon（工作）稳定的：*For the moment, his job is secure.* 目前，他工作稳定。
4 feeling safe and happy, and not worried about life 安心的；无忧无虑的：*She felt secure when she was with him.* 和他在一起时她感到安心。

security /sɪˈkjʊərɪti/ *uncountable noun* 不可数名词
1 everything that you do to protect a place 保安措施；安全工作：*They are improving airport security.* 他们在加强机场的保安措施。
2 a feeling of being safe and free from worry 安全感；无忧无虑：*He loves the security of a happy home life.* 他喜欢幸福家庭生活带来的安全感。

see /siː/ *verb* 动词 (**sees, seeing, saw, seen**)
1 to notice something using your eyes 看见：*The fog was so thick we couldn't see anything.* 浓雾弥漫，我们什么也看不见。□ *Have you seen my keys?* 你看见我的钥匙了吗？
2 to visit or meet someone 拜访；遇见：*I saw him yesterday.* 我昨天见过他。
3 to watch a play, film or sports match 观看：*I saw a great film last night.* 我昨晚看了一部精彩的电影。
4 to understand something 明白；理解：*Oh, I see what you're saying.* 哦，我明白你说什么了。
5 to find out information or a fact about something 察看；弄清：*She looked around to see if anyone was listening.* 她环顾四周看看是否有人在听。
6 to experience a particular event 经历；见证：*I have seen many changes here over the past decade.* 在过去的十年里我目睹了这里的许多变化。
I'll see or **we'll see** used for saying that you will decide something later 看看再说吧（表示暂不决定）：*'Can we go swimming tomorrow?' — 'We'll see. Maybe.'* "我们明天能去游泳吗？"——"再说吧，也许可以。"
let's see used when you are trying to remember something 让我想想（表示试图想起某事）：*Let's see. Where did I leave my purse?* 让我想想，我把钱包放哪儿了？
see someone off to go with someone who is leaving, to the station or airport, to say goodbye to them 送别某人：*Ben saw Jackie off on her plane.* 本送杰姬上了飞机。
see you used for saying goodbye to someone (*informal* 非正式) 再见：*'Talk to you later.' — 'All right. See you.'* "回头再和你聊。"——"好的，再见。"

seed /siːd/ *noun* 名词
the small, hard part of a plant which a new plant grows 种子：*Plant the seeds in small plastic pots.* 把种子种在小塑料花盆里。

seek /siːk/ *verb* 动词 (**seeks, seeking, sought**)
to try to find or get something (*formal* 正式) 寻找；物色：*They are seeking work in hotels and bars.* 他们在找旅馆和酒吧的工作。

seem /siːm/ *verb* 动词 (**seems, seeming, seemed**)
to give the impression of being a particular thing or of being a particular way 好像；似乎；看上去：*The thunder seemed quite close.* 那声巨响似乎就在附近。□ *They seemed a perfect couple to everyone who knew them.* 在相识的人眼中，他们似乎是一对模范夫妻。

seen /siːn/
→ see 见 see

ˈsee-saw *countable noun* 可数名词
a long board that children play on. One child sits at each end, and they go up and down. 跷跷板

segment /ˈsegmənt/ *countable noun* 可数名词
one part of something 部分；片段：*These people come from the poorer segments of society.* 这些人来自社会中较贫困的阶层。

segregation /ˌsegrɪˈgeɪʃən/ *uncountable noun* 不可数名词
the official practice of separating people, especially based on race or religion（尤指基于种族或宗教的）隔离政策，隔离措施：*The report criticized the racial segregation of pupils in the school.* 该报道谴责了学校对小学生实行种族隔离的做法。

seize /siːz/ *verb* 动词 (**seizes, seizing, seized**)
to take hold of something quickly and firmly（快速有力地）抓住：*He seized my arm and pulled me closer.* 他一把抓住我的胳膊，把我拽得更靠近些。

seldom /ˈseldəm/ *adverb* 副词
not very often 不常；很少：*They seldom speak to each other.* 他们彼此很少说话。 ◻ *I've seldom felt so happy.* 我难得觉得这么高兴。

select /sɪˈlekt/ *verb* 动词 (**selects, selecting, selected**)
to choose one particular person or thing from a group of similar people or things 选择；挑选：*Only three players were selected for the team.* 仅有 3 名运动员入选该队。 ◻ *Select 'Save' from the File menu.* 从文件菜单上选择"保存"这一项。

selection /sɪˈlekʃən/ *countable noun* 可数名词
a set of people or things that someone has chosen, or that you can choose from 选出的一批人（或物）；可供选择的一批人（或物）：*The singer will perform a selection of his favourite songs.* 那名歌手将演唱他最喜欢的几首歌曲。 ◻ *Choose from a selection of delicious dishes prepared by our chefs.* 从我们厨师准备的一系列美味菜肴中选择。

self /self/ *countable noun* 可数名词 (**selves**)
your own personality or nature 自身；本我；本性：*You're looking like your usual self again.* 你看起来又像平时的样子了。

self-ˈconfident *adjective* 形容词
behaving confidently because you feel sure of your abilities or value 自信的：*She's become a very self-confident young woman.* 她成了一名非常自信的年轻女子。
▶ **self-ˈconfidence** *uncountable noun* 不可数名词：*I lost all my self-confidence.* 我丧失了全部自信。

self-ˈconscious *adjective* 形容词
easily embarrassed because you feel that everyone is judging you 难为情的；不自然的：*I felt a bit self-conscious in my bikini.* 穿着比基尼我觉得有些不好意思。

self-conˈtrol *uncountable noun* 不可数名词
the ability to control yourself and your feelings 自制力；自我克制：*She was told she must learn self-control.* 有人告诉她一定要学会自我克制。

self-deˈfence *uncountable noun* 不可数名词
the use of force to protect yourself against someone who is attacking you 自卫；自我保护：*Use your gun only in self-defence.* 只有在自卫时才能用枪。

self-emˈployed *adjective* 形容词
working for yourself, rather than for someone else 个体经营的；自由职业的：*If you are self-employed, it is easy to change the time you start work.* 如果你是自由职业者，就可以随时更改开始工作的时间。

selfie /ˈselfi/ *countable noun* 可数名词 (**selfies**)
a photograph you take of yourself by turning your phone or camera towards your face 自拍（照）：*The square was full of tourists taking selfies.* 广场上到处是自拍的游客。

ˈselfie stick *countable noun* 可数名词
a long device with a holder for your phone at one end and a button at the other that you can press to take a photograph of yourself 自拍杆：*The gallery banned selfie sticks.* 美术馆禁止使用自拍杆。

selfish /ˈselfɪʃ/ *adjective* 形容词
caring only about yourself, and not about other people 自私的：*I realize now that I've been very selfish.* 我现在意识到我一直都太自私了。
▶ **selfishly** /ˈselfɪʃli/ *adverb* 副词：*Someone has selfishly finished all the milk.* 有人只顾自己，把牛奶都喝了。
▶ **selfishness** /ˈselfɪʃnəs/ *uncountable*

noun 不可数名词: *Julie's selfishness shocked us.* 朱莉的自私让我们震惊。

ˌself-reˈspect *uncountable noun* 不可数名词
confidence in your own ability and value 自尊(心): *They have lost their jobs, their homes and their self-respect.* 他们失去了工作，失去了家园，失去了自尊。

ˌself-ˈstudy *uncountable noun* 不可数名词
study that you do on your own, without a teacher 自学: *She's started a self-study course.* 她开始学习一门自学课程。

sell /sel/ *verb* 动词 (**sells, selling, sold**)
1 to let someone have something that you own in return for money 卖；转让: *Emily sold the paintings to an art gallery.* 埃米莉把这些画卖给了一家美术馆。 □ *The directors sold the business for £14.8 million.* 董事们以 1,480 万英镑卖掉了公司。
2 to be available for people to buy 出售: *The shop sells newspapers and sweets.* 这家商店出售报纸和糖果。

sell out to not have any tickets left because they have all been sold 售完；售罄: *Football games often sell out fast.* 足球比赛的票经常很快就卖光了。

sell out of something to sell all of your supply of something 卖光某物: *The supermarket sold out of milk yesterday.* 这家超市昨天卖光了牛奶。

Sellotape /ˈseləˌteɪp/ *uncountable noun* 不可数名词
a sticky strip of plastic used for sticking things together (*trademark* 商标)
*Sellotape 透明胶带

selves /selvz/
→ see 见 **self**

semester /səˈmestə/ *countable noun* 可数名词
half of a school or a college year 学期: *February 22nd is when the spring semester begins.* 春季学期于 2 月 22 日开学。

semicircle /ˈsemiˌsɜːkəl/ *countable noun* 可数名词
one half of a circle 半圆: *They sit in a semicircle and share stories.* 他们坐成半圆形分享故事。

semicolon /ˌsemiˈkəʊlɒn/ *countable noun* 可数名词
the mark (;) that you use in writing to separate different parts of a sentence 分号

semifinal /ˌsemiˈfaɪnəl/ *countable noun* 可数名词
one of the two games in a competition that are played to decide who will play in the final part 半决赛: *The football team lost in their semifinal yesterday.* 这支足球队输掉了昨天的半决赛。

seminar /ˈsemɪnɑː/ *countable noun* 可数名词
a class at a college or university in which the teacher and a small group of students discuss a topic (学院或大学里的)研讨班，研讨课: *Students are asked to prepare material for the weekly seminars.* 学生们需要为每周的研讨课准备材料。

send /send/ *verb* 动词 (**sends, sending, sent**)
1 to make a message or a package go to someone 寄；发送: *I sent her an email this morning.* 我今早给她发了一封电子邮件。 □ *Hannah sent me a letter last week.* 汉娜上周给我寄了一封信。
2 to make someone go somewhere 派遣，打发: *His parents sent him to the supermarket to buy a few things.* 他父母打发他去超市买点儿东西。

send for someone to send someone a message asking them to come and see you 请某人来: *If her temperature goes up, send for the doctor.* 如果她体温升高，就请医生来。

senior /ˈsiːnjə/ *adjective* 形容词
having an important job in an organization (在组织中)级别高的，资深的: *He was a senior official in the Italian government.* 他是意大利政府的一名高级官员。

ˌsenior ˈcitizen *countable noun* 可数名词
an older person, especially someone over 65 (尤指 65 岁以上的)老年人: *We want to improve healthcare services for senior citizens.* 我们想改善老年人的医疗保健服务。

sensation /senˈseɪʃən/ *countable noun* 可数名词
a physical feeling 感觉；知觉: *Floating can be a pleasant sensation.* 漂浮会给人一种惬意的感觉。

be a sensation to cause great excitement or interest 引起轰动: *The film was an overnight sensation.* 那部电影一夜之间火了。

sensational /senˈseɪʃənəl/ *adjective* 形容词
causing great excitement and interest 轰动的；引起哄然的: *a sensational victory* 轰动一时的胜利

sense /sens/ *noun* 名词
1 *countable* 可数 your physical ability to

see, smell, hear, touch or taste 感觉官能（即视觉、嗅觉、听觉、触觉和味觉）: We are studying the five senses at school. 我们在学校研究5种感官。
2 singular 单数 a feeling of something 感觉；意识: She felt a sense of relief as she crossed the finish line. 她越过终点线时感到如释重负。
3 uncountable 不可数 the ability to think carefully about something and to do the right thing 良好的判断力；理智: Now that he's older, he has a bit more sense. 现在他年长了些，也有点儿头脑了。
4 countable 可数 one of the possible meanings of a word 意思；含义: This noun has four senses. 这个名词有4个意思。
make sense to be able to be understood 可理解；有意义；讲得通: Do these figures make sense to you? 你能看懂这些数字吗？

sense of 'humour singular noun 单数名词 the ability to find things funny and not to be serious all the time 幽默感: She has a good sense of humour. 她很有幽默感。

sensible /ˈsensɪbəl/ adjective 形容词 based on reasons rather than emotions 明智的；理智的；合理的: It might be sensible to get a lawyer. 找个律师也许是明智的。□ The sensible thing is to leave them alone. 明智的做法是不理会他们。
▶ **sensibly** /ˈsensɪbli/ adverb 副词: He sensibly decided to hide for a while. 他明智地决定暂不露面。

> **LANGUAGE HELP** 语言提示
> If you want to talk about someone whose emotions are strongly affected by their experiences, use **sensitive**. 表示情绪易受个人经历影响，用 sensitive: He's a highly sensitive child. 他是个非常敏感的孩子。

sensitive /ˈsensɪtɪv/ adjective 形容词
1 easily affected by something 敏感的；易受影响的: This chemical is sensitive to light. 这种化学品对光敏感。□ He is very sensitive to the cold. 他对寒冷很敏感。
2 showing that you understand other people's feelings 体贴的；善解人意的: The classroom teacher must be sensitive to a child's needs. 任课教师必须对学童的需求体察入微。
3 easily worried and offended about something when people talk about it 易担忧；易生气；神经过敏的: Young people are sensitive about their appearance. 年轻人很在意自己的外表。

sent /sent/
→ see 见 **send**

sentence /ˈsentəns/ noun 名词
1 countable 可数 a group of words that tells you something or asks a question 句子: After I've written each sentence, I read it aloud. 每写完一个句子，我都会大声念出来。
→ Look at picture on P3 参见彩插第3页
2 the punishment that a person receives in a law court 判决；判刑: He was given a four-year sentence. 他被判处4年徒刑。
● **sentence** verb 动词 (**sentences, sentencing, sentenced**): The court sentenced him to five years in prison. 法庭判他5年徒刑。

sentimental /ˌsentɪˈmentəl/ adjective 形容词 feeling or showing too much pity or love 多情的；多愁善感的: I'm trying not to be sentimental about the past. 我努力不再为过去而感伤。

separate¹ /ˈsepərət/ adjective 形容词 apart and not connected to another thing 分开的；单独的；独立的: Use separate surfaces for cutting raw meats and cooked meats. 切生肉和熟肉要用不同的台面。□ In this gym, men and women have separate exercise rooms. 在这家体育馆，男女健身房是分开的。
▶ **separately** /ˈsepərətli/ adverb 副词: Cook each vegetable separately. 将每种蔬菜分别烹制。

separate² /ˈsepəˌreɪt/ verb 动词 (**separates, separating, separated**)
1 to move people or things apart 使分开；使分离: The police tried to separate the two groups. 警察试图将两伙人分开。
2 to decide to live apart 分居: Her parents separated when she was very young. 她很小的时候父母就分居了。
▶ **separated** /ˈsepəˌreɪtɪd/ adjective 形容词: Rachel's parents are separated. 蕾切尔的父母分居了。
3 to exist between two people, groups or things 隔开；阻离；分隔: The white fence separated the garden from the field. 白色围栏将花园和田野隔开。

September /sepˈtembə/ noun 名词 the ninth month of the year 九月: Her son was born in September. 她儿子出生在9月。

sequence /ˈsiːkwəns/ *countable noun* 可数名词
a number of events or things that come one after another 一系列；一连串：*This is the sequence of events that led to the murder.* 这是导致谋杀发生的一系列事件。

sergeant /ˈsɑːdʒənt/ *countable noun* 可数名词
an officer in the army or the police（陆军）中士；（英国警察的）巡佐；（美国警察的）警佐：*A police sergeant patrolling the area noticed the fire.* 在该地区巡逻的一名警佐发现了火情。

serial /ˈsɪəriəl/ *countable noun* 可数名词
a story that is told in a number of parts on television or radio, or in a magazine or newspaper 电视连续剧；广播连续剧；连载小说：*The book was filmed as a six-part TV serial.* 这本书被拍成 6 集电视连续剧。

series /ˈsɪəriːz/ *countable noun* 可数名词 (series)
1 a number of things or events that come one after another 一连串；一系列：*There will be a series of meetings with political leaders.* 即将与政治领袖举行一系列会议。
2 a set of radio or television programmes （广播或电视的）系列节目：*The long-running TV series is filmed in Manchester.* 这部长篇电视连续剧拍摄于曼彻斯特。

serious /ˈsɪəriəs/ *adjective* 形容词
1 very bad; making people worried or afraid 不好的；严重的：*Crime is a serious problem in our society.* 犯罪是我们社会中的一个严重问题。
▶ **seriously** /ˈsɪəriəsli/ *adverb* 副词：*This law could seriously damage my business.* 这条法律会使我的生意损失严重。
▶ **seriousness** /ˈsɪəriəsnəs/ *uncountable noun* 不可数名词：*They don't realize the seriousness of the crisis.* 他们没有意识到这场危机的严重性。
2 important that people need to think about carefully 重要的；需认真考虑的：*This is a very serious matter.* 这是件重要的事情。
3 not joking, and really meaning what you say 郑重的；认真的；当真的：*You really are serious about this, aren't you?* 你对此的确是认真的，是不是？
▶ **seriously** /ˈsɪəriəsli/ *adverb* 副词：*'I followed him home,' he said. 'Seriously?'* "我跟着他回家了。"他说。"真的吗？"

seriously /ˈsɪəriəsli/ *adverb* 副词
take someone/something seriously to believe that someone or something is important and that they deserve attention 认真对待某人／某事物：*The company takes all complaints seriously.* 那家公司认真对待所有投诉。

sermon /ˈsɜːmən/ *countable noun* 可数名词
a talk that a religious leader gives as part of a religious service 布道；讲道：*Cardinal Murphy will deliver the sermon on Sunday.* 枢机主教墨菲将在星期日布道。

servant /ˈsɜːvənt/ *countable noun* 可数名词
someone who works at another person's home, doing work like cooking or cleaning 仆人：*The family employed several servants.* 那家人雇用了几名仆人。

serve /sɜːv/ *verb* 动词 (serves, serving, served)
1 to give people food and drinks 提供，端上（食物或饮料）：*The restaurant serves breakfast, lunch and dinner.* 这家餐厅供应早餐、午餐和晚餐。
2 to help customers in a shop or a bar and to provide them with what they want to buy 接待，服务（顾客）：*They refused to serve me as I looked too young.* 我看上去年纪很小，他们拒绝招待我。
3 to do useful work for your country, an organization or a person 为⋯效力；为⋯工作：*He spoke of the fine character of those who serve their country.* 他谈到那些为国效忠者的优良品质。

server /ˈsɜːvə/ *countable noun* 可数名词
a computer that stores information and supplies it to a number of computers on a network（计算机网络的）服务器：*They couldn't send any emails because the mail server was down.* 他们发不了邮件，因为邮件服务器崩溃了。

service /ˈsɜːvɪs/ *noun* 名词
1 *countable* 可数 something that the public needs, such as transport or energy supplies 公共服务系统；公共事业：*There is a regular local bus service to Yorkdale.* 当地有一趟开往约克代尔购物中心的班车。
2 *uncountable* 不可数 the help that people in a restaurant or a shop give you（饭店或商店提供的）服务：*We always receive good service in that restaurant.* 我们在那家餐厅总是得到很好的服务。
3 *uncountable* 不可数 the time that you

spend working for a person or an organization 任职期；服务期：*Most employees had long service with the company.* 大多数员工在公司供职多年。
4 countable 可数 a religious ceremony 宗教礼仪；礼拜仪式：*After the service, his body was taken to a cemetery.* 宗教仪式结束后，他的遗体被送往公墓。

session /ˈseʃən/ **countable noun** 可数名词 a period of a particular activity（某项活动的）一段时间：*The two leaders arrived for a photo session.* 两位领导人前来接受拍照。

set¹ /set/ **countable noun** 可数名词
1 a number of things that belong together 一套；一组；一系列：*The table and chairs are normally bought as a set.* 桌椅通常成套购买。□ *I got a chess set for my birthday.* 我生日时给自己买了一副国际象棋。
2 the place where a film is made（电影的）拍摄场地：*The place looked like the set of a James Bond movie.* 这地方看起来像某部詹姆斯·邦德电影的拍摄场地。

set² /set/ **verb** 动词 (**sets, setting, set**)
1 to put something somewhere carefully（小心地）放，置：*She set the vase down gently on the table.* 她轻轻地把花瓶放在桌子上。
2 to make a clock ready to use 设置，调好（钟表）：*I set my alarm clock for seven o'clock every morning.* 我设定了每天早晨7点的闹钟。
3 to decide what a date or a price will be 决定，确定（日期或价格）：*They have finally set the date of their wedding.* 他们最终定下了婚礼的日子。
4 when the sun sets, it goes down in the sky（太阳）落山：*They watched the sun set behind the hills.* 他们望着太阳落下山。
5 to prepare the table for a meal by putting plates, glasses, knives, forks, and spoons on it 在（桌子）上摆放餐具：*Could you set the table for dinner, please?* 请你摆放餐具准备开饭，好吗？

set fire to something or **set something on fire** to make something burn 放火烧某物：*Angry protestors threw stones and set cars on fire.* 愤怒的抗议者投掷石块并放火焚烧汽车。□ *I struck a match and set fire to the papers.* 我划着一根火柴，将文件点燃。

set off to start going somewhere 动身；出发：*Nick set off for his farmhouse in Connecticut.* 尼克动身前往他在康涅狄格的农舍。

set someone free to cause someone to be free 释放某人：*They agreed to set the prisoners free.* 他们同意释放犯人。

set something up to start or arrange something 创建某事物；建立某事物：*He plans to set up his own business.* 他打算自己创业。

set³ /set/ **adjective** 形容词
1 fixed and not able to be changed 固定的；确定的：*The kids have to be home at a set time every evening.* 孩子们每天晚上必须在固定的时间回家。
2 happening in a particular place or time 位于（某地）的；处于（某个时间）的：*The play is set in a small seaside town.* 这出戏以一个海滨小镇为背景。

set square **countable noun** 可数名词 a thin flat piece of plastic or metal with three straight sides, used for drawing lines and measuring angles 三角板
→ Look at picture on P1 参见彩插第1页

settle /ˈsetəl/ **verb** 动词 (**settles, settling, settled**)
1 to decide what to do about an argument or a problem by talking about it 解决，结束（争端或问题）：*They agreed to try again to settle the dispute.* 他们同意再次尝试解决纠纷。
2 to start living in a place permanently 定居：*He visited Paris and eventually settled there.* 他造访了巴黎，并最终在那里定居。
3 to sit down and make yourself comfortable 舒舒服服地坐下：*Brandon settled in front of the television.* 布兰登舒舒服服地坐到了电视机前。

settle down to become calm after being excited 平静下来：*Come on, kids. Time to settle down and go to sleep now.* 来吧，孩子们。是时候安静下来去睡觉了。

settle in to become used to living in a new place, doing a new job, or going to a new school 安顿下来；习惯（新地方）；适应（新工作、新学校等）：*I enjoyed school once I settled in.* 适应学校生活后，我就喜欢上了上学。

settled /ˈsetəld/ **adjective** 形容词 decided and arranged 已决定的；已安排好的：*We feel the matter is now settled.* 我们觉得事情现在已经解决了。

settlement /ˈsetəlmənt/ **countable noun** 可数名词
1 an official agreement between two

people or groups after they have disagreed about something（争议双方的）正式协议，和解：*Officials are hoping for a peaceful settlement of the crisis.* 官员们希望和平解决危机。

2 a place where people have come to live and have built homes 定居点：*The village is a settlement of just fifty houses.* 这个村子只有 50 户人家。

seven /ˈsevən/
the number 7 七

seventeen /ˌsevənˈtiːn/
the number 17 十七

▶ **seventeenth** /ˌsevənˈtiːnθ/ *adjective* 形容词，*adverb* 副词：*I had a big party for my seventeenth birthday.* 我为自己的 17 岁生日举办了一场盛大的派对。

seventh[1] /ˈsevənθ/ *adjective* 形容词，*adverb* 副词
counted as number seven in a series 第七：*I was the seventh child in the family.* 我是家里第 7 个孩子。

seventh[2] /ˈsevənθ/ *countable noun* 可数名词
one of seven equal parts of something (1/7) 七分之一

seventy /ˈsevənti/
the number 70 七十

▶ **seventieth** /ˈsevəntiəθ/ *adjective* 形容词，*adverb* 副词：*It's my grandad's seventieth birthday next week.* 下周是我爷爷七十大寿。

several /ˈsevrəl/ *adjective* 形容词
used for talking about a number of people or things that is not large but is greater than two 几个；数个；一些：*I spent several years in France.* 我在法国待过几年。□ *There were several blue boxes on the table.* 桌子上有几个蓝盒子。● **several** *pronoun* 代词：*The cakes were delicious, and we ate several.* 蛋糕很美味，我们吃了一些。

severe /sɪˈvɪə/ *adjective* 形容词 (**severer, severest**)
1 very bad 严重的；恶劣的：*The business is having severe financial problems.* 这家公司有严重的财务问题。

▶ **severely** /sɪˈvɪəli/ *adverb* 副词：*An aircraft crashed on the runway and was severely damaged.* 一架飞机在跑道上坠毁，严重受损。

2 very strong 严厉的；苛刻的：*A severe sentence is necessary for this type of crime.* 对这类犯罪必须从重量刑。

▶ **severely** /sɪˈvɪəli/ *adverb* 副词：*They want to punish dangerous drivers more severely.* 他们希望加大对危险驾车者的处罚力度。

sew /səʊ/ *verb* 动词 (**sews, sewing, sewed, sewn**)
to join pieces of cloth together using a needle and thread 缝；缝制：*Anyone can sew a button onto a shirt.* 谁都会给衬衫缝纽扣。

▶ **sewing** /ˈsəʊɪŋ/ *uncountable noun* 不可数名词：*She lists her hobbies as cooking, sewing and going to the cinema.* 她列出了自己的爱好，如做饭、缝纫和看电影。

sewer /ˈsuːə/ *countable noun* 可数名词
a large pipe under the ground that carries waste and rain water away 污水管道；下水道；阴沟：*The rain water drains into the city's sewer system.* 雨水流入城市排水系统。

sewn /səʊn/
→ see 见 **sew**

sex /seks/ *noun* 名词 (**sexes**)
1 *countable* 可数 one of the two groups, male and female, into which you can divide people and animals 男性；女性；雄性；雌性：*This movie appeals to both sexes.* 这部电影男女都喜欢。

2 *countable* 可数 the characteristic of being either male or female 性别；性别特征：*We can identify the sex of your unborn baby.* 我们可以确定你未出生婴儿的性别。

3 *uncountable* 不可数 the physical activity by which people can produce children 性行为；性交：*He was very open in his attitudes about sex.* 他对性行为的态度非常开放。

have sex to perform the act of sex 发生性关系；做爱

sexual /ˈsekʃuəl/ *adjective* 形容词
1 connected with the physical act of sex 性行为的；性的：*The clinic can provide information about sexual health.* 这家诊所可以提供性健康的相关信息。

2 relating to the differences between male and female people 性别的；性别差异的；两性间的：*There are laws against sexual discrimination.* 有禁止性别歧视的法律。

3 relating to the biological process by which people and animals produce young 生殖的；有性繁殖的：*Girls usually reach sexual maturity earlier than boys.* 女孩通常

比男孩性成熟得早。
▶ **sexually** /ˈsekʃuəli/ *adverb* 副词: *These organisms can reproduce sexually.* 这些生物可以有性繁殖。

sexy /ˈseksi/ *adjective* 形容词 (**sexier, sexiest**)
sexually attractive 性感的；引起性欲的: *She is the sexiest woman I have ever seen.* 她是我见过的最性感的女人。

shabby /ˈʃæbi/ *adjective* 形容词 (**shabbier, shabbiest**)
old and in bad condition 破旧的；破败的；破烂的: *His clothes were old and shabby.* 他的衣服又旧又破。

shade /ʃeɪd/ *noun* 名词
1 countable 可数 one of the different forms of a particular colour (色彩的) 浓淡, 深浅, 色度: *The walls were painted in two shades of green.* 墙壁刷了一深一浅两种绿色。
2 uncountable 不可数 an area where direct sunlight does not reach 阴凉处；背阴: *Alexis was reading in the shade of a tree.* 亚历克西丝在树荫下看书。

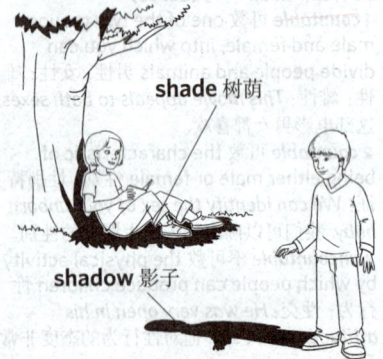
shade 树荫
shadow 影子

shadow /ˈʃædəʊ/ *countable noun* 可数名词
a dark shape on a surface that is made when something blocks the light 影子；阴影: *The long shadows of the trees fell across their path.* 长长的树影落在他们脚下的小路上。

shady /ˈʃeɪdi/ *adjective* 形容词 (**shadier, shadiest**)
not in bright sunlight 阴凉的；背阴的: *We stopped in a shady place under some trees.* 我们在一片树荫下停了下来。

shake /ʃeɪk/ *verb* 动词 (**shakes, shaking, shook, shaken**)
1 to move quickly backward and forward or up and down 发抖；颤抖: *My whole body was shaking with fear.* 我吓得浑身发抖。
2 to hold something and move it quickly up and down 摇动；抖动；摇晃: *Always shake the bottle before you pour out the medicine.* 每次倒药之前先摇一摇瓶子。
● **shake** *countable noun* 可数名词: *We gave the children a gentle shake to wake them.* 我们轻轻地摇了摇孩子，把他们叫醒。
3 to move your head from side to side to say 'no' (表示否定) 摇 (头): *'Did you see Crystal?' Kathryn shook her head.* "你见到克里斯特尔了吗？"凯瑟琳摇了摇头。
shake hands to say hello or goodbye to someone by holding their right hand in your own right hand and moving it up and down (问好或道别时) 握手: *Michael shook hands with Burke.* 迈克尔和伯克握了握手。 □ *The two men shook hands.* 那两个男人握了握手。

shaken /ˈʃeɪkən/
→ see 见 **shake**

shaky /ˈʃeɪki/ *adjective* 形容词 (**shakier, shakiest**)
not able to control your voice or your body because you are ill or afraid (声音或身体) 颤抖的: *Her voice was shaky and she was close to tears.* 她的声音颤抖着，几乎要哭了。
▶ **shakily** /ˈʃeɪkɪli/ *adverb* 副词: *'I don't feel well,' she said shakily.* "我觉得不舒服。"她颤抖着声音说。

shall /ʃəl, STRONG 强读 ʃæl/ *modal verb* 情态动词
1 used with 'I' and 'we' in questions to make offers or suggestions (在疑问句中与 I 或 we 连用，表示提出建议) 好吗，可以吗: *Shall I get the keys?* 我去拿钥匙好吗？ □ *Well, shall we go?* 嗯，我们可以走了吗？
2 usually used with 'I' and 'we', when you are talking about something that will happen to you in the future (*formal* 正式) (通常与 I 或 we 连用，表示将来) 将要, 将会: *We shall be landing in Paris in sixteen minutes.* 我们将于 16 分钟后在巴黎降落。 □ *I shall know more tomorrow.* 明天我会了解到更多情况。

shallow /ˈʃæləʊ/ *adjective* 形容词 (**shallower, shallowest**)
not deep 浅的: *The river is very shallow here.* 这里的河水很浅。

shame /ʃeɪm/ *noun* 名词
1 uncountable 不可数 the very

uncomfortable feeling that you have when you have done something wrong or stupid 羞耻；羞愧；惭愧: *I was filled with shame.* 我满心羞愧。
2 *singular* 单数 something that you feel sad or disappointed about 令人惋惜的事；让人遗憾的事: *It was a shame about the weather, but the party was still a great success.* 令人遗憾的是天气不好，但聚会还是很成功的。

shameful /ˈʃeɪmful/ *adjective* 形容词
very bad 可耻的；丢脸的: *The government's treatment of the refugees was shameful.* 政府对待难民的态度真是可耻。

shampoo /ʃæmˈpuː/ *noun* 名词
a liquid soap that you use for washing your hair 洗发剂；香波: *Don't forget to pack a towel, soap, and shampoo.* 别忘了装上毛巾、肥皂和洗发水。● **shampoo** *verb* 动词 (**shampoos, shampooing, shampooed**): *I shampooed my hair and dried it, then I got dressed.* 我用洗发水洗了头后擦干，然后穿上衣服。

shan't /ʃɑːnt/
short for (缩写 =) 'shall not'

shape /ʃeɪp/ *countable noun* 可数名词
1 the form or appearance of the outside edges or surfaces of something 外形；轮廓: *Pasta comes in all different shapes and sizes.* 意大利面有各种不同的形状和大小。
2 something such as a circle, a square or a triangle 形状；图形 ● **shape** *verb* 动词 (**shapes, shaping, shaped**): *Shape the dough into a ball and place it in the bowl.* 把面团揉成球，放进碗里。
in bad shape in a bad state of health or in

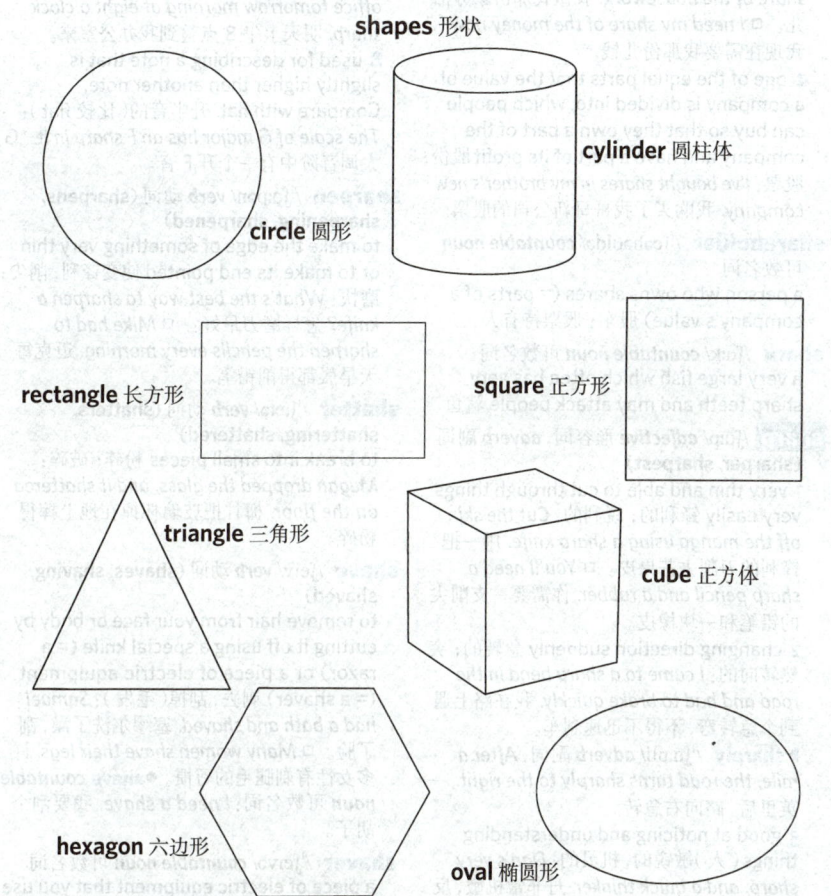

shapes 形状

circle 圆形

cylinder 圆柱体

rectangle 长方形

square 正方形

triangle 三角形

cube 正方体

hexagon 六边形

oval 椭圆形

a bad condition 身体不健康的；情况糟糕的：*The company is in bad shape.* 公司状况堪忧。
in (good) shape in a good state of health or in a good condition 身体健康的；情况良好的：*He's 76 and still in good shape.* 他 76 岁了，身体依然硬朗。

share¹ /ʃeə/ *verb* 动词 (**shares, sharing, shared**)
to have or use something with another person 共享；共有；合用：*Jose shares an apartment with six other students.* 乔斯和其他 6 名学生合住一间公寓。口 *Maria and I shared a dessert.* 我和玛丽亚把甜点分着吃了。

share² /ʃeə/ *countable noun* 可数名词
1 the part of something that you do or have 应做的一份；应得的一份：*I do my share of the housework.* 我做我那份家务活儿。口 *I need my share of the money now.* 我现在需要我那份儿钱。
2 one of the equal parts that the value of a company is divided into, which people can buy so that they own a part of the company and have a part of its profit 股份；股票：*I've bought shares in my brother's new company.* 我购买了我哥新公司的股票。

shareholder /ʃeəhəʊldə/ *countable noun* 可数名词
a person who owns shares (= parts of a company's value) 股东；股票持有人

shark /ʃɑːk/ *countable noun* 可数名词
a very large fish which often has very sharp teeth and may attack people 鲨鱼

sharp /ʃɑːp/ *adjective* 形容词, *adverb* 副词 (**sharper, sharpest**)
1 very thin and able to cut through things very easily 锋利的；锐利的：*Cut the skin off the mango using a sharp knife.* 用一把锋利的刀削去芒果皮。口 *You'll need a sharp pencil and a rubber.* 你需要一支削尖的铅笔和一块橡皮。
2 changing direction suddenly 急转的；突然转向的：*I came to a sharp bend in the road and had to brake quickly.* 我在路上遇到个急转弯，不得不迅速刹车。
▶ **sharply** /ʃɑːpli/ *adverb* 副词：*After a mile, the road turns sharply to the right.* 一英里后，路向右急转。
3 good at noticing and understanding things（人）敏锐的，机灵的：*Dan's very sharp, and a quick thinker.* 丹非常机敏，反应很快。
4 sudden and angry（言语）尖锐的，尖刻的：*His sharp reply surprised me.* 他尖锐的回答让我吃惊。
▶ **sharply** /ʃɑːpli/ *adverb* 副词：'Why didn't you tell me?' she asked sharply. "你为什么不告诉我？"她厉声问道。
5 big or strong and sudden 急剧的；骤然的；大幅度的：*There's been a sharp rise in oil prices.* 油价大涨。口 *I felt a sharp pain in my right leg.* 我的右腿感到一阵剧痛。
▶ **sharply** /ʃɑːpli/ *adverb* 副词：*Unemployment rose sharply last year.* 去年失业率大幅上升。
6 very clear and easy to see 清晰的；鲜明的：*Digital TV offers sharper images than analogue TV.* 数字电视比模拟电视成像更清晰。
7 exactly (…点)整；准时地：*Be in my office tomorrow morning at eight o'clock sharp.* 明天上午 8 点整到我办公室来。
8 used for describing a note that is slightly higher than another note. Compare with **flat**. 升半音的（比较 flat）：*The scale of G major has an F sharp in it.* *G 大调音阶中有一个升 F 音。

sharpen /ʃɑːpən/ *verb* 动词 (**sharpens, sharpening, sharpened**)
to make the edge of something very thin or to make its end pointed 使变锋利；削尖；磨快：*What's the best way to sharpen a knife?* 怎样磨刀最好？ 口 *Mike had to sharpen the pencils every morning.* 迈克每天早晨都得削铅笔。

shatter /ʃætə/ *verb* 动词 (**shatters, shattering, shattered**)
to break into small pieces 粉碎；破碎：*Megan dropped the glass, and it shattered on the floor.* 梅甘把玻璃杯掉在地上摔得粉碎。

shave /ʃeɪv/ *verb* 动词 (**shaves, shaving, shaved**)
to remove hair from your face or body by cutting it off using a special knife (= a razor) or a piece of electric equipment (= a shaver) 剃去，刮掉（毛发）：*Samuel had a bath and shaved.* 塞缪尔洗了澡，刮了脸。口 *Many women shave their legs.* 许多女性有剃腿毛的习惯。● **shave** *countable noun* 可数名词：*I need a shave.* 我要刮个胡子。

shaver /ʃeɪvə/ *countable noun* 可数名词
a piece of electric equipment that you use

for shaving hair from your face and body 电动剃须刀: *In 1937 the company introduced the world's first electric shaver.* *1937 年，这家公司推出了世界上第一款电动剃须刀。

shawl /ʃɔːl/ *countable noun* 可数名词
a large piece of cloth that a woman wears over her shoulders or head（女用）披巾，披肩

she /ʃi, STRONG 强读 ʃiː/ *pronoun* 代词
used for talking about a female person or animal when they are the subject of a sentence（用作句子主语）她: *She's seventeen years old.* 她 17 岁。

shed /ʃed/ *countable noun* 可数名词
a small building where you store things 小屋，棚（用于储藏物品）: *The house has a large shed in the backyard.* 房子后院有个大棚子。

she'd /ʃiːd, ʃɪd/
1 short for（缩写 =）'she had'
2 short for（缩写 =）'she would'

sheep /ʃiːp/ *countable noun* 可数名词 (sheep)
a farm animal with thick hair called wool, that is kept for its wool or for its meat 羊；绵羊

sheet /ʃiːt/ *countable noun* 可数名词
1 a large piece of cloth that you sleep on or cover yourself with in bed 被单；床单: *Once a week, we change the sheets.* 我们每星期换一次床单。
2 a piece of something flat such as paper （纸等薄片类物品的）张，片: *Sean folded the sheets of paper and put them in his briefcase.* 肖恩把这几张纸折叠好放进公文包里。

shelf /ʃelf/ *countable noun* 可数名词 (shelves /ʃelvz/)
a long flat piece of wood on a wall or in a cupboard that you can keep things on（固定在墙上的或橱柜的）架子，搁板: *Dad took a book from the shelf.* 爸爸从架子上拿了本书。

shell /ʃel/ *countable noun* 可数名词
1 the hard part of something, such as a nut or an egg, that surrounds it and protects it（坚果、鸡蛋等的）壳: *They cracked the nuts and removed their shells.* 他们砸裂坚果，剥去硬壳。
2 the hard part that covers the back of an animal such as a snail and protects it（蜗牛等的）壳
3 the hard part of a small sea creature that you find on beaches 贝壳: *I have gathered shells since I was a child.* 我从小就收集贝壳。

she'll /ʃiːl, ʃɪl/
short for（缩写 =）'she will'

shellfish /ˈʃelfɪʃ/ *noun* 名词 (shellfish)
a small creature that lives in the ocean and has a shell（海生）贝类: *The restaurant serves local fish and shellfish.* 这家餐厅供应当地的鱼和贝类。

shelter[1] /ˈʃeltə/ *noun* 名词
1 *countable* 可数 a place that protects you from bad weather or danger 遮蔽物；庇护处；掩体: *a bus shelter* 公共汽车候车亭
2 *uncountable* 不可数 protection from bad weather or danger 遮蔽；庇护；掩蔽: *They took shelter under a tree.* 他们躲在树下。

shelter[2] /ˈʃeltə/ *verb* 动词 (shelters, sheltering, sheltered)
to stay in a place to be protected from bad weather or danger 躲避；避难: *They sheltered from the rain under a tree.* 他们在树下躲雨。

she's /ʃiːz, ʃɪz/
1 short for（缩写 =）'she is'
2 short for（缩写 =）'she has'

shield[1] /ʃiːld/ *verb* 动词 (shields, shielding, shielded)
to protect someone or something from danger or injury 保护；保卫: *I shielded my eyes from the sun with my hands.* 我用手遮住眼睛不被阳光照到。

shield[2] /ʃiːld/ *countable noun* 可数名词
a large piece of metal or leather that soldiers carried in the past to protect their bodies 盾；盾牌
→ Look at picture on P10 参见彩插第 10 页

shift[1] /ʃɪft/ *verb* 动词 (shifts, shifting, shifted)
to move something from one place to another 移动；挪动；转移: *Please would you help me shift the table over to the window?* 你可以帮我把桌子挪到窗边吗？

shift[2] /ʃɪft/ *countable noun* 可数名词
one of the fixed periods of work in a factory or a hospital 轮班；轮班工作时间: *Nick works night shifts at the hospital.* 尼克在医院上夜班。

shin /ʃɪn/ *countable noun* 可数名词
the front part of your leg between your knee and your ankle 胫部；小腿: *Ken suffered a bruised left shin.* 肯的左小腿磕青了。

shine /ʃaɪn/ *verb* 动词 (**shines, shining, shone**)
1 to give out bright light 发光；照耀: *Today it's warm and the sun is shining.* 今天很暖和，阳光灿烂。
2 to point a light somewhere 把(光)照向；使(光)投向: *The guard shone a light in his face.* 警卫把灯照向他的脸。
3 to reflect light (因反射而)发光，发亮: *The sea shone in the silver moonlight.* 大海在银色的月光下波光粼粼。

shiny /ˈʃaɪni/ *adjective* 形容词 (**shinier, shiniest**)
bright and reflecting light 发亮的；闪光的；有光泽的: *Her blonde hair was shiny and clean.* 她的金发洁净而有光泽。

ship¹ /ʃɪp/ *countable noun* 可数名词
a large boat that carries people or goods 轮船: *The ship was ready to sail.* 轮船准备起航了。

ship² /ʃɪp/ *verb* 动词 (**ships, shipping, shipped**)
to send goods somewhere 运送；运输: *Our company ships orders worldwide.* 我们公司向世界各地运送订购的货物。

shirt /ʃɜːt/ *countable noun* 可数名词
a piece of clothing with a collar and buttons, that you wear on the top part of your body 衬衫

shiver /ˈʃɪvə/ *verb* 动词 (**shivers, shivering, shivered**)
to shake because you are cold, frightened or sick (因寒冷、恐惧或生病而)哆嗦，颤抖: *She shivered with cold and fear.* 她又冷又害怕，身体直发抖。 • **shiver** *countable noun* 可数名词: *She gave a small shiver.* 她微微一颤。

shock¹ /ʃɒk/ *countable noun* 可数名词
1 when you suddenly feel very upset because something unpleasant has happened 震惊；惊愕: *William never recovered from the shock of his brother's death.* 威廉从未从他哥哥去世的打击中恢复过来。
2 → see 见 **electric shock**

shock² /ʃɒk/ *verb* 动词 (**shocks, shocking, shocked**)
to be very unpleasant and suddenly make someone feel very upset 使震惊；使惊愕: *After forty years as a police officer, nothing shocks me.* 当了40年警察，没有什么能让我感到震惊的了。
▶ **shocked** /ʃɒkt/ *adjective* 形容词: *She was deeply shocked when she heard the news.* 她听到这个消息时深感震惊。
→ Look at picture on P15 参见彩插第15页

shocking /ˈʃɒkɪŋ/ *adjective* 形容词
very bad or morally wrong, and making you feel very upset and surprised 极坏的；不道德的；令人震惊的: *Everyone found the photos shocking.* 所有人都觉得这些照片令人发指。

shoe /ʃuː/ *countable noun* 可数名词
things that you wear on your feet 鞋: *I need a new pair of shoes.* 我需要一双新鞋。 □ *I don't usually wear high-heeled shoes.* 我通常不穿高跟鞋。

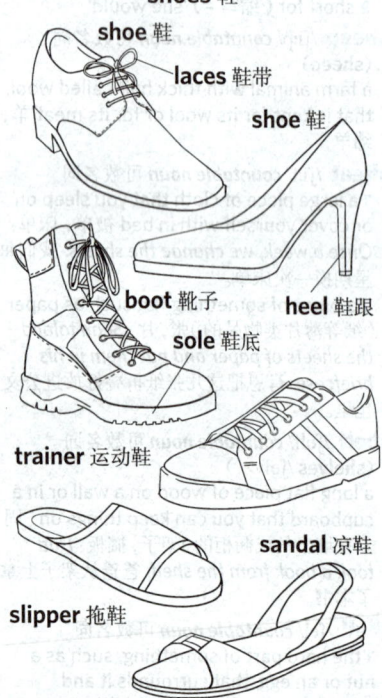

shoes 鞋
shoe 鞋
laces 鞋带
shoe 鞋
boot 靴子
heel 鞋跟
sole 鞋底
trainer 运动鞋
sandal 凉鞋
slipper 拖鞋

shoelace /ˈʃuːleɪs/ *countable noun* 可数名词
a long, thick string that you use to fasten your shoe 鞋带: *He began to tie his shoelaces.* 他开始系鞋带。

shone /ʃɒn/
→ see 见 **shine**

shook /ʃʊk/
→ see 见 **shake**

shoot¹ /ʃuːt/ *verb* 动词 (**shoots, shooting, shot**)
1 to kill or injure a person or an animal by firing a gun at them 枪杀；射伤: *The gunmen shot two policemen before they escaped.* 持枪歹徒开枪射伤两名警察后逃跑。▫ *A man was shot dead during the robbery.* 一名男子在抢劫案中中枪身亡。
2 to fire a bullet from a weapon 开枪；射击: *He raised his arms above his head, and shouted, 'Don't shoot!'* 他双臂举过头，喊道：" 不要开枪！"
3 to make a film 拍摄: *Tim wants to shoot his new film in Mexico.* 蒂姆想在墨西哥拍摄他的新电影。
4 to kick or throw the ball toward the goal or net in football or basketball 射门；投篮: *Brennan shot and missed.* 布伦南把球射偏了。

shoot² /ʃuːt/ *countable noun* 可数名词
a new part that is growing from a plant or tree 幼苗；嫩芽；新枝: *It was spring, and new shoots began to appear.* 时值春天，草木初萌。

shop¹ /ʃɒp/ *countable noun* 可数名词
a place where you buy things 商店；店铺: *Paul and his wife run a flower shop.* 保罗和他妻子开了一家花店。

shop² /ʃɒp/ *verb* 动词 (**shops, shopping, shopped**)
to go to shops and buy things 购物: *He always shops on Saturday mornings.* 他总是在星期六上午去采购。
▸ **shopper** /ʃɒpə/ *countable noun* 可数名词: *The streets were filled with crowds of shoppers.* 街上挤满了成群的购物者。

shop assistant *countable noun* 可数名词 (American 美国英语: **clerk**)
a person who works in a shop 店员；售货员
→ Look at picture on P16 参见彩插第 16 页

shopping /ʃɒpɪŋ/ *uncountable noun* 不可数名词
the activity of going to shops to buy things 购物: *I'll do the shopping this afternoon.* 今天下午我会去买东西。

shopping centre *countable noun* 可数名词 (American 美国英语: **mall**)
a large building with lots of shops and restaurants inside it 购物中心

shopping trolley *countable noun* 可数名词
a large metal or plastic basket on wheels that you put your shopping in while you are in a shop 购物车

shore /ʃɔː/ *countable noun* 可数名词
the land along the edge of the sea or a lake 海岸；湖滨: *They walked slowly down to the shore.* 他们慢慢地走到湖滨。

short /ʃɔːt/ *adjective* 形容词 (**shorter, shortest**)
1 not lasting very long 短暂的；短促的；短期的: *Last year we all went to Brighton for a short holiday.* 去年我们全都去布赖顿度了个短假。
2 not tall 矮的: *She's a short woman with grey hair.* 她个子不高，头发灰白。
3 measuring only a small amount from one end to the other (距离、长度等) 短的，不长的，不远的: *The restaurant is only a short distance away.* 餐厅离得不远。▫ *She has short, curly hair.* 她有一头卷曲的短发。
be short for something to be a shorter way of saying something 是某事物的简称: *Her name's Jo — it's short for Josephine.* 她名叫约——是约瑟芬的简称。
be short of something not having enough of something 缺乏某物: *His family is very short of money.* 他家经济很拮据。

shortage /ʃɔːtɪdʒ/ *noun* 名词
when there is not enough of something 不足；短缺；缺乏: *In this town there is a great shortage of cheap housing.* 在这个镇上，廉价住房严重短缺。

shorten /ʃɔːtən/ *verb* 动词 (**shortens, shortening, shortened**)
to make something shorter 使缩短: *The treatment shortens the length of the illness.* 治疗缩短了病程。

shortly /ʃɔːtli/ *adverb* 副词
soon 不久；立刻: *'Please take a seat. Dr Garcia will see you shortly.'* " 请坐。加西亚博士马上就来见你。"

shorts /ʃɔːts/ *plural noun* 复数名词
trousers with very short legs 短裤: *She was wearing pink shorts and a black T-shirt.* 她穿着粉色短裤、黑色 T 恤。

short-term *adjective* 形容词
lasting only for a short time, or having an effect soon 短期的；近期的: *This is only a*

short-term solution. 这只是个短期的解决方案。

shot¹ /ʃɒt/
→ see 见 **shoot**

shot² /ʃɒt/ *countable noun* 可数名词
1 an act of firing a gun 开枪；射击：*The man was killed with a single shot.* 那人被一枪毙命。
2 in sports, when you kick, hit or throw the ball, to try to score a point 射门；击球；投篮：*Grant missed two shots at the goal.* 格兰特射失了两球。
3 a photograph 照片：*The photographer got some great shots of the bride.* 摄影师给新娘拍了几张很美的照片。

should /ʃəd, STRONG 强读 ʃʊd/ *modal verb* 情态动词
1 used for saying what is the right thing to do 应该；应当：*I should exercise more.* 我应该加强锻炼。 □ *You shouldn't stay up so late.* 你不应该这么晚才睡。
2 used for saying that something is probably true or will probably happen（表示预期或可能性）应该会，可能：*The doctor said I should be fine by next week.* 医生说下周我就会好了。 □ *You should have no problems with this exercise.* 这种练习你应该没有问题。
3 used in questions when you are asking someone for advice（用于疑问句中表示征求意见）可以，该：*Should I ask for more help?* 我应该寻求更多帮助吗？ □ *What should I do?* 我应该做些什么？

shoulder /ˈʃəʊldə/ *countable noun* 可数名词
one of the two parts of your body between your neck and the tops of your arms 肩膀：*She put her arm round his shoulders.* 她搂着他的肩膀。
→ Look at picture on P4 参见彩插第 4 页

shouldn't /ˈʃʊdənt/
short for（缩写 =）'should not'

should've /ˈʃʊdəv/
short for（缩写 =）'should have'

shout /ʃaʊt/ *verb* 动词 (**shouts, shouting, shouted**)
to say something very loudly 大叫，嚷；高呼：*'She's alive!' he shouted.* "她还活着！"他大声叫道。 □ *Andrew ran out of the house, shouting for help.* 安德鲁跑出屋子，大声呼救。● **shout** *countable noun* 可数名词：*There were angry shouts from the crowd.* 人群中发出愤怒的呼声。

shove /ʃʌv/ *verb* 动词 (**shoves, shoving, shoved**)
to push someone or something roughly 猛推；乱挤：*The woman shoved the other customers out of the way.* 那个女人推开了其他顾客。

shovel /ˈʃʌvəl/ *countable noun* 可数名词
a flat tool with a handle that is used for lifting and moving earth or snow 铲；铁锹：*I'll need the coal shovel.* 我需要煤铲。● **shovel** *verb* 动词 (**shovels, shovelling, shovelled**)：*He had to shovel the snow away from the door.* 他不得不把门前的雪铲掉。

shovel 铁锹

show¹ /ʃəʊ/ *verb* 动词 (**shows, showing, showed, shown**)
1 to prove that a situation exists 显示；表明，证明：*Research shows that certain foods can help prevent headaches.* 研究表明，某些食物可以帮助预防头痛。
2 to let someone see something 给…看；出示：*She showed me her engagement ring.* 她向我展示了她的订婚戒指。
3 to teach someone how to do something 向…演示：*Claire showed us how to make pasta.* 克莱尔给我们示范了如何做意大利面。
4 to be easy to notice 显示；流露：*When I feel angry, it shows.* 我是个怒形于色的人。
show off to try to make people admire you 炫耀；卖弄：*He spent the entire evening showing off.* 他整个晚上都在炫耀。
show something off to show something to a lot of people because you are proud of it 炫耀某物；卖弄某物：*Naomi was showing off her engagement ring.* 娜奥米正在炫耀她的订婚戒指。
show up to arrive at the place where you agreed to meet someone 如约赶到；露面：*We waited until five, but he didn't show up.* 我们一直等到了 5 点，但是他没有露面。

show² /ʃəʊ/ *countable noun* 可数名词
1 a programme on television or radio（电视或广播）节目：*I never missed his TV show when I was a kid.* 我小时候从不错过他的电视节目。
2 a performance in a theatre 演出：*How*

about going to see a show tomorrow? 明天去看演出怎么样？

show business uncountable noun 不可数名词
the entertainment industry of films, theatre and television 娱乐行业；演艺界：His show business career lasted more than 45 years. 他的演艺生涯超过了 45 年。

shower /ʃaʊə/ countable noun 可数名词
1 a short period of rain 阵雨：A few showers are expected in the south on Saturday. 预计周六南部将有几场阵雨。
2 a thing that you stand under, that covers you with water so you can wash yourself 花洒；淋浴喷头：I was in the shower when the phone rang. 电话响的时候我正在洗澡。
3 an occasion when you wash yourself by standing under the water that comes from a shower 淋浴：I think I'll take a shower. 我要洗个澡。 • **shower** verb 动词 (showers, showering, showered) : I was late and there wasn't time to shower. 我晚了，没时间洗澡了。

shown /ʃəʊn/
→ see 见 **show**

shrank /ʃræŋk/
→ see 见 **shrink**

shriek /ʃriːk/ verb 动词 (shrieks, shrieking, shrieked)
to give a short, very loud cry 尖叫：Gwen shrieked with excitement when she heard the news. 格温听到这个消息激动地尖叫起来。 • **shriek** countable noun 可数名词：She let out a shriek and leapt out of the way. 她尖叫一声，跳到了一边。

shrimp /ʃrɪmp/ countable noun 可数名词 (shrimp) (American 美国英语）
→ see 见 **prawn** : Add the shrimp and cook for 30 seconds. 加入小虾，煮 30 秒钟。

shrine /ʃraɪn/ countable noun 可数名词
a religious place where people go to remember a holy person or event 圣地；圣坛；圣殿：They visited the holy shrine of Mecca. 他们拜访了麦加圣地。

shrink /ʃrɪŋk/ verb 动词 (shrinks, shrinking, shrank, shrunk)
to become smaller in size 缩水，收缩：Dad's trousers shrank after just one wash. 爸爸的裤子才洗过一次就缩水了。

shrub /ʃrʌb/ countable noun 可数名词
a small bush 灌木：This book tells you how to choose shrubs for your garden. 本书告诉你如何为自己的花园挑选灌木。

shrug /ʃrʌɡ/ verb 动词 (shrugs, shrugging, shrugged)
to move your shoulders up to show that you do not know or care about something 耸肩（表示不知道或不在乎）：Melissa just shrugged and replied, 'I don't know.' 梅利莎只是耸了耸肩回答道：“我不知道。” • **shrug** countable noun 可数名词：'Who cares?' said Anna with a shrug. "管他呢。"安娜耸了耸肩说道。

shrunk /ʃrʌŋk/
→ see 见 **shrink**

shudder /ʃʌdə/ verb 动词 (shudders, shuddering, shuddered)
to shake because you are frightened or cold, or because you feel disgust（因害怕、寒冷或厌恶而）发抖，打战：Some people shudder at the idea of injections. 有些人一想到打针就发抖。 • **shudder** countable noun 可数名词：'It was terrifying,' she says with a shudder. "太可怕了。"她说的时候抖了一下。

shuffle /ʃʌfəl/ verb 动词 (shuffles, shuffling, shuffled)
1 to walk without lifting your feet off the ground 拖着脚走：Moira shuffled across the kitchen. 莫伊拉拖着脚走过厨房。
2 to mix up playing cards before you begin a game 洗（牌）：Aunt Mary shuffled the cards. 玛丽姑妈洗了牌。

shut /ʃʌt/ verb 动词 (shuts, shutting, shut)
to close something 关闭；合上：Please shut the gate. 请关上大门。 ☐ Lucy shut her eyes and fell asleep at once. 露西闭上眼睛，随即睡着了。 • **shut** adjective 形容词：The police have told us to keep our doors and windows shut. 警察告诉过我们要紧闭门窗。 ☐ Her eyes were shut and she seemed to be asleep. 她眼睛闭着，似乎睡着了。
shut down to close and stop working（工厂、商店等）关闭，歇业
shut up used for telling someone, in a rude way, to stop talking 住口；闭嘴：Just shut up, will you? 请闭嘴，好吗？

shutter /ʃʌtə/ countable noun 可数名词
a wooden or metal cover on the outside of a window 百叶窗：She opened the shutters and looked out of the window. 她打开百叶窗向外看。

shuttle /ʃʌtəl/ countable noun 可数名词
1 → see 见 **space shuttle**

2 a plane, bus, or train that makes regular trips between two places 往返运行航班（或公共汽车、火车）: *There is a free shuttle between the airport terminals.* 机场航站楼之间有免费班车。

shy /ʃaɪ/ *adjective* 形容词 (**shyer**, **shyest**) nervous and embarrassed about talking to people that you do not know well 害羞的；腼腆的: *She was a shy, quiet girl.* 她是个腼腆、安静的姑娘。◻ *I was too shy to say anything.* 我太害羞了，一句话也说不出来。
▶ **shyly** /ˈʃaɪli/ *adverb* 副词: *The children smiled shyly.* 孩子们害羞地笑了。
▶ **shyness** /ˈʃaɪnəs/ *uncountable noun* 不可数名词: *His shyness made it difficult for him to make friends.* 他很害羞，很难交到朋友。

sibling /ˈsɪblɪŋ/ *countable noun* 可数名词 your brother or sister (*formal* 正式) 兄弟姐妹: *I often had to take care of my five younger siblings.* 我经常要照顾5个弟弟妹妹。

sick /sɪk/ *adjective* 形容词 (**sicker**, **sickest**) not well 生病的；有病的: *He's very sick. He needs a doctor.* 他病得很重，需要看医生。
be sick of something to be very annoyed by something that has been happening for a long time (*informal* 非正式) 厌倦某事物；厌烦某事物: *I am sick of all your complaints!* 我听腻了你的那些抱怨！
off sick not at work because you are sick 因病缺勤: *Tom is off sick today.* 今天汤姆请病假了。

sickness /ˈsɪknəs/ *uncountable noun* 不可数名词 the state of being unwell or unhealthy 生病；有病: *Grandpa had only one week of sickness in fifty-two years.* *52年以来，祖父只生过一个星期的病。

side /saɪd/ *countable noun* 可数名词
1 a position to the left or right of something 一边；一侧；一旁: *On the left side of the door there's a door bell.* 门的左侧有个门铃。
2 any part of an object that is not its front, back, top or bottom 侧面: *He took me along the side of the house and into the garden.* 他带我沿着房子的一侧走进花园。
3 the edge of something 边；边缘: *We parked on the side of the road.* 我们把车停在路边。
4 one of the flat surfaces of something (扁平物体的)一面: *You should write on both sides of the paper.* 你应该在纸的正反两面书写。
5 the part of your body from under your arm to the top of your leg 体侧；胁: *Hold your arms by your sides and bend your knees.* 将双臂放在身体两侧，屈膝。
6 a group of people who are fighting in a war or playing against another group in a game (战争或比赛中的)一方，一派: *Both sides want the war to end.* 双方都希望停战。
on someone's side supporting someone in an argument (争论中)支持某人，赞成某人: *Whose side are you on?* 你站哪一边？
side by side next to each other 并排；并肩: *The children were sitting side by side on the sofa.* 孩子们并排坐在沙发上。
take someone's side to support someone in an argument (争论中)支持某人，赞成某人: *Mum took my side in the argument.* 这次争论妈妈站在我这边。

sidebar /ˈsaɪdbɑːr/ *noun* 名词 the narrow area at the side of a web page where you find more information or links to other pages (网页的)侧边栏，边注栏

sidewalk /ˈsaɪdwɔːk/ *countable noun* 可数名词 (*American* 美国英语)
→ see 见 **pavement**

sideways /ˈsaɪdweɪz/ *adverb* 副词 from or towards the side 往(或从、向)一侧: *Pete looked sideways at her.* 皮特斜眼看她。● **sideways** *adjective* 形容词: *Alfred gave him a sideways look.* 艾尔弗雷德斜眼看了他一下。

siege /siːdʒ/ *countable noun* 可数名词 a situation in which soldiers or police officers surround a place in order to force the people there to come out (军队或警方对某地的)围困，包围，围攻: *The siege has been going on for three days.* 围攻已经持续了3天。

sieve /sɪv/ *countable noun* 可数名词 a tool with a fine metal net, that you use for separating solids from liquids 筛子；漏勺；笊篱: *Pour the soup through a sieve to remove any lumps.* 把汤过筛，滤去食物块儿。● **sieve** *verb* 动词 (**sieves**, **sieving**, **sieved**): *Sieve the flour into a bowl.* 把面粉筛进碗里。

sigh /saɪ/ *verb* 动词 (**sighs**, **sighing**, **sighed**) to let out a deep breath because you are disappointed, tired or pleased 叹气；叹息: *Roberta sighed with relief.* 罗伯塔舒了口

气。● **sigh** *countable noun* 可数名词: *Maria kicked off her shoes and sat down with a sigh.* 玛丽亚踢掉鞋子，叹了口气坐了下来。

sight /saɪt/ *noun* 名词
1 *uncountable* 不可数 the ability to see 视力；视觉: *Grandpa has lost the sight in his right eye.* 祖父的右眼看不见了。
2 *singular* 单数 the act of seeing something 看见；目睹: *Liz can't bear the sight of blood.* 利兹看到血就受不了。
3 [**sights**] *plural* 复数 places that are interesting to see and that tourists often visit 名胜；景点: *We saw the sights of Paris.* 我们游览了巴黎的风景名胜。
catch sight of someone/something to suddenly see someone or something for a short period of time 突然看见某人／某事物: *He caught sight of Helen in the crowd.* 他突然在人群中看到了海伦。
in sight/within sight/out of sight used for saying that you can or cannot see something 看得见／在视野内／看不见: *At last the town was in sight.* 最后小镇映入眼帘。
lose sight of someone/something used for saying that you can no longer see someone or something（视野内）看不见某人／某事物: *The man ran off and I lost sight of him.* 那人跑开，我看不见他了。

sightseeing /ˈsaɪtsiːɪŋ/ *uncountable noun* 不可数名词
the activity of travelling around visiting the interesting places that tourists usually visit 观光；旅游: *During our holiday, we had a day's sightseeing in Venice.* 度假期间，我们来了个威尼斯一日游。

sign¹ /saɪn/ *noun* 名词
1 *countable* 可数 a mark, a shape or a movement that has a particular meaning 符号；记号；示意动作: *In maths, + is a plus sign and = is an equals sign.* 数学中，+ 表示加号，= 表示等号。 □ *They gave me a sign to show that everything was OK.* 他们向我做了个手势，表示一切都好。
2 *countable* 可数 a piece of wood, metal or plastic with words or pictures on it that warn you about something, or give you information or an instruction 招牌；标牌；告示牌: *The road signs here are in both English and French.* 这里的路标是英法双语的。 □ *The sign said, 'Welcome to Glasgow'.* 牌子上写着: "欢迎来到格拉斯哥"。
3 something that shows that something

else exists or is happening 迹象；征兆；痕迹: *Matthew showed no sign of fear.* 马修一点儿害怕的表现都没有。

sign² /saɪn/ *verb* 动词 (**signs, signing, signed**)
to write your name on a document 在…上签字；签署: *World leaders have signed an agreement to protect the environment.* 各国首脑签署了一项保护环境的协议。

signal /ˈsɪɡnəl/ *countable noun* 可数名词
a movement, a light, or a sound that gives a particular message to the person who sees or hears it 信号；暗号: *The captain gave the signal for the soldiers to attack.* 上尉向战士们发出进攻的信号。 ● **signal** *verb* 动词 (**signals, signalling, signalled**): *Mandy signalled to Jesse to follow her.* 曼迪示意杰西跟着她。

signature /ˈsɪɡnətʃə/ *countable noun* 可数名词
your name, written in your own special way 签字；签名；署名: *I put my signature at the bottom of the page.* 我在那页纸底部签了字。

significance /sɪɡˈnɪfɪkəns/ *uncountable noun* 不可数名词
the importance or meaning of something 重要性；意义: *What do you think is the significance of this event?* 你觉得这件事的意义是什么？

significant /sɪɡˈnɪfɪkənt/ *adjective* 形容词
important or large 重要的；显著的: *There has been a significant increase in the price of oil.* 油价大幅上涨。
▶ **significantly** /sɪɡˈnɪfɪkəntli/ *adverb* 副词: *The temperature dropped significantly.* 气温大幅下降。

Sikh /siːk/ *countable noun* 可数名词
a person who follows the Indian religion called Sikhism 锡克教教徒: *Rebecca's husband is a Sikh.* 丽贝卡的丈夫是锡克教教徒。 □ *a Sikh temple* 锡克教庙宇

silence /ˈsaɪləns/ *noun* 名词
1 when no one is speaking 沉默；默不作声: *They stood in silence.* 他们默默地站着。 □ *There was a long silence before Sarah replied.* 萨拉沉默了良久才回应。
2 complete quietness, with no sound at all 寂静；无声: *She breathed deeply, enjoying the silence.* 她深深地吸了口气，享受着这宁静。

silent /ˈsaɪlənt/ *adjective* 形容词
1 not speaking 沉默的；默不作声的:

silhouette – simplify

Jessica was silent because she did not know what to say. 杰茜卡沉默不语，因为她不知道说什么。
- ▶ **silently** /ˈsaɪləntli/ *adverb* 副词：*She and Ned sat silently, enjoying the peace.* 她和内德默默地坐着，享受着平静。

2 completely quiet, with no sound at all 寂静的；无声的：*The room was silent except for the TV.* 屋子里一片寂静，只有电视的声音。
- ▶ **silently** /ˈsaɪləntli/ *adverb* 副词：*The thief moved silently across the room.* 小偷悄悄地穿过房间。

silhouette /ˌsɪluˈet/ *countable noun* 可数名词
the dark shape that you see when someone or something has a bright light behind them 暗色轮廓：*She could see the distant silhouette of a castle.* 她能看到远处一座城堡的轮廓。

silk /sɪlk/ *uncountable noun* 不可数名词
a smooth, shiny cloth that is made from very thin threads 丝绸：*Pauline was wearing a beautiful silk dress.* 保利娜穿着一条漂亮的丝绸连衣裙。

silky /ˈsɪlki/ *adjective* 形容词 (**silkier, silkiest**)
smooth, soft and shiny, like silk 丝绸般的；柔滑光洁的：*This shampoo makes your hair beautifully silky.* 这款洗发水会让头发丝滑亮丽。

silly /ˈsɪli/ *adjective* 形容词 (**sillier, silliest**)
not behaving in a sensible or serious way 傻的；愚蠢的；可笑的：*'Don't be so silly, darling!'* "别这么傻，亲爱的！"

silver[1] /ˈsɪlvə/ *uncountable noun* 不可数名词
a valuable pale grey metal that is used for making jewellery 银：*He bought her a bracelet made from silver.* 他给她买了一个银手镯。

silver[2] /ˈsɪlvə/ *adjective* 形容词
shiny and pale grey in colour 银色的；银灰色的：*He had thick silver hair.* 他有一头浓密的银发。

silver medal *countable noun* 可数名词
an award made of silver metal that you get as second prize in a competition 银牌：*Gillingham won the silver medal in the 200 metres.* 吉林厄姆获得了 200 米银牌。

SIM card /ˈsɪm ˌkɑːd/ *countable noun* 可数名词
a small piece of electronic equipment in a mobile phone that connects it to a particular phone network. SIM is short for (缩写 =) 'Subscriber Identity Module'.（手机的）SIM 卡，用户识别模块

similar /ˈsɪmɪlə/ *adjective* 形容词
the same in some ways but not in every way 相似的；相近的；类似的：*This cake tastes similar to carrot cake.* 这种蛋糕味道和胡萝卜蛋糕相似。□ *Nowadays, cars all look very similar.* 如今，汽车看上去都差不多。

similarity /ˌsɪmɪˈlærɪti/ *countable noun* 可数名词 (**similarities**)
something that is the same about two people or things 相似点；相似处：*There are many similarities between the two country's cultures.* 两国文化有许多相似之处。

simile /ˈsɪmɪli/ *countable noun* 可数名词
an expression that describes a person or a thing by comparing it with another person or thing, using the words 'like' or 'as'. An example of a simile is 'She swims like a fish'. 明喻；直喻

simmer /ˈsɪmə/ *verb* 动词 (**simmers, simmering, simmered**)
to cook gently in water that is just boiling 煨；炖；文火炖：*Let the soup simmer for 15-20 minutes.* 用小火炖汤 15 至 20 分钟。

simple /ˈsɪmpəl/ *adjective* 形容词 (**simpler, simplest**)
1 easy to understand 简单的；易懂的：*The recipes in the book are simple and easy to follow.* 这本书上的食谱简单好上手。□ *Just follow the simple instructions below.* 只需遵循下面的简单指令即可。
- ▶ **simply** /ˈsɪmpli/ *adverb* 副词：*He explained his views simply and clearly.* 他简单明了地解释了自己的看法。

2 having all the basic necessary things, but nothing more 简朴的；简易的；朴素的：*He ate a simple dinner of rice and beans.* 他晚饭简单地吃了点米饭和豆子。□ *Amanda was wearing a simple black silk dress.* 阿曼达穿了一条朴素的黑色丝绸连衣裙。
- ▶ **simply** /ˈsɪmpli/ *adverb* 副词：*Her house is decorated simply.* 她家房子装修简单。

simplicity /sɪmˈplɪsɪti/ *uncountable noun* 不可数名词
the quality of being simple 简单；质朴：*I love the simplicity of his designs.* 我喜欢他质朴的设计风格。

simplify /ˈsɪmplɪfaɪ/ *verb* 动词 (**simplifies, simplifying, simplified**)
to make something easier to understand or to do 简化；使易懂：*This program*

simplifies the task of searching for information. 这个程序简化了信息检索任务。
▶ **simplified** /'sɪmplɪˌfaɪd/ *adjective* 形容词: We read a simplified version of Shakespeare's 'Hamlet'. 我们读了莎士比亚所著《哈姆莱特》的简写本。

simply /'sɪmpli/ *adverb* 副词
used to emphasize what you are saying（用于强调）简直，根本: Your behaviour is simply unacceptable. 你的行为简直令人无法接受。

sin /sɪn/ *noun* 名词
an action or a type of behaviour that breaks a religious law（违反宗教戒律的）罪，罪过，罪孽: They believe that lying is a sin. 他们认为撒谎是一种罪过。● **sin** *verb* 动词 (**sins, sinning, sinned**): The Bible says that we have all sinned.《圣经》上说我们都有罪。

since¹ /sɪns/ *preposition* 介词
used for talking about a time or an event that started in the past, and that has continued from then until now 从…起；自…以来: My uncle has lived in India since 1995. 自1995年起我叔叔就一直住在印度。● **since** *adverb* 副词: They worked together in the 1980s, and have been friends ever since. 他们在20世纪80年代共事，从此便成了朋友。● **since** *conjunction* 连词: I've lived here since I was six years old. 我自打6岁起就一直住在这里。

since² /sɪns/ *conjunction* 连词
because 因为；由于；既然: I'm always on a diet, since I put on weight easily. 我一直在节食，因为我很容易长胖。

sincere /sɪnˈsɪə/ *adjective* 形容词
honest and really meaning what you say 真诚的；诚恳的: Do you think Ryan's being sincere? 你觉得瑞安是诚心诚意的吗？

sincerely /sɪnˈsɪəli/ *adverb* 副词
used for showing that you really mean or feel something 真诚地；诚恳地: 'Well done!' he said sincerely. "干得好！"他真诚地说。
Yours sincerely written before your signature at the end of a formal letter when you have addressed it to someone by their name（用于以收信人姓名相称呼的正式书信末尾，署名之前）谨启，谨上: Yours sincerely, Robbie Weinz. 谨上，罗比·魏因兹

sing /sɪŋ/ *verb* 动词 (**sings, singing, sang, sung**)
to make music with your voice 唱；唱歌: I love singing. 我喜欢唱歌。 □ My brother and I used to sing this song. 我和弟弟过去唱过这首歌。

singer /'sɪŋə/ *countable noun* 可数名词
a person who sings, especially as a job 歌者；(尤指)歌手，歌唱家: My mother was a singer in a band. 我妈妈曾是一支乐队的歌手。

single /'sɪŋɡəl/ *adjective* 形容词
1 used for showing that you are talking about only one thing 单一的；单个的: She hasn't said a single word about what happened. 她只字不提发生了什么。 □ We sold over two hundred pizzas in a single day. 我们一天之内卖了200多份比萨。
2 not married 单身的；未婚的: Joseph is a single man in his early twenties. 约瑟夫是个20出头的单身汉。
3 for one person only 单人的；供单人用的: Would you like to reserve a single or a double room? 你想订单人间还是双人间？

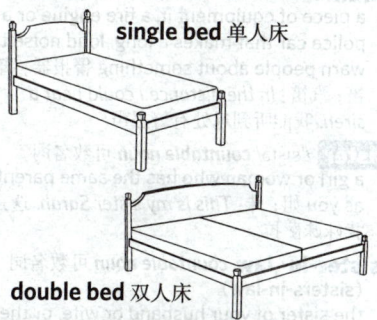

single bed 单人床

double bed 双人床

singular /'sɪŋɡjʊlə/ *adjective* 形容词
used for describing the form of a word that you use when you are talking about one person or thing 单数的；单数形式的: The singular form of 'mice' is 'mouse'. *mice 的单数形式是 mouse. ● **singular** *singular noun* 单数名词: What is the singular of 'geese'? *geese 的单数形式是什么？

sink¹ /sɪŋk/ *countable noun* 可数名词
a large fixed container in a kitchen or a bathroom that you can fill with water 洗涤槽；洗碗池；盥洗池: The sink was filled with dirty dishes. 洗碗池里堆满了脏盘子。□ The bathroom has a toilet, a shower and a sink. 卫生间里有马桶、淋浴和盥洗池。

sink² /sɪŋk/ *verb* 动词 (**sinks, sinking, sank, sunk**)
1 to go below the surface of the water 沉没；下沉: The boat hit the rocks and began

to sink. 船撞上了礁石，开始下沉。
2 to move slowly down, to a lower level 缓缓下降；沉降：*The sun was sinking in the west.* 夕阳在缓缓西下。

sip /sɪp/ *verb* 动词 (**sips, sipping, sipped**)
to drink something slowly, taking a small amount at a time 小口慢饮；抿：*Jessica sipped her drink slowly.* 杰茜卡慢慢地小口喝着饮料。● **sip** *countable noun* 可数名词：*Harry took a sip of tea.* 哈里抿了一口茶。

sir /sɜː/ *noun* 名词
used as a polite way of talking to a man （对男子的敬称）先生：*Excuse me sir, is this your car?* 先生，请问这是您的车吗？
Dear Sir written at the beginning of a formal letter or a business letter when you are writing to a man（正式书信或商务信函开头对男士的称呼语）亲爱的先生，尊敬的阁下：*Dear Sir, Thank you for your letter.* 尊敬的阁下，感谢您的来信。

siren /ˈsaɪərən/ *countable noun* 可数名词
a piece of equipment in a fire engine or a police car that makes a long, loud noise to warn people about something 警报器；警笛；汽笛：*In the distance I could hear a siren.* 我能听到远处有警报声。

sister /ˈsɪstə/ *countable noun* 可数名词
a girl or woman who has the same parents as you 姐；妹：*This is my sister Sarah.* 这是我妹妹萨拉。

sister-in-law *countable noun* 可数名词 (**sisters-in-law**)
the sister of your husband or wife, or the woman who is married to your brother 大（或小）姑子；大（或小）姨子；嫂子；弟媳

sit /sɪt/ *verb* 动词 (**sits, sitting, sat**)
1 to have the lower part of your body resting on a chair and the upper part straight 坐：*Mother was sitting in her chair in the kitchen.* 妈妈坐在厨房的椅子上。□ *They sat watching television all evening.* 他们坐着看了一晚上电视。
2 to move your body down until you are sitting on something 就座；坐下：*Kelly sat down on the bed and took off her shoes.* 凯莉坐到床上脱了鞋。□ *Mom sat down beside me.* 妈妈在我身旁坐了下来。
sit up to change the position of your body, so that you are sitting instead of lying down 坐起来；坐直：*She felt dizzy when she sat up.* 她坐起来时感到头晕。

site /saɪt/ *countable noun* 可数名词
1 a place where a particular thing happens 场地；场所：*Dad works on a building site.* 爸爸在建筑工地干活儿。□ *This city was the site of a terrible earthquake.* 这座城市曾发生过一场可怕的地震。
2 → see 见 **website**：*The site contains advice for new teachers.* 网站上有对新教师的建议。

ˈsitting room *countable noun* 可数名词
a room in a house where people sit and relax 客厅；起居室

situated /ˈsɪtʃueɪtɪd/ *adjective* 形容词
in a particular place 位于…的；坐落于…的：*The hotel is situated in the centre of Berlin.* 这家酒店位于柏林市中心区。

situation /ˌsɪtʃuˈeɪʃən/ *countable noun* 可数名词
what is happening in a particular place at a particular time 形势；情况；局面：*Army officers said the situation was under control.* 军方官员称局势得到了控制。

six /sɪks/
the number 6 六

sixteen /ˌsɪksˈtiːn/
the number 16 十六
▸ **sixteenth** /ˌsɪksˈtiːnθ/ *adjective* 形容词, *adverb* 副词：*I'm having a party for my sixteenth birthday.* 我要开个派对庆祝自己16岁生日。

sixth¹ /sɪksθ/ *adjective* 形容词, *adverb* 副词
counted as number six in a series 第六：*The sixth round of the competition begins tomorrow.* 第6轮竞赛将于明天开始。

sixth² /sɪksθ/ *countable noun* 可数名词
one of six equal parts of something (1/6) 六分之一

sixty /ˈsɪksti/
the number 60 六十
▸ **sixtieth** /ˈsɪkstiəθ/ *adjective* 形容词, *adverb* 副词：*Dad had a big party for his sixtieth birthday.* 爸爸60岁生日时办了个盛大的聚会。

size /saɪz/ *noun* 名词
1 how big or small something is 大小；规模：*The size of the room is about 10 feet by 15 feet.* 这间屋子大约长15英尺、宽10英尺。□ *The shelves contain books of various sizes.* 书架上摆着各种开本的书。
▸ **-sized** /saɪzd/ *adjective* 形容词：*I work for a medium-sized company in Chicago.* 我在芝加哥一家中型公司工作。
2 *countable* 可数 one of a series of

particular measurements for clothes and shoes(衣服、鞋子的)尺寸，尺码：*My sister is a size 12.* 我妹妹穿 12 码。▫ *What size are your feet?* 你的脚穿多大码的鞋？▫ *Do you have these shoes in a size nine?* 这款鞋有 9 码的吗？

skate[1] /skeɪt/ *countable noun* 可数名词
1 (also 亦作 **ice-skate**) a boot with a long, sharp piece of metal on the bottom, for moving quickly and smoothly on ice 冰鞋
2 (also 亦作 **roller-skate**) a boot with wheels on the bottom, for moving quickly on the ground 轮滑鞋

skate[2] /skeɪt/ *verb* 动词 (**skates, skating, skated**)
to move around wearing skates 滑冰；溜冰：*When the pond froze, we skated on it.* 池塘结冰时，我们在上面溜冰。
▶ **skating** /ˈskeɪtɪŋ/ *uncountable noun* 不可数名词：*They all went skating together in the winter.* 冬天他们一起去滑冰。
▶ **skater** /ˈskeɪtə/ *countable noun* 可数名词：*The ice-rink was full of skaters.* 冰场里满是滑冰的人。

skateboard /ˈskeɪtbɔːd/ *countable noun* 可数名词
a narrow board with wheels at each end that you can stand on and ride 滑板

skatepark /ˈskeɪtpɑːk/ *noun* 名词
an area designed for people to ride on skateboards 滑板场；滑板公园

skeleton /ˈskelɪtən/ *countable noun* 可数名词
all the bones in a person's or an animal's body(人或动物的)骨骼：*a human skeleton* 人体骨骼

sketch /sketʃ/ *countable noun* 可数名词 (**sketches**)
a drawing that you do quickly, without a lot of details 草图；速写：*He did a quick sketch of the building.* 他快速地画了一幅这栋楼的草图。● **sketch** *verb* 动词 (**sketches, sketching, sketched**)：*She started sketching designs when she was six years old.* 她 6 岁开始画设计图。

→ Look at picture on P13 参见彩插第 13 页

ski[1] /skiː/ *countable noun* 可数名词
a long, flat, narrow piece of wood, metal or plastic that you fasten to your boot so that you can move easily on snow or water 滑雪板；水橇；滑水板

ski[2] /skiː/ *verb* 动词 (**skis, skiing, skied**)
to move over snow or water on skis 滑雪；滑水：*They tried to ski down the mountain.* 他们试图滑雪下山。
▶ **skier** /ˈskiːə/ *countable noun* 可数名词：*My dad's a very good skier.* 我爸爸滑雪滑得很好。
▶ **skiing** /ˈskiːɪŋ/ *uncountable noun* 不可数名词：*My hobbies are skiing and swimming.* 我爱好滑雪和游泳。
→ Look at picture on P14 参见彩插第 14 页

skid /skɪd/ *verb* 动词 (**skids, skidding, skidded**)
to slide sideways 侧滑；打滑：*The car skidded on the icy road.* 汽车在结冰的路上打滑。

skilful /ˈskɪlfʊl/ *adjective* 形容词
able to do something very well 有技巧的；熟练的：*He was a highly skilful football player.* 他是一名技术高超的足球运动员。
▶ **skilfully** /ˈskɪlfʊli/ *adverb* 副词：*The story is skilfully written.* 这个故事写得很巧妙。

skill /skɪl/ *noun* 名词
1 *countable* 可数 a job or an activity that needs special training and practice 技术性工作；手艺：*You're never too old to learn new skills.* 学习新手艺从不嫌晚。
2 *uncountable* 不可数 your ability to do something well 技能；技巧；本领：*He shows great skill on the football field.* 他在足球场上展现了高超的技巧。

skilled /skɪld/ *adjective* 形容词
having the knowledge and ability to do something well 有技能的；熟练的：*We need more skilled workers.* 我们需要更多熟练工人。

skim /skɪm/ *verb* 动词 (**skims, skimming, skimmed**)
to move quickly just above a surface 掠过；擦过；滑过：*We watched seagulls skimming the waves.* 我们看着海鸥掠过海浪。

skin /skɪn/ *noun* 名词
1 *uncountable* 不可数 the substance that covers the outside of a person's or an animal's body 皮肤；皮：*His skin is pale*

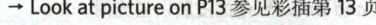

skeleton 骨骼
skull 颅骨
rib cage 胸廓

and smooth. 他的皮肤白皙光滑。▫ *a crocodile skin handbag* 鳄鱼皮手提包
2 the outer part that covers a fruit or a vegetable 果皮；(蔬菜、水果等)表皮：*a banana skin* 香蕉皮

skinny /ˈskɪni/ *adjective* 形容词 (**skinnier, skinniest**)
extremely thin or too thin (*informal* 非正式) 皮包骨头的；骨瘦如柴的：*He was a skinny little boy.* 他是一个骨瘦如柴的小男孩。

skip /skɪp/ *verb* 动词 (**skips, skipping, skipped**)
1 to move forward quickly, jumping from one foot to the other 蹦跳着前行：*We skipped down the street, talking and laughing.* 我们沿着街道蹦蹦跳跳地前行，说着笑着。
2 to jump repeatedly over a rope 跳绳：*She took the rope and began to skip.* 她拿起绳子开始跳起来。
3 to decide not to do something that you usually do 跳过，略过，不做(常做的事)：*Don't skip breakfast.* 早餐不能省。

¹skipping rope *countable noun* 可数名词
a piece of rope that you jump over, with handles at each end that you use to turn the rope 跳绳

skirt /skɜːt/ *countable noun* 可数名词
a piece of clothing for women and girls that hangs down from the waist and covers part of the legs 短裙；半身裙

skull /skʌl/ *countable noun* 可数名词
the bones of a person's or an animal's head 颅骨；头骨：*After the accident, they X-rayed his skull.* 事故之后，他们给他的颅骨做了 X 光检查。

sky /skaɪ/ *noun* 名词 (**skies**)
the space above the Earth that you can see when you stand outside and look upwards 天；天空：*The sun was shining in the sky.* 太阳当空照。▫ *Today we have clear blue skies.* 今天天空明净蔚蓝。

Skype /skaɪp/ *uncountable noun* 不可数名词
a computer program that you can use to make voice calls or video calls on the Internet (*trademark* 商标) 讯佳普网络电话软件：*After she moved away they spoke regularly on Skype.* 她搬走之后，他们经常在讯佳普上聊天。● **Skype** *verb* 动词 (**Skypes, Skyping, Skyped**) (*trademark* 商标)：*She Skypes her grandchildren in Australia.* 她用讯佳普和在澳的孙女们聊天。

skyscraper /ˈskaɪskreɪpə/ *countable noun* 可数名词
a very tall building in a city 摩天大楼

slab /slæb/ *countable noun* 可数名词
a thick, flat piece of something 板；平板：*slabs of stone* 石板

slack /slæk/ *adjective* 形容词 (**slacker, slackest**)
1 loose 松弛的：*Suddenly, the rope went slack.* 突然，绳子松了。
2 not busy 不忙的；冷清的：*The shop has busy times and slack periods.* 店铺时忙时闲。

slam /slæm/ *verb* 动词 (**slams, slamming, slammed**)
1 to shut a door very noisily and roughly 砰地关上，使劲关上(门)：*She slammed the door behind her.* 她砰的一声摔门而去。
2 to close very noisily (门等)砰的一声关上：*He walked out and the door slammed behind him.* 他走出去后门砰的一声关上了。
3 to put something down somewhere quickly and roughly 猛地放下：*Lauren slammed the phone down angrily.* 劳伦愤怒地啪的一声挂断了电话。

slang /slæŋ/ *uncountable noun* 不可数名词
informal words that you can use when you are talking to people you know very well 俚语：*'A quid' is slang for 'a pound (£1)'.* *a quid* 是 *a pound* (1英镑)的俚语说法。

slant /slɑːnt/ *verb* 动词 (**slants, slanting, slanted**)
to have one side higher than the other 倾斜；歪斜；偏斜：*The roof of the house slants sharply.* 这所房子的屋顶斜度很大。

slap /slæp/ *verb* 动词 (**slaps, slapping, slapped**)
to hit someone with the flat inside part of your hand 掴；扇：*I slapped him hard across the face.* 我朝他脸上狠狠地扇了一巴掌。● **slap** *countable noun* 可数名词：*She gave him a slap on the face.* 她打了他一耳光。

slash¹ /slæʃ/ *verb* 动词 (**slashes, slashing, slashed**)
to make a long, deep cut in something 劈；砍；划破：*Someone slashed my car tyres in the night.* 夜里有人划破了我的车胎。

slash² /slæʃ/ *countable noun* 可数名词 (**slashes**)
a line (/) that separates numbers, letters or words in writing 斜线；斜杠

slaughter /ˈslɔːtə/ *verb* 动词 (**slaughters, slaughtering, slaughtered**)
1 to kill a very large number of people violently 屠杀；杀戮: *So many innocent people have been slaughtered.* 这么多无辜者惨遭屠杀。● **slaughter** *uncountable noun* 不可数名词: *The slaughter of women and children was common.* 屠杀妇孺那时很常见。
2 to kill animals for their meat 屠宰，宰杀（动物）: *The farmers here slaughter their own sheep.* 这里的农夫自己养羊自己宰。
● **slaughter** *uncountable noun* 不可数名词: *The sheep were taken away for slaughter.* 羊被带去屠宰。

slave¹ /sleɪv/ *countable noun* 可数名词
a person who belongs to another person and who works for them without being paid 奴隶
▶ **slavery** /ˈsleɪvəri/ *uncountable noun* 不可数名词: *The United States abolished slavery in 1865.* 美国于 1865 年废除奴隶制。

slave² /sleɪv/ *verb* 动词 (**slaves, slaving, slaved**)
(also 亦作 **slave away**) to work very hard 辛苦工作；卖力干活儿: *He was slaving away in the hot kitchen.* 他在热气腾腾的厨房里忙得热火朝天。

slave trade *singular noun* 单数名词
the business of buying and selling slaves (= servants who are forced to work for someone) 奴隶贸易: *Many people made money from the slave trade.* 许多人从奴隶贸易中赢利。

sledge /sledʒ/ *countable noun* 可数名词
an object that you sit on in order to travel over snow 雪橇: *We pulled the children across the snow on a sledge.* 我们用雪橇拉着孩子们过雪地。

sleep¹ /sliːp/ *noun* 名词
1 *uncountable* 不可数 a person's or an animal's natural state of rest when their eyes are closed, and their body is not active 睡眠；睡觉: *You should try to get as much sleep as possible.* 你应该尽可能多睡会儿。
2 *countable* 可数 a period of sleeping 睡眠时间: *Good morning, Pete. Did you have a good sleep?* 早上好，皮特。你睡得好吗？
go to sleep to start sleeping 入睡: *Be quiet and go to sleep!* 安静，睡觉!

LANGUAGE HELP 语言提示
When you go to bed at night, you **go to sleep** or **fall asleep**. If you have difficulty sleeping, you can say that you cannot **get to sleep**. 晚间上床睡觉用 go to sleep 或 fall asleep，表示入睡有困难可以用 cannot get to sleep。

sleep² /sliːp/ *verb* 动词 (**sleeps, sleeping, slept**)
to rest with your eyes closed and with no activity in your mind or body 睡；睡觉: *I didn't sleep well last night — it was too hot.* 我昨晚没有睡好——太热了。

sleeping bag *countable noun* 可数名词
a large warm bag for sleeping in when you go camping（野营用的）睡袋

sleepless /ˈsliːpləs/ *adjective* 形容词
without sleep 不睡觉的；不眠的: *I have sleepless nights worrying about her.* 我好几宿都睡不着，一直担心她。

sleepy /ˈsliːpi/ *adjective* 形容词 (**sleepier, sleepiest**)
very tired and almost asleep 困倦的；瞌睡的: *The pills made me sleepy.* 这药令我昏昏欲睡。

sleet /sliːt/ *uncountable noun* 不可数名词
a mixture of snow and rain 雨夹雪: *The snow and sleet will continue overnight.* 雪和雨夹雪将持续一夜。

sleeve /sliːv/ *countable noun* 可数名词
one of the two parts of a piece of clothing that cover your arms 袖子: *Rachel wore a blue dress with long sleeves.* 蕾切尔穿了一条蓝色的长袖连衣裙。

slender /ˈslendə/ *adjective* 形容词
used to describe a person who is thin in a graceful, attractive way（人）苗条的，修长的: *She was tall and slender, like her mother.* 她身材颀长苗条，像她母亲。

slept /slept/
→ see 见 **sleep**

slice /slaɪs/ *countable noun* 可数名词
a thin piece of something that you cut from a larger piece 切片；薄片: *Would you like a slice of bread?* 你要来片面包吗? □ *Nicole had a cup of coffee and a large slice of chocolate cake.* 妮科尔喝了一杯咖啡，吃了一大片巧克力蛋糕。● **slice** *verb* 动词 (**slices, slicing, sliced**): *I blew out the candles and Mum sliced the cake.* 我吹灭了蜡烛，妈妈切了蛋糕。

slid /slɪd/
→ see 见 **slide**

slide¹ /slaɪd/ *verb* 动词 (**slides, sliding, slid**)
to move quickly and smoothly over a surface 滑动；溜：*She slid across the ice on her stomach.* 她趴着滑过冰面。

slide² /slaɪd/ *countable noun* 可数名词
a large metal frame that children can play on. They climb the steps at one side, and move down a smooth slope on their bottom. 滑梯

slide 滑梯

slight /slaɪt/ *adjective* 形容词
small and not important or serious 小的；轻微的；些微的：*The sun was shining and there was a slight breeze.* 阳光明媚，微风轻拂。 □ *The company has announced a slight increase in sales.* 公司宣布销售额略有增长。

slightly /ˈslaɪtli/ *adverb* 副词
just a little 略微；稍微：*We've moved to a slightly larger house.* 我们搬到了一所稍大一点儿的房子里。

slim¹ /slɪm/ *adjective* 形容词 (**slimmer, slimmest**)
thin in an attractive way 苗条的；纤细的：*The young woman was tall and slim.* 那名年轻女子身材高挑。

slim² /slɪm/ *verb* 动词 (**slims, slimming, slimmed**)
(also 亦作 **slim down**) to lose weight and become thinner 瘦身；瘦下来：*I've slimmed down a size or two.* 我瘦了一两个尺码。

slime /slaɪm/ *uncountable noun* 不可数名词
a thick, wet substance that looks or smells unpleasant 烂泥；黏泥；黏垢：*The rocks are slippery with mud and slime.* 岩石很滑，上面有泥巴和黏垢。

sling¹ /slɪŋ/ *verb* 动词 (**slings, slinging, slung**)
to throw something in a careless way（随便地）扔，丢：*She slung the sack over her shoulder.* 她把麻袋甩上肩头。

sling² /slɪŋ/ *countable noun* 可数名词
a piece of cloth that you wear around your neck and arm, to hold up your arm when it is broken or injured（悬吊受伤手臂的）悬带：*Emily had her arm in a sling.* 埃米莉用悬带吊着胳膊。

slip¹ /slɪp/ *verb* 动词 (**slips, slipping, slipped**)
1 to accidentally slide and fall 滑跤；滑倒：*He slipped on the wet grass.* 他在湿漉漉的草地上滑倒了。

slip 滑倒

2 to slide out of position 滑落；脱落：*Grandpa's glasses slipped down his nose.* 爷爷的眼镜从鼻梁上滑了下来。
3 to go somewhere quickly and quietly 溜；悄然疾行：*In the morning she quietly slipped out of the house.* 早上她悄悄溜出了家门。
4 to put something somewhere quickly and quietly 悄然迅速放置；偷偷塞：*I slipped the letter into my pocket.* 我悄悄将信一把塞进了口袋。

slip up to make a mistake 出错；出现疏失：*We slipped up a few times, but no one noticed.* 我们有几次疏失，但没人注意到。

slip² /slɪp/ *countable noun* 可数名词
1 a small mistake 小差错；失误：*Even a tiny slip could spoil everything.* 哪怕是一个微不足道的小差错也有可能毁掉一切。
2 a small piece of paper 小纸片；纸条：*He wrote our names on slips of paper.* 他在纸条上写下了我们的名字。

slipper /ˈslɪpə/ *countable noun* 可数名词
a loose, soft shoe that you wear indoors 拖鞋：*She put on a pair of slippers and went downstairs.* 她穿上拖鞋下了楼。

slippery /ˈslɪpəri/ *adjective* 形容词
smooth or wet, and difficult to walk on or to hold 滑的；滑溜的：*Be careful — the floor is slippery.* 小心——地滑。

slit /slɪt/ *verb* 动词 (**slits, slitting, slit**)
to make a long narrow cut in something

割；剖；切：*He slit open the envelope.* 他割开信封。● **slit** *countable noun* 可数名词：*Make a slit about half an inch long.* 切一道约半英寸长的口子。

slither /ˈslɪðə/ *verb* 动词 (**slithers, slithering, slithered**)
to move along the ground, sliding from side to side, like a snake 蜿蜒滑行；蛇行：*Robert slithered down into the water.* 罗伯特摇摇晃晃跌进了水里。

slogan /ˈsləʊɡən/ *countable noun* 可数名词
a short phrase that you can remember easily, that is used in advertisements and by political parties 口号；标语：*His campaign slogan was 'Time for Action'.* 他的竞选口号是"行动起来"。

slope[1] /sləʊp/ *countable noun* 可数名词
the side of a mountain, hill or valley 坡；山坡；斜坡：*A steep slope leads to the beach.* 一个陡坡通向海滩。

slope[2] /sləʊp/ *verb* 动词 (**slopes, sloping, sloped**)
1 having one end higher than the other 倾斜：*The land sloped down sharply to the river.* 这片土地向河边倾斜得厉害。
▶ **sloping** /ˈsləʊpɪŋ/ *adjective* 形容词：*Our house has a sloping roof.* 我们家房子是斜顶。
2 to lean to the right or to the left rather than being straight 歪斜：*John's writing slopes backwards.* 约翰的字迹朝右倾斜。

sloppy /ˈslɒpi/ *adjective* 形容词 (**sloppier, sloppiest**)
done in a careless and lazy way 马虎的；敷衍的；草率的：*All teachers hate sloppy work from their students.* 所有老师都讨厌学生敷衍了事的作业。

slot /slɒt/ *countable noun* 可数名词
a long, narrow hole in something 槽；狭缝；缝隙：*He dropped a coin into the slot and pressed the button.* 他往投币口里投了一枚硬币，按下按钮。□ *Please place your credit card in the slot.* 请将信用卡插入卡槽。

slow[1] /sləʊ/ *adjective* 形容词 (**slower, slowest**)
1 not moving or happening quickly 慢的；缓慢的：*His bike was heavy and slow.* 他的自行车沉，速度慢。□ *The investigation was a long and slow process.* 调查的过程漫长而缓慢。□ *They danced to the slow rhythm of the music.* 他们伴着缓慢的音乐节奏跳舞。
▶ **slowly** /ˈsləʊli/ *adverb* 副词：*He spoke slowly and clearly.* 他说话缓慢而清晰。
2 showing a time that is earlier than the correct time (钟表) 慢的：*The clock is five minutes slow.* 这钟慢了5分钟。

slow[2] /sləʊ/ *verb* 动词 (**slows, slowing, slowed**)
slow down to start to move or happen more slowly 减速；放缓：*The bus slowed down for the next stop.* 公交车减速准备停靠下一站。

slow motion also 亦作 **slow-motion** *uncountable noun* 不可数名词
when film or television pictures are shown much more slowly than normal 慢动作；慢镜头：*They played it again in slow motion.* 他们又用慢镜头放了一遍。

slug /slʌɡ/ *countable noun* 可数名词
a small animal with a long soft body and no legs that moves very slowly 蛞蝓；鼻涕虫

slug 蛞蝓

slum /slʌm/ *countable noun* 可数名词
an area of a city where the buildings are in bad condition and the people are very poor 贫民窟；贫民区：*More than 2.4 million people live in the city's slums.* 有240多万人住在城里贫民区。

slump /slʌmp/ *verb* 动词 (**slumps, slumping, slumped**)
1 to fall suddenly and by a large amount 急剧下降；暴跌：*The company's profits slumped by 41% in a single year.* 公司利润一年间就暴跌了 41%。● **slump** *countable noun* 可数名词：*There has been a slump in house prices.* 房价暴跌。
2 to fall or sit down suddenly and heavily 猛然倒下；跌坐：*She slumped into a chair and burst into tears.* 她重重地瘫坐在椅子上，突然大哭起来。

slung /slʌŋ/
→ see 见 **sling**

slur /slɜː/ *verb* 动词 (**slurs, slurring, slurred**)
to speak without saying each word clearly, because you are drunk, ill or very tired 含糊不清地说：*He was slurring his words and I couldn't understand what he was saying.* 他说话含糊不清，我不明白他在说什么。
▶ **slurred** /slɜːd/ *adjective* 形容词：*Her*

speech was slurred and she was very pale. 她说话口齿不清，脸色惨白。

sly /slaɪ/ *adjective* 形容词
showing that you know something that other people do not know or that was meant to be a secret 诡秘的（表示自己知道别人不知道的秘密）: *He gave a sly smile.* 他诡秘地笑了。
▶ **slyly** /ˈslaɪli/ *adverb* 副词: *Anna grinned slyly.* 安娜诡秘地咧嘴一笑。

smack /smæk/ *verb* 动词 (**smacks, smacking, smacked**)
to hit someone with your hand（用手）打，拍: *He smacked me on the side of the head.* 他挥手打了我脑袋一侧。

small /smɔːl/ *adjective* 形容词 (**smaller, smallest**)
1 not large in size or amount（尺寸或数量）小的: *My daughter is small for her age.* 我女儿要比同龄人个头小。 □ *Fry the onions in a small amount of butter.* 用少量黄油煎一下洋葱。
2 young 幼小的；年纪小的: *I have two small children.* 我有两个小孩。
3 not very serious or important 不太严重的；不太重要的: *It's a small problem, and we can easily solve it.* 这是个小问题，我们能轻松解决掉。

small-ˈscale *adjective* 形容词
small in size 小型的；小规模的: *Most of the world's coffee beans are grown by small-scale farmers.* 世界上大部分咖啡豆都是由小农场主种植的。

smart /smɑːt/ *adjective* 形容词 (**smarter, smartest**)
1 right for a formal occasion or activity; clean and tidy 衣着讲究的；（衣服）得体的，整洁的: *He looked very smart in his new uniform.* 他穿上新制服显得很有精神。 □ *Members must wear a smart jacket and tie in the restaurant.* 会员在饭店内必须着考究的西服领带。
▶ **smartly** /ˈsmɑːtli/ *adverb* 副词: *a tall, smartly dressed young man* 一名衣冠楚楚的高个儿年轻人
2 (*American* 美国英语) clever or intelligent 机灵的；聪明的: *He's a very smart, intelligent player.* 他是一名非常聪明机智的选手。
3 able to do many of the things that a computer does, for example to connect with the Internet and use software 智能的: *A smart meter can show how much electricity you have used and calculate your bill.* 智能电表可以显示用电量、计算电费。

smartphone /ˈsmɑːtfəʊn/ *countable noun* 可数名词
a type of mobile phone that can do many of the things that a computer does 智能手机

smash /smæʃ/ *verb* 动词 (**smashes, smashing, smashed**)
1 to break something into many pieces 打烂，打碎（某物）: *The gang started smashing windows in the street.* 那帮小混混儿开始在街上打砸窗户。
2 to break into many pieces（某物）摔碎，打碎: *I dropped the bottle and it smashed on the floor.* 我把瓶子掉在地上摔碎了。
● **smash** *countable noun* 可数名词: *I heard the smash of glass and I shouted, 'Get down!'* 我听到玻璃打碎的声音，于是喊道："趴下！"

smear /smɪə/ *verb* 动词 (**smears, smearing, smeared**)
to spread a sticky substance all over a surface 涂，抹（黏性物）: *My little sister smeared jam all over her face.* 我妹妹涂了一脸果酱。● **smear** *countable noun* 可数名词: *There were smears of oil on his face.* 他脸上有油污。

smell¹ /smel/ *countable noun* 可数名词
the quality of something that you notice when you breathe in through your nose 气味: *I just love the smell of freshly baked bread.* 我特别喜欢新出炉面包的香味。 □ *There was a horrible smell in the refrigerator.* 冰箱里有一股难闻的气味。

smell² /smel/ *verb* 动词 (**smells, smelling, smelled** or 或 **smelt**)
1 to have a quality that you notice by breathing in through your nose 散发气味；闻起来: *The room smelled of lemons.* 这屋里有股柠檬味儿。 □ *The soup smells delicious!* 汤闻起来真香！
2 to smell unpleasant 散发异味（或臭味）: *My girlfriend says my feet smell.* 我女朋友说我的脚很臭。
3 to notice something when you breathe in through your nose 嗅到；闻到: *As soon as we opened the front door, we could smell smoke.* 我们一打开前门就能闻到烟味儿。

smelly /ˈsmeli/ *adjective* 形容词 (**smellier, smelliest**)
having an unpleasant smell 气味难闻的；

发臭的: *smelly socks* 臭袜子
smelt /smelt/
→ see 见 **smell**

smile /smaɪl/ *verb* 动词 (**smiles, smiling, smiled**)
to curve up the corners of your mouth because you are happy or you think that something is funny 微笑；笑: *When he saw me, he smiled.* 看到我时，他笑了。□ *The children were all smiling at her.* 孩子们都冲她笑。● **smile** *countable noun* 可数名词: *She gave a little smile.* 她微微一笑。

smoke¹ /sməʊk/ *uncountable noun* 不可数名词
the black or white clouds of gas that you see in the air when something burns 烟；烟雾: *Thick black smoke blew over the city.* 浓浓的黑烟在城市上空弥漫开来。

smoke² /sməʊk/ *verb* 动词 (**smokes, smoking, smoked**)
1 to suck the smoke from a cigarette into your mouth and blow it out again 吸，抽（香烟）: *He smokes 20 cigarettes a day.* 他一天抽 20 根香烟。
2 to regularly smoke cigarettes（经常性）吸烟，抽烟: *Do you smoke?* 你抽烟吗？
▶ **smoker** /ˈsməʊkə/ *countable noun* 可数名词: *Smokers have a much higher risk of developing this disease.* 吸烟者患这种疾病的风险要高得多。
▶ **smoking** /ˈsməʊkɪŋ/ *uncountable noun* 不可数名词: *Smoking is banned in many restaurants.* 许多饭店都禁烟。

smoky /ˈsməʊki/ *adjective* 形容词 (**smokier, smokiest**)
with a lot of smoke in the air 烟雾弥漫的: *The bar was dark, noisy and smoky.* 酒吧里光线昏暗，众声嘈杂，烟雾缭绕。

smooth /smuːð/ *adjective* 形容词 (**smoother, smoothest**)
1 flat, with no rough parts, lumps or holes 光滑的；平滑的: *The baby's skin was soft and smooth.* 宝宝的皮肤柔软光滑。□ *The surface of the water is as smooth as glass.* 水面平滑如镜。
2 without lumps 匀和的；不结块的: *Stir the mixture until it is smooth.* 把混合物搅匀。
3 without sudden changes in direction or speed 平稳的；流畅的: *The pilot made a very smooth landing.* 飞行员着陆时非常平稳。
▶ **smoothly** /ˈsmuːðli/ *adverb* 副词: *The boat was travelling smoothly through the water.* 船在水面上平稳航行。
4 happening without any problems 顺利的；无困难的: *We hope for a smooth move to our new home.* 我们希望能顺利地搬进新家。
▶ **smoothly** /ˈsmuːðli/ *adverb* 副词: *I hope your trip goes smoothly.* 我希望你一路顺风。

smoothie /ˈsmuːði/ *countable noun* 可数名词
a thick drink made by crushing fruit or vegetables, and sometimes mixing them with milk, yogurt, or ice cream 思慕雪（压榨果蔬制成的一种浓稠饮料）: *Try a nutritious spinach and avocado smoothie.* 尝尝营养丰富的菠菜牛油果思慕雪。

smother /ˈsmʌðə/ *verb* 动词 (**smothers, smothering, smothered**)
1 to cover a fire with something in order to stop it burning 把（火）闷熄: *She tried to smother the flames with a blanket.* 她试图用毯子将火扑灭。
2 to cover something with too much of a substance（用某物）厚厚地覆盖: *Don't smother the pasta in sauce.* 不要在意大利面上浇太多酱汁。

smudge /smʌdʒ/ *countable noun* 可数名词
a dirty mark 污点；污迹: *There was a dark smudge on his forehead.* 他额头上有一块黑乎乎的污迹。● **smudge** *verb* 动词 (**smudges, smudging, smudged**): *Jennifer rubbed her eyes, smudging her make-up.* 珍妮弗揉了揉眼睛，把妆给弄花了。

smudge 弄花   **smudge** 弄污

smug /smʌɡ/ *adjective* 形容词
very pleased with yourself, in a way that other people find annoying 自鸣得意的；沾沾自喜的: *'I have everything I need,' he said with a smug little smile.* "我要啥有啥。"他得意地微笑着说。
▶ **smugly** /ˈsmʌɡli/ *adverb* 副词: *Sue smiled smugly and sat down.* 休得意地笑了笑，坐了下来。

smuggle /ˈsmʌɡəl/ *verb* 动词 (**smuggles, smuggling, smuggled**)
to take things or people into a place or out of it illegally or secretly 走私；偷运：*They smuggled goods into the country.* 他们向该国走私货物。
▶ **smuggler** /ˈsmʌɡələ/ *countable noun* 可数名词：*The police arrested the diamond smugglers yesterday.* 警方昨天逮捕了钻石走私犯。
▶ **smuggling** /ˈsmʌɡəlɪŋ/ *uncountable noun* 不可数名词：*A pilot was arrested and charged with smuggling.* 一名飞行员被捕并被控走私。

snack /snæk/ *countable noun* 可数名词
a simple meal that is quick to prepare and to eat or something you eat between meals 快餐；便餐；小吃；点心：*The children have a snack when they come in from school.* 孩子们放学回来会吃顿便餐。● **snack** *verb* 动词 (**snacks, snacking, snacked**)：*During the day, I snack on fruit and drink lots of water.* 白天，我吃点水果，大量喝水。

snag /snæɡ/ *countable noun* 可数名词
a small problem or difficulty 小问题；小困难：*There is one possible snag in his plans.* 他的计划可能存在一个小问题。

snail /sneɪl/ *countable noun* 可数名词
a small animal with a long, soft body, no legs and a round shell on its back 蜗牛

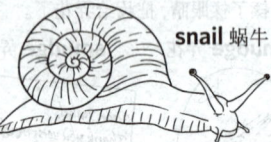
snail 蜗牛

snake /sneɪk/ *countable noun* 可数名词
a long, thin animal with no legs, that slides along the ground 蛇

snap /snæp/ *verb* 动词 (**snaps, snapping, snapped**)
1 to break with a short, loud noise (某物) 啪的一声断裂，咔嚓一声折断：*The rope snapped, and he fell to his death.* 绳子啪的一声断了，他摔死了。
2 to break something in this way 啪的一声弄断，咔嚓一声折断 (某物)：*Angrily, Matthew snapped the plastic pen in two.* 马修一气之下把塑料笔咔嚓撅成了两截。
● **snap** *singular noun* 单数名词：*I heard a snap and a crash as the tree fell.* 我先是听到咔嚓一声，接着树哗啦一下倒地。
3 to speak to someone in a sharp, angry way 声色俱厉地说；怒气冲冲地说：*Sorry, I didn't mean to snap at you.* 对不起，我不是有意对你凶的。
4 to try to bite someone (动物) 试图咬：*The dog snapped at my ankle.* 狗冲我脚踝咬来。

snatch /snætʃ/ *verb* 动词 (**snatches, snatching, snatched**)
to take something away quickly and roughly 夺；抢：*Michael snatched the cards from Archie's hand.* 迈克尔一把夺过阿奇手里的牌。

sneak /sniːk/ *verb* 动词 (**sneaks, sneaking, sneaked**)
1 to go somewhere very quietly 溜；悄悄地走；潜行：*He sneaked out of his house late at night.* 深夜，他偷偷溜出家门。
2 to secretly have a quick look at something 偷看：*She sneaked a look at her watch.* 她偷偷看了一眼手表。

sneaker /ˈsniːkə/ *countable noun* 可数名词 (*American* 美国英语)
→ see 见 **trainer**：*a pair of sneakers* 一双运动鞋

sneer /snɪə/ *verb* 动词 (**sneers, sneering, sneered**)
to show on your face that you do not like someone or something 讥笑；嘲讽；讥讽：*'I don't need any help from you,' he sneered.* "我不需要你的任何帮助。"他不屑地说。
□ *I could see her sneering at me.* 我看得出她在嘲笑我。

sneeze /sniːz/ *verb* 动词 (**sneezes, sneezing, sneezed**)
to suddenly take in your breath and then blow it down your nose noisily, for example, because you have a cold 打喷嚏：*Cover your nose and mouth when you sneeze.* 打喷嚏时要捂住口鼻。● **sneeze** *countable noun* 可数名词：*The disease is passed from person to person by a sneeze.* 这种病通过喷嚏在人际间传播。

sniff /snɪf/ *verb* 动词 (**sniffs, sniffing, sniffed**)
to suddenly and quickly breathe in air through your nose 抽鼻子：*She dried her eyes and sniffed.* 她擦干眼泪，抽了抽鼻子。
● **sniff** *countable noun* 可数名词：*I could hear quiet sobs and sniffs.* 我能听到微弱的抽泣声。

snigger /ˈsnɪɡə/ *verb* 动词 (**sniggers, sniggering, sniggered**)
to laugh quietly in an unpleasant way (不怀好意地) 暗笑，窃笑：*Three kids started*

sniggering. *3个孩子偷笑起来。● **snigger** *countable noun* 可数名词：*I heard a snigger, and looked around.* 我听到有人在窃笑，于是看了看四周。

snip /snɪp/ *verb* 动词 (**snips, snipping, snipped**)
to cut something quickly using sharp scissors（迅速地）剪，剪开：*Snip off the dead flowers with a pair of scissors.* 用剪刀把枯萎的花剪下来。

snob /snɒb/ *countable noun* 可数名词
someone who feels that they are better than other people because of their behaviour or social class 势利者；自命不凡者：*Her parents did not like him because they were snobs.* 她爸妈不喜欢他，因为他们都是势利眼。

snooker /ˈsnuːkə/ *uncountable noun* 不可数名词
a game that is played on a special table. Players use a long stick to hit a white ball so that it knocks coloured balls into holes around the edge of the table. 斯诺克

snore /snɔː/ *verb* 动词 (**snores, snoring, snored**)
to make a loud noise each time you breathe when you are asleep 打鼾；打呼噜：*His mouth was open, and he was snoring.* 他张着嘴，打着呼噜。● **snore** *countable noun* 可数名词：*We heard loud snores coming from the next room.* 我们听见隔壁屋传来响亮的呼噜声。

snorkel /ˈsnɔːkəl/ *countable noun* 可数名词
a tube that a person swimming just under the surface of the sea can breathe through（浮潜用的）呼吸管，通气管
▶ **snorkelling** /ˈsnɔːkəlɪŋ/ *uncountable noun* 不可数名词：*We went snorkelling at the nearby beach.* 我们去了附近海滩浮潜。

snorkel 呼吸管

snort /snɔːt/ *verb* 动词 (**snorts, snorting, snorted**)
to breathe air noisily out through your nose 喷鼻息；哼鼻子；打响鼻：*Harrell snorted with laughter.* 哈勒尔扑哧一声笑了。● **snort** *countable noun* 可数名词：*Yana gave a snort of laughter.* 亚娜发出一声嗤笑。

snout /snaʊt/ *countable noun* 可数名词
the long nose of an animal such as a pig（猪等动物的）吻部，口鼻部，长鼻子：*Two alligators rest their snouts on the water's surface.* 两只美洲鳄将鼻子露出水面。

snow /snəʊ/ *uncountable noun* 不可数名词
soft white frozen water that falls from the sky 雪：*Six inches of snow fell.* 雪下了6英寸厚。● **snow** *verb* 动词 (**snows, snowing, snowed**)：*It snowed all night.* 雪下了一整夜。

snowball /ˈsnəʊbɔːl/ *countable noun* 可数名词
a ball of snow 雪球

snowboard /ˈsnəʊbɔːd/ *countable noun* 可数名词
a board that you stand on and travel down slopes that are covered with snow 滑雪板
▶ **snowboarding** /ˈsnəʊbɔːdɪŋ/ *uncountable noun* 不可数名词：*He loves skiing and snowboarding.* 他喜欢双板滑雪和单板滑雪。
▶ **snowboarder** /ˈsnəʊbɔːdə/ *countable noun* 可数名词：*He's one of the world's top snowboarders.* 他是世界顶级单板滑雪运动员之一。

snowman /ˈsnəʊmæn/ *countable noun* 可数名词 (**snowmen** /ˈsnəʊmen/)
a large shape like a person that is made out of snow 雪人

snowy /ˈsnəʊi/ *adjective* 形容词 (**snowier, snowiest**)
covered with snow 积雪覆盖的：*snowy mountains* 白雪皑皑的山脉
→ Look at picture on P8 参见彩插第8页

snuggle /ˈsnʌɡəl/ *verb* 动词 (**snuggles, snuggling, snuggled**)
to get into a warm, comfortable position, especially by moving closer to another person（温暖而舒适地）依偎，蜷伏：*Jane snuggled up against his shoulder.* 简依偎在他肩头。

so[1] /səʊ/ *adverb* 副词
1 used for talking about something that has just been mentioned 如此，这样（指刚提到的事）：*'Do you think they will stay*

together?' — 'I hope so.' "你觉得他们会在一起吗？" —— "我希望如此。" □ *If you don't like it, then say so.* 你要是不喜欢，就说出来。
2 used when you are saying that something is also true 同样，也一样（指后者跟前者一样）: *I enjoy Ann's company and so does Martin.* 我喜欢和安在一起，马丁也是。□ *They had a wonderful time and so did I.* 他们玩得很开心，我也一样。
3 used in conversations to introduce a new subject（用于引出新话题）那么，这么: *So how was your day?* 那么，你今天过得怎么样？
4 used in front of adjectives and adverbs to make them stronger（用于形容词和副词前，表示强调）太，如此，这么: *I'm surprised they're married — they seemed so different.* 我很惊讶他俩居然结婚了——他们太不一样了。
▸ **or so** used when you are giving an approximate amount 左右；上下: *A ticket will cost you £20 or so.* 一张票卖 20 英镑左右。

so² /səʊ/ *conjunction* 连词
1 used for introducing the result of a situation 因此；所以: *I am shy and so I find it hard to talk to people.* 我很腼腆，所以我觉得跟别人交流很困难。
2 (also 亦作 **so that**) used for introducing the reason for doing something 以便；这样: *Come to dinner so we can talk about what happened.* 来吃晚饭吧，这样我们可以聊一聊发生的事儿。□ *They moved to the corner of the room so that nobody would hear them.* 他们挪到房间角落里，这样就没人听得见他们说什么了。

soak /səʊk/ *verb* 动词 (**soaks, soaking, soaked**)
1 to put something into a liquid and leave it there 浸；泡: *Soak the beans for 2 hours.* 将豆子浸泡两个小时。
2 to make something very wet 浸湿；使湿透: *The water soaked his jacket.* 水浸湿了他的夹克。
▸ **soaked** /səʊkt/ *adjective* 形容词: *The tent got completely soaked in the storm.* 帐篷在风暴中湿透了。
▸ **soaking** /ˈsəʊkɪŋ/ *adjective* 形容词: *My raincoat was soaking wet.* 我的雨衣湿淋淋的。
3 to pass through something 渗透；浸透: *Blood soaked through the bandages.* 血浸透了绷带。
▸ **soak something up** to take in a liquid 吸收（液体）: *Use a towel to soak up the water.* 用毛巾吸水。

soap /səʊp/ *uncountable noun* 不可数名词
a substance that you use with water for washing yourself or for washing clothes 肥皂: *a bar of soap* 一块肥皂

ˈsoap ˌopera *countable noun* 可数名词
a popular television series about the daily lives and problems of a group of people who live in a particular place 肥皂剧

soar /sɔː/ *verb* 动词 (**soars, soaring, soared**)
1 to quickly increase 激增；骤增: *Prices soared in the first half of the year.* 上半年物价飞涨。
2 to go quickly upwards 急升；跃升: *A golden eagle soared overhead.* 一只金雕在头顶展翅直飞高空。

sob /sɒb/ *verb* 动词 (**sobs, sobbing, sobbed**)
to cry in a noisy way 呜咽；啜泣: *She began to sob.* 她啜泣起来。 • **sob** *countable noun* 可数名词: *She heard quiet sobs from the next room.* 她听到隔壁房间传来微弱的啜泣声。

sober /ˈsəʊbə/ *adjective* 形容词
1 not drunk 清醒的；未醉的: *He was completely sober.* 他当时完全清醒。
2 plain and not bright 素淡的；素净的: *He dresses in sober grey suits.* 他穿着素净的灰西服。

ˈso-ˌcalled *adjective* 形容词
used for showing that you think a word or an expression is in fact wrong（表示不认同）所谓的: *This so-called miracle never actually happened.* 所谓的奇迹从未真正发生过。

soccer /ˈsɒkə/ *uncountable noun* 不可数名词
→ see 见 **football**: *My father played soccer for Manchester United.* 我父亲在曼联队踢球。
→ Look at picture on P14 参见彩插第 14 页

sociable /ˈsəʊʃəbl/ *adjective* 形容词
friendly, and enjoying talking to other people 友善的；喜欢交际的: *She was extremely sociable.* 她特别爱交际。

social /ˈsəʊʃl/ *adjective* 形容词
1 relating to society 社会的: *He sings about social problems like poverty.* 他唱的是贫穷之类的社会问题。

▶ **socially** /ˈsəʊʃəli/ *adverb* 副词: *It wasn't socially acceptable to eat in the street.* 街头吃东西有违社会规范。
2 relating to enjoyable activities that involve meeting other people 社交的；交际的: *We organize social events.* 我们组织社交活动。
▶ **socially** /ˈsəʊʃəli/ *adverb* 副词: *We have known each other socially for a long time.* 我们在社交场合相识已久。

socialism /ˈsəʊʃəˌlɪzəm/ *uncountable noun* 不可数名词
a set of political principles whose general aim is to create a system in which everyone has equal chances to gain wealth and to own the country's main industries 社会主义

socialist /ˈsəʊʃəlɪst/ *adjective* 形容词
based on socialism or to do with socialism 社会主义的: *He's a member of the Socialist Party.* 他是一名社会党党员。● **socialist** *countable noun* 可数名词: *His grandparents were socialists.* 他祖父母都是社会主义者。

socialize /ˈsəʊʃəˌlaɪz/ *verb* 动词 (**socializes, socializing, socialized**)
to meet other people socially, for example at parties 社交；交际；交往: *I like socializing and making new friends.* 我喜欢交际，爱结交新朋友。

ˈ**social** ˈ**life** *countable noun* 可数名词 (**social lives**)
the time someone spends with their friends 社交生活；社会生活: *I was popular and had a busy social life.* 我人缘不错，应酬很多。

ˌ**social** ˈ**media** *uncountable noun* 不可数名词
websites that are used for sharing information about yourself and contacting and making friends 社交媒体: *Companies try to build loyalty via social media.* 各家公司试图通过社交媒体来培养客户的忠诚度。

ˌ**social** ˈ**networking** *uncountable noun* 不可数名词
the activity of contacting friends, sharing information and making new friends using links on particular websites 网络社交: *Have you used a social networking site such as Instagram or Facebook?* 你使用过影思馆、脸书这样的社交网站吗？

ˌ**social** ˌ**worker** *countable noun* 可数名词
a person whose job is to help people who have social problems 社会福利工作者

society /səˈsaɪəti/ *noun* 名词 (**societies**)
1 all the people in a country, when you think about their general behaviour or problems 社会: *These are common problems in today's society.* 这些都是当今社会的常见问题。 ☐ *We live in an unequal society.* 我们生活在一个不平等的社会里。
2 *countable* 可数 an organization for people who have the same interest or aim 社；协会；学会: *He's a member of the historical society.* 他是这个历史学会的会员。

sock /sɒk/ *countable noun* 可数名词
a piece of clothing that covers your foot and ankle and that you wear inside shoes 短袜: *a pair of red socks* 一双红色短袜

socket /ˈsɒkɪt/ *countable noun* 可数名词
a hole that something fits into to make a connection 插座；灯座: *He took the light bulb out of the socket.* 他把灯泡从灯座上取了下来。 ☐ *There's an electric socket by every seat on the train.* 火车上每一个座位边上都有一个电源插座。

soda /ˈsəʊdə/ *uncountable noun* 不可数名词
water with bubbles that is used for mixing with other drinks 苏打水；汽水: *orange juice and soda* 橙汁和苏打水

sodium /ˈsəʊdiəm/ *uncountable noun* 不可数名词
a silvery white chemical element that combines with other chemicals to form compounds such as salt 钠

sofa /ˈsəʊfə/ *countable noun* 可数名词
a long, comfortable seat with a back, and usually with arms, that two or three people can sit on (两人或三人坐的)长沙发

soft /sɒft/ *adjective* 形容词 (**softer, softest**)
1 pleasant to touch, and not rough or hard 柔软的；柔滑的: *Body lotion will keep your skin soft.* 润肤露会保持皮肤柔滑。 ☐ *She wiped the baby's face with a soft cloth.* 她用一块柔软的布给宝宝擦了脸。
2 changing shape easily when pressed 软的；易塑形的: *Add milk to form a soft dough.* 加入牛奶，揉成软面团。
3 very gentle 轻柔的；柔和的: *There was a soft tapping on my door.* 有人在轻敲我的房门。 ☐ *Her skin was glowing in the soft light.* 她的皮肤在柔和的灯光下光彩照人。

▶**softly** /'sɒftli/ *adverb* 副词: *She walked into the softly lit room.* 她走进一间灯光柔和的房间。

soft 'drink *countable noun* 可数名词
a cold drink that does not contain alcohol, such as lemonade or fruit juice 软饮料（指不含酒精的冷饮）: *Can I get you some tea or coffee, or a soft drink?* 我给你弄点茶、咖啡或软饮料好吗？

soften /'sɒfən/ *verb* 动词 (**softens, softening, softened**)
to become, or make something less hard 软化；（使）变软: *Soften the butter in a small saucepan.* 在小炖锅里将黄油化软。

software /'sɒftweə/ *uncountable noun* 不可数名词
computer programs. Compare with **hardware**. 软件（比较 hardware）: *He writes computer software.* 他编写计算机软件。

soggy /'sɒgi/ *adjective* 形容词 (**soggier, soggiest**)
unpleasantly wet 湿乎乎的；湿漉漉的: *The cheese and tomato sandwiches were soggy.* 干酪番茄三明治湿乎乎的。

soil /sɔɪl/ *noun* 名词
the substance on the surface of the Earth in which plants grow 土壤: *The soil here is good for growing vegetables.* 这儿的土壤适合种菜。

solar /'səʊlə/ *adjective* 形容词
used for describing power that is obtained from the sun's light and heat 太阳能的: *The visitor centre runs on solar power.* 游客中心使用的是太阳能。

sold /səʊld/
→ see 见 **sell**

soldier /'səʊldʒə/ *countable noun* 可数名词
a member of an army 士兵；军人
→ Look at picture on P10 参见彩插第 10 页

sole¹ /səʊl/ *adjective* 形容词
used for describing the only thing or person of a particular type 仅有的；唯一的: *Their sole aim is to win.* 他们唯一的目标就是取得胜利。
▶**solely** /'səʊlli/ *adverb* 副词: *The money that you earn belongs solely to you.* 你挣的钱只属于你一个人。

sole² /səʊl/ *countable noun* 可数名词
the lower surface of your foot or of a shoe or sock 脚掌；鞋底；袜底: *Wear shoes with thick soles.* 穿鞋底厚的鞋子。

solemn /'sɒləm/ *adjective* 形容词
very serious rather than cheerful or amusing 严肃的；庄严的；郑重的: *His face looked solemn.* 他神色肃穆。
▶**solemnly** /'sɒləmli/ *adverb* 副词: *Her listeners nodded solemnly.* 她的听众郑重地点了点头。

solicitor /sə'lɪsɪtə/ *countable noun* 可数名词
a lawyer who gives legal advice, prepares legal documents, and arranges for people to buy and sell land 事务律师（提供法律咨询，准备法律文件，安排土地的买卖等）

solid¹ /'sɒlɪd/ *adjective* 形容词
1 hard; not like liquid or gas 硬的；固体的；固态的: *The pure oil is solid at room temperature.* 纯油在室温下是固态的。
□ *The lake was frozen solid.* 湖水冻上了。
2 with no holes or space inside 实心的；坚实的；无孔隙的: *They had to cut through 50 feet of solid rock.* 他们必须凿开 50 英尺厚的坚硬岩石。

solid 实心的   **hollow** 空心的

solid² /'sɒlɪd/ *countable noun* 可数名词
a hard substance 固体: *Solids turn to liquids at certain temperatures.* 在特定温度下固体会变成液体。
→ Look at picture on P6 参见彩插第 6 页

solitary /'sɒlɪtri/ *adjective* 形容词
1 spending a lot of time alone 喜欢独处的；习惯独居的: *Paul was a shy, solitary man.* 保罗是一个喜欢独来独往的腼腆男人。
2 done alone 独自的；单独的: *He spent his evenings in solitary reading.* 夜晚他都是在独自阅读中度过的。

solo /'səʊləʊ/ *countable noun* 可数名词
a piece of music or a dance performed by one person 独奏；独唱；独舞: *The music teacher asked me to sing a solo.* 音乐老师要我独唱。 • **solo** *adjective* 形容词: *He has just recorded his first solo album.* 他刚刚录制了首张个人专辑。 • **solo** *adverb* 副词: *Lindbergh flew solo across the Atlantic.* 林

白独自飞越了大西洋。

solution /səˈluːʃən/ ***countable noun*** 可数名词
a way of dealing with a problem 解决办法: *They both want to find a peaceful solution to the conflict.* 他们都想找到一种和平解决这场冲突的方案。

solve /sɒlv/ ***verb*** 动词 (**solves, solving, solved**)
to find an answer to a problem or a question 解决（问题）；解（题）: *They have not solved the problem of unemployment.* 他们还没有解决失业问题。

some /səm, STRONG 强读 sʌm/ ***adjective*** 形容词
1 used for talking about an amount of something or a number of people or things 一些；若干: *Would you like some orange juice?* 你要来些橙汁吗？ □ *He went to buy some books.* 他去买了一些书。 □ *Some of the workers will lose their jobs.* 有些工人会失业。 □ *Put some of the sauce onto a plate.* 往盘子里倒一些酱油。
● **some** ***pronoun*** 代词: *The apples are ripe, and we picked some today.* 苹果熟了，我们今天摘了一些。
2 used for showing that you do not know exactly which person or thing you are talking about 某个: *She wanted to talk to him about some problem she was having.* 她想和他谈谈她现在遇到的某个问题。

somebody /ˈsʌmbədi/ ***pronoun*** 代词
→ see 见 **someone**

someday /ˈsʌmdeɪ/ ***adverb*** 副词
a time in the future that you do not yet know 将来；有朝一日: *Someday I hope to become a pilot.* 我希望自己有朝一日成为一名飞行员。

somehow /ˈsʌmhaʊ/ ***adverb*** 副词
used when you do not know or cannot say how something was done or will be done 不知怎么；用某种方法: *We'll manage somehow, I know we will.* 我们总能应付过去的，我知道我们会的。 □ *I somehow managed to finish the race.* 我设法坚持完成了比赛。

someone /ˈsʌmwʌn/ ***pronoun*** 代词

> **LANGUAGE HELP** 语言提示
> You can also say **somebody**. 也可用 **somebody**。

used for talking about a person without saying exactly who you mean 某人；有人：

I got a call from someone who wanted to rent the flat. 我接到一个电话，是一个想租公寓的人打来的。 □ *I need someone to help me.* 我需要个人来帮我。

something /ˈsʌmθɪŋ/ ***pronoun*** 代词
used for talking about a thing or a situation, without saying exactly what it is 某物；某事: *He knew that there was something wrong.* 他知道有问题了。 □ *Was there something you wanted to ask me?* 你有什么事儿想问我吗？

sometime /ˈsʌmtaɪm/ ***adverb*** 副词
used for talking about a time in the future or the past that you do not yet know（将来或过去的）某个时间: *We will finish sometime next month.* 我们会在下个月某个时间完成。 □ *Why don't you come and see me sometime?* 为什么不找个时间来看我呢？

sometimes /ˈsʌmtaɪmz/ ***adverb*** 副词
on some occasions rather than all the time 有时；不时: *I sometimes sit out in the garden and read.* 我有时会坐在花园里看书。 □ *Sometimes he's a little rude.* 他有时候有点儿粗鲁。

somewhat /ˈsʌmwɒt/ ***adverb*** 副词
a little (*formal* 正式) 稍微；有几分: *She behaved somewhat differently when he was there.* 他在时，她表现得有几分异样。

somewhere /ˈsʌmweə/ ***adverb*** 副词
used for talking about a place without saying exactly where you mean 某个地方；某处: *I've seen him before somewhere.* 我之前在哪儿见过他。 □ *I needed somewhere to live.* 我需要个住的地方。

son /sʌn/ ***countable noun*** 可数名词
your male child 儿子: *Sam is the seven-year-old son of Eric Davies.* 萨姆是埃里克·戴维斯 7 岁的儿子。 □ *I have two daughters and a son.* 我有两个女儿，一个儿子。

song /sɒŋ/ ***countable noun*** 可数名词
1 words and music sung together 歌；歌曲: *She sang a Spanish song.* 她唱了一首西班牙歌曲。
2 the pleasant musical sounds that a bird makes（鸟的）鸣啭，啼鸣: *It's lovely to hear a blackbird's song in the evening.* 夜听乌鸫鸣啭好不惬意。

son-in-law ***countable noun*** 可数名词 (**sons-in-law**)
the husband of your daughter 女婿

soon /suːn/ *adverb* 副词 (**sooner, soonest**) after a short time 很快；不久：*I'll call you soon.* 我很快就会给你打电话的。□ *He arrived sooner than I expected.* 他到得要比我预料的快。

as soon as used for saying that one thing happens immediately after something else ……就……：*As soon as the weather improves we will go.* 天气一转好我们就走。

soothe /suːð/ *verb* 动词 (**soothes, soothing, soothed**)
1 to make someone who is angry or upset feel calmer 安慰；抚慰；劝慰：*He sang to her to soothe her.* 他给她唱歌来抚慰她。
▶ **soothing** /ˈsuːðɪŋ/ *adjective* 形容词：*Put on some nice soothing music.* 播放一些柔和舒缓的音乐。
2 to make a painful part of your body feel better 减轻，缓和（身体的疼痛或不适）：*Use this lotion to soothe dry skin.* 用这种乳液滋润干燥的皮肤。
▶ **soothing** /ˈsuːðɪŋ/ *adjective* 形容词：*Cold tea is very soothing for burns.* 凉的茶水能有效减轻烧伤灼痛。

sophisticated /səˈfɪstɪˌkeɪtɪd/ *adjective* 形容词
1 complicated and highly developed 复杂的；高级的；精密的：*Bees use a very sophisticated communication system.* 蜜蜂的交流系统非常复杂。
2 knowing about things like culture and fashion 练达的；见过世面的：*Claude was a charming, sophisticated man.* 克劳德是个有魅力、练达老成的男人。

sore /sɔː/ *adjective* 形容词 (**sorer, sorest**) painful and uncomfortable 疼的；不舒服的：*I had a sore throat and a cough.* 我嗓子疼，还咳嗽。

sorrow /ˈsɒrəʊ/ *uncountable noun* 不可数名词 a feeling of deep sadness 悲伤；哀伤：*Words cannot express my sorrow.* 语言无法表达我的哀伤。

sorry /ˈsɒri/ *adjective* 形容词 (**sorrier, sorriest**)
feeling regret, sadness or disappointment 遗憾的；难过的；失望的：*I'm sorry he's gone.* 他离开了，我很难过。
feel sorry for someone to feel sadness for someone 为某人感到难过；同情某人：*I felt sorry for him because nobody listened to him.* 我很同情他，因为没有人听他讲话。

sorry or **I'm sorry**
1 used for apologizing for something that you have done 对不起；抱歉：*'You're making too much noise.' — 'I'm sorry.'* "你太吵了。" —— "对不起。" □ *Sorry I took so long.* 抱歉，我花了这么长时间。
2 used when you have not heard what someone has said（用于没听清对方所说的话时）不好意思，请再说一遍：*'My name's Thea.' — 'Sorry?'* "我叫西娅。" —— "不好意思，能再说一遍吗？"
3 used to express your regret and sadness when you hear sad or unpleasant news（用于听到悲伤或不快的消息时）我很遗憾：*'Robert's sick today.' — 'I'm sorry to hear that.'* "罗伯特今天生病了。" —— "真是遗憾。"

sort¹ /sɔːt/ *countable noun* 可数名词 a type or kind of person or thing 种类；类型：*What sort of school did you go to?* 你上的是哪类学校？

sort² /sɔːt/ *verb* 动词 (**sorts, sorting, sorted**)
to separate things into different groups 把…分类；整理：*He sorted the materials into their folders.* 他把材料分门别类地放进了不同的文件夹中。
sort of used when your description of something is not very accurate（informal 非正式）有几分；有那么点；近似：*'What's a sub?' — 'Well, it's sort of a sandwich.'* "潜艇三明治是什么？" —— "呃，就是种三明治。"

sort someone/something out
1 to separate people or things into different groups 把（某人／某事物）分类（或分组）：*Sort out all your bills as quickly as possible.* 把你的账单尽快整理出来。
2 to deal with a problem successfully 解决（问题）：*The two countries have sorted out their disagreement.* 两国已经解决了他们之间的分歧。

sought /sɔːt/
→ see 见 **seek**

soul /səʊl/ *noun* 名词
1 *countable* 可数 the part of you that consists of your mind, character, thoughts and feelings. Many people believe that your soul continues existing after your body is dead. 灵魂：*She prayed for the soul of her dead father.* 她为亡父的灵魂祈祷。
2 *uncountable* 不可数 → see 见 **soul music**：*The show stars American soul*

singer Anita Baker. 这场演出的主角是美国灵乐歌手安妮塔·贝克。

¹soul ˌmusic *uncountable noun* 不可数名词 a type of pop music performed mainly by African-American musicians, which often expresses deep emotions 灵乐（一种主要由美国非裔音乐家表演的流行乐）

sound¹ /saʊnd/ *countable noun* 可数名词 something that you hear 声音；响声：*Peter heard the sound of a car engine outside.* 彼得听到了外面汽车发动机的声音。

sound² /saʊnd/ *verb* 动词 (sounds, sounding, sounded)
1 used for describing a noise（声音）听起来：*They heard something that sounded like a huge explosion.* 他们听见一声像爆炸一样的巨响。
2 used for describing how someone seems when they speak（某人）听上去好像：*She sounds very angry.* 听她说话好像很生气。
3 used for describing your opinion of something（用于表达观点）听起来，看上去：*It sounds like a wonderful idea to me.* 我听着这个主意特别好。
4 to produce a sound 发出声响；鸣响：*The fire alarm sounded at about 3.20 a.m.* 凌晨3点20分左右火险报警器响了。

sound³ /saʊnd/ *adjective* 形容词 (sounder, soundest)
1 in good condition 完好的；无损的：*The building is perfectly sound.* 该建筑物完好无损。
2 sensible; that you can trust 明智的；可靠的；合理的：*Our experts will give you sound advice.* 我们的专家会给你可靠的建议。

sound⁴ /saʊnd/ *adverb* 副词
sound asleep in a deep sleep 熟睡的：*He was lying in bed, sound asleep.* 他躺在床上，睡得很熟。

soundly /ˈsaʊndli/ *adverb* 副词
sleep soundly to sleep deeply, without waking during your sleep 酣睡；熟睡：*How can he sleep soundly at night?* 他晚上怎么能睡安稳？

soup /suːp/ *uncountable noun* 不可数名词 a liquid food made by boiling meat, fish or vegetables in water 汤；羹：*home-made chicken soup* 自制鸡汤

sour /ˈsaʊə/ *adjective* 形容词
1 with a sharp, unpleasant taste like the taste of a lemon 酸的；酸味的：*The stewed apple was sour.* 炖苹果味道发酸。
2 tasting bad; not fresh 发馊的；酸臭的：*I can smell sour milk.* 我能闻出馊牛奶的味道。

source /sɔːs/ *countable noun* 可数名词
1 the person, place or thing that something comes from 来源；出处：*Many adults use television as their major source of information.* 电视是许多成年人主要的信息来源。 □ *We are developing new sources of energy.* 我们在开发新能源。
2 the place where a river or a stream begins（河流或溪水的）源头：*the source of the Tiber* 台伯河的源头

south /saʊθ/ also 亦作 **South** *uncountable noun* 不可数名词 the direction that is on your right when you are looking at the sun in the morning 南；南方：*The town lies ten miles to the south.* 那个小镇在往南10英里处。 □ *We organize vacations in the south of Mexico.* 我们组织在墨西哥南部度假。 ● **south** *adjective* 形容词, *adverb* 副词：*We live on the south coast of Ireland.* 我们住在爱尔兰南部海岸。 □ *I drove south on the M1 motorway.* 我在M1高速公路上向南行驶。
→ Look at picture on P9 参见彩插第9页
▶ **southern** /ˈsʌðən/ *adjective* 形容词：*The Everglades National Park stretches across southern Florida.* 大沼泽地国家公园横贯佛罗里达州南部。

south-east /ˌsaʊθˈiːst/ *uncountable noun* 不可数名词 the direction that is between south and east 东南；东南方：*The train left Colombo for Galle, 70 miles to the south-east.* 火车从科伦坡开往位于东南方70英里处的加勒。 ● **south-east** *adjective* 形容词：*South-east Asia* 东南亚
→ Look at picture on P9 参见彩插第9页
▶ **south-eastern** /ˌsaʊθˈiːstən/ *adjective* 形容词：*The city is on the south-eastern edge of the United States.* 这座城市位于美国东南部边缘。

southerly /ˈsʌðəli/ *adjective* 形容词
1 to or towards the south 朝南的；向南的：*We travelled in a southerly direction towards Italy.* 我们朝着意大利一路向南旅行。
2 blowing from the south（风）来自南方的：*a strong southerly wind* 强劲的南风

south-west /ˌsaʊθˈwest/ *uncountable noun* 不可数名词 the direction that is between south and

souvenir – spaghetti

west 西南；西南方：*He lives about 500 miles to the south-west of Johannesburg.* 他住在约翰内斯堡西南方 500 英里的地方。● **south-west** *adjective* 形容词：*south-west France* 法国西南部
→ Look at picture on P9 参见彩插第 9 页
▶ **south-western** /ˌsaʊθˈwestən/ *adjective* 形容词：*They come from a small town in the south-western part of the country.* 他们来自该国西南部的一个小镇。

souvenir /ˈsuːvəˈnɪə/ *countable noun* 可数名词
something that you buy or keep to remind you of a place or an event 纪念品；纪念物：*He had a shop selling souvenirs and postcards.* 他开了一家出售纪念品和明信片的商店。

sovereignty /ˈsɒvrɪnti/ *uncountable noun* 不可数名词
the power that a country has to govern itself 主权：*It is important to protect our national sovereignty.* 保护我们国家的主权很重要。

sow /səʊ/ *verb* 动词 (**sows, sowing, sowed, sown**)
to plant seeds in the ground 播（种）：*Sow the seed in a warm place in early March.* *3 月初在温暖的地方种下种子。

sown /səʊn/
→ see 见 **sow**

soya /ˈsɔɪə/ *uncountable noun* 不可数名词
used for describing flour, oil or sauce that is made using **soya beans** 豆制品；大豆食品：*soya sauce* 酱油

soya bean *countable noun* 可数名词
a bean that can be eaten, or used for making flour, oil or sauce 大豆

spa /spɑː/ *countable noun* 可数名词
1 a place where water comes out of the ground 矿泉疗养地：*Buxton is a spa town that is famous for its water.* 巴克斯顿是一个以水闻名的矿泉小镇。
2 a place where people go to exercise and have special treatments in order to improve their health 休闲健身中心；温泉疗养中心：*Hotel guests may use the health spa.* 酒店的客人可以使用温泉疗养中心。

space¹ /speɪs/ *noun* 名词
1 an area that is empty 空地；空间：*They cut down trees to make space for houses.* 他们把树砍了了以留出空地建房子。 □ *The space under the bed could be used as a* storage area. 床底下的空间可用来储物。
2 *singular* 单数 a period of time 一段时间；期间：*They've come a long way in a short space of time.* 他们很快就从大老远赶了过来。
3 *uncountable* 不可数 the area beyond the Earth's atmosphere, where the stars and planets are 太空：*The six astronauts will spend ten days in space.* *6 名航天员将在太空中度过 10 天。

space² /speɪs/ *verb* 动词 (**spaces, spacing, spaced**)
(also 亦作 **space something out**) to separate a series of things so that they are not all together 分隔；使有间隔：*Write the words down, spacing them evenly.* 把这些词写下来, 单词之间的间隔要均匀。
□ *He talks quite slowly and spaces his words out.* 他说得很慢，每个词之间都有停顿。

spacecraft /ˈspeɪskrɑːft/ *countable noun* 可数名词 (**spacecraft**)
a vehicle that can travel in space 航天器；宇宙飞船：*This is the world's largest and most expensive spacecraft.* 这是世界上最大、造价最高的航天器。

spaceship /ˈspeɪsʃɪp/ *countable noun* 可数名词
→ see 见 **spacecraft**

¹space shuttle *countable noun* 可数名词
a vehicle that is designed to travel into space and back to Earth several times 航天飞机

space shuttle 航天飞机

spacious /ˈspeɪʃəs/ *adjective* 形容词
large, with a lot of space 广阔的；宽敞的：*The house has a spacious kitchen and dining area.* 这座房子有宽敞的厨房和用餐区。

spade /speɪd/ *countable noun* 可数名词
a tool that is used for digging 铲；锹：*a garden spade* 园艺铲

spaghetti /spəˈɡeti/ *uncountable noun* 不可数名词
a type of pasta (= a food made from flour and water) that looks like long pieces of

string 意大利面条

spam /spæm/ *uncountable noun* 不可数名词
advertising messages that are sent automatically by email to large numbers of people 垃圾电子邮件: *Spam is becoming a major problem for many Internet users.* 垃圾邮件日益成为许多因特网用户面临的一个主要问题。

span[1] /spæn/ *countable noun* 可数名词
1 a period of time 持续时间: *The batteries had a life span of six hours.* 这些电池的寿命是 6 个小时。
2 the total width of something from one side to the other 宽度；宽长: *The butterfly has a 2-inch wing span.* 这只蝴蝶的翼展是 2 英寸。

span[2] /spæn/ *verb* 动词 (**spans, spanning, spanned**)
1 to last for a particular period of time 持续；跨越: *His professional career spanned 16 years.* 他的职业生涯持续了 16 年。
2 to stretch right across something such as a river 横跨，跨越（河流等）: *There is a footbridge that spans the little stream.* 小溪上横跨着一座步行桥。

spanner /ˈspænə/ *countable noun* 可数名词
a metal tool that you use for turning small pieces of metal (= nuts) to make them tighter 扳手；扳钳

spare[1] /speə/ *adjective* 形容词
used for describing extra things that you keep in case you need them 备用的；预备的: *It's useful to have a spare pair of glasses.* 多备一副眼镜很有用。 □ *I'll give you the spare key.* 我会给你备用钥匙。

spare[2] /speə/ *verb* 动词 (**spares, sparing, spared**)
to make time or money available 抽出，拨出（时间或金钱）: *I can only spare 35 minutes for this meeting.* 我只能抽出 35 分钟来参加这次会议。

spare time *uncountable noun* 不可数名词
the time when you do not have to work 业余时间: *In her spare time she read books on cooking.* 业余时间里她看了一些烹饪方面的书。

spark /spɑːk/ *countable noun* 可数名词
1 a very small piece of burning material that comes out of something that is burning 火花；火星: *Sparks flew out of the fire in all directions.* 火星从火堆中四下飞溅。
2 a flash of light caused by electricity 电

火花: *I saw a spark when I connected the wires.* 我连接电线时看到了火花。

sparkle /ˈspɑːkəl/ *verb* 动词 (**sparkles, sparkling, sparkled**)
to shine clearly and brightly, with a lot of very small points of light 闪闪发光；闪耀: *The jewels on her fingers sparkled.* 她手指上的珠宝闪闪发光。 □ *His bright eyes sparkled.* 他一双明眸闪着光。

sparkling /ˈspɑːklɪŋ/ *adjective* 形容词
containing bubbles 起泡的: *a glass of sparkling water* 一杯气泡水

sparrow /ˈspærəʊ/ *countable noun* 可数名词
a small very common brown bird 麻雀

sparse /spɑːs/ *adjective* 形容词 (**sparser, sparsest**)
spread out in small amounts over an area 稀疏的；稀少的: *He was a fat little man in his fifties, with sparse hair.* 他是一个矮胖的男人，50 多岁，头发稀疏
▶ **sparsely** /ˈspɑːsli/ *adverb* 副词: *This is a sparsely populated mountain region.* 这里是人烟稀少的山区。

spat /spæt/
→ see 见 **spit**

speak /spiːk/ *verb* 动词 (**speaks, speaking, spoke, spoken**)
1 to use your voice in order to say something 说话；讲话: *He opened his mouth to speak.* 他张嘴说话。 □ *I called the hotel and spoke to Louie.* 我打电话到酒店，跟路易通了话。 □ *He often speaks about his mother.* 他经常讲起他妈妈。
→ Look at picture on P3 参见彩插第 3 页
▶ **spoken** /ˈspəʊkən/ *adjective* 形容词: *They took tests in written and spoken English.* 他们参加了英语笔试和口试。
2 to make a speech 发言: *He will speak at the Democratic Convention.* 他将在民主党大会上发言。
3 to know a foreign language and be able to have a conversation in it 会说，会讲（某种语言）: *He speaks English.* 他会讲英语。

speak up to speak more loudly 大声说；提高嗓门: *I'm quite deaf — you'll have to speak up.* 我耳背——你得大声说。

LANGUAGE HELP 语言提示
See note at **talk**. 见 **talk** 的语言提示。

speaker /ˈspiːkə/ *countable noun* 可数名词
1 a piece of electrical equipment that

sound comes out of 喇叭；扬声器：*I bought a pair of speakers for my computer.* 我给电脑买了一对扬声器。
2 a person who makes a speech 发言人；演讲者：*Bruce Wyatt will be the guest speaker at next month's meeting.* 布鲁斯·怀亚特将是下个月会议的特邀发言人。

spear /spɪə/ ***countable noun*** 可数名词
a weapon consisting of a long pole with a sharp metal point at the end 矛；标枪
→ Look at picture on P10 参见彩插第 10 页

special /ˈspeʃəl/ ***adjective*** 形容词
1 better or more important than other people or things 特别的；非同寻常的：*You're very special to me.* 你对我来说是与众不同的。 □ *My special guest will be Zac Efron.* 我的特别嘉宾是扎克·埃弗龙。
2 different from normal 特殊的；异常的：*In special cases, a child can be educated at home.* 在特殊情况下，孩子可以在家接受教育。

specialist /ˈspeʃəlɪst/ ***countable noun*** 可数名词
a person who knows a lot about a particular subject 专家：*Peckham is a cancer specialist.* 佩卡姆是癌症专家。

speciality /ˌspeʃiˈælɪti/ ***countable noun*** 可数名词 (**specialities**)
1 a particular type of work that someone does, or a subject that they know a lot about 专业；专长：*My father's speciality was the history of Germany.* 我父亲的专长是德国史。
2 a special food or product that is always very good in a particular place 特色菜；特产：*Paella is a speciality of the restaurant.* 西班牙海鲜饭是这家餐馆的特色菜。

specialize /ˈspeʃəˌlaɪz/ ***verb*** 动词 (**specializes**, **specializing**, **specialized**)
to concentrate a lot of your time and energy on a subject 专攻；专门从事；专门研究：*He's a professor who specializes in Russian history.* 他是一名专门研究俄罗斯历史的教授。

specially /ˈspeʃəli/ ***adverb*** 副词
1 only for a particular person 特别地；专门地：*This soap is specially designed for sensitive skin.* 这种香皂专门为敏感皮肤设计。
2 more than usual (*informal* 非正式) 特别；格外；超常地：*On his birthday I got up specially early.* 他生日那天我起得特别早。

species /ˈspiːʃiːz/ ***countable noun*** 可数名词 (**species**)
a related group of plants or animals 物种；种：*Many species could disappear from our Earth.* 许多物种可能会从地球上消失。

specific /spɪˈsɪfɪk/ ***adjective*** 形容词
1 particular 特定的；特别的：*Do you have pain in any specific part of your body?* 你哪个身体部位感到疼痛吗？ □ *There are several specific problems.* 有几个特定的问题。
2 exact and clear 明确的；具体的；确切的：*She refused to be more specific about her plans.* 她拒绝透露计划中更具体的内容。

specifically /spɪˈsɪfɪkli/ ***adverb*** 副词
used for showing that something is being considered separately 特别地；特意地；专门地：*The show is specifically for children.* 这场演出是专给孩子们看的。

specify /ˈspesɪfaɪ/ ***verb*** 动词 (**specifies**, **specifying**, **specified**)
to explain something in an exact and detailed way 明确地说；具体指明：*Does the recipe specify the size of egg to be used?* 菜谱上有没有明确地说用多大的鸡蛋？

specimen /ˈspesɪmɪn/ ***countable noun*** 可数名词
an example or a small amount of something 样品；样本；标本：*Job applicants have to give a specimen of handwriting.* 求职者必须提交一份书写样稿。

speck /spek/ ***countable noun*** 可数名词
a very small mark or piece of something 痕迹；斑点；小块：*There was a speck of dirt on his collar.* 他的领子上有一块污迹。

spectacle /ˈspektəkəl/ ***countable noun*** 可数名词
a big, wonderful sight or event 壮观的场面；盛大的活动：*The fireworks were an amazing spectacle.* 燃放烟火的场面极为壮观。

spectacles /ˈspektəkəlz/ ***plural noun*** 复数名词 (*formal* 正式)
→ see 见 **glasses** : *a pair of spectacles* 一副眼镜

spectacular /spekˈtækjʊlə/ ***adjective*** 形容词
big and dramatic 壮观的；引人注目的：*We had spectacular views of Mount Qomolangma.* 我们欣赏到了珠穆朗玛峰壮丽的景观。

▶**spectacularly** /spek'tækjʊləli/ *adverb* 副词: *Our sales increased spectacularly.* 我们的销售额大幅上升。

spectator /spek'teɪtə/ *countable noun* 可数名词
someone who watches a sports event（体育比赛的）观众: *Thirty thousand spectators watched the game.* 有 3 万名观众观看了这场比赛。

speculate /'spekjʊleɪt/ *verb* 动词 (**speculates, speculating, speculated**)
to make guesses about something 推测；猜测: *Everyone has been speculating about why she left.* 每个人都在猜测她为什么离开。

▶**speculation** /ˌspekjʊ'leɪʃən/ *uncountable noun* 不可数名词: *There has been a lot of speculation about the future of the band.* 关于乐队的未来有很多猜测。

sped /sped/
→ see 见 **speed**

speech /spiːtʃ/ *noun* 名词 (**speeches**)
1 *uncountable* 不可数 the ability to speak or the act of speaking 说话的能力；说话；言语: *We are studying the development of speech in children.* 我们正在研究儿童言语能力的发展。 □ *The medicine can affect speech.* 这种药物会对说话能力产生影响。
2 *uncountable* 不可数 the way in which you speak 说话方式: *His speech became slow and unclear.* 他说话慢了下来，而且变得不清楚。
3 *countable* 可数 a formal talk that someone gives to a group of people 演讲；讲话；致辞: *The president gave a speech to the nation.* 总统向全国人民发表了讲话。

speech 讲话

The president gave a speech to the nation. 总统向全国人民发表了讲话。

¹**speech marks** *plural noun* 复数名词
→ see 见 **quotation mark**

¹**speed** /spiːd/ *noun* 名词
1 how fast something moves or is done 速度；速率: *He drove off at high speed.* 他驱车飞驰而去。 □ *He invented a way to measure wind speeds.* 他发明了一种测风速的方法。
2 *uncountable* 不可数 very fast movement or travel（指运动、运行的）高速，快速: *Speed is essential for all athletes.* 速度对于所有运动员来说都很关键。

²**speed** /spiːd/ *verb* 动词 (**speeds, speeding, sped** or 或 **speeded**)

> **LANGUAGE HELP 语言提示**
> Use **sped** in meaning 1 and **speeded** for the phrasal verb. Meaning 2 is usually used as **be speeding**. 义项 1 的过去式和过去分词用 sped，短语动词的过去式和过去分词用 speeded。义项 2 常用进行式。

1 to move or travel somewhere quickly, usually in a vehicle 快速行进: *Trains speed through the tunnel at 186 mph.* 火车以每小时 186 英里的速度穿过隧道。
2 to drive a vehicle faster than the legal speed limit 超速驾驶: *Police stopped him because he was speeding.* 他因超速驾驶被警察拦下。

▶**speeding** /'spiːdɪŋ/ *uncountable noun* 不可数名词: *He was fined for speeding.* 他因超速驾驶被罚款。

speed something up to make something happen more quickly than before 使某事物进度加快: *We need to speed up a solution to the problem.* 我们需要加快速度解决这个问题。

speed up to happen more quickly than before 加速: *My breathing speeded up a bit.* 我的呼吸有些急促。

¹**speed limit** *countable noun* 可数名词
the highest speed at which you are legally allowed to drive on a particular road（道路的）限速，最高时速

speedy /'spiːdi/ *adjective* 形容词 (**speedier, speediest**)
happening or done very quickly 迅速的: *We wish Bill a speedy recovery.* 我们祝愿比尔早日康复。

¹**spell** /spel/ *verb* 动词 (**spells, spelling, spelled** or 或 **spelt**)
1 to write or speak each letter of a word in the correct order 拼写出；拼读出: *He*

spell - spirit

spelled his name. 他将自己的名字拼了出来。▫ How do you spell 'potato'? *potato 这个词怎么拼写？
2 to know the correct order of letters in words 能拼出，会拼（单词）: He can't spell his own name. 他不会拼写自己的名字。

spell² /spel/ **countable noun** 可数名词
a set of magic words 咒语: They say that a witch cast a spell on her. 他们说女巫给她施了咒语。

spelling /ˈspelɪŋ/ **countable noun** 可数名词
the correct order of the letters in a word 拼法；拼写: I'm not sure about the spelling of his name. 我不确定他的名字如何拼写。

spelt /spelt/
→ see 见 **spell**

spend /spend/ **verb** 动词 (**spends, spending, spent**)
1 to pay money for things that you want or need 花费，用（钱）: I have spent all my money. 我花光了我所有的钱。
2 to use your time doing something 花费（时间）: She spends hours working on her garden. 她花好几个小时打理她的花园。

spent /spent/
→ see 见 **spend**

sphere /sfɪə/ **countable noun** 可数名词
an object that is completely round in shape, like a ball 球体；球形: A tennis ball is a regular sphere shape. 网球是一种规则的球体。

spice /spaɪs/ **noun** 名词
a part of a plant that you put in food to give it flavour 香料: herbs and spices 香草和香料

spicy /ˈspaɪsi/ **adjective** 形容词 (**spicier, spiciest**)
strongly flavoured with spices（食物）加有香料的，辛辣的: Thai food is hot and spicy. 泰国菜味道辛辣浓烈。

spider /ˈspaɪdə/ **countable noun** 可数名词
a small animal with eight legs 蜘蛛

spike /spaɪk/ **countable noun** 可数名词
a long piece of metal with a sharp point 金属钉状物；尖锥: There was a high wall around the building with iron spikes at the top. 建筑物周围有一面高墙，墙头装有铁刺。

spill /spɪl/ **verb** 动词 (**spills, spilling, spilled** or 或 **spilt**)
to accidentally make a liquid flow over the edge of a container（使）溢出；（使）洒出: He always spilled the drinks. 他总是将饮料洒出来。▫ Oil spilt into the sea. 石油溢出，流入大海。

spilt /spɪlt/
→ see 见 **spill**

spin /spɪn/ **verb** 动词 (**spins, spinning, spun**)
1 to turn quickly around a central point（使）旋转: The disc spins 3,600 times a minute. 光盘的转速为每分钟 3,600 转。▫ He spun the steering wheel and turned the car around. 他旋转方向盘，掉转了车头。
2 to make thread by twisting together pieces of wool or cotton 将…纺成线: It's a machine for spinning wool. 这是一台羊毛纺线机。

spinach /ˈspɪnɪdʒ, -ɪtʃ/ **uncountable noun** 不可数名词
a vegetable with large dark green leaves 菠菜

spine /spaɪn/ **countable noun** 可数名词
the row of bones down a person's or an animal's back 脊椎；脊柱: He suffered injuries to his spine. 他的脊柱有伤。

spiral /ˈspaɪərəl/ **countable noun** 可数名词
a shape that winds around and around, with each curve above or outside the one before 螺旋（形）● **spiral adjective** 形容词: a spiral staircase 螺旋形楼梯

spiral 螺旋形

spirit /ˈspɪrɪt/ **noun** 名词
1 *singular* 单数 the part of you that is not physical and that consists of your character and feelings 精神；心灵: The human spirit is hard to destroy. 人的精神是难以摧毁的。
2 *countable* 可数 the part of a person that some people believe remains alive after their death 灵魂: He is gone, but his spirit is still with us. 他走了，但是他的灵魂依然

与我们在一起。

3 [spirits] *plural* 复数 your feelings at a particular time, especially feelings of happiness or unhappiness 情绪；心情；兴致：*At supper, everyone was in high spirits.* 晚餐时，所有的人都兴致勃勃。

4 [spirits] *plural* 复数 strong alcoholic drinks 烈性酒：*I don't drink beer, wine, or spirits.* 我不喝啤酒、葡萄酒和烈性酒。

spiritual /ˈspɪrɪtʃuəl/ *adjective* 形容词
1 relating to people's thoughts and beliefs, rather than to their bodies 精神的；心灵的：*She is a very spiritual person.* 她是一个精神丰富的人。
2 relating to people's religious beliefs 宗教的：*He is the spiritual leader of the world's Catholics.* 他是天主教世界里的精神领袖。

spit /spɪt/ *verb* 动词 (spits, spitting, spat) to force a small amount of liquid or food out of your mouth 吐出（少量液体或食物）：*Spit out that gum.* 把口香糖吐出来。

spite /spaɪt/ *uncountable noun* 不可数名词 a feeling that makes you do something because you want to hurt or upset someone 恶意；怨恨：*I said those things out of spite I suppose.* 我想我说这些话是出于怨恨。
in spite of something used to introduce a fact that makes the rest of what you are saying seem surprising 尽管…；虽然…：*He hired her in spite of her lack of experience.* 虽然她缺乏经验，他还是雇用了她。

splash /splæʃ/ *verb* 动词 (splashes, splashing, splashed)
1 to hit water in a noisy way 戏水；哗哗地玩水：*People were splashing around in the water.* 人们在水中戏水玩耍。
2 if a liquid splashes, it moves or hits something, making a noise（液体）飞溅，哗啦作响：*A little wave splashed in my face.* 一个小小的浪打到了我的脸上。
● **splash** *singular noun* 单数名词：*There was a splash as something fell into the water.* 有东西扑通一声掉进了水里。

splendid /ˈsplendɪd/ *adjective* 形容词 very good 极好的；绝妙的；出色的：*The book includes some splendid photographs.* 这本书里有一些非常美丽的照片。

splinter /ˈsplɪntə/ *countable noun* 可数名词 a thin, sharp piece of wood or glass that has broken off from a larger piece 碎片；裂片：*We found splinters of the glass in our clothes.* 我们在自己的衣服里发现了玻璃碎片。

split /splɪt/ *verb* 动词 (splits, splitting, split)
1 to break into two or more parts 断裂；裂开：*The ship split in two during a storm.* 船在风暴中断成了两截。
2 to divide something into two or more parts 使断裂；使裂开：*Split the chicken in half.* 把这只鸡切成两半。
3 to break, producing a long crack or tear 撕裂；扯裂：*My trousers split while I was climbing over the wall.* 我翻墙的时候把裤子扯裂了。
4 to share something between two or more people 分享；分担：*Let's split the bill.* 我们分摊账单吧。
split up to stop being in a relationship together 分手；决裂；离婚：*His parents split up when he was ten.* 他的父母在他10岁时离了婚。

spoil /spɔɪl/ *verb* 动词 (spoils, spoiling, spoiled or 或 spoilt)
1 to prevent something from being successful 弄糟；破坏：*Don't let mistakes spoil your life.* 别让错误毁了你的一生。
2 to give children everything they want or ask for 溺爱，宠坏（小孩）：*Grandparents often like to spoil their grandchildren.* 祖父母常常喜欢宠溺孙辈。

spoilt /spɔɪlt/
→ see 见 **spoil**

spoke¹ /spəʊk/
→ see 见 **speak**

spoke² /spəʊk/ *countable noun* 可数名词 a bar that connects the outer ring of a wheel to the centre 辐条；轮辐：*Her feet got caught in the spokes of the bike wheel.* 她的双脚卡在了自行车车轮的辐条中。

spoken /ˈspəʊkən/
→ see 见 **speak**

spokesman /ˈspəʊksmən/ *countable noun* 可数名词 (spokesmen /ˈspəʊksmən/) a man who speaks as the representative of a group or an organization 男发言人：*A spokesman said that food is on its way to the region.* 一名男发言人表示食品正在运往该地区的路上。

spokesperson /ˈspəʊkspɜːsən/ *countable noun* 可数名词 (spokespersons or 或

spokespeople /ˈspəʊkspiːpəl/
a person who speaks as the representative of a group or an organization 发言人: *a White House spokesperson* 白宫发言人

spokeswoman /ˈspəʊkswʊmən/ *countable noun* 可数名词 (**spokeswomen** /ˈspəʊkswɪmɪn/)
a woman who speaks as a representative of a group or an organization 女发言人: *A hospital spokeswoman said he was recovering well.* 医院的女发言人透露他恢复得很好。

sponge /spʌndʒ/ *countable noun* 可数名词
a piece of a very light soft material with lots of little holes in it, that you use for washing yourself or for cleaning things 海绵: *He wiped the table with a sponge.* 他用一块海绵擦了桌子。

sponsor /ˈspɒnsə/ *verb* 动词 (**sponsors, sponsoring, sponsored**)
1 to pay for an event 赞助 (活动): *A local bank is sponsoring the race.* 一家当地的银行赞助这次比赛。
2 to agree to give money to someone who is doing something to raise money, if they succeed in doing it 为 (某人) 捐款; 资助 (某人): *The children asked friends and family to sponsor them.* 孩子们要求朋友和家人资助他们。

spontaneous /spɒnˈteɪniəs/ *adjective* 形容词
done because someone suddenly wants to do it 自发的; 自然的: *He gave her a spontaneous hug.* 他不由自主地拥抱了她。
▶ **spontaneously** /spɒnˈteɪniəsli/ *adverb* 副词: *People spontaneously stood up and cheered.* 人们自发地站起来欢呼。

spooky /ˈspuːki/ *adjective* 形容词 (**spookier, spookiest**)
seeming frightening (*informal* 非正式) 阴森恐怖的; 闹鬼似的: *The house has a slightly spooky atmosphere.* 这座房子的氛围有点阴森恐怖。

spoon /spuːn/ *countable noun* 可数名词
a long object with a round end that is used for eating, serving or mixing food 勺子; 匙; 调羹: *He stirred his coffee with a spoon.* 他用勺子搅拌咖啡。

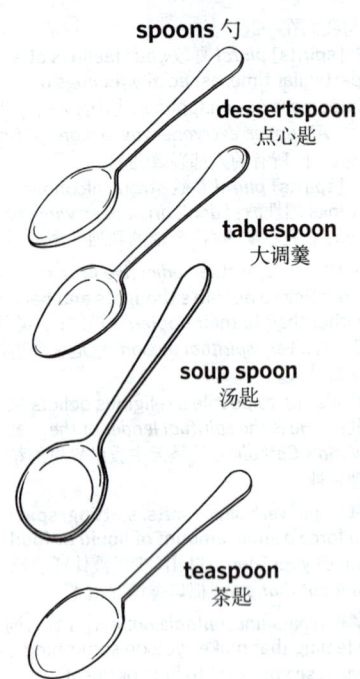

spoons 勺
dessertspoon 点心匙
tablespoon 大调羹
soup spoon 汤匙
teaspoon 茶匙

spoonful /ˈspuːnfʊl/ *countable noun* 可数名词
an amount of food that a spoon holds 一匙之量; 一满勺: *He took a spoonful of the stew and ate it.* 他舀了一勺炖菜吃。

sport /spɔːt/ *noun* 名词
a game or other activity that needs physical effort and skill 运动; 体育运动: *Basketball is my favourite sport.* 篮球是我最喜欢的体育运动。 □ *She is very good at sports.* 她非常擅长体育运动。
→ Look at picture on P14 参见彩插第 14 页

¹sports centre *countable noun* 可数名词
a building where you can go to do sports and other activities 体育中心

spot¹ /spɒt/ *countable noun* 可数名词
1 a small, round coloured area on a surface 小圆点; 斑点: *The leaves are yellow with orange spots.* 叶子是黄色的, 上面带着橙色的斑点。
2 a particular place 地点; 位置; 处所: *This is one of the country's top tourist spots.* 这是该国最著名的旅游景点之一。
3 a small red lump or mark on a person's skin (皮肤上的) 小肿块, 斑点: *I've got a big spot on my nose.* 我的鼻子上长了一大块斑。
on the spot immediately 立刻; 当场: *They*

offered him the job on the spot. 他们当场就给了他这份工作。

spot² /spɒt/ ***verb*** 动词 (**spots, spotting, spotted**)
to notice something or someone 发现；注意到：*I didn't spot the mistake in his essay.* 我没有发现他文章中的这处错误。

spotlight /ˈspɒtlaɪt/ ***countable noun*** 可数名词
a powerful light that can be directed so that it lights up a small area 聚光灯

spotty /ˈspɒti/ ***adjective*** 形容词
1 with small red lumps on your skin 有粉刺的：*a spotty face* 长满粉刺的脸
2 with a pattern of spots 带斑点图案的：*a spotty dress* 带圆点的连衣裙

spouse /spaʊs/ ***countable noun*** 可数名词
someone's husband or wife 配偶：*You and your spouse must both sign the contract.* 你和你的配偶都必须签这份合同。

sprang /spræŋ/
→ see 见 **spring**

spray /spreɪ/ ***noun*** 名词
1 a lot of small drops of water that are thrown into the air 水花；飞沫：*We were hit by spray from the waterfall.* 瀑布溅起的水花打到了我们身上。
2 a liquid that comes out of a can or other container in very small drops when you press a button 喷雾；喷剂：*hair spray* 发胶
● **spray** ***verb*** 动词 (**sprays, spraying, sprayed**)：*Firefighters sprayed water on the fire.* 消防员往火里喷水。

spread /spred/ ***verb*** 动词 (**spreads, spreading, spread**)
1 (also 亦作 **spread something out**) to open something out over a surface 摊开；铺开：*She spread a towel on the sand and lay on it.* 她把毛巾铺在沙滩上，然后躺了下来。
2 (also 亦作 **spread something out**) to stretch out parts of your body until they are far apart 伸出，伸开（身体部位）：*Sit on the floor, and spread your legs.* 坐在地板上，伸开你的双腿。
3 to put a substance all over a surface 涂；抹；敷：*She was spreading butter on the bread.* 她在面包上涂了黄油。
4 to gradually reach a larger area 传播；扩散；蔓延：*Information technology has spread across the world.* 信息技术已在全世界传播开来。● **spread** ***singular noun*** 单数名词：*We closed schools to stop the spread of the disease.* 我们关闭了学校来阻止疾病的蔓延。
spread something out
1 to open something out over a surface 摊开某物；铺开某物：*He spread the papers out on a table.* 他把报纸摊在了桌子上。
2 to stretch out parts of your body until they are far apart 伸出，伸开（身体部位）：*David spread out his hands.* 戴维伸出了双手。

spreadsheet /ˈspredʃiːt/ ***countable noun*** 可数名词
a computer program that deals with numbers. Spreadsheets are mainly used for financial planning. 电子表格（主要用于制订财务计划的计算机程序）

spring¹ /sprɪŋ/ ***noun*** 名词
1 the season between winter and summer when the weather becomes warmer and plants start to grow again 春天；春季：*They are getting married next spring.* 他们将在明年春天结婚。
→ Look at picture on P8 参见彩插第 8 页
2 ***countable*** 可数 a long piece of metal that goes round and round. It goes back to the same shape after you pull it. 弹簧：*The springs in the bed were old and soft.* 这床上的弹簧又旧又软。
3 ***countable*** 可数 a place where water comes up through the ground 泉；泉水：*The town is famous for its hot springs.* 这座小镇因温泉而闻名。

spring² /sprɪŋ/ ***verb*** 动词 (**springs, springing, sprang, sprung**)
to jump suddenly or quickly 跳；跃；蹦：*He sprang to his feet.* 他跳了起来。

spring onion ***countable noun*** 可数名词
a small onion with long green leaves 洋葱苗

sprinkle /ˈsprɪŋkəl/ ***verb*** 动词 (**sprinkles, sprinkling, sprinkled**)
to drop a bit of liquid or powder over the surface of something 往…上撒（或洒）：*Sprinkle the meat with salt before you cook it.* 在烹饪之前，往肉上撒些盐。

sprinkler /ˈsprɪŋklə/ ***countable noun*** 可数名词
a machine that spreads drops of water over an area of grass or onto a fire 喷洒器；消防喷淋

sprint /sprɪnt/ ***verb*** 动词 (**sprints, sprinting, sprinted**)
to run as fast as you can over a short

sprout - squid

distance（短距离内）快速奔跑，冲刺：
Sergeant Adams sprinted to the car. 亚当斯中士全力冲向那辆汽车。● **sprint** *singular noun* 单数名词：*Rob Harmeling won the sprint.* 罗布·哈梅林获得了短跑冠军。

sprout¹ /spraʊt/ *verb* 动词 (**sprouts, sprouting, sprouted**)
to start to grow out of the ground 发芽；抽芽：*It only takes a few days for beans to sprout.* 豆子长芽只需几天的时间。

sprout² /spraʊt/ *countable noun* 可数名词 (also 亦作 **Brussels sprout**) a small round green vegetable 抱子甘蓝；球芽甘蓝

sprung /sprʌŋ/
→ see 见 **spring**

spun /spʌn/
→ see 见 **spin**

spy¹ /spaɪ/ *countable noun* 可数名词 (**spies**)
a person whose job is to find out secret information about another country or organization 间谍：*He used to be a spy.* 他过去是一名间谍。

spy² /spaɪ/ *verb* 动词 (**spies, spying, spied**)
1 to try to find out secret information about another country or organization 从事间谍活动；当间谍：*The two countries are still spying on one another.* 这两个国家仍在互相进行间谍活动。
2 to watch someone secretly 秘密监视：*He spied on her while she was on her way to work.* 他在她上班的路上秘密监视着她。

square¹ /skweə/ *countable noun* 可数名词
1 a shape with four straight sides that are all the same length 正方形；四方形：*Cut the cake into squares.* 把蛋糕切成若干四方形。
→ Look at picture on P2 参见彩插第 2 页
2 an open place with buildings around it in a town or city 广场：*The restaurant is in the town square.* 这家餐馆在镇广场上。
3 the number you get when you multiply a number by itself 平方：*The square of 4 is 16.* *4 的平方是 16。

square² /skweə/ *adjective* 形容词
1 used for describing a shape that has four straight sides that are all the same length 正方形的；四方形的：*They sat at a square table.* 他们坐在一张方桌旁。
2 used for talking about the area of something（用于表示面积）平方的：*The house covers an area of 3,000 square feet.* 这座房子占地 3,000 平方英尺。

square ˈroot *countable noun* 可数名词
a number that you multiply by itself to produce another number 平方根：*The square root of 36 is 6.* *36 的平方根是 6。

squash¹ /skwɒʃ/ *verb* 动词 (**squashes, squashing, squashed**)
to push or press someone or something hard 挤压；压扁；压碎：*Robert was squashed against a fence by a car.* 罗伯特被一辆小汽车顶到了栅栏上。

squash² /skwɒʃ/ *uncountable noun* 不可数名词
1 a game in which two players hit a small rubber ball against the walls of a court 壁球：*I play squash once a week.* 我一周打一次壁球。
2 a drink that is made from fruit juice, sugar, and water 果汁饮料：*a glass of orange squash* 一杯橙汁

squeak /skwiːk/ *verb* 动词 (**squeaks, squeaking, squeaked**)
to make a short, high sound 发出短而尖的声音；发出吱吱声：*My boots squeaked as I walked.* 我走路时靴子发出嘎吱嘎吱的声音。● **squeak** *countable noun* 可数名词：*I heard a squeak, like a mouse.* 我听到了吱吱声，就像老鼠的叫声。

squeal /skwiːl/ *verb* 动词 (**squeals, squealing, squealed**)
to make a long, high sound 发出长而尖的声音：*Jennifer squealed with pleasure.* 珍妮弗高兴地尖叫起来。● **squeal** *countable noun* 可数名词：*There was a squeal of brakes as the car suddenly stopped.* 汽车突然停了下来，发出一阵尖厉刺耳的刹车声。

squeeze /skwiːz/ *verb* 动词 (**squeezes, squeezing, squeezed**)
1 to press something firmly, usually with your hands 挤；压；捏：*He squeezed her arm gently.* 他轻轻地捏了捏她的胳膊。
● **squeeze** *countable noun* 可数名词：*She took my hand and gave it a squeeze.* 她握着我的手，捏了捏。
2 to get a soft substance out of a container by pressing 压榨；挤出：*Joe squeezed some toothpaste out of the tube.* 乔从管子里挤出一些牙膏。

squid /skwɪd/ *noun* 名词

> **LANGUAGE HELP** 语言提示
> The plural can also be **squid**. 复数形式也可用 **squid**。

1 countable 可数 a sea animal that has a long soft body and many soft arms called tentacles 枪乌贼；鱿鱼
2 uncountable 不可数 this animal eaten as food（供食用的）枪乌贼，鱿鱼：*Cook the squid for 2 minutes.* 将鱿鱼烹制两分钟。

squirrel /ˈskwɪrəl/ **countable noun** 可数名词
a small animal with a long thick tail. Squirrels live mainly in trees. 松鼠

squirt /skwɜːt/ **verb** 动词 (**squirts, squirting, squirted**)
1 to make a liquid come out of a narrow opening very quickly 使喷出（或喷射）：*Norman squirted tomato sauce onto his plate.* 诺曼把番茄酱挤到了盘子里。
2 to come out of a narrow opening very quickly 喷射；射出：*The mustard squirted all over the front of my shirt.* 芥末酱喷满了我衬衫的前襟。 ● **squirt countable noun** 可数名词：*It needs a little squirt of oil.* 需要喷一点油。

stab /stæb/ **verb** 动词 (**stabs, stabbing, stabbed**)
to push a knife or sharp object into someone's body 刺；戳；捅：*Someone stabbed him in the stomach.* 有人朝他肚子上捅了一刀。

stable¹ /ˈsteɪbəl/ **adjective** 形容词 (**stabler, stablest**)
1 not likely to change suddenly 稳定的；平稳的：*The price of oil has remained stable this month.* 这个月的油价保持稳定。
▶ **stability** /stəˈbɪlɪti/ **uncountable noun** 不可数名词：*It was a time of political stability.* 这是一段政治稳定的时期。
2 firmly fixed in position 稳固的；牢固的：*Make sure the ladder is stable.* 确保梯子稳固。

stable² /ˈsteɪbəl/ **countable noun** 可数名词
(also 亦作 **stables**) a building in which horses are kept 马厩

stack /stæk/ **countable noun** 可数名词
a pile of things 一堆；一叠：*There were stacks of books on the floor.* 地板上有几摞书。 ● **stack verb** 动词 (**stacks, stacking, stacked**)：*He asked me to stack the dirty dishes.* 他要我把脏盘子摞起来。

stadium /ˈsteɪdiəm/ **countable noun** 可数名词
a large sports pitch with rows of seats all around it（周围设有看台的）体育场，运动场：*a football stadium* 足球场

staff /stɑːf/ **countable noun** 可数名词
the people who work for an organization（某一机构的）全体职员：*The hospital staff were very good.* 这家医院的员工都很不错。 □ *staff members* 职员

stag /stæg/ **countable noun** 可数名词
an adult male deer (= a large wild animal that eats grass and leaves, and has horns that look like branches)（成年的）牡鹿，雄鹿

stage /steɪdʒ/ **countable noun** 可数名词
1 one part of an activity or process 时期；阶段：*We are completing the first stage of the plan.* 我们正在完成计划的第一阶段。
2 the area in a theatre where people perform 舞台：*The band walked onto the stage.* 乐队走上了舞台。

stagger /ˈstæɡə/ **verb** 动词 (**staggers, staggering, staggered**)
to walk as if you are going to fall, for example because you are ill 蹒跚而行；摇摇晃晃地走：*He staggered back and fell over.* 他往后趔趄了一下，然后摔倒了。

stain /steɪn/ **countable noun** 可数名词
a mark on something that is difficult to remove 污迹；污渍：*How do you remove tea stains?* 你怎么去除茶渍？ ● **stain verb** 动词 (**stains, staining, stained**)：*Some foods can stain the teeth.* 有些食物会形成牙渍。
▶ **stained** /steɪnd/ **adjective** 形容词：*His clothing was stained with mud.* 他的衣服沾上了泥。

stair /steə/ **countable noun** 可数名词
one of a set of steps inside a building 一级楼梯；梯级：*Terry was sitting on the bottom stair.* 特里正坐在最下面的一级楼梯上。

staircase /ˈsteəkeɪs/ **countable noun** 可数名词
a set of stairs inside a building（建筑物内的）楼梯：*They walked down the staircase together.* 他们一起走下楼梯。

stairs /steəz/ **plural noun** 复数名词
a set of steps inside a building that go from one level to another（上下楼层之间的）楼梯：*Nancy began to climb the stairs.* 南希开始爬楼梯。 □ *We walked up the stairs to the second floor.* 我们走楼梯上了 3 楼。

stale /steɪl/ **adjective** 形容词 (**staler, stalest**)
no longer fresh 不新鲜的：*stale bread* 不新鲜的面包

stalk /stɔːk/ **countable noun** 可数名词
the thin part of a flower, leaf or fruit that joins it to the plant or tree 柄；蒂；茎；梗：*A single flower grows on each long stalk.* 每

根长长的茎上都长着一朵花。

stammer /ˈstæmə/ *verb* 动词 (**stammers, stammering, stammered**)
to find it difficult to speak without repeating words or sounds 结巴；口吃：*'F-f-forgive me,' I stammered.* "原——原——原谅我。"我结巴着说。

stamp¹ /stæmp/ *countable noun* 可数名词
1 a small piece of paper that you stick on an envelope before you post it 邮票：*She put a stamp on the corner of the envelope.* 她在信封角上贴了一枚邮票。
2 a small block of wood or metal with words, numbers or a pattern on it. You put ink on it, then press it onto a piece of paper. 章；戳；印：*a date stamp* 日期戳

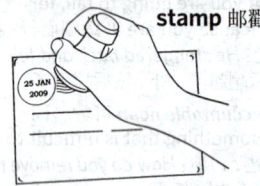

stamp 邮戳

stamp 邮票

stamp² /stæmp/ *verb* 动词 (**stamps, stamping, stamped**)
to press a mark or a word onto an object using a stamp 盖（章、戳、印）：*They stamp a special number on new cars.* 他们给新车加盖特殊数字戳。

stamp your foot to put your foot down very hard on the ground 跺脚：*I stamped my foot in anger.* 我气得直跺脚。

stand¹ /stænd/ *verb* 动词 (**stands, standing, stood**)
1 to be on your feet 站；立；站立：*She was standing beside my bed.* 她站在我床边。
2 (also 亦作 **stand up**) to move so that you are on your feet 起立；站起来：*Becker stood and shook hands with Ben.* 贝克尔起身同本握手。
3 to be in a place 处于；位于；坐落：*The house stands alone on top of a hill.* 房子孤零零地坐落在一座小山顶上。

can't stand someone/something used for saying that you dislike someone or something very strongly (*informal* 非正式) 无法容忍某人／某事物：*I can't stand that awful man.* 我受不了那个可恶的男人。 □ *I can't stand that smell.* 我受不了那种气味。

stand aside/stand back to move a short distance away 靠边站／往后站：*I stood aside to let her pass me.* 我让开叫她过去。

stand by
1 to be ready to help 待命；随时备用：*Police officers are standing by in case of trouble.* 警察随时待命，以备万一。
2 to not do anything to stop something bad from happening 袖手旁观；坐视不管：*I will not stand by and watch people suffering.* 我不会坐视不管，眼看着人民受苦。

stand for something to be a short form of a word 是某词的缩略形式；代表某词：*U.S. stands for United States.* *U.S. 代表 United States（美国）

stand out to be very easy to see 显眼；突出：*The black necklace stood out against her white dress.* 黑项链配她的白连衣裙特别显眼。

stand up to move so that you are on your feet 起立；站起来：*When I walked in, they all stood up.* 我一进门，他们便集体起立。

stand up for someone/something to support a person or a belief 挺身支持某人／某信念：*Nelson Mandela stood up for his people and his beliefs.* 纳尔逊·曼德拉为人民和自己的信念挺身而出。

stand up to someone to defend yourself against someone who is more powerful than you 对抗某人：*He was too afraid to stand up to her.* 他太害怕，不敢顶撞她。

stand² /stænd/ *countable noun* 可数名词
1 a small structure where you can buy things like food, drink and newspapers 货摊；摊位：*I bought a magazine from a newspaper stand.* 我从报摊买了一本杂志。
2 a small piece of furniture that you use to hold a particular thing 架；座；托：*Take the television set off the stand.* 把电视从架子上取下来。

standard¹ /ˈstændəd/ *noun* 名词
1 *countable* 可数 a level of quality 水平；水准：*The standard of his work is very low.* 他的活儿做得很糙。
2 [**standards**] *plural* 复数 moral principles that guide people's behaviour 道德标准：*My father always had high moral*

standards. 我父亲始终坚守着很高的道德标准。

standard² /ˈstændəd/ *adjective* 形容词
usual and normal 常规的；普通的；标准的：*It's just a standard size car.* 这不过是一辆标准尺寸的汽车。

standby /ˈstændbaɪ/ *countable noun* 可数名词
something or someone that is always ready to be used if they are needed 备用物；备用人选：*Canned vegetables are a good standby.* 蔬菜罐头是不错的备用品。
on standby ready to be used if needed 备用的；待命的：*Five ambulances are on standby.* *5 辆救护车随时待命。

stank /stæŋk/
→ see 见 **stink**

staple¹ /ˈsteɪpəl/ *countable noun* 可数名词
a small piece of bent wire that holds sheets of paper together firmly. You put the staples into the paper using a stapler. 订书钉 ● **staple** *verb* 动词 (**staples, stapling, stapled**)：*Staple some sheets of paper together.* 把一些纸订起来。

staple² /ˈsteɪpəl/ *adjective* 形容词
important in people's lives（在人们生活中）主要的，重要的：*Rice is the staple food of more than half the world's population.* 大米是世界半数以上人口的主食。

stapler /ˈsteɪplə/ *countable noun* 可数名词
a small piece of equipment that is used for attaching sheets of paper together 订书机
→ Look at picture on P1 参见彩插第 1 页

star¹ /stɑː/ *countable noun* 可数名词
1 a large ball of burning gas in space. Stars look like small points of light in the sky. 星；恒星：*Stars lit the sky.* 星星点亮了天空。
2 a shape that has four, five or more points sticking out of it in a regular pattern 星形：*How many stars are there on the American flag?* 美国国旗上有多少颗星星？
3 a famous actor, musician or sports player 明星：*He's one of the stars of the TV series 'Friends'.* 他是电视连续剧《老友记》里的明星之一。

star² /stɑː/ *verb* 动词 (**stars, starring, starred**)
1 to have one of the most important parts in a play or a film 主演；担任主角：*Meryl Streep stars in the movie 'The Devil Wears Prada'.* 梅里尔·斯特里普在影片《穿普拉达的女王》里担任主角。
2 to have a famous actor or actress in one of the most important parts in a play or film 由（知名演员）担任主角：*The movie stars Brad Pitt.* 影片由布拉德·皮特主演。

stare /steə/ *verb* 动词 (**stares, staring, stared**)
to look at someone or something for a long time 凝视；盯着看：*Ben continued to stare out the window.* 本继续盯着窗外。
□ *She was staring at me angrily.* 她气呼呼地瞪着我。● **stare** *countable noun* 可数名词：*Harry gave him a long stare.* 哈里盯着他看了好一会儿。

starfish /ˈstɑːfɪʃ/ *countable noun* 可数名词 (**starfish**)
a flat creature in the shape of a star, that lives in the sea 海星

start /stɑːt/ *verb* 动词 (**starts, starting, started**)
1 to do something that you were not doing before 开始（做事）：*Susanna started working in TV four years ago.* 苏珊娜 4 年前进入电视圈。
2 to take place from a particular time 开始（发生）：*The fire started in an upstairs room.* 火是从楼上一个房间燃起来的。
● **start** *singular noun* 单数名词：*It was 1918, four years after the start of the Great War.* 那是 1918 年，距离第一次世界大战爆发已经过去 4 年。
3 to create something or cause it to begin 创办；开办：*She has started a child care centre in Leeds.* 她已经在利兹创办了一家儿童护理中心。
4 to make an engine, a car or a machine begin to work 发动；启动：*He started the car and drove off.* 他发动汽车开走了。
start off to do something as the first part of an activity（从做某事）开始，着手：*She started off by clearing some space on the table.* 她先在桌上清理出一些空间。
to start with used for introducing the first of a number of things 首先；第一：*To start with, you need her name and address.* 首先，你得知道她的名字和地址。

starter /ˈstɑːtə/ *countable noun* 可数名词
a small amount of food that you eat as the first part of a meal 开胃小吃：*There was a choice of three starters and three main courses on the menu.* 菜单上开胃小吃、主

startle – statistic

菜各有 3 道可选。

startle /ˈstɑːtəl/ verb 动词 (startles, startling, startled)
to suddenly surprise and frighten someone slightly 使受惊吓；使吓一跳: *The telephone startled him.* 电话吓了他一跳。
▶ **startled** /ˈstɑːtəld/ adjective 形容词: *Martha gave her a startled look.* 玛莎吃惊地看了她一眼。

starve /stɑːv/ verb 动词 (starves, starving, starved)
to suffer greatly or die from lack of food 挨饿；饿死: *A number of the prisoners are starving.* 一些犯人快饿死了。
▶ **starvation** /stɑːˈveɪʃən/ uncountable noun 不可数名词: *Over three hundred people died of starvation.* 300 多人死于饥饿。
starve yourself to eat very little or no food over a long period of time 节食: *He was starving himself.* 他在节食。

starving /ˈstɑːvɪŋ/ adjective 形容词
very hungry (informal 非正式) 非常饿的；饿得要命的: *Does anyone have any food? I'm starving.* 哪位有吃的？我快饿死了。

state¹ /steɪt/ noun 名词
1 countable 可数 a country, especially when it is considered politically (尤指政治意义上的) 国家: *a socialist state* 社会主义国家
2 countable 可数 a smaller area that some large countries such as the United States are divided into (国家行政区划的) 州，邦: *Leaders of the Southern states are meeting in Louisville.* 南方诸州领导人在路易斯维尔会面。
3 singular 单数 the government of a country 政府；国家: *In Sweden, child care is provided by the state.* 在瑞典，儿童保育由国家负责。
4 countable 可数 the condition that someone or something is in 状况；状态；情况: *After Daniel died, I was in a state of shock.* 丹尼尔去世后，我处于震惊之中。
the States the United States of America (informal 非正式) 美国: *She bought it in the States.* 这个是她在美国买的。

state² /steɪt/ verb 动词 (states, stating, stated)
to say or write something in a formal or definite way 陈述；声明；宣称: *Clearly state your address and telephone number.* 清楚地报出你的地址和电话号码。

statement /ˈsteɪtmənt/ countable noun 可数名词
something that you say or write that gives information in a formal way 陈述；声明；说明: *I was very angry when I made that statement.* 我发表那份声明时非常生气。

static¹ /ˈstætɪk/ adjective 形容词
not moving or changing 静止的；不变的: *House prices were static last month.* 上个月房价未有变化。

static² /ˈstætɪk/ uncountable noun 不可数名词
(also 亦作 **static electricity**) electricity that collects on things such as your body or metal objects 静电

station /ˈsteɪʃən/ countable noun 可数名词
1 a place where trains stop so that people can get on or off 火车站: *Ingrid went with him to the train station.* 英格丽德陪他去了火车站。
2 a place in a town or a city where a lot of buses stop 公共汽车站: *I walked to the bus station and bought a ticket.* 我走到公共汽车站买了张票。
3 a company that broadcasts programmes on radio or television 电台；电视台: *a local radio station* 地方广播电台

stationary /ˈsteɪʃənri/ adjective 形容词
not moving 静止的；不动的: *A bus crashed into the back of a stationary vehicle.* 一辆巴士追尾了一辆静止不动的车辆。

> **LANGUAGE HELP 语言提示**
> **Stationary** or **stationery**? 用 stationary 还是 stationery？
> **Stationary** is an adjective; it means 'not moving'. **Stationery** is a noun; it means 'paper products used for writing and typing'. *stationary 是形容词，意为"静止的"，stationery 是名词，意为"文具"。

stationery /ˈsteɪʃənri/ uncountable noun 不可数名词
paper, envelopes and other materials or equipment used for writing and typing 文具: *office stationery* 办公用品

statistic /stəˈtɪstɪk/ countable noun 可数名词
a fact that is expressed in numbers 统计数字: *Statistics show that wages are rising.* 统计数字显示工资在上涨。

statue /ˈstætʃuː/ *countable noun* 可数名词
a large model of a person or an animal, made of stone or metal 雕像；雕塑：*She gave me a stone statue of a horse.* 她给我了一尊石马雕塑。
→ Look at picture on P10 参见彩插第 10 页

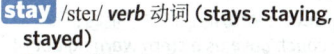
statue 雕像

status /ˈsteɪtəs/
uncountable noun 不可数名词
the importance that people give to someone or something 地位：*Older family members enjoy high status in many societies.* 在很多社会里，年长的家庭成员享有的地位高。

stay /steɪ/ *verb* 动词 (**stays, staying, stayed**)
1 to continue to be where you are, and not to leave 待在原地；停留：*'Stay here,' Trish said. 'I'll bring the car to you.'* "待这儿别动，"特里希说，"我把车给你开过来。"
2 to live somewhere for a short time 待；暂住：*Gordon stayed at The Park Hotel, Milan.* 戈登下榻在米兰的帕克酒店。 □ *Can't you stay for a few more days?* 你不能多待几天吗？ ● **stay** *countable noun* 可数名词：*Please contact the hotel reception if you have any problems during your stay.* 入住期间遇到问题请联系宾馆前台。
3 to continue to be in a particular state or situation 保持；维持：*Exercise is one of the best ways to stay healthy.* 锻炼是保持健康的最佳方式之一。
stay away to not go to a place 远离；不去：*Most workers stayed away from work during the strike.* 罢工期间大多数工人不上班。
stay in to remain at home and not go out 待在家里：*We decided to stay in and have dinner at home.* 我们决定待在家里吃晚饭。
stay up not to go to bed at your usual time 熬夜：*I used to stay up late with my mum and watch films.* 我以前常和妈妈熬夜看电影。

steady /ˈstedi/ *adjective* 形容词 (**steadier, steadiest**)
1 continuing or developing gradually and not likely to change quickly 稳步的；稳健的：*Despite these problems there has been steady progress.* 尽管存在这些问题，但是推进工作一直在稳步进行。
▶ **steadily** /ˈstedɪli/ *adverb* 副词：*Prices have been rising steadily.* 物价稳步上涨。
2 firm, and not moving around 稳定的；稳固的：*Hold the camera steady.* 拿稳相机。
● **steady** *verb* 动词 (**steadies, steadying, steadied**)：*Two men were steadying the ladder.* 两名男子扶着梯子。

steak /steɪk/ *noun* 名词
1 a large flat piece of beef without much fat on it 牛排：*There was a steak cooking on the grill.* 烤架上烤着一块牛排。
2 *countable* 可数 a large piece of fish that does not contain many bones 鱼排：*fresh salmon steaks* 新鲜的鲑鱼排

steal /stiːl/ *verb* 动词 (**steals, stealing, stole, stolen**)
to take something from someone without their permission 偷窃；窃取；盗窃：*They said he stole a small boy's bicycle.* 他们说他偷了一个小男孩的自行车。 □ *It's wrong to steal.* 偷东西是不对的。 □ *Give me back the money that you stole from me.* 把你偷我的钱还给我。
▶ **stolen** /ˈstəʊlən/ *adjective* 形容词：*We have now found the stolen car.* 我们现在已经找到了被盗车辆。

steam¹ /stiːm/ *uncountable noun* 不可数名词
the hot gas that forms when water boils 蒸汽；水蒸气：*The heat converts water into steam.* 水加热后转化为蒸汽。

steam² /stiːm/ *verb* 动词 (**steams, steaming, steamed**)
to cook food in steam rather than in water 蒸（食物）：*Steam the carrots until they are slightly soft.* 把胡萝卜蒸到微微发软。

steel /stiːl/ *uncountable noun* 不可数名词
a very strong metal that is made mainly from iron 钢；钢材：*steel pipes* 钢管 □ *the steel industry* 钢铁工业

steep /stiːp/ *adjective* 形容词 (**steeper, steepest**)
1 rising at a very sharp angle 陡的；陡峭的：*Some of the hills in San Francisco are very steep.* 旧金山有些小山非常陡。
▶ **steeply** /ˈstiːpli/ *adverb* 副词：*The road climbs steeply.* 公路陡然向上。
2 very big 非常大的：*There have been steep price increases.* 价格急剧走高。
▶ **steeply** /ˈstiːpli/ *adverb* 副词：*Unemployment is rising steeply.* 失业率急

剧上升。

steer /stɪə/ *verb* 动词 (steers, steering, steered)
to control a vehicle so that it goes in the direction that you want 驾驶（汽车等）: *What is it like to steer a big ship?* 驾驶一艘大轮船是什么感觉？

'steering ˌwheel *countable noun* 可数名词
the wheel in a car or other vehicle that the driver holds when he or she is driving 方向盘；转向盘；操舵轮

stem /stem/ *countable noun* 可数名词
the long, thin part of a plant that the flowers and leaves grow on 茎；梗；柄: *He cut the stem and gave her the flower.* 他剪断茎，把花递给她。

step¹ /step/ *countable noun* 可数名词
1 the action of lifting your foot and putting it down in a different place 步；脚步；步伐: *I took a step towards him.* 我朝他迈了一步。□ *She walked back a few steps.* 她后退了几步。
2 a raised flat surface that you put your feet on in order to walk up or down to a different level 台阶；梯级: *We went down some steps into the garden.* 我们走下台阶进入花园。□ *A girl was sitting on the bottom step.* 一个女孩儿坐在最下面的台阶上。
3 one of a series of actions that you take in a process（一系列行动中的）一步；举措: *We have taken the first step towards peace.* 我们已经朝着和平迈出了第一步。
step by step progressing gradually from one stage to the next 一步步；稳步地；逐步地: *I am not rushing things. I'm taking it step by step.* 我不会急于求成。我会一步一步地来。

step² /step/ *verb* 动词 (steps, stepping, stepped)
1 to move somewhere by lifting your foot and putting it down in a different place 迈步；跨步: *He stepped carefully over the sleeping cat.* 他小心翼翼地迈过熟睡的猫。
2 to put your foot on something 踩；踏足: *Neil Armstrong was the first man to step on the Moon.* 尼尔·阿姆斯特朗是第一个踏足月球的人。

stepfather /'stepfɑːðə/ *countable noun* 可数名词
the man who has married someone's mother but who is not their father 继父；后爸

stepmother /'stepmʌðə/ *countable noun* 可数名词
the woman who has married someone's father but who is not their mother 继母；后妈

stereo /'steriəʊ/ *countable noun* 可数名词
a machine that plays music, with two parts (= speakers) that the sound comes from 立体声音响: *a car stereo* 车载立体声音响

sterile /'steraɪl/ *adjective* 形容词
1 completely clean 无菌的；灭菌的: *Cover the cut with a sterile bandage and keep it dry.* 用无菌绷带包扎伤口，保持干燥。
2 unable to produce babies 不育的: *The tests showed that George was sterile.* 检测结果显示乔治没有生育能力。

stern /stɜːn/ *adjective* 形容词 (sterner, sternest)
1 very severe 严厉的；非常严重的: *Our rugby coach gave us a stern warning about our behaviour.* 我们橄榄球教练对我们的行为予以严厉的警告。
▶ **sternly** /'stɜːnli/ *adverb* 副词: *'We will punish anyone who breaks the rules,' she said sternly.* "凡破坏规则者，严惩不贷。" 她严厉地说。
2 very serious and not friendly 冷峻的；非常严肃的: *Her father was a stern man.* 她父亲是个冷峻的人。

stew¹ /stjuː/ *noun* 名词
a meal that you make by cooking meat and vegetables in liquid 炖菜: *She gave him a bowl of stew.* 她给他端了一碗炖菜。

stew² /stjuː/ *verb* 动词 (stews, stewing, stewed)
to cook meat, vegetables, or fruit slowly in liquid 炖: *Stew the apples for half an hour.* 把苹果炖上半个小时。

steward /'stjuːəd/ *countable noun* 可数名词
a man whose job is to look after passengers on a ship, a plane, or a train （船、飞机或列车上的）男乘务员

stewardess /ˌstjuːəˈdes/ *countable noun* 可数名词 (stewardesses)
a woman whose job is to look after passengers on a ship, a plane, or a train （船、飞机或列车上的）女乘务员

stick¹ /stɪk/ *countable noun* 可数名词
1 a thin branch from a tree 细枝；小树枝；柴枝: *She put some dry sticks on the fire.* 她给火添了些干树枝。

2 a long thin piece of wood that is used for a particular purpose（具特定用途的）棍，杖，棒: *He picked up his walking stick and walked away.* 他捡起拐杖走开了。

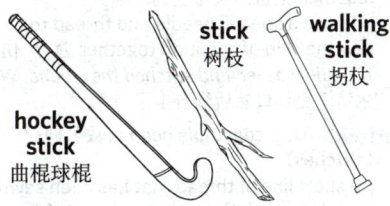

sticks 棍；杖；树枝

stick 树枝
walking stick 拐杖
hockey stick 曲棍球棍

stick² /stɪk/ *verb* 动词 (**sticks, sticking, stuck**)

1 to join one thing to another using a sticky substance（用胶）粘，粘贴: *Now stick your picture on a piece of paper.* 现在把你的照片贴到一张纸上。

2 to push a pointed object into something 刺；扎；插；戳: *The doctor stuck the needle into Joe's arm.* 医生把针头扎进乔的胳膊。

3 to put something somewhere (*informal* 非正式) 搁；放置: *He folded the papers and stuck them in his desk.* 他将文件折起来塞进书桌里。

4 to become joined to something and be difficult to remove 黏附；附着: *The paper sometimes sticks to the bottom of the cake.* 纸有时粘在蛋糕底上。

stick by someone to continue to give someone support 继续支持某人: *All my friends stuck by me during the difficult times.* 困难时期朋友们对我不离不弃。

stick out to continue further than the main part of something（某物）突出，伸出: *His two front teeth stick out slightly.* 他的两颗门牙有点儿翘。

stick something out to push something forwards or away from you 伸出某物: *She stuck out her tongue at him.* 她冲他吐舌头。

stick to something to not change your mind about a promise or a decision 遵守，坚守（承诺或决定）: *We are waiting to see if he sticks to his promise.* 我们等着看他说话算不算数。

stick up for someone/something to support someone or something, and say that they are right 维护某人/某事物: *My father always sticks up for me.* 父亲总是给我撑腰。

sticker /'stɪkə/ *countable noun* 可数名词 a small piece of paper with writing or a picture on one side, that you can stick onto a surface 贴纸: *I bought a sticker that said, 'I love Florida'.* 我买了一张贴纸，上面印着"我爱佛罗里达"。

sticky /'stɪki/ *adjective* 形容词 (**stickier, stickiest**)

1 sticking to other things 黏的；黏性的: *The floor was sticky with spilled orange juice.* 地板上洒了橙汁，黏黏的。 □ *If the mixture is sticky, add more flour.* 混合物黏的话，再加点面粉。

2 involving problems (*informal* 非正式) 麻烦的；棘手的: *There were some sticky moments.* 有些时刻很棘手。

stiff /stɪf/ *adjective* 形容词 (**stiffer, stiffest**)

1 firm or not bending easily 硬的；挺的；不易弯曲的: *His jeans were new and stiff.* 他的牛仔裤又新又挺。

▶ **stiffly** /'stɪfli/ *adverb* 副词: *Moira sat stiffly in her chair.* 莫伊拉直挺挺地坐在椅子上。

2 with muscles or joints that hurt when you move（肌肉或关节）僵硬的: *A hot bath is good for stiff muscles.* 泡热水澡对缓解肌肉僵硬有好处。

bored stiff/worried stiff extremely bored or worried (*informal* 非正式) 厌烦透顶的/担心得要命的: *Anna tried to look interested, but she was bored stiff.* 安娜努力装出感兴趣的样子，可心里烦透了。

stifle /'staɪfəl/ *verb* 动词 (**stifles, stifling, stifled**) to stop something from happening or continuing 阻止；遏制；抑制: *He stifled a laugh.* 他憋住笑。

still¹ /stɪl/ *adverb* 副词

1 used for showing that a situation that existed in the past has continued and exists now（表示状况持续至今）还，仍旧，依然: *Do you still live in Newcastle?* 你还住在纽卡斯尔吗？□ *Donald is still teaching at the age of 89.* 唐纳德 89 岁还在教书。

2 used for saying that something is true, despite something else（虽然…）还是，仍然: *She says she still loves him even though he treats her badly.* 她说虽然他对她不好，她还是爱他。

3 used for making another word stronger（加强语气）更，还要: *It's good to travel, but it's better still to come home.* 旅行好，不过回家更好。

still² /stɪl/ *adjective* 形容词 (**stiller, stillest**)
1 not moving 静止的；不动的：*Please stand still and listen to me!* 请站着别动，听我说！
2 without any wind 无风的：*It was a warm, still evening.* 那是一个温暖无风的夜晚。
3 without bubbles 无泡泡的；不起泡的：*Would you like still or sparkling mineral water?* 矿泉水你要有气泡的还是没气泡的？

stimulate /ˈstɪmjʊˌleɪt/ *verb* 动词 (**stimulates, stimulating, stimulated**)
1 to make something more active 刺激；使更活跃：*America is trying to stimulate its economy.* 美国在想办法刺激经济。
2 to make someone feel full of ideas and enthusiasm 激励；使振奋：*Bill was stimulated by the challenge.* 这一挑战让比尔受到了激励。
▶ **stimulating** /ˈstɪmjʊˌleɪtɪŋ/ *adjective* 形容词：*It is a stimulating book.* 这是一本令人振奋的书。
▶ **stimulation** /ˌstɪmjʊˈleɪʃən/ *uncountable noun* 不可数名词：*Children need stimulation, not relaxation.* 孩子需要督促，而不是放任。

sting /stɪŋ/ *verb* 动词 (**stings, stinging, stung**)
1 if a plant, an animal or an insect stings you, a pointed part of it is pushed into your skin so that you feel a sharp pain（植物）刺；（动物或昆虫）叮，蜇：*She was stung by a bee.* 她被蜜蜂蜇了一下。
2 to feel a sharp pain in a part of your body 感到刺痛（或剧痛）：*His cheeks were stinging from the cold wind.* 他两颊被冷风吹得生疼。● **sting** *countable noun* 可数名词：*This won't hurt — you will just feel a little sting.* 这个不疼——就跟被轻轻叮了一下似的。

stink /stɪŋk/ *verb* 动词 (**stinks, stinking, stank, stunk**)
to smell very bad 发臭；发出难闻气味：*We all stank and nobody cared.* 我们都发臭了，没人在乎。□ *The kitchen stinks of fish.* 厨房里有鱼腥味儿。● **stink** *singular noun* 单数名词：*He was aware of the stink of onions on his breath.* 他注意到了口气里的洋葱味儿。

stir /stɜː/ *verb* 动词 (**stirs, stirring, stirred**)
1 to mix a liquid in a container using a spoon 搅；搅拌；搅和：*Stir the soup for a few seconds.* 把汤搅一会儿。
2 to move slightly in your sleep（睡眠中）微动：*Eileen shook him, and he started to stir.* 艾琳摇晃他，他身子动了几下。

stitch¹ /stɪtʃ/ *verb* 动词 (**stitches, stitching, stitched**)
1 to sew cloth using a needle and thread 缝；缝补：*Stitch the two pieces of fabric together.* 把这两块布缝到一起。
2 to use a special needle and thread to sew the skin of a wound together 缝合（伤口）：*Jill washed and stitched the wound.* 吉尔清洗完伤口然后缝合上了。

stitch² /stɪtʃ/ *countable noun* 可数名词 (**stitches**)
1 a short line of thread that has been sewn in a piece of cloth 针脚：*Sew a row of straight stitches.* 缝一溜儿直直的针脚。
2 a short line of thread that has been used for sewing the skin of a wound together（伤口的）缝针：*He had six stitches in the cut.* 他那处伤口缝了6针。

stock¹ /stɒk/ *noun* 名词
1 *uncountable* 不可数 the total amount of goods that a shop has available to sell（店铺的）存货，库存：*Most of the stock was destroyed in the fire.* 大部分存货毁于大火。
2 *countable* 可数 one part of the value of a business that may be bought and sold 股票：*She works for a bank, buying and selling stocks and shares.* 她在银行工作，负责股票买卖。

in stock available for you to buy 有货：*Check that your size is in stock.* 查查你的尺码有没有货。

out of stock not available for you to buy 没货；售罄：*Sorry. The TV you are looking for is out of stock.* 对不起。您找的电视卖光了。

stock² /stɒk/ *verb* 动词 (**stocks, stocking, stocked**)
to keep a supply of a particular product to sell（店铺）备有，存有（货物）：*The shop stocks everything from pens to TV sets.* 这家店货品齐全，从钢笔到电视机一应俱全。

stock exchange *countable noun* 可数名词 a place where people buy and sell stocks in companies 证券交易所；股票交易所：*the New York Stock Exchange* 纽约证券交易所

stocking /ˈstɒkɪŋ/ *countable noun* 可数名词 a piece of women's clothing that fits closely over the foot and leg 长筒女袜：*a pair of nylon stockings* 一双尼龙长筒袜

stock market *countable noun* 可数名词 the activity of buying shares (= parts of a company's value）股市；股票市场：*This book is a practical guide to investing in the stock market.* 本书是股市投资的实用指南。

stole /stəʊl/
→ see 见 **steal**

stolen /ˈstəʊlən/
→ see 见 **steal**

stomach /ˈstʌmək/ *countable noun* 可数名词
1 the organ inside your body where food goes when you eat it 胃：*He has stomach problems.* 他有胃病。
2 the front part of your body below your waist 腹部；肚子：*The children lay down on their stomachs.* 孩子们趴了下来。
→ Look at picture on P4 参见彩插第 4 页

stone /stəʊn/ *noun* 名词
1 *uncountable* 不可数 a hard solid substance that is found in the ground and is often used for building 石头：*a stone floor* 石头地面
2 *countable* 可数 a small piece of rock that is found on the ground 石子；石块：*He removed a stone from his shoe.* 他倒掉鞋子里的一颗石子。
3 *countable* 可数 a piece of beautiful and valuable rock that is used in making jewellery 宝石：*He gave her a diamond ring with three stones.* 他送她一枚镶着 3 颗宝石的钻戒。

stood /stʊd/
→ see 见 **stand**

stool /stuːl/ *countable noun* 可数名词
a seat with legs and no support for your arms or back 凳子：*Kate sat on a stool in the corner of the room.* 凯特坐在房间角落的凳子上。

stop[1] /stɒp/ *verb* 动词 (**stops, stopping, stopped**)
1 to not do something any more 停止；停下；不再做：*Stop throwing those stones!* 别再扔那些石子了！□ *She stopped eating and started to laugh.* 她停止吃东西，大笑了起来。
2 to prevent something from happening 阻止；终止；结束：*They are trying to find a way to stop the war.* 他们在努力想办法结束战争。
3 to not happen any more 停；止住；不再发生：*The rain has stopped.* 雨已经停了。
4 to be no longer working 停止工作；不再运转：*The clock stopped at 11.59 on Saturday night.* 钟表停在了星期六夜里 11 点 59 分。
5 to not move any more 停住；停下；不再动：*The car failed to stop at a traffic light.* 汽车在一个红绿灯处没能停下来。□ *He stopped and waited for her.* 他停下来等她。

LANGUAGE HELP 语言提示
Stop doing or **stop to do something**? 用 stop doing something 还是 stop to do something？
When an action comes to an end, you say that someone **stops doing** it. 表示结束行动，用 stop doing something：*She stopped reading and closed the book.* 她停止阅读，合上了书。
If you say that someone **stops to do** something, you mean that they interrupt their activity in order to do that thing. 而 stop to do something 则表示中止活动去做某事：*I stopped to read the notices on the bulletin board.* 我停下来读布告栏上的告示。

stop[2] /stɒp/ *countable noun* 可数名词
a place where buses or trains regularly stop so that people can get on and off（公交车或列车的）停靠站：*Ann started to walk towards the bus stop.* 安迈步走向公交站。
come to a stop to slow down and no longer move 停住；停下来：*Do not open the door before the train comes to a stop.* 列车停稳前不要打开车门。
put a stop to something to prevent something from continuing 终止某事：*Our leaders must put a stop to the war.* 我们的领导人必须终止这场战争。

storage /ˈstɔːrɪdʒ/ *uncountable noun* 不可数名词
when you keep something in a special place until it is needed 储备；储藏；储存：*This room is used for storage.* 这间屋子作储藏室用。

store[1] /stɔː/ *countable noun* 可数名词
1 a large shop that sells many different products 商场；（大型）百货商店：*The company has 100 stores across the country.* 该公司在全国拥有 100 家百货商店。□ *This is my favourite high-street store.* 这是我最喜欢的一家商业区商场。
2 (*American* 美国英语) a shop of any size 商店，店铺（规模可大可小）：*a grocery store* 杂货店

store² /stɔː/ *verb* 动词 (**stores, storing, stored**)
to put things somewhere and leave them there until they are needed 储备；储藏；储存：*Store the biscuits in a tin.* 把饼干储存在罐子里。

storey /ˈstɔːri/ *countable noun* 可数名词
one of the different levels of a building（建筑物的）层：*Our block of flats is 25 storeys high.* 我们的公寓楼有25层高。

storm /stɔːm/ *countable noun* 可数名词
very bad weather, with heavy rain and strong winds 风暴：*There will be violent storms along the coast tonight.* 今夜沿海地区将有猛烈的风暴。

stormy /ˈstɔːmi/ *adjective* 形容词 (**stormier, stormiest**)
with strong winds and heavy rain 有风暴的：*Expect a night of stormy weather, with heavy rain and strong winds.* 预计将迎来一个风暴肆虐的夜晚，大雨滂沱，狂风大作。
→ Look at picture on P8 参见彩插第8页

story /ˈstɔːri/ *countable noun* 可数名词 (**stories**)
1 a description of imaginary people and events, that is intended to entertain people 故事：*I'm going to tell you a story about four little rabbits.* 我要给你们讲一个4只小兔子的故事。
2 a description of something that has happened 说法；叙述；描述：*The parents all had interesting stories about their children.* 家长们都讲了些儿女们的趣事。

stove /stəʊv/ *countable noun* 可数名词
a piece of equipment that provides heat, either for cooking or for heating a room 炉子：*She put the saucepan on the gas stove.* 她把炖锅放到燃气炉上。□ *There's a wood-burning stove in the living room.* 客厅里有一个烧柴的炉子。

straight /streɪt/ *adjective* 形容词, *adverb* 副词 (**straighter, straightest**)
1 continuing in one direction; not bending or curving 直的（地）；笔直的（地）：*Keep the boat moving in a straight line.* 让船走直线。□ *Grace had long straight hair.* 格雷丝的头发又长又直。□ *Stand straight and hold your arms out to the side.* 身体站直，双臂向两侧张开。□ *When he arrived, he went straight to his office.* 他赶到时，径直去了办公室。
2 clear and honest 直率的；直截了当的：*She tells lies all the time. I can't get a straight answer from her.* 她老是撒谎。我从她那里得不到直截了当的回答。
get something straight to make sure that you understand something properly (*informal* 非正式) 把某事物弄清楚；明确某事物：*Now, let me get this straight: you say that you were here all evening?* 好，让我把这事儿明确一下：你说你整晚都在这儿？

straighten /ˈstreɪtən/ *verb* 动词 (**straightens, straightening, straightened**)
1 to make something neat or put it in its proper position 整理；收拾；摆正…的位置：*She straightened a picture on the wall.* 她把墙上的一幅画扶正。
2 (also 亦作 **straighten up**) to make your back or body straight when you are standing 端正站姿；挺直身子：*The three men straightened and stood waiting.* *3名男子挺直身子，站着等候。□ *He straightened up and took his hands out of his pockets.* 他挺直身子，双手从兜里抽了出来。
3 to make something straight 弄直；使变直：*Straighten both legs.* 伸直双腿。

strain¹ /streɪn/ *noun* 名词
1 the state of having to do more than you are able to do 过劳；过度紧张：*She couldn't cope with the stresses and strains of her career.* 她应付不了事业的压力。
2 an injury to a muscle in your body, caused by using it too much（肌肉的）劳损：*Avoid muscle strain by taking rests.* 注意休息，避免肌肉劳损。

strain² /streɪn/ *verb* 动词 (**strains, straining, strained**)
1 to injure a muscle by using it too much 使（肌肉）劳损；拉伤：*He strained his back playing tennis.* 他打网球拉伤了背肌。
2 to make a great effort to do something 费力；竭力：*The music was so loud that I had to strain to hear what she was saying.* 音乐太聒噪，我得费很大力气听她说话。
3 to separate the liquid part of food from the solid parts 粗滤；过滤（食物）：*Strain the soup and put it back into the pan.* 滤掉汤然后放回锅里。

strange /streɪndʒ/ *adjective* 形容词 (**stranger, strangest**)
1 unusual or unexpected 奇怪的；出乎意料的：*There was something strange about the way she spoke.* 她说话的样子有点儿怪怪的。

▶**strangely** /ˈstreɪndʒli/ *adverb* 副词: *She noticed he was acting strangely.* 她注意到他表现怪怪的。
2 that you have never been to before 陌生的: *I was alone in a strange city.* 我孤身一人在一座陌生的城市。

stranger /ˈstreɪndʒə/ *countable noun* 可数名词
someone who you have never met before 陌生人: *We don't want a complete stranger staying with us.* 我们不想和一个素昧平生的陌生人待在一起。

strangle /ˈstræŋgəl/ *verb* 动词 (**strangles, strangling, strangled**)
to kill someone by pressing their throat tightly so that they cannot breathe 掐死；勒死；扼杀: *He tried to strangle a policeman.* 他企图勒死一名警察。

strap¹ /stræp/ *countable noun* 可数名词
a long, narrow piece of leather or other material 带子: *Nancy held the strap of her bag.* 南希抓着包带。□ *Her shoes had elastic ankle straps.* 她的鞋有弹性踝带。

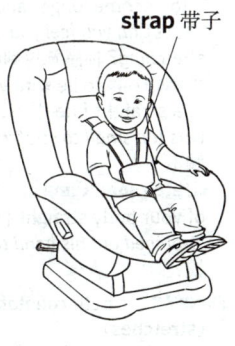
strap 带子

strap² /stræp/ *verb* 动词 (**straps, strapping, strapped**)
to fasten something somewhere with a strap 用带子固定；绑；系: *She strapped the baby seat into the car.* 她把婴儿座椅系到车上。

strategy /ˈstrætədʒi/ *noun* 名词 (**strategies**)
a general plan or set of plans for the future 战略；策略；规划: *Do you have a strategy for solving this type of problem?* 你们有解决这类问题的规划吗？

straw /strɔː/ *noun* 名词
1 *uncountable* 不可数 the dried, yellow stems of crops 禾秆；稻草: *The floor of the barn was covered with straw.* 谷仓地上尽是稻草。□ *a straw hat* 草帽
2 *countable* 可数 a thin tube that you use to suck a drink into your mouth 吸管: *I drank from a bottle of lemonade with a straw in it.* 我用吸管喝一瓶柠檬汽水。
the last straw or **the final straw** the last in a series of bad events that makes you feel that the situation is now impossible 最后一根稻草（指压垮人的最后一件坏事）: *When both children started crying, it was the last straw for their mother.* 两个孩子都哭了起来，做母亲的终于受不了了。

strawberry /ˈstrɔːbri/ *countable noun* 可数名词 (**strawberries**)
a small soft red fruit that has a lot of very small seeds on its skin 草莓: *strawberries and cream* 奶油草莓（一种甜点）

stray¹ /streɪ/ *verb* 动词 (**strays, straying, strayed**)
to go away from where you are supposed to be 偏离；走失；迷失: *Be careful not to stray into dangerous parts of the city.* 小心别误入城内的危险地段。

stray² /streɪ/ *adjective* 形容词
far away from home, or not having a home 流浪的；离家在外的: *A stray dog came up to him.* 一条流浪狗走到他跟前。● **stray** *countable noun* 可数名词: *The dog was a stray.* 这是条流浪狗。

streak /striːk/ *countable noun* 可数名词
a long mark on a surface 条纹；条痕: *There are dark streaks on the surface of the moon.* 月亮上有深色的条纹。

stream¹ /striːm/ *countable noun* 可数名词
1 a small narrow river 溪流；小河: *There was a small stream at the end of the garden.* 园子尽头有一条小溪。
2 a large number of things that come one after another 一连串: *The TV show caused a stream of complaints.* 这个电视节目招致一连串投诉。

stream² /striːm/ *verb* 动词 (**streams, streaming, streamed**)
1 to move somewhere in large amounts 涌流；涌动: *Tears streamed down their faces.* 眼泪顺着他们的脸颊往下流。□ *Sunlight was streaming into the room.* 阳光倾泻进屋里。
2 to play films, television programmes, or music directly over the Internet 流播（影片、电视节目或音乐）: *You can stream music to your stereo system from your mobile phone.* 你可以将音乐从手机流播到立体声音响。

street /striːt/ *countable noun* 可数名词
a road in a city or a town 街；街道: *The*

streets were crowded with shoppers. 街头购物者熙熙攘攘。▫ He lives at 66 Bingfield Street. 他住在宾菲尔德街 66 号。

strength /streŋθ/ *noun* 名词
1 *uncountable* 不可数 how physically strong you are 力量；力气；体力：*Swimming builds up the strength of your muscles.* 游泳可以增强肌肉力量。▫ *He threw the ball forward with all his strength.* 他用尽浑身力气把球扔向前方。
2 *uncountable* 不可数 your confidence or courage 信心；勇气：*He copes with his illness very well. His strength is amazing.* 他非常从容地面对疾病。他的勇气令人赞叹。
3 how strong something is 强度：*He checked the strength of the rope.* 他检查了一下绳子的强度。
4 the qualities and abilities that you have 强项；优点；长处：*Make a list of your strengths and weaknesses.* 列举一下你的优缺点。
5 *uncountable* 不可数 how deeply people feel or believe something（情感或信念的）强烈程度：*He was surprised at the strength of his own feeling.* 他讶异于自己情感之强烈。

strengthen /ˈstreŋθən/ *verb* 动词 (**strengthens, strengthening, strengthened**)
to make something stronger 增强；加强；强化：*Cycling strengthens all the muscles of the body.* 自行车运动可以强化人体所有肌肉。

stress¹ /stres/ *noun* 名词
1 an unpleasant feeling of worry caused by difficulties in life 精神压力；紧张情绪：*She's away from work suffering from stress.* 她不堪压力，休假了。▫ *I cannot think clearly when I'm under stress.* 我一紧张脑子就乱了。
2 when you say a word or part of a word slightly more loudly 重读；重音：*The stress is on the first part of the word 'animal'.* 重音在 animal 这个词的第一部分。

stress² /stres/ *verb* 动词 (**stresses, stressing, stressed**)
1 to make it clear that something is very important 强调；着重：*He stressed that the problem was not serious.* 他强调问题不严重。
2 to say something slightly more loudly 重读：*She stressed the words 'very important'.* 她重读了 very important（非常重要）这几个词。

stressed /strest/ *adjective* 形容词
feeling very worried because of difficulties in your life 紧张不安的；忧心忡忡的：*What situations make you feel stressed?* 什么情况让你焦虑不安？

stressful /ˈstresfl/ *adjective* 形容词
making you feel worried or upset 压力大的；令人紧张的：*She's got a very stressful job.* 她找了份压力很大的工作。

stretch¹ /stretʃ/ *verb* 动词 (**stretches, stretching, stretched**)
1 to cover all of a particular distance 延伸；绵延：*The queue of cars stretched for several miles.* 汽车队伍排了好几英里。
2 to put your arms or legs out very straight 伸展，舒展（胳膊或腿）：*He yawned and stretched.* 他打了个哈欠，伸了伸懒腰。
3 to become longer and thinner 拉伸；变细长：*Can you feel your leg muscles stretching?* 你感觉得到腿部肌肉拉伸吗？
stretch out to lie with your legs and body in a straight line 平躺；躺直：*The bath was too small to stretch out in.* 浴缸太小，躺不下。
stretch something out to hold out a part of your body straight 伸出（身体部位）：*He stretched out his hand to touch me.* 他伸手摸我。

stretch² /stretʃ/ *countable noun* 可数名词 (**stretches**)
a length or an area of land or water（土地或水域的）一段，一片：*It's a very dangerous stretch of road.* 这段路非常危险。

stretcher /ˈstretʃə/ *countable noun* 可数名词
a long piece of strong material with a pole along each side, used for carrying an injured or ill person 担架：*They put him on a stretcher and lifted him into the ambulance.* 他们把他放上担架，抬进了救护车。

strict /strɪkt/ *adjective* 形容词 (**stricter, strictest**)
1 very clear; that you must obey completely 明确的；严明的：*She gave them strict instructions not to get out of the car.* 她严令他们不要下车。▫ *The school's rules are very strict.* 该校校规非常严格。
▸ **strictly** /ˈstrɪktli/ *adverb* 副词：*The number of new members each year is strictly controlled.* 每年会员人数有严格控制。
2 expecting rules to be obeyed and people

to behave properly 严格的；严厉的：*My parents were very strict.* 我爸妈非常严厉。
▶ **strictly** /ˈstrɪktli/ ***adverb*** 副词：*They brought their children up very strictly.* 他们对孩子从小到大的管教都很严格。

stride /straɪd/ ***verb*** 动词 (**strides, striding, strode**)
to walk with long steps 大步走：*The farmer came striding across the field.* 农场主大步流星地穿过田地走来。● **stride** *countable noun* 可数名词：*He crossed the street with long, quick strides.* 他迈开大步快速过了马路。

strike¹ /straɪk/ ***verb*** 动词 (**strikes, striking, struck**)
1 to hit something (*formal* 正式) 击打；撞击：*She took two steps forward and struck him across the face.* 她上前两步打了他一耳光。□ *His head struck the bottom when he dived into the pool.* 他往泳池里扎时头撞到了池底。
2 to have a quick and violent effect 侵袭；袭击：*A storm struck the northeastern United States on Saturday.* 星期六一场风暴袭击了美国东北部。
3 to come suddenly into your mind 闪现在⋯脑海：*A thought struck her. Was she jealous of her mother?* 一个想法突然冒了出来。她嫉妒自己的母亲吗？
4 when a clock strikes, it makes a sound so that people know what the time is（钟）敲响：*The clock struck nine.* 时钟敲响9点。
5 to stop working, usually in order to try to get more money 罢工：*Workers have the right to strike.* 工人有权利罢工。
strike a match to make a match produce a flame by moving it against something rough 划火柴：*Duncan struck a match and lit the fire.* 邓肯划着一根火柴点着火。

strike² /straɪk/ ***countable noun*** 可数名词
a period of time when workers stop working, usually in order to try to get more money 罢工：*Staff at the hospital went on strike yesterday.* 医院员工昨天罢工了。

string /strɪŋ/ ***noun*** 名词
1 very thin rope that is made of twisted threads 线绳；细绳；线；带子：*He held out a small bag tied with string.* 他拿出一个系着细绳的小袋子。
2 *countable* 可数 a number of things on a piece of thread 串：*She wore a string of pearls around her neck.* 她脖子上戴着一串珍珠。
3 *countable* 可数 one of the thin pieces of wire that are stretched across a musical instrument and make sounds when the instrument is played（乐器的）弦：*Suddenly one of his guitar strings snapped.* 突然他的吉他断了一根弦。

stringed ˈinstrument ***countable noun*** 可数名词
any musical instrument that has strings 弦乐器
→ Look at picture on P12 参见彩插第 12 页

strip¹ /strɪp/ ***countable noun*** 可数名词
1 a long, narrow piece of something 条；带：*The rugs are made from strips of fabric.* 这些小地毯是用布条做成的。
2 a long narrow area of something 条状（或带状）区域：*He owns a narrow strip of land along the coast.* 他在海边有一块狭长的地。

strip² /strɪp/ ***verb*** 动词 (**strips, stripping, stripped**)
(also 亦作 **strip off**) to take off your clothes 脱衣：*They stripped and jumped into the pool.* 他们脱掉衣服跳进泳池。□ *The children were stripping off and running into the sea.* 孩子们在脱衣服往海里冲。

stripe /straɪp/ ***countable noun*** 可数名词
a long line that is a different colour from the areas next to it 条纹；斑纹：*She wore a blue skirt with white stripes.* 她穿了一条蓝底白条纹的半身裙。

striped /straɪpt/ ***adjective*** 形容词
having stripes 有条纹的：*a striped tie* 条纹领带

strode /stroʊd/
→ see 见 **stride**

stroke¹ /stroʊk/ ***verb*** 动词 (**strokes, stroking, stroked**)
to move your hand slowly and gently over someone or something 轻抚；抚摸：*Carla was stroking her cat.* 卡拉抚摸着她的猫。

stroke² /stroʊk/ ***countable noun*** 可数名词
1 a movement or mark that you make with a pen or a brush 一笔；一画；笔画：*She added a few brush strokes to the painting.* 她给这幅画添了几笔。
2 a movement that you make with your arms when you are swimming or playing some sports 划水；挥臂；挥击：*I turned and swam a few strokes further out to sea.*

我转身朝海里又游了几下。
3 a serious illness where the blood does not flow through your brain properly（脑）卒中；中风：*He had a stroke last year, and now he can't walk.* 他去年中风了，现在走不了路。

stroll /strəʊl/ *verb* 动词 (**strolls, strolling, strolled**)
to walk in a slow, relaxed way 散步；溜达；慢悠悠地走：*We love strolling along by the river.* 我们喜欢在河边散步。● **stroll** *countable noun* 可数名词：*After dinner, I took a stroll around the city.* 饭后，我在城里溜达了一会儿。

strong /strɒŋ/ *adjective* 形容词 (**stronger** /ˈstrɒŋɡə/, **strongest** /ˈstrɒŋɡɪst/)
1 healthy, with good muscles 强壮的；强健的；健壮的：*I'm not strong enough to carry him.* 我力气不够，背不动他。
2 confident and determined 坚决的；坚定的：*You have to be strong and do what you believe is right.* 你得坚决、认准的事就去做。
3 not breaking easily 结实的；坚固的：*This strong plastic will not crack.* 这种结实的塑料不会破裂。
▶ **strongly** /ˈstrɒŋli/ *adverb* 副词：*The wall was very strongly built.* 这堵墙建得很坚固。
4 that you will not change easily 坚定的；强硬的；不易改变的：*She has strong views on environmental issues.* 她在环境问题上态度很强硬。□ *He has strong beliefs and ideas.* 他的思想根深蒂固。
▶ **strongly** /ˈstrɒŋli/ *adverb* 副词：*Obviously you feel very strongly about this.* 显然你对此看法很坚定。
5 containing a lot of a particular substance in order to be effective 浓烈的；强效的：*a cup of strong coffee* 一杯浓咖啡 □ *The doctor gave me some strong painkillers.* 大夫给我开了些强效止痛药。
6 easily noticed 明显的；易察觉的：*Onions have a strong flavour.* 洋葱味儿很大。□ *There was a strong smell of paint in the house.* 房子里油漆味儿很大。
▶ **strongly** /ˈstrɒŋli/ *adverb* 副词：*He smelled strongly of sweat.* 他身上汗味儿很重。

struck /strʌk/
→ see 见 **strike**

structure /ˈstrʌktʃə/ *noun* 名词
1 the way in which something is made, built or organized 结构；构造：*The typical family structure was two parents and two children.* 典型的家庭结构是一对父母、两个孩子。
2 *countable* 可数 something that consists of parts that are connected together in an ordered way 结构体：*She had beautiful bone structure and great big eyes.* 她骨架漂亮，眼睛又大又好看。□ *This week's lesson is about the structure of the human brain.* 本周讲的是人脑结构。
3 *countable* 可数 something that has been built 建筑物：*This modern brick and glass structure was built in 1905.* 这座砖块玻璃的现代建筑建于 1905 年。

struggle¹ /ˈstrʌɡəl/ *verb* 动词 (**struggles, struggling, struggled**)
1 to try hard to do something that you find very difficult 努力；奋力；争取：*She struggled to find the right words.* 她搜索枯肠寻找恰当的词。
2 to try very hard to get away from someone who is holding you 挣扎；努力挣脱：*I struggled, but she was too strong for me.* 我使劲挣扎，但她太壮了。

struggle² /ˈstrʌɡəl/ *noun* 名词
1 *singular* 单数 something that is very difficult to do 难事：*Losing weight was a terrible struggle.* 减肥是一件非常难的事。
2 a long and difficult attempt to achieve something such as freedom 斗争；奋斗：*The movie is about a young boy's struggle to survive.* 影片讲述了一个小男孩奋力求生的故事。

stubborn /ˈstʌbən/ *adjective* 形容词
determined to do what you want 倔强的；固执的；执拗的：*I am a very stubborn and determined person.* 我是个非常倔强而坚定的人。
▶ **stubbornly** /ˈstʌbənli/ *adverb* 副词：*He stubbornly refused to tell her the truth.* 他固执地拒绝告诉她真相。

stuck¹ /stʌk/
→ see 见 **stick**

stuck² /stʌk/ *adjective* 形容词
unable to move 被卡住了的；动弹不得的：*His car was stuck in the snow.* 他的车陷进了雪里。

be/get stuck
1 to want to get away from somewhere boring or from an unpleasant situation, but to be unable to do so 被困（某地）；陷入（窘境）：*I don't want to get stuck in another job like that.* 我不想陷入又一份类

似的工作。□ *The airport's closed, so we're stuck in this hotel.* 机场关闭了，我们被困在这家宾馆。
2 to be unable to continue doing something because it is too difficult 被难住；难以继续：*The teacher will help if you get stuck.* 被难住的话，老师会帮忙。

student /ˈstjuːdənt/ *countable noun* 可数名词
a person who is studying at a university, college, or school 学生：*Warren's eldest son is an art student.* 沃伦的大儿子在读艺术专业。
→ Look at picture on P1 参见彩插第 1 页

studies /ˈstʌdiz/ *plural noun* 复数名词
the activity of learning about a particular subject（特定主题的）学习，研究：*In 1924, he went to Paris where he continued his studies in painting, sculpture and drawing.* *1924 年，他前往巴黎继续学习油画、雕塑和素描。

studio /ˈstjuːdiəʊ/ *countable noun* 可数名词
1 a room where someone paints, draws or takes photographs（绘画、摄影等的）工作室：*She was in her studio, painting on a large canvas.* 她在画室里，正在一块大画布上作画。
2 a room where people make radio or television programmes, record CDs, or make films 录音室；演播室；摄影棚：*a New York recording studio* 纽约的一个录音棚

study¹ /ˈstʌdi/ *verb* 动词 (**studies, studying, studied**)
1 to spend time learning about a particular subject 学习；攻读：*She spends most of her time studying.* 她大部分时间用在学习上。□ *He studied History and Economics at university.* 他在大学学习历史和经济。
2 to look at or consider something very carefully 审视；细致考虑：*Debbie studied her friend's face.* 黛比审视了友人的脸。

study² /ˈstʌdi/ *noun* 名词 (**studies**)
1 the activity of studying 学习；研究：*'What is the study of animals called?' — 'Zoology.'* "对动物的研究叫什么？" ——"动物学。"
→ Look at picture on P1 参见彩插第 1 页
2 *countable* 可数 a room in a house that is used for reading, writing and studying 书房：*We sat together in his study.* 我们一起坐在他的书房里。

stuff¹ /stʌf/ *uncountable noun* 不可数名词
things in general (*informal* 非正式)（泛指）东西，物品：*He pointed to a bag. 'That's my stuff.'* 他指着一个袋子说："那是我的东西。" □ *There is a huge amount of useful stuff on the Internet.* 因特网上有用的东西非常多。

stuff² /stʌf/ *verb* 动词 (**stuffs, stuffing, stuffed**)
1 to push something somewhere quickly and roughly 塞：*I stuffed the money into my pocket.* 我把钱塞进口袋。
2 to put a mixture of one type of food inside another type of food 给…填馅（或加填料）：*Stuff the mushrooms with cheese and put them in the oven for 5 minutes.* 给蘑菇填上干酪，放烤箱里烤 5 分钟。
□ *stuffed olives* 酿橄榄

stuffy /ˈstʌfi/ *adjective* 形容词 (**stuffier, stuffiest**)
warm; without enough fresh air 暖烘烘的；憋闷的：*It was hot and stuffy in the classroom.* 教室里又热又闷。

stumble /ˈstʌmbəl/ *verb* 动词 (**stumbles, stumbling, stumbled**)
to nearly fall down while you are walking or running 绊脚；趔趄；踉跄：*He stumbled on the pavement and almost fell.* 他在人行道上绊了一下，差点儿摔倒。

stump /stʌmp/ *countable noun* 可数名词
a small part of something that remains when the rest of it has been removed or broken off 茬；残根；残余部分：*a tree stump* 树桩

tree stump 树桩

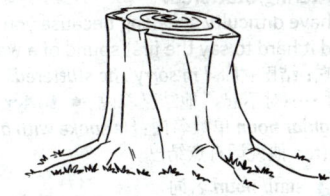

stun /stʌn/ *verb* 动词 (**stuns, stunning, stunned**)
1 to shock or surprise someone so much that they are unable to speak 使惊呆；使目瞪口呆：*We were stunned by his sudden death.* 他的突然死亡让我们震惊。
2 to make you unconscious for a short time 打昏；使昏迷：*The blow to his head stunned him.* 他头上挨了一击，昏迷过去。

stung /stʌŋ/
→ see 见 **sting**

stunk /stʌŋk/
→ see 见 **stink**

stunning /ˈstʌnɪŋ/ *adjective* 形容词
extremely beautiful 极美的；令人惊艳的：*She was 55 and still a stunning woman.* 她时年55岁，依然魅力四射。

stunt /stʌnt/ *countable noun* 可数名词
a dangerous piece of action in a film (影片中的) 特技：*This movie has some amazing stunts.* 这部影片有一些令人叫绝的特技。

stupid /ˈstjuːpɪd/ *adjective* 形容词 (**stupider, stupidest**)
not sensible 傻的；愚蠢的：*I'll never do anything so stupid again.* 我再也不做这么蠢的事了。 □ *I made a stupid mistake.* 我犯了一个愚蠢的错误。
▶ **stupidly** /ˈstjuːpɪdli/ *adverb* 副词：*I'm sorry. I behaved stupidly.* 对不起。我表现得真傻。
▶ **stupidity** /stjuːˈpɪdɪti/ *uncountable noun* 不可数名词：*I was surprised by his stupidity.* 他的愚蠢让我惊讶。

sturdy /ˈstɜːdi/ *adjective* 形容词 (**sturdier, sturdiest**)
strong; unlikely to be easily hurt or damaged 强壮的；结实的；坚固的：*She was a short, sturdy woman.* 她是一个矮小结实的女人。□ *Bring a hat, sunscreen and wear sturdy shoes.* 带上帽子、防晒霜，穿上结实的鞋子。
▶ **sturdily** /ˈstɜːdɪli/ *adverb* 副词：*The table was strong and sturdily built.* 桌子很结实，做得很牢固。

stutter /ˈstʌtə/ *verb* 动词 (**stutters, stuttering, stuttered**)
to have difficulty speaking because you find it hard to say the first sound of a word 口吃；结巴：*'I ... I'm sorry', he stuttered.* "对……对不起。"他结巴着说。● **stutter** *singular noun* 单数名词：*He spoke with a stutter.* 他说话有点结巴。

style /staɪl/ *noun* 名词
1 *countable* 可数 the way in which something is done 方式；风格；作风：*Children have different learning styles.* 孩子们的学习方式不同。□ *I prefer the Indian style of cooking.* 我喜欢印式烹饪。
2 the design of something 设计；款式；样式：*These kids want everything in the latest style.* 这些孩子什么都想要最新款式的。

stylish /ˈstaɪlɪʃ/ *adjective* 形容词
attractive and fashionable 时髦的；时尚的；入时的：*She was an attractive, stylish woman.* 她是个有魅力的时髦女人。

subject /ˈsʌbdʒɪkt/ *countable noun* 可数名词
1 the thing that is being discussed in a conversation or a book (谈话或图书的) 主题，题目，话题：*I'd like to hear the president's own views on the subject.* 我想听听总统本人对这个问题的看法。
2 an area of knowledge that you study in school, university or college 学科；科目；课程：*Maths is my favourite subject.* 数学是我最喜欢的科目。
3 in grammar, the noun that talks about the person or thing that is doing the action expressed by the verb. For example, in 'My cat keeps catching birds', 'my cat' is the subject. 主语
4 the person or thing that is shown in a piece of art (艺术表现的) 对象，题材：*Spring flowers are a perfect subject for painting.* 春花是绘画的绝佳题材。

subjective /səbˈdʒektɪv/ *adjective* 形容词
based on personal opinions and feelings rather than on facts 主观的：*Art is very subjective.* 艺术非常主观。

submarine /ˌsʌbməˈriːn/ *countable noun* 可数名词
a type of ship that can travel below the surface of the sea 潜艇：*a nuclear submarine* 核潜艇

submit /səbˈmɪt/ *verb* 动词 (**submits, submitting, submitted**)
to formally send something to someone, so that they can consider it 提交；递交；呈递：*They submitted their reports yesterday.* 他们昨天提交了报告。

subscription /səbˈskrɪpʃən/ *countable noun* 可数名词
an amount of money that you pay regularly in order to belong to an organization or to receive a service 会员费；订购费：*Members pay a subscription every year.* 会员每年要交会费。

subsidy /ˈsʌbsɪdi/ *countable noun* 可数名词 (**subsidies**)
money that a government pays in order to help an industry or a business (政府) 补贴：*farming subsidies* 农业补贴

substance /ˈsʌbstəns/ *countable noun* 可数名词
a solid, a powder, a liquid or a gas 物质：

The waste contained several unpleasant substances. 这种废弃物含有几种有害物质。

substantial /səbˈstænʃəl/ *adjective* 形容词 very large (*formal* 正式) 巨大的；庞大的：A substantial number of people disagree with the new plan. 很多人不赞成这个新方案。

substitute /ˈsʌbstɪˌtjuːt/ *verb* 动词 (**substitutes**, **substituting**, **substituted**) to make one person or thing take the place of another person or thing (用…)替代，替换，替补：You can substitute wholewheat flour for white flour. 你可以用全麦面代替白面。□ Goalkeeper Aidan Davison was substituted at half-time because of an injury. 半场时守门员艾丹·戴维森因伤被替换下场。● **substitute** *countable noun* 可数名词：Many teachers worry that pupils are using calculators as a substitute for thinking. 许多教师担心学生用计算器代替思考。□ Jefferson entered as a substitute for the injured player. 杰斐逊替补受伤队员登场。

subtle /ˈsʌtəl/ *adjective* 形容词 (**subtler**, **subtlest**)
1 not immediately obvious 不明显的；细微的：Subtle changes take place in all living things. 所有生物都会发生细微变化。
▶ **subtly** /ˈsʌtəli/ *adverb* 副词：The truth is subtly different. 真相略有出入。
2 pleasant and delicate in smell, taste, sound or colour (气味或味道) 清淡的；(声音或色彩) 淡淡的：Brown, grey or subtle shades of purple suit you best. 褐色、灰色或淡紫色系最适合你。

subtract /səbˈtrækt/ *verb* 动词 (**subtracts**, **subtracting**, **subtracted**) to take one number away from another number. For example, if you subtract 3 from 5, you get 2. 减；减去
▶ **subtraction** /səbˈtrækʃən/ *uncountable noun* 不可数名词：She's ready to learn subtraction. 她准备好学减法了。

suburb /ˈsʌbɜːb/ *countable noun* 可数名词 one of the areas on the edge of a city where many people live 郊区；城郊：Anna was born in a suburb of Philadelphia. 安娜出生于费城郊区。□ His family lives in the suburbs. 他们家住在郊区。

suburban /səˈbɜːbən/ *adjective* 形容词 in or relating to the suburbs 郊区的；城郊的：They have a comfortable suburban home. 他们有一套舒适的郊区住房。

subway /ˈsʌbweɪ/ *noun* 名词
1 *countable* 可数 a path that goes under a road so that people can cross safely 地下通道
2 *uncountable* 不可数 (*American* 美国英语) → see 见 **underground**

succeed /səkˈsiːd/ *verb* 动词 (**succeeds**, **succeeding**, **succeeded**) to get the result that you wanted 成功；达到目的：We have already succeeded in starting our own company. 我们已经成功开办了自己的公司。□ Do you think he will succeed? 你觉得他会成功吗？

success /səkˈses/ *noun* 名词 (**successes**)
1 *uncountable* 不可数 when you do well and get the result that you wanted 成功；胜利：Hard work is the key to success. 勤奋乃成功之钥。□ We were surprised by the play's success. 我们对该剧的成功感到惊讶。
2 *countable* 可数 someone or something that does very well, or that is admired very much 成功的人 (或事物)：We hope the movie will be a success. 我们希望影片取得成功。

successful /səkˈsesful/ *adjective* 形容词 doing or getting what you wanted 成功的；达到目的的：Kate's job application was successful. 凯特求职成功了。
▶ **successfully** /səkˈsesfuli/ *adverb* 副词：The disease can be successfully treated with drugs. 这种病可以用药物治好。

such /sʌtʃ/ *adjective* 形容词
1 like this or like that 这样的；那样的；此类的：How could you do such a thing? 你怎么能做这种事呢？
2 used for making an uncountable or plural noun stronger (用于不可数或复数名词前以加强语气) 这么的，如此的：These roads are not designed for such heavy traffic. 这些道路的设计交通量没这么大。

such a(n) used for making a noun stronger (用于名词前以加强语气) 这么一个：It was such a pleasant surprise. 那真是一个大大的惊喜。

such as used for introducing an example 例如；比如：Avoid fatty food such as butter and red meat. 避免吃黄油、红肉等高脂食物。

suck /sʌk/ *verb* 动词 (**sucks**, **sucking**, **sucked**)
1 to hold something in your mouth for a

long time 含；吮：*They sucked their sweets noisily.* 他们吧唧吧唧地含着糖果。▫ *Many young children suck their thumbs.* 许多小孩儿吮拇指。
2 to pull liquid into your mouth through your lips 吸；咂：*The baby sucked the milk from his bottle.* 宝宝吮吸奶瓶子里的奶。

sudden /ˈsʌdən/ *adjective* 形容词
happening quickly and unexpectedly 突然的；骤然的；猝然的：*He was shocked by the sudden death of his father.* 他对父亲猝亡感到震惊。▫ *It was all very sudden.* 这一切都非常突然。
▶ **suddenly** /ˈsʌdənli/ *adverb* 副词：*Suddenly, she looked ten years older.* 突然之间，她看上去老了 10 岁。▫ *Her expression suddenly changed.* 她突然脸色一变。
all of a sudden quickly and unexpectedly 突然；*All of a sudden she didn't look tired anymore.* 她似乎一下子没了倦意。

sudoku /suˈdəʊkuː/ *noun* 名词
a puzzle that involves putting the numbers 1 to 9 in squares, without repeating any of the numbers in the same row, column or box of nine squares 数独（游戏）

sue /suː/ *verb* 动词 (**sues, suing, sued**)
to start a legal case against someone, usually in order to get money from them because they have harmed you（通常为索赔）起诉，控告：*The couple are suing the company for $4.4 million.* 夫妇俩起诉公司索赔 440 万美元。

suffer /ˈsʌfə/ *verb* 动词 (**suffers, suffering, suffered**)
1 to feel pain, sadness or worry 遭受，经受（疼痛、悲伤或忧虑）：*She was very sick, and suffering great pain.* 她病得很重，疼得厉害。▫ *He has suffered terribly the last few days.* 他过去几天遭了大罪。
2 to be affected by an illness（因病）受影响，受罪：*He was suffering from cancer.* 他遭受着癌症之苦。
▶ **sufferer** /ˈsʌfərə/ *countable noun* 可数名词：*asthma sufferers* 哮喘患者

suffering /ˈsʌfərɪŋ/ *noun* 名词
the pain, sadness or worry that someone feels 痛苦；苦难；折磨：*They began to recover from their pain and suffering.* 他们开始走出痛苦和苦难。

sufficient /səˈfɪʃənt/ *adjective* 形容词
as much of something as you need or want 足够的；充足的：*The food we have is sufficient for 12 people.* 我们的食物够 12 个人吃。
▶ **sufficiently** /səˈfɪʃəntli/ *adverb* 副词：*She recovered sufficiently to go on holiday.* 她恢复得不错，可以去度假了。

suffix /ˈsʌfɪks/ *countable noun* 可数名词 (**suffixes**)
a letter or a group of letters, for example '-ly' or '-ness', that is added to the end of a word in order to form a different word, often of a different word class. For example, the suffix '-ly' is added to 'quick' to form 'quickly'. Compare with **prefix**. 后缀（比较 prefix）

suffocate /ˈsʌfəkeɪt/ *verb* 动词 (**suffocates, suffocating, suffocated**)
to die because there is no air to breathe 窒息而死；闷死：*He either suffocated, or froze to death.* 他不是闷死的，就是冻死的。

suffragist /ˈsʌfrədʒɪst/ *countable noun* 可数名词
a person who believes that all adults in a particular country should have the right to vote. Suffragists often fight for women to be allowed to vote.（常指为女性）争取平等选举权者

sugar /ˈʃʊɡə/ *uncountable noun* 不可数名词
a sweet substance used for making food and drinks taste sweet 食糖：*Do you take sugar in your coffee?* 您的咖啡放糖吗？▫ *a bag of brown sugar* 一袋红糖

suggest /səˈdʒest/ *verb* 动词 (**suggests, suggesting, suggested**)
to tell someone what you think they should do 建议；提议：*I suggest you ask him some questions about his past.* 我建议你问他一些关于他过去的问题。▫ *I suggested we go for a walk in the park.* 我提议我们到公园里走一走。

> **LANGUAGE HELP** 语言提示
> Note that you **suggest something to someone**. 注意，向某人提建议要用 suggest something to someone：*John suggested this idea to me.* 约翰给我提了这个建议。
> Note also that you **suggest that someone does something**. 还要注意，suggest 后接 that 从句时，从句中的动词用现在式：*I suggest that you put some of the money in a bank account.* 我建议你把一些钱存进银行账户。

suggestion /səˈdʒestʃən/ *countable noun* 可数名词
something that you tell someone they should do 建议；提议：*Do you have any suggestions for improving the service we provide?* 您对我们提供的服务有什么改进意见吗？ □ *May I make a suggestion?* 我说个提议好吗？

suicide /ˈsuːɪsaɪd/ *noun* 名词
the act of killing yourself 自杀：*She tried to commit suicide several times.* 她曾几次试图自杀。 □ *It was obviously a case of attempted suicide.* 这显然是自杀未遂。

suit¹ /suːt/ *countable noun* 可数名词
1 a jacket and trousers or a jacket and skirt that are both made from the same cloth 套装：*a dark business suit* 深色商务套装
2 a piece of clothing that you wear for a particular activity（参加特定活动时穿的）服装：*The divers wore special rubber suits.* 潜水员穿了专门的橡胶服。

suit² /suːt/ *verb* 动词 (**suits, suiting, suited**)
1 to make you look attractive 适合；与…相配；使显得好看：*Green suits you.* 绿色适合你。 □ *Isabel's soft woollen dress suited her very well.* 伊莎贝尔柔软的羊毛连衣裙非常适合她。
2 to be convenient for you 对…方便：*With online shopping, you can do your shopping when it suits you.* 有了在线购物，你随时可以买东西。

> **LANGUAGE HELP** 语言提示
> **Suit** or **fit**? 用 suit 还是 fit？
> If something looks attractive on a person, use **suit**. 表示某物由某人穿戴起来很好看，用 suit：*Do you think green suits me?* 你觉得我穿绿色好看吗？
> If clothes are the right size for someone, use **fit**. 表示衣物尺寸合适，用 fit：*These gloves fit me perfectly.* 这副手套我戴着大小正合适。

suitable /ˈsuːtəbl/ *adjective* 形容词
right for a particular purpose or occasion 合适的；适当的；适宜的：*This film is suitable for young children.* 这部影片适合少儿观看。
▶ **suitably** /ˈsuːtəbli/ *adverb* 副词：*He was suitably dressed for the occasion.* 他的着装很适合这个场合。

suitcase /ˈsuːtkeɪs/ *countable noun* 可数名词
a case for carrying your clothes when you are travelling（旅行用的）手提箱：*It did not take Andrew long to pack a suitcase.* 安德鲁没花多长时间就打包好了手提箱。

sulk /sʌlk/ *verb* 动词 (**sulks, sulking, sulked**)
to be silent for a while because you are angry about something 生闷气：*He turned his back and sulked.* 他转过身生起了闷气。
▶ **sulky** /ˈsʌlki/ *adjective* 形容词：*I was a sulky, 14-year-old teenager.* 我当时是个闷闷不乐的 14 岁少年。

sum /sʌm/ *noun* 名词
1 *countable* 可数 an amount of money 金额；钱数：*Large sums of money were lost.* 亏了很多钱。
2 *singular* 单数 in mathematics, the number that you get when you add two or more numbers together 和；总数：*Fourteen is the sum of eight and six.* 14 是 8 和 6 之和。

summarize /ˈsʌməraɪz/ *verb* 动词 (**summarizes, summarizing, summarized**)
to give the most important points about something 总结；概括；概述：*Now summarize the article in three sentences.* 现在用三句话总结一下这篇文章。

summary /ˈsʌməri/ *countable noun* 可数名词 (**summaries**)
a short description of something that gives the main points but not the details 总结；概述；摘要：*Here is a short summary of the news.* 下面是简短的新闻摘要。

summer /ˈsʌmə/ *noun* 名词
the season between spring and autumn. In the summer the weather is usually warm or hot. 夏天；夏季：*I went to France this summer.* 我今年夏天去了法国。 □ *It was a perfect summer's day.* 那是一个美好的夏日。
→ Look at picture on P8 参见彩插第 8 页

summit /ˈsʌmɪt/ *countable noun* 可数名词
1 a meeting between the leaders of two or more countries 峰会；首脑会议：*The topic will be discussed at next week's Washington summit.* 这个话题将在下周华盛顿峰会上讨论。
2 the top of a mountain 山顶；顶峰：*He wanted to be the first man to reach the summit of Mount Qomolangma.* 他想成为第一个登顶珠峰的人。

summon /ˈsʌmən/ *verb* 动词 (**summons, summoning, summoned**)
to order someone to come to you (*formal*

正式）召唤；召见；传唤：The queen summoned her guards. 女王召唤卫士。▫ Suddenly we were summoned to his office. 我们突然被召集到了他的办公室。

sun /sʌn/ *noun* 名词
1 *singular* 单数 the ball of fire in the sky that gives us heat and light 太阳；日：The sun was now high in the sky. 太阳此刻高挂在天上。▫ Suddenly, the sun came out. 突然，太阳出来了。
2 *uncountable* 不可数 the heat and light that comes from the sun 阳光；日光：They went outside to sit in the sun. 他们出门坐在阳光下。

sunbathe /ˈsʌnbeɪð/ *verb* 动词 (**sunbathes, sunbathing, sunbathed**)
to sit or lie in a place where the sun shines on you, so that your skin becomes browner 晒太阳；晒日光浴：Frank swam and sunbathed at the pool every morning. 弗兰克每天早上在泳池游泳、晒日光浴。
▸ **sunbathing** /ˈsʌnbeɪðɪŋ/ *uncountable noun* 不可数名词：The beach is perfect for sunbathing. 沙滩特别适合日光浴。

sunburn /ˈsʌnbɜːn/ *uncountable noun* 不可数名词
pink sore skin that you get when you have spent too much time in the sun 晒伤：Sunburn can damage your skin. 晒伤会损伤皮肤。

sunburned /ˈsʌnbɜːnd/ *also* 亦作 **sunburnt** /ˈsʌnbɜːnt/ *adjective* 形容词
having pink, sore skin because you have spent too much time in the sun 晒伤的：A badly sunburned face is extremely painful. 脸被严重晒伤时特别疼。

sundae /ˈsʌndeɪ/ *countable noun* 可数名词
a tall glass of ice cream (= a frozen sweet food) with cream and nuts or fruit on top 圣代冰激凌：We had ice cream sundaes for dessert. 我们甜点吃了圣代冰激凌。

Sunday /ˈsʌndeɪ, -di/ *noun* 名词
the day after Saturday and before Monday 星期日：We went for a walk on Sunday. 我们周日出门散了个步。

sunflower /ˈsʌnflaʊə/ *countable noun* 可数名词
a very tall plant with large yellow flowers 向日葵

sung /sʌŋ/
→ see 见 **sing**

sunglasses /ˈsʌnɡlɑːsɪz/ *plural noun* 复数名词
dark glasses that you wear to protect your eyes from bright light 太阳镜；墨镜：She put on a pair of sunglasses. 她戴上了一副太阳镜。

sunk /sʌŋk/
→ see 见 **sink**

sunlight /ˈsʌnlaɪt/ *uncountable noun* 不可数名词
the light that comes from the sun 阳光：Sunlight filled the room. 阳光洒满了房间。

sunny /ˈsʌni/ *adjective* 形容词 (**sunnier, sunniest**)
1 with the sun shining brightly 晴朗的；阳光明媚的：The weather was warm and sunny. 天气温暖，阳光明媚。
→ Look at picture on P8 参见彩插第 8 页
2 being brightly lit by the sun 阳光照耀的；被阳光照亮的：a sunny window seat 阳光充足的靠窗座位

sunrise /ˈsʌnraɪz/ *uncountable noun* 不可数名词
the time in the morning when the sun first appears in the sky 日出：The rain began before sunrise. 日出前开始下雨。

sunscreen /ˈsʌnskriːn/ *uncountable noun* 不可数名词
a cream that protects your skin from the sun 防晒霜；防晒油：Use a sunscreen when you go outside. 出门要抹防晒霜。

sunset /ˈsʌnset/ *uncountable noun* 不可数名词
the time in the evening when the sun goes down 日落：The party began at sunset. 聚会在日落时分开始。

sunshine /ˈsʌnʃaɪn/ *uncountable noun* 不可数名词
the light and heat that comes from the sun 阳光；日光：She was sitting outside a cafe in bright sunshine. 她坐在一个咖啡馆外面明媚的阳光下。

suntan /ˈsʌntæn/ *countable noun* 可数名词
when your skin becomes darker because you have been outside in the sun 晒黑：They want to go to the Bahamas and get a suntan. 他们想去巴哈马把皮肤晒黑。

super /ˈsuːpə/ *adjective* 形容词, *adverb* 副词
1 very good 非常好的；超级棒的：That was a super concert. 那是一场超级棒的音乐会。
2 having a lot of a particular quality 十分；特别；格外：Beverly Hills, home of the rich

and the super rich 贝弗利山庄，有钱人和超级有钱人的住宅区

superb /suːˈpɜːb/ *adjective* 形容词
very good 非常好的：*There is a superb golf course 6 miles away.* 离这儿 6 英里有座特别棒的高尔夫球场。
- **superbly** /suːˈpɜːbli/ *adverb* 副词：*The orchestra played superbly.* 管弦乐队的演奏非常精彩。

superior¹ /suːˈpɪəriə/ *adjective* 形容词
better than other similar people or things 优于他人的；优质的：*We want to create superior products for our customers.* 我们想给顾客生产出高质量的产品。▫ *superior quality coffee* 品质卓越的咖啡
- **superiority** /suːˌpɪəriˈɒrɪti/ *uncountable noun* 不可数名词：*Belonging to a powerful organization gives them a feeling of superiority.* 作为一个强大组织的成员，他们有种优越感。

superior² /suːˈpɪəriə/ *countable noun* 可数名词
a person who has a higher position than you at work 上司；上级：*They do not have much communication with their superiors.* 他们和上司沟通不多。

superlative /suːˈpɜːlətɪv/ *adjective* 形容词
used in grammar when talking about the form of an adjective or an adverb that shows that something has more of a quality than anything else in a group. For example, 'biggest' is the superlative form of 'big'. Compare with **comparative**.（语法中）最高级的（比较 comparative）
- **superlative** *countable noun* 可数名词：*His writing contains many superlatives.* 他的文章里使用了很多最高级形式。

supermarket /ˈsuːpəmɑːkɪt/ *countable noun* 可数名词
a large shop that sells all kinds of food and other products for the home 超市：*We mostly do our food shopping in the supermarket.* 我们大多数时候去超市采购食品。

superstition /ˌsuːpəˈstɪʃən/ *noun* 名词
a belief that things such as good and bad luck exist, even though they cannot be explained 迷信：*Many people have superstitions about numbers.* 许多人对数字有迷信。

superstitious /ˌsuːpəˈstɪʃəs/ *adjective* 形容词

believing in things that cannot be explained 迷信的：*Jean was superstitious and believed that the colour green brought bad luck.* 琼这人迷信，认为绿色不吉利。

supervise /ˈsuːpəˌvaɪz/ *verb* 动词
(**supervises, supervising, supervised**)
to make sure that an activity is done correctly 监督；指导：*She cooks the supper, supervises the children's homework, and puts them to bed.* 她做晚饭，辅导孩子作业，安顿他们上床睡觉。
- **supervision** /ˌsuːpəˈvɪʒən/ *uncountable noun* 不可数名词：*Young children need close supervision.* 小孩儿需要看紧些。
- **supervisor** /ˈsuːpəˌvaɪzə/ *countable noun* 可数名词：*He got a job as a supervisor at a factory.* 他在一家工厂谋到了个监工的职位。

supper /ˈsʌpə/ *noun* 名词
a meal that people eat in the evening 晚餐；晚饭：*Would you like to join us for supper?* 你要不要和我们共进晚餐？

supplement /ˈsʌplɪmənt/ *verb* 动词
(**supplements, supplementing, supplemented**)
to add one thing to another thing in order to improve it 增补；补充：*Some people do extra jobs to supplement their incomes.* 有些人做兼职贴补收入。
- **supplement** *countable noun* 可数名词：*These classes are a supplement to school study.* 这些课是对学校学习的一种补充。

supplier /səˈplaɪə/ *countable noun* 可数名词
a company that sells something such as goods or equipment to customers 供方；供应商：*We are one of the country's biggest food suppliers.* 我们是全国最大的食品供应商之一。

supplies /səˈplaɪz/ *plural noun* 复数名词
food, equipment and other important things that are provided for people 物资；物料；供应物：*What happens when there are no more food supplies?* 食品一旦供应不上会怎么样？

supply /səˈplaɪ/ *verb* 动词 (**supplies, supplying, supplied**)
to give someone an amount of something 供应；供给；提供：*The pipeline will supply Greece with Russian natural gas.* 这条管道将向希腊输送俄罗斯的天然气。
- **supply** *uncountable noun* 不可数名词：*The brain needs a constant supply of oxygen.* 大脑需要持续的氧气供应。

support¹ /sə'pɔːt/ *verb* 动词 (supports, supporting, supported)
1 to agree with someone or their ideas, and perhaps help them because you want them to succeed 支持；支援；拥护：We haven't found any evidence to support that idea. 我们还没有找到支持那个想法的证据。
▶ **supporter** /sə'pɔːtə/ *countable noun* 可数名词：the president's supporters 总统的支持者
2 to provide someone with money or the things that they need 养活；供养；抚养：I have three children to support. 我要供养 3 个孩子。
3 to be under an object and holding it up 支撑；支承：Thick wooden posts supported the roof. 粗粗的木柱支撑着房顶。

support² /sə'pɔːt/ *noun* 名词
1 *uncountable* 不可数 actions that help someone 支援；帮助：She gave me a lot of support when my partner died. 我爱人去世后，她给了我很多帮助。
2 *uncountable* 不可数 actions or words that show that you agree with someone 拥护；支持：The president gave his full support to the reforms. 总统全力支持改革。
3 *countable* 可数 a bar or another object that supports something 支柱；支座；支撑物：Each piece of metal was on wooden supports. 每块金属下都有木头支座。

supportive /sə'pɔːtɪv/ *adjective* 形容词 kind and helpful to someone at a difficult or unhappy time in their life 支持的；热心帮忙的：They were always supportive of each other. 他们始终互相支持。

suppose /sə'pəʊz/ *verb* 动词 (supposes, supposing, supposed)
1 used before talking about a situation that could happen 假定；假设；设想：Suppose someone gave you a cheque for £6 million. What would you do with it? 假设有人给你一张 600 万英镑的支票。你会拿它做什么？
2 to imagine that something is probably true 料想；揣测；推断：I suppose you'll going back to New York. 我觉得你要回纽约了。

be supposed to do something used when someone expects you to do something, especially when this does not happen 应该（或应当）做某事（尤指实际未做）：She was supposed to be home at six. 她本应 6 点到家。

I suppose used for showing that you are slightly uncertain about something（表示不太确定）我想，我觉得：I suppose you're right. 我觉得你是对的。 □ 'Is that the right way?' — 'Yeah. I suppose so.' "这么做对吗？" —— "嗯，我觉得对。"

sure¹ /ʃʊə/ *adjective* 形容词 (surer, surest) certain 确定的；有把握的：He was not sure that he wanted to be a teacher. 他拿不准自己想不想当老师。 □ I'm not sure where he lives. 我不确定他住哪儿。
for sure definitely true 肯定；确定：One thing's for sure, women still love Barry Manilow. 有一点是肯定的，女人们依然爱巴里·马尼洛。
make sure to check that something is the way that you want it to be 核实；查明；弄清：He looked in the bathroom to make sure that he was alone. 他往浴室里看了看，确保就自己一个人。

sure² /ʃʊə/ *exclamation* 感叹词 used as an informal way of saying 'yes' or 'all right'（非正式用法，表示 yes 或 all right）是，好，没问题：'Can you show me where she lives?' — 'Sure.' "你能给我指指她住哪儿吗？" —— "行。"

surely /'ʃʊəli/ *adverb* 副词 used for showing that you think something should be true 想必；当然；肯定：You surely haven't forgotten Dr Walters? 你想必没有忘记沃尔特斯博士吧？

surf¹ /sɜːf/ *uncountable noun* 不可数名词 the mass of white bubbles on the top of waves in the sea（激浪的）浪花：We watched the surf rolling onto the white sandy beach. 我们看着浪花翻卷着涌上白色的沙滩。

surf² /sɜːf/ *verb* 动词 (surfs, surfing, surfed) to ride on big waves in the sea on a special board 冲浪：I'm going to buy a board and learn to surf. 我要去买块冲浪板学习冲浪。
▶ **surfer** /'sɜːfə/ *countable noun* 可数名词：This small fishing village continues to attract surfers. 这个小渔村持续吸引着冲浪者。
▶ **surfing** /'sɜːfɪŋ/ *uncountable noun* 不可数名词：My favourite sport is surfing. 我最喜欢的运动是冲浪。

surf the Internet to spend time looking at different websites on the Internet 上网：No one knows how many people surf the Internet. 谁也不知道有多少人上网。

surface /'sɜːfɪs/ *countable noun* 可数名词 the flat top part or the outside of something 表面：There were pen marks on the table's surface. 桌面上有笔迹。▫ Small waves moved on the surface of the water. 水面微波荡漾。

surfboard /'sɜːfbɔːd/ *countable noun* 可数名词
a long narrow board that people use for surfing (= riding on waves in the sea) 冲浪板

surge /sɜːdʒ/ *verb* 动词 (**surges, surging, surged**)
to move forward suddenly 涌动；猛然前冲：*The crowd surged forward into the shop.* 众人一窝蜂涌进了店里。 ● **surge** *countable noun* 可数名词：*a surge in prices* 物价飞涨

surgeon /'sɜːdʒən/ *countable noun* 可数名词
a doctor who is specially trained to perform operations 外科医师：*a heart surgeon* 心脏外科医生

surgery /'sɜːdʒəri/ *uncountable noun* 不可数名词
a process in which a doctor cuts open a patient's body in order to repair, remove or replace a diseased or damaged part 外科手术：*His father just had heart surgery.* 他父亲刚刚做了心脏外科手术。

surgical /'sɜːdʒɪkl/ *adjective* 形容词
relating to the process in which a doctor cuts open a patient's body to repair, remove or replace a diseased or damaged part 外科手术的：*a collection of surgical instruments* 一套外科手术器械

surname /'sɜːneɪm/ *countable noun* 可数名词
the name that you share with other members of your family 姓氏：'*And what's your surname, please?*' — '*Mitchell.*' "请问您贵姓？" —— "米切尔。"

surplus /'sɜːpləs/ *noun* 名词 (**surpluses**)
more than you need of a particular thing 盈余；过剩；剩余：*The world has a surplus of food, but still people are hungry.* 世界粮食有富余，可是还有人挨饿。 ● **surplus** *adjective* 形容词：*Few people have large sums of surplus cash.* 没多少人手头富余大笔现金。

surprise /sə'praɪz/ *noun* 名词
1 *countable* 可数 an unexpected event, fact or piece of news 令人吃惊（或意外）的事物：*I have a surprise for you: we are moving to Switzerland!* 我有个惊喜告诉你：我们要移民瑞士了！ ● **surprise** *adjective* 形容词：*Baxter arrived this afternoon, on a surprise visit.* 巴克斯特今天下午到的，来了个突然袭击。

2 *uncountable* 不可数 the feeling that you have when something that you do not expect happens 吃惊；惊讶；诧异：*The prime minister has expressed surprise at his comments.* 首相已经对他的言论表示了诧异。 ● **surprise** *verb* 动词 (**surprises, surprising, surprised**)：*We'll do the job ourselves and surprise everyone.* 这活儿我们自己干，叫所有人都吃一惊。 ▫ *It surprised me that he should make such a stupid mistake.* 他竟然犯了这么愚蠢的错误，真叫我吃惊。

surprised /sə'praɪzd/ *adjective* 形容词
having a feeling of surprise when something happens, because you did not expect it to happen 吃惊的；惊讶的；诧异的：*I was surprised at how easy it was.* 我吃惊于此事之容易。
→ Look at picture on P15 参见彩插第 15 页

surprising /sə'praɪzɪŋ/ *adjective* 形容词
not expected and making you feel surprised 惊人的；令人惊讶的；叫人诧异的：*It is not surprising that children learn to read at different rates.* 儿童识字有快有慢，这不足为怪。
▸ **surprisingly** /sə'praɪzɪŋli/ *adverb* 副词：*The party was surprisingly good.* 派对办得出人意料得好。

surrender /sə'rendə/ *verb* 动词 (**surrenders, surrendering, surrendered**)
to stop fighting because you cannot win 投降：*The army finally surrendered.* 军队最后投降了。

surround /sə'raʊnd/ *verb* 动词 (**surrounds, surrounding, surrounded**)
to be or go all around something 围绕；环绕；包围：*Bodyguards surrounded the president.* 警卫人员围着总统。 ▫ *The cottage was surrounded by a low wall.* 小房子周围有一圈矮墙。

surround 环绕

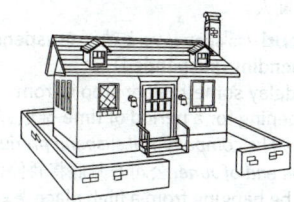

The cottage was surrounded by a low wall.
小房子周围有一圈矮墙。

surroundings /səˈraʊndɪŋz/ *plural noun* 复数名词
everything around you or the place where you live（周围）环境：*He soon felt at home in his new surroundings.* 他不久便适应了新环境。

survey /ˈsɜːveɪ/ *countable noun* 可数名词
the process of finding out information about a lot of different people, in a formal way, by asking them questions 调查：*They conducted a survey to see how students study.* 他们搞了一次调查，看学生是如何学习的。

survival /səˈvaɪvəl/ *uncountable noun* 不可数名词
when someone or something still exists after a difficult or dangerous time 存活；幸存；生存：*Many of these companies are now struggling for survival.* 目前这些公司中的很多都在挣扎求生。

survive /səˈvaɪv/ *verb* 动词 (survives, surviving, survived)
to still exist after a difficult or dangerous time 存活；幸存；生存：*It's a miracle that anyone survived.* 有人活下来真是奇迹。□ *He survived heart surgery.* 他挺过了心脏手术。

▶ **survivor** /səˈvaɪvə/ *countable noun* 可数名词：*There were no survivors of the plane crash.* 那次坠机事故中无人幸存。

suspect /səˈspekt/ *verb* 动词 (suspects, suspecting, suspected)
1 to think that something is true although you are not certain about it 疑心；觉得：*He suspected that she was telling lies.* 他疑心她在撒谎。
2 to believe that someone probably did something wrong 怀疑（某人做坏事）：*The police did not suspect him of anything.* 警方没有对他产生任何怀疑。● **suspect** /ˈsʌspekt/ *countable noun* 可数名词：*Police have arrested a suspect.* 警方已经逮捕了一名嫌疑人。

suspend /səˈspend/ *verb* 动词 (suspends, suspending, suspended)
1 to delay something or stop it from happening for a period of time 推迟；暂停；暂缓：*The company will suspend production at the end of June.* 公司 6 月底将暂停生产。
2 to be hanging from a high place 悬；吊；悬挂：*Three television screens were suspended from the ceiling.* 3 块电视屏幕悬挂在天花板上。

suspense /səˈspens/ *uncountable noun* 不可数名词
a state of excitement about something that is going to happen very soon 悬念；悬疑；挂虑：*The suspense ended when the judges gave their decision.* 法官作出裁决后，悬念尘埃落定。

suspicion /səˈspɪʃən/ *noun* 名词
a belief or a feeling that someone has done something wrong 怀疑；疑心；猜疑：*Don't do anything that might cause suspicion.* 不要做任何可能引起怀疑的事。

suspicious /səˈspɪʃəs/ *adjective* 形容词
1 not trusting someone or something 怀疑的；不信任的；有疑虑的：*He was suspicious of me at first.* 他起初对我有怀疑。
▶ **suspiciously** /səˈspɪʃəsli/ *adjective* 形容词：*'What is it you want me to do?' Adams asked suspiciously.* "你想要我做什么？"亚当斯狐疑地问。
2 making you feel that something is wrong 可疑的；令人怀疑的：*Please contact the police if you see any suspicious person in the area.* 在这一带看到任何可疑人物，请报警。
▶ **suspiciously** /səˈspɪʃəsli/ *adverb* 副词：*Has anyone been acting suspiciously over the last few days?* 最近几天有没有谁形迹可疑？

sustain /səˈsteɪn/ *verb* 动词 (sustains, sustaining, sustained)
1 to continue something for a period of time 保持；维持：*He has difficulty sustaining relationships.* 他每次恋爱都难长久。
2 to have something bad happen to you (*formal* 正式) 遭受；蒙受：*The aircraft sustained some damage.* 飞机受到了一些损坏。

sustainable /səˈsteɪnəbəl/ *adjective* 形容词
using natural products in a way that does not damage the environment 可持续的；对环境无害的：*The government introduced a program of sustainable development.* 政府推出了可持续发展规划。
▶ **sustainability** /səˌsteɪnəˈbɪlɪti/ *uncountable noun* 不可数名词：*environmental sustainability* 环境的可持续性

swallow[1] /ˈswɒləʊ/ *verb* 动词 (swallows, swallowing, swallowed)
to make something go from your mouth

down into your stomach 吞；咽: *Polly took a bite of the apple and swallowed it.* 波莉咬了一口苹果咽了下去。

swallow² /ˈswɒləʊ/ *countable noun* 可数名词
a type of small bird with pointed wings and a split tail 燕子

swam /swæm/
→ see 见 **swim**

swan /swɒn/ *countable noun* 可数名词
a large, usually white, bird with a very long neck, that lives on rivers and lakes 天鹅

swap /swɒp/ *verb* 动词 (**swaps, swapping, swapped**)
1 to give something to someone and to receive a different thing back from them 交换；互换: *We swapped phone numbers.* 我们互换了电话号码。
2 to remove one thing and replace it with another thing 调换；更换: *He swapped his jeans and T-shirt for a suit and tie.* 他脱掉牛仔裤 T 恤衫，换上了西装领带。

sway /sweɪ/ *verb* 动词 (**sways, swaying, swayed**)
to move slowly from one side to the other 摇晃；摇摆；晃荡: *The people swayed from side to side, singing.* 人们左右摇摆着，唱着歌。 □ *The tall grass was swaying in the wind.* 高高的草在风中摇曳。

swear /sweə/ *verb* 动词 (**swears, swearing, swore, sworn**)
1 to use language that is considered to be offensive 骂人；咒骂；说脏话: *It's wrong to swear and shout.* 叫骂是不对的。
2 to promise in a serious way that you will do something 发誓；起誓: *I swear to do everything I can to help you.* 我发誓尽我所能帮你。

sweat /swet/ *verb* 动词 (**sweats, sweating, sweated**)
to produce liquid from your skin when you are hot, ill or afraid 出汗；冒汗: *It's really hot. I'm sweating.* 天真热。我直冒汗。
● **sweat** *uncountable noun* 不可数名词: *Both horse and rider were dripping with sweat.* 马匹和骑手都大汗淋漓。

sweater /ˈswetə/ *countable noun* 可数名词
a warm piece of clothing that covers the upper part of your body and your arms 毛衣；毛线衫；针织衫

sweatshirt /ˈswetʃɜːt/ *countable noun* 可数名词
a loose, warm piece of clothing, made of thick cotton, that covers the upper part of your body 运动衫

sweaty /ˈsweti/ *adjective* 形容词 (**sweatier, sweatiest**)
covered with sweat 满是汗的；汗淋淋的: *hot, sweaty hands* 热乎乎、汗津津的双手 □ *sweaty socks* 汗湿的袜子

sweep /swiːp/ *verb* 动词 (**sweeps, sweeping, swept**)
1 to push dirt off an area using a brush with a long handle (用扫帚)扫，清扫: *The owner of the shop was sweeping his floor.* 店主在扫地。 □ *She was in the kitchen sweeping food off the floor.* 她在厨房里清扫地上的饭菜。
2 to push objects off something with a quick smooth movement of your arm (用手臂)拂去，扫掉: *She swept the cards from the table.* 她把桌上的牌都划拉到了地上。

sweet¹ /swiːt/ *adjective* 形容词 (**sweeter, sweetest**)
1 containing a lot of sugar 甜的；含糖多的: *a cup of sweet tea* 一杯甜茶 □ *If the sauce is too sweet, add some salt.* 酱汁要是太甜，就加点盐。
2 having a pleasant smell 芳香的；芬芳的: *I recognized the sweet smell of her perfume.* 我闻出了她身上香水的香味。
3 having a pleasant, smooth and gentle sound (声音)甜美的，悦耳的: *The young girl's voice was soft and sweet.* 那个少女的声音柔美动听。
4 kind and gentle toward other people 和善的；温和的；温柔的: *He was a sweet man.* 他是个温和的人。
▶ **sweetly** /ˈswiːtli/ *adverb* 副词: *I just smiled sweetly and said no.* 我只是和气地笑了笑，说不行。
5 attractive in a simple way (*informal* 非正式) 可爱的；讨人喜欢的: *a sweet little baby* 讨人喜欢的小宝宝

sweet² /swiːt/ *countable noun* 可数名词
a food such as a chocolate that contains a lot of sugar 糖；糖果: *Eat more fruit and vegetables and fewer sweets.* 多吃果蔬，少吃糖。

sweetcorn /ˈswiːtkɔːn/ *uncountable noun* 不可数名词
a long round vegetable covered in small yellow seeds. The seeds are also called sweetcorn. 甜玉米(粒)

swell /swel/ *verb* 动词 (**swells, swelling, swelled, swollen**)
(also 亦作 **swell up**) to become larger and thicker than normal 膨胀；肿胀；鼓胀：*Do your legs swell at night?* 你的双腿夜里肿吗？ □ *His eye swelled up.* 他的一只眼睛肿了起来。

swept /swept/
→ see 见 **sweep**

swerve /swɜːv/ *verb* 动词 (**swerves, swerving, swerved**)
to suddenly change direction 急转弯；突然转向：*Her car swerved off the road.* 她的车猛一转向冲出了公路。

swift /swɪft/ *adjective* 形容词 (**swifter, swiftest**)
1 happening very quickly or without delay 迅速的；毫不耽搁的：*We need to make a swift decision.* 我们得从速决断。
▶ **swiftly** /ˈswɪftli/ *adverb* 副词：*We have to act as swiftly as we can.* 我们必须尽快行动。
2 moving very quickly 迅疾的；迅捷的：*With a swift movement, Matthew sat up.* 马修一骨碌坐了起来。
▶ **swiftly** /ˈswɪftli/ *adverb* 副词：*Lenny moved swiftly and silently across the grass.* 伦尼不声不响快速穿过了草地。

swim /swɪm/ *verb* 动词 (**swims, swimming, swam, swum**)
to move through water by making movements with your arms and legs 游泳：*She learned to swim when she was 10.* 她10岁学会游泳。 □ *I swim a mile a day.* 我每天游1英里。● **swim** *singular noun* 单数名词：*When can we go for a swim?* 我们什么时候能去游个泳？
▶ **swimmer** /ˈswɪmə/ *countable noun* 可数名词：*I'm a good swimmer.* 我是游泳好手。

swimming /ˈswɪmɪŋ/ *uncountable noun* 不可数名词
the activity of swimming, especially as a sport or for pleasure 游泳：*Swimming is a great form of exercise.* 游泳是一种很好的锻炼方式。
→ Look at picture on P14 参见彩插第 14 页

swimming costume *countable noun* 可数名词
a piece of clothing that is worn for swimming, especially by women and girls（尤用于女式）泳衣：*Don't forget to pack a swimming costume and a towel.* 别忘了带上泳衣和毛巾。

swimming pool *countable noun* 可数名词
a large hole filled with water that people can swim in 游泳池

swimming trunks *plural noun* 复数名词
a piece of clothing that is worn for swimming by men and boys（男式）泳裤：*The boys changed into their swimming trunks.* 男孩子们换上了泳裤。

swimsuit /ˈswɪmsuːt/ *countable noun* 可数名词
→ see 见 **swimming costume**

swing¹ /swɪŋ/ *verb* 动词 (**swings, swinging, swung**)
to move repeatedly backwards and forwards or from side to side through the air 摇摆；摆动；摇荡：*Amber walked beside him, her arms swinging.* 安伯摆着双臂走在他身旁。

swing² /swɪŋ/ *countable noun* 可数名词
a seat, hanging by two ropes, that you can sit on and move forwards and backwards through the air 秋千：*I took the kids to the park to play on the swings.* 我带孩子们到公园玩秋千。

swipe /swaɪp/ *verb* 动词 (**swipes, swiping, swiped**)
1 to pass a bank card through a machine so that it can read information on the card 刷（银行卡）：*Swipe your card through the phone, then dial.* 先在电话机上刷卡，然后拨号。
2 to move your finger sideways across the screen of a phone or computer in order to give it an instruction（在触摸屏上）滑动手指：*Swipe right to answer the call.* 向右滑接听电话。

switch¹ /swɪtʃ/ *countable noun* 可数名词 (**switches**)
a small control for turning electricity on or off 开关：*She shut the dishwasher and pressed the switch.* 她关上洗碗机，按下开关。
→ Look at picture on P6 参见彩插第 6 页

switch² /swɪtʃ/ *verb* 动词 (**switches, switching, switched**)
1 to change to something different 转换；转变；改变：*Companies are switching to cleaner fuels.* 公司正在转用更清洁的燃料。
2 to replace one thing with another thing 交换；调换；互换：*They switched the keys, so Karen had the key to my room*

and I had the key to hers. 他们调换了钥匙，这样卡伦就拿着我房间的钥匙，我拿着她的。

switch something off to stop electrical equipment from working by operating a switch 关掉（电气设备）: *She switched off the coffee machine.* 她关掉了咖啡机。

switch something on to make electrical equipment start working by operating a switch 打开（电气设备）: *He switched on the lamp.* 他打开电灯。

swollen¹ /ˈswəʊlən/
adjective 形容词
larger and thicker than normal 膨胀的；肿胀的；鼓胀的: *My eyes were swollen and I could hardly see.* 我双眼肿得几乎看不见东西。

swollen 肿胀的

swollen² /ˈswəʊlən/
→ see 见 **swell**

sword /sɔːd/ *countable noun* 可数名词
a weapon with a handle and a long sharp blade 剑；刀

swore /swɔː/
→ see 见 **swear**

sworn /swɔːn/
→ see 见 **swear**

swum /swʌm/
→ see 见 **swim**

swung /swʌŋ/
→ see 见 **swing**

syllable /ˈsɪləbəl/ *countable noun* 可数名词
a part of a word that contains a single vowel sound and that is pronounced as a unit. So, for example, 'book' has one syllable, and 'reading' has two syllables. 音节

syllabus /ˈsɪləbəs/ *countable noun* 可数名词 (**syllabuses**)
a list of the subjects to be covered in a school, university or college course 教学大纲: *The course syllabus consists mainly of novels by American writers.* 该课程大纲主要涵盖美国作家的小说。

symbol /ˈsɪmbəl/ *countable noun* 可数名词
a number, a letter or a shape that represents a particular thing 符号: *The chemical symbol for hydrogen is 'H'.* 氢的化学符号是 H。

symmetrical /sɪˈmetrɪkəl/ *adjective* 形容词
having two halves that are exactly the same 对称的: *The rows of windows were perfectly symmetrical.* 一排排窗户完全对称。

symmetrical 对称的

sympathetic /ˌsɪmpəˈθetɪk/ *adjective* 形容词
kind and able to understand other people's feelings 有同情心的；体恤他人的: *Try talking about your problem with a sympathetic teacher.* 找一位善解人意的老师聊聊你的问题。

▶ **sympathetically** /ˌsɪmpəˈθetɪkli/ *adverb* 副词: *She nodded sympathetically.* 她同情地点了点头。

sympathize /ˈsɪmpəˌθaɪz/ *verb* 动词 (**sympathizes, sympathizing, sympathized**)
to show that you are sorry for someone who is in a bad situation 同情: *It's terrible when a parent dies. I sympathize with you.* 父母去世可谓晴天霹雳。我理解你的感受。

sympathy /ˈsɪmpəθi/ *uncountable noun* 不可数名词
the feeling of being sorry for someone who is in a bad situation, or the act of showing them that you feel sorry for them 同情: *I get no sympathy from my family when I'm sick.* 我生病时家人一点儿也不同情我。□ *I have great sympathy for these refugees.* 我非常同情这些难民。

symphony /ˈsɪmfəni/ *countable noun* 可数名词 (**symphonies**)
a piece of music that has been written to be played by an orchestra 交响曲；交响乐: *Beethoven's Ninth Symphony* 贝多芬《第九交响曲》

symphony ˈorchestra *countable noun* 可数名词
a large orchestra that plays classical music 交响乐团: *the London Symphony Orchestra* 伦敦交响乐团

symptom /ˈsɪmptəm/ *countable noun* 可数名词
something that is wrong with you that is a sign of a particular illness 症状: *All these patients have flu symptoms.* 这些患者都有流感症状。

synagogue /ˈsɪnəgɒg/ *countable noun* 可数名词
a building where Jewish people go to pray（犹太教的）会堂

syndrome /ˈsɪndrəʊm/ *countable noun* 可数名词
a medical condition 综合征: *No one knows what causes Sudden Infant Death Syndrome.* 谁也不知道婴儿猝死综合征因何发生。

synonym /ˈsɪnənɪm/ *countable noun* 可数名词
a word or an expression that means the same as another word or expression 同义词；同义语: *'Afraid' is a synonym for 'frightened'.* *afraid 是 frightened 的同义词。

synthetic /sɪnˈθetɪk/ *adjective* 形容词
made from chemicals or artificial substances rather than from natural ones 合成的；人造的；人工的: *synthetic rubber* 合成橡胶

syringe /sɪˈrɪndʒ/ *countable noun* 可数名词
a small tube with a thin hollow needle at the end that is used for putting medicine into a part of the body or for taking blood from your body 注射器

syrup /ˈsɪrəp/ *noun* 名词
a sweet liquid made by cooking sugar with water 糖浆；糖水: *tinned fruit with syrup* 糖水水果罐头

system /ˈsɪstəm/ *countable noun* 可数名词
1 a way of working, organizing or doing something that follows a plan 制度；体制: *You need a better system for organizing your DVDs.* 你们需要改进一下 DVD 管理制度。
2 a set of equipment, parts or instruments（设备等的）系统: *There's something wrong with the computer system.* 计算机系统出了点问题。□ *a heating system* 供暖系统
3 a network of things that are linked together so that people or things can communicate with each other or travel from one place to another（通信或交通）系统: *Australia's road and rail system* 澳大利亚的公路和铁路系统

Tt

table /ˈteɪbəl/ *countable noun* 可数名词
1 a piece of furniture with a flat top that you put things on or sit at 桌子：*Mum was sitting at the kitchen table.* 妈妈坐在餐桌旁。
2 a set of facts or numbers that you arrange in neat rows 表；表格：*See the table on page 104.* 参阅第 104 页的表格。

tablecloth /ˈteɪbəlklɒθ/ *countable noun* 可数名词
a cloth that you use to cover a table 桌布；台布

tablespoon /ˈteɪbəlspuːn/ *countable noun* 可数名词
a large spoon that you use when you are cooking 大汤匙；大调羹

tablet /ˈtæblət/ *countable noun* 可数名词
1 a small solid piece of medicine that you swallow 药片：*The doctor gave me a sleeping tablet to help me sleep.* 医生给了我一片安眠药助眠。

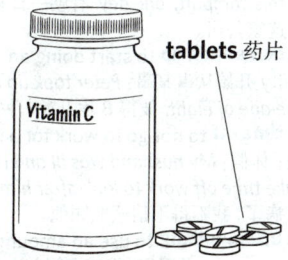
tablets 药片

2 a small, flat computer that you use by touching the screen 平板电脑
→ Look at picture on P11 参见彩插第 11 页

ˈtable ˌtennis *uncountable noun* 不可数名词
a game in which one or two players on either side of a table hit a small light ball across a low net across the table 乒乓球运动

tabloid /ˈtæblɔɪd/ *countable noun* 可数名词
a newspaper that has small pages, short news stories, and a lot of photographs 通俗小报

tackle /ˈtækəl/ *verb* 动词 (tackles, tackling, tackled)
1 to deal with a problem 应对，处理（难题）：*We discussed the best way to tackle the situation.* 我们商讨应对此局面的最佳办法。
2 to try to take the ball away from someone in a sports game（球类比赛中）抢断，抢截，擒抱：*Foley tackled the defender.* 福利阻截了防守队员。● **tackle** *countable noun* 可数名词：*A great tackle from Beckham saved the game.* 贝克汉姆一次漂亮抢断拯救了比赛。

tactful /ˈtæktfʊl/ *adjective* 形容词
very careful not to do or say anything that will upset or embarrass other people 考虑周全的；圆通的：*Dan obviously heard our argument but he was too tactful to mention it.* 丹明显听到了我们的争执，但他很有分寸，没有提及此事。
▶ **tactfully** /ˈtæktfʊli/ *adverb* 副词：*Tactfully, Jessica changed the subject.* 杰茜卡巧妙地转移了话题。

tactic /ˈtæktɪk/ *countable noun* 可数名词
the way that you choose to do something when you are trying to succeed in a particular situation 手法；策略：*Things weren't going well, so I decided to change my tactics.* 事情进展不顺，于是我决定改变策略。

tadpole /ˈtædpəʊl/ *countable noun* 可数名词
a small water animal that looks like a black fish, and that develops into a frog or a toad (= a small green or brown animal with long back legs) 蝌蚪

tag /tæɡ/ *countable noun* 可数名词
a small piece of cardboard or cloth that is attached to something. It has information written on it. 标签；标牌：*The staff all wear name tags.* 工作人员都佩戴姓名牌。
□ *There's no price tag on this purse.* 这个钱包没有价格标签。

tail /teɪl/ *countable noun* 可数名词
1 the long thin part at the end of an

tailor – takeaway

animal's body（动物的）尾巴：*The dog barked and wagged its tail.* 那只狗叫了几声，摇了摇尾巴。
2 the end or the back of something 尾部；末端：*The plane's tail hit the runway while it was landing.* 飞机降落时，尾部与跑道相撞。

tailor /ˈteɪlə/ ***countable noun*** 可数名词
a person whose job is to make and repair clothes 裁缝

take /teɪk/ ***verb*** 动词 **(takes, taking, took, taken)**
1 to hold or remove something 拿；取：*Let me take your coat.* 我来帮你拿大衣。□ *He took a pen from his pocket.* 他从口袋里取出一支笔。
2 to carry something with you 带；携带：*Don't forget to take a map with you.* 别忘了带地图。

> **LANGUAGE HELP 语言提示**
> See note at **bring**. 见 bring 的语言提示。

3 to transport someone somewhere 送；运送：*Michael took me to the airport.* 迈克尔把我送到机场。
4 to steal something 偷走；（擅自）拿走：*They took my wallet.* 他们拿走了我的钱包。
5 to need an amount of time 花费（时间）：*The sauce takes 25 minutes to prepare.* 准备酱汁需要 25 分钟。
6 to accept something that someone offers you 接受；采纳：*Sylvia has taken a job in Tokyo teaching English.* 西尔维娅接受了一份在东京教英语的工作。□ *I think you should take my advice.* 我认为你该采纳我的建议。
7 to choose to travel along a road 走（某条路）：*Take a right at the traffic lights.* 在红绿灯处右拐。
8 to use a vehicle to go from one place to another 乘坐；搭乘：*She took the train to New York.* 她乘火车到纽约。
9 used for saying that someone does something 做（某个动作）：*She was too tired to take a bath.* 她累得没有力气洗澡了。□ *Betty took a photograph of us.* 贝蒂给我们拍了一张照片。
10 to study a subject at school 学习，读（课程）：*Students can take European history and American history.* 学生可以选修欧洲史和美国史。
11 to do an examination 参加（考试）：*She took her driving test yesterday and passed.* 她昨天参加了驾照考试，结果通过。
12 to swallow medicine 服用，使用（药物）：*I try not to take pills of any kind.* 我尽量不服用任何药物。
take after someone to look or behave like an older member of your family 像（家中长辈）：*Your mum was a clever, brave woman. You take after her.* 你妈妈是个聪明、勇敢的女人，你很像她。
take off used for saying that an aeroplane leaves the ground and starts flying 起飞：*We took off at 11 o'clock.* 我们 11 点起飞。
take someone out to take someone somewhere enjoyable 带某人外出消遣：*Sophia took me out to lunch today.* 索菲娅今天请我出去吃的午餐。
take something away to remove something 拿走某物；移开某物：*The waitress took away the dirty dishes.* 女服务员收走了脏盘子。
take something back to return something 退回某物：*If you don't like it, I'll take it back to the shop.* 你要是不喜欢，我就拿去商店退货。
take something off to remove clothes 脱下（衣物）：*Come in and take off your coat.* 进来脱掉大衣。
take something over to get control of something 接管某事物：*I'm going to take over this company one day.* 有朝一日我将接手这家公司。
take something up to start doing an activity 开始从事某事：*Peter took up tennis at the age of eight.* 彼得 8 岁开始打网球。
take time off to not go to work for a time 请假；休假：*My husband was ill and I had to take time off work to look after him.* 我丈夫生病了，我不得不请假照顾他。
take up something to use an amount of time or space 占用（时间或空间）：*I don't want to take up too much of your time.* 我不想占用你太多时间。□ *The round wooden table takes up most of the kitchen.* 那个圆木桌占了厨房大部分空间。

takeaway /ˈteɪkəˌweɪ/ ***countable noun*** 可数名词（**American** 美国英语：**takeout**）
1 hot cooked food that you buy from a shop or a restaurant and eat somewhere else 外卖食品：*a Chinese takeaway* 中式外卖● **takeaway** ***adjective*** 形容词：*a takeaway pizza* 外卖比萨饼
2 a shop or a restaurant which sells hot cooked food that you eat somewhere else

外卖店；外卖餐馆

taken /ˈteɪkən/
→ see 见 **take**

takeoff /ˈteɪkɒf/ also 亦作 **take-off** noun 名词
the time when an aircraft leaves the ground and starts to fly 起飞：*What time is takeoff?* 什么时候起飞？

takeout /ˈteɪkaʊt/ countable noun 可数名词
(American 美国英语)
→ see 见 **takeaway**

tale /teɪl/ countable noun 可数名词
a story 传说；故事：*It's a tale about the friendship between two boys.* 这个故事讲的是两个男孩之间的友谊。

talent /ˈtælənt/ noun 名词
your natural ability to do something well 天赋；天资：*Both her children have a talent for music.* 她的两个孩子都很有音乐天赋。 □ *He's got lots of talent, but he's rather lazy.* 他特别有天分，但很懒惰。

talented /ˈtæləntɪd/ adjective 形容词
having a natural ability to do something well 天资聪颖的；有天赋的：*Howard is a talented pianist.* 霍华德是位天才钢琴家。

talk[1] /tɔːk/ verb 动词 (talks, talking, talked)
to say words, or speak to someone about your thoughts, ideas or feelings 讲话；谈话：*After the fight, Mark was too upset to talk.* 争辩过后，马克心烦意乱，闭口不言。 □ *Tom didn't talk until he was three years old.* 汤姆直到 3 岁才开口说话。 □ *They were all talking about the film.* 他们都在谈论那部影片。 □ *I talked to him yesterday.* 我昨天和他说过话。

LANGUAGE HELP 语言提示
Talk or **speak**? 用 talk 还是 speak？
When you **speak**, you say things. *speak 表示说话：*Did someone speak?* 有人说话了吗？
Talk is used for describing a conversation or discussion. *talk 表示交谈或讨论：*I talked about it with my family at dinner.* 吃饭的时候我和家人讨论了这件事。

talk[2] /tɔːk/ noun 名词
1 countable 可数 when two or more people talk together 交谈；讨论：*I had a long talk with my father.* 我和父亲长谈了一次。
2 countable 可数 when someone speaks to a group of people 演讲；讲话：*She gave a brief talk on the history of the building.* 她简要介绍了一下那栋建筑的历史。
3 [talks] plural 复数 formal discussions between different groups, to try to reach an agreement 谈判；会谈：*peace talks* 和平谈判

tall /tɔːl/ adjective 形容词 (taller, tallest)
1 higher than other people or things 高的；高大的：*John is very tall.* 约翰个子很高。 □ *The lighthouse is a tall square tower.* 灯塔是一座高高的方形塔。
2 used when you are asking or talking about the height of someone or something（用于指高度）有…高的，身高…的：*'How tall are you?'* — *'I'm six foot five.'* "你有多高？" —— "我身高 6 英尺 5 英寸。"

tambourine /ˌtæmbəˈriːn/ countable noun 可数名词
a round musical instrument that you shake or hit with your hand 铃鼓
→ Look at picture on P12 参见彩插第 12 页

tame /teɪm/ adjective 形容词 (tamer, tamest)
used for describing an animal that is not afraid of humans（动物）驯化的，驯服的

tan[1] /tæn/ singular noun 单数名词
when your skin has become darker because you have spent time in the sun 晒黑的肤色：*She is tall and blonde, with a tan.* 她高个儿金发，皮肤晒得黝黑。

tan[2] /tæn/ verb 动词 (tans, tanning, tanned)
to become darker because you have spent time in the sun 晒黑：*I have very pale skin that never tans.* 我皮肤很白，怎么也晒不黑。
▶ **tanned** /tænd/ adjective 形容词：*Becky's skin was deeply tanned.* 贝姬的皮肤晒得黝黑。

tangle /ˈtæŋɡəl/ countable noun 可数名词
a mass of something that has become twisted together in a messy way 缠结的一团：*A tangle of wires connected the two computers.* 乱糟糟的一团电线将两台电脑连在了一起。

tangle（头发）打结

● **tangle** verb 动词 (tangles, tangling, tangled)：*Her hair is curly and tangles easily.* 她一头鬈发，很容易打结。

tank /tæŋk/ countable noun 可数名词
1 a large container for holding liquid or

gas（盛放液体或气体的）箱，罐：*a fuel tank* 燃油箱
2 a heavy, strong military vehicle, with large guns. It moves on metal tracks that are fixed over the wheels. 坦克

tanker /ˈtæŋkə/ **countable noun** 可数名词
a large ship or lorry that carries large amounts of gas or liquid 油轮；油罐车：*an oil tanker* 油轮

tap¹ /tæp/ **verb** 动词 (**taps, tapping, tapped**)
to hit or touch something quickly and lightly 轻敲；轻拍：*He tapped the table nervously with his fingers.* 他不安地用手指敲了敲桌子。□ *Karen tapped on the bedroom door and went in.* 卡伦轻轻敲了敲卧室门，走了进去。

tap² /tæp/ **countable noun** 可数名词
1 (*American* 美国英语：**faucet**) an object that controls the flow of a liquid or a gas from a pipe 龙头；阀门：*When people turn the tap on, they have good, drinkable water.* 人们打开水龙头就有优质的饮用水。
2 when someone hits or touches something quickly and lightly 轻敲；轻拍：*There was a tap on the door.* 传来轻轻的叩门声。

tape¹ /teɪp/ **noun** 名词
1 uncountable 不可数 a sticky strip of plastic used for sticking things together 胶带；胶条：*Attach the picture to the cardboard using sticky tape.* 用胶条把照片贴在硬纸板上。
2 a long narrow plastic strip that you use to record music, sounds or moving pictures 磁带；录音带；录像带
3 countable 可数 a small, flat plastic case containing tape that is used for recording and playing sound or pictures（盒式）磁带，录像带：*Her brother found an old tape of her music under the bed.* 她哥哥在床下找到了一盘录有她音乐的旧磁带。

tape² /teɪp/ **verb** 动词 (**tapes, taping, taped**)
1 to record music, sounds or moving pictures on a tape（用磁带）录制：*Ms Pringle secretly taped her conversation with her boss.* 普林格尔女士偷偷录下了她与老板的对话。
2 to stick two things together using tape（用胶条）粘贴：*I taped the envelope shut.* 我把信封粘上了。

ˈtape ˌrecorder also 亦作 **tape-recorder** **countable noun** 可数名词
a machine that you use for recording and playing sound or music 录音机

tar /tɑː/ **uncountable noun** 不可数名词
a thick, black, sticky substance that is used for making roads 柏油；沥青：*It was so hot that the tar melted on the roads.* 天气太热了，柏油马路都融化了。

target /ˈtɑːɡɪt/ **countable noun** 可数名词
1 something that you try to hit with a weapon or other object 靶子；目标：*One of the missiles missed its target.* 其中一枚导弹没有命中目标。
2 the result that you are trying to achieve 目标；指标：*We failed to meet our sales targets last year.* 我们去年没有完成销售指标。

Tarmac /ˈtɑːmæk/ **uncountable noun** 不可数名词
a black substance used for making road surfaces (*trademark* 商标) *Tarmac 柏油碎石（铺路用）

tart /tɑːt/ **noun** 名词
a case made of flour, fat and water (= pastry) that you fill with fruit or vegetables and cook in an oven（水果或蔬菜）馅饼：*We had apple tarts, served with fresh cream.* 我们吃了苹果馅饼配鲜奶油。

task /tɑːsk/ **countable noun** 可数名词
a piece of work that you have to do 任务；工作：*I had the task of cleaning the kitchen.* 我得清理厨房。

taskbar /ˈtɑːskbɑː/ also 亦作 **task bar countable noun** 可数名词
a narrow strip at the bottom of a computer screen that shows you which windows are open（计算机屏幕下方的）任务栏

taste¹ /teɪst/ **noun** 名词
1 uncountable 不可数 your ability to recognize the flavour of things with your tongue 味觉：*Over the years my sense of taste has disappeared.* 这么多年过去，我已经没有味觉了。
2 countable 可数 the particular quality that something has when you put it in your mouth, for example whether it is sweet or salty 味道；口味：*I like the taste of chocolate.* 我喜欢巧克力的味道。□ *This medicine has a nasty taste.* 这药真难喝。
3 uncountable 不可数 someone's choice in all the things that they like or buy 品味；

鉴赏力: Will's got great taste in clothes. 威尔的衣服品味很高。
4 *singular* 单数 a small amount of food or drink that you try in order to see what the flavour is like 品尝的少许东西；一小口: Have a taste of this pie. 尝一点儿这个馅饼。

taste² /teɪst/ *verb* 动词 (**tastes, tasting, tasted**)
1 to have a particular flavour 有…的味道: The water tasted of metal. 这水有股金属味儿。▫ The pizza tastes delicious. 比萨饼很美味。
2 to eat or drink a small amount of food or drink in order to see what the flavour is like 尝；品尝: Don't add salt until you've tasted the food. 品尝过食物之后再加盐。
3 to be aware of the flavour of something that you are eating or drinking 尝出…的味道: Can you taste the onions in this dish? 你能吃出这道菜里有洋葱味吗？

tasteful /ˈteɪstfʊl/ *adjective* 形容词
attractive, having a good design and being of good quality 高雅的；有品味的: Sarah was wearing a purple suit and tasteful jewellery. 萨拉身穿紫色套装，戴着雅致的珠宝。
▸ **tastefully** /ˈteɪstfʊli/ *adverb* 副词: They live in a large and tastefully decorated home. 他们住在装饰别致的大房子里。

tasteless /ˈteɪstləs/ *adjective* 形容词
1 unattractive, badly designed and of poor quality 俗气的；没品味的: Jim's house is full of tasteless furniture. 吉姆家摆满了俗不可耐的家具。
2 that upsets people 粗俗的；不雅的: That was a very tasteless remark. 那话说得非常粗俗。
3 having no flavour 无味的；没滋味的: The fish was tasteless. 那鱼淡而无味。

tasty /ˈteɪsti/ *adjective* 形容词 (**tastier, tastiest**)
having a pleasant flavour and being good to eat 可口的；美味的: The food here is tasty and good value. 这儿的食物美味还划算。

tattoo /tæˈtuː/ *countable noun* 可数名词
a design on a person's skin made with a needle and coloured ink 文身；刺青: He has a tattoo on his arm. 他的胳膊上有个文身。 ● **tattoo** *verb* 动词 (**tattoos, tattooing, tattooed**): She has had three small stars tattooed on one of her shoulders. 她肩膀的一侧文了三颗小星星。

taught /tɔːt/
→ see 见 **teach**

tax¹ /tæks/ *noun* 名词 (**taxes**)
an amount of money that you have to pay to the government so that it can pay for public services such as roads and schools 税；税款: No one enjoys paying tax. 没人喜欢缴税。▫ The government has promised not to raise taxes this year. 政府承诺今年不增税。

tax² /tæks/ *verb* 动词 (**taxes, taxing, taxed**)
to make a person or a company pay a part of their income to the government 对…征税: We are the most heavily taxed people in Europe. 我们是欧洲税负最重的。

taxation /tækˈseɪʃn/ *uncountable noun* 不可数名词
when a government takes money from people and spends it on things such as education, health and defence 征税；课税: The council wants major changes in taxation. 政务委员会希望对税收进行重大改革。

taxi /ˈtæksi/ *countable noun* 可数名词
a car that you can hire, with its driver, to take you where you want to go 出租车；的士: We took a taxi back to our hotel. 我们坐出租车回到酒店。

ˈtaxi rank *countable noun* 可数名词
a place where taxis wait for passengers, for example at an airport 出租车候客点；出租车站；的士站

taxpayer /ˈtækspeɪə/ *countable noun* 可数名词
a person who pays tax 纳税人: The government has wasted taxpayers' money. 政府浪费了纳税人的钱。

tea /tiː/ *uncountable noun* 不可数名词
1 a drink that you make by pouring boiling water on the dry leaves of a plant called the tea bush 茶；茶水: I made myself a cup of tea and sat down to watch TV. 我给自己泡了杯茶，然后坐下来看电视。▫ Would you like some tea? 你喝茶吗？
2 the chopped dried leaves of the plant that tea is made from 茶叶
3 a meal that some people eat in the late afternoon or the early evening (傍晚时吃的)晚点，便餐

teach /tiːtʃ/ *verb* 动词 (**teaches, teaching, taught**)
1 to give someone instructions so that they know about something or know how to do it 教；教会: She taught me to read.

team – tedious

她教我识字。▫ *George taught him how to ride a horse.* 乔治教他骑马。
2 to give lessons in a subject at a school or a college 教…课程；教书： *Christine teaches biology at Piper High.* 克里斯蒂娜在派珀高中教生物。▫ *Mrs Green has been teaching part-time for 16 years.* 格林夫人兼职教书已经 16 年了。

▶ **teacher** /ˈtiːtʃə/ *countable noun* 可数名词： *I was a teacher for 21 years.* 我当了 21 年老师。
→ Look at pictures on P1 and P16 参见彩插第 1 页和第 16 页

▶ **teaching** /ˈtiːtʃɪŋ/ *uncountable noun* 不可数名词： *The quality of teaching in the school is excellent.* 该校教学质量一流。

team /tiːm/ *countable noun* 可数名词
1 a group of people who play a particular sport or game against other groups of people (体育运动或游戏的) 队： *Kate was in the school hockey team.* 凯特在校曲棍球队。
2 any group of people who work together 工作组；工作队： *A team of doctors visited the hospital yesterday.* 一队医生昨日到访医院。

teamwork /ˈtiːmwɜːk/ *uncountable noun* 不可数名词
the ability that a group of people have to work well together 合作；协作： *She knows the importance of teamwork.* 她知晓团队合作的重要性。

teapot /ˈtiːpɒt/ *countable noun* 可数名词
a container that is used for making and serving tea 茶壶

tear[1] /tɪə/ *countable noun* 可数名词
a drop of the liquid that comes out of your eye when you are crying 眼泪；泪水： *Her eyes filled with tears.* 她眼中噙满了泪水。
burst into tears to suddenly start crying 突然哭起来： *She burst into tears and ran from the kitchen.* 她突然大哭着跑出了厨房。
in tears crying 流眼泪的： *By the end of the film, we were all in tears.* 电影结束时，我们都哭了。

tear[2] /teə/ *verb* 动词 (**tears, tearing, tore, torn**)
to pull something into pieces or make a hole in it 撕破；划破；戳破： *I tore my coat on a nail.* 我的大衣被钉子钩破了。▫ *She tore the letter into several pieces.* 她把信撕成了碎片。● **tear** *countable noun* 可数名词： *I looked through a tear in the curtains.* 我从窗帘的破洞看过去。

tear something up to tear something such as a piece of paper into small pieces 把 (纸等) 撕碎： *He tore up the letter and threw it in the fire.* 他把信撕碎扔进了火里。

tease /tiːz/ *verb* 动词 (**teases, teasing, teased**)
to laugh at someone or make jokes about them in order to embarrass or annoy them 嘲笑；取笑： *Amber's brothers are always teasing her.* 安伯的哥哥们总是取笑她。

teaspoon /ˈtiːspuːn/ *countable noun* 可数名词
a small spoon that you use for putting sugar into tea or coffee 茶匙： *Use a teaspoon to remove the seeds from the fruit.* 用茶匙剔除水果的籽儿。

technical /ˈteknɪkəl/ *adjective* 形容词
involving machines, processes and materials that are used in science and industry 技术的；工艺的： *We still have to solve a number of technical problems.* 我们还得解决一些技术问题。

▶ **technically** /ˈteknɪkli/ *adverb* 副词： *It is a very technically advanced car.* 这是一辆工艺非常先进的车。

technician /tekˈnɪʃən/ *countable noun* 可数名词
someone who works with scientific or medical equipment or machines 技术人员；技师： *Joseph works as a laboratory technician at St Thomas's Hospital.* 约瑟夫在圣托马斯医院做实验室技术员。

technique /tekˈniːk/ *countable noun* 可数名词
a special way of doing something practical 技巧；方法： *Doctors have recently developed these new techniques.* 医生近来开发了这些新技术。

technology /tekˈnɒlədʒi/ *noun* 名词 (**technologies**)
the way that scientific knowledge is used in a practical way 科技；工艺： *Computer technology has developed fast during the last 10 years.* 在过去 10 年中，计算机技术的发展日新月异。
→ Look at picture on P11 参见彩插第 11 页

teddy bear *countable noun* 可数名词
(also 亦作 **teddy**) a soft toy that looks like a bear 泰迪熊 (一种玩具)

tedious /ˈtiːdiəs/ *adjective* 形容词
continuing for too long, and not

interesting 冗长的；枯燥乏味的：*The film was very tedious.* 那部影片十分冗长乏味。

teenage /ˈtiːneɪdʒ/ *adjective* 形容词
aged between thirteen and nineteen years old 十几岁的；青少年的：*Taylor is a typical teenage girl.* 泰勒是个典型的十几岁的女孩子。

teenager /ˈtiːneɪdʒə/ *countable noun* 可数名词
someone who is between thirteen and nineteen years old 青少年；少男；少女

teens /tiːnz/ *plural noun* 复数名词
in your teens between thirteen and nineteen years old 在十几岁时：*I met my husband when I was in my teens.* 我十几岁时遇到了我的丈夫。

teeth /tiːθ/
the plural of **tooth**（tooth 的复数形式）
→ Look at picture on P4 参见彩插第 4 页

telephone¹ /ˈtelɪfəʊn/ *countable noun* 可数名词
the piece of equipment that you use for speaking to someone who is in another place 电话：*He got up and answered the telephone.* 他起身接了电话。
on the telephone speaking to someone by telephone 在打电话；在通话：*Linda was on the telephone for three hours this evening.* 琳达今晚打了 3 个小时的电话。

telephone² /ˈtelɪfəʊn/ *verb* 动词
(**telephones, telephoning, telephoned**)
to speak to someone using a telephone（给…）打电话：*I telephoned my boyfriend to say I was sorry.* 我打电话给男友，跟他说对不起。□ *He telephoned for a taxi to take him to the airport.* 他打电话叫出租车送他去机场。

telescope /ˈtelɪskəʊp/ *countable noun* 可数名词
an instrument shaped like a tube. It has special glass inside it that makes things that are far away look bigger and nearer when you look through it. 望远镜

telescope 望远镜

television /ˈtelɪˌvɪʒən, ˌtelɪˈvɪʒ-/ 或 **TV** *noun* 名词
1 *countable* 可数 a piece of electrical equipment with a screen on which you watch moving pictures with sound 电视：*She turned the television on.* 她打开电视。
2 *uncountable* 不可数 the moving pictures and sounds that you watch and listen to on a television 电视节目：*Michael spends too much time watching television.* 迈克尔花太多时间看电视了。□ *What's on television tonight?* 今晚有什么电视节目？ □ *My favourite television programme is about to start.* 我最喜欢的电视节目要开始了。

tell /tel/ *verb* 动词 (**tells, telling, told**)
1 to give someone information 告诉；告知：*I told Rachel I got the job.* 我告诉蕾切尔我找到工作了。□ *I called Anna to tell her how angry I was.* 我打电话告诉安娜我有多生气。□ *Claire made me promise to tell her the truth.* 克莱尔要我保证把真相告诉她。□ *He told his story to The Times.* 他向《泰晤士报》的记者讲述了自己的故事。

LANGUAGE HELP 语言提示
See note at **say**. 见 say 的语言提示。

2 to order someone to do something 命令；吩咐：*The police officer told him to get out of his car.* 警察叫他下车。
3 to be able to judge correctly what is happening or what is true 判断；看出：*I could tell that Tom was tired and bored.* 我看得出汤姆又累又烦。
tell someone off to speak to someone in an angry or serious way because they have done something wrong 斥责某人；训斥某人：*He never listened to us when we told him off.* 我们教训他的时候，他从来都听不进去。

telly /ˈteli/ *noun* 名词 (**tellies**) (*informal* 非正式)
→ see 见 **television**

temper /ˈtempə/ *noun* 名词
have a temper to become angry very easily 脾气坏；脾气大：*Their mother had a terrible temper.* 他们的妈妈脾气特别不好。
in a temper angry 在生气；在气头上：*I was in a temper last night because I was so tired.* 我昨晚因为太累了情绪不好。
lose your temper to suddenly become angry 发脾气：*Simon lost his temper and hit me.* 西蒙大发雷霆，还打了我。

temperature /ˈtemprətʃə/ *noun* 名词
1 how hot or cold something is 温度；气温：

At night here, the temperature drops below freezing. 这里晚上的温度降至冰点以下。
2 uncountable 不可数 how hot someone's body is 体温: *The baby's temperature continued to rise.* 婴儿的体温持续上升。
have a temperature to have a temperature that is higher than it should be 发烧
take someone's temperature to use an instrument (= a thermometer) to measure the temperature of someone's body 量某人的体温: *The nurse took my temperature.* 护士给我量了体温。

temple /ˈtempəl/ **countable noun** 可数名词 a building where people pray to their god or gods 寺庙；庙宇；神殿: *We visited the biggest Sikh temple in India.* 我们参观了印度最大的锡克教庙宇。

temporary /ˈtempərəri/ **adjective** 形容词 lasting for only a certain time 暂时的；临时的: *His job here is only temporary.* 他在这里的工作只是临时的。
▶ **temporarily** /ˈtempərəli/ **adverb** 副词: *Her website was temporarily shut down yesterday.* 她的网站昨天被临时关闭了。

tempt /tempt/ **verb** 动词 (**tempts, tempting, tempted**) to make someone want something, even though it may be wrong or harmful 引诱；诱惑: *Credit cards can tempt people to buy things they can't afford.* 信用卡会让人购买超过自己支付能力的东西。 ▫ *I was tempted to lie, but in the end I told the truth.* 我忍不住想撒谎，但最后我还是说了实话。
▶ **tempting** /ˈtemptɪŋ/ **adjective** 形容词: *The berries look tempting to children, but they're poisonous.* 对孩子们来说浆果看起来很诱人，但它们是有毒的。

temptation /tempˈteɪʃən/ **noun** 名词 the feeling that you want to do something or have something, when you know that it is wrong 引诱；诱惑: *Exercise regularly and resist the temptation to eat snacks.* 定期锻炼，抵挡住吃零食的诱惑。

tempted /ˈtemptɪd/ **adjective** 形容词 feeling that you would like to do something although it may not be a good idea (受诱惑而)想做⋯的: *I was tempted to buy a car, but I paid off my debts instead.* 我本想买车动了心，但我还是去还清了借款。

ten /ten/ the number 10 十

tenant /ˈtenənt/ **countable noun** 可数名词 someone who pays money to use a house or an office 租户；房客: *Each tenant in the flat pays £200 a week.* 公寓里每位租客每周要付 200 英镑。

tend /tend/ **verb** 动词 (**tends, tending, tended**)
tend to to usually do or be something 往往会；经常就: *Women tend to live longer than men.* 女性往往比男性长寿。

tendency /ˈtendənsi/ **countable noun** 可数名词 (**tendencies**) something that usually happens, or something a person usually does 倾向；偏好: *Laura has a tendency to gossip.* 劳拉总爱说长道短。

tender /ˈtendə/ **adjective** 形容词 (**tenderer, tenderest**)
1 kind and gentle 慈爱的；温柔的: *Her voice was tender.* 她的声音很温柔。
▶ **tenderly** /ˈtendəli/ **adverb** 副词: *He kissed her tenderly.* 他温柔地亲了亲她。
2 easy to cut or bite 软的；嫩的: *Cook for about 2 hours, until the meat is tender.* 煮两个小时，直到肉质松软为止。
3 painful when touched 一触即痛的: *My cheek felt very tender.* 我的脸颊一碰就很疼。

tennis /ˈtenɪs/ **uncountable noun** 不可数名词 a game for two or four players, who use rackets (= special bats) to hit a ball across a net between them 网球运动
→ Look at picture on P14 参见彩插第 14 页

tense[1] /tens/ **adjective** 形容词 (**tenser, tensest**)
1 anxious and nervous, and not feeling relaxed 紧张的；焦虑的: *The team were very tense before the game.* 这支队伍赛前非常紧张。
2 when your muscles are tight and not relaxed (肌肉)紧张的，绷紧的: *A bath can relax tense muscles.* 洗个澡可以放松紧张的肌肉。

tense[2] /tens/ **countable noun** 可数名词 the form of a verb that shows whether something is happening in the past, present or future (动词的)时，时态

tension /ˈtenʃən/ **uncountable noun** 不可数名词 a feeling of worry and anxiety that makes it impossible for you to feel relaxed 紧张；焦虑: *Physical exercise can reduce tension.* 体育锻炼可以缓解紧张情绪。

tent /tent/ *countable noun* 可数名词
a shelter made of cloth that is held up by poles and ropes. You sleep in a tent when you go camping. 帐篷

tent 帐篷

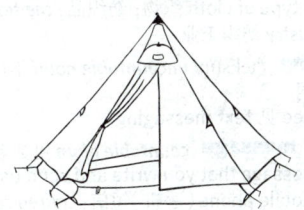

tenth¹ /tenθ/ *adjective* 形容词, *adverb* 副词
counted as number ten in a series 第十：*She's having a party for her tenth birthday.* 她要为她的 10 岁生日办个聚会。

tenth² /tenθ/ *countable noun* 可数名词
one of ten equal parts of something (1/10) 十分之一：*She won the race by a tenth of a second.* 她以领先 0.1 秒的优势赢得了比赛。

term /tɜːm/ *noun* 名词
1 *countable* 可数 a special word or expression that is used by experts in a particular subject 术语；学科用语：*Sodium chloride is the scientific term for table salt.* 氯化钠是食盐的学名。
2 one of the periods of time that a school, college or university year is divided into 学期：*The school's headteacher, Mrs Johnson, will retire at the end of the term.* 该校校长约翰逊夫人将在学期末退休。
3 [**terms**] *plural* 复数 the conditions that all of the people involved in an arrangement must agree to（协议的）条款，条件：*The terms of the agreement are quite simple.* 协议的条款相当简单。

terminal /ˈtɜːmɪnəl/ *countable noun* 可数名词
a place where people begin or end a trip by bus, aircraft or ship 客运站；公交场站；航站楼；码头：*Port Authority is one of the world's busiest bus terminals.* 港务局公共汽车总站是世界上最繁忙的公共汽车站之一。

terminate /ˈtɜːmɪneɪt/ *verb* 动词 (**terminates, terminating, terminated**)
to end something (*formal* 正式) 终止；结束：*His contract was terminated early.* 他的合同提早终止了。

terrace /ˈterɪs/ *countable noun* 可数名词

1 a flat area next to a building, where people can sit（房屋外的）露天平台：*Our house has a terrace overlooking the sea.* 我们家有眺望海景的露台。
2 a line of houses that are joined together by their side walls 排房，排屋（边墙相连的一排房屋）

terraced house /ˌterɪst ˈhaʊs/ *countable noun* 可数名词
one of a row of houses that are joined together by both of their side walls 排房（边墙相连的一排房屋中的一幢）

terrible /ˈterɪbl/ *adjective* 形容词
1 extremely bad 差劲的；糟糕的：*I have a terrible singing voice.* 我唱歌极难听。
▶ **terribly** /ˈterɪbli/ *adverb* 副词：*Our team played terribly today.* 我们队今天打得极差劲。
2 causing great pain or sadness 造成极大痛苦（或悲伤）的：*Thousands of people suffered terrible injuries.* 上千人受了重伤。
▶ **terribly** /ˈterɪbli/ *adverb* 副词：*These people have suffered terribly during the war.* 这些人在战争中受尽磨难。

terrific /təˈrɪfɪk/ *adjective* 形容词
very good (*informal* 非正式) 极好的；绝妙的：*What a terrific idea!* 多棒的点子啊！

terrify /ˈterɪfaɪ/ *verb* 动词 (**terrifies, terrifying, terrified**)
to make someone feel extremely afraid 使恐惧；使受惊吓：*Flying terrifies him.* 他害怕坐飞机。
▶ **terrified** /ˈterɪfaɪd/ *adjective* 形容词：*Jacob is terrified of spiders.* 雅各布怕蜘蛛。

terrifying /ˈterɪfaɪɪŋ/ *adjective* 形容词
making you very afraid 吓人的；令人胆战心惊的：*That was a terrifying experience.* 那是一次可怕的经历。

territory /ˈterətri/ *noun* 名词 (**territories**)
all the land that a particular country owns 领土；领地

terror /ˈterə/ *uncountable noun* 不可数名词
very great fear 恐惧；惊恐：*I shook with terror.* 我吓得直发抖。

terrorism /ˈterəˌrɪzəm/ *uncountable noun* 不可数名词
the use of violence to force a government to do something 恐怖主义：*We need new laws to fight terrorism.* 我们需要制定新法律与恐怖主义作斗争。

terrorist /ˈterərɪst/ *countable noun* 可数名词
a person who uses violence to achieve

their aims 恐怖分子：*terrorist attacks* 恐怖袭击 ◻ *The president called for all nations to come together to defeat terrorists.* 总统号召所有国家共同打击恐怖分子。

test /test/ *verb* 动词 (**tests, testing, tested**)
1 to use or touch something to find out what condition it is in, or how well it works 测试；试验：*Test the temperature of the water with your wrist before you put your baby in the bath.* 把宝宝放进澡盆前要先用手腕测试水温。◻ *The drug has only been tested on mice.* 这种药物只在老鼠身上做过试验。●**test** *countable noun* 可数名词：*The car achieved great results in crash tests.* 这款车在碰撞试验中表现出色。
2 to ask someone questions to find out how much they know about something 测验；考察：*The students were tested on grammar, spelling and punctuation.* 学生们接受了语法、拼写和标点用法的考试。●**test** *countable noun* 可数名词：*Only 15 of the 25 students passed the test.* 25 名学生中只有 15 人通过了测试。

'test ,tube *countable noun* 可数名词
a long thin glass container that is used in scientific experiments 试管

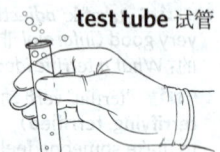

test tube 试管

text[1] /tekst/ *noun* 名词
1 *uncountable* 不可数 all the words in a book, document, newspaper or magazine 文本：*You can insert text, delete text or move text around.* 你可以添加、删除或移动文本。
2 *countable* 可数 an academic or scientific book or short piece of writing（学术或科学方面的）文献，文本：*The bookshelves were filled with religious texts.* 书架上摆满了宗教文献。
3 *countable* 可数 → see 见 **text message**：*The new system can send a text to a mobile phone.* 新系统可以给手机发送短信。

text[2] /tekst/ *verb* 动词 (**texts, texting, texted**)
to send someone a text message on a mobile phone（用手机）给⋯发短信：*Mary texted me when she got home.* 玛丽回到家后给我发了条短信。

textbook /'tekstbʊk/ *also* 亦作 **text book** *countable noun* 可数名词
a book containing facts about a particular subject that is used by people studying that subject 课本；教材：*Amy was in the library reading a textbook on international law.* 埃米在图书馆阅读一本国际法方面的教材。
→ Look at picture on P1 参见彩插第 1 页

textile /'tekstaɪl/ *countable noun* 可数名词 any type of cloth 织物；纺织品：*the textile industry* 纺织工业

texting /'tekstɪŋ/ *uncountable noun* 不可数名词
→ see 见 **text messaging**

'text ,message *countable noun* 可数名词
a message that you write and send using a mobile phone（手机）短信：*Lauren sent her boyfriend a text message asking him to meet her at the restaurant at eight.* 劳伦给男友发短信，让他 8 点在饭店与她见面。
→ Look at picture on P11 参见彩插第 11 页

'text ,messaging *uncountable noun* 不可数名词
sending messages in writing using a mobile phone 发送（手机）短信：*Mobile phones and text messaging make it easy to stay in touch.* 打手机和发短信方便人们保持联系。

texture /'tekstʃə/ *noun* 名词
the way that something feels when you touch it 质地；质感；手感：*The cheese has a soft, creamy texture.* 奶酪的口感柔软滑腻。

than /ðən, STRONG 强读 ðæn/ *preposition* 介词
used when you are comparing two people or things（用于引出比较的第二个人或事物）比：*Tom is taller than his dad.* 汤姆比他爸爸高。◻ *Children learn faster than adults.* 儿童比成人学得快。●**than** *conjunction* 连词：*He should have helped her more than he did.* 他本应该更多地帮助她。

thank /θæŋk/ *verb* 动词 (**thanks, thanking, thanked**)
to say 'thank you' to someone to show that you are grateful to them for something 感谢；向⋯表示感谢：*I thanked them for all their kindness to me.* 我对他们的一番好意表示感谢。

thankful /'θæŋkfʊl/ *adjective* 形容词
grateful and glad that something has happened 感激的；感谢的：*I'm so thankful that they are all safe.* 他们都平安无事，我感到很欣慰。

thankfully /'θæŋkfʊli/ *adverb* 副词
used in order to express approval or happiness about something 幸亏；幸好：

Thankfully, she was not injured. 幸好她没有受伤。

thanks /θæŋks/
1 *exclamation* 感叹词 used when you want to show that you are grateful for something (*informal* 非正式) 谢谢；多谢：*Thanks for the information.* 多谢提供这个信息。▫ *'Tea?' — 'No thanks.'* "喝茶吗？" —— "不了，谢谢。"
2 *plural noun* 复数名词 things that you say when you are grateful to someone for something 感谢；谢意：*I would like to express my thanks to the wonderful hospital staff.* 我想对了不起的医院医护人员表示感谢。
thanks to someone/something because of a particular person or thing 感谢某人／某事物；多亏某人／某事物：*Thanks to Sean's courage, his dad survived.* 多亏了肖恩的勇敢，他父亲才活了下来。

'thank you *exclamation* 感叹词 used when you want to show that you are grateful for something that someone has done for you 谢谢；感谢：*Thank you very much for inviting me to your birthday party.* 非常感谢你邀请我参加你的生日聚会。▫ *'Would you like a cup of coffee?' — 'Thank you, I'd love one.'* "要喝杯咖啡吗？" —— "谢谢，我想来一杯。"

that¹ /ðət, STRONG 强读 ðæt/ *adjective* 形容词 used for talking about someone or something that is a distance away from you in position or time 那，那个：*Look at that guy over there.* 瞧那边的那个家伙。
not that not as much as might be possible 不太；不那么：*Well, actually, it's not that expensive.* 啊，其实也不是那么贵。

that² /ðət, STRONG 强读 ðæt/ *pronoun* 代词
1 used for talking about someone or something that is a distance away from you in position or time（指在空间或时间距离上较远的人或事物）那，那个：*What's that?* 那是什么？
2 used for talking about something that you have mentioned before（指已提及的内容）那，那个：*They said you wanted to talk to me. Why was that?* 他们说你想和我谈谈。为什么？
3 used for showing which person or thing you are talking about（指正在谈论的人或事物）那个：*There's the girl that I told you about.* 那就是我跟你说过的那个女孩。▫ *He hates the town that he lives in.* 他厌恶自己所居住的小镇。

that's that used for saying that you have finished with a particular subject (*informal* 非正式) 就是这样，就这么定了（表示结束某一话题）：*If that's your final decision, I guess that's that.* 如果那就是你最后的决定，我想那就这样吧。

that³ /ðət, STRONG 强读 ðæt/ *conjunction* 连词
1 used for joining two parts of a sentence（用于引导从句）：*He said that he and his wife were coming to New York.* 他说他和妻子要来纽约。▫ *I felt sad that he was leaving.* 他要走了，我很难过。
2 used after 'so' and 'such' to talk about the result of something（用在 so、such 之后，引出某事的结果）：*I shouted so that they could hear me.* 我大声呼喊，以便他们能听见我的话。

that's /ðæts/
short for（缩写 =) 'that is'

thaw /θɔː/ *verb* 动词 (**thaws, thawing, thawed**)
1 to warm something that is frozen until it becomes soft or liquid 使（冷冻食品）解冻：*How long does it take to thaw a frozen chicken?* 化开冻鸡肉要多长时间？
2 to become warm enough to become soft or liquid（冰雪）融化：*We will leave when the snow thaws.* 雪化了我们就走。

thaw（冰雪）融化

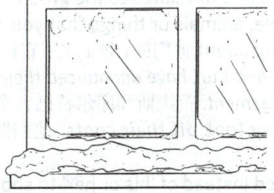

the *article* 冠词

PRONUNCIATION HELP 发音提示
Pronounce **the** /ði/ before a vowel.
Pronounce **the** /ðə/ before a consonant.
*the 在元音前读作 /ði/，在辅音前读作 /ðə/。

1 used before a noun when it is clear which person or thing you are talking about（用于名词之前，指明确提及的人或事物）：*The office staff here are all British.* 这里的办公室职员全都是英国人。▫ *It's always hard to think about the future.* 未来总是难以想象。▫ *The doctor's on his way.*

医生在路上。
2 used before a singular noun to talk about things of that type in general（用于单数名词之前，表示一类事物）: *The computer has developed very fast in recent years.* 计算机近年来发展非常迅速。
3 used with adjectives and plural nouns to talk about all people of a particular type or nationality（与形容词或复数名词连用，表示某一类人或某一国人）: *the British and the French* 英国人和法国人
4 used in front of dates（用于日期之前）: *The meeting should take place on the fifth of May.* 会议应于5月5日召开。
5 used in front of superlative adjectives and adverbs（用于形容词和副词的最高级前）: *Daily walks are the best exercise.* 每天散步是最好的锻炼。

theatre /ˈθiːətə/ *countable noun* 可数名词
a place where you go to see plays or shows 剧场；戏院: *Last night, we went to the theatre to see a play by Chekhov.* 我们昨晚去剧院看了一出契诃夫的戏剧。

theft /θeft/ *noun* 名词
the crime of stealing 偷窃；盗窃罪: *Martinez was arrested for car theft and assault.* 马丁内斯因盗窃车辆罪和侵犯人身罪而被捕。

their /ðeə/ *adjective* 形容词
1 used for showing that something belongs to or relates to the group of people, animals or things that you are talking about 他们的；她们的；它们的: *Janis and Kurt have announced their engagement.* 贾妮斯和库尔特已宣布订婚。□ *They took off their coats.* 他们脱下了大衣。
2 used instead of 'his or her' to show that something belongs or relates to a person, without saying if that person is a man or a woman（代替 his or her，不指明其性别）: *Each student works at their own pace.* 每个学生都按自己的节奏学习。

theirs /ðeəz/ *pronoun* 代词
used for showing that something belongs or relates to the group of people, animals or things that you are talking about 他们的，她们的，它们的（东西）: *The people at the table next to theirs were talking loudly.* 坐在他们邻桌的人正大声交谈着。

them /ðəm, STRONG 强读 ðem/ *pronoun* 代词
1 used for talking about more than one person, animal or thing 他们；她们；它们: *I've lost my keys. Have you seen them?* 我钥匙找不到了。你见到了吗？
2 used instead of 'him or her', to talk about a person without saying whether that person is a man or a woman（代替 him or her，不指明其性别）: *If anyone calls, tell them I'm out.* 如果有人来电，告诉他们我不在。

theme /θiːm/ *countable noun* 可数名词
the most important idea of a piece of writing or a discussion, or its subject 主题；题目: *Progress was the main theme of his speech.* 他演讲的主题是进步。

themselves /ðəmˈselvz/ *pronoun* 代词
1 used for talking about people, animals or things that you have just talked about（指提到过的人、事物或动物）他们自己，她们自己，它们自己: *They all seemed to be enjoying themselves.* 他们似乎都玩得很开心。
2 used for saying that certain people did something, and not anyone else（用于强调）他们自己，她们自己，它们自己: *My parents designed our house themselves.* 我们家是我父母亲自设计的。

then /ðen/ *adverb* 副词
1 at a particular time in the past or in the future（指过去）当时，那时；（指将来）届时: *I bought this flat two years ago. Since then, house prices have fallen.* 我两年前买的这套公寓。从那以后，房价就跌了。
2 used for saying that one thing happens after another 然后；接着: *Add the onion and then the garlic.* 放入洋葱，然后放大蒜。
3 used for starting the second part of a sentence that begins with 'if' 那么；因此: *If you are not sure about this, then you must say so.* 如果你对此不确定，那你就必须这么说。

theory /ˈθɪəri/ *noun* 名词 (**theories**)
an idea or a set of ideas that tries to explain something 理论；学说: *The Big Bang Theory explains the beginning of the universe.* 大爆炸理论解释了宇宙的起源。

therapist /ˈθerəpɪst/ *countable noun* 可数名词
a person who helps people who have emotional or physical problems 治疗师: *Scott saw a therapist after his daughter died.* 斯科特在女儿去世后去看了治疗师。

therapy /ˈθerəpi/ *noun* 名词 (**therapies**)
1 uncountable 不可数 the process of

talking to a person with special training about your problems and your relationships so that you can understand them and then change the way you feel and behave 心理治疗: *He returned to work, but he was still having therapy.* 他回到了工作岗位, 但还在接受心理治疗。 **2** a treatment for a particular illness or condition (对某特定病情的)治疗, 疗法: *Scientists are working on a therapy to slow down the aging process.* 科学家正在研究减缓衰老进程的疗法。

there¹ /ðə/ *pronoun* 代词
used with the verb 'be' to say that something exists or is happening (与动词 be 连用, 表示存在或发生): *There is a swimming pool in the garden.* 花园里有一个游泳池。 □ *Are there any biscuits left?* 还有饼干剩下吗?

there² /ðə, STRONG 强读 ðeə/ *adverb* 副词
1 used for talking about a place that has already been mentioned (指已提及的地方)那儿: *I'm going back to California. My family have lived there for many years.* 我要回加利福尼亚了。 我家人在那里生活了许多年。
2 used for talking about a place that you are pointing to or looking at (表示指向或看向的地方)那儿, 那边: '*Where is Mr Hernandez?*' — '*He's sitting over there.*' "埃尔南德斯先生在哪儿?" —— "他坐在那里。" □ *There she is, at the corner of the street.* 她在那儿, 在街的拐角。
3 used when you are speaking on the telephone, to ask if someone is available to speak to you (用于打电话询问某人在不在)在: *Hello, is Tony there, please?* 你好, 请问托尼在吗?

here you are or **there you are** used when you are offering something to someone (*informal* 非正式)给你; 拿去吧: '*There you are, Mr Walters,*' *she said, giving him his documents.* "给你, 沃尔特斯先生。"她边说边把他的文件递给他。

therefore /ˈðeəfɔː/ *adverb* 副词
used when you are talking about the result of an action or a situation 所以; 因此: *Matthew is injured and therefore will not play in Saturday's game.* 马修受伤了, 因此不会参加周六的比赛。

there's /ðəz/
short for (缩写 =) 'there is'

thermometer /θəˈmɒmɪtə/ *countable noun* 可数名词
an instrument for measuring how hot or cold something is 温度计; 体温计

thermometer 温度计

these /ðiːz/ *adjective* 形容词
1 used for talking about people or things that are near you, especially when you touch them or point to them (指离自己近的人或事物)这些: *These scissors are heavy.* 这把剪刀很沉。 ● **these** *pronoun* 代词: *Do you like these?* 你喜欢这些吗?
2 used for talking about someone or something that you have already mentioned (指已提及的人或事物)这些: *These people need more support.* 这些人需要更多的支持。
3 used for introducing people or things that you are going to talk about (用于引出将要提及的人或事物)这些: *If you're looking for a builder, these phone numbers will be useful.* 如果你在找建筑工人, 这些电话号码能用上。

they /ðeɪ/ *pronoun* 代词
1 used when you are talking about more than one person, animal or thing 他们; 她们; 它们: *She said goodbye to the children as they left for school.* 孩子们离开去上学时, 她向他们道别。 □ '*Where are your toys?*' — '*They're in the garden.*' "你的玩具呢?" —— "它们在花园里。"
2 used instead of 'he or she' when you are talking about a person without saying whether that person is a man or a woman (代替 he or she, 不指明其性别): '*Someone phoned. They said they would call back later.*' "有人来过电话, 说晚点儿会再打过来。"

they'd /ðeɪd/
1 short for (缩写 =) 'they had'
2 short for (缩写 =) 'they would'

they'll /ðeɪl/
short for (缩写 =) 'they will'

they're /ðeə, ðeɪə/
short for (缩写 =) 'they are'

they've /ðeɪv/
short for (缩写 =) 'they have', especially when 'have' is an auxiliary verb (尤当 have 为助动词时)

thick /θɪk/ *adjective* 形容词 (**thicker, thickest**)

1 having a large distance between one side and the other 厚的；粗的：*I cut a thick slice of bread.* 我切了一片厚厚的面包。

thick 厚的
thin 薄的

2 used for saying or asking how wide or deep something is *…宽的；…深的；…厚的：*The book is two inches thick.* 这本书有两英寸厚。 □ *How thick are these walls?* 这些墙有多厚？

▶ **thickness** /ˈθɪknəs/ *uncountable noun* 不可数名词：*The cooking time depends on the thickness of the steaks.* 烹饪时长取决于牛排的厚度。

3 consisting of a lot of hairs growing closely together（毛发）浓密的：*Jessica has thick dark curly hair.* 杰茜卡有一头乌黑浓密的卷发。

4 difficult to see through 浓的；混浊的：*The crash happened in thick fog.* 碰撞事故发生于浓雾中。

5 not flowing easily（液体）浓的，稠的：*Cook the sauce until it is thick and creamy.* 将酱汁烹煮至浓稠细腻。

thief /θiːf/ *countable noun* 可数名词 (**thieves** /θiːvz/)
a person who steals something from another person 小偷；窃贼：*The thieves took his camera.* 窃贼偷走了他的相机。

thigh /θaɪ/ *countable noun* 可数名词
the top part of your leg, above your knee 股；大腿：*She's broken her thigh bone.* 她大腿骨骨折了。
→ Look at picture on P4 参见彩插第 4 页

thin /θɪn/ *adjective* 形容词 (**thinner, thinnest**)

1 having a small distance between one side and the other 薄的；细的：*The book is printed on very thin paper.* 这本书是用很薄的纸印刷的。

2 having no extra fat on your body（身体）瘦的：*Bob was a tall, thin man.* 鲍勃是个又高又瘦的男人。 □ *His arms and legs were very thin.* 他的胳膊和腿都很瘦。

3 flowing easily（液体）稀的，淡的：*The soup was thin and tasteless.* 这汤淡而无味。

thing /θɪŋ/ *noun* 名词

1 *countable* 可数 an object 东西；物品：*What's that thing in the middle of the road?* 路中间那个是什么东西？

2 [**things**] *plural* 复数 possessions 财物；财产：*She told him to take all his things and not to return.* 她让他带着他全部家当离开，再也别回来。

3 *countable* 可数 something that happens or something that you think or talk about 事情；事件：*They were driving home when a strange thing happened.* 他们开车回家时，一件奇怪的事情发生了。 □ *We had so many things to talk about.* 我们有太多事情要聊。

4 [**things**] *plural* 复数 used for talking about life in general（泛指）情况：*How are things with you?* 你近来怎么样？

think /θɪŋk/ *verb* 动词 (**thinks, thinking, thought**)

1 to believe something or have an opinion about it 想；认为；觉得：*I think that it will snow tomorrow.* 我觉得明天会下雪。 □ *What do you think of my idea?* 你觉得我的想法如何？

2 to use your mind to consider something 想，思考，考虑：*She closed her eyes for a moment, trying to think.* 她闭了一会儿眼睛，努力思考着。 □ *What are you thinking about?* 你在想什么？

think of doing something or **think about doing something** to consider doing something 考虑做某事：*I'm thinking of going to college next year.* 我考虑明年上去大学。

think of something used for saying that something comes into your mind 想出（或想起）某事物：*I know who he is but I can't think of his name.* 我知道他是谁，但是我想不起他的名字。

think something over to consider something carefully before you make a decision about it 认真考虑某事物；仔细思考某事物：*They've offered her the job but she said she needs time to think it over.* 他们给了她这份工作，但她说要仔细考虑一下。

third¹ /θɜːd/ *adjective* 形容词, *adverb* 副词
the item in a series that you count as number three 第三: *My office is the third door on the right.* 我的办公室是从右数第三间。 □ *Katie came third in the race.* 凯蒂在比赛中得了第三名。

third² /θɜːd/ *noun* 名词
one of three equal parts of something (1/3) 三分之一
→ Look at picture on P2 参见彩插第 2 页

thirst /θɜːst/ *uncountable noun* 不可数名词
the feeling that you want to drink something 渴；口渴: *Drink water to satisfy your thirst.* 喝点水解解渴。

thirsty /ˈθɜːsti/ *adjective* 形容词 (**thirstier, thirstiest**)
wanting to drink something 渴的；口渴的: *Drink some water whenever you feel thirsty.* 感到口渴时就喝水。

thirteen /ˌθɜːˈtiːn/
the number 13 十三
▶ **thirteenth** /ˌθɜːˈtiːnθ/ *adjective* 形容词, *adverb* 副词: *It's my thirteenth birthday tomorrow.* 明天是我 13 岁生日。

thirty /ˈθɜːti/
the number 30 三十
▶ **thirtieth** /ˈθɜːtiəθ/ *adjective* 形容词, *adverb* 副词: *We celebrated the thirtieth anniversary of my parents' wedding.* 我们给我父母庆祝了 30 周年结婚纪念日。

this¹ /ðɪs/ *adjective* 形容词
1 used for talking about a person or a thing that is near you, especially when you touch them or point to them（指较近的人或事物）这，这个: *I like this room much better than the other one.* 这个房间比另一间让我中意多了。
2 used for talking about someone or something that you have already mentioned（指先前提及的人或事物）这，这个: *How can we solve this problem?* 我们如何才能解决这个问题呢？
3 used for talking about the next day, month or season（指接下来的日、月或季）本，今，这个: *We have tickets for this Sunday's performance.* 我们有这周日演出的门票。□ *We're getting married this June.* 我们将在今年 6 月结婚。

this² /ðɪs/ *pronoun* 代词
1 used for talking about a person or a thing that is near you, especially when you touch them or point to them（指较近的人或事物）这位，这个: *'Would you like a different one?' — 'No, this is great.'* "你要换一个别的吗？" —— "不用了，这个挺好。"
2 used for introducing someone or something that you are going to talk about（引出将要谈论的人或事物）这个: *This is what I will do. I will telephone Anna and explain.* 这是我要做的：我会给安娜打电话解释清楚。
this is used for saying who you are when you are speaking on the telephone（通话时介绍自己）我是，这里是: *Hello, this is John Thompson.* 喂，我是约翰·汤普森。

thorn /θɔːn/ *countable noun* 可数名词
a sharp point on some plants and trees（某些草木的）刺，棘刺: *He removed a thorn from his foot.* 他从脚上拔下一根刺。

thorough /ˈθʌrə/ *adjective* 形容词
done completely, and with great attention to detail 彻底的；全面的；详尽的: *There will be a thorough investigation into the cause of the crash.* 发生撞击事故的原因将得到彻查。
▶ **thoroughly** /ˈθʌrəli/ *adverb* 副词: *The food must be thoroughly cooked.* 食物必须彻底煮熟。

those /ðəʊz/ *adjective* 形容词
1 used when you are talking about people or things that are a distance away from you in position or time, especially when you point to them（指时间或空间上较远的人或事物）那些: *What are those buildings?* 那些是什么建筑？ ● **those** *pronoun* 代词: *Those are nice shoes.* 那双鞋子不错。
2 used for talking about people or things that have already been mentioned（指已经提及的人或事物）那些: *I don't know any of those people you mentioned.* 你说的那些人我一个也不认识。

though /ðəʊ/ *conjunction* 连词
1 although, or despite the fact that 尽管；虽然: *I love him though I do not know him.* 我爱他，尽管我不了解他。 □ *Ashley plays in adult tennis games even though she is only 15.* 阿什莉打成人网球赛，尽管她只有 15 岁。
2 but 不过；然而: *I think I left home at about seven thirty, though I could be wrong.* 我觉得我是 7 点半左右离开家的，但也可能不是。

thought¹ /θɔːt/
→ see 见 **think**

thought² /θɔːt/ *noun* 名词
1 countable 可数 an idea or an opinion 想法；主意: *The thought of Nick made her sad.* 一想到尼克，她就伤心。 ◻ *I just had a thought. Why don't you have a party?* 我刚刚有个想法。你们为什么不开场派对呢？ ◻ *What are your thoughts about the political situation?* 你对政局有什么看法？
2 uncountable 不可数 the activity of thinking, especially deeply and carefully 思考；（尤指）沉思: *Alice was deep in thought.* 艾丽斯陷入了沉思。

thoughtful /ˈθɔːtfʊl/ *adjective* 形容词
1 quiet and serious because you are thinking about something 沉思的；深思的: *Nancy paused, looking thoughtful.* 南希顿了一下，若有所思。
▶ **thoughtfully** /ˈθɔːtfʊli/ *adverb* 副词: *Daniel nodded thoughtfully.* 丹尼尔若有所思地点点头。
2 thinking and caring about other people's feelings 考虑周到的；体贴的: *Ben is a thoughtful and caring boy.* 本是个体贴周到的男孩。

thoughtless /ˈθɔːtləs/ *adjective* 形容词
not caring or thinking about other people's feelings 不为他人着想的；欠考虑的: *It was thoughtless of me to forget your birthday.* 我太粗心了，竟然忘了你的生日。

thousand /ˈθaʊzənd/

> **LANGUAGE HELP 语言提示**
> The plural form is **thousand** after a number. 用在数字后，复数形式为 thousand。

the number 1,000 一千: *Over five thousand people attended the conference.* 逾五千人出席了此次大会。
thousands of a very large number of things or people 成千上万的；数以千计的: *I have been there thousands of times.* 我去过那儿很多次。

thread¹ /θred/ *noun* 名词
a long, very thin piece of cotton, nylon or silk that you use for sewing（缝纫用的）细线: *a needle and thread* 针线

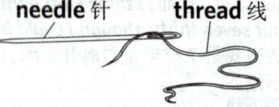
needle 针　　thread 线

thread² /θred/ *verb* 动词 (**threads, threading, threaded**)
to put a piece of thread through the hole in the top of a needle so that you can sew with it 穿（针）: *I threaded a needle and sewed the button on the shirt.* 我穿好针，把扣子缝到衬衫上。

threat /θret/ *noun* 名词
1 when you say that something bad will happen to someone if they do not do what you want 威胁；恐吓: *The journalist received a death threat.* 这位记者收到一份死亡威胁。
2 countable 可数 something that can harm someone or something 形成威胁的事物: *Stress is a threat to people's health.* 压力威胁人们健康。

threaten /ˈθretən/ *verb* 动词 (**threatens, threatening, threatened**)
1 to say that you will hurt someone if they do not do what you want 威胁；恐吓: *Army officers threatened to destroy the town.* 陆军军官威胁要摧毁那座小镇。 ◻ *If you threaten me, I will go to the police.* 如果你威胁我，我就去报警。
▶ **threatening** /ˈθretənɪŋ/ *adjective* 形容词: *He was arrested for using threatening behaviour toward police officers.* 他因威胁警察而被捕。
2 to be likely to harm people or things 可能危害到；威胁到: *The fire threatened more than 1,000 homes.* 大火威胁到1,000多户人家。

three /θriː/
the number 3 三: *We waited three months before going back.* 我们等了3个月才回去。

three-dimensional /ˌθriːdaɪˈmenʃənəl, -dɪ-/ *adjective* 形容词
1 solid rather than flat. The short form '3D' is also used. 三维的，立体的（缩写形式为 3D）: *We made a three-dimensional model.* 我们制作了一个三维模型。
2 looking deep or solid rather than flat 三维的；有立体感的: *The software generates three-dimensional images.* 该软件能生成三维图像。

threw /θruː/
→ see 见 **throw**

thrill¹ /θrɪl/ *countable noun* 可数名词
a sudden feeling of great excitement 狂喜；激动；兴奋: *I can remember the thrill of opening my birthday presents when I was a child.* 我还记得小时候打开生日礼物时的兴

奋劲儿。

thrill² /θrɪl/ *verb* 动词 (**thrills, thrilling, thrilled**)
to give you a feeling of great excitement 使狂喜；使激动不已: *Manchester United thrilled the crowd with a 5-3 victory.* 曼联队以 5 比 3 赢得胜利，这令观众兴奋不已。

thrilled /θrɪld/ *adjective* 形容词
very happy and excited about something 欣喜若狂的；兴奋不已的: *I was so thrilled to get a good mark for my maths exam.* 我数学考试得了高分，感到非常兴奋。

thriller /ˈθrɪlə/ *countable noun* 可数名词
an exciting book, film or play about a crime 惊险小说；惊悚电影；惊险戏剧: *The book is a historical thriller.* 这本书是一部历史惊险小说。

thrilling /ˈθrɪlɪŋ/ *adjective* 形容词
very exciting and enjoyable 扣人心弦的；激动人心的: *It was a thrilling finish to the tournament.* 锦标赛结尾真是激动人心。

thrive /θraɪv/ *verb* 动词 (**thrives, thriving, thrived**)
to do well and be successful, healthy or strong 兴旺；欣欣向荣: *Some plants thrive in the shade.* 有些植物喜阴。 □ *Their national film industry is thriving. It produces thousands of films each year.* 他们国家的电影业蓬勃发展，每年制作数千部影片。

throat /θrəʊt/ *countable noun* 可数名词
1 the back of your mouth and inside your neck, where you swallow 咽喉；喉咙: *He spent two days at home with a sore throat.* 他嗓子疼，在家待了两天。
2 the front part of your neck 喉部；颈前部: *Mr Williams grabbed him by the throat.* 威廉斯先生掐住了他的喉咙。

throb /θrɒb/ *verb* 动词 (**throbs, throbbing, throbbed**)
1 to beat regularly and very strongly, or to make a regular sound, like your heart 悸动；(强烈而有节奏地)跳动，搏动: *His heart throbbed with excitement.* 他的心激动得怦怦直跳。 □ *The ship's engines throbbed.* 轮船的发动机隆隆地震动着。
2 to beat regularly with pain (有规律地)抽动，抽痛: *Kevin's head throbbed.* 凯文头抽痛。

throne /θrəʊn/ *countable noun* 可数名词
the special chair where a king or a queen sits on important official occasions (国王或女王的)宝座，御座

through /θruː/ *preposition* 介词
1 from one side of something to the other side 穿过；通过: *The bullet went through the front windscreen.* 子弹穿了前挡风玻璃。 □ *We walked through the crowd.* 我们穿过了人群。 □ *Alice looked through the window.* 艾丽斯透过窗户往外看。
● **through** *adverb* 副词: *There was a hole in the wall and water was coming through.* 墙上有个洞，水从洞里进来。
2 from the beginning until the end of a period of time 自始至终；从头到尾: *She kept quiet all through breakfast.* 早餐时，她从头到尾都沉默不语。
3 because of 因为；由于: *I only succeeded through hard work.* 我全凭努力工作才成功的。

throughout /θruːˈaʊt/ *preposition* 介词
1 during all of a particular period of time 贯穿…期间: *It rained heavily throughout the game.* 整个比赛期间都下着大雨。
2 in all parts of a place 遍及；在…各处: *Thousands of children throughout Africa suffer from the condition.* 整个非洲数以千计的儿童患有此病。 ● **throughout** *adverb* 副词: *The flat is painted white throughout.* 这套公寓全部刷成了白色。

throw /θrəʊ/ *verb* 动词 (**throws, throwing, threw, thrown**)
to move your hand or arm quickly and let go of an object that you are holding, so that it moves through the air 扔；抛；掷: *The crowd began throwing stones at the police.* 众人开始朝警察扔石头。 ● **throw** *countable noun* 可数名词: *That was a good throw.* 那一下扔得好。

throw something away or **throw something out** to get rid of something that you do not want 扔掉某物；丢弃某物: *I never throw anything away.* 我从不扔东西。 □ *I've decided to throw out all the clothes I never wear.* 我决定扔掉所有从来不穿的衣服。

thrown /θrəʊn/
→ see 见 **throw**

thud /θʌd/ *countable noun* 可数名词
the sound that a heavy object makes when it hits the ground (重物撞击地面发出的)砰的一声: *She tripped and fell with a thud.* 她绊了一跤，砰的一声摔倒了。

thumb /θʌm/ *countable noun* 可数名词
the short thick finger on your hand 拇指；

thump – tie

O'Donnell missed the game because of a broken thumb. 奥唐奈拇指骨折了，未能参加比赛。

thump /θʌmp/ *verb* 动词 (**thumps, thumping, thumped**)
1 to hit something hard with your hand (用手) 捶打，重击: *Kazuo thumped the table with his fist.* 和雄挥拳捶桌子。
2 used for saying that someone's heart beats strongly and quickly because they are afraid or excited (心脏因恐惧或激动而) 怦怦地跳，悸动: *Her heart was thumping loudly in her chest.* 她的心在胸口怦怦直跳。

thunder /'θʌndə(r)/ *uncountable noun* 不可数名词
the loud noise that you sometimes hear from the sky during a storm 雷；雷声: *Last night there was thunder and lightning.* 昨晚电闪雷鸣。

thunderstorm /'θʌndəstɔːm/ *countable noun* 可数名词
a very noisy storm 雷暴；雷雨: *The tree was hit by lightning during a thunderstorm last night.* 那棵树在昨晚的雷暴中被闪电击中。

Thursday /'θɜːzdeɪ, -di/ *noun* 名词
the day after Wednesday and before Friday 星期四: *On Thursday Barbara invited me to her house for lunch.* 周四芭芭拉邀请我去她家吃午饭。 □ *We go to the supermarket every Thursday morning.* 我们每周四上午去超市。

tick /tɪk/ *verb* 动词 (**ticks, ticking, ticked**)
1 to make a regular series of short sounds 发出嘀嗒声: *An alarm clock ticked loudly on the bedside table.* 闹钟在床头柜上嘀嗒地走着，声音很大。 • **tick** *countable noun* 可数名词: *I could hear the tick of the clock in the hall.* 我能听见大厅里钟的嘀嗒声。
2 (*American* 美国英语: **check**) to put a written mark √ on a piece of paper to show that something is correct or that it has been done 打钩；勾选: *Tick the correct answer.* 勾选出正确答案。 • **tick** (*American* 美国英语: **check mark**) *countable noun* 可数名词: *Put a tick in the box.* 在方框内打钩。

ticket /'tɪkɪt/ *countable noun* 可数名词
a small piece of paper that shows that you have paid to go somewhere or to do something 票；入场券: *Where are the tickets for tonight's game?* 今晚比赛的门票

在哪里？ □ *He had a first-class plane ticket for London.* 他有一张飞伦敦的头等舱机票。

tickle /'tɪkəl/ *verb* 动词 (**tickles, tickling, tickled**)
to move your fingers lightly over a part of someone's body to make them laugh 胳肢；轻挠(身体部位)使人发笑: *Stephanie was cuddling the baby and tickling her toes.* 斯蒂芬妮抱着那个婴儿，挠着她的脚趾。

tide /taɪd/ *countable noun* 可数名词
the regular change in the level of the sea towards the land and away from the land that happens twice a day 潮；潮汐；潮水: *The tide was going out.* 要退潮了。

tidy¹ /'taɪdi/ *adjective* 形容词 (**tidier, tidiest**)
1 liking everything to be in its correct place 爱整洁的；爱整齐的: *I'm not a very tidy person.* 我不是个特别爱整洁的人。
2 neat, and arranged in an organized way 整洁的；整齐的；井井有条的: *The room was neat and tidy.* 房间干净整洁。

tidy² /'taɪdi/ *verb* 动词 (**tidies, tidying, tidied**) (also 亦作 **tidy up**) to organize a place by putting things in their proper places 整理；收拾: *She tidied her room.* 她打扫了她的房间。 □ *You relax while I tidy up the house.* 我打扫屋子，你好好休息。

tie¹ /taɪ/ *verb* 动词 (**ties, tying, tied**)
1 (also 亦作 **tie up**) to fasten or fix something, using string or a rope 系；拴；绑: *He tied the dog to the fence.* 他把狗拴在栅栏上。 □ *She tied the ends of the two ropes together.* 她把两条绳子的末端系在一起。 □ *She tied her scarf over her head.* 她用围巾包着头。 □ *His hands were tied with rope.* 他的双手被绳子绑着。 □ *I bent down to tie my shoelaces.* 我弯下腰系鞋带。 □ *The woman tied up her dog outside the shop.* 那个女人把她的狗拴在商店外面。
2 to have the same number of points at the end of a game (比赛中) 打成平局: *The teams tied 2-2.* 两队打成2比2平。

tie² /taɪ/ *countable noun* 可数名词
1 a long narrow piece of cloth that you wear around your neck with a shirt 领带: *Jason took off his jacket and loosened his tie.* 贾森脱下夹克，松了松领带。
2 when teams have the same number of points at the end of a game (比赛的) 平局，平分: *The first game ended in a tie.* 第一场比赛打成了平局。

3 a connection that you have with people or a place（与某人或某地的）关系，联系: *Quebec has close ties to France.* 魁北克与法国关系密切。

tiger /ˈtaɪɡə/ *countable noun* 可数名词
a large wild animal of the cat family. Tigers are usually orange with black stripes. 虎；老虎

tight /taɪt/ *adjective* 形容词, *adverb* 副词 **(tighter, tightest)**
1 small, and fitting closely to your body 紧身的: *Amanda was wearing a tight black dress.* 阿曼达穿着一条黑色的紧身连衣裙。
▸ **tightly** /ˈtaɪtli/ *adverb* 副词: *Her jacket fastened tightly at the waist.* 她的夹克腰部收得很紧。
2 very firm or firmly 紧紧的（地）；牢牢的（地）: *He kept a tight hold of her arm.* 他紧紧地抓着她的胳膊。□ *Richard put his arms around her and held her tight.* 理查德搂住她，紧紧地抱着。□ *Just hold tight to my hand and don't let go.* 就紧紧地握着我的手，不要松开。
▸ **tightly** /ˈtaɪtli/ *adverb* 副词: *The children hugged me tightly.* 孩子们紧紧地搂住我。

tighten /ˈtaɪtən/ *verb* 动词 **(tightens, tightening, tightened)**
to make something tighter 使变紧；使更牢固: *She tightened the belt on her robe.* 她紧了紧浴袍的腰带。□ *He tightened the last screw.* 他将最后一颗螺丝拧紧。

tights /taɪts/ *plural noun* 复数名词
a piece of tight clothing that covers the lower body, worn by women, girls and dancers（女子或舞蹈者穿的）紧身裤袜，紧身下装

tile /taɪl/ *noun* 名词
a flat, square object that is used for covering floors, walls or roofs 瓷砖；墙砖；地砖

till[1] /tɪl/ *preposition* 介词
until 直到: *They had to wait till Monday to phone the bank.* 他们不得不等到周一再打电话给银行。● **till** *conjunction* 连词: *I didn't leave home till I was nineteen.* 我 19 岁时才离开家。

till[2] /tɪl/ *countable noun* 可数名词
a machine that holds money in a shop（商店的）现金出纳机，收银机

tilt /tɪlt/ *verb* 动词 **(tilts, tilting, tilted)**
to have one end higher than the other 倾斜；倾侧: *The boat tilted as Eric leaned over the side.* 埃里克身体一探出船舷，船就倾斜了。

timber /ˈtɪmbə/ *uncountable noun* 不可数名词
wood that is used for building and making things 木材: *There are timber floors throughout the house.* 整座房子都铺了木地板。

time[1] /taɪm/ *noun* 名词
1 *uncountable* 不可数 something that we measure in minutes, hours, days and years 时间: *Time passed, and still Mary did not come back.* 时间一点点流逝，玛丽仍然没有回来。□ *I've known Mr Martin for a long time.* 我认识马丁先生很久了。□ *Listen to me. I haven't got much time.* 听我说，我没有多少时间。
2 *singular* 单数 used when you are talking about a particular point in the day, that you describe in hours and minutes 钟点；时刻: *'What time is it?' — 'Eight o'clock.'* "几点了？" —— "8 点。" □ *He asked me the time.* 他问我几点了。
3 the point in the day when something happens（某事发生的）时刻: *Departure times are 08.15 from London, and 10.15 from Birmingham.* 伦敦的发车时间为 8 点 15 分，伯明翰的发车时间为 10 点 15 分。□ *It's time to go home.* 该回家了。
4 *countable* 可数 used for talking about a particular period of time in the past（过去的）时期，时代: *At that time there were no cars.* 那个年代没有汽车。
5 *countable* 可数 used for talking about an experience that you had（个人经历的）时光，时日: *Sarah and I had a great time at the party.* 我和萨拉在聚会上玩得很愉快。
6 *countable* 可数 used for talking about how often you do something 次；回: *Try to exercise at least three times a week.* 尽量一周至少锻炼 3 次。

> **LANGUAGE HELP** 语言提示
> Do not say 不要说 'one time a day/week/month/year' or 或 'two times a day/week/month/year'; instead, say 而要说: **'once a day/week/month/year'**（一天 / 周 / 月 / 年一次）or **'twice a day/week/month/year'**（一天 / 周 / 月 / 年两次）。

7 [**times**] *plural* 复数 used after numbers when you are showing how much bigger or smaller one thing is than another 倍: *The sun is 400 times bigger than the moon.* 太阳的大小是月球的 400 倍。

all the time continually or very often 一直；始终：*We can't be together all the time.* 我们不能一直在一起。
at a time together 一次；每次：*Patients may have two visitors at a time.* 患者每次可以有两位探视者。
at times sometimes 有时；偶尔：*Every job is boring at times.* 任何工作都会偶尔让人感到厌烦。
for the time being now, but only for a short time 眼下；暂时：*The situation is calm for the time being.* 局势暂时平静。
from time to time sometimes but not often 偶尔；有时：*Her daughters visited her from time to time.* 她的女儿们偶尔来看望她。
in a few minutes'/days'/weeks' time after a few minutes/days/weeks 几分钟／几天／几周后：*Presidential elections will be held in a few days' time.* 总统选举将于数日后举行。
in time not late 及时：*I arrived just in time for my flight to Bristol.* 我将将赶上了前往布里斯托尔的航班。
on time not late or early 准时；按时：*The train arrived at the station on time at eleven thirty.* 火车于 11 点 30 分准时到站。
take your time to do something slowly 不着急；慢慢来：*'Take your time,' Ted told him. 'I'm in no hurry.'* "慢慢来。"特德跟他说，"我不急。"

time² /taɪm/ *verb* 动词 (**times, timing, timed**) to measure how long an activity lasts 测定⋯⋯所需的时间：*Practise your speech and time yourself, so that you don't talk for too long.* 练习演讲并计时，这样就不会讲太长时间。

timeline /ˈtaɪmlaɪn/ also 亦作 **time line** *countable noun* 可数名词
a picture that shows the order of historical events 大事记；大事年表：*The timeline shows important events from the Earth's creation to the present day.* 大事记展示了地球自创世至今的重大事件。

times /taɪmz/ *conjunction* 连词
used when you are multiplying numbers. Three times five is written 3 x 5. 乘；乘以：*Four times six is 24.* *4 乘以 6 等于 24。

timetable /ˈtaɪmteɪbəl/ *countable noun* 可数名词
a list of the times when trains, buses or planes arrive and depart, or when something happens 时刻表；运行时刻表：*Have you checked the bus timetable?* 你查过公共汽车时刻表了吗？ □ *a school timetable* 课程表
→ Look at picture on P1 参见彩插第 1 页

time zone *countable noun* 可数名词
one of the areas that the world is divided into for measuring time 时区：*We were tired after a long flight across several time zones.* 经过穿越几个时区的长途飞行，我们感到很累。

timid /ˈtɪmɪd/ *adjective* 形容词
shy and nervous, and lacking confidence in yourself 羞怯的；胆小的：*I was a timid child.* 我是个胆小的孩子。
▶ **timidly** /ˈtɪmɪdli/ *adverb* 副词：*The little boy stepped forward timidly.* 小男孩怯生生地向前走。

timing /ˈtaɪmɪŋ/ *uncountable noun* 不可数名词
the skill of judging the right moment to do something 时机掌握；时间选择：*'Am I too early?' — 'No, your timing is perfect.'* "我来得太早了吗？"——"不，你来得正是时候。"

tin /tɪn/ *noun* 名词
1 *uncountable* 不可数 a type of soft metal 锡：*a tin can* 锡罐
2 *countable* 可数 a metal container used for keeping food or drink fresh（保存食品或饮料的）金属罐：*a tin of soup* 一罐汤

tin-opener *countable noun* 可数名词
a tool that you use for opening tins 开罐器；罐头刀

tiny /ˈtaɪni/ *adjective* 形容词 (**tinier, tiniest**)
extremely small 极小的；微小的：*The living room is tiny.* 客厅极小。

tip¹ /tɪp/ *countable noun* 可数名词
1 the end of something long and narrow 末梢；尖端：*He pressed the tips of his fingers together.* 他将指尖捏在一起。
2 a useful piece of advice 忠告；建议；指点：*The article gives tips on applying for jobs.* 这篇文章提供了求职建议。
3 money that you give someone to thank them for a job they have done for you 小费：*I gave the waiter a tip.* 我给了侍者小费。

tip² /tɪp/ *verb* 动词 (**tips, tipping, tipped**)
1 to move so that one end is higher than the other 倾斜；侧倾：*The pram can tip backwards if you hang bags on the handles.* 如果把包挂在把手上，婴儿车可能会向后倒。

2 to pour something somewhere 倾倒；倒出：*I picked up the bowl of cereal and tipped it over his head.* 我端起那碗麦片粥倒在了他的头上。
3 to give someone some money to thank them for a job they have done for you 给…小费：*At the end of the meal, he tipped the waiter.* 饭后他给了侍者小费。
tip something over to make something fall over 打翻某物；使某物倾覆：*He tipped the table over.* 他把桌子打翻了。

tiptoe¹ /ˈtɪptəʊ/ *verb* 动词 (**tiptoes, tiptoeing, tiptoed**)
to walk somewhere very quietly on your toes 踮着脚尖走；蹑手蹑脚地走：*Emma got out of bed and tiptoed to the window.* 埃玛下了床，蹑手蹑脚地走到窗边。

tiptoe² /ˈtɪptəʊ/ *noun* 名词
on tiptoe on your toes and not putting your heels on the ground 踮着脚尖：*She stood on tiptoe to look over the wall.* 她踮着脚尖向墙那边看。

tire /taɪə/ *verb* 动词 (**tires, tiring, tired**)
to make you feel that you want to rest or sleep 使感到累（或疲劳）：*If driving tires you, take the train instead.* 如果觉得开车累，就坐火车吧。

tired /ˈtaɪəd/ *adjective* 形容词
feeling that you want to rest or sleep 累的；疲倦的：*Michael is tired after his long flight.* 长途飞行后，迈克尔感到很累。
→ Look at picture on P15 参见彩插第 15 页
tired of something not wanting something to continue because you are bored with it 对某事感到厌倦的：*I'm tired of waiting for him.* 我厌倦了等他。

tiring /ˈtaɪərɪŋ/ *adjective* 形容词
making you feel tired so that you want to rest or sleep 使人疲劳的；累人的：*It was a long and tiring day.* 那是漫长而累人的一天。 □ *Travelling is tiring.* 旅行很累人。

tissue /ˈtɪʃuː, ˈtɪsjuː/ *noun* 名词
1 *uncountable* 不可数 one of the substances that humans, animals and plants are made of（人、动植物的）组织：*brain tissue* 脑组织
2 *uncountable* 不可数 (also 亦作 **tissue paper**) thin paper that you use for wrapping things that break easily（包装碎品的）纸；绵纸：*The parcel was wrapped in pink tissue paper.* 包裹用粉色的薄纸包着。
3 *countable* 可数 a piece of thin, soft paper that you use to wipe your nose 纸巾；面巾纸：*He passed me a box of tissues.* 他递给我一盒纸巾。

title /ˈtaɪtəl/ *countable noun* 可数名词
1 the name of a book, a play, a film or a piece of music 标题；题目：*What is the title of the poem?* 这首诗的题目是什么？
→ Look at picture on P3 参见彩插第 3 页
2 a word such as 'Mr' or 'Dr' that is used in front of someone's own name 头衔；称谓

to¹ *preposition* 介词

PRONUNCIATION HELP 发音提示
To is usually pronounced /tə/ before a consonant and /tu/ before a vowel, but pronounced /tuː/ when you are emphasizing it. 通常情况下，to 在辅音前读作 /tə/，元音前读作 /tu/，但强调时读作 /tuː/。

1 used when you are talking about the position or direction of something 在；向；朝；到：*Two friends and I drove to Wales.* 我和两个朋友开车去威尔士。 □ *She went to the window and looked out.* 她走到窗边向外望去。 □ *The bathroom is to the right.* 浴室在右边。
2 used for saying that someone receives something 给；予：*He picked up the knife and gave it to me.* 他捡起刀递给我。
3 used when you are talking about how something changes（表示变化）倾向于，趋于：*The shouts of the crowd changed to laughter.* 众人的叫喊声变成了笑声。
4 used before the last thing in a range 至；到：*I worked there from May to December.* 我在那里从 5 月工作到 12 月。 □ *I can count from 1 to 100 in Spanish.* 我可以用西班牙语从 1 数到 100。
5 used when you are saying how many minutes there are until the next hour（表示时间）差，在…之前：*At twenty to six I was waiting by the entrance to the station.* 6 点差 20 分时，我在进站口等着。

to²

PRONUNCIATION HELP 发音提示
To is usually pronounced /tə/ before a consonant and /tu/ before a vowel, but pronounced /tuː/ when you are emphasizing it. 通常情况下，to 在辅音前读作 /tə/，元音前读作 /tu/，但强调时读作 /tuː/。

1 used before the infinitive (= the simple form of a verb)（用于动词原形前构成不定式）: *We just want to help.* 我们只是想帮个忙。 □ *It was time to leave.* 该离开了。
2 used for giving the reason for doing something（表示动作的目的）: *I went out to buy some milk.* 我出门买点牛奶。

toad /təʊd/ *countable noun* 可数名词
a small brown or green animal with long legs, that lives in water 蟾蜍；癞蛤蟆

toast¹ /təʊst/ *noun* 名词
1 *uncountable* 不可数 slices of bread that you have heated until they are brown 烤面包片；吐司: *a slice of toast* 一片吐司
2 *countable* 可数 when you lift up your glass, wish someone happiness and drink 祝酒，敬酒；干杯: *We drank a toast to the bride and groom.* 我们为新郎新娘干杯。

toast² /təʊst/ *verb* 动词 (**toasts, toasting, toasted**)
1 to lift up your glass, wish someone happiness, and drink 为…举杯祝福: *We all toasted the baby's health.* 我们都为宝宝的健康干杯。
2 to heat bread so that it becomes brown 烘，烤（面包）: *Mum made us some delicious toasted sandwiches.* 妈妈给我们做了些可口的烤三明治。

toaster /ˈtəʊstə/ *countable noun* 可数名词
a piece of electrical equipment that you use to heat bread 烤面包片机

tobacco /təˈbækəʊ/ *uncountable noun* 不可数名词
the dried leaves of a plant that people smoke in cigarettes 烟叶；烟草

today /təˈdeɪ/ *adverb* 副词
1 used when you are talking about the actual day on which you are speaking or writing 在今天: *How are you feeling today?* 你今天感觉怎么样？ ● **today** *uncountable noun* 不可数名词: *Today is Friday, September 14th.* 今天是9月14日，星期五。
2 used when you are talking about the present period of history 现今；如今；时下: *More people have cars today.* 如今有车的人多了起来。

toddler /ˈtɒdlə/ *countable noun* 可数名词
a young child who has only just learned to walk 学步儿童: *Toddlers love activities that involve music and singing.* 学步儿童喜欢有音乐和唱歌的活动。

toe /təʊ/ *countable noun* 可数名词
one of the five parts at the end of your foot 脚趾: *He is in hospital with a broken toe.* 他脚趾骨折住院了。

toenail /ˈtəʊneɪl/ *countable noun* 可数名词
one of the hard parts that cover the ends of each of your toes 趾甲

toffee /ˈtɒfi/ *noun* 名词
a sticky brown sweet 太妃糖

together /təˈgeðə/ *adverb* 副词
1 with each other 一起；共同: *We went on long walks together.* 我们一起走了很长的路。 □ *Richard and I went to school together.* 我和理查德一起上学。
2 touching each other or making a single object, group or mixture 合在一起；到一起: *Beat the butter and sugar together.* 把黄油和糖搅在一起。 □ *He joined the two pieces of wood together.* 他把两块木头接了起来。 □ *We added all the numbers together.* 我们把所有的数字加了起来。
3 in the same place and very near to each other（位置）在一起，紧挨着: *The trees grew close together.* 那些树长得很密。 □ *Carol and Nick live together in Manhattan.* 卡萝尔和尼克一起住在曼哈顿。
4 at the same time 同时；一齐: *Patrick and Amanda arrived at the party together.* 帕特里克和阿曼达一齐到了聚会现场。

toilet /ˈtɔɪlət/ *countable noun* 可数名词
1 a large bowl with a seat that you use when you want to get rid of waste from your body 抽水马桶；坐便器: *She flushed the toilet and went back into the bedroom.* 她冲了马桶，回到卧室里。
2 (*American* 美国英语: **restroom**) (also 亦作 **toilets**) a room that contains one or more toilets 厕所；卫生间；洗手间: *She ran to the toilet and locked the door.* 她跑进厕所，锁上了门。

ˈtoilet ˌpaper or 或 **ˈtoilet ˌtissue** *uncountable noun* 不可数名词
the thin, soft paper that you use for cleaning yourself after using the toilet 卫生纸；手纸

toiletries /ˈtɔɪlətriz/ *plural noun* 复数名词
the things that you use when you are washing or taking care of your body, such as soap and toothpaste 洗漱用品；盥洗用品

toiletries 洗漱用品

- **deodorant** 除臭剂
- **hairbrush** 发刷
- **toothpaste** 牙膏
- **toothbrush** 牙刷
- **soap** 香皂

token /ˈtəʊkən/ *countable noun* 可数名词
a round, flat piece of metal or plastic that you use in a machine instead of money 代用币: *The machine uses plastic tokens rather than coins.* 这台机器使用塑料代用币，不用硬币。

told /təʊld/
→ see 见 **tell**

tolerant /ˈtɒlərənt/ *adjective* 形容词
happy for other people to say, think and do what they like even though you do not agree with them 宽容的；容忍的: *We all need to be tolerant of different points of view.* 我们都需要包容不同的观点。
▶ **tolerance** /ˈtɒlərəns/ *uncountable noun* 不可数名词: *They promote tolerance of all religions.* 他们提倡对所有宗教都持包容态度。

tolerate /ˈtɒləˌreɪt/ *verb* 动词 (**tolerates, tolerating, tolerated**)
to accept something or someone although you do not like them very much 容忍；包容: *The college will not tolerate such behaviour.* 学院不会容忍这种行为。

tomato /təˈmɑːtəʊ/ *noun* 名词 (**tomatoes**)
a soft, red fruit that you can eat raw in salads or cook like a vegetable 番茄；西红柿

tomb /tuːm/ *countable noun* 可数名词
a stone grave where the body of a dead person is placed 坟墓；冢: *In Xi'an, we visited the emperor's tomb.* 我们在西安参观了皇帝的陵墓。

tombstone /ˈtuːmstəʊn/ *countable noun* 可数名词
a large stone on a person's grave, with words written on it, telling their name and the date that they were born and died 墓碑

tomorrow /təˈmɒrəʊ/ *adverb* 副词
1 used for talking about the day after today 在明天: *Bye, see you tomorrow.* 再见，明天见。 • **tomorrow** *uncountable noun* 不可数名词: *What's on your schedule for tomorrow?* 你明天是什么安排？
2 in the future 来日；在未来: *What is the world going to be like tomorrow?* 世界未来会是什么样子？ • **tomorrow** *uncountable noun* 不可数名词: *The children of today are the adults of tomorrow.* 今日的孩子们便是来日的成年人。

ton /tʌn/ *countable noun* 可数名词
a unit of weight. There are 2,240 pounds (≈ 1,016 kilos) in a British ton and 2,000 pounds (≈ 907 kilos) in an American ton. 吨（重量单位，1英吨 = 2,240 磅 ≈ 1,016 千克，1美吨 = 2,000 磅 ≈ 907 千克）: *Hundreds of tons of oil spilled into the sea.* 数百吨石油溢出流入大海。

tone /təʊn/ *countable noun* 可数名词
1 the particular quality of a sound 音质；音色: *Lisa has a deep tone to her voice.* 莉萨的声音很低沉。
2 the quality in someone's voice that shows what they are feeling or thinking 语气；口气；腔调: *I didn't like his tone of voice; he sounded angry.* 我不喜欢他说话的语气，听起来他很生气。

tongue /tʌŋ/ *countable noun* 可数名词
the soft part inside your mouth that moves when you speak or eat 舌；舌头

tonight /təˈnaɪt/ *adverb* 副词
used for talking about the evening of today 在今晚: *I'm at home tonight.* 我今晚在家。 □ *Tonight he showed what a great player he is.* 今晚，他展示了自己是一个多么伟大的运动员。 • **tonight** *uncountable noun* 不可数名词: *Tonight is a very important night for him.* 今晚对他而言是一个非常重要的夜晚。

too /tuː/ *adverb* 副词
1 also 也；亦: *I like swimming and tennis*

too. 我喜欢游泳，也喜欢打网球。 □ *'Can we come too?'* '我们也能来吗？" □ *'I'm excited about the party.' — 'Me too.'* "这聚会真让我兴奋。" —— "我也是。"

LANGUAGE HELP 语言提示
See note at **also**. 见 **also** 的语言提示。

2 more than you want or need 太；过于：*She talks too much.* 她说得太多了。 □ *Sorry, I can't stop. I'm too busy.* 抱歉，我不能停下来。我太忙了。

took /tʊk/
→ see 见 **take**

tool /tuːl/ *countable noun* 可数名词
anything that you hold in your hands and use to do a particular type of work 工具：*Do you have the right tools for the job?* 你有适合这个活计的工具吗？
→ Look at picture on P10 参见彩插第 10 页

toolbar /ˈtuːlbɑː/ *countable noun* 可数名词
a narrow strip across a computer screen that contains pictures (= icons) that represent different things that the computer can do (计算机屏幕上的) 工具栏

toot /tuːt/ *verb* 动词 (**toots, tooting, tooted**)
if a car horn toots, or if you toot it, it makes a short sound (汽车喇叭) 发出嘟嘟声 (鸣) (笛)：*The cars passed by with their horns tooting.* 汽车鸣笛驶过。 □ *The driver behind tooted his horn.* 后面的司机按了喇叭。● **toot** *countable noun* 可数名词：*The driver gave me a wave and a toot.* 司机跟我挥了挥手，鸣了一声喇叭。

tooth /tuːθ/ *noun* 名词 (**teeth**)
1 *countable* 可数 one of the hard white objects in your mouth, that you use for biting and eating 牙；牙齿：*Brush your teeth at least twice a day.* 每天至少要刷牙两次。
→ Look at picture on P4 参见彩插第 4 页
2 [**teeth**] *plural* 复数 the parts of a comb that stick out in a row on its edge (梳子的) 齿

toothache /ˈtuːθeɪk/ *uncountable noun* 不可数名词
a pain in your tooth 牙痛

toothbrush /ˈtuːθbrʌʃ/ *countable noun* 可数名词 (**toothbrushes**)
a small brush that you use for cleaning your teeth 牙刷

toothpaste /ˈtuːθpeɪst/ *uncountable noun* 不可数名词
a thick substance that you put on a toothbrush and use for cleaning your teeth 牙膏

top¹ /tɒp/ *countable noun* 可数名词
1 the highest point of something 顶点；顶端：*We climbed the path up to the top of the hill.* 我们沿着小路爬上山顶。
2 the lid of something 盖子：*He twisted the top off the bottle and handed it to her.* 他拧开瓶盖，把瓶子递给她。
3 a piece of clothing that you wear on the upper half of your body (*informal* 非正式) 上衣：*I was wearing a black skirt and a red top.* 我当时穿着黑裙子红上衣。
on top of something on the highest part of something 在某物顶部：*There was a clock on top of the television.* 电视顶上有个时钟。

top² /tɒp/ *adjective* 形容词
highest 最高的；顶端的：*I can't reach the top shelf.* 我够不着最上面的架子。

topic /ˈtɒpɪk/ *countable noun* 可数名词
a particular subject that you discuss or write about 话题；主题；题目：*What is the topic of your essay?* 你的文章主题是什么？

torch /tɔːtʃ/ *countable noun* 可数名词 (**torches**)
1 a small electric light that you carry in your hand 手电筒
2 a long stick or object that has a flame at one end 火炬；火把：*Wood carried the famous Torch into the stadium.* 伍德手持那把著名的火炬进了体育场。

tore /tɔː/
→ see 见 **tear**

torn /tɔːn/
→ see 见 **tear**

tornado /tɔːˈneɪdəʊ/ *countable noun* 可数名词 (**tornadoes** or 或 **tornados**)
a storm with strong winds that spin around very fast and cause a lot of damage 龙卷风

tortoise /ˈtɔːtəs/ *countable noun* 可数名词
an animal with a shell on its back. Tortoises move very slowly. 陆龟；乌龟

torture /ˈtɔːtʃə/ *verb* 动词 (**tortures, torturing, tortured**)
to deliberately cause someone terrible pain 折磨；虐待；拷打 ● **torture** *uncountable noun* 不可数名词：*The use of torture is prohibited by international law.* 国际法禁止严刑拷问。

toss /tɒs/ *verb* 动词 (**tosses, tossing, tossed**)
1 to throw something 扔；抛；掷：*Kate*

tossed the ball to Jessica. 凯特把球扔给杰茜卡。
2 (also 亦作 **toss something about** or **toss something around**) to make something move up and down, or from side to side, quickly and suddenly 使颠簸；使摇晃：*The strong winds tossed the plane up and down.* 强风使飞机上下颠簸。▫ *The huge waves tossed the boat about.* 巨浪使小船摇来晃去。
toss a coin to decide something by throwing a coin into the air and guessing which side of the coin will face upwards when it lands 抛硬币（以决定某事）：*We tossed a coin to decide who should go first.* 我们抛硬币决定谁先开始。

total¹ /ˈtəʊtəl/ ***countable noun*** 可数名词
the number that you get when you add several numbers together 总数；总额：*Add all the amounts together, and subtract ten from the total.* 把所有数量加起来，再从总数中减去 10。▫ *The three companies have a total of 1,776 employees.* 这 3 家公司共有 1,776 名雇员。

total² /ˈtəʊtəl/ ***adjective*** 形容词
1 when you add all the numbers together 总的；总计的：*The total cost of the project was £240 million.* 该项目共花费 2.4 亿英镑。
2 complete 完全的；彻底的：*When I failed all my exams, I felt like a total failure.* 当我各门考试全都不及格时，我觉得自己是个彻底的失败者。
▶ **totally** /ˈtəʊtəli/ ***adverb*** 副词：*I accept that I am totally to blame.* 我同意由我来负全责。

totalitarian /təʊˌtælɪˈteəriən/ ***adjective*** 形容词
used for describing a political system in which there is only one political party that controls everything 极权主义的：*He promised that the country would never return to its totalitarian past.* 他承诺这个国家的极权主义时代不会复返了。

touch¹ /tʌtʃ/ ***verb*** 动词 (**touches, touching, touched**)
1 to put your hand onto something（用手）碰，触摸：*Her little hands gently touched my face.* 她的小手轻轻触摸我的脸庞。
2 to be so close to another thing or person that there is no space between the two 接触；触及：*Their knees were touching.* 他们的膝盖挨着。▫ *Her feet just touched the floor.* 她的双脚刚触到地板。

touch² /tʌtʃ/ ***noun*** 名词 (**touches**)
1 countable 可数 when someone puts their hand onto something 碰；触摸：*She felt the touch of his hand on her arm.* 她感觉到他在摸自己的胳膊。
2 uncountable 不可数 your ability to tell what something is like when you feel it with your hands 触觉；触感：*A baby's sense of touch is fully developed at birth.* 婴儿的触觉在出生时就发育完全了。
be in touch or **keep in touch** or **stay in touch** to write or speak to someone regularly 保持联系：*My brother and I keep in touch by phone.* 我和哥哥保持着电话联系。
get in touch to write to someone or telephone them 取得联系：*We'll get in touch with you if we have any news of your brother.* 一有你哥哥的消息我们就联系你。
lose touch to gradually stop writing or speaking to someone 失去联系：*When he went to college, I lost touch with him.* 他上大学后，我们就失去了联系。

tough /tʌf/ ***adjective*** 形容词 (**tougher, toughest**)
1 strong and determined 坚强的；意志坚定的：*Paul has a reputation as a tough businessman.* 保罗以铁面商人著称。
2 difficult to do 难办的；棘手的：*We will have to make some tough decisions.* 我们将不得不作出一些艰难的决定。
3 strong, and difficult to break or cut 坚固的；结实的：*The bag is made from a tough and waterproof nylon material.* 这个包是用结实防水的尼龙料做的。▫ *The meat was tough and chewy.* 这肉太老，很难嚼。

tour¹ /tʊə/ ***noun*** 名词
1 a trip to several different places in order to perform a concert or a show 巡回演出：*The band is planning a national tour.* 该乐队正计划在全国进行巡回演出。▫ *Next year, the orchestra will be going on tour.* 明年这支管弦乐队将进行巡回演出。
2 countable 可数 a trip to an interesting place or around several interesting places 旅游；旅行；参观：*Michael took me on a tour of the nearby islands.* 迈克尔带我游览了附近的岛屿。▫ *We went on a tour of the new office building.* 我们参观了新办公楼。

tour² /tʊə/ ***verb*** 动词 (**tours, touring, toured**)
1 to go to several different places in order to perform a concert or a show 在（某地）作巡回演出：*A few years ago the band*

toured Europe. 几年前该乐队在欧洲进行巡回演出。
2 to go on a trip around a place 游览；参观：*Tour the museum with a guide for £5 per person.* 由导游带领游览博物馆每人收费 5 英镑。

tour guide *countable noun* 可数名词
someone whose job is to help people who are on holiday, or to show them round a place 导游：*A tour guide will organize activities every day.* 每天由导游组织各种活动。

tourism /ˈtʊərɪzəm/ *uncountable noun* 不可数名词
the business of providing hotels, restaurants, trips and activities for people who are on holiday 旅游业：*Tourism is the island's main industry.* 旅游业是该岛的主要产业。

tourist /ˈtʊərɪst/ *countable noun* 可数名词
a person who is visiting a place on holiday 游客；观光者：*About 75,000 tourists visit the town each year.* 每年约有 75,000 名游客来此镇观光。

tourist information *uncountable noun* 不可数名词
details of hotels and places to visit in an area 旅游信息

tourist information centre *countable noun* 可数名词
a place that provides details of hotels and places to visit in an area for people who are on holiday 旅游信息咨询处

tournament /ˈtʊənəmənt/ *countable noun* 可数名词
a sports competition. Each player who wins a game plays another game, until just one person or team remains. They win the competition. 锦标赛：*They were the best team in the tournament.* 他们是此次锦标赛的最佳球队。

tow /təʊ/ *verb* 动词 (**tows**, **towing**, **towed**)
to pull another vehicle along behind 牵引，拖，拉（车辆）：*He uses the lorry to tow his trailer.* 他用大卡车牵引他的拖车。

towards /təˈwɔːdz/ *also* 亦作 **toward** /təˈwɔːd/ *preposition* 介词
1 in the direction of something or someone 朝；向：*They drove towards Lake Ladoga in silence.* 他们默默地朝拉多加湖开去。
2 used for describing the way you feel about something or someone 对于；关于：*How do you feel towards the man who stole your handbag?* 对于偷你手提包的人，你有什么看法？
3 just before a particular time 将近，临近（某一时刻）：*We're having another meeting towards the end of the month.* 临近月底时我们会再开一次会。
4 to help pay for something（钱）用于：*My parents gave us £50,000 towards our first house.* 我父母给了我们 5 万英镑用于买首套房。

towel /ˈtaʊəl/ *countable noun* 可数名词
a piece of thick soft cloth that you use to dry yourself 毛巾：*I've put clean towels in the bathroom.* 我在浴室里放了干净毛巾。

tower /ˈtaʊə/ *countable noun* 可数名词
a tall, narrow building, or a tall part of another building 塔；塔楼：*He looked up at the clock in the church tower. It was ten o'clock.* 他抬头看了看教堂塔楼上的钟。10 点了。

town /taʊn/ *countable noun* 可数名词
a place with many streets, buildings and shops, where people live and work 镇；城镇：*Larry comes from a small town near the Canadian border.* 拉里来自加拿大边境附近的一个小镇。□ *We met in town at around eight.* 我们 8 点左右在镇上见面。

toxic /ˈtɒksɪk/ *adjective* 形容词
poisonous 有毒的：*The leaves of the plant are highly toxic.* 这种植物的叶子有剧毒。

toy /tɔɪ/ *countable noun* 可数名词
an object that children play with 玩具：*Sophie went to sleep holding her favourite toy.* 索菲抱着最喜欢的玩具睡着了。

trace /treɪs/ *verb* 动词 (**traces**, **tracing**, **traced**)
1 to find someone or something after looking for them 追踪；追查：*The police quickly traced the owner of the car.* 警方很快就追查到了车主。
2 to copy a picture by covering it with a piece of thin paper and drawing over the lines 描摹：*Linda learned to draw by tracing pictures in books.* 琳达通过描摹书上的图画学会了画画。

track[1] /træk/ *noun* 名词
1 *countable* 可数 a rough road or path 小路；小径：*We walked along a track in the forest.* 我们在森林中沿着小路行进。
2 *countable* 可数 a piece of ground that is

used for races 跑道；赛道：*The university's facilities include a 400-metre running track.* 这所大学的设施包括一条 400 米的跑道。
3 *countable* 可数 one of the metal lines that trains travel along 铁轨；火车轨道：*a railway track* 铁路轨道
4 *countable* 可数 one of the songs or pieces of music on a CD*（CD 上的）歌曲，乐曲：*I only like two of the tracks on this CD.* 这张 CD 中只有两首歌是我喜欢的。
5 **[tracks]** *plural* 复数 the marks that an animal leaves on the ground（动物的）足迹，踪迹：*William found fresh bear tracks in the snow.* 威廉在雪地上发现了熊刚刚留下的足迹。
keep track of someone/something to have information about someone or something all the time 了解某人／某事物的动态：*Keep track of what you spend while you're on holiday.* 把度假花销记录下来。
lose track of someone/something to no longer know where someone or something is or what is happening 不再了解某人／某事物的动态：*I'm sorry I'm late. I lost track of time.* 对不起，我迟到了。我忘了时间。

track² /træk/ *verb* 动词 (**tracks, tracking, tracked**)
to try to find animals or people by following the signs or marks that they leave behind 追踪；跟踪：*We all got up early to track deer in the woods.* 我们都早早起来去林间追寻鹿的踪迹。
track someone/something down to find someone or something after a difficult or long search 追查到某人／某物：*She spent years trying to track down her parents.* 她花了好几年时间试图找到她的父母。

tractor /ˈtræktə/ *countable noun* 可数名词
a vehicle that a farmer uses to pull farm machinery 拖拉机

trade /treɪd/ *verb* 动词 (**trades, trading, traded**)
1 to buy and sell goods 做买卖；做生意：*We have been trading with this company for over thirty years.* 我们和这家公司做了三十多年生意了。● **trade** *uncountable noun* 不可数名词：*Texas has a long history of trade with Mexico.* 得克萨斯和墨西哥的贸易往来历史悠久。
2 to give someone one thing and get something else from them in exchange 交换：*He traded his car for a motorcycle.* 他用

汽车换了一辆摩托车。

trademark /ˈtreɪdmɑːk/ *countable noun* 可数名词
a special name or symbol that a company owns and uses on its products 商标：*Kodak is a trademark of Eastman Kodak Company.* *Kodak 是伊士曼柯达公司的商标。

tradition /trəˈdɪʃən/ *noun* 名词
a type of behaviour or a belief that has existed for a long time 传统；习俗：*Afternoon tea is a British tradition.* 喝下午茶是英国的传统。
▶ **traditional** /trəˈdɪʃənəl/ *adjective* 形容词：*The band plays a lot of traditional Scottish music.* 这个乐队演奏许多苏格兰传统音乐。
▶ **traditionally** /trəˈdɪʃənəli/ *adverb* 副词：*Christmas is traditionally a time for families.* 圣诞节传统上是家庭团聚的日子。

traffic /ˈtræfɪk/ *uncountable noun* 不可数名词
1 all the vehicles that are on a particular road at one time 交通；车流：*There was heavy traffic on the roads.* 路上交通繁忙。□ *Yesterday, traffic was light on the motorway.* 昨天高速公路上车不多。
2 the movement of ships, trains or aircraft between one place and another（轮船、火车或飞机在两地间的）交通，往来：*No air traffic was allowed out of the airport.* 飞机不准飞离机场。

ˈtraffic ˌjam *countable noun* 可数名词
a long line of vehicles that cannot move forward, or can only move very slowly 交通堵塞

ˈtraffic ˌlights *plural noun* 复数名词
coloured lights that control the flow of traffic 交通信号灯；红绿灯

tragedy /ˈtrædʒɪdi/ *noun* 名词 (**tragedies**)
1 an extremely sad event or situation 不幸；惨剧：*They have suffered a terrible personal tragedy.* 他们有过一次悲惨的遭遇。
2 a type of serious play, that usually ends with the death of the main character 悲剧；悲剧作品：*the tragedies of Shakespeare* 莎士比亚的悲剧作品

tragic /ˈtrædʒɪk/ *adjective* 形容词
extremely sad 不幸的；悲惨的：*It was a tragic accident.* 那是一场不幸的事故。
▶ **tragically** /ˈtrædʒɪkli/ *adverb* 副词：*He died tragically in a car accident.* 他在一场车祸中不幸丧生。

trail /treɪl/ *countable noun* 可数名词
  1 a series of marks that is left by someone or something as they move around 痕迹；踪迹：*Everywhere in the house was a sticky trail of orange juice.* 家里到处是橙汁黏糊糊的痕迹。
  2 a path through the countryside（乡间的）小路：*He was walking along a trail through the trees.* 他正沿着一条林间小路行进。

trailer /ˈtreɪlə/ *countable noun* 可数名词
  1 a large container on wheels that is pulled by a lorry or other vehicle 拖车；挂车
  2 (*American* 美国英语)→ see 见 **caravan**

train¹ /treɪn/ *countable noun* 可数名词
  a long vehicle that is pulled by an engine along a railway 火车：*We caught the early-morning train.* 我们赶上了早班火车。□ *He came to Glasgow by train.* 他乘火车来到格拉斯哥。

train² /treɪn/ *verb* 动词 (**trains, training, trained**)
  1 to learn the skills that you need in order to do something 训练；培训：*Stephen is training to be a teacher.* 斯蒂芬正受训成为一名老师。
  ▶ **training** /ˈtreɪnɪŋ/ *uncountable noun* 不可数名词：*Kennedy had no formal training as an artist.* 肯尼迪没有接受过正规的美术培训。
  2 to prepare for a sports competition（为体育赛事）训练：*She spent six hours a day training for the race.* 为了备战赛跑她每天训练 6 个小时。
  ▶ **training** /ˈtreɪnɪŋ/ *uncountable noun* 不可数名词：*He keeps fit through exercise and training.* 他通过运动和锻炼保持健康。

trainer /ˈtreɪnə/ *countable noun* 可数名词
  (*American* 美国英语：**sneaker**)
  a shoe that you wear for running and other sports, or with informal clothes 运动鞋：*a pair of trainers* 一双运动鞋

traitor /ˈtreɪtə/ *countable noun* 可数名词
  someone who harms a group that they belong to by helping its enemies 叛徒：*Traitors were sending messages to the enemy.* 叛徒在给敌人通风报信。

tram /træm/ *countable noun* 可数名词
  an electric vehicle that travels along rails in the surface of a street 有轨电车：*You can get to the beach by tram.* 你可以乘有轨电车前往海滨。

transfer /trænsˈfɜː/ *verb* 动词 (**transfers, transferring, transferred**)
  to make something or someone go from one place to another 转移：*Transfer the meat to a dish.* 把肉盛到盘子里。● **transfer** /ˈtrænsfɜː/ *noun* 名词：*Arrange for the transfer of medical records to your new doctor.* 安排一下把病历转交给你的新医生。

transform /trænsˈfɔːm/ *verb* 动词 (**transforms, transforming, transformed**)
  to change someone or something completely 彻底改变：*The railway transformed America.* 铁路建设使美国发生了翻天覆地的变化。□ *Your body transforms food into energy.* 身体将食物转化为能量。
  ▶ **transformation** /ˌtrænsfəˈmeɪʃən/ *noun* 名词：*The TV show follows the transformation of a bedroom into an office.* 这是一档关于将卧室改造成办公室的电视节目。

transitive /ˈtrænzɪtɪv/ *adjective* 形容词
  used for describing a verb that has a direct object（动词）及物的

translate /trænzˈleɪt/ *verb* 动词 (**translates, translating, translated**)
  to say or write something again in a different language 翻译：*A small number of Kadare's books have been translated into English.* 卡达雷的书有一小部分译成了英文。
  ▶ **translator** /trænzˈleɪtə/ *countable noun* 可数名词：*She works as a translator.* 她是做翻译的。

translation /trænzˈleɪʃən/ *countable noun* 可数名词
  a piece of writing or speech that has been put into a different language 译本；译文：*a translation of the Bible* 《圣经》的一个译本

transparent /trænsˈpærənt/ *adjective* 形容词
  used for describing an object or a substance that you can see through（物体或物质）透明的：*We used a sheet of transparent plastic.* 我们用了一块透明塑料。

transplant /ˈtrænsplɑːnt/ *noun* 名词
  a medical operation in which a part of a person's body is replaced because it has a disease（器官的）移植：*a heart transplant* 心脏移植

transport¹ /ˈtrænspɔːt/ *uncountable noun* 不可数名词
  a system for taking people or things from one place to another in a vehicle 交通运输系统：*We will spend the money on improving public transport.* 我们将把钱用

于改善公共交通运输系统。

transport² /trænsˈpɔːt/ *verb* 动词 (**transports, transporting, transported**)
to take people or goods from one place to another in a vehicle 运输；运送：*Buses transported passengers to the town.* 公共汽车将乘客运送到城里。

trap¹ /træp/ *countable noun* 可数名词
1 a piece of equipment for catching animals（捕捉动物的）陷阱，罗网，夹子：*Nathan's dog got caught in a trap.* 内森的狗落入了陷阱。
2 a trick that is intended to catch someone 诡计；圈套：*He hesitated, wondering if there was a trap in the question.* 他迟疑着，想知道这个问题里是不是有圈套。

trap² /træp/ *verb* 动词 (**traps, trapping, trapped**)
1 to catch animals using traps 设陷阱捕捉（动物）：*They survived by trapping and killing wild animals.* 他们靠设陷阱捕杀野兽才活了下来。
2 to trick someone so that they do or say something that they do not want to do or say 诱骗；使上当：*Were you trying to trap her into confessing?* 你刚才是想诱使她招供吗？
3 to prevent someone from moving 困住；使无法动弹：*The car turned over, trapping both men.* 汽车翻了，把两个人都困住了。

trash /træʃ/ *uncountable noun* 不可数名词 (American 美国英语)
→ see 见 **rubbish**

travel¹ /ˈtrævəl/ *verb* 动词 (**travels, travelling, travelled**)
to go from one place to another, often to a place that is far away（常指长途）旅行，出行：*I've been travelling all day.* 我整整一天都在赶路。 □ *People often travel hundreds of miles to get here.* 人们常常赶数百英里路来到这里。

travel² /ˈtrævəl/ *uncountable noun* 不可数名词
the activity of travelling（常指长途的）旅行，出行：*He hated air travel.* 他讨厌坐飞机。

LANGUAGE HELP 语言提示
Travel, journey or **trip**? 用 travel、journey 还是 trip？
The uncountable noun **travel** is used for talking about the general activity of travelling. *travel 是不可数名词，泛指出行。*
If you want to talk about a particular occasion when someone goes somewhere, use **journey**. *journey 特指某次出行：a journey by train from Berlin 从柏林出发的火车之旅。*
Use **trip** to talk about the whole experience of going somewhere, staying there and returning. *trip 表示整个旅程，包括去程、当地停留和回程：He suggested I cancel my trip to China.* 他建议我取消去中国的行程。

travel agency *countable noun* 可数名词 (**travel agencies**)
a company or a shop that sells holidays 旅行社

travel agent *countable noun* 可数名词
a person who works for a company or a shop that sells holidays 旅行代办人；旅游代理人

traveller /ˈtrævələ/ *countable noun* 可数名词
a person who is on a trip or a person who travels a lot 旅行者；旅客：*airline travellers* 航空旅客

tray /treɪ/ *countable noun* 可数名词
a flat piece of wood, plastic or metal that is used for carrying things, especially food and drinks（尤指放饮食的）托盘

tread /tred/ *verb* 动词 (**treads, treading, trod, trodden**)
to walk in a particular way（以某种方式）行走：*There is no safety railing here, so tread carefully.* 这里没有安全围栏，走路要小心。

treasure /ˈtreʒə/ *uncountable noun* 不可数名词
a collection of valuable old objects in children's stories, such as gold coins and jewellery 宝物；宝藏：*buried treasure* 埋藏的宝物

treat /triːt/ *verb* 动词 (**treats, treating, treated**)
1 to behave towards someone or something in a particular way 对待；看待：*Stop treating me like a child.* 别把我当小孩对待了。
2 to try to make a patient well again 治疗；医治：*Doctors treated the boy for a minor head wound.* 医生给那个男孩治疗了头部的轻伤。
3 to buy or arrange something special for someone 请（客）；款待：*She treated him*

to ice cream. 她请他吃冰激凌。● **treat** countable noun 可数名词: *Lesley returned from town with a special treat for him.* 莱斯莉从城里回来，给他带了一个特别的礼物。

treatment /ˈtriːtmənt/ noun 名词
1 medical attention that is given to an ill or injured person or animal 治疗；疗法: *Many patients are not getting the medical treatment they need.* 很多病人没有得到需要的治疗。
2 *uncountable* 不可数 the way you behave towards someone or deal with them 对待方式；待遇: *We don't want any special treatment.* 我们不想要任何特殊待遇。

treaty /ˈtriːti/ countable noun 可数名词 (**treaties**)
a written agreement between countries （国家间的）条约，协定: *a treaty on global warming* 关于全球变暖问题的条约

tree /triː/ countable noun 可数名词
a tall plant that lives for a long time. It has a hard central part (= a trunk), branches and leaves. 树；树木: *apple trees* 苹果树

trek /trek/ verb 动词 (**treks, trekking, trekked**)
to go on a journey across difficult country, usually on foot（通常指徒步）远足，跋涉: *We trekked through the jungle.* 我们徒步过丛林。● **trek** countable noun 可数名词: *We went on a trek through the desert.* 我们徒步穿越沙漠。

tremble /ˈtrembəl/ verb 动词 (**trembles, trembling, trembled**)
to shake slightly 颤抖；哆嗦: *Lisa was white and trembling with anger.* 丽萨气得脸色发白，浑身发抖。□ *He felt the earth tremble under him.* 他感到大地在脚下颤动。

tremendous /trɪˈmendəs/ adjective 形容词
1 very big or very great 巨大的；极大的: *My students have all made tremendous progress recently.* 我的学生最近都取得了巨大的进步。
▶ **tremendously** /trɪˈmendəsli/ adverb 副词: *I thought they played tremendously well, didn't you?* 我认为他们发挥得非常棒，你不觉得吗？
2 very good 极好的；出色的: *I thought her performance was absolutely tremendous.* 我认为她的表演精彩极了。

trend /trend/ countable noun 可数名词
a change or a development towards something different 趋势；倾向: *The restaurant is responding to the trend toward healthier eating.* 这家餐馆正在顺应健康饮食的趋势。

trendy /ˈtrendi/ adjective 形容词 (**trendier, trendiest**)
fashionable and modern (*informal* 非正式) 时髦的；现代的: *a trendy Manchester nightclub* 曼彻斯特一家时尚的夜总会

trial /ˈtraɪəl/ noun 名词
1 a formal meeting in a law court, at which people decide whether someone is guilty of a crime 审判；审理: *New evidence showed that the witness lied at the trial.* 新证据表明证人在审讯中撒了谎。□ *He is on trial for murder.* 他因涉嫌谋杀而受审。
2 an experiment in which you test something by using it or doing it for a period of time to see how well it works 试用；试验: *The drug is being tested in clinical trials.* 这种药正用于临床试验中。

triangle /ˈtraɪæŋɡəl/ countable noun 可数名词
a shape with three straight sides 三角形
→ Look at picture on P2 参见彩插第 2 页
▶ **triangular** /traɪˈæŋɡjʊlə/ adjective 形容词: *a triangular roof* 三角形屋顶

tribe /traɪb/ countable noun 可数名词
used for talking about a group of people of the same race, language and culture, especially in a developing country. Some people disapprove of this use.（尤指发展中国家的）部落，部族（一些人不赞成此用法）: *three hundred members of the Xhosa tribe* 300 名科萨人
▶ **tribal** /ˈtraɪbəl/ adjective 形容词: *tribal lands* 部族属地

tribute /ˈtrɪbjuːt/ noun 名词
something that you say, do or make to show that you admire and respect someone 颂词；致敬: *The song is a tribute to Roy Orbison.* 那首歌是对罗伊·奥比森的致敬。

trick[1] /trɪk/ verb 动词 (**tricks, tricking, tricked**)
to do something dishonest in order to make someone do something 欺骗: *Stephen is going to be very upset when he finds out how you tricked him.* 如果斯蒂芬发现你是如何欺骗他的，他会非常气愤。□ *They tricked him into signing the contract.* 他们骗他在合同上签了字。

trick[2] /trɪk/ countable noun 可数名词
1 something dishonest that you do in order to make someone do something 诡计；花招

2 a clever or skilful action that someone does in order to entertain people 戏法；把戏：*a card trick* 纸牌戏法

trickle /ˈtrɪkəl/ *verb* 动词 (**trickles, trickling, trickled**)
to flow slowly in small amounts 滴；淌：*A tear trickled down the old man's cheek.* 一滴眼泪顺着老人的脸颊淌了下来。● **trickle** *countable noun* 可数名词：*There was not even a trickle of water.* 连一道细流都没有。

tricky /ˈtrɪki/ *adjective* 形容词 (**trickier, trickiest**)
difficult 难办的；棘手的：*Parking can be tricky in the town centre.* 在市镇中心很难找到停车的地方。

tricycle /ˈtraɪsɪkəl/ *countable noun* 可数名词
a bicycle with three wheels 三轮车

trigger /ˈtrɪɡə/ *countable noun* 可数名词
the part of a gun that you pull to make it shoot（枪的）扳机：*A man pointed a gun at them and pulled the trigger.* 一名男子用枪指着他们，然后扣动了扳机。

trim /trɪm/ *verb* 动词 (**trims, trimming, trimmed**)
to cut off small amounts of something in order to make it look tidy 修剪；修整：*My friend trims my hair every eight weeks.* 我朋友每 8 个星期给我修剪一次头发。● **trim** *singular noun* 单数名词：*His hair needed a trim.* 他该理发了。

trio /ˈtriːəʊ/ *countable noun* 可数名词
a group of three people, especially musicians or singers 三人组合；（尤指）三重唱，三重奏

trip[1] /trɪp/ *countable noun* 可数名词
a journey that you make to a particular place and back again 旅行；出行：*She has just returned from a trip to Switzerland.* 她去瑞士旅行刚回来。

trip[2] /trɪp/ *verb* 动词 (**trips, tripping, tripped**)
to knock your foot against something and fall or nearly fall 绊；绊倒：*She tripped and broke her hip.* 她绊了一跤，髋骨骨折了。

triple[1] /ˈtrɪpəl/ *adjective* 形容词
consisting of three things or parts 三个的；三部分的：*The property includes a triple garage.* 这处房产有 3 个车库。

triple[2] /ˈtrɪpəl/ *verb* 动词 (**triples, tripling, tripled**)
to become three times as large 增至三倍：

I got a fantastic new job and my salary tripled. 我找到了一份非常棒的新工作，工资涨到了原来的 3 倍。

triplet /ˈtrɪplət/ *countable noun* 可数名词
one of three children that are born at the same time to the same mother 三胞胎之一

triumph /ˈtraɪʌmf/ *noun* 名词
1 a great success 巨大成功；伟大胜利：*The championships were a personal triumph for the coach.* 这次锦标赛中该教练取得了非凡的个人成就。
2 *uncountable* 不可数 a feeling of great satisfaction after a great success 成功的满足，胜利的喜悦：*She felt a sense of triumph.* 她感受到了成功的喜悦。

trivial /ˈtrɪviəl/ *adjective* 形容词
not important or serious 不重要的；琐碎的：*I was not interested in the trivial details of his life.* 我对他生活中的细碎琐事不感兴趣。

trod /trɒd/
→ see 见 **tread**

trodden /ˈtrɒdən/
→ see 见 **tread**

trolley /ˈtrɒli/ *countable noun* 可数名词
(*American* 美国英语：**cart**) a large container with wheels that you use for moving heavy things such as shopping or luggage 手推车：*a supermarket trolley* 超市手推车 □ *She pushed her cases on a trolley.* 她用手推车推着箱子。

trombone /trɒmˈbəʊn/ *noun* 名词
a metal musical instrument that you play by blowing into it and sliding part of it backwards and forwards 长号：*Her husband plays the trombone.* 她丈夫吹长号。
→ Look at picture on P12 参见彩插第 12 页

troops /truːps/ *plural noun* 复数名词
armed forces or soldiers 军队；部队；士兵：*35,000 troops from a dozen countries are already there.* 来自 12 个国家的 35,000 名士兵已经到达那里。

trophy /ˈtrəʊfi/ *countable noun* 可数名词 (**trophies**)
a prize, such as a silver cup, that is given to the winner of a competition（颁发给竞赛获胜者的）奖品，奖杯：*The special trophy for the best rider went to Chris Read.* 克里斯·里德获得了最佳骑手的特别奖杯。

tropical /ˈtrɒpɪkəl/ *adjective* 形容词
belonging to or typical of the hot, wet

areas of the world 热带的: *tropical diseases* 热带疾病

tropics /'tropɪks/ *plural noun* 复数名词
the tropics the hottest parts of the world, where it is hot and wet 热带;热带地区

trot /trɒt/ *verb* 动词 (**trots, trotting, trotted**)
1 to move at a speed between walking and running 小跑;疾走: *I trotted down the steps and out to the garden.* 我快步走下台阶,奔向外面的花园。
2 used for saying that an animal such as a horse moves fairly fast, taking quick small steps (马等) 小跑: *My horse was soon trotting around the field.* 我的马很快就在田野间小跑起来。

trouble¹ /'trʌbəl/ *noun* 名词
1 problems or difficulties 问题;困难;麻烦: *I had trouble parking.* 我很难找到停车的地方。□ *You've caused us a lot of trouble.* 你给我们找了很多麻烦。
2 *uncountable* 不可数 a situation where people are arguing or fighting 纷争;骚乱: *Police were sent to the city to prevent trouble.* 警察被派往城里驻守,以防止发生骚乱。
in trouble having broken a rule or a law, and likely to be punished 有麻烦的;将受罚的: *He was in trouble with his teachers.* 老师们想好好教训他。

trouble² /'trʌbəl/ *verb* 动词 (**troubles, troubling, troubled**)
1 to make someone feel worried 使烦恼;使担忧: *Is anything troubling you?* 有什么事情让你烦恼吗?
2 to disturb someone 打扰;烦扰: *Sorry to trouble you, but can I borrow your pen?* 抱歉打扰一下,能借用一下你的钢笔吗?

trousers /'traʊzəz/ *plural noun* 复数名词 (*American* 美国英语: **pants**)
a piece of clothing that covers the body from the waist downwards, and that covers each leg separately (*formal* 正式) 裤子: *He was dressed in a shirt, dark trousers and boots.* 他身穿衬衫和深色裤子,脚踩靴子。

truck /trʌk/ *countable noun* 可数名词 (*American* 美国英语)
→ see 见 **lorry**

true /truː/ *adjective* 形容词 (**truer, truest**)
based on facts, and not invented or imagined 真的;真实的: *Everything she said was true.* 她说的都是真的。□ *The film is based on a true story.* 这部电影是根据真实故事改编的。
come true to actually happen 实现;变成现实: *When I was 13, my dream came true and I got my first horse.* *13 岁时,我梦想成真,拥有了第一匹马。

truly /'truːli/ *adverb* 副词
really and completely 真正;完全: *We want a truly democratic system.* 我们想要真正民主的制度。□ *Believe me, Susan, I am truly sorry.* 相信我,苏珊,我真的感到抱歉。
Yours truly (*American* 美国英语)
→ see 见 **Yours faithfully**

trumpet /'trʌmpɪt/ *noun* 名词
a metal musical instrument that you blow 小号;喇叭: *I played the trumpet in the school orchestra.* 我在学校的管弦乐队吹过小号。
→ Look at picture on P12 参见彩插第 12 页

trunk /trʌŋk/ *noun* 名词
1 *countable* 可数 the large main stem of a tree from which the branches grow 树干: *The tree trunk was more than two metres across.* 这个树干直径超过两米。
2 *countable* 可数 (*American* 美国英语) the **boot** of a car (汽车的) 行李舱,行李厢
3 *countable* 可数 a large, strong box that is used for storing things 大箱子;大衣箱: *Maloney unlocked his trunk and took out some clothing.* 马洛尼打开大衣箱,取出一些衣服。
4 *countable* 可数 the long nose of an elephant 象鼻
5 [**trunks**] *plural* 复数 → see 见 **swimming trunks**

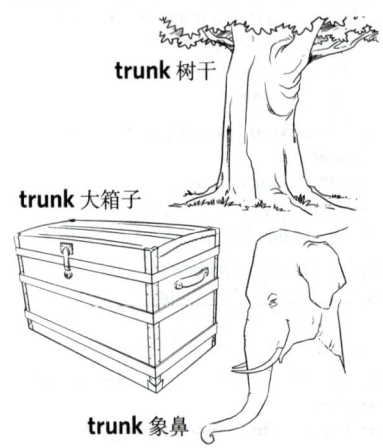

trunk 树干

trunk 大箱子

trunk 象鼻

trust /trʌst/ *verb* 动词 (**trusts, trusting, trusted**)
1 to believe that someone is honest and that they will not deliberately do anything to harm you 信任；信赖: *'I trust you completely,' he said.* "我完全信任你。"他说。● **trust** *uncountable noun* 不可数名词: *He destroyed my trust in men.* 他毁了我对男人的信任。□ *There was a shared feeling of trust amongst the members of the team.* 团队成员之间彼此信任。
2 to believe that someone will do something 相信（某人会做某事）: *I trust you to keep this secret.* 我相信你会保守这个秘密。

trustworthy /ˈtrʌstwɜːði/ *adjective* 形容词
responsible and able to be trusted completely 可信赖的；可靠的: *He is a trustworthy leader.* 他是一位值得信赖的领导。

truth /truːθ/ *uncountable noun* 不可数名词
all the facts about something, rather than things that are imagined or invented 真相；实情: *There is no truth in this story.* 这个故事纯属虚构。□ *Are you telling me the truth?* 你跟我说的是实话吗？

truthful /ˈtruːθfʊl/ *adjective* 形容词
honest 诚实的: *She was always completely truthful with us.* 她每次跟我们讲的全是真话。□ *The truthful answer is that I don't know.* 说实话，我不知道。
▶ **truthfully** /ˈtruːθfʊli/ *adverb* 副词: *I answered all their questions truthfully.* 我诚实地回答了他们所有的问题。
▶ **truthfulness** /ˈtruːθfʊlnəs/ *uncountable noun* 不可数名词: *I can say, with absolute truthfulness, that I did my best.* 我可以绝对坦诚地说，我尽力了。

try /traɪ/ *verb* 动词 (**tries, trying, tried**)
1 to make an effort to do something 试图；设法: *He tried to help her at work.* 他试图在工作上帮助她。□ *She doesn't seem to try hard enough.* 她似乎还不够努力。□ *I must try and see him.* 我必须设法见到他。● **try** *countable noun* 可数名词 (**tries**): *It was a good try.* 这是一次很好的尝试。

> **LANGUAGE HELP** 语言提示
> **Try and** is often used instead of **try to** in spoken English. 英语口语中，常用 **try and** 替代 **try to**: *Just try and stop me!* 来阻止我呀！

2 to use or do something new or different in order to discover what it is like 试用；试做: *You could try a little cheese melted on the top.* 你可以尝一点上面融化的奶酪。● **try** *countable noun* 可数名词 (**tries**): *All we're asking is that you give it a try.* 我们只是想让你试一试。
3 to go to a particular place or person because you think that they may be able to give you what you need 到（某处）试试；找（某人）试试: *Have you tried the local music shops?* 你到当地的音像店找过了吗？
4 to decide in a law court if someone is guilty of a crime 审判；审理: *They were arrested and tried for murder.* 他们被捕了，并因涉嫌谋杀而受审。
try something on to put on a piece of clothing in order to see if it fits you or if it looks nice 试穿某物: *Try on the shoes to make sure they fit.* 试穿一下鞋子，看看是否合适。
try something out to test something in order to find out how useful or effective it is 试验某物: *I want to try the boat out next weekend.* 下周末我想把船开出去试一下。

¹T-shirt also 亦作 **tee-shirt** *countable noun* 可数名词
a simple shirt with no collar and short sleeves *T 恤衫；短袖无领衫

tsunami /tsʊˈnɑːmi/ *countable noun* 可数名词
a very large wave that flows onto the land and can cause a lot of damage 海啸

tub /tʌb/ *countable noun* 可数名词
a deep container 桶；缸；盆: *We ate four tubs of ice cream between us.* 我们一起吃了4桶冰激凌。

tuba /ˈtjuːbə/ *noun* 名词
a large round metal musical instrument with one wide end, that produces very low notes when you blow into it 大号
→ Look at picture on P12 参见彩插第 12 页

tube /tjuːb/ *countable noun* 可数名词
1 a long hollow object that is usually round, like a pipe 管；管子: *He is fed by a tube that enters his nose.* 他靠鼻饲管进食。
2 a long, thin container that you can press in order to force the substance out 管状容器: *a tube of toothpaste* 一管牙膏

the ¹Tube *singular noun* 单数名词
the underground railway in London（伦敦的）地铁: *I took the Tube and then the train.*

我先坐了地铁，然后坐火车。

tuck /tʌk/ *verb* 动词 (**tucks, tucking, tucked**)
to put something somewhere so that it is safe, comfortable or tidy 把…塞入；把…掖入：*He tucked his shirt inside his trousers.* 他把衬衫掖进裤子里。

Tuesday /'tjuːzdeɪ, -di/ *noun* 名词
the day after Monday and before Wednesday 星期二：*He phoned on Tuesday, just before you arrived.* 他星期二来电话了，就在你来之前。▫ *Work on the project will start next Tuesday.* 这个项目的工作将在下周二启动。

tug /tʌɡ/ *verb* 动词 (**tugs, tugging, tugged**)
to give something a quick, strong pull 猛拉；猛拽：*A little boy tugged at his sleeve excitedly.* 一个小男孩激动地拽着他的袖子。● **tug** *countable noun* 可数名词：*I felt a tug at my sleeve.* 我感觉袖子被拽了一下。

tulip /'tjuːlɪp/ *countable noun* 可数名词
a flower that grows in the spring and is shaped like a cup 郁金香

tumble /'tʌmbəl/ *verb* 动词 (**tumbles, tumbling, tumbled**)
to fall with a rolling movement 滚落；跌落：*A small boy tumbled off the step.* 一个小男孩从台阶上滚了下来。

tummy /'tʌmi/ *countable noun* 可数名词 (**tummies**)
your stomach 肚子：*Your baby's tummy should feel warm, but not hot.* 婴儿的肚子摸起来应该是暖暖的，不应该发烫。

tumour /'tjuːmə/ *countable noun* 可数名词
an unusual lump that has grown in a person's or an animal's body 肿瘤：*a brain tumour* 脑瘤

tuna /'tjuːnə/ *or* 或 **'tuna ˌfish** *noun* 名词 (**tuna** *or* 或 **tunas**)
1 a large fish that lives in warm seas 金枪鱼
2 *uncountable* 不可数 this fish when it is eaten as food 金枪鱼肉：*She opened a can of tuna.* 她打开一听金枪鱼罐头。

tune¹ /tjuːn/ *countable noun* 可数名词
a series of musical notes that is pleasant to listen to 曲调；曲子：*She was humming a little tune.* 她哼着一支小曲。
in tune/out of tune producing or not producing exactly the right notes 在调子上／不在调子上：*It was just an ordinary voice, but he sang in tune.* 他嗓音一般，但唱得也在调子上。

tune² /tjuːn/ *verb* 动词 (**tunes, tuning, tuned**)
to adjust a musical instrument so that it produces the right notes 为（乐器）调音：*We tune our guitars before we go on stage.* 登台前我们要为吉他调音。
tune something up same meaning as **tune** 同 tune：*Others were quietly tuning up their instruments.* 其他人在默默地为乐器调音。

tunnel /'tʌnəl/ *countable noun* 可数名词
a long passage that has been made under the ground, usually through a hill or under the sea 地道；隧道

turkey /'tɜːki/ *noun* 名词
1 *countable* 可数 a large bird that is kept on a farm for its meat 火鸡
2 *uncountable* 不可数 the meat of this bird when it is eaten as food 火鸡肉

turn¹ /tɜːn/ *verb* 动词 (**turns, turning, turned**)
1 to move in a different direction 转向；转弯：*He turned and walked away.* 他转身走开了。▫ *Then we turned right, off the motorway.* 然后我们右转，下了高速公路。
2 to move around in a circle 旋转；转动：*The wheels turned very slowly.* 轮子转得很慢。▫ *Turn the key to the right.* 向右转动钥匙。
3 to move a page in a book so that you can look at the next page 翻动（书页）：*He turned the pages of his photo album.* 他翻看相册。
4 to open a book and find a particular page 翻页：*Please turn to page 236.* 请翻到第 236 页。
5 to become something different 变成；成为：*The sky turned pale pink.* 天空变成了淡粉色。
6 to reach a particular age 达到（某个年龄）：*He made a million dollars before he turned thirty.* 他未满 30 岁就赚了 100 万美元。
turn into something to become something different 变成某事物：*In the story, the prince turns into a frog.* 在这个故事中，王子变成了青蛙。
turn out to happen 结果是；最终为：*I didn't know my life was going to turn out like this.* 我不知道我的生活会变成这个样子。
turn something down
1 to refuse an offer 拒绝（提议）：*The company offered me a new contract, but I*

turned it down. 公司提出和我签新合同，但我拒绝了。
2 to make a piece of equipment produce less sound or heat 把（设备）关小；把（设备）调低：*Please turn the TV down!* 请把电视音量调小点儿！ ▫ *I'll turn down the central heating.* 我要把中央供暖系统的温度调低些。
turn something off to make a piece of equipment stop working 关闭（设备）：*The light's a bit bright. Can you turn it off?* 灯光有点儿刺眼，你能把灯关掉吗？ ▫ *When the bath was full, she turned off the tap.* 浴缸里放满水后，她关掉了水龙头。
turn something on to make a piece of equipment start working 打开（设备）：*I turned on the television.* 我打开了电视。
turn something out to switch off a light 关（灯）：*Remember to turn the lights out when you leave the building.* 离开大楼时记得把灯都关掉。
turn something over to move something so that the top part is on the bottom 翻转某物；使某物颠倒：*Liz picked up the envelope and turned it over.* 利兹拿起信封，把它翻了过来。 ▫ *The car turned over and landed in a river.* 汽车翻了，掉进了河里。
turn something up to make a piece of equipment produce more sound or heat 把（设备）开大；把（设备）调高：*I turned the volume up.* 我调高了音量。
turn to someone to ask someone for their help 向某人求助：*She turned to him for support when she lost her job.* 她丢了工作后向他求助。
turn up to arrive 出现；到来：*They finally turned up at nearly midnight.* 几近午夜时他们终于到了。

turn² /tɜːn/ *countable noun* 可数名词
1 a move in a different direction 转向；转弯：*You can't do a right-hand turn here.* 此处禁止右转。
2 the time when you can do something 轮到的机会：*Tonight it's my turn to cook.* 今晚该我做饭了。
take turns to do something one after the other several times 轮流；交替：*It's a long way to Washington, so we took turns driving.* 去华盛顿很远，所以我们轮流开车。

turning /ˈtɜːnɪŋ/ *countable noun* 可数名词
a place where two roads join 转弯处；岔道口：*Take the next turning on the right.* 在下一个路口向右拐。

turnip /ˈtɜːnɪp/ *noun* 名词
a round white vegetable that grows under the ground 蔓菁；芜菁

turnover /ˈtɜːnəʊvə/ *noun* 名词
the value of the goods or services that are sold by a company during a particular period of time 营业额：*The company had a turnover of £3.8 million.* 那家公司的营业额为 380 万英镑。

turquoise /ˈtɜːkwɔɪz/ *adjective* 形容词
of a light greenish-blue colour 青绿色的：*the clear turquoise sea* 清澈碧蓝的大海
● **turquoise** *noun* 名词：*The door is painted a bright turquoise.* 门被漆成了鲜艳夺目的青绿色。

turtle /ˈtɜːtəl/ *countable noun* 可数名词
an animal that has a thick shell around its body and mainly lives in water 海龟：*Seabirds and turtles live on the island.* 海鸟和海龟生活在这个岛上。

tusk /tʌsk/ *countable noun* 可数名词
a very long, curved, pointed tooth that grows beside the mouth of some animals, such as an elephant (= a very large grey animal that lives in Africa and Asia)（象等动物的）獠牙

tutor /ˈtjuːtə/ *countable noun* 可数名词
someone who gives private lessons to one student or a very small group of students 家庭教师；私人教师：*a maths tutor* 数学家教

TV /ˌtiː ˈviː/ *noun* 名词 (**TVs**)
→ see 见 **television** : *The TV was on.* 电视开着。 ▫ *What's on TV?* 电视里演什么呢？ ▫ *They watch too much TV.* 他们老看电视。

tweezers /ˈtwiːzəz/ *plural noun* 复数名词
a small tool that you use for picking up or removing small objects. Tweezers consist of two thin pieces of metal joined together at one end. 镊子；小夹钳：*a pair of tweezers* 一把镊子

twelfth¹ /twelfθ/ *adjective* 形容词, *adverb* 副词
the item in a series that you count as number twelve 第十二：*They're celebrating the twelfth anniversary of the revolution.* 他们在庆祝革命 12 周年。 ▫ *She came twelfth in the competition.* 她在竞赛中得了第 12 名。

twelfth² /twelfθ/ *countable noun* 可数名词
one of twelve equal parts of something (1/12) 十二分之一：*She will get a twelfth of*

her father's money. 她将得到父亲财产的十二分之一。

twelve /twelv/
the number 12 十二

twenty /'twenti/
the number 20 二十

24-7 /ˌtwentifɔː 'sevən/ also 亦作 **twenty-four seven** adverb 副词
all the time; twenty-four hours a day, seven days a week (informal 非正式) 每时每刻；一周七天一天二十四小时：I feel like sleeping 24-7. 我想白天黑夜一直睡下去。
● **24-7** adjective 形容词：a 24-7 radio station 全天候广播电台

twice /twaɪs/ adverb 副词
two times 两次；两倍：He visited me twice last week. 上周他来看过我两次。□ I phoned twice a day. 我一天打两次电话。□ Budapest is twice as big as my home town. 布达佩斯是我家乡的两倍大。

twig /twɪɡ/ countable noun 可数名词
a small thin branch of a tree or a bush 细枝；嫩枝

twilight /'twaɪlaɪt/ uncountable noun 不可数名词
the time just before night when the light of the day has almost gone 黄昏；暮色：They returned at twilight. 他们黄昏时分回来了。

twin /twɪn/ countable noun 可数名词
one of two people who were born at the same time to the same mother 双胞胎之一：Sarah was looking after the twins. 萨拉当时在照看双胞胎。

twinkle /'twɪŋkəl/ verb 动词 (**twinkles, twinkling, twinkled**)
to shine with a light that continuously becomes brighter and then weaker 闪烁；闪耀：Lights twinkled across the valley. 整个山谷灯光闪闪。

twirl /twɜːl/ verb 动词 (**twirls, twirling, twirled**)
to turn or make something turn around several times very quickly（使）快速转动；（使）轻快地旋转：Bonnie twirled her empty glass in her fingers. 邦妮晃了晃手中握着的空玻璃杯。□ The dancers twirled around the dance floor. 舞者们在舞池中旋转。

twist /twɪst/ verb 动词 (**twists, twisting, twisted**)
1 to turn something to make it into a different shape 拧；使弯曲：She sat twisting the handles of the bag, and looking worried. 她坐着，手指绞着手提包的包带，看上去忧心忡忡。
2 to turn part of your body such as your head or your shoulders while keeping the rest of your body still 扭动，转动（身体部位）：She twisted her head around to look at him. 她扭过头去看他。
3 to injure a part of your body by turning it too suddenly, or in an unusual direction 扭伤：He fell and twisted his ankle. 他摔了一跤，扭伤了脚踝。
4 to turn something so that it moves around 转动，旋转（某物）：She was twisting the ring on her finger. 她转动着指上的戒指。

twitch /twɪtʃ/ verb 动词 (**twitches, twitching, twitched**)
to make a little jumping movement 抽搐；抽动：Her right eye began to twitch. 她的右眼开始跳。 ● **twitch** countable noun 可数名词 (**twitches**)：He had a nervous twitch. 他紧张得直抽搐。

two /tuː/
the number 2 二

two-dimensional /ˌtuː daɪ'menʃənəl, -dɪ-/ adjective 形容词
used for describing an object or a figure that is flat（物体或图形）平面的，二维的

type¹ /taɪp/ countable noun 可数名词
a particular kind of something 类型；种类：I like most types of music. 大部分音乐类型我都喜欢。□ Have you done this type of work before? 你以前做过这类工作吗？

type² /taɪp/ verb 动词 (**types, typing, typed**)
to write something using a machine like a computer（用计算机等）打（字）：I can type your essays for you. 我可以帮你把文章打出来。□ You should learn to type properly. 你应该学会如何正确打字。

typewriter /'taɪpraɪtə/ countable noun 可数名词
a machine with keys that you press in order to print writing onto paper 打字机

typical /'tɪpɪkəl/ adjective 形容词
1 used for describing a good example of a type of person or thing 典型的；有代表性的：Tell me about your typical day. 给我讲讲你每天都是怎么过的。□ In some ways, Jo is just a typical 12-year old. 从某些方面来看，乔就是个典型的 12 岁的孩子。

2 showing the usual qualities or characteristics of someone or something 特有的；独特的：*The bear had thick, white fur, typical of polar bears.* 这只熊长着北极熊特有的又厚又白的皮毛。

typically /ˈtɪpɪkəli/ *adverb* 副词
1 used for saying that something is a good example of a particular type of person or thing 典型地；具有代表性地：*The food is typically American.* 这是典型的美国食物。
2 usually 通常；一般：*The day typically begins with swimming.* 每天通常要先游泳。

typist /ˈtaɪpɪst/ *countable noun* 可数名词
someone who works in an office typing letters and other documents 打字员

tyrant /ˈtaɪərənt/ *countable noun* 可数名词
someone who has a lot of power and treats people in a cruel and unfair way 暴君；暴虐的统治者：*His staff all thought he was a tyrant.* 他的员工都认为他是个暴君。

tyre /ˈtaɪə/ *countable noun* 可数名词
a thick round piece of rubber that fits around the wheels of cars and bicycles 轮胎

Uu

ugly /ˈʌgli/ *adjective* 形容词 (**uglier**, **ugliest**)
very unpleasant to look at 丑陋的；难看的: *The museum is a rather ugly building.* 这家博物馆建得真难看。

ultimate /ˈʌltɪmət/ *adjective* 形容词
used for describing the final result of a long series of events 最后的；最终的: *Our ultimate goal is to win the gold medal.* 我们的终极目标是赢得金牌。

ultimately /ˈʌltɪmətli/ *adverb* 副词
finally, after a long series of events 最后；最终: *Who, ultimately, is going to pay?* 最后，谁来买单？

umbrella /ʌmˈbrelə/ *countable noun* 可数名词
a thing that you hold over your head to protect yourself from the rain 伞；雨伞: *She put up her umbrella and headed back to the car.* 她撑开伞，掉头向汽车走去。

umbrella 伞

umpire /ˈʌmpaɪə/ *countable noun* 可数名词
a person who watches a game such as tennis or cricket to make sure that the players do not break the rules（网球、板球等体育运动的）裁判员: *The umpire's decision is final.* 裁判的裁定不可更改。

unable /ʌnˈeɪbəl/ *adjective* 形容词
not able to do something 不能的；无法的: *After the car accident, Jacob was unable to walk.* 车祸后，雅各布不能走路了。

unacceptable /ˌʌnəkˈseptəbəl/ *adjective* 形容词
used for describing something that is so bad or wrong that you cannot accept it or allow it 不能接受的；不能容忍的: *This behaviour is unacceptable and will be punished.* 这种行为不可容忍，必将受到惩罚。

unanimous /juːˈnænɪməs/ *adjective* 形容词
with everyone agreeing about something 全体同意的；无异议的: *Their decision was unanimous.* 他们的决定是全体一致通过的。
▶ **unanimously** /juːˈnænɪməsli/ *adverb* 副词: *The board unanimously approved the project last week.* 上周董事会一致同意批准了这个项目。

unattractive /ˌʌnəˈtræktɪv/ *adjective* 形容词
not beautiful or attractive 难看的；不吸引人的: *I felt lonely and unattractive.* 我感到孤独，长得也不好看。 □ *The walls were painted an unattractive orange colour.* 墙被漆成了难看的橘色。

unavailable /ˌʌnəˈveɪləbəl/ *adjective* 形容词
busy and unable to meet you or talk to you 不方便的；没空见面的；没空交谈的: *The actress was making a film in Canada, and was unavailable for comment.* 这位女演员正在加拿大拍电影，不便发表评论。

unavoidable /ˌʌnəˈvɔɪdəbəl/ *adjective* 形容词
impossible to avoid or prevent 不可避免的；无法阻止的: *The accident was unavoidable.* 这起事故无法避免。

unaware /ˌʌnəˈweə/ *adjective* 形容词
not knowing about or not seeing someone or something 不知道的；未察觉的: *Many people are unaware that they have the disease.* 许多人并不知道自己得了这种病。 □ *She said she was unaware of the incident.* 她说她不知道这件事。

unbearable /ʌnˈbeərəbəl/ *adjective* 形容词
used for describing something that is so unpleasant that you cannot deal with it 不堪忍受的；无法容忍的；难以承受的: *The pain was unbearable.* 疼痛难忍。
▶ **unbearably** /ʌnˈbeərəbli/ *adverb* 副词: *In the afternoon, the sun became unbearably hot.* 下午阳光变得酷热难当。

unbelievable /ˌʌnbɪˈliːvəbəl/ *adjective* 形容词
1 very hard to believe 不可信的；不像真的: *The film was good, but the plot was*

unbelievable. 电影不错，但情节不可信。
2 very good or very bad (*informal* 非正式) 非常好(或坏)的：*It's a beautiful island, with unbelievable views.* 这是座美丽的小岛，景色美得超乎想象。▫ *The pain was unbelievable.* 这种痛实在让人受不了。
▶ **unbelievably** /ˌʌnbɪˈliːvəbli/ *adverb* 副词：*Jarrod is an unbelievably brave guy.* 贾罗德异常勇敢。

unborn /ˌʌnˈbɔːn/ *adjective* 形容词
not born yet 未降生的；未出世的：*This disease can harm an unborn child.* 这种疾病会危害胎儿。

uncertain /ʌnˈsɜːtən/ *adjective* 形容词
not sure; not decided 无把握的；不确定的：*If you're uncertain about anything, you must ask.* 有任何拿不准的地方务必提出来。

uncertainty /ʌnˈsɜːtənti/ *uncountable noun* 不可数名词
a feeling that bad things might happen 不确定；不安：*a time of political uncertainty* 政治动荡时期

uncle /ˈʌŋkəl/ *countable noun* 可数名词
the brother of your mother or father, or the husband of your aunt 伯父；叔父；舅舅；姑父；姨父：*My uncle was the mayor of Liverpool.* 我的伯父是利物浦市长。▫ *An email from Uncle Fred arrived.* 收到了弗雷德舅舅的一封邮件。

unclear /ʌnˈklɪə/ *adjective* 形容词
1 not known (事情)不清楚的：*It is unclear who tried to kill the president.* 尚不清楚谁试图刺杀总统。
2 not understanding or being sure about something (人)不理解的，不确定的：*People are unclear about the present situation.* 人们不清楚当前形势。

uncomfortable /ʌnˈkʌmftəbəl/ *adjective* 形容词
1 slightly worried or embarrassed, and not relaxed and confident 不自在的；不安的；尴尬的：*The request for money made them feel uncomfortable.* 索要金钱让他们有些不安。▫ *She was uncomfortable with the situation.* 这个场面让她觉得很不自在。
▶ **uncomfortably** /ʌnˈkʌmftəbli/ *adverb* 副词：*Sam's face was uncomfortably close.* 萨姆的脸靠得很近，让人不自在。
2 not pleasant to sit on, lie on or wear 让人不舒服的；令人不舒适的：*This is an extremely uncomfortable chair.* 这把椅子坐着很不舒服。

uncommon /ʌnˈkɒmən/ *adjective* 形容词
not happening very often 不平常的；罕见的：*It's not uncommon to get rain, snow and sun, all in one day.* 一天当中既有雨雪天气又出太阳的情况并不少见。

unconscious /ʌnˈkɒnʃəs/ *adjective* 形容词
not awake and not aware of what is happening around you because of illness or a serious injury 不省人事的；失去知觉的：*When the ambulance arrived, he was unconscious.* 救护车到达时，他已不省人事了。
▶ **unconsciousness** /ʌnˈkɒnʃəsnəs/ *uncountable noun* 不可数名词：*Breathing in this gas can cause unconsciousness and death.* 吸入这种气体会导致昏迷和死亡。

uncontrollable /ˌʌnkənˈtrəʊləbəl/ *adjective* 形容词
impossible to stop or control 无法控制的；控制不住的：*She felt an almost uncontrollable excitement.* 她的兴奋之情几乎难以抑制。
▶ **uncontrollably** /ˌʌnkənˈtrəʊləbli/ *adverb* 副词：*I started shaking uncontrollably.* 我开始控制不住地发抖。

uncountable /ʌnˈkaʊntəbəl/ *adjective* 形容词
used for describing nouns such as 'gold' or 'information' that have only one form and that cannot be used with 'a' or 'an' (名词)不可数的

uncover /ʌnˈkʌvə/ *verb* 动词 (uncovers, uncovering, uncovered)
1 to take away something that is on top of another thing 揭开…的盖子；除去…上的覆盖物：*Uncover the dish and cook the chicken for about 15 minutes.* 揭开盘子，将鸡肉煮15分钟左右。
2 to find out about something secret 揭露；发现：*They want to uncover the truth of what happened that night.* 他们想揭露那晚所发生之事的真相。

undecided /ˌʌndɪˈsaɪdɪd/ *adjective* 形容词
not having decided about something yet 未拿定主意的；犹豫不决的：*Mary is still undecided about her future.* 对于未来，玛丽依然犹豫不决。

under /ˈʌndə/ *preposition* 介词
1 below something 在…下面；在…下方；在…底下：*There are hundreds of tunnels under the ground.* 地下有上百条隧道。▫ *The two girls were sitting under a tree.* 那

两个女孩坐在树下。▫ *There was a big splash and she disappeared under the water.* 扑通一声,她消失在水下。 **2** less than a particular age or amount(年龄或数量)不足,低于: *Sarah has three children under ten years of age.* 萨拉有 3 个不满 10 岁的孩子。● under *adverb* 副词: *Children (14 years and under) get into the show free.* 儿童(14 岁及以下)免费入场。

undergo /ˌʌndəˈɡəʊ/ *verb* 动词 (**undergoes, undergoing, underwent, undergone**)
to have an unpleasant experience 经历;遭受;忍受: *Mia is undergoing treatment for cancer.* 米娅正在接受癌症治疗。

undergone /ˌʌndəˈɡɒn/
→ see 见 **undergo**

undergraduate /ˌʌndəˈɡrædʒuət/ *countable noun* 可数名词
a university or college student who has not yet passed their final exams(在读的)本科生,大学生: *More than 55 per cent of undergraduates are female.* *55% 以上的本科生是女性。

underground¹ *adjective* 形容词, *adverb* 副词

> **PRONUNCIATION HELP** 发音提示
> *adverb* /ˌʌndəˈɡraʊnd/; *adjective* /ˈʌndəˌɡraʊnd/. 副词读作 /ˌʌndəˈɡraʊnd/, 形容词读作 /ˈʌndəˌɡraʊnd/。

below the surface of the ground 在地下(的);在地面下(的): *The new library has an underground car park for 143 vehicles.* 新图书馆有一个地下停车场,可停放 143 辆汽车。 ▫ *Much of the castle is built underground.* 这座城堡大部分建在地下。

underground² /ˈʌndəˌɡraʊnd/ *singular noun* 单数名词
(*American* 美国英语: **subway**) in a city, the railway system in which electric trains travel below the ground in tunnels 地铁: *The underground is the best way of getting to work in Milan.* 在米兰,乘地铁是最佳的通勤方式。

underline /ˌʌndəˈlaɪn/ *verb* 动词 (**underlines, underlining, underlined**)
to draw a line under a word or a sentence 在…下画线: *She underlined her name.* 她在自己的名字下画线。

underneath /ˌʌndəˈniːθ/ *preposition* 介词
below or under something 在…下面;在…底下: *The bomb exploded underneath a van.* 炸弹在一辆厢式汽车底下爆炸了。 ● **underneath** *adverb* 副词: *He was wearing a blue sweater with a white T-shirt underneath.* 他穿着蓝色毛衣,里面是一件白色 T 恤。

underpants /ˈʌndəˌpænts/ *plural noun* 复数名词
a short piece of underwear that covers the area between a man's or a boy's waist and the top of his legs 男用内裤: *Richard packed a spare shirt, socks and underpants.* 理查德装了一件备用衬衫、袜子和内裤。

understand /ˌʌndəˈstænd/ *verb* 动词 (**understands, understanding, understood**)
1 to know what something means 理解,懂,领会(意思): *Toni can speak and understand Russian.* 托尼会说俄语,也听得懂。 ▫ *'Do you understand what I'm telling you, Sean?'* "肖恩,你明白我在和你说什么吗?"
2 to know why or how something happens 清楚,明白(某事): *The children are too young to understand what is going on.* 孩子们太小,不明白发生了什么。 ▫ *I don't understand why you're so afraid of her.* 我想不通你为什么那么怕她。
3 to believe that something is true because you have heard it or read it somewhere 听说;获悉: *I understand that you're leaving tomorrow.* 我听说你明天就要走了。

understanding¹ /ˌʌndəˈstændɪŋ/ *uncountable noun* 不可数名词
when you know about something 了解;掌握: *Children need to have an understanding of right and wrong.* 孩子得会分辨是非。

understanding² /ˌʌndəˈstændɪŋ/ *adjective* 形容词
kind to other people and thinking about how they feel 能谅解的;宽容的;通情达理的: *He was very understanding when we told him about our mistake.* 当我们告诉他我们犯的错误时,他非常理解。

understood /ˌʌndəˈstʊd/
→ see 见 **understand**

undertake /ˌʌndəˈteɪk/ *verb* 动词 (**undertakes, undertaking, undertook, undertaken**)
to start doing some work 着手做;从事;承担: *The company has undertaken two large projects in Dubai.* 这家公司在迪拜承

接了两个大型项目。

undertaken /ˌʌndəˈteɪkən/
→ see 见 **undertake**

undertook /ˌʌndəˈtʊk/
→ see 见 **undertake**

underwater /ˌʌndəˈwɔːtə/ *adjective* 形容词, *adverb* 副词
below the surface of the sea, a river or a lake 在水下(的); 在水中(的): *The divers were using underwater cameras.* 潜水员正在使用水下摄影机。□ *Submarines are able to travel at high speeds underwater.* 潜艇能够在水下高速行进。

underwear /ˈʌndəˌweə/ *uncountable noun* 不可数名词
clothes that you wear next to your skin, under your other clothes 内衣: *I bought some new underwear for the children.* 我给孩子们买了几件新内衣。

underwent /ˌʌndəˈwent/
→ see 见 **undergo**

undid /ʌnˈdɪd/
→ see 见 **undo**

undo /ʌnˈduː/ *verb* 动词 (**undoes, undoing, undid, undone**)
to untie something or make it loose 解开; 打开; 松开: *I managed to undo a corner of the package.* 我设法拆开了包裹的一角。□ *I undid the buttons of my shirt.* 我解开了衬衫纽扣。

undone /ʌnˈdʌn/
→ see 见 **undo**

undoubtedly /ʌnˈdaʊtɪdli/ *adverb* 副词
used for emphasizing that something is true 无疑地; 确定地: *Hanley is undoubtedly a great player.* 毋庸置疑, 汉利是一名伟大的运动员。

undress /ʌnˈdres/ *verb* 动词 (**undresses, undressing, undressed**)
to take off your clothes or another person's clothes (给⋯)脱衣服: *Emily undressed, got into bed and turned off the light.* 埃米莉脱了衣服上床, 然后关了灯。□ *Often young babies don't like being undressed and bathed.* 小宝宝往往不喜欢别人给他们脱衣洗澡。
▶ **undressed** /ʌnˈdrest/ *adjective* 形容词: *Fifteen minutes later Brandon was undressed and in bed.* *15 分钟后布兰登便脱衣上床了。

uneasy /ʌnˈiːzi/ *adjective* 形容词

anxious or afraid about something 焦虑的; 不安的: *Emma looked uneasy and refused to answer questions.* 埃玛看上去很不安, 拒绝回答问题。
▶ **uneasily** /ʌnˈiːzɪli/ *adverb* 副词: *Meg looked at her watch and moved uneasily on her chair.* 梅格看了看表, 在椅子上焦躁不安地动来动去。

unemployed /ˌʌnɪmˈplɔɪd/ *adjective* 形容词
able to work but without a job 失业的; 未受雇用的: *Millions of people are unemployed.* 数百万人失业。□ *This course helps young unemployed people to find work.* 该课程帮助年轻的失业者找到工作。
the unemployed people who are able to work but are without a job 失业者: *We want to create jobs for the unemployed.* 我们想为失业者创造就业岗位。

unemployment /ˌʌnɪmˈplɔɪmənt/ *uncountable noun* 不可数名词
when people who want to work cannot work, because there are not enough jobs 失业: *Robert's family live in an area of high unemployment.* 罗伯特一家住在高失业率地区。

unequal /ʌnˈiːkwəl/ *adjective* 形容词
not equal in quality or quantity 不平等的; 不均衡的: *Unequal pay is a serious problem in this industry.* 工资不平等是这个行业一个严重的问题。

uneven /ʌnˈiːvən/ *adjective* 形容词
not flat or smooth 不平坦的; 不平滑的: *The ground was uneven and he fell off his bike.* 地面高低不平, 他从自行车上摔了下来。

unexpected /ˌʌnɪkˈspektɪd/ *adjective* 形容词
surprising, because you did not expect it to happen 想不到的; 未意料到的; 意外的: *Scientists have made an unexpected discovery.* 科学家们有了意想不到的发现。
▶ **unexpectedly** /ˌʌnɪkˈspektɪdli/ *adverb* 副词: *April was unexpectedly hot.* 四月出乎意料地热。

unfair /ʌnˈfeə/ *adjective* 形容词
not treating people in an equal way or in the right way 不公正的; 不公平的: *It's unfair to expect a child to behave like an adult.* 期望孩子表现得像个成年人, 这不公平。□ *They claimed that the test was unfair.* 他们声称这次测验不公正。
▶ **unfairly** /ʌnˈfeəli/ *adverb* 副词: *She feels*

they treated her unfairly. 她觉得他们对她不公平。

▶ **unfairness** /ʌnˈfeənəs/ *uncountable noun* 不可数名词: I joined the police to tackle unfairness in society. 我当警察是为了解决社会上的不公平问题。

unfamiliar /ˌʌnfəˈmɪliə/ *adjective* 形容词
that you do not know; strange 不熟悉的；陌生的: The woman's voice was unfamiliar to me. 那个女人的声音我不熟悉。

unfit /ʌnˈfɪt/ *adjective* 形容词
1 not good enough for a particular purpose 不胜任的；不合格的: The water was unfit for drinking. 这水不宜饮用。
2 not healthy or strong 不健康的；不强健的: Many children are so unfit they cannot do even basic exercises. 许多孩子身体很差，甚至连基本的运动都做不了。

unfold /ʌnˈfəʊld/ *verb* 动词 (**unfolds, unfolding, unfolded**)
1 to open something that has been folded, to make it flat 使展开: Mum unfolded the piece of paper. 妈妈展开那张纸。
2 to open out and become flat 展开；打开: The sofa unfolds to form a double bed. 沙发展开成了一张双人床。

unfollow /ʌnˈfɒləʊ/ *verb* 动词 (**unfollows, unfollowing, unfollowed**)
to choose to stop seeing messages and pictures that someone posts on a social media website (在社交网站上)取消对…的关注: His posts were annoying so I unfollowed him. 他发布的信息很烦人，我取消了对他的关注。

unfortunate /ʌnˈfɔːtʃʊnət/ *adjective* 形容词
1 unlucky 不幸的；倒霉的: We were very unfortunate to lose the game. 我们不幸输了比赛。
2 talking about something that you wish had not happened 令人遗憾的；可惜的: We've made some unfortunate mistakes in the past. 过去我们犯了一些令人遗憾的错误。

unfortunately /ʌnˈfɔːtʃʊnətli/ *adverb* 副词
used for showing that you are sorry about something 不幸地；遗憾地: Unfortunately, I don't have time to stay. 遗憾的是，我没有时间停留。

unfriend /ʌnˈfrend/ *verb* 动词 (**unfriends, unfriending, unfriended**)
to stop being someone's friend on a social media website (在社交网站上)将…从好友列表删除: I don't know why she unfriended me. 我不知道她为什么把我从好友列表里删了。

unfriendly /ʌnˈfrendli/ *adjective* 形容词
not friendly; behaving in an unkind or unpleasant way 不友好的；不友善的；冷漠的: The people he met there were unfriendly and rude. 他在那里遇到的人既冷漠又粗鲁。

ungrateful /ʌnˈɡreɪtfʊl/ *adjective* 形容词
not showing that you want to thank someone who has helped you or been kind to you 不感恩的；忘恩负义的

unhappy /ʌnˈhæpi/ *adjective* 形容词 (**unhappier, unhappiest**)
1 sad 不快乐的；不幸福的；难过的: Christopher was a shy, unhappy man. 克里斯托弗生性腼腆、郁郁寡欢。
▶ **unhappily** /ʌnˈhæpɪli/ *adverb* 副词: Jean shook her head unhappily. 琼不开心地摇了摇头。
▶ **unhappiness** /ʌnˈhæpɪnəs/ *uncountable noun* 不可数名词: There was a lot of unhappiness in my childhood. 我的童年经历过很多不幸。
2 not pleased about something or satisfied with it 不高兴的；不满意的: We were unhappy with the way we played on Friday. 我们对自己周五的表现不满意。

unhealthy /ʌnˈhelθi/ *adjective* 形容词 (**unhealthier, unhealthiest**)
1 ill or not in good physical condition (身体)不健康的: The man looked pale and unhealthy. 那人面色苍白，满脸病容。
2 likely to make you ill or harm your health 会致病的；损害健康的: Avoid unhealthy foods such as hamburgers and chips. 不要吃不健康食品，如汉堡包和薯条。

unhelpful /ʌnˈhelpfʊl/ *adjective* 形容词
not helping you or making things better 不予帮助的；无益的: Josh was rude and unhelpful to Della. 乔希对德拉很无礼，而且一点儿忙也不帮。

uniform /ˈjuːnɪˌfɔːm/ *noun* 名词
the special clothes that some people wear to work, and that some children wear at school 制服: The police wear blue uniforms. 警察穿着蓝色制服。◻ Daniel was dressed in his school uniform. 丹尼尔穿着校服。

uniform 制服
school uniform 校服
police officer's uniform 警服

unimportant /ˌʌnɪmˈpɔːtənt/ *adjective* 形容词
not important 不重要的: *Abigail always remembers unimportant details.* 阿比盖尔总是记得一些无关紧要的细节。

union /ˈjuːnjən/ *noun* 名词
1 *countable* 可数 a workers' organization that tries to improve working conditions for the workers 工会: *Ten new members joined the union last week.* 上周有 10 名新成员加入工会。
2 *singular* 单数 a group of people or countries that have joined together 联盟；共同体: *the European Union* 欧盟

unique /juːˈniːk/ *adjective* 形容词
different from every other person or thing 独一无二的；独特的: *Each person's signature is unique.* 每个人的签名都是独一无二的。

unit /ˈjuːnɪt/ *countable noun* 可数名词
1 a single, complete thing that can belong to something larger（构成更大整体的）单位，单元: *The building is divided into twelve units.* 大楼分成 12 个单元。
2 a measurement（计量）单位: *A centimetre is a unit of measurement.* 厘米是计量单位。

unite /juːˈnaɪt/ *verb* 动词 (**unites, uniting, united**)
to join together and act as a group 联合；团结: *The world must unite to fight this disease.* 全世界必须联手抗击这种疾病。 □ *The president can unite the people.* 总统能将人们团结起来。

universal /ˌjuːnɪˈvɜːsəl/ *adjective* 形容词
including or affecting everyone 普遍的；全体的: *Love is a universal emotion.* 爱是一种普遍的情感。

▸ **universally** /ˌjuːnɪˈvɜːsəli/ *adverb* 副词: *Reading is universally accepted as being good for kids.* 人们普遍认为阅读对儿童有益。

universe /ˈjuːnɪvɜːs/ *singular noun* 单数名词
the universe everything that exists in space, including the Earth, the sun, the moon, the planets and the stars 宇宙: *Can you tell us how the universe began?* 你可以跟我们说说宇宙的起源吗？

university /ˌjuːnɪˈvɜːsɪti/ *noun* 名词 (**universities**)
a place where you can study after you leave school 大学: *I started my degree at the University of St Andrews last year.* 我从去年开始在圣安德鲁斯大学攻读学位。 □ *Robert's mother is a university professor.* 罗伯特的母亲是一名大学教授。

unjust /ʌnˈdʒʌst/ *adjective* 形容词
not fair or right 不公平的；不公正的: *He was an unjust ruler, responsible for the deaths of thousands of people.* 他是个不公正的统治者，成千上万的人因他丧命。
▸ **unjustly** /ʌnˈdʒʌstli/ *adverb* 副词: *Megan was unjustly accused of stealing money.* 梅甘被冤枉偷钱。

unkind /ʌnˈkaɪnd/ *adjective* 形容词 (**unkinder, unkindest**)
unpleasant and unfriendly 不仁慈的；刻薄的；不友好的: *Tyler was unkind to his sister all evening.* 泰勒一整晚都没给妹妹好脸色。

unknown /ʌnˈnəʊn/ *adjective* 形容词
1 not known 不明了的；未知的: *The child's age is unknown.* 这个孩子的年龄不得而知。
2 not famous 不出名的；不为人知的: *Ten years ago he was an unknown writer but now he is a celebrity.* 10 年前他还是个名不见经传的作家，现在已然是个名人。

unleaded /ʌnˈledɪd/ *adjective* 形容词
unleaded fuel contains a smaller amount of lead (= a metal) than most types of fuel（燃料）无铅的: *He filled up his car with unleaded petrol.* 他给车加满了无铅汽油。

unless /ənˈles/ *conjunction* 连词
used for saying what will happen if another thing does not happen 除非: *Ryan says he won't go to the party, unless I go too.* 瑞安说，除非我也去参加聚会，否则他不会去。

unlike /ʌnˈlaɪk/ *preposition* 介词
different from 不像；与…不同: *You're so unlike your father!* 你和你父亲太不一样了！

unlikely /ʌnˈlaɪkli/ *adjective* 形容词 (**unlikeliest**)
not likely to happen 不太可能的: *The boys are unlikely to arrive before nine o'clock.* 男孩们不太可能在 9 点前到达。

unload /ʌnˈləʊd/ *verb* 动词 (**unloads, unloading, unloaded**)
to remove goods from a ship or a vehicle 卸下（货物）; 从…上卸货: *We unloaded everything from the car.* 我们把所有东西从车上卸了下来。 □ *The men started unloading the lorry.* 那些人开始从卡车上卸货。

unlock /ʌnˈlɒk/ *verb* 动词 (**unlocks, unlocking, unlocked**)
to open something using a key（用钥匙）打开, 开启: *Taylor unlocked the car and got in.* 泰勒用钥匙打开车门上了车。

unlucky /ʌnˈlʌki/ *adjective* 形容词 (**unluckier, unluckiest**)
1 having something bad happen to you when it is not your fault 不幸的; 倒霉的: *Michael was unlucky to break his leg in the tournament in Rotterdam.* 迈克尔在鹿特丹的锦标赛中不幸摔断了腿。
2 bringing bad luck 不吉利的; 晦气的: *Four is an unlucky number in East Asia.* 在东亚, 4 是个不吉利的数字。

unmarried /ʌnˈmærid/ *adjective* 形容词
not married 未婚的; 独身的: *an unmarried couple* 未婚情侣

unmistakable /ˌʌnmɪsˈteɪkəbəl/ also 亦作 **unmistakeable** *adjective* 形容词
very obvious and easy to recognize 清楚明白的; 确定无疑的: *A few minutes later, we heard Shirley's unmistakable voice.* 几分钟后, 我们真真切切地听到了雪利的声音。

unnatural /ʌnˈnætʃərəl/ *adjective* 形容词
different from what you usually expect 反常的; 异常的: *His eyes were an unnatural shade of blue.* 他的眼睛呈一种异样的蓝色。

unnecessary /ʌnˈnesəsri/ *adjective* 形容词
not needed or that you do not need to do 不需要的; 没必要的: *It is unnecessary to spend huge amounts of money on Christmas presents.* 没必要在圣诞节礼物上花大钱。

unofficial /ˌʌnəˈfɪʃəl/ *adjective* 形容词
not organized or approved by an official person or group 未经正式批准的; 非官方的; 非正式的: *Unofficial reports say that one police officer was killed.* 非官方报道称一名警官被杀。

unpack /ʌnˈpæk/ *verb* 动词 (**unpacks, unpacking, unpacked**)
to take things out of a suitcase or a box 打开（箱、盒等）取出物品: *He unpacked his bag.* 他打开包取出东西。 □ *Bill helped his daughter to unpack.* 比尔帮女儿打开行李。

unpaid /ʌnˈpeɪd/ *adjective* 形容词
1 without receiving any money for something 无偿的; 没有薪水的: *Most of the work I do is unpaid.* 我做的大部分工作都是无偿的。
2 not yet paid 未付的: *His telephone was disconnected because of an unpaid bill.* 他的电话欠费停机了。

unpleasant /ʌnˈplezənt/ *adjective* 形容词
1 making you feel upset or uncomfortable 令人不快的; 令人不舒服的: *The plant has an unpleasant smell.* 这种植物有股难闻的气味。
▸ **unpleasantly** /ʌnˈplezəntli/ *adverb* 副词
She stayed until the water became unpleasantly cold. 她一直待到水冷得让人不舒服。
2 very unfriendly and rude 不友好的; 粗鲁的: *He is such an unpleasant man!* 他真是个粗鲁的人！

unplug /ʌnˈplʌɡ/ *verb* 动词 (**unplugs, unplugging, unplugged**)
to take a piece of electrical equipment from its electrical supply, so that it stops working 拔掉…的电源插头: *Whenever there's a storm, I unplug my computer.* 每当有风暴, 我就会把电脑的插头拔掉。

unpopular /ʌnˈpɒpjʊlə/ *adjective* 形容词
not liked by most people; not popular 不受欢迎的; 不得人心的: *It was an unpopular decision.* 那是个不得人心的决定。□ *I was very unpopular at school.* 我在学校很不受欢迎。

unpredictable /ˌʌnprɪˈdɪktəbəl/ *adjective* 形容词
always behaving in a way that you do not expect 不可预测的; 难以预料的: *Jim was unpredictable — he could get angry about anything.* 吉姆让人捉摸不透——任何事都可能让他发火。□ *The British weather is unpredictable.* 英国的天气变幻莫测。

unprepared /ˌʌnprɪˈpeəd/ *adjective* 形容词
not ready for something 无准备的: *I'm totally unprepared for my English exam tomorrow.* 对于明天的英语考试我毫无准备。

unreasonable /ˌʌnˈriːzənəbəl/ *adjective* 形容词
not fair or sensible 不公平的；不合理的：*It's unreasonable to expect a child to behave well all the time.* 期待孩子一直表现良好并不合理。

unreliable /ˌʌnrɪˈlaɪəbəl/ *adjective* 形容词
that you cannot trust or depend on 不可靠的；不能信赖的：*My old car is very slow and unreliable. It's always breaking down.* 我这辆旧车又慢又不可靠，总是出故障。□ *The law protects people from unreliable builders.* 这条法律保护人们免受不可靠建筑商的侵害。

unruly /ʌnˈruːli/ *adjective* 形容词
difficult to control 难控制的；难管束的：*Police arrested 60 people after the unruly crowd began throwing rocks and bottles.* 在失控人群开始投掷石块和瓶子后，警方逮捕了 60 人。

unsafe /ʌnˈseɪf/ *adjective* 形容词
dangerous; not safe 危险的；不安全的：*The building is unsafe and beyond repair.* 那栋大楼不安全，也无法再修复了。□ *The water here is unsafe to drink.* 饮用这里的水不安全。

unsatisfactory /ˌʌnsætɪsˈfæktəri/ *adjective* 形容词
not good enough 不够好的；不能令人满意的：*His boss said that his work was unsatisfactory.* 他老板说他的工作做得不够好。□ *Our accommodation was unsatisfactory.* 我们的住处让人不满意。

unsteady /ʌnˈstedi/ *adjective* 形容词
likely to fall 不稳的；摇晃的：*My grandma is unsteady on her feet.* 我奶奶站不稳。

unsuccessful /ˌʌnsəkˈsesful/ *adjective* 形容词
failing to do what you wanted and tried to do 不成功的；失败的：*They tried to save the man's life, but they were unsuccessful.* 他们试图挽救那人的性命，但是失败了。

unsuitable /ʌnˈsuːtəbəl/ *adjective* 形容词
not right for someone or something 不适宜的；不合适的：*This film is unsuitable for children.* 这部电影不适合儿童观看。

unsure /ʌnˈʃʊə/ *adjective* 形容词
not certain about something 不确定的；不清楚的：*Police are unsure exactly when the items were stolen.* 警方不清楚物品被盗的确切时间。

unsympathetic /ˌʌnsɪmpəˈθetɪk/ *adjective* 形容词
not kind or helpful to someone who is having problems 冷漠的；无同情心的：*Jane's friends were unsympathetic and she felt she had no one to talk to.* 简的朋友们都很冷漠，她觉得无人可倾诉。

untidy /ʌnˈtaɪdi/ *adjective* 形容词
not well arranged 不整齐的；凌乱的：*The place quickly became untidy.* 这地方很快变得凌乱不堪。□ *He was a thin man with untidy hair.* 他身形消瘦，头发蓬乱。□ *Clothes were thrown in the luggage in an untidy heap.* 衣服被胡乱扔进了行李箱里。

untie /ˌʌnˈtaɪ/ *verb* 动词 (**unties, untying, untied**)
to open a knot, or something that is tied with a knot 解开；松开：*She untied the laces on one of her shoes.* 她解开了一只鞋的鞋带。□ *They untied his hands.* 他们给他的手松绑。

until /ənˈtɪl, ʌnˈtɪl/ *preposition* 介词
1 happening before a particular time and then stopping at that time 直到，在⋯之前（表示某事在某个时间停止）：*Until 2004, Julie lived in Canada.* 2004 年以前，朱莉生活在加拿大。● **until** *conjunction* 连词：*I waited until it got dark.* 我一直等到天黑。
2 not happening before a particular time and only starting to happen at that time 直到⋯之前，除非（表示某事直到某个时间才发生）：*I won't arrive in Dublin until Saturday.* 我要到星期六才到都柏林。● **until** *conjunction* 连词：*They won't be safe until they get out of the country.* 除非离开这个国家，否则他们不会安全。

> **LANGUAGE HELP** 语言提示
> You only use **until** when you are talking about time. When you are talking about place or position, use **as far as** or **up to**.
> *until 只用于表示时间，表示地点或位置用 as far as 或 up to：Will you come with us as far as the village?* 你能陪我们到那个村子吗？□ *We walked up to the gate, but we didn't go in.* 我们走到了大门口，但没有进去。

untrue /ʌnˈtruː/ *adjective* 形容词
not true or correct 不真实的；假的：*Bryant said the story was untrue.* 布赖恩特声称这个故事不实。

unusual /ʌnˈjuːʒəl/ *adjective* 形容词
not happening very often or not seen or heard very often 不寻常的；罕见的：*It's unusual for our teacher to make a mistake.* 很少见我们老师犯错。
▶ **unusually** /ʌnˈjuːʒəli/ *adverb* 副词：*It was an unusually cold winter.* 那年冬天异常寒冷。

unwanted /ʌnˈwɒntɪd/ *adjective* 形容词
not wanted or loved 无人要的；没人爱的：*Delete unwanted emails from your computer.* 删去电脑上不需要的邮件。 □ *Emily felt unwanted and unloved.* 埃米莉觉得自己很多余，也无人疼爱。

unwelcome /ʌnˈwelkəm/ *adjective* 形容词
used for describing something or someone that you are not happy to have or to see 不受欢迎的；讨人嫌的：*We were clearly unwelcome guests.* 我们的到来显然不受欢迎。

unwell /ʌnˈwel/ *adjective* 形容词
not well; ill 不适的；不舒服的：*Grandpa was feeling unwell and had to stay at home.* 爷爷感觉不舒服，只能待在家里。

unwilling /ʌnˈwɪlɪŋ/ *adjective* 形容词
not happy or keen to do something 不愿意的；不情愿的：*Many people are unwilling to change their email addresses.* 许多人不愿意更改自己的电子邮件地址。

unwind /ʌnˈwaɪnd/ *verb* 动词 (**unwinds, unwinding, unwound**)
1 to loosen and straighten something that has been wrapped around something else 解开；展开：*She unwound the scarf from her neck.* 她把围巾从脖子上解开。
2 to do something relaxing after you have been working hard or worrying about something 放松；减压：*You need to unwind after a busy day at work.* 在一天忙碌的工作后，你需要放松自己。

unwise /ʌnˈwaɪz/ *adjective* 形容词
not sensible 不明智的；轻率的：*It would be unwise of me to comment.* 我发表评论非明智之举。
▶ **unwisely** /ʌnˈwaɪzli/ *adverb* 副词：*She understands that she acted unwisely.* 她知道自己之前的举动不明智。

unwound /ʌnˈwaʊnd/
→ see 见 **unwind**

unwrap /ʌnˈræp/ *verb* 动词 (**unwraps, unwrapping, unwrapped**)
to take off the paper or plastic that is around something 打开（或拆开）…的包装：*I untied the ribbon and unwrapped the small box.* 我解开带子，拆开小盒子的包装。

unzip /ʌnˈzɪp/ *verb* 动词 (**unzips, unzipping, unzipped**)
1 to undo the metal strip (= a zip) that fastens a piece of clothing 拉开…的拉链：*Pete unzipped his leather jacket and sat down.* 皮特拉开皮夹克的拉链，坐了下来。
2 to make a computer file go back to its original size after it has been zipped (= reduced in size using a special program) 给（文档）解压缩：*Use the 'Unzip' command to unzip the file.* 使用 Unzip 指令解压文件。

up[1] /ʌp/ *preposition* 介词
1 towards a higher place 向上；朝上；往上：*They were climbing up a mountain road.* 他们沿着一条山路向上爬。□ *I ran up the stairs.* 我跑上楼梯。
2 along a road 沿着；顺着：*A dark blue lorry came up the road.* 一辆深蓝色的卡车沿路驶来。

up[2] /ʌp/ *adjective* 形容词, *adverb* 副词
1 towards a higher place 向上；朝上；往上：*Keep your head up.* 抬起你的头。
2 from sitting or lying down to standing （站）起：*He stood up and went to the window.* 他起身走向窗户。
3 to the place where someone or something is 往；朝：*He came up to me and gave me a big hug.* 他朝我走来，给了我一个大大的拥抱。
4 not in bed 起床的：*'Did I wake you?' — 'No, I'm up.'* "我吵醒你了吗？" —— "没有，我已经起床了。"
be up to come to an end （时间）到了，结束：*When the half-hour was up, Brian left.* 半小时一到，布赖恩便离开了。
be up against someone/something to have a difficult person or situation to deal with 遭遇（强敌）/面临（困难）：*They were up against a good team, but did very well.* 他们遇到了一支强队，但他们表现很出色。
be up to someone to do something to be the person who must do or decide something 由某人负责某事；由某人决定某事：*It's up to you to solve your own problems.* 你自己的问题自己来解决。
What's up? used for asking someone what is wrong (*informal* 非正式) 出什么

事啦？出什么问题啦？：'What's up?' I said to him. 'Nothing much,' he answered. "出什么事啦？"我对他说。"没什么事。"他答道。

upbringing /ˈʌpbrɪŋɪŋ/ ***countable noun*** 可数名词
the way that your parents treat you and the things that they teach you when you are growing up 抚育；培育；教养：*I had a strict upbringing.* 我家教很严。

update[1] /ʌpˈdeɪt/ ***verb*** 动词 (**updates, updating, updated**)
to make something more modern or add new information to it 更新；使现代化：*We update our news reports regularly.* 我们定期更新新闻报道。

update[2] /ˈʌpdeɪt/ ***countable noun*** 可数名词
the most recent information about a particular situation 最新消息；快讯：*Now here's a weather update.* 现在播报最新天气状况。

upgrade[1] /ʌpˈɡreɪd/ ***verb*** 动词 (**upgrades, upgrading, upgraded**)
to improve something or replace it with a better version 改良；更新；升级：*The road into town is being upgraded.* 进城的道路正在整修中。 □ *I recently upgraded my computer.* 我最近升级了我的电脑。

upgrade[2] /ˈʌpɡreɪd/ ***countable noun*** 可数名词
a piece of equipment or a program that makes a computer more powerful（计算机的）升级装置, 升级程序：*a software upgrade* 软件升级程序

uphill /ʌpˈhɪl/ ***adverb*** 副词
up, towards the top of a slope 上坡；向山上：*He ran uphill a long way.* 他跑了一段很长的上坡路。

upload /ʌpˈləʊd/ ***verb*** 动词 (**uploads, uploading, uploaded**)
to move a document or a program from your computer to another one, using the Internet 上传；上载：*Next, upload the files on to your website.* 接下来，把文件上传到你的网站。 ● **upload** /ˈʌpləʊd/ ***noun*** 名词：*Her blog features regular updates and picture uploads for her fans.* 她的博客定期为粉丝更新博文并上传照片。

upon /əˈpɒn/ ***preposition*** 介词
on (*formal* 正式) 在…上：*The decision was based upon science and fact.* 这个决定是根据科学和事实作出的。

upper /ˈʌpə/ ***adjective*** 形容词
in a higher position（位置）较上的, 较高的：*There is a good restaurant on the upper floor of the building.* 这栋大楼的高层有一家不错的餐厅。 □ *The soldier was shot in the upper back.* 这名士兵的上背部中弹了。

ˌupper ˈcase ***uncountable noun*** 不可数名词
the larger form of letters at the beginning of sentences or people's names. These are also called 'capital letters'. Compare with **lower case**. 大写字母（比较 lower case）：*Typing an email using upper case is like shouting at someone instead of talking to them.* 用大写字母写邮件就像是在冲人吼叫, 不像是在与人谈话。

upright /ˈʌpraɪt/ ***adjective*** 形容词
standing up and not lying down 挺直的；笔直的：*John offered Andrew a seat, but he remained upright.* 约翰请安德鲁坐下, 但他依旧站得笔直。 □ *The ladder was upright against the wall.* 梯子靠墙直立着。

upset[1] /ʌpˈset/ ***adjective*** 形容词
unhappy because something bad has happened 心烦的；苦恼的；沮丧的：*After Grandma died, I was very, very upset.* 祖母去世后, 我悲痛万分。 □ *Marta looked upset.* 马尔塔看起来很沮丧。
have an upset stomach to have a mild illness that affects your stomach, often because of something that you have eaten 肠胃不适：*Paul was sick last night with an upset stomach.* 保罗昨晚病了, 肚子不舒服。

upset[2] /ʌpˈset/ ***verb*** 动词 (**upsets, upsetting, upset**)
1 to make you feel worried or unhappy 使心烦意乱；使心情不悦：*What you said in your letter really upset me.* 你在信里说的话真让我心烦。
2 to make your plans go wrong 打乱；搅乱：*Heavy rain upset our plans for a barbecue on the beach.* 大雨打乱了我们在海滩上烧烤的计划。

upsetting /ʌpˈsetɪŋ/ ***adjective*** 形容词
making you feel unhappy or worried 令人不快的；令人心烦的：*The death of a family pet is always upsetting.* 家里养的宠物死去总是令人难过。

upside down /ˌʌpsaɪd ˈdaʊn/ *adverb* 副词
with the bottom part of something at the top 颠倒地；倒置地: *The painting was hanging upside down.* 这幅画挂倒了。

upside down 颠倒地

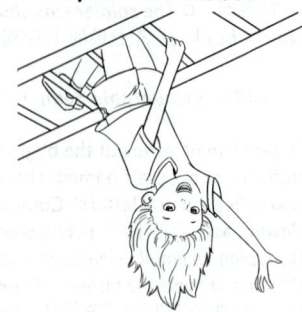

upstairs /ˌʌpˈsteəz/ *adverb* 副词
on or to a higher floor of a building 在楼上；往楼上: *He went upstairs and changed his clothes.* 他上楼换了衣服。 □ *The restaurant is upstairs.* 餐厅在楼上。● **upstairs** *adjective* 形容词: *Mark lived in the upstairs flat.* 马克住在楼上的公寓里。

up-to-date also 亦作 **up to date** *adjective* 形容词
1 most recent 新近的；最新的: *Our company uses the most up-to-date technology.* 我们公司使用最先进的技术。
2 having the latest information about something 掌握最新信息的: *We'll keep you up to date with any news.* 一有新消息我们就会告诉你。 □ *We need some up-to-date weather information.* 我们需要一些最新的天气信息。

upwards /ˈʌpwədz/ or 或 **upward** /ˈʌpwəd/ *adverb* 副词
moving or looking up 向上；朝上: *She turned her face upwards.* 她仰起头来。

urban /ˈɜːbən/ *adjective* 形容词
relating to a city or a town 城市的；城镇的: *We are recruiting young adults from both rural and urban areas all over the country.* 我们向全国的农村和城市招募年轻人。

urge¹ /ɜːdʒ/ *verb* 动词 (**urges, urging, urged**)
to try hard to persuade someone to do something 敦促；力劝: *Doctors urged my uncle to change his diet.* 医生们敦促我叔叔改变饮食习惯。

urge² /ɜːdʒ/ *countable noun* 可数名词
a strong feeling that you want to do or have something 强烈的欲望；冲动: *He felt a sudden urge to phone Mary.* 他突然很想给玛丽打个电话。

urgent /ˈɜːdʒənt/ *adjective* 形容词
needing attention as soon as possible 紧迫的；紧急的；紧要的: *The refugees have an urgent need for food and water.* 难民急需食物和水。 □ *I've got to take an urgent telephone call.* 我有个要紧的电话要打。
▶ **urgently** /ˈɜːdʒəntli/ *adverb* 副词: *These people urgently need medical supplies.* 这些人急需医疗用品。

URL /ˌjuː ɑːr ˈel/ *countable noun* 可数名词 (**URLs**)
an address that shows where you can find a particular page on the World Wide Web 统一资源定位地址

us /əs, STRONG 强读 ʌs/ *pronoun* 代词
used for talking about yourself and the person or people with you 我们: *William's girlfriend has invited us for lunch.* 威廉的女友邀请我们去吃午餐。 □ *Heather went to the kitchen to get drinks for us.* 希瑟去厨房给我们拿喝的。

USB /ˌjuː es ˈbiː/ *countable noun* 可数名词 (**USBs**)
a part of a computer where you can attach another piece of equipment. **USB** is short for (缩写 =) 'Universal Serial Bus'. 通用串行总线

USB stick *countable noun* 可数名词
a small object for storing digital information that you can connect to the USB port of a computer or other device 优盘: *Just load your images onto a USB stick and take them with you.* 把照片传到优盘里随身带着。

use¹ /juːz/ *verb* 动词 (**uses, using, used**)
1 to do something with a particular thing 使用；应用；运用: *They wouldn't let him use the phone.* 他们不会让他用电话的。 □ *She used the money to buy food for her family.* 她用这笔钱给家人买吃的。
2 to finish something so that none of it is left 耗尽；用光: *She used all the shampoo.* 她把洗发水用完了。
use up to finish something so that none of it is left 耗尽；用光: *If you use up the milk, please buy some more.* 如果你把牛奶用完了，请再买一些。

use² /juːs/ *noun* 名词
1 *uncountable* 不可数 the action of using

something 使用；应用；运用：*We encourage the use of computers in the classroom.* 我们鼓励在教室里使用计算机。**2** the way in which you can use something 用途；用处：*Bamboo has many uses — it provides food, shelter and medicine.* 竹子用途繁多——既可食用，又能遮风挡雨，还能入药。
have the use of something to be allowed to use something that belongs to someone else 有某物的使用权：*My older sister has the use of Mum's car one night a week.* 我姐姐每周有一个晚上可以用妈妈的车。
it's no use doing something something that you say when you stop doing something because you believe that it is impossible to succeed 做某事没有用：*'It's no use asking him what happened,' said Kate. 'He won't tell us.'* "问他发生了什么没有用，"凯特说，"他不会告诉我们的。"
make use of something to use something for a particular purpose 使用某物；利用某物：*You can make use of the leisure facilities in the nearby hotel.* 你可以使用附近宾馆的休闲设施。

used¹ /juːst/ *adjective* 形容词
be used to something to be familiar with something because you have done it many times before 习惯于某事：*I'm used to hard work.* 我习惯了努力工作。 *I am used to travelling First Class.* 我习惯了坐头等舱出行。
get used to something to become familiar with something 开始习惯于某事：*This is how we do things here. You'll soon get used to it.* 我们这儿就是这么做事的。你很快就会习惯。

used² /juːzd/ *adjective* 形容词
not new 旧的；二手的：*If you are buying a used car, you will need to check it carefully.* 如果要买二手车，你需要仔细检查一番。

used to /ˈjuːs tə/ *modal verb* 情态动词
used for talking about something that was true in the past but is not true now 过去常常；曾经：*I used to live in Los Angeles.* 我过去住在洛杉矶。 *He used to be one of my teachers.* 他曾是我的老师。

useful /ˈjuːsfʊl/ *adjective* 形容词
helpful 有用的；有益的：*The book is full of useful advice about growing fruit and vegetables.* 这本书里全是关于种植果蔬的有用建议。

▶**usefully** /ˈjuːsfʊli/ *adverb* 副词：*The students used their extra time usefully, doing homework or playing sports.* 学生们有效利用了课余时间，不是做作业，就是做运动。

useless /ˈjuːsləs/ *adjective* 形容词
1 not helpful or useful in any way 无用的；无价值的：*My leather jacket is useless in the rain.* 我的皮夹克在雨天毫无用处。**2** not having the result you would like 无益的；无效的：*Christina knew it was useless to argue with the police officer.* 克里斯蒂娜知道和警官争论无济于事。**3** very bad at something (*informal* 非正式) 差劲的；不行的：*I was always useless at maths.* 我数学一向很差。

user /ˈjuːzə/ *countable noun* 可数名词
a person who uses something 使用者；用户：*Some young Internet users spend up to 70 hours a week online.* 有些年轻的因特网用户一周的上网时间长达 70 个小时。 *I'm a regular user of the underground.* 我经常乘地铁。

user-friendly *adjective* 形容词
well designed and easy to use 易使用的；用户友好的：*This is a well designed and user-friendly website.* 这个网站设计美观、用户友好。

username /ˈjuːzəˌneɪm/ *noun* 名词
the name that you type onto your screen each time you open a particular computer program or website 用户名：*You have to log in with a username and a password.* 必须使用用户名和密码登录。

usual /ˈjuːʒuəl/ *adjective* 形容词
happening or found most often 通常的；惯常的：*It is a large city with the usual problems.* 这是个有着常见问题的大城市。 *February was warmer than usual.* 那年 2 月比往年暖和。
as usual happening in the way that it normally does 像平常一样；照例：*Dad's late, as usual.* 爸爸照例迟到了。

usually /ˈjuːʒuəli/ *adverb* 副词
in the way that most often happens 通常地；惯常地：*We usually eat in the kitchen.* 我们通常在厨房吃饭。

utensil /juːˈtensəl/ *countable noun* 可数名词
a tool or an object that you use when you are preparing or eating food（厨房）用具，器皿：*Always wash cooking utensils thoroughly.* 每次都要把炊具洗得干干净净。

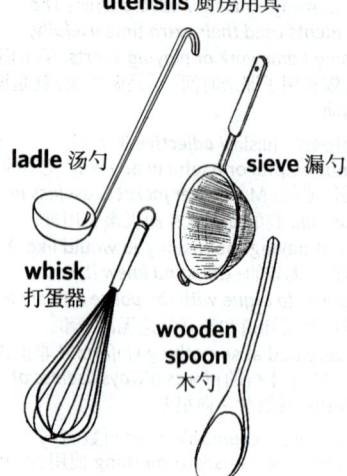

utensils 厨房用具
ladle 汤勺
sieve 漏勺
whisk 打蛋器
wooden spoon 木勺

uterus /ˈjuːtərəs/ *countable noun* 可数名词 (**uteruses**)
the part of the female body where babies grow 子宫

utter[1] /ˈʌtə/ *verb* 动词 (**utters, uttering, uttered**)
to say something or to make a sound (*formal* 正式) 说；讲；发出（声音）: *He finally uttered the words 'I'm sorry.'* 他终于说了一声"对不起"。▫ *He uttered a cry of pain.* 他痛得叫了起来。

utter[2] /ˈʌtə/ *adjective* 形容词
complete 完全的；彻底的；十足的: *This is utter nonsense.* 真是一派胡言。

utterly /ˈʌtəli/ *adverb* 副词
completely or very 完全地；彻底地；十足地: *Their behaviour was utterly stupid.* 他们的行为愚蠢至极。▫ *Patrick felt completely and utterly alone.* 帕特里克感到孤独至极。

Vv

v.
short for (缩写 =) versus

vacancy /ˈveɪkənsi/ *countable noun* 可数名词 (**vacancies**)
1 when a room in a hotel is empty 旅馆空房：*The hotel still has a few vacancies.* 这家旅馆还有几间空房。
2 a job that has not been filled 职位空缺：*We have a vacancy for an assistant.* 我们有一个助理职位空缺。

vacant /ˈveɪkənt/ *adjective* 形容词
not being used by anyone 空着的；闲置的；未占用的：*They saw two vacant seats in the centre.* 他们看到当中有两个空座。

vacation /vəˈkeɪʃən/ *countable noun* 可数名词 (*American* 美国英语)
→ see 见 **holiday**

vaccinate /ˈvæksɪneɪt/ *verb* 动词 (**vaccinates, vaccinating, vaccinated**)
to give a person or an animal a substance to prevent them from getting a disease 给⋯接种疫苗；给⋯打防疫针：*Has your child been vaccinated against measles?* 你的孩子接种麻疹疫苗了吗？
▶ **vaccination** /ˌvæksɪˈneɪʃən/ *noun* 名词：*I got my flu vaccination last week.* 我上周接种了流感疫苗。

vaccine /ˈvæksiːn/ *noun* 名词
a substance containing a very small amount of the thing that causes a particular disease. It is given to people to prevent them from getting that disease. 疫苗：*The flu vaccine is free for those aged 65 years and over.* *65 岁及以上的人可免费接种流感疫苗。

vacuum¹ /ˈvækjuːm/ *verb* 动词 (**vacuums, vacuuming, vacuumed**)
to clean a room or a surface using a vacuum cleaner 用真空吸尘器清扫：*I had to vacuum the carpet and clean the bathrooms.* 我得用吸尘器吸地毯，还得打扫浴室。

vacuum² /ˈvækjuːm/ *countable noun* 可数名词
a space that contains no air or other gas 真空：*When the machine is switched on, a vacuum is created.* 机器启动时，就产生了真空。

vacuum cleaner *countable noun* 可数名词
(also 亦作 **vacuum**)
an electric machine that cleans surfaces by sucking up dust and dirt 真空吸尘器

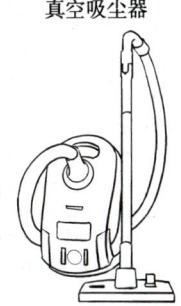
vacuum cleaner 真空吸尘器

vagina /vəˈdʒaɪnə/ *countable noun* 可数名词
the passage that leads from the outside of a woman's or girl's body to the uterus (= the place where babies grow) 阴道

vague /veɪg/ *adjective* 形容词 (**vaguer, vaguest**)
not explaining things clearly 模糊的；含糊的；不确切的：*The description was pretty vague.* 描述相当模糊。

vaguely /ˈveɪgli/ *adverb* 副词
slightly 略微；稍微：*The voice on the phone was vaguely familiar.* 电话里的声音似曾相识。

vain /veɪn/ *adjective* 形容词 (**vainer, vainest**)
1 not successful 无用的；徒劳的；枉然的：*She made a vain attempt at a smile.* 她试图微笑，但没笑出来。
2 too proud of the way you look 虚荣的；自负的：*He was so vain he spent hours in front of the mirror.* 他太虚荣了，在镜子前照了好几个小时。

in vain without success 徒劳；枉然：*She tried in vain to open the door.* 她想把门打开，但没有成功。

valentine /ˈvælənˌtaɪn/ *countable noun* 可数名词
(also 亦作 **valentine card, valentine's**

card) a card that you send to someone who you are in love with, or who you like very much, on Valentine's Day, February 14 * 圣瓦伦廷节情人卡: *I didn't receive any valentine cards this year.* 今年我没有收到任何圣瓦伦廷节卡片。

valid /ˈvælɪd/ *adjective* 形容词
used for saying that a ticket can be used and will be accepted 有效的；认可的: *All tickets are valid for two months.* 所有票的有效期均为两个月。

valley /ˈvæli/ *countable noun* 可数名词
a low area of land between hills 谷；山谷: *a steep mountain valley* 陡峭的山谷

valuable /ˈvæljuəbəl/ *adjective* 形容词
1 very useful 非常有用的: *Television can be a valuable tool in the classroom.* 教室里的电视有时是一种非常有用的工具。
2 worth a lot of money 很值钱的；贵重的: *Do not leave any valuable items in your hotel room.* 不要把贵重物品留在酒店房间里。

value¹ /ˈvæljuː/ *noun* 名词
1 *uncountable* 不可数 the importance or usefulness of something 重要性；好处: *They didn't recognize the value of language learning.* 他们没有认识到语言学习的重要性。
2 how much money you can get if you sell something (物品的)价值: *The value of the house rose by £50,000 in a year.* 这房子一年间升值了 5 万英镑。
3 *uncountable* 不可数 how much money something is worth compared with its price (价格的)划算程度: *This restaurant is extremely good value.* 这家餐厅的价格非常划算。
4 [values] *plural* 复数 the moral principles and beliefs of a person or group 是非标准；生活准则；价值观: *The countries of South Asia share many common values.* 南亚各国有许多共同的价值观念。

value² /ˈvæljuː/ *verb* 动词 (**values, valuing, valued**)
to think that something or someone is important 珍视；重视: *I value my sister's opinion.* 我重视我姐姐的意见。

valve /vælv/ *countable noun* 可数名词
an object that controls the flow of air or liquid through a tube 阀；阀门；气门

vampire /ˈvæmpaɪə/ *countable noun* 可数名词
a monster in stories that comes out at night and sucks the blood of living people 吸血鬼

van /væn/ *countable noun* 可数名词
a vehicle like a large car or a small lorry with space for carrying things in the back 厢式汽车；客货车

vandal /ˈvændəl/ *countable noun* 可数名词
someone who deliberately damages property 故意破坏财物者: *The street lights were broken by vandals.* 有人故意毁坏了路灯。

vandalism /ˈvændəˌlɪzəm/ *uncountable noun* 不可数名词
the act of deliberately damaging property 故意破坏财物的行为: *What can be done to stop school vandalism?* 我们能做些什么来制止校园破坏行为?

vandalize /ˈvændəˌlaɪz/ *verb* 动词 (**vandalizes, vandalizing, vandalized**)
to damage something on purpose 故意破坏: *The walls were vandalized with spray paint.* 墙壁被人故意喷漆搞破坏。

vanilla /vəˈnɪlə/ *uncountable noun* 不可数名词
a flavour used in some sweet foods, such as ice cream 香草香精(用于甜食调味)

vanish /ˈvænɪʃ/ *verb* 动词 (**vanishes, vanishing, vanished**)
to go away suddenly or in a way that cannot be explained 消失；不见踪影: *He vanished ten years ago and was never seen again.* 他 10 年前失踪了，再也没人见过他。

vapour /ˈveɪpə/ *uncountable noun* 不可数名词
tiny drops of water or other liquids in the air 蒸气；雾气: *Water vapour rises from earth and falls again as rain.* 水蒸气从地面升起，又以雨的形式落下。

variable /ˈveəriəbəl/ *adjective* 形容词
changing quite often 多变的: *The quality of his work is very variable.* 他的工作质量时好时坏。

variation /ˌveəriˈeɪʃən/ *noun* 名词
1 *countable* 可数 a similar thing in a slightly different form 变异的东西；变种；变体: *This is a delicious variation on an omelette.* 这是改良版煎蛋饼。
2 a change or difference in a level or amount (水平或数量的)变化，变更，变异: *Can you explain the wide variation in your prices?* 你能解释一下你们价格的巨大变化吗?

varied /ˈveərid/ *adjective* 形容词
consisting of different types of things 各种各样的；形形色色的：*Your diet should be varied.* 饮食应该多样化。

variety /vəˈraɪəti/ *uncountable noun* 不可数名词
when something consists of things that are different from each other 多种多样：*Susan wanted variety in her lifestyle.* 苏珊希望自己的生活方式多样化。

various /ˈveəriəs/ *adjective* 形容词
of several different types 不同的；各种各样的：*He spent the day doing various jobs around the house.* 他那天一整天都在家里做各种各样的工作。

varnish /ˈvɑːnɪʃ/ *uncountable noun* 不可数名词
a thick, clear liquid that is painted onto things to give them a shiny surface 清漆；罩光漆

vary /ˈveəri/ *verb* 动词 (**varies, varying, varied**)
1 to be different from each other 有差别：*The bowls are handmade, so they vary slightly.* 这些碗是手工制作的，所以它们略有不同。
2 to change something or make it different 变更；改变：*Be sure to vary the topics you write about.* 写作主题一定要有变化。
3 to become different or changed 变化：*Here in the village, the temperature never varied a great deal.* 在这个村子里，气温一直变化不大。

vase /vɑːz/ *countable noun* 可数名词
a container that is used for holding flowers 花瓶：*There was a small vase of flowers on the table.* 桌上有一小瓶花。

vast /vɑːst/ *adjective* 形容词 (**vaster, vastest**)
extremely large 庞大的；巨大的；浩大的：*Australia is a vast continent.* 澳大利亚是一片广阔的大陆。□ *Suddenly they have a vast amount of cash.* 突然间他们有了一大笔现金。

vegetable /ˈvedʒtəbəl/ *countable noun* 可数名词
a plant that you can cook and eat 蔬菜
→ Look at picture on P5 参见彩插第 5 页

vegetarian[1] /ˌvedʒɪˈteəriən/ *countable noun* 可数名词
someone who never eats meat or fish 素食者；吃素的人：*When did you decide to become a vegetarian?* 你什么时候决定开始吃素的？

vegetarian[2] /ˌvedʒɪˈteəriən/ *adjective* 形容词
not containing meat or fish 素食的：*They did not follow a strict vegetarian diet.* 他们没有遵循严格的素食饮食。□ *a vegetarian dish* 素菜

vegetation /ˌvedʒɪˈteɪʃən/ *uncountable noun* 不可数名词
plants, trees and flowers (*formal* 正式) 植被；植物；植物群落：*tropical vegetation* 热带植物

vehicle /ˈviːɪkəl/ *countable noun* 可数名词
a machine that carries people or things from one place to another 交通工具；车辆：*There are too many vehicles on the road.* 路上的车辆太多了。□ *The car hit another vehicle that was parked nearby.* 小汽车撞上了停在附近的另一辆车。

veil /veɪl/ *countable noun* 可数名词
a piece of thin soft cloth that women sometimes wear over their heads to cover their faces (女用) 面纱：*She wore a veil over her face.* 她脸上戴着面纱。

veil 面纱

vein /veɪn/ *countable noun* 可数名词
a thin tube in your body that carries blood to your heart. Compare with **artery**. 静脉 (比较 artery)
→ Look at picture on P5 参见彩插第 5 页

velvet /ˈvelvɪt/ *noun* 名词
soft cloth that is thick on one side 丝绒；天鹅绒：*red velvet curtains* 红色天鹅绒窗帘

vent /vent/ *countable noun* 可数名词
a hole that allows clean air to come in, and smoke or gas to go out 通风口；排放口：*Vents in the walls allow fresh air to enter the house.* 墙壁上的通风口使得新鲜空气进入屋中。

ventilate /ˈventɪˌleɪt/ *verb* 动词 (**ventilates, ventilating, ventilated**)
to allow fresh air to get into a room 使(房间)通风；使空气流通：*You must ventilate the room well when painting.* 油漆时房间必须通风良好。

▶ **ventilation** /ˌventɪˈleɪʃən/ *uncountable noun* 不可数名词：*The only ventilation* came from one small window. 唯一的通风口是一扇小窗。

venue /'venjuː/ *countable noun* 可数名词
the place where an event or an activity will happen 活动场地: *Fenway Park will be used as a venue for the rock concert.* 芬威公园将被用作摇滚音乐会的场地。

verb /vɜːb/ *countable noun* 可数名词
a word such as 'sing', 'feel' or 'eat' that is used for saying what someone or something does 动词

verbal /'vɜːbəl/ *adjective* 形容词
used for showing that something is expressed in speech 文字的；言语的；词语的: *We will not tolerate verbal abuse.* 我们不会容忍恶语谩骂。
▶ **verbally** /'vɜːbəli/ *adverb* 副词: *We complained both verbally and in writing.* 我们口头和书面上都进行了投诉。

verdict /'vɜːdɪkt/ *countable noun* 可数名词
the decision that is given in a court of law（法庭的）裁定，裁决: *The jury delivered a verdict of 'not guilty'.* 陪审团作出了"无罪"的裁决。

verge /vɜːdʒ/ *noun* 名词
be on the verge of something to be about to do something 濒于…；接近于…；行将…: *Carole was on the verge of tears (= she was nearly crying).* 卡萝尔几乎要哭出来了。

verify /'verɪfaɪ/ *verb* 动词 (**verifies, verifying, verified**)
to check that something is true (*formal* 正式) 核实；查对；核准: *We haven't yet verified his information.* 我们还没有核实他的信息。

versatile /'vɜːsətaɪl/ *adjective* 形容词
having many different skills or uses 有多种技能的；多才多艺的；多用途的: *He was one of our most versatile athletes.* 他是我们技术最全面的运动员之一。

verse /vɜːs/ *noun* 名词
1 *uncountable* 不可数 poetry 诗；韵文: *The story was written in verse.* 这个故事是用韵文写的。
2 *countable* 可数 one of the groups of lines in a poem or song 诗节；歌曲的段落

version /'vɜːʃən, -ʒən/ *countable noun* 可数名词
1 a particular form of something 版本；变体: *He is bringing out a new version of his book.* 他将要出版他那本书的新版。
2 someone's own description of an event（对所发生事件的）说法，描述: *Her version of the story was different from Jack's.* 她对这个故事的描述与杰克不同。

versus /'vɜːsəs/ *preposition* 介词
used for showing that two teams or people are on different sides in a sports event. The short forms **vs.** and **v.** are also used.（表示体育运动中双方对阵）对（缩写形式为 vs. 或 v.）: *It will be Scotland versus Belgium in tomorrow's game.* 明天的比赛将是苏格兰对比利时。

vertebrate /'vɜːtɪˌbrət/ *countable noun* 可数名词
an animal that has a spine (= bones in its back). Compare with **invertebrate**. 脊椎动物（比较 invertebrate）

vertical /'vɜːtɪkəl/ *adjective* 形容词
standing or pointing straight up 竖的；垂直的；直立的: *The climber moved up a vertical wall of rock.* 攀登者沿垂直的岩壁向上爬。

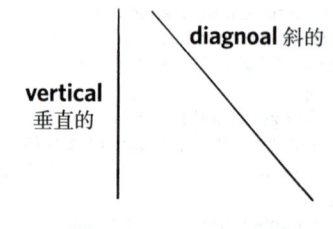

very /'veri/ *adverb* 副词
used before an adjective or an adverb to make it stronger 很；非常；十分: *The answer is very simple.* 答案很简单。 □ *I'm very sorry.* 我很抱歉。

vest /vest/ *countable noun* 可数名词
1 a piece of clothing that you wear under your shirt or T-shirt in order to keep warm（贴身穿的）背心，汗衫
2 (*American* 美国英语)→ see 见 **waistcoat**

vet /vet/ *countable noun* 可数名词
(*American* 美国英语: **veterinarian**)
a person whose job is to treat ill or injured animals (*informal* 非正式) 兽医
→ Look at picture on P16 参见彩插第 16 页

veterinarian /ˌvetərɪˈneəriən, ˌvetrɪ-/ *countable noun* 可数名词 (*American* 美国英语)
→ see 见 **vet**

veto¹ /ˈviːtəʊ/ *verb* 动词 (**vetoes, vetoing, vetoed**)
to stop something from happening 否决；否定：*The president vetoed the proposal.* 总统否决了这项提议。

veto² /ˈviːtəʊ/ *uncountable noun* 不可数名词
the power that someone has to stop something from happening 否决权：*The president has power of veto over the matter.* 总统对此事拥有否决权。

via /ˈvaɪə, ˈviːə/ *preposition* 介词
through one place on the way to another 经，经由（某地方）：*I'm flying to New York via Sweden.* 我要经瑞典飞往纽约。

vibrate /vaɪˈbreɪt/ *verb* 动词 (**vibrates, vibrating, vibrated**)
to shake with repeated small, quick movements 震动；颤动：*There was a loud bang and the ground seemed to vibrate.* 一声巨响，地面似乎在震动。
▶ **vibration** /vaɪˈbreɪʃən/ *noun* 名词：*Vibrations from the train made the house shake.* 火车造成的震动使房子晃动起来。

vice /vaɪs/ *noun* 名词
1 uncountable 不可数 criminal activity connected with sex and drugs（与性或毒品有关的）犯罪活动，罪行
2 countable 可数 a bad habit or weakness 恶行；恶习；不道德行为：*My only vice is spending too much on clothes.* 我唯一不好的习惯就是花太多钱买衣服。

vice versa /ˌvaɪsə ˈvɜːsə/ *adverb* 副词
showing the opposite of what you have said 反过来也一样；反之亦然：*The government exists to serve us, and not vice versa.* 政府的存在是为了服务我们，而不是反过来。

vicious /ˈvɪʃəs/ *adjective* 形容词
1 violent and cruel 狂暴的；残酷的：*He was a cruel and vicious man.* 他是一个残忍狠毒的人。
2 cruel and intended to upset someone 恶毒的：*That wasn't true; it was just a vicious rumour.* 这不是真的，只是一个恶毒的谣言。

victim /ˈvɪktɪm/ *countable noun* 可数名词
someone who has been hurt or killed 受害者；罹难者：*The driver apologized to the victim's family.* 司机向受害者家属道歉。

victorious /vɪkˈtɔːriəs/ *adjective* 形容词
describing someone who has won in a war or a competition 胜利的；获胜的：*The French team was victorious in all four games.* 法国队在 4 场比赛中全部获胜。

victory /ˈvɪktəri/ *noun* 名词 (**victories**)
a success in a war or a competition 胜利：*The team are celebrating their victory.* 这支队伍正在庆祝他们的胜利。

video /ˈvɪdiəʊ/ *noun* 名词
1 countable 可数 an event that has been recorded, that you can watch on a television using a special machine 录像：*We watched a video of my first birthday party.* 我们看了我第一次生日聚会的录像。
2 countable 可数 a film that you can watch at home 录像带：*You can rent a video for £3 and watch it at home.* 你可以花 3 英镑租个录像带在家里看。
3 uncountable 不可数 the system of recording films and events in this way 录像系统：*She has watched the show on video.* 她看了那个节目的录像。
4 countable 可数 (also 亦作 **video recorder**) a machine for playing videos 录像机

ˈvideo ˌgame *countable noun* 可数名词
an electronic game that you play on your television or on a computer screen 电子游戏

view /vjuː/ *countable noun* 可数名词
1 an opinion that you have about something 观点；看法；见解：*We have similar views on politics.* 我们有相似的政治见解。
2 everything that you can see from a place 景观；视野：*From our hotel room we had a great view of the sea.* 从我们的酒店房间能看到大海的美景。 ▫ *He stood up to get a better view of the blackboard.* 他站起来以便看黑板看得更清楚些。
on view in a public place for people to look at 在展出：*Her paintings are on view at the Portland Gallery.* 她的画作正在波特兰美术馆展出。

viewer /ˈvjuːə/ *countable noun* 可数名词
a person who is watching a particular programme on television 电视观众：*Twelve million viewers watch the show every week.* 每周有 1,200 万观众观看这个节目。

vigorous /ˈvɪgərəs/ *adjective* 形容词
using a lot of energy 剧烈的；强度大的：*You should have an hour of vigorous exercise three times a week.* 你应该每周剧

烈运动 3 次，每次 1 小时。
▶ **vigorously** /ˈvɪɡərəsli/ *adverb* 副词：*He shook his head vigorously.* 他使劲摇了摇头。

village /ˈvɪlɪdʒ/ *countable noun* 可数名词
a very small town in the countryside 村；乡村；村庄

villain /ˈvɪlən/ *countable noun* 可数名词
someone who deliberately harms other people or breaks the law 坏人；坏蛋：*They called him a villain and a murderer.* 他们称他为恶棍、杀人犯。

vine /vaɪn/ *noun* 名词
a plant that grows up or over things 藤本植物；攀缘植物：*a grape vine* 葡萄藤

vinegar /ˈvɪnɪɡə/ *noun* 名词
a sour, sharp-tasting liquid that is used in cooking 醋

vinyl /ˈvaɪnɪl/ *uncountable noun* 不可数名词
a strong plastic that is used for making things like floor coverings and furniture 乙烯基；乙烯基塑料：*vinyl floor covering* 乙烯基地板

viola /viˈəʊlə/ *noun* 名词
a musical instrument with four strings that produces low notes. You hold it under your chin, and play it by moving a long stick (= a bow) across the strings. A viola is larger than a violin. 中提琴：*She plays the viola in several different orchestras.* 她在几个不同的管弦乐队中演奏中提琴。
→ Look at picture on P12 参见彩插第 12 页

violate /ˈvaɪəˌleɪt/ *verb* 动词 (**violates, violating, violated**)
to break an agreement or a law (*formal* 正式) 违反，违犯，违背（协议或法律）：*The company has violated international law.* 这家公司违反了国际法。
▶ **violation** /ˌvaɪəˈleɪʃən/ *noun* 名词：*This is a violation of the law.* 这违反了法律。

violence /ˈvaɪələns/ *uncountable noun* 不可数名词
behaviour that is intended to hurt or kill people 暴力；暴行：*Twenty people died in the violence.* 20 人死于这起暴力事件。

violent /ˈvaɪələnt/ *adjective* 形容词
using physical force to hurt or kill other people 暴力的；狂暴的：*These men have committed violent crimes.* 这些人犯下了暴力罪行。
▶ **violently** /ˈvaɪələntli/ *adverb* 副词：*The woman was violently attacked while out walking.* 这名女性在外出散步时遭到暴力袭击。

violet¹ /ˈvaɪəlɪt/ *noun* 名词
1 *countable* 可数 a small plant that has purple or white flowers in the spring 堇菜；紫罗兰
2 a blue-purple colour 蓝紫色；紫罗兰色：*The sky turned purple and violet as the sun set.* 太阳下山时，天空中紫色和蓝紫色交错。

violet² /ˈvaɪəlɪt/ *adjective* 形容词
of a blue-purple colour 蓝紫色的；紫罗兰色的：*a violet dress* 蓝紫色的连衣裙

violin /ˌvaɪəˈlɪn/ *noun* 名词
a musical instrument made of wood with four strings. You hold it under your chin, and play it by moving a long stick (= a bow) across the strings. 小提琴：*Lizzie plays the violin.* 莉齐拉小提琴。
→ Look at picture on P12 参见彩插第 12 页

VIP /ˌviː aɪ ˈpiː/ *countable noun* 可数名词 (**VIPs**)
someone who receives better treatment than ordinary people because they are famous or important. VIP is short for (缩写 =) 'very important person'. 要人；贵宾

virtual /ˈvɜːtʃuəl/ *adjective* 形容词
1 used for showing that something is nearly true 几乎…的；事实上的；实际上的：*He was a virtual prisoner in his own home.* 他实际上就是个被囚禁在家的囚徒。
▶ **virtually** /ˈvɜːtʃuəli/ *adverb* 副词：*She does virtually all the cooking.* 几乎所有的饭都是她做的。
2 made by a computer to seem like real objects and activities（计算机）虚拟的：*The virtual world sometimes seems more attractive than the real one.* 虚拟世界有时似乎比真实世界更有吸引力。

ˌvirtual reˈality *uncountable noun* 不可数名词
a situation that is produced by a computer to seem almost real to the person who is using it（计算机）虚拟现实：*a virtual reality game* 一款虚拟现实游戏

virtue /ˈvɜːtʃuː/ *noun* 名词
1 *uncountable* 不可数 good thoughts and behaviour 高尚的道德；美德；善行：*The headmaster talked to us about virtue.* 校长给我们讲美德。
2 *countable* 可数 a good quality or way of acting 美德；优秀品质；良好习惯：*His greatest virtue is patience.* 他最大的美德是

耐心。

virus /ˈvaɪərəs/ *countable noun* 可数名词 (viruses)
1 a very small living thing that can enter your body and make you ill 病毒: *There are thousands of different types of virus, and they change all the time.* 病毒有成千上万种，它们一直都在变化。
2 a program that enters a computer system and changes or destroys the information that is there 计算机病毒: *You should protect your computer against viruses.* 你应该保护你的电脑不受病毒侵害。

visa /ˈviːzə/ *countable noun* 可数名词 an official document or a stamp in your passport that allows you to enter a particular country 签证

visibility /ˌvɪzɪˈbɪlɪti/ *uncountable noun* 不可数名词 how far or how clearly you can see in particular weather conditions 可见度；能见度；能见距离: *Visibility was poor.* 能见度很差。

visible /ˈvɪzɪbəl/ *adjective* 形容词 able to be seen 看得见的；可见的: *The warning lights were clearly visible.* 警示灯清晰可见。

vision /ˈvɪʒən/ *noun* 名词
1 *countable* 可数 what you imagine or hope a future situation or society will be like 幻想；想象: *I have a vision of world peace.* 我有一个世界和平的愿景。
2 *uncountable* 不可数 your ability to see clearly with your eyes 视力；视觉: *He's suffering from loss of vision.* 他正遭受视力丧失之苦。

visit /ˈvɪzɪt/ *verb* 动词 (visits, visiting, visited)
1 to go to see someone in order to spend time with them 访问；拜访；看望: *He wanted to visit his brother.* 他想去看望哥哥。 □ *In the evenings, friends often visit.* 晚上，朋友们经常来拜访。 ● **visit** *countable noun* 可数名词: *I recently had a visit from an English relative.* 最近有一位英国亲戚来看我。
2 to go to a place for a short time 参观；游览: *He'll be visiting four cities on his trip.* 他这次旅行要去 4 个城市。

visitor /ˈvɪzɪtə/ *countable noun* 可数名词 someone who is visiting a person or place 访问者；来访者；参观者；游客: *We had some visitors from Australia.* 我们有一些来自澳大利亚的访客。

visual /ˈvɪʒuəl/ *adjective* 形容词 relating to sight, or to things that you can see 视觉的: *The film's visual effects are amazing.* 这部电影的视觉效果令人惊叹。

vital /ˈvaɪtəl/ *adjective* 形容词 very important 极其重要的；必不可少的: *It is vital that children attend school regularly.* 孩子上学一定要规律。

vitamin /ˈvɪtəmɪn/ *countable noun* 可数名词 a substance in food that you need in order to stay healthy 维生素: *These problems are caused by lack of vitamin D.* 这些问题是由缺乏维生素 D 引起的。

vivid /ˈvɪvɪd/ *adjective* 形容词
1 very clear and detailed 生动的；清晰的: *I had a very vivid dream last night.* 昨天晚上我做了一个非常逼真的梦。 ▶ **vividly** /ˈvɪvɪdli/ *adverb* 副词: *I can vividly remember the first time I saw him.* 我清楚地记得我第一次见到他的情景。
2 very bright in colour（颜色）鲜明的，鲜艳的: *She was dressed in a vivid pink jacket.* 她穿着一件鲜艳的粉红色夹克衫。

vlog /vlɒg/ *countable noun* 可数名词 a set of videos that someone regularly posts on the Internet in which they record their thoughts or experiences or talk about a subject 视频博客: *He has his own lifestyle vlog.* 他有记录自己生活方式的视频博客。 ▶ **vlogger** /ˈvlɒgə/ *countable noun* 可数名词: *She is a successful YouTube beauty vlogger.* 她是 YouTube 视频网站上一位成功的美妆博主。

vocabulary /vəʊˈkæbjʊləri/ *noun* 名词 (vocabularies)
1 all the words a person knows in a particular language（个人掌握的）词汇，词汇量: *He has a very large vocabulary.* 他的词汇量很大。
2 *singular* 单数 all the words in a language（某一语言的）词汇: *Which language has the biggest vocabulary?* 哪种语言词汇量最大？

vocal /ˈvəʊkəl/ *adjective* 形容词
1 giving your opinion very strongly 大声表达的；直言不讳的: *Local people were very vocal about the problem.* 当地人对这个问题直言不讳。
2 using the human voice, especially in

singing 嗓音的；发声的：*She has an interesting vocal style.* 她的发声方式很有趣。

voice /vɔɪs/ *countable noun* 可数名词
the sound that comes from someone's mouth when they speak or sing 说话声；嗓音：*She spoke in a soft voice.* 她用柔和的声音说话。□ *Lucinda sings in the choir and has a beautiful voice.* 露辛达在合唱团唱歌，声音很好听。

voicemail /ˈvɔɪsmeɪl/ *uncountable noun* 不可数名词
an electronic system that records spoken messages 语音信箱；电话留言：*a voicemail message* 一条语音信息

volcano /vɒlˈkeɪnəʊ/ *countable noun* 可数名词 (**volcanoes**)
a mountain that throws out hot liquid rock and fire 火山：*The volcano erupted last year.* 这座火山去年爆发了。

volcano 火山

volleyball /ˈvɒlibɔːl/ *uncountable noun* 不可数名词
a game in which two teams hit a large ball over a high net with their arms or hands 排球运动

volt /vəʊlt/ *countable noun* 可数名词
a unit used for measuring electricity 伏，伏特（电压单位）

volume /ˈvɒljuːm/ *noun* 名词
1 *countable* 可数 the amount of space that an object contains 体积；容积；容量：*What is the volume of a cube with sides 3 cm long?* 一个边长 3 厘米的立方体的体积是多少？
→ Look at picture on P2 参见彩插第 2 页
2 *countable* 可数 one book in a series of books（一套书的）卷，册：*We read the first volume of his autobiography.* 我们读了他自传的第 1 卷。
3 *uncountable* 不可数 how loud or quiet a sound is 音量：*He turned down the volume.* 他把音量关小了。

voluntary /ˈvɒləntri/ *adjective* 形容词
1 done because someone wants to, and not because they must 自愿的；主动的：*Participation is completely voluntary.* 是否参与完全自愿。
▶ **voluntarily** /ˈvɒləntərəli/ *adverb* 副词：*I would never leave here voluntarily.* 我永远不会主动离开这里。
2 used for describing work that is done by people who are not paid, but who do it because they want to 义务的；无偿的：*I do voluntary work with children who have disabilities.* 我为残疾儿童做义工。

volunteer¹ /ˌvɒlənˈtɪə/ *countable noun* 可数名词
someone who does work without being paid, because they want to do it 志愿者；义务工作者：*She helps in a local school as a volunteer.* 她在当地的一所学校做志愿者。

volunteer² /ˌvɒlənˈtɪə/ *verb* 动词 (**volunteers, volunteering, volunteered**)
to offer to do something that you do not have to do, or that you will not be paid for 自愿，志愿，主动（做某事）：*Mary volunteered to clean up the kitchen.* 玛丽自愿打扫厨房。

vomit¹ /ˈvɒmɪt/ *verb* 动词 (**vomits, vomiting, vomited**)
if you vomit, food and drink comes up from your stomach and out through your mouth 呕吐：*Milk made him vomit.* 他喝牛奶会吐。

vomit² /ˈvɒmɪt/ *uncountable noun* 不可数名词
food and drink that comes up from your stomach and out of your mouth when you vomit 呕吐物

vote¹ /vəʊt/ *countable noun* 可数名词
a choice made by a particular person or group in a meeting or an election 投票；表决：*Mr Reynolds won the election by 102 votes to 60.* 雷诺兹先生以 102 票对 60 票赢得了选举。

vote² /vəʊt/ *verb* 动词 (**votes, voting, voted**)
to show your choice officially at a meeting or in an election 投票；表决：*The workers voted to strike.* 工人们投票赞成罢工。
▶ **voter** /ˈvəʊtə/ *countable noun* 可数名词：*The region has 2.1 million registered voters.* 该地区有 210 万注册选民。

vow /vaʊ/ *verb* 动词 (**vows, vowing, vowed**) to make a serious promise or decision that you will do something 起誓；立誓；发誓：*She vowed to continue the fight.* 她发誓要继续战斗。□ *I vowed that someday I would go back to Europe.* 我发誓有一天我会回到欧洲。● **vow** *countable noun* 可数名词：*I made a vow to be more careful in the future.* 我发誓以后要更加小心。

vowel /ˈvaʊəl/ *countable noun* 可数名词
1 a sound such as the ones written as **a, e, i, o** and **u**, and sometimes **y** 元音；母音
2 one of the letters **a, e, i, o** and **u** 元音字母

voyage /ˈvɔɪɪdʒ/ *countable noun* 可数名词 a long trip on a ship or in a spacecraft 航行；航海；航天：*They began the long voyage down the river.* 他们开始了沿河而下的长途航行。

vs.
short for (缩写 =) **versus**

vulnerable /ˈvʌlnərəbəl/ *adjective* 形容词 weak and without protection 脆弱的；易受伤害的：*Older people are particularly vulnerable to colds and flu in cold weather.* 在寒冷的天气里，老年人特别容易患感冒和流感。

Ww

wade /weɪd/ *verb* 动词 (**wades, wading, waded**)
to walk through water with difficulty 涉水；蹚水：*I waded across the river to reach them.* 我蹚水过河与他们会合。

wade 蹚水

waffle /ˈwɒfl/ *countable noun* 可数名词
a flat, sweet cake with a pattern of squares on it 华夫饼

wag /wæɡ/ *verb* 动词 (**wags, wagging, wagged**)
when a dog wags its tail, it moves it from side to side（狗）摇，摆动（尾巴）

wage /weɪdʒ/ *countable noun* 可数名词
the amount of money that is paid to someone for the work that they do 工资：*His wages have gone up.* 他的工资涨了。

> **LANGUAGE HELP** 语言提示
> See note at **salary**. 见 salary 的语言提示。

wagon /ˈwæɡən/ *countable noun* 可数名词
a strong vehicle with four wheels, usually pulled by animals 四轮载重马车

waist /weɪst/ *countable noun* 可数名词
1 the middle part of your body 腰；腰部：*Ricky put his arm around her waist.* 里基揽住她的腰。
→ Look at picture on P4 参见彩插第 4 页
2 the part of a pair of trousers that goes around the middle part of your body（裤子的）腰部，腰：*The waist of these trousers is a little tight.* 这条裤子的腰有点儿紧。

waistcoat /ˈweɪstkəʊt/ *countable noun* 可数名词（**American** 美国英语：**vest**）
a piece of clothing without sleeves that people usually wear over a shirt 西服背心

wait /weɪt/ *verb* 动词 (**waits, waiting, waited**)
1 to spend time doing very little, before something happens 等候；等待：*I walked to the street corner and waited for the school bus.* 我走到街道拐角处等校车。 □ *I waited to hear what she said.* 我等着听她说什么。 □ *We had to wait a week before we got the results.* 我们不得不等了一个星期才得到结果。● **wait** *countable noun* 可数名词：*There was a four-hour wait at the airport.* 在机场等了 4 个小时。
2 to be ready for someone to use, have or do 准备妥当；在手边；可使用：*There'll be a car waiting for you.* 会有辆车等着你。
can't wait or **can hardly wait** to be very excited about something 迫不及待：*We can't wait to get started.* 我们等不及要开始了。
something can wait used to say that something is not very important, so you will do it later 某事能推迟：*I want to talk to you, but it can wait.* 我想和你谈谈，但不着急。

waiter /ˈweɪtə/ *countable noun* 可数名词
a man whose job is to serve food in a restaurant（餐馆）服务员
→ Look at picture on P16 参见彩插第 16 页

waiting room *countable noun* 可数名词
a room where people can sit down while they wait 等候室：*She sat for half an hour in the dentist's waiting room.* 她在牙医的候诊室里坐了半个小时。

waitress /ˈweɪtrəs/ *countable noun* 可数名词 (**waitresses**)
a woman whose job is to serve food in a restaurant（餐馆）女服务员
→ Look at picture on P16 参见彩插第 16 页

wake /weɪk/ *verb* 动词 (**wakes, waking, woke, woken**)
1 (also 亦作 **wake up**) to stop sleeping 睡

醒；醒来：*It was cold and dark when I woke at 6.30.* 当我 6 点半醒来时，天又冷又黑。□ *We woke up early to a perfect summer morning.* 我们在一个美好的夏日早晨早早醒来。

2 (also 亦作 **wake someone up**) to make someone stop sleeping 唤醒；弄醒：*Betty woke me when she left.* 贝蒂离开时叫醒了我。□ *She went upstairs to wake Jack up.* 她上楼去叫醒杰克。

walk¹ /wɔːk/ *verb* 动词 (**walks, walking, walked**)

to move forwards by putting one foot in front of the other 走路；行走；步行：*She walked two miles to school every day.* 她每天步行两英里去上学。□ *We walked into the hall.* 我们走进大厅。□ *I walked a few steps toward the fence.* 我朝篱笆走了几步。

walk out to leave a situation suddenly, to show that you are angry or bored（因气愤或无聊而）突然离开，退场：*Several people walked out of the meeting in protest.* 有几个人在会议中离场以示抗议。

walk² /wɔːk/ *countable noun* 可数名词

a trip that you make by walking, usually for pleasure 步行；散步：*I went for a walk after lunch.* 午饭后我去散步。

wall /wɔːl/ *countable noun* 可数名词

1 one of the sides of a building or a room（建筑物或房间的）墙：*His bedroom walls are covered with pictures of cars.* 他卧室的墙上挂满了汽车的照片。

2 a long narrow structure made of stone or brick that divides an area of land 城墙；围墙；隔墙：*He sat on the wall in the sun.* 他坐在围墙上晒太阳。

wallet /ˈwɒlɪt/ *countable noun* 可数名词

a small case in which you can keep money and cards 钱包

wallpaper /ˈwɔːlpeɪpə/ *uncountable noun* 不可数名词

coloured or patterned paper that is used for decorating the walls of rooms 壁纸；墙纸● **wallpaper** *verb* 动词 (**wallpapers, wallpapering, wallpapered**)：*Every wall was wallpapered with a different colour.* 每面墙都贴上了不同颜色的墙纸。

walnut /ˈwɔːlnʌt/ *noun* 名词

a nut that is hard and round, with a rough texture 核桃；胡桃

walnut 核桃

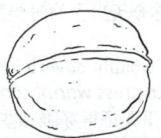

wander /ˈwɒndə/ *verb* 动词 (**wanders, wandering, wandered**)

to walk around, often without intending to go in any particular direction 漫游；闲逛；游荡：*When he got bored he wandered around the park.* 他感到无聊时就在公园里闲逛。

want /wɒnt/ *verb* 动词 (**wants, wanting, wanted**)

to feel a need for something 想要；要：*I want a drink.* 我想喝一杯饮料。□ *People wanted to know who she was.* 人们想知道她是谁。

war /wɔː/ *noun* 名词

a period of fighting between countries or groups 战争；战时：*He spent part of the war in France.* 战争期间他在法国待过一段时间。

ward /wɔːd/ *countable noun* 可数名词

a room in a hospital that has beds for many people 病房：*They took her to the children's ward.* 他们把她送到儿童病房。

wardrobe /ˈwɔːdrəʊb/ *countable noun* 可数名词 (**American** 美国英语: **closet**)

a cupboard where you hang your clothes 衣柜；衣橱

warehouse /ˈweəhaʊs/ *countable noun* 可数名词

a large building where goods are stored before they are sold 仓库；货仓

warfare /ˈwɔːfeə/ *uncountable noun* 不可数名词

the activity of fighting a war 战事；作战：*His men were trained in desert warfare.* 他的部下受过沙漠作战的训练。

warm¹ /wɔːm/ *adjective* 形容词 (**warmer, warmest**)

1 having some heat, but not hot 温暖的；暖和的：*On warm summer days, she would sit outside.* 在温和的夏日，她会在外面坐坐。□ *Because it was warm, David wore only a white cotton shirt.* 因为天气暖和，戴维只穿了一件白色的棉衬衫。

2 made of a material that protects you from the cold（衣服）暖和的，保温的：*You*

need to wear warm clothes when you go out today. 你今天出去的时候需要穿暖和的衣服。
▶ **warmly** /ˈwɔːmli/ *adverb* 副词: *Remember to dress warmly on cold days.* 在寒冷的日子里要记得穿暖和些。
3 friendly 友好的；热情的: *She was a warm and loving mother.* 她是一位热情而慈爱的母亲。
▶ **warmly** /ˈwɔːmli/ *adverb* 副词: *We warmly welcome new members.* 我们热烈欢迎新成员。

warm² /wɔːm/ *verb* 动词 (**warms, warming, warmed**)
warm something up to make something less cold 使某物变暖；使某物暖和: *He blew on his hands to warm them up.* 他向双手哈气使它们暖和起来。

warmth /wɔːmθ/ *uncountable noun* 不可数名词
1 the heat that something produces 温暖；暖和: *Feel the warmth of the sun on your skin.* 感受阳光照在皮肤上带来的温暖。
2 friendly behaviour towards other people 热情；友善: *They treated us with warmth and kindness.* 他们对我们热情友好。

warm-up *countable noun* 可数名词
a period of gentle exercise that you do to prepare yourself for a particular sport or activity (体育运动等的)准备活动，适应性活动: *Training consists of a 20-minute warm-up, followed by ball practice.* 训练包括 20 分钟的热身，然后是球类练习。

warn /wɔːn/ *verb* 动词 (**warns, warning, warned**)
to tell someone about something such as a possible danger 提醒…注意；警告: *They warned him of the dangers of sailing alone.* 他们提醒他独自航行的危险。

warning /ˈwɔːnɪŋ/ *noun* 名词
something that tells people of a possible danger 警告；警示: *It was a warning that we should be careful.* 这是一个警告，提醒我们要小心。 □ *Suddenly and without warning, a car crash changed her life.* 一场突如其来、毫无预兆的车祸改变了她的生活。

warrant /ˈwɒrənt/ *countable noun* 可数名词
a legal document that allows someone to do something 执行令；授权令: *Police have a warrant for his arrest.* 警方有对他的逮捕令。

warranty /ˈwɒrənti/ *countable noun* 可数名词 (**warranties**)
a promise by a company that if you buy something that does not work, they will repair it or replace it (商品)保用单: *The TV comes with a twelve-month warranty.* 这台电视机有 12 个月的保修期。

wary /ˈweəri/ *adjective* 形容词 (**warier, wariest**)
careful because you do not know much about something or someone, and you think they may be dangerous 小心的；谨慎的；留神的: *People teach their children to be wary of strangers.* 人们教育自己的孩子要提防陌生人。

was /wəz, STRONG 强读 wɒz/
→ see 见 **be**

wash¹ /wɒʃ/ *verb* 动词 (**washes, washing, washed**)
1 to clean something using water and soap 洗；洗涤: *She finished her dinner and washed the dishes.* 她吃完晚饭洗了碗。 □ *It took a long time to wash the dirt out of his hair.* 洗掉他头发上的脏东西花了很长时间。
2 to clean your body using soap and water 洗澡；洗(身体部位): *I haven't washed for days.* 我好几天没洗澡了。 □ *She washed her face with cold water.* 她用冷水洗脸。
wash up to wash dishes 洗餐具；洗碗: *You cooked, so I'll wash up.* 你做饭了，我来洗碗。

wash² /wɒʃ/ *uncountable noun* 不可数名词
in the wash being washed (*informal* 非正式) (衣物)在洗涤中: *Your jeans are in the wash.* 你的牛仔裤正在洗。

washbasin /ˈwɒʃbeɪsən/ *countable noun* 可数名词
a large bowl in a bathroom for washing your hands and face 洗手池；洗脸盆

washing /ˈwɒʃɪŋ/ *uncountable noun* 不可数名词
clothes and other things that you need to wash, or that you have just washed 待洗 (或洗好)的衣物: *a bag full of dirty washing* 装满待洗衣服的袋子

ˈwashing maˌchine *countable noun* 可数名词
a machine that you use to wash clothes in 洗衣机: *Dan put his shirts in the washing machine.* 丹把他的衬衫放进了洗衣机。

ˈwashing-up *uncountable noun* 不可数名词
the activity of washing the plates, cups and other things that you have used for cooking and eating a meal 洗餐具；洗碗；

washing-'up ,liquid uncountable noun 不可数名词
a thick liquid that you put into hot water to wash dirty dishes (餐具的)洗涤剂

wasn't /'wɒzənt/
short for (缩写 =) 'was not'

wasp /wɒsp/ countable noun 可数名词
an insect with wings and yellow and black stripes across its body. Wasps can sting people. 黄蜂；胡蜂

waste¹ /weɪst/ verb 动词 (**wastes, wasting, wasted**)
to use too much of something such as time, money or energy doing something that is not important 浪费；滥用: *She didn't want to waste time looking at old cars.* 她不想浪费时间看旧汽车。◻ *I decided not to waste money on a hotel room.* 我决定不把钱浪费在旅馆房间上。
● **waste** singular noun 单数名词: *It is a waste of time complaining about it.* 抱怨那件事是浪费时间。

waste² /weɪst/ uncountable noun 不可数名词
material that is no longer wanted because the valuable or useful part of it has been taken out 废料；废物；弃物: *Waste materials such as paper and aluminium cans can be recycled.* 像纸和铝罐这样的废料可以被回收利用。

'waste,paper ,basket countable noun 可数名词
a container where you put things like paper that you do not need any more 废纸篓；废纸筐

watch¹ /wɒtʃ/ verb 动词 (**watches, watching, watched**)
1 to look at someone or something for a period of time 注视；观看: *A man stood in the doorway, watching me.* 一个男人站在门口，注视着我。◻ *I stayed up late to watch the film.* 我熬夜看了那部电影。

LANGUAGE HELP 语言提示
See note at **look**. 见 **look** 的语言提示。

2 to take care of someone or something for a period of time 照看；照管: *Could you watch my bags? I need to go to the bathroom.* 你能帮我看一下包吗？我要去洗手间。
keep watch to keep looking and listening so that you can warn other people of danger 放哨；看守: *Josh climbed a tree to keep watch.* 乔希爬上一棵树放哨。
watch for someone/something or **watch out for someone/something** to pay attention so that you will notice something if it happens 当心某人 / 某事；密切注意某人 / 某事: *You should watch carefully for signs of the illness.* 你应该密切注意发病迹象。◻ *Police warned shoppers to watch out for thieves.* 警方警告购物者当心小偷。
watch out used for warning someone to be careful 当心；小心: *You must watch out because this is a dangerous city.* 你必须小心，因为这是一个危险的城市。

watch² /wɒtʃ/ countable noun 可数名词 (**watches**)
a small clock that you wear on your wrist 手表: *Dan gave me a watch for my birthday.* 丹送给我一块手表作为生日礼物。

water¹ /'wɔːtə/ uncountable noun 不可数名词
a clear, thin liquid that has no colour or taste. It falls from clouds as rain. 水: *Could I have a glass of water, please?* 请给我一杯水好吗？

water² /'wɔːtə/ verb 动词 (**waters, watering, watered**)
1 to pour water over plants in order to help them to grow 给…浇水；灌溉: *Make sure you water the plants before you go on holiday.* 你去度假前一定要给植物浇水。
2 when your eyes water, tears appear in them (眼睛)含泪: *His eyes were watering in the smoke.* 他的眼睛被烟熏得直流泪。

watercolour /'wɔːtəˌkʌlə/ noun 名词
1 a coloured paint that is mixed with water and used for painting pictures 水彩(颜料): *Campbell painted with watercolours.* 坎贝尔用水彩作画。
2 countable 可数 a picture that has been painted with watercolours 水彩画: *a watercolour by Andrew Wyeth* 一幅安德鲁·怀斯的水彩画

waterfall /'wɔːtəˌfɔːl/ countable noun 可数名词
a place where water flows over the edge of a steep part of hills or mountains, and falls into a pool below 瀑布
→ Look at picture on P7 参见彩插第 7 页

watermelon /'wɔːtəˌmelən/ noun 名词
a large, heavy fruit with green skin, pink

flesh and black seeds 西瓜

waterproof /'wɔːtəˌpruːf/ *adjective* 形容词
not letting water pass through 不透水的；防水的：*You'll need to take waterproof clothing when you go camping.* 你去野营时需要带防水的衣服。

watt /wɒt/ *countable noun* 可数名词
a unit of power 瓦，瓦特（功率单位）：*The lamp takes a 60-watt lightbulb.* 这盏灯要装 60 瓦的灯泡。

wave¹ /weɪv/ *verb* 动词 (**waves, waving, waved**)
1 to hold your hand up and move it from side to side, usually in order to say hello or goodbye to someone 挥手；招手；摆手：*Jessica saw Lois and waved to her.* 杰茜卡看见洛伊丝，向她招了招手。 □ *She waved her hand in the air.* 她举起手挥了挥。

wave 招手

2 to hold something up and move it from side to side 挥动；挥舞：*More than 4,000 people waved flags and sang songs.* 4,000 多人挥舞着旗帜，唱着歌。

wave² /weɪv/ *countable noun* 可数名词
1 a higher part of water on the surface of the sea. Waves are caused by the wind blowing on the surface of the water. 海浪；波浪：*I fell asleep to the sound of waves hitting the rocks.* 我在海浪拍击岩石的声音中睡着了。
2 when you hold your hand up and move it from side to side 挥手；招手；摆手：*Steve stopped him with a wave of his hand.* 史蒂夫挥手叫他停下来。
3 the form in which things such as sound, light and radio signals travel（声音、光、无线电信号等的）波：*sound waves* 声波 □ *radio waves* 无线电波

wavelength /'weɪvleŋθ/ *countable noun* 可数名词 the size of a radio wave that a particular radio station uses to broadcast its programmes（广播电台的）波长：*She found the station's wavelength on her radio.* 她在收音机上找到了该电台的波长。
on the same wavelength finding it easy to understand someone because you share similar interests or opinions 具有相同思路的；合拍的：*We often finished each other's sentences — we were on the same wavelength.* 我们经常接着把对方的话说完——我们志趣相投。

wavy /'weɪvi/ *adjective* 形容词 (**wavier, waviest**)
not straight or curly, but curving slightly 波浪似的；拳曲的：*She had short, wavy, brown hair.* 她有一头卷曲的棕色短发。

wax /wæks/ *uncountable noun* 不可数名词
a solid, slightly shiny substance that is used for making candles (= sticks that you burn for light) and polish for furniture 蜡：*The candle wax melted in the heat.* 蜡烛的蜡在高温下熔化了。

way /weɪ/ *noun* 名词
1 *countable* 可数 the action that you take to do something 方法；方式；手段；途径：*One way of making friends is to go to an evening class.* 交朋友的一种途径是去上夜校。 □ *She smiled in a friendly way.* 她友善地笑了笑。
2 *countable* 可数 the route that you take in order to get to a place 路线；路径；通路：*Do you know the way to the post office?* 你知道去邮局的路吗？
3 *singular* 单数 a direction 方向：*Which way do we go now — left or right?* 我们现在走哪条路？向左还是向右？
a long way a long distance 很长的距离：*It's a long way from New York to Nashville.* 从纽约到纳什维尔距离很远。
by the way used when you are going to talk about something different（用于转换话题）顺便提一下，附带说一句：*By the way, how is your back?* 顺便问一下，你后背怎么样了？
get your way or **have your way** to do what you want to do without anyone stopping you 一意孤行；为所欲为：*He likes to get his own way.* 他喜欢随心所欲。
in the way in the same place as you, and stopping you from doing something 挡道：*Please can you move? You're in the way.* 请问你能挪一下吗？你挡道了。

out of the way no longer stopping another person from doing something 不再挡道；不再碍事：*Get out of the way of the ambulance!* 别挡救护车的路！

we /wɪ, STRONG 强读 wiː/ **pronoun** 代词
used for talking about both yourself and one or more other people as a group 我们；咱们：*We said we would be friends for ever.* 我们说过我们将永远是朋友。▫ *We bought a bottle of lemonade.* 我们买了一瓶柠檬汽水。

weak /wiːk/ **adjective** 形容词 (**weaker, weakest**)
1 not healthy, or not having strong muscles 虚弱的；无力的：*I was too weak to move.* 我太虚弱了，动弹不得。
▸ **weakly** /ˈwiːkli/ **adverb** 副词：*'I'm all right,' Max said weakly.* "我没事。"马克斯虚弱地说。
▸ **weakness** /ˈwiːknəs/ **uncountable noun** 不可数名词：*Symptoms of the disease include weakness in the arms.* 这种疾病的症状包括手臂无力。
2 containing very little of a particular substance 稀的；淡的：*We drank weak coffee.* 我们喝了淡咖啡。
3 not having much determination, and easy to influence 易受影响的；懦弱的；软弱的：*He was weak, but he was not a bad man.* 他很懦弱，但他不是一个坏人。
▸ **weakness** /ˈwiːknəs/ **uncountable noun** 不可数名词：*Some people think that crying is a sign of weakness.* 有些人认为哭是软弱的表现。

weaken /ˈwiːkən/ **verb** 动词 (**weakens, weakening, weakened**)
to become less strong 虚弱；减弱：*The economy weakened after the election.* 选举后经济疲软。

weakness /ˈwiːknəs/ **countable noun** 可数名词 (**weaknesses**)
the amount, usually a lot, that you like something 喜爱；迷恋：*Stephen had a weakness for chocolate.* 斯蒂芬爱吃巧克力。

wealth /welθ/ **uncountable noun** 不可数名词
a large amount of money, property or other valuable things 财富；财产：*He used his wealth to help others.* 他利用他的财富帮助别人。

wealthy /ˈwelθi/ **adjective** 形容词 (**wealthier, wealthiest**)
having a large amount of money, property or valuable possessions 富有的；富裕的；富饶的：*She's going to be a very wealthy woman someday.* 她总有一天会成为一个非常富有的女人。

weapon /ˈwepən/ **countable noun** 可数名词
an object such as a gun, that is used for killing or hurting people 武器；兵器；凶器：*He was charged with carrying a dangerous weapon.* 他被指控携带危险武器。

wear[1] /weə/ **verb** 动词 (**wears, wearing, wore, worn**)
to have something such as clothes, shoes or jewellery on your body 穿；戴；佩戴：*He was wearing a brown shirt.* 他穿着一件棕色的衬衫。

> **LANGUAGE HELP 语言提示**
> After getting up in the morning, you **get dressed** by **putting on** your clothes. 早上起床穿衣用 get dressed 或 put on one's clothes：*I got up, got dressed, and went downstairs.* 我起床，然后穿上衣服下了楼。▫ *He put on his shoes and socks.* 他穿上鞋袜。
> When you **are dressed**, you **are wearing** your clothes, or you **have** them **on**. 穿着衣物用 be dressed、be wearing one's clothes 或 have one's clothes on：*Cheryl was wearing a short black dress.* 谢里尔穿着一条短款黑连衣裙。▫ *Edith still had her hat on.* 伊迪丝仍旧戴着帽子。

wear down to become flatter or smoother because of rubbing against something (因摩擦而) 变平，变光滑：*The heels on my shoes have worn down.* 我的鞋跟已经磨平了。
wear off to disappear slowly 变弱；减弱：*The excitement of having a new job soon wore off.* 找到新工作的兴奋感很快就消失了。
wear someone out to make someone feel extremely tired (*informal* 非正式) 使某人疲乏；使某人筋疲力尽：*The kids wore themselves out playing football.* 孩子们踢足球累坏了。

wear[2] /weə/ **uncountable noun** 不可数名词
1 used to talk about clothes that are suitable for a certain time or place 衣着；穿着：*Jeans are perfect for everyday wear.* 牛仔裤非常适合日常穿着。
2 the damage or change that is caused by something being used a lot 磨损；耗损：*The suit showed signs of wear.* 这套衣服看起来有些磨损了。

weary - weekly

weary /ˈwɪəri/ *adjective* 形容词 (**wearier, weariest**)
very tired 疲劳的；疲倦的：*Rachel looked pale and weary.* 雷切尔脸色苍白，疲惫不堪。
be weary of something to have become tired of something 对某事物不再感兴趣；厌倦某事物：*They were all growing a bit weary of the game.* 他们都有点厌倦这个游戏了。

weather /ˈweðə/ *uncountable noun* 不可数名词
the temperature and conditions outside, for example if it is raining, hot or windy 天气；气象：*The weather was bad.* 天气很糟糕。 □ *I like cold weather.* 我喜欢寒冷的天气。 □ *Have you heard the weather forecast this morning?* 你今天早上听天气预报了吗？
→ Look at picture on P8 参见彩插第 8 页

weave /wiːv/ *verb* 动词 (**weaves, weaving, wove, woven**)
to make cloth by crossing threads over and under each other 编织：*We gathered wool and learned how to weave it into cloth.* 我们收集羊毛，然后学会如何把它织成布。

web /web/ *countable noun* 可数名词
the thin net made by a spider from a string that comes out of its body 蜘蛛网：*a spider's web* 蜘蛛网

web 蜘蛛网

the ˈweb *singular noun* 单数名词
(also 亦作 **the World Wide Web**) a computer system that helps you find information. You can use it anywhere in the world. 万维网：*The handbook is available on the Web.* 该指南可以在万维网上找到。

webcam /ˈwebkæm/ *countable noun* 可数名词
a camera on a computer that produces images that can be seen on a website 网络摄像机；网络摄影机；网络摄像头
→ Look at picture on P11 参见彩插第 11 页

ˈweb ˌpage *countable noun* 可数名词
a set of information that you can see on a computer screen as part of a website 网页

website /ˈwebsaɪt/ also 亦作 **web site** *countable noun* 可数名词
a set of information about a particular subject that is available on the Internet 网站

wedding /ˈwedɪŋ/ *countable noun* 可数名词
a marriage ceremony and the party that often takes place after the ceremony 婚礼：*Many couples want a big wedding.* 许多夫妇想要一个盛大的婚礼。

Wednesday /ˈwenzdeɪ, -di/ *noun* 名词
the day after Tuesday and before Thursday 星期三：*Come and have supper with us on Wednesday.* 星期三来和我们一起吃晚饭吧。

weed¹ /wiːd/ *countable noun* 可数名词
a plant that grows where you do not want it 杂草；野草：*The garden was full of weeds.* 花园里长满了杂草。

weed² /wiːd/ *verb* 动词 (**weeds, weeding, weeded**)
to remove the weeds from an area 除草：*Try not to walk on the flowerbeds while you are weeding.* 除草时，尽量不要在花坛上行走。

week /wiːk/ *countable noun* 可数名词
1 a period of seven days 星期；周；礼拜：*I thought about it all week.* 整个礼拜我都在想这件事。
2 the hours that you spend at work during a week 工作周：*I work a 40-hour week.* 我每周工作 40 小时。

weekday /ˈwiːkdeɪ/ *countable noun* 可数名词
any of the days of the week except Saturday and Sunday 工作日（周一至周五任何一天）

weekend /ˌwiːkˈend/ *countable noun* 可数名词
Saturday and Sunday 周末（星期六和星期日）：*I had dinner with Tim last weekend.* 上周末我和蒂姆共进了晚餐。

weekly /ˈwiːkli/ *adjective* 形容词, *adverb* 副词
happening once a week or every week 每

周(的); 每周一次(的): We do the weekly shopping every Thursday. 我们每周会在周四购物一次。 □ They are paid weekly. 他们领周薪。

weep /wiːp/ *verb* 动词 (**weeps, weeping, wept**)
to cry 哭泣: She wept tears of joy. 她喜极而泣。

weigh /weɪ/ *verb* 动词 (**weighs, weighing, weighed**)
1 to have a particular weight 重量为: She weighs nearly 10 stone. 她体重近 10 英石。
2 to measure how heavy something or someone is 称…的重量: Lisa weighed the boxes for postage. 莉萨称了这些箱子的重量来算邮资。

weight /weɪt/ *noun* 名词
1 how heavy a person or thing is 重量: What is your height and weight? 你的身高和体重是多少?
→ Look at picture on P2 参见彩插第 2 页
2 *countable* 可数 an object that people lift as a form of exercise 哑铃; 杠铃: I was in the gym lifting weights. 我在健身房举杠铃。
lose weight/gain weight or **put on weight** to become thinner or become fatter 体重减轻/长胖: I'm lucky because I never put on weight. 我很幸运, 因为我从不发胖。

weird /wɪəd/ *adjective* 形容词 (**weirder, weirdest**)
strange (*informal* 非正式) 奇怪的; 怪异的: He's a very weird guy. 他是个很奇怪的家伙。

welcome¹ /ˈwelkəm/ *verb* 动词 (**welcomes, welcoming, welcomed**)
to act in a friendly way when someone arrives somewhere 欢迎; 迎接: She was there to welcome him home. 她在那儿欢迎他回家。● **welcome** *countable noun* 可数名词: They gave him a warm welcome. 他们热烈欢迎他。

welcome² /ˈwelkəm/ *exclamation* 感叹词
used for being friendly to someone who has just arrived somewhere 欢迎: Welcome to Washington! 欢迎来到华盛顿!

welcome³ /ˈwelkəm/ *adjective* 形容词
you're welcome used for answering someone who has thanked you for something 别客气; 不用谢: 'Thank you for dinner.' — 'You're welcome.' "谢谢你的晚餐。" —— "不客气。"

welfare /ˈwelfeə/ *uncountable noun* 不可数名词

the health and happiness of a person or a group 福祉; 健康; 幸福: I don't believe he is thinking of Emma's welfare. 我不相信他会考虑埃玛的幸福。

well¹ /wel/ *exclamation* 感叹词
used before you begin to speak, or when you are surprised about something (用于开始说话或对某事感到惊讶时) 嗯, 噢, 哎呀: Well, it's a pleasure to meet you. 噢, 很高兴认识你。 □ Well, I didn't expect to see you here! 哎呀, 我没想到会在这儿见到你!
oh well used for showing that you accept a situation, even though you are not very happy about it (用于表示接受不愉快的事) 好吧, 算了: Oh well, I suppose it could be worse. 唉, 好吧。我想事情可能会更糟。

well² /wel/ *adverb* 副词 (**better, best**)
1 in an effective way 好: The team played well last week. 这个队上星期打得很好。 □ He speaks English well. 他英语说得很好。 □ Did you sleep well last night? 你昨晚睡得好吗?
2 in a complete way 完全; 彻底: Mix the butter and sugar well. 把黄油和糖充分混合。 □ Do you know him well? 你对他一清二楚吗?
as well also 也; 还: Everywhere he went, I went as well. 他去哪里, 我也去哪里。
as well as and also 以及: Adults as well as children will enjoy the film. 大人和小孩都会喜欢这部电影的。
do well to be successful 成功; 做得好: If she does well in her exams, she will go to college. 如果她考试考得好, 她就会上大学。
may as well or **might as well** used for saying that you will do something because there is nothing better to do 不妨: Anyway, you're here now — you may as well stay. 不管怎样, 你现在在这儿了——你不妨留下来吧。
well done! said to someone when they have done something good (表示赞赏) 干得好!: This is excellent work. Well done! 这项工作完成得很出色。做得好!

well³ /wel/ *adjective* 形容词
healthy 健康的: 'How are you?' — 'I'm very well, thank you.' "你好吗?" —— "我很好, 谢谢你。" □ He said he wasn't feeling well. 他说他感觉不舒服。

well⁴ /wel/ *countable noun* 可数名词
a deep hole in the ground from which people take water or oil 井; 水井; 油井: The women and children were carrying

water from the well. 妇女和孩子们正在从井里打水。

we'll /wɪl, STRONG 强读 wiːl/
short for (缩写 =) 'we shall' or 'we will'

well-be'haved *adjective* 形容词
behaving in a correct way 品行端正的；规规矩矩的：*well-behaved children* 有规矩的孩子们

well 'done *adjective* 形容词
cooked thoroughly 熟透的；全熟的：*I like lamb well done.* 我喜欢熟透的羔羊肉。

wellies /ˈweliz/ *plural noun* 复数名词 (*informal* 非正式)
→ see 见 **wellingtons**

wellingtons /ˈwelɪŋtənz/ *plural noun* 复数名词
(also 亦作 **wellington boots**) long rubber boots that you wear to keep your feet dry 威灵顿长筒靴；长筒橡胶雨靴

well-'known *adjective* 形容词
famous 著名的；知名的：*She was a very well-known author.* 她是一位非常著名的作家。

well-'off *adjective* 形容词
rich (*informal* 非正式) 有钱的；富裕的：*She comes from a reasonably well-off family.* 她出身于一个还算富裕的家庭。

went /went/
→ see 见 **go**

wept /wept/
→ see 见 **weep**

were¹ /wə, STRONG 强读 wɜː/
→ see 见 **be**

were² /wə, STRONG 强读 wɜː/
sometimes used instead of 'was' in conditional sentences or after the verb 'wish' (*formal* 正式) (有时代替 was，用在条件句中或动词 wish 后)：*Jerry wished he were back in Britain.* 杰里希望他回到了英国。

we're /wɪə/
short for (缩写 =) 'we are'

weren't /wɜːnt/
short for (缩写 =) 'were not'

west¹ /west/ also 亦作 **West** *uncountable noun* 不可数名词
the direction that is in front of you when you look at the sun in the evening 西；西部；西方：*Many of the buildings in the west of the city are on fire.* 这座城市西部的许多建筑物都着火了。

the West the United States, Canada and the countries of Western Europe 西方国家 (指美国、加拿大以及欧盟诸国)：*relations between Japan and the West* 日本与西方国家的关系
→ Look at picture on P9 参见彩插第 9 页

west² /west/ also 亦作 **West** *adjective* 形容词, *adverb* 副词
1 towards the west 朝西 (的)；向西 (的)：*We are going west to Glasgow.* 我们向西去格拉斯哥。
2 coming from the west 来自西方的；来自西部的

westerly /ˈwestəli/ *adjective* 形容词
1 to the west or towards the west 西面的；朝西的；向西的：*They walked in a westerly direction along the riverbank.* 他们沿着河岸向西走。
2 blowing from the west 从西方吹来的：*a strong westerly wind* 强劲的西风

western¹ /ˈwestən/ also 亦作 **Western** *adjective* 形容词
1 in or from the west of a place 西方的；西部的：*Western Europe* 西欧
2 used for describing things, people or ideas that come from the United States, Canada and the countries of Western Europe 西方的；西方国家的：*They need billions of dollars from Western governments.* 他们需要西方政府出数十亿美元。

western² /ˈwestən/ also 亦作 **Western** *countable noun* 可数名词
a film about life in the western United States in the past (美国) 西部电影

wet¹ /wet/ *adjective* 形容词 (**wetter**, **wettest**)
1 covered in liquid 湿的：*He dried his wet hair with a towel.* 他用毛巾把湿头发擦干。
2 raining 下雨的：*It's cold and wet outside.* 外面很冷，正下着雨。

wet² /wet/ *verb* 动词 (**wets**, **wetting**, **wet** or 或 **wetted**)
to put water or some other liquid over something 使潮湿；把…弄湿：*She wet a cloth and wiped the child's face.* 她把一块布弄湿，给孩子擦了脸。

we've /wɪv, STRONG 强读 wiːv/
short for (缩写 =) 'we have'

whale /weɪl/ *countable noun* 可数名词
a very large mammal that lives in the sea 鲸

what /wɒt/ *pronoun* 代词
used in questions when you ask for information（用于问句）什么: *What do you want?* 你想要什么？ □ *'Has something happened?' — 'Yes.' — 'What?'* "发生什么事情了吗？"——"是的。"——"什么事情？" ● **what** *adjective* 形容词: *What time is it?* 几点了？ ● **what** *conjunction* 连词: *I want to know what happened to Norman.* 我想知道诺曼出了什么事。
what (a/an) used in exclamations to make an opinion or a reaction stronger（用于感叹句）多么，真，太: *What a horrible thing to do!* 这么做太可怕了！ □ *What pretty hair she has!* 她的头发真漂亮！
what about...? used when you make a suggestion, an offer or a request（用于提议或要求）⋯怎么样？: *What about going to see a film?* 去看电影怎么样？
what if...? used at the beginning of a question when you ask about something that might happen 要是⋯会怎么样呢？: *What if this doesn't work?* 如果这行不通怎么办？

whatever /wɒt'evə/ *conjunction* 连词
1 used for talking about anything or everything of a particular type 任何事物；一切事物: *Frank was free to do whatever he wanted.* 弗兰克想干什么就干什么。
● **whatever** *adjective* 形容词: *He has to accept whatever punishment they give him.* 他们给他什么惩罚他都不得不接受。
2 used to say that something is the case in all situations（表示在任何情况下都一样）无论什么，不管什么: *I will always love you, whatever happens.* 无论发生什么，我都会永远爱你。

what's /wɒts/
short for (缩写 =) 'what is' or 'what has'

wheat /wiːt/ *uncountable noun* 不可数名词
a crop that is grown for food. It is made into flour and used for making bread. 小麦；麦子

wheel¹ /wiːl/ *countable noun* 可数名词
1 one of the round objects under a vehicle that allow it to move along the ground 轮子；车轮: *The car's wheels slipped on the wet road.* 汽车轮子在湿滑的路上打滑了。
2 the round object on a vehicle that you turn to make the vehicle go in different directions 方向盘；转向盘: *He sat down behind the wheel and started the engine.* 他坐到方向盘后面发动了引擎。

wheel² /wiːl/ *verb* 动词 (wheels, wheeling, wheeled)
to push an object along on its wheels 推（有轮之物）: *He wheeled his bike into the alley.* 他把自行车推到小巷里。

wheelbarrow /'wiːlbærəʊ/ *countable noun* 可数名词
an open container with one wheel and two handles, that is used for moving things such as bricks, earth or plants 独轮手推车

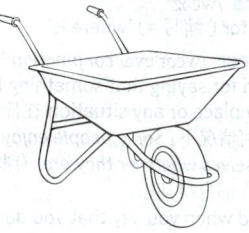

wheelbarrow 独轮手推车

wheelchair /'wiːltʃeə/ *countable noun* 可数名词
a chair with wheels that you use if you cannot walk very well 轮椅

when¹ /wen/ *adverb* 副词
used for asking questions about the time at which things happen（用于问句）什么时候，何时: *When are you going home?* 你什么时候回家？ □ *When did you get married?* 你什么时候结婚的？

when² /wen/ *conjunction* 连词
1 used for talking about something that happens during a situation 在⋯时候；当⋯时；在⋯期间: *When I met Jill, I was living on my own.* 遇到吉尔时，我正独自生活。
2 used for introducing the part of the sentence where you mention the time at which something happens 一⋯就；刚⋯就: *I asked him when he was coming back.* 他一回来我就问他了。

whenever /wen'evə/ *conjunction* 连词
used for talking about any time or every time that something happens 在任何时候；无论何时；每当；每次: *Whenever I talked to him, he seemed quite nice.* 我每次和他说话，他都显得很和蔼可亲。 □ *You can stay at my house whenever you like.* 你愿意什么时候来我家住一下都可以。

where¹ /weə/ *adverb* 副词
used for asking questions about the place

someone or something is in（用于问句）在哪里, 到哪里: *Where did you meet him?* 你在哪里遇见他的？▫ *Where's Anna?* 安娜在哪里？

where² /weə/ *conjunction* 连词
used for talking about the place in which something happens ⋯的那个地方: *People were looking to see where the noise was coming from.* 人们都在找噪音是从哪里来的。▫ *He knew where Henry was.* 他知道亨利在哪里。▫ *This is the room where I work.* 这是我工作的房间。

where's /weəz/
short for（缩写 =）'where is'

wherever /weər'evə/ *conjunction* 连词
1 used for saying that something happens in any place or any situation 在任何地方；在任何情况下: *Some people enjoy themselves wherever they are.* 有些人在任何地方都自得其乐。
2 used when you say that you do not know where a person or a place is 无论在哪里；无论在何处: *I'd like to be with my children, wherever they are.* 我想和我的孩子们在一起,无论他们在哪里。

whether /'weðə/ *conjunction* 连词
1 used when you are talking about a choice between two or more things（表示选择）⋯还是⋯: *They now have two weeks to decide whether or not to buy the house.* 他们现在有两周时间决定是否买这所房子。
2 used for saying that something is true in any of the situations that you mention（表示两种情况都不会改变事实）是⋯（还是）, 或者⋯（或者）, 不管⋯（还是）: *You are part of this family whether you like it or not.* 不管你喜不喜欢,你都是这个家庭的一员。

which¹ /wɪtʃ/ *adjective* 形容词
used for talking about a choice between two or more possible people or things 哪一个: *I want to know which school you went to.* 我想知道你上的是哪所学校。▫ *'You go down that road.' — 'Which one?'* "你沿着那条路走。" —— "哪一条？" ▫ *Which teacher do you like best?* 你最喜欢哪位老师？

which² /wɪtʃ/ *pronoun* 代词
1 used when you want to show the exact thing that you are talking about（用于指明所谈及的事物）⋯的那个: *Police followed a car which didn't stop at a red light.* 警察跟踪一辆闯红灯的汽车。
2 used for talking about something that you have just said（用于指刚谈及的内容）这, 那个, 那些: *She spoke extremely good English, which was not surprising.* 她英语说得非常好, 这并不奇怪。

whichever /wɪtʃ'evə/ *adjective* 形容词
any person or thing 无论哪个: *Whichever way we do this, it isn't going to work.* 不管我们怎么做, 都行不通。● **whichever** *conjunction* 连词: *You can order by phone or from our website — whichever you prefer.* 您可以通过电话或我们的网站订购——随您选择。

while¹ /waɪl/ *conjunction* 连词
used for saying that two things are happening at the same time 当⋯时候；与⋯同时: *His wife got up while he was in bed asleep.* 他在床上睡觉时, 妻子起身下床。

while² /waɪl/ *singular noun* 单数名词
a period of time 一段时间；一会儿: *They walked on in silence for a while.* 他们默默地走了一会儿。

whine /waɪn/ *verb* 动词 (**whines, whining, whined**)
1 to make a long, high noise that sounds sad or unpleasant 哀鸣；惨叫: *He could hear the dog barking and whining in the background.* 在一片背景音中, 他能听到狗在吠叫哀嚎。
2 to complain in an annoying way about something unimportant 哼哼唧唧地抱怨；哀诉: *People were complaining and whining.* 人们怨声不断, 哭哭啼啼。

whip¹ /wɪp/ *countable noun* 可数名词
a long, thin piece of material attached to a handle. It is used for hitting people or animals. 鞭子

whip² /wɪp/ *verb* 动词 (**whips, whipping, whipped**)
1 to hit a person or an animal with a whip 鞭打: *Mr Melton whipped the horse several times.* 梅尔顿先生抽了那匹马好几下。
2 to stir cream very fast until it is thick or stiff 搅打（奶油）: *Whip the cream until it is thick.* 把奶油打稠。

whirl /wɜːl/ *verb* 动词 (**whirls, whirling, whirled**)
to turn around very quickly 快速旋转；急转: *She whirled around to look at him.* 她猛地转过身来看他。

whisk¹ /wɪsk/ *verb* 动词 (**whisks, whisking, whisked**)
1 to take or move someone or something somewhere quickly 匆匆带走；迅速移走：*He whisked her across the dance floor.* 他带着她飞快地穿过舞池。
2 to stir eggs or cream very fast 快速搅打（鸡蛋或奶油）

whisk² /wɪsk/ *countable noun* 可数名词
a kitchen tool used for whisking eggs or cream 打蛋器；搅打器

whisker /ˈwɪskə/ *countable noun* 可数名词
one of the long, stiff hairs that grow near the mouth of an animal such as a cat or a mouse（猫、鼠等的）须

whisky /ˈwɪski/ *uncountable noun* 不可数名词
a strong alcoholic drink made from grain 威士忌：*a bottle of whisky* 一瓶威士忌

whisper /ˈwɪspə/ *verb* 动词 (**whispers, whispering, whispered**)
to say something very quietly 低语；小声说：*'Be quiet,' I whispered.* "安静。"我低声说。□ *He whispered in her ear.* 他在她耳边低语。● **whisper** *countable noun* 可数名词：*People were talking in whispers.* 人们在窃窃私语。

whistle¹ /ˈwɪsəl/ *verb* 动词 (**whistles, whistling, whistled**)
to make musical sounds by blowing your breath out between your lips 吹口哨儿：*He was whistling softly to himself.* 他正自娱自乐地轻声吹着口哨儿。

whistle² /ˈwɪsəl/ *countable noun* 可数名词 whistle 哨子
a small tube that you blow into in order to produce a loud sound 哨子：*The guard blew his whistle and the train started to move.* 列车长吹响哨子，火车开动了。

white¹ /waɪt/ *adjective* 形容词 (**whiter, whitest**)
1 having the colour of snow or milk 白的；白色的：*He had nice white teeth.* 他有一口整齐洁白的牙齿。
→ Look at picture on P13 参见彩插第 13 页
2 having a pale skin 白种人的；白人的：*A family of white people moved into a house up the street.* 一户白人家庭搬进了这条街前头的一栋房子里。
3 white wine is a pale-yellow colour（葡萄酒）白的：*a glass of white wine* 一杯白葡萄酒
4 white coffee or tea has milk in it（咖啡或茶）加牛奶的

white² /waɪt/ *noun* 名词
the colour of snow or milk 白色：*He was dressed in white from head to toe.* 他从头到脚穿着一身白。

whiteboard /ˈwaɪtbɔːd/ *countable noun* 可数名词
a shiny, white board that you can draw or write on, using special pens. Teachers often use whiteboards. 白板
→ Look at picture on P1 参见彩插第 1 页

whizz /wɪz/ *verb* 动词 (**whizzes, whizzing, whizzed**)
to move somewhere very fast (*informal* 非正式) 快速移动：*Stewart felt a bottle whizz past his head.* 斯图尔特感到有一个瓶子从他的头边嗖地飞过。

who /huː/ *pronoun* 代词
used in questions when you ask about the name of a person or a group of people（用于问句）谁，什么人：*Who's there?* 谁在那儿？□ *Who is the strongest man around here?* 谁是这儿附近最强壮的人？□ *'You remind me of someone.' — 'Who?'* "你使我想起了一个人。"——"谁？" ● **who** *conjunction* 连词：*Police have not found out who did it.* 警方还没有查出是谁干的。

who'd /huːd/
1 short for (缩写 =) 'who had'
2 short for (缩写 =) 'who would'

whoever /huːˈevə/ *conjunction* 连词
1 used for talking about someone when you do not know who they are …的那个人；…的任何人：*Whoever wins the prize is going to be famous for life.* 得奖的人将毕生成名。
2 used for talking about any person 无论谁；不管什么人：*You can have whoever you like visit you.* 你想让谁来拜访你都可以。

whole /həʊl/ *noun* 名词
all of something 所有；全部；全体：*This is a problem for the whole of society.* 这是一个关系到整个社会的问题。● **whole** *adjective* 形容词：*We spent the whole summer in Italy that year.* 那年我们在意大

who'll - wiggle

利度过了整个夏天。
on the whole in general 总的说来；大体上：*On the whole I agree with him.* 总的来说，我同意他的意见。

who'll /huːl/
short for (缩写 =) 'who will' or 'who shall'

whom /huːm/ *pronoun* 代词
used in formal or written English instead of 'who' when it is the object of a verb or a preposition (在正式或书面英语中代替 who，用作动词或介词的宾语) 谁，什么人：*The article was about the people whom she met at her brother's wedding.* 这篇文章讲的是她在哥哥婚礼上遇到的那些人。□ *To whom am I speaking?* 我在跟谁说话？

who's /huːz/
short for (缩写 =) 'who is' or 'who has'

whose /huːz/ *pronoun* 代词
1 used in questions to ask about the person that something belongs to (用于询问物品的所有人) 谁的：*'Whose is this?' — 'It's mine.'* "这是谁的？"——"是我的。"
● **whose** *adjective* 形容词：*Whose daughter is she?* 她是谁的女儿？□ *I can't remember whose idea it was.* 我记不得这是谁的主意了。
2 used when you mention something that belongs to the person or the thing mentioned before (表示已经提到过的) 那个人的，那一个的，其：*That's the driver whose car was blocking the street.* 那就是把汽车挡在道上的那个司机。

who've /huːv/
short for (缩写 =) 'who have'

why /waɪ/ *adverb* 副词
used when you ask or talk about the reasons for something 为什么；为何：*Why is she here?* 她为什么在这里？□ *Why are you laughing? I liked him — I don't know why.* 你为什么笑？我喜欢他——我不知道为什么。● **why** *conjunction* 连词：*He wondered why she was late.* 他想知道她为什么迟到。

Why not?
1 used for agreeing with a suggestion (表示赞同建议) 为什么不呢？：*'Would you like to spend the afternoon with me?' — 'Why not?'* "你愿意和我一起度过下午时光吗？"——"为什么不呢？"
2 used for introducing a suggestion (表示提出建议) 为什么不…？何不…？：*Why not give Jenny a call?* 为什么不给珍妮打个电话呢？

wicked /ˈwɪkɪd/ *adjective* 形容词
very bad 很坏的；邪恶的：*That's a wicked lie!* 那是一个恶毒的谎言！

wide /waɪd/ *adjective* 形容词 (**wider, widest**)
1 having a large distance from one side to the other 宽的；宽阔的：*The bed is too wide for this room.* 这张床放这个房间太宽了。
2 as far as possible 全张开的：*'It was huge,' he announced, spreading his arms wide.* "它很大。"他郑重其事地说，同时张开双臂比画着。
3 used to talk or ask about how much something measures from one side to the other 宽度为…的；有…宽的：*The lake was over a mile wide.* 这个湖宽1英里多。

widen /ˈwaɪdən/ *verb* 动词 (**widens, widening, widened**)
to make something bigger from one side or edge to the other 使变宽；加宽；拓宽：*They are planning to widen the road.* 他们正在计划拓宽这条路。

widespread /ˈwaɪdspred/ *adjective* 形容词
happening over a large area, or to a great extent 普遍的；广泛的：*Food shortages are widespread.* 食品短缺现象普遍存在。

widow /ˈwɪdəʊ/ *countable noun* 可数名词
a woman whose husband has died 寡妇；孀妇：*She became a widow a year ago.* 她一年前成了寡妇。

widower /ˈwɪdəʊə/ *countable noun* 可数名词
a man whose wife has died 鳏夫

width /wɪdθ/ *noun* 名词
the distance from one side of something to the other 宽度；广度：*Measure the full width of the window.* 量一下窗户的全宽。

wife /waɪf/ *countable noun* 可数名词 (**wives**)
the woman that someone is married to 妻子；太太；夫人：*He married his wife, Jane, 37 years ago.* 37 年前，他与妻子简结婚。

wig /wɪɡ/ *countable noun* 可数名词
a covering of artificial hair that you wear on your head 假发

wiggle /ˈwɪɡəl/ *verb* 动词 (**wiggles, wiggling, wiggled**)
to make something move up and down or from side to side in small quick movements 使扭动；使摆动；使摇动；使

起伏: She wiggled her finger. 她摆动手指。

wild /waɪld/ *adjective* 形容词 (**wilder, wildest**)
1 used for describing animals or plants that live or grow in nature, and are not taken care of by people (动植物) 自然生长的, 野生的: *We could hear the calls of wild animals in the jungle.* 我们可以听到丛林里野兽的叫声。
2 uncontrolled or excited 激动的; 失控的: *The crowds went wild when they saw him.* 人们看到他时欣喜若狂。
▶ **wildly** /ˈwaɪldli/ *adverb* 副词: *As she finished each song, the crowd clapped wildly.* 她每唱完一首歌, 众人就疯狂地鼓掌。

wilderness /ˈwɪldənəs/ *countable noun* 可数名词 (**wildernesses**)
a desert or other area of natural land that is not used by people 荒野: *There will be no wilderness left on the planet within 30 years.* 30 年内, 地球上将不再有荒野。

wildlife /ˈwaɪldlaɪf/ *uncountable noun* 不可数名词
used for talking about the animals and other living things that live in nature 野生动植物; 野生生物: *The area is rich in wildlife.* 这个地区野生生物丰富多样。

will¹ /wɪl/ *modal verb* 情态动词

> **LANGUAGE HELP 语言提示**
> When you are speaking, you can use the short forms **I'll** for **I will** and **won't** for **will not**. 口语中, I will 可缩作 I'll, will not 可缩作 won't。

1 used for talking about things that are going to happen in the future (表示将来) 将, 会: *I'm sure things will get better.* 我相信情况会好转的。 □ *The concert will finish at about 10.30 p.m.* 音乐会将在晚上 10 点 30 分左右结束。 □ *One day I will come to visit you in York.* 有朝一日我会去约克看你。
2 used when you are asking someone to do something (表示请求): *Please will you be quiet?* 请你安静点好吗?
3 used when you offer to do something (表示主动提出做某事): *No, don't call a taxi. I'll drive you home.* 不, 不要叫出租车。我开车送你回家。

will² /wɪl/ *noun* 名词
1 the ability that someone has to decide to do something difficult 意志; 毅力: *I have a strong will and I'm sure I'll succeed.* 我有坚强的意志, 我相信我会成功。

2 *countable* 可数 a legal document that says who will receive someone's money when they die 遗嘱: *He left £8 million in his will to the University of Edinburgh.* 他在遗嘱中留下了 800 万英镑赠予爱丁堡大学。

willing /ˈwɪlɪŋ/ *adjective* 形容词
happy to do something 愿意的; 乐意的: *He was a natural and willing learner.* 他生来善学、爱学。 □ *She's willing to answer questions.* 她愿意回答问题。
▶ **willingly** /ˈwɪlɪŋli/ *adverb* 副词: *Bryant talked willingly to the police.* 布赖恩特积极地和警察谈了起来。
▶ **willingness** /ˈwɪlɪŋnəs/ *uncountable noun* 不可数名词: *She showed her willingness to work hard.* 她表现出努力工作的意愿。

win /wɪn/ *verb* 动词 (**wins, winning, won**)
1 to do better than everyone else involved in a race, a game, or a competition 获胜; 赢: *He does not have a chance of winning the fight.* 他没有机会赢得这场战斗。 □ *The four local teams all won their games.* 当地 4 支球队都赢得了比赛。 ● **win** *countable noun* 可数名词: *They played eight games without a win.* 他们打了 8 场比赛, 无一胜绩。
2 to get a prize because you have done better than everyone else 赢得; 获得: *The first correct answer wins the prize.* 第一个答对者将会获得奖品。

wind¹ /wɪnd/ *noun* 名词
air that moves 风: *A strong wind was blowing from the north.* 一阵强风从北方吹来。

wind² /waɪnd/ *verb* 动词 (**winds, winding, wound**)
1 to have a lot of bends 蜿蜒; 曲折: *From here, the river winds through attractive countryside.* 这条河从这里蜿蜒流过迷人的乡村。
2 to wrap something long around something else several times 缠; 绕: *She wound the rope around her waist.* 她把绳子绕在腰间。
3 to turn part of a clock or a watch several times in order to make it work 给 (钟表) 上发条: *Did you remember to wind the clock?* 你记得给钟上发条了吗?

'wind ,instrument *countable noun* 可数名词
any musical instrument that you blow into

to produce sounds 管乐器；吹奏乐器

windmill /ˈwɪndmɪl/ *countable noun* 可数名词
a building with long, flat parts on the outside that turn as the wind blows to make machinery move inside. Windmills are used for grinding grain or to pump water. 风车

window /ˈwɪndəʊ/ *countable noun* 可数名词
1 a space in the wall of a building or in the side of a vehicle that has glass in it 窗；窗户；窗口: *He looked out of the window.* 他向窗外望去。
2 one of the work areas that a computer screen can be divided into (计算机屏幕的) 窗口: *Open the document in a new window.* 在新窗口中打开文档。
→ Look at picture on P11 参见彩插第 11 页

windscreen /ˈwɪndskriːn/ *countable noun* 可数名词 (*American* 美国英语: **windshield**)
the glass window at the front of a car or other vehicle (车辆的) 前窗玻璃, 前风挡玻璃

windscreen wiper *countable noun* 可数名词
a thing that cleans rain from a vehicle's windscreen 刮水器；刮雨器

windshield /ˈwɪndʃiːld/ *countable noun* 可数名词 (*American* 美国英语)
→ see 见 **windscreen**

windsurfing /ˈwɪndsɜːfɪŋ/ *uncountable noun* 不可数名词
a sport in which you move across water on a long narrow board with a sail on it 帆板运动

windy /ˈwɪndi/ *adjective* 形容词 (**windier**, **windiest**)
with a lot of wind 多风的；风大的: *It was a wet and windy day.* 那是一个风雨交加的日子。
→ Look at picture on P8 参见彩插第 8 页

wine /waɪn/ *uncountable noun* 不可数名词
an alcoholic drink made from grapes (= small green or purple fruit) 葡萄酒: *a bottle of white wine* 一瓶白葡萄酒

wing /wɪŋ/ *countable noun* 可数名词
1 one of the two parts of the body of a bird or an insect that it uses for flying (鸟或昆虫的) 翅膀, 翼: *The bird flapped its wings.* 鸟振了振翅膀。
2 one of the long flat parts at the side of an aeroplane that support it while it is flying 机翼

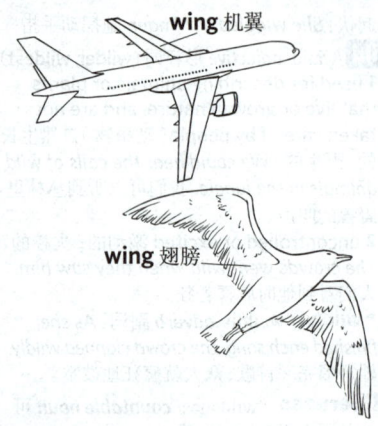

wing 机翼

wing 翅膀

wink /wɪŋk/ *verb* 动词 (**winks**, **winking**, **winked**)
to look at someone and close one eye quickly, usually as a sign that something is a joke or a secret 眨单眼示意；使眼色
● **wink** *countable noun* 可数名词: *I gave her a wink.* 我冲她使了个眼色。

winner /ˈwɪnə/ *countable noun* 可数名词
the person who wins a prize, a race or a competition 获胜者；优胜者: *She will present the prizes to the winners.* 她将为获胜者颁奖。

winter /ˈwɪntə/ *noun* 名词
the season between autumn and spring. In winter the weather is usually cold. 冬天；冬季: *In winter the nights are long and cold.* 冬天夜晚又长又冷
→ Look at picture on P8 参见彩插第 8 页

wipe /waɪp/ *verb* 动词 (**wipes**, **wiping**, **wiped**)
1 to rub the surface of something with a cloth to remove dirt or liquid from it 擦；拭；抹: *I'll just wipe my hands.* 我擦擦手就行了。● **wipe** *countable noun* 可数名词: *The table's dirty — could you give it a wipe, please?* 桌子脏了——请你擦一擦好吗？
2 to remove dirt or liquid from something by using a cloth or your hand 擦掉；抹掉: *Gary wiped the sweat from his face.* 加里擦去脸上的汗水。

wipe something out to destroy something completely 彻底消灭某物；摧毁某物: *The disease wiped out thousands of birds.* 这种疾病使成千上万的鸟死亡。

wire /waɪə/ *noun* 名词
1 a long, thin piece of metal 金属丝；金属

线: *Eleven birds were sitting on a telephone wire.* 11只鸟栖落在电话线上。▫ *a wire fence* 铁丝栅栏
2 a long thin piece of wire that carries electricity 电线；导线: *A wire connects the device to your mobile phone.* 一根电线可以把设备连接到手机上。

wireless /ˈwaɪələs/ *adjective* 形容词
using radio waves (= a form of power that travels through the air) instead of wires 无线的: *I have a wireless Internet connection for my laptop.* 我的笔记本电脑可以无线上网。

wisdom /ˈwɪzdəm/ *uncountable noun* 不可数名词
the ability to use your experience and knowledge to make sensible decisions or judgements 智慧；才智: *He has the wisdom that comes from old age.* 他有漫长岁月积淀下来的智慧。

wise /waɪz/ *adjective* 形容词 (**wiser, wisest**)
able to use your experience and knowledge to make sensible decisions and judgements 智慧的；明智的；聪明的: *She's a wise woman.* 她是个聪明的女人。
▸ **wisely** /ˈwaɪzli/ *adverb* 副词: *They spent their money wisely.* 他们花钱很精明。

wish¹ /wɪʃ/ *noun* 名词 (**wishes**)
1 *countable* 可数 something that you would like 愿望；志向: *Her wish is to become a doctor.* 她的愿望是成为一名医生。
2 *countable* 可数 when you say in your mind that you want something, and then hope that it will happen 愿；心愿: *Did you make a wish?* 你许愿了吗？
3 [**wishes**] *plural* 复数 polite and friendly feelings that you express to someone 祝福；祝愿: *Please give him my best wishes.* 请代我向他致以最良好的祝愿。

wish² /wɪʃ/ *verb* 动词 (**wishes, wishing, wished**)
1 to want to do something (*formal* 正式) 希望，想要（做某事）: *I wish to leave a message.* 我想留个口信。
2 to want something to be true, even though you know that it is impossible or unlikely 希望（没有可能或不太可能的事发生）: *I wish I could do that.* 我真希望我能做那件事。
wish for something to say in your mind that you want something, and then hope that it will happen 盼望得到某事物: *Every* *birthday I closed my eyes and wished for a guitar.* 每年生日我都闭上眼睛，盼着能得到一把吉他。
wish someone something to express the hope that someone will be lucky or happy 祝愿某人…: *I wish you both a good trip.* 祝你们俩旅途愉快。

wit /wɪt/ *uncountable noun* 不可数名词
the ability to use words or ideas in an amusing and clever way 机智；才思；风趣: *He writes with great wit.* 他的文笔特别诙谐。

witch /wɪtʃ/ *countable noun* 可数名词 (**witches**)
a woman in children's stories who has magic powers that she uses to do bad things（童话故事中的）女巫，巫婆

with /wɪð/ *preposition* 介词
1 together in one place 和…在一起: *Her son and daughter were with her.* 她的儿子和女儿跟她在一起。
2 used for saying that two people or groups are both involved in a discussion, a fight or an argument（一方）与，和（另一方）: *We didn't discuss it with each other.* 我们没有和彼此讨论这件事。▫ *About a thousand students fought with police.* 大约1,000名学生与警察发生了冲突。
3 using something 用；使用: *Turn the meat over with a fork.* 用叉子把肉翻过来。▫ *I don't allow my children to eat with their fingers.* 我不允许我的孩子用手抓饭吃。
4 carrying something 携带: *A woman came in with a cup of coffee.* 一个女人端着一杯咖啡走了进来。
5 having a feature or a possession 有；具有；带有: *He was tall, with blue eyes.* 他高个子，蓝眼睛。

withdraw /wɪðˈdrɔː/ *verb* 动词 (**withdraws, withdrawing, withdrew, withdrawn**)
1 to remove or take something away from a place (*formal* 正式) 抽回；移开；撤回: *He reached into his pocket and withdrew a sheet of paper.* 他把手伸进口袋，掏出来一张纸。
2 to leave the place where you are fighting and return nearer home 撤离；撤退: *The army will withdraw as soon as the war ends.* 战争一结束军队就会撤出。
3 to take money out of a bank account（从银行账户里）提取: *He withdrew £750 from his account.* 他从账户里提取了750英镑。

withdrawn - wonder

4 to stop taking part in an activity or an organization 退出（活动或组织）: *She's the second tennis player to withdraw from the games.* 她是第二个退赛的网球运动员。

withdrawn /wɪðˈdrɔːn/
→ see 见 **withdraw**

withdrew /wɪðˈdruː/
→ see 见 **withdraw**

within /wɪˈðɪn/ *preposition* 介词
1 inside or surrounded by a place, an area or an object (*formal* 正式) 在…里: *The sports fields must be within the city.* 运动场必须在市内。
2 less than a particular distance from a place 在（特定距离）之内: *The man was within a few feet of him.* 那个男人离他只有几英尺远。
3 before the end of a particular length of time 在（特定时段）之内: *Within twenty-four hours I had the money.* 24 小时之内我拿到了钱。

without /wɪˈðaʊt/ *preposition* 介词
1 used for showing that someone or something does not have or use the thing mentioned 不用；缺乏: *I prefer tea without milk.* 我喜欢不加牛奶的茶。 □ *You shouldn't drive without a seat belt.* 你不应该不系安全带就开车。
2 used for saying that the second thing mentioned does not happen 未，没有（做某事）: *He left without speaking to me.* 他没和我说话就走了。 □ *They worked without stopping.* 他们不停地工作。
3 used for saying that someone else is not in the same place as you are, or they are not involved in the same action as you 未与…一起: *I told Frank to start dinner without me.* 我让弗兰克自己先吃晚饭，不用等我。

witness /ˈwɪtnəs/ *countable noun* 可数名词 (**witnesses**)
1 a person who saw a particular event such as an accident or a crime 目击者；见证人: *Witnesses say they saw an explosion.* 目击者称他们看到了一次爆炸。
2 someone who appears in a court of law to say what they know about a crime or other event（出庭作证的）证人: *Eleven witnesses appeared in court.* 11 名证人出庭作证。● **witness** *verb* 动词 (**witnesses, witnessing, witnessed**): *Anyone who witnessed the attack should call the police.* 任何目击这场袭击的人都应该报警。

witty /ˈwɪti/ *adjective* 形容词 (**wittier, wittiest**)
amusing in a clever way 机智的；诙谐的: *His books were very witty.* 他的书非常诙谐。

wives /waɪvz/
the plural of **wife**（wife 的复数形式）

wizard /ˈwɪzəd/ *countable noun* 可数名词
a man in children's stories who has magic powers（童话故事中的）巫师，魔法师

wobble /ˈwɒbəl/ *verb* 动词 (**wobbles, wobbling, wobbled**)
a person or thing wobbles when they make small movements from side to side as if they are going to fall 摇摆；摇晃: *The bike wobbled, but I didn't fall.* 自行车摇晃了几下，但我没有摔下来。

wobbly /ˈwɒbli/ *adjective* 形容词 (**wobblier, wobbliest**)
not steady, and moving from side to side 不稳的；摇摇晃晃的: *He sat on a wobbly plastic chair.* 他坐在一把摇摇晃晃的塑料椅子上。

woke /wəʊk/
→ see 见 **wake**

woken /ˈwəʊkən/
→ see 见 **wake**

wolf /wʊlf/ *countable noun* 可数名词 (**wolves** /wʊlvz/)
a wild animal that looks like a large dog 狼

woman /ˈwʊmən/ *countable noun* 可数名词 (**women**)
an adult female human being 成年女子；女人；妇女: *She was a tall, dark woman, with an unusual face.* 她身材高大，皮肤黝黑，面相奇特。

women /ˈwɪmɪn/
the plural of **woman**（woman 的复数形式）

won /wʌn/
→ see 见 **win**

wonder¹ /ˈwʌndə/ *verb* 动词 (**wonders, wondering, wondered**)
to think about something, and try to guess or understand more about it 想知道；想弄明白: *I wondered what the noise was.* 我想知道那是什么声音。

wonder² /ˈwʌndə/ *noun* 名词
1 *singular* 单数 a very surprising and unexpected thing 令人惊奇的事: *It's a wonder that we're still friends.* 奇怪的是我们还是朋友。

2 uncountable 不可数 a feeling of great surprise and pleasure 惊奇；惊异；惊叹：*My eyes opened wide in wonder at the view.* 看到这景色，我惊奇地睁大了眼睛。
3 countable 可数 something that causes people to feel great surprise or admiration 奇迹；奇观；奇妙事物：*He loved to read about the wonders of nature.* 他喜欢读讲述自然奇观的书。

wonderful /ˈwʌndəful/ *adjective* 形容词 extremely good 极好的；绝妙的；精彩的：*The cold air felt wonderful on his face.* 冷空气拂面，他感觉神清气爽。▫ *It's wonderful to see you.* 见到你真是太好了。

won't /wəʊnt/
short for (缩写 =) 'will not'

wood /wʊd/ *noun* 名词
1 uncountable 不可数 the hard material that trees are made of 木头；木材：*Some houses are made of wood.* 有些房子是木头的。
2 countable 可数 (also 亦作 **woods**) a large area of trees growing near each other 树林；林子：*We went for a walk in the woods.* 我们去树林里散了会儿步。

wooden /ˈwʊdən/ *adjective* 形容词 made of wood 木制的；木头的：*She sat in a wooden chair.* 她坐在一把木椅上。

woodwind /ˈwʊdwɪnd/ *noun* 名词 the group of musical instruments that are mainly made of wood, that you play by blowing into them 木管乐器
→ Look at picture on P12 参见彩插第 12 页

wool /wʊl/ *uncountable noun* 不可数名词
1 the hair that grows on sheep and on some other animals (绵羊等的) 毛，绒
2 a material made from animal's wool that is used for making things such as clothes 毛料；毛织物：*The socks are made of wool.* 这双袜子是羊毛的。

woollen /ˈwʊlən/ *adjective* 形容词 made from wool 毛纺的；毛制的：*thick woollen socks* 厚厚的羊毛袜子

woolly /ˈwʊli/ *adjective* 形容词 made from wool or looking like wool 毛制的；羊毛似的：*a woolly hat* 毛线帽

word /wɜːd/ *countable noun* 可数名词 a unit of language with meaning 单词；词：*The Italian word for 'love' is 'amore'.* 意大利语中的 "爱" 是 amore 这个词。
→ Look at picture on P3 参见彩插第 3 页
a word something that you say 说的话；话

语；言语：*John didn't say a word all the way home.* 回家时约翰一路上一句话也没说。
have a word with someone to have a short conversation with someone 和某人说会儿话：*Could I have a word with you in my office, please?* 可以在我办公室和你谈谈吗？
in other words said before you repeat something in a different way 换句话说；也就是说：*Ray is in charge of the office. In other words, he's my boss.* 雷负责这个办公室。换句话说，他是我的老板。
word for word using exactly the same words 一字不差地；逐字地：*I learned the song word for word.* 我逐字学了这首歌。

Word document *countable noun* 可数名词 a document that you create on a computer using a program for writing text (*trademark* 商标) *Word 文档

wore /wɔː/
→ see 见 **wear**

work¹ /wɜːk/ *verb* 动词 (**works, working, worked**)
1 to have a job and earn money for it 工作：*He worked as a teacher for 40 years.* 他当了 40 年教师。▫ *I can't talk to you right now — I'm working.* 我现在不能和你说话——我在工作。
2 to do an activity that uses a lot of your time or effort 卖力干活：*You should work harder at school.* 你在学校应该加倍努力。
3 to operate correctly 运转；运行：*My mobile phone isn't working.* 我的手机坏了。
4 to be successful 成功；奏效：*Our plan worked perfectly.* 我们的计划很成功。
5 to use or control a machine 使用；操作；控制：*Do you know how to work the DVD player?* 你知道怎么用 DVD 播放机吗？
work out
1 to develop in a way that is good for you 进展顺利：*I hope everything works out for you in Australia.* 我希望你在澳大利亚一切顺利。
2 to do physical exercises in order to make your body healthy 锻炼身体；做运动：*I work out at a gym twice a week.* 我每周去健身房锻炼两次。
work something out to discover the solution to a problem by thinking 找到 (问题) 的解决办法：*It took me some time to work out the answer.* 我花了一些时间才找到问题的答案。

work out 锻炼身体

They were working out at the gym. 他们在健身房锻炼身体。

work² /wɜːk/ *noun* 名词
1 *uncountable* 不可数 the job that you do to earn money 工作；职业：*I start work at 8.30 a.m. and finish at 7 p.m.* 我早上 8 点半开始工作，晚上 7 点收工。
2 *uncountable* 不可数 the place where you do your job 工作地点；工作场所：*I'm lucky. I can walk to work.* 我很幸运，我可以走路去上班。
3 *uncountable* 不可数 any activity that uses a lot of your time or effort（耗费大量时间或精力的）活动，活计：*I did some work in the garden this weekend.* 这个周末我在花园里干了些活计。
4 *countable* 可数 a painting, a book or a piece of music that someone has produced 作品（指绘画、图书或音乐）：*My uncle bought me the complete works of William Shakespeare for Christmas.* 我叔叔给我买了威廉·莎士比亚的全部作品作为圣诞节礼物。 □ *a work of art* 一件艺术品

worker /ˈwɜːkə/ *countable noun* 可数名词
1 a person who works, who is not a manager 工人；工作者：*His parents were factory workers.* 他父母是工厂工人。
2 used for saying how well or badly someone works 干活…的人：*He is a hard worker.* 他是个努力做事的人。

workforce /ˈwɜːkfɔːs/ *countable noun* 可数名词
1 the total number of people in a country or a region who are able to do a job and who are available for work（国家或地区的）劳动力，劳动人口：*Half the workforce is unemployed.* 一半劳动力处于失业状态。
2 the total number of people who are employed by a particular company（某一公司的）员工总数：*The company employs a very large workforce.* 这家公司雇用了大量员工。

workout /ˈwɜːkaʊt/ *countable noun* 可数名词
a period of physical exercise or training 锻炼；健身：*She does a 35-minute workout every day.* 她每天锻炼 35 分钟。

workplace /ˈwɜːkpleɪs/ *countable noun* 可数名词
the place where you work 工作场所：*This new law will make the workplace safer for everyone.* 这部新法律将使每个人的工作场所更安全。

workshop /ˈwɜːkʃɒp/ *countable noun* 可数名词
1 a time when people share their knowledge or experience on a particular subject 研讨会；研习班：*A music workshop for beginners will be held in the town hall.* 市政厅将举办一个初学者音乐工作坊。
2 a place where people make or repair things 车间；作坊；维修厂：*He works as a mechanic in the workshop.* 他在维修厂做机修工。

world /wɜːld/ *singular noun* 单数名词
1 the planet that we live on 世界；地球：*Scotland is a beautiful part of the world.* 苏格兰是世界上一个美丽的地方。
2 a particular area of activity, and the people who are involved in it（某一活动的）领域，界：*We have the latest news from the fashion world.* 我们有来自时尚界的最新消息。

worldwide /ˌwɜːldˈweɪd/ *adverb* 副词
throughout the world 在全世界：*His books have sold more than 20 million copies worldwide.* 他的书在世界范围内卖出了 2,000 多万册。● **worldwide** *adjective* 形容词：*They made £20 billion in worldwide sales last year.* 他们去年全球销售额达 200 亿英镑。

World Wide Web *noun* 名词
a computer system that allows you to see information from all over the world on your computer. The short forms **WWW** and **the Web** are often used. 万维网（缩写形式为 WWW 或 the Web）

worm /wɜːm/ *countable noun* 可数名词
a small animal with a long, thin body, no bones and no legs 蠕虫

worn¹ /wɔːn/
→ see 见 **wear**

worn² /wɔːn/ *adjective* 形容词
used for describing something that is damaged or thin because it is old and you have used it a lot 用坏的；用旧的；磨损的：*There was a worn blue carpet on the floor.* 地板上有一块破旧的蓝色地毯。

worn 'out also 亦作 **worn-out** *adjective* 形容词
1 damaged after being used a lot 用坏了；磨损的：*old, worn-out tyres* 又旧又破的轮胎
2 very tired after hard work 疲惫不堪的；精疲力竭的：*After the race, he was worn out.* 比赛结束后，他筋疲力尽。

worry¹ /'wʌri/ *verb* 动词 (**worries, worrying, worried**)
1 to keep thinking about problems that you have or about unpleasant things that might happen 担心；担忧：*Don't worry, I'm sure he'll be fine.* 别担心，我相信他会没事儿的。□ *I worry about her all the time.* 我一直为她担心。□ *They worry that he works too hard.* 他们担心他工作太拼命了。
▶ **worried** /'wʌrid/ *adjective* 形容词：*He seemed very worried.* 他显得很担心。
2 to make someone anxious 使担心；使担忧；使发愁：*'Why didn't you tell us?' — 'I didn't want to worry you.'* "你为什么不告诉我们？" —— "我不想让你们担心。"

worry² /'wʌri/ *noun* 名词 (**worries**)
1 *uncountable* 不可数 the state or feeling of anxiety and unhappiness caused by the problems that you have or by thinking about unpleasant things that might happen 担心；忧虑；发愁：*Modern life is full of worry.* 现代生活充满了忧虑。
2 *countable* 可数 a problem that you keep thinking about and that makes you unhappy 令人担忧的事；让人发愁的事：*My parents had a lot of worries.* 我父母有很多烦恼。

worse /wɜːs/ *adjective* 形容词, *adverb* 副词
1 a form of the adjective **bad**, used for saying that one thing is of a lower standard than another thing (bad 的比较级) 更差的，更糟的：*The situation is even worse than we imagined.* 情况比我们想象的还要糟。
2 a form of the adverb **badly**, used for saying that one thing is done or happens in a way that is of a lower standard than

another thing (badly 的比较级) 更差，更糟：*I did worse in my exam than last time.* 我这次考得比上次还差。

worship /'wɜːʃɪp/ *verb* 动词 (**worships, worshipping, worshipped**)
1 to show your respect to God or a god, for example, by saying prayers 崇拜，敬仰（上帝或神）；做礼拜：*He likes to worship in his own home.* 他喜欢在自己家里做礼拜。□ *We talked about different ways of worshipping God.* 我们讨论了崇拜上帝的不同方式。● **worship** *uncountable noun* 不可数名词：*This was his family's place of worship.* 这是他家的礼拜场所。
2 to love or admire someone or something very much 热爱；爱慕；崇拜：*She worshipped him for many years.* 她崇拜他很多年了。

worst¹ /wɜːst/ *adjective* 形容词, *adverb* 副词
1 a form of the adjective **bad**, used for saying that one thing is of the lowest possible standard (bad 的最高级) 最差的，最糟的：*That was the worst meal I've ever had.* 那是我吃过的最糟糕的一顿饭。
2 a form of the adverb **badly**, used for saying that one thing is done or happens in a way that is of the lowest possible standard (badly 的最高级) 最差，最糟，最严重：*The areas outside the city were worst affected by the fires.* 城外地区受火灾影响最为严重。

worst² /wɜːst/ *singular noun* 单数名词
the most unpleasant thing that could happen or does happen 最糟糕的事物：*Many people still fear the worst.* 许多人仍然担心最坏的情况。

worth¹ /wɜːθ/ *adjective* 形容词
1 having a particular value 有…价值的；值（…钱）的：*The picture is worth £500.* 这幅画价值 500 英镑。
2 pleasant or useful, and a good thing to have 值得的：*He decided to see if the house was worth buying.* 他决定看看这座房子是否值得买。

worth² /wɜːθ/ *uncountable noun* 不可数名词
used for saying how much of something you can buy for a particular amount of money 价值…的量：*I put twenty pounds' worth of petrol in the car.* 我给汽车加了 20 英镑的汽油。

worthless /'wɜːθləs/ *adjective* 形容词
having no value or use 毫无价值的；无用

的: He had nothing but a worthless piece of paper. 他除了一张毫无价值的纸一无所有。

worthwhile /ˌwɜːθˈwaɪl/ *adjective* 形容词
enjoyable or useful, and worth the time, money or effort that you spend on it 值得花时间（或金钱、气力等）的: *The president's trip was worthwhile.* 总统不虚此行。

would /wəd, STRONG 强读 wʊd/ *modal verb* 情态动词
1 used for asking questions in a polite way（表示客气地请求）: *Would you mind if I opened the window?* 你介意我打开窗户吗？
2 often used in questions with 'like', when you are making a polite offer or invitation（常在疑问句中与 like 连用，表示客气地建议或邀请）: *Would you like a drink?* 你要来一杯饮料吗？
3 used for talking about situations that are not real（表示想象）会: *If I had more money, I would go travelling.* 如果我有更多的钱，我就去旅行。
4 used when you are saying what someone believed, hoped or expected to happen（表示愿意）会，将会: *We all hoped you would come.* 我们都希望你能来。
5 used for saying that someone was willing to do something. You use **would not** to say that someone refused to do something.（表示愿意）肯，会: *He said he would help her.* 他说他会帮助她。 □ *She wouldn't say where she bought her shoes.* 她不肯说她在哪儿买的鞋。
6 used for talking about something that someone often did in the past（表示过去经常发生的情况）总是，老是: *He would sit by the window, watching people go by.* 他会坐在窗边，看着人来人往。

wouldn't /ˈwʊdənt/
short for（缩写 =）'would not'

would've /ˈwʊdəv/
short for（缩写 =）'would have'

wound¹ /waʊnd/
→ see 见 **wind**

wound² /wuːnd/ *countable noun* 可数名词
damage to part of your body caused by a gun or something sharp like a knife（枪炮或利器造成的）伤，伤口: *The wound is healing nicely.* 伤口愈合得很好。 ● **wound** *verb* 动词 (**wounds, wounding, wounded**): *He killed one man with a knife and wounded five other people.* 他持刀杀死 1

人，刺伤 5 人。

> **LANGUAGE HELP 语言提示**
> **Injured** or **wounded**? 用 injured 还是 wounded？
> When someone is hurt accidentally, for example in a car accident, or when they are playing sport, you say that they **are injured**. 表示在车祸、运动等中意外受伤，用 be injured: *A man was injured in the explosion.* 一名男子在爆炸中受伤。
> **Wounded** is normally used for talking about soldiers who are injured in battle, or someone who has been physically attacked. *wounded 一般用于表示士兵在战斗中负伤，或某人遭殴打致伤: *a wounded soldier* 伤兵

wove /wəʊv/
→ see 见 **weave**

woven /ˈwəʊvən/
→ see 见 **weave**

wow /waʊ/ *exclamation* 感叹词
used for saying that you think something is very good or surprising (*informal* 非正式)（表示惊奇和高兴）哇，呀: *I thought, 'Wow, what a good idea.'* 我想: "哇，真是个好主意。"

wrap /ræp/ *verb* 动词 (**wraps, wrapping, wrapped**)
1 (also 亦作 **wrap something up**) to fold paper or cloth tightly around something to cover it 包; 裹: *Diana is wrapping up the presents.* 黛安娜正在包装礼物。
2 to put something such as a piece of paper or cloth around another thing 用…缠绕（或围紧）: *She wrapped a cloth around her hand.* 她用一块布缠住手。

wrapper /ˈræpə/ *countable noun* 可数名词
a piece of paper or plastic that covers something that you buy, especially food（尤指食品的）包装纸，包装塑料: *There were sweet wrappers on the floor.* 地板上有糖纸。

wrapping paper *uncountable noun* 不可数名词
special paper that is used for covering presents（礼品的）包装纸

wreck¹ /rek/ *verb* 动词 (**wrecks, wrecking, wrecked**)
to completely destroy or ruin something 毁坏; 破坏; 损坏: *The storm wrecked the garden.* 风暴毁坏了花园。

wreck² /rek/ *countable noun* 可数名词
something such as a ship, a car, a plane or a building that has been destroyed, usually in an accident（通常指事故中）严重受损的船（或汽车、飞机、建筑物等）: *The car was a total wreck.* 这辆车完全报废了。

wrestle /ˈresəl/ *verb* 动词 (**wrestles, wrestling, wrestled**)
to fight someone by trying to throw them to the ground. Some people wrestle as a sport. 摔跤: *My father taught me to wrestle.* 父亲教我摔跤。

wriggle /ˈrɪgəl/ *verb* 动词 (**wriggles, wriggling, wriggled**)
to twist and turn your body, or part of your body, with quick movements 扭动（身体或身体部位）: *She pulled off her socks and wriggled her toes.* 她扯下袜子，扭动起脚趾。

wrinkle¹ /ˈrɪŋkəl/ *countable noun* 可数名词
one of the lines that form on your face as you grow old（脸上的）皱纹

wrinkle² /ˈrɪŋkəl/ *verb* 动词 (**wrinkles, wrinkling, wrinkled**)
to develop folds or lines 起褶皱: *Her stockings wrinkled at the ankles.* 她长袜的脚踝处起了褶皱。
▶ **wrinkled** /ˈrɪŋkəld/ *adjective* 形容词: *His suit was wrinkled and he looked very tired.* 他的西装皱巴巴的，人看上去很疲倦。

wrist /rɪst/ *countable noun* 可数名词
the part between your hand and your arm that bends when you move your hand 手腕: *She fell over and broke her wrist.* 她跌倒摔断了手腕。
→ Look at picture on P4 参见彩插第 4 页

write /raɪt/ *verb* 动词 (**writes, writing, wrote, written**)
1 to use a pen or a pencil to produce words, letters or numbers 写；书写: *Write your name and address on a postcard and send it to us.* 把你的名字和地址写在明信片上寄给我们。 □ *I'm teaching her to read and write.* 我在教她读书写字。
2 to create something such as a book, a poem or a piece of music 写（书、诗歌等）;作（曲）: *She wrote articles for French newspapers.* 她为法国报纸写文章。
3 to give someone information, ask them something or express your feelings in a letter or an email（给…）写信；写（信）: *She wrote to her aunt asking for help.* 她写信向姑妈求助。 □ *I wrote a letter to the manager.* 我给经理写了一封信。
write something down to record something on a piece of paper using a pen or a pencil 写下某事物；记下某事物: *He took out a small notebook and wrote down the number.* 他掏出一个小笔记本，写下了号码。

writer /ˈraɪtə/ *countable noun* 可数名词
a person whose job is to write books, stories or articles 作家: *She enjoys reading detective stories by American writers.* 她喜欢读美国作家写的侦探小说。

writing /ˈraɪtɪŋ/ *uncountable noun* 不可数名词
1 something that has been written or printed（书写或印刷的）文字: *Joe tried to read the writing on the next page.* 乔试着读下一页上的文字。
2 used for describing any piece of written work, especially when you are considering the style of language used in it 著作；文字作品；文章: *The writing is very funny.* 这篇文章很有趣。
3 the activity of writing, especially of writing books for money（尤指专职）写作: *She was a little bored with novel writing.* 她有些厌倦了写小说。
→ Look at picture on P3 参见彩插第 3 页
4 the way that you write with a pen or a pencil 笔迹；字迹；书法: *It's difficult to read your writing.* 你的字迹很难认。

written /ˈrɪtən/
→ see 见 **write**

wrong¹ /rɒŋ/ *adjective* 形容词
1 not as it should be 有毛病的；不正常的: *Pain is the body's way of telling us that something is wrong.* 疼痛是身体在告诉我们出了问题。 □ *What's wrong with him?* 他怎么了？
2 chosen by mistake 选错的: *He went to the wrong house.* 他走错了门。
3 not the best or most suitable 不是最好的；并非最合适的: *I made the wrong decision.* 我做了一个错误的决定。
4 not correct 错误的；不对的；不正确的: *I did not know if Mark's answer was right or wrong.* 我不知道马克的回答是对还是错。
● **wrong** *adverb* 副词: *I must have added it up wrong.* 我一定是加错了。
▶ **wrongly** /ˈrɒŋli/ *adverb* 副词: *He is an innocent man who was wrongly accused of*

stealing. 他是一个无辜的人，被冤枉盗窃。
5 bad 坏的；不正当的：*She was wrong to leave her child alone.* 她不该把孩子单独留下。
go wrong to stop progressing, and become worse 出问题；出毛病：*We will do everything to make sure that nothing goes wrong.* 我们将尽一切努力确保一切顺利。

wrong² /rɒŋ/ *uncountable noun* 不可数名词 activities or actions that are considered to be morally bad 恶；坏事；错误：*He can't tell the difference between right and wrong.* 他分不清是非。

wrote /rəʊt/
→ see 见 **write**

WWW /ˌdʌbljuː dʌbljuː ˈdʌbljuː/ short for (缩写 =) **World Wide Web**. It appears at the beginning of website addresses in the form www. 万维网（用于网址开头时写作 www）

Xmas /'eksməs, 'krɪsməs/ *noun* 名词 (**Xmases**)
short for (缩写 =) **Christmas**

X-ray¹ /'eks ˌreɪ/ also 亦作 **x-ray** *countable noun* 可数名词
a picture of the inside of someone's body that is made by using a special type of light *X 光片: *She had a chest X-ray at the hospital.* 她在医院拍了一张胸部 X 光片。

X-ray² /'eks ˌreɪ/ *verb* 动词 (**X-rays, X-raying, X-rayed**) also 亦作 **x-ray**
to take an X-ray picture of someone or something 给⋯拍摄 X 光片；对⋯进行 X 光检查: *All hand luggage must be x-rayed.* 所有手提行李都要接受 X 光检查。

xylophone /'zaɪləˌfəʊn/ *countable noun* 可数名词
a musical instrument with a row of wooden bars of different lengths that you play with special hammers 木琴
→ Look at picture on P12 参见彩插第 12 页

xylophone 木琴

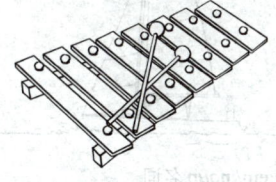

Yy

yacht /jɒt/ *countable noun* 可数名词
a large boat with sails or a motor, used for racing or for pleasure trips 帆船；游艇

yacht 帆船

yam /jæm/ *noun* 名词
a vegetable that is similar to a sweet potato 薯蓣；山药：*Peel and boil the yams, and then mash them.* 将山药去皮煮一下，然后捣成泥。

yank /jæŋk/ *verb* 动词 (**yanks, yanking, yanked**)
to pull someone or something hard 猛拉；猛拽：*She yanked open the drawer.* 她猛地拉开了抽屉。

yard /jɑːd/ *countable noun* 可数名词
1 a unit for measuring length. There are around 91.4 centimetres in a yard. 码（长度单位，1 码 ≈ 91.4 厘米）：*The bomb exploded 500 yards from where he was standing.* 炸弹在距离他所站位置 500 码的地方爆炸了。
2 (*American* 美国英语) a garden next to a house 院子；庭院

yarn /jɑːn/ *uncountable noun* 不可数名词
thick cotton or wool thread 纱；纱线；毛线：*She brought me a bag of yarn and some knitting needles.* 她给我带来了一包毛线和几根编织针。

yawn /jɔːn/ *verb* 动词 (**yawns, yawning, yawned**)
to open your mouth very wide and breathe in more air than usual because you are tired 打哈欠：*She yawned, and stretched lazily.* 她打了个哈欠，伸了个懒腰。● **yawn** *countable noun* 可数名词：*Sophia woke and gave a huge yawn.* 索菲娅醒过来，打了个大哈欠。

yeah /jeə/
yes (*informal* 非正式) 是；好；对：*'Don't forget your library book.' — 'Oh, yeah.'* "不要忘了你图书馆的书。" —— "嗯，好。" □ *'Anybody want my ice cream?' — 'Um, yeah, sure.'* "有人想吃我的冰激凌吗？" —— "嗯，有，当然了。"

year /jɪə/ *noun* 名词
1 *countable* 可数 a period of twelve months, beginning on the first of January and ending on the thirty-first of December 年：*The year was 1840.* 那年是 1840 年。 □ *We had an election last year.* 去年我们举行了一次选举。
2 *countable* 可数 any period of twelve months 一年时间：*The castle has more than 650,000 visitors a year.* 这座城堡一年的游客量超过 65 万人次。
3 *countable* 可数 the period of time in the year when schools or universities are open 学年：*the last academic year* 上一学年
4 [**years**] *plural* 复数 used for talking about a long time 很久；很长时间：*I lived here years ago.* 我很久以前住在这儿。
all year round for the whole year 一年到头；终年：*The hotel is open all year round.* 这家酒店终年营业。

yearly /ˈjɪəli/ *adjective* 形容词, *adverb* 副词
happening once a year or every year 一年一度（的）；每年（的）：*The company dinner is a yearly event.* 公司晚宴是一年一度的活动。 □ *Students may pay fees yearly or each term.* 学生可以按年或者按学期交学费。

yeast /jiːst/ *uncountable noun* 不可数名词
the substance that makes bread rise 酵母；酵母菌：*Add the yeast to the flour in the bowl.* 给盆里的面粉加上酵母。

yell /jel/ *verb* 动词 (**yells, yelling, yelled**)
to shout loudly 大喊；吼叫：*'Eva!' he yelled.* "伊娃！" 他大喊道。● **yell** *countable noun*

可数名词: *I heard a yell and the sound of something falling.* 我听到一声叫喊和东西坠落的声音。

yellow /ˈjeləʊ/ *adjective* 形容词
of the colour of lemons or butter 黄色的: *She was wearing a yellow dress.* 她穿着一条黄色连衣裙。● **yellow** *noun* 名词: *Her favourite colour is yellow.* 她最喜欢的颜色是黄色。
→ Look at picture on P13 参见彩插第 13 页

Yellow ˈPages *uncountable noun* 不可数名词
a book that has the telephone numbers for businesses and organizations in a particular area (*trademark* 商标) 黄页（企业机构电话号码簿）: *I looked for a plumber in the Yellow Pages.* 我在黄页上找一个管工。

yes /jes/
1 used for giving a positive answer to a question（用于肯定回答）是的, 对: *'Are you a friend of Nick's?' — 'Yes.'* "你是尼克的朋友吗？"——"是的。"
2 used for accepting an offer or a request, or for giving permission（用于接受提议、请求或表示许可）可以, 好的: *'More coffee?' — 'Yes please.'* "再来点儿咖啡？"——"好的，麻烦了。" □ *'Could you help me, please?' — 'Yes, of course.'* "请问您能帮帮我吗？"——"好的，当然。" □ *'Can I borrow your pen?' — 'Yes, of course.'* "我能借一下你的钢笔吗？"——"当然可以。"

yesterday /ˈjestədeɪ, -di/ *adverb* 副词
used for talking about the day before today 昨天: *She left yesterday.* 她昨天走了。● **yesterday** *uncountable noun* 不可数名词: *In yesterday's game, the Cowboys were the winners.* 在昨天的比赛中，牛仔队获胜了。

yet¹ /jet/ *adverb* 副词
1 used when something has not happened up to the present time, although it probably will happen（用于否定句中表示某事尚未发生，但有可能发生）尚, 还, 仍: *They haven't finished yet.* 他们还没有完成。□ *They haven't yet set a date for their wedding.* 他们还没有定下婚礼的日期。
2 used in questions to ask if something has happened before the present time（在疑问句中用来询问某事是否已发生）: *Have they finished yet?* 他们完成了吗？
3 not now, but at a later time（用于否定，表示现在尚不能做某事）: *Don't get up yet.* 先别起来。□ *You can't go home yet.* 你还不能回家。

yet² /jet/ *conjunction* 连词
but 但是; 可是: *He's a champion tennis player yet he is very modest.* 他是网球冠军，但是为人很谦虚。

yield /jiːld/ *verb* 动词 (**yields, yielding, yielded**)
1 to produce crops, fruit or vegetables 出产（作物或果蔬）: *Each tree yields about 20 kilos of apples.* 每棵树结约 20 千克苹果。
2 to finally agree to do what someone wants you to do 屈服; 屈从; 让步: *Finally, he yielded to his parents' demands.* 最后，他屈从了父母的要求。

yoga /ˈjəʊɡə/ *uncountable noun* 不可数名词
a type of exercise in which you move your body into various positions in order to become more fit, and to relax your body and your mind 瑜伽: *I do yoga twice a week.* 我一周做两次瑜伽。

yogurt /ˈjɒɡət/ also 亦作 **yoghurt** *noun* 名词
a thick, liquid food that is made from milk 酸奶: *Frozen yogurt is £2 per cup.* 冻酸奶每杯 2 英镑。

yolk /jəʊk/ *noun* 名词
the yellow part in the middle of an egg 蛋黄

you /juː/ *pronoun* 代词
1 the person or people that you are talking to or writing to 你; 您; 你们: *Hurry up! You are really late.* 快点儿！你真的迟到了。□ *I'll call you tonight.* 我今晚给你打电话。
2 any person; people in general（泛指）人, 任何人: *Getting good results gives you confidence.* 取得好成绩给人以信心。□ *In those days you did what you were told.* 那时候，你只是听命于人。

you'd /juːd/
1 short for（缩写 =）'you had'
2 short for（缩写 =）'you would'

you'll /juːl/
short for（缩写 =）'you will'

young¹ /jʌŋ/ *adjective* 形容词 (**younger** /ˈjʌŋɡə/, **youngest** /ˈjʌŋɡɪst/)
not having lived for very long 幼小的; 年轻的; 年幼的: *There is plenty of information on this for young people.* 对于年轻人来说，这方面的信息很多。□ *a field of young corn* 一片玉米苗田

young² /jʌŋ/ *plural noun* 复数名词
an animal's babies 幼崽; 幼兽; 幼禽: *You*

can watch birds feed their young with this wireless camera. 你可以用这台无线摄像机观察鸟儿给雏鸟喂食。

the young people who are young 年轻人；青年人：*Everyone from the young to the young at heart can enjoy yoga.* 年轻人和内心年轻的人都可以享受瑜伽。

youngster /ˈjʌŋstə/ *countable noun* 可数名词

a young person, especially a child 年轻人；（尤指）儿童，少年：*The children's club will keep the youngsters occupied.* 儿童俱乐部会让孩子们有事儿干。

your /jɔː/ *adjective* 形容词
1 belonging to or relating to the person or people that you are talking or writing to 你的；您的；你们的：*Are you taller than your brother?* 你比你弟弟高吗？ □ *I left your newspaper on your desk.* 我把你的报纸放到你桌上了。
2 belonging to or relating to people in general（泛指）人的，任何人的：*You should always wash your hands after touching raw meat.* 碰过生肉之务必洗手。

you're /jɔː/
short for (缩写 =) 'you are'

yours /jɔːz/ *pronoun* 代词
something that belongs or relates to the person or people that you are talking to 你的；您的；你们的：*I believe Paul is a friend of yours.* 我认为保罗是你的朋友。
Yours or **Yours sincerely** or **Yours faithfully** (*American* 美国英语：**Yours truly**) written at the end of a letter before you sign your name（用于书信末尾签名前）你的，您诚挚的，您忠实的：*I hope to see you soon. Yours, George.* 我希望早日见到你。你的，乔治。

yourself /jɔːˈself/ *pronoun* 代词
(**yourselves** /jɔːˈselvz/)
1 the person that you are talking or writing to（指谈话或写信的对象）你自己，您自己，你们自己：*Be careful with that knife — you might cut yourself.* 小心那把刀——你有可能切到自己。
2 used for making 'you' stronger（用于加强语气）你自己，你本人，你们自己：*You don't know anything about it — you said so yourself.* 你什么都不知道——你自己这么说的。
3 done by you, and not by anyone else 你独自；你一个人：*Don't do all of that yourself — let me help you.* 不要自己全做了——让我帮帮你。

youth /juːθ/ *noun* 名词 (**youths** /juːðz/)
1 *uncountable* 不可数 the period of someone's life when they are a child, before they become an adult 青年时期；青少年时期：*In my youth, my ambition was to be a dancer.* 我青年时期的志向是成为一名舞蹈家。
2 *uncountable* 不可数 the quality or state of being young 青春；朝气；年轻：*Youth is not an excuse for bad behaviour.* 年轻不是行为不轨的借口。
3 *countable* 可数 a young man 青年；小伙子：*A 17-year-old youth was arrested yesterday.* 昨天一个 17 岁的青年被捕了。
the youth young people when they are considered as a group（统称）青年，年轻人：*The youth of today are just as caring as we were.* 如今的年轻人和我们当年一样有爱心。

you've /juːv/
short for (缩写 =) 'you have'

yo-yo /ˈjəʊjəʊ/ *countable noun* 可数名词   yo-yo 悠悠球
a round wooden or plastic toy that you hold in your hand. You make it go up and down on a piece of string. 悠悠球

Zz

zebra /ˈzebrə, ˈziː-/ *countable noun* 可数名词 (**zebras** or 或 **zebra**)
a wild horse with black and white stripes that lives in Africa 斑马

ˌzebra ˈcrossing *countable noun* 可数名词
a place on the road that is painted with black and white lines, where vehicles should stop so that people can cross the road safely 斑马线

zero /ˈzɪərəʊ/ *uncountable noun* 不可数名词
1 the number 0 零
2 the temperature of 0°C, at which water freezes(气温的)零摄氏度: *a few degrees above zero* 零上几度

zigzag /ˈzɪgzæg/ also 亦作 **zig-zag** *countable noun* 可数名词
a line that has angles in it like a lot of Ws 之字线；Z 字线

zinc /zɪŋk/ *uncountable noun* 不可数名词
a blue-white metal 锌

zip¹ /zɪp/ *countable noun* 可数名词
a long metal or plastic object with two rows of teeth that join together, and a small part that you pull in order to open and close clothes or bags 拉链；拉锁

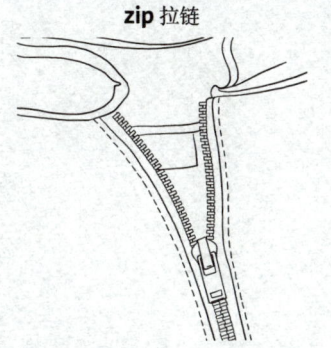

zip 拉链

zip² /zɪp/ *verb* 动词 (**zips, zipping, zipped**)
to use a special program to reduce the size of a computer file so that it is easier to send it to someone using the Internet 压缩(计算机文档): *This is how to zip files so that you can send them via email.* 这便是如何压缩文件，压缩后就可以通过电子邮件发送了。

zip something up to fasten something such as a piece of clothing using its zip 拉上某物的拉链: *He zipped up his jeans.* 他拉上牛仔裤的拉链。

ˈzip ˌcode *countable noun* 可数名词 (*American* 美国英语)
→ see 见 **postcode**

zone /zəʊn/ *countable noun* 可数名词
an area where something particular happens(发生特定事件的)地带，地区: *The area is a disaster zone.* 这个地区是灾区。

zoo /zuː/ *countable noun* 可数名词
a park where animals are kept and people can go to look at them 动物园: *He took his son to the zoo.* 他带着儿子去了动物园。

zoom /zuːm/ *verb* 动词 (**zooms, zooming, zoomed**)
to go somewhere very quickly (*informal* 非正式)疾行；快速移动: *Lorries zoomed past at 70 miles per hour.* 卡车以 70 英里的时速疾驰而过。

zucchini /zuːˈkiːni/ *noun* 名词 (**zucchini** or 或 **zucchinis**) (*American* 美国英语)
→ see 见 **courgette**

Reference Pages
附录

Irregular verbs 不规则动词

Infinitive 不定式	Past Tense 过去式	Past Participle 过去分词	Infinitive 不定式	Past Tense 过去式	Past Participle 过去分词
arise	arose	arisen	feel	felt	felt
be	was, were	been	fight	fought	fought
beat	beat	beaten	find	found	found
become	became	become	fly	flew	flown
begin	began	begun	forbid	forbade	forbidden
bend	bent	bent	forget	forgot	forgotten
bet	bet	bet	freeze	froze	frozen
bind	bound	bound	get	got	got or gotten
bite	bit	bitten			
bleed	bled	bled	give	gave	given
blow	blew	blown	go	went	gone
break	broke	broken	grind	ground	ground
bring	brought	brought	grow	grew	grown
build	built	built	hang	hung or hanged	hung or hanged
burn	burned or burnt	burned or burnt			
burst	burst	burst	have	had	had
buy	bought	bought	hear	heard	heard
catch	caught	caught	hide	hid	hidden
choose	chose	chosen	hit	hit	hit
cling	clung	clung	hold	held	held
come	came	come	hurt	hurt	hurt
cost	cost	cost	keep	kept	kept
creep	crept	crept	kneel	kneeled or knelt	kneeled or knelt
cut	cut	cut			
deal	dealt	dealt	know	knew	known
dig	dug	dug	lay	laid	laid
dive	dived	dived	lead	led	led
do	did	done	lean	leaned or leant	leaned or leant
draw	drew	drawn			
dream	dreamed or dreamt	dreamed or dreamt	leap	leaped or leapt	leaped or leapt
			learn	learned or learnt	learned or learnt
drink	drank	drunk			
drive	drove	driven	leave	left	left
eat	ate	eaten	lend	lent	lent
fall	fell	fallen	let	let	let
feed	fed	fed	lie	lay	lain

Infinitive 不定式	Past Tense 过去式	Past Participle 过去分词	Infinitive 不定式	Past Tense 过去式	Past Participle 过去分词
light	lit *or* lighted	lit *or* lighted	speed	sped *or* speeded	sped *or* speeded
lose	lost	lost	spell	spelled *or* spelt	spelled *or* spelt
make	made	made	spend	spent	spent
mean	meant	meant	spill	spilled *or* spilt	spilled *or* spilt
meet	met	met	spit	spat	spat
pay	paid	paid	spoil	spoiled *or* spoilt	spoiled *or* spoilt
put	put	put	spread	spread	spread
quit	quit	quit	spring	sprang	sprung
read	read	read	stand	stood	stood
ride	rode	ridden	steal	stole	stolen
ring	rang	rung	stick	stuck	stuck
rise	rose	risen	sting	stung	stung
run	ran	run	stink	stank	stunk
say	said	said	strike	struck	struck
see	saw	seen	swear	swore	sworn
seek	sought	sought	sweep	swept	swept
sell	sold	sold	swell	swelled	swollen
send	sent	sent	swim	swam	swum
set	set	set	swing	swung	swung
shake	shook	shaken	take	took	taken
shine	shone	shone	teach	taught	taught
shoot	shot	shot	tear	tore	torn
show	showed	shown	tell	told	told
shrink	shrank	shrunk	think	thought	thought
shut	shut	shut	throw	threw	thrown
sing	sang	sung	wake	woke	woken
sink	sank	sunk	wear	wore	worn
sit	sat	sat	weep	wept	wept
sleep	slept	slept	win	won	won
slide	slid	slid	wind	wound	wound
smell	smelled *or* smelt	smelled *or* smelt	write	wrote	written
speak	spoke	spoken			

Key words 重点词汇

Here is a list of the 1,544 most common and useful words you need to know. 以下为 1,544 个必须掌握的最常用、最有用的词语。

a, an	airport	as	begin	budget
ability	album	ask	behaviour	build
able	all	aspect	behind	building
about	allow	asset	believe	burn
above	all right	association	below	business
absolutely	almost	assume	benefit	but
abuse	alone	at	best	buy
accept	along	attack	better	by
according to	already	attempt	between	cabinet
account	also	attend	beyond	call
accuse	alternative	attention	bid	camera
achieve	although	attitude	big	camp
across	always	attract	bill	campaign
act	among	audience	billion	can
action	amount	August	bird	cancer
active	and	aunt	bit	capital
activity	animal	author	bite	captain
actually	announce	authority	black	car
add	annual	available	blame	card
addition	another	average	block	care
address	answer	avoid	blood	career
admit	any	award	blow	careful
adopt	anyone	aware	blue	carry
adult	anything	away	board	case
advance	anyway	baby	boat	cash
advantage	apart	back	body	catch
advice	apparently	bad	bomb	cause
affair	appeal	bag	bond	cell
affect	appear	balance	book	central
after	appearance	ball	border	centre
afternoon	apply	ban	born	century
again	approach	band	boss	certainly
against	approve	bank	both	chair
age	April	bar	bottle	challenge
agency	area	base	bottom	chance
agent	aren't	basic	box	change
ago	argue	basis	boy	channel
agree	argument	battle	brain	charge
agreement	arm	be	break	cheap
ahead	army	bear	bridge	check
aid	around	beat	brief	chemical
AIDS	arrest	beautiful	bright	chief
aim	arrive	because	bring	child
air	art	become	broad	choice
aircraft	artichoke	bed	brother	choose
airline	artist	before	brown	church

circle	cost	depend	dry	evening
city	could	describe	due	event
claim	count	design	during	eventually
class	country	desire	duty	ever
clean	couple	desk	each	every
clear	course	despite	early	everybody
close	court	destroy	earn	everyone
clothes	cousin	detail	earth	everything
club	cover	determine	east	evidence
coach	crash	develop	eastern	exact
coast	cream	development	easy	examine
coffee	create	didn't	eat	example
cold	credit	die	economic	excellent
collapse	crime	diet	economy	except
colleague	criminal	difference	edge	exchange
collect	crisis	different	editor	exercise
collection	criticism	difficult	education	exist
college	cross	difficulty	effect	expect
colour	crowd	digital	effective	expensive
come	cry	dinner	effort	experience
comment	culture	direct	egg	expert
commercial	cup	direction	eight	explain
commit	customer	director	eighteen	express
commitment	cut	discover	eighth	extra
committee	daily	discuss	eighty	eye
common	damage	discussion	either	face
community	dance	disease	elect	fact
company	danger	dispute	election	factor
competition	dangerous	distance	eleven	factory
complain	dark	district	else	fail
complete	data	divide	email	failure
complex	date	division	emerge	fair
computer	daughter	do	emergency	fall
concerned	day	doctor	employee	family
condition	dead	document	encourage	famous
conduct	death	doesn't	end	fan
conference	debt	dog	energy	far
confidence	decade	dollar	engine	farmer
confident	December	door	English	fashion
confirm	decide	double	enjoy	fast
conflict	decision	doubt	enough	fat
consider	declare	down	ensure	father
constant	decline	dozen	enter	favour
contact	deep	Dr	entire	favourite
contain	defeat	dramatic	entry	fear
continue	defence	draw	environment	feature
contract	defend	dream	equipment	February
control	degree	dress	escape	fee
cook	delay	drink	especially	feed
cool	deliver	drive	establish	feel
copy	demand	driver	estimate	feeling
corner	deny	drop	European	female
correct	department	drug	even	festival

few	from	hardly	in	justice	
field	front	have	incident	keep	
fifteen	fruit	he	include	key	
fifth	fuel	head	including	kick	
fifty	full	health	income	kid	
fight	fully	health care	increase	kill	
figure	fun	hear	increasingly	kind	
file	function	heart	indeed	king	
fill	fund	heat	independent	kitchen	
film	future	heavy	indicate	know	
final	gain	help	individual	knowledge	
finally	game	her	industrial	lack	
financial	garden	here	industry	lady	
find	gas	herself	inflation	land	
fine	gather	high	influence	language	
finger	general	highly	information	large	
finish	generally	him	injury	largely	
fire	generation	himself	inside	last	
firm	get	his	insist	late	
first	girl	history	instance	later	
fish	give	hit	instead	latest	
fit	glass	hold	institution	laugh	
five	glasses	hole	insurance	launch	
flat	go	holiday	intend	law	
flight	goal	home	interest	lawyer	
floor	god	hope	interested	lay	
flow	going	horse	international	lead	
flower	gold	hospital	internet	leader	
fly	gone	host	interview	leadership	
focus	good	hot	into	leading	
follow	goods	hotel	introduce	learn	
following	government	hour	investigate	least	
food	grand	house	investment	leave	
foot	great	how	invite	leg	
football	green	however	involve	legal	
for	ground	huge	involved	length	
force	group	human	island	less	
foreign	grow	hundred	issue	let	
forget	growth	hurt	it	letter	
form	guard	husband	I.T.	level	
formal	guess	I	item	liberal	
former	guest	ice	its	lie	
forty	guide	idea	itself	life	
forwards	gun	identify	January	lift	
four	guy	if	job	light	
fourteen	hair	ignore	join	like	
fourth	half	ill	joint	likely	
free	hand	image	journalist	limit	
freedom	handle	imagine	judge	line	
frequent	hang	impact	July	link	
fresh	happen	important	jump	list	
Friday	happy	impossible	June	listen	
friend	hard	improve	just	little	

live	military	new	operate	physical
loan	million	news	operation	pick
local	mind	newspaper	opinion	picture
long	mine	next	opportunity	piece
look	minority	nice	option	pink
lose	minute	night	or	place
loss	miss	nine	orange	plan
lot	Miss	nineteen	order	plane
love	mission	ninety	organization	plant
low	mistake	ninth	organize	play
lunch	mix	no	original	player
machine	model	nobody	other	please
magazine	modern	none	otherwise	plus
main	moment	no one	our	point
mainly	Monday	nor	out	police
maintain	money	normal	outside	policy
major	month	north	over	political
majority	more	north-east	own	politician
make	morning	north-west	owner	politics
male	most	not	pack	poor
man	mother	note	package	popular
manage	motor	nothing	page	population
management	mountain	notice	pain	position
manager	mouth	novel	paint	positive
many	move	November	painting	possibility
March	movement	now	pair	possible
mark	movie	nuclear	paper	possibly
market	MP	number	parent	post
marriage	Mr	object	park	potential
marry	Mrs	obvious	part	pound
match	Ms	obviously	particular	power
material	much	occasion	particularly	powerful
matter	mum	occupy	partner	practice
may	murder	occur	party	practise
May	museum	October	pass	prefer
maybe	music	odd	past	prepare
me	must	of course	patient	prepared
mean	my	off	pattern	presence
means	myself	offer	pay	present
meanwhile	name	office	payment	president
measure	narrow	officer	peace	press
media	national	official	people	pressure
medical	natural	often	per cent	pretty
meet	nature	oh	perfect	prevent
meeting	near	oil	perform	previous
member	nearly	okay	performance	price
memory	necessary	old	perhaps	prime minister
mention	need	on	period	prince
message	neighbour-	once	person	princess
method	hood	one	personal	principle
middle	neither	online	phone	print
might	network	only	photo	prison
mile	never	open	photograph	prisoner

7

private	real	rich	sentence	slightly
prize	reality	ride	separate	slip
probably	realize	right	September	slow
problem	really	ring	series	small
process	reason	rise	serious	smile
produce	recall	risk	serve	smoke
product	receive	rival	service	so
production	recent	river	set	social
professional	recently	road	settle	society
professor	recognize	rock	seven	soft
profit	recommend	role	seventeen	soldier
program	record	roll	seventh	solution
programme	red	room	seventy	some
progress	reduce	round	several	somebody
project	refer	route	severe	someone
promise	reflect	royal	shake	something
promote	reform	rule	shall	sometimes
property	refugee	run	shape	son
proposal	refuse	sad	share	song
propose	regard	safe	sharp	soon
protect	region	safety	she	sorry
protection	regular	sale	ship	sort
protest	reject	same	shock	sound
prove	relation	Saturday	shoot	source
provide	relationship	save	shop	south
public	release	say	short	south-east
publish	relief	scale	shot	south-west
pull	religious	scales	should	space
purchase	remain	scene	shoulder	speak
purple	remember	schedule	show	special
purpose	remove	scheme	side	specific
push	repeat	school	sight	speech
put	replace	science	sign	speed
quality	reply	scientist	significant	spend
quarter	report	score	similar	spirit
queen	reporter	screen	simple	split
question	represent	sea	simply	sport
quick	request	search	since	spot
quiet	require	season	sing	spread
quite	research	seat	single	spring
race	reserve	second	sir	square
radio	resident	secret	sister	stable
rain	resource	secretary	sit	staff
raise	respect	section	site	stage
range	respond	secure	situation	stand
rapid	response	security	six	standard
rate	responsibility	see	sixteen	star
rather	responsible	seed	sixth	start
reach	rest	seem	sixty	state
reaction	restaurant	sell	size	statement
read	result	send	skill	station
reader	return	senior	skin	stay
ready	reveal	sense	sleep	step

stick	team	to	useful	while
still	tear	today	usual	white
stone	technique	together	usually	who
stop	technology	tomorrow	value	whole
store	telephone	tonight	variety	whom
storey	television	too	various	whose
story	tell	top	vehicle	why
straight	ten	total	version	wide
strange	tend	touch	very	wife
street	tenth	tough	victim	wild
strength	terrible	tour	victory	will
stress	test	towards	video	willing
strike	than	town	view	win
strong	thank	track	village	wind
structure	thanks	trade	violence	window
struggle	thank you	train	visit	wing
student	that	transport	voice	winner
study	the	travel	volume	wish
stuff	theatre	treat	vote	with
style	their	treatment	wait	within
subject	them	tree	walk	without
succeed	themselves	trial	wall	woman
success	then	trip	want	wonder
successful	theory	trouble	war	wonderful
such	there	true	warm	wood
suffer	therefore	trust	warn	word
suggest	these	truth	waste	work
suit	the Web	try	watch	world
summer	they	Tuesday	water	worry
sun	thing	turn	wave	worth
Sunday	think	TV	way	would
supply	third	twelfth	we	wound
support	thirteen	twelve	weak	write
suppose	thirty	twenty	weapon	writer
sure	this	twice	wear	writing
surface	those	two	weather	wrong
surprise	though	type	website	yard
surround	thought	uncle	Wednesday	year
survive	thousand	under	week	yellow
suspect	threat	understand	weekend	yes
system	threaten	unit	weight	yesterday
table	three	university	welcome	yet
take	through	unless	well	you
talk	throughout	unlikely	west	young
tape	throw	until	western	your
target	Thursday	up	what	yourself
task	ticket	upon	whatever	youth
taste	tie	us	when	
tax	tight	use	where	
tea	time	used	whether	
teach	title	used to	which	

Study vocabulary 学科词汇

Technology 技术

account
address
address book
analogue
app
application
artificial
    intelligence
attachment
back up
backup
bit
blog
blogosphere
Bluetooth
bookmark
boot
broadband
browse
browser
bug
bulletin board
byte
camera phone
CD
CD burner
CD player
CD-ROM
chat
chat room
click
code
command
compact disc
computer
corrupt
crash
cursor
cut and paste
cyberbully
cyberspace
data
database
delete
desktop
dialogue box
digital
disk
disk drive
document
domain name
double-click
down
download
downloadable
drag and drop
drop-down menu
DVD
DVD burner
DVD player
e-book
email
emoji
FAQ
file
filename
file-sharing
flash drive
folder
follow
font
format
forward slash
game console
gigabyte
Google
graphics
hard disk
hard drive
hardware
HDTV
home page
HTML
hyperlink
icon
IM
inbox
information
    technology
instant messaging
internet
intranet
ISP
I.T.
KB
key
keyboard
keyword
kilobyte
laptop
laser printer
log
magnetic
mailbox
megabyte
memory
memory card
memory stick
menu
message board
microchip
mobile phone
modem
mouse
mouse mat
MP3
MP3 player
navigate
net
network
notebook
notification
offline
online
operating system
outbox
password
PC
PDF
plasma screen
podcast
post
profile
program
RAM
reboot
satellite
satellite dish
satellite television
satnav
save
scanner
screensaver
scroll
search engine
selfie
selfie stick
server
sidebar
site
Skype®
smart
smartphone
social media
social networking
software
spam
spreadsheet
stream
surf
swipe
tablet
taskbar
texting
text message
text messaging
unfollow
unfriend
unzip
upload
URL
USB
USB stick
username
video
virtual
virus
vlog
the Web
webcam
web page
website
window
Word document
World Wide Web
WWW
zip

Geography 地理

altitude

atlas
avalanche
bay
beach
canal
canyon
cape
capital
channel
cliff
coast
coastline
compass
continent
country
desert
dune
earth
earthquake
east
easterly
eastern
equator
equatorial
estuary
forest
geography
globe
gulf
hemisphere
hill
island
lake
land
landform
latitude
longitude
map
marsh
mountain
mouth
north-east
northerly
north-west
oasis
ocean
peninsula
plateau
pole
port
rainforest
region
reservoir

ridge
river
satnav
scale
shore
south
south-east
southerly
south-west
stream
time zone
tropical
valley
village
volcano
waterfall
wave
west
westerly
western
world

Language 语言

abbreviation
accent
acknowledgments
active
acute accent
adjective
adverb
alphabet
antonym
apostrophe
appendix
author
autobiography
auxiliary verb
biography
book
brackets
capital
chapter
character
clause
colon
comedy
comma
comparative
compound
conclusion
conditional
conjunction
consonant

continuous
contraction
countable noun
dash
definite article
definition
dialogue
dictionary
direct object
draft
drama
dramatist
e-book
emphasis
English
epic
epilogue
essay
exclamation
exclamation mark
fable
fairy tale
feminine
fiction
foreword
form
future tense
glossary
grammar
grammatical
hero
heroine
hyphen
idiom
imperative
indefinite article
index
indirect object
infinitive
intransitive
introduction
irony
irregular
journal
language
legend
letter
literature
lower case
main clause
manga
masculine
metaphor

modal
moral
mystery
myth
narrator
negative
nonfiction
noun
novel
novelist
object
paragraph
parody
participle
part of speech
passage
passive
past tense
perfect tense
period
phrasal verb
phrase
playwright
plot
plural
poem
poet
poetry
possessive
preface
prefix
preposition
present continuous
present perfect
present tense
prologue
pronoun
pronunciation
proper noun
prose
punctuation
punctuation marks
question mark
quotation
quotation mark
read
reader
reflexive pronoun
reflexive verb
regular
rhyme
romance
satire

scene	diameter	ml	time
script	digit	mm	triangle
semicolon	dimensions	mph	two
sentence	divide	multiply	unit
simile	division	negative	volume
singular	eight	nine	
slash	eighteen	nineteen	**Music 音乐**
speech marks	eighth	ninety	accompany
spell	eighty	ninth	accordion
story	equal	nought	band
stress	equals sign	number	banjo
subject	even	numeral	bass
summary	fifteen	oblong	bassoon
superlative	fifth	odd	baton
syllable	fifty	one	beat
symbol	figure	ounce	the blues
synonym	five	oz.	bow
tense	formula	parallel	brass
title	forty	pentagon	carol
tragedy	four	per cent	cello
upper case	fourteen	percentage	choir
verb	fourth	perimeter	chord
verse	fraction	plus	chorus
vocabulary	gallon	positive	clarinet
vowel	geometry	power	classical
word	gram	probability	compose
write	graph	protractor	composer
writer	half	pyramid	composition
writing	hemisphere	quarter	concert
	hexagon	radius	conduct
Maths 数学	hundred	ratio	conductor
acute angle	inch	rectangle	cymbal
add	kg	right angle	double bass
addition	kilo	ruler	drum
algebra	kilogram	second	duet
angle	kilometre	semicircle	duo
area	km	set square	flat
arithmetic	lb.	seven	flute
average	litre	seventh	folk music
axis	mathematical	seventy	French horn
calculate	mathematics	six	guitar
calculation	maths	sixth	guitarist
circle	mean	square	harmony
circumference	median	square root	harp
compasses	meter	subtract	hip-hop
cone	metric	sum	horn
cube	mg	ten	hymn
cubic	mile	tenth	instrument
cylinder	milligram	third	instrumental
decimal	millilitre	thirteen	jazz
decimal point	millimetre	thirty	key
degree	million	thousand	keyboard
diagonal	minus	three	lyrics

major
melody
minor
music
musical
musical instrument
musician
note
oboe
octave
opera
orchestra
organ
percussion
pianist
piano
piccolo
play
player
plectrum
quartet
rap
reggae
rhythm
rock and roll
saxophone
scale
sharp
sing
singer
solo
song
soul
soul music
string
stringed instrument
symphony
symphony
   orchestra
tambourine
trio
trombone
trumpet
tuba
tune
viola
violin
wind instrument
woodwind

Science 科学

abdomen
absorb
acid
air
air pollution
alkali
animal
antenna
antler
anus
appendix
artery
artichoke
astronaut
astronomy
atmosphere
atom
atomic
attract
axis
backbone
bacteria
bark
beam
biceps
big bang theory
biological
bladder
blood
blood vessel
boiling point
bone
botany
bowels
brain
breast
breathe
breed
bud
bulb
calorie
carbohydrate
carbon dioxide
carbon monoxide
carnivore
cave
cell
Celsius
centrifugal force
charge
chemical
chemist
chemistry
chest
cholesterol
chromosome
circuit
circulation
climate
climate change
coast
coastline
cocoon
collarbone
colon
comet
compound
conduct
conservation
core
crater
crystal
current
cycle
degree
dense
density
dental
desert
digest
dilute
dissect
dissolve
drug
eardrum
echo
eclipse
ecology
ecosystem
electric
electricity
element
embryo
endangered
   species
energy
environment
erupt
evaporate
evolution
experiment
extinct
eyeball
Fahrenheit
female
fertile
filter
foetus
food chain
force
formula
fossil
fossil fuel
freeze
frequency
fungus
galaxy
gas
gene
genetic
genetically
   modified
genetics
genus
geology
glacier
global warming
gravity
greenhouse effect
greenhouse gas
gum
habitat
hail
heart
heartbeat
herbivore
hibernation
hill
hormone
human being
humidity
hurricane
iceberg
insulate
invertebrate
iris
island
jaw
joint
kHz
kidney
kilohertz
kilowatt
kW
lab
laboratory
laser
lava
lens
life cycle
light
lightning

liquid	respiration	amendment	globalization
live	rib	ancestor	govern
liver	rib cage	archaeology	government
lung	ridge	assassinate	gross national
magnet	river	BC	product
male	rock	BCE	history
mammal	saliva	bill	holocaust
mass	sand	border	human rights
mate	scalp	boycott	ideal
melting point	skeleton	cabinet	immigrant
mercury	skin	capitalism	imperialism
meteor	sodium	capitalist	import
metric ton	soil	CE	independence
microbe	solar	cease-fire	industrial
microscope	solid	census	industry
milk	source	charter	king
mineral	spacecraft	citizen	kingdom
mix	spaceship	civilization	knight
molecule	space shuttle	civil rights	labour
monsoon	species	civil war	mayor
moon	specimen	classics	medieval
mountain	speed	Cold War	Middle Ages
mouth	spine	colony	middle class
muscle	star	communism	migrant
nature	stomach	communist	migrate
nostril	sun	conquer	monarchy
nuclear	test tube	constituency	monopoly
nucleus	thigh	constitution	monument
nutrient	throat	country	nation
omnivore	tide	crown	nationality
organ	tissue	culture	neutral
organic	tongue	currency	parliament
organism	tornado	delegate	pass
oxygen	tsunami	democracy	petition
the ozone layer	tumour	democrat	policy
pelvis	universe	democratic	political
photosynthesis	uterus	dictator	political party
physics	vacuum	discriminate	population
planet	vapour	discrimination	prejudice
plant	vertebrate	eastern	president
pollen	volt	economics	prime minister
power	watt	economist	propaganda
predator	wavelength	economy	queen
pressure	weather	elect	racism
prey	wind	election	rebellion
psychology	X-ray	emperor	reform
pulse	zero	empire	reign
radar	zinc	ethnic	representative
radiation		export	republic
radio wave	**History and**	feminism	revenue
rain	**Social Studies**	feminist	revolution
rainfall	历史与社会科学	general election	right
ray		global economy	ruler
reproduce	AD		

segregation
settlement
slave trade
socialism
sovereignty
state
suffragist
territory
timeline
totalitarian
treaty
veto
vote
western

Sport 体育

aerobics
athlete
backstroke
badminton
ball
baseball
basketball
bat
baton
batter
beat
bicycle
bike
box
boxing
breaststroke
captain
catch
champion
championship
cheerleader
climber
climbing
coach
course
court
crawl
cross
cycle
cyclist
darts
defence
defend
defender
discus
dive
diving board
draw
exercise
field
fielder
final
fishing
fishing rod
football
footballer
foul
game
goal
goalkeeper
goalpost
golf
golf club
golf course
gym
gymnasium
gymnastics
halftime
high jump
hockey
hockey stick
horse racing
horse riding
hurdles
ice hockey
javelin
jockey
jog
judo
karate
lap
league
long jump
marathon
match
mountain bike
opponent
paddle
penalty
physical education
play
player
race
racket
referee
relay
rider
riding
rink
row
rugby
run
runner
sail
sailing
save
score
semifinal
shoot
skate
skatepark
ski
soccer
sport
squash
stadium
stroke
surf
surfboard
swim
swimming
swimming costume
swimming pool
swimming trunks
table tennis
tackle
team
tennis
tie
tournament
track
train
umpire
versus
volleyball
vs.
win
windsurfing
wrestle
yoga

Art 美术

abstract
acrylic
acrylics
aesthetic
animation
art
art gallery
artist
background
canvas
carve
ceramic
ceramics
chalk
charcoal
clay
collage
culture
design
designer
draw
drawing
easel
exhibit
exhibition
fine art
foreground
gallery
graphics
landscape
manga
marble
media
medium
model
mosaic
multimedia
museum
nude
oil painting
paint
painter
painting
pastel
pattern
pencil
perspective
photograph
photography
picture
pottery
primary colour
proportion
sculptor
sculpture
sketch
statue
studio
subject
texture
theatre
three-dimensional
two-dimensional
watercolour

Classroom vocabulary 课堂语汇

Useful verbs 有用的动词

clear something **up** 整理；收拾
The children always clear up the classroom at the end of the day. 孩子们每天放学时都会打扫教室。

colour something **in** 给…上色
Colour the picture in with crayons. 用蜡笔给画儿涂色。

go over something 仔细查看
Let's go over the answers now. 咱们现在核对一下答案。

go through something 将…过一遍
Go through your work and check it carefully. 把作业过一遍，仔细检查下。

hand something **out** 分发
Can you hand out the books please? 请你发一下书好吗？

hand something **in** 提交
Hand in your homework on Tuesday. 周二交家庭作业。

jot something **down** 匆匆写下
Jot down your answers while you listen. 边听边快速写下答案。

look something **up** 查找；查阅
You can look your answers up in the back of the book. 可以翻到书后查对一下答案。

put something **away** 收起
Please put your things away now. 现在请把你们的东西收起来。

rub something **out** 用橡皮擦掉
Jenna rubbed her answer out and tried again. 詹娜擦掉答案又做了一遍。

take something **out** 取出
Take out your books. 拿出课本。

turn something **off** 关闭
Turn off the computer, please. 请关掉电脑。

turn something **on** 打开
Please turn on the lights. 请开灯。

write something **down** 写下
Write your answers down in the space. 在空白处作答。

Useful phrases 有用的短语

do your homework/an exercise/a sum/ a project 做家庭作业／练习／计算／项目
It is important to do your homework every week. 每周务必做家庭作业。

take/make notes 做笔记
You should take notes while you are listening. 你应该边听边做笔记。

take a test (= do it) / **pass** a test (= succeed in it) 参加／通过考试
The students all took the test, but only three of them passed it. 学生们都参加了考试，但只有3人通过。

work in pairs/groups/3s 结对／分组／3人一组练习
They were asked to work in groups of 4. 他们被要求4人一组练习。

Phrases you might hear 可能会听到的语句

Instructions & questions 指令与询问

Any questions? 有问题吗？
Can everyone see the board? 大家都能看到黑板吗？
Check your answers with a partner. 跟同伴对一下答案。
Come up to the front, please. 请到前面来。
Copy the sentence from the board. 抄写黑板上的句子。
Discuss your ideas with a partner. 跟同伴讨论一下自己的想法。
Do you understand? 听懂了吗？
Fill in the gaps in the text. 将文中空白处填写完整。
Find the answers in the text. 从文中寻找答案。

Give me an example. 给我举个例子。
Go back to your seat, please. 请回座位。
Listen to the recording. 听录音。
Look at the board/your book/page 10/me. 看黑板 / 看着书 / 看第 10 页 / 看着我。
Open your books at page 10, please. 请把书打开，翻到第 10 页。
Put the words in the right order. 将这些词语正确排序。
Read the instructions carefully. 认真阅读说明。
Read your answer out loud. 大声报出答案。
Swap your work with a partner. 跟同伴交换一下作业。
Turn to page 10, please. 请翻到第 10 页。
Write the questions into your book. 把这些问题记到书上。

In the gym 在体育馆

Cross your arms/legs. 交叉两臂 / 双腿。
Face your partner. 面向同伴。
Find a partner. 找个同伴。
Freeze! 别动！
Get into a line/a circle/pairs/groups/teams. 排成一队 / 围成一圈 / 两两一组 / 分成小组 / 分成队伍。
Hold hands. 手拉手。
Sit down. 坐下。
Stand up. 起立。
Turn round. 向后转。

Requests 要求

Face the front, please. 请面向前方。
Get on with your work, please. 请接着做作业。
I'm waiting for quiet. 我等你们安静下来。
Less chat, please. 请少聊天。
Look at the board, please. 请看黑板。
Pay attention, please. 请注意听讲。
Please be quiet. 请保持安静。
Please don't interrupt. 请不要插嘴。
Settle down now, please. 请马上安静下来。
Stop being silly, please. 请不要犯傻了。
Stop messing around, please. 请不要胡闹了。
Stop talking and listen now, please. 请马上停止说话，注意听讲。
Stop what you're doing and listen to me, please. 请停下来听我讲。

Feedback 反馈

Can you try again? 你能再试一下吗？
Go on. 来吧。
Good job! 干得好！
Have another think. 再想一下。
That's nearly right. 快对了。
That's not quite right. 不太对。
That's right. 对了。
Very good! 很好！
Well done! 太棒了！

Opinions 观点

Can you explain that? 你能解释一下吗？
Can you think of a reason for that? 你觉得那是为什么呢？
Do you agree? 你同意吗？
What do you think? 你觉得呢？
Why do you think that is? 你觉得那是为什么呢？

At the end of the lesson 快下课时

Clean the board. 擦一下黑板。
Collect your jackets. 带上你们的夹克衫。
Hand in your books, please. 请把书交上来。
Have a good weekend/holiday! 周末 / 假期愉快！
Log off, please. 请注销计算机。
Push your chairs in (= put your chairs under the table). 把椅子推到桌子下面。
Put your chairs up (= put your chairs on the table). 把椅子放到桌子上。
Put your rubbish in the bin. 把垃圾放到垃圾桶里。
Put/Tidy your things away now, please. 请马上收拾好自己的物品。
See you tomorrow/on Monday/after the holidays! 明天 / 下周一 / 假期后见！

Phrases you might use 可能会用到的语句

Asking for help 求助

Can you help me with this? 你能帮我看一下这个吗？
Can you spell that for me? 你能帮我拼出那个吗？
How do you say ...? *……怎么说？
I don't get it. 我没听懂。
I don't understand. 我不懂。
Is this right/OK? 这样行吗？
I've forgotten the word for ... 我忘了……那个词怎么说。
Sorry? 什么？
What does ... mean? *……什么意思？
What's the difference between ... and ...? *……和……有什么区别？
What's the word for ...? *……那个词怎么说？

Making a request 提出请求

Can you pass me a dictionary, please? 请递给我一本词典好吗？
Could I borrow your pencil, please? 请问，我能借一下你的铅笔吗？
Do you have a ruler I could use? 能借给我一把尺子吗？
May I open the window, please? 请问，我能开一下窗户吗？
May I sharpen my pencil, please? 请问，我能削一下铅笔吗？
Please may I go to the toilet? 请问，我能上个洗手间吗？

Numbers and measurements 数字与度量衡

Cardinal numbers 基数

1	one		20	twenty
2	two		21	twenty-one
3	three		22	twenty-two
4	four		30	thirty
5	five		40	forty
6	six		50	fifty
7	seven		60	sixty
8	eight		70	seventy
9	nine		80	eighty
10	ten		90	ninety
11	eleven		100	a hundred
12	twelve		101	a hundred and one
13	thirteen		1,000	a thousand
14	fourteen		10,000	ten thousand
15	fifteen		100,000	a hundred thousand
16	sixteen		1,000,000	a million
17	seventeen			
18	eighteen			
19	nineteen			

Ordinal numbers 序数

1st	first		20th	twentieth
2nd	second		21st	twenty-first
3rd	third		22nd	twenty-second
4th	fourth		30th	thirtieth
5th	fifth		40th	fortieth
6th	sixth		50th	fiftieth
7th	seventh		60th	sixtieth
8th	eighth		70th	seventieth
9th	ninth		80th	eightieth
10th	tenth		90th	ninetieth
11th	eleventh		100th	hundredth
12th	twelfth		101st	hundred and first
13th	thirteenth		200th	two hundredth
14th	fourteenth		1,000th	thousandth
15th	fifteenth		10,000th	ten thousandth
16th	sixteenth		100,000	hundred thousandth
17th	seventeenth		1,000,000	millionth
18th	eighteenth			
19th	nineteenth			

Roman numerals 罗马数字

I	1	VIII	8	XV	15	L	50
II	2	IX	9	XVI	16	C	100
III	3	X	10	XVII	17	D	500
IV	4	XI	11	XVIII	18	M	1,000
V	5	XII	12	XIX	19	MM	2,000
VI	6	XIII	13	XX	20	MMI	2,001
VII	7	XIV	14	XL	40	MMX	2,010

Length 长度

millimetre (mm) 毫米
centimetre (cm) 厘米
metre (m) 米
kilometre (km) 千米
mile (≈ 1.61 kilometres) 英里

Weight 重量

milligram (mg) 毫克
gram (g) 克
kilogram (kg) 千克
tonne (=1,000 kilograms) 吨

Capacity 容积

millilitre (ml) 毫升
litre (l) 升
pint (≈ 0.57 litres) 品脱
gallon (≈ 4.55 litres) 加仑

Numbers and measurements 數字與度量衡

Cardinal numbers 基數

1	one
2	two
3	three
4	four
5	five
6	six
7	seven
8	eight
9	nine
10	ten
11	eleven
12	twelve
13	thirteen
14	fourteen
15	fifteen
16	sixteen
17	seventeen
18	eighteen
19	nineteen
20	twenty
21	twenty-one
22	twenty-two
30	thirty
40	forty
50	fifty
60	sixty
70	seventy
80	eighty
90	ninety
100	a hundred
101	a hundred and one
1,000	a thousand
10,000	ten thousand
100,000	a hundred thousand
1,000,000	a million

Ordinal numbers 序數

1st	first
2nd	second
3rd	third
4th	fourth
5th	fifth
6th	sixth
7th	seventh
8th	eighth
9th	ninth
10th	tenth
11th	eleventh
12th	twelfth
13th	thirteenth
14th	fourteenth
15th	fifteenth
16th	sixteenth
17th	seventeenth
18th	eighteenth
19th	nineteenth
20th	twentieth
21st	twenty-first
22nd	twenty-second
30th	thirtieth
40th	fortieth
50th	fiftieth
60th	sixtieth
70th	seventieth
80th	eightieth
90th	ninetieth
100th	hundredth
200th	two hundredth
1,000th	thousandth
10,000th	ten thousandth
100,000th	hundred thousandth
1,000,000th	millionth

Roman numerals 羅馬數字

I	1	VIII	8	XV	15	L	50
II	2	IX	9	XVI	16	C	100
III	3	X	10	XVII	17	D	500
IV	4	XI	11	XVIII	18	M	1,000
V	5	XII	12	XIX	19	MM	2,000
VI	6	XIII	13	XX	20	MMI	2,001
VII	7	XIV	14	XL	40	MMX	2,010

Length 長度

millimetre (mm) 毫米
centimetre (cm) 厘米
metre (m) 米
kilometre (km) 千米
mile (= 1.6 kilometres) 英哩

Weight 重量

milligram (mg) 毫克
gram (g) 克
kilogram (kg) 千克
tonne (= 1,000 kilograms) 噸

Capacity 容量

millilitre (ml) 毫升
litre (l) 升
pint (= 0.57 litres) 品脫
gallon (= 4.55 litres) 加侖